LITERARY
RESEARCH
GUIDE

LITERARY RESEARCH GUIDE

An Annotated Listing of Reference
Sources in English Literary Studies

FIFTH EDITION

JAMES L. HARNER

THE MODERN LANGUAGE ASSOCIATION OF AMERICA

NEW YORK 2008

For information about obtaining permission to reprint material from
MLA book publications, send your request by mail (see address below),
e-mail (permissions@mla.org), or fax (646 458-0030).

Library of Congress Cataloging-in-Publication Data

Harner, James L.
Literary research guide : an annotated listing of reference sources
in English literary studies / James L. Harner. — 5th ed.
p.   cm
Includes bibliographical references and indexes.
978-0-87352-808-5 (pbk. : alk. paper)
1. English literature — Information resources.
2. American literature — Information resources.
3. Commonwealth literature (English) — Information resources.
4. English literature — Research — Methodology.
5. American literature — Research — Methodology.
6. Commonwealth literature (English) — Research — Methodology.   I. Title.
Z2011.H34   2007
[PR83]
016.8209 — dc22   2007044727

Printed on recycled paper

Published by The Modern Language Association of America
26 Broadway, New York, NY 10004-1789
www.mla.org

Contents

Acknowledgments

A work such as this depends on the assistance of a multitude of individuals who patiently answered requests for information, recommended works for inclusion, or offered advice and other assistance. In particular, I want to thank the following for their help with the original edition of this *Guide*: Jessica Wade and Mary Jo Smith tended a recalcitrant printer as it cranked out draft after draft of the manuscript. The staffs of libraries at Bowling Green State University, the University of Michigan, Indiana University, the University of Toledo, the University of Illinois at Urbana, the University of Texas at Austin, Texas A&M University, and the University of Toronto were invariably helpful. Kausalya Padmaraj and Catherine Sandy of the interlibrary loan office at Bowling Green were typically efficient in securing copies of elusive works. My former colleagues Lester Barber, Thomas Wymer, and Thomas Klein generously allocated a portion of their NEH grant to defray some of my travel costs. The Bowling Green State University Faculty Research Committee granted me an uninterrupted semester for editing the manuscript, and the English department at Texas A&M allowed me a course reduction so that I could make final revisions. Walter Achtert, a model editor, provided sound guidance on a host of problems, and Susan Joseph, my copyeditor, gave careful attention to my manuscript. In my work on the second edition, I benefited from the assistance of librarians at the University of Texas at Austin and Texas A&M University. At the latter, the interlibrary services staff were remarkably efficient and inventive in securing works that are rarely loaned by libraries. Once again, I enjoyed the opportunity of profiting from the editorial skills and advice of Joe Gibaldi, Judith Altreuter, Elizabeth Holland, and David Cloyce Smith in the MLA's publications division and editorial office. And Karla Reganold's blue pencil prevented a number of errors.

In preparing the third edition, I was fortunate to have the assistance of librarians at the Library of Congress (where Abby Yochelson's expert guidance saved me many hours), the University of Texas at Austin, and Texas A&M University. At the last, the incomparable interlibrary services office made it possible for me to examine a number of elusive works. And, as in the previous editions, I derived considerable pleasure from working with Judith Altreuter, David Cloyce Smith, Paul Banks, and James Poniewozik of the MLA staff.

Preparation of the fourth edition was made considerably easier by a Texas A&M University faculty development leave and the bursary from the Samuel Rhea Gammon Professorship in Liberal Arts. As in earlier editions, I enjoyed the assistance of librarians at several research libraries, especially Texas A&M University (with its incomparable interlibrary loan staff), the University of Texas at Austin, Rice University, Indiana University, and the Library of Congress (where once again I benefited from Abby

Yochelson's expertise). Once again, I benefited from the expertise of Judith Altreuter, Paul Banks, Elizabeth Holland, and Angela Gibson of the MLA staff.

As with the fourth edition, my work on the current one was facilitated by a faculty development leave from Texas A&M University and the bursary from the Samuel Rhea Gammon Professorship in Liberal Arts. The bursary was especially important to supporting my work in research libraries: Harvard University (where Helene Williams expedited my work), the University of Texas at Austin, Rice University, Indiana University, the University of Illinois at Urbana, the University of Toronto, the Library of Congress (where I have come to rely on Abby Yochelson's expertise), and Texas A&M University (where for eighteen years I have been the beneficiary of an incomparable interlibrary loan staff). As in the previous editions, I profited from the advice and editorial skills of the MLA staff, especially Judith Altreuter and Sara Pastel.

Darinda Harner and Lenée Harner Pennington, who have reconciled themselves to sharing their lives with a bibliographer, made valued contributions to all five editions. My greatest debt, however, is to those who read portions of the manuscript of the first edition and generously responded with encouragement and valuable suggestions: Richard D. Altick, Carl T. Berkhout, Florence S. Boos, Jerome S. Dees, Donald C. Dickinson, John H. Fisher, Willard Fox, Hal W. Hall, Robert D. Hume, Nancy M. Ide, W. J. Keith, Paul J. Klemp, Raoul Kulberg, Alan Lawson, Virginia Leland, J. A. Leo Lemay, Michael Marcuse, Jack W. Marken, Harrison T. Meserole, Eric L. Montenyohl, David J. Nordloh, Robert M. Philmus, Frances Povsic, Fred C. Robinson, Harris Ross, Brownell Salomon, Patrick Scott, Jack Stillinger, G. Thomas Tanselle, Mary Helen Thuente, Marshall B. Tymn, Rosemary T. VanArsdel, Ulrich Weisstein, and Joe Weixlmann. (Of these, both Harry Meserole and Skip Fox deserve a special note of thanks, for they read, in various stages, the entire manuscript of the first edition.)

In revising the original edition, I again profited from the advice of many of the same people (Richard D. Altick, Willard Fox, Hal W. Hall, Robert D. Hume, Paul J. Klemp, Harrison T. Meserole, Harris Ross, and Rosemary T. VanArsdel) as well as of the following: Richard R. Centing, John Goldfinch, Maura Ives, Craig Kallendorf, Susan Koppelman, Steven E. Smith, William Proctor Williams, and George T. Worth. In preparing the third edition, I drew on the advice of Sandra Donaldson, Hal W. Hall, Gerard Lowe, and Herman Saatkamp. And, in my revisions for the fourth edition, I called again on Robert D. Hume and Alan Lawson, as well as some new scholars: Wendi Arant-Kaspar and Robert Clarke. In preparing this edition, I have drawn on conversations with or presentations by members of the Literatures in English Section of the Association of College and Research Libraries—especially Helene Williams, Rob Melton, Marcia Pankake, Madeline Copp, Kathleen Kluegel, Lindsey Schell, Abby Yochelson, and Steven Harris. In addition, extended conversations with Martha Brogan sharpened my thoughts on several electronic resources.

That I benefited from the advice of these people is an understatement, but they must not be held accountable, individually or collectively, for the selection or evaluation of works or for any errors; the responsibility for these—especially the errors—is mine alone.

Prefaces

Second Edition

Along with adding important reference tools that appeared after February 1989 and deleting discussions of superseded works or journals that have ceased publication, I have revised about one-half of the original entries. This second edition includes 1,194 entries, refers to an additional 1,248 books and articles in annotations and headnotes, and cites 745 reviews.

Third Edition

In preparing the third edition, I assessed anew each of the works cited in the second edition and evaluated reference works, print and electronic, that appeared after April 1992. I deleted 47 entries, added 60, and revised 560. The resulting edition includes 1,207 entries; refers to 1,331 additional books, articles, and electronic resources in annotations and headnotes; and cites 752 reviews.

Although I cite URLs for Internet sites related to printed works, databases, and online library catalogs, I have admitted few resources that exist only as World Wide Web sites. As I write (April 1997), the Web is too unstructured, unregulated, and unstable to offer many literary reference sources of value.

Fourth Edition

In preparing the fourth edition, I assessed anew each of the works cited in the third edition and evaluated reference works, print and electronic, that appeared after April 1997. I deleted 25 entries, added 41, conflated a few existing entries, and revised 568. The resulting edition includes 1,217 entries; refers to 1,496 additional books, articles, and electronic resources in annotations and headnotes; and cites 730 reviews. Many of the new entries reflect the expansion of literary study into gay, lesbian, and transgendered studies and postcolonial theory; other cutting-edge fields (e.g., cultural studies) have not yet produced reference works of sufficient focus or quality to warrant inclusion in this *Guide*.

Although this edition includes substantially more electronic resources, I generally include only those related to printed works, subscription sites, or resources sponsored by an academic institution or learned society. I admit very few Web sites maintained by individuals: the Web remains too unstructured, unregulated, and unstable to offer many free literary reference sources of value. Users familiar with the protean nature of the Web will realize that many URLs I cite will have changed by the time this copy sees print, and they will thus resort to a good search engine (I recommend Google) to locate a current URL. Revisions and additions for the next edition of the *Guide* will be available on my Web site (http://www-english.tamu.edu/pubs/lrg).

Fifth Edition

In preparing the current edition, I reassessed each of the works included in the fourth edition and evaluated reference sources, print and electronic, that appeared after May 2001. Readers of earlier editions will notice some major changes in the fifth edition: the inclusion of far more electronic resources and the wholesale deletion of entries for scholarly journals and background studies as well as the section on encyclopedias in the Literature-Related Topics and Sources division. The reason for the electronic additions is obvious: the proliferation of bibliographic databases, text archives, and other online resources. As in the fourth edition, I favor subscription-based resources or those sponsored by a professional organization or university. The wholesale deletion arose from the need make room for the entries on electronic resources and to sharpen the focus on *reference* sources. I have added a section on cultural studies. In numerical terms, I deleted 236 entries, added 78, and revised 482. The *Guide* now includes 1,059 entries; refers to 1,555 additional books, articles, and electronic resources in annotations and headnotes; and cites 723 reviews.

Since the electronic version of the *Guide* will be updated regularly, I shall no longer post revisions and additions for the next edition at my Web site (http://www-english .tamu.edu/index.php?id=924).

Introduction

Scope. The *Literary Research Guide* is a selective, annotated guide to reference sources essential to the study of British literature, literatures of the United States, other literatures in English, and related topics. In it I describe and, in most instances, evaluate important bibliographies, abstracts, surveys of research, indexes, databases, catalogs, general histories and surveys, annals, chronologies, dictionaries, encyclopedias, and handbooks. When possible, I am rigorously selective, admitting only works that are reasonably thorough, accurate, effectively organized, and adequately indexed or accessible (in the case of electronic resources); in many instances I have had to include works that fail to meet one or more of these criteria because they are the only available resources in their fields. I have based decisions about what to include—as well as evaluations—on my own experience in using these works and on published surveys of research, authoritative reviews, the advice of scholars from a variety of fields, and existing guides to literary reference sources. (In addition to my own publications, I have ties to three other works listed in this *Guide*: I have been a field bibliographer for the *MLA International Bibliography* [G335] since 1974 and served twice on its advisory board; I am a member of the advisory board of *Literature Online* [I527]; and I was a member of the advisory panel for *Early English Prose Fiction* [M2103]. I trust that none of these affiliations has swayed my evaluations of these works.)

Limitations. Since the *Guide* is intended as a vade mecum for researchers—from advanced undergraduates to experienced scholars—pursuing a topic at a more than superficial level, I have omitted elementary works (such as collections of plot synopses or excerpts from criticism and handbooks that consist of little more than brief critical commentary). Readers who lack basic library skills or require an orientation to using literary reference works should begin with Baker, *Research Guide for Undergraduate Students* (B80). I have omitted general critical studies as well as publications devoted to a single author or literary work, since such materials are readily identifiable in library catalogs and in the sources listed in various period sections.

Although a majority of the entries are for works published and available by October 2006, I have included some significant works in progress or in press when authors have provided detailed descriptions or extensive samples. In some few instances I have listed works announced for publication when it appears that they will be important reference sources. Users should watch for these unpublished works but regard my citations and annotations as provisional.

Organization. The *Guide* is organized in divisions for general literary reference works, national literatures, and topics or sources related to literature. Each division is variously subdivided, and each subdivision classified by type of reference work. The table of contents offers a detailed overview of the divisions and subdivisions, each of which begins with an outline of its organization. Where possible, I use the following organization:

Research Methods
Guides to Reference Works
Histories and Surveys
Literary Handbooks, Dictionaries, and Encyclopedias
Annals
Bibliographies of Bibliographies
Guides to Primary Works
  Guides to Collections
  Manuscripts
  Printed Works
Guides to Scholarship and Criticism
  Surveys of Research
  Serial Bibliographies
  Other Bibliographies
  Abstracts
  Dissertations and Theses
  Review Indexes
  Related Topics
Language
  Guides to Primary Works
  Guides to Scholarship
  Dictionaries
  Thesauruses
  Concordances
  Studies of Language
Biographical Dictionaries
Microform Collections
Periodicals
  Research Methods
  Histories and Surveys
  Guides to Primary Works
  Guides to Scholarship
Background Reading
Genres
  Fiction
    (Research Methods, Guides to Reference Works, Histories and Surveys, etc.)
  Drama
  Poetry
  Prose

Under each heading, truly seminal works appear first, followed by important works that, while not seminal, are noteworthy for their accuracy and value as research tools, then the remainder in alphabetical order by author, editor, or title (for an anonymous work or an edited one better known by its title). I use the letter-by-letter system to alphabetize entries.

Entry numbers. At a late stage of work on the first edition, I numbered entries in increments of five and left two or three entry numbers open at the end of each section or division to accommodate insertions as well as to preclude complete renumbering in succeeding editions.

The entries. I describe a work fully under the most appropriate classification and provide cross-references in related ones. (Cross-references cite entry numbers; a number followed by *a* means that the work appears in the annotation rather than citation.) Thus users of this *Guide* must be certain to examine the *See also* references in each classification and consult appropriate headings in the subject index.

An entry consists of two parts: the citation and the annotation. Citations follow the form recommended in the *MLA Style Manual* (U6400) but add the following: a commonly used acronym or short title, pagination for a single-volume work, the URL for a World Wide Web site, and Library of Congress and Dewey Decimal Classification numbers. For pagination, I cite the final printed arabic page number in a book. My sources for Library of Congress and Dewey numbers are Library of Congress Cataloging-in-Publication information or Library of Congress cataloging records in *WorldCat* (E225); in some few instances I have had to rely on less accurate sources. I omit classification numbers for microform publications and CD-ROMs because most libraries have individual systems of cataloging and storing works in these media. Users should remember that these classification numbers are merely general guides, since libraries vary in their cataloging practices.

The citations. I cite the most recent edition or corrected reprint of a work, noting an earlier one only when it retains independent value. For unrevised works, I cite the earliest edition (making no attempt to list reprints). For works published independently in two or more countries, I give the publication information for the copy I consulted (although I do record a variant title). For multivolume works published over a number of years, place and publisher are those of the most recent volume. Rather than give the editor, edition, and year of works revised annually or biennially, I cite the title, place, and publisher of the most recent edition, the year of initial publication, and the frequency. I generally record separately published supplements or continuations in the citation; where appropriate, titles of individual volumes of a multivolume work appear in a list following the citation. In some instances, I include a parenthetical note on revisions or new editions in progress or announced for publication—some of which will be delayed or will never appear. For electronic resources, I cite—when needed and if known—the title, author or editor; version number, publisher, date of access, URL or medium (CD-ROM), and frequency of updating. For Internet resources, I attempt to cite the URL of the log-in page (alternatively, a home or information page); most researchers, however, will access subscription-based sites through a library's OPAC or electronic resources page. I give the current title of a resource and usually record up to two earlier titles; for those with numerous title changes, I simply note that the title varies.

The annotations. The second part of an entry is the annotation, which does the following:

1. describes the type of work; its scope, major limitations (with particular attention to criteria governing selection), and basic organization (with details of significant changes in a multivolume work); parts of a typical entry; type and number of indexes; electronic version and its interface; and aids to its use (such as detailed evaluations; historical studies; and separately published supplements, indexes, or lists of additions and corrections);

2. offers an evaluation (with particular attention to coverage, organization, accuracy, or accessibility) combined, usually, with a description of the work's important uses in research;

3. lists significant reviews that more fully define the importance or uses of the work or its place in a scholarly tradition, detail its deficiencies or strengths, or provide significant additions and corrections;

4. notes related works, including supplementary, complementary, or superseded ones not accorded separate entries in the *Guide.*

Because many electronic reference resources are available from more than one purveyor, I evaluate the standard search interfaces of the major database aggregators or vendors (entries 510-35). In evaluating an electronic resource, I kept in mind the following questions (some of which are borrowed or adapted from the *Minimal Guidelines for Authors of Web Pages* [http://www.mla.org/resources/documents/rep_it/web_guidelines] prepared by the Modern Language Association's Committee on Information Technology).

Does the resource

identify author(s) or editor(s) and provide contact information?

identify, if appropriate, designer(s) and contact information?

identify the institution, group, or organization funding, sponsoring, or publishing the database and contact information?

provide a statement of copyright (and contact information for copyright permissions)?

provide a privacy statement that indicates what information is collected on users and how that information is used?

note any special software requirements (and provisions for users with special needs)?

provide a precise description of scope (e.g., what kinds of documents are included or excluded; what years are covered; what languages, if any, are excluded)?

offer a description of sources of data (e.g., are records based on firsthand examination of documents or are they taken secondhand from other sources [a list of which should be included])?

indicate who (author, professional abstracter, volunteer) writes abstracts for and indexes documents?

describe editorial practices that might affect search strategies and capabilities?

spell out the frequency of updates?

explain record structure?

explain the relation to any print version (e.g., what is omitted, what is added)?

provide a way for users to report errors and omissions?

explain how the database complements, supersedes, or mirrors other resources?

provide a help file that explains search techniques and alerts users to quirks in searching?

provide a site map?

offer a description of the taxonomy of the database if it replicates a print source and allows browsing based on the taxonomy?

provide a way of sorting records by accession number or date and identifying records added within each update?

My initial plan was to provide a kind of scorecard (based on the preceding questions) for each electronic resource, but it soon became apparent that only a miniscule number of the Web sites or CD-ROMs would receive more than five affirmative responses. To avoid lengthy repetitions of the litany "This site does not identify or provide . . . ," I discuss such omissions only when they substantially affect the quality or accessibility of a resource. Because many electronic resources based on a print ancestor inexcusably fail to offer an adequate discussion of editorial policy or scope, I have retained my discussions of printed versions.

Although I attempt to keep annotations to a reasonable size by emphasizing major points, important or particularly complex works receive lengthier treatment. The annotations—which will offer too much information for some users and too little for others—are meant to allow researchers to determine what works will best suit their needs (and at the same time alert them to major strengths and deficiencies), but the annotations cannot substitute for a careful perusal of the works themselves.

Indexes. The index of persons includes authors, editors, compilers, and others responsible for any of the works I include in citations or annotations. The title index cites all titles referred to in the entries. The subject index includes entries for kinds of reference works as well as other appropriate headings. Each index is alphabetized according to the letter-by-letter system. Most index entries cite entry numbers (an *a* following a number means that the person or title is referred to in the annotation rather than in the citation). In the few instances where I refer to a page, the abbreviation *p.* or *pp.* precedes the number.

It is the fate of every bibliographer to produce a work that includes errors and is outdated before the last keystroke of the final draft is saved. Even worse is the lot of one who prepares a selective critical bibliography, for he or she will inevitably omit important works, misjudge others, and fail to notice every new work or revised edition. I therefore append the bibliographer's infrequently heeded plea that those who use the *Guide* inform me of outright errors, suggest additions and deletions, and point out disagreements in matters of judgment.

How to Use This *Guide*

When we begin a new research project, we must first identify the types of reference sources that will include the data we are seeking and then determine specific titles within each type. Although we will likely be familiar with a few major general reference tools (see the list at the end of this section) or those important to a discipline we know well, we will want to consult a reputable guide to reference works, Thus, the resources evaluated in this *Literary Research Guide* are organized by types of reference works within chapters on resources that cover several national literatures, on genres, on national literatures, and on literature-related topics. Identifying specific resources requires an understanding of the kinds of information found in and uses associated with these types of works.

Guides to research methods offer essential introductions to the methods and tools associated with the kinds of research done within a discipline. Such works are especially important to scholars engaged in interdisciplinary projects.

Guides to reference works identify and (in the better ones) evaluate the handbooks, dictionaries, encyclopedias, bibliographies of bibliographies, national bibliographies, surveys of research, bibliographic databases, review indexes, and other resources—print and electronic—important to research within a discipline. Once we have identified the kinds of reference sources we need to consult, we use guides to reference works (such as this *Guide*) to discover what specific works exist and to plan the order in which we will consult them. In other words, these are the essential first sources a scholar consults when planning how to approach a research topic.

Histories and surveys offer an overview of a national literature, period, genre, or topic and thus can offer an important orientation to an unfamiliar subject.

Literary handbooks, dictionaries, and encyclopedias are useful for finding brief biographies of authors; descriptions of literary characters; plot summaries; definitions of terms; and information about events, groups, places, and institutions of literary interest. They are meant for quick access to factual information.

Annals place a publication, person, or event within a chronological context and thus are essential to studying the intellectual milieu of a work.

Bibliographies of bibliographies are essential sources for identifying subject, title, genre, and author bibliographies; they are among the first resources a researcher consults when setting out to discover what primary and secondary works are related to a topic. Failing to identify an existing bibliography will result in replicating work already done.

Guides to primary works are essential sources for identifying what has been written by an individual or within a genre or literary form. *Guides to collections* identify institutions that hold significant collections built around an author, genre, or subject. *Guides to manuscripts* identify the locations of manuscript material. *Guides to printed works*, which record published works, include *national bibliographies*, which list documents printed within a country or region and thus are essential works for identifying editions of a work, investigating printing history, and re-creating the intellectual and cultural milieu of a work. *Union catalogs*, which record the holdings of several libraries, are indispensable for identifying and locating copies of editions and translations of almost any book; some also include manuscripts. *Digital archives* make accessible large numbers of documents and typically support keyword searching.

Guides to scholarship and criticism identify what has been written about an author, work, genre, form, or other literary topic. *Surveys of research* are important resources for keeping abreast of scholarship on a national literature, literary period, genre, or author. Over the long term, such surveys are valuable for tracing fluctuations in the academic reputation of an author, work, critical approach, or theory. *Serial bibliographies, indexes,* and *abstracts* (print and electronic) that are published or updated at regular intervals are important resources for literature and language scholars since they guide researchers to the most recent scholarship. At the first stage of a project, researchers should identify the pertinent serial bibliographies, indexes, and abstracts; become thoroughly familiar with their scope, limitations, taxonomy, and record structure; master the advanced search interface (especially any strategy that allows identification of records added since a previous search); and plan to search each at intervals. *Abstracts* collect and index summaries of published works and thus are valuable resources for identifying studies of an author or topic buried within a larger work or an obscurely-titled one and for making a preliminary decision about what books, articles, and dissertations to obtain. *Book review indexes* are essential tools for locating reviews of a book and tracing the critical reception of an author or work.

Biographical dictionaries offer basic information about the life, career, and accomplishments of individuals. Those that include living persons will sometimes provide an address or other contact information.

In addition to being able to identify specific titles of kinds of reference works, any scholar working in literatures in English should be familiar with the following:

Harmon, William. *A Handbook to Literature* (C105).
The Oxford Classical Dictionary (C115).
WorldCat (E225).
Year's Work in English Studies (G330).
MLA International Bibliography (G335).
Annual Bibliography of English Language and Literature (G340).
Essay and General Literature Index (G380).
ProQuest Dissertations and Theses (H465).
MLA Directory of Periodicals (K615).
New Princeton Encyclopedia of Poetry and Poetics (L1230).
Columbia Granger's World of Poetry (L1235).
Oxford Companion to English Literature (M1330).
Index of English Literary Manuscripts (M1365).
The New Cambridge Bibliography of English Literature (M1385).
Oxford English Dictionary Online (M1410).
Oxford Dictionary of National Biography (M1425).
Hart, James D. *The Oxford Companion to American Literature* (Q3210).
Blanck, Jacob. *Bibliography of American Literature* (Q3250).
American Literary Scholarship (Q3265).
Dictionary of American Regional English (Q3350).
American National Biography Online (Q3378).

A

Research Methods

Guides to research methods offer essential introductions to the methods and tools associated with the kinds of research done within a discipline.

General Guides

A5   Altick, Richard D., and John J. Fenstermaker. *The Art of Literary Research.*
      4th ed. New York: Norton, 1993. 353 pp.   PR56.A68   807'.2.
      A guide to research techniques, emphasizing "the irreducible element of brain work that lies at the heart of productive research" and the ways in which traditional methods of research and "historically oriented literary scholarship" can work in tandem with recent theoretical and critical approaches. The discussions of the vocation and spirit of scholarship, scholarly occupations (biography, textual study, authorship attribution, source investigation, reception and influence study, and historical research), the tracking down of materials (some information is outdated and computer-accessible resources need fuller treatment), major libraries, note taking (the discussion on mechanics is more applicable to the era of fountain pens than to that of laptops), and the composing process are full of sound practical advice and leavened with instructive examples. Concludes with a selective bibliography and exercises keyed to the text. Indexed by persons, titles, and subjects. The standard vade mecum of methods of literary research, *The Art of Literary Research* should be among the well-thumbed volumes in every literary critic or scholar's personal library.
      In contrast, *A Handbook to Literary Research,* ed. Simon Eliot and W. R. Owens (London: Routledge in assn. with Open U, 1998, 240 pp.) should be avoided. More properly A Handbook to Literary Research in the Literature of England, Primarily after 1700, for Students Enrolled in a Post-graduate Programme of the Open University, this book overlooks a substantial number of resources essential for literary research, offers cursory and sometimes misguided descriptions of important tools, devotes about

a third of the volume to introductions to recent theoretical approaches, and betrays a lack of awareness of numerous electronic resources and their uses.

Sporting an equally promising title, *Research Methods for English Students*, ed. Gabriele Griffin (Edinburgh: Edinburgh UP, 2005, 248 pp.) is long on anecdote and fatally deficient on practical advice and discussion of basic methodology (e.g., the chapter on archives focuses on the "romance" of the archive, the chapter on textual analysis uses a painting as an example, and there is a discussion of "Creative Writing as a Research Method").

For an entertaining and instructive account of the literary detective work behind some major scholarly discoveries, see Altick, *The Scholar Adventurers*, rpt. with a new pref. (Columbus: Ohio State UP, 1987, 338 pp.).

A10   Barzun, Jacques, and Henry F. Graff. *The Modern Researcher*. 6th ed.
        Belmont: Wadsworth, 2004. 322 pp.   D13.B334   001.4'32.

A multidisciplinary guide that emphasizes techniques important in historical research. Of most use to literature scholars are the discussions of note taking, the researcher's virtues (accuracy, love of order, logic, honesty, self-awareness, imagination), verification, the establishment of dates, kinds of evidence, and bias. Indexed by persons and subjects. Some chapters suffer from discursiveness and an attempt to address both the experienced scholar and the neophyte (who will be hampered by numerous incomplete and sometimes inaccurate citations for basic sources and will be misled by the shameless hyping of resources published by the Gale Group and Scribner's, which — like the publisher of this edition — are subsidiaries of Thomson), and overall the current edition gives short shrift to electronic resources. This guide offers an instructive overview of research techniques, but literary scholars will find Altick, *Art of Literary Research* (A5), more concise and immediately helpful.

The third edition of Thomas Mann's *The Oxford Guide to Library Research* (New York: Oxford UP, 2005, 293 pp.) — a substantial improvement over the second edition (1998, 316 pp.) and its predecessor (*A Guide to Library Research Methods* [New York: Oxford UP, 1987, 199 pp.]) — is organized "around nine different *methods* of subject searching," including controlled vocabulary searching, browsing classified book stacks, keyword searching, and related record searching. His advice on locating literary criticism (pp. 248–50) should be ignored, however. David Beasley's *Beasley's Guide to Library Research* (Toronto: U of Toronto P, 2000, 206 pp.), an inadequately updated version of *How to Use a Research Library* (New York: Oxford UP, 1988, 164 pp.), is an elementary, frequently inaccurate, outdated, and untrustworthy guide addressed to novices.

A25   Nicholls, David G., ed. *Introduction to Scholarship in Modern Languages and
        Literatures*. 3rd ed. New York: MLA, 2007. 370 pp.   PB29.I58   407.2.

A collection of fifteen essays, each by a major scholar, designed as an introduction to selected fields of linguistic and literary study: linguistics; language, culture, and society; language acquisition and language learning; rhetoric; composition; poetics; textual scholarship; literary interpretation; historical scholarship; comparative literature; cultural studies; feminist and gender studies; ethnic and minority studies; border studies; and translation studies. A concluding essay addresses the issue of scholar in society. The authors typically "discuss the nature, value, philosophy, and underlying assumptions of their subjects; outline the history of relevant scholarship; survey major issues and approaches of the past, present, and foreseeable future; and conclude with suggestions for further reading." Although directed to a student audience, the essays offer authoritative and balanced introductions for all nonspecialists.

Specialized Topics

A30   Harner, James L. *On Compiling an Annotated Bibliography.* 2nd ed., 2nd
        printing. New York: MLA, 2001. 48 pp.   Z1001.H33   010'.44.

A succinct guide to planning, organizing, researching, writing, editing, and indexing a comprehensive or selective bibliography on a literary subject or author. The second
printing of the second edition adds an appendix, Annotation Verbs, by Ken Bugajski.
Although directed to those preparing an annotated bibliography for publication either
in print or online, the practical advice on planning research and identifying scholarly
works is valuable for anyone compiling a preliminary bibliography for other scholarly
or critical studies.

D. W. Krummel, *Bibliographies: Their Aims and Methods* (London: Mansell, 1984,
192 pp.), which ranges beyond literary bibliographies, also offers useful advice on compilation and organization.

A40   Love, Harold. *Attributing Authorship: An Introduction.* Cambridge:
        Cambridge UP, 2002. 271 pp.   PN171.F6 L68   809.

Evaluates the potential and limits of traditional and modern methods of attributing
authorship, including the use of external evidence, internal evidence (including stylistic
elements, self-reference within the work, and evidence from "themes, ideas, beliefs and
conceptions of genre manifested in the work"), statistical methods, stylometrics, and
bibliographical evidence; also addresses methods of detecting gender and forgery. Concludes with a chapter on arguing attribution. Drawing on a wide range of authorship
studies and thoroughly conversant with the methods discussed, Love is essential reading
for anyone investigating the authorship of a document or evaluating the evidence behind
an attribution.

A45   Latham, Sean, and Robert Scholes. "The Rise of Periodical Studies." *PMLA*
        121 (2006): 517–31.   PB6.M6.

A description of the emerging field of periodical studies, its methodologies, and
the problems attendant on its dependence on digital archives. Focuses on the "hole in
the archive," that is, the failure to preserve advertising pages in bound print runs and
digital copies; the unreliability of optical character recognition (OCR) scanning and its
implications for searching full text; and the need to "[g]enerate metadata for advertisements along with other features." "The Rise of Periodical Studies" is required reading
for anyone working with digital archives.

B

Guides to Reference Works

Guides to reference works identify and (in the better ones) evaluate the handbooks, dictionaries, encyclopedias, bibliographies of bibliographies, national bibliographies, surveys of research, bibliographic databases, review indexes, and other resources—print and electronic—important to research within a discipline. They are the essential first sources a scholar consults when planning how to approach a research problem.

General Guides

B60   *Guide to Reference Books.* 11th ed. Ed. Robert Balay. Chicago: Amer. Lib. Assn., 1996. 2,020 pp. (A new edition—*Guide to Reference Sources*—is in progress.)   Z1035.1.G89   011′.02.

A guide to general and specialized reference works published through 1993 (along with a few later ones). Entries are organized alphabetically by author, editor, or title in five extensively classified sections: general works; humanities; social and behavioral sciences; history and area studies; and science, technology, and medicine. Indexed by persons, titles, and subjects (but subject indexing is not as detailed or complete as it should be). Although descriptions are now more evaluative than those in previous editions (the level of evaluation is not uniform across sections), the annotations overall still rely too uncritically on quotations from prefatory matter to describe scope or purpose, and too few compare similar works; many annotations ignore important limitations or weaknesses. The cutoff date of 1993—far too early in a work that many see as the bible of North American reference librarians—means that many important new works and editions are omitted, as are a host of electronic resources; indeed, the major failing of the eleventh edition is its inadequate treatment of databases, CD-ROMs, and other electronic resources. And though the guide is "pitch[ed] . . . toward research libraries," far too many works of dubious value continue to clutter the pages of a volume that is now too large to use comfortably. Despite its manifold shortcomings, *Guide to Reference Books* remains useful to literature scholars for its general coverage of reference works essential to research in areas related to literature. The move to an online-only resource should reduce substantially the gap between coverage and publication; however, it is clear from reports posted at the *Guide to Reference Sources* Web site (http://www.haverford.edu/library/grb) that the twelfth edition is not progressing as expeditiously as planned. "Selected Reference Books" in various issues of *College and Research Libraries* updates this edition. For the genesis and publishing history of *Guide to Reference Books* (along with a selective bibliography of studies and reviews), see Stuart W. Miller, " 'Monument': *Guide to Reference Books*," *Distinguished Classics of Reference Publishing*, ed. James Rettig (Phoenix: Oryx, 1992) 129–37.

Complemented by *Walford's Guide to Reference Material* (B65). Although now dated, Louise-Noëlle Malclès, *Les sources du travail bibliographique*, 3 vols. in 4 (Genève: Droz, 1950–58), is an occasionally useful supplement to *Guide to Reference Books* because of its extensive coverage of Continental publications and older works. More current but less thorough is Malclès, *Manuel de bibliographie*, 4th ed., rev. Andrée Lhéritier (Paris: PU de France, 1985, 448 pp.). Researchers should ignore *Bowker's Best Reference Books: Arranged by LC Classification Number*, 3 vols. (New Providence: Best Books–Bowker, 2005), which offers an uncritical list that includes in the literature section a substantial number of works that are not reference books. For timely notices of new and revised reference books, see *American Reference Books Annual* (K745) and *Choice* (K750).

B65   *The New Walford Guide to Reference Resources* (*TNW*). Ed. Ray Lester. 3 vols. London: Facet, 2005– .   Z1035.1.W33   001'.02.

      Vol. 1: *Science, Technology, and Medicine.* 2005. 827 pp.

      Vol. 2: *Walford's Guide to Reference Material: Social and Historical Sciences, Philosophy and Religion.* Ed. Alan Day and Michael Walsh. 8th ed. London: Lib. Assn., 2000. 794 pp. (A new edition—*Social Sciences*—is scheduled for 2007.)

      Vol. 3: *Walford's Guide to Reference Material: Generalia, Language and Literature, the Arts.* Ed. Anthony Chalcraft, Ray Prytherch, and Stephen Willis. 7th ed. 1998. 1,186 pp. (A new edition—*Arts, Humanities, and General Reference*—is scheduled for 2008.)

The British counterpart to *Guide to Reference Books* (B60), but more international and comprehensive in coverage. Entries in vols. 2–3 are organized by the Universal Decimal Classification system; those in *New Walford* are organized by "subject parts, subject groupings and subject fields." Annotations are sometimes evaluative and helpfully identify related works, especially supplements or titles that have been superseded. Three indexes in vols. 2–3: authors and titles, subjects, electronic resources; two in vol. 1: topics (i.e., subjects) and authors and titles. Vol. 3, the one of most interest to literary researchers, is judicious in its selection and evaluation of works, is current through early 1998, and has been carefully proofread (unlike the volume's fourth edition). Unfortunately, however, many works that exhibit major shortcomings are accompanied by only a brief descriptive comment.

Although *Walford's* and *Guide to Reference Books* are ultimately complementary works, *Walford's* is more current and accurate; offers broader, more extensive coverage (including reference works on individual authors); supplies more evaluation; and relies less on reviews of dubious authority. The *Literary Research Guide* offers more current coverage of sources for the study of language and literature, but both *Guide to Reference*

Books and, especially, *Walford's* are essential guides to reference sources necessary to research in related areas.

Specialized Guides

B70   *The Reader's Adviser.* 14th ed. Ed. Marion Sader. 6 vols. New Providence: Bowker, 1994.   Z1035.B7   016.028. CD-ROM.

> Vol. 1: *The Best in Reference Works, British Literature, and American Literature.* Ed. David Scott Kastan and Emory Elliott. 1994. 1,472 pp.
> Vol. 2: *The Best in World Literature.* Ed. Robert DiYanni. 1994. 1,122 pp.
> Vol. 3: *The Best in Social Sciences, History, and the Arts.* Ed. John G. Sproat. 1994. 1,127 pp.
> Vol. 4: *The Best in Philosophy and Religion.* Ed. Robert S. Ellwood. 1994. 1,054 pp.
> Vol. 5: *The Best in Science, Technology, and Medicine.* Ed. Carl Mitcham and William F. Williams. 1994. 975 pp.
> Vol. 6: *Indexes.* 1994. 823 pp.

Ostensibly a guide to the best editions, studies, biographies, and reference books in print at the time of compilation (along with a few out of print); however, the lack of discrimination in the selection of works, the variable quality of evaluations, and the emphasis on books in print render this work virtually useless as a critical guide, especially for the lay reader. In effect, *Reader's Adviser* is a repackaging of noncurrent information from *Books in Print* (Q4225a). Indexed in vol. 6 by persons, titles, and subjects. Author sections are also indexed in *Biography and Genealogy Master Index* (J565).

Even more useless is *The Best Books for University Libraries*, 10 vols. in multiple pts. (Temecula: Best Books, 2002), an egregious waste of paper that uncritically lists titles by Library of Congress classification. See Bateson, *Guide to English and American Literature* (B85), *Year's Work in English Studies* (G330), *Year's Work in Critical and Cultural Theory* (U6133), and *American Literary Scholarship* (Q3265) instead.

B75   Taylor, Archer. *General Subject-Indexes since 1548.* Publications of the A. S. W. Rosenbach Fellowship in Bibliography. Philadelphia: U of Pennsylvania P, 1966. 336 pp.   Z695.T28   017.

A historical and critical account of important subject indexes in Latin and European vernacular languages published through the 1950s. Organized by century, the full descriptions, which illustrate uses in modern scholarship, offer helpful introductions to earlier reference works now little known but still essential to research in many periods.

See also

Carter, *Women's Studies* (U6580).

Literature Guides

The following works cover two or more national literatures. Guides devoted to a single national literature or period appear in appropriate sections under the heading "Guides to Reference Works."

For a discussion of 71 literary reference works that need to be written or revised, see James L. Harner, "Literary Reference Works: Some Desiderata," *Scholarly Publishing* 21 (1990): 171–83.

B80   Baker, Nancy L., and Nancy Huling. *A Research Guide for Undergraduate Students: English and American Literature.* 6th ed. New York: MLA, 2006. 96 pp.   PR56.B34   820.72.

An introduction for undergraduate students to the use of electronic and print versions of major bibliographies of bibliographies, bibliographies and indexes of criticism, book review indexes, text archives, biographical dictionaries, concordances and quotation indexes, dictionaries, and literary encyclopedias. Particularly noteworthy is the detailed explanation of how to search an OPAC. The thorough explanations are accompanied by screen shots and reproductions of entries from the reference works. An appendix provides a highly selective, descriptively annotated bibliography of reference sources, including several not discussed in the text. Sound selection and clear, helpful explanations make this an ideal guide for introducing undergraduate English majors to library research.

B85   Bateson, F. W., and Harrison T. Meserole. *A Guide to English and American Literature.* 3rd ed. London: Longman, 1976. 334 pp.   Z2011.B32 [PR83] 016.82.

An evaluative survey of the best editions and criticism of important authors as well as the reference works, literary histories, anthologies, and special studies essential to the study of a period. In addition, there are chapters on general works, modern literary criticism, and research techniques, as well as "interchapters" offering historical perspectives on the medieval, Renaissance, Augustan, and Romantic periods. Readers will disagree with some of the frequently trenchant evaluations; many authors are treated more fully elsewhere; and all sections are outdated; but no single work encompasses so much, so successfully, and so conveniently. Literature scholars sorely need a new edition. Review: Rodney L. Smith, *Seventeenth-Century News* 36 (1978): 23–24.

For recent works see *Year's Work in English Studies* (G330), *Year's Work in Critical and Cultural Theory* (U6133), and *American Literary Scholarship* (Q3265). *Reader's Adviser* (B70) offers broader, but far less discriminating, coverage.

B90   Marcuse, Michael J. *A Reference Guide for English Studies.* Berkeley: U of California P, 1990. 790 pp.   PR56.M37   016.82′09.

A selective guide to reference works (current through 1985 but with some publications as late as 1989) important to the study of the English language and literatures in English. Entries are organized in 24 variously classified divisions for general reference works; libraries; retrospective and current national bibliographies; guides to serial publications; miscellaneous topics (including dissertations, microforms, reviews, indexes to anonymous and pseudonymous works, and films); historical sources; biography and biographical references; archives and manuscripts; language, linguistics, and philology; literary materials and contexts (including folklore, mythology, the Bible, proverbs, quotations, and symbols); literature (a miscellany including sections for literary dictionaries, various foreign literatures, children's literature, and women and literature); English literature (with sections for general works as well as various new literatures in English); medieval literature; Renaissance and early seventeenth century; Restoration and eighteenth century; nineteenth century; twentieth century; American literature; poetry and versification; theater, drama, and film; prose and prose fiction; literary theory and criticism, rhetoric, and composition; bibliography; and the profession of English (including sections on research guides, scholarly writing and publishing, computers, and careers). Within a typical section, guides and reviews of research appear first, then bibliographies, and then other reference works; many sections also include unannotated lists of journals and frequently recommended studies. Reference sources are fully annotated, usually with descriptions of a work's history, purpose, scope, and organization; comments on uses; a judicious evaluation; and references to related works, many of which are not entered separately. Three indexes: persons, titles, subjects (with works appearing in the lists of recommended studies indexed in only the last). Given the principles determining placement of a work and the sometimes confusing organization, the subject index offers the best access to contents. Thorough in its annotations, usually judicious in selection and evaluation, and covering some non-English language works, *Reference Guide for English Studies* is a valuable complement to the present *Literary Research Guide* and a trustworthy companion for the novice as well as for the advanced scholar. Users must remember that Marcuse is current only through 1985 and thus cites many superseded editions or works and describes editorial policies or taxonomies that are now quite different.

    For a comparison of the first edition of this *Literary Research Guide* and Marcuse see the review by Robert Schweik, *Analytical and Enumerative Bibliography* ns 4 (1990): 171–83.

See also

> ALS (Q3265): Chapter on reference works since the volume for 1977.
> Thompson, *Key Sources in Comparative and World Literature* (S4850).
> YWES (G330): Chapter on Reference, Literary History, and Bibliography in vols. 66–72 (for 1985–91); in addition, some chapters survey reference works, and the Bibliography and Textual Criticism chapter (which begins with vol. 76 [for 1995]) evaluates some reference works.

C

Literary Handbooks, Dictionaries, and Encyclopedias

Literary handbooks, dictionaries, and encyclopedias are useful for finding brief biographies of authors; descriptions of literary characters; plot summaries; definitions of terms; and information about events, groups, places, and institutions of literary interest. Some also include potted critical commentary. The best ones offer accurate, concise entries written by established scholars and overseen by an editor who exercises judicious selectivity and a firm editorial hand.

This section is limited to works devoted to literary terminology or more than one national literature. For an evaluative overview of 20 handbooks, several of which are omitted from this *Guide*, see Thomas Clayton, "Literary Handbooks: A Critical Survey," *Literary Research Newsletter* 5 (1980): 67–87.

The best one-volume general encyclopedia is *The Columbia Encyclopedia*, 6th ed, ed. Paul Lagassé (New York: Columbia UP, 2000, 3,156 pp.), which is updated at http://www.bartleby.com/65; the best multivolume one is *Encyclopædia Britannica Online* (http://www.britannica.com).

This *Guide* excludes collections of plot summaries; those needing to locate a synopsis of a specific work can consult Carol Koehmstedt Kolar, comp., *Plot Summary Index*, 2nd ed., rev. and enl. (Metuchen: Scarecrow, 1981, 526 pp.), or Barbara K. Adams et al., eds., *Plot Locator: An Index to Summaries of Fiction and Nonfiction*, Garland Reference Lib. of the Humanities 1437 (New York: Garland, 1991, 704 pp.).

Literary Terminology

C105   Harmon, William. *A Handbook to Literature*. 10th ed. Upper Saddle River: Pearson, 2006. 675 pp.   PN41.H355   803.

A dictionary of places, groups, movements, isms, critical terms, forms, genres, periods, character types, concepts, and other literary terms associated with English and American literature. Each entry provides a succinct, admirably clear definition, frequently accompanied by examples, liberal cross-references, and citations to important scholarship. Concludes with a chronology of English and American literary history (through early 2005) and five appendixes: English monetary terms and values; Nobel prizes in literature (through 2004); Pulitzer prizes for fiction, poetry, and drama (through 2005). Indexed by persons. The *Companion Website for* A Handbook to Literature (http://wps.prenhall.com/hss_harmon_handbook_10) is designed for teachers and students. The most authoritative and clear of the numerous general handbooks to English and American literature, *Handbook to Literature* is the classic in its field and an essential desktop companion.

Chris Baldick, *The Concise Oxford Dictionary of Literary Terms*, 2nd ed. (Oxford: Oxford UP, 2001, 280 pp.), is a more concise, but quite serviceable, compilation, with succinct, clearly written definitions that frequently—but inconsistently—include pronunciation (e.g., for *lyric* but not for *préciosité*).

C107   Cuddon, J. A. *A Dictionary of Literary Terms and Literary Theory*. 4th ed.
        Rev. C. E. Preston. Oxford: Blackwell, 1998. 991 pp.   PN41.C83   803.
    A dictionary of technical terminology, forms, genres, kinds, groups, schools, movements, phrases, isms, motifs, themes, character types, modes, styles, objects, and concepts associated with classical and modern literatures and currently in regular use. Along with a brief definition or description, many entries provide an etymology, examples, or an illustrative passage; some cite major studies. Although its entries on literary theories are uneven and definitions are frequently vague or too diffuse, Cuddon is the most international and inclusive of single-volume dictionaries of literary terms. Review (3rd ed.): Peter Barry, *English* 40 (1991): 275–84.

See also

> Dupriez, *Dictionary of Literary Devices* (U5560a).
> *International Dictionary of Theatre Language* (L1135).
> Lanham, *Handlist of Rhetorical Terms* (U5560a).

General Literary Guides

C115   *The Oxford Classical Dictionary*. 3rd ed. rev. Ed. Simon Hornblower and
        Antony Spawforth. Oxford: Oxford UP, 2003. 1,640 pp.   DE5.O9
        913.38003. Online (Intelex; 24 Feb. 2005 <http://www.library.nlx.com>)
        and through *Oxford Reference Online* (I530); CD-ROM (Intelex).
    A dictionary of classical civilization through the early Christian era (c. 337), with entries for authors and other important persons, places, peoples, mythological figures, themes, deities, written works, forms, genres, historical events, and literary terms. The third edition emphasizes interdisciplinary studies over literature (its revision corrects errors and adds one new entry consisting of two lines). The 6,251 signed entries by established scholars range from a few lines to several pages, but even the brief ones are replete with information. Almost all conclude with references to important scholarship through the early 1990s. The Intelex electronic versions (which are static texts with hyperlinks) can be browsed by entry or searched by keyword; however, the Folio search

interface on the CD-ROM is cumbersome to use. See entry I530 for an evaluation of the *Oxford Reference Online* interface. Authoritative and informative, the work is the best single-volume classical dictionary in English and an essential desktop reference for deciphering classical allusions in literary works; it truly has, as its editors claim, "no competitor in any language."

Although less authoritative and offering briefer discussions, *The Oxford Companion to Classical Literature*, 2nd ed. rpt. with corrections, ed. M. C. Howatson (Oxford: Oxford UP, 1991, 615 pp.), is a useful complement because of its entries on individual works. Indexed in *Biography and Genealogy Master Index* (J565). Review: Keith Hopkins, *TLS: Times Literary Supplement* 14 Feb. 1997: 6.

Fuller discussions of mythological figures are offered by Pierre Grimal, *The Dictionary of Classical Mythology*, trans. A. R. Maxwell-Hyslop, corrected rpt. (Oxford: Blackwell, 1987, 603 pp.), which prints a helpful set of genealogical tables. Women mentioned in classical myths are accorded fuller treatment in Robert E. Bell, *Women of Classical Mythology: A Biographical Dictionary* (New York: Oxford UP, 1991, 462 pp.), which has a concluding list of cross-references to men in the women's lives.

C118   Reid, Jane Davidson. *The Oxford Guide to Classical Mythology in the Arts, 1300–1990s*. 2 vols. New York: Oxford UP, 1993.   NX650.M9 R45 700.

An encyclopedic catalog of treatments of themes and figures from classical Greek and Roman mythology in more than 30,000 works from the fine arts, music, dance, and literature of the Western world. In addition to mythological figures and themes "that have inspired an appreciable number of artistic treatments," the *Guide* includes some subjects that derive from classical myths and some stories based on classical literature; it excludes "subjects from classical history and the post-*Aeneid* legends of early Rome" and allegorical personifications. The 205 main entries (the more extensive ones, such as those for Aphrodite and Odysseus, are thematically subdivided) begin with a headnote that briefly describes the subject and lists major classical sources and, occasionally, scholarly books on the subject; the note is followed by a chronological list (usually organized by date of composition) of works in which the subject is central or prominent or that contain an especially famous or seminal brief treatment of the subject. (The chronological order is, however, violated when works by the same artist are grouped under the date of the earliest work.) For each work, provides — as appropriate — author; title; explanation of the work's relation to the subject; genre or medium; date of composition (or first publication, exhibition, or performance); publication or performance details; present location; and citations to other versions, translations, copies, or revisions related to the original. Indexed by artists. The breadth of coverage, the wealth of information, the careful attention to significant details, and the clear organization make the *Guide* an impressive achievement that will both stimulate and make feasible a variety of studies — interdisciplinary, iconographic, comparative, thematic, historical — of the influence of classical mythology on Western art. We are all in Reid's debt for what is obviously a labor of love. Review: Alexander P. MacGregor, *Classical Bulletin* 70 (1994): 89–96.

C119   Ferber, Michael. *A Dictionary of Literary Symbols*. Cambridge: Cambridge UP, 1999. 263 pp.   PN56.S9 F47   809'.915. Online through *Gale Virtual Reference Library* (I535).

A dictionary of traditional symbols in Western literature that emphasizes those appearing in canonical British poetry. A typical entry, replete with examples spanning classical literature to the present, traces the origin or etymology of a symbol, surveys its history and associations, and examines the range of contexts in which it appears. Although necessarily very selective in what he can include, Ferber offers valuable advice (p.5) on how to investigate symbols excluded. Readers, whether novice or erudite, who consult the *Dictionary* for such symbols as rose, dolphin, labyrinth, swallow, or worm will come away with their understanding enriched by the judicious, informative, and readable explanations (and will invariably be seduced into browsing, ultimately wishing that the Cambridge editors had not imposed such a restricted word limit).

C120   *Benét's Reader's Encyclopedia.* Ed. Bruce Murphy. 4th ed. New York:
        HarperCollins, 1996. 1,144 pp.   PN41.B4   803.

   A general dictionary of authors, works, terms, groups and organizations, movements, concepts, literary characters, and historical and mythological figures from all periods and a variety of literatures. Indexed in *Biography and Genealogy Master Index* (J565). Earlier editions remain useful for entries omitted in the fourth edition. For a history of the work, see Gary L. Ferguson, "The Domain of Learning and Imagination: William Rose Benét and *The Reader's Encyclopedia*," *Reference Services Review* 18.1 (1990): 31–37. Although limited in its treatment of modern literature and not always accurate, *Benét's* offers the broadest coverage of any single-volume literary dictionary in English.

C125   *The Cambridge Guide to Literature in English.* 3rd ed. Ed. Dominic Head.
        Cambridge: Cambridge UP, 2006. 1,241 pp.   PR85.C29   820'.90003.

   A dictionary of American, British, Canadian, Irish, Australian, New Zealand, Indian, African, and Caribbean literatures in English. The approximately 4,500 entries treat writers (living and dead), major works, literary journals, genres, movements, groups, critical and rhetorical terms, theaters and theater companies, and literary concepts. The third edition emphasizes contemporary writers. Although the entries are not signed, the list of contributors includes a number of established scholars. The remarkable breadth of coverage makes *Cambridge Guide* a valuable complement to those literary dictionaries confined to a single national literature.

   Readers should avoid Michael Stapleton, *The Cambridge Guide to English Literature* (Cambridge: Cambridge UP; Feltham, Middlesex: Newnes, 1983, 992 pp.), an unbalanced, untrustworthy attempt to cover works, characters, and authors of literature of the English-speaking world.

C130   *Kindlers neues Literatur Lexikon.* Ed. Walter Jens. 21 vols. München:
        Kindler, 1988–96. *Supplement.* 2 vols. Ed. Rudolf Radler. 1998.
        PN44.K54   016.808. CD-ROM.

   A dictionary of literary works—along with some important philosophical, historical, and scholarly ones—from all literatures and eras. This new edition, while borrowing from *Kindlers Literatur Lexikon,* 7 vols., and *Supplement* (Zürich: Kindler, 1965–74), significantly expands the earlier edition's scope to include more poets and Third World, women, and contemporary authors. Organized alphabetically by author, the signed entries provide a synopsis and lists of selected editions, translations, and studies (many bibliographies were badly dated before publication, and far too many ignore important studies; these problems do not plague the *Supplement*). Vols. 18–20 print general essays on national literatures and indexes; vol. 21 provides additional bibliographies and a necrology. The most international in scope and extensive in coverage of any dictionary of literary works, *Kindlers* is valuable for its succinct summaries of major and minor works, but the bibliographies in the main volumes cannot be trusted to guide users to the most important or representative studies.

Useful complements are:

Dizionario letterario Bompiani delle opere e dei personaggi di tutti i tempi e di tutte le letterature. 9 vols. Milano: Bompiani, 1947–50. *Appendice.* 3 vols. 1964–79. The model for *Kindlers,* the *Dizionario* includes signed entries for literary and musical works before about 1900 from all literatures, entries for literary characters (in vol. 8), and brief (and generally superficial) essays (in vol. 1) on intellectual and artistic movements. Works are alphabetized by Italian titles, characters by the Italian form of the given name. Three indexes in vol. 9: original titles; literary authors; illustrations. *Dizionario Bompiani degli autori di tutti i tempi e di tutte le letterature,* 4 vols. (Milano: Bompiani, 1987), summarizes the careers of about 9,000 writers, from the classical period to the late 1980s.

Dictionnaire universel des littératures. Ed. Béatrice Didier. 3 vols. Paris: PUF, 1994. A dictionary of the literatures, classical to modern, of the world (but with special focus on French and European literatures), with signed articles on writers (the majority from the twentieth century); movements; national, ethnic, or regional literatures; scholarly organizations; periods, genres and forms, places, anonymous works, and literary topics. Each entry concludes with a selective list of editions or studies. Users should be certain to consult the "Présentation des secteurs" for discussion of the scope of the treatment of individual literatures; unfortunately, most of the selective bibliographies appended to these sections are outdated or ignore important recent publications. Seven indexes: entries (organized by national literature, language, or region); authors (organized by literary period); entries on literatures in specific languages; genres (organized by national literature, language, or region); anonymous works (organized by national literature, language, or region); themes and myths; and schools, movements, and groups (organized by period).

See also

Enzyklopädie des Märchens (U5830).

D

Bibliographies of Bibliographies

Bibliographies of bibliographies are essential sources for identifying subject, title, genre, and author bibliographies; they are among the first resources a researcher consults when setting out to discover what has been written about a topic.

Those sources restricted to a single national literature appear under the heading "Bibliographies of Bibliographies" in appropriate sections of this *Guide*. For an evaluative survey of early works, see Archer Taylor, *A History of Bibliographies of Bibliographies* (New Brunswick: Scarecrow, 1955, 147 pp.).

General Bibliographies of Bibliographies

Serial Bibliographies

D145   *Bibliographic Index Plus.* Online. Wilson. 24 June 2005 <http://vnweb.hwwilsonweb.com/hww/>. Updated daily.

   Bibliographic Index: A Cumulative Bibliography of Bibliographies. New York: Wilson, 1937– . 3/yr., inc. annual cumulation.   Z1002.B595   016.016.

A subject index to bibliographies that are published separately, as parts of books, or in about 2,800 periodicals (currently). Concentrates on works in Germanic and Romance languages and is now limited to bibliographies with at least 50 entries. Like other Wilson indexes, *Bibliographic Index* offers generous subdivisions and cross-references for easy location of entries. Entries since 1982 can be searched through *Bibliographic Index Plus* (which also includes the full text of some 100,000 bibliographies). The advanced search screen allows users to search by keyword, author, title, journal, document language, publisher, and a variety of other document fields. See entry I525 for an evaluation of the *WilsonWeb* search interface, which all of the Wilson databases use. Especially valuable for its inclusion of parts of books, *Bibliographic Index* is the most current and thorough subject index to bibliographies.

An essential complement for 1956–87 is *Bibliographische Berichte/Bibliographical Bulletin*, 30 vols. (Frankfurt: Klostermann, 1959–88), a bibliography of bibliographies (including books, essays in collections, and journal articles) published for the most part in German, English, Romance, and East European languages. Bibliographies are listed by author or title (for edited and anonymous works) in 18 divisions, most of them extensively classified: general; education; geography; history; information science, librarianship, and museums; the arts (including theater and film); agriculture; mathematics; medicine; natural sciences; language and literature; philosophy; psychology; law; religion; social sciences (including folklore); sport and games; and technology. The language and literature division is classified by language or geographical area. Entries, which provide basic bibliographic information, are based on acquisitions of a small number of German libraries or copied from national bibliographies. Indexed by subject in each volume through vol. 13 (1971); cumulative indexes: vols. 1–5 (1965, 140 pp.); vols. 6–10 (1970, 176 pp.); vols. 11–29, as vol. 30 (1988): 664 pp. Although *Bibliographische Berichte* is not comprehensive and is sometimes inaccurate, its demise deprived researchers of a resource especially valuable for its extensive coverage of European publications.

See also

>   *ABELL* (G340): In the volumes for 1973–84, the Bibliography section has a subdivision for Subject, Genre, and Period Bibliographies, Checklists, and Indexes, and in the volumes for 1973–76, a subdivision for author bibliographies.
>   *Bibliographie der Buch- und Bibliotheksgeschichte* (U5280).

Other Bibliographies

D150   *BibSite*. Bibliographical Society of America. Online. 24 Mar. 2006 <http://www.bibsocamer.org/BibSite/bibsite.htm>. Updated irregularly.

A World Wide Web site devoted to hosting or linking to original bibliographies and supplements, updates, and corrections to existing bibliographies. Although it is in its infancy, the site has the potential to become an important gateway to bibliographies that are not commercially viable and to revisions to published ones.

D155   Besterman, Theodore. *A World Bibliography of Bibliographies, and of Bibliographical Catalogues, Calendars, Abstracts, Digests, Indexes, and the Like.* 4th ed. 5 vols. Lausanne: Societas Bibliographica, 1965–66. Z1002.B5685   016.01.

A World Bibliography of Bibliographies, 1964–1974. 2 vols. Comp. Alice F. Toomey. Totowa: Rowman, 1977.   Z1002.T67   016.011.

A subject guide to 117,187 bibliographies (published through 1963) on all subjects. Ostensibly, only separately published bibliographies are admitted; however, issues of periodicals and offprints of journal articles haphazardly find their way into the listings. Booksellers' and auction catalogs, art lists, general library catalogs, and works printed in Oriental languages are excluded. Arranged chronologically under subject headings, entries record the number of items in a bibliography as well as the first and last, but usually not intervening, editions. Indexed in vol. 5 by persons, titles of anonymous bibliographies, and libraries. Although noteworthy for its broad coverage, Besterman must be supplemented with *Bibliographic Index* (D145). For a detailed critique, see Roderick Cave, "Besterman and Bibliography: An Assessment," *Journal of Librarianship* 10 (1978): 149–61.

The supplement uncritically reproduces, sometimes illegibly, about 18,000 Library of Congress catalog cards in a subject list without an index. Of the various sections that have been extracted from Besterman and published by Rowman in the Besterman World Bibliographies series, the two of most interest to the literature scholar are *Literature: English and American: A Bibliography of Bibliographies* (1971, 457 pp.) and *Music and Drama: A Bibliography of Bibliographies* (1971, 365 pp.). Because they include articles and parts of books, the following are occasionally useful supplements to Besterman:

> Courtney, William P. *A Register of National Bibliography.* 3 vols. London: Constable, 1905–12.
>
> Northup, Clark Sutherland. *A Register of Bibliographies of the English Language and Literature.* Cornell Studies in English. New Haven: Yale UP; London: Oxford UP, 1925. 507 pp.
>
> Van Patten, Nathan. *An Index to Bibliographies and Bibliographical Contributions Relating to the Work of American and British Authors, 1923–1932.* Stanford: Stanford UP, 1934. 324 pp.

D160   Arnim, Max. *Internationale Personalbibliographie, 1800–1943.* 2nd ed., expanded and rev. 2 vols. Stuttgart: Hiersemann, 1944–52. Gerhard Bock and Franz Hodes. Vol. 3: *1944–1959.* 1961–63. 659 pp. Hodes. *1944–1975.* 2nd ed. of vol. 3. 3 vols. 1978–87.   Z8001.A1 I57   016.012.

A bibliography of bibliographies of works by and about writers and scholars from 1800 through c. 1986. Although international in scope and covering all disciplines, the work emphasizes German authors. Under each writer is a list of bibliographies, including books, articles, and entries in a wide range of biographical dictionaries, handbooks, registers, and sections of other bibliographies of bibliographies published through the early 1980s. *Internationale Personalbibliographie, 1850–1935, in der preussischen Staatsbibliothek* (Leipzig: Hiersemann, 1936, 572 pp.) indexes a few works omitted in the second edition. Although it is not comprehensive, the scope and coverage of foreign publications and collective works make *Internationale Personalbibliographie* an important complement to the other bibliographies of bibliographies in this section. Because of the nature of many of the collective works indexed, it is also a useful source for locating biographies and obituaries.

D165   Bewsey, Julia J. "Festschriften Bibliographies and Indexes." *Bulletin of Bibliography* 42 (1985): 193–202   Z1007.B94

An annotated guide to 63 bibliographies and indexes (including journal articles but excluding serial bibliographies) of Festschriften published worldwide. Bewsey is noteworthy because standard serial bibliographies frequently overlook such collections.

See also

Ballou, *Women: A Bibliography of Bibliographies* (U6585).
Gray, *Guide to Book Review Citations* (G410).
Reynolds, *Guide to Theses and Dissertations* (H455).
Wortman, *Guide to Serial Bibliographies* (G325).

Indexes

D170   Weiner, Alan R., and Spencer Means. *Literary Criticism Index.* 2nd ed.
         Metuchen: Scarecrow, 1994. 559 pp.   Z6511.W44 [PN523]   016.809.

An index to 146 period and genre bibliographies (published between 1958 and 1991) principally of literatures in English. After an initial section for anonymous works, entries are arranged by author, then by literary works, with page references cited for individual bibliographies. A time-saving source for determining which specialized bibliographies include sections on a work or an author.

National Bibliographies

National bibliographies attempt to record documents printed within a country or region; as such, they are essential works for identifying editions of a work, investigating printing history, and re-creating the intellectual and cultural milieu of a work.

Bibliographies

D180   Domay, Friedrich. *Bibliographie der nationalen Bibliographien/Bibliographie mondiale des bibliographies nationales/A World Bibliography of National Bibliographies.* Hiersemanns Bibliographische Handbücher 6. Stuttgart: Hiersemann, 1987. 557 pp.   Z1002.A1 D65.

A bibliography of approximately 3,000 retrospective and current national bibliographies (and related works) published by the end of 1980 (with coverage of some countries extending through mid-1982). Organized by continent, then region, countries variously and inconsistently include divisions for a variety of reference works (e.g., historical overviews, bibliographies of bibliographies, guides to reference books, lists of auction catalogs, biographical dictionaries, lists of dissertations) besides the national bibliographies and trade lists (listed by initial year of coverage). The annotations describe content, organization, and scope; cite cumulations or related works and scholarship; and occasionally offer an evaluative comment. Indexed by persons and titles (but with numerous errors and inconsistencies). Although admitting numerous works that are hardly national bibliographies, inexplicably omitting New Zealand, haphazardly organized within several countries, citing numerous superseded works, and less current than one should expect, *Bibliographie der nationalen Bibliographien* nonetheless offers the fullest guide to national bibliographies worldwide.

For more-current and better organized—but generally less-thorough—coverage, see:

> Beaudiquez, Marcelle, ed. *Inventaire général des bibliographies nationales rétrospectives/Retrospective National Bibliographies: An International Bibliography.* IFLA Publications 35. München: Saur, 1986. 189 pp. An inventory of retrospective national bibliographies for all countries except European socialist ones, with French or English annotations that describe sources, scope, coverage, and organization. The quality of annotations varies with the contributor, much information is taken secondhand, and there are significant omissions, but this work defines national bibliography more narrowly than Domay does and describes some works omitted by him.

> Bell, Barbara L. *An Annotated Guide to Current National Bibliographies.* 2nd ed. UBCIM Publications ns 18. Munich: Saur, 1998. 487 pp. A bibliography of national bibliographies that record current publications within a country. A typical annotation identifies scope, coverage, contents, cataloging rules and classification scheme, content of an entry, arrangement, indexing, predecessors, supplementary works, published guides, currency, print and electronic formats, current deposit laws, and selected scholarship. The extensive commentary under most countries offers a wealth of information about current and, in some cases, retrospective national bibliographies. Review: (Beaudiquez and Bell [1986 ed.]) D. W. Krummel, *Libraries and Culture* 24 (1989): 217–30.

Background Reading

D185   Linder, LeRoy Harold. *The Rise of Current Complete National Bibliography.* New York: Scarecrow, 1959. 290 pp.   Z1001.3.L5   015.

A history of current national bibliographies published in England, France, Germany, and the United States from the sixteenth century through 1939. Limited to current complete national bibliographies (and thus excluding retrospective ones such as the *Short-Title Catalogues* [M1990 and M1995] and Evans, *American Bibliography* [Q4005]), Linder also covers some periodical indexes and lists of newspapers and dissertations. After an initial definition of national bibliographies and discussion of their importance, chapters proceed chronologically, surveying by country the content, organization, and development of individual works. Concludes with three appendixes (the most useful one being a chronological list of national bibliographies by country, with dates of coverage and symbols indicating scope and organization) and a selected bibliography. Indexed by titles and persons. The chronological organization means that the discussion of some works is split between two or more chapters; the focus is blurred by the admission of numerous works that hardly qualify as national bibliographies; there is little evaluation; and the work still reads like the dissertation it originally was. Nonetheless, it is the most complete history of current national bibliographies through 1939. Review: Archer Taylor, *Library Quarterly* 30 (1960): 150–52.

E

Libraries and Library Catalogs

Research Libraries

Although most public, national, and academic libraries in North America and Europe are open to qualified researchers, many require some kind of professional identification for admission and a few require advance application. Researchers planning to work in an unfamiliar library—especially in special collections or at a European institution—should inquire well in advance about admission procedures, restrictions on materials in special collections, and hours of operation.

Becoming familiar with a major research library can occupy the better part of a morning, but researchers can reduce this lost time by requesting in advance a copy of any locally produced guide (which usually prints maps and a stack guide) and consulting the library's Web site and published descriptions of collections or catalogs. For example, one can save considerable time in the Main Reading Room of the Library of Congress by copying out call numbers in advance from the *Library of Congress Online Catalog* (E260); many libraries sponsor journals that print articles on their holdings and news of acquisitions; and most allow public access over the Internet to their electronic catalogs. Most library Web sites and commercial Web search engines provide links to library

OPACs (online public-access catalogs) worldwide. For valuable advice on preparing to visit an unfamiliar library, see Thorpe, *Use of Manuscripts in Literary Research* (F275).

Major general research libraries in the United States, Canada, and Great Britain include the following:

Boston Public Library (http://www.bpl.org).

British Library (http://www.bl.uk). See especially the Collections page (http://www.bl.uk/collections/listings.html) and *Directory of Rare Book and Special Collections* (E210), pp. 132–80. *British Library Journal.* 1975–99. 2/yr. Preceded by *British Museum Quarterly.* 1926–73.

University of California, Berkeley (http://www.lib.berkeley.edu).

University of California, Los Angeles (http://www2.library.ucla.edu).

Cambridge University (http://www.lib.cam.ac.uk). See the section on Cambridge libraries in *Directory of Rare Book and Special Collections* (E210), pp. 25–40. Researchers who need to use the college and other libraries associated with the university should consult the University of Cambridge Libraries Directory at the above URL for information on access to collections.

Library and Archives Canada (http://www.collectionscanada.gc.ca).

Center for Research Libraries, Chicago (http://www.crl.edu).

University of Chicago (http://www1.lib.uchicago.edu/e/index.php3).

Columbia University (http://www.columbia.edu/cu/lweb).

Cornell University (http://www.library.cornell.edu).

Duke University (http://library.duke.edu).

Harvard University (http://lib.harvard.edu). *Harvard Library Bulletin.* 1947– . Quarterly.

University of Illinois (http://www.library.uiuc.edu/index.html).

Indiana University (http://www.libraries.iub.edu).

Library of Congress (http://www.loc.gov/index.html).

University of Michigan (http://www.lib.umich.edu).

National Library of Scotland (http://www.nls.uk). For an overview of collections, see *Directory of Rare Book and Special Collections* (E210), pp. 631–44.

Newberry Library (http://www.newberry.org).

New York Public Library (http://www.nypl.org). *Biblion: The Bulletin of the New York Public Library.* 1902–2001. Title varies. 2/yr.

University of North Carolina, Chapel Hill (http://www.lib.unc.edu).

Ohio State University (http://www.lib.ohio-state.edu).

Oxford University (http://www.lib.ox.ac.uk). For college and other libraries see the Individual Libraries link at the above URL. *The Bodleian Library: A Subject Guide to the Collections.* Ed. Gregory Walker, Mary Clapinson, and Lesley Forbes. Oxford: Bodleian Lib., 2004. 240 pp. See also *Directory of Rare Book and Special Collections* (E210), pp. 490–541. *Bodleian Library Record.* 1938– . Irregular. Preceded by *Bodleian Quarterly Record,* 1914–38.

University of Pennsylvania (http://www.library.upenn.edu).

Pennsylvania State University (http://www.libraries.psu.edu).

Princeton University (http://library.princeton.edu). *Princeton University Library Chronicle.* 1939– . 3/yr.

Stanford University (http://library.stanford.edu).

University of Texas (http://www.lib.utexas.edu).

University of Toronto (http://main.library.utoronto.ca).

University of Washington (http://www.lib.washington.edu).

University of Wisconsin (http://www.library.wisc.edu).

Yale University (http://www.library.yale.edu). *Yale University Library Gazette.* 1926– . 2/yr.

Important specialized libraries include the following:

American Antiquarian Society (http://www.americanantiquarian.org).

Folger Shakespeare Library (http://www.folger.edu). The following remain essential complements to the Folger's OPAC: *Catalog of Printed Books of the Folger Shakespeare Library, Washington, DC.* 28 vols. Boston: Hall, 1970. *First Supplement.* 3 vols. 1976. *Second Supplement.* 2 vols. 1981. *Catalog of Manuscripts of the Folger Shakespeare Library, Washington, DC.* 3 vols. 1971. *First Supplement.* 1987. 524 pp.

Huntington Library (http://www.huntington.org). *Huntington Library Quarterly: Studies in English and American History and Literature.* 1931– . Quarterly. Former title: *Huntington Library Bulletin* (1931–37).

Marcuse, *Reference Guide for English Studies* (B90), pp. 21–33, has a valuable annotated list of major research libraries.

Guides to Libraries

E200   *World Guide to Libraries.* München: Saur, 1966– . Biennial.   Z721.I63
         027'.0025.
         A guide to 41,826 research, national, governmental, public, and academic libraries in 205 countries. Entries are organized alphabetically by country, then type of library (national, general research, academic, professional school, government, ecclesiastical, corporate and business, special, and public), then place, and then name of library (with academic libraries listed by institution). A typical entry includes the name of the library; address; telephone, fax, and telex numbers; Web site; e-mail address; director or head; main departments (with descriptions of important holdings or special collections in a few instances); special divisions; statistics on holdings; and indication of participation in interlibrary loan. Indexed by libraries (with academic libraries entered by institution). Since the material is based on questionnaires, the detail, accuracy, and currency of descriptions vary, but the *World Guide to Libraries* is the fullest international source for basic information on libraries worldwide.
         More-thorough guides to individual countries include the following:

American Library Directory. Medford: Information Today, 1923– . Annual. Online. A guide to public, academic, government, and special libraries in the United States, Mexico, Puerto Rico and other regions administered by the United States, and Canada (along with a smattering in foreign countries). Within divisions for each of the four areas, libraries are listed alphabetically by state, region, or province, then city, then library or institution name. A typical entry includes name, address, telephone and fax numbers, Internet address and World Wide Web URL, major administrative personnel and subject specialists, statistics on holdings, lists of special collections, automation information, and names of departmental libraries with addresses and information on holdings. Indexed by names. The directory is the most thorough general guide to North American libraries.

Special libraries, divisions of academic libraries, archives, and research centers in the United States and Canada are more exhaustively covered in the most recent edition of *Directory of Special Libraries and Information Centers* (Detroit: Gale, 1963– , irregular; updated between editions by *New Special Libraries*). The best approach is through the subject index.

Aslib Directory of Information Sources in the United Kingdom. 13th ed. Ed. Michael Chapman. London: Europa–Taylor and Francis, 2004. 1,580 pp. A directory that ranges beyond libraries to include institutions, repositories, archives, groups, art galleries, charities, and other organizations. Organized alphabetically by name of organization, entries typically include address, telephone and fax numbers, e-mail address, URL, description of the organization, restrictions on admission, subject interests, special collections (citing name or giving a brief description), OPAC access, and publications. Two indexes: abbreviations and acronyms; subjects. Unfortunately, the minimal space allocated to describing subject interests and special collections and the lack of sufficiently full subject indexing make the directory much less useful than it might be. Although less thorough in coverage, *Directory of Rare Book and Special Collections* (E210) is superior as a guide to collections.

Guides to Collections

E205   Ash, Lee, and William G. Miller, comps. *Subject Collections: A Guide to Special Book Collections and Subject Emphases as Reported by University, College, Public, and Special Libraries and Museums in the United States and Canada.* 7th ed., rev. and enl. 2 vols. New Providence: Bowker, 1993. Z731.A78   026′.00025′7.

A subject guide to specialized collections in North American libraries and other institutions. Most local history collections and those in separate departmental units of large academic libraries are excluded. Under subject headings, entries are listed alphabetically by state (with United States territories and Canadian provinces appearing after states), then city, and then library. A typical entry includes library address; kinds of holdings and cataloging status; and notes on specific holdings, size of the collection, guides or catalogs, and restrictions on use. Because most entries are based on questionnaires, the sophistication and specificity of the descriptions vary considerably. Although many subject headings are frustratingly broad, there are numerous headings for individual authors and literary topics. *Subject Collections* is the best guide to identifying specialized library collections, but it retains some unrevised entries from the preceding edition, omits or inadequately describes collections in several major research libraries, and includes disproportionately lengthy descriptions of holdings that hardly justify the appellation "collection."

Collections in some European libraries are described in:

Gallico, Alison, ed. *Directory of Special Collections in Western Europe.* London: Bowker, 1993. 146 pp. Entries (organized by country, then alphabetically by city) include the name of the collection, address, a brief description of subjects, details of the kinds and size of holdings, information on access to the collection, and a list of finding aids and catalogs. Of the 343 collections described, 131 are from the United Kingdom, which is more thoroughly covered in *Directory of Rare Book and Special Collections* (E210). Two indexes: institutions; subjects (in English, French, and German).

> Lewanski, Richard C., comp. *Subject Collections in European Libraries.* 2nd ed. London: Bowker, 1978. 495 pp. Organized alphabetically by broad Dewey Decimal Classification, then alphabetically by country, then city, and then library, entries include address, information on cataloging status, and notes on the size and content of holdings, restrictions, and published finding aids. Indexed by subject headings. Although many important collections are omitted or incompletely described and subject headings are frequently too broad, this is a useful preliminary guide to subject collections in European libraries, especially those with no published descriptions of their collections.

Although these two directories omit or incompletely describe several important collections, they can be useful preliminary guides to defined collections in European libraries, especially those not described in print elsewhere.

E210   *A Directory of Rare Book and Special Collections in the United Kingdom and the Republic of Ireland.* 2nd ed. Ed. B. C. Bloomfield. London: Lib. Assn., 1997. 740 pp.   Z791.A1 D58   027'.0025'41.

A guide to collections in public, national, academic, church, and institutional libraries (along with a very few private collections that are accessible to researchers). Manuscript holdings are noted only when closely related to rare book collections. Organized by country, roughly by county (in the case of England), city, and then institution, entries typically include address, telephone number, hours, requirements for admission, research facilities, and sometimes a brief history of the library. Each collection is then described separately, typically with a note on its origin and history, indication of size, summary of content and major holdings, and citations to finding aids. The thoroughness and quality of the descriptions vary considerably; the better ones cite specific works by referring to standard bibliographies such as the *Short-Title Catalogues* (M1990 and M1995), note unrecorded works, and comment on provenance. Indexed by persons, places, and subjects; however, the indexing is insufficiently thorough. For some cities (notably London) and individual libraries (such as the British Library and the Bodleian), the entries offer the best available general descriptions of collections. While the second edition redresses most of the serious flaws of the first (significant omissions, uneven descriptions, frequent typographical errors), it remains incompletely indexed. For additions and corrections, see Bloomfield, "*A Directory of Rare Books and Special Collections*: Some Corrections and Additions," *Rare Books Newsletter* 59 (1998): 41–42.

The following identify some additional collections:

> *The Aslib Directory of Literary and Historical Collections in the UK.* Ed. Keith W. Reynard. London: Aslib, 1993. 287 pp. The descriptions of the more than 1,000 collections tend to be brief and, inevitably, depend on questionnaire responses for accuracy and informativeness, but the subject index seems reasonably thorough.
>
> *Directory of Literary Societies and Author Collections.* Ed. Roger Sheppard. London: Lib. Assn., 1994. 288 pp. Although a rather hit-or-miss affair (especially in the coverage of literary societies), this directory does identify

a few additional collections. Although ostensibly limited to English literature and related topics, it includes a number of non-English-language authors.

Additional information on theater collections is available in Diana Howard, comp., *Directory of Theatre Resources: A Guide to Research Collections and Information Services*, 2nd ed. ([London:] Lib. Assn. Information Services Group and Soc. for Theatre Research, 1986, 144 pp.), a guide to public and private collections in libraries, museums, and record offices, as well as information services provided by organizations in England, Scotland, and Wales. Few collections housed in theaters are included, and the descriptions, based on questionnaires, vary considerably in precision and detail; nonetheless, this is an important guide to collections of theater material.

See also

> Field, *Special Collections in Children's Literature* (U5460).
> Geist, *Directory of Popular Culture Collections* (U6290).
> Schatz, *Directory of Afro-American Resources* (Q3730).

Interlibrary Loan

From time to time, researchers need to obtain books, dissertations, articles, or microforms through interlibrary loan. While each institution will have its own procedures and forms, most United States libraries comply with the National Interlibrary Loan Code of 2001 (http://www.ala.org/ala/rusa/rusaprotools/referenceguide/interlibrary .cfm), which requires that requests include full bibliographic information and be verified in a standard bibliography (such as the *National Union Catalogs* [E235, E240, and E245], *MLA International Bibliography* [G335], or *Annual Bibliography of English Language and Literature* [G340]) or database (such as *WorldCat* [E225] or RLG Union Catalog [E230], which are particularly good sources, since each includes an interlibrary loan subsystem). Many libraries now have Web forms that allow researchers to file requests electronically, and several bibliographic databases can automatically generate requests.

Filling a request sometimes takes several weeks; however, the process can be expedited if researchers specify exactly the edition required or discriminate between journals with the same or similar titles. Some research libraries do not lend any of their holdings and most will not send rare, valuable, fragile, or unique books; manuscripts; or reference books. Most libraries, however, will photocopy or film manuscripts or rare items if their physical condition or restrictions on use permit reproduction. Although some libraries will lend dissertations, copies must usually be obtained through UMI (formerly University Microfilms International) or the British Library Document Supply Centre.

Library Catalogs

Published library catalogs and OPACs are essential sources for locating copies, identifying unique items, building a preliminary bibliography, and conducting subject searches. Researchers who have only rudimentary skill in searching an OPAC should read the chapter on using library catalogs (pp. 9–26) in Baker, *A Research Guide for Undergraduate Students* (B80).

Bibliographies and Guides

E215   Downs, Robert B. *American Library Resources: A Bibliographical Guide.*
        Chicago: Amer. Lib. Assn., 1951. 428 pp. *Supplement, 1950–1961.* 1962.
        226 pp. *Supplement, 1961–1970.* 1972. 244 pp. *Supplement, 1971–1980.*
        1981. 209 pp. American Library Resources: *Cumulative Index, 1870–1970.*
        Comp. Clara D. Keller. 1981. 89 pp.   Z1002.D6   016.016.

        ———. *British and Irish Library Resources: A Bibliographical Guide.*
        London: Mansell, 1981. 427 pp.   Z791.A1 D68   016.0252′07.

The works list printed catalogs, guides to libraries, union lists, descriptions of collections, calendars, indexes, surveys of holdings, and exhibition catalogs, along with some library reports, miscellaneous bibliographies, and unpublished works. Users must remember that the *Library Resources* volumes are guides to published materials and not to collections themselves. Entries are listed alphabetically by library or author within classified subject divisions, including ones for general works (with sections for general library catalogs, manuscripts, rare books, and printing history), social sciences (including folklore), linguistics, literature (organized by national literatures, with subsections in the American volumes for general works, genres, and individual authors), and biography and genealogy. The British volume is more extensively and precisely classified and includes a division for individuals (predominantly literary authors), but it is far less thorough than the American volumes. Some entries are accompanied by a brief description of content. Indexed in each American volume and the *Cumulative Index* by persons, subjects, and libraries; the British volume has two indexes: authors, compilers, and editors; subjects. Because of inadequate subject indexing, inconsistencies in classifying items, and a lack of cross-references, users must exercise considerable ingenuity to locate all works on a topic or library. Although incomplete in covering journal articles and general bibliographies that cite locations, the *Library Resources* volumes are valuable for identifying works that provide important access to special collections and describe unique items. They are especially strong in covering local publications that usually are not listed in the standard bibliographies and indexes given in section G, in *American Book Publishing Record* (Q4110), or in *GlobalBooksinPrint.com* (Q4225). Review: (British) R. J. Roberts, *Notes and Queries* ns 31 (1984): 252–53.

E220   Nelson, Bonnie R. *A Guide to Published Library Catalogs.* Metuchen:
        Scarecrow, 1982. 342 pp.   Z710.N44   019.

A classified list of important general and specialized catalogs, the majority of which are multivolume works published since 1960 and representing the holdings of North American or Western European libraries. The approximately 429 entries are listed alphabetically by main entry in 33 divisions, with the following of most interest to literature researchers: general catalogs of major research libraries; manuscripts, rare books, and book arts; anthropology, American Indians, and folklore; American West; Continental languages and literatures; English and American literature; African and black studies; women's studies; performing arts; and education and children's books. A majority of the entries are accompanied by annotations that describe the organization of a catalog, its library classification and subject indexing system, and special features. Two indexes: subjects; libraries. Although Nelson omits some important catalogs published before 1960 and includes a few serial bibliographies that are not library catalogs, it is the best guide to published library catalogs (most of which have been superseded by publicly accessible OPACs).

See also

> Secs. E: Libraries and Library Catalogs/Research Libraries/Guides to Collections and U: Literature-Related Topics and Sources/Bibliography and Textual Criticism/Guides to Scholarship/Serial Bibliographies.
> *ABELL* (G340): Bibliography/Book Production, Selling, Collecting, Librarianship, the Newspaper (with variations in the title) in the volumes for 1934 through 1972; Bibliography/Booksellers', Exhibition, and Sale Catalogues in the volumes for 1973 through 1984; and Bibliography/Collecting and the Library in the volumes for 1973 to the present.
> *MLAIB* (G335): See the headings Collection Study and Collections in the index to post-1980 volumes and the online Thesaurus.
> Taylor, *Book Catalogues: Their Varieties and Uses* (U5395).

Union Catalogs

Union catalogs are indispensable for identifying and locating copies of editions and translations of almost any book. Since entries reflect the cataloging practices of a variety of libraries, union catalogs generally include a number of ghosts and duplicate records for the same edition and must be used with care for verification of dates, titles, publishers, editions, or series. Although *WorldCat* (E225) and RLG Union Catalog (E230) are more efficient, accessible, and (for recent books) comprehensive sources than the *National Union Catalogs* (E235, E240, and E245), the following databases and printed catalogs are complementary research tools.

DATABASES

The following databases are designed for cataloging, interlibrary loan, serials control, acquisitions, and production of online catalogs by libraries, but their widespread availability through the World Wide Web offers researchers access to records of reported holdings of books, manuscripts, maps, audiovisual media, machine-readable data files, software, microforms, musical scores, serials, and sound recordings. The extensive coverage (which for works published after 1956 generally surpasses that of *NUC* [E240] and *NUC: Books* [E245]), variety of access points, continual updating of information, interlibrary loan subsystems, and general ease of use make *WorldCat* and RLG Union Catalog more efficient to search than the *NUCs*. Given the magnitude and versatility of the databases, no researcher can afford to ignore *WorldCat* or RLG Union Catalog, but users must remember that, despite the size of the databases, their coverage—especially of materials in languages other than English—becomes less thorough as one moves back in time.

E225   *WorldCat.* OCLC: Online Computer Library Center. Online. 20 Mar.
        2006 <http://www.firstsearch.org>. Updated daily. <http://
        www.oclc.org>.

A database whose several million records for books, e-books, journals, manuscripts, audio and video recordings, and software form the largest union catalog. Available through OCLC's FirstSearch service, *WorldCat* can be searched at three levels:

> Basic Search allows users to search keyword, author, title, ISBN, and date fields. Users should note that records are sorted by the number of libraries holding copies.
>
> Advanced Search allows users to search a combination of fields: keyword, access method (e.g., URL), accession number, author, language, type of material, notes, publisher, place of publication, ISBN, ISSN, subject, and title. For each of these fields, users can browse an index list. Searches can be limited by date, language, number of libraries holding a work, type of document, audience, content (e.g., fiction, musical score), format (e.g., manuscript, LP recording), and documents held by a particular library. Records can be sorted by number of libraries holding copies, relevance, date, or accession number (essential for users who run the same search at intervals and want to determine what has been newly added to the database). The default sort is number of libraries (usually the worst choice for a search that returns a large number of records); unfortunately, users wanting to change the default must do so during each search. Users who set up an account (click My Account) can both save searches and change sort options permanently for a session; the Options link and the Sort button also allow sorting by ascending or descending author, title, date, or number of libraries.
>
> Expert Search offers command-line searching of all records fields. Searches can be limited and records sorted the same as in Advanced Search.

WorldCat records typically indicate if the subscribing institution has the document in its collection and provide a link for requesting the item through interlibrary loan. Previous searches can be rerun or combined. Records can be marked for printing, e-mailing, or downloading as a text file or into bibliographic software. Researchers should avoid the public version of *WorldCat* (http://worldcat.org), which offers much less sophisticated search interfaces. Searches of this do not identify all editions of a work in the *WorldCat* database.

Because of differences in cataloging practices by contributors, several records for the same edition may appear in a list. *WorldCat* also includes Cataloging-in-Publication records for books that were never actually published.

WorldCat is an invaluable resource for literary and linguistic research: using it, a researcher can identify separately published works about a topic (and, increasingly, parts of books, thanks to the inclusion of tables of contents in many recently added records), by or about an author, by a publisher, or in a series and—depending on the reported holdings of cooperating libraries—can discover what libraries hold copies and can expedite interlibrary loan by using *WorldCat*'s ordering subsystem.

In addition to *WorldCat* FirstSearch also allows access to other databases, including *Alternative Press Index* (G400a), *Article First* (G400a), *Art Abstracts* (U5145a), *Art Index* (U5145), *Arts and Humanities Citation Index* (G365), *ATLA Religion Database* (U6350), *Biography Index* (J540), *Book Review Digest* (G415a), *Books in Print* (Q4225a), *ECO* (an archive of about 5,000 full-text journals since 1995), *Education Abstracts* (U5590a), *Education Index* (U5590a), *ERIC* (U5590), *Essay and General Literature Index* (G380),

Humanities Abstracts (G385a), *Humanities Index* (G385a), *MLAIB* (G335), *PapersFirst* (a bibliographic database of conference proceedings received by the British Library Document Supply Centre since 1993), *Periodical Abstracts* (G387a), *Philosopher's Index* (U6275), *PsycINFO* (U6530), *Readers' Guide Abstracts* (G400), *RILM Abstracts* (U6240), *Social Sciences Abstracts* (U6470), *Social Sciences Index* (U6470), and *Sociological Abstracts* (U6560). Access is through a version of the *WorldCat* interface that is adapted to the record fields of the individual database.

E230   RLG Union Catalog. Research Libraries Group (RLG). Online. 19 Mar.
        2006. (On 1 July 2006 RLG merged with OCLC [E225]; the RLG Union
        Catalog and some RLG databases have been merged into *WorldCat* or
        FirstSearch.)
   A union catalog of several million unique records representing the holdings of participating libraries or included in several special databases. Eureka, RLG's search interface, offers three levels of searching: the basic level allows author, title, subject, or keyword searches; Advanced Search lets users combine searches of author, title, subject, keyword, form and genre, ISBN, ISSN, LC card number, publisher, and record number and limit searches by date, language, and type of material; Command Line. In personal name searches, a comma must separate surname and forename. By clicking on Preferences, users can control how records are displayed, sorted (author, title, or date [descending]), and exported. Users can rerun or combine searches by clicking on Previous Searches. Because of differences in cataloging practices by contributors, several records for the same edition may appear in a list.
   Both RLG Union Catalog and *WorldCat* (E225) allow a researcher to identify separately published works about a topic, by or about an author, or in a series; to determine (depending on reported holdings) what libraries own a work; and to expedite interlibrary loan. Although coverage overall is not as extensive as WorldCat and the search options are not as flexible, RLG offers access to additional databases of particular importance to literature scholars:

   1. ArchiveGrid (http://archivegrid.org) contains more than one million records
      (as of early 2006), including those in *Location Register of English Literary Manuscripts and Letters: Eighteenth and Nineteenth Centuries* (M2227), the print version of *Location Register of Twentieth-Century English Literary Manuscripts and Letters* (M2765a), and those prepared since 1986 for the *National Union Catalog of Manuscript Collections* (F295).
   2. *English Short Title Catalogue* database (M1377). Users should note that the version available through RLG is outdated and does not transfer to FirstSearch.
   3. The Hand Press Book (HPB) file offers a union catalog of hand press books
      (c. 1455 to c. 1830) cataloged by members of the Consortium of European Research Libraries.
   4. SCIPIO: Art and Rare Book Sales Catalogs is a union catalog of auction catalogs issued by North American and European auction houses since 1599.

In addition, RLG offers access to *BHA: Bibliography of the History of Art* (U5138), *Chicano Database* (Q3973a), and *FRANCIS* (G345).

See also

   Copac (E250a)

PRINTED CATALOGS

E235   *National Union Catalog, Pre-1956 Imprints (NUC, Pre-56).* 754 vols.
        London: Mansell, 1968–81. Microfiche ed. Chicago: Amer. Lib. Assn.,
        1983.   Z881.A1 U518   021.6'4.
    An author catalog of reported holdings of the Library of Congress and about 1,000
other North American libraries. The majority of the 11,000,000 or so author entries
are for printed works, although some manuscripts, theses, and dissertations are listed.
Since entries reproduce catalog cards from many libraries, information ranges from
detailed analytic descriptions to truncated records, but each entry identifies at least one
library that owns an item. Users should keep the following points in mind:

1. A work can be located only by author, title for an anonymous publication, or
   (sometimes) editor for an anthology or collection; RLG Union Catalog
   (E230), *WorldCat* (E225), *Library of Congress Shelflist* (E260a), and *LC Subject
   Catalog* (E260a) provide subject access to some entries, and RLG Union Catalog, *WorldCat*, and *Cumulative Title Index to the Library of Congress Shelflist*
   (E260a) offer title access.
2. There are numerous errors and ghosts, particularly because a card that includes
   even a minor variation is frequently treated as representing an "edition."
3. Not all holdings of cooperating libraries are listed (e.g., works in non-Latin
   alphabets are included only if represented by a printed LC card).
4. Listings for prolific major authors are subclassified.
5. The supplement (vols. 686–754) corrects errors, provides the only adequate
   cross-references in the work, and records new titles, editions, and locations.
6. Additional locations are recorded in *National Union Catalog: Register of
   Additional Locations* (1963–96, microform only after the volumes for 1979
   [1980]).

    Unfortunately, the widespread availability of *WorldCat* and RLG Union Catalog
and the erroneous assumption that these two union catalogs include everything in *NUC,
Pre-56* have prompted many libraries to move their set into storage or deaccession it.
One study determined that 27.8% of the records in *NUC, Pre-56* were not in *WorldCat*
(Jeffrey Beall and Karen Kafadar, "The Proportion of NUC Pre-56 Titles Represented
in OCLC WorldCat," *College and Research Libraries* 66 [2005]: 431–35).
    For an account of the history and editing of the *NUC, Pre-56*, see David A. Smith,
"*The National Union Catalog, Pre-1956 Imprints,*" *Book Collector* 31 (1982): 445–62.
Continued by *National Union Catalog* (E240) and *NUC: Books* (E245).
    Libraries unable to afford *NUC, Pre-56* will probably have one or more of the
following:

> *Library of Congress and National Union Catalog Author Lists, 1942–1962: A
> Master Cumulation.* 152 vols. Detroit: Gale, 1969–71. (This work incorporates
> the following catalogs.)
> *A Catalog of Books Represented by Library of Congress Printed Cards Issued to July
> 31, 1942.* 167 vols. Ann Arbor: Edwards, 1942–46. *Supplement: Cards Issued
> August 1, 1942–December 31, 1947.* 42 vols. 1948.
> *Library of Congress Author Catalog: A Cumulative List of Works Represented by Library
> of Congress Printed Cards, 1948–52.* 24 vols. Ann Arbor: Edwards, 1953.
> *The National Union Catalog . . . 1953–57.* 28 vols. Ann Arbor: Edwards,
> 1958.

For comprehensive searches involving several works or editions by an author, begin with *NUC, Pre-56* and supplement its listings with *WorldCat* and RLG Union Catalog; for interlibrary loan requests or searches for a few specific works or editions, begin with the databases.

E240   *National Union Catalog: A Cumulative Author List Representing Library of*
        Congress Printed Cards and Titles Reported by Other American Libraries
        (*NUC*). Washington: Lib. of Congress, 1958–83. 9/yr., with quarterly,
        annual, and quinquennial cumulations.   Z881.A1 U372   018.1.

An author catalog that continues *NUC, Pre-56* (E235) for works published after 1956. Since a work is not listed until a cooperating library prepares a catalog card, a book published outside the United States may not be entered until several years after its publication date. Additional locations are recorded in *National Union Catalog: Register of Additional Locations* (1963–96, microform only after the volumes for 1979 [1980]). Continued by *NUC: Books* (E245).

Cumulative Title Index to the Library of Congress Shelflist (E260a), *WorldCat* (E225), and RLG Union Catalog (E230) offer title access to many works recorded in *NUC*; and *LC Subject Catalog* (E260a), RLG Union Catalog, *WorldCat*, and *Library of Congress Shelflist* (E260a) provide subject access to many listings. For author, title, or location searches, researchers will find *WorldCat* or RLG Union Catalog more efficient and generally more comprehensive than *NUC*.

E245   *NUC: Books.* Washington: Lib. of Congress, 1983–2002. Microfiche.
        Published in five parts: *Register,* monthly; *Name Index, Title Index, Series*
        Index, Subject Index, quarterly, with annual and larger cumulations. *NUC:*
        US Books extracts records for books published in the United States.

A continuation of the *National Union Catalog* (E240). The *Register*—to which the other four parts are keyed—lists books by *NUC* number and is the only part that records full cataloging information. For locations other than the library that contributed the record, users must consult *National Union Catalog: Register of Additional Locations* (1963–96, microform only after the volumes for 1979 [1980]). The other parts are alphabetical indexes to the *Register* and, except for the *Subject Index,* print abbreviated entries. Although the four indexes remedy access problems that plague users of the earlier *NUCs,* they are time-consuming to search because of the necessity of consulting the numerically arranged *Register* and *Register of Additional Locations* for full cataloging and locations. Users would be better served if each index printed complete information and locations. Literary researchers will find *WorldCat* (E225) and RLG Union Catalog (E230) more efficient to use and generally more comprehensive than *NUC: Books,* especially beginning in 1990, when records were no longer included from *WorldCat,* RLG Union Catalog, and Western Library Network.

See also

New Serial Titles (K640).
Serials in the British Library (K645).

Catalogs of National Libraries

Because of copyright deposit privileges and the magnitude and quality of their general collections, which transcend national boundaries, the major national libraries are among the great research centers. Their catalogs—many of which are available online—are essential complements to the union catalogs.

E250   *British Library Integrated Catalogue.* British Library. Online. 19 Mar. 2006
        <http://catalogue.bl.uk>.
A catalog of the majority of the printed books and periodicals held by the British Library that, for the most part, supersedes an unwieldy array of printed catalogs that were frequently difficult to search by anyone unfamiliar with the complex British Library cataloging rules. The main page of the *Catalogue* Web site lists materials not included; for manuscripts, see *British Library Manuscripts Catalogue* (F300). Basic Search allows keyword searches of author, title, date, publisher, subject, LC subject heading, ISSN, ISBN, or British Library shelfmark. Advanced Search allows users to combine the preceding fields (along with ones for place of publication, type of work, and notes) and to limit a search by language, date, or type of work. Users can also browse most fields and search subsets of the *Catalogue.*

Those interested in the origin and evolution of the printed *General Catalogue of Printed Books* and its bewildering cataloging rules should consult A. H. Chaplin, *GK: 150 Years of the General Catalogue of Printed Books in the British Museum* (Aldershot: Scolar, 1987, 177 pp.). Researchers using specialized collections should consult the Collections page at the British Library Web site (http://www.bl.uk/collections/listings .html).

Because of the British Library's extensive holdings, the *British Library Integrated Catalogue* is an invaluable source for identifying works by and about authors and allows readers to request copies in advance. Anyone not holding a current reader's pass must read Applying for a Reader's Pass (click on Information on Using Our Reading Rooms).

Holdings of the British Library can also be searched through *Copac* (http:// copac.ac.uk), a union catalog of 24 university libraries in the United Kingdom and the national libraries of Scotland and Wales.

E255   *Catalogs de la BnF.* Bibliothèque Nationale. Online. 19 Mar. 2006 <http://
        www.bnf.fr/pages/catalogues.htm>. Updated weekly. The online catalogs of
        the Bibliothèque Nationale (BN) relieve researchers from having to consult
        a bewildering array of printed catalogs (listed in part at the library's Web
        site).
        BN-OPALE PLUS includes books, periodicals, and some other materials.
        BN-OPALINE includes manuscripts and other specialized collections.

The catalogs of the Bibliothèque Nationale, whose extensive collections of French publications (including translations of British and American works) along with important holdings in other national literatures rank it among the great research libraries. Recherche Simple allows users to restrict an author, title, or subject search by type of document. Recherche Avancée allows searchers to combine fields (author, title, subject, Dewey Decimal number, imprint, performance place, ISSN, and ISBN) and limit searches by date, language, country, city, and collection. Recherche Experte adds fields for artistic collaborator, participant, other standard numbers and provides subfields for some fields (e.g., title), but otherwise it offers the same access as Recherche Avancée.

Anyone finding it necessary to consult the printed catalogs should first read Annick Bernard, *Guide de l'utilisateur des catalogues des livres imprimés de la Bibliothèque Nationale* (Paris: Chadwyck-Healey France, 1986, 60 pp.).

E260   *Library of Congress Online Catalog.* Online. 19 Mar. 2006 <http://
        catalog.loc.gov>. Updated daily.

A catalog of the print, multimedia, manuscript, and electronic resources held by the Library of Congress.

In Basic Search users can search by title, keyword, standard number (LC card number, ISBN, ISSN), author, call number, or series title. Guided Search allows searchers to combine two fields: all those in Basic Search plus publication information, notes, and credits or performers. Clicking Set Search Limits allows users to limit searches by date, language, type of work, LC collection, and place of publication. (Users should note that these limits can be set in Basic Search only for title, keyword, or standard number searches and that the limits apply to searches in a session until cleared by the user.) When viewing records, users should note where to request a copy (see the "Request in:" line) and remember that holdings information for older records (especially for journals) is not complete.

Public access to the LC online catalog relieves researchers from tedious searches through generally inadequate print records of holdings:

> *Main Catalog of the Library of Congress: Titles Cataloged through December 1980.* München: Saur, 1984–89. Microfiche. A reproduction of the author, title, and subject cards for works cataloged by the Library of Congress between c. 1898 and 1980.
>
> *Library of Congress Shelflist* (*LC Shelflist*). Ann Arbor: Univ. Microfilms Int. 1979. *Supplement, 1978–79.* 1980. Microfiche. Since the *Shelflist* reproduces Library of Congress catalog cards by LC classification number, it offers broad subject access to many works listed in *NUC, Pre-56* (E235) and *National Union Catalog* (E240). Users should be aware that some changes in the classification schedule have resulted in the separation or juxtaposition of subjects in the shelflist. Linda K. Hamilton, ed., *The Library of Congress Shelflist: A User's Guide to the Microfiche Edition,* 2 vols. (Ann Arbor: Univ. Microfilms Int. 1979), provides a basic introduction to the use of the shelflist.
>
> *Cumulative Title Index to the Library of Congress Shelflist: A Combined Listing of the MARC and REMARC Databases through 1981.* 158 vols. Arlington: Carrollton, 1983. Also available on microfiche. A title list of works cataloged by the Library of Congress through 1981.
>
> *Library of Congress Catalogs: Subject Catalog* (*LC Subject Catalog*). Washington: Lib. of Congress, 1950–83. Quarterly, with annual and quinquennial cumulations. Former title: *Library of Congress Catalog: Books: Subjects.* Continued by *NUC: Books: LC Subject Index* (E245).

Anyone using the Library of Congress for the first time should peruse the Library of Congress Researchers page (http://www.loc.gov/rr), especially the Preparing for Your Visit and Hold, Reserve Services links.

F

Guides to Manuscripts and Archives

Guides to manuscripts and archives are essential sources for identifying collections of manuscripts and locating specific manuscripts.

This section includes general works on manuscripts and archives, as well as guides, catalogs, and other finding aids that cover two or more national literatures. Works limited to a single national literature appear under the "Manuscripts" heading in appropriate sections in this *Guide*.

For additional works see Marcuse, *Reference Guide for English Studies* (B90), pp. 119–35.

Research Methods

F275   Thorpe, James. *The Use of Manuscripts in Literary Research: Problems of Access and Literary Property Rights*. 2nd ed. New York: MLA, 1979. 40 pp. Z692.M28 T47   026′.091.

An introduction to locating, gaining access to, and obtaining permission to publish manuscripts. Beginning with the essential but frequently unheeded dictum that "much work should precede any effort to use manuscript materials," Thorpe offers practical advice on locating manuscripts, corresponding with libraries, preparing to visit a collection, approaching a private collector, gaining admittance to a collection (with a survey of common regulations and courtesies), obtaining photocopies (with notes on typical and atypical restrictions), acquiring permission to publish, and understanding literary property rights (principally in the United States). Although it cites some outdated sources, the work is essential preliminary reading for anyone who needs to consult manuscripts in public or private hands.

Guides to Repositories and Archives

F280   *ArchivesUSA.* UMI-ProQuest. Online. 17 Mar. 2006 <http://archives
.chadwyck.com>. Updated regularly. (Selected records can be searched
through *C19: The Nineteenth Century Index* [M2466].)
   Consists of:

> A guide to 5,596 archives and repositories that hold manuscripts (including microfilms of originals in foreign or private collections), photographs, sound recordings, films, drawings, and other materials. Entries include address and telephone number; e-mail address and URL; information on access; statistics on holdings; a brief general description of the collection; and references to catalogs, guides, or descriptions.
> Records from *NUCMC* (F295) and the *Index to Personal Names* (F295a) and *Index to Subjects and Corporate Names* (F295a).
> Records from *National Inventory of Documentary Sources in the United States* (*NIDS*; Ann Arbor: UMI, 1982–).
> Records submitted directly by repositories.
> Links to online finding aids.

   Repositories can be searched by name, location (city or state), and holdings keyword. Collections can be searched by keyword, collection name, repository name, repository location (city or state), *NIDS* number, *NUCMC* number, and date; searches can be limited to *NIDS* records, *NUCMC* records, or submitted records.
   Since this is a guide to repositories and archives, holdings are described in general terms; however, researchers will find the work an essential source for identifying institutions that might own manuscripts related to an author or a subject. Review: Sarah Spurgin Witte, *College and Research Libraries* 59 (1998): 179–81.
   Although now largely superseded by *ArchivesUSA, Directory of Archives and Manuscript Repositories in the United States,* 2nd ed. (Phoenix: Oryx, 1988, 853 pp.) and Philip M. Hamer, ed., *A Guide to Archives and Manuscripts in the United States* (New Haven: Yale UP, 1961, 775 pp.) — the original version of the *Directory* containing fuller descriptions of holdings — remain useful for information about institutions that did not return a questionnaire for *ArchivesUSA.*

F283   Foster, Janet, and Julia Sheppard, eds. *British Archives: A Guide to Archive
Resources in the United Kingdom.* 4th ed. Basingstoke: Palgrave, 2002.
      815 pp.   CD1040.F67   027.541.
   A guide to the archival holdings, as of late 2001, of British record offices, libraries, public and private institutions, associations, businesses, and societies. Organized alphabetically by town, then by repository name, entries typically provide address, phone and fax numbers, e-mail addresses, Web site, and contact person; hours of operation and details of any restrictions on access; a brief history of the organization or repository; an overview of acquisitions policies, archival holdings, major collections, and important nonmanuscript holdings; a list of finding aids and publications about the repository or holdings; and information on available facilities (e.g., photocopying). Since entries are

based on responses to a questionnaire, descriptions, especially of holdings and collections, inevitably vary in thoroughness and specificity. Concludes with three appendixes: organizations whose archives are deposited elsewhere; organizations without archives; and organizations on whose archives the editors could supply no information. Two indexes: repository names, organizations, and collections; subjects (derived from a checklist sent to repositories). Although reflecting the shortcomings attendant upon any guide necessarily dependent on questionnaires, *British Archives* offers a wealth of information and is the essential starting place for identifying repositories and archival collections in the British Isles.

More current information about hours, contact information (including e-mail address and Web site URL), access policy, and location (some entries link to a digital streetmap)—as well as links to National Register of Archives (F285a) resources for an archive—can be found at the Historical Manuscripts Commission ARCHON Directory (http://www.nationalarchives.gov.uk/archon/).

F285   The National Archives. Kew, Richmond, Surrey. 19 Mar. 2006 <http://www.nationalarchives.gov.uk>.

A repository of government, legal, institutional, and family records and manuscripts associated with the United Kingdom or relating to British history from the eleventh century to the present. The National Archives was formed in April 2003 by amalgamating the Public Record Office (PRO) and the Royal Commission on Historical Manuscripts.

With its extensive holdings of governmental, political, civil, legal, and ecclesiastical records, the National Archives is an essential and sometimes lengthy stop for many literary biographers. In advance of any visit, researchers can save valuable time by consulting the institution's informative Web site, where they can:

1. find current information for readers (click on the Visit Us tab for valuable advice on planning a visit and instructions on preregistering for the required reader's ticket);
2. receive valuable guidance for the researcher new to the National Archives (path: Getting Started/Academic Research);
3. learn about the nature and organization of the classes of records they need to consult (an essential prelude to searching the catalog effectively) and identify any published or digital transcripts and finding aids (path: Search Our Collections/The Catalogue/Research Guides: A to Z);
4. search the online catalog and request documents in advance;
5. search other catalogs (especially the National Register of Archives and ARCHON [a directory of other repositories in the United Kingdom]).

For an illuminating discussion of the public records as a source of literary texts and biographical information, see A. D. Harvey, "The Public Record Office in London as a Source for English Literary Studies," *Etudes anglaises* 43 (1990): 303–16. For an introduction to the investigation of suits in the Court of Exchequer (and their heretofore-unrecognized value to literary researchers and biographers), see Judith Milhous and Robert D. Hume, "Eighteenth-Century Equity Lawsuits in the Court of Exchequer as a Source for Historical Research," *Historical Research* 70 (1997): 231–46.

Although now subsumed in the National Archives, the Royal Commission on Historical Manuscripts (Historical Manuscripts Commission; HMC) has published (since 1870) an important but bewildering array of reports, appendixes, calendars, and editions of collections that are not available in electronic form. The best conspectus of these publications is offered by Mullins, *Texts and Calendars* (M1375), and Mortimer, *Texts and Calendars* (M1375). In addition, four guides broadly index places and persons mentioned in documents described or calendared in published volumes:

> *A Guide to Reports on Collections of Manuscripts of Private Families, Corporations, and Institutions in Great Britain and Ireland.* Pt. 1: Topographical. London: HMSO, 1914. 233 pp.
>
> *Guide to the Reports of the Royal Commission on Historical Manuscripts, 1870– 1911.* Pt. 2: *Index of Persons.* Ed. Francis Bickley. 2 vols. 1935–38.
>
> *Guide to the Reports of the Royal Commission on Historical Manuscripts, 1911– 1957.* Pt. 1: *Index of Places.* Ed. A. C. S. Hall. 1973. 536 pp.
>
> *Guide to the Reports of the Royal Commission on Historical Manuscripts, 1911– 1957.* Pt. 2: *Index of Persons.* Ed. Hall. 3 vols. 1966.

Users must remember that these works are only general indexes and not cumulations of indexes in individual volumes. The reports on collections range from hastily prepared brief descriptions in haphazard order to full calendars that carefully transcribe entire documents or generous extracts. Although varying widely in accuracy and thoroughness, the guides and reports provide the best access to important private collections (some of which are now in public repositories), and many preserve the only record of documents subsequently destroyed, lost, or inaccessible to researchers. For current locations, researchers should consult *Guide to the Location of Collections Described in the Reports and Calendars Series, 1870–1980,* Guides to Sources for British History 3 (London: HMSO, 1982, 69 pp.).

In 1945 the Royal Commission on Historical Manuscripts established the National Register of Archives (NRA) to collect and index lists and reports of private collections. These finding aids, which vary considerably in detail and sophistication, can be identified through the NRA catalog at the National Archives Web site (users should note that the catalog includes only the finding aids and not the collections' contents). For a description of the National Register of Archives and accessibility to its holdings, see Dick Sargent, ed., "The National Register of Archives," *The National Register of Archives: An International Perspective,* (London: U of London, Inst. of Historical Research, 1995) 1–43.

F290   *Guide to Federal Records in the National Archives of the United States.* Online. National Archives. 15 Mar. 2006 <http://www.archives.gov/ research/guide-fed-records/index.html>. Regularly updated. An online, updated version of *Guide to Federal Records in the National Archives of the United States.* Comp. Robert B. Matchette. 3 vols. Washington: Natl. Archives and Records Administration, 1995.

A descriptive guide to governmental and other records under the jurisdiction of the National Archives. This excludes material held in presidential libraries. Organized by record group (i.e., government agency), the brief entry for each group or class of records typically includes a descriptive title, inclusive dates, quantity, location, notes (on content, type or purpose of documents, completeness, or organization), and finding aids. Each agency or department is prefaced by a description of the history, administration, organization, or other details necessary to understanding the nature of its records. Indexed by names, organizations, and subjects. The text can be searched by keyword or browsed by the index or record group number. Accessions and the opening of records are reported in *Prologue: Quarterly of the National Archives and Records Administration* (1969– , quarterly), which also prints articles on holdings; in the *Record: News from the National Archives and Records Administration* (1994–98, 5/yr.); and at http://www.archives.gov/research/accessions/index.html. The bulk of this massive accumulation of documents relates to administrative matters, but there is considerable material on individuals that is too rarely explored by literary biographers. Although lacking the tradition of important discoveries made in the Public Record Office and thus not as well known to literary researchers, the National Archives repositories are an obligatory stop for biographers of writers associated with the federal government, whether by election, through employment, or under surveillance.

The *Guide to Federal Records in the National Archives of the United States* is gradually being replaced by *Archival Research Catalog* (*ARC*) (http://www.archives.gov/research/arc).

Prucha, *Handbook for Research in American History* (Q3185a), has a useful overview of the National Archives, and Sears, *Using Government Information Sources, Electronic and Print* (Q3190), outlines strategies for searching National Archives materials.

See also

Sec. E: Libraries and Library Catalogs/Research Libraries/Guides to Libraries.
Albinski, "Guide to the Archives of Publishers, Journals, and Literary Agents in North American Libraries" (U5242).
Brodersen, *A Guide to Book Publishers' Archives* (U5242a).
Canadian Publishers' Records database (U5242a).
Fraser, *Children's Authors and Illustrators* (U5465).
Schatz, *Directory of Afro-American Resources* (Q3730).
Weedon, *British Book Trade Archives, 1830–1939* (U5243).

Guides to Collections

Bibliographies and Guides

F293   *Guides to Archives and Manuscript Collections in the United States.* Comp.
         Donald L. DeWitt. Bibliographies and Indexes in Library and Information
         Science 8. Westport: Greenwood, 1994. 478 pp.   CD3022.A2 D48
         016.973.

An annotated bibliography of separately published finding aids (through c. 1990) to collections of unpublished materials (including archives and collections of maps, photographs, oral histories, and films) held in repositories in the United States. Unfortunately, coverage excludes journal articles, exhibition catalogs, accession reports, discussions of individual documents, dissertations, dictionary catalogs (except those incorporating unpublished materials), and "indexes to large collections or bodies of records." Guides to foreign repositories are included if they "describe records or papers relating specifically to United States history." Entries are listed alphabetically by author, editor, or compiler in classified divisions for general collections, business collections, collections on ethnic minorities and women, federal archives, fine arts collections (with a section for drama, theater, and motion pictures), literary collections, military collections, political collections, collections of professional groups and organizations, regional collections, collections of religious groups, foreign repositories holding records related to the United States, and United States repositories of foreign records and manuscripts. The literary collections division records bibliographies, indexes, calendars, catalogs, checklists, and other guides to the papers of authors (United States and foreign). The brief annotations typically describe content and organization. and indicate whether the work is indexed. Indexed by persons and subjects. Because of the unfortunate exclusion of journal articles, exhibition catalogs, electronic resources, and unpublished finding aids (frequently the most valuable guides to archival material), *Guides to Archives* is merely a preliminary resource for identifying frequently elusive and locally produced finding aids to collections of an author's papers or to collections on literary subjects. Review: Carole Elizabeth Nowicke, *Library Quarterly* 65 (1995): 134–35.

The exclusion of periodical articles is remedied by DeWitt, comp., *Articles Describing Archives and Manuscript Collections in the United States: An Annotated Bibliography*, Bibliographies and Indexes in Library and Information Science 11 (Westport: Greenwood, 1997, 458 pp.), with coverage extending to the mid-1990s.

Union Catalogs

F295   *National Union Catalog of Manuscript Collections* (*NUCMC*). Library of Congress. Online. 22 Mar. 2007 <http://www.loc.gov/coll/nucmc>. Updated daily.

   Library of Congress National Union Catalog of Manuscript Collections (*NUCMC*). 29 vols. Washington: Lib. of Congress, 1962–94. Former title: *National Union Catalog of Manuscript Collections* (1962–85). Z6620.U5 N3.

A union catalog of collections of manuscripts held in public or quasi-public libraries, archives, historical societies, museums, and other institutions in the United States. Users must remember that *NUCMC* is not a catalog of individual manuscripts (although a few exceptions are made for important items) but of collections of papers formed about an individual, subject, or organization or by an individual, group, or institution. Although the collections encompass many periods and countries, the bulk of them are of English-language materials. Along with original manuscripts, transcripts, photocopies, microforms, facsimiles, and transcripts of sound recordings are included. A typical entry includes person, family, organization, or collector who formed the collection or is its focus; collection title; physical description in linear feet or number of items; repository; location of original manuscripts if the collection consists of copies; description of scope and content, mentioning principal subjects and individuals (including sometimes the writers and recipients of letters); and notes on restrictions, provenance, and available descriptions, catalogs, indexes, or calendars. Entries for some extensive collections merely refer users to published finding aids. The best access is offered by *ArchivesUSA* (F280), which includes all *NUCMC* records, and by the RLG ArchiveGrid database (E230a), which includes records since 1986 and which can be accessed for free through the *NUCMC* Web site.

Those who must consult the printed *NUCMC* should note that it is indexed by persons, places, and subjects in each volume; there are cumulative indexes for volumes covering 1959–62, 1963–66, 1967–69, 1970–74, 1975–79, 1980–84, 1986–90, and 1991–93 (the volume for 1985 is not included in the cumulative indexes). Scholars searching for manuscripts by or about individuals should begin with *Index to Personal Names in the* National Union Catalog of Manuscript Collections*, 1959–1984*, 2 vols. (Alexandria: Chadwyck-Healey, 1988); subject access is offered by *Index to Subjects and Corporate Names in the* National Union Catalog of Manuscript Collections*, 1959–1984*, 3 vols. (1994); both incorporate numerous corrections and additions to the interim indexes.

Prepared from reports, indexes, and other sources, the entries vary considerably in detail, sophistication, and accuracy. Inevitably, the length of many descriptions is disproportionate to their content. Although collections at numerous major repositories are either omitted or incompletely reported, the breadth of coverage—especially of little-known or uncataloged collections—makes *NUCMC* one of the indispensable sources for locating manuscripts and letters by (and sometimes about) authors and literary-related subjects.

See also

> *Archives Canada* (R4590).
> *Union List of Manuscripts in Canadian Repositories* (R4590a).

Catalogs of Major Collections

F300   *British Library Manuscripts Catalogue.* British Library. Online. 15 Mar. 2006
         <http://molcat.bl.uk>. Typically updated every six months.
A catalog of accessions in Western languages since 1753 in the Department of Manuscripts, British Library, the single most important collection of literary manuscripts. Created by scanning print indexes and incorporating recent cataloging entries, the *Manuscripts Catalogue* is very much a work-in-progress that is subject to continual editing. (For the current status of the conversion of printed indexes to the online catalog, see "About the *Manuscripts Catalogue*" at the *Catalogue* Web site [click About].) Users should note that the indexes and descriptions have separate search screens (be sure to consult Search Tips for an explanation of the search descriptors for the index screen). Although edited for consistency and corrected as much as possible, the entries reflect the variations in accuracy, thoroughness, and cataloging practices of their sources; in addition, scanning of catalogs with poor print quality has introduced errors.
Until all of the printed catalogs are incorporated, researchers may have to consult the following:

> *Index of Manuscripts in the British Library.* 10 vols. Cambridge: Chadwyck-Healey, 1984–86. A person and place index to manuscripts acquired through 1950 by the British Library Department of Manuscripts. The *Index* is an amalgamation of the indexes in the printed catalogs and unprinted working indexes as well as of cards for collections first indexed herein.
>
> *"Rough Register" of Acquisitions of the Department of Manuscripts, British Library, 1961–1965.* List and Index Society Special Series 7. London: Swift, 1974, 172 pp. *1966–1970.* List and Index Society Special Series 8. 1975, n. pag.; *1971–1975.* List and Index Society Special Series 10. 1977, 246 pp. *1976–1980.* List and Index Society Special Series 15. 1982, 242 pp. Lists manuscripts acquired since 1960.
>
> *Catalogue of Additions to the Manuscripts [1756–]: Additional Manuscripts [4104–].* London: British Lib., 1843– . The individual volumes vary in cataloging practices, accuracy, and thoroughness, but recent ones provide full descriptions of individual documents and summary descriptions of larger archives (some of which will eventually have their own catalogs); revisions are stored in electronic form, and details are available on inquiry.

For a description of the collection of plays submitted to the lord chamberlain, see entry M1540.

Recent acquisitions are listed or described in various handlists and loose-leaf catalogs in the Department of Manuscripts. The most current guide to the catalogs and other finding aids (especially for manuscripts acquired after 1950) is M. A. E. Nickson, *The British Library: Guide to the Catalogues and Indexes of the Department of Manuscripts*, 3rd ed., rev. J. Conway (London: British Lib., 1998, 24 pp.); Alston, comp., *Handlist of Unpublished Finding Aids to the London Collections of the British Library* (E250a), identifies a few additional lists. Somewhat fuller descriptions are in T. C. Skeat, *The Catalogues of the Manuscript Collections, The British Museum*, rev. ed. (London: British Museum, 1962, 45 pp.).

Other catalogs of significant collections include the following:

> *Catalogue of Manuscripts in the Houghton Library, Harvard University.* 8 vols. Alexandria: Chadwyck-Healey, 1986–87. Covers acquisitions as of April 1985. Many finding aids for individual collections are accessible through OASIS (http://oasis.harvard.edu/oasis/deliver/advancedsearch?_collection=oasis).
>
> Madan, Falconer, et al. *A Summary Catalogue of Western Manuscripts in the Bodleian Library at Oxford.* 7 vols. Oxford: Clarendon–Oxford UP, 1895–1953. To sort out the various catalogs and classification schemes, users must consult vol. 1, which also includes lists of current and obsolete shelf marks. Two indexes in vol. 7: persons, places, some subjects; owners.
>
> Clapinson, Mary, and T. D. Rogers. *Summary Catalogue of Post-medieval Western Manuscripts in the Bodleian Library, Oxford: Acquisitions 1916–1975 (SC 37300–55936).* 3 vols. Oxford: Clarendon–Oxford UP, 1991. A continuation of Madan (see above). Five indexes in vol. 3: persons and places mentioned in manuscripts; owners and donors; manuscripts owned by Sir Thomas Phillipps; auctioneers and booksellers; binders. Details of additional catalogs can be found at the Department of Special Collections and Western Manuscripts Web site (http://www.bodley.ox.ac.uk/dept/scwmss/wmss/wmss.htm#cats).

See also

> Sec. E: Libraries and Library Catalogs/Research Libraries.
> Crum, *First-Line Index of English Poetry, 1500–1800, in Manuscripts of the Bodleian Library* (M1590).

General Indexes

F305   Schoenberg, Lawrence J. *Schoenberg Database of Manuscripts.* Online. 26 July 2006 <http://dewey.library.upenn.edu/sceti/sdm/index.cfm>. Updated regularly.

A database of c. 75,000 manuscripts (as of early 2006) of at least five leaves written between 1200 BC and 1600 AD and included in the catalogs of more than 400 auction houses and book dealers since 1800. The amount of information in a record depends on the catalog description: a full record includes author, title, comments, provenance (which can include the current owner), artist, date of creation, number of folios (as well as lines and columns), historiated and illuminated initials, miniatures, language, place of composition, dimensions, material (i.e., paper or vellum), liturgical use, seller, catalog, lot number, date of catalog, price, and record number. Records, which can be searched by a combination of the preceding fields, can be sorted by record number, author, title, date of composition, seller, artist, or language. In addition, records can be browsed by author, seller, provenance, or seller and catalog list. An important resource that is making accessible data buried in thousands of catalogs, Schoenberg is an essential tool for locating manuscripts, tracing their provenance, reconstructing collections, and studying social and economic aspects of the manuscript trade.

See

> *American Book Prices Current* (U5415).
> *Book Auction Records* (U5420).

G

Serial Bibliographies, Indexes, and Abstracts

Serial bibliographies, indexes, and abstracts (print and electronic) that are published or updated at regular intervals are important resources for literature and language scholars since they guide researchers to the most recent scholarship. At the first stage of a project, researchers should identify the pertinent serial bibliographies, indexes, and abstracts; become thoroughly familiar with their scope, limitations, taxonomy, and record structure; master the advanced search interface (especially any strategy that allows identification of records added since a previous search); and plan to search each at intervals. The best of the electronic resources allow users to save searches for running at regular intervals and offer an alert service that generates e-mail notices when new records related to a search are added. Unfortunately, many specialized serial bibliographies and indexes have been discontinued during the last decade because of financial constraints, the inability to move from print to electronic form, or the unfounded assumption that the presence of such electronic bibliographical behemoths as *WorldCat* (E225) or *MLAIB* (G335) and Internet search engines have rendered more specialized bibliographies obsolete.

This section includes works covering more than one national literature or discipline. Works devoted to a single national literature or subject appear in appropriate sections of the *Guide*. Although there is considerable overlapping among the following sources, each — because of its scope, organization, or indexing features — cites studies omitted from or not readily accessible in the others. (The extent of duplication in literature serial bibliographies has never been satisfactorily established. The existing studies are based on seriously flawed methodologies and an inadequate grasp of the scope, editorial principles, and taxonomies of the major bibliographies. See, for example, Lewis Sawin, "The Integrated Bibliography for English Studies: Plan and Project," *Pennsylvania Library Association Bulletin* 19 [1964]: 7–19; Abigail A. Loomis, "Dickens Duplications: A Study of Overlap in Serial Bibliographies in Literature," *RQ* 25 [1986]: 348–55.)

Bibliographies of Bibliographies

G325   Wortman, William A. *A Guide to Serial Bibliographies for Modern Literatures.* 2nd ed. New York: MLA, 1995. 333 pp.   Z6519.W67 [PN695]   016.805.

A guide to serial bibliographies published separately or in journals (generally excluding those that ceased publication before c. 1960). Organized in divisions for comprehensive bibliographies and general indexes, literatures in English, non-English literatures, subjects, and authors, the 777 titles include bibliographies for periods, genres, subjects, themes, and literature-related topics (such as psychology, music, art, and religion). Many sections are preceded by a helpful evaluative overview. A typical annotation briefly describes basic organization and scope (users should note that Wortman uses the term *comprehensive* in reference to breadth of coverage rather than thoroughness [see p. 6]), but discontinued bibliographies are not always identified. Additions and corrections are listed at http://adler.lib.muohio.edu/serial-bibliographies. Wortman is the best source for identifying specialized serial bibliographies that are frequently more extensive in coverage than—or at least essential supplements to—comparable parts of standard general works such as *MLAIB* (G335) and *ABELL* (G340).

Bibliographic Index (D145) lists new serial bibliographies as well as a number of discontinued ones omitted by Wortman. Richard A. Gray, comp., *Serial Bibliographies in the Humanities and Social Sciences* (Ann Arbor: Pierian, 1969, 345 pp.), covers philosophy, religion, the social sciences, language, the arts, history, and literature, but is now outdated.

G327   Balay, Robert. *Early Periodical Indexes: Bibliographies and Indexes of Literature Published in Periodicals before 1900.* Lanham: Scarecrow, 2000. 315 pp.   Z6941.B35 [PN4801]   011'.34.

An annotated bibliography of approximately 400 indexes and bibliographies, print and electronic and dating from 1790 to 1999, that index periodicals published before 1900. The scope is international, but resources in Western European languages predominate. Entries are organized in six divisions: general works, humanities (with sections on language and literature), history and area studies, social and behavioral sciences, science and technology, and library and information sciences. Annotations fully describe scope, content, and organization; establish the relation to other resources; and are exacting in evaluations. Four indexes: authors; titles; subjects; dates of coverage. Drawing on the author's extensive experience as a reference librarian who frequently dealt with the vexing question of how to identify the contents of periodicals before 1900, *Early Periodical Indexes* is an invaluable guide.

Serial Bibliographies

Surveys of Research

Surveys of research are important resources for keeping abreast of scholarship on a national literature, literary period, genre, or author. Over the long term, such surveys are valuable for tracing fluctuations in the academic reputation of an author, work, critical approach, or theory. The best are judiciously evaluative essays by established scholars who place a study within a critical tradition; the worst are strings of uncritical descriptions of whatever came the reviewer's way.

G330   *Year's Work in English Studies (YWES)*. Oxford: Oxford Journals–Oxford
        UP for the English Assn., 1921– . Annual.   PE58.E6   820.9. Oxford
        UP. Online. 28 Aug. 2006 <http://ywes.oxfordjournals.org>. Updated
        regularly.
        A selective, evaluative review of scholarship on English, American, and some other literatures in English. Coverage of American literature began in vol. 35 (for 1954); a chapter on African, Caribbean, and Canadian literature in English was added in vol. 63 (for 1982) and expanded to include Australian, New Zealand, and Indian literature in vol. 64 (for 1983) and South Pacific literature in vol. 81 (2000). African literature disappears from the chapter in vol. 81 (for 2000). Each volume is organized by individual essays devoted to periods, national literatures, major authors (Chaucer, Shakespeare, Milton), the English language, and bibliography and textual criticism. Some volumes include chapters on reference works, literary history, and literary theory (with coverage of the last now relegated to *Year's Work in Critical and Cultural Theory* [U6133]). The scope of some chapters varies over the years.
        Coverage is necessarily selective (sometimes erratic, idiosyncratic, or restricted because of the unavailability of works) and emphasizes Anglo-American scholarship. The quality, objectivity, rigor of evaluation, and breadth of individual chapters vary, depending on the contributor(s), but most attempt to evaluate judiciously the most significant scholarship. To offer representative coverage of the steadily increasing number of studies, contributors in recent volumes tend to be more succinct in discussing an individual work. Citations to books and articles do not include complete bibliographical information until vol. 68 (for 1987). A volume now appears about three years after the year of scholarship it covers; the classified list of books received for future review lasted only from vol. 64 (for 1983) through vol. 73 (for 1992). The online version, which includes all volumes, publishes chapters as they are edited and typeset. Two indexes: critics; subjects and literary authors. Since vol. 47 (for 1966) the subject indexing has been more detailed and includes titles of literary works.
        Chapters have been reproduced in three collections (published in 1998 by Blackwell [Oxford] for the English Assn.): *A Critical Bibliography of American Literature Studies*, 4 vols. (covering 1964–94); *A Critical Bibliography of Twentieth-Century Literature Studies*, 4 vols. (covering 1964–94); and *A Critical Bibliography of English Language Studies*, 3 vols. (covering 1939–94). Other than convenience, the only value of the series is that each *Critical Bibliography* is cumulatively indexed.
        Because it offers the most comprehensive evaluative survey of important studies, *YWES* can be an invaluable guide to significant scholarship (particularly in English literature; *American Literary Scholarship* [Q3265] provides more exhaustive coverage of American literature). In vols. 66–69 (for 1985–88), the year's best books and articles

are identified in a separate list. Together, the annual volumes offer an incomparable record of scholarly and critical trends as well as of the fluctuations of academic reputations of literary works and authors.

Literature Bibliographies

G335   *MLA International Bibliography of Books and Articles on the Modern Languages and Literatures* (*MLAIB*; sometimes called *PMLA Bibliography*). New York: MLA, 1922– . Annual.   Z7006.M64   016.8. Mod. Lang. Assn. Online. 7 Mar. 2006 <http://www.mla.org>. Updated ten times per year.

A classified bibliography of literary, linguistic, and folklore scholarship published in print or electronically throughout the world. Its scope is extensive: *all* human languages (living and dead) and many invented ones; *all* literatures (except classical Greek and Latin, which are covered in *L'année philologique* [S4890]); *all* aspects of folklore; and, beginning in the volume for 2000, rhetoric and composition and the teaching of all aspects of language and literature. Although many bibliographies listed in this *Guide* offer more exhaustive coverage of a single literature, period, genre, or subject, many achieve their superiority by relying heavily on the *MLAIB*, and none approaches its breadth and few its currency.

Effective use of the *Bibliography* requires close familiarity with the many alterations over the years in editorial policy, scope, and organization. Because of the extensive changes instituted with the 1981 *Bibliography* and the general similarity of the organization of the earlier volumes, a separate consideration of the two periods is appropriate.

MLAIB for 1921–80. Originally titled the "American Bibliography," published in essay format, nominally limited to scholarship by Americans, and covering English, Romance, Germanic, and American languages and literatures, the bibliography gradually expanded its scope to cover other literatures and languages, and to become "international" in the volume for 1956. Volumes covering 1921–68 were published as a part of *PMLA*; however, many libraries will have these volumes in the separate reprints published by Kraus or New York University Press. With the 1969 volume the *Bibliography* became a separate publication issued in four parts (each with its separate index of scholars). Pt. 1: General, English, American, Medieval and Neo-Latin, and Celtic Literatures; pt. 2: General Romance, French, Italian, Spanish, Portuguese and Brazilian, Romanian, General Germanic, German, Netherlandic, Scandinavian, Modern Greek, Oriental, African, and East European Literatures; pt. 3: Linguistics; pt. 4: ACTFL Annual Bibliography on Pedagogy in Foreign Languages. (Most libraries will have the bound library edition.) In the 1970 volume, Folklore became a separate section in pt. 1; pt. 4 was discontinued after the 1972 *MLAIB*.

The continual expansion was accompanied by numerous changes in the organization of sections and refinements in the classification of entries (especially in the bibliographies for 1926, 1928, 1953, 1956, 1957, 1967, and 1969); consequently, users must be certain to check the table of contents at the beginning of each volume. In general, scholarship on literary works is organized by national literature, then (after a general section) by period, and then by genre and literary author; some literatures, however, are grouped by language rather than geography (e.g., Cornish and Welsh are under Celtic Literatures; French-Canadian and West Indian are listed with French Literature). Studies not assignable to a national literature, general discussions of themes or genres, and works about criticism and theory are listed in the General Literature section (which for many years also served as a catchall and included several national literatures, folklore, and general linguistics). Folklore scholarship is classified by broad topics (e.g., Folk Poetry, Folk Games and Toys, Material Culture), then by types (e.g., Folk Poetry includes headings for Oral Epics, Ballads, Songs, and Rhymes and Verses), and then continent. (Folklore scholarship appears in the various national literature divisions through the volume for 1927 and in the General division in the volumes for 1928–68; even after Folklore became a separate division, several national literatures continued to include a Folklore section.) The Linguistics part includes classified sections for linguistic topics (e.g., Theoretical and Descriptive Linguistics includes a subdivision for Grammar, which is further subdivided into General and Miscellaneous, Morphophonemics, Morphology, Syntax, Word Classes and Categories, and Discourse Analysis) and language groups (subdivided by specific languages, with further subdivisions for General Studies, Bibliography, Dialectology, Graphemics, Lexis, Morphology, Onomastics, Phonology, Semantics, Stylistics, Syntax, and Translation). Until the volume for 1967 (which marks the beginning of systematic coverage of linguistic studies), linguistic scholarship was included with individual languages; general linguistic studies were listed in the General section.

A publication is listed only once in each part, with up to five cross-references; any work that requires more is relegated, without cross-references, to the most appropriate general heading (e.g., a book on several English plays, medieval through modern, would usually be listed only under Drama in the General section of the English Literature division; an article surveying plays from several national literatures would usually appear only under Drama in the General IV: Themes and Types section). Thus scholars must be certain to search appropriate general sections.

Most journals and series are cited by acronyms keyed to the Master List of Periodicals found at the front of each part. (Serials on the Master List are fully described in *MLA Directory of Periodicals* [K615].) Essays from a collection or Festschrift (identifiable by a bracketed number preceded by F) are keyed to the Festschriften and Other Analyzed Collections entries at the beginning of each part. In the volumes for 1970–75, an asterisk preceding an entry number means that an abstract is printed in the corresponding volume of *MLA Abstracts of Articles in Scholarly Journals* (New York: MLA, 1972–77, annual). Indexed by scholars' names in most volumes since 1948.

MLAIB for 1981– . Since the introduction of a sophisticated computerized classification and indexing system in the volume for 1981, the *Bibliography* has been published in five parts (with variations in some titles). Pt. 1: British and Irish, Breton, Commonwealth, English Caribbean, and American Literatures; pt. 2: European, Asian, African, and Latin American Literatures; pt. 3: Linguistics; pt. 4: General Literature, Humanities, Teaching of Literature, and Rhetoric and Composition; pt. 5: Folklore. Most libraries will subscribe to the library edition, which includes all five parts and comprehensive scholar and subject indexes. National literature sections are classified chronologically in pts. 1 and 2; depending on the scholarship covered in a volume, chronological spans range from a single century to several centuries. For example, a book on English drama from the Renaissance to the modern period would appear in a division headed "English Literature/1500–1999"; an article on Black Mountain poets would appear in "American Literature/1900–1999." Chronological divisions encompassing more than a century include subdivisions for general studies and genres; those limited to a century or, for some literatures, a broader early period (e.g., Old English, medieval, Old Russian, Ch'ing Dynasty period) are further classified by literary author. Individual authors have subdivisions for general studies, bibliographies, genres, and literary works. In general, the post-1980 volumes are more consistent than their predecessors in distinguishing national literatures. The remaining inconsistencies—for example, there are no separate sections for Swiss or Austrian literature—are generally ameliorated by the national literature headings in the subject index.

Studies on general literature and related topics are currently classified in pt. 4 under fifteen broad divisions: General Literature, Comparative Literature, Humanities, Research Tools, Bibliographical, Censorship, Dramatic Arts, Figures of Speech, Genres, Literary Forms, Literary Movements, Literary Theory and Criticism, Themes and Figures, Teaching of Literature, Rhetoric and Composition. Each includes appropriate subdivisions, again depending on the nature of the scholarship covered in a given volume (e.g., the Poetry subdivision of the Genres division might include headings for Concrete Poetry, Elegy, Haiku, Lyric Poetry, and Prose Poem).

Linguistic scholarship is organized by broad topics (Linguistics, History of Linguistics, Theory of Linguistics, Applied Linguistics, Areal Linguistics, Comparative Linguistics, Diachronic Linguistics, Language Interaction, Mathematical Linguistics, Paralinguistics, Psycholinguistics, Sociolinguistics, Teaching of Linguistics), by aspects of language (Dialectology, Grammar, Lexicology, Morphology, Morphophonology, Onomastics, Phonetics, Phonology, Pragmatics, Prosody, Semantics, Stylistics, Syntax, Translation, Writing Systems), and by specific language. Each section includes appropriate divisions and subdivisions (e.g., Sociolinguistics has subdivisions for Ethnolinguistics, Language Attitudes, Language Policy, Social Dialects, and Speech Registers; Stylistics has a subdivision for Rhetoric). Folklore studies are listed in pt. 5 under general studies and under headings for History and Study of Folklore, Folk Literature, Ethnomusicology, Folk Belief Systems, Folk Rituals, and Material Culture. Each is subdivided by type or genre and then by geographical area (continent, region, country); for example, Folk Literature has subdivisions for Folk Speech Play, Folk Narrative, and Folk Poetry (the last with headings for such forms as ballad, epic, and folk song).

A study is listed only once in each part; there are no cross-references in the classified listings, since the subject index provides access to related authors, genres, or subjects. Acronyms are still used for most journal and series titles, but an entry for an essay from a collection provides full bibliographical information (and thus does away with the [F] numbers that mystified so many users of the pre-1981 bibliography). Since index terms are printed within brackets following a citation, researchers can usually get some sense of the content of a study.

Of most benefit is the subject indexing made possible by the new system. Each separately published part or combination thereof includes self-contained subject and scholar indexes, but for comprehensive searches users must consult the integrated indexes to the library edition. All searches should begin with the subject index because the classified listings include no cross-references. The subject index provides access to literary authors, genres, groups, themes, literary movements, motifs, literary characters, theories, critics, scholars, linguistic features, techniques (such as characterization, allusion), languages, folklore genres, literary features (e.g., structure, point of view), and processes (e.g., textual revision). In addition, the subject index provides access to national literatures that do not have their own sections in the classified listings as well as literatures that do not fall within the primary language of a given country. For example, literature in Spanish by American writers is found under the heading Spanish-Language Literature; all medieval Latin references can be located as a group in the subject index under Latin-Language Literature. Similar principles apply to Yiddish-language literature, French-language literature (e.g., in Africa), and English-language literature (e.g., in India and South Africa). Each subject heading is followed by the citations in which it appears. Since each citation prints its full list of subject terms, a user can frequently judge the probable relevance of a book or article before looking it up in the classified listing. Many subject headings also refer users to related headings.

MLAIB Database. The *MLAIB* database includes the records in the volumes for 1926 to the present as well as additional ones derived from the indexing of JSTOR's language and literature journals back to the 1880s. Including more than 1,990,000 citations (as of 3 June 2006), the database is available online through FirstSearch (E225a), EBSCO (I512), Gale Literature Resource Center (I528), Gale Infotrac (G387), ProQuest (I519 and through *Literature Online* [I527]), and CSA (I510). For a comparison of features offered by these distributors, see http://www.mla.org/bib_ dist_comparison; users should note many of these features are modified over time. For an evaluation of the individual search interfaces, see the entries above. Updated ten times a year, the database is more current than the printed *Bibliography*, and, since 1981, entries are retrievable by several groups of terms only through the database— terms that are too numerous to list in a printed subject index, such as *edition, interview,* and various scholarly approaches (e.g., *biographical*). The MLA's *How to Use the* MLA International Bibliography (http://www.mla.org/howtouse_ mlabiblio) explains how to perform searches, includes a table of field codes used by vendors, and provides links to vendors' guides. Users must be aware that a distributor's search interface will determine how the database can be searched, affect the number of records that a search returns, and govern how search results appear and can be manipulated. For an instructive over- view of how distributor packaging of the *MLAIB Database* can affect searching, see Jody Condit Fagan, "Comparative Review of the *MLA International Bibliography* on EBSCO, InfoTrac, and OVID," *Charleston Advisor* 5.1 (2003): 12–17.

The lack of subject indexing has always been a major impediment to the use of the print volumes for 1921 through 1980. However, free text searching of the database makes some subject access possible for entries from 1926 on (e.g., searchers can retrieve all studies with "Joyce" and "*Ulysses*" in their respective titles or that have been classified under Irish Literature/1900–1999/Joyce, James).

Online searching of post-1980 entries offers some advantages (besides speed) over manual searches of the printed classified listings and subject indexes. Using combina- tions of descriptors (e.g., codes for genre, literary technique, theme, place, or time period), a researcher can narrow a search to various levels (e.g., one could quickly isolate journal articles written in English between 1982 and 1985 and employing an archetypal approach to Joyce's use of the journey motif in *Ulysses*). Although some descriptors were added and classification discrepancies resolved when listings from 1926 through 1980 were added to the database, online searching of these entries will never allow the flexibility and specificity possible with post-1980 citations. Those using the online file should watch the MLA Web site for updates on search techniques or consult the guides associated with the vendor interfaces.

Despite the dramatic increase in accessibility to the post-1980 listings, a search of the printed subject indexes or online file must be supplemented by a reading of appro- priate sections in the classified volumes. Although the number of index terms has grown steadily each year, many broad studies can be described in only the most general terms, and some publications, lacking a thesis or any discernible focus, cannot be given any descriptors. Subject indexing, at its best, is an imperfect art. A book or essay usually requires an MLA bibliographer to choose among a range of indexing possibilities, and no two people are likely to index any but the most straightforward study in the same way.

No reference work of this magnitude, especially one that relies heavily in its earlier years on a network of volunteer contributors, is without its limitations and faults. Before 1956 the *Bibliography* was generally (but never completely, as some descriptions erro- neously assert) restricted to scholarship by American authors. Although it became "in- ternational" in 1956 and includes books, essays from edited collections, journal articles, review essays (but not reviews), and published abstracts of dissertations, coverage has never been exhaustive. The classification system—sometimes maddeningly quirky and inconsistent—requires considerable time to master. (For a discussion of inconsistencies involving literatures in English, see Reed Way Dasenbrock, "English Department Geography: Interpreting the *MLA Bibliography*," *Pedagogy Is Politics: Literary Theory and Critical Teaching*, ed. Maria-Regina Kecht [Urbana: U of Illinois P, 1992] 193–214. However, the solutions proposed in the article would result in an unwieldy classification scheme and are largely obviated by the subject index and the wide electronic dissemination of the *Bibliography*.) Until 1981 there is no convenient way of determining what serials listed in the Master List of Periodicals are actually covered in a given volume; in the bibliographies since that for 1989, an asterisk preceding an acronym in the Master List denotes that at least one issue of the journal or volume in the series is indexed (those with access to the database can search by journal and year to determine which volumes were actually covered); issues of journals whose coverage lapses for a year or more are frequently left unanalyzed. New journals are not always added in a timely manner; when they are, retrospective coverage is haphazard. For coverage of single-author monographs, which is particularly weak, researchers should rely instead on *WorldCat* (E225) and RLG Union Catalog (E230); for an analysis of one year's coverage of single-author monographs, see James L. Harner, Letter to the Editor, *MLA Newsletter* 34.3 (2002): 18. Access to (but not the coverage of) the content of single-author monographs has improved with the introduction of a searchable table of contents field beginning with records added in 2003. For suggestions about how the *MLAIB* can redress some weaknesses in coverage, see Harner, "Some Suggestions for the Future of the *MLA International Bibliography*," *Bibliography in Literature, Folklore, Language, and Linguistics: Essays on the Status of the Field*, ed. David William Foster and James R. Kelly (Jefferson: McFarland, 2003) 153–60. Since MLA bibliographers must actually have a work in hand before listing it, studies are overlooked or entered years after publication. And there are the inevitable number of outright errors. Yet no researcher can afford to ignore the *MLAIB*.

The most detailed critique of the print and electronic versions of *MLAIB* and comparison of coverage with *ABELL* is offered by Jost Hindersmann, MLAIB *und* ABELL*: Periodische Fachbibliographien, CD-ROM- und Online-Datenbanken zur Anglistik*, Anglistik/Amerikanistik 4 (Münster: Lit, 1997, 93 pp.), with an English summary in Horst Weinstock, ed., *English and American Studies in German 1997: Summaries of Theses and Monographs. A Supplement to* Anglia (Tübingen: Niemeyer, 1998) 52–54; Hindersmann's discussion of the CD-ROM version is updated in a review in *Zeitschrift für Bibliothekswesen und Bibliographie* 4 (1997): 439–42 (available in an electronic version at http://www.klostermann.de/zeitsch/osw_444.htm). See also Stebelman, "Retrieval Performance and Citation Characteristics of the *MLA International Bibliography* and the *Annual Bibliography of English Language and Literature*: A Comparative Study" (G340a). For a comparison of *MLAIB* and *ABELL*, see the following entry.

Although the *MLAIB* is frequently the single most valuable aid to research, its coverage must be supplemented with other serial bibliographies and reference works. For a documentation of this necessity, see Charles A. Carpenter, "Tracking Down Shaw Studies: The Effective Use of Printed and Online Bibliographical Sources," *Shaw* 25 (2005): 165–78.

G340   *Annual Bibliography of English Language and Literature* (*ABELL*; sometimes
       called *MHRA Bibliography*). Chadwyck-Healey-ProQuest. Online. 7 Mar.
       2006 <http://collections.chadwyck.com/home/home_abell.jsp>. Updated
       monthly. CD-ROM. Updated annually.

Annual Bibliography of English Language and Literature. Leeds: Maney for
Mod. Humanities Research Assn., 1921– . Annual.   Z2011.M69
016.82. <http://www.mhra.org.uk/Publications/Journals/abell.html>.

An international bibliography of scholarship about the English language and literatures in English (British, American, Canadian, Australian, African, Asian); recent
volumes also cover selectively film, travel writing, and cultural studies. Although a
number of subdivisions have been added, deleted, or combined over the years (especially
in vols. 48 [for 1973], 51 [for 1976], and 60 [for 1985]), the scope and basic organization have remained fairly stable (although coverage of unpublished dissertations was
discontinued with 75 [for 2000]). Entries are currently organized in divisions for bibliography; scholarly method; language, literature, and the computer; newspapers and
other periodicals; English language; traditional culture, folklore, and folklife; English
literature. This last division has sections for general studies and periods (Old English,
Middle English and fifteenth century, then by century), with subsections for general
studies, genres, children's literature, literary theory, related studies, and individual authors; the twentieth and twenty-first century sections also have subsections for cinema
and radio, television, and interactive media. Entries are efficiently cross-referenced, and
uninformative titles are occasionally glossed. When searching for reviews, users must
remember that a book is relisted only in the first section in which it originally appeared;
e.g., a book on Shakespeare's language, originally classified in the Literary Stylistics and
Poetics section, would, in subsequent volumes, appear only in that section (without
cross-references and without inclusion in the subject index). Beginning with vol. 66
(for 1991) the Sources and Abbreviations list includes only those serials actually
searched; an asterisk denotes a title from which an item was indexed. Two indexes:
authors and film directors; scholars. Coverage is reasonably thorough (indeed, it improves markedly with vol. 66 [for 1991]); the editors have embarked on a retrospective
indexing program going back to 1991 (works published before 2003 will appear only
in the database since bound volumes are at capacity). The broad subject classifications,
failure to distinguish among national literatures (the sections for the nineteenth and
twentieth centuries are particularly unwieldy), and inadequate subject indexing (essentially listings of the classification and author heads) make the print version a cumbersome work to search for studies other than those restricted to a specific author.

Fortunately, the CD-ROM and online versions (which include records since 1921,
although the Web version is more current) substantially improve the accessibility of
ABELL. Both electronic versions allow searches by keyword (that is, any word in the
database), title keyword, subject (unfortunately limited to subject headings, including
authors' names, used in the print version; subject headings have been standardized),
document author or reviewer, publication details (including series title), journal, ISBN,
ISSN, date; searches can be limited to articles, books, and reviews. Records—which
are sorted by year (descending), then alphabetically by author (ascending)—can be
marked for e-mailing or printing, and citations can be exported into several kinds of
bibliographic software. Entries for reviews of a book are not conflated; thus searchers
must sometimes work through several entries to identify all the reviews included. And,
since it is not possible to limit a search by accession number or update code, users must
frequently read through the full list of records to identify those added since a previous
search on the same subject.

The more detailed classification system, subject indexing in recent volumes, and
greater flexibility of online access render *MLAIB* (G335) a more efficient source to
search for post-1980 publications; for publications before 1980, the electronic versions
of *ABELL* and *MLAIB* offer essentially equivalent accessibility. Regardless of where one

begins, any search of *MLAIB* must be complemented by a search of *ABELL*, and vice versa, for each volume of these two resources includes scores of works omitted from the other, a fact underscored by Scott Stebelman, "Retrieval Performance and Citation Characteristics of the *MLA International Bibliography* and the *Annual Bibliography of English Language and Literature*: A Comparative Study," *Journal of Documentation* 56 (2000): 332–40, and Hindersmann, MLAIB *und* ABELL*: Periodische Fachbibliographien, CD-ROM- und Online-Datenbanken zur Anglistik* (G335a), who offer the most thorough critique of the overlap between the two works (although Stebelman's data is skewed by failing to consider the effect of the greater level of indexing in *MLAIB* and although Hindersmann was able to evaluate only the obsolete telnet version of the electronic *ABELL*). Precise comparison of coverage of areas common to the two serial bibliographies is difficult because of differences in scope, level of indexing, and organization. Comparing the number of entries in similar sections is an invalid measure, since *ABELL* numbers separately all cross-references and entries for books reviewed and does not distinguish among national literatures in literary period sections; comparing the number of hits a search generates is equally invalid because of the greater level of indexing in *MLAIB*. Before 1956—when *MLAIB* was generally restricted to scholarship by American authors—the duplication is frequently quite low. Although recent volumes of *MLAIB* are overall more comprehensive than *ABELL* in their common areas of coverage, *ABELL* lists British theses until vol. 75 (for 2000; only those abstracted in *ProQuest Dissertations and Theses* [H465] are indexed in *MLAIB*) and reviews (however, coverage of reviews is not thorough even within issues of journals indexed; *MLAIB* includes only some review essays); its coverage of books published solely in Great Britain and smaller British journals is superior; and it includes a selective list of related studies for each historical period. Used together, *ABELL* and *MLAIB* will lead researchers to the bulk of scholarship since 1921 on the English language and literatures in English. (ProQuest [I519] is the only distributor that allows cross-searching of *ABELL* and *MLAIB* and thus provides a basis for a detailed study of overlap between the two databases.)

G343   *ABES: Annotated Bibliography for English Studies.* Lisse: Swets, 1997– . Online. 22 Mar. 2007 <http://abes.tandf.co.uk/abes>. CD-ROM. (Routledge plans to relaunch *ABES* in 2007, with the focus restricted to literature.)

     A selective annotated guide to important studies of the English language, literatures in English, cultural studies, women's studies, gender studies, film, and literary theory. As of 1999 the database included about 25,000 records grouped by topical chapters (contributed by a wide range of scholars, with the breadth and depth of coverage varying widely) within volumes (e.g., Renaissance and Seventeenth Century, English Fiction and Prose 1890–1945, and History and Theory of Genre); coverage will continually change to reflect developments in scholarship and criticism. A typical record provides a citation; an annotation that offers a description of contents and a brief evaluative comment (and frequently identifies theoretical orientation); an indication of level (introductory, core, specialist, reference); and index terms. The search engine allows keyword searches and offers a list of index fields; searches can be limited by genre, period, language, and level (but not by date). Unfortunately, there is no way to view a "chapter" directly and skim the contents (and thus judge the soundness of coverage of a topic), and the inclusion in the search menu of primary and secondary index fields will skew results for those who don't consult the help file. Annotations are inevitably uneven, a few outdated editions are cited, several records are for studies that can hardly be termed "the most valuable" in their respective field, and not all the chapters include reference works and critical editions. The database is still very much a work-in-progress, but if *ABES* can ultimately achieve the ambitious coverage outlined in its prospectus and maintain the level of contributors and chapter editors, it will be an invaluable research tool, fulfilling a long-standing need for a trustworthy, current guide to the most important books and articles on literatures in English and related fields. However, until coverage expands substantially, users must be certain to search other serial bibliographies in section G.

G345   *FRANCIS.* Centre National de la Recherche Scientifique (CNRS). Online.
        17 May 2005 <http://www.inist.fr/en/PRODUITS/francis.php>. Updated
        monthly. CD-ROM. Updated quarterly.
        Francis bulletin signalétique, 523: Histoire et sciences de la littérature.
        Vandœuvre-lès-Nancy: Institut de l'Information Scientifique et Technique,
        1947–94. Former titles: *Bulletin analytique* (1947–55); *Bulletin
        signalétique: Philosophie, sciences humaines* (1956–60); *Bulletin signalétique C
        (19–24): Sciences humaines* (1961–68).   Z6513.B82   800.

   A database of articles from journals (currently about 4,300) and edited collections that are devoted to the humanities, linguistics, social sciences, and history of art. Since 1988, the literature portion has focused on English- and French-language literatures, comparative literature, and literary theory and history; before 1988 coverage extended to European as well as to non-English-language South American and African literatures. Coverage begins c. 1980 in the database. Most North American users will access *FRAN-CIS* through RLG's (E230) Eureka interface, which offers three search levels: basic (keyword, author, title, subject, abstract term, or journal searches); advanced (which allows combinations of the preceding kinds of searches plus ISSN and ISBN to be limited by date and language); and command line. Records include bibliographical information, a brief summary in French, and a list of indexing terms (in English and French). Records, which are returned in no apparent order (and cannot be sorted), can be printed or emailed. The CNRS site includes records since 1972; coverage in the RLG file and the CD-ROM begins with 1984. For earlier studies, users will have to consult the print version, which organizes entries in three extensively classified divisions: general studies, sciences of literature (including literary theory, genre studies, and comparative literature), history of literature (with sections for general studies, literary periods and movements, and national literatures). Four indexes: subjects; literary authors and anonymous works; scholars and critics; journals listed. Although especially useful for its coverage of French publications and subject indexing (which frequently cites only passing mention of a subject or literary author and sometimes employs terms that are too general), *FRANCIS* is much less comprehensive and current than *MLAIB* (G335) and (for British and American literature) *ABELL* (G340).

G355   *Literature and Language Bibliographies from the* American Year Book. *1910–
        1919.* Introd. and indexes by Arnold N. Rzepecki. Cumulated Bibliography
        Series 1. Ann Arbor: Pierian, 1970. 259 pp.   Z7001.L57 [P121]   016.41.
   A convenient reprint of the annual surveys, useful now because they cover a period before publication of *MLAIB* (G335) and *ABELL* (G340). The highly selective essay reviews, restricted largely to American scholarship, cover classical and European languages and literatures. The American literature sections treat creative, rather than scholarly, works. The one-page subject index lists only literature and language divisions; the "Personal Name and Main Entry" index, contrary to its title, includes only scholars, literary authors, and an occasional anonymous work.

See also

> "Check List of Explication" (L1255a).
> *Linguistics and Language Behavior Abstracts* (U6015).

General Bibliographies

Although the following indexes are much less extensive in their coverage of language and literature studies, their interdisciplinary scope and subject indexing make them important complements to *MLAIB* (G335) and *ABELL* (G340).

G360   *Humanities International Complete*. EBSCO. Online. 25 July 2006
          <http://www.epnet.com>.
     A bibliographic database of articles and creative works (primarily in English) in about 1,000 journals (overall), with full-text for several titles; the database is also available without full-text links as *Humanities International Index*. The database incorporates and continues *American Humanities Index* (*AHI*) (Albany: Whitston, 1976–2004), which was not limited to American journals or subjects and whose focus was overwhelmingly on literature. Except for a few little magazines and author newsletters, periodicals covered in *AHI* are more adequately indexed by the other serial bibliographies. (*AHI*'s claim that "most of the journals and magazines in the *AHI* are not indexed elsewhere, or are found only in indexing services not universally available" is inaccurate.) With the move to electronic-only publication, a substantial number of journals has been added (including more nonliterary ones) along with a few books (although the basis for their inclusion is unclear), abstracts are provided, citation indexing for full-text records is added, and the subject indexing is improved. *Humanities International Complete* uses the standard EBSCO interface (see entry I512) but does not utilize many of its features; users must consult the database-specific Help file to identify the codes for searchable fields. The extensive duplication with other databases; imprecise, superficial subject indexing of many early records; and limited search options rank *Humanities International Complete* among the least satisfactory indexes in this section.

G365   *Arts and Humanities Citation Index, [1976–]* (*AHCI*). Philadelphia:
          Thomson, 1978– . Semiannual, with some annual cumulations and an
          expanded quinquennial one covering 1975–79 (14 vols., 1987).   AI3.A63
          016.05. Online. 26 June 2005 <http://portal.isiknowledge.com>. Updated
          weekly. CD-ROM.
     Subject, author, and citation indexes to journals (currently about 1,130) and a few books in archaeology, dance, history, music, architecture, film, language, philosophy, art, television, radio, linguistics, theater, classics, folklore, religion, and literature. (An additional 7,000 journals surveyed for *Science Citation Index* [1961–] and *Social Sciences Citation Index* [1966–] are selectively covered.) The contents of *AHCI* are indexed in four ways:

1. The Source Index, to which entries in the other three indexes are keyed, is an author list of articles, reviews, notes, illustrations, letters, and creative works. Each entry includes basic publication information, the author's address (a useful feature for those wishing to request an offprint), and a list of works cited. The latter sometimes indicates the focus of an article and yields sources relevant to its topic.

2. The Permuterm Subject Index indexes keywords in titles of entries in the Source Index. Although "title enrichment terms" are added for uninformative titles, the value of this part as a subject index is restricted because of the reliance on title words for index terms.

3. The Citation Index lists (by author or artist) books, articles, dissertations, reviews, works of art, music, and films mentioned in the text, notes, or bibliography of works in the Source Index. Thus users can identify (a) scholarship relevant to a topic by locating studies that cite a pertinent book or article; (b) discussions of literary authors buried in vaguely titled or broad studies. Because indexers do not discriminate between passing references and substantial discussions, users frequently will waste time tracking down insignificant citations (especially in the case of a major, frequently cited author). Also, the uncritical reliance on endnotes and footnotes results in numerous misattributions and variant titles.

4. The Corporate Index, which lists authors in the Source Index by organizational affiliation (e.g., a department in a university), is useful principally when a researcher knows that a particular organization is involved in work relevant to a search.

The numerous errors and false leads, very small print, abbreviated entries and cross-references, the use of initials for first and middle names, and the need to refer continually to the Source Index make *AHCI* a cumbersome, time-consuming work to use.

Access to the post-1974 records in the *AHCI* database (which includes a substantial number of items not in the print version) is offered by the ISI Web of Science search interface. This search interface allows users to perform a keyword cross-search of *AHCI* and other resources or to open the Web of Knowledge search interface, which offers three options: General Search (keyword, author [type the last name first], journal title, and author's affiliation), Cited Reference Search (cited author, cited work, and cited date), and a command-line search screen. Search results can be limited by date and marked for printing, e-mailing, or saving. (Users must remember to submit marked records before moving to a new list of records screen.) Searches can be saved as alerts. The electronic version, with its poorly designed user interface, does not make searching the work as straightforward as it should be.

Index to Social Sciences and Humanities Proceedings (ISSHP) (1980– , quarterly, with annual cumulation; online and CD-ROM, with coverage beginning in 1991) indexes the published proceedings of conferences, seminars, and symposia by author or editor, topic, permuterm subject, sponsor, and geographic area. Volumes are needlessly swollen by the inclusion of journal articles derived from conference papers and already indexed in *AHCI*. The publisher offers a reprint service for indexed journal articles published after 1980 and for some papers listed in *ISSHP*.

Although *AHCI* represents a largely unsuccessful attempt to apply science and social science indexing practices to the humanities, it occasionally uncovers important discussions of individuals buried in obscurely titled articles. Review: Sandy Petrey, *French Review* 54 (1980): 117–21.

G370   *BHI: British Humanities Index.* CSA. Online. 6 Mar. 2006 <http://www.csa.com>. Updated monthly.

British Humanities Index (*BHI*). Bethesda: CSA, 1963– . Quarterly, with annual cumulation and author index.   AI3.B7   011′.34.

A subject index to about 400 British and Commonwealth periodicals and newspapers that continues *Subject Index to Periodicals* (1915–62). Beginning with the volume for 1990, most titles are followed by a brief description of contents, which in subsequent volumes is a full abstract. Starting with the volume for 1993, entries appear under a single subject heading, followed by subject, author, and source indexes. Records in the electronic version, which includes publications since 1962, can be searched by title, author, journal title, ISSN, CODEN, abstract, document language, date of publication, descriptors (the subject headings used in the print version), British Library shelf mark, update code, and accession number (see the evaluation of the CSA interface [I510] for a full discussion of search options). *BHI* is useful because of its good subject indexing, abstracts, and inclusion of some publications (mostly weeklies and newspapers) not covered by other bibliographies in this section.

G380   *Essay and General Literature Index (EGLI)*. New York: Wilson, 1931– .
        Semiannual, with annual, quinquennial, and larger cumulations extending
        coverage to 1900.   AI3.E752   080.1'6. Online. H. W. Wilson. 6 Mar.
        2006 <http://vnweb.hwwilsonweb.com/hww>. Updated daily. CD-ROM.
        Updated annually.
       An author and subject index to essays and chapters in books—both single-author volumes and edited collections—and some annual publications, with emphasis on the humanities and social sciences. Entries for literary authors include works by and about a writer (with the latter classified by literary work). Books indexed are listed in the back of each issue; a cumulative list was published in 1972 (Essay and General Literature Index: *Works Indexed, 1900–1969* [New York: Wilson, 1972, 437 pp.]). Although highly selective and limited to English-language publications, *EGLI* is the only serial bibliography devoted to the indexing of chapters of books and essays in a collection by a single author. (In 2003, the *MLAIB* began including a searchable table of contents field in records for single-author monographs.) It is also a good source for locating a reprint of an essay. Entries since January 1985 can be searched in the electronic versions. See entry I525 for an evaluation of the WilsonWeb search interface, which all of the Wilson databases use.
       For discussions of authors that occupy only a portion (at least six pages) of a chapter in a single-author monograph or of an essay in an edited collection, see Richard E. Combs and Nancy R. Owen, *Authors: Critical and Biographical References*, 2nd ed. (Metuchen: Scarecrow, 1993, 478 pp.). Although limited to English-language books and lacking any discernable rationale for the selection of works, *Authors* is the only reference identifying discussions of authors buried within many of the 1,158 volumes indexed.
       English-language books before 1900 are indexed by subject in the *"A. L. A." Index: An Index to General Literature: Bibliographical, Historical, and Literary Essays and Sketches, Reports and Publications of Boards and Societies Dealing with Education, Health, Labor, Charities, and Corrections, Etc., Etc.*, 2nd ed., by William I. Fletcher (Boston: Amer. Lib. Assn., 1901, 679 pp.). Some of the books in the *Supplement, 1900–1910* (Chicago: Amer. Lib. Assn., 1914, 223 pp.) are reindexed in *EGLI*. For authors, see *A. L. A. Index to General Literature Cumulative Author Index*, comp. and ed. C. Edward Wall, Cumulative Author Index Series 4 (Ann Arbor: Pierian, 1972, 192 pp.).

G383   Google. Online. Google. 31 May 2006 <http://www.google.com>.
       A popular Internet search engine that offers two specialized databases of interest to language and literature scholars:
        Google Scholar. Beta version. Google. 31 May 2006 <http://scholar
        .google.com>. A multidisciplinary database of "scholarly literature

[, including] . . . peer-reviewed papers, theses, books, abstracts and articles, from academic publishers, professional societies, preprint repositories, universities and other scholarly organizations." However, the Web site offers no explanation of editorial procedures or chronological scope; update frequency; how content is chosen; or what specific journals, publishers, repositories, and organizations are covered. The default search screen offers basic keyword searching; the Advanced Scholar Search screen allows searchers to search by author and title and to restrict keyword searches to full-text or citation, by date, and by broad subject fields. Records, which are ordered by relevance and cannot be otherwise sorted, include a basic citation and sometimes provide information and library links. Of the fields covered, humanities fares the worst: an important study of coverage (Chris Neuhaus et al., "The Depth and Breadth of Google Scholar: An Empirical Study," *Portal: Libraries and the Academy* 6.2 [2006]: 127–41) reveals that *Google Scholar* includes only 8% of the citations in *MLAIB* (G335). Unless coverage improves dramatically, *Google Scholar* will be a marginally useful resource for literature and language scholars.

Google Book Search. Online. Beta version. Google. 31 May 2006 <http://books.google.com>. A full-text database intended to include substantial portions of the holdings of five major research libraries (Harvard, Michigan, New York Public Library, Bodleian, and Stanford) and books published by cooperating publishers. As is the case with *Google Scholar,* the *Google Book Search* Web site offers minimal information about the status of the database and editorial procedures. The default search screen offers basic keyword searching; Advanced Book Search allows searchers to restrict keyword searches to books with full-text available or by date and to search by author, title, publisher, and ISBN. Records—which are returned in no discernible order—appear in three forms: Snippet View (a few words of the text including the search term[s] and a citation); Sample Pages View (books under copyright for which the copyright owner has given permission to display sample pages); Full Book View (for works in the public domain). If it can overcome copyright restrictions, *Google Book Search* could offer unparalleled access to the content of books across the disciplines.

G385   *Humanities Full Text.* Wilson. Online. 6 Mar. 2006 <http://vnweb.hwwilsonweb.com/hww>. Updated daily. CD-ROM. Updated monthly.

Humanities and Social Sciences Index Retrospective. Wilson. Online 2 Aug. 2006 <http://vnweb.hwwilsonweb.com/hww>. CD-ROM.

Humanities Index. New York: Wilson, 1975– . Quarterly, with annual cumulation. (An expanded continuation of humanities coverage in *Social Sciences and Humanities Index* [1966–74], itself a continuation of *International Index to Periodicals* [1916–65, with coverage beginning with 1907].)   AI3.H85   016.0013.

An author and subject index to English-language articles, creative works, and reviews in about 450 journals (as of March 2006) devoted to archaeology, classical studies, area studies, folklore, history, language, literature, performing arts, philosophy, religion, and related fields. Book reviews, listed by author of the book reviewed, are grouped separately at the back. Since 1974, author and title (but not subject) entries for short stories are repeated in *Short Story Index* (L1085). Listings since February 1984 can be searched through three electronic versions: *Humanities Index*; *Humanities Abstracts* (includes the index entries from *Humanities Index* along with abstracts since March 1994); *Humanities Full Text* (which includes the data in the two preceding works as well as the full text of selected journals since January 1995). Coverage back to 1907 is available through *Humanities and Social Sciences Index Retrospective* or *Humanities Index Retrospective*. See entry I525 for an evaluation of the WilsonWeb search interface, which all of the *Humanities Index* databases use. Although highly selective, the work is useful for its interdisciplinary coverage and subject indexing.

G387   Infotrac. Gale. Online. 11 June 2006 <http://infotrac.galegroup.com/
             default>. Updated daily.
      A database that indexes a variety of popular, general interest, and scholarly periodicals, newspapers, and wire services through several systems, the most valuable of which to researchers is *InfoTrac OneFile*. Coverage extends to some 10,200 publications from 1980 to the present. Basic Search allows users to search by keyword; Subject Guide Search allows users to limit subject searches by date, publication title, or publication subject and to documents with full text, peer-reviewed journals, or documents with images. Advanced Search allows keyword searches of record fields (e.g., abstract, author, title, ISSN) to be limited as in Subject Guide Search. Results appear in tabbed lists—academic journals, magazines, reference works, news, and multimedia—and can be sorted by date (descending) or relevance. To the left of the results screen is a pane with searchable subject terms associated with the records returned. Records can be marked for downloading, e-mailing, or printing. In addition, InfoMark lets users save links to searches, results lists, documents, and marked item lists.
      The breadth of coverage, user-friendliness, excellent subject access, and speed make Infotrac the best periodical index for searching recent issues of general interest and some scholarly periodicals; however, its severely limited and unrepresentative coverage of many subject areas (especially language and literature) means that it must be supplemented by other indexes in this section.
      Periodical Abstracts (Ann Arbor: UMI, 1988– ; online) currently offers 25-word abstracts for about 612 general interest periodicals (with coverage beginning January 1986).

G390   *IBZ: Internationale Bibliographie der geistes- und sozialwissenschaftlichen
             Zeitschriftenliteratur/International Bibliography of Periodical Literature in the
             Humanities and Social Sciences/Bibliographie internationale de la littérature
             périodique dans les sciences humaines et sociales [1965–] (IBZ, Dietrich).*
             Munich: Saur, 1965– . 2 multivol. pts./yr. (A merger of *Internationale
             Bibliographie der Zeitschriftenliteratur. Abteilung A: Bibliographie der
             deutschen Zeitschriftenliteratur [1896–1964]* and Abteilung B: *Bibliographie
             der fremdsprachigen Zeitschriftenliteratur [1911–64].*) Former title:
             *Internationale Bibliographie der Zeitschriftenliteratur aus allen gebieten des
             Wissens/International Bibliography of Periodical Literature Covering All Fields
             of Knowledge/Bibliographie internationale de la littérature périodique dans tous
             les domaines de la connaissance* (1965–2000).   AI9.I5   016.

             *IBZ: Internationale Bibliographie der geistes- und sozialwissenschaftlichen
             Zeitschriftenliteratur/International Bibliography of Periodical Literature.* Saur.

Online. 15 Mar. 2006 <http://gso.gbv.de>. Updated monthly. CD-ROM. Updated twice per year.

An international bibliography of periodical articles on the humanities and social sciences (though until the middle of the volumes for 1999 all subjects were included). Coverage, now extending to several thousand serials published worldwide, emphasizes those in English and German and excludes only those in Oriental languages. Currently each half-year part has three main divisions:

1. The Subject Index is a keyword index to article titles. Author, title, and publication information are listed only under German headings, with cross-references in English and French. Periodical titles are keyed by number to the periodical index (an irritating feature that wastes a searcher's time). The keyword and author indexes refer to subject headings in this index.
2. The Author Index consists of an alphabetical list of authors of articles cited in the Subject Index. An author entry cites the heading under which the article is listed.
3. The Periodical Index contains an alphabetical list of periodicals cited in the Subject Index.

The electronic versions include records since 1983. The basic search screen allows users to search by keyword (subject, author, and title fields), article title, author, periodical title, subject headings (most are in German; browsing leads to a meaningless list of classification numbers), classification, place of publication, publisher, or ISSN. Advanced Search allows users to combine the preceding fields and limit a search by date and language. Results can be sorted by date (descending) or relevance (a useless option for sorting a large number of records). Results can be e-mailed or saved to the screen for printing or downloading. Although the search interface has improved dramatically since the electronic versions were first released, the current version lacks an adequate help file and does not allow searchers to manipulate results in a sophisticated way.

The most useful feature of *IBZ, IJBF* (G395), and *IJBK* (G395a)—all share the same interface and indexing procedures—is the subject indexing; however, researchers must devote considerable time to mastering terminology and identifying appropriate headings and must remember that indexing is dependent on title words and is sometimes too broad to be useful (e.g. "englische literatur" or "theater").

The criteria governing selection of journals and articles have never been explained; coverage of a journal is often erratic (and grossly incomplete); many issues are only partially indexed; and the compilation procedures and editing (as described by Broadwin—see below) hardly inspire confidence in accuracy or thoroughness. However, the breadth of coverage makes *IBZ* an occasionally useful complement to the other works in this section. Currently, however, coverage of English and American literature is not particularly thorough.

For a discussion of editorial procedures and evaluation of *IBZ*, see John A. Broadwin, "An Analysis of the *Internationale Bibliographie der Zeitschriftenliteratur*," *Journal of Documentation* 32 (1976): 26–31; and B. J. McMullin, "Indexing the Periodical Literature of Anglo-American Bibliography," *Studies in Bibliography* 33 (1980): 1–17.

G395   *Internationale Jahresbibliographie der Festschriften/International Annual Bibliography of Festschriften/Bibliographie internationale annuelle des mélanges [1980–] (IJBF)*. Munich: Saur, 1982– . Annual.   Z1033.F4.

IJBF: Internationale Jahresbibliographie der Festschriften/International Annual Bibliography of Festschriften. Saur. Online. 16 Mar. 2006 <http:// gso.gbv.de>.

An international index to Festschriften (including those published as an issue of a periodical) in all subjects. Each annual bibliography has five divisions:

1. The Festschriften list by honoree is an index with publication information for the collection and a list of contents. The following divisions are keyed to this one.
2. The Festschriften list by fields of knowledge classifies the collections in 17 fields of knowledge, including general, book and documentation, literature and linguistics, and fine arts.
3. The subject index is a keyword index, in German with English and French cross-references, to titles of contributions.
4. The keyword index lists, by field of knowledge, the headings used in the subject index.
5. The author index is an index of contributors listed in the Festschriften entries.

Divisions 1 and 5 are cumulatively indexed in *Internationale Jahresbibliographie der Festschriften/International Annual Bibliography of Festschriften/Bibliographie internationale annuelle des mélanges: Alphabetisches Register 1980–1989/Alphabetical Register 1980– 1989; Index alphabétique 1980–1989,* 2 vols., ed. Otto Zeller and Wolfram Zeller (1992) and *Alphabetisches Register 1990–1999/Alphabetical Register 1990–1999/ Index alphabétique 1990–1999,* 3 vols., ed. Zeller and Zeller (1999).

A companion index — *Internationale Jahresbibliographie der Kongressberichte/International Annual Bibliography of Congress Proceedings/Bibliographie internationale annuelle des actes de congrès [1984–94]* (*IJBK*) (1987–96); online [16 Mar. 2006 <http:// gso.gbv.de>] and CD-ROM only since 1996) — is organized in the same divisions (except that the first organizes collections by German-language subject groups, with English and French cross-references).

The most useful feature of both bibliographies is the subject indexing; however, researchers must devote considerable time to mastering terminology and identifying appropriate headings and must remember that indexing is dependent on title words and is sometimes too broad to be useful (e.g. "englische literatur" or "theater").

The online *IJBF* (with coverage since 1986) and *IJBK* (with coverage since 1984) are much easier to search than the print version. The search interface is the same as that for *IBZ* (G390) — with additional fields for honoree, title of festschrift, and date of publication in *IBJF* and for title of conference and ISBN in *IJBK*—and is subject to the same limitations.

Although both *IJBF* and *IJBK* are marred by compilation and editorial procedures that hardly inspire confidence in accuracy or thoroughness, by the lack of an adequate explanation of scope and criteria governing selection, and by awkward organization, the breadth of the works makes them potentially useful sources for identifying essays on language and literature appearing in collections of essays in disciplines other than language and literature. Indexing is now about three years in arrears except for the online *IJBF,* which is more current. *MLAIB* (G335) offers superior and more current coverage of collections devoted to language and literature.

Festschriften published through 1979 are indexed in Otto Leistner, *Internationale Bibliographie der Festschriften von den Anfängen bis 1979 mit Sachregister/International Bibliography of Festschriften from the Beginnings until 1979 with Subject-Index,* 2nd enl. ed., 3 vols. (Osnabrück: Biblio, 1984–89). The first part lists collections by honoree;

the second indexes volumes (but not individual essays) by subject under German and English headings; the third supplements and indexes by subject entries in the preceding parts. For other bibliographies of Festschriften, see Bewsey, "Festschriften Bibliographies and Indexes" (D165).

G397   *Periodicals Index Online.* Chadwyck-Healey. Online. 4 Mar. 2006
        <http://pio.chadwyck.com>. Updated regularly. CD-ROM. (Former title:
        PCI: Periodicals Contents Index.)
        Periodicals Archive Online. Chadwyck-Healey. 31 July 2006
        <http://pao.chadwyck.com>. Updated regularly. (Former title: *PCI Full Text.*)

   An index to the contents of arts, humanities, and social sciences periodicals (popular and academic) published since 1770, for the most part in North America and Western Europe. Coverage, which (as of March 2006) encompasses more than 15 million records from 4,698 journals published through 1996, will eventually extend to more than 20 million records from about 5,000 journals. The full text of articles in 636 journals (as of 31 July 2006) can be searched through *Periodicals Archive Online.* To discover what issues of a journal are actually indexed, users must search by journal title or browse the list on the Find Journals page. In both the *Index* and *Archive*, records can be searched by keyword (in the full text in *Archive*), title keyword, author, language, journal title, subject of journal, ISSN, and date (and any combination thereof); searchers can elect to exclude or search only book reviews. Users can also browse the contents of volumes of journals. Search results can be sorted by relevance, alphabetically by journal title, or date (ascending or descending); in addition, results of a search can be filtered by journal title, language, date ranges, or journal subjects. Records—which include basic bibliographical information—can be marked for e-mailing, downloading, printing, or storing in a personal archive. Indexing is based on tables of contents (which are not always reliable) rather than on a perusal of articles and reviews, the names of authors are not regularized, keyword access is not based on a controlled thesaurus, some records lack full bibliographical information, and coverage of topics is haphazard. Before using *Periodicals Index Online*, researchers should consult Robert Balay's evaluation (pp. 13–20) in *Early Periodical Indexes* (G327), keeping in mind that the current search interface is substantially better than earlier ones. In their current state, *Archive* and *Index* are primarily useful to language and literature researchers as a supplement to the other serial bibliographies in this section.

   Records from 1770 through 1919 in *Index* can be searched through *C19: The Nineteenth Century Index* (M2466).

G400   *Readers' Guide Full Text, Mega Edition.* H. W. Wilson. Online. 4 Mar.
        2006 <http://vnweb.hwwilsonweb.com/hww>. Updated daily.
        Readers' Guide Abstracts. H. W. Wilson. Online. 6 Feb. 2005 <http://
        vnweb.hwwilsonweb.com/hww>. Updated daily. CD-ROM. Updated
        monthly.
        Readers' Guide to Periodical Literature: An Author and Subject Index (*RG;
        Readers' Guide*). New York: Wilson, 1901– . Monthly, with annual
        cumulation. Subtitle varies.   AI3.R4   051. Online. 6 Feb. 2005 <http://
        vnweb.hwwilsonweb.com/hww>. Updated daily. CD-ROM. Updated
        monthly.
        Readers' Guide Retrospective: 1890-1992. H. W. Wilson. Online. 4 Mar.
        2006 <http://vnweb.hwwilsonweb.com/hww>.

An author and subject index to about 230 popular magazines (as of March 2006) published in English (with full-text access to about 165 of the magazines covered). *Readers' Guide Full Text* also includes abstracts and index entries from *Readers' Guide Abstracts*, which in turn incorporates the index entries since January 1983 in *Readers' Guide to Periodical Literature*. Users searching the print version of *Readers' Guide to Periodical Literature* for reviews should consult the prefatory "Suggestions for . . . Use" for an explanation of indexing practices. Since 1974, author and title (but not subject) entries for short stories are repeated in *Short Story Index* (L1085). *Readers' Guide Retrospective*—which replicates the data in the print version of *Readers' Guide to Periodical Literature*—indexes 375 magazines published between 1890 and 1992. See entry I525 for an evaluation of the WilsonWeb search interface, which all of the *Readers' Guide* databases use.

Among indexes to popular magazines, *Readers' Guide* offers the most extensive retrospective coverage; however, the following indexes include additional publications:

> *Academic Search Premier.* EBSCO. Online. 4 Mar. 2006 <http://web .ebscohost.com>. Indexes more than 8,200 journals in a wide variety of disciplines (including language and literature), with full-text access to 4,650 publications. For a list of journals covered and dates of coverage, click the Publications tab. See entry I512 for a discussion of the EBSCO search interface.

> *Access: The Supplementary Index to Periodicals.* Evanston: Burke, 1976– . Annual. Online. Mar. 2006 <http://www.jgburkepub.com/access .html>. Indexes, by author and subject, about 75 periodicals not covered by *Readers' Guide* or (since 25 [1999]) by any other Wilson index.

> *Alternative Press Index.* Baltimore: Alternative Press Center, 1970– . Quarterly. Title varies. Online. 4 Mar. 2006 <http://www.firstsearch.org>. Updated quarterly. Indexes by subject between 200 and 400 radical, alternative, and leftist English-language magazines. Unfortunately, the online version does not offer a list of journals indexed or explanation of coverage. See entry E225 for an evaluation of the search interface.

> *ArticleFirst.* Online. 4 Mar. 2006 <http://www.firstsearch.org>. Updated daily. Indexes the tables of contents of several thousand journals in a multitude of disciplines. Coverage extends at least back to 1990. Like other FirstSearch databases, this offers no explanation of scope or editorial principles, and to identify what issues of journals have been indexed, a searcher must find a title through Browse Journals and Magazines, click on Available Issues, and then skim the entire list since volumes and issues are not listed in numerical order. In addition, there are frequently gaps in coverage of a journal. See entry E225 for an evaluation of the search interface.

For nineteenth-century periodicals, see Helen Grant Cushing and Adah V. Morris, eds., *Nineteenth Century Readers' Guide to Periodical Literature, 1890–1899: With Supplementary Indexing, 1900–1922,* 2 vols. (New York: Wilson, 1944); *Wellesley Index* (M2545); and *Poole's Index to Periodical Literature* (Q4150).

These sources are occasionally useful to literary researchers for locating creative works, articles, interviews, and reviews of books, films, and plays in periodicals not covered by the standard literature indexes.

See also

> *19th Century Masterfile* (Q4147).
> *Poole's Index to Periodical Literature* (Q4150).

Book Review Indexes

Bibliographies of Bibliographies

G410   Gray, Richard A., comp. *A Guide to Book Review Citations: A Bibliography of Sources.* Ohio State University Libraries Publications 2. Columbus: Ohio State UP, 1968. 223 pp.   Z1035.A1 G7   016.0281.

A bibliography of serial bibliographies and indexes, closed bibliographies, and other works (through the mid-1960s) that cite reviews from more than one periodical. The 512 entries are organized by author or title in eight variously classified subject divisions: general works (including general book review indexes); philosophy and psychology; religion; social sciences (with a section for anthropology and folklore); ancient, Oriental, and African civilizations; modern languages, philology, and literature; geography and history; fine arts (with sections for the performing arts and theater and drama); and science and technology. In the language and literature division, sections for general indexes, comparative literature, and periods are followed by sections for various languages, with that for English subdivided by period. Additions are printed on pp. 194–97. Annotations first describe the general scope of a work, then the organization of review citations. Five indexes: subjects; persons who are the subjects of bibliographies; titles; works indexing reviews before 1900 and before 1800; country of origin (listing works that review or cite periodicals published in a single country). The lack of headings for sections leaves readers unable to skim effectively or locate a work easily, but the full descriptions and international coverage make Gray an indispensable guide to identifying sources that index reviews. A revised, updated edition that evaluates sources is badly needed, however.

Supplemented by Donald Altschiller and Sarah G. Wenzel, "Finding Book Reviews in Print and Online," *Reference and User Services Quarterly* 42 (2002–03): 193–98, 200–05.

Indexes

Book review indexes are essential tools for locating reviews of a book and tracing the critical reception of an author or work. Unfortunately, there is no adequate current index of reviews of belles lettres or of books on literary and linguistic topics. Most vendors of collections of electronic journals fail to identify adequately book reviews in tables of contents: some merely use the label *book reviews*, others cite reviewer and short title (sometimes within brackets to distinguish a review from an article), and yet others make no distinction between a book review and an article.

G415   *Book Review Index.* Detroit: Gale, 1965–69, 1972– . 3/yr., with annual cumulation and ones for 1965–84, 1985–92, 1993–97, and 1998–2002. Z1035.A1.B6. Online. 29 June 2006 <http://web4.infotrac.galegroup.com>.

An index of reviews of books and serials in about 400 (as of June 2006) newspapers, library and popular periodicals, and scholarly journals. Books reviewed are listed by author or editor; periodicals and some reference works, by title; all are included in the title index. Although *Book Review Index* lists numerous brief mentions and uncritical summaries and at one time covered few serials that offer substantial and substantive evaluations of scholarly books, it is the best source for identifying reviews of creative works and thus for tracing their critical reception; recent volumes have substantially increased the number of reviews of scholarly books.

Reviews since 1965 can be searched online through three search screens: Author (of book review); Title; Advanced Search. Searches in each can be limited to refereed journals and by date, journal, type of review, length of review, and reading level of book reviewed; in addition, Advanced Search allows record field searches to be limited by reviewer and publisher. Records are returned in descending order by date of review.

Entries for children's books are repeated in *Children's Book Review Index* (U5495), but this clone and two cumulations — *Book Review Index: Reference Books, 1965–1984* (1986, 700 pp.) and *Book Review Index: Periodical Reviews, 1976–1984* (1987, 295 pp.) — are hardly essential for those with access to the 1965–84 cumulation.

To locate reviews before 1965, see *Book Review Digest* (New York: Wilson, 1905– , 10/yr., with annual cumulation). Because of its weak coverage of the humanities, limited scope (currently, about 109 periodicals, many of them popular), and numerous restrictions — books must be published or distributed in the United States, reviews must appear within 18 months of publication, a nonfiction work must have two reviews (fiction, three) in the periodicals indexed, at least one review must be published in the United States — *Book Review Digest* is more useful for identifying reviews of popular fiction and nonfiction than scholarly works. Since brief excerpts from three or four reviews are re-printed and citations indicate the approximate number of words, users are generally spared from searching out the brief uncritical summaries. Cumulatively indexed in *Author/Title Index, 1905–1974*, ed. Leslie Dunmore-Leiber, 4 vols. (1976); *1975–1984*, ed. Robert E. Klaum (1986, 1,488 pp.); and *1985–1994*, ed. Martha T. Mooney (1996, 1, 261 pp.). Entries can be searched most efficiently through *Book Review Digest Plus* (online; 1 Mar. 2006 <http://vnweb.hwwilsonweb.com/hww>; updated daily; CD-ROM), which expands coverage of the print version to include reviews indexed in several other Wilson publications and the full-text of many reviews, and *Book Review Digest Retro-spective: 1905–1982* (online; 1 Mar. 2006 <http://vnweb.hwwilsonweb.com/hww>). Entries, which bring together all reviews under a citation to the book reviewed, can be searched by such fields as keyword, title, author, reviewer, and ISBN. (For a full dis-cussion of the WilsonWeb search interface, see entry I525.)

G420   *Combined Retrospective Index to Book Reviews in Humanities Journals, 1802–1974*. Ed. Evan Ira Farber et al. 10 vols. Woodbridge: Research, 1982–84.
        Z6265.C65 [AZ221] 001.3.

An index to reviews in about 150 philosophy, classics, folklore, linguistics, music, and (primarily) literature journals, all but a few of them published in English in Great Britain or North America. Although the criteria determining the choice of journals are never revealed, most of the important literature journals are indexed. The work excludes brief summaries or annotated listings, and — unfortunately — review articles whose titles do not cite the books reviewed. Organized alphabetically by primary authors or editors and then by book titles, reviews are listed by journal title and cite publication infor-mation and reviewer. Users searching for anything other than a single-author mono-graph should begin with the title index (vol. 10) because names are not thoroughly edited for consistency, critical editions are inconsistently entered under author or editor, authors are confused (see, e.g., Robert Herrick), reference works are usually listed by primary editor, and there are no cross-references. Unfortunately, there are numerous omissions of reviews in journals that are supposedly fully indexed. Although flawed in organization and untrustworthy in coverage, *Combined Retrospective Index* is undeniably valuable as the only source offering retrospective indexing of reviews in a significant number of scholarly humanities journals. For reviews published between 1960 and 1974, *Index to Book Reviews in the Humanities* (G425) usually offers fuller, more accurate indexing. Researchers should also check *ABELL* (G340) for reviews of scholarly books.

Some additional reviews can be found in *Combined Retrospective Index to Book Reviews in Scholarly Journals, 1886–1974*, ed. Evan Ira Farber, 15 vols. (Arlington: Carrollton, 1979–82), which indexes about one million reviews in 459 scholarly periodicals in history, political science, and sociology.

G425   *An Index to Book Reviews in the Humanities [1960–89].* 30 vols.
      Williamstown: Thomson, 1960–90. Annual.   Z1035.A1 I63   028.1.

An index to reviews in scholarly journals devoted to literature (primarily), language, philosophy, the arts, travel, biography, dance, folklore, and sports and pastimes. Coverage underwent a major change with vol. 12 (for 1971): history and social science journals were dropped; journals in major foreign languages were added; the emphasis became more literary; and except for those of children's books, all reviews—not just of humanities books—were indexed. Organized for the most part by author or editor—but occasionally by title for some reference works, with cross-references for compilers or editors—entries cite title and reviews. (Since names of authors are taken from reviews and not edited for consistency, users must check all forms of a name, including pseudonyms.) An asterisk following a title indicates that reviews are cited in the preceding volume. Since most review citations identify journals by a number code (with many omitting the *MLAIB* [G335] acronym that the compiler claims to use when possible) and cite date but not volume number, users must continually flip to the prefatory list of journals (and issues) indexed and then waste time hunting out issues by date rather than the more convenient volume number. Although it omits numerous important journals, is difficult to scan in the volumes printed from uppercase computer printout, is inconsistent in covering titles, and lacks an adequate statement of criteria governing the selection of journals, *Index to Book Reviews in the Humanities* was by far the best, most trustworthy source for locating scholarly reviews of books on language and literature; its demise leaves no remotely adequate index to reviews of scholarly books in the two fields.

G430   *IBR: International Bibliography of Book Reviews/Internatioinale Bibliographie*
      der Rezensionen. Saur. Online. 28 July 2005 <http://gso.gbv.de>. CD-
      ROM.
      Internationale Bibliographie der Rezensionen geistes- und
      sozialwissenschaftlicher Literatur/International Bibliography of Book Reviews of
      Scholarly Literature in the Humanities and Social Sciences (IBR). München:
      Saur, 1971– . Title varies. Online. 22 Mar. 2007 <http://gso.gbv.de>;
      CD-ROM.   Z5051.I64 [AS9]   001.2.

A database of more than 990,000 reviews published since c. 1984 of books primarily in the social sciences and humanities; according to the publisher, 65% are in English, 23% in German, and the remainder in other European languages. In the Basic Search screen users can limit keyword searches of the full text or of the following fields: book author, reviewer, article title, journal, broad classification, year of publication, publisher, place of publication, or ISSN. The Advanced Search screen allows users to perform keyword searches of combinations of the above fields and to limit results to a single language. In both Basic and Advanced Search, results can be sorted by year of publication of reviews or relevance (avoid this option when dealing with large numbers of records). A maximum of 100 records can be marked for e-mailing, printing, or saving. Although not an especially sophisticated interface, it is far superior to the original one, which caused most users to exit in frustration before extracting anything.

The print version indexes reviews (published since c. 1969) in journals devoted to the arts, humanities, and social sciences. Coverage extends to more than 10,000 journals published worldwide, excluding only those in Asian languages; until vol. 27 (1996) coverage extended to all topics (and included reviews of belles lettres). The last few half-year parts of the print version have five divisions:

1. Books reviewed (organized by author, with a full citation for the book and a list of reviews but, unfortunately, with periodical titles keyed by number to the periodicals indexed). The next three indexes are keyed to this one.
2. Reviewers.
3. Titles of books reviewed.
4. Subjects of books reviewed (with headings generally too broad to be of much use).
5. Periodicals.

The work is needlessly complicated and time-consuming to use, since a researcher must consult two indexes to locate all publication information for a review. The criteria governing selection of journals and reviews have never been explained; coverage of a journal is often erratic and issues incompletely indexed; and the compilation procedures and editing hardly inspire confidence in the accuracy and thoroughness. However, the breadth of coverage—the most wide-ranging of any single index—makes *IBR* a useful complement to the other review indexes in this section.

IBR continues *Internationale Bibliographie der Zeitschriftenliteratur, Abteilung C: Bibliographie der Rezensionen [1900–1943]*, 77 vols. (Osnabrück: Dietrich, 1901–44), which inconsistently covers non-German periodicals.

See also

Sec. G: Serial Bibliographies, Indexes, and Abstracts/Serial Bibliographies/General Bibliographies.
ABELL (G340): Coverage of reviews is neither thorough nor consistent, however.
Index to Book Reviews in Religion (U6350a).
Index to Reviews of Bibliographical Publications (U5275a).

Abstracts

Abstracts collect and index summaries of published works and thus are valuable re-sources for identifying studies of an author or topic buried within a larger work or an obscurely titled one and for making a preliminary decision about what books, articles, and dissertations to obtain. In general, abstracts by trained abstractors are preferable to those written by authors, who sometimes do not describe what they actually wrote.

A major lacunae in reference works for literatures in English is a thorough, current, fully indexed abstract. Because of the discontinuation of *MLA Abstracts of Articles in Scholarly Journals* (G335a) and the dim prospect that libraries could afford to support a private venture, literature scholars will likely never enjoy a resource comparable to *Psychological Abstracts* (U6530).

The following include summaries of scholarship on more than one national literature. Those limited to a single national literature or subject will be found under the heading Abstracts in appropriate sections.

G435   *Abstracts of English Studies* (*AES*). 34 vols. Oxford: Blackwell for Dept. of English, U of Calgary, 1958–94. Quarterly.   PE25.A16   820′.5.

Abstracts of articles published in a core list of about 500 journals (at its demise), all but a few publishing in English. Originally restricted to articles on English and American literature, coverage was eventually extended to world literature in English and related literatures (defined by the editors as any "literature that has had marked influence on English literature and language"). With vol. 13 (1969), the unwieldy organization of entries by journal was replaced by a classified arrangement. Users should consult the front matter of each volume for the then-current organization. The descriptive summaries tend to be brief but frequently alert researchers to discussions of authors or topics buried in vaguely titled or general studies. Two indexes (subjects; scholars) in each issue; cumulated annually in the last issue, which also prints a list of journals abstracted in the volume. Except for literary authors and titles of anonymous works, the subject indexing is inadequate. Coverage is erratic (with unfilled gaps for many major periodicals) and includes few articles in foreign languages.

G440   *English and American Studies in German: Summaries of Theses and Monographs: A Supplement to* Anglia. Tübingen: Niemeyer, 1969– .   Annual.   PE3.A6   420′.5.

Publishes English summaries of dissertations, collections of essays, and books (primarily in German) on the English language and literatures in English. Coverage begins with 1967. Currently organized in five sections: language, English literature, American and Canadian literatures, new literatures in English, and teaching of English. Indexed by author and subject. Since *English and American Studies in German* relies on authors and editors for abstracts, coverage is incomplete but does include many studies overlooked in the standard bibliographies.

See also

> Because of their international, interdisciplinary scope, the following works abstract a considerable number of literature- and language-related studies not included or inadequately indexed in standard literature and language bibliographies: *America: History and Life* (Q3310), *Historical Abstracts* (U6500), *PsycINFO* (U6530), *Sociological Abstracts* (U6560), *Women Studies Abstracts* (U6610).
> *Children's Literature Abstracts* (U5490).

H

Guides to Dissertations and Theses

This section includes bibliographies, indexes, and abstracts of dissertations on more than one national literature. Those devoted to a single literature, period, or topic appear in appropriate sections.

Bibliographies of Bibliographies

H455   Reynolds, Michael M. *A Guide to Theses and Dissertations: An International Bibliography of Bibliographies.* Rev. and enl. ed. Phoenix: Oryx, 1985. 263 pp.   Z5053.A1 R49   011′.7.

A bibliography of bibliographies, abstracts, and indexes (through mid-1984) of dissertations and theses. Reynolds includes separately published works as well as periodical contributions but excludes general lists of theses and dissertations accepted by a single institution. The entries are generally organized by date of publication within 19 classified divisions; of most interest to language and literature scholars are the universal and national divisions (with the latter classified by country), which list the general indexes, abstracts, and bibliographies; area studies (with a section for Anglo-American studies); special and racial groups; fine arts (with a section on theater); and language and literature, with sections for general lists, African languages and literature, Anglo-American language and literature (subdivided by country), Arabic literature, Austronesian linguistics, Chinese linguistics, children's literature, classical studies, comparative literature, folklore, Germanic languages and literature, Hebrew literature, Indian languages and literature, Japanese language and literature, languages and linguistics, Philippine literature, Romance languages and literature, science fiction, Slavic and East European languages and literature, speech, and individual authors. The annotations clearly describe scope, organization, and content. Three indexes: institutions; names and journal titles; subjects. Although the introduction is unduly murky, *Guide to Theses and Dissertations* is the essential, time-saving source for identifying both the well-known and the obscure indexes, bibliographies, and abstracts that must be searched for theses and dissertations relevant to a topic.

General Abstracts

H465   *ProQuest Dissertations and Theses.* ProQuest. Online. 28 Feb. 2006 <http:// proquest.umi.com>. Updated monthly. (Title varies.)

Dissertation Abstracts Online. Online (available through Ovid [I515], SilverPlatter [I523], and FirstSearch [E225a]). Updated monthly.

Dissertation Abstracts Ondisc. CD-ROM. Updated quarterly.

Available in print form as:

> *Dissertation Abstracts International* (*DAI*). Ann Arbor: UMI-ProQuest, 1938– . Monthly. Former titles: *Dissertation Abstracts* (*DA*) (1952–69); *Microfilm Abstracts* (1938–51).   Z5053.D57   011′.7.
>
>> Pt. A: *The Humanities and Social Sciences.* 1966– . Monthly.
>> Pt. B: *The Sciences and Engineering.* 1966– . Monthly.
>> Pt. C: *Worldwide.* 1976– . Quarterly.
>
> *Masters Abstracts International.* 1962– . 6/yr. (Former title: *Masters Abstracts* (1962–85).
>
> *American Doctoral Dissertations* [1933–] (*ADD*). Ann Arbor: ProQuest, 1934– . Annual. Former titles: *Index to American Doctoral Dissertations* [1955–63] (1957–64); *Doctoral Dissertations Accepted by American Universities* [1933–55] (*DDAU*).
>
> *Comprehensive Dissertation Index, 1861–1972* (*CDI*). 37 vols. Ann Arbor: UMI, 1973. Annual supplements, with cumulations for 1973–82 and 1983–87.   Z5053.X47   013′.379.

A database of doctoral dissertations and master's theses accepted by North American and some foreign institutions since 1861. The database now cites dissertations from most United States and Canadian institutions (and, since 1988, many British ones), but coverage in the early years is considerably less thorough, and some universities still do not submit abstracts or dissertations for reproduction. Coverage of dissertations outside North America is superficial. A list of participating institutions is printed at the beginning of each issue of *DAI* (some lists cite the year an institution began submitting dissertations).

Because of the massive number of records and the inadequacies of the indexing and organization of the print versions, the electronic versions offer the best access; however, since these do not include abstracts before July 1980 for dissertations and before 1988 for theses or include records from *DAI* pt. C before vol. 49 (1988), researchers will frequently find themselves digging through stacks of the print versions. In addition, effective searching of the electronic versions requires a familiarity with the scope, organization, and editorial principles of *DAI*.

In *DAI* abstracts are now organized in classified subject divisions. Currently, the language and literature division is in two parts: (1) language, with sections for general studies, ancient languages, linguistics, modern languages, and rhetoric and composition;

(2) literature, with sections for general, classical, comparative, medieval, modern, African, American, Asian, Canadian, Caribbean, English, Germanic, Latin American, Middle Eastern, Romance, and Slavic and East European literatures. Theater and cinema appear as sections in the communication and the arts division; folklore and women's studies, in the social sciences division. Since placement is determined by the dissertation author, subject classification is frequently inconsistent or imprecise. Within each section, abstracts are now listed alphabetically by author.

An entry consists of title, UMI order number, author, degree, institution, date of degree, number of pages, sometimes the dissertation adviser, and an abstract written by the author. In recent volumes, many titles have keywords added parenthetically to facilitate electronic searches—e.g., "Working Fictions: Narratives of Women and Labor in Early Modern England (William Shakespeare, Mary, Lady Wroth, Thomas Heywood, Aemilia Lanyer)"—abstracts sometimes include untranslated HTML codes, and copyediting is negligent. Entries in pt. C add an English translation of a foreign language title and ISBN for a published dissertation or information on location or availability of a reference copy if the work is unavailable from UMI. In recent years, UMI's rigorous enforcement of a 350-word limit results in some abstracts being cut off in mid-sentence.

Since vol. 30 (1969), each issue of *DAI* has keyword title and dissertation author indexes, with the latter cumulated at the end of a volume. Earlier issues and volumes have a dissertation author index, and vols. 22–29 (1961–69) are indexed by subject. *Dissertation Abstracts International Retrospective Index, Volumes I–XXIX*, 9 vols. (Ann Arbor: Xerox, 1970), is superseded by the electronic versions. The keyword access to abstracts is particularly welcome because of the sometimes imprecise subject classification of *DAI* and the recent trend toward uninformative, imprecise dissertation titles.

Researchers without access to one of the electronic versions should consult *Comprehensive Dissertation Index*, a keyword index to the titles of dissertations in the *Dissertation Abstracts Database*. Entries are organized by broad subject divisions, then alphabetically by keyword, then chronologically by date (with the most recent first), then alphabetically by institution, and then alphabetically by author. An entry cites title, author, degree, date, institution, number of pages, source of entry, and UMI order number. Indexed by dissertation author in each cumulation and annual issue. Users must bear in mind the following:

1. The subject organization has changed during the course of publication (e.g., in the 1861–1972 cumulation, theater is a subdivision of communications and the arts, and folklore a subdivision of social sciences; in the 1973–82 cumulation and subsequent issues, theater and folklore studies are incorporated into the language and literature division).
2. Because of the sources, there are duplicate and misclassified entries as well as numerous errors.
3. Cumulations and annual issues correct earlier entries and offer some retrospective coverage (e.g., *Canadian Theses* and its predecessors are first indexed in the 1973–82 cumulation).
4. Because *CDI* is an index of title keywords, users must check for variant spellings of names or terms, must keep in mind that many titles do not lend themselves to keyword indexing, and, if possible, should search for narrow rather than broad terms (e.g., in 1861–1972, "novel" and related terms occupy 37 columns). Foreign-language titles are only indexed by their English-language translations.

ProQuest's database is available in a variety of electronic forms: *ProQuest Dissertations and Theses, Dissertation Abstracts Online,* and *Dissertation Abstracts Ondisc.* All allow users to narrow a search by combining or excluding keywords and to limit it by such fields as degree date, adviser, language, or institution. *ProQuest Dissertations and Theses* offers two search screens. Basic Search allows keyword searches of the citation, index terms, subjects, and abstract fields to be limited by date, degree-granting institution, subject, and language. Advanced Search allows users to search by several Boolean combinations of citation and abstract, abstract, adviser, author, degree, title, index terms, ISBN, language, publication or order number, institution, date, or subject. Searches in both modes can be limited to dissertations only and to documents with full text available; results can be returned by date or relevance (although there is no explanation about how the latter is established); and searches can be saved as alerts. In both modes, users should consult the Search Tips screen for search syntax and for additional ways to limit searches (e.g., by *DAI* volume and issue). Inexperienced searchers should begin with ProQuest's quick reference guide (http://training.proquest.com/trc/training/en/pqdd.pdf).

A typical record consists of citation (title, author, degree, institution, date, number of pages, and publication number), along with fields for adviser, institution, location of institution, index terms, *DAI* citation, type of document, subjects, publication number, document URL, ProQuest document number, and abstract. (Users should note that titles of dissertations are not in title case; that an italicized title-within-a-title is enclosed within double quotation marks; and that as of the middle of 66.10 [2006], page numbers are rarely cited because the database is now updated before *DAI* or *MAI* page numbers are assigned.) For many dissertations after 1997, searchers can view a 24-page preview or—if their institutional subscription allows—read the entire document as a PDF file. Records can be marked for printing, e-mailing, exporting (in a variety of forms), or downloading as a Web page. Records printed or e-mailed can be formatted in several citation styles, including MLA and Chicago; however, citations formatted in MLA style require substantial editing. Although allowing for sophisticated searching of the database and offering extensive output options, *Proquest Dissertations and Theses* offers no description of the scope of the database or editorial principles underlying the records.

Copies of many dissertations deposited with UMI can be purchased in microform or on paper (directly through *ProQuest Dissertations and Theses* or see the Dissertation Express Web site for details (http://il.proquest.com/products_umi/dissertations/disexpress.shtml). Some dissertations are restricted, and others must be ordered from the degree-granting institution. For information on how to obtain British and Irish dissertations and theses, see *Index to Theses* (H475). D. H. Borchardt and J. D. Thawley, comps., *Guide to the Availability of Theses*, IFLA Publications 17 (München: Saur, 1981, 443 pp.), and G. G. Allen and K. Deubert, comps., *Guide to the Availability of Theses, II: Non-university Institutions*, IFLA Publications 29 (1984, 124 pp.), outline policies governing the borrowing or copying of theses and dissertations accepted by 750 institutions in 85 countries.

Although frequently imprecise in subject classification and incomplete in coverage, *ProQuest Dissertations and Theses* database offers an invaluable service in making available abstracts of so many dissertations. For the genesis and publishing history of *DAI* (along with a selective bibliography of studies and reviews), see Mary W. George, "Controlling the Beasties: *Dissertation Abstracts International*," *Distinguished Classics of Reference Publishing*, ed. James Rettig (Phoenix: Oryx, 1992) 66–76.

North American dissertations not abstracted in *DAI* are listed in *American Doctoral Dissertations* and *A List of American Doctoral Dissertations Printed in [1912–38]* (Washington: GPO, 1913–40). Entries from both are incorporated into *ProQuest Dissertations and Theses* database.

Masters Abstracts International is similar in organization to *DAI* but abstracts a relatively small percentage of the annual output of master's theses even in the United States. Each volume has cumulative author and subject indexes, and titles can be searched by keyword through *ProQuest Dissertations and Theses.*

National Bibliographies and Abstracts

H470   *Canadian Theses/Thèses canadiennes [1961–96].* Ottawa: Natl. Lib. of
         Canada, 1963–97. 2/yr., with cumulative index. Microfiche only since
         1980–1981 (1984–97). *1947–1960.* 2 vols. 1973.   Z5055.C2 O883
         013′.375′0971.

A bibliography of theses and dissertations accepted by Canadian institutions since 1947 or microfilmed by the National Library since 1981 and, beginning with the *1980–1981* volumes, foreign theses and dissertations by Canadians or related to Canada. Beginning with *1980–1981* entries are listed in processing order in two parts: works accepted by Canadian institutions; those by Canadians or about the country accepted by foreign institutions. Entries cite author, title, degree, institution, and date. Access to the parts is provided by four indexes (which cumulate with each issue): author and title; title keywords; Dewey Decimal Classification; ISBN. Before *1980–1981,* entries are organized by Dewey Decimal Classification.

This work continues *Canadian Graduate Theses in the Humanities and Social Sciences, 1921–1946/Thèses des gradués canadiens dans les humanités et les sciences sociales* (Ottawa: Cloutier, 1951, 194 pp.). Together, the two sources provide the fullest coverage of theses and dissertations accepted by Canadian institutions through 1996; however, researchers will find those on literature easier to identify in Antoine Naaman and Léo A. Brodeur, *Répertoire des thèses littéraires canadiennes de 1921 à 1976,* Collection "Bibliographies" 3 (Sherbrooke: Naaman, 1978, 453 pp.), a subject list that includes a few works in progress as of March 1976 and some written by Canadians at foreign universities. Canadian theses and dissertations on Canadian literature are covered by Gabel, *Canadian Literature* (R4660); several on British or American literature are listed in McNamee, *Dissertations in English and American Literature* (H490). Many Canadian dissertations—especially those received by the National Library of Canada since February 1991—are listed in *American Doctoral Dissertations* (H465a) and abstracted in *ProQuest Dissertations and Theses* (H465). *Theses/Thèses Canada* (http://www.collectionscanada.gc.ca/thesescanada/index-e.html) allows users to search theses and dissertations in the Library and Archives Canada collection, to borrow copies, and to view a limited number in electronic form. For other bibliographies of Canadian dissertations and theses, see Denis Robitaille and Joan Waiser, *Theses in Canada: A Bibliographic Guide/Thèses au Canada: Guide bibliographique* (Ottawa: Natl. Lib. of Canada, 1986, 72 pp.).

The quickest way to search *Canadian Theses* (through the volume for 1969–70) and its predecessor is through the *ProQuest Dissertations and Theses* (H465).

H475   *Index to Theses.* Expert Information. Online. 28 Feb. 2006
         <http://www.theses.com>. Updated regularly.

A database of bachelor's, master's, and doctoral theses accepted since 1716 by academic institutions in the British Isles. Records are taken from two publications:

> *Index to Theses with Abstracts Accepted for Higher Degrees by the Universities
> of Great Britain and Ireland.* London: Expert Information, 1953– . Fre-

quency and title vary. A list of theses accepted since 1950. Currently, entries are listed alphabetically by author within classified subject divisions, including one for arts and humanities, with subdivisions for theater, cinema, and broadcasting; linguistics; and literature. The last has sections for general, classical, English (divided by period), American, Celtic, Romance (divided by language), Germanic (divided by language), Slavonic, and other languages. The organization has changed over the years. An entry includes title, author, institution, degree, date, and—since vol. 35 (1986)—an abstract (sometimes edited for length) for most PhD and DPhil theses; the microfilm abstracts for 1970–85 are available as PDF files through the database. Variations in institutional policies mean that the date can refer to submission, acceptance, or award of degree. Indexed by authors in each issue; the subject index was discontinued with vol. 48 (1999).

> *Retrospective Index to Theses of Great Britain and Ireland, 1716–1950.* Ed. Roger R. Bilboul. 5 vols. Santa Barbara: ABC-Clio, 1975–77. *Addenda.* 1977. 26 pp. Entries citing author, title, degree, date, and institution appear in two parts: (1) a subject index, which is based largely but not exclusively on title keywords, offers liberal cross-references, and provides several multiple entries; and (2) an author list. Since *Retrospective Index* is compiled from information supplied by institutions, there are inconsistencies and errors.

The online version offers four ways of searching the database:

Quick Search: keyword search of (presumably) all searchable record fields.
Simple Search: keyword search of title, author, abstract; pull-down menu searches of university, classification scheme used by *Index to Theses with Abstracts*, and year (as designated in the *Index to Theses with Abstracts* record). Fields must be combined by the Boolean "and" or "or."
Standard Search. Combination keyword and pull-down menu searches of title, author, degree, classification, year, university, and any field. Fields must be combined by "and" or "or."
Advanced Search. Command line searches of title, author, university, classification, year, degree, and abstract. Help screen links (Search Tips and Various Examples) appear on only this page.

Records are returned in no discernible order, although it is possible to limit the results of a search to records added or modified between two dates (for the search syntax, click the Various Examples link on the Advanced Search page). Unfortunately, the site does not allow users to mark records for printing, exporting, or downloading; indeed, the only way to extract a record is through a Web browser's print or copy functions. Although lacking adequate help screens, awkward to navigate (Simple Search and Standard Search should be combined into a single screen), and time-consuming to use if a researcher needs to examine and copy a large number of records, the online *Index to Theses* is the essential resource for identifying British and Irish theses, especially since they are no longer included in *ABELL* (G340).

Since 1988, many British doctoral dissertations are abstracted in *ProQuest Dissertations and Theses* (H465) and available through UMI. The best general source for copies, however, remains the British Thesis Service (http://www.bl.uk/britishthesis).

H480   *Union List of Higher Degree Theses in Australian University Libraries: Cumulative Edition to 1965.* Hobart: U of Tasmania Lib., 1967. 568 pp.

Supplement, [1966–89]. 1971–91. Irregular. Since the supplement for
1974, the main title omits *University.*   Z5055.A698 U5   011′.7.

A union list of master's theses and doctoral dissertations accepted by Australian
universities and held by at least one Australian university library. Works are organized
alphabetically by author within extensively classified subject divisions (including, in the
later supplements, folklore, language, literature, and theater). Two indexes: authors;
subject headings (the supplements have an additional one for title keywords). Although
the subject classification is sometimes imprecise because it is based largely on titles and
although coverage is not exhaustive, *Union List* offers the fullest record of theses and
dissertations accepted by Australian universities. The National Library of Australia's
plan to assume publication of the *Union List* was never realized.

The prefatory matter of the last supplement discusses the availability of theses in
Australian university libraries. For additional information, see *How to Locate Australian
Theses: A Guide to Theses in Progress or Completed at Australian Universities and the
University of Papua New Guinea* (Canberra: Lib., Australian Nat. U, 1979, 41 pp.).

The best resource for identifying Australian theses accepted after 1985 is *Libraries
Australia* (http://librariesaustralia.nla.gov.au/apps/kss).

See also

   English and American Studies in German (G440).

Other Bibliographies

H485   Gabel, Gernot U., and Gisela R. Gabel. *Catalogue of Austrian and Swiss
       Dissertations (1875–1995) on English and American Literature.* Hürth:
       Gemini, 1997. 222 pp.   Z2011.G24 [PR83]   016.8209.

A bibliography of doctoral-level theses compiled from the standard national dissertation bibliographies (and university lists in the case of Austria) of the two countries.
The earlier versions—*Dissertations in English and American Literature: Theses Accepted
by Austrian, French, and Swiss Universities, 1875–1970* (Hamburg: Gabel, 1977, 198
pp.) and *Dissertations in English and American Literature: A Bibliography of Theses Accepted by Austrian, French, and Swiss Universities: Supplement, 1971–1975, and Additions* (Köln: Gemini, 1982, 56 pp.)—include French dissertations. Dissertations are
listed chronologically in nine classified divisions: general literary history and criticism,
Old and Middle English literature, then by century for English literature, American
literature to 1900, and twentieth-century American literature. The period divisions have
sections for general studies or individual authors. Two indexes: scholars; literary authors
and anonymous works. A time-saving compilation that offers the single fullest list of
dissertations on English and American literature accepted by universities in the two
countries.

H490   McNamee, Lawrence F. *Dissertations in English and American Literature:
       Theses Accepted by American, British, and German Universities, 1865–1964.*
       New York: Bowker, 1968. 1,124 pp. *Supplement One, 1964–1968.* 1969.
       450 pp. *Supplement Two: Theses Accepted by American, British, British
       Commonwealth, and German Universities, 1969–1973.* 1974. 690 pp.
       Z5053.M32   016.82.

A subject bibliography of dissertations written in English departments of institutions in the United States, Great Britain, East and West Germany, Canada (beginning in the first supplement and including retrospective coverage), Australia (beginning in the first supplement), and New Zealand (in the second supplement). Derived from lists supplied or checked by the institutions, the 25,953 entries are organized by date of acceptance in 35 classified divisions: Anglo-Saxon; English language and linguistics; Chaucer; Middle English; Renaissance; Shakespeare; seventeenth century; Milton; eighteenth century; Romantic period; Victorian period; twentieth century; drama and theater; English novel; poetry; comparative literature; literary criticism, rhetoric, and genre studies; creative dissertations; teaching of English; Empire literature; magazines, newspapers, and publishing; religion and literature; colonial American; National period; post–Civil War period; twentieth-century American literature; American novel and fiction; American drama and theater; literary criticism in the United States; language in the United States; regional literature; African American literature; American poetry; American literary relationships; miscellaneous topics in American literature. Most divisions are extensively classified by subjects, groups, genres, movements, or individual authors. An entry consists of author, title, date of acceptance, a code number that identifies the institution, and, in the 1969–73 supplement, number of pages. Two indexes in each volume: a cross-index of literary authors in the titles of multiple-author studies; dissertation writers. McNamee must be used with due regard for its numerous limitations and deficiencies:

1. The work falls far short of the complete list it claims to be. Restricted to studies written in English departments, it ignores numerous dissertations on English and American literature produced in history, comparative literature, and (especially) theater or drama departments. And there are many omissions of dissertations accepted by English departments.

2. Dissertations are frequently difficult to locate because titles determine placement in divisions and classified sections, many of which are insufficiently exclusive. Particularly vexing are the numerous classified sections that are frequently imprecise in heading, inconsistent across divisions, and organized in no discernible manner (e.g., related topics are rarely grouped together). Because a dissertation is listed in only one section and multiple-author studies are placed under the first author mentioned, users searching for dissertations on specific writers must be certain to check the cross-index of authors, which is unhelpfully keyed to the numbered sections rather than to pages. The vagueness and inconsistencies in subject classifications and inadequate indexing mean that researchers must exercise considerable ingenuity to locate dissertations.

3. There are numerous typographical errors, and the combination of uppercase computer print and poor layout makes for inefficient scanning.

Because of these serious limitations and deficiencies, McNamee is now principally useful for identifying the occasional dissertation overlooked in a search of the more thorough and easily accessible *ProQuest Dissertations and Theses* (H465) and the other bibliographies and abstracts in this section.

H495   Mummendey, Richard. *Language and Literature of the Anglo-Saxon Nations as Presented in German Doctoral Dissertations, 1885–1950/Die Sprache und Literatur der Angelsachsen im Spiegel der deutschen Universitätsschriften, 1885–1950.* Bonn: Bouvier; Charlottesville: Bibliographical Soc. of the U of Virginia, 1954. 200 pp.   Z2011.M8   016.82.

A classified list of doctoral dissertations on the English language and literature in English accepted by German universities between 1885 and 1950, by the University of Strassburg up to 1918, and by Austrian universities from 1938 to 1945. The approximately 3,000 entries are organized in three divisions: linguistics, with dissertations listed by year of acceptance within sections for general studies, phonetics, orthography, morphology, etymology, syntax, dialect and slang, stylistics, and prosody; literature, with sections for Great Britain (including subsections for genres, motifs and topics, influences, and individual periods), the Commonwealth, and the United States (including subsections for general studies and individual periods); theater. In the literature and theater divisions, dissertations are organized alphabetically by a title keyword, which is set in spaced type. An entry cites author, title, number of pages, publication information for dissertations published in a series or periodical, an indication of manuscript ("HS") or typescript ("MS") for those not printed, institution, and year of acceptance. Indexed by dissertation authors and title keywords.

The subject indexing by title keyword is frequently imprecise or misleading (and the spaced type is not immediately recognizable), but the poor subject indexing is a minor deficiency in comparison to the frequent errors in citations and numerous omissions. (In *Guide to Doctoral Dissertations in Victorian Literature* [M2510], Altick reports that he discovered about 130 dissertations overlooked by Mummendey.) While useful for compiling a preliminary list of German dissertations on a topic, Mummendey must be supplemented by a laborious search through *Jahresverzeichnis der Hochschulschriften der DDR, der BRD und Westberlins [1885–1987]* (Leipzig: VEB Bibliographisches Institut, 1887–90; title varies).

See also

Dundes, *Folklore Theses and Dissertations in the United States* (U5885).
Fielding, *Bibliography of Theses and Dissertations on the Subject of Film, 1916–1979* (U5795).
Gilbert, *Women's Studies: A Bibliography of Dissertations, 1870–1982* (U6615).

I

Internet Resources

The proliferation of electronic journals and discussion groups, text archives, and informational World Wide Web sites; the accessibility of online library catalogs; the ability to communicate and exchange drafts of documents within seconds with colleagues around the world; the availability of online databases; and the possibilities offered by electronic publication — all mean that a literary scholar with only elementary knowledge of computers and the Internet is at a serious disadvantage. Those who need to learn how to use electronic mail, the World Wide Web, and FTP should see their academic computing service about short courses. Those who do not know how to use Boolean operators, truncation, wildcards, nesting, phrase searching, proximity operators, or relevancy searching should consult the admirably clear "Basics of Online Searching" chapter (pp. 1-17) in Keeran, *Literary Research and the British Romantic Era* (M2445).

Internet Resources

The phenomenal growth of the Internet and especially the World Wide Web has led to a proliferation of electronic resources for literary research. The overwhelming amount of material available — including far too many dubious reference tools — and its frequently ephemeral nature have led to the creation of World Wide Web metapages, that is, clearinghouses of links to resources in a discipline or subject. Because World Wide Web sites constantly appear, disappear, change URLs, become inactive, or vary in quality, metapages that judiciously evaluate — rather than indiscriminately link to — sites serve as essential gateways to Internet resources.

Internet Metapages

I500   *Intute.* Resource Discovery Network. Online. 29 Aug. 2006
        <http://www.intute.ac.uk>. Updated daily.
    A selective, annotated catalog of online resources that supersedes *Humbul Humanities Hub*. Among the 40 subjects covered in Arts and Humanities pages are humanities computing, manuscript studies, American literature, English studies, comparative literature, and linguistics. Records, which can be searched by keyword or browsed by subject, include such fields as: title, alternative title, description, controlled keywords, uncontrolled keywords, URL, classification, intended audience, editor and other persons responsible for the site, publisher, type of resource, dates of coverage, historical period, country of origin, record creation date, references to the site or awards, and special technical requirements (including an indication if the site requires a subscription). Basic Search allows simple keyword searches; Advanced Search allows users to restrict a keyword search to the title, alternative title, and description fields, and to narrow the results of a search by subject area or type of resource. The browse screen allows users to browse subjects by all entries, by type of entry (e.g., primary sources or bibliographic resources), or by historical period, but the inability to refine searches further leaves users to scroll through lengthy screens (e.g., 478 records—alphabetized by title—under English Studies/Bibliographic Databases). Although *Intute* sets itself apart from other metapages by being maintained by a full-time staff that creates records and vets those submitted by contributors, many records are seriously outdated (the *ABELL* [G340] record was created on 24 Jan. 2002), much of dubious value is included (e.g., Anniina's Alice Walker page), a disconcerting number of URLs are dead or outdated, and there is little in the way of evaluation in the descriptions. *Intute* has the potential to become the principal gateway to online humanities sources; to realize this potential will require redesigning the browse screen, maintaining currency of information (especially for major resources) and weeding out defunct sites, and paying more attention to evaluating—rather than merely cataloging—sites.

I503   *Literary Resources on the Net.* Online. 27 Feb. 2006 <http://andromeda
        .rutgers.edu/~jlynch/Lit>. Updated regularly. Maintained by Jack Lynch
        (jlynch@andromeda.rutgers.edu).
    As of 27 February 2006, this metapage, which offers links to Internet sites related to English and American literature, includes the following categories: classical and biblical, medieval, Renaissance, eighteenth century, Romantic, Victorian (British), twentieth century (British and Irish), American, theater and drama, theory, women's literature and feminism, ethnicities and nationalities, other national literatures, bibliography and history of the book, hypertext, and miscellaneous. This site is the best of the selective metapages.

I505   *Voice of the Shuttle: Web Page for Humanities Research.* Online. 27 Feb.
        2006 <http://vos.ucsb.edu>. Updated regularly. Maintained by Alan Liu
        (ayliu@english.ucsb.edu).
    As of 27 February 2006, this metapage covers general humanities resources along with resources in such areas as anthropology, art history, classical studies, cultural studies, gender and sexuality studies, history, linguistics, literary theory, media studies, minority studies, music, philosophy, technology of writing, and women's studies. The

Literature (in English) subpage includes the following categories: general resources (including pedagogy); Anglo-Saxon and medieval; Renaissance and seventeenth century; Restoration and eighteenth century; Romantic; Victorian; modern (with subsections for British and American); contemporary (with subsections for British and American); American (with subsections for colonial and nineteenth century); minority literatures; other literatures in English (with subsections for African, Asian, Australian, Canadian, Caribbean, Irish, Scottish, Subcontinental, and Welsh); genres (with subsections for drama and theater, fiction, and poetry); creative writing; and history of the book. This site is the best of the inclusive metapages and fully deserves the praise accorded it by scholars and Web aficionados.

See also

> *NetFirst* (E225a).

Database Vendors

The following vendors offer access to electronic versions of several reference sources in this *Guide*. *NetFirst* (E225a) identifies Internet resources.

I510   Cambridge Scientific Abstracts (CSA). 25 Feb. 2006 <http://
            www.csa.com>.
        Offers online access to *ARTbibliographies Modern* (U5140), *ATLA Religion Database* (U6350), *BHA: Bibliography of the History of Art* (U5138), *BHI: British Humanities Index* (G370), ERIC (U5590), *FRANCIS* (G345), *Linguistics and Language Behavior Abstracts* (U6015), *MLAIB* (G335), *Philosopher's Index* (U6275), *PsycINFO* (U6530), *RILM Abstracts of Music Literature* (U6240), and *Sociological Abstracts* (U6560).
        CSA's Illumina search interface offers three search options: Quick Search, Advanced Search, Search Tools. The Quick Search option allows basic keyword or phrase searching of all default fields (users must insert a Boolean operator; otherwise two or more words will be searched as a phrase) and offers date limits only in broad ranges. Advanced Search lets searchers limit searches to or combine (by Boolean operators) a variety of record fields (e.g., author, title, abstract, ISBN, ISSN, language, publisher, and year); restrict searches to a year or year range, journal articles only, the latest update, and English-language titles; and choose the format in which records appear. Search Tools allows users to execute a command search (easily done thanks to a pull-down menu of field codes); to browse any thesaurus or index associated with a database; to create alerts; and to view a search history and combine, save, or edit searches. (Users can also browse journals and books in the Illumina databases.) Users can isolate records returned by type of publication (journal article, dissertation, book chapter, book) to articles from peer-reviewed journals, books, or Web sites. Unfortunately, there are only two choices for sorting records: chronological (descending); relevance (determined by the first eight terms in the Descriptor field). Users can mark records for printing, saving to disk, or e-mailing (with the option of formatting records in a variety of citation styles including MLA and Chicago; however, the output in both requires substantial editing). Researchers must take particular care in searching for publications in languages other than English: in some databases, titles are translated into English in the Title field (the foreign-language title appears in the Original Title field); diacritics are omitted in the

Author field (and in the entire record in some databases). Illumina allows cross-searching of its databases included in an institution's subscription.

I512   EBSCO. 25 Feb. 2006 <http://www.ebsco.com>.

Offers access to the following databases of interest to language and literature scholars: *Academic Search Premier* (G400a), *ATLA Religion Database* (U6350), *Columbia Granger's Poetry Database* (L1235), ERIC (U5590), *Film and Television Literature Index* (U5780), *Gender Studies Database* (U6610a), *Humanities International Index* and *Humanities International Complete* (G360), *International Bibliography of Theatre and Dance* (L1160), *International Political Science Abstracts* (U6520), *MLAIB* (G335), *Music Index* (U6240a), *PsycINFO* (U6530), *RILM Abstracts of Music Literature* (U6240), and *Women's Studies International* (U6610a).

The EBSCO search interface offers three search screens: Basic Search allows a keyword search to be limited by date, type of publication, and language and to journals that are peer reviewed and linked to full text (in addition, users can elect to expand searches to related words and to full text [if available] and to link terms with "and"); Advanced Search allows users to combine keyword searches of individual record fields (identified in pull-down lists) and adds genre, time period, and electronic publication to the Basic Search options for limiting or expanding a search; Visual Search creates a visual representation of a keyword search by mapping results by topic (circles represent categories and can have subcategories within them; squares are links to individual documents—the larger the number of hits, the less Visual Search is effective at organizing the results). The searchable fields vary depending on the content of individual databases. Depending on the database being searched, users can browse a thesaurus, a list of names as subjects, and a list of indexes; these options are especially important features for searching *MLAIB* (though the list of indexes would be more useful if each index were mapped to a list of searchable terms).

Results of a search can be sorted (by date, author, title, and relevancy rank), marked, and custom formatted for printing, e-mailing, downloading, or saving to a user's account. Sophisticated searching requires that users become familiar with the Searchable Fields section of Database Help; unfortunately, in the case of *MLAIB*, the explanation of some fields is too imprecise to allow users to exploit fully the *MLAIB*'s indexing of records.

I515   Ovid. 25 Feb. 2006 <http://www.ovid.com>.

Offers access to the following databases of interest to language and literature scholars: *ATLA Religion Database* (U6350), *BHA: Bibliography of the History of Art* (U5138), *Books in Print* (Q4225a), *ProQuest Dissertations and Theses* (H465), ERIC (U5590), *Philosopher's Index* (U6275), *PsycINFO* (U6530), *Ulrich's Periodicals Directory* (K625), and a few of the databases available through *WilsonWeb* (I525).

The Ovid search interface offers three search options: Basic Search (with fields for keyword and author); Advanced Search (a confusingly-designed screen that allows a user to choose a keyword, author, title, or journal field; or to click on More Options for a screen that allows a search of individual record fields; or to click on Search Tools, which allows searches of an index or thesaurus associated with a database); and Find Citation, which allows users to search for articles, has fields for title, author, year of publication, journal, volume number, issue number, and beginning page. Basic and Advanced Search offer several options—e.g., date, full text sources, latest update—for limiting a search.

Results of a search can be sorted by a substantial number of record fields, and the record display can be customized. Records can be selected for e-mailing, saving, or printing (in a variety of formats). The Ovid interface is far less user-friendly than and does not offer the same level of sophistication in searching as those of the other vendors in this section of the *Guide*; fortunately no major literature databases are offered through Ovid.

I519   ProQuest (including Chadwyck-Healey and UMI). 26 Feb. 2006
        <http://il.proquest.com>.

Offers access to the following databases and text archives of interest to language and literature scholars: *AABD: African American Biographical Database* (Q3765); *African American Poetry* (Q3848); *American Drama 1714–1915* (Q3514); *AFI Catalog* (U5760); *American Poetry* (Q3536); *ABELL* (G340); *Bibliography of American Literature* (Q3250); *C19: The Nineteenth Century Index* (M2466); *Canadian Poetry* (R4753); *ProQuest Dissertations and Theses* (H465); *Early American Fiction, 1789–1875* (Q4183); *Early English Books Online* (M2009); *Early English Prose Fiction* (M2103); *Eighteenth-Century Fiction* (M2339); *English Drama* (M1553); *English Poetry Database* (M1593); *Film Index International* (U5767a); ERIC (U5590); *International Index to Black Periodicals Full Text* (Q3740a); *International Index to Music Periodicals* (U6240a); *Literature Online* (I527); *MLAIB* (G335); *Nineteenth-Century Fiction* (M2663); *Nineteenth Century Short Title Catalogue* (M2475); *Periodicals Index Online* (G397); *ProQuest Historical Newspapers*; *PsycINFO* (U6530); *Twentieth-Century African-American Poetry* (Q3848a); *Twentieth-Century American Poetry* (Q4333); *Twentieth-Century Drama* (L1158); and *Twentieth-Century English Poetry* (M2894). Many of the preceding use the *Literature Online* (I527) interface or one that differs from the following.

The ProQuest search interface offers two search screens: Basic Search allows users to limit a keyword search by date, to full-text documents, and to scholarly or peer-reviewed journals; Advanced Search allows keyword searches of specific record fields (to see all fields, users must click on More Search Options, which adds two fields—journal title and document type—to a series that otherwise repeats fields already on the pull-down lists and which offers additional options for limiting a search). Both search screens include a Browse Topics link; the window that opens also includes a link to any thesaurus attached to a database. In addition, a Topics tab opens a screen that offers the same search capability as the Browse Topics link (but lacks the link to a thesaurus), and a Publications tab allows users to browse issues of journals indexed. The results of a search (which can be saved as an alert) can be grouped by type of document, restricted to full-text documents, and sorted only by descending date and relevancy. Marked records can be e-mailed (with options for determining record content and citation style, including Chicago and MLA; users should note that MLA-formatted citations require substantial editing) or downloaded (with options for exporting directly into bibliographic management software). Users can cross-search ProQuest databases included in an institution's subscription (although historical databases cannot be searched with nonhistorical ones). Although ProQuest's search interface sports redundant features, it does not allow for the level of sophistication that expert searchers expect and is too restrictive in the options it offers for managing results of a search, but it is the only vendor that offers cross-searching of *MLAIB* and *ABELL* (see the discussion of *Literature Online* [I527]).

I523   SilverPlatter. 22 Feb. 2006 <http://www.ovid.com/site/products/tools/
        silverplatter>.

Offers access to: *American Library Directory* (E200a), *BHA: Bibliography of the History of Art* (U5138), *Books in Print with Book Reviews* (Q4225a), *Choice* (K750), *ProQuest Dissertations and Theses* (H465), ERIC (U5590), *FIAF International Film-Archive Database* (U5785), *FRANCIS* (G345), *Marquis Who's Who* (Q3395), *Philoso-*

pher's Index (U6275), *PsycINFO* (U6530), *ATLA Religion Database* (U6350), *RILM Abstracts of Music Literature* (U6240), *Sociological Abstracts* (U6560), *Ulrich's Periodicals Directory* (K625), and most databases available through *WilsonWeb* (I525).

WebSPIRS, the SilverPlatter search interface, offers five search screens (though not all can be used with every database):

> Search allows keyword searches of full-text, titles, subjects, or authors.
>
> Advanced allows searchers to combine searches of record fields used by a database (e.g., author, title, journal, ISSN, or publisher). The pull-down menu identifies fields specific to a database when users simultaneously search more than one database.
>
> Index allows users to search or browse alphabetic or numeric lists (such as accession numbers, languages, journal titles, or authors). As in Advanced, the pull-down menu identifies lists specific to a database when users simultaneously search more than one database.
>
> Find Citation, which allows users to search for articles, has fields for title, author, year of publication, journal, and ISSN. Users can perform the same search on the Advanced page.
>
> Thesaurus. This screen is available only if the database has a thesaurus; when cross-searching databases, all must share the same thesaurus.

Searches through the Search, Advanced, and Index screens can be limited in a variety of ways (e.g., by update code, document type, language, and date); however, users must set these limits by clicking More beneath the Limit Search To: box. Users can also control how records are displayed and sorted by clicking on Change Display. Search History allows users to rerun, combine, or save searches.

Records can be marked for printing, e-mailing, or downloading (although the icons for these tasks are not as easily found as they should be); users can select which fields to display in exported records.

The WebSPIRS search interface has improved markedly over the years to the point where it now allows sophisticated searches and substantial control over the display of · records. Some features (such as setting limits, displaying marked records, and clearing a search) are not easily identifiable, however.

I524   Thomson Gale. Online. 27 Feb. 2006 <http://www.gale.com>.
Offers online access to several text archives and databases of interest to literature scholars: *American History and Culture Online: Sabin Americana 1500–1926* (Q4015a), *Biography and Genealogy Master Index* (J565), *Biography Resource Center* (J572), *Book Review Index Online* (G415), *Contemporary Authors* (J595), *Dictionary of Literary Biography* (J600), *Eighteenth Century Collections Online* (M2238), *Expanded Academic ASAP*, and *InfoTrac OneFile* (G387), and *MLAIB* (through *Literature Resource Center* [I528]). Since Thomson Gale does not use a common search interface for all of its databases and digital archives, see the individual entries for evaluation of the interface.

I525   *WilsonWeb*. H. W. Wilson. Online. 22 Feb. 2006 <http://vnweb
            .hwwilsonweb.com/hww/>.
Offers online access to several of the popular Wilson indexes: *Art Index* databases (U5145), *Bibliographic Index Plus* (D145), *Biography Index* (J540), *Book Review Digest Plus* (G415a), *Book Review Digest Retrospective: 1905–1982* (G415a), *Children's Catalog* (U5475a), *Current Biography* databases (J585), *Education Index* (U5590a), *Essay and General Literature Index* (G380), *Fiction Catalog* (L835), *Humanities Index* (G385), *Middle and Junior High School Catalog* (U5475a), *Play Index* (L1155), *Readers' Guide*

databases (G400), *Senior High School Library Catalog* (U5475a), *Short Story Index* (L1085), *Social Sciences* databases (U6470), and the Wilson author biographies (J595a). The *WilsonWeb* search screen offers four search options:

> Basic Search (users can search by keyword, with the option of extending the search to the full-text of articles);
>
> Advanced Search (users can combine up to three fields — smart search [all fields], keyword, subject, title, personal author, corporate author, abstract, artist, books reviewed, document type, form review [i.e., a combination of title, abstract, and subject fields], historical subject, ISSN, journal issue, journal title, language, materials and date [i.e., of works of art], materials and technique [i.e., of works of art], other titles, and physical description [e.g., illustration or map] — and can limit searches by date, document type, physical description, subject area [if the search is across several databases], full-text article, PDF file, peer-reviewed journal; in addition, a search can be expanded to include full text);
>
> Browse (users can browse a series of alphabetic or numeric lists within a pull-down list of fields); and
>
> Thesaurus.

Searches can be saved for use in another session. Before searching, users should click the Customize Display link to set display options, sort order, record fields displayed, and record sets; Advanced Search allows users to set a descending (but not ascending) sort order. When sorting records in chronological order, users should note that some records are labeled "Record in process" (which seems to identify a document that will eventually have a full-text HTML or PDF file linked to it). Users can search across the Wilson databases included in an institution's subscription (but the maximum number of records that can be displayed is 10,000). Although users can use the Customize Display page to determine what records fields will be displayed, the default display (which varies somewhat depending on the source database) typically includes title, author, basic bibliographical information, peer-review status, ISSN, language, abstract, document type, source database, and persistent URL to the citation or — for full-text documents — to the HTML or PDF file. For an explanation of the fields used in a database, go to Help and click the Database Description/Details tab which will bring to the screen a pull-down list of databases.

When printing, e-mailing, saving, or exporting records to bibliographic software, users must be certain to scan all options for each choice; for example, E-mail and Save can format data in a variety of citation styles (including MLA, though the records still require substantial editing).

Most Wilson databases have a Journal Directory that lists journals and dates for coverage for both indexing and full-text availability.

The Help file includes full explanations and offers a feedback form. In general the search interface is user-friendly, offers an array of options that allows for sophisticated searching, and supports an admirable range of output options.

I527   *Literature Online* (*LiOn*). ProQuest. Online. 13 June 2006
         <http://lion.chadwyck.com>.
    A text archive that also offers access to a few databases (notably *MLAIB* [G335] and *ABELL* [G340]), reference works (notably Blanck, *Bibliography of American Literature* [Q3250], *Webster's Third New International Dictionary* [Q3365], and *New Princeton Encyclopedia of Poetry and Poetics* [L1230]), links to Web sites, commissioned biographies for c. 3,500 authors, and 180 full-text journals. The bulk of *LiOn* consists

of rekeyed texts of more than 350,000 English-language poems, plays, and works of fiction grouped in collections: *English Poetry* (M1593), *African American Poetry* (Q3848), *American Poetry* (Q3536), *Canadian Poetry* (R4753), *Twentieth-Century American Poetry* (Q4333), *Twentieth-Century English Poetry* (M2894), *Twentieth-Century African American Poetry* (Q3848a), *English Drama* (M1553), *American Drama 1714–1915* (Q3514), *Eighteenth-Century Fiction* (M2339), *Early English Prose Fiction* (M2103), *Nineteenth-Century Fiction* (M2663), *Early American Fiction 1789–1875* (Q4183), *Twentieth-Century Drama* (L1158), *Literary Theory*, and *African Writers Series*. (Users should note that many institutions that offer *LiOn* do not subscribe to all of the preceding, that each of the collections also has its own site with a separate—and some-times superior—search engine, and that there is no way in *LiOn* to restrict a search to a particular collection.)

Quick Search offers keyword searching of the entire content of *LiOn*. The regular Search offers three options: Authors (users can restrict a search by date, gender, ethnicity, literary movement, and literary period; most fields allow users to select from a list); Texts (users can restrict searches to keyword-in-text, title/first line of poem, and author by genre); Criticism and Reference (users can restrict keyword, author, and subject searches to criticism or reference works). When searching through the Texts screen, searchers must be certain to checkmark the Variant Spellings and Typographical Var-iants boxes. Users can also browse a list of authors (alphabetically or by period, nation-ality, literary movement, ethnicity, or gender) as well as nested lists of collections, reference and critical works, multimedia sites, and full-text journals. Users can save searches and records in My Archive and sign up for alerts. Depending on what content is being searched, results are displayed chronologically (descending order) or alphabet-ically (ascending order). Citations (but not the full text) can be marked for e-mailing, downloading, or printing; each citation includes a durable URL to the full text. Because of the variety of search screens and options, users new to *LiOn* should peruse the beginners' guide (Research Centre/Getting Started).

Some works are rekeyed from textually unsound editions; however, the biblio-graphic record for each work identifies the source of the text and any omissions (e.g., preliminary matter), and the site is refreshingly forthcoming in its explanations of ed-itorial procedures and revision history. Besides being a useful source for identifying an elusive quotation or locating allusions, the scope of *LiOn*'s text archive makes feasible a variety of kinds of studies (stylistic, thematic, imagistic, and topical). In addition, *LiOn* has proven valuable in authorship attribution studies. Currently, ProQuest is the only vendor that allows cross-searching of *MLAIB* and *ABELL* (search Criticism and Reference; limit the search to Criticism). Besides saving time, since users no longer have to integrate separate searches of the two databases, cross-searching provides the basis for a valid study of the overlap between the two.

I528   *Literature Resource Center*. Thomson Gale. Online. 21 June 2006
           <http://infotrac.galegroup.com/galenet>.
        A reference database that includes *MLAIB* (G335), links to more than 5,000 Web sites, and the full text of c. 260 journals (some of which are not peer-reviewed) and several multivolume reference works published by Thomson Gale (e.g., *Contemporary Authors* [J595] and *Dictionary of Literary Biography* [J600], which, however, lacks the illustrations in the print edition). Users can search through five search screens: Author; Title (and author); Keyword; Advanced Search (which allows author, title, critic, full-text, keyword, and document number searches to be limited by document type and specific database); and Authors by Type (which allows an author search to be limited by gender, year of birth, year of death, ethnicity, genre, literary movement or period,

nationality, and theme). Results appear on tabbed pages: Biographies; Literary Criticism, Articles, and Work Overviews; Bibliographies; Additional Resources (e.g., Web sites); and Literary-Historical Timeline. Since the majority of the full-text journals are available through other distributors (as is *MLAIB*), the chief value of *Literature Resource Center* is as an index to a variety of Thomson Gale publications (many of which are designed for an undergraduate audience).

I530   Oxford Reference Online. Oxford UP. Online. 9 May 2005
        <http://www.oxfordreference.com>.
        A database that offers electronic versions of *Oxford Companion to American Literature* (Q3210), *Oxford Companion to English Literature* (M1330), *Oxford Companion to American Theatre* (Q3500), *Oxford Companion to Music* (U6235a), *Dictionary of English Folklore* (U5838), *Oxford Companion to Australian Literature* (R4450), *Oxford Companion to Canadian Literature* (R4567), *Oxford Dictionary of English*, *Oxford Companion to New Zealand Literature* (R4807), *Oxford Companion to Twentieth-Century Poetry in English* (M2893), *Oxford Companion to Women's Writing in the United States* (Q3213), *Oxford Classical Dictionary* (C115), *Oxford Dictionary of Quotations* (U6315a), and a variety of other Oxford University Press reference books. The well-designed interface offers two search modes: quick search (keyword) and advanced search (keyword, Boolean, or pattern searches of full text, entry headings, people, or dates, with the option of limiting searches to subject groups or to specific titles). Results of searches can be e-mailed.

I535   *Gale Virtual Reference Library.* Gale. Online. 10 June 2006
        <http://galegroup.com>.
        Offers online access to a variety of reference works published by Thomson Gale and other publishers. Basic Search allows users to search across all works by document title, keyword, or entire document or to select individual works and volumes to search separately. Advanced Search allows users to search by keyword, document title, image caption, entire document, publication title, ISBN, author, publisher, start page, document number, and previous searches; searches can be limited to documents with images or by date, publication title, subject area, or target audience. CCL Advanced Search offers command-line searching of the same fields Advanced Search offers. Results can be sorted by document title or publication title. Individual documents can be displayed as HTML or PDF files for reading, printing, or downloading. The following works listed in this *Guide* are accessible through *Gale Virtual Reference Library: Acronyms, Initialisms, and Abbreviations Dictionary* (U5045); *American Women Writers* (Q3390); *Cambridge Guide to Children's Books in English* (U5450); *Cambridge Guide to Women's Writing in English* (J593a); *Contemporary Authors* (J595); *Contemporary Authors: New Revision Series* (J595a); *Contemporary Novelists* (M2845); *Contemporary Poets* (M2895); Ferber, *A Dictionary of Literary Symbols* (C119); *Encyclopedia of African-American Culture and History* (Q3714); *LGBT: Encyclopedia of Lesbian, Gay, Bisexual, and Transgender History in America* (U5928); *Encyclopedia of Religion* (U6340); *New Catholic Encyclopedia* (U6345); *New Dictionary of the History of Ideas* (U5960); and *Who's Who among African Americans* (Q3770a).

See also

        FirstSearch (E225a).
        RLG Union Catalog (E230).

J

Biographical Sources

This section includes the important general bibliographies, indexes, and biographical dictionaries. Those devoted to residents of a single country are listed with the appropriate national literature.

General Bibliographies and Indexes

Guides to Biographies

SERIAL BIBLIOGRAPHIES

J540   *Biography Index.* H. W. Wilson. Online. 15 Aug. 2006 <http://vnweb .hwwilsonweb.com/hww>. Updated daily. CD-ROM. Updated quarterly.

Biography Index: Past and Present. H. W. Wilson. Online. 15 Aug. 2006 <http://vnweb.hwwilsonweb.com/hww>. Updated daily.

Biography Index. New York: Wilson, 1946– . Quarterly, with annual and larger cumulations. Subtitle varies.   Z5301.B5   016.92.

A biographee index to biographical material and obituaries in about 2,800 periodicals (as of August 2006; almost all are in English and covered by other Wilson indexes), a few books (including chapters therein), and some collective biographies and biographical dictionaries. A majority of the individuals covered are Americans. Indexed in each issue and cumulation by professions and occupations. Highly selective and providing no explanation of the criteria governing the selection process and citing many publications that are only remotely biographical, the source is useful principally for locating biographical material in periodicals.

Coverage in *Biography Index: Past and Present* begins with 1946; *Biography Index* includes only entries since July 1984. Both employ the standard Wilson search interface (see entry I525). Indexed in *Biography and Genealogy Master Index* (J565).

OTHER BIBLIOGRAPHIES

J550   *Biographical Books, 1876–1949.* New York: Bowker, 1983. 1,768 pp.
        Z5301.B48 [CT104]   016.92′002. *Biographical Books, 1950–1980.* New
        York: Bowker, 1980. 1,557 pp.   Z5301.B68 [CT104]   016.92′002.

A biographee and subject index to biographical books (including biographies, autobiographies, collective biographies, collections of letters, diaries, journals, and biographical dictionaries) published, reprinted, or distributed in the United States between 1876 and 1980. Each entry prints card-catalog copy as it appears in Bowker's *American Book Publishing Record* (Q4110) database. Three indexes: vocations (at the beginning); authors; titles. (The *1950–1980* volume prints a superfluous list of books in print.) The total reliance on card-catalog tracings to generate biographee and subject headings leads to the placement of numerous books under vague or general subject heads, the failure to list many works under biographees, the needless duplication of entries, and an incomplete index of vocations. The uncritical reliance on computer-generated indexing and utter lack of editing has produced a seriously flawed work that, while occasionally useful, cannot be relied on to identify biographical books about an individual.

J555   Jarboe, Betty M. *Obituaries: A Guide to Sources.* 2nd ed. Boston: Hall,
        1989. 362 pp.   Z5305.U5 J37 [CT214]   016.920073.

A bibliography of indexes through c. 1987—including serial publications, books, articles, and a few manuscripts—of tombstone inscriptions and obituaries in newspapers and periodicals. Although international in coverage, *Obituaries* emphasizes indexes of American sources. The 3,547 entries are organized variously by title, author, or corporate author in three divisions: international sources, United States (with sections for general studies and for each state), and foreign (with sections for Great Britain, France, Germany, and other countries). A few entries are accompanied by a brief description of scope. Appendixes list by state the location of obituary card files for the United States and online databases that index obituaries. Indexed by subject (but so incompletely that users must scan all possibly relevant sections). Although the work is inconsistently organized, inadequately indexed, too reliant on other sources rather than personal examination, and sketchy in covering foreign sources, Jarboe leads researchers to the major—as well as several obscure and local—indexes to obituaries.

Guides to Scholarship and Criticism

J557   Rollyson, Carl. *Biography: An Annotated Bibliography.* Magill Bibliographies.
         Pasadena: Salem, 1992. 215 pp.   Z5301.R57 [CT21]   016.808′066.

An annotated bibliography of English-language publications about biography (but
fortunately not, as the introduction claims, limited to items "published in the United
States"). The approximately 700 entries are organized in eight divisions: biographers
on biography, historical and critical studies (with sections for general studies and historical periods), Johnson and Boswell, Leon Edel, psychobiography, feminist biography,
innovations in biography, and fictional works that depict biographers. Two indexes:
biographical subjects; authors and subjects. Since entries are not numbered, users must
search an entire page to track down an index reference and can easily overlook other
references to a person or subject on the same page. Although poorly indexed and lacking
a clear statement of principles guiding the selection of studies, *Biography* is the best
guide to English-language publications on the theory and practice of biography.

Biographical Dictionaries

Biographical dictionaries offer basic information about the life, career, and accomplishments of individuals. Those that include living persons will sometimes provide an address or other contact information. Accuracy and reliability vary widely among these
works, especially those that rely on information supplied by biographees.

There is no adequate evaluative guide to the hundreds of biographical dictionaries
that compete for space on library shelves. *Guide to Reference Books* (B60) and vol. 2 of
Walford's Guide to Reference Material (B65) describe—but too rarely compare or eval-
uate—major current and retrospective ones. For dictionaries published since c. 1965,
Bohdan S. Wynar, ed., *ARBA Guide to Biographical Dictionaries* (Littleton: Libraries
Unlimited, 1986, 444 pp.), and Robert L. Wick and Terry Ann Mood, eds., *ARBA
Guide to Biographical Resources, 1986–1997* (Englewood: Libraries Unlimited, 1998,
604 pp.), offer some guidance. Both are composed largely of entries from *American
Reference Books Annual* (K745); neither selection nor evaluation is as rigorous as it should
be (especially in the 1986 volume), and *1986–1997* includes in the literature section
a number of works that are only marginally biographical resources.

Indexes

J565   *Biography and Genealogy Master Index.* Thomson Gale. Online. 25 Feb.
         2006 <http://infotrac.galegroup.com/galenet>. Updated twice a year.

         *Biography and Genealogy Master Index: A Consolidated Index to More Than
         3,200,000 Biographical Sketches in Over 350 Current and Retrospective
         Biographical Dictionaries* (*BGMI*). Ed. Miranda C. Herbert and Barbara
         McNeil. 2nd ed. 8 vols. Gale Biographical Index Series 1. Detroit:
         Gale, 1980. Annual supplements, with quinquennial cumulations.
         Z5305.U5 B56 [CT214]   920′.073.

A name index to entries in a wide variety of popular and scholarly English-language biographical dictionaries, most of which are regularly updated compilations published in the United States, along with some collections of excerpts from literary criticism, general indexes, and subject encyclopedias. As of 2006, some 16,300,000 entries on living and dead individuals, the majority of whom are American or British, are listed. Users can search the database from three screens: a basic name search; Advanced Search (with fields for name, prefix or suffix, year of birth, year of death, printed source, and full-text keyword; searches can be limited to entries with portraits); Expert Search (which offers essentially the same access as Advanced Search). An entry provides name, birth and death dates, and a list of dictionaries (the online version provides a full bibliographical citation; the print version offers a sometimes daunting mass of codes). Since variations in the form and spelling of names and discrepancies in dates are not edited for consistency, numerous individuals have several entries; thus users of either the print or electronic version must be certain to check all variant spellings, discrepancies in birth and death dates, and combinations of prename, middle name, initials, and surname. Accessibility would be improved by some judicious editing, and the *Master Index* omits some of the major retrospective works (such as the main volumes of *Dictionary of National Biography* [M1425a]), while including several works that hardly qualify as biographical compendia (but are published by Gale). But it is a valuable, time-saving source for determining in which of the numerous general and specialized biographical dictionaries an individual would be found. Coverage of literary figures is especially strong. Because of the sheer size of the work, the best access is offered by the electronic version, even though the search interface is poorly designed and printing or downloading entries can be done only through a Web browser's print or save functions. Review: Bruce Bonta and Frances Cable, *RSR: Reference Services Review* 10.1 (1982): 25–33.

Gale has used this database to produce several clones, some of which include additional entries; those of most interest to literary researchers are the following:

> *Almanac of Famous People: A Comprehensive Reference Guide to More Than 36,000 Famous and Infamous Newsmakers from Biblical Times to the Present.* Ed. Jennifer Mossman. 8th ed. 2 vols. Detroit: Gale, 2004.
> *Artist Biographies Master Index.* Ed. Barbara McNeil. 1986. 700 pp.
> *Author Biographies Master Index.* Ed. Geri Speace. 5th ed. 2 vols. 1997.
> *Children's Authors and Illustrators* (U5500).
> *Historical Biographical Dictionaries Master Index.* Ed. McNeil and Miranda C. Herbert. 1980. 1,003 pp.
> *Performing Arts Biography Master Index.* Ed. McNeil and Herbert. 2nd ed. 1982. 701 pp.
> *Twentieth-Century Author Biographies Master Index.* Ed. McNeil. 1984. 519 pp.
> *Writers for Young Adults: Biographies Master Index* (U5500a).

Although the work has largely been superseded, Patricia Pate Havlice, *Index to Literary Biography*, 2 vols. (Metuchen: Scarecrow, 1975), and *First Supplement*, 2 vols. (1983), does index some biographical dictionaries of foreign authors that are omitted from *Biography and Genealogy Master Index*.

J570   *IBN: Index Bio-bibliographicus Notorum Hominum* (*IBN*). Ed. Jean-Pierre Lobies et al. 5 pts. Mettingen: Zeller, 1972– .   Z5301.L7 [CT104] 016.92. CD-ROM.

Pars A: *Allgemeine Einführung/General Introduction/Introduction générale.* In progress.

Pars B: *Catalogus Operum Examinatorum/Liste der ausgewerteten bio-bibliographischen Werke/List of the Evaluated Bio-bibliographical Works/Liste des ouvrages bio-bibliographiques dépouillés.* 1973– .

Pars C: *Corpus Alphabeticum.*

I. *Sectio Generalis.* 1974– .
II. *Sectio Islamica.*
III. *Sectio Armeniaca.* 4 vols. 1982–87.
IV. *Sectio Indica.*
V. *Sectio Japonica.*
VI. *Sectio Sinica.* 1976– .

Pars D: *Supplementum.*

Pars E: *Gesamtregister der Verweisungen/General Index of References/Table générale des renvois.*

A massive index to entries on more than 3 million people (as of mid-2005) in several thousand universal and specialized biographical dictionaries published throughout the world. The sources are listed in pt. B, with periodic supplements in volumes of the *Corpus Alphabeticum* (see *Sectio Generalis,* vols. 23–25, 40, 47, 99). In the *Corpus Alphabeticum,* a typical entry cites name; birth and death dates; occupation, residence, birthplace, or other information that distinguishes between persons with the same name; and coded references to the sources listed in *List of the Evaluated Bio-bibliographical Works.* Supplementary listings for the portion of the alphabet already covered appear at intervals in volumes of *Corpus Alphabeticum.* Entries, alphabetized by the 24-letter Latin alphabet, follow sources in forms of names, with cross-references for variant forms and pseudonyms. Because the *General Introduction* (which will explain principles of compilation, guidelines for using the work, and transliteration practices) has not been published, the scope, organization, and criteria governing selection of sources remain unclear. It appears that *Corpus Alphabeticum: Sectio Generalis* covers persons of all nationalities other than those accorded a separate sectio. In contrast to *Biography and Genealogy Master Index* (J565), *IBN* emphasizes retrospective dictionaries rather than regularly updated compilations and is far more international in scope; however, publication of *Corpus Alphabeticum: Sectio Generalis* had reached only the middle of *J* by mid-2005. When finished, *IBN* will provide an invaluable, time-saving source for identifying which biographical dictionaries print an entry on an individual.

J572   *Biography Resource Center (BioRC).* Thomson Gale. Online. 18 Feb. 2006
        <http://infotrac.galegroup.com/galenet>. Updated regularly.

A database that indexes and provides full-text access to biographical data about more than 335,000 individuals (as of early 2006). Among the print sources included are *Baker's Biographical Dictionary of Musicians* (U6235a); *Contemporary Authors* (J595); *Contemporary Authors: New Revision Series* (J595a); *Contemporary Dramatists* (M2880); *Contemporary Novelists* (M2845); *Contemporary Poets* (M2895); *Contemporary Theatre, Film, and Television* (Q4305); *Dictionary of American Biography* (Q3380); *Directory of American Scholars* (U5070a); *Marquis Who's Who on the Web* (Q3395); *Merriam-Webster's Biographical Dictionary* (J580); *Who's Who among African Americans* (Q3770a); *Who's Who in the Theatre* (17th ed.; Q4305a); and more than 538,000 articles from a variety of magazines. Users can chose from three search screens: Name; Biographical Facts (with fields for name, occupation, ethnicity, nationality, gender, birth year, death year, place of birth, and place of death); Advanced Search (with fields for name, full text, keyword, source [title of magazine or book indexed in the database], date of publication, and document number). Searching any of the preceding will lead to a tabbed screen (Narrative Biographies; Thumbnail Biographies; Articles; Web sites) that displays a person's name (including variant forms), occupation, and lifespan, along with links to resources that include the person. A biography cites its source, indicates date of last update (if necessary), and includes a link that allows the biographee to update the information. Users can e-mail or print an entry or save it to a list for e-mailing with other entries; when e-mailing a list of entries, users must remember that the List View button generates an e-mail with citations only while the Each Document Separately button will send the full text of each entry. Although depending heavily on Thomson Gale publications for content, *Biography Resource Center* does offer a convenient way of searching a group of standard biographical dictionaries.

See also

> Arnim, *Internationale Personalbibliographie* (D160).
> Wearing, *American and British Theatrical Biography* (L1175).

General Biographical Dictionaries

RETROSPECTIVE DICTIONARIES

J575   *Biographie universelle (Michaud) ancienne et moderne, ou histoire, par ordre alphabétique, de la vie publique et privée de tous les hommes qui se sont fait remarquer par leurs écrits, leurs actions, leurs talents, leurs vertus ou leurs crimes* (Michaud). [Ed. J. F. Michaud, L. G. Michaud, and E. E. Desplaces.] New ed. 45 vols. Paris: Desplaces; Leipzig: Brockhaus, 1843–65.   CT143.M5.
        An extensive universal biographical dictionary of eminent and notorious persons. The signed articles, ranging from a few lines to several pages, frequently include a list of works by the entrant. Although badly dated, Michaud is the best of the older universal dictionaries and remains a useful source of information on numerous minor figures. Less trustworthy but including more minor figures through the letter *M* is *Nouvelle biographie générale depuis les temps les plus reculés jusqu'à nos jours*, ed. [Jean Chrétien Ferdinand] Hoefer, 46 vols. (Paris: Didot, 1857–66).
        For a detailed evaluation and comparison of the two works—along with a summary of the legal action brought by Michaud and Desplaces against Didot for plagiarism—see [R. C. Christie, "Biographical Dictionaries,"] *Quarterly Review* 157 (1884): 187–230.

J580   *Merriam-Webster's Biographical Dictionary.* Springfield: Merriam, 1995. 1,170 pp.   CT103.W4   920'.02. Online (through *Biography Resource Center* [J572]); CD-ROM.
        A compilation of biographical data on some 30,000 dead individuals who were "important, celebrated, or notorious" from c. 2925 BC to the twentieth century. A revision of the venerable *Webster's Biographical Dictionary* (Springfield: Merriam, with several revised printings from 1943 to 1980), this edition—like its immediate predecessor (*Webster's New Biographical Dictionary* [Springfield: Merriam, 1983, 1,130 pp.])—omits living persons and increases coverage of non-English-speaking

countries, especially in the Third World. The brief entries provide surname (indicating end-of-line division and pronunciation); prenames; titles, epithets, pseudonyms, or nicknames; birth and death dates; nationality or ethnic group; occupations; birthplace (primarily for Americans and Canadians); and brief career details. Concludes with a guide to pronunciation of name elements, titles, and prenames. Although vague about criteria determining selection, *Merriam-Webster's Biographical Dictionary* remains the best desktop source of basic biographical information and pronunciation of names for important individuals.

   Chambers Biographical Dictionary, ed. Una McGovern, 7th ed. (Edinburgh: Chambers–Chambers Harrap, 2002, 1,650 pp.) covers fewer persons (ca. 17,500) but offers fuller, albeit not always accurate and current, information and gives more prominence to twentieth-century figures, women, and individuals from popular spheres of life. David Crystal, *The Cambridge Biographical Encyclopedia*, 2nd ed. (Cambridge: Cambridge UP, 1998, 1,179 pp.) includes even fewer (about 16,500) and briefer entries, emphasizes twentieth-century individuals (especially politicians and those involved in sports), offers a pronunciation guide (except, inexplicably, for those accorded the longer, boxed entries), and concludes with a "ready-reference" section that lists—by field, country, position, award, or sport—numerous people not given entries. Entrants are indexed in *Biography and Genealogy Master Index* (J565).

CURRENT DICTIONARIES

J585   *Current Biography*. Bronx: Wilson, 1940– . 11/yr., with annual cumulation and revision as *Current Biography Yearbook*.   CT100.C8   920'.009'04.

   Current Biography Illustrated. H. W. Wilson. Online. 10 May 2005 <http://vnweb.hwwilsonweb.com/hww>. Updated monthly.

   Biographies of persons throughout the world who are currently "prominent in the news." Issues also include revised biographies and obituaries of previous entrants. Based on popular sources and information from the biographees, the approximately 2,500-word sketches provide basic biographical data, address, an interpretative account of the person's career and achievements, and a list of sources. The annual cumulations update entries, classify entrants by profession, and provide a cumulative index for the current decade. Cumulatively indexed in *Current Biography Cumulated Index, 1940–1990*, ed. Jill Kadetsky (1991, 133 pp.); the yearbooks are also indexed in *Biography and Genealogy Master Index* (J565).

   Current Biography Illustrated allows data from the yearbooks to be searched by keyword, biographee, date of birth or death, gender, birthplace, profession or vocation, race, and works by the biographee. The database is also available online at the URL above as part of *Wilson Biographies Plus Illustrated, Biography Reference Bank*, and without illustrations as *Current Biography 1940 to Present* (CD-ROM). See entry I525 for an evaluation of the WilsonWeb search interface, which all of the *Current Biography* databases use. Although formulaic in organization, predictable in style, usually uncritical in interpretation, and relying largely on popular sources and information supplied by biographees, *Current Biography* does treat a substantial number of writers from throughout the world.

J590   *The International Who's Who*. Europa Biographical Reference Series. London: Routledge–Taylor and Francis, 1935– . Annual.   CT120.I5 920.01. Online. 3 Sept. 2006 <http://www.worldwhoswho.com>.

A biographical dictionary of living notable and eminent individuals from throughout the world (including some 25,000 persons in the 69th ed., 2005). The compact entries provide basic biographical and career information, selected publications and awards, and address. A list of reigning royal families appears at the beginning. Starting with the 38th edition, entrants are indexed in *Biography and Genealogy Master Index* (J565).

In the online version, users can search the full text by keyword, surname, first name, nationality, profession, place of birth, and date of birth or death; searches can be restricted by gender and status (i.e., living or deceased). Results are ordered by surname in ascending alphabetical order and cannot be sorted or searched. Users can also browse an alphabetic list of entrants. An entry can be printed or downloaded only through a Web browser's print or save commands.

This work is generally accounted the best of the who's who dictionaries that attempt international coverage. Among others of this kind, *Who's Who in the World* (New Providence: Marquis, 1970– , biennial; online as part of *Marquis Who's Who on the Web* [Q3395]) is sometimes useful.

Dictionaries of Writers

J593   Blain, Virginia, Patricia Clements, and Isobel Grundy, eds. *The Feminist Companion to Literature in English: Women Writers from the Middle Ages to the Present.* New Haven: Yale UP, 1990. 1,231 pp.   PR111.B57 820.9′0003.

A biographical dictionary of English-language belletristic and popular writers, diarists, autobiographers, and critics, along with a few foreign-language authors and some entries on related genres, critical theories, topics, and institutions. Although covering Africa, North America, the British Isles, Asia, the Caribbean, New Zealand, and the South Pacific through 1985, the majority of the approximately 2,700 individually authored but unsigned entries are for British and United States writers born after 1800. The entries, which are alphabetized by the best-known form of an author's name and which range from about 50 to 500 words, sketch an entrant's personal and professional career and stress her connections with other women. Most entries conclude with references to standard biographies or critical studies; the abbreviated—sometimes cryptic—citations require a user to consult both the prefatory list of abbreviations as well as the concluding list of works cited. Three indexes: topics; chronology; variant forms of names and women referred to but without separate entries. Entrants are also indexed in *Biography and Genealogy Master Index* (J565). Although lacking any explanation of how entrants were selected, *The Feminist Companion* is the most thorough biographical dictionary devoted to women writing in English. The breadth of coverage and the well-edited entries combine to make this a rare example of an informative and—despite the inevitable abbreviations—readable biographical dictionary. Reviews: Maureen E. Mulvihill, *Scriblerian* 24 (1992): 211–14; John Sutherland, *London Review of Books* 11 July 1991: 18–19; Sharon Valiant, *Analytical and Enumerative Bibliography* ns 4 (1990): 190–94.

Complementing *The Feminist Companion,* but including fewer writers, are Todd, *British Women Writers* (M1433a), Bell, *Biographical Dictionary of English Women Writers, 1580–1720* (M1433a), Todd, *Dictionary of British and American Women Writers* (M2265), Schlueter, *Encyclopedia of British Women Writers* (M1433), and Lorna Sage, ed., *The Cambridge Guide to Women's Writing in English* (Cambridge: Cambridge UP,

1999, 696 pp.; online through *Gale Virtual Reference Library* [I535]), which sports an impressive array of contributors but which lacks an explanation of scope and criteria governing selection.

J595   *Contemporary Authors: A Bio-bibliographical Guide to Current Writers in Fiction, General Nonfiction, Poetry, Journalism, Drama, Motion Pictures, Television, and Other Fields.* Detroit: Gale, 1962– .   Z1224.C6   928.1. Online. 8 Feb. 2006 <http://galenet.galegroup.com>. Updated biweekly. Also searchable through *Biography Resource Center* (J572) and *Literature Resource Center* (I528).

A dictionary of twentieth-century writers, scholars, and critics whose books have been published by legitimate publishers. Although emphasizing living authors who write in English, *Contemporary Authors* includes those authors whose works have been translated into English as well as many persons who died since 1900. (Until vol. 104 [1982], the only deceased persons included were those who died after 1959.) Entries are of two types:

1. Sketches are full entries that provide basic biographical and career information; home, office, or agent address; memberships; awards and honors; publications; work in progress; sidelights (e.g., a comment by the biographee or quotations from reviews or criticism); avocational interests; selected biographical and critical sources; and occasionally an interview.
2. Obituaries of both previous entrants and other writers include references to obituaries in other publications or biographical sources; many obituaries are expanded or revised as sketches in subsequent volumes.

Many volumes through 131 (1991) include brief entries that give basic biographical details and a list of selected publications; many of the brief entries are expanded into sketches in subsequent volumes.

All entries in vols. 1–44 are revised or reprinted in *Contemporary Authors: First Revision*, 44 vols. (1967–79). A few early entries for writers who later died or became inactive are revised or reprinted in *Contemporary Authors: Permanent Series*, 2 vols. (1975–78). Revised or updated entries now appear in *Contemporary Authors: New Revision Series* (1981–). (All the preceding are included in the electronic versions; *New Revision Series* is searchable through *Biography Resource Center* [J572] and [beginning with vol. 114 (2003)] through *Gale Virtual Reference Library* [I535], as is *Contemporary Authors* [beginning with vol. 206 (2003)].) All these sources are complemented by the following:

Contemporary Authors: Autobiography Series. 30 vols. 1984–99. A collection of extensively illustrated autobiographical essays of 10,000 words written especially for the series.

Contemporary Authors: Bibliographical Series. 3 vols. 1986–89.

Vol. 1: *American Novelists.* Ed. James J. Martine. 1986. 431 pp.

Vol. 2: *American Poets.* Ed. Ronald Baughman. 1986. 387 pp.

Vol. 3: *American Dramatists.* Ed. Matthew C. Roudané. 1989. 484 pp.

A collection of surveys of research and bibliographies of works by and English-language scholarship about post–World War II authors. Each separately authored essay is organized in three divisions: a list of primary works, a list of important studies (with sections for bibliographies, biographies, interviews, and criticism), and an evaluative survey of major scholarship (which occasionally offers suggestions for further research).

Although highly selective in coverage of scholarship and varying in quality, their typically rigorous evaluative surveys make these bibliographies useful starting points for research on the authors covered. It is indeed unfortunate that Gale terminated such a valuable series.

Because of the numerous series and frequent revisions, users must consult the most recent *Contemporary Authors: Cumulative Index* to locate the most current entry on a writer. (The cumulative index also includes other Gale biographical dictionaries such as *Dictionary of Literary Biography* [J600].) The various *Contemporary Authors* volumes are also indexed in *Biography and Genealogy Master Index* (J565). The electronic version includes the most recent entry on a writer, and some printed entries have been updated, albeit haphazardly. Because unrevised entries unaccountably fail to identify the original publication date, users must take care not to associate the copyright date accompanying an entry with the currency of the information. While the electronic version speeds up access, it needs a clear explanation of its relation to its print ancestors and of the nature and extent of revision. Right now it offers little more than a transfer of data from a print to an electronic medium. For a comparison of the print and electronic versions, see the review by Susan Herzog, *Against the Grain* 12.4 (2000): 30, 32, 34, 36.

Although a majority of the entries are based on information supplied (and subsequently checked) by a biographee, agent, or family member, there are omissions and errors; however, currency and scope make *Contemporary Authors* a valuable source for information about and addresses of living British and American writers.

Other useful, but less comprehensive, sources for biographical information on writers include the following:

> *World Authors, 1900–1950.* Ed. Martin Seymour-Smith and Andrew C. Kimmens. 4 vols. Wilson Authors Series. New York: Wilson, 1996. CD-ROM. (A revision of *Twentieth Century Authors: A Biographical Dictionary of Modern Literature*, ed. Stanley J. Kunitz and Howard Haycraft [1942, 1,577 pp.] and *First Supplement*, ed. Kunitz and Vineta Colby [1955, 1,123 pp.].) The work is continued as *World Authors, 1950–1970*, ed. John Wakeman, Authors Series (1975, 1,594 pp.); *World Authors, 1970–1975*, ed. Wakeman, Wilson Authors Series (1980, 894 pp.); *World Authors, 1975–1980*, ed. Colby, Wilson Authors Series (1985, 829 pp.); *World Authors, 1980–1985*, ed. Colby, Wilson Authors Series (1991, 938 pp.); *World Authors, 1985–1990*, ed. Colby, Wilson Authors Series (1995, 970 pp.); *World Authors, 1990–1995*, ed. Clifford Thompson (1999, 863 pp.); *World Authors, 1995–2000*, ed. Thompson and Mari Rich (2003, 872 pp.). Selection in the preceding works is based on importance or popularity. Others in the series—*American Authors, 1600–1900: A Biographical Dictionary of American Literature*, ed. Kunitz and Haycraft (1938, 846 pp.); *British Authors before 1800: A Biographical Dictionary*, ed. Kunitz and Haycraft (1952, 584 pp.); *British Authors of the Nineteenth Century*, ed. Kunitz and Haycraft (1936, 677 pp.); and *European Authors, 1000–1900: A Biographical Dictionary of European Literature*, ed. Kunitz and Colby, Authors Series (1967, 1,016 pp.)—are too dated to be of much value. All the preceding are available (some with updated bibliographies) in electronic form as *Wilson Biographies Plus Illustrated* and as *Biography Reference Bank* (both online at http://vnweb.hwwilsonweb.com/hww). All the preceding works are indexed in *Biography and Genealogy Master Index* (J565) and (except for *World Authors, 1995–2000*) in *Index to the Wilson Authors Series*, [rev. ed.] (1997,

136 pp.). For a history of the series and its critical reception, see Gary L. Ferguson, "Lives of the Poets, Novelists, and Dramatists: The Wilson Authors Series," *Reference Services Review* 16.3 (1988): 31–44.

J600   *Dictionary of Literary Biography (DLB)*. Detroit: Gale, 1978– .   PS221.D5. Online. Thomson Gale. 8 Feb. 2006 <http://galenet.galegroup.com>. Updated quarterly. Also searchable through Gale's *Literature Resource Center* (I528).

Separately edited volumes of commissioned biographical-bibliographic-critical essays that trace the careers of selected authors, critics, screenwriters, journalists, scholars, and publishers. Most volumes are organized around a genre, group, or type of writer within a historical period of a national literature (e.g., *American Novelists since World War II*; *American Humorists, 1800–1950*; *Victorian Novelists before 1885*; *American Newspaper Journalists, 1926–1950*; *Canadian Writers since 1960*; *British Mystery Writers, 1860–1919*; *Chicano Writers*); the majority of the 324 volumes published by June 2006 are devoted to literatures in English. The extensively illustrated discussions integrate biographical information with brief synopses and critical estimates of major works within the designated genre or topic, describe the author's importance and reputation, note manuscripts, and list primary works and selected scholarship. Each volume concludes with a list of important general studies. Because of the organization by genre or group within a period, some writers appear in more than one volume. Cumulatively indexed by writer (along with the *Yearbooks* and *Documentary Series*—see below) in each volume; volumes are also indexed in *Biography and Genealogy Master Index* (J565) and *Contemporary Authors* (J595).

The online version, which omits illustrations and some other copyrighted content, can be searched by literary author, title of work, birth year, death year, nationality, genre, essay topic (for essays about anonymous works, printers, publishers, magazines, and other non-author-centered topics), full text, ethnicity, gender, and *DLB* volume title.)

Although varying widely in quality, the essays are generally superior to those in similar collections, offer a convenient summary of a writer's career, and for several minor authors provide the fullest available discussions.

Dictionary of Literary Biography: Yearbook [1980–2002] (1981–2003) includes reports on conferences; discussions and lists of literary prizes and awards; interviews; obituaries; descriptions of new literary periodicals; essays on a variety of literary topics; and surveys of the year's publications in fiction, poetry, drama, and literary biography. The *Yearbooks* through 1987 (1988) update entries or add new ones to published volumes of *Dictionary of Literary Biography*. *Dictionary of Literary Biography: Documentary Series: An Illustrated Chronicle* (1982–99) reprints biographical and background materials (including letters, diary entries, interviews, book reviews, and excerpts from criticism) on selected authors or topics; beginning in 1999, documentary volumes appear in the regular *DLB* series. Cumulatively indexed by author (along with the *Dictionary* and *Yearbooks*) in each volume. The *Concise Dictionary of American Literary Biography*, 6 vols. (1987–89) and *Concise Dictionary of British Literary Biography*, 8 vols. (1992), collections of *DLB* articles (some updated) on major authors, are designed for high school and junior college libraries.

See also

Allibone, *Critical Dictionary of English Literature* (M1430).
Benét's Reader's Encyclopedia (C120).
Cambridge Guide to Literature in English (C125).
Dizionario Bompiani degli autori (C130a).

K

Periodicals

This section is limited to works not restricted to a national literature, genre, or subject.

Directories

K615   *MLA Directory of Periodicals: A Guide to Journals and Series in Languages and Literatures* [1978–]. New York: MLA, 1979– . Online (available only through vendors of the *MLAIB* [G335]). Updated biannually.

A directory to c. 5,500 print and electronic serials devoted to studies of language or literatures (other than classical Greek or Latin) and included at some point on the *MLAIB* Master List of Periodicals (see http://www.mla.org/masterlistper07pdf or the front matter of the print volumes of *MLAIB* [G335]). Entries typically include *MLAIB* acronym, scope (articles, notes, reviews, bibliographies), subjects covered, language published, publication information (including ISSN, frequency, circulation, format), indication whether the journal is peer reviewed, editorial and subscription information, and submission details (restrictions on contributors; submission fees and page charges;

manuscript length and number of copies required; style manual; time interval between submission and editorial decision and between acceptance and publication; whether a journal has a blind or anonymous submissions policy; number of referees; and number of manuscripts submitted, accepted, and published each year). Since some editors do not respond to requests for verification, information carried over from earlier updates may be outdated. The accessibility of the data in these records varies markedly depending on the vendor.

Although it is not comprehensive and is outdated in some of its information, the *MLA Directory* is the best source for identifying serials that specialize in an author or topic and for determining where to submit a manuscript. Authors should, of course, verify submission requirements by consulting the most recent copy of the serial or visiting its Web site.

See also

> Patterson, *Author Newsletters and Journals* (K620).
> *Ulrichsweb.com* (K625).

K620   Patterson, Margaret C. *Author Newsletters and Journals: An International Annotated Bibliography of Serial Publications Concerned with the Life and Works of Individual Authors.* American Literature, English Literature, and World Literatures in English: An Information Guide Series 19. Detroit: Gale, 1979. 497 pp.   Z6513.P37 [PN4836]   016.809.

A bibliography of 1,129 currently published and defunct serials, arranged alphabetically by author (with additions on pp. 357–65). Entries typically include bibliographical, editorial, and subscription information; description of contents; languages published; reprint availability; and indexing information (in both the publication and standard serial bibliographies and abstracts). Seven appendixes analyze listings in a variety of ways (e.g., by centuries and authors, and by indexing and abstracting services). Title index. Updated by Patterson's "Author Newsletters and Journals: Supplement 1 [2, 3]," *Serials Review* 8.4 (1982): 61–72; 10.1 (1984): 51–59; 11.3 (1985): 31–44. Patterson provides a wealth of detail on specialized serials, many of which are not indexed by the standard serial bibliographies and indexes in section G of this *Guide*. A revised edition is now needed.

Additional current author journals are listed in Bracken, *Reference Works in British and American Literature* (M1357).

K625   *Ulrichsweb.com.* Online. ProQuest CSA. 30 Mar. 2006 <http://www.ulrichsweb.com>. Updated weekly.

Ulrich's on Disc. CD-ROM. Quarterly.

Ulrich's Periodicals Directory: Including Irregular Serials and Annuals (Ulrich's). New Providence: Bowker, 1932– . Annual. Title varies. Z6941.U5   011.

A bibliographic database of information on regularly and irregularly published serials (print and electronic) published worldwide. The Quick Search box allows users to search by title (both exact and keyword), ISSN, keyword within a record, and subject. The Advanced Search screen allows users to combine record fields (such as title, ISSN, publisher, language, and subject) and to limit searches in a variety of ways (e.g., refereed publications, date, language, availability through document vendors, and publisher).

Searchers can also browse several indexes, with the Subject and LC Classification Number being of most interest to language and literature researchers. Each entry provides basic editorial and subscription information, ISSN, e-mail address, URL, electronic and other formats, an indication whether the journal is refereed (not always accurate), an incomplete (and sometimes inaccurate) list of serial bibliographies and abstracts that index the publication, and—for some periodicals—a brief description of contents or editorial focus, a link to tables of contents, and reviews published in a limited number of journals. The CD-ROM version includes less information and restricted search capability.

Ulrich's Periodicals Directory classifies by subject only active serials and those which ceased publication within the past three years, includes much less information than the electronic versions, and is cumbersome to search. Following the subject classification are indexes of providers of online serials, providers of serials published on CD-ROM, of serials that have ceased publication within the past three years, of publications by international organizations, of ISSNs, and of titles.

Given the ephemerality of many periodicals, the ease with which they begin and cease publication, and their proneness to frequent changes in editorial personnel or publisher, it is hardly surprising that directories such as Ulrichsweb.com are so full of errors or outdated information and omit so many publications.

See also

> Anson, "Journals in Composition" (U5605).
> *Dictionary of Literary Biography: Yearbook* (J600a).
> *Directory of Literary Societies and Author Collections* (E210a).

Related Works

K630   *Periodical Title Abbreviations: Covering Periodical Title Abbreviations, Database Abbreviations, and Selected Monograph Abbreviations in Science, the Social Sciences, the Humanities, Law, Medicine, Religion, Library Science, Engineering, Education, Business, Art, and Many Other Fields.* Comp. and ed. Leland G. Alkire, Jr. 16th ed. 3 vols. Detroit: Gale, 2006.   Z6945.A2 P47 [PN4832]   050'.148.

A dictionary of periodical acronyms and abbreviations used by some of the major serial bibliographies, indexes, and abstracts. Coverage is limited primarily to North American and British publications and does not include all works in section G: Serial Bibliographies, Indexes, and Abstracts. Vol. 1 is an acronym list; vol. 2, a title list. Although coverage is far from exhaustive and includes some serial bibliographies that no longer use acronyms, the work is occasionally useful for interpreting the acronym or abbreviated title for a journal not included in the *MLA Directory of Periodicals* (K615) or the lists prefacing *MLAIB* (G335), *ABELL* (G340), or other standard language or literature bibliographies.

Acronyms and abbreviations of journals in classical studies are more fully covered in Wellington, *Dictionary of Bibliographic Abbreviations Found in the Scholarship of Classical Studies* (S4890a). A useful supplement for foreign journals is *ITA: Internationale Titelabkürzungen von Zeitschriften, Zeitungen, wichtigen Handbüchern, Wörterbüchern, Gesetzen, Institutionen, usw./International Title Abbreviations of Periodicals,*

Newspapers, Important Handbooks, Dictionaries, Laws, Institutions, etc., 10th ed., 3 vols. (Munich: Saur, 2005; CD-ROM).

Union Lists

Union lists of journals are essential tools for finding out what libraries hold a specific journal (and sometimes the volumes or issues held).

In records for journals, *WorldCat* (E225) both lists holdings in many libraries and provides a link to an institution's OPAC; RLG Union Catalog (E230) provides a link to the OPAC or holdings record of selected institutions.

Many library consortia or state associations produce regional union lists of serials. A reference or interlibrary loan librarian is usually the best source for information on the local lists.

Although now dated, Ruth S. Freitag, comp., *Union Lists of Serials: A Bibliography* (Washington: Reference Dept., Lib. of Congress, 1964, 150 pp.), is still useful for identifying union lists published before c. 1962.

K640   *New Serial Titles: A Union List of Serials Held by Libraries in the United States and Canada* (*NST*). Washington: Lib. of Congress, 1953–99. Monthly, with quarterly, annual, and larger cumulations, including one for 1950–70. Available on microfiche since 1984.   Z6945.U5 S42 [PN4832] 016.05.

A title list of serials from throughout the world held by libraries in the United States and Canada. Until 1981, *NST* includes only works first published after 1949; since 1981, it admits newly cataloged serials regardless of initial date of publication; and, since April 1996, it includes only printed serials. *NST* continues *Union List of Serials in Libraries of the United States and Canada* (*ULS*), ed. Edna Brown Titus, 3rd ed., 5 vols. (New York: Wilson, 1965), which records holdings for more than 156,000 serials published before 1950. *NST* and *ULS* are essential for identifying libraries that own lengthy or complete runs (but there are numerous errors and omissions in the records of holdings, and after the 1976–80 cumulation *NST* does not designate specific volumes held). For subject access, see *New Serial Titles, 1950–1970: Subject Guide*, 2 vols. (New York: Bowker, 1975).

K645   *Serials in the British Library.* Wetherby: British Lib., 1981– . Quarterly, with annual and larger cumulations.   Z6945.B874 [PN4832]   011.34.

From 1987 on, this source is restricted to new serials acquired by the British Library, with entries providing title, publication details, and ISSN. Indexed by subject. From 1981 through 1986, it is a union list of serials acquired since 1976 by the British Library and 16 other major libraries in the United Kingdom and Republic of Ireland. *Serials in the British Library* succeeds *British Union-Catalogue of Periodicals Incorporating World List of Scientific Periodicals: New Periodical Titles* (London: Butterworths, 1964–81, quarterly, with annual and larger cumulations), which records periodicals that were first published, began a new series, or ceased publication from 1960 through 1980, and lists the holdings of a significantly larger number of libraries. The holdings of earlier periodicals are recorded in *British Union-Catalogue of Periodicals: A Record of the Periodicals of the World, from the Seventeenth Century to the Present Day, in British*

Libraries (*BUCOP*), ed. James D. Stewart, 4 vols. (New York: Academic; London: Butterworths, 1955–58); a supplement (1962) extends coverage to 1960.

Digital Archives

This section is limited to digital archives that include journals from more than a single publisher. Several publishers (e.g., Cambridge University Press, Oxford University Press, and Blackwell) maintain their own archives, and several vendors (especially EBSCO [I512] and Wilson [I525]) offer access to a substantial number of titles. (For titles in common, EBSCO is preferable to Wilson, which does not consistently list contents— or even issues—seriatim.) The lack of a common standard for indexing journal issues can frustrate searchers. Some tables of content include an abstract; some do not distinguish between articles and reviews; some do not identify the author of the book reviewed; some are inconsistent from volume to volume about how and what information is supplied; some do not list separately reviews (requiring that a searcher open and skim the HTML or PDF text of the entire review section); some do not provide a full citation on the first page of the HTML or PDF text of an article; some do not include front matter or back matter that appears in the print version of an issue.

K700   *JSTOR.* JSTOR. Online. 12 June 2006 <http://www.jstor.org>. Updated
        regularly.
        A digital archive of 513 titles (with an additional 300 scheduled to be added by 2008), with individual issues added three to five years after publication and with the goal of offering a complete back file for each journal. Unfortunately, a few publishers have stopped allowing new issues to be added (for a list see About JSTOR/The Moving Wall). Before searching or browsing, users should click the Set Preferences button to choose at least printing and downloading options. Journals can be browsed by discipline or alphabetically by title. Basic Search allows users to search author, title, or full text (users must read the Quick Tips below the search box). Advanced Search allows users to limit a search to one or more Fields (author, title, caption, abstract), to one or more Types (article, review, opinion piece, other), to a date range, and to one or more journals or disciplines. Results can be sorted by relevance, date (ascending or descending), or journal title (ascending). Expert Search allows command-line searching with the same limits as Advanced Search. Article Locator allows users to search author, title, journal, ISSN, volume number, issue number, start page, month, day, and year. A record allows users to go directly to the full text, view or save a citation (which includes a stable URL for the document), go directly to the page with the first match of the search term, or print or download the text. Documents open one page at a time. Although the search interface is not as clean and intuitive as it should be, *JSTOR* offers full-text searching to several important language and literature journals and remedies some of the major frustrations of working with printed volumes (incomplete runs and missing, misshelved, or vandalized volumes).

K705   *Project Muse* (*Muse*). Johns Hopkins UP. Online. 3 June 2006 <http://
        muse.jhu.edu>. Updated weekly.
        A digital archive of more than 300 journals in the arts, humanities, and social sciences. For journals that also appear in print, *Muse* digitizes all content except advertisements and covers. Users can browse a journal by volume and issue or search all journals. Basic Search allows users to limit a keyword search to all fields with text, all

fields except text, article text, author, title, Library of Congress subject headings, journal title, reviewer, or title reviewed. Advanced Search allows users to combine the preceding fields, include articles from selected *JSTOR* (K700) back files, and limit searches by document type (e.g., review, poetry), date, titles in an institution's subscription, and specific journal. Results—which can be ordered chronologically (ascending or descending), alphabetically (ascending or descending) by journal title, or by relevance rank—provide the full table-of-contents citation (including any abstract); unfortunately, records marked for export or e-mailing include only a basic citation. Users can sign up for alerts.

The typical table-of-contents page identifies sections of an issue, cites authors and titles (but not pagination), includes Library of Congress subject headings for articles and reviews, prints an abstract if supplied by the journal, and clearly identifies reviewer and author and title of the work reviewed. Most content can be accessed in HTML or PDF files. A clean, well-designed display and powerful search engine make *Project Muse* one of the top text archives of journals.

K710   *IngentaConnect.* Ingenta. Online. 2 July 2006
        <http://www.ingentaconnect.com>. Updated daily (electronic content); updated weekly (fax content).

A bibliographic database that indexes and provides full-text access (either digitally or by fax) to more than 20 million articles, book chapters, and books covering a wide spectrum of fields and published, for the most part, since 1991. Quick Search allows users to limit basic keyword searches of citations to journal title, documents available digitally, documents available by fax, or documents included in an institution's subscription. Advanced Search allows users to combine searches of citation, author, journal title, volume, and issue and to limit searches by date and the same document options as in Quick Search. Users can also browse journals by title, subject area, or publisher. Records (which are returned in descending chronological order and cannot be otherwise sorted) can be marked for printing, exporting, or e-mailing. Users can save searches and create alerts. Although coverage of the arts and humanities is not particularly broad and the search interface requires users to search digital and fax content separately, *IngentaConnect* is useful for identifying articles in journals not covered by the literature bibliographies in Section G.

Book Reviews

Included in this section are serials whose primary content is reviews. For indexes to book reviews, see sec. G: Serial Bibliographies, Indexes, and Abstracts/Book Review Indexes.

K745   *American Reference Books Annual [1970–]* (*ARBA*). Westport: Libraries Unlimited–Greenwood, 1970– . Annual.   Z1035.1.A55   011'.02.
        ARBAonline. Online. 19 Apr. 2006 <http://arba.lu.com>. Updated monthly.

Prints brief reviews (typically 150–400 words) of English-language reference works (print and electronic) published or distributed in the United States or Canada (with decent coverage of the latter beginning in vol. 18 [1987]). Although claiming comprehensive coverage, *ARBA* actually overlooks or ignores each year a substantial number of major works within its scope. Reviews are organized in four extensively classified divisions: general reference works (organized by types of works, including bibliographies, biographical sources, directories, encyclopedias, and indexes), social sciences (including sections for ethnic studies and anthropology; genealogy; history; library science, publishing, and bookselling; and women's studies), humanities (including general works; language and linguistics; literature; mythology, folklore, and popular culture; and performing arts), and science and technology. The literature section has subdivisions for general works, children's literature, drama, fiction, poetry, and national literatures (with each of the national literatures having sections, as needed, for general works, genres, and individual authors). Most reviews conclude with citations to others in library journals. Two indexes: authors and titles; subjects. Cumulative indexes: Joseph W. Sprug, *Index to* American Reference Books Annual*, 1970–1974: A Cumulative Index to Subjects, Authors, and Titles* (1974, 364 pp.); Christine L. Wynar, *1975–1979* (1979, 407 pp.); Ruth Blackmore, *1980–1984* (1984, 402 pp.); Anna Grace Patterson, comp., *1985–1989* (1989, 275 pp.); Patterson, comp., *1990–1994* (1994, 288 pp.); Susan D. Strickland, comp., *1995–1999* (1999, 346 pp.); Martin Dillon and Shannon Graff Hysell, comps., *2000–2004* (2004, 332 pp.).

ARBAonline includes reviews from vol. 28 (1997) forward, with new reviews added each month. Users can search by keyword, author or editor, ISBN or ISSN, publisher, subject, and title; searches can be limited to classified divisions and their subheadings (see above), *ARBA* volume, monthly update (important for those who want to keep current with new reference works), and publication date of the work reviewed. Users can also browse records by subject or by update. Results—which can be sorted by author or editor, publication date, publisher, *ARBA* volume, or title—can be saved to a list for printing (but not downloading or e-mailing), but each review must be printed separately. *ARBAonline* saves researchers from having to consult the individual print volumes and is more current than *ARBA*, but users who want to retrieve more than a couple records will justifiably chafe at having to print (or save through a Web browser) one review at a time.

Although the quality of the reviews has improved a bit over the years, too many remain essentially descriptive, and many that attempt evaluation are simply inaccurate or insufficiently rigorous. Omitting too many significant publications within its scope and insufficiently rigorous in evaluations, *ARBA* is primarily useful for alerting researchers to some new reference books and to changes in serial ones (which are examined at intervals).

Selected reviews are reprinted in *Best Reference Books, 1970–1980: Titles of Lasting Value Selected from* American Reference Books Annual, ed. Susan Holte and Bohdan S. Wynar (1981, 480 pp.); *1981–1985*, ed. Wynar (1986, 504 pp.); and *1986–1990*, ed. Wynar (1992, 544 pp.). None fulfills the claim of the works' common title and subtitle.

K750   *Choice: Current Reviews for College Libraries.* 1964– . 11/yr.   Z1035.C5
           028.

           ChoiceReviews.online. Ed. 1.3. Assn. of College and Research Libraries.
           Online. 28 Jan. 2006 <http://www.cro2.org>. Updated monthly. <http://
           www.ala.org/ala/acrl/acrlpubs/choice/home.cfm>.

A selection guide for libraries, each issue prints approximately 600 brief notices of English-language books published or distributed in North America (for the most part), electronic resources, a few new journals, and some nonprint materials. (For a full statement of the selection policy, see http://www.ala.org/ala/acrl/acrlpubs/choice/selectionpolicy/

selectionpolicy.cfm.) Most issues also feature an extended bibliographical essay on a topic of current interest, and the January issue lists "Outstanding Academic Titles" drawn from works reviewed during the past year. The notices, which have been signed only since vol. 22 (1984), are organized by subject areas, including the humanities, language and literature (classified by language), performing arts (with sections for film and theater), and reference works (although coverage of the last is weak). Two indexes in each issue (authors; titles); annual cumulative index.

Reviews (but not the front matter or advertisements) since September 1988 can be searched through *ChoiceReviews.online*; however the poorly designed interface is cumbersome to navigate, requires too much mouse clicking, and displays annoying ads that hog bandwidth and slow what is frequently a sluggish site. The Site License edition does not allow users to save searches. Before moving to a new page, users must remember to e-mail, print, or save selected records. The publisher has announced a new search interface for 2007.

The notices are too seldom by recognized scholars, reviewers are allowed insufficient space for more than a cursory report, and too many important books are ignored or overlooked. Nonetheless, the sheer number of publications noticed, coupled with the abundance of publishers' advertisements, makes *Choice* one of the better sources for identifying new and forthcoming English-language books published in North America.

Current *Choice* reviews are included in *globalbooksinprint.com* (Q4225).

K765   TLS: Times Literary Supplement (*TLS*). 1902–. Weekly. Former title: *Times Literary Supplement* (1902–68).   AP4.T45   072′.1. Online. 28 Jan. 2006 <http://tls.timesonline.co.uk>. Updated weekly.

Publishes reviews of books in a variety of fields (but with a decided emphasis on the humanities, especially literature) and, in recent years, of art exhibitions, television programs, movies, operas, and productions of plays; occasional essays on literary and other topics; a lively, sometimes contentious, letters section; reports on book auctions; and requests for information from biographers, editors, and other scholars (with much fewer appearing in recent years). Since 7 June 1974, reviews are signed. Long regarded as the best general review publication, *TLS* is valuable for its broad, literate coverage; however, it frequently still betrays a British bias, the quality of reviews and qualifications of reviewers vary considerably, and the occasional reference work accorded space is rarely subjected to rigorous examination. Author index in each issue. TLS *Archive* (http://tls.timesonline.co.uk/section/0,,25332,00.html), which begins with 1994 and is free to *TLS* subscribers, excludes advertisements and some copyrighted material. Users can search by keyword only; contrary to the Search Tips, proper nouns are not case sensitive. Although *TLS* is indexed since 1973 in the Times *Index* (M1450), fuller, more convenient access is offered by the cumulative indexes: Times Literary Supplement *Index, 1902–1939*, 2 vols. (Reading: Newspaper Archive Developments, 1978); *1940–1980*, 3 vols. (Reading: Research 1982); and *1981–1985* (1986, 407 pp.). Most of these indexes are superseded by the TLS *Archive* and TLS *Centenary Archive* (http://www.tls.psmedia.com), which covers 1902-90, identifies many of the anonymous contributors, and allows searching by any combination of keyword, title of article or book reviewed, author, subject, publisher, type of publication (e.g., lead article, poem, book review), date, and contributor (the last can be searched on a separate screen by keyword, name, gender, date of birth or death, occupation, non-*TLS* journalism [which is keyed to a list of publications in a contributor's profile], and subjects or languages reviewed). Records are sorted chronologically (ascending) and cannot be re-sorted. Primary Source Media no longer plans to extend coverage to the original terminal date (1994); thus, there is no electronic access to the *TLS* for 1991–93.

For the history of the weekly, see Derwent May, *Critical Times: The History of the Times Literary Supplement* (London: Harper, 2001, 606 pp.).

The *Times Higher Education Supplement* (1971–, weekly) also reviews a number of books of interest to literature researchers.

Little Magazines

Guides to Reference Works

K767   Kempcke, Ken, Diana Ramirez, and Steven Smith. "Reference Sources for the Study of Little Magazines." *Popular Culture in Libraries* 5.2 (1999): 1–28.   Z688.P64 P68.

A guide to essential reference sources—overviews, guides to scholarship, bibliographies of magazines, directories, union lists and catalogs, periodicals about little magazines, and indexes—for the study of little magazines. The annotations are typically descriptive (though some offer an evaluative comment).

Histories and Surveys

K770   Hoffman, Frederick J., Charles Allen, and Carolyn F. Ulrich. *The Little Magazine: A History and a Bibliography.* 2nd ed. Princeton: Princeton UP, 1947. 450 pp.   PN4836.H6   052.

A survey rather than a history proper of selected little magazines published since c. 1912, principally in the United States but also including a few from Great Britain and Ireland. The narrative part emphasizes the place of these publications in literary and cultural history, with chapters on individual magazines, types of publications, poetry, regionalism, politics, and psychoanalysis. The selective bibliography of United States, Canadian, British, and Irish magazines (from 1891 through 1946) is organized chronologically by date of first issue. Entries provide title; publication information; frequency; a record of mergers and suspensions; editors; and notes on history, scope, editorial policy, important contributors, and contents (although some information is taken from sources other than the magazines themselves). The bibliography includes a supplementary list of periodicals that are similar to little magazines. (For some additions to both lists, see Carolyn F. Ulrich and Eugenia Patterson, comps., "Little Magazines," *Bulletin of the New York Public Library* 51 [1947]: 3–25.) Concludes with a list of secondary sources, which must be supplemented by Charles L. P. Silet, "An Annotated Checklist of Articles and Books on American Little Magazines," *Bulletin of Bibliography* 34 (1977): 157–66, 208. Indexed by persons, titles, and a few subjects. This remains the fullest survey and bibliography of little magazines. Reviews: Louis Filler, *American Literature* 18 (1947): 334–35; Robert Wooster Stallman, *Poetry* 70 (1947): 274–78.

Although many supplements or new histories have been contemplated, none has appeared. For magazines since c. 1940, the best general source is Elliott Anderson and Mary Kinzie, eds., *The Little Magazine in America: A Modern Documentary History* (Yonkers: Pushcart, 1978, 770 pp.; also published as *Triquarterly* 43 [1978], 750 pp., but without the index), a collection of essays, interviews, and memoirs treating individual titles and kinds of magazines. *The Little Magazine in America* also includes an annotated bibliography (modeled on the one in Hoffman) of 84 little magazines since c. 1950, with a valuable preliminary discussion of sources for the study of little magazines in the United States.

Guides to Primary Works

Despite the importance of little magazines in twentieth-century literature, their use is hampered by the lack of adequate bibliographies of magazines and indexes to their content. Consequently, researchers must depend heavily on incomplete collections in various libraries. Willard Fox, "The Archives: An Analysis of Little Magazine Collections in the United States and Canada" (Chielens, *American Literary Magazines: The Twentieth Century* [Q3410], pp. 439–58), offers an overview of the collections, finding aids, and complementary holdings of 28 repositories.

The fullest—but by no means comprehensive—list of little magazines is *Catalog of Little Magazines: A Collection in the Rare Book Room, Memorial Library, University of Wisconsin—Madison*, comp. and ed. Robert F. Roeming (Madison: U of Wisconsin P, 1979, 137 pp.). Profiles of several American little magazines are included in Chielens, *American Literary Magazines: The Twentieth Century* (Q3410).

DIRECTORIES

K775   *The International Directory of Little Magazines and Small Presses*. Paradise: Dustbooks, 1965– . Annual. Former title: *Directory of Little Magazines and Small Presses* (1965–73).   Z6944.L5 D5   015'.025.

A directory of English-language little magazines and small presses, the majority of them in the United States, Canada, and the United Kingdom. Presses and magazines are listed alphabetically by name or title, with a typical entry recording such information as press or publisher (for magazines), editor, address, telephone number, e-mail address, Web site, type of material published, notes (on content of recent issues or publications, contributors, editorial policies, and sometimes artistic credos or pleas for submissions), submission requirements, production method, and subscription information. Based on information supplied by publishers or editors, entries vary in fullness, accuracy, and currency. Two indexes: subjects; regional (by state, then city; foreign countries follow states). The *Directory* is the best source for identifying current little magazines and active small presses; earlier editions remain valuable for information about defunct publications and presses, especially alternative and underground ones. Between editions, new listings appear in *Small Press Review* (1967– , bimonthly).

Two complementary publications based on the *Directory* are *Directory of Small Press / Magazine Editors and Publishers* (1971– , annual) and *Directory of Poetry Publishers* (1985– , annual).

For earlier English-language little magazines and small presses, *Trace* (1952–70) remains a valuable source of information, although locating within issues the variously titled "Directory" and its supplements is exasperating.

See also

Sullivan, *British Literary Magazines* (M1445).
Warwick, *Commonwealth Literature Periodicals* (R4385).

BIBLIOGRAPHIES

K777   *British Poetry Magazines, 1914-2000: A History and Bibliography of "Little*
        Magazines." Comp. David Miller and Richard Price. London: British Lib.;
        New Castle: Oak Knoll, 2006. 452 pp.   Z2014.P7 B758   016.80881.

    A bibliography of little magazines, originating in the United Kingdom or Republic
of Ireland, that focus on the publication of poetry or, in a few instances, that publish
prose or illustrations with "a strong connection to poetry." Entries are organized by
date of first issue (then alphabetically by title) within chronological periods: 1914–39,
1940–49, 1950–59, 1960–75, and 1976–2000; each section begins with a brief
overview, but taken together these do not justify the *History* of the book's subtitle. A
full entry includes title; editor; publication information; dates of publication and issue
numbering; references to indexes, studies, anthologies, Web sites, and reprints; notes
on related publications (e.g., continuations); commentary on content, ideological bent,
and key contributors; location of any surviving archive; and location of copies (usually
with shelf mark). Entries for magazines published in Ireland are less full because of their
coverage in Clyde, *Irish Literary Magazines* (N3003).
    Concludes with a timeline of notable magazines and four indexes: places; subjects;
names (including publishers and associations); titles. Replete with information on nearly
2,000 titles, *British Poetry Magazines* is the essential resource for identifying and tracking
down copies of these frequently scarce publications and a valuable complement to such
indexes of little magazines as Bloomfield, *Author Index to Selected British "Little Magazines"* (K785), and Sader, *Comprehensive Index to English-Language Little Magazines*
(K790).

INDEXES

K780   *Access: The Index to Little Magazines, [1976–78].* N.p.: Burke, 1977–79.
        Annual.   AI3.A24.

    Author, title, and subject indexes to selected little magazines published, for the
most part, in the United States. The title index covers only fiction and poetry; the
subject index is limited to nonfiction, including book reviews that are listed by the
author of the book. Offering no explanation of the criteria governing selection, covering
a very limited number of magazines (69 in the 1978 volume), and weak in its subject
indexing, *Access* is principally useful because no other bibliography indexes most of the
magazines for these years.

K785   Bloomfield, B. C. *An Author Index to Selected British "Little Magazines,"*
        1930–1939. London: Mansell, 1976. 153 pp.   AI3.B56   052.

    An author index to 73 little magazines, all but one of them published in Great
Britain. Magazines not included—those indexed in general periodical indexes, without
literary merit, or unlocated—are listed on pp. vii–viii. The approximately 11,000
entries cite title, publication information, and type of work (verse, prose, illustration);
at the end of each author entry is a list of books by that author reviewed in magazines
indexed. Although lacking subject access (except for the heading "Films Reviewed")
and encompassing only 73 magazines within a decade, Bloomfield is valuable for the
access it provides to magazines otherwise unindexed.

K790   *Comprehensive Index to English-Language Little Magazines, 1890–1970:*
        Series One. Ed. Marion Sader. 8 vols. Millwood: Kraus, 1976.
        Z6944.L5 S23 [PN4836]   016.051.

An author index to 100 periodicals, 59 of which are published in the United States
and most of the remainder in Great Britain. Ostensibly limited to the "best" works, the
Index does include several publications (such as *Modern Fiction Studies* and *Twentieth
Century Literature*) that hardly qualify as "little magazines." Under each author, primary
works appear first, followed by works about the author (including reviews). In addition
to recording basic publication information, each entry identifies the type of work (see
vol. 1, p. xv for a list of abbreviations). Since unsigned works that cannot be attributed
are omitted, Sader is not the "comprehensive" index claimed by the title; however, it
does offer the fullest access to a minuscule number of twentieth-century little magazines.

K795   *Index to Commonwealth Little Magazines, 1964–1965.* By Stephen H.
        Goode. New York: Johnson Rpt., 1966. 187 pp. *1966–1967.* 1968.
        251 pp. *1968–1969.* Troy: Whitston, 1970. 216 pp. *1970–1973.* 1975.
        550 pp. *1974–1975.* 1976. 491 pp. *1976–1979.* Comp. Sarah V. Gray.
        2 vols. 1984. *1980–1982.* 1986. 926 pp. *1983–1984.* 1987. 575 pp.
        1985–1986. 1989. 280 pp. *1987–1989.* 1991. 434 pp. *1990–1992.*
        1993. 308 pp. AI3.I48   051.

A highly selective author and subject index to articles, original works, review essays,
and substantial reviews in 15 to 42 English-language little magazines, many of them
published in the British Isles. Canadian publications are excluded. Although offering
no explanation of the criteria governing selection, including some periodicals that hardly
qualify as little magazines, and utilizing inexact subject headings, the work at least
provides access to a few little magazines indexed nowhere else. Reviews: (1964–65)
Charles L. Dwyer, *English Literature in Transition, 1880–1920* 10 (1967): 96; (1974–
75) Joan Stockard, *Literary Research Newsletter* 3 (1978): 186–90.

K800   *Index to Little Magazines [1948–67].* Chicago: Swallow, 1949–70.
        Compilers and frequency vary.   AI3.I54.

Retrospective volumes have been compiled by Stephen H. Goode:

> *Index to Little Magazines, 1943–1947.* Denver: Swallow, 1965. 287 pp.
> *Index to Little Magazines, 1940–1942.* New York: Johnson Rpt., 1967.
>   234 pp.
> *Index to American Little Magazines, 1920–1939.* Troy: Whitston, 1969.
>   346 pp.
> *Index to American Little Magazines, 1900–1919: To Which Is Added a Selected
>   List of British and Continental Titles for the Years 1900–1950, Together
>   with Addenda and Corrigenda to Previous Indexes.* 3 vols. Troy: Whitston,
>   1974.

Contains author and subject indexes to selected little magazines, the majority published in the United States. Volumes typically cover between 31 and 57 important
magazines not indexed by general periodical bibliographies such as *Readers' Guide*
(G400) and *Humanities Index* (G385). Besides covering 102 magazines, the *1900–
1919* index supplements and corrects Goode's other volumes. The subject indexing is
usually too imprecise to be of much use, book reviews are not always indexed, and the
coverage extends to only a small percentage of little magazines published before 1967.
Still, these works remain the only indexes to many of the magazines.

See also

> *American Humanities Index* (G360).
> *Annual Index to Poetry in Periodicals* (Q4325a).
> *British Poetry Magazines, 1914–2000* (K777).
> *Humanities Index* (G385).
> *Index of American Periodical Verse* (Q4325).
> *Index to Poetry in Periodicals* (Q4325a).
> Messerli, *Index to Periodical Fiction in English, 1965–1969* (L1085a).

Guides to Scholarship and Criticism

K803   Glazier, Loss Pequeño. *Small Press: An Annotated Guide.* Westport:
          Greenwood, 1992. 123 pp.   Z472.G58   016.0705'0973.

A selective annotated bibliography of important works, published in the United States between 1960 and 1992, that treat aspects of literary publishing involving small presses and little magazines in the United States (principally since 1960). Excluded are bibliographies and most studies of individual presses, discussions of fine printing and vanity publishing, and material about nonliterary publishing by minority, ethnic, and other groups. The 174 entries are listed alphabetically in five divisions: directories, indexes, and guides; trade journals; studies of cultural aspects of small presses; commercial topics; catalogs, lists, and bibliographies. The thorough annotations are packed with essential information and frequently offer trustworthy evaluations. Indexed by persons, title, and subjects. Although selective and limited to English-language resources published after 1960, *Small Press* is the essential guide to contemporary literary small presses and little magazines.

See also

> Chielens, *Literary Journal in America, 1900–1950* (Q4250).

L

Genres

Only works that encompass more than one national literature are included here. Works limited to a single literature are listed in the genre portion of national literature sections. All of the guides to scholarship and criticism in this section should be supplemented by the serial bibliographies, indexes, and abstracts in section G.

General

Guides to Scholarship and Criticism

L820   Ruttkowski, Wolfgang. *Bibliographie der Gattungspoetik für den Studenten der Literaturwissenschaft: Ein abgekürztes Verzeichnis von über 3,000 Büchern, Dissertationen, und Zeitschriftenartikeln in Deutsch, Englisch, und Französisch/ Bibliography of the Poetics of Literary Genres for the Student of Literature: A Short-Title Catalogue of More Than 3,000 Books, Dissertations, and Articles in English, French, and German/Bibliographie de la poétique des genres littéraires pour l'étudiant de la littérature: Une bibliographie de plus que 3,000 livres, thèses, et articles en français, en allemand, et en anglais.* München: Hueber, 1973. 246 pp. Z6511.R86.
A selective bibliography of studies on genres and forms. Ruttkowski emphasizes English, French, and German publications from 1940 to 1970 but includes, albeit unsystematically, earlier studies as well as works in other European languages. Entries are arranged alphabetically by author in three sections: literary dictionaries containing articles on genres, general and multiple genre studies, and works on particular genres. Since the last section is classified by German terminology for genres and forms, use of the trilingual genre index is mandatory. Many entries are taken from other bibliographies; both selection and classification seem based primarily on title keywords; and the extensive use of abbreviations, especially in titles, requires constant reference to the list of abbreviations. Two indexes: genres (which indexes only the classified section on individual forms and genres); authors. Although the work is uneven in coverage, inadequately subject-indexed, and now badly dated—given the attention accorded genre study since 1970—Ruttkowski provides the most extensive list of studies on genres and forms, and thus offers a convenient starting point for research.

See also

> *ABELL* (G340): [English] Literature/General through the volume for 1972, Literary History and Criticism division in the volume for 1973, and English Literature/General in later volumes.
> "Check List of Explication" (L1255a).
> *MLAIB* (G335): General VII: Literature, General and Comparative in the volumes for 1953–55; General II: Literature, General and Comparative in the volume for 1956; General IV in the volumes for 1957–80; and the Genres and Literary Forms divisions in pt. 4 of the later volumes.

Fiction

General

BIBLIOGRAPHIES OF BIBLIOGRAPHIES

L833   Hartman, Donald K., and Jerome Drost, comps. *Themes and Settings in*
        Fiction: A Bibliography of Bibliographies. Bibliographies and Indexes in
        World Literature 14. New York: Greenwood, 1988. 223 pp.   Z5916.H28
        [PN3353]   016.01680883'93.
        An annotated bibliography of English-language bibliographies (published 1900 –
87) of themes, topics, persons, or places treated in adult fiction, regardless of language
or publication date. Included are books, parts of books, articles, review essays, and
dissertations that refer to more than five works of fiction by two or more authors. The
1,412 entries are divided among three sequences, each organized alphabetically by author, editor, or title of anonymous work: sources covering several themes or settings;
bibliographies devoted to a single theme, person, topic, or setting; and works published
1986 – 87. Accompanying each entry is a brief, but generally adequate, description of
the subject or person treated. Two indexes: joint authors; subjects (which would benefit
from more-thorough cross-referencing). Although Hartman overlooks several bibliographies, it is an essential starting point for identifying fictional treatments of persons,
places, or subjects.

GUIDES TO PRIMARY WORKS

L835   *Fiction Catalog.* Ed. John Greenfieldt. 15th ed. Standard Catalog Series.
        New York: Wilson, 2006. 1,317 pp. Annual supplements.   Z5916.F5
        [PN3451]   016.80883. H. W. Wilson. Online. 29 June 2006
        <http://vnweb.hwwilsonweb.com/hww>. Updated daily.
        A highly selective author, title, and subject index to more than 8,000 English-
language works (including translations). Although emphasizing novels, *Fiction Catalog*
includes some short story and novella collections. Pt. 1 is an author catalog, and entries
include publication information; plot summary; list of contents; and extracts from reviews, literary dictionaries, or a publisher's description. Pt. 2 is a title and subject index.
Designed as a selection aid for libraries and thus emphasizing established authors, *Fiction*
Catalog is useful to the literary researcher needing to identify novels about a topic or
representing a genre or literary form. Earlier editions cite works subsequently dropped.
In addition to the online version of the current edition, users can search noncurrent
entries in *Fiction Catalog Archive* (although it is unclear from the Web site whether this
includes all previous editions). See entry I525 for an evaluation of the *WilsonWeb* search
interface, which all of the Wilson databases use.
        A useful complement for works published since 1945 is *Cumulated Fiction Index,*
1945 – 1960, comp. G. B. Cotton and Alan Glencross (London: Assn. of Assistant
Librarians, 1960, 552 pp.); *1960 – 1969,* comp. Raymond Ferguson Smith (1970, 307
pp.); *1970 – 1974,* comp. Smith and Antony John Gordon (1975, 192 pp.); *1975 –*
1979, comp. Marilyn E. Hicken (1980, 225 pp.); *1980 – 1989,* comp. Hicken (1990,
495 pp.); *1990 – 1994,* comp. Hicken (1996, 269 pp.); *1995 – 1999,* comp. Hicken

([London?]: Career Dev. Group–The Lib. Assn., [2000?], 194 pp.). *Fiction Index [1945–95]: A Guide to Works of Fiction Available during the Year and Not Previously Indexed in the Fiction Index Series* (Halifax: Career Dev. Group, 1952–98) — the annual supplements between cumulations — ceased with the volume covering 1995. Although *Cumulated Fiction Index* covers more titles than *Fiction Catalog,* many subject headings are vague, the criteria governing selection are unclear, and entries unhelpfully cite only author and abbreviated title.

See also

> Adams, *Plot Locator* (p. 11).

GUIDES TO SCHOLARSHIP AND CRITICISM

See

> *ABELL* (G340): [English] Literature/General through the volume for 1967; Literature, General/Literary History/Fiction, and Literature, General/Literary Criticism/Fiction in the volumes for 1968–72; Literary History and Criticism/ Fiction in the volume for 1973; and English Literature/General/Fiction in later volumes.
> "Check List of Explication" (L1255a).
> *MLAIB* (G335): General VII: Literature, General and Comparative in the volumes for 1953–55; General II: Literature, General and Comparative in the volume for 1956; General IV/Prose Fiction in the volumes for 1957–80; and the Literary Forms division and Genres/Fiction section in pt. 4 of the later volumes. Researchers must also check the "Fiction" heading in the subject index to post-1980 volumes and in the online thesaurus.

Gothic and Horror Fiction

Many works in section L: Genres/Fiction/Science and Fantasy Fiction are useful for research in horror fiction.

GUIDES TO REFERENCE WORKS

See

> Burgess, *Reference Guide to Science Fiction, Fantasy, and Horror* (L952).

GUIDES TO PRIMARY WORKS

L860   Bleiler, Everett F. *The Guide to Supernatural Fiction: A Full Description of 1,775 Books from 1750 to 1960, Including Ghost Stories, Weird Fiction, Stories of Supernatural Horror, Fantasy, Gothic Novels, Occult Fiction, and Similar Literature.* Kent: Kent State UP, 1983. 723 pp.   PN56.S8 B57 809.3'937.

A collection of summaries of about 7,200 stories. Books are organized by author, editor, or title of anonymous work, then chronologically by publication date, with a separate summary for each story within a collection. Most summaries conclude with a brief evaluative comment. Three indexes: motifs and story types; persons; titles. Offering fuller but less discriminating coverage than Tymn, *Horror Literature* (below), Bleiler is primarily valuable for its extensive indexing of motifs and story types.

The following are useful complements to Bleiler:

> Barron, Neil, ed. *Fantasy and Horror: A Critical and Historical Guide to Literature, Illustration, Film, TV, Radio, and the Internet* (L1015a). A revision of Barron, ed., *Fantasy Literature: A Reader's Guide* (L1015a), and Barron, ed., *Horror Literature: A Reader's Guide* (L1015a), this copies the format, organization, and indexing of Barron, *Anatomy of Wonder* (L1015), and cites many of the same reference works (updating information where necessary). Judicious in its selection and evaluation, *Fantasy and Horror* is the best selective guide to primary works and scholarship.
>
> Frank, Frederick S. *The First Gothics: A Critical Guide to the English Gothic Novel.* Garland Reference Library of the Humanities 710. New York: Garland, 1987. 496 pp. Offers extensive summaries of 500 representative English Gothic romances from 1764 to the 1820s.
>
> ————. *Through the Pale Door: A Guide to and through the American Gothic.* Bibliographies and Indexes in American Literature 11. New York: Greenwood, 1990. 338 pp. Provides a critical synopsis (along with a list of reprints and studies) of 509 Gothic novels and short stories from 1786 through 1988. Concludes with a chronology, a bibliography of general studies, and three indexes: persons; titles; themes, motifs, events, and characters. Review: Benjamin Franklin Fisher IV, *Resources for American Literary Study* 21 (1995): 286–89.
>
> Summers, Montague. *A Gothic Bibliography.* London: Fortune, 1941. 620 pp. Although notoriously unreliable, Summers does include some works not in Bleiler.
>
> Tymn, Marshall B., ed. *Horror Literature: A Core Collection and Reference Guide.* New York: Bowker, 1981. 559 pp. A selective guide to primary works and research materials in Gothic and horror literature through the late 1970s. Although the incomplete, poorly organized chapters on criticism and reference works have been superseded by Barron, *Horror Literature* (above), Tymn remains useful to the literary researcher for its annotated lists of major primary works.

Far inferior to the preceding is Elsa J. Radcliffe, *Gothic Novels of the Twentieth Century: An Annotated Bibliography* (Metuchen: Scarecrow, 1979, 272 pp.), which is too inconsistent, idiosyncratic, and error-ridden to recommend to researchers.

GUIDES TO SCHOLARSHIP AND CRITICISM

Serial Bibliographies

See

> *ABELL* (G340): [English] Literature/General through the volume for 1967; Literature, General/Literary History/Fiction, and Literature, General/Literary

Criticism/Fiction in the volumes for 1968–72; Literary History and Criticism/
Fiction in the volume for 1973; and English Literature/General/Fiction in later
volumes.

MLAIB (G335): General VII: Literature, General and Comparative in the volumes for 1953–55; General II: Literature, General and Comparative in the
volume for 1956; General IV/Prose Fiction in the volumes for 1957–80; and
Genres/Fiction/Gothic Fiction, Genres/Fiction/Horror Fiction, Genres/Novel/
Gothic Novel, and Genres/Escape Literature/Horror Literature sections in pt. 4
of the later volumes. Researchers must also check the headings beginning
"Gothic" and "Horror" in the subject index to post-1980 volumes and in the
online thesaurus.

Other Bibliographies

L875   Frank, Frederick S. *Guide to the Gothic: An Annotated Bibliography of
        Criticism.* Metuchen: Scarecrow, 1984. 421 pp. *Guide to the Gothic II: An
        Annotated Bibliography of Criticism, 1983–1993.* Lanham: Scarecrow, 1995.
        523 pp. *Guide to the Gothic III: An Annotated Bibliography of Criticism,
        1994–2003.* 2 vols. 2005.   Z5917.G66 F7 [PN3435]   016.8093′872.

Guide to the Gothic is a descriptively annotated guide to criticism from 1900 to
1982. The approximately 2,500 entries are organized in classified divisions for bibliographies, national literatures (English, American, Canadian, French, and German, with
sections for individual authors listed chronologically), and subjects (e.g., parodies, vam-
pire, death by spontaneous combustion, film). Two indexes: critics; authors, artists,
actors.

Guide to the Gothic II is both a sequel to and expansion of its parent volume. The
1,547 entries, which offer fuller, more evaluative annotations, are organized in divisions
for reference works, general studies, English literature (in which Canadian writers are
inexplicably included), American writers, other national literatures, and subjects. Two
indexes: critics; authors and titles of Gothic fiction.

Guide to the Gothic III continues the preceding but wastes an inordinate amount
of paper by including short entries for the 4,055 entries in its predecessors. With one
exception, the 1,651 new entries are organized in the same divisions as *Gothic II*:
Canadian literature has its own division. Users should note that each volume, inexplicably, is indexed separately by critics and authors or titles of Gothic fiction. Despite
these quirks (and the italicization of authors of dissertations and theses), *Gothic III*
continues to offer full, evaluative annotations (the value of which are compromised by
the lack of a subject index).

Some additional studies through 1987 are listed in Frank, *Gothic Fiction: A Master
List of Twentieth Century Criticism and Research,* Meckler's Bibliographies on Science
Fiction, Fantasy, and Horror 3 (Westport: Meckler, 1988, 193 pp.), which rearranges
entries (minus annotations) from *Guide to the Gothic* (without, of course, acknowledging
its ancestry).

A necessary complement is Benjamin Franklin Fisher IV, *The Gothic's Gothic: Study
Aids to the Tradition of the Tale of Terror,* Garland Reference Library of the Humanities
567 (New York: Garland, 1988, 485 pp.). Emphasizing British and American writers,
Fisher includes much nineteenth-century criticism; is more thorough than Frank in
covering many authors and topics; offers brief evaluations in many annotations; and
provides indexes of subjects, scholars, and titles of literary works. Users will, however,

regret the ill-advised decisions to exclude a number of important studies because they appear in other bibliographies of the Gothic and to conclude with 1977 because of the presence of "Bibliography of Gothic Studies [1978–80]," published in or as a supplement to *Gothic* (which appeared irregularly between 1979 and 1987 and is not widely held). Review: James P. Carson, *South Central Review* 7.1 (1990): 81–83.

   Guide to the Gothic, Guide to the Gothic II, Guide to the Gothic III, Gothic Fiction, and *Gothic's Gothic* must be used together for any extensive study of literary Gothicism.

See also

   Greenwood Guide to American Popular Culture (U6295).
   Spector, *English Gothic* (M2345).
   Tymn, *Horror Literature* (L860a).

Historical Fiction

GUIDES TO PRIMARY WORKS

There is no adequate general guide to historical fiction; the following are the best reference sources available.

L885   Baker, Ernest A. *A Guide to Historical Fiction.* London: Routledge; New
         York: Macmillan, 1914. 566 pp.   Z5917.H6 B2   016.80883'81.
   A selective guide, arranged by chronological periods within country divisions, mainly to novels in English (including translations). The bulk of the entries are devoted to British, American, and French history. The summary annotations are frequently quite full. Indexed by authors, titles, and subjects. Like Nield, *Guide to the Best Historical Novels and Tales* (L900), Baker is dated but still useful for its subject indexing.

L890   Adamson, Lynda G. *American Historical Fiction: An Annotated Guide to
         Novels for Adults and Young Adults.* Phoenix: Oryx, 1999. 405 pp.
         Z1231.F4 D47 [PS374.H5]   016.813'08109.
   A selective guide to 3,387 English-language novels published through 1998 and depicting some aspect of American history. Classified by historical period, entries include a one-sentence summary that outlines the plot and identifies major characters, locale, any sequels or prequels, and series; a list of awards; and an indication of genre. Many of the summaries are apparently based on a review or publisher's description. Appendixes list books by award and works suitable for young adults. Five indexes: authors; titles; genres; locales; subjects. Although lacking an adequate explanation of the criteria governing selection, Adamson is valuable for its indexing, which allows identification by ethnic group, geographical location, historical figure or event, and genre.
   Although *American Historical Fiction* is cataloged as a revised and expanded edition of Virginia Brokaw Gerhardstein, *Dickinson's American Historical Fiction*, 5th ed. (Metuchen: Scarecrow, 1986, 352 pp.), Adamson omits many titles included by Gerhardstein. Some additional works on American history are listed in the following:

         Coan, Otis W., and Richard G. Lillard. *America in Fiction: An Annotated
         List of Novels That Interpret Aspects of Life in the United States, Canada,*

and Mexico. 5th ed. Palo Alto: Pacific, 1967. 232 pp. A selective guide to English-language novels, volumes of short stories, and folklore collections that treat some aspect of American life. Other than a preference for "substantial, realistic books over those that are romantic or sentimental or melodramatic or that merely broke ground," criteria governing selection are vague. Works are listed by author in seven variously classified divisions: pioneering, farm and village life, industrial America, politics and institutions, religion, minority ethnic groups, and Mexico. A brief descriptive annotation accompanies each entry. Indexed by authors.

VanDerhoof, Jack. *A Bibliography of Novels Related to American Frontier and Colonial History.* Troy: Whitston, 1971. 501 pp. Although VanDerhoof offers more thorough coverage of novels treating colonial and frontier history, the lack of subject classification or indexing means that a user must search all 6,439 entries to locate works on a particular topic.

L895   Adamson, Lynda G. *World Historical Fiction: An Annotated Guide to Novels for Adults and Young Adults.* Phoenix: Oryx, 1999. 719 pp.
        Z5917.H6 A33 [PN3377.5.H57]   016.80883'81.

A selective guide to 6,116 English-language novels published, for the most part, after 1972 and treating historical events outside the United States (which is covered in Adamson, *American Historical Fiction* [L890]). Entries are organized by time period (prehistory and the ancient world; Roman empire—with each subdivided by geographic area) or by geographic area (subdivided by chronological period); within each subdivision, novels are listed alphabetically by author. Entries include a one-sentence summary that outlines the plot and identifies major characters, locale, any sequels or prequels, and series; a list of awards; and an indication of genre. Many of the summaries are apparently based on a review or publisher's description. Appendixes list books by award and works suitable for young adults. Five indexes: authors; titles; genres; locales and time periods; subjects. Although lacking an adequate explanation of the criteria governing selection, Adamson is valuable for its indexing, which allows identification by time period, geographical location, historical figure or event, and genre.

A good complement to Adamson is Sarah L. Johnson, *Historical Fiction: A Guide to the Genre,* Genreflecting Advisory Series (Westport: Libraries Unlimited–Greenwood, 2005, 813 pp.), which covers c. 3,800 English-language titles or series written for adults and published, for the most part, in the United States between 1995 and mid-2004. Entries are organized by subgenre (e.g., traditional historical novels, sagas, historical novels of the American West, literary historical novels, and Christian historical fiction), then by subcategories or themes. Annotations are typically fuller than is usual for guides to historical fiction. Four indexes: authors; titles, series; historical characters; places and times; subjects.

For books published before 1972, Daniel D. McGarry and Sarah Harriman White, *World Historical Fiction Guide: An Annotated, Chronological, Geographical, and Topical List of Selected Historical Novels,* 2nd ed. (Metuchen: Scarecrow, 1973, 629 pp.), remains of some use. However, the one-sentence annotations are frequently inaccurate and rarely provide an adequate sense of content.

L900   Nield, Jonathan. *A Guide to the Best Historical Novels and Tales.* 5th ed.
        New York: Macmillan, 1929. 424 pp.   Z5917.H6 N6   016.80883'81.

A chronological guide, largely devoted to novels in English (including translations). Entries do not provide complete bibliographical information, but the succinct summaries clearly delineate content. Includes a brief bibliography of publications on historical fiction. Three indexes: authors; titles; subjects. Like Baker, *Guide to Historical Fiction* (L885), Nield is dated but still useful for its subject indexing.

GUIDES TO SCHOLARSHIP AND CRITICISM

See

> *ABELL* (G340): [English] Literature/General through the volume for 1967; Literature, General/Literary History/Fiction, and Literature, General/Literary Criticism/Fiction in the volumes for 1968–72; Literary History and Criticism/Fiction in the volume for 1973; and English Literature/General/Fiction in later volumes.
>
> Inge, *Handbook of American Popular Literature* (U6295a).
>
> *MLAIB* (G335): General VII: Literature, General and Comparative in the volumes for 1953–55; General II: Literature, General and Comparative in the volume for 1956; General IV/Prose Fiction in the volumes for 1957–80; and the Genres/Fiction/Historical Fiction and Genres/Novel/Historical Novel sections in pt. 4 of the later volumes. Researchers must also check the "Historical Fiction" and "Historical Novel" headings in the subject index to post-1980 volumes and in the online thesaurus.

Mystery Fiction

GUIDES TO REFERENCE WORKS

L903   Bleiler, Richard J. *Reference and Research Guide to Mystery and Detective Fiction*. 2nd ed. Reference Sources in the Humanities Series. Westport: Libraries Unlimited–Greenwood, 2004. 828 pp.   Z5917.D5 B59 [PN3448.D4]   016.80883′872.

An evaluative guide to print and electronic reference works (published by 2002) devoted to mystery and detective fiction, with chapters on dictionaries and encyclopedias, general guides and genre or theme bibliographies, general bibliographies and library catalogs, national bibliographies, geographical guides, lists of awards, bibliographies of publishers, indexes to magazines and anthologies (with a guide to where specific magazines are indexed), biographical resources, author bibliographies, character indexes, bibliographies of secondary studies, cataloging guides, studies of artists, calendars, directories of booksellers and publishers, guides to quotations, electronic sources, and current periodicals. The full annotations thoroughly describe works; most welcome are the uncompromisingly frank, authoritative evaluations—a feature noticeably absent from most reference works of this kind. Indexed by authors and titles (but, unfortunately, not by subjects). An appendix indexes entries for writers in the biographical dictionaries and handbooks listed by Bleiler (and cites selected author Web sites). Although some chapters would benefit from a hierarchical, rather than alphabetical, organization, *Reference and Research Guide to Mystery and Detective Fiction*—based on an intimate knowledge of the works listed — is the essential first source for anyone engaged in more than cursory research in the field.

LITERARY HANDBOOKS, DICTIONARIES, AND ENCYCLOPEDIAS

L905   *Oxford Companion to Crime and Mystery Writing.* Ed. Rosemary Herbert.
       New York: Oxford UP, 1999. 535 pp.   PN3488.D4 H37   809.3'872'03.
    An encyclopedia of canonical authors, characters and character types, works, genres and forms, national traditions, geographic settings, conventions, themes, and other topics that emphasizes English-language crime and mystery writing. The signed entries tend to be fuller than those in the typical *Oxford Companion*; most include cross-references and suggestions for additional reading. Concludes with a glossary and an index of names of persons and characters. In *Reference and Research Guide to Mystery and Detective Fiction* (L903), Bleiler calls this the best encyclopedia in the field.

GUIDES TO PRIMARY WORKS

L910   Cook, Michael L., comp. *Monthly Murders: A Checklist and Chronological
       Listing of Fiction in the Digest-Size Mystery Magazines in the United States
       and England.* Westport: Greenwood, 1982. 1,147 pp.   Z1231.F4 C67
       [PS374.D4]   016.813'0872'08.
    A list of the stories published in American and English mystery magazines from 1941 through 1980. Magazines are organized alphabetically by title, with stories listed chronologically by issue. Two indexes: titles of magazines (including variant and alternate titles); authors (followed by titles of stories). Although not comprehensive, *Monthly Murders* is the fullest single index to the contents of these periodicals. Continued by William G. Contento, *Mystery Short Fiction: [1990–]: An Index to Mystery Magazines, Anthologies, and Single-Author Collections* (http://www.philsp.com/homeville/msf/0start.htm; also included in Contento, *Mystery Short Fiction Miscellany: An Index*, CD-ROM [Oakland: Locus, 2002]).
    A companion work indexes American pulp magazines: Michael L. Cook and Stephen T. Miller, *Mystery, Detective, and Espionage Fiction: A Checklist of Fiction in U.S. Pulp Magazines, 1915–1974*, 2 vols., Garland Reference Library of the Humanities 838: Fiction in the Pulp Magazines 1 (New York: Garland, 1988). Vol. 1 organizes 360 magazines alphabetically by title; an entry lists publication information, title change(s), and the fiction printed in each surviving issue. Additions, including a few magazines published outside the United States, appear on pp. 662–66. The author index in vol. 2 is plagued by a poorly conceived coding system and by inconsistencies in alphabetization (users must note that several authors have two separate — and separated — sequences of index headings). Despite the indexing flaws, *Mystery, Detective, and Espionage Fiction* draws extensively on private collections to offer a pioneering index to these elusive magazines.

L915   Hubin, Allen J. *Crime Fiction, IV: A Comprehensive Bibliography 1749–
       2000.* [Rev. ed.] CD-ROM. Oakland: Locus, 2005. A new edition is in
       progress.

Indexes 4,600 films and 106,549 separately published English-language novels, collections of short stories or novellas, plays, and poems of mystery, detective, suspense, thriller, romantic suspense, police, and spy fiction. Access is inhibited because users must navigate a series of cross-linked indexes rather than access a search interface (a result of the failure to divorce the electronic from the five-volume print version [Shelbourne: Battered Silicon Dispatch Press, 2003]). Most users will begin with the books listed by author or stories listed by author index, each of which lists works by name on title page with cross-references between pseudonym and real name. In the books listed by author index, entries identify setting, series character, and film adaptation; in the stories listed by author index, short stories are linked to the collections in which they appear. Entries in the books and stories listed by author indexes are linked to an array of indexes: titles of books; titles of stories; titles of movies; authors of movies; publishers; studios; authors (with titles listed chronologically, and the only place where works are identified by genre); series characters; and settings. Additions and corrections are contained in three separate addenda; some of the other addenda published in *Mystery*File* (which is held by only two libraries in the United States) are available at http://www.mysteryfile.com. The corrections and additions at http://www.locusmag.com/index/cf4cd.htm appear to have been incorporated into recent issues of the CD-ROM. To obtain full details about a work, users must cut and paste from too many indexes; access would be measurably improved by conflating many of the separate lists, expanding abbreviations, and providing a basic search engine. Like its predecessors — *Crime Fiction, 1749–1980: A Comprehensive Bibliography*, Garland Reference Library of the Humanities 371 (1984, 712 pp.); *1981–1985 Supplement*, Garland Reference Library of the Humanities 766 (1988, 260 pp.); *Crime Fiction, II: A Comprehensive Bibliography 1749–1995*, rev. and updated ed., 2 vols., Garland Reference Library of the Humanities 1353 (1994); and *Crime Fiction, III: A Comprehensive Bibliography 1749–1995*, rev. ed., CD-ROM (Oakland: Locus, 2001) — *Crime Fiction IV* is an indispensable guide to the subject but one that many users will avoid because poor design and inadequate search features make extracting information so needlessly frustrating and time-consuming.

Users will find locating stories in collections easier in William G. Contento and Martin H. Greenberg, *Index to Crime and Mystery Anthologies* (Boston: Hall, 1991, 736 pp.; also included in Contento, *Mystery Short Fiction Miscellany: An Index*, CD-ROM [Oakland: Locus, 2002]), which indexes 1,031 English-language volumes (published between 1875 and 1990 in the United States, Great Britain, Canada, and Australia) in five lists: an author or editor list of collections; a title list of collections; an author list of stories (with the earliest printing of a story noted when possible); a title list of stories; and an author or editor list of books with full contents. Combining the first four lists would make the work more accessible. Continued by William G. Contento, *Mystery Short Fiction: [1990–]* (L910a).

Albert J. Menendez, *The Subject Is Murder: A Selective Guide to Mystery Fiction*, 2 vols. (with vol. 2 subtitled *A Selective Subject Guide to Mystery Fiction*), Garland Reference Library of the Humanities 627 and 1060 (New York: Garland, 1986–90), classifies about 5,900 works under 29 subjects (e.g., academe, literary people, bookshops and libraries, weddings and honeymoons, and gardening). Readers new to mystery fiction will find useful guidance in Jacques Barzun and Wendell Hertig Taylor, *A Catalogue of Crime*, rev. and enl. ed. (New York: Harper, 1989, 952 pp.), whose listings of novels, short stories, plays, critical studies, true crime stories, and Sherlockiana are accompanied by succinct evaluations.

Most issues of *Armchair Detective* 1–30 (1967–97) include "Checklist of Mystery, Detective, and Suspense Fiction Published in the United States."

GUIDES TO SCHOLARSHIP AND CRITICISM

L920   Albert, Walter. *Detective and Mystery Fiction: An International Bibliography of Secondary Sources.* 3rd ed. CD-ROM. Oakland: Locus, 2003.

A classified, annotated bibliography of studies (published through 2000) on crime, detective, mystery, suspense, and espionage fiction that excludes Sherlockiana. Although the subtitle denominates this an "international bibliography," coverage of non-English-language sources is inconsistent. The 10,721 entries are arranged alphabetically by scholar in five divisions: reference works; general studies (books); general studies (articles); dime novels, juvenile series, and pulps; and authors. An additional section on magazines updates Cook, *Mystery, Detective, and Espionage Magazines* (L925). Annotations are frequently extensive and evaluative. The CD-ROM provides a series of static pages that can only be navigated by clicking through a series of alphabetical files. There are hyperlinks, but it is not possible to search across files. Indexed by scholars, authors, series characters, magazines, and publishers. To obtain full details about a work, users must cut and paste from too many indexes; access would be measurably improved by conflating many of the separate lists and providing a basic search engine. Although frustratingly inaccessible, *Detective and Mystery Fiction* is the most thorough bibliography of the subject and is superior to the following:

> Breen, Jon L. What about Murder? *A Guide to Books about Mystery and Detective Fiction.* Metuchen: Scarecrow, 1981. 157 pp. *What about Murder? 1981–1991.* 1993. 376 pp. Supplemented by "What about Murder," Breen's regular column in *Armchair Detective* 18–30 (1984–97). This work remains valuable for its detailed evaluations.
>
> Johnson, Timothy W., and Julia Johnson, eds. *Crime Fiction Criticism: An Annotated Bibliography.* Garland Reference Library of the Humanities 233. New York: Garland, 1981. 423 pp.
>
> Skene Melvin, David, and Ann Skene Melvin, comps. *Crime, Detective, Espionage, Mystery, and Thriller Fiction and Film: A Comprehensive Bibliography of Critical Writing through 1979.* Westport: Greenwood, 1980. 367 pp.

See also

> *ABELL* (G340): [English] Literature/General through the volume for 1967; Literature, General/Literary History/Fiction, and Literature, General/Literary Criticism/Fiction in the volumes for 1968–72; Literary History and Criticism/Fiction in the volume for 1973; and English Literature/General/Fiction in later volumes.
>
> Inge, *Handbook of American Popular Literature* (U6295a).
>
> *MLAIB* (G335): General VII: Literature, General and Comparative in the volumes for 1953–55; General II: Literature, General and Comparative in the volume for 1956; General IV/Prose Fiction in the volumes for 1957–80; and the Genres/Fiction/Crime Fiction, Genres/Fiction/Detective Fiction, Genres/Fiction/Mystery Fiction, Genres/Novel/Crime Novel, Genres/Novel/Detective Novel, and Genres/Novel/Mystery Novel sections in pt. 4 of the later volumes. Researchers must also check the headings beginning "Crime," "Detective," and "Mystery" in the subject index to post-1980 volumes and in the online thesaurus.

PERIODICALS

Guides to Primary Works

L925   Cook, Michael L., [ed.]. *Mystery, Detective, and Espionage Magazines.*
         Historical Guides to the World's Periodicals and Newspapers. Westport:
         Greenwood, 1983. 795 pp.   PN3448.D4 C56   809.3'872.
     A collection of separately authored profiles of English-language fiction and non-
fiction magazines (including scholarly journals and fanzines) published in North America and England, along with selective overviews of foreign-language periodicals. Excludes
publications restricted to members of Sherlock Holmes organizations. Organized alphabetically by title (with cross-references for variants), the entries for the English-
language periodicals include a discussion of publishing history and general content; a
selected list of studies, indexing sources, and locations (with many citing only private
collections); and information on title changes, volume and issue numbering and dates,
publisher(s), editor(s), price, size and pagination, and current status. Two other divisions
offer basic overviews and lists by country of foreign-language magazines and discussions
of book clubs. Seven appendixes: United States, English, and Canadian magazines,
classified by country, then format for fiction and subject for nonfiction publications;
major writers and the magazines that published them; chronology of English-language
periodicals and book clubs; American true-detective magazines; Canadian true-detective
magazines; Sherlock Holmes scion society periodicals; other periodicals of interest to
the collector. Concludes with a selected bibliography. The index of titles, persons,
publishers, and some subjects excludes the division listing foreign-language magazines.
Given the ephemeral nature and short lives of many of these publications, the lack of
publishing details and few locations for many entries is not surprising. Although the
essays vary substantially in quality and accuracy, Cook is the single best guide to the
important English-language periodicals. Review: Fred Erisman, *Resources for American
Literary Study* 13 (1983): 109–11.
     The section on magazines in the 3rd ed. of Albert, *Detective and Mystery Fiction*
(L920), updates some information in Cook.

Picaresque Fiction

GUIDES TO SCHOLARSHIP AND CRITICISM

L950   Laurenti, Joseph L. *Catálogo bibliográfico de la literatura picaresca siglos XVI–
         XX.* 2nd ed. 2 vols. Teatro del Siglo de Oro: Bibliografías y catálogos 27–
         28. Kassel: Reichenberger, 2000.   Z2694.P5 L38.
     A bibliography of editions and translations of Spanish picaresque fiction first pub-
lished between 1554 and 1743 and of studies through 1998 of picaresque fiction worldwide. Entries are listed chronologically in sections on bibliographies, etymology of
pícaro, anthologies, general studies, literary relations (subdivided by country), and individual Spanish novels (with subdivisions for bibliographies, editions, translations
[grouped by language], and studies). Two indexes: persons; subjects. Users should note
that the list of abbreviations and acronyms appears at the end of the book. Although

the organization impedes access to the contents, no other source collects so handily the widely dispersed scholarship on the picaresque.

See also

> *ABELL* (G340): [English] Literature/General through the volume for 1967; Literature, General/Literary History/Fiction, and Literature, General/Literary Criticism/Fiction in the volumes for 1968 72; Literary History and Criticism/Fiction in the volume for 1973; and English Literature/General/Fiction in later volumes.
>
> *MLAIB* (G335): General VII: Literature, General and Comparative in the volumes for 1953–55; General II: Literature, General and Comparative in the volume for 1956; General IV/Prose Fiction in the volumes for 1957–80; and the Genres/Fiction/Picaresque Fiction and Genres/Novel/Picaresque Novel sections in pt. 4 of the later volumes. Researchers must also check the headings beginning "Picaresque" in the subject index to post-1980 volumes and in the online thesaurus.

Science and Fantasy Fiction

This section lists only the major general reference works on science and fantasy fiction. It excludes works devoted to film and television; illustration; chronological periods; a single national literature; and individual forms, types, or themes. For these specialized reference works, consult Tymn, *Research Guide to Science Fiction Studies* (L1015a); *Barron, Anatomy of Wonder* (L1015); and, especially, Burgess, *Reference Guide to Science Fiction, Fantasy, and Horror* (L952).

GUIDES TO REFERENCE WORKS

L952   Burgess, Michael, and Lisa R. Bartle. *Reference Guide to Science Fiction, Fantasy, and Horror.* 2nd ed. Reference Sources in the Humanities Series. Westport: Libraries Unlimited – Greenwood, 2002. 605 pp. Z5917.S36 B87 [PN3433.5]   016.8093'876.

An evaluative guide to bibliographies, indexes, dictionaries, encyclopedias, and other reference works published through 1999 (with a few from 2000) devoted to fantastic literature. The 699 entries are organized in divisions for encyclopedias and dictionaries; atlases and gazetteers; cataloging guides; yearbooks, annuals, and almanacs; annual directories; statistical sources; awards lists; pseudonyms lists; biographical directories; readers' and critical guides; guides to secondary sources; library catalogs and collection guides; magazine and anthology indexes; general bibliographies; national bibliographies; subject bibliographies; publisher bibliographies; author bibliographies; artist bibliographies; character dictionaries and author encyclopedias; film and television catalogs; printed guides to the Internet; calendars and chronologies; quotation dictionaries; collectors' and price guides; fan guides; online resources; core periodicals; professional organizations; and core collections. Three indexes: authors; titles; subjects. Although some chapters would benefit from a hierarchical, rather than alphabetical, organization, the extensive annotations offer a thorough description of content and organization, comparisons with similar or related works, and a rigorous, uncompromising evaluation of strengths and weaknesses (though the entry on Summers, *A Gothic Bibliography* [L860a] fails to warn readers about the notorious unreliability of this work). With one of the foremost bibliographers of the field as an author, this work supersedes or is superior to the sections on reference works in Tymn, *Horror Literature* (L860a), Barron, *Horror Literature* (L1015a), Barron, *Anatomy of Wonder* (L1015), and Justice, *Science Fiction, Fantasy, and Horror Reference* (L1015a) and is the essential guide to reference works in a field beset by more than its share of shoddy bibliographies, dictionaries, and the like.

HISTORIES AND SURVEYS

For an evaluative annotated list of histories and surveys, see Gary K. Wolfe, "History and Criticism" (pp. 523–612), in Barron, *Anatomy of Wonder* (L1015); and Marshall B. Tymn, "Science Fiction: A Brief History and Review of Criticism," *American Studies International* 23.1 (1985): 41–66.

For a chronological overview of science fiction criticism since the seventeenth century, see "A History of Science Fiction Criticism," a special section in *Science-Fiction Studies* 26 (1999): 161–283.

L955   Aldiss, Brian W., and David Wingrove. *Trillion Year Spree: The History of Science Fiction.* New York: Atheneum, 1986. 511 pp.   PR830.S35 A38 823'.0876'09.

A critical history from Shelley's *Frankenstein* through the mid-1980s that locates the origin of science fiction in the Gothic romance and emphasizes its development as a genre (primarily in Britain and the United States). Indexed by author, title, and some subjects. Although some assertions are controversial and although the treatment of post-1970 works is not up to the standard of the earlier part, *Trillion Year Spree* remains the fullest history of science fiction and a worthy successor to Aldiss, *Billion Year Spree: The True History of Science Fiction* (Garden City: Doubleday, 1973, 339 pp.). Reviews: John Clute, *TLS: Times Literary Supplement* 31 Oct. 1986: 1223; Veronica Hollinger, *Science-Fiction Studies* 15 (1988): 102–05; Roz Kaveney, *Foundation: The Review of Science Fiction* 38 (1986–87): 69–76, with responses by Wingrove and Malcolm Edwards and a reply by Kaveney, 40 (1987): 72–81.

L960   Suvin, Darko. *Metamorphoses of Science Fiction: On the Poetics and History of a Literary Genre.* New Haven: Yale UP, 1979. 317 pp.   PN3448.S45 S897 809.3'876.

An attempt to legitimatize science fiction by establishing a poetics of the genre and tracing its early evolution. Based on Marxist ideology, the first part presents the theoretical foundation, which defines science fiction as "the literature of cognitive estrangement" and emphasizes utopian literature while largely excluding myth and fantasy. The second part traces the evolution of European and American science fiction from More through Wells, with a brief excursion into early-twentieth-century Russian works and a chapter on Karel Čapek. Concludes with a selected bibliography. Indexed by persons. Although reviewers justifiably find the discussion of poetics too restrictive, most agree that Suvin is an important, provocative contribution to the study of the genre. Reviews: Dagmar Barnouw, *MLN* 95 (1980): 1461–66; John R. Reed, *Modern*

Philology 78 (1981): 338–40; George Slusser, *Nineteenth-Century Fiction* 35 (1980): 73–76.

LITERARY HANDBOOKS, DICTIONARIES, AND ENCYCLOPEDIAS

L965   *Multimedia Encyclopedia of Science Fiction.* CD-ROM. Danbury: Grolier Electronic, 1995.

Encyclopedia of Science Fiction. [Updated 2nd ed.] Ed. John Clute and Peter Nicholls. New York: St. Martin's Griffin, 1995. 1,386 pp.   PN3433.4.E53 809.3'8762'03.

Encyclopedia of Science Fiction *Edited by John Clute and Peter Nicholls: New Data, Typographical Errors, Factual Corrections, and Miscellanea.* Ed. David Langford. Online. 16 Jan. 2006 <http://www.dcs.gla.ac.uk/SF-Archives/Misc/sfec.html>.

Prints more than 4,360 signed entries on authors, themes, films and television programs, magazines and fanzines, illustrators, editors, critics, filmmakers, publishers, pseudonyms, series, anthologies, comics, terminology, and awards. The updated 2nd edition reprints the 1993 edition (New York: St. Martin's, 1993, 1,370 pp.) together with a 16-page section of additions and corrections; the CD-ROM incorporates these changes, updates about 600 entries, and adds more than 150 entries and numerous illustrations and film clips. Prefaced by an admirably clear statement of editorial principles and coverage and replete with evaluative, well-written, information-packed entries, *Encyclopedia of Science Fiction* and its CD-ROM counterpart are the essential desktop references for the subject. Complemented by *Encyclopedia of Fantasy* (L967). Review: Edward James, *Foundation: The Review of Science Fiction* 58 (1993): 100–03.

James Gunn, ed., *The New Encyclopedia of Science Fiction* (New York: Viking, 1988, 524 pp.), emphasizes American and British science fiction in signed entries for writers and others (such as illustrators, film directors, and actors), organizations, films, serial publications, and a variety of related topics. Unfortunately, *New Encyclopedia* is so error-ridden that it cannot be trusted. Reviews: Gregory Feeley, *Foundation: The Review of Science Fiction* 45 (1989): 81–83; Gary K. Wolfe, *Science-Fiction Studies* 16 (1989): 379–83.

Both works are indexed in *Biography and Genealogy Master Index* (J565).

L967   *The Encyclopedia of Fantasy.* Ed. John Clute and John Grant. New York: St. Martin's, 1997. 1,049 pp.   PN3435.E53   809.3'8766'03.

Encyclopedia of Fantasy *Edited by John Clute and John Grant: New Data, Typographical Errors, Factual Corrections, and Miscellanea.* Ed. David Langford. Online. 16 Jan. 2006 <http://www.dcs.gla.ac.uk/SF-Archives/Misc/fec.html>.

An encyclopedia of authors, artists, movies, motifs, themes, genres, art, characters, television series, printed works, concepts, periodicals, critics, awards, and the like associated with fantasy. Many of the more than 4,000 entries conclude with suggestions for further reading. Like its counterpart *Encyclopedia of Science Fiction* (L965) — to which there are numerous cross-references — *Encyclopedia of Fantasy* is replete with evaluative, well-written, information-packed entries and is the essential desktop companion for fantasy literature. Review: Andy Sawyer, *Foundation: The International Review of Science Fiction* 70 (1997): 86–89.

GUIDES TO PRIMARY WORKS

For an overview of bibliographies of primary works of science fiction, see Hal W. Hall and Wendi Arant, "The Bibliographic Control of Science Fiction: A Quarter-Century of Change," *Extrapolation* 40 (1999): 304–13.

Serial Bibliographies

L980   *NESFA Index to Short Science Fiction for [1987–89].* Cambridge: NESFA, 1989–92.   Z5917.S36 I55   808.83.

   NESFA Index to the Science Fiction Magazines and Original Anthologies [1971–86]. Cambridge: NESFA, 1973–88. Annual. Title varies. Z5917.S36 I55 [PN3433]   813'.0876'016.

   An author and title index to English-language "professional" science fiction magazines, anthologies, and single-author collections. The last volumes were organized in four divisions: separate lists of magazines, anthologies, and collections indexed; contents of issues or volumes indexed (listed alphabetically by periodical or collection title); author index (keyed to the contents list); title index (keyed to the author index). The space devoted to the superfluous list of magazines, anthologies, and collections indexed could be better utilized for fuller citations in the author and title indexes. Anyone consulting the title index must move to the author index and then to the list of contents to gather sufficient information to locate a story. Nonetheless, *NESFA Index* remains the standard index for 1971–89.

   It appeared that *NESFA Index* would be rendered superfluous by Charles N. Brown and William G. Contento, *Science Fiction, Fantasy, and Horror [1985–90]: A Comprehensive Bibliography of Books and Short Fiction Published in the English Language* (Oakland: Locus, 1986–91). Although hardly "comprehensive" and inefficiently organized, it was the work that came closest to providing a list of current science fiction publications and was a useful continuation of Contento, *Index to Science Fiction Anthologies and Collections* (L985). *Science Fiction, Fantasy, and Horror* is cumulated and continued, in truncated form, in the annual *Locus Index to Science Fiction [1984–   ]* (online; 16 Jan. 2006 <http://www.locusmag.com/index/0start.html>; CD-ROM [combined with *Index to Science Fiction Anthologies and Collections* (L985)]), a series of hyperlinked indexes structured much like the pages of *Index to Science Fiction Anthologies and Collections: Combined Edition* (L985) and suffering from the same deficiencies.

   The best coverage of magazines is provided by Miller, *Science Fiction, Fantasy, and Weird Fiction Magazine Index* (L987).

Other Bibliographies

L985   Contento, William. *Index to Science Fiction Anthologies and Collections: Combined Edition.* Online. 6 Jan. 2006 <http://contento.best.vwh.net>. CD-ROM (combined with *Locus Index to Science Fiction* [L980a]).

An expanded, corrected electronic version of Contento, *Index to Science Fiction Anthologies and Collections*, 2 vols., Reference Publication in Science Fiction (Boston: Hall, 1978–84), which is an author and title index to the contents of English-language collections, anthologies, and novels developed out of three or more stories. Vol. 1 (covering works published through June 1977) is restricted to science fiction that deals "with social and technical extrapolation and invention," but the second volume (primarily covering works published from July 1977 through December 1983) admits more horror, weird, and fantasy fiction. The second volume offers a significantly improved layout, but both volumes are plagued by an unduly confusing system of abbreviations.

The *Combined Edition* reformats the data into six static lists (titles of books, authors of books, titles of short stories, authors of short stories, chronological list of novels and short stories for each author, and series titles) that users must navigate by hyperlinks. As of the 29 Oct. 2005 update, the site indexed 3,900 collections containing more than 38,000 stories by 3,880 authors. Although the electronic version reduces the number of abbreviations, enough remain that users will need frequent recourse to the list; because the list has to be accessed through the Table of Contents page, searchers should load the Abbreviations page in a separate browser tab. To obtain full details about a work, users must cut and paste from too many indexes; access would be measurably improved by conflating many of the separate lists, expanding abbreviations, and providing a basic search engine. Although not comprehensive and lacking full publication details for some entries, *Index to Science Fiction Anthologies and Collections: Combined Edition* is the best single index to science fiction anthologies and collections.

Continued (for collections published December 1984–90) by Brown, *Science Fiction, Fantasy, and Horror* (L980a).

Many (but not all of the collections) in the preceding are also indexed in Mike Ashley and Contento, *The Supernatural Index: A Listing of Fantasy, Supernatural, Occult, Weird, and Horror Anthologies*, Bibliographies and Indexes in Science Fiction, Fantasy, and Horror 5 (Westport: Greenwood, 1995, 933 pp.). The 2,100 volumes cited herein are needlessly relegated to separate lists of editors, anthology titles, authors, short story titles, and anthology contents. Although the author index includes information on length of a story, original publication information, and a chronological list of collections that reprint it, the separate indexes make the work awkward to consult.

L987   Miller, Stephen T., and William G. Contento. *Science Fiction, Fantasy, and Weird Fiction Magazine Index: 1890– *. CD-ROM. Oakland: Locus, 2001– . Annual.

An index to English-language science fiction, fantasy, and weird fiction magazines (including some that were assembled but not published). The 2006 release covers more than 16,400 issues for 1,171 publications, with separate indexes of magazine titles, authors and artists, stories listed alphabetically by author, stories listed by title, works about authors, stories listed chronologically by author, series, cover artists, and magazines with issues listed by date. Given the extensive hyperlinking and the lack of any search capability beyond that of the user's Web browser, several of the separate indexes could be conflated so that users don't have to click through successive indexes in order to assemble a full citation for a story. Titles are followed by an abbreviation that identifies genre or type of work (e.g., interview, letter, cartoon); since space is not a concern on the CD-ROM, users would be better served by expanded abbreviations instead of having to consult the list of abbreviations. Concludes with a list of missing issues, a hyperlink to an online addendum (last updated in 1999), and a notes section, which includes a poorly identified and murky user's guide; the last, along with a clear explanation of the scope and editorial procedures, should be at the very top of the opening screen. Although in need of proofreading, conflation of some of the separate lists, and an embedded search capability, *Science Fiction, Fantasy, and Weird Fiction Magazine Index* (which is based on a perusal of tables of contents or information from collectors) offers the best access to these fugitive publications.

L990   Reginald, R. *Science Fiction and Fantasy Literature: A Checklist, 1700–1974, with Contemporary Science Fiction Authors II.* 2 vols. Detroit: Gale, 1979.
         Science Fiction and Fantasy Literature 1975–1991: A Bibliography of Science Fiction, Fantasy, and Horror Fiction Books and Nonfiction Monographs. 1992.
         1,512 pp.   Z5917.S36 R42 [PN3448.S45]   016.823′0876.

Lists about 38,000 English-language first editions by author, with accompanying title and series indexes. There are, of course, omissions, and the introduction suggests that some information is taken from union catalogs and other secondhand sources. Review: (*1975–1991*) Andrew M. Butler, *Foundation: The Review of Science Fiction* 63 (1995): 105–07.

Although Reginald is the standard bibliography of separately published fantasy, science, and weird supernatural fiction, it does not completely supersede E. F. Bleiler, *The Checklist of Science-Fiction and Supernatural Fiction* (Glen Rock: Firebell, 1978, 266 pp.). L. W. Currey, *Science Fiction and Fantasy Authors: A Bibliography of First Printings of Their Fiction and Selected Nonfiction,* rev. ed., CD-ROM (St. Olathe: RB, 2002), is the most accurate source for identifying first printings through 1977 of separately published works by 215 writers. For detailed critical synopses of several thousand works (including novels, novellas, short stories, and plays) published in English through 1936, see Everett F. Bleiler, *Science-Fiction: The Early Years* (Kent: Kent State UP, 1990, 998 pp.) and *Science-Fiction: The Gernsback Years: A Complete Coverage of the Genre Magazines* Amazing, Astounding, Wonder, *and Others from 1926 through 1936* (Kent: Kent State UP, 1998, 730 pp.). Based on firsthand acquaintance with each work, the summaries are admirably full and usually conclude with an evaluative comment. Running heads and better page design would have allowed users to locate entries more readily. Three indexes: titles; persons; motifs and themes (an especially valuable feature).

Vol. 2, a revision of *Contemporary Science Fiction Authors* (New York: Arno, 1975, 365 pp.), provides biographical information on 1,443 twentieth-century authors. All the volumes of *Science Fiction and Fantasy Literature* are indexed in *Biography and Genealogy Master Index* (J565). Since details were compiled from questionnaires and *Contemporary Authors* (J595), entries are uneven.

L995   Schlobin, Roger C. *The Literature of Fantasy: A Comprehensive, Annotated Bibliography of Modern Fantasy Fiction.* Garland Reference Library of the Humanities 176. New York: Garland, 1979. 425 pp.   Z2014.F4 S33 [PR830.F3]   016.823′0876.

A selective guide to major works published between 1837 and April 1979 by English and American authors and a few foreign writers important to the Anglo-American tradition. *Literature of Fantasy* includes primarily adult prose fiction published in book form in English. The first part is a list of novels and collections—as well as bibliographies—accompanied by summaries, with occasional evaluative comments, for novels and lists of contents for collections. The second part lists anthologies (along with contents) alphabetically by editor. Two indexes: authors, compilers, editors, translators; titles. Although hardly the comprehensive bibliography claimed in the subtitle, Schlobin is the fullest guide to important fantasy fiction.

Although more selective, Barron, *Fantasy and Horror* (L1015a), is valuable for its annotations. Barron supersedes Marshall B. Tymn, Kenneth J. Zahorski, and Robert H. Boyer, *Fantasy Literature: A Core Collection and Reference Guide* (New York: Bowker, 1979, 273 pp.).

L1000   Tuck, Donald H. *The Encyclopedia of Science Fiction and Fantasy through
          1968.* 3 vols. Chicago: Advent, 1974–82.   Z5917.S36 T83
          016.80883'876.

Vols. 1 and 2 constitute an international who's who of science, fantasy, and weird fiction. Entries include basic biographical information, but the focus of each is a bibliography of collections (including contents), novels (originally published or reprinted 1945–68), and translations. (For earlier novels see Reginald, *Science Fiction and Fantasy Literature* [L990].) Vol. 2 prints a title index to the listings. Vol. 3 includes a title bibliography of magazines (with publication and historical information on many ephemeral periodicals); an author list of paperback editions from the 1940s through 1968; a list of paperback publishers with titles published under imprints; a pseudonym and real-name list; and a list of series, connected stories, and sequels. Tuck records a wealth of information, although parts are superseded by recent bibliographies of primary works in this section and by more current but less comprehensive biographical dictionaries.

See also

   Barron, *Anatomy of Wonder* (L1015).
   Bleiler, *Guide to Supernatural Fiction* (L860).
   "Cross-Referenced Index of Short Fiction Anthologies" (L1085a). Science fiction
      anthologies have been included since the index for 1978–79 in *Studies in Short
      Fiction* 16.2 (1979).

GUIDES TO SCHOLARSHIP AND CRITICISM

For an overview of bibliographies of secondary works on science fiction, see Hal W. Hall and Wendi Arant, "The Bibliographic Control of Science Fiction: A Quarter-Century of Change," *Extrapolation* 40 (1999): 304–13; for an evaluation of Web sites, see Arant and Hall, "Science Fiction and Fantasy: A Guide to Resources on the Web," *College and Research Library News* 63 (2002): 652–55.

Serial Bibliographies

L1013   Hall, Hal W., ed. *Science Fiction and Fantasy Research Database.* Online.
          31 Aug. 2006 <http://library.tamu.edu/cushing/sffrd>. Updated quarterly.

A database of about 73,191 (as of 31 Aug. 2006) books, articles, parts of books, and newspaper articles on science, fantasy, horror, supernatural, and weird fiction (with science fiction predominating). Although the index is international in scope, coverage is fullest for English-language publications (an inevitable consequence of the elusiveness or limited distribution of so much secondary literature on science fiction). Records can be searched by title keyword, author, date, publisher, place, journal title, or subject (or any combination of the preceding). Records can be sorted by author, title, subject, or imprint, but not by date; selected records (which are sorted by author) can be e-mailed or printed (only by using a Web browser's print function). The database is still evolving and—like so many other databases—bears traces of its print ancestors, but it already is the preeminent bibliography of studies of science fiction. In its currency, accessibility, and thoroughness, it stands among the very best online nonsubscription literature databases.

Science Fiction and Fantasy Research Database supersedes Hall, *Science Fiction Index: Criticism* (Bryan: the author, 1980, microfiche); the augmented cumulation of *Science Fiction and Fantasy Research Index* in Hall, *Science Fiction and Fantasy Book Review Index, 1980–1984* (L1020), pp. 347–761; Hall, comp., *Science Fiction and Fantasy Research Index* (San Bernardino: Borgo, 1981–88); Hall, "Research Index," in the 1988–90 volumes of Brown, *Science Fiction, Fantasy, and Horror* (L980a); Hall, *Science Fiction and Fantasy Reference Index, 1878–1985: An International Author and Subject Index to History and Criticism,* 2 vols. (Detroit: Gale, 1987) and its two supplements: *1985–1991* (Englewood: Libraries Unlimited, 1993, 677 pp.) and *1992–1995* (1997, 503 pp.); and the following (though some remain useful for their annotations):

> "The Year's Scholarship in Fantastic Literature and the Arts 1988." *Journal of the Fantastic in the Arts* 2.3 (1990): 63–128.
> "The Year's Scholarship in Fantastic Literature [1972–79, 1983–87]." *Extrapolation* 17–22, 26–29 (1975–81, 1985–88). Title varies.
> Tymn, Marshall B., ed. *The Year's Scholarship in Science Fiction, Fantasy, and Horror Literature, [1980, 1981, 1982].* Kent: Kent State UP, 1983–84.

The bibliographies for 1972–79 are cumulated and expanded as the following:

> Tymn, Marshall B., and Roger C. Schlobin, eds. *The Year's Scholarship in Science Fiction and Fantasy, 1976–1979.* Serif Series 41. Kent: Kent State UP, 1982. 251 pp.
> *The Year's Scholarship in Science Fiction and Fantasy, 1972–1975.* Serif Series 36. 1979. 222 pp.

See also

> *ABELL* (G340): [English] Literature/General through the volume for 1967; Literature, General/Literary History/Fiction, and Literature, General/Literary Criticism/Fiction in the volumes for 1968–72; Literary History and Criticism/Fiction in the volume for 1973; and English Literature/General/Fiction in later volumes.
> *MLAIB* (G335): General VII: Literature, General and Comparative in the volumes for 1953–55; General II: Literature, General and Comparative in the volume for 1956; General IV/Prose Fiction in the volumes for 1957–80; and the Genres/Fiction/Fantasy Fiction, Genres/Fiction/Futuristic Fiction, Genres/Fiction/Science Fiction, Genres/Novel/Fantasy Novel, and Genres/Novel/Science Fiction Novel sections in pt. 4 of the later volumes. Researchers must also check the headings beginning with "Fantasy" and "Science Fiction" in the subject index to post-1980 volumes and in the online thesaurus.
> "Relations of Science to Literature and the Arts" (U6440).

Other Bibliographies

L1015   Barron, Neil, ed. *Anatomy of Wonder: A Critical Guide to Science Fiction.* 5th ed. Westport: Libraries Unlimited, 2004. 995 pp.   Z5917.S36 A52 [PN3433.8]   016.80883′876.

A selective, evaluative guide to primary works, scholarship, and reference sources. The first part consists of historical surveys of periods: the beginnings to 1914, 1915–39, 1940–63, 1964–83, 1984–2004. The second part consists of critical summaries of 1,400 novels and collections. The third part is devoted to lists of research aids, with chapters on library selection; general reference works; history and criticism; books about individual authors; film, television, and radio; illustration; teaching materials; magazines; and library collections. The full annotations are rigorously evaluative and frequently offer helpful comparisons. (In parts 2 and 3 an asterisk denotes an especially significant work.) The third edition (1987, 874 pp.) remains useful for its coverage of foreign-language science fiction. Three indexes: authors and subjects; titles; themes.

Neil Barron, ed., *Fantasy and Horror: A Critical and Historical Guide to Literature, Illustration, Film, TV, Radio, and the Internet* (Lanham: Scarecrow, 1999, 816 pp.) — a revision of Barron, ed., *Fantasy Literature: A Reader's Guide*, Garland Reference Library of the Humanities 874 (New York: Garland, 1990, 874 pp.), and Barron, ed., *Horror Literature: A Reader's Guide*, Garland Reference Library of the Humanities 1220 (New York: Garland, 1990, 596 pp.) — copies the format, organization, and indexing of *Anatomy of Wonder 4: A Critical Guide to Science Fiction*, 4th ed. (New Providence: Bowker, 1995, 912 pp); cites many of the same reference works; and offers the same rigorously evaluative, comparative annotations.

Usually judicious in selection and pointed in evaluation, *Anatomy of Wonder* and *Fantasy and Horror* are the best guides to important scholarship and reference works.

Although now dated, the following selective guides remain occasionally useful:

> Clareson, Thomas. *Science Fiction Criticism: An Annotated Checklist.* Serif Series 23. Kent: Kent State UP, 1972. 225 pp. The work remains useful for its inclusion of articles, which both Barron and Tymn (see below) omit.
>
> Tymn, Marshall B., Roger C. Schlobin, and L. W. Currey, comps. and eds. *A Research Guide to Science Fiction Studies: An Annotated Checklist of Primary and Secondary Sources for Fantasy and Science Fiction.* Garland Reference Library of the Humanities 87. New York: Garland, 1977. 165 pp. A selective, classified guide to about 400 important bibliographies, reference works, biographical dictionaries, indexes, surveys and histories, studies of individual authors, and periodicals published in the United States and England through 1976. The annotations are only occasionally evaluative but usually indicate when a work supersedes an earlier one. (The separate list of North American dissertations, compiled by Douglas R. Justus, is not annotated.)

Although Keith L. Justice, *Science Fiction, Fantasy, and Horror Reference: An Annotated Bibliography of Works about Literature and Film* (Jefferson: McFarland, 1989, 266 pp.), is purportedly a guide to reference materials, the majority of its 304 entries are for critical and historical books. The extensive annotations are frequently rigorous in evaluating works, but *Science Fiction, Fantasy, and Horror Reference* is untrustworthy as a guide to reference materials because of its inclusion of so many superseded publications (e.g., only the first edition of Barron, *Anatomy of Wonder* [L1015] appears), incomplete coverage of multivolume works (e.g., only the 1923–73 volume of *Science Fiction Book Review Index* [L1020], the 1972–75 cumulation of "The Year's Scholarship in Fantastic Literature" [L1013], and vol. 1 of Contento, *Index to Science Fiction Anthologies and Collections* [L985] are admitted), and inexcusable omission of numerous essential guides and bibliographies (e.g., Hall, *Science Fiction and Fantasy Research Index* [L1013a], and Tymn, *Science Fiction, Fantasy, and Weird Fiction Magazines* [L1025]).

See also

> Greenwood Guide to American Popular Culture (U6295).
> Schatzberg, *Relations of Literature and Science* (U6445).

Review Indexes

L1020   *Science Fiction and Fantasy Book Review Index* (*SFFBRI*). Comp. Hal W.
   Hall. Bryan: SFBRI, 1970–90. Annual. Former title: *SFBRI: Science Fiction
   Book Review Index* (1970–84).   PN3433.S29   813.
   The work is cumulated and augmented in the following:

> Hall, Hal W. *Science Fiction and Fantasy Book Review Index, 1980–1984.*
> Detroit: Gale, 1985. 761 pp.
> ———. *Science Fiction Book Review Index, 1974–1979.* 1981. 391 pp.
> ———. *Science Fiction Book Review Index, 1923–1973.* 1975. 438 pp.

An author list, with title index, of works reviewed in science fiction, fantasy, and
a few general-interest periodicals. Although entries before vol. 15 (1985) do not include
full bibliographic information and many are taken from other indexes, *SFFBRI* was the
fullest guide to reviews of science fiction works and scholarship. The cumulation of
Science Fiction and Fantasy Research Index, vols. 1–5 (L1013a) in the 1980–84 cumulation of *SFBRI*, is superseded by Hall, *Science Fiction and Fantasy Reference Index,
1878–1985* (L1013a). Review: (1980–84) Gary K. Wolfe, *Science-Fiction Studies* 14
(1987): 252–60.

See also

> Sec. G: Serial Bibliographies, Indexes, and Abstracts/Book Review Indexes.

BIOGRAPHICAL DICTIONARIES

For an evaluatively annotated list of biographical reference works, see Neil Barron,
"General Reference Works" (pp. 502–15) and Barron, Richard L. McKinney, and
Michael A. Morrison, "Author Studies" (pp. 613–77), in Barron, *Anatomy of Wonder*
(L1015).

See also

> *Contemporary Authors* (J595).
> *Dictionary of Literary Biography* (J600).
> *Multimedia Encyclopedia of Science Fiction* (L965).
> Reginald, *Science Fiction and Fantasy Literature*, vol. 2 (L990).
> Tuck, *Encyclopedia of Science Fiction and Fantasy through 1968* (L1000).

PERIODICALS

For an evaluative, but highly selective, list of reference works and periodicals, see Joe
Sanders, "Science Fiction Magazines and Fandom" (pp. 775–92), in Barron, *Anatomy
of Wonder* (L1015).

Guides to Primary Works

L1025   Tymn, Marshall B., and Mike Ashley, eds. *Science Fiction, Fantasy, and
         Weird Fiction Magazines*. Historical Guides to the World's Periodicals and
         Newspapers. Westport: Greenwood, 1985. 970 pp.   PN3433.T9
         809.3'876.
         A guide to magazines, fanzines, and scholarly journals from 1882 through 1983.
The entries are organized in four divisions: 279 English-language magazines, 15 paperback English-language anthology series associated with magazines, 72 scholarly journals
and major fanzines, and 184 foreign-language magazines. The first three divisions are
organized alphabetically by title (with cross-references for variant titles); the last by
country, then title. In the first and second divisions, the separately authored profiles
consist of a discussion of publishing history, editorial policies, contents, personnel, and
significance; a selective list of scholarship, indexing sources, reprints, and locations; and
details of title changes, volume and issue data, publisher(s), editor(s), format, and price.
Entries in the other divisions offer much less detailed information on scope, contents,
beginning and ending dates, and publishing information. Concludes with two appendixes (index to major cover artists; chronology of English-language magazines from 1882
through 1983) and a selective bibliography. The persons, titles, and awards index excludes foreign-language magazines. Although the entries vary in amount of detail and
degree of assessment, Tymn and Ashley offers the fullest guide to the important magazines. Review: Gary K. Wolfe, *Science-Fiction Studies* 14 (1987): 252–60.

Utopian Fiction

Many works in the preceding part on science and fantasy fiction are important for
research in utopian literature.

GUIDES TO PRIMARY WORKS

L1055   Sargent, Lyman Tower. *British and American Utopian Literature, 1516–
         1985: An Annotated, Chronological Bibliography*. Garland Reference Library
         of the Humanities 831. New York: Garland, 1988. 559 pp.
         Z2014.U84 S28 [PR149.U8]   016.82'08'0372.
         An annotated list of fictional and nonfictional works that describe "a non-existent
society . . . in considerable detail." The utopias, dystopias, eutopias, and utopian sat-
ires are arranged chronologically by year of first publication. Entries provide basic bibliographic information, location of one or two copies of rare editions, and brief annotations on content or type of work. Two indexes: authors; titles. The annotations are
too frequently telegraphic in their brevity, and the lack of a subject index hampers
usability; yet Sargent remains the best guide to English-language utopian works.
         Complemented by a series of specialized lists by Sargent:
              "Australian Utopian Literature: An Annotated, Chronological Bibliography,
              1667–1999." *Utopian Studies* 10.2 (1999): 138–173.
              New Zealand Utopian Literature: An Annotated Bibliography. Occasional Pa-
              per 97/1. Wellington: Stout Research Centre for the Study of New Zea-

land History, Culture, and Society, Victoria U of Wellington, 1996. 20 pp.

"Utopian Literature in English Canada: An Annotated, Chronological Bibliography, 1852-1999." *Utopian Studies* 10.2 (1999): 174–206.

The earlier edition (*British and American Utopian Literature, 1516–1975: An Annotated Bibliography*, Reference Publication in Science Fiction [Boston: Hall, 1979, 324 pp.]) remains useful for its list of studies of utopian literature worldwide. Unfortunately, the list is segregated into books, articles, and dissertations and is unindexed.

Although Glenn Negley, *Utopian Literature: A Bibliography, with a Supplementary Listing of Works Influential in Utopian Thought* (Lawrence: Regents P of Kansas, 1977, 228 pp.), includes European fiction, it is more restrictive in defining utopian literature and marred by a number of deficiencies (see the review by R. D. M[ullen], *Science-Fiction Studies* 5 [1978]: 184–86).

GUIDES TO SCHOLARSHIP AND CRITICISM

There is no adequate guide to studies of utopian literature. Paul G. Haschak, *Utopian/ Dystopian Literature: A Bibliography of Literary Criticism* (Metuchen: Scarecrow, 1994, 370 pp.) is a mishmash of studies that, like the primary authors included, are selected according to no apparent criteria; indeed, several studies included give little attention to utopian or dystopian elements.

See also

> *MLAIB* (G335): Genres/Fiction/Utopian Fiction, Genres/Novel/Utopian Novel, and Themes and Figures/Utopia sections of pt. 4 of the post-1980 volumes. Researchers must also check the headings beginning "Utopia," "Utopian," and "Utopianism" in the subject index to post-1980 volumes and in the online thesaurus.

Novel

GUIDES TO PRIMARY WORKS

L1060   Wright, R. Glenn, comp. *Author Bibliography of English Language Fiction in the Library of Congress through 1950.* 8 vols. Boston: Hall, 1973. *Chronological Bibliography of English Language Fiction in the Library of Congress through 1950.* 8 vols. 1974. *Title Bibliography of English Language Fiction in the Library of Congress through 1950.* 9 vols. 1976.   Z5918.W74 016.823′008.

Reproductions of catalog cards from the Library of Congress shelflist PZ3 classification, which lists individual works of English-language prose fiction, including translations, by authors whose first work was published before 31 December 1950. The *Author Bibliography* arranges cards alphabetically under the author's nationality (Australia, Canada, East and Southeast Asia, Europe, Latin America, New Zealand, South Africa, United Kingdom, United States, and unknown). Vol. 7 includes a pseudonym index; vol. 8 is an author list of English-language translations (with a translator index).

The *Chronological Bibliography* is also organized by nationality of the author and then by date of edition (although many editions are actually classified by country of publication). Vol. 7 includes an index of joint authors, and lists of pseudonyms, real names, and unidentified pseudonymous authors (all classified by nationality); vol. 8 prints chronological indexes to translations and translators and alphabetical indexes to joint authors of translations and joint translators. Users can construct their own chronological lists by searching the PZ3 classification through the Library of Congress online catalog (E260); searches must be limited by date ranges to avoid exceeding the 10,000 record limit.

Like the other works, the *Title Bibliography* is organized by nationality of the author, then alphabetically by title, with cross-references for variant titles; however, many works are actually classified by country of publication. Vol. 8 includes an index of joint authors, list of pseudonyms, list of real names, list of unidentified pseudonymous authors and their works, and index of translations; vol. 9 has an index of translators and joint translators.

Wright's compilations are principally useful as catalogs of American editions of English-language novels (largely by Americans) but limited by their restriction to the Library of Congress holdings, which are extensive but not comprehensive. The *Author* and *Title* bibliographies are superseded by *WorldCat* (E225), RLG Union Catalog (E230), and more specialized works such as Wright, *American Fiction* (Q4180). The *Chronological Bibliography* is a convenient preliminary source for charting trends in the publishing of fiction in the United States (particularly in the twentieth century); however, its ascriptions of nationality cannot be trusted.

GUIDES TO SCHOLARSHIP AND CRITICISM

See

ABELL (G340): [English] Literature/General through the volume for 1967; Literature, General/Literary History/Fiction, and Literature, General/Literary Criticism/Fiction in the volumes for 1968–72; Literary History and Criticism/ Fiction in the volume for 1973; and English Literature/General/Fiction in later volumes.

MLAIB (G335): General VII: Literature, General and Comparative in the volumes for 1953–55; General II: Literature, General and Comparative in the volume for 1956; General IV/Prose Fiction in the volumes for 1957–80; and Genres/Fiction and Genres/Novel sections in pt. 4 of the later volumes. Researchers must also check the headings beginning "Fiction" and "Novel" in the subject index to post-1980 volumes and in the online thesaurus.

Short Fiction (Short Story, Novella)

GUIDES TO PRIMARY WORKS

L1085   *Short Story Index: An Index to Stories in Collections and Periodicals (SSI).*
New York: Wilson, 1953– . Annual, with quinquennial and other
cumulations extending coverage to 1900.   Z5917.S5 C62   016.80883′1.

H. W. Wilson. Online. 24 June 2005 <http://vnweb.hwwilsonweb.com/hww>. Updated daily. CD-ROM. Updated quarterly.

An author, title, and subject index to short stories published in anthologies and (since 1974) in periodicals covered by *Readers' Guide* (G400) and *Humanities Index* (G385). (Those from periodicals are not indexed by subject.) The coverage emphasizes established authors. Entries are keyed to a list of anthologies at the back and in the cumulation *Short Story Index: Collections Indexed, 1900–1978*, ed. Juliette Yaakov (1979, 349 pp.). The electronic versions, which include the indexes since 1984, can be searched by keyword, subject (including genre or form), author, and/or journal title. The online version includes the full text of more than 3,000 stories. The standard Wilson search interface (see entry I525) does not fully exploit the information available in the print version of the index. *SSI* is the best source for identifying stories on a theme or subject and for locating reprints.

Less comprehensive but occasionally useful are the following:

> Chicorel, Marietta, ed. *Chicorel Index to Short Stories in Anthologies and Collections.* 4 vols. Chicorel Index Series 12. New York: Chicorel, 1974. Supplement: *1975/76.* 2 vols. 1977. An author and title list only.
>
> "Cross-Referenced Index of Short Fiction Anthologies." *Studies in Short Fiction* 7.1 (1970); 8 (1971): 351–409; updated annually in 13–31 (1976–94). Indexes fiction anthologies by author and anthology.
>
> Messerli, Douglas, and Howard N. Fox, comps. *Index to Periodical Fiction in English, 1965–1969.* Metuchen: Scarecrow, 1977. 746 pp. An author list of 11,077 works of short fiction in a variety of journals (popular and little magazines, university reviews, scholarly journals) published throughout the world (but emphasizing American publications). Although several periodicals are not fully searched and coverage is restricted to five years, a majority of the entries are not indexed elsewhere.

See also

> Sec. K: Periodicals/Little Magazines.
> *American Humanities Index* (G360).
> *Arts and Humanities Citation Index* (G365).
> *Humanities Index* (G385).
> *Readers' Guide* (G400).

GUIDES TO SCHOLARSHIP AND CRITICISM

L1090   *Twentieth-Century Short Story Explication: Interpretations 1900–1975 of Short Fiction since 1800.* 3rd ed. Comp. Warren S. Walker. Hamden: Shoe String, 1977. 880 pp. *Supplement I.* 1980. 257 pp. *Supplement II.* 1984. 348 pp. *Supplement III.* 1987. 486 pp. *Supplement IV.* 1989. 342 pp. *Supplement V.* 1991. 401 pp. *An Index to the Third Edition and Its Five Supplements, 1961–1991.* 1992. 254 pp.   Z5917.S5 W33 [PN3373] 016.8093′1.

   Twentieth-Century Short Story Explication New Series [1989–]. 1989–1990. Ed. Walker. 1993. 366 pp. *1991–1992.* Ed. Wendell M. Aycock. 1995. 295 pp. *1993–1994.* 1997. 347 pp. *1995–1996.* 1999. 342 pp. *1997–*

1998. 2002. 399 pp. *1999–2000.* 2004. 382 pp. (EBSCO [I512] plans to offer an electronic version.)   Z5917.S5 W35 [PN3373]   016.8093′1.

A selective bibliography of articles and parts of books (primarily in English and published since 1900) on short stories printed after 1800 by some 3,838 (as of the volume for 1999–2000) authors worldwide. Since the focus is explication ("interpretation or explanation of the meaning of a story, including observations on theme, symbol, and sometimes structure"), source, biographical, and background studies are excluded. Entries are organized by writer, then by individual work, with citations to books keyed to a list at the back. For abbreviations of journal titles in the main volume, users must consult the list in the first supplement. *Twentieth-Century Short Story Explication* incorporates listings from "Annual Bibliography of Short Story Explication" in *Studies in Short Fiction* 1–31 (1963–94). The volumes offer no explanation of the criteria for selecting journals and books to search and many entries repeat the same essay under several short-story headings or refer to passing mentions (e.g., in *1991–1992* four of the five entries under Lycia Fagundes Telles refer to the same two pages). But *Twentieth-Century Short Story Explication* is a useful starting point for research, especially since it indexes parts of books.

See also

> *ABELL* (G340): [English] Literature/General through the volume for 1967; Literature, General/Literary History/Fiction, and Literature, General/Literary Criticism/Fiction in the volumes for 1968–72; Literary History and Criticism/Fiction in the volume for 1973; and English Literature/General/Fiction in later volumes.
>
> *MLAIB* (G335): General VII: Literature, General and Comparative in the volumes for 1953–55; General II: Literature, General and Comparative in the volume for 1956; General IV/Prose Fiction in the volumes for 1957–80; and the Genres/Fiction, Novella, and Short Story sections in pt. 4 of the later volumes. Researchers must also check the "Novella," "Short Fiction," and "Short Story" headings in the subject index to post-1980 volumes and in the online thesaurus.
>
> Thurston, *Short Fiction Criticism* (Q3480a).

Drama and Theater

Guides to Reference Works

L1115   Bailey, Claudia Jean. *A Guide to Reference and Bibliography for Theatre Research.* 2nd ed. Columbus: Publications Committee, Ohio State U Libraries, 1983. 149 pp.   Z5781.B15 [PN1620.A1]   016.792.

A classified, descriptively annotated guide to general and specialized reference works on drama and theater. Although the emphasis is overwhelmingly on the United States and Western Europe, and the annotations are sometimes less thorough than they could be, Bailey remains the only introduction to reference works for theater research. A replacement is badly needed. Review: Robert H. Hethmon, *Theatre Research International* 9 (1984): 260–61.

L1120   Whalon, Marion K. *Performing Arts Research: A Guide to Information
        Sources.* Performing Arts Information Guide Series 1. Detroit: Gale, 1976.
        280 pp.   Z6935.W5 [PN1584]   016.7902.

A selective guide to reference works (in several languages and published through
1973) useful to research in the performance aspects of theater, dance, music, musical
theater, film, and other entertainments. Entries are organized alphabetically in seven
variously classified divisions for types of works: basic guides and general reference works;
dictionaries, encyclopedias, and handbooks; directories of organizations, institutions,
and persons; play indexes and finding lists; sources for reviews of plays and films; bibliographies, indexes, and abstracts; sources for illustrations and audiovisual material.
The numerous cross-references compensate somewhat for imprecise classification of
several entries. Many of the descriptive annotations offer helpful evaluative comments.
Indexed by authors, titles, and subjects. Although it lacks an adequate statement of
scope and explanation of criteria governing selections, omits some important works,
and is now badly dated, *Performing Arts Research* remains the best general guide to
reference works important to research in the performing arts.

It is not superseded by Linda Keir Simons, *The Performing Arts: A Guide to the
Reference Literature*, Reference Sources in the Humanities Series (Englewood: Libraries
Unlimited, 1994, 244 pp.). Although some annotations offer brief evaluative comments,
Simons is marred by inconsistent organization and coverage (especially of non-English-
language resources), omission of several important works, and lack of rigor in assessing
key tools.

Some additional resources on film, theater, popular music, and broadcast media
are identified in Barbara J. Pruett, *Popular Entertainment Research: How to Do It and
How to Use It* (Metuchen: Scarecrow, 1992, 579 pp.). Unfortunately, because of numerous errors and omissions, untrustworthy evaluations, insufficient annotations, inadequate subject indexing, and poor organization, this work must be used with care.

Literary Handbooks, Dictionaries, and Encyclopedias

L1125   *Cambridge Guide to Theatre.* Ed. Martin Banham. Cambridge: Cambridge
        UP, 1995. 1,233 pp. (Rev. of *Cambridge Guide to World Theatre*, ed.
        Banham, 1988, 1,104 pp.)   PN2035.C27   792.'03.

An international dictionary of theater, classical to contemporary, that emphasizes
performance, popular entertainment, and traditions outside Europe and North America.
The signed entries cover traditions, theories, acting companies, playwrights, performers,
designers, directors, movements, folk drama, types of performance, television and radio
drama, playhouses, and the theatrical aspects of ballet and opera; those on national
traditions and general topics conclude with a brief bibliography. Indexed in *Biography
and Genealogy Master Index* (J565). Although imbalance in coverage of forms and
geographical areas is inevitable in a work of this scope, the *Cambridge Guide* is the most
thorough and authoritative single-volume encyclopedia of world theater. Review: Anton
Wagner, *Theatre History in Canada* 12 (1991): 213–18.

The entries in the first edition for Asia have been revised and expanded as *The
Cambridge Guide to Asian Theatre*, ed. James R. Brandon (Cambridge: Cambridge UP,
1993, 252 pp.).

L1130   *Enciclopedia dello spettacolo.* Ed. Silvio d'Amico and Francesco Savio. 9 vols.
        Roma: Maschere, 1954–62. *Aggiornamento, 1955–1965.* Roma: Unione,

1966. 1,292 cols. *Indice-Repertorio.* 1968. 1,024 pp. *Cinema, teatro, balletto, tv.* Roma: Garzanti, 1978. 782 pp.   PN1625.E7   792.03.

An international encyclopedia of all forms of dramatic and musical theater, opera, cinema, television, and circus from classical antiquity to 1965. Concerts, sports, and civil and religious ceremonies are excluded. The more than 30,000 signed entries encompass dramatists, composers, librettists, performers, cinematographers, directors, producers, critics, various other theater personnel, terminology, genres and forms, national and ethnic literatures, places, technical matters, movements, groups, and themes. The entries, which range from a paragraph to several pages, are organized alphabetically by Italian-language term; most conclude with a brief bibliography, and many are accompanied by illustrations. Indexed by title in the index volume. Entries in *Appendice di aggiornamento: Cinema* (Roma: Istituto per la Collaborazione Culturale, 1963, 178 cols.) are revised in the supplement for 1955–65, but the former includes some different plates. Although now dated, the *Enciclopedia* and companion volumes remain the fullest international guide to all aspects of the theatrical arts.

An important complement to *Enciclopedia dello spettacolo, The World Encyclopedia of Contemporary Theatre,* 6 vols., ed. Don Rubin (London: Routledge, 1994–2000), surveys national theatrical activity since 1945. The national surveys (ranging from 3,000 to 30,000 words) typically cover history, structure of the national theater community, major artistic trends, music theater, dance theater, young adult theater, puppet theater, design, theatrical space and architecture, training, and scholarship and criticism; each concludes with a selective bibliography (which are cumulated, updated, and expanded in vol. 6). The section on scholarship and criticism—which identifies major research centers, important collections, and periodicals—is of particular importance. Indexed in each volume—and cumulatively in vol. 6—by persons, titles, and subjects.

L1135   *An International Dictionary of Theatre Language.* Gen. ed. Joel Trapido.
          Westport: Greenwood, 1985. 1,032 pp.   PN2035.I5   792'.03'21.

A dictionary of some 10,000 English-language and 5,000 foreign-language terms, historical and current, covering drama and theater worldwide. Definitions are very brief but do cite works in the accompanying bibliography that offer fuller definitions or discussions. "A Brief History of Theatre Glossaries and Dictionaries" (pp. xxxiii–xxxvi) surveys related works. Although not exhaustive—since only foreign-language terms "used in the English-speaking world" are admitted and since some technical aspects of production are excluded (see the detailed explanation of scope in the prefatory matter)—the work is the most extensive dictionary of drama and theater terminology.

L1140   *The Oxford Companion to the Theatre.* Ed. Phyllis Hartnoll. 4th ed. Oxford:
          Oxford UP, 1983. 934 pp.   PN2035.O9   792'.03'21.

Emphasizes established legitimate theater, classical to contemporary, with factual entries on actors, actresses, producers, directors, designers, dramatists, groups, movements, theatrical techniques and technology, theaters, acting companies, and national drama. Concludes with a highly selective bibliography. Individuals with separate entries in the third and fourth editions are indexed in *Biography and Genealogy Master Index* (J565). Coverage of ballet, opera, and dance was dropped, and several entries were condensed in the fourth edition, but this volume remains a standard source for quick reference. Because they are riddled with errors, earlier editions must be used with care. Some entries are updated in *The Concise Oxford Companion to the Theatre,* ed. Hartnoll and Peter Found (Oxford: Oxford UP, 1992, 568 pp.), which excludes individuals under age forty.

Among the numerous other encyclopedic works on drama and theater, the following are reasonably trustworthy:

> *The Encyclopedia of World Theater.* Ed. Martin Esslin. New York: Scribner's, 1977. 320 pp. A translation and revision of Karl Gröning and Werner Kliess, *Friedrichs Theaterlexikon*, ed. Henning Rischbieter (Hannover: Friedrich, 1969, 462 pp.), that covers theater, classical to contemporary, in brief entries on performers, theatrical personnel, forms, genres, theaters, movements, terms, groups, characters and character types, and critics. Entrants are indexed in *Biography and Genealogy Master Index* (J565).
>
> *McGraw-Hill Encyclopedia of World Drama.* Ed. Stanley Hochman. 2nd ed. 5 vols. New York: McGraw, 1984. Emphasizes dramatists but also includes entries on terms, anonymous plays, genres, national literatures, and movements. The lengthy entries on major dramatists include biographical information, critical commentary, synopses of selected plays, a list of plays, and selected bibliography. Entrants are indexed in *Biography and Genealogy Master Index* (J565).

L1145   *Piper's Enzyklopädie des Musiktheaters: Oper, Operette, Musical, Ballett.* Ed. Carl Dalhaus and Sieghart Döhring. 7 vols. München: Piper, 1986–97. ML102.O6 P5   782′.03′31.

An encyclopedia of musicals, melodramas, ballets, operas, and operettas in the modern repertory as well as some works of historical importance. Although the work emphasizes European theater, there is substantial coverage of the rest of the world. In vols. 1–6, signed entries on about 3,000 works are organized by author, composer, or choreographer. When possible, an entry identifies the author and source of the libretto, composer of the music, date and place of premiere and later important versions, characters, and orchestral requirements; provides a lengthy synopsis; analyzes the historical or current significance of the work; traces influence; locates the original manuscript and important copies; and cites printed versions, copyright holders, and selected scholarship. Indexed by titles in each volume; vol. 7 is a cumulative index of titles and persons. The handbook of terminology relating to all aspects of musical theater (originally planned as vols. 7–8) has been abandoned. Offering considerably more detail than one typically encounters in an encyclopedic work, *Piper's* is the fullest single guide to international musical theater.

More closely focused on musical drama, Kurt Gänzl, *The Encyclopedia of the Musical Theatre*, 2nd ed., 3 vols. (New York: Schirmer–Gale, 2001), excludes opera, pantomime, music-hall and vaudeville pieces, and musicals for video and concentrates on France, Austria, Great Britain, the United States, Hungary, Australia, and Germany. The majority of the approximately 4,000 entries are devoted to shows and writers; entrants are indexed in *Biography and Genealogy Master Index* (J565).

Guides to Primary Works

BIBLIOGRAPHIES AND INDEXES

L1150   Connor, Billie M., and Helene G. Mochedlover. *Ottemiller's Index to Plays in Collections: An Author and Title Index to Plays Appearing in Collections*

Published between 1900 and 1985. 7th ed. Metuchen: Scarecrow, 1988. 564 pp.   Z5781.O8 [PN1655]   016.80882.

An author index to 6,548 titles in various languages (including translations) by 2,555 authors in 1,350 collections published for the most part in the United States or England. Plays are keyed by an awkward system of symbols to the list of anthologies. Indexed by title. Similar indexes include the following:

> Chicorel, Marietta, ed. *Chicorel Theater Index to Plays in Anthologies, Periodicals, Discs, and Tapes.* 2 vols. New York: Chicorel, 1970–71. *Chicorel Theater Index to Plays in Anthologies and Collections, 1970–1976.* Chicorel Index Series 25. 1977. 479 pp. An author and title list, with minimal subject indexing, of English-language plays.

> Samples, Gordon. *The Drama Scholars' Index to Plays and Filmscripts: A Guide to Plays and Filmscripts in Selected Anthologies, Series, and Periodicals.* 3 vols. Metuchen: Scarecrow, 1974–86. A selective author and title index to plays and scripts of radio, television, and film productions in a variety of languages. Entries are keyed to lists of periodicals and collections. A useful complement to the other indexes listed in this entry, since coverage extends from eighteenth-century collections through the early 1980s and includes periodicals; however, the number of entries is needlessly swollen by the indexing of many standard collected editions of individual authors. Poor typography and layout make this a frustrating work to use.

There is considerable overlapping among these indexes, which are principally useful for locating anthologized reprints of plays.

Dean H. Keller, *Index to Plays in Periodicals,* rev. ed. (Metuchen: Scarecrow, 1979, 824 pp.), and *1977–1987* (1990, 391 pp.), each an author list with title index, supplement periodical coverage of the preceding works and locate many plays not separately published or anthologized. Users should note that a majority of the entries in the *1977–1987* volume comes from pre-1977 issues of periodicals.

L1155   *Play Index.* New York: Wilson, 1953– . Irregular.   Z5781.P53 016.80882. H. W. Wilson. Online. 15 Aug. 2006 <http:// vnweb.hwwilsonweb.com/hww>.

A selective author, title, and subject index to English-language plays and translations—classical through contemporary—published separately or in collections since 1949. Entries, which include a brief plot summary and production specifications, are keyed to a list of collections at the back.

The Web version offers four ways to search records: Basic Search allows keyword searches of fields; Advanced Search allows users to search by play title, author, subject, keyword, genre, number in cast, and audience level; Browse allows users to browse record fields (author, document type, ISBN, LC control number, language, physical description, subject, publication date, series, or update code); Thesaurus. A record for a play in a collection is linked to the entry for the collection (click Find This Play in a Book); the Related Web Resources link merely executes a Gigablast.com search whose results frequently are unrelated to the play. For a full discussion of the Wilson search interface, see entry I525.

Although *Play Index* overlaps with the sources listed in entry L1150, this is the only work of its kind that indexes plays by subject (although some subject headings are too broad to be useful). Ina Ten Eyck Firkins, comp., *Index to Plays, 1800–1926* (New York· Wilson, 1927, 307 pp.) and *Supplement* (1935, 140 pp.), selectively cover plays first published between 1800 and 1934.

See also

   Howard, *Directory of Theatre Resources* (E210a).

TEXT ARCHIVES

L1158   *Twentieth-Century Drama.* Rel. 5. ProQuest. Online. 18 June 2006
          <http://collections.chadwyck.com>.
   An archive of rekeyed texts that, when complete, will include 2,500 English-language dramatic works (published in book form since 1890) from throughout the world. Editions were selected according to the following criteria: a collected edition; if no collected edition exists, "either the first reliable edition of each play, or . . . a later edition incorporating revisions by the author."
   Standard Search allows simple keyword, first line or title, and author searches to be limited by date of first performance, publication date, genre, gender, and nationality. Advanced Search offers additional ways of limiting a search: speaker, number and gender of speakers, place of first performance, director, theatrical company, designer, number of acts, and subject. Find Monologues allows users to search by gender of speaker, name of speaker, title, date of first performance, genre, subject, gender of playwright, nationality, ethnicity, and verse or prose drama. Searchers can also browse an author list of the contents of the database. Results appear in ascending alphabetical order and cannot be re-sorted. Citations (but not the full text) can be marked for e-mailing, downloading, or printing; each citation includes a durable URL to the full text.
   Some works are rekeyed from textually unsound editions; however, the bibliographic record for each work identifies the source of the text and any omissions (e.g., preliminary matter). Besides being a useful source for identifying an elusive quotation or half-remembered line, the scope of *Twentieth-Century Drama*'s text archive makes feasible a variety of kinds of studies (stylistic, thematic, imagistic, generic, and topical).
   The contents of *Twentieth-Century Drama* can also be searched through *LiOn* (I527), which offers a less versatile search interface.

Guides to Scholarship and Criticism

SERIAL BIBLIOGRAPHIES

L1160   *International Bibliography of Theatre and Dance with Full Text.* EBSCO.
          Online. 27 July 2006 <http://www.epnet.com>. Updated regularly.
   A bibliographic database of books, articles, dissertations, and other documents on all aspects of theatrical performance worldwide, with full text available for some 100 journals; the database is also available without full-text links as *International Bibliography of Theatre and Dance.* The database cumulates and continues *International Bibliography of Theatre [1982–99]* (*IBT*) (New York: Theatre Research Data Center, Brooklyn Coll., City U of New York, 1985–2002). While the move to electronic-only publication has resulted in a much-improved currency in coverage and accessibility as well as the inclusion of reviews of individual books and performances, it has also led to the uncritical admission of much that is inconsequential (e.g., lists of books received or contributors) or has no discussion of performance, as well as a precipitous decline in

documents in languages other than English (a problem that the Theatre Research Data Center is working to remedy). The standard EBSCO search interface (see entry I512) does not take full advantage of *IBT*'s elaborate classification system (outlined in the prefatory matter to each volume). Users must consult the database-specific Help file to identify the codes for searchable fields; however, the explanation for some fields is too imprecise to allow identification of parts of an *IBT* record. Inexplicably, the only document languages that can be searched are English, French, German, Portuguese, and Spanish— a major impediment to searching a work once notable for its international scope. Indeed, users should not even bother limiting a search by document language since many entries from *IBT* have no language code or an inaccurate one. If *International Bibliography of Theatre and Dance* is to regain its place as an essential resource for the study of performance arts, it will need a substantial refinement of its search interface, attention to non-English language publications, a firmer editorial hand, and a return to a clear focus on performance (an area not effectively covered by the serial bibliographies and indexes in section G of this *Guide*).

Some additional coverage is offered by *International Index to Performing Arts Full Text* (*IIPA*; online, Chadwyck-Healey, 1 Aug. 2006 <http://iipaft.chadwyck.com>, updated monthly), which is a database of journal articles covering dance, film, drama, television, the performing arts industry, stagecraft, musical theater, and performance art. Although coverage ranges from 1864 to the present, indexing of a substantial number of the c. 240 journals commenced with volumes published in the late 1990s, and there are unexplained gaps in the coverage of some journals. Users should click on Browse Journals to locate details of coverage for each title. Although the publisher claims that the database is updated monthly, the *IIPA* site provides no record of updates. Users can search by a combination of keyword, title, author, subject categories, subject terms, document type, special features, journal title (ambiguously labeled Publication), language, country of publication, date, ISSN, and *IIPA* citation number. Searches can be limited to full-text and peer-reviewed articles; users can elect to exclude reviews. Records provide basic bibliographical information; those since 1998 include a brief abstract, and full-text coverage extends to about 85 journals. Researchers must use this resource with due regard for the gaps in coverage.

See also

> *ABELL* (G340): [English] Literature/General through the volume for 1967; Literature, General/Literary History/Drama and Theatre History, and Literature, General/Literary Criticism/Drama [and Theatre History] in the volumes for 1968–72; Literary History and Criticism/Drama and Theatre History in the volume for 1973; and English Literature/General/Drama and the Theatre in later volumes.
>
> Carpenter, *Modern Drama Scholarship and Criticism* (M2875).
>
> *MLAIB* (G335): General VII: Literature, General and Comparative in the volume for 1953–55; General II: Literature, General and Comparative in the volume for 1956; General IV/Drama in the volumes for 1957–80; the General Literature/Theater section in pt. 4 of the volumes for 1981–91; the Dramatic Arts/Theater section in pt. 4 of the volumes for 1992–present; and the Genres/Drama sections in pt. 4 of the volumes for 1981–present. Researchers must also check the headings beginning "Theater," "Theatrical," "Dramatic," or "Drama" in the subject index to post-1980 volumes and in the online thesaurus.
>
> "Modern Drama Studies: An Annual Bibliography" (M2870).
>
> *RILM Abstracts* (U6240).

OTHER BIBLIOGRAPHIES

L1165   *Cumulated Dramatic Index, 1909–1949: A Cumulation of the F. W. Faxon
        Company's* Dramatic Index. 2 vols. Boston: Hall, 1965.   Z5781.C8
        016.8082.
    Reprints, in a single alphabetical sequence, the annual *Dramatic Index* subject
indexes to English-language books and articles, illustrations, and plays published in
about 150 British and American periodicals between 1909 and 1949. Opera, dance,
and ballet as well as plays are covered. Except for play titles and dramatists, the subject
headings are quite general. Three appendixes: author list of books; title list of plays;
author list of plays. Although there are numerous errors, the work is useful for locating
reviews and articles in periodicals not indexed in standard bibliographies and indexes
in section G. Coverage continues as "Dramatic Index," *Bulletin of Bibliography* 20.1–
21.1 (1950–53).

L1170   Palmer, Helen H., comp. *European Drama Criticism, 1900–1975.* 2nd ed.
        Hamden: Shoe String; Folkestone: Dawson, 1977. 653 pp.   Z5781.P2
        [PN1721]   016.809′2.
    A selective bibliography of articles, parts of books, and abstracts from *ProQuest
Dissertations and Theses* (H465) in a variety of languages on plays, classical through
modern, by "outstanding" playwrights (except Shakespeare). Except for the limitation
to studies, regardless of merit, devoted to a play as a whole, the entries seem to represent
what the compiler could locate. Studies are listed under individual plays arranged alphabetically by dramatist; citations to parts of books are keyed to a list at the back. A
separate list of journals does not identify volumes actually searched. Indexed by playwrights and plays. Although selection criteria are vague, the bibliography is useful for
its indexing of parts of books.
    Less comprehensive and current but occasionally supplementing Palmer are the
following:

> Adelman, Irving, and Rita Dworkin. *Modern Drama: A Checklist of Critical
> Literature on 20th Century Plays* (M2875a).
> Breed, Paul F., and Florence M. Sniderman, comps. and eds. *Dramatic Crit-
> icism Index: A Bibliography of Commentaries on Playwrights from Ibsen to
> the Avant-Garde* (M2875a).
> Coleman, Arthur, and Gary R. Tyler. *Drama Criticism.* Vol. 1: *A Checklist
> of Interpretation since 1940 of English and American Plays.* Vol. 2: *A Checkl-
> ist of Interpretation since 1940 of Classical and Continental Plays* (M2875a).

    For scholarship between 1966 and 1990 on twentieth-century drama, researchers
should begin with Carpenter, *Modern Drama Scholarship and Criticism* (M2875).

See also

    Wildbihler, *The Musical: An International Annotated Bibliography* (Q4295).

REVIEW INDEXES

See

    Salem, *Guide to Critical Reviews* (Q4300).

Biographical Dictionaries

INDEXES

L1175   Wearing, J. P. *American and British Theatrical Biography: A Directory.*
          Metuchen: Scarecrow, 1979. 1,007 pp.   PN2285.W42   792'.0295.
   A finding list of entries on dramatists and theatrical personnel in about 55 popular
and scholarly biographical dictionaries and reference works from the mid-eighteenth
century to the late 1970s. Each entry includes name, cross-references to married or stage
name or pseudonym, dates of birth and death, nationality, theatrical occupation, and
coded references to the dictionaries and reference works. Because of the works indexed,
coverage is fuller for those who lived after c. 1800. A time-saving source for determining
which of the numerous standard biographical sources include an individual. Reviews:
Sandra Billington, *Theatre Research International* 7 (1982): 152–53; Joseph Donohue,
Theatre Journal 32 (1980): 406–08; Cecil Price, *Notes and Queries* ns 28 (1981): 569–70.

See also

   Sec. J: Biographical Sources/Biographical Dictionaries/Indexes.

DICTIONARIES

See

   Sec. L: Genres/Drama and Theater/Literary Handbooks, Dictionaries, and En-
      cyclopedias.
   Contemporary Theatre, Film, and Television (Q4305).

Poetry

Literary Handbooks, Dictionaries, and Encyclopedias

L1230   *New Princeton Encyclopedia of Poetry and Poetics.* Ed. Alex Preminger and
          T. V. F. Brogan. Princeton: Princeton UP, 1993. 1,383 pp.   PN1021.N39
          808.1'03. Online through *LiOn* (I527).
   A guide to the history, theory, technique, and criticism of poetry, ancient to modern, Eastern and Western. The approximately 950 signed entries, written by an impressive array of scholars, cover the history of poetry (by language, school, movement,
and country), technique, genres, forms, prosody, poetic theory and criticism (including
critical terminology), related forms, and the relationship of poetry to other fields (e.g.,
music, religion, philosophy). A typical entry includes a definition, discussion of historical development, examples, and a brief bibliography. The electronic version in *LiOn*
can be searched by keyword (path: Criticism and Reference/Reference) or browsed by
entry (path: Complete Contents/Criticism and Reference/Reference Works). Almost
completely rewritten and substantially enlarged, *New Princeton Encyclopedia* supersedes
its predecessor (*Princeton Encyclopedia of Poetry and Poetics*, enl. ed., ed. Preminger
[1974, 992 pp.]). The most thorough, erudite, and authoritative of the numerous poetry

encyclopedias, *New Princeton Encyclopedia* is an essential companion for serious readers and scholars and—as one of the very finest examples of its kind—a model for similar, much needed encyclopedias of drama and fiction. Selected entries on prosodic and poetic terms are reprinted in *The New Princeton Handbook of Poetic Terms*, ed. Brogan (Princeton: Princeton UP, 1994, 339 pp.); entries on national literatures and cultures are reprinted—but few seem to have "been brought completely up to date, with a greatly augmented bibliography" as the preface claims—in *The Princeton Handbook of Multicultural Poetries*, ed. Brogan (Princeton: Princeton UP, 1996, 366 pp.).

Although neither as comprehensive nor as thorough as the *New Princeton Encyclopedia*, the following are also useful:

> Deutsch, Babette. *Poetry Handbook: A Dictionary of Terms.* 4th ed. New York: Funk, 1974. 203 pp.
>
> Myers, Jack, and Michael Simms. *Longman Dictionary and Handbook of Poetry.* Longman English and Humanities Series. New York: Longman, 1985. 366 pp. Reprinted as *The Longman Dictionary of Poetic Terms* (1989), with no acknowledgment of its ancestry or correction of the numerous factual and typographical errors (see the review by Basil Cottle, *Review of English Studies* ns 40 [1989]: 398–99). Even its third incarnation—Myers and Don C. Wukasch, *Dictionary of Poetic Terms* (Denton: U of North Texas P, 2003, 434 pp.)—does not correct many of the errors Cottle identified, fails to provide an adequately updated bibliography, and (even with a host of entries for what can hardly be called *poetic* terms [e.g., colophon, id, verso]) is hardly "the most comprehensive list of poetic terms that has yet been compiled."
>
> Turco, Lewis. *The Book of Forms: A Handbook of Poetics.* 3rd ed. Hanover: UP of New England, 2000. 337 pp.
>
> Williams, Miller. *Patterns of Poetry: An Encyclopedia of Forms.* Baton Rouge: Louisiana State UP, 1986. 203 pp. Stanza patterns and poetic forms—including a few not in *New Princeton Encyclopedia*—are more fully illustrated in this and the preceding work.

See also

> Malof, *Manual of English Meters* (M1585).
> Shapiro, *Prosody Handbook* (M1585a).

Guides to Primary Works

L1235   *Columbia Granger's Index to Poetry in Anthologies* (*Granger's Index*). Ed. Tessa Kale. 12th ed. New York: Columbia UP, 2002. 2,219 pp. Former titles: *Granger's Index to Poetry* (1904–86); *Columbia Granger's Index to Poetry* (1990–94).   PN1022.H39   016.80881.

   Columbia Granger's World of Poetry. (Also called *Columbia Granger's Poetry Database.*) Columbia UP. Online 5 May 2005 <http://www.columbiagrangers.org>. Also available online through EBSCO (I512).

Title/first-line/last-line, author, and subject indexes to some 81,000 English-language poems (including translations) in the most accessible anthologies published through 2001. Subject indexing, although expanded in recent editions, relies heavily on title keywords, and thus form and genre headers are virtually useless (e.g., under "sonnets" Shakespeare does not appear). The indexes are cumbersome to use because the author and subject listings are keyed to the title/first-line/last-line entries, which are in turn keyed to the list of anthologies. Users must remember to check for variant titles and first lines. Since the current edition is not fully cumulative, earlier editions are still useful. *A Compilation of Works Listed in* Granger's Index to Poetry, *1904–1978* (Great Neck: Granger, 1980, 217 pp.) indexes anthologies by Granger symbol, title, and editor or compiler. Although highly selective and emphasizing established writers, *Granger's Index* is valuable for identifying poems on a topic or anthologized reprints. A companion volume— *The Columbia Granger's Index to Poetry in Collected and Selected Works,* 2nd ed., ed. Keith Newton (2004, 1,847 pp.)—indexes more than 65,000 poems in collections by 266 authors. While the likelihood that a volume will be found on library shelves is Newton's primary selection criterion, the editorial board also considered a poet's reputation and a collection's editorial standards.

Granger's can be searched most efficiently through *Columbia Granger's World of Poetry* database, which incorporates the 8th through the 12th editions of *Granger's Index,* the first two editions of *Columbia Granger's Index to Poetry in Collected and Selected Works,* and *The Columbia Granger's Index to African-American Poetry* (Q3840), in addition to the full texts of nearly 50,000 poems, more than 1,100 potted explications accompanied by a selective bibliography, and c. 500 biographies. *Columbia Grangers* search interface allows for a Quick Search (by author; title, first line, last line; subject; or keywords in the text of poems) or an Advanced Search (combinations of the preceding along with an uninformatively titled "author category" field [e.g., nationality, ethnicity, literary period]). Keyword searches of texts of poems frequently return several false hits since the interface does not allow exact matching. Results appear in no apparent order and cannot be re-sorted. Although in need of a more flexible search interface, *Columbia Granger's World of Poetry* allows users to locate quickly poems about a particular subject or to identify half-remembered lines from a poem. Unfortunately, the online version offered by EBSCO offers no explanation of its relation to the printed editions; see entry I512 for a discussion of the search interface. The CD-ROM offers a smaller database that is updated less frequently.

Fuller coverage of recent anthologies was offered for a time by *Poetry Index Annual: A Title, Author, First Line, Keyword, and Subject Index to Poetry in Anthologies* (Great Neck: Poetry Index, 1982–94). Although more thorough than *Granger's Index* in covering small-press publications, it hardly achieved the exhaustiveness it sometimes claimed ("all poetry anthologies as they are published").

See also

> *American Humanities Index* (G360).
> *Humanities Index* (G385).
> *Index to Children's Poetry* (U5540).
> *Readers' Guide* (G400).

Guides to Scholarship and Criticism

L1245 Coleman, Arthur. *Epic and Romance Criticism.* 2 vols. Searingtown: Watermill, 1973–74. Z7156.E6 C64 016.8091.

> Vol. 1: *A Checklist of Interpretations, 1940–1972, of English and American Epics and Metrical Romances.* 1973. 387 pp.

Vol. 2: *A Checklist of Interpretations, 1940–1973, of Classical and Continental Epics and Metrical Romances.* 1974. 368 pp.

A selective bibliography of English-language articles and parts of books organized by title of poem. Inconsistencies abound in the inclusion of several works that can hardly be classified as epic or romance, in the alphabetization of titles, and in the transcription of bibliographical information. Despite the inconsistencies, errors, and omissions, the focus on long poems makes Coleman — if used with considerable caution — a useful complement to Kuntz, *Poetry Explication* (L1255), Cline, *Index to Criticisms of British and American Poetry* (L1255a), and Alexander, *American and British Poetry* (L1255a). Review: John Keith Wikeley, *Literary Research Newsletter* 1 (1976): 117–21.

L1250   Donow, Herbert S., comp. *The Sonnet in England and America: A Bibliography of Criticism.* Westport: Greenwood, 1982. 477 pp.
Z2014.S6 D66 [PR509.S7]   821′.042′09.

A bibliography of studies, anthologies, and editions of British and American sonneteers from the Renaissance through the nineteenth century. Coverage of English, French, and German scholarship is reasonably thorough; that of other languages is admittedly less so. Entries are listed alphabetically in four classified sections: general studies and anthologies, Renaissance, Shakespeare, and eighteenth and nineteenth centuries; the period sections have subdivisions for general studies, anthologies, and poets. Approximately half of the 4,191 entries are annotated, but usually with a brief sentence that rarely offers an adequate indication of content. Of the three indexes (scholars, poets, subjects) only the first is adequate: neither the poet index — essential to discovering studies that discuss more than one writer — nor the subject index, which utilizes unconventional headings, is thorough. Despite its shortcomings, Donow is a valuable compilation of the widely scattered scholarship on the sonnet.

L1255   Kuntz, Joseph M., and Nancy C. Martinez. *Poetry Explication: A Checklist of Interpretation since 1925 of British and American Poems Past and Present.*
[3rd ed.] Boston: Hall, 1980. 570 pp.   Z2014.P7 K8 [PR502]
016.821′009.

A selective list of English-language articles and parts of books (published between 1925 and 1977) that explicate poems of generally less than 500 lines. Contemporary authors who are not widely recognized are not included. Entries are classified by poet, then by title, with parts of books keyed to a list at the back (which also identifies volumes of journals searched). The focus is explication; therefore, source, analogue, and most metrical studies are excluded, as are studies devoted to only part of a poem or books limited to one author. Long a standard source, particularly because of its indexing of parts of books, *Poetry Explication* is now largely superseded by a series of volumes published by Hall (New York):

Ruppert, James. *Guide to American Poetry Explication,* vol. 1: *Colonial and Nineteenth-Century.* Reference Publication in Literature. 1989. 252 pp.

Leo, John R. *Guide to American Poetry Explication,* vol. 2: *Modern and Contemporary.* Reference Publication in Literature. 1989. 546 pp.

Martinez, Nancy C., and Joseph G. R. Martinez. *Guide to British Poetry Explication,* vol. 1: *Old-English-Medieval.* Reference Publication in Literature. 1991. 310 pp.

———. *Guide to British Poetry Explication,* vol. 2: *Renaissance.* Reference Publication in Literature. 1992. 540 pp.

Martinez, Nancy C., Joseph G. R. Martinez, and Erland Anderson. *Guide to British Poetry Explication*, vol. 3: *Restoration-Romantic*. Reference Publication in Literature. 1993. 576 pp.

——. *Guide to British Poetry Explication*, vol. 4: *Victorian-Contemporary*. Reference Publication in Literature. 1995. 720 pp.

These volumes incorporate entries from the three editions of *Poetry Explication* and follow its structure but extend coverage (through 1987–92, depending on the publication date of a volume) and expand the scope of the earlier work by admitting interviews and books devoted to a single poet and including poems of more than 500 lines and (in the second American volume) writers from throughout North America. Reviews: (*Renaissance*) William C. Johnson, *Analytical and Enumerative Bibliography* ns 6 (1992): 45–49; (*Restoration-Romantic*) Madeline A. Copp, *Analytical and Enumerative Bibliography* ns 8 (1994): 78–80.

Similar indexes that supplement the preceding checklists include Gloria Stark Cline and Jeffrey A. Baker, *An Index to Criticisms of British and American Poetry* (Metuchen: Scarecrow, 1973, 307 pp.), covering studies published between 1960 and 1970 in 30 journals and a few books; and Harriet Semmes Alexander, comp., *American and British Poetry: A Guide to the Criticism, 1925–1978* (Athens: Swallow, 1984, 486 pp.) and *1979–1990* (Athens: Swallow–Ohio UP, 1996, 465 pp.), which include articles and parts of books that range beyond explication but are based on an unstated selection policy. In addition, an annual "Check List of Explication" appears in *Explicator* 3–41 (1944–45 through 1990–91). For studies of long poems, see Coleman, *Epic and Romance Criticism* (L1245).

See also

> *ABELL* (G340): [English] Literature/General through the volume for 1967; [English] Literature/General/[Study of] Metre in the volumes for 1926–72; Literature, General/Literary History/Poetry, and Literature, General/Literary Criticism/Poetry in the volumes for 1968–72; Literary History and Criticism/Poetry, and Literary History and Criticism/Versification in the volume for 1973; and English Literature/General/Poetry in later volumes.
>
> *MLAIB* (G335): General VII: Literature, General and Comparative in the volumes for 1953–55; General II: Literature, General and Comparative in the volume for 1956; General IV/Poetry in the volumes for 1957–80; and the Literary Forms division and Genres/Poetry section in pt. 4 of the later volumes. Researchers must also check the headings beginning "Poetry" in the subject index to post-1980 volumes and in the online thesaurus.
>
> *RILM Abstracts* (U6240).

Prose

General

GUIDES TO SCHOLARSHIP AND CRITICISM

See

> *ABELL* (G340): [English] Literature/General through the volume for 1967; Literature, General/Literary History/Prose, and Literature, General/Literary Crit-

icism/Prose in the volumes for 1968–72; Literary History and Criticism/Prose in the volume for 1973; and English Literature/General/Prose in later volumes. *MLAIB* (G335): General VII: Literature, General and Comparative in the volumes for 1953–55; General II: Literature, General and Comparative in the volume for 1956; General IV/Prose in the volumes for 1957–80; and the Literary Forms division and Genres/Prose section in pt. 4 of the later volumes. Researchers must also check the headings beginning "Prose" in the subject index to post-1980 volumes and in the online thesaurus.

Biography and Autobiography

RESEARCH METHODS

L1275   Edel, Leon. *Writing Lives: Principia Biographica.* New York: Norton, 1984. 270 pp.   CT21.E33   808′.06692.
An exploration of the theory and problems of writing a biography of a literary author. Successive chapters examine the basic principles of biography since c. 1920, the relationship between biographer and subject, the search for materials, the role of criticism in biography, the application of psychoanalytic concepts to biography, and types of biographies. An appendix reprints some papers on Edel's research for his biography of James. Indexed by persons, titles, and subjects. An expansion of *Literary Biography*, rpt. of rev. ed., with new foreword (Bloomington: Indiana UP, 1973, 170 pp.), *Writing Lives* is one of the best introductions to the art of literary biography by one of its masters.
An important complement is Paula R. Backscheider, *Reflections on Biography* (Oxford: Oxford UP, 1999, 289 pp.), which examines some of the decisions that biographers must make (including choosing a subject, establishing a voice, using evidence, and employing a theory of personality).

L1280   Runyan, William McKinley. *Life Histories and Psychobiography: Explorations in Theory and Method.* New York: Oxford UP, 1982. 288 pp. BF38.5.R86   155.
An examination of the methodological and conceptual problems of psychobiography, with particular attention to descriptive, conceptual, and interpretive issues. The chapters are organized in three parts: problems of description and explanation (with discussions of alternative explanations in biographies, social influences, and the structure of biographical narrative), models for conceptualization of the life course, and theory and method in the study of individual lives (with examinations of the case-study, idiographic, and psychobiographic methods). Indexed by persons and subjects. Although addressed to psychologists and social scientists, Runyan is important preliminary reading for the literary biographer who would employ psychobiography or the reader evaluating a product of the approach.

HANDBOOKS, DICTIONARIES, AND ENCYCLOPEDIAS

L1283   *Encyclopedia of Life Writing: Autobiographical and Biographical Forms.* Ed. Margaretta Jolly. 2 vols. London: Fitzroy Dearborn, 2001.   CT21.E53   920′.003.

An encyclopedia of life writing, including its genres, forms, themes, significant practitioners, important exemplars (such as major national biographies), history, geographical practice, and major "social, political, religious, and academic contexts" from the classical era to the present. The signed entries—a refreshing number of which are by authors who have published on their topics—employ a variety of disciplinary approaches in combining description and criticism; each entry concludes with a decent-size bibliography and a biography (in entries on individuals). Indexed by authors, titles, and subjects of life writings, along with key concepts. The quality of the entries and the breadth of coverage—geographical, chronological, and topical—make *Encyclopedia of Life Writing* an essential guide to the field.

GUIDES TO SCHOLARSHIP AND CRITICISM

There is no adequate bibliography of scholarship on the theory and practice of biography and autobiography. Given the interest in life writing, such a bibliography is a major desideratum.

L1285   "Annual Bibliography of Works about Life Writing, [1977–]." *Biography*
         1 (1978)– . CT100.B54   920′.005.
   A selective list of studies, mostly in English, about biography, autobiography, and related topics. Works are currently organized in four author lists: books; collections of essays, issues of journals devoted to biography, and biographical dictionaries (with contents listed under the first two); articles; dissertations. In most installments, entries are accompanied by brief descriptive annotations. The lack of a subject index means that users must scan every entry; however, researchers with access to the electronic version of the journal can use their Web browser to search the bibliographies beginning with the one for 1999–2000. Although far from comprehensive—with several entries based on advertisements or sources other than the works themselves—and hardly accessible, this bibliography does isolate studies that are sometimes difficult to identify in the standard serial bibliographies and indexes in section G.

See also

   ABELL (G340): Biography [and Autobiography] division through the volume
      for 1974; and English Literature/General/Biography and Autobiography in
      later volumes.
   MLAIB (G335): General IV/Biography [and Autobiography] in the volumes for
      1957–80; and Genres/Autobiography and Biography sections in pt. 4 of the
      later volumes. Researchers must also check the headings beginning "Autobi-
      ography," "Biography," or "Life Writing" in the subject index to post-1980
      volumes and in the online thesaurus.

Travel Writing

GUIDES TO PRIMARY WORKS

L1295   Cox, Edward Godfrey. *A Reference Guide to the Literature of Travel:*
         Including Voyages, Geographical Descriptions, Adventures, Shipwrecks, and

    Expeditions. 3 vols. University of Washington Publications in Language and
Literature 9–10, 12. Seattle: U of Washington P, 1935–49.   Z6011.C87
016.91.

       Vol. 1: *The Old World.* 1935. 404 pp.
       Vol. 2: *The New World.* 1938. 591 pp.
       Vol. 3: *Great Britain.* 1949. 732 pp.

    A bibliography of travel literature printed before 1800 in Great Britain. Cox in-
cludes English-language translations, some European-language versions of English
works, and accounts written before 1800 but first published later. Vol. 3 goes beyond
separately published works to cite a host of letters, diaries, and miscellaneous documents
printed in larger works or collections. Each volume is organized by topical or geographical divisions; within each division, works are listed chronologically by publication date.
Many entries are accompanied by a note that variously refers to translations or other
editions, offers biographical information, or comments on contents. Many notes quote
from other sources, some of them of dubious authority. Indexed by persons (vols. 1–2
in vol. 2, vol. 3 in vol. 3). The projected volume on Ireland was never published.
Organization by date of publication combined with a lack of subject indexing makes
the work less accessible than it should be. Despite the numerous errors and heavy
reliance on other sources, Cox remains the best guide to travel literature in English
before 1800.

M

English Literature

Section M includes works devoted primarily to literature in England or the British Isles generally. Works limited to Irish, Scottish, or Welsh literature will be found in their respective sections.

General

This part includes works that encompass several periods of English literature. Works limited to a movement, century, or period will be found in the appropriate parts of section M. Users should note that most of the reference works in sections A–L of the *Guide* are useful to research in English literature.

Histories and Surveys

LITERARY HISTORIES

M1310   *The Oxford History of English Literature* (*OHEL*). Ed. F. P. Wilson et al. 15
   vols. Oxford: Clarendon–Oxford UP, 1945–97.   PR823.09   820.9.
    Vol. 1, pt. 2: Bennett, J. A. W. *Middle English Literature*. Ed. and completed
     by Douglas Gray. 1986. (M1785).
    Vol. 2, pt. 1: Bennett, H. S. *Chaucer and the Fifteenth Century*. 1947.
     (M1780).
    Vol. 2, pt. 2: Chambers, E. K. *English Literature at the Close of the Middle
     Ages.* 2nd impression with corrections. 1947. (M1790).
    Vol. 3: Lewis, C. S. *English Literature in the Sixteenth Century Excluding
     Drama.* 1954. (M1975).
    Vol. 4, pt. 1: Wilson, F. P. *The English Drama, 1485–1585*. Ed. G. K.
     Hunter. 1969. (M2125).
    Vol. 4, pt. 2: Hunter, G. K. *The English Drama, 1586–1642: The Age of
     Shakespeare.* 1997. (M2117).
    Vol. 5: Bush, Douglas. *English Literature in the Earlier Seventeenth Century,
     1600–1660.* 2nd ed. rev. 1962. (M1970).
    Vol. 6: Sutherland, James. *English Literature of the Late Seventeenth Century.*
     1969. (M2215).
    Vol. 7: Dobrée, Bonamy. *English Literature in the Early Eighteenth Century,
     1700–1740.* Corrected rpt. 1964. (M2210).
    Vol. 8: Butt, John. *The Mid-Eighteenth Century.* Ed. and completed by Geof-
     frey Carnall. 1979. (M2205).
    Vol. 9: Renwick, W. L. *English Literature, 1789–1815.* 1963. (M2460).
    Vol. 10: Jack, Ian. *English Literature, 1815–1832.* 1963. (M2455).
    Vol. 11, pt. 1: Turner, Paul. *English Literature, 1832–1890, Excluding the
     Novel.* 1989. 522 pp.
    Vol. 11, pt. 2: Horsman, Alan. *The Victorian Novel.* 1990. 465 pp.
    Vol. 12: Stewart, J. I. M. *Eight Modern Writers.* 1963. 704 pp.
  In 1990 Oxford University Press needlessly complicated the lives of researchers
and bibliographers by reprinting, without revision but with new volume numbers and
titles, 14 of the published volumes:
    Vol. 1: Bennett. *Middle English Literature, 1100–1400.*
    Vol. 2: Bennett. *Chaucer and Fifteenth-Century Verse and Prose.*
    Vol. 3: Chambers. *Malory and Fifteenth-Century Drama, Lyrics, and Ballads.*
    Vol. 4: Lewis. *Poetry and Prose in the Sixteenth Century.*
    Vol. 5: Wilson. *English Drama, 1485–1585.*
    Vol. 7: Bush. *The Early Seventeenth Century, 1600–1660: Jonson, Donne,
     and Milton.*
    Vol. 8: Sutherland. *Restoration Literature, 1660–1700: Dryden, Bunyan, and
     Pepys.*
    Vol. 9: Dobrée. *The Early Eighteenth Century, 1700–1740: Swift, Defoe, and
     Pope.*
    Vol. 10: Butt. *The Age of Johnson, 1740–1789.*
    Vol. 11: Renwick. *The Rise of the Romantics, 1789–1815: Wordsworth, Cole-
     ridge, and Jane Austen.*

Vol. 12: Jack. *English Literature, 1815–1832: Scott, Byron, and Keats.*
Vol. 13: Horsman. *The Victorian Novel.*
Vol. 14: Turner. *Victorian Poetry, Drama, and Miscellaneous Prose, 1832–1890.*
Vol. 15: Stewart. *Writers of the Early Twentieth Century: Hardy to Lawrence.*

A traditional history of English literature, with each volume by a distinguished scholar. Most volumes open with a chapter on the social, scientific, political, and religious background; examine major and minor writers; include a chronology (with sections for public events, literary history, verse, prose, and drama); and conclude with a highly selective bibliography (with sections for reference works, collections and anthologies, literary history and criticism, studies of topics and subjects, background studies, and authors). Indexed by persons, anonymous works, and a few subjects. Although their bibliographies are dated in varying degrees, many volumes rank among the better histories of their respective periods; a few are classics (especially those by Bush and Lewis); but others have met with a mixed reception (such as those by Dobrée and Butt) or are clearly inadequate (such as those by Stewart and Renwick). See the individual entries for fuller discussions of volumes not superseded by *Oxford English Literary History* (see below). The manifold inadequacies of the original vol. 12 are detailed in the review by Robert Martin Adams, *Hudson Review* 16 (1963–64): 594–600.

To replace *OHEL*, Oxford University Press is publishing the *Oxford English Literary History*:

Vol. 1: Linda Georgianna and Katherine O'Brien O'Keeffe. *To 1350: The Literary Cultures of Early England.*
Vol. 2: James Simpson. *1350–1547:Reform and Cultural Revolution.* 2002. (M1778).
Vol. 3: Colin Burrow. *1533–1603: The Elizabethans.*
Vol. 4: Katharine Eisaman Maus. *1603–1660: Literary Cultures of the Early Seventeenth Century.*
Vol. 5: Margaret Ezell. *1645–1714: The Later Seventeenth Century.*
Vol. 6: John Mullan. *1709–1784: The Eighteenth Century.*
Vol. 7: Fiona Robertson. *1785–1832: The Romantic Period.*
Vol. 8: Philip Davis. *1830–1880: The Victorians.* 2002. (M2462).
Vol. 9: Joseph Bristow. *1875–1914: From "Victorian" to "Edwardian."*
Vol. 10: Chris Baldick. *1910–1940: The Modern Movement.* 2004. (M2752).
Vol. 11: Rick Rylance. *1930–1970: Literature among the Wars.*
Vol. 12: Randall Stevenson. *1960–2000: The Last of England?* 2004. (M2753).
Vol. 13: Bruce King. *1948–2000: The Internationalization of English Literature.* 2004. (M2753a).

While each volume "offers an individual scholar's vision of a discrete period of literary history," all give attention to the institutions associated with literary creation, forms and genres, and "the relationship between literature and broader historical continuities and transformations." The selective bibliographies that conclude each volume vary substantially in their quality: some (e.g., Simpson) are little more than inadequate—and sometimes untrustworthy—lists of editions and studies; others (e.g., Davis) offer fuller, evaluative guides to further reading. Indexed by persons and subjects.

For an overview of the *OHEL* and discussion of the principles undergirding it, see Jonathan Bate, "The History of Literary History," Oxford UP, online, 9 Oct. 2005 <http://www.oup.co.uk/academic/humanities/literature/oelhist/bate>.

Some of the individual chapters in the *Cambridge History of English Literature* (*CHEL*), ed. A. W. Ward and A. R. Waller, 15 vols. (Cambridge: Cambridge UP, 1907–27; online as *The Cambridge History of English and American Literature* <http://www.bartleby.com/cambridge>), have never been completely superseded, although the work as a whole is outdated. George Sampson, *The Concise Cambridge History of English Literature*, rev. R. C. Churchill, 3rd ed. (Cambridge: Cambridge UP, 1970, 976 pp.), is a revised digest of *CHEL* that extends coverage to the mid-twentieth century for British literature and adds discussions of Commonwealth and American literature (through James).

M1315   Baugh, Albert C., ed. *A Literary History of England.* 2nd ed. New York:
          Appleton-Century-Crofts, 1967. 1,605 pp.   PR83.B3   820.9.
     A traditional history in four books written (and then updated with bibliographical supplements) by eminent scholars: Kemp Malone and Albert C. Baugh, the Middle Ages (to 1500); Tucker Brooke, Renaissance (1500–1660), supplemented by Matthias A. Shaaber; George Sherburn, Restoration and eighteenth century (1660–1789), supplemented by Donald F. Bond; Samuel C. Chew, nineteenth century and after (1789–1939), supplemented by Richard D. Altick. The second edition reprints with minor corrections the text of the 1948 edition with bibliographical supplements at the back. Indexed by authors and titles. Although dated in many respects, the work is still the best single-volume history of English literature. Review: René Wellek, *Modern Philology* 47 (1949): 39–45.

OTHER HISTORIES

M1323   *New Oxford History of England.* Ed. J. M. Roberts. 16 vols. Oxford:
          Clarendon–Oxford UP, 1989– .
          Bartlett, Robert. *England under the Norman Kings, 1075–1225.* 2000.
               772 pp.   DA195.B28   942.02.
          Prestwich, Michael. *Plantagenet England, 1225–1360.* 2005. 638 pp.
               DA225.P744   942.03.
          Harriss, Gerald. *Shaping the Nation: England, 1360–1461.* 2005. 705 pp.
               DA245.H3155   942.04.
          Williams, Penry. *The Later Tudors: England, 1547–1603.* 1995. 606 pp.
               DA355.W4835   942.05.
          Hoppit, Julian. *A Land of Liberty? England, 1689–1727.* 2000. 580 pp.
               DA460.H66   941.06'8'092.
          Langford, Paul. *A Polite and Commercial People: England, 1727–1783.* 1989.
               803 pp.   DA480.L26   941.07'2.
          Hilton, Boyd. *A Mad, Bad, and Dangerous People? England, 1783–1846.*
               2006. 755 pp.   DA520.H64   941.07.
          Searle, G. R. *A New England? Peace and War, 1886–1918.* 2004. 951 pp.
               DA560.S396   941.081.
          Hoppen, K. Theodore. *The Mid-Victorian Generation, 1846–1886.* 1998.
               787 pp.   DA560.H58   941.081.
     A general history of England that focuses on the political but that also treats, as the period demands, military, demographic, cultural, religious, economic, and govern-

mental topics. Each volume concludes with a chronology, selective bibliography, and an index of persons and subjects. *New Oxford History of England* is gradually superseding the following:

> The Oxford History of England. Ed. George N. Clark. 17 vols. Oxford: Clarendon–Oxford UP, 1936–91.
>
> > Vol. 1a: Salway, Peter. *Roman Britain.* 1981. 824 pp.   DA145.S26 936.1′04.
> >
> > Vol. 1b: Myres, J. N. L. *The English Settlements.* 1986. 248 pp. DA152.M97   942.01. (This and the preceding volume replace R. G. Collingwood and Myres, *Roman Britain and the English Settlements,* 2nd ed. [1937, 515 pp.].)
> >
> > Vol. 2: Stenton, F. M. *Anglo-Saxon England.* 3rd ed. 1971. 765 pp. DA152.S74   942.01.
> >
> > Vol. 3: Poole, Austin Lane. *From Domesday Book to Magna Carta, 1087– 1216.* 2nd ed. 1955. 541 pp.   DA175.P6   942.02.
> >
> > Vol. 4: Powicke, Maurice. *The Thirteenth Century, 1216–1307.* 2nd ed. 1962. 829 pp.   DA225.P65   942.034.
> >
> > Vol. 5: McKisack, May. *The Fourteenth Century, 1307–1399.* 1959. 598 pp.   DA230.M25   942.037.
> >
> > Vol. 6: Jacob, E. F. *The Fifteenth Century, 1399–1485.* 1961. 775 pp.   DA245.J3   942.05.
> >
> > Vol. 7: Mackie, J. D. *The Earlier Tudors, 1485–1558.* Rpt. with corrections. 1978. 699 pp.   DA325.M3   942.05.
> >
> > Vol. 8: Black, J. B. *The Reign of Elizabeth, 1558–1603.* 2nd ed. 1959. 539 pp.   DA355.B65   942.055.
> >
> > Vol. 9: Davies, Godfrey. *The Early Stuarts, 1603–1660.* 2nd ed. 1959. 458 pp.   DA390.D3   942.06.
> >
> > Vol. 10: Clark, George N. *The Later Stuarts, 1660–1714.* 2nd ed., rpt. with corrections. 1961. 479 pp.   DA435.C55   942.06.
> >
> > Vol. 11: Williams, Basil. *The Whig Supremacy, 1714–1760.* 2nd ed., rev. C. H. Stuart. 1962. 504 pp.   DA498.W5   942.071.
> >
> > Vol. 12: Watson, J. Steven. *The Reign of George III, 1760–1815.* 1960. 637 pp.   DA505.W38   942.073.
> >
> > Vol. 13: Woodward, Llewellyn. *The Age of Reform, 1815–1870.* 2nd ed. 1962. 681 pp.   DA530.W6   942.07.
> >
> > Vol. 14: Ensor, R. C. K. *England, 1870–1914.* 1936. 634 pp. DA560.E6   942.08.
> >
> > Vol. 15: Taylor, A. J. P. *English History, 1914–1945.* 1965. 708 pp. DA566.T38   942.083.
> >
> > Raper, Richard, comp. *The Oxford History of England: Consolidated Index.* 1991. 622 pp.   DA32.A1 R36   016.942.

A general economic, social, political, and military history. Individual volumes are variously organized, but each includes a selective bibliography, maps, and an index of persons and subjects.

M1325   *The Victoria History of the Counties of England* (*Victoria County History,* *VCH*). Woodbridge: Boydell and Brewer for Inst. of Historical Research, 1900– .   DA670   942. Online. <http://www.victoriacountyhistory.ac.uk>.

   A collaborative history, with several volumes devoted to each county. Among the topics covered are the physical environment; prehistory; archaeology; schools; industries;

sports and pastimes; topography (with descriptions of manors, estates, and other places); and natural, political, social, and economic history. Some volumes have an index of persons, places, and subjects; a cumulative index is planned for each county when all the volumes are published. The quality of the essays varies considerably, but coverage has generally become more thorough over the years; however, there is no consistency in the publication schedule of volumes for each county. Although frequently pedestrian, the volumes offer an incomparable accumulation of local history. The *General Introduction*, ed. R. B. Pugh (1970, 282 pp.), and *Supplement*, ed. C. R. Elrington (1990, 67 pp.), offer a thorough discussion of the origin and history of the project; an overview of changes in titles, publishers, and printers; and a detailed list of contents of all volumes published by 1990. For the status of the work on each county and a description of the planned online version, consult the Victoria County History Web site.

For a county-by-county survey of histories, see *English County Histories: A Guide: A Tribute to C. R. Elrington*, ed. C. R. J. Currie and C. P. Lewis (Stroud: Sutton, 1994, 483 pp.).

Literary Handbooks, Dictionaries, and Encyclopedias

M1330   *The Oxford Companion to English Literature*. Ed. Margaret Drabble. 6th ed. rev. Oxford: Oxford UP, 2006. 1,172 pp.   PR19.D73   820'.9. Online through *Oxford Reference Online* [I530].

A wide-ranging encyclopedia, with entries for authors, works, characters, literary prizes, movements, critical theories, periods, groups, historical figures and foreign writers important to English literature, critics, theaters, periodicals, terminology, places, prosody, and allusions (although the last two are treated less fully than in the fourth edition). The sixth edition is more inclusive in admitting young writers than was the preceding edition, which excluded anyone born after 1939, and offers more entries on literary theory, women writers, and postcolonial authors. There is no explanation of the revisions made in the revised sixth edition. Entries emphasize information rather than critical evaluation, although the latter is inevitably present. Discussions of authors are very inconsistent in directing readers to standard editions and critical works. Like the fifth edition, this one concludes with a chronology, a list of poets laureate, and a list of literary awards, which unfortunately replace the valuable appendixes that conclude earlier editions ("Censorship and the Law of the Press"; "Notes on the History of English Copyright"; "The Calendar," with tables for the Gregorian and Julian calendars, movable feast days, and saints' days—all essential to dating documents). Individuals with separate entries in the fourth, fifth, revised fifth, and sixth editions are indexed in *Biography and Genealogy Master Index* (J565). Despite omissions, errors, and inconsistencies, the *Oxford Companion* retains its stature as the most reliable and readable single source for essential information on English literary culture. Reviews: (5th ed.) Basil Cottle, *Review of English Studies* ns 37 (1986): 620–23; Harold Fromm, *American Scholar* 55 (1986): 410–18; James R. Kincaid, *New York Times Book Review* 14 July 1985: 11; Iain McGilchrist, *TLS: Times Literary Supplement* 26 Apr. 1985: 455–56.

The Continuum Encyclopedia of British Literature, ed. Steven R. Serafin and Valerie Grosvenor Myer (New York: Continuum, 2003, 1,184 pp.) offers lengthier entries on some 1,200 authors and topics associated with British literature; however, it is not even remotely the "comprehensive survey" or "most extensive single-volume treatment of its subject" and far too few contributors can legitimately be called "literary authorities."

The Oxford Encyclopedia of British Literature, ed. David Scott Kastan, 5 vols. (New York: Oxford UP, 2006; online, 17 Aug. 2006 (<http://www.oxford-british literature.com>) offers even longer entries on more than 500 themes, genres, movements, institutions, and (predominantly) "major authors." Written for the most part by established scholars, entries conclude with suggestions for further reading. The electronic version (available as part of *The Oxford Digital Reference Shelf* [http://www.oxford-digitalreference.com]) can be searched by keyword or browsed by entry; entries can be e-mailed. There will be quibbles over admissions (e.g., Richard Barnfield) and omissions (e.g., Nicholas Rowe), but *Oxford Encyclopedia* will be welcomed by those who need more information than *Oxford Companion* can offer.

M1335 Eagle, Dorothy, and Hilary Carnell, comps. and eds. *The Oxford Literary Guide to Great Britain and Ireland*. [Rev. paperback ed.] Rev. Eagle and Meic Stephens. Oxford: Oxford UP, 1993. 467 pp., 13 maps. (A corrected, amplified edition of *The Oxford Illustrated Literary Guide to Great Britain and Ireland*, 2nd ed., rev. Eagle and Stephens [1992], 322 pp., 12 maps.) PR109.E18   820.9.

An alphabetical guide to 1,349 places, real and imaginary, associated with some 1,064 dead authors. Although the bulk of the places are in England, the second edition increases coverage of Ireland, Scotland, and Wales. The entries, which are keyed to a series of maps, succinctly identify associations with writers and works (occasionally quoting relevant passages) and provide directions for locating places. Indexed by authors. Based on visits to most of the places described, the work offers the fullest, most authoritative general guide to British literary topography.

M1340 Goode, Clement Tyson, and Edgar Finley Shannon. *An Atlas of English Literature*. New York: Century, 1925. 136 pp.   PR109.G6   820′.9.

A series of historical maps, each accompanied by a list of writers and associated places. The maps and lists for England and Wales are organized by period (449–1066, 1066–1500, 1500–1660, 1660–1798, and 1798–1900); a single map and list cover each of the following: Scotland, Ireland, London, and Italian locales associated with British authors. Two indexes: places (with authors listed under each); authors. Although in need of revision, the *Atlas* remains useful for identifying the literary associations of locales as they existed in various periods.

Although lacking this historical perspective, Michael Hardwick, *A Literary Atlas and Gazetteer of the British Isles* (Detroit: Gale, 1973, 216 pp.), prints detailed county maps (keyed to terse explanatory notes on literary associations) and is more current.

See also

Sec. C: Literary Handbooks, Dictionaries, and Encyclopedias.

Annals

LITERATURE

M1345 *Oxford Chronology of English Literature*. Ed. Michael Cox. 2 vols. Oxford: Oxford UP, 2002.   Z2011.O98   016.82. CD-ROM.

A selected chronological record of printed works authored, for the most part, by British writers and printed between 1474 and 2000 in Britain, but the approximately 4,000 individuals include some foreign authors who made their home in the British Isles, some colonial writers who were published primarily by British publishers, and some postcolonial writers influential in the United Kingdom. The focus is imaginative writing, but some translations, periodicals, works for children, and nonfictional works are admitted (by the editor's count, there are approximately "30,000 works — over 11,000 works of fiction, nearly 6,000 poetry titles, 2,500 dramatic works, and over 6,500 works of non-fiction"). Entries are organized chronologically by date of publication (which can differ from the imprint date and, sometimes substantially, from date of composition), then alphabetically (first by title of anonymous works, then by author); a typical entry includes date of birth (and date of death if the work was published posthumously), category (e.g., fiction, prose satire, verse), title, imprint, and a note (including, e.g., date of first performance for a play, bibliographical information, names of illustrators, references to later editions, or cross-references to related works). Three indexes: authors (with titles listed chronologically under each); titles; translated authors (with titles listed chronologically under each).

Although a work that is so catholic in its scope will always invite carping over who or what did or did not survive the editorial delete key, coverage seems even-handed and representative. Users must remember, however, that titles and bibliographical information are not based on copies in hand.

A substantially expanded successor to *Annals of English Literature, 1475–1950: The Principal Publications of Each Year Together with an Alphabetical Index of Authors with Their Works,* [ed. R. W. Chapman and W. K. Davin], 2nd ed. rpt. with corrections (Oxford: Clarendon–Oxford UP, 1965, 380 pp.), *Oxford Chronology of English Literature* is the best print-based resource for placing a work in its literary milieu, tracing changes in reading tastes, and charting more clearly the outlines of a literary period; however, the chronological sorting capabilities of several electronic databases (e.g., *English Short Title Catalogue* [M1377]) can provide a much more detailed conspectus of the print record for many periods.

RELATED TOPICS

M1350 *Handbook of British Chronology.* 3rd ed., corr. Ed. E. B. Fryde et al. Royal Historical Society Guides and Handbooks 2. Cambridge: Cambridge UP, 1996. 605 pp.   DA34.P6   942.002.

A chronology of rulers, officers of state, archbishops, and bishops to 1985 and of peers, parliaments, and church councils for earlier periods. Entries are organized in six divisions: rulers (by country, with details of "parentage, birth, accession, death [or removal], marriage and issue" as well as changes in titles and regents); officers of state (by country, office, then ruler, with dates of assumption and demission); archbishops and bishops (by country, see, then date of accession); dukes, marquesses, and earls (by country, then title, but covering only 1066 to 1714 for England); English and British parliaments and related assemblies to 1832; and provincial and national councils of the church in England, c. 600–1536. An introduction to each division (and to many sections) fully explains content, organization, limitations, and sources. Although access is hampered by the lack of an index and information is provisional for the period to 1066, the *Handbook* is the standard chronology and an indispensable source for dating documents.

Equally important for dating documents is *A Handbook of Dates for Students of British History*, ed. C. R. Cheney, new ed. rev. Michael Jones, Royal Historical Society Guides and Handbooks 4 (Cambridge: Cambridge UP, 2000, 246 pp.), which provides tables listing rulers of England and regnal years, popes, saints' days and festivals, law terms, and dates of Easter.

Bibliographies of Bibliographics

M1355   Howard-Hill, T. H. *Index to British Literary Bibliography.* Oxford: Clarendon–Oxford UP, 1969– .   Z2011.A1 H68 [PR83]   016.82.

Vol. 1: *Bibliography of British Literary Bibliographies.* 2nd ed., rev. and enl. 1987. 886 pp.

Vol. 2: *Shakespearian Bibliography and Textual Criticism: A Bibliography.* 2nd ed. rev. and enlarged. Signal Mountain: Summertown, 2000. 290 pp. A final revised edition is in progress.

Vol. 3: *British Literary Bibliography to 1890: A Bibliography.* In progress.

Vol. 4: *British Bibliography and Textual Criticism: A Bibliography.* 1979. 732 pp.

Vol. 5: *British Bibliography and Textual Criticism: A Bibliography (Authors).* 1979. 488 pp.

Vol. 6: *British Bibliography and Textual Criticism, 1890–1969: An Index.* 1980. 409 pp.

Vol. 7: *British Literary Bibliography, 1970–1979.* 1992. 912 pp.

Vol. 8: *Dissertations on British Literary Bibliography to 2000.* In progress. A preliminary version was published as *British Book Trade Dissertations to 1980* (Signal Mountain: Summerton, 1998, 314 pp.).

Vol. 9: *British Literary Bibliography, 1980–1989: A Bibliography (Authors).* 1999. 591 pp.

Additions and corrections to all volumes are posted at Bib Site, online, Bibliog. Soc. of Amer., 15 Apr. 2007 <http://www.bibsocamer.org/BibSite/HowardHill/>.

Also planned are decennial supplements covering 1980–2000, revised editions of vols. 2 and 8 that extend coverage to the year 2000, and an index to all volumes.

The work is a broad-ranging index of bibliographies and bibliographical and textual studies originally intended to cover books, substantial parts of books, and periodical articles written in English and published in the English-speaking Commonwealth and the United States after 1890, on the bibliographical and textual examination of English manuscripts, books, printing and publishing, and any other books published in English in Great Britain or by British authors abroad, from the establishment of printing in England, except for material on modern (post-1890) printing and publishing not primarily of bibliographical or literary interest.

Among kinds of publications initially excluded are bibliographical and textual discussions in editions; catalogs of manuscripts; and most library, auction, booksellers', and private library catalogs. During the course of publication, Howard-Hill has included some studies in foreign languages and on foreign-language books published in Britain; has added coverage of manuscripts before 1475 by authors for whom studies of printed books are listed; has included some material on some modern private presses, studies published before 1890, and discussions in editions; and has modified organization and citation form. For a full discussion of changes in scope, see his "The *Index to British*

Literary Bibliography," TEXT: Transactions of the Society for Textual Scholarship 2 (1985): 1–12.

In general, entries are organized by date of publication within sections. The brief descriptive annotations frequently note contents and selected reviews. Since a work is usually entered only once and seldom cross-referenced, users must check the index volume (vol. 6) to locate all entries relevant to an author or topic.

Vol. 1 classifies enumerative bibliographies (published c. 1890–1969) in divisions for general bibliographies, periods, regions (generally works printed at or written by inhabitants of—rather than those about—a place), book production and distribution, forms and genres (e.g., ballads, emblem books, forgeries, poetry, unfinished books), subjects (e.g., alchemy, circus, fencing, tobacco, witchcraft), and authors. Under some literary authors, the bibliographies of primary works are preceded by a selective list of bibliographies of scholarship; both are organized by date of publication, and the latter sometimes admits works belonging to the former list. The brief descriptive annotations frequently note organization, type of bibliography, content of bibliographical descriptions, revised editions or supplements published after 1969, and reviews. Indexed by persons and subjects; vol. 6 also indexes most entries in the revised edition of vol. 1.

Vol. 2 organizes Shakespearean textual and bibliographical research (published c. 1890 through 1995) in divisions for general bibliographies and guides, editions (with sections on quartos and the various folios), and textual studies (with sections on handwriting and paleography, collected emendations, and individual works). Bibliographies appear first in each section, followed by studies in chronological order. Coverage of suggested emendations is not complete. Two indexes: persons; subjects.

Vols. 4 and 5 classify bibliographical and textual studies (published c. 1890– c. 1969) on printed works and manuscripts in divisions for bibliography and textual criticism; general and period bibliography; regional bibliography; book production and distribution; forms, genres, and subjects; and authors. Only a very few entries are annotated. Corrections appear in vol. 6 (pp. xvii–xix).

Vol. 6 indexes vols. 1 (including most entries in the revised edition), 2 (the original 1971 edition), 4, and 5 in two sequences: persons and titles of anonymous works; subjects. The organization of the subject index requires considerable study before it can be used efficiently, as it must be if all entries on an author or subject are to be located.

Vol. 7 continues the coverage of vols. 1, 2 (the original 1971 edition), 4, and 5 but excludes most publications in Asian languages.

Vol. 8 includes doctoral dissertations, master's theses, and other diploma theses.

Vol. 9 continues the coverage of vols. 1, 2, 4, 5, and 7.

Mastering indexing principles and changes in scope and organization amply rewards a user's perseverance because Howard-Hill offers the fullest single guide to bibliographical scholarship on and bibliographies of English literature. Review: (vols. 4– 6) Peter Davison, *Library* 6th ser. 4 (1982): 185–87.

For bibliographies published before 1890, see Besterman, *World Bibliography of Bibliographies* (D155); for those after 1969, see *Bibliographic Index* (D145); for recent bibliographical and textual studies, see *ABHB: Annual Bibliography of the History of the Printed Book* (U5275).

M1357   Bracken, James K. *Reference Works in British and American Literature.* 2nd
        ed. Reference Sources in the Humanities. Englewood: Libraries Unlimited,
        1998. 726 pp.   Z2011.B74 [PR83]   016.8209.

An annotated bibliography of "bibliographies (including exhibition, book dealer's, and library catalogs); dictionaries, encyclopedias, and handbooks (ranging from chronologies and gazetteers to companions and prefaces); indexes and concordances (including topical indexes and collections of quotations, proverbs, symbolic language, and critical terminology); and currently published, or recently ceased periodicals (ranging from yearbooks to newsletters, but excluding monographic series)" and a few electronic resources devoted to one of about 1,500 British or American authors or anonymous works (such as *Beowulf*). The most important or useful separately published English-language works (through early 1997) receive full entries, with annotations frequently citing journal articles and sections of composite or collective reference sources (such as *NCBEL* [M1385] or *BAL* [Q3250]). The annotations are thorough (with nicely succinct descriptions of scope, organization, contents, kinds of annotations, and indexing), helpfully cite related or superseded works, usually compare works when two or more are listed under an author, and—unlike in the first edition—are more pointedly evaluative. Unfortunately, the indexing is inadequate: main entries are indexed by persons and titles; titles of books (but not their authors or editors) cited in annotations are indexed (unaccountably by page rather than entry number like other titles); journal articles mentioned in annotations are not indexed. Nonetheless, Bracken is an invaluable starting place for identifying and sorting through published book-length single-author reference works, and it serves to highlight the many authors awaiting a bibliographer.

Important complements are several volumes in the Undergraduate Companion Series:

> Bracken and Larry G. Hinman. *The Undergraduate's Companion to American Writers and Their Web Sites.* Englewood: Libraries Unlimited, 2001. 309 pp.
>
> Dean, Katharine A., Miriam Conteh-Morgan, and Bracken. *The Undergraduate's Companion to Women Writers and Their Web Sites.* Westport: Libraries Unlimited–Greenwood, 2002. 182 pp.
>
> Galbraith, Steven K. *The Undergraduate's Companion to English Renaissance Writers and Their Web Sites.* Westport: Libraries Unlimited–Greenwood, 2004. 144 pp.
>
> Stevens, Jen. *The Undergraduate's Companion to Children's Writers and Their Web Sites.* Westport: Libraries Unlimited–Greenwood, 2004. 154 pp.

These offer trustworthy guidance to good free Web sites for established writers and, in their unannotated lists of bibliographies, occasionally update *Reference Works in British and American Literature.*

See also

Sec. D: Bibliographies of Bibliographies.

Guides to Primary Works

MANUSCRIPTS

M1365   *Index of English Literary Manuscripts.* Ed. P. J. Croft, Theodore Hofmann, and John Horden. 5 vols. London: Mansell; New York: Bowker, 1980– . Z6611.L7 I5 [PR83]   016.82908.

> Vol. 1: *1450–1625.* Comp. Peter Beal. 2 pts. 1980. (M1985).
> Vol. 2: *1625–1700.* Comp. Beal. 2 pts. 1987–93. (M1985).
> Vol. 3: *1700–1800.* Comp. Margaret M. Smith and Alexander Lindsay. 1986–97. (M2225).

Vol. 4: *1800–1900.* Comp. Barbara Rosenbaum and Pamela White. 1982– . (M2465).

Vol. 5: *Indexes of Titles, First Lines, Names, Repositories.* In progress.

A descriptive catalog of extant literary manuscripts by about 300 British and Irish writers who flourished between 1450 and 1900. The authors included are essentially those listed in *Concise Cambridge Bibliography of English Literature, 600–1950,* ed. George Watson, 2nd ed. (Cambridge: Cambridge UP, 1965, 270 pp.). The emphasis is on *literary* manuscripts, including an author's typescripts, corrected proof sheets, diaries, notebooks, and marginalia in printed books, but excluding letters; scribal copies to c. 1700 are also included. The individual volumes are organized alphabetically by author, with entries listed as the nature of the surviving manuscripts and canon demands. An introduction to each author describes the manuscripts generally, summarizes scholarship, alerts researchers to special problems, comments on nonliterary papers, discusses canon, and concludes with an outline of the arrangement of entries. A typical entry provides a physical description, dates composition of the manuscript, lists editions and facsimiles, notes provenance, cites relevant scholarship, and identifies location (with shelf mark). Additions and corrections will be printed in vol. 5. Since some entries are based on inquiries to libraries and collectors, on bibliographies and other reference works, and on booksellers' and auction catalogs, rather than on personal examination by a compiler, the descriptions vary in fullness and accuracy. Terminology and format also vary somewhat from volume to volume. Although there are inevitable errors and omissions, and although the scope is unduly restricted by reliance on the *Concise Cambridge Bibliography,* the *Index* has brought to light a number of significant unrecorded manuscripts and is an essential, if limited, source for the identification and location of manuscripts. It must, however, be supplemented by the works listed in section F: Guides to Manuscripts and Archives.

M1375   Mullins, E. L. C. *Texts and Calendars: An Analytical Guide to Serial Publications.* Rpt. with corrections. Royal Historical Society Guides and Handbooks 7. London: Royal Historical Soc., 1978. 674 pp. *Texts and Calendars II: An Analytical Guide to Serial Publications, 1957–1982.* Royal Historical Society Guides and Handbooks 12. 1983. 323 pp.   Z2016.M82 [DA30]   016.941.

Mortimer, Ian, ed. *Texts and Calendars since 1982: A Survey.* Historical Manuscripts Commission. Online. No longer available (see below).

An annotated guide to the contents of serial publications issued by government bodies or learned societies since the eighteenth century and devoted to printing texts or calendars of records and documents important to the history of England and Wales. In the print volumes, serials are grouped by issuing body in four divisions: official bodies (including the Public Record Office and Royal Commission on Historical Manuscripts, which merged to form the National Archives [F285]), national societies (e.g., Hakluyt Society), English local societies (including records, antiquarian, historical, and archaeological societies), and Welsh societies. Vol. 2 adds a division for series begun after 1957. The citation to each publication is accompanied by a full description of contents and, in vol. 2, a summary of prefatory matter. Corrections to the corrected reprint appear in vol. 2, pp. 317–20. Indexed in each volume by persons, places, subjects, and types of documents. *Texts and Calendars since 1982* (which does not cover local-history societies and which was to serve as the basis for an eventual *Texts and Calendars III* is no longer online; data from it will be incorporated into the *Royal Historical Society Bibliography* [M1400]) listed issuing bodies alphabetically and offered only the occasional sparse comment on the contents of publications. Besides being the only source that indexes many of these volumes, *Texts and Calendars* offers an invaluable conspectus of the numerous publications of the Public Record Office (in the print volumes) and Royal Commission on Historical Manuscripts.

See also

Sec. F: Guides to Manuscripts and Archives.
Storey, *Primary Sources for Victorian Studies* (M2450).

PRINTED WORKS

M1376   *The Cambridge Bibliography of English Literature* (*CBEL*). 3rd ed. 6 vols.
Cambridge: Cambridge UP, 1999– .   Z2001.N45 [PR83]   016.82.

Vol. 1: *600–1500.* Ed. Peter Brown.
Vol. 2: *1500–1700.* Ed. Douglas Sedge.
Vol. 3: *1700–1800.* Ed. Shef Rogers. <http://www.otago.ac.nz/english/ cbel>.
Vol. 4: *1800–1900.* Ed. Joanne Shattock. 1999. 2,995 cols. (M2467).
Vol. 5: *1900–2000.*
Vol. 6: *Index.*

More a reconceptualization than a revision of *NCBEL* (M1385), *CBEL* now focuses on primary works, textual and bibliographical studies, biographies, the initial reception of an author's works, and critical studies before 1920. Although it is intended as "a definitive primary bibliography," thoroughness of coverage varies widely; only extended use will reveal how adequate an individual part is.

Entries are organized into major divisions, with each extensively subdivided and classified as its subject and period require; volumes typically include divisions for book production and distribution, literary relations with the Continent, poetry, novel, drama, prose, history, political economy, philosophy and science, religion, travel, household books, sport, education, and newspapers and magazines. The genre divisions are no longer separated into major and minor writers, and Scottish, Irish, and Welsh literatures in English are integrated into the divisions instead of having ones of their own.

The main entry for an author who writes in several genres or on a variety of subjects is located under the genre or subject with which he or she is most closely associated; briefer entries appear under other genres or subjects, with a cross-reference to the main one. A full author entry consists of two parts: primary works (with sections, as needed, for manuscripts; bibliographies and reference works; collected editions; selective editions; individual works [listed chronologically by date of first publication, with each followed by significant English-language editions, translations, and contemporary reviews]; contributions to periodicals and collaborative works; published letters, journals, diaries, notebooks, and marginalia; translations, editions, introductions, and prefaces; pseudonymous works; attributed or spurious works; imitations or -ana); and secondary works (a selective list of studies published before 1920 — though, in fact, many entries cite later scholarship and criticism), including textual studies and selected biographies. Within each section, works are listed by date of publication; mercifully, *CBEL* discontinues *NCBEL*'s vexing practice of interrupting the chronological sequence to group all studies by a scholar under the year of the first one cited. As in *NCBEL*, scholars are identified by surname and initial(s), titles are sometimes shortened, and page numbers are not given for essays in periodicals—all of which deter users from actually laying hands on works cited. Individual volumes are provisionally indexed by writers and a few subdivision headings; fuller indexing will be offered by vol. 6. Predictably, entries for authors and subjects vary in their thoroughness, consistency, accuracy, and currency, but if vol. 4 is representative, *CBEL* will add coverage of hundreds of writers and broaden the notion of "literature." For many authors and subjects, it will offer the fullest information available on primary works, but the general exclusion of post-1920 secondary works (based on the unfounded assumption that such studies are adequately covered and easily identified in *MLAIB* [G335] and *ABELL* [G340]) means that *CBEL*—unlike *NCBEL*—is no longer one of the principal starting points for research.

M1377   *English Short Title Catalogue (ESTC; EngSTC)*; formerly *The Eighteenth-Century Short-Title Catalogue.* London: British Lib.; Riverside: U of California. Online. 11 Dec. 2006 <http://estc.bl.uk/F/?func=file&file_name=login-bl-list>. Updated daily. <http://estc.ucr.edu>; <http://www.bl.uk/collections/early/estc1.html>. (The *ESTC* database available through RLG Union Catalog [E230] is outdated and does not transfer to FirstSearch [E225a]).

A bibliographic database and union list of editions; issues; impressions; and variant states of books, serials, pamphlets, bookplates, and single sheets printed in any language in the British Isles, North America, and British territories and printed in English throughout the rest of the world between c. 1473 and 1800. Excludes engraved single sheets without letterpress (unless the text is significant), forms intended to be completed in manuscript, trade cards, tickets, playbills, concert and theater programs, playing cards, maps, and games. The database includes records of the North American Imprints Program (Q4010) as well as expanded, edited *RSTC* (M1990) and Wing (M1995) entries.

A typical record includes author; title; edition; imprint; pagination; illustrations; format; notes on authorship, language, type of work, and content (if not clear from the title) and bibliographical and publication details; references to other bibliographies; identification of microform copies; and locations (with call number or shelf mark and notes on provenance or imperfections); many records also include a subject field. The amount of detail and degree of bibliographical sophistication vary; many records taken over from *RSTC* and Wing are placeholders that will eventually be expanded. Users should be aware that information included in entries is frequently not precise enough to identify reprints and variant issues, that imprints for eighteenth-century publications are not fully recorded, and that the list of locations of copies is frequently seriously incomplete. For an informative analysis of the errors and omissions in records for eighteenth-century publications, see James E. May, "Who Will Edit the ESTC? (and Have You Checked OCLC Lately?)," *Analytical and Enumerative Bibliography* ns 12 (2001): 288–304. For a convenient summary of cataloging practices, see R. C. Alston, *The First Phase: An Introduction to the Catalogue of the British Library Collections for* ESTC, Occasional Paper 4, *Factotum: Newsletter of the XVIIIth Century STC* (London: British Lib., 1983, 29 pp.); fuller details are provided in J. C. Zeeman, *The Eighteenth Century Short Title Catalogue: The Cataloguing Rules*, 1991 ed. (London: British Lib., 1991, 140 pp.).

Basic Search allows users to search by keyword, author, title, place of publication, publisher, date, subject (i.e., Library of Congress subject heading), shelf mark, library, or *ESTC* number. Advanced Search allows users to combine the preceding fields with ones for language, genre, notes, and format and to restrict searches by language, date, format, and country of publication. Users can also browse lists of authors, titles, places of publication, subjects, genres, bibliographical citations (such as *RSTC* or Wing), shelf marks, and libraries. Results, which are listed in ascending order by author then by date of publication, can be sorted by title or date and can be marked for e-mailing, printing, downloading, or moving to a personal folder at the site. (If a search returns more than 1,000 records, they will appear in *ESTC* number order and cannot be re-sorted.) Searchers should consult the most recent help screen for search instructions. The guides published by *ESTC*—M. J. Crump, *Searching* ESTC *on Blaise-Line: A Brief Guide*, Occasional Paper 6, *Factotum: Newsletter of the XVIIIth Century STC* ([London: British Lib., 1989,] 37 pp.); and John Bloomberg-Rissman, *Searching* ESTC *on RLIN*, Occasional Paper 7, *Factotum: Newsletter of the English STC, Incorporating the XVIIIth Century STC* (1996, 22 pp.; also available at the project's Web site [http://estc.ucr.edu/factotum.html]); and *Searching the* ESTC (http://estc.ucr.edu/estcsrch.html)—are obsolete.

A portion of the database was published as *The Eighteenth Century Short Title Catalogue 1990* (*ESTC 1990*) (London: British Lib., 1990, microfiche), an author-title list of about 284,000 entries from the database, with indexes for date and place of publication and five types of publications (advertisements, almanacs, directories, prospectuses, and single-sheet verse); the 2003 CD-ROM has about 465,000 records. On the vagaries of the search interface for the 2003 CD-ROM, see the review by E. Thomson Shields, Jr., *Early Modern Literary Studies* 10.3 (M2005): 9 pars. 10 Apr. 2005 <http://purl.oclc.org/emls/10-3/revshiel.html>.

Factotum: Newsletter of the English STC, Incorporating the XVIIIth Century STC (1978–c. 1996) carried progress reports as well as notes derived from research in *ESTC* records. (From 1978 to 1980, *ESTC Facsimile: The Newsletter of the Eighteenth-Century Short Title Catalogue in America* recorded the progress of the North American group.) For a history of the project and examples of research based on *ESTC*, see M. Crump and M. Harris, eds., *Searching the Eighteenth Century: Papers Presented at the Symposium on the* Eighteenth Century Short Title Catalogue *in July 1982* (London: British Lib. in association with Dept. of Extra-mural Studies, U of London, 1983, 104 pp.) and Henry L. Snyder and Michael S. Smith, eds., The English Short-Title Catalogue: *Past, Present, Future* (New York: AMS, 2003, 290 pp.). R. C. Alston also recounts the history of the project in "The History of *ESTC*," *Age of Johnson* 15 (2004): 269–329.

The *ESTC* is the most sophisticated and accessible of the short-title catalogs, and supplants—but does not supersede—*RSTC* and Wing. Since the database can be searched in a variety of ways and is continually updated to reflect corrections and additions, it is an important source for identifying extant works by an author, about a topic, or published within a time period and for locating copies. A major international cooperative project that has already unearthed a number of unknown works and unrecorded editions, the *ESTC* is effecting a revolution in all areas of pre-nineteenth-century studies, and it has precipitated similar projects such as the *ISTC* (M1820a). Users must, however, be aware that the disparate nature of the records brought together in this database means that there are substantial inconsistencies and hundreds of errors (for which, see the exchange of letters between Peter W. M. Blayney, and Henry L. Snyder and M. J. Crump in *Library* 7th ser. 1 [2000]: 72–78). For important strictures on using *ESTC* records for 1475–1700, see William Proctor Williams and William Baker, "*Caveat Lector*, English Books 1475–1700 and the Electronic Age," *Analytical and Enumerative Bibliography* ns 12 (2001):1–29.

M1380   Records of the Worshipful Company of Stationers and Newspaper Makers. Stationers' Hall, London EC4M 7DD. <http://www.stationers.org/>.

The records, which date from 1554, are in three main groups: the court books (valuable for biographical research on printers and publishers and essential sources for publishing history); miscellaneous documents; and—of primary interest to literary researchers—the registers of printed books, usually called the Stationers' Register (SR). The registers are virtually complete for 1554–1911, when compulsory registration halted. For 1554–1708, the registers consist of works entered for ownership by a member of the company; for 1710–1911, of works entered for copyright. The so-called voluntary register (1920–2000) is not available to researchers. Arranged chronologically, the registers identify the member claiming ownership or copyright, title (frequently descriptive in the early registers), author (but infrequently in the early years), and registration fee.

The registers for 1554–1842 and other records of the company are available to researchers at Stationers' Hall (by appointment only); the registers for 1842–1911 are held by the National Archives (F285). In addition, many records can be consulted in microfilm (Robin Myers, ed., *Records of the Stationers' Company, 1554–1920* [Cambridge: Chadwyck-Healey, 1987]) or in various published transcripts:

> 1554–1640: *Transcript of the Registers of the Company of Stationers* (M2000).
>
> 1640–1708: *Transcript of the Registers of the Worshipful Company of Stationers* (M2005).
>
> (David Foxon has unfortunately had to abandon his transcript of the registers for the period 1710–46.)
>
> The court books of the company have been indexed in Alison Shell and Alison Emblow, *Index to the Court Books of the Stationers' Company, 1679–1717* (London: Bibliog. Soc., 2007), 433 pp.

Review: (microfilm) Michael Robertson, *Microform Review* 20 (1991): 85–88.

Since the records are the property of the company, scholars should seek permission to cite them in books and articles.

Essential reading for those consulting the records is Robin Myers, *The Stationers' Company Archive: An Account of the Records, 1554–1984* (Winchester: St. Paul's Bibliographies; Detroit: Omnigraphics, 1990, 376 pp.), which offers a brief history of the archives, an essential glossary, an analytical catalog of records in the muniment room (together with references to editions, indexes, and published commentary), and registers of documents (together with a name index). For a history of the company, see Cyprian Blagden, *The Stationers' Company: A History, 1403–1959* (Cambridge: Harvard UP, 1960, 321 pp.), portions of which are superseded by *The Stationers' Company: A History of the Later Years, 1800–2000*, ed. Robin Myers (London: Worshipful Company of Stationers and Newspaper Makers, 2001, 265 pp.) and Peter W. M. Blayney, *The Stationers' Company before the Charter, 1403–1557* (London: Worshipful Company of Stationers and Newspapermakers [sic], 2003, 62 pp.).

Researchers must remember that the registers are records of ownership or copyright by members of the company and thus do not include everything actually printed or published in England, and that many works entered were never published or appeared under a different title. See entry M2000 for a further discussion of problems in the use of the early registers. The records—many of which await adequate exploration—are essential sources for identifying lost works, aiding in dating composition or publication, and researching all aspects of printing or publishing history.

See also

> Sec. U: Literature-Related Topics and Sources/Anonymous and Pseudonymous Works/Dictionaries.

Guides to Scholarship and Criticism

SURVEYS OF RESEARCH

M1383   Greenblatt, Stephen, and Giles Gunn, eds. *Redrawing the Boundaries: The Transformation of English and American Literary Studies.* New York: MLA, 1992. 595 pp.   PR21.R43   820.9'0001.

A collection of surveys of conceptual, methodological, and theoretical shifts since the 1960s in literary studies. Essays—which typically examine significant developments in the field, comment on major studies, and conclude with a selective annotated bibliography—cover historical periods in English and American literature; composition studies; and feminist, gender, African American, Marxist, psychoanalytic, deconstruction, new historicist, cultural, and postcolonial criticism (but not textual criticism). The omission of a subject index is inexplicable in a volume devoted to shifts and interdisciplinarity in literary studies; limiting the index to persons makes it impossible to use the collection to trace across periods or critical schools the effects of a methodology, concept, approach, ideology, or critical school. Despite this drawback, the volume does offer a convenient overview of the evolution of literary studies from the 1960s to the early 1990s.

OTHER BIBLIOGRAPHIES

M1385   *The New Cambridge Bibliography of English Literature* (*NCBEL*). Ed. George Watson and I. R. Willison. 5 vols. Cambridge: Cambridge UP, 1969–77. Z2011.N45 [PR83]   016.82.
  Vol. 1: *600–1660.* Ed. Watson. 1974. 2,476 cols. (M1675, M1840, and M2035).
  Vol. 2: *1660–1800.* Ed. Watson. 1971. 2,082 cols. (M2255).
  Vol. 3: *1800–1900.* Ed. Watson. 1969. 1,948 cols. (M2505).
  Vol. 4: *1900–1950.* Ed. Willison. 1972. 1,408 cols. (M2785).
  Vol. 5: *Index.* Comp. J. D. Pickles. 1977. 542 pp.

A selective, but extensive, bibliography of works by and about "literary authors native to or mainly resident in the British Isles" from the Old English period through those established by 1950. Because of the scope, coverage of scholarship is necessarily selective and excludes unpublished dissertations, ephemeral publications, encyclopedia articles, insignificant notes, and superseded studies. Parts of books are omitted from the lists of secondary materials, thus leading researchers to overlook important studies. Otherwise, the thoroughness of coverage and terminal date (from c. 1962 to 1969) vary widely from section to section, with only extended use revealing how adequate an individual part is.

Entries are organized by literary period and then by six major divisions (each extensively subdivided and classified as its subject and the period require): introduction, poetry, novel, drama, prose, and Scottish or Anglo-Irish. For a fuller account of the organization of each period, see entries for the individual volumes.

Listings under individual authors are divided into bibliographies, collections, primary works, and secondary materials. Headnotes sometimes locate manuscripts or unique items. The full entry for an author who writes in several genres appears under the genre with which he or she is most closely associated; briefer entries emphasizing primary works usually appear under other genres or forms. Since these entries are not always cross-referenced, users must check the index volume (vol. 5) to locate all listings for an author. In the various subdivisions and author entries, primary and secondary works are listed chronologically by date of publication. Editions and translations follow, in chronological order, a primary work. When a list of secondary materials includes more than one study by a scholar, the chronological sequence is unnecessarily violated by grouping all the studies under the earliest publication date of those cited. This practice, which requires considerable backtracking in lengthy lists (since scholars are not indexed), is almost universally condemned by reviewers and users.

Scholars are identified by surname and initial(s); titles are short titles, with only the first word capitalized and no designation of a title within a title; bibliographical information is incomplete. Although these conventions save space and create an un-cluttered page, they also frequently prolong searches in library catalogs and volumes of journals.

The index (vol. 5) lists literary authors, major anonymous works, and some head-ings for subdivisions but is insufficiently detailed to provide adequate access to the wealth of information in vols. 1–4. To be certain of locating all sections on an author, form, or genre, users must consult vol. 5 rather than the provisional index in each volume. Entrants are also indexed in *Biography and Genealogy Master Index* (J565).

Although the *NCBEL* is a revision of *The Cambridge Bibliography of English Lit-erature (CBEL)*, ed. F. W. Bateson, 4 vols. (Cambridge: Cambridge UP, 1940), and *Supplement*, ed. George Watson (1957), the *CBEL* is still occasionally useful for its sections on political and social background and Commonwealth literature dropped from the *NCBEL*. See the entries on individual volumes for details of differences in coverage. For a discussion of the significance and history of *CBEL* and *NCBEL*, see George Watson, *CBEL: The Making of the Cambridge Bibliography* (Los Angeles: School of Lib. Service, U of California, 1965, 13 pp.).

Although its coverage of primary works is being superseded by *CBEL* (M1376), *NCBEL*, despite its unevenness, errors, inconsistencies, and deficiencies in organization, remains frequently the best starting point for research, especially for authors, forms, genres, and subjects that are not themselves subjects of bibliographies.

Reviews: (vol. 1) Fred C. Robinson, *Anglia* 97 (1979): 511–17; (vol. 2) *TLS: Times Literary Supplement* 15 Oct. 1971: 1296; Eric Rothstein, *Modern Philology* 71 (1973): 176–86; (vol. 3) Richard D. Altick, *JEGP: Journal of English and Germanic Philology* 70 (1971): 139–45; (vol. 4) *TLS: Times Literary Supplement* 29 Dec. 1972: 1582; T. A. Birrell, *Neophilologus* 59 (1975): 306–15.

Addressed to the student and general reader, *The Shorter New Cambridge Bibli-ography of English Literature*, ed. George Watson (Cambridge: Cambridge UP, 1981, 1,612 cols.), emphasizes the traditional canon of English literature by reprinting, with few changes, the sections on primary works by major authors and several minor ones, listing only a very few basic studies about each author, and completely cutting or severely trimming other sections. Although the *Shorter NCBEL* includes a few additions and corrections, it is, as Peter Davison points out in his review, "an unimaginative scissors-and-paste job which shows little thought for the needs of" its intended audience (*Library* 6th ser. 4 [1982]: 188–89).

M1390   Baer, Florence E. *Folklore and Literature of the British Isles: An Annotated Bibliography.* Garland Reference Library of the Humanities 622: Garland Folklore Bibliographies 11. New York: Garland, 1986. 355 pp. Z2014.F6 B34 [PR149.F64]   016.82′09.

A bibliography of studies that discuss folklore elements in literary works written in English in the British Isles. Baer includes scholarly and popular studies (all but a few in English and published between 1890 and 1980) as well as dissertations after 1950 but excludes most of the standard reference works. Listed alphabetically by scholar, the 1,039 entries are accompanied by descriptive annotations offering clear, informative summaries that isolate significant elements of a study; cite tale-types, motifs, or Child numbers for ballads; provide appropriate cross-references; and sometimes include an astute evaluation. Because of the organization, users must approach the contents through the detailed general index, which covers literary and folklore genres, literary authors, titles, subjects, theoretical approaches, and theorists. Three additional indexes cover tale-types, folklore motifs, and Child ballad numbers. Although the work is not comprehensive, the careful annotations and thorough indexing make it a valuable, time-saving source for identifying studies of the folklore content and relationships of British literature. Until *MLAIB* for 1981 (G335), such studies are not easily identified in the standard serial bibliographies and indexes in section G.

See also

> Secs. G: Serial Bibliographies, Indexes, and Abstracts and U: Literature-Related Topics and Sources/Folklore and Literature/Guides to Scholarship and Criticism.
> *ABELL* (G340): English Literature division.
> Bailey, *English Stylistics* (U6080).
> Hayes, *Sources for the History of Irish Civilisation* (N2980).
> Horner, *Historical Rhetoric* (U5600).
> Horner, *Present State of Scholarship in Historical and Contemporary Rhetoric* (U5565).
> Kallendorf, *Latin Influences on English Literature from the Middle Ages to the Eighteenth Century* (S4895).
> Kirby, *America's Hive of Honey* (Q4190).
> *MLAIB* (G335): English Language and Literature (or English Literature) division through the volume for 1980; the Literatures of the British Isles/General and English Literature sections in the volumes for 1981–90; the British and Irish Literatures/General and English sections in the volumes for 1991–present. Researchers must also check the "English Literature" and "British and Irish Literatures" headings in the subject index to post-1980 volumes and in the online thesaurus.
> Ross, *Film as Literature, Literature as Film* (U5800).
> Schwartz, *Articles on Women Writers* (U6605).
> *YWES* (G330) has a chapter on general literary history and criticism.

DISSERTATIONS AND THESES

M1395   Howard, Patsy C., comp. *Theses in English Literature, 1894–1970.* Ann Arbor: Pierian, 1973. 387 pp.   Z2011.H63 [PR83]   016.82.
      A list of baccalaureate and master's theses accepted by American and some foreign institutions. Includes a limited number of institutions (whether completely is unclear) and apparently only theses on an identifiable author. Entries are organized alphabetically

under literary authors. Cross-references identify studies of multiple authors. Two indexes: subject (inadequate); thesis author. Although marred by an insufficient explanation of scope and coverage, *Theses in English Literature* will save some hunting through elusive institutional lists. A companion volume is devoted to *Theses in American Literature* (Q3315).

See also

Sec. H: Guides to Dissertations and Theses.

RELATED TOPICS

M1400   *The Royal Historical Society Bibliography: A Guide to Writing about British
        and Irish History.* Royal Historical Society. Online. 6 Dec. 2005 <http://
        www.rhs.ac.uk:80/bibwel.html>. Updated three times a year.
   A bibliographic database of historical writings about the British Isles, (including their relations with the British Empire and Commonwealth) from 55 BC to the present. Coverage is more complete for publications after 1900 than before. The database incorporates and supersedes the following:

> *Annual Bibliography of British and Irish History: Publications of [1975–2002].*
> Oxford: Oxford UP, 1976–2003. Annual.Coverage is highly selective,
> with many entries taken at second hand.
> *Writings on British History, [1946–74]: A Bibliography of Books and Articles
> on the History of Great Britain from about 450 A. D. to 1939.* 12 vols.
> London: Institute of Historical Research, U of London, 1973–86.
> *Writings on British History, [1934–45]: A Bibliography of Books and Articles
> on the History of Great Britain from about 450 A. D. to 1914, Published
> during the Year [1934–45], with an Appendix Containing a Select List of
> Publications . . . on British History since 1914.* Comp. Alexander Taylor
> Milne. 8 vols. London: Cape, 1937–60.
> *Writings on British History, 1901–1933: A Bibliography of Books and Articles
> on the History of Great Britain from about 400 A. D. to 1914, Published
> during the Years 1901–1933 Inclusive, with an Appendix Containing a
> Select List of Publications in These Years on British History since 1914.* 5
> vols. London: Cape, 1968–70. An important complementary work is
> E. L. C. Mullins, comp., *A Guide to the Historical and Archaeological
> Publications of Societies in England and Wales, 1901–1933* (London: Athlone, 1968, 850 pp.).
> *Royal Historical Society Bibliography on CD-ROM.* Oxford: Oxford UP, 1998.
> Covers 1901–1992.

Entries can be searched by author, title keyword, journal, date, keyword, and subject classification; these fields can also be combined on a Search Builder screen. Although the search interface has improved substantially since the initial version, there is still no provision for exporting records and printing must be done through a browser's print function. *Royal Historical Society Bibliography* offers the most current list of publications on British history and is useful for literature researchers because of its inclusion of several literary studies from periodicals not covered by the standard bibliographies and indexes in section G.

Language

GUIDES TO PRIMARY WORKS

M1405   Alston, R. C., comp. *A Bibliography of the English Language from the Invention of Printing to the Year 1800: A Systematic Record of Writings on English, and on Other Languages in English, Based on the Collections of the Principal Libraries of the World.* 20 vols. N.p.: Privately printed, 1965– . Z2015.A1 A4.

> Vol. 1: *English Grammars Written in English and English Grammars Written in Latin by Native Speakers.* 1965. 119 pp.
>
> Vol. 2: *Polyglot Dictionaries and Grammars; Treatises on English Written for Speakers of French, German, Dutch, Danish, Swedish, Portuguese, Spanish, Italian, Hungarian, Persian, Bengali, and Russian.* 1967. 311 pp.
>
> Vol. 3, pt. 1: *Old English, Middle English, Early Modern English: Miscellaneous Works; Vocabulary.* 1970. 205 pp.
>
> Vol. 3, pt. 2: *Punctuation, Concordances, Works on Language in General, Origins of Language, Theory of Grammar.* 1971. 66 pp.
>
> Vol. 4: *Spelling Books.* 1967. 277 pp.
>
> Vol. 5: *The English Dictionary.* 1966. 195 pp.
>
> Vol. 6: *Rhetoric, Style, Elocution, Prosody, Rhyme, Pronunciation, Spelling Reform.* 1969. 202 pp.
>
> Vol. 7: *Logic, Philosophy, Epistemology, Universal Language.* 1967. 115 pp.
>
> Vol. 8: *Treatises on Short-Hand.* 1966. 152 pp.
>
> Vol. 9: *English Dialects, Scottish Dialects, Cant and Vulgar English.* 1971. 178 pp.
>
> Vol. 10: *Education and Language-Teaching.* 1972. 75 pp.
>
> Supplement: *Additions and Corrections, Volume I–X; List of Libraries; Cumulative Indexes.* 1973. 117 pp.
>
> Vol. 11: *Place Names and Personal Names.* 1977. 148 pp.
>
> Vol. 12, pt. 1: *The French Language: Grammars, Miscellaneous Treatises, Dictionaries.* 1985. 208 pp.
>
> Vol. 12, pt. 2: *The Italian, Spanish, Portuguese, and Romansh Languages: Grammars, Dictionaries, Miscellaneous Treatises.* 1987. 55 pp.
>
> Vol. 13: *The Germanic Languages.* 1999. 208 pp.
>
> Vol. 14: *The British Isles; Hebrew; Eastern Europe; Africa; South Asia; Australasia; The Americas; Pacific Islands.* 2000. 561 pp.
>
> Vol. 15: *Greek; Latin to 1500.* 2001. 454 pp.
>
> Vol. 16: *Latin 1651–1800.* 2 vols. 2002.
>
> Vol. 17: *Botany, Horticulture, Agriculture.* 2 vols. 2003.
>
> Vol. 18, pt. 1: *Zoology, Geology, Chemistry, Medicine, Veterinary Medicine, Mathematics, Astronomy, Miscellaneous.* 2 vols. 2004.
>
> Vol. 18, pt. 2: *Law, Art, Architecture, Building, Heraldry.* 2 vols. 2004.
>
> Vol. 18, pt. 3: *Military and Naval Arts and Sciences.* 2 vols. 2005.
>
> Vol. 18, pt. 4: *Commerce, Classics, Cookery, Technology, Religion, Recreation, Music.* In progress.
>
> Vol. 19: *Periodical Literature; Essays.* In progress.
>
> Vol. 20: *Material in Manuscript.* In progress.
>
> Vol. 21: *Addenda, Corrigenda.* In progress.
>
> Vol. 22: *Indexes.* In progress.

(The compiler's annotated copies of vols. 1–10 were reprinted, without the facsimiles, in a single volume [Ilkley: Janus, 1974]. The corrections and additions are incorporated into the printed supplement to the first ten volumes.)

A massive bibliography of English-language works through 1800 related to the history of the English language. Works are organized by publication date within various subject classifications; subsequent editions follow, in chronological order, the first. A typical entry provides author, short title, publication information, format, pagination, citations to standard bibliographies, locations, references to important scholarship and contemporary reviews, and occasional notes on content. Most volumes print several facsimiles of title pages and other printed material. Each volume has up to four indexes: titles; authors; subjects and other persons; places (however, indexing is less thorough in recent volumes). Based on research in an extensive number of libraries, Alston is an indispensable guide to the identification and location of works essential for the study of the early history of the English language. Review: (rpt. of vols. 1–10) *TLS: Times Literary Supplement* 8 Nov. 1974: 1267.

When complete, Alston will supersede (for publications before 1800) Arthur G. Kennedy, *A Bibliography of Writings on the English Language from the Beginning of Printing to the End of 1922* (Cambridge: Harvard UP; New Haven: Yale UP, 1927, 517 pp.). For extensive additions and corrections to Kennedy, see the following reviews: Arvid Gabrielson, "Professor Kennedy's *Bibliography of Writings on the English Language:* A Review with a List of Additions and Corrections," *Studia Neophilologica* 2 (1929): 117–68; Rudolph Brotanek, "Englische Sprachbücher aus frühneuenglischer Zeit," *Zeitschrift für Anglistik und Amerikanistik* 4 (1956): 5–18; and Hermann M. Flasdieck, *Anglia Beiblatt* 39 (1928): 166–74.

GUIDES TO SCHOLARSHIP

See

> Sec. U: Literature-Related Topics and Sources/Linguistics and Literature/General Linguistics/Guides to Scholarship.
>
> *ABELL* (G340): English Language division.
>
> *MLAIB* (G335): English Language and Literature division in the volumes for 1922–25; English Language and Literature I/Linguistics in the volumes for 1926–66; Indo-European C/Germanic Linguistics IV/English in those for 1967–80; and Indo-European Languages/Germanic Languages/West Germanic Languages/English Language in later volumes. Researchers must also check "British English Dialect" in the subject index to post-1980 volumes and in the online thesaurus.

DICTIONARIES

M1410   *Oxford English Dictionary Online.* Oxford UP. Online. 4 Dec. 2005
        <http://www.oed.com>. Updated quarterly.

        Oxford English Dictionary (OED). 2nd ed. Ed. J. A. Simpson and E. S. C. Weiner. 20 vols. Oxford: Clarendon–Oxford UP, 1989. CD-ROM. *The Compact Oxford English Dictionary.* New ed. Ed. Simpson and Weiner. New York: Oxford UP, 1991. (A micrographic reprint of the second edition.)

(A third edition is in progress; a draft of the preface is at the *OED* Web site.)   PE1625.O87   423.

Oxford English Dictionary Additions. Ed. John Simpson and Edmund Weiner. Oxford: Clarendon–Oxford UP, 1993– .

An integrated expansion of:

> *The Oxford English Dictionary (OED).* Ed. James A. H. Murray et al. 12 vols. and supplement. Oxford: Clarendon–Oxford UP, 1933. (A corrected reissue of *A New English Dictionary on Historical Principles* [*NED*], originally published in 125 fascicles between 1884 and 1928.) CD-ROM.
> *A Supplement to the Oxford English Dictionary.* Ed. R. W. Burchfield. 4 vols. Oxford: Clarendon–Oxford UP, 1972–86.
> *The New Shorter Oxford English Dictionary on Historical Principles.* Ed. Lesley Brown. 2 vols. Oxford: Clarendon–Oxford UP, 1993. CD-ROM.

A historical dictionary that attempts to record all English words (including obsolete ones, dialect terms before 1500, and archaisms, as well as a considerable number of scientific, technical, and slang terms) used since c. 1150. Words obsolete by 1150 and dialect terms new after 1500 are excluded. Although the *OED* emphasizes standard British usage and vocabulary, it admits meanings and senses used in English worldwide (especially for words added in the *Supplement* and second edition). The entries for more than 500,000 words are based on several million excerpts from written works (a majority of which are belles lettres).

The best access to the *OED* is offered by *OED Online*, which allows parallel searching of the text of the second edition and the database containing additions and revisions for the third edition; searches display earlier versions of revised entries. The online version can be searched (in the Advanced Search screen) by any combination of headword, definition, etymology, part of speech, date, author, source, and text of quotations. Entries consist of two parts: the headword section (which includes status [e.g., obsolete], pronunciation, variant spellings, etymology, and label indicating context in which the word is used); the sense section (which includes definitions that list quotations in which the word appears, compound forms, and derivatives). To search the *OED Online* efficiently and thoroughly, users must read the Help with Using *OED Online* page.

For an overview of the principles guiding the revision of the etymology and other linguistic elements appearing in brackets at the beginning of an entry, see Philip N. R. Durkin, "Root and Branch: Revising the Etymological Component of the *Oxford English Dictionary*," *Transactions of the Philological Society* 97 (1999): 1–49; for a critique of the plan to rely on *MED* (M1860) and *DOST* (O3090a) for Middle English etymologies, see William Rothwell, "*OED, MED, AND*: The Making of a New Dictionary of English," *Anglia* 119 (2001): 527–53. For examples of the kind of revision being undertaken in the third edition, see John Simpson, Edmund Weiner, and P. Durkin, "The *Oxford English Dictionary* Today," *Transactions of the Philological Society* 102 (2004): 335–91.

In the printed *OED* there are three classifications of headwords: main words (all single words, whether radical or derivative, as well as compounds requiring separate treatment), subordinate words (mostly obsolete and variant forms, irregular inflections, or alleged words), and combined forms. Entries for subordinate words and combinations typically refer users to related main words for fuller information. A typical entry for a main word consists of four parts: (1) identification, with the headword appearing in its current or most usual spelling, pronunciation, part of speech, any specification of vocation, status, earlier spellings (with indication of chronological range), and inflected forms; (2) morphology, with etymology, history of the form, and notes on the history of the word; (3) signification, with senses organized from the earliest to most recent; (4) dated illustrative quotations listed chronologically (averaging one per century for words in the first edition and one per decade for those added in the *Supplement* or later). Each grammatical form of a main word is accorded a separate entry. New entries (including headwords as well as new senses and collocations) are also recorded in *Oxford English Dictionary Additions*, each volume of which prints words from throughout the alphabet. Cumulatively indexed beginning with vol. 2.

The 1933 corrected reissue adds a supplement that records new words and senses, corrections, and spurious words and lists the sources of illustrative quotations. Except for the list of sources, the 1933 supplement is superseded by the four-volume *Supplement*, which records new words or senses since 1884–1928 to 1965–85 (depending on when the part of the alphabet was sent to the printer), includes several words (especially "taboo" terms) and senses omitted from or overlooked in the original volumes and offers more substantial coverage of colloquialisms and English outside the British Isles. The necessity of having the original volumes in hand for effective use of the *Supplement* is remedied by the second edition, which integrates (but does not correct or revise) the original volumes and *Supplement*, adds 5,000 new words or senses, and converts Murray's phonetic system to the International Phonetic Alphabet. (For an explanation of the phonetic theory behind and practice in the original edition and *Supplement*, see M. K. C. MacMahon, "James Murray and the Phonetic Notation in the *New English Dictionary*," *Transactions of the Philological Society* [1985]: 72–112.)

To make effective use of the *OED* users must study the introductory explanation (in the 1933 reissue, *Supplement*, second edition, and *OED Online*) of principles of compilation and editorial practices and must keep in mind the following points:

1. The *OED* is not exhaustive in its coverage of standard vocabulary and is limited in its treatment of slang, dialect, scientific, and technical terms. Thus, it must be supplemented by more specialized dictionaries such as Eric Partridge, *A Dictionary of Slang and Unconventional English: Colloquialisms and Catch-Phrases, Solecisms and Catachreses, Nicknames and Vulgarisms*, ed. Paul Beale, 8th ed. (New York: Macmillan, 1984, 1,400 pp.; for an important discussion of the strengths and weaknesses of this edition, see the review by Richard A. Spears, *American Speech* 62 [1987]: 361–68); *UrbanDictionary.com* (http://www.urbandictionary.com); *Dictionary of Old English* (M1690); *Middle English Dictionary* (M1860); *Dictionary of the Scots Language* (O3090); *Dictionary of American English* (Q3355); *Dictionary of Americanisms* (Q3360); *Webster's Second* and *Third* (Q3365); *Dictionary of American Regional English* (Q3350); and *English Dialect Dictionary* (M1415). For an important account of the day-to-day editing of the original *OED* (including decisions to drop words and to restrict coverage of scientific terminology), see Lynda Mugglestone, *Lost for Words: The Hidden History of the* Oxford English Dictionary (New Haven: Yale UP, 2005, 273 pp.).

2. Each grammatical form of a main word has a separate entry; thus, explicators in search of a definition must be certain to locate the entry for the grammatical form of the word as it is used in the literary work.

3. Subsequent research has corrected several etymologies; since erroneous ones are not revised in the *Supplement* or second edition, users must consult a good etymological dictionary such as *The Oxford Dictionary of English Etymology*,

ed. C. T. Onions, G. W. S. Friedrichsen, and R. W. Burchfield, rpt. with corrections (Oxford: Clarendon–Oxford UP, 1969, 1,024 pp.). For others, see Anatoly Liberman, "An Annotated Survey of English Etymological Dictionaries and Glossaries," *Dictionaries* 19 (1998): 21–96.

4. Dates of first recorded uses are frequently incorrect (for an important study of the unreliability of first citations, see Jürgen Schäfer, *Documentation in the O. E. D.: Shakespeare and Nashe as Test Cases* [Oxford: Clarendon–Oxford UP, 1980, 176 pp.]).

5. Additions of new words and senses, corrections, and antedatings are regularly published in a variety of journals (especially *Notes and Queries* and *American Speech*; several of these are indexed in Wall, *Words and Phrases Index* [U6025]). More than 5,000 additions, antedatings, and corrections from the period 1475–1640 make up Jürgen Schäfer, *Early Modern English Lexicography*, vol. 2: *Additions and Corrections to the* OED (Oxford: Clarendon–Oxford UP, 1989, 227 pp.). Neither the *Supplement* nor the second edition records antedatings before 1820; the *OED Online* includes numerous antedatings.

For a detailed critique of the unreliability of readers, selection of source material, and editorial processing of data from readers in the first edition and *Supplement* and of the implications of merging first-edition entries unrevised into the second edition, see Charlotte Brewer, "The Second Edition of the *Oxford English Dictionary*," *Review of English Studies* ns 44 (1993): 313–42. Users should also consult John Willinsky, *Empire of Words: The Reign of the* OED (Princeton: Princeton UP, 1994, 258 pp.), which explores the prejudices underlying the compilation and questions the assumptions behind the ongoing revision.

Novices—and those who have never bothered to read the introduction to the *OED*—will benefit from Donna Lee Berg, *A Guide to the* Oxford English Dictionary (Oxford: Oxford UP, 1993, 206 pp.), a remarkably clear guide to the parts and types of entries, with a glossary of terms used in and related to the dictionary.

One of the truly great dictionaries, the *OED* is an indispensable source for the historical study of the English language and for the explication of literary works. Reviews of *Supplement*: (vol. 1) Fred C. Robinson, *Yale Review* 62 (1973): 450–56; Donald B. Sands, *College English* 37 (1976): 710–18; (vol. 2) Robinson, *Yale Review* 67 (1977): 94–99; (vol. 3) Roy Harris, *TLS: Times Literary Supplement* 3 Sept. 1982: 935–36; Thomas M. Paikeday, *American Speech* 60 (1985): 74–79; (vol. 4) Pat Rogers, *TLS: Times Literary Supplement* 9 May 1986: 487–88; Gabriele Stein, *Anglia* 107 (1989): 482–91. Reviews of 2nd ed.: John Algeo, *Transactions of the Philological Society* 88 (1990): 131–50; Geoffrey Hill, *TLS: Times Literary Supplement* 21–27 Apr. 1989: 411–14; E. G. Stanley, *Review of English Studies* ns 41 (1990): 76–88 (with a rejoinder by I. S. Asquith, ns 42 [1991]: 81–82, and a reply by Stanley, 82–83). Reviews of 2nd ed. and CD-ROM: Andreas H. Jucker, *Literary and Linguistic Computing* 9 (1994): 149–54; Edward Mendelson, *Yale Review* 81.4 (1993): 111–23.

An informative and entertaining account of the inception, editing, and publication of *OED* is K. M. Elizabeth Murray, *Caught in the Web of Words: James A. H. Murray and the* Oxford English Dictionary (New Haven: Yale UP, 1977, 386 pp.); an equally entertaining account of one individual's contributions is Simon Winchester, *The Professor and the Madman: A Tale of Murder, Insanity, and the Making of the* Oxford English Dictionary (New York: Harper, 1998, 242 pp.). More scholarly are the essays in Lynda Mugglestone, ed., *Lexicography and the* OED *: Pioneers in the Untrodden Forest* (Oxford: Oxford UP, 2000, 288 pp.), which focus on the first edition.

In addition to those noted above, the following are important complementary works:

> Richard W. Bailey, *Michigan Early Modern English Materials* (Ann Arbor: Xerox U Microfilms, 1975, microfiche) and Bailey, ed., *Early Modern English: Additions and Antedatings to the Record of English Vocabulary 1475–1700* (Hildesheim: Olms, 1978, 367 pp.)—both of which can be searched at http://quod.lib.umich.edu/m/mcmem or http://etext.virginia.edu/memem.query.html. These works are derived from data collected for the *Early Modern English Dictionary, 1475–1700*, the materials for which are being incorporated into the third edition of the *OED*.
>
> *The Barnhart Dictionary Companion* (Q3365a) updates several standard dictionaries, including the *OED*, *Supplement*, and Partridge, *Dictionary of Slang*.
>
> H. W. Fowler, *The New Fowler's Modern English Usage*, rev. 3rd ed., ed. R. W. Burchfield (Oxford: Clarendon–Oxford UP, 1998, 873 pp.; reissued in 2004 with the title *Fowler's Modern English Usage*) offers a fuller guide than the *OED* to usage; the third edition is less prescriptive and idiosyncratic than its predecessors. Reviews: Herbert C. Morton, *American Speech* 73 (1998): 313–25 (an important comparison of Fowler's and Burchfield's editions); L. C. Mugglestone, *Notes and Queries* 44 (1997): 437–43.
>
> Ian Lancashire, ed., *LEME: Lexicons of Early Modern English* (U of Toronto P, online, 26 June 2006 <http://leme.library.utoronto.ca>) allows searches of 156 dictionaries, hard-word glossaries, and similar works from 1480 to 1702.

The best single-volume dictionary of British English is *The Chambers Dictionary* [new ed.] (Edinburgh: Chambers, 2003, 1,825 pp.).

M1415   *The English Dialect Dictionary: Being the Complete Vocabulary of All Dialect Words Still in Use, or Known to Have Been in Use during the Last Two Hundred Years.* Ed. Joseph Wright. 6 vols. London: Frowde; New York: Putnam's, 1898–1905. (Originally issued in parts.)   PE1766.W8.

A dictionary of dialect terms (as distinct from those appearing in "the literary language") and Americanisms used in Great Britain and Ireland. A typical entry consists of headword, geographical area, variant spellings, pronunciation, definitions organized by parts of speech, illustrative dated quotations taken from printed sources and organized by area, and etymology. Vol. 6 includes a supplement (179 pp.), bibliography of sources (59 pp.), and grammar of English dialect (187 pp.). Although incomplete and dated, the work remains the fullest English dialect dictionary and, for literary scholars, an essential source for explicating dialect terms in English literature.

Two essential complements, both based on data collected for the Survey of English Dialects, are:

> Orton, Harold, Stewart Sanderson, and John Widdowson, eds. *The Linguistic Atlas of England.* London: Croom Helm; Atlantic Highlands: Humanities, 1978. N. pag. With maps illustrating the distribution of phonological, morphological, lexical, and syntactic features. Review: K. M. Petyt, *English World-wide* 7 (1986): 287–310.

Viereck, Wolfgang, and Heinrich Ramisch, dialectological eds. *The Computer Developed Linguistic Atlas of England.* 2 vols. Tübingen: Niemeyer, 1991– 97. With maps that illustrate in a more sophisticated fashion the distribution of morphological, lexical, and syntactic features. Unfortunately, the laid-in transparent overlay of localities will likely disappear from most library copies. Review: Ossi Ihalainen and Juhani Klemola, *Neuphilologische Mitteilungen* 94 (1993): 377–81.

THESAURUSES

M1420   *The Historical Thesaurus of English.* Ed. M. L. Samuels et al. London: Oxford UP. In progress.

A historical thesaurus of standard British English words arranged according to sense and with synonymous forms dated and listed in chronological order. The *Historical Thesaurus* differs from Roget and other modern thesauruses by including Old and Middle English as well as obsolete words and senses from Modern English. It will eventually be accessible online and as a CD-ROM; in the interim, a portion has been published and is available as Edmonds, *Thesaurus of Old English* (M1707). For a description of the project and a sample entry, see the project's Web site (http://www.arts.gla.ac.uk/SESLl/EngLang/thesaur/homepage.htm). When published, the *Historical Thesaurus* will be a valuable tool for studying the evolution of meaning of words as well as explicating literary works.

The standard general thesaurus remains *Roget's International Thesaurus*, 5th ed., ed. Robert L. Chapman (New York: Harper, 1992, 1,141 pp.).

Biographical Dictionaries

M1425   *Oxford Dictionary of National Biography in Association with the British Academy: From the Earliest Times to the Year 2000 (ODNB).* Ed. H. G. C. Matthew and Brian Harrison. 60 vols. and *Index of Contributors.* Oxford: Oxford UP, 2004.   DA28.O95   920.041. Online. 7 Jan. 2006 <http://www.oxforddnb.com>. Updated three times a year.

A biographical dictionary of dead individuals of some eminence, celebrity, or notoriety born or resident in the British Isles or the colonies (when under British rule). Of the 54,922 persons in the print edition, 50,113 receive individual entries while the others appear in family entries or in subsidiary notices appended to an individual entry. Included among these are revised or rewritten entries for the 38,607 persons in the *ODNB*'s predecessor, the *Dictionary of National Biography from the Earliest Times to 1900 (DNB)*, ed. Leslie Stephen and Sidney Lee, 22 vols. (London: Oxford UP, 1967– 68; originally published in 63 parts between 1885 and 1900) and its supplements. Many of the new entries are from "fields that were poorly represented in the *DNB*: women; people in business and the world of labour; Britain's Roman rulers . . . ; preindependence Americans; and twentieth-century subjects." The signed entries typically provide standard details of an individual's personal life, relationships, and career, along with an assessment of character, reputation, and importance; when possible, they end with a list of primary and secondary sources, the location of archives (manuscript, sound,

and film) and important papers, an enumeration of likenesses or portraits, and an indication of wealth at death (sometimes with precise amounts from probate records;
sometimes with generalizations, e.g., "died in debtor's prison"); approximately 20 per-
cent include a portrait or likeness. The introduction supplies a full account of the
inception, organization, editorial principles and practices, and production of the work.
For the publishing history of the *DNB* and its relationship to the *ODNB*, see Robert
Faber and B. Harrison, "The *Dictionary of National Biography*: A Publishing History,"
Lives in Print: Biography and the Book Trade from the Middle Ages to the 21st Century,
ed. Robin Myers, Michael Harris, and Giles Mandelbrote, Publishing Pathways (New
Castle: Oak Knoll; London: British Lib., 2000) 171–92.

The online *ODNB*—which incorporates corrections to the print volumes, adds
entries for those who died after 31 December 2000 as well as essays on groups and
includes the original text of rewritten or revised articles—allows users to browse entries
(alphabetically or by date of birth or death, with the option of limiting the results to
males, females, families, or illustrated entries), isolate entries by themes (e.g., Olympic
titleholders, poets laureate, or consorts of monarchs), and search the database through
six screens: Quick Search (persons and keyword or phrase); People (with the ability to
limit a search by combinations of name, field of interest [users should choose the Open
Full List option with its nested lists that offer quite narrow fields, e.g. bibliographer,
duelist, and forger], sex, birth and death dates, places, date, life events, religious affiliation, presence of a likeness, and keyword or phrase); Full Text (with pull-down menus
allowing restriction to specific fields of an entry); Images reproduced in the *ODNB* (by
artist, date, present location, and copyright holder); References (primary and secondary
sources, archives, likenesses [i.e., portraits and pictures cited, but not necessarily reproduced, in *ODNB*], wealth at death); and Contributors. Most search fields support the
* and ? wildcards; no search field allows for Boolean operators. Most search functions
are intuitive, but users wanting to perform sophisticated searches—especially in the
People search screen—will want to study the clear explanations of search protocols in
the Help screen or read Rupert Mann, "Searching the *Oxford Dictionary of National
Biography*" (*Indexer* 25 [2006]: 16–18), an explanation of the metadata that supports
searches. Users must remember (1) to type names in normal order or to insert a comma
between surname and forename(s) or initial(s) and (2) to use the Images screen to locate
portraits and pictures reproduced in the *ODNB* and the References/likenesses box to
search for pictures and portraits cited in the entries. In general, the user interface is well
designed and easily navigated; the database design allows for sophisticated ways of min-
ing the enormous amount of data.

Besides its superior search capabilities, the online *ODNB* offers other advantages
over the print version: it is updated and corrected three times per year (though the lists
of newly added entries are hidden in the Themes screen, with the first alphabetized
under *J* [January 2005: additions to the *Oxford DNB*]), hyperlinks allow for easy nav-
igation between related articles (and within longer ones) and for connections to other
electronic sources that provide additional information on the biographee, and images
are in color.

For an analysis of the place of the *ODNB* in the evolution of collective national
biography, see Keith Thomas, *Changing Conceptions of National Biography:* The Oxford
DNB *in Historical Perspective*, Leslie Stephen Special Lecture (Cambridge: Cambridge
UP, 2005, 56 pp.)

Any biographical dictionary—even one of the magnitude and quality of the
ODNB—is destined to contain factual errors and wrongheaded conclusions and to be
criticized for omitting some while including others, but no other national biography

measures up to this one: it is both a scholar's first resource and a browser's delight. Reviews: Nicolas Barker, *TLS: Times Literary Supplement* 10 Dec. 2004: 5–7; Stefan Collini, *London Review of Books* 20 Jan. 2005: 3+; John Gross, *TLS: Times Literary Supplement* 17 Dec. 2004: 12–13.

With all of the original articles in the *DNB* and its supplements accessible in the online *ODNB*, the earlier print version is largely of historical interest. Anyone consulting it needs to be aware that unflattering details were frequently suppressed in the original dictionary and early supplements; however, recent supplements and the *ODNB* are more candid about the foibles of entrants (e.g, in the *ODNB* one person is described as a "duelist, gambler, and womanizer"; another as a "bibliographer and forger"). For an important discussion of biases, editorial intervention in the original contributions, and unacknowledged revisions made in successive printings, see Laurel Brake, "The *DNB* and the *DNB* 'Walter Pater,' " *Subjugated Knowledges: Journalism, Gender, and Literature in the Nineteenth Century* (New York: New York UP, 1994) 169–87 (a revision of "Problems in Victorian Biography: The *DNB* and the *DNB* 'Walter Pater,' " *Modern Language Review* 70 [1975]: 731–42). For the treatment of women in the *DNB*, see Gillian Fenwick, *Women and the* Dictionary of National Biography *: A Guide to* DNB *Volumes 1885–1985 and* Missing Persons (Aldershot: Scolar, 1994, 181 pp.).

Among major dictionaries that cover a more restricted period but incorporate additional lives, the most important are the following:

> Baylen, Joseph O., and Norbert J. Gossman, eds. *Biographical Dictionary of Modern British Radicals [1770–1914].* 3 vols. Hemel Hempstead: Harvester, 1979–88. Vol. 1 covers 1770–1830; vol. 2, 1830–70; and vol. 3, 1870–1914.
>
> Boase, Frederic. *Modern English Biography: Containing Many Thousand Concise Memoirs of Persons Who Have Died between the Years 1851–1900.* 6 vols. Truro: Netherton, for the author, 1892–1921. Indexed by subject in each volume; women are indexed in Peter Bell, comp., *Index to Biographies of Women in Boase's* Modern English Biography (Edinburgh: Bell, 1986, n. pag.).
>
> Valentine, Alan. *The British Establishment, 1760–1784: An Eighteenth-Century Biographical Dictionary.* 2 vols. Norman: U of Oklahoma P, 1970. About one-half of the approximately 3,000 entries are for people not in the *DNB*.

For members of the aristocracy, see:

> C[okayne], G[eorge] E[dward], ed. *Complete Baronetage.* 6 vols. Exeter: Pollard, 1900–09. Covers only the period 1611–1800. (The microreprint edition [Gloucester: Sutton, 1983] includes an introduction on the Order of the Baronetage by Hugh Montgomery-Massingberd.)
>
> Cokayne, George Edward, ed. *The Complete Peerage of England, Scotland, Ireland, Great Britain, and the United Kingdom, Extant, Extinct, or Dormant.* Ed. Vicary Gibbs et al. New ed. 13 vols. London: St. Catherine P, 1910–59. Records "particulars of the parentage, birth, honours, orders, offices, public services, politics, marriage, death and burial, of every holder of a Peerage."

M1430   Allibone, S. Austin. *A Critical Dictionary of English Literature, and British and American Authors, Living and Deceased, from the Earliest Accounts to the Middle of the Nineteenth Century.* 3 vols. Philadelphia: Lippincott; London:

Trübner, 1859–71. Online. 3 Dec. 2005 <http://quod.lib.umich.edu/cgi/
b/bib/bibperm?q1=AHN9011.0001.001>.

Kirk, John Foster. *A Supplement to Allibone's Critical Dictionary of English
Literature and British and American Writers.* 2 vols. Philadelphia: Lippincott,
1892.   Z2010.A44   820.3

A dictionary of British and American writers through 1888. The approximately
83,000 entries provide biographical details, a list of books by the entrant, and references
to other biographical dictionaries, all interspersed with biographical and critical comments extracted from the major nineteenth-century periodicals and other sources. The
supplement provides less biographical information and fewer extracts. The original dictionary is indexed in vol. 3 by broad topic, but the supplement is not indexed; entrants
in both are indexed in *Biography and Genealogy Master Index* (J565). Although saddled
with one of the most tedious introductions of any reference work, riddled with inaccuracies (partly because of its heavy reliance on untrustworthy sources), and thoroughly
outdated in its treatment of authors of any note, Allibone remains occasionally useful
for its inclusion of a host of minor writers nowhere else listed and extracts from nineteenth-century periodicals. Information taken from Allibone must always be verified.

M1433   *Orlando: Women's Writing in the British Isles from the Beginnings to the
        Present.* Ed. Susan Brown, Patricia Clements, and Isobel Grundy.
        Cambridge UP. Online. 25 Oct. 2006 <http://orlando.cambridge.org>.
        Updated semiannually.

A database of biographical, critical, and bibliographical information on more than
850 dead and living British women writers, along with entries on literary and historical
events and some males and non-British females of importance to women's writing.
People can be searched by name, occupation, genre, or place (the last three can be
combined); tags (i.e., an extensive set of semantic or conceptual tags dealing with an
author's life and literary production and reception) can be searched in sections of entries
(lives, writings, bibliographies, and full text); and chronologies can be created by date,
keyword(s), or tags. Many search options provide pull-down lists. Searches can be limited by date and scope (with the latter depending on the type of search). To make full
use of this resource, users must consult the search tutorials.

An entry for an author presents information in a series of tabbed screens: Overview
(with a list of milestones and links to writings and life highlights); Writing (content
varies with the writer, but an outline appears at the top left of the screen); Life; Writing
and Life (the content of the Writing and Life tabs presented side-by-side); Timeline;
Links (i.e., a hyperlinked list of semantic tags included in the entry); and Works By (a
list of published works).

The tagging allows for extensive hyperlinking and for sophisticated searches of the
data; for example, users can identify governesses who wrote poetry, authors for whom
press run data is cited, or entrants with the same political affiliation or sexual identity.
In addition, users can create timelines by various elements, such as genre, place, or
theme. Occasional indiscriminate tagging does bring inessential data to the screen (e.g.,
in the chronology for Jane Austen, the first three entries include two for books owned
by Austen and a comment by a modern scholar that Austen was not influenced by a
particular work).

Because of the ways in which the extensive data can be mined or formulated,
Orlando offers the best access to information on British women writers and serves as a
model for similar databases that will supplant printed literary dictionaries, encyclopedias, and handbooks.

Those without access to *Orlando* will have to make do with the static content of the following;

> Schlueter, Paul, and June Schlueter, eds. *An Encyclopedia of British Women Writers.* Rev. and expanded ed. New Brunswick: Rutgers UP, 1998. 741 pp. A collection of separately authored biographical and critical discussions of approximately 600 writers who were born in or were residents of Great Britain from the Middle Ages to the present. Entries provide an overview of the subject's life and career, as well as a critical estimate of major works, and conclude with lists of books by and works about the entrant. Indexed by persons and subjects; entrants in the first edition are indexed in *Biography and Genealogy Master Index* (J565). Although lacking an adequate explanation of the basis of selection, Schlueter offers the fullest printed guide to British women writers.
>
> Todd, Janet, ed. *British Women Writers: A Critical Reference Guide.* New York: Ungar-Continuum, 1989. 762 pp. A collection of separately authored biographical and critical discussions of approximately 440 writers since the Middle Ages. The entries — ranging from approximately 500 to 2,500 words — provide an overview of the subject's life and career, as well as a critical estimate of major works, and conclude with lists of works by and about the entrant. Indexed by names (including alternate forms and pseudonyms) and subjects (including genres and forms). Although marred by an utterly inadequate explanation of editorial procedures and criteria governing selection, Todd frequently offers the most-extensive entries of any biographical-critical dictionary devoted solely to British women writers. Blain, *Feminist Companion to Literature in English* (J593), includes far more writers, but the entries rarely exceed 500 words. For Restoration and eighteenth-century authors, see Todd, *Dictionary of British and American Women Writers* (M2265).

For those writing between 1580 and 1700, the most thorough source is Maureen Bell, George Parfitt, and Simon Shepherd, *A Biographical Dictionary of English Women Writers, 1580–1720* (Boston: Hall, 1990, 298 pp.), whose approximately 550 brief entries include women "whose only known writing is a single surviving manuscript letter"; entrants are also indexed in *Biography and Genealogy Masher Index* (J565).

For a comparison of Todd, Blain, and the first edition of Schlueter, see the review of Schlueter by Joyce Zonana, *Analytical and Enumerative Bibliography* ns 4 (1990): 186–89.

M1435   *Who's Who: An Annual Biographical Dictionary.* London: Black, 1849– .
        Annual.   DA28.W6   920.042. Online. <http://corp.credoreference.com>.

A biographical dictionary of living persons of distinction and influence primarily in the British Isles and current and former Commonwealth countries. The compact entries provide basic biographical, family, and career information; a list of publications, awards, and honors; and address. Indexed in *Biography and Genealogy Master Index* (J565). This is the best general source for biographical data and addresses of notable residents of the British Isles.

Biographies of dead entrants are reprinted with corrections in *Who Was Who: A Companion to* Who's Who *Containing the Biographies of Those Who Died during the Period [1897–]* (London: Black, 1920–). Volumes are now issued for each five-year period; several early volumes have been published in revised editions. Cumulatively indexed in *Who Was Who: A Cumulated Index, 1897–2000* (2002, 908 pp.).

See also

    Sec. J: Biographical Sources.
    Oxford Companion to English Literature (M1330).

Periodicals

See section K: Periodicals.

DICTIONARIES, ENCYCLOPEDIAS, AND HANDBOOKS

M1437   *The Encyclopedia of the British Press, 1492–1992.* Ed. Dennis Griffiths.
     New York: St. Martin's, 1992. 694 pp.   PN5114.E53 072'.09.
    An encyclopedia of representative national and local newspapers, journalists and
other persons associated with newspapers, and "terms, ideas, places and events associated
with the British press." The approximately 3,000 entries are preceded by six historical
overviews and followed by a chronology, circulation figures as of 1991, lists of women
and Fleet Street editors, and miscellaneous brief essays on, for example, professional
and trade organizations, the British Library Newspaper Library, newspaper collecting,
and women in British journalism. *Encyclopedia of the British Press* is a convenient source
for facts on all aspects of the British press (including addresses of current newspapers).

GUIDES TO PRIMARY WORKS

Bibliographies

M1440 *Bibliography of British Newspapers.* Gen. ed. Charles A. Toase. London:
     British Lib., 1975– . Z6956.G6 B5 [PN5114] 016.079'41.
    Vol. 1: *Wiltshire.* Ed. R. K. Bluhm. 1975. 28 pp.
    Vol. 2: *Kent.* Ed. Winifred E. Bergess, Barbara R. M. Riddell, and John
       Whyman. 1982. 139 pp.
    Vol. 3: *Durham and Northumberland.* Ed. F. W. D. Manders. 1982. 65 pp.
    Vol. 4: *Derbyshire.* Ed. Anne Mellors and Jean Radford. 1987. 74 pp.
    Vol. 5: *Nottinghamshire.* Ed. Michael Brook. 1987. 62 pp.
    Vol. 6: *Cornwall; Devon.* Ed. Jean Rowles and Ian Maxted, resp. 1991.
       123 pp.
    A bibliography of current and defunct newspapers, with individual volumes de-
voted to a single county or related counties according to boundaries before the 1974
reorganization (and in the case of greater London, the pre-1965 boundaries). Titles are
organized geographically by "main area of news coverage or . . . principal area of
circulation," then (depending on the volume) chronologically by date of first issue or
alphabetically by title. Defunct newspapers are listed by earliest title; others by current
title. A typical entry records place of publication, publisher, address (if still being published), dates of publication, mergers and name changes, locations of copies (with information on completeness of holdings), and references to historical studies. Two in-

dexes: places; titles. When complete, this bibliography will offer the fullest, most current general record of British newspapers and the locations of copies.

As part of the NEWSPLAN program to microfilm all newspapers published in the United Kingdom, many participating regional library systems have established databases that supply basic bibliographical information and locations of copies. (For the databases, see http://www.bl.uk/collections/nplan.html.) The amount of information and user interfaces vary from site to site.

The single fullest list of newspapers published in England and Wales is *Tercentenary Handlist of English and Welsh Newspapers, Magazines, and Reviews,* [comp. J. G. Muddiman] (London: The Times, 1920, 324 pp.), which covers 1620 through 1919. Based on the British Library holdings, the *Handlist* is far from complete (especially for the eighteenth century) and lists titles chronologically by date of the first issue extant in the library's collection. Numerous additions and corrections are scattered throughout *Notes and Queries* 12th ser. 8 (1921), 12th ser. 10 (1922), and 161 (1931). Although covering briefer periods, the following are superior in thoroughness and accuracy:

> Crane, *Census of British Newspapers and Periodicals, 1620–1800* (M2270).
> Nelson, *British Newspapers and Periodicals, 1641–1700* (M2060).
> North, *Waterloo Directory of English Newspapers and Periodicals, 1800–1900* (M2540).
> ———, *Waterloo Directory of Irish Newspapers and Periodicals, 1800–1900* (N3000).
> ———, *Waterloo Directory of Scottish Newspapers and Periodicals, 1800–1900* (O3103).
> Ward, *Index and Finding List of Serials Published in the British Isles, 1789–1832* (M2535).

M1445   Sullivan, Alvin, ed. *British Literary Magazines.* 4 vols. Historical Guides to the World's Periodicals and Newspapers. Westport: Greenwood, 1983–86. PN5124.L6 B74   820′.8.

> Vol. 1: *The Augustan Age and the Age of Johnson, 1698–1788.* 1983. 427 pp.
> Vol. 2: *The Romantic Age, 1789–1836.* 1983. 491 pp. (Errata in vol. 3, p. xii.)
> Vol. 3: *The Victorian and Edwardian Age, 1837–1913.* 1984. 560 pp.
> Vol. 4: *The Modern Age, 1914–1984.* 1986. 628 pp.

Profiles of major and representative minor literary magazines. Each volume includes an introductory survey, essays on 80 to 90 magazines, and a chronology of social and literary events and literary magazines; vols. 1 and 3 list other magazines with literary content, and vol. 4, Scottish literary periodicals and magazines with short runs. The individual essays, which vary widely in quality, survey publishing history, characterize content, note important literary contributions, and provide publication details (title changes, volume and issue data, frequency of publication, publishers, and editors) and selective lists of studies, indexes, reprints, and locations. Indexed by persons and magazine titles. Although the lack of clear criteria governing selection leads to the inclusion of some magazines that can hardly qualify as literary, Sullivan is a serviceable compilation of basic information on a number of periodicals. Reviews: (vols. 1–2) Hugh Amory, *Book Collector* 34 (1985): 386–92; G. E. Bentley, Jr., *Victorian Periodicals Review* 17 (1984): 109–13; (vol. 3) Charles Brownson, *English Literature in Transition, 1880–1920* 29 (1986): 340–42; Rosemary T. VanArsdel, *Victorian Periodicals Review*

18 (1985): 99.–101; (vol. 4) Joel H. Wiener, *English Literature in Transition, 1880–1920* 30 (1987): 504–06.

Indexes

M1450   *The Times Index [1906–]*. Reading: Primary Source Microfilm–Thomson, 1907– . Monthly, with annual cumulations. Former titles: *The Annual Index to the* Times (1907–13); *The Official Index to the* Times (1914–57). AI21.T46   072′.1. CD-ROM.

A subject and author index to the final editions of the *Times* and, since 1973, *Sunday Times, TLS: Times Literary Supplement, Times Educational Supplement, Times Scottish Educational Supplement,* and *Times Higher Education Supplement* (coverage of *Times Educational Supplement Cymru* began in 2004). Users should watch for changes in coverage and indexing practices over the years, and note that annual cumulations do not begin until 1977. In most volumes, books reviewed are listed by title under the heading "Books" as well as under the authors. The *Index* offers the best access to one of the world's great newspapers, which for literature scholars is a valuable source of biographical information (especially in obituaries). And, like other indexes of major newspapers, the source can be used to narrow dates for searching unindexed papers. The CD-ROM covers 1906–80.

For issues before 1906, see *Palmer's Index to the* Times *Newspaper [10 October 1790–30 June 1941]* (Corsham: Palmer, 1868–1943; the indexes for 1790–1905 are also searchable through *C19: The Nineteenth Century Index* [M2466] and on CD-ROM [Cambridge: Chadwyck-Healey, 1994]; the indexes for 1880–1890 can be searched in *19th Century Masterfile* [Q4147]), which is much less thorough and more idiosyncratic in indexing practices, and *The* Times *Index [1785–90]*, 6 vols. (Reading: Newspaper Archive Developments, 1978–84). *Times Literary Supplement Index* (K765a) offers superior access to *TLS: Times Literary Supplement* (K765).

Doreen Morrison, "Indexes to the *Times* of London: An Evaluation and Comparative Analysis," *Serials Librarian* 13.1 (1987): 89–106, offers a useful comparison of the two indexes and discussion of the difficulties in using *Palmer's Index*.

Issues since 1 January 1995 can be searched at the newspaper's Web site (http://www.timesonline.co.uk); earlier issues can be searched through *The* Times *Digital Archive 1775–1985* in *Infotrac* (G387).

See the British Library Newspaper Library Web site (http://www.bl.uk/collections/newspapers.html#newspaper) for links to United Kingdom newspapers and indexes.

GUIDES TO SCHOLARSHIP AND CRITICISM

M1455   Linton, David, and Ray Boston, eds. *The Newspaper Press in Britain: An Annotated Bibliography*. London: Mansell, 1987. 361 pp.   Z6956.G6 L56 [PN5114]   016.072.

A bibliography of published studies (through c. 1985), dissertations, theses, and a few manuscripts (although the latter are inadequately identified and unlocated). The approximately 2,900 entries are listed alphabetically by author. Unfortunately the citations do not record pagination for articles or essays in collections, there are inconsistencies in citation form, and many of the brief descriptive annotations fail to provide an adequate sense of contents. Two appendixes: a chronology of British newspaper history from 1476 through 1986; locations of papers and archives of newspapers and persons connected with the trade. Indexed by subjects (including newspapers). Although *Newspaper Press in Britain* is the fullest general list of scholarship on British newspapers, it omits numerous important studies, and the lack of a classified organization, frequently inadequate annotations, and insufficiently thorough subject indexing make the work far less accessible than it should be. Review: Donald Munro, *Journal of Newspaper and Periodical History* 3.3 (1987): 33–39.

Partially expanded by Linton, *The Twentieth-Century Newspaper Press in Britain: An Annotated Bibliography* (London: Mansell, 1994, 386 pp.). The 3,799 entries exclude studies in the 1987 volume published before 1900 and those concerned with only pre-twentieth-century topics. Coverage extends through 1994 (many of the most recent studies are relegated to the section "Late Entries"). Except for an initial section listing reference works, the organization is the same as the earlier volume's; the chronology begins at 1900; and the appendix listing archives and collections of papers has disappeared. And *Twentieth-Century Newspaper Press in Britain* suffers the same shortcomings as its parent volume.

M1460   White, Robert B. *The English Literary Journal to 1900: A Guide to
         Information Sources.* American Literature, English Literature, and World
         Literatures in English: An Information Guide Series 8. Detroit: Gale, 1977.
         311 pp.   Z6956.G6 W47 [PN5114]   016.81′05.

An annotated bibliography of English-language studies (published between c. 1890 and c. 1973) and modern critical editions of literary periodicals. Entries are organized in five chapters: bibliographies, general studies, periodicals, persons (including authors), and places. Few annotations are adequately informative, and many entries are unannotated. Of the four indexes (authors, periodicals, persons, places), only the first is necessary; the others merely repeat classified listings without incorporating cross-references. Because the lack of clarity in the selection policy and definition of the term *literary periodical* results in considerable unevenness of coverage (which is more thorough for eighteenth- than nineteenth-century periodicals), White is little more than a place to begin research. For nineteenth-century periodicals, see Madden, *Nineteenth-Century Periodical Press* (M2560). Reviews: Richard Haven, *Analytical and Enumerative Bibliography* 1 (1977): 250–55; Lionel Madden, *Victorian Periodicals Newsletter* 11 (1978): 108–10; Joanne Shattock, *Yearbook of English Studies* 10 (1980): 230–32.

Genres

Most of the works in section L: Genres are useful for research in English literature.

FICTION

Most of the works in section L: Genres/Fiction are important to research in English fiction.

Histories and Surveys

M1505   Baker, Ernest A. *The History of the English Novel*. 10 vols. London:
Witherby, 1924–39.   PR821.B3   823.09.

>   Vol. 1: *The Age of Romance; from the Beginnings to the Renaissance*. 1924.
336 pp.
>   Vol. 2: *The Elizabethan Age and After*. 1929. 303 pp.
>   Vol. 3: *The Later Romances and the Age of Realism*. 1929. 278 pp.
>   Vol. 4: *Intellectual Realism: From Richardson to Sterne*. 1930. 297 pp.
>   Vol. 5: *The Novel of Sentiment and the Gothic Romance*. 1934. 300 pp.
>   Vol. 6: *Edgeworth, Austen, Scott*. 1929. 277 pp.
>   Vol. 7: *The Age of Dickens and Thackeray*. 1936. 404 pp.
>   Vol. 8: *From the Brontës to Meredith: Romanticism in the English Novel*. 1937.
411 pp.
>   Vol. 9: *The Day before Yesterday*. 1938. 364 pp.
>   Vol. 10: *Yesterday*. 1939. 420 pp.
>   Vol. 11: Stevenson, Lionel. *Yesterday and After*. New York: Barnes, 1967.
431 pp.

A descriptive history, ranging from Anglo-Saxon fiction through the mid-twentieth
century, with an emphasis on major authors. Each volume includes a highly selective
bibliography (now outdated) and is indexed by author, anonymous work, and subject.
Although pedestrian and predictable, Baker remains the most comprehensive general
history of the English novel. More compact surveys include Lionel Stevenson, *The
English Novel: A Panorama* (Boston: Houghton, 1960, 539 pp.); Edward Wagenknecht,
Cavalcade of the English Novel (New York: Holt, 1954, 686 pp., with a supplementary
bibliography); and Walter Allen, *The English Novel: A Short Critical History* (New York:
Dutton, 1955, 454 pp.). Major desiderata are a multivolume history that would replace
Baker and a good general compact history of the novel.

Literary Handbooks, Dictionaries, and Encyclopedias

M1507   *Dictionary of British Literary Characters: 18th- and 19th-Century Novels*. Ed.
John R. Greenfield. New York: Facts on File, 1993. 655 pp.
PR830.C47 D5   823'.80927'03.

>   *Dictionary of British Literary Characters: 20th-Century Novels*. Ed.
Greenfield. New York: Facts on File, 1994. 583 pp.   PR888.C47 D53
823'.910927'03.

A dictionary of major characters and those who contribute significantly to plot or
theme in 1,172 British novels, from 1678 to around 1980. Coverage includes established novelists and a representative sampling of lesser-known writers; the selection of
individual titles is based on the work's significance, its popularity, and its critical reception. Organized alphabetically by surname (if there is one), first name, or salient characteristic of an unnamed character (such as the Gentleman of Bath in *Moll Flanders*),
the succinct entries provide information about "characters' occupations, family relations,
relations with other characters, class, and gender roles as well as the characters' contributions to the novels' plot and themes." Indexed in each volume by author (including
novels and a list of characters therein that are indexed); in addition, the twentieth-
century volume includes a title index for both volumes. Although the lack of a subject

index will inhibit its use for "various historical, sociological, or thematic studies," the
Dictionary allows researchers to identify characters and the novels in which they appear.

Guides to Scholarship and Criticism

Surveys of Research

M1510   Dyson, A. E., ed. *The English Novel: Select Bibliographical Guides.* London:
        Oxford UP, 1974. 372 pp.   Z2014.F5 D94   016.823'03.
    A collection of evaluative surveys of the best editions, critical studies, biographies
and collections of letters, bibliographies, and background studies (published through
the early 1970s) for 22 novelists: Bunyan, Defoe, Swift, Richardson, Fielding, Sterne,
Smollett, Scott, Austen, Thackeray, Dickens, Trollope, the Brontë sisters, Eliot, Hardy,
James, Conrad, Forster, Lawrence, and Joyce. The quality of individual essays varies
widely, but Dyson is a serviceable guide to important scholarship published through
the early 1970s. See *Year's Work in English Studies* (G330) for evaluations of later works.
Review: David Leon Higdon, *Modern Fiction Studies* 20 (1974–75): 607–08.

Other Bibliographies

M1515   Bell, Inglis F., and Donald Baird. *The English Novel, 1578–1956: A*
        Checklist of Twentieth-Century Criticisms. Denver: Swallow, 1958. 168 pp.
        Z2014.F4 B4   016.82309.
    Continued by:
        Palmer, Helen H., and Anne Jane Dyson, comps. *English Novel Explication:*
            Criticisms to 1972. Hamden: Shoe String, 1973. 329 pp.
        Supplement I. Comp. Peter L. Abernethy, Christian J. W. Kloesel, and Jeffrey
            R. Smitten. 1976. 305 pp.
        Supplement II. Comp. Kloesel and Smitten. 1981. 326 pp.
        Supplement III. Comp. Kloesel. 1986. 533 pp.
        Supplement IV. Comp. Kloesel. 1990. 351 pp.
        Supplement V. Comp. Kloesel. 1994. 431 pp.
        Supplement VI. Comp. Kloesel. 1997. 478 pp.
        Supplement VII. Comp. Kloesel. North Haven: Archon–Shoe String, 2002.
            597 pp.   Z2014.F5 P26 [PR821]   016.823'009.
    Bell and Baird provide a highly selective list of English-language books, parts of
books, and articles published from c. 1900 to c. 1957, with entries organized alphabetically by novelist and then by novel. The emphasis is rather loosely on explication,
but the criteria for selection are unclear. The degree of selectivity, typographical errors,
lack of indexing, and inadequate explanation of editorial policy render Bell and Baird
the least useful of these checklists.
    Palmer and Dyson interpret "novel" more broadly, range beyond explication, ex-
tend coverage back to Malory's *Morte Darthur,* and include dissertation abstracts, some
book reviews, and foreign-language criticism. Their work covers studies published between 1958 and 1972, with selection apparently based on what the compilers could
discover. Indexed by literary authors and novel titles.
    The first supplement lists books, parts of books, and articles published between
1972 and 1974 (with some earlier works and some from 1975), is more precisely limited
to explication, and coordinates coverage with *Twentieth-Century Short Story Explication*
(L1090). The supplements extend coverage through early 2000.

Although *English Novel* and *English Novel Explication* (and supplements) make a handy set of volumes for preliminary work (especially because of the inclusion of parts of books), many novelists are more adequately treated in author bibliographies.

M1520   *The English Novel: Twentieth Century Criticism*. Vol. 1: *Defoe through Hardy*. Ed. Richard J. Dunn. Chicago: Swallow, 1976. 202 pp. Vol. 2: *Twentieth Century Novelists*. Ed. Paul Schlueter and June Schlueter. Athens: Swallow–Ohio UP, 1982. 380 pp.   Z2014.F4 E53 [PR821] 016.823'91'09.

Highly selective lists of English-language books, parts of books, and articles (published through 1974 in vol. 1; 1975 in vol. 2). Vol. 1 covers general studies of the novel and 45 novelists, each with sections for general studies (an alphabetical hodgepodge), bibliographies, and works on individual novels. Vol. 2 covers 80 established writers, each with sections for bibliographies, interviews, general studies, and works on individual novels. Both volumes fail to clarify selection criteria, and the second hardly bears out its editors' claim as "the most nearly complete bibliography of criticism of the twentieth century British novel yet published." Although these volumes are occasionally useful as a starting point, most of the novelists included are more adequately treated in period and author bibliographies.

See also

> *ABELL* (G340): English Literature/General/Fiction section.
>
> *MLAIB* (G335): English III/Prose Fiction section in pre-1981 volumes; Literatures of the British Isles/Fiction, Novel, English Literature/Fiction, and Novel sections in pt. 1 of the volumes for 1981–90; and the British and Irish Literatures/Fiction, Novel, English Literature/Fiction, and Novel sections in pt. 1 of the later volumes. Researchers must also check the "British Fiction," "British Novel," "English Fiction," "English Novel," and "English Novelists" headings in the subject index to post-1980 volumes and in the online thesaurus.

DRAMA AND THEATER

Most works in section L: Genres/Drama and Theater are important to research in English drama.

Histories and Surveys

M1525   Nicoll, Allardyce. *A History of English Drama, 1660–1900*. 6 vols. Cambridge: Cambridge UP, 1952–59.   PR625.N52   822.09.

> Vol. 1: *Restoration Drama*. 4th ed. 1952. (M2360).
>
> Vol. 2: *Early Eighteenth Century Drama*. 3rd ed. 1952. (M2360).
>
> Vol. 3: *Late Eighteenth Century Drama, 1750–1800*. 2nd ed. 1952. (M2360).
>
> Vol. 4: *Early Nineteenth Century Drama, 1800–1850*. 2nd ed. 1955. (M2670).
>
> Vol. 5: *Late Nineteenth Century Drama, 1850–1900*. 2nd ed. 1959. (M2670).

Vol. 6: *A Short-Title Alphabetical Catalogue of Plays Produced or Printed in England from 1660 to 1900.* 1959. (M1545).

Emphasizes the history of the stage and dramatic forms of the legitimate and popular theater. Each volume includes a chapter on the theater, discussions of genres or kinds of dramatic entertainments, an appendix on playhouses, and an author list of plays first printed or produced during the respective period. Readers should watch for the supplementary sections containing revisions that could not be incorporated into the text. Each volume is indexed by persons and subjects; vol. 6 indexes by title plays in the author list to each volume and includes numerous additions and corrections. Although the history of the stage is now dated and the production details for 1660–1800 are now largely superseded by *London Stage* (M2370), the volumes include a wealth of information, especially on minor writers, not readily available elsewhere. Continued by Nicoll, *English Drama, 1900–1930* (M2855). See the individual entries for a fuller description of each volume. Reviews: Rudolf Stamm, *English Studies* 37 (1956): 220–22; 42 (1961): 46–48.

Although more current, *The Cambridge History of British Theatre*, gen. ed. Peter Thomson, 3 vols. (Cambridge: Cambridge UP, 2004) eschews a "seamless narrative" in favor of allowing contributors "to use a searchlight rather than a floodlight to illuminate the past." The result is a series of disconnected essays and case studies, albeit ones written by major scholars. Each volume concludes with a list of works cited (not a bibliography as the list is denominated in vols. 2–3). Indexed by persons and subjects in each volume.

M1530   *The Revels History of Drama in English.* Gen. eds. Clifford Leech, T. W. Craik, and Lois Potter. 8 vols. London: Methuen, 1975–83.   PR625.R44 822'.009.

Each volume includes a chronology; essays that examine the social or literary context, actors and the stage, and the plays and playwrights; an evaluative survey of important scholarship; and an index of authors, titles, and subjects. The *Revels History* offers a useful synthesis of scholarship rather than a connected history of the drama, with many volumes justly faulted for unevenness and inconsistencies.

Annals

M1535   Harbage, Alfred. *Annals of English Drama, 975–1700: An Analytical Record of All Plays, Extant or Lost, Chronologically Arranged and Indexed by Authors, Titles, Dramatic Companies, &c.* Rev. S. Schoenbaum. 3rd ed. rev. Sylvia Stoler Wagonheim. London: Routledge, 1989. 375 pp.   Z2014.D7 H25 016.822008.

A chronology of dramatic and quasidramatic works (including translations) written in England or by English writers in other countries. Entries are organized according to the known or probable date of first performance: under each century (to 1495) or year (1495–1700), plays of known authorship are listed alphabetically by author, followed by anonymous plays listed by title. Information is presented in tabular format, with columns for author, title, date of first performance (when known), type of play, auspices of first production (including acting company and place), date of first edition or manuscript, and date of most recent modern edition (which is not always the best edition). To decipher information in the columns, users must refer continually to the explanation of symbols in the introduction (some symbols can be deciphered only by consulting the second edition). Following the chronology are supplementary lists of plays omitted because of uncertain date or identity, of selected collections of medieval drama texts, and of theaters. An appendix lists extant play manuscripts, with location and shelf number. Five indexes: English playwrights (including collected editions); English plays (including modern editions, both printed and in dissertations); foreign playwrights; foreign plays translated or adapted; dramatic companies. The third edition incorporates scholarship through the late 1980s but remains as conservative as its predecessor in dating and attributing works. The second edition (1964) with its supplements (1966, 1970) of the *Annals* was an authoritative accumulation of factual information and an essential source for investigating the environment of a play or the evolution of the early drama; the same cannot be said for the third edition, which is so rife with errors, misprints, omissions, and inconsistencies that it cannot be trusted. Researchers must consult the second edition and its supplements, along with *London Stage, 1660–1800* (M2370) for 1660–1700, and Kawachi, *Calendar of English Renaissance Drama* (M2130), for 1558–1642. Anyone who uses the third edition should first study Anne Lancashire's account of its deficiencies in her review in *Shakespeare Quarterly* 42 (1991): 225–30.

   For an instructive discussion of how the *Annals* led to the discovery of a "lost" play, see Arthur H. Scouten and Robert D. Hume, eds., introd., The Country Gentleman: *A "Lost" Play and Its Background* (Philadelphia: U of Pennsylvania P, 1976) 10–17.

Guides to Primary Works

Manuscripts

M1540 *Catalogue of Additions to the Manuscripts: Additional Manuscripts 42865–
        43038: Plays Submitted to the Lord Chamberlain, 1824–1851.* London:
        British Museum, 1964. 357 pp.   Z6621.B8422   016.091.
   One result of the Licensing Act of 1737, which required that every play intended for performance be approved by the lord chamberlain, is an unrivaled collection of manuscripts and printed acting copies and editions documenting English theater and drama since the early eighteenth century. Unfortunately, the collection is split between the Huntington Library and the British Library, and only plays submitted between 1737 and 1851 have published catalogs.

   1737–January 1824. Held in the Huntington Library and cataloged in *Catalogue of the Larpent Plays in the Huntington Library,* comp. Dougald MacMillan, Huntington Library Lists 4 (San Marino: Huntington Lib., 1939, 442 pp.).

   February 1824–December 1851. Held in the Department of Manuscripts, British Library. The catalog lists plays in order of submission, with a typical entry recording manuscript title, any alternate title, author (frequently taken from Nicoll, *History of English Drama,* vol. 4 [M2670]), and the presence of an autograph copy. Two indexes: authors; titles. *British Library Manuscripts Catalogue* (F300) offers the best access to the contents of this catalog.

   1852–1967. Held in the Department of Manuscripts, British Library, and indexed by title in a card index there.

   1968– . Since 1968, plays no longer must be licensed, but a copy of the script of every play produced in Great Britain must be deposited in the Department of Manuscripts. Indexed by authors and titles in a card index there. Unfortunately, the Modern Playscripts Collection (as the post-1967 deposits are called) is missing more than 1,000 works produced between 1968 and April 2005 because of a lack of compliance with the deposit provision of the Theatres Act of 1968. Fortunately, though, *Theatre Archive*

Project (http://www.bl.uk/projects/theatrearchive/homepage.html) is sponsoring a Scripts Collection project that is devoted to identifying and recovering copies of the missing playscripts (click on Scripts at the above Web site).

An invaluable collection that preserves hundreds of unique copies of dramatic presentations, legitimate and popular, London and provincial, and whose existence is too little known among researchers.

Printed Works

Bibliographies and Indexes

M1545   Nicoll, Allardyce. *A Short-Title Alphabetical Catalogue of Plays Produced or Printed in England from 1660 to 1900*. Vol. 6 of *A History of English Drama, 1660–1900* (M1525). Cambridge: Cambridge UP, 1959. 565 pp. PR625.N52   822.09.

More than a title index to the author lists of plays in vols. 1–5, this is an independent record of plays and dramatic entertainments (excluding most Italian operas and "the repertoire of the French and Italian comedians") first produced or printed in England from 1660 to 1900. The entries, which identify authors and dates of first productions, include corrections and additions to the individual lists. Of particular value is the inclusion of alternate titles and subtitles along with main titles. Although not exhaustive and partly superseded by *London Stage* (M2370) for the period 1660–1800, the *Catalogue* remains the most complete list of dramatic works for the period 1660–1900.

M1550   Stratman, Carl J., C. S. V., comp. and ed. *Bibliography of English Printed Tragedy, 1565–1900*. Carbondale: Southern Illinois UP; London: Feffer, 1966. 843 pp.   Z2014.D7 S83   016.822051.

A bibliography of editions published between 1565 and the early 1960s of 1,483 tragedies written in English and first printed between 1565 and 1900. Stratman excludes Shakespeare's tragedies (but includes adaptations of them), translations, one-act plays unless the author also wrote full-length plays, and works existing only in manuscript. Plays are organized alphabetically by author, then title, with editions listed chronologically. Additions and corrections appear on pp. 837–43. An entry typically includes title, imprint, pagination, notes (principally bibliographical or textual, with references to standard bibliographies), and locations. Useful features include a list of anthologies and collections, a chronological list of plays by date of first edition, and a list of locations of manuscripts of works included in the bibliography. Indexed by titles. Although not comprehensive (especially for nineteenth-century works), Stratman is valuable for identifying and locating editions and for studying the genre. Review: Inga-Stina Ewbank, *Shakespeare Studies* 5 (1969): 366–69.

See also

Davis, *Drama by Women to 1900* (Q3513).

Text Archives

M1553   *English Drama*. ProQuest. Online. 15 June 2006 <http://collections .chadwyck.com>.

An archive of rekeyed texts of about 3,900 English-language plays, in verse and prose and intended for the stage, by British writers and ranging from the thirteenth to the twentieth century. Being listed in *NCBEL* (M1385) is the criterion on which drama-tists or anonymous works were admitted. Editions—preferably not modernized—were selected according to the following criteria: "the first authorised edition"; a later edition if an early one is unreliable or if a work were significantly revised; a collected edition.

Simple keyword, title, and author searches can be limited by speaker, date of performance, date of publication, genre, gender, literary period, verse or prose drama, notes, and part of a work (e.g., prologues, stage directions). Searchers must be certain to checkmark the Include Typographical Variants box but must be aware that this feature works on simple variants (e.g. "glove/gloue") but not more complicated ones ("dogs/dogges/doges"). Searchers can also browse an author list of the contents of the database. Results appear in ascending alphabetical order and cannot be re-sorted. Ci-tations (but not the full text of plays) can be marked for e-mailing, downloading, or printing; each citation includes a durable URL to the full text.

Some works are rekeyed from textually unsound editions; however, the biblio-graphic record for each work identifies the source of the text and any omissions (e.g., preliminary matter). Besides being a useful source for identifying an elusive quotation or half-remembered line, the scope of *English Drama*'s text archive makes feasible a variety of kinds of studies (stylistic, generic, thematic, imagistic, and topical).

The contents of *English Drama* can also be searched through *LiOn* (I527), which offers a less-versatile search interface.

Guides to Scholarship and Criticism

Surveys of Research

M1555   Wells, Stanley, ed. *English Drama (Excluding Shakespeare): Select Bibliographical Guides.* London: Oxford UP, 1975. 303 pp.
Z2014.D7 E44 [PR625]   822'.009.
A collection of essays that delineate trends in criticism, evaluate the best editions and studies published through the early 1970s, and frequently suggest work that needs to be undertaken on medieval through contemporary drama. Chapters are devoted to reference works and general studies; medieval drama; Tudor and early Elizabethan drama; Marlowe; Jonson and Chapman; Marston, Middleton, and Massinger; Beau-mont and Fletcher, Heywood, and Dekker; Webster, Tourneur, and Ford; the court masque; Davenant, Dryden, Lee, and Otway; Etherege, Shadwell, Wycherley, Con-greve, Vanbrugh, and Farquhar; Gay, Goldsmith, Sheridan, and other eighteenth-century dramatists; nineteenth-century drama; Shaw; the Irish School; English drama, 1900–45; and English drama since 1945. Shakespeare occupies a separate volume: *Shakespeare: A Bibliographical Guide,* new ed., ed. Stanley Wells (Oxford: Clarendon–Oxford UP, 1990, 431 pp.). Indexed by dramatists and anonymous plays. The judicious (sometimes pointed) evaluations serve as useful guides through the mass of scholarship. See *Year's Work in English Studies* (G330) for evaluations of works published after c. 1970, and Logan and Smith (M2145) for more thorough treatment of Renaissance dramatists.

Other Bibliographies

M1560   Arnott, James Fullarton, and John William Robinson. *English Theatrical Literature, 1559–1900. A Bibliography Incorporating Robert W. Lowe's*

A Bibliographical Account of English Theatrical Literature *Published in
1888*. London: Soc. for Theatre Research, 1970. 486 pp.   Z2014.D7 A74
016.792'0942.

A bibliography of works published between 1559 and 1900 on British theater
(including opera, pantomime, and music hall, but not ballet or circus). Studies are
organized chronologically within classified divisions for bibliography, government regulation of the theater, theater arts (e.g., acting, costume, playwriting), general history,
London theater, theater out of London, a national theater, opera, irregular forms (pantomime, music hall, etc.), societies, amateur theater, biography, theory and criticism,
and periodicals (see Stratman, *Britain's Theatrical Periodicals* [M1565] for a fuller list
of periodicals). Only British editions are fully described; only one location is cited for
each work; and the notes generally deal with bibliographical matters. Three indexes:
authors; titles; places of publication. The classified organization and cross-references do
not compensate for the absence of a subject index. Although limited by its exclusion of
articles (unless also separately printed) and terminal date, Arnott is still the best single
guide to early publications, many of which are indexed nowhere else. Coverage is continued by Cavanagh, *British Theatre* (M1563).

M1562   *Guide to British Drama Explication.* 2 vols. Reference Publication in
         Literature. New York: Hall–Simon and Schuster Macmillan; London:
         Prentice, 1996– .   Z2014.D7 D68 [PR625]   016.822009.

   Vol. 1: *Beginnings to 1640.* Krystan V. Douglas. 1996. 552 pp.

A highly selective guide to English-language articles (of more than one page) and
parts of books (published between the early 1940s and 1991) that offer a close reading
of a dramatic text. Entries are classified by poet, then by title, and parts of frequently
cited books are keyed to a list at the back (which also identifies volumes of journals
searched). Nearly half of vol. 1 is devoted to Shakespeare. The focus is explication;
therefore, studies of theater history, productions, and authorship are excluded. Although
the guide lacks an adequate explanation of the selection criteria for books and journals,
is based on only a partial examination of a majority of the journals listed at the back,
is poorly proofread in many parts, and is current through 1991 for only a few of the
journals covered, *British Drama Explication* is useful for its indexing of parts of books.

M1563   Cavanagh, John. *British Theatre: A Bibliography, 1901 to 1985.* Motley
         Bibliographies 1. Mottisfont, Eng.: Motley, 1989. 510 pp.
         Z2014.D7 C38 [PN2581]   016.792'0941.

A continuation through December 1985 of Arnott, *English Theatrical Literature*
(M1560) that, like its predecessor, is limited to separately published works (including
some periodicals) on the theater, medieval to modern, in the British Isles, but expands
the scope to include master's theses, dissertations, and books published outside Great
Britain and in languages other than English and to place more emphasis on drama (as
it relates to the stage). Users must be certain to study the admirably clear explanation
(pp. 9–11) of scope and coverage for the bibliography generally as well as for individual
sections, several of which supplement (but do not duplicate coverage in) existing bibliographies. The 9,310 entries—which usually cite the "best" edition—are divided
among three classified divisions: theater (with sections for reference works; government
intervention; religion; theater arts; history; theater in London; theater outside London;
theater companies, clubs, and societies; biography; criticism; pantomime; music hall,
revues, and concert parties; amateur theater; and pedagogy); drama (with sections for
history, foreign influences, and dramatic biography and criticism [including studies not

cited in *NCBEL* (M1385) of individual dramatists]); and music (with sections on music in the dramatic theater and opera, operetta, and musical comedy). Within each section, books are listed chronologically (by date of edition cited, which may not be the first edition), then alphabetically by author within a year. Some entries are accompanied by brief annotations that provide bibliographical information, list contents, or elucidate an unclear title; for all but the most obscure or ephemeral works, locating the copy described at one of 18 institutions is superfluous. The indexing needlessly confuses users: only the first author or editor is listed in the author index; all others — including writers of prefatory matter or of essays mentioned in annotations — appear in the subject index. Neither index is thorough. Although it excludes articles, is very selective in some sections, and omits several foreign-language publications, *British Theatre* is especially valuable for its coverage of pamphlets and publications of limited distribution, is accurately and attractively printed, and offers the best general list of separately published books on all aspects of British theater. Review: Thomas Postlewait, *Theatre History Studies* 11 (1991): 207–10.

See also

ABELL (G340): English Literature/General/Drama and the Theatre section.
MLAIB (G335): English III/Drama section in the pre-1981 volumes; Literatures of the British Isles/Drama, Theater, English Literature/Drama, and Theater sections in pt. 1 of the volumes for 1981–90; and the British and Irish Literatures/Drama, Theater, English Literature/Drama, Theater sections in pt. 1 of the later volumes. Researchers must also check the "English Drama" and "English Theater" headings in the subject index to post-1980 volumes and in the online thesaurus.

Biographical Dictionaries

Indexes

See

Wearing, *American and British Theatrical Biography* (L1175).

Periodicals

Guides to Primary Works

M1565 Stratman, Carl J., C. S. V. *Britain's Theatrical Periodicals, 1720–1967: A Bibliography.* 2nd ed. New York: New York Public Lib., 1972. 160 pp. Z6935.S76 016.792'0942.

A chronological bibliography of periodicals devoted to the theater and published in Great Britain between 1720 and 1967. Entries are listed by date of original issue and include title, publication information, and locations. Indexed by titles, editors, and places of publication. *Britain's Theatrical Periodicals* remains useful for identifying periodicals and locating complete (or the most complete) runs. For additional locations, consult *WorldCat* (E225), RLG Union Catalog (E230), *New Serial Titles* (K640), *Union List of Serials* (K640a), and *Serials in the British Library* (K645). Review: J. W. Robinson, *Victorian Periodicals Newsletter* 8 (1975): 109–10.

POETRY

Most of the works listed in section L: Genres/Poetry are important to research in English poetry.

Histories and Surveys

M1575   Courthope, W. J. *A History of English Poetry.* 6 vols. New York: Macmillan, 1895–1910.   PR502.C8   821.09.
　　A historical survey of the development of poetry (including dramatic poetry) through the Romantic movement. In treating poetry as an aspect of intellectual history, Courthope emphasizes the impact of political and social history but gives little attention to minor figures. Cumulative index of authors and titles in vol. 6. Although uneven in places and generally superseded by surveys limited to individual periods, the work remains the most extensive connected history of English poetry.

M1583   *The Columbia History of British Poetry.* Ed. Carl Woodring. New York: Columbia UP, 1994. 732 pp.   PR502.C62   821.009.
　　A collection of separately written essays on periods, groups of poets, kinds of poetry, and individuals. Employing a variety of critical approaches, the contributors consider "voices long suppressed" as well as resituate "some of the more celebrated poets within more sharply defined social and literary contexts." Each essay concludes with a brief list of related studies, and the volume concludes with brief biographies of some of the poets discussed. Indexed by authors and titles. Sporting an impressive array of contributors, the *Columbia History* covers a substantial range of English, Scottish, Welsh, and Irish poets; but, since it is a collaborative volume, it does not offer a seamless history of the subject.

Literary Handbooks, Dictionaries, and Encyclopedias

M1585   Malof, Joseph. *A Manual of English Meters.* Bloomington: Indiana UP, 1970. 236 pp.   PE1505.M3   426.
　　A technical manual of metrical forms and techniques of scansion. After a preliminary discussion of basic terms and symbols, chapters define and illustrate the patterns and forms of foot verse, stress verse, syllabic verse, and free verse; a section on the application of scansion in critical reading concludes the body of the manual. Appendixes include common stanza forms, checklist of rhymes, glossary of additional terms, selected bibliography, and summary of metrical forms. Indexed by subjects. Clear explanations combined with aptly chosen examples make Malof the best manual for learning scansion.
　　A useful complementary handbook for the analysis of English prosody is Karl Shapiro and Robert Beum, *A Prosody Handbook* (New York: Harper, 1965, 214 pp.), which moves from syllable to stanza.

Guides to Primary Works

Bibliographies and Indexes

M1590   Crum, Margaret, ed. *First-Line Index of English Poetry, 1500–1800, in Manuscripts of the Bodleian Library, Oxford.* 2 vols. Oxford: Clarendon–Oxford UP, 1969.   Z2014.P7 F5   821'.0016.

An index to poems in manuscripts acquired before April 1961. Entries, arranged alphabetically according to the initial word of the first line, include first and last line, author, title of poem, references to printed versions, and a list of Bodleian manuscripts containing the poem. Five indexes: Bodleian manuscripts by shelf marks; poets; names mentioned; authors of works translated, paraphrased, or imitated; composers of settings and of tunes named or quoted. Crum is the essential index to the most important collection of English poetry manuscripts of the three centuries. Manuscripts acquired after April 1961 are described in Clapinson, *Summary Catalogue of Post-medieval Western Manuscripts in the Bodleian Library* (F300a); significant manuscripts are also described in the "Notable Acquisitions" section of *Bodleian Library Record* (1938– , 2/yr.).

Michael Londry (see below) reports that a supplemental card index and an interleaved copy of Crum "noting later identifications and other information concerning individual manuscript versions of poems" are available in Duke Humfrey's Library at the Bodleian.

For important guides to other works—print, manuscript, and electronic—that index first-lines of poems, see Londry, "On the Use of First-Line Indices for Researching English Poetry of the Long Eighteenth Century, c. 1660–1830, with Special Reference to Women Poets," *Library* 7th ser. 5 (2004): 12–38; and James Woolley, "First-Line Indexes of English Verse, 1650-1800: A Checklist," *BibSite*, Bibliog. Soc. of Amer., online, 29 Feb. 2004 <http://www.bibsocamer.org/BibSite/Woolley/index.html>.

See also

Davis, *Poetry by Women to 1900* (Q3534).

Text Archives

M1593   *English Poetry.* 2nd ed. ProQuest. Online. 14 June 2006 <http://
collections.chadwyck.com>.
An archive of rekeyed texts of more than 183,000 English-language poems by writers of the British Isles from the Anglo-Saxon era to the end of the nineteenth century. English-language translations and hymns published after 1800 are excluded as are verse dramas intended for performance and unpublished poems or ones that appeared only in periodicals or miscellanies. Editions were selected according to the following criteria: "editions published during the author's lifetime or shortly afterwards"; "later editions" if "the early editions of a poet's work are unreliable or incomplete"; copyrighted editions if rights were available. Being listed as a poet in *NCBEL* (M1385) or being recommended by the editorial board are the criteria on which poets were admitted. Simple keyword, first line or title, and author searches can be limited by date during an author's lifetime, gender, literary period, to rhymed or unrhymed poems, and to parts. Searches must be certain to checkmark the Include Typographical Variants box but must be aware that this feature works on simple variants (e.g., "glove/gloue") but not on more complicated ones ("dogs/dogges/doges"). Searchers can also browse an author list of the contents of the database. Results appear in ascending alphabetical order and cannot be re-sorted. Citations (but not the full text of poems) can be marked for e-mailing, downloading, or printing; each citation includes a durable URL to the full text.

Some works are rekeyed from textually unsound editions; however, the bibliographic record for each work identifies the source of the text and any omissions (e.g., preliminary matter), and the site is refreshingly forthcoming in its explanations of editorial procedures and revision history. Besides being a useful source for identifying an elusive quotation or half-remembered line, the scope of *English Poetry's* text archive makes feasible a variety of kinds of studies (stylistic, thematic, imagistic, and topical). The contents of *English Poetry* can also be searched through *LiOn* (I527), which offers a less-versatile search interface. Continued by *Twentieth-Century English Poetry* (M2894).

Guides to Scholarship and Criticism

Surveys of Research

M1595   Dyson, A. E., ed. *English Poetry: Select Bibliographical Guides.* London: Oxford UP, 1971. 378 pp.   Z2014.P7 E53   016.821.

A collection of essays that evaluate the best editions, critical studies, biographies and collections of letters, bibliographies, and background studies published before 1970 on 20 major poets (Chaucer, Spenser, Donne, Herbert, Milton, Marvell, Dryden, Pope, Blake, Wordsworth, Coleridge, Byron, Shelley, Keats, Tennyson, Browning, Arnold, Hopkins, Yeats, and Eliot). *English Poetry* remains useful for its generally judicious evaluations of scholarship before 1970. See *Year's Work in English Studies* (G330) for later editions and studies.

Other Bibliographies

M1600   Brogan, T. V. F. *English Versification, 1570–1980: A Reference Guide with a Global Appendix.* Baltimore: Johns Hopkins UP, 1981. 794 pp.
Z2015.V37 B76 [PE1505]   016.821′009.

A classified annotated bibliography of studies published from 1570 through 1979 on all aspects of versification in British and American poetry in English. An appendix selectively annotates major studies on versification in other languages. Pt. 1 treats modern poetry (since Wyatt), with sections, classified as the topic requires, on histories and bibliographies, general studies, sound, rhythm, meter, syntax and grammar, stanza structures, visual structures, and the poem in performance. Pt. 2 divides studies between sections for Old and Middle English verse. The appendix has sections for other languages as well as comparative studies, poetry and music, and classical versification. The lengthy annotations usually offer a trenchant evaluation, place a work in its theoretical or historical context, and cite selected reviews. Two indexes: British and American poets and anonymous works; scholars. Since classifications are sometimes ambiguous, access would be improved by a subject index (even though liberal cross-references conclude each section). An authoritative guide with admirably full coverage, *English Versification* deserves the acclaim of all those working in a field heretofore plagued by a lack of bibliographical control and standardized terminology.

Some additions and corrections appear in Brogan, "Addenda and Corrigenda to *English Versification, 1570–1980,*" *Modern Philology* 81 (1983): 50–52. Coverage is continued by Brogan as "Studies of Verseform [1979–89]," *Eidos: The International Prosody Bulletin* 1–3 (1984–90). Originally called "Current Bibliography," "Studies of Verseform" is not annotated but provides fuller coverage of other languages.

In *Verseform: A Comparative Bibliography* (Baltimore: Johns Hopkins UP, 1989, 122 pp.), Brogan selects the most important studies through 1987 of poetic form in the major languages. Unlike *English Versification,* however, very few of the 1,494 entries are annotated and most of those with only a brief descriptive sentence or two.

See also

    ABELL (G340): English Literature/General/Poetry section.

    MLAIB (G335): English III/Poetry section in the pre-1981 volumes; Literatures of the British Isles/Poetry and English Literature/Poetry sections in pt. 1 of the volumes for 1981–90; and British and Irish Literatures/English Literature/ Poetry section in pt. 1 of the later volumes. Researchers must also check the "English Poetry" heading in the subject index to post-1980 volumes and in the online thesaurus.

PROSE

Many works listed in section L: Genres/Prose are important to research in English prose.

Biography and Autobiography

Histories and Surveys

M1605   Stauffer, Donald A. *English Biography before 1700.* Cambridge: Harvard UP, 1930. 392 pp.   CT34.G7 S7   920.002.

    A critical history of published biographical works in prose and verse by English writers in any language to 1700. Emphasizing the place of biography in English literature and focusing on works important in themselves or to the development of biography, chapters treat the Middle Ages, Renaissance, ecclesiastical biography, Izaak Walton, intimate biography, autobiography, and biography as a form. The extensive bibliography is divided into two parts. The first is an author list, with cross-references to subjects, of biographical works before 1700. Each entry cites the most important modern edition; several entries provide notes on the importance, quality, or content of a work. The second part is a selected, evaluatively annotated list of scholarship. Concludes with a chronology of the most important biographies. Indexed by names and some titles. Although its bibliographies are incomplete and outdated, Stauffer is still the most comprehensive treatment of early English biography.

    Continued by Stauffer, *Art of Biography in Eighteenth Century England* (M2430).

Guides to Primary Works

M1610   Matthews, William, comp. *British Autobiographies: An Annotated Bibliography of British Autobiographies Published or Written before 1951.* Berkeley: U of California P, 1955. 376 pp.   Z2027.A9 M3   016.920042.

    A bibliography of English-language autobiographies, published and in manuscript, written by a British subject and treating a significant portion of the writer's life. Matthews excludes works restricted to a single event (such as religious conversion); fiction; and discussions of life in Canada, South Africa, New Zealand, Australia, and the United States. The majority of the works date from the nineteenth and twentieth centuries. Listed alphabetically by autobiographer or title of anonymous work, entries provide title, publication information or location of manuscript, dates of coverage, and a very brief note on content. Most descriptions are based on personal examination, but some are taken from reviews. Indexed by subjects (but utilizing headings that are sometimes too general). Although incomplete and offering briefer notes on content than Matthews's other compilations (M1615, Q3540a, and R4765), this work remains an important initial source for identifying British autobiographies. Many of its entries are repeated or revised in Handley, *An Annotated Bibliography of Diaries Printed in English* (M1615a). Autobiographies by British subjects are also included in Matthews, *Canadian Diaries and Autobiographies* (R4765), Davis, *Personal Writings by Women to 1900* (Q3545a), and Arksey, *American Diaries* (Q3540).

Much fuller descriptions of 1,040 published autobiographies by British women since the eighteenth century are offered by Barbara Penny Kanner, *Women in Context: Two Hundred Years of British Women Autobiographers: A Reference Guide and Reader* (New York: Hall-Simon; London: Prentice, 1997, 1,049 pp.). Entries, which are listed alphabetically by autobiographer, include a citation, biographical note, lengthy synopsis, and concluding sociohistorical commentary. Three indexes: authors (organized chronologically by 20-year segments); vocations and avocations; subjects. The detailed synopses offer a wealth of information that is, unfortunately, not easily accessible because of inadequate subject indexing.

M1615   Matthews, William, comp. *British Diaries: An Annotated Bibliography of British Diaries Written between 1442 and 1942.* Berkeley: U of California P, 1950. 339 pp.   Z5305.G7 M3   016.920042.

An annotated bibliography of published and manuscript English-language diaries written by British citizens in the British Isles, in Europe, and on the high seas, and by foreigners traveling in the British Isles. Besides diaries by British travelers in the United States (listed in Arksey, *American Diaries* [Q3540]), it excludes works that are not primarily daily accounts, explorers' journals, ships' logs, and parliamentary diaries. Although the majority of the works have been published separately or in periodicals, Matthews includes several manuscripts in public collections and private hands. Entries are organized chronologically by the New Style calendar according to the year of initial entry and then alphabetically by diarist. Annotations cite type of diary and inclusive dates, briefly describe content (major places, persons, and events), sometimes evaluate style or coverage, and give publication information or location of manuscript (including shelf number). Two indexes: diaries extending more than 10 years (at the beginning); diarists (at the end). Although incomplete (especially in its coverage of unpublished diaries) and lacking a subject index, it remains the fullest record of British diaries and an essential source for identifying where they were published or are held in manuscript. Reviews: T. A. Birrell, *English Studies* 33 (1952): 264–66; Hilary Jenkinson, *American Historical Review* 56 (1951): 552–54.

For manuscript diaries between 1800 and 1899, Matthews is superseded by John Stuart Batts, *British Manuscript Diaries of the Nineteenth Century: An Annotated Listing* (Totowa: Rowman, 1976, 345 pp.), a chronological list of unpublished diaries held primarily in public collections in Great Britain. There are numerous errors and inconsistencies in the entries, however.

Some additional published British diaries are listed in Patricia Pate Havlice, *And So to Bed: A Bibliography of Diaries Published in English* (Metuchen: Scarecrow, 1987, 698 pp.); however, its chief feature is the combined index of diarists in Matthews, *British Diaries*; *American Diaries* (Q3540a); and *Canadian Diaries* (R4765).

Many of the entries in Arksey, *American Diaries* (Q3540) and Matthews's *British Diaries, British Autobiographies* (M1610), *American Diaries* (Q3540a), and *Canadian Diaries* (R4765) are repeated or revised in C. S. Handley, *An Annotated Bibliography of Diaries Printed in English*, 3rd ed., 8 vols. (Tyne and Wear: Hanover, 2002; CD-ROM); however, this work is not widely held.

A rekeyed full text of some of the diaries listed in the preceding and begun before 1950 can be searched in *British and Irish Women's Letters and Diaries* (Alexandria: Alexander Street, online, 15 Feb. 2006 <http://www.alexanderstreet2.com/bwldlive>). A companion to *North American Women's Letters and Diaries* (Q3540a), it shares many of its features and shortcomings but includes only about 332 documents.

See also

Davis, *Personal Writings by Women to 1900* (Q3545a).

Old English Literature

Many works listed in section M: English Literature/General are useful for research in Old English literature. In "Anglo-Saxon Studies: Present State and Future Prospects," *Mediaevalia* 1.1 (1975): 62–77, Fred C. Robinson suggests a number of reference works still needed by Anglo-Saxonists.

Research Methods

M1625 O'Keeffe, Katherine O'Brien, ed. *Reading Old English Texts.* Cambridge: Cambridge UP, 1997. 231 pp.   PR73.O38   829.

A collection of essays that outline approaches to reading Old English texts, including comparative approaches, source study, philology, historicist approaches, oral tradition, textual criticism, feminist criticism, poststructuralist criticism, and computer-assisted approaches. The essays typically outline and define the approach, provide examples of the approach (with attention to noteworthy applications), and suggest topics for further research. Indexed by persons, titles, and some subjects. An exemplary collection by a virtual who's who of Old English studies, *Reading Old English Texts* is a model of the kind of work needed for every period of English and American literature.

See also

Powell, *Medieval Studies* (M1755).

Histories and Surveys

For an evaluative review of literary histories and surveys from the seventeenth century through 1977, see Daniel G. Calder, "Histories and Surveys of Old English Literature: A Chronological Review," *Anglo-Saxon England* 10 (1982): 201–44. Particularly valuable are Calder's analysis of trends in scholarship and trenchant evaluations of individual works.

LITERARY HISTORIES AND SURVEYS

M1635 Greenfield, Stanley B., and Daniel G. Calder. *A New Critical History of Old English Literature.* With a Survey of the Anglo-Latin Background by

Michael Lapidge. New York: New York UP, 1986. 370 pp.   PR173.G73
829'.09.

A critical history of Anglo-Saxon poetry and prose that incorporates important
scholarship and criticism in its readings of texts. Chapters are devoted to the Anglo-
Latin background; Alfredian translations and related prose; Ælfric, Wulfstan, and other
late prose; the nature and quality of Old English poetry; secular heroic poetry; the
Christian saint as hero; Christ as poetic hero; Old Testament narrative poetry; miscellaneous religious and secular poetry; lore and wisdom verse; and elegiac poetry. The
extensive list of works cited also serves as the best selective bibliography of scholarship
on Old English literature through the early 1980s. Indexed by literary authors and
anonymous works (but unfortunately not by scholars). Like its predecessor—Greenfield, *A Critical History of Old English Literature* (New York: New York UP, 1965, 237
pp.)—this is an authoritative history that has had a profound impact on Old English
scholarship. Review: E. G. Stanley, *Comparative Literature* 40 (1988): 286–89.

R. D. Fulk and Christopher M. Cain, *A History of Old English Literature*, Blackwell
Histories of Literature (Oxford: Blackwell, 2003, 346 pp.) is an important complement
because it emphasizes scholarship since the mid-1980s and offers a fuller treatment of
prose.

See also

Sec. M: English Literature/General/Histories and Surveys.
Greenfield, *Bibliography of Publications on Old English Literature* (M1670), lists
histories and surveys (entries 530–611 in Greenfield).

RELATED TOPICS

M1637   Hill, David. *An Atlas of Anglo-Saxon England.* Toronto: U of Toronto P,
1981. 180 pp. (A second edition was announced for 2002 but has not been
published as of March 2007.)   G1812.21.S2.H5   912'.42.

A series of maps, tables, diagrams, chronologies, and graphs that organize information on topography, demography, physical geography, historical events and periods,
political administration, the economy, and the church. Indexed by place. An essential
complement to narrative histories. Reviews: Rebecca V. Colman, *Canadian Journal of
History* 17 (1982): 515–16; Simon Keynes, *Antiquity* 57 (1983): 66–67.

Literary Handbooks, Dictionaries, and Encyclopedias

M1640   *Reallexikon der germanischen Altertumskunde.* 2nd ed. Ed. Heinrich Beck et
al. Berlin: Gruyter, 1968– . (Published in parts [through *Stil–Tissø* as of
March 2006]).   DD51.R42. <http://www.hoops.uni-goettingen.de>.

An encyclopedia of pre-Christian Germanic culture, including Anglo-Saxon England. The signed entries—predominantly in German, but with some in English and
a few lengthy ones in a mixture of the two languages—range from single paragraphs
to extensive essays on persons, places, material culture, folklore, languages, archaeological discoveries, literary works, numismatics, religion, historical events, commerce, do-
mestic matters, art works, and politics. The lengthy entries are helpfully subdivided and
sometimes consist of separately authored divisions. All conclude with references to im-

portant scholarship. Generous cross-references guide users to appropriate headings. When complete, the *Reallexikon* will offer the fullest encyclopedic coverage of Anglo-Saxon culture. Until then, the earlier edition edited by Johannes Hoops (4 vols., Strassburg: Trübner, 1911–19) remains useful. *Lexikon des Mittelalters* (M1800) and *Dictionary of the Middle Ages* (M1795) include some Anglo-Saxon topics.

More compact is *Blackwell Encyclopaedia of Anglo-Saxon England*, ed. Michael Lapidge, John Blair, Simon Keynes, and Donald Scragg (Oxford: Blackwell, 1999, 537 pp.), which has signed entries that cover persons, places, objects, architecture, manuscripts, language, religion, literary works in both Old English and Latin, and subjects. The generous entries conclude with a list of related studies. Sporting many of the leading Anglo-Saxon scholars among its contributors, *Blackwell Encyclopaedia of Anglo-Saxon England* offers a sure-handed, interdisciplinary introduction to Anglo-Saxon culture; unfortunately, it is marred by an inexcusable lack of discussion of scope and editorial procedures.

See also

> *Dictionary of the Middle Ages* (M1795).
> *Lexikon des Mittelalters* (M1800).

Bibliographies of Bibliographies

See

> Rouse, *Serial Bibliographies for Medieval Studies* (M1805).

Guides to Primary Works

M1645   Ker, N. R. *Catalogue of Manuscripts Containing Anglo-Saxon.* Oxford: Clarendon–Oxford UP, 1990. 579 pp. (A reissue of the 1957 edition with Ker's "Supplement" [see below].)   Z6605.A56 K4   015.4203.

A descriptive catalog of more than 400 manuscripts written before c. 1200 entirely or partly in Old English. Ker includes fragments, Latin–Old English glossaries, and Latin manuscripts that contain even a single gloss (other than a tag phrase) in Old English but excludes cartularies and charters. Entries are organized alphabetically by the city in which a collection is located or the surname of private owner, then by title of collection, then by shelf mark. Concludes with a section listing lost and untraced manuscripts and an appendix with brief descriptions of "manuscripts containing Anglo-Saxon written by foreign scribes." Manuscripts entirely or substantially in Old English receive full descriptions, with references to significant scholarship and editions, and discussion of date, content, physical characteristics, script and decorations, and provenance. Ker's "Supplement to *Catalogue of Manuscripts Containing Anglo-Saxon*," *Anglo-Saxon England* 5 (1976): 121–31, is reprinted in the 1990 reissue (see above), but not Mary Blockley's "Addenda and Corrigenda to N. R. Ker's 'A Supplement to *Catalogue of Manuscripts Containing Anglo-Saxon*,'" *Notes and Queries* ns 29 (1982): 1–3, with corrections by the editors, 533; Blockley subsequently expanded the "Addenda and Corrigenda" as "Further Addenda and Corrigenda to N. R. Ker's *Catalogue*," *Anglo-Saxon Manuscripts: Basic Readings*, ed. Mary P. Richards, Garland Reference Library of the Humanities 1434: Basic Readings in Anglo-Saxon England 2 (New York: Garland, 1994) 79–85.

The *Catalogue of Manuscripts Containing Anglo-Saxon* is the essential source for information about the location, dating, localization, and paleographic details of Anglo-Saxon manuscripts. Like Ker's *Medieval Manuscripts in British Libraries* (M1810), it is a magisterial achievement informed by an incomparable knowledge of early manuscripts. Reviews: Kenneth Sisam, *Review of English Studies* ns 10 (1959): 68–71; Rudolph Willard, *JEGP: Journal of English and Germanic Philology* 59 (1960): 129–37.

For complementary lists, especially of Latin manuscripts, see Helmut Gneuss, *Handlist of Anglo-Saxon Manuscripts: A List of Manuscripts and Manuscript Fragments Written or Owned in England up to 1100*, Medieval and Renaissance Texts and Studies (Tempe: Arizona Center for Medieval and Renaissance Studies, 2001, 188 pp.), "Addenda and Corrigenda to the *Handlist of Anglo-Saxon Manuscripts*," *Anglo-Saxon England* 32 (2003): 293–305, and "Liturgical Books in Anglo-Saxon England and Their Old English Terminology," *Learning and Literature in Anglo-Saxon England: Studies Presented to Peter Clemoes on the Occasion of His Sixty-Fifth Birthday*, ed. Michael Lapidge and Helmut Gneuss (Cambridge: Cambridge UP, 1985) 91–141. These works represent preliminary stages in the compilation of *Sources of Anglo-Saxon Literary Culture*, a summary of current scholarship on the sources, written and oral, of Anglo-Saxon and Anglo-Latin literary works. For a description of the project and sample entries, see Frederick M. Biggs, Thomas D. Hill, and Paul E. Szarmach, eds., *Sources of Anglo-Saxon Literary Culture: A Trial Version*, Medieval and Renaissance Texts and Studies 74 (Binghamton: Center for Medieval and Early Renaissance Studies, State U of New York, Binghamton, 1990, 256 pp.) and the project's Web site (http://www.wmich.edu/ medieval/research/saslc). Until completion of that project, J. D. A. Ogilvy, *Books Known to the English, 597– 1066* (Cambridge: Mediaeval Acad. of Amer., 1967, 300 pp.) and "*Books Known to the English, A. D. 597– 1066*: Addenda et Corrigenda," *Mediaevalia* 7 (1981): 281–325 (rpt. in *Old English Newsletter* 11, subsidia [1985]), offer the fullest record. For iconographic descriptions of illustrations, see Thomas H. Ohlgren, comp. and ed., *Insular and Anglo-Saxon Illuminated Manuscripts: An Iconographic Catalogue, c. A.D. 625 to 1100*, Garland Reference Library of the Humanities 631 (New York: Garland, 1986, 400 pp.), which is revised and expanded as Ohlgren, *Corpus of Insular, Anglo-Saxon, and Early Anglo-Norman Manuscript Art: A Hypertext System*, HyperShell vers. 1.0, CD-ROM (West Lafayette: ScholarWare, 1994); a supplement, *Anglo-Saxon Textual Illustration: Photographs of Sixteen Manuscripts with Descriptions and Index* (Kalamazoo: Medieval Inst., 1992, 576 pp.) is also available on CD-ROM as *ASTI: A Hypertext System for Anglo-Saxon Textual Illustration: Descriptions and Index*, HyperShell vers. 1.0, CD-ROM (West Lafayette: ScholarWare, 1994). Other major catalogs of Anglo-Saxon manuscripts are listed in Greenfield, *Bibliography of Publications on Old English Literature* (M1670), entries 108–28.

See also

Cameron, "A List of Old English Texts" (M1705a).

Guides to Scholarship and Criticism

SURVEYS OF RESEARCH

M1655   "The Year's Work in Old English Studies, [1967–]." *Old English Newsletter* 2 (1968)– .   PE101.O44   829'.09.

An evaluative survey of research based on the "Old English Bibliography" (M1665). The commentary by various scholars is currently arranged in nine classified divisions: general; memorials, tributes, and history of the discipline; language; literature; Anglo-Latin and ecclesiastical works; manuscripts and illumination; history and culture; onomastics; and archaeology and numismatics. Most sections concludes with a list of works not seen, which may be discussed in a following survey. Like the "Old English Bibliography" and the annual bibliography in *Anglo-Saxon England* (M1660), "The Year's Work in Old English Studies" is an essential source for current scholarship and one that is more thorough and critical than the chapter on Old English literature in *Year's Work in English Studies* (G330); unfortunately, coverage is now far in arrears. For a history and evaluation of this annual survey, see *Twenty Years of the "Year's Work in Old English Studies,"* ed. Katherine O'Brien O'Keeffe, *Old English Newsletter* 15, subsidia (1989): 57 pp.

See also

YWES (G330) has a chapter on Old English literature.

SERIAL BIBLIOGRAPHIES

M1660   "Bibliography for [1971–]." *Anglo-Saxon England* 1 (1972)– .
        DA152.2.A75   942.01'05.
   An international classified bibliography of books, articles, and significant reviews on all aspects of Anglo-Saxon studies. Entries are currently classified in 10 divisions: general; Old English language; Old English literature; Anglo-Latin, liturgy, and other ecclesiastical texts; paleography, diplomatics, and illumination; history; numismatics; onomastics; archaeology; reviews. This bibliography, "Old English Bibliography" (M1665), and "The Year's Work in Old English Studies" (M1655)are essential sources for identifying current scholarship.

M1665   "Old English Bibliography [1969–]." *Old English Newsletter* 3 (1970)– .
        PE101.O44   829'.09.
        OEN *Bibliography Database*. Online. 2 Apr. 2006 <http://www
        .oenewsletter.org/OENDB/index.php>. Updated regularly.
   An international bibliography of scholarship on England before 1066 in ten divisions: general; memorials, tributes, and history of the profession; language; literature; Anglo-Latin and ecclesiastical works; manuscripts and illumination; history and culture; names; archaeology and related subjects; and reviews. Many of the works are subsequently evaluated in "The Year's Work in Old English Studies" (M1655). The bibliographies since 1975 can be searched online in OEN *Bibliography Database*, which allows users to browse records organized by the taxonomy of the print "Bibliography"; to search by keyword; or (in Advanced Search) to search by personal name, title, journal title, keyword, type of publication, and language. Each of these methods allows users to restrict searches by date and to sort results in ascending order by date, author, or title. Records can be marked for e-mailing or printing. Anglo-Saxon scholars are fortunate to have nearly all of the installments of "Old English Bibliography" searchable through a well-designed interface. Like the annual bibliography in *Anglo-Saxon England* (M1660), this work is an essential source for current scholarship that offers fuller coverage than the serial bibliographies and indexes in section G.

See also

> Sec. G: Serial Bibliographies, Indexes, and Abstracts.
> *ABELL* (G340): English Literature/Old English section and, through the volume
>   for 1933, English Literature/Old and Middle English: Subsidiary.
> *BREPOLiS Medieval Bibliographies: International Medieval Bibliography Online*
>   (M1835).
> *MLAIB* (G335): English Language and Literature division in the volumes for
>   1921–25; English V in the volumes for 1926–56; English IV in the volumes
>   for 1957–80; and the English Literature/400–1099: Old English section (as
>   well as any larger chronological sections encompassing the period) in later
>   volumes. Researchers must also check the headings beginning "Old English"
>   in the subject index to post-1980 volumes and in the online thesaurus.

OTHER BIBLIOGRAPHIES

M1670   Greenfield, Stanley B., and Fred C. Robinson. *A Bibliography of Publications*
            on Old English Literature to the End of 1972. Toronto: U of Toronto P,
            1980. 437 pp.   Z2012.G83 [PR173]   016.829.
    The closest we are likely to come to an exhaustive bibliography of books, editions,
articles, notes, and reviews published from the fifteenth century through 1972 (with a
few later publications) on Old English literature. Since the focus is literature in Old
English, Greenfield and Robinson exclude discussions of Anglo-Latin literature as well
as linguistic, historical, and archaeological studies that do not bear directly on an Old
English literary text; they also exclude unpublished dissertations as well as general anthologies and surveys of English literature. Entries are listed chronologically in three
variously classified divisions: general works, poetry, and prose. Many entries are accompanied by a brief annotation that clarifies the topic or place of a study in a scholarly
controversy; entries for books list reviews. The liberal cross-references exclude works
within the same section and standard texts in collections. Two indexes: authors and
reviewers; subjects. A magisterial achievement whose accuracy and comprehensiveness
fully deserve the praise accorded it by reviewers. Reviews: Carl T. Berkhout, *Speculum*
57 (1982): 897–99; Donald K. Fry, *Analytical and Enumerative Bibliography* 6 (1982):
183–86; Fry, *English Language Notes* 20 (1982): 11–20.
    A discursive examination of "the changing aims and achievements of [Anglo-
Saxon] scholars" occasioned by the Greenfield and Robinson *Bibliography*, E. G. Stanley's "The Scholarly Recovery of the Significance of Anglo-Saxon Records in Prose and
Verse: A New Bibliography," *Anglo-Saxon England* 9 (1981): 223–62, notes important
sources for research in areas outside Greenfield and Robinson's scope (as does *New
Cambridge Bibliography of English Literature* [M1675]). For supplementary coverage of
prose (principally by King Alfred and his circle), see Carl T. Berkhout, "Research on
Early Old English Literary Prose, 1973–1982," *Studies in Earlier Old English Prose*, ed.
Paul E. Szarmach (Albany: State U of New York P, 1986) 401–09, and Karen J. Quinn
and Kenneth P. Quinn, *A Manual of Old English Prose*, Garland Reference Library of
the Humanities 453 (New York: Garland, 1990, 439 pp.), with coverage through 1982.
For studies published after 1972, see the annual bibliographies in *Anglo-Saxon England*
(M1660) and *Old English Newsletter* (M1655 and M1665). North American dissertations through 1986 are conveniently found in Phillip Pulsiano, *An Annotated Bibliog-*

raphy of North American Doctoral Dissertations on Old English Language and Literature, Medieval Texts and Studies 3 (East Lansing: Colleagues, 1988, 317 pp.).

For a description of a database that would incorporate and continue Greenfield and Robinson, see Berkhout, "The Bibliography of Old English: Back to the Future," *Old English Scholarship and Bibliography: Essays in Honor of Carl T. Berkhout,* ed. Jonathan Wilcox, *Old English Newsletter* Subsidia 32 ([Kalamazoo:] Medieval Inst., Western Michigan U, 2004) 107–14.

Areas not covered in existing or planned bibliographies constitute the principal subjects of *Annotated Bibliographies of Old and Middle English Literature* (Woodbridge: Brewer, 1992–):

> Vol. 1: Burnley, David, and Matsuji Tajima. *The Language of Middle English Literature.* 1994. 280 pp.
>
> Vol. 2: Millett, Bella. Ancrene Wisse, *the Katherine Group, and the Wooing Group.* 1996. 260 pp.
>
> Vol. 3: Easting, Robert. *Visions of the Other World in Middle English.* 1997. 119 pp.
>
> Vol. 4: Hollis, Stephanie, and Michael Wright. *Old English Prose of Secular Learning.* 1992. 404 pp.
>
> Vol. 5: Poole, Russell. *Old English Wisdom Poetry.* 1998. 418 pp.
>
> Vol. 6: Waite, Greg. *Old English Prose Translations of King Alfred's Reign.* 2000. 394 pp.
>
> Vol. 7: Greentree, Rosemary. *The Middle English Lyric and Short Poem.* 2001. 570 pp.
>
> Vol. 8: Scahill, John. *Middle English Saints' Legends.* 2005. 209 pp.

The volumes typically include an evaluative overview of trends in scholarship along with extensively annotated entries (arranged by date of publication).

M1675   *The New Cambridge Bibliography of English Literature* (*NCBEL*). Vol. 1:
              600–1660. Ed. George Watson. Cambridge: Cambridge UP, 1974. 2,476
              cols.   Z2011.N45 [PR83]   016.82.

(For a full discussion of *NCBEL,* see entry M1385.) The part devoted to the Anglo-Saxon period (to 1100) has two major divisions: Old English Literature and Writings in Latin. The first includes sections for general works (subdivided by bibliographies, histories, anthologies, general studies, and ancillary studies), poetry (dictionaries, collections, manuscript studies, general criticism, and individual poems and authors), and prose (collections, general criticism, major translators of King Alfred's reign, major writers of the later period, other religious prose, chronicles, laws and charters, and secular prose). Writings in Latin includes sections for general works, British Celtic writers, Irish writers, and Anglo-Saxon writers. The general introduction for the volume as a whole lists bibliographies, histories, anthologies, and works about prosody, prose rhythm, and language that include the Anglo-Saxon period. Vol. 1 of *Cambridge Bibliography of English Literature* (M1385a) is still occasionally useful for its coverage of the social and political background (which *NCBEL* drops).

Users must familiarize themselves with the organization, remember that there is considerable unevenness of coverage in subdivisions, and consult the index volume (vol. 5) rather than the provisional index in vol. 1. Review: Fred C. Robinson, *Anglia* 97 (1979): 511–17.

Although Greenfield, *Bibliography of Publications on Old English Literature* (M1670), is the source for research on Old English literature, *NCBEL* is still useful for studies outside the scope of the former.

RELATED TOPICS

M1680   Rosenthal, Joel T. *Anglo-Saxon History: An Annotated Bibliography, 450–*
        1066. AMS Studies in the Middle Ages 7. New York: AMS, 1985. 177 pp.
        Z2017.R67 [DA152]   016.94201.

A highly selective bibliography of primary and secondary sources for the study of
Anglo-Saxon history. Confined largely to English-language works published through
the early 1980s, *Anglo-Saxon History* excludes most Celtic and literary topics. Entries
are organized alphabetically in 11 variously classified divisions: reference works and
collections of essays; primary sources and scholarship on them (including chronicles,
biography and hagiography, and constitutional and administrative history); general and
political history (including secular biography and Vikings); constitutional and administrative history; ecclesiastical history; social and economic history; science, technology,
and agriculture; place and personal names; numismatics; archaeology; and fine arts, arts,
and crafts (including manuscripts). Rarely do annotations adequately describe a work
(although some do offer evaluative comments). Indexed by person. Although highly
selective, poorly organized in many divisions, and lacking an adequate statement of
editorial policy, the work is the most current guide to scholarship on Anglo-Saxon
history. For more-thorough coverage of recent scholarship on some topics, see "Old
English Bibliography" (M1665), "The Year's Work in Old English Studies" (M1655),
and the annual bibliography in *Anglo-Saxon England* (M1660). Older bibliographies
still of value are the following:

> Altschul, Michael. *Anglo-Norman England, 1066–1154.* Conference on Brit-
> ish Studies Bibliographical Handbooks. Cambridge: Cambridge UP for
> the Conf. on British Studies, 1969. 83 pp. Coverage extends through mid-
> 1968.
> Bonser, Wilfrid. *An Anglo-Saxon and Celtic Bibliography (450–1087).* 2 vols.
> Berkeley: U of California P, 1957. Coverage extends through 1953.

See also

> Graves, *Bibliography of English History to 1485* (M1845).
> *Royal Historical Society Bibliography* (M1400).

Language

GUIDES TO SCHOLARSHIP

M1685   Cameron, Angus, Allison Kingsmill, and Ashley Crandell Amos. *Old English*
        Word Studies: A Preliminary Author and Word Index. Toronto Old English
        Series 8. Toronto: U of Toronto P in association with Centre for Medieval
        Studies, U of Toronto, 1983. 192 pp. and 5 microfiche.   Z2015.S4 C35
        [PE265]   016.429.

An interim bibliography of Old English vocabulary studies (published through
1980) compiled as part of the *Dictionary of Old English* project (M1690). Entries are
listed by author in three sections: sixteenth- and seventeenth-century manuscript dictionaries; dictionaries, encyclopedias, concordances, and glossaries; and vocabulary studies. The third section is indexed (in the accompanying microfiche) by words discussed

(see pp. xiv–xv for an explanation of the indexing of variant forms). Although not exhaustive, *Old English Word Studies* is an essential source for the study of Old English vocabulary. A revised edition is planned after publication of the *Dictionary*. Reviews: Susan Cooper, *Medium Ævum* 54 (1985): 290–91; Constance B. Hieatt, *English Studies in Canada* 11 (1985): 231–32; Ilkka Mönkkönen, *Neuphilologische Mitteilungen* 86 (1985): 599–601.

M1687   Tajima, Matsuji, comp. *Old and Middle English Language Studies: A Classified Bibliography, 1923–1985.* Amsterdam Studies in the Theory and History of Linguistic Science, Ser. 5: Library and Information Sources in Linguistics 13. Amsterdam: Benjamins, 1988. 391 pp.   Z2015.A1 T3 [PE123]   016.429.

A bibliography of studies, including dissertations and book reviews but excluding works in Slavic languages and most Japanese studies, published between 1923 and 1985 about Old and Middle English language. The approximately 3,900 entries are organized in 14 divisions (each with sections for general or historical studies, Old English, and Middle English): bibliographies; dictionaries, concordances, and glossaries; histories of the English language; grammars; general works; studies of the language of individual authors or works (however, numerous author studies appear without cross-references in other sections); orthography and punctuation; phonology and phonetics; morphology; syntax; lexicology, lexicography, and word formation; onomastics; dialectology; and stylistics. A few entries include a brief note on content or a list of later editions and reprints. Indexed by scholars. The lack of a subject index and cross-references means that users searching for studies of an author, an anonymous work, or a topic will find themselves skimming all entries. Although it is less accessible than it should be (with some entries not seen by the compiler) and although it excludes important studies published within critical editions, Tajima provides the fullest list of twentieth-century scholarship on Old and Middle English language. Review: George Jack, *Diachronica* 6 (1989): 151–54.

See also

> *ABELL* (G340): Old English heading in the subdivisions of the English Language section in the volumes for 1934–84; in earlier and later volumes, studies treating Old English appear throughout the English Language division.
> Mitchell, *Critical Bibliography of Old English Syntax* (M1710a).
> *MLAIB* (G335): English Language and Literature division in the volumes for 1922–25; Old English headings in English I/Linguistics section in the volumes for 1926–66; Indo-European C/Germanic Linguistics IV/English/Old English section in the volumes for 1967–80; and the Indo-European Languages/Germanic Languages/West Germanic Languages/English Language/English Language (Old) section in pt. 3 of the later volumes. Researchers should also check the "English Language (Old)" heading in the subject index to post-1980 volumes and in the online thesaurus.
> *YWES* (G330): The chapter on English language covers Old English.

DICTIONARIES

M1690   *Dictionary of Old English A-F (DOE).* Ed. Angus Cameron, Ashley Crandell Amos, and Antonette diPaolo Healey. CD-ROM. Ver. 1.0.

Toronto: Pontifical Inst. of Mediaeval Studies for Dictionary of Old English Project, Centre for Medieval Studies, U of Toronto, 2003. Also published on microfiche, which are revised in the CD-ROM. (Publication began in 1986 with fascicle *D*; when complete, *DOE* will be issued in hard copy.) <http://www.doe.utoronto.ca>.

A dictionary of Old English (600–1150) that excludes only place and personal names. There are three types of entries: common words receive full entries; rarer words, exhaustive ones; and grammar words, special entries. A full entry consists of headword (usually in late West-Saxon spelling), grammatical details, variant spellings, occurrence and usage information, definitions, illustrative citations (with hyperlinks to the full bibliographical information on texts and editions used; citations in the microfiches are keyed to the accompanying *List of Texts and Index of Editions* and to Pauline A. Thompson, *Abbreviations for Latin Sources and Bibliography of Editions* [1992, 50 pp.]), Latin equivalents in the same manuscript, typical collocations, and references to the *Middle English Dictionary* (M1860), *English Dialect Dictionary* (M1415), *Dictionary of the Older Scottish Tongue* (O3090a), and *Oxford English Dictionary* (M1410). The CD-ROM, which includes revisions to the *A–E* microfiche, offers HTML, SGML, and XML texts. Those using the search engine that accompanies the HTML text must read the Search Tips screen before initiating a pattern search. Editorial practices are outlined in the *Preface* (1987, 14 pp.) and in prefaces to the individual microfiche fascicles but (inexplicably) not in the CD-ROM. Progress reports appear regularly in *Old English Newsletter*; a discussion of the research for and possible uses of the *Dictionary* may be found in A. C. Amos, "The Dictionary of Old English," *Sources of Anglo-Saxon Culture*, ed. Paul E. Szarmach, Studies in Medieval Culture 20 (Kalamazoo: Medieval Inst., Western Michigan U, 1986) 407–13, and in two essays by A. Healey: "The Search for Meaning," *The Editing of Old English: Papers from the 1990 Manchester Conference*, ed. D. G. Scrazz and Paul E. Szarmach (Woodbridge: Brewer, 1994) 85–96, and "Reasonable Doubt, Reasoned Choice: The Letter *A* in the *Dictionary of Old English*," *Studies in English Language and Literature: "Doubt Wisely": Papers in Honour of E. G. Stanley*, ed. M. J. Toswell and E. M. Tyler (London: Routledge, 1996) 71–84. For the importance of the *DOE* to the study of Old English syntax, see William F. Koopman, "The Study of Old English Syntax and the Toronto *Dictionary of Old English*," *Neophilologus* 76 (1992): 605–15. Although *DOE* omits etymologies, it is an invaluable resource for linguists and literary scholars that will, when complete, supersede the Bosworth-Toller *Dictionary* (M1695). Reviews: Janet Bately, *Notes and Queries* 40 (1993): 510–12; Daniel Donoghue, *Speculum* 64 (1989): 155–57; R. D. Fulk, *JEGP: Journal of English and Germanic Philology* 90 (1991): 125–28; Mark Griffith, *Medium Ævum* 59 (1990): 148–52, and 63 (1994): 121–23; Joy Jenkyns, *Review of English Studies* ns 42 (1991): 380–416; Lucia Kornexl, *Anglia* 112 (1994): 421–53; Hans Sauer, *Mitteilungen des Verbandes deutscher Anglisten* 3.2 (1992): 41–53; Jonathan Wilcox, *Philological Quarterly* 71 (1992): 127–30.

The *DOE* project has been the source of other important reference works: Dictionary of Old English *Old English Corpus* (M1705); Cameron, "A List of Old English Texts" (M1705a); and Cameron, *Old English Word Studies* (M1685).

M1695   Bosworth, Joseph. *An Anglo-Saxon Dictionary.* Ed. and enl. by T. Northcote Toller. 4 pts. Oxford: Clarendon-Oxford UP, 1882–98. Rpt. in 1 vol., 1898. 1,302 pp. Toller. *Supplement.* 3 pts. 1908–21. Rpt. in 1 vol., 1921.

768 pp. Alistair Campbell. *Enlarged Addenda and Corrigenda to the Supplement.* 1972. 68 pp.   PE279.B5   429.3.

The most complete Anglo-Saxon dictionary currently available. A typical entry includes part of speech, definition, Latin equivalents, illustrative passages (with modern English translation), etymology, and cross-references to variant and related forms. Campbell's *Enlarged Addenda* incorporates Toller's additions published in *Modern Language Review* 17 (1922): 165–66; 19 (1924): 200–04. Inconsistencies and unevenness in treatment occur, since editorial practices changed during the course of publication (e.g., in the *Dictionary* different forms are listed separately in the earlier part of the alphabet but grouped under a single form in the latter part); there are errors and omissions; and definitions of rare or difficult words are not always accurate. But until *Dictionary of Old English* (M1690) is complete, Bosworth-Toller remains the most authoritative dictionary. Reviews: Edward M. Brown, *JEGP: Journal of English and Germanic Philology* 3 (1901): 505–09; Otto B. Schlutter, *JEGP: Journal of English and Germanic Philology* 18 (1919): 137–43.

The best concise dictionary is John R. Clark Hall, *A Concise Anglo-Saxon Dictionary,* 4th ed. (Cambridge: Cambridge UP, 1960, 432 pp.), which includes a supplement by Herbert D. Meritt.

The best source for etymology is F. Holthausen, *Altenglisches Etymologisches Wörterbuch,* Germanische Bibliothek, Reihe 4: Wörterbücher 7 (Heidelberg: Winter, 1934, 428 pp.), with additions and corrections in Alfred Bammesberger, *Beiträge zu einem etymologischen Wörterbuch des Altenglischen,* Anglistische Forschungen 139 (Heidelberg: Winter, 1979, 156 pp.).

M1700   *Dictionary of Medieval Latin from British Sources.* Ed. R. E. Latham and
        D. R. Howlett. London: Oxford UP for British Acad., 1975– . (Published in
        fascicles.)   PA2891.L28   473'.21.

A dictionary of the Latin language used in Great Britain from c. 550 to c. 1550, but excluding most personal and place names as well as Irish sources before 1200 because of their inclusion in *Dictionary of Medieval Latin from Celtic Sources* (in progress; see http://journals.eecs.qub.ac.uk/DMLCS/index.html) and covering Welsh sources very selectively. Classical Latin words used with little change are given brief entries; fuller treatment is accorded postclassical words and usages, with the fullest entries going to distinctly British words and usages. An entry provides basic meaning(s), accompanied by an extensive list of quotations to illustrate nuances of meaning. Arabic etymologies in the *Dictionary* are more fully explained in J. D. Latham, "Arabic into Medieval Latin," *Journal of Semitic Studies* 17 (1972): 30–67; 21 (1976): 120–37; 34 (1989): 459–69. Users should note that the original prefatory matter is reprinted along with a supplementary bibliography at the end of fasc. 5; this is meant to replace the prefatory matter to fasc. 1 when fascs. 1–5 are bound as vol. 1. The indispensable source for interpreting early British writings in Latin. Until the work is complete, R. E. Latham, ed., *Revised Medieval Latin Word-List from British and Irish Sources* (London: Oxford UP for British Acad., 1980, 535 pp., a reprint of the 1965 edition along with a supplement listing additions and corrections), provides basic meanings for words. Review: (fasc. 1) A. B. Scott, *Medium Ævum* 46 (1977): 105–08.

See also

Greenfield, *Bibliography of Publications on Old English Literature* (M1670), lists other dictionaries (entries 52–82).

CONCORDANCES

M1705   Dictionary of Old English *Old English Corpus*. 2004 release. *Dictionary of Old English* Project. Online. 3 Apr. 2006 <http://quod.lib.umich.edu/o/oec>.

An electronic corpus of all extant Old English texts (except for some variants in manuscripts of individual works) as well as of the Latin texts attached to them. The search engine allows users to create their own concordances of words or phrases (though users must search all spelling variants to construct a full list; variants are listed in the Old English Word Wheel in *Old English Corpus*). Basic, Boolean, and proximity searches can be limited to a class (prose, verse, or gloss) and to a specific work; doing the latter requires that one know the entry number or short title used in Cameron, "A List of Old English Texts" (see below), which can be found through the site's Bibliography Searches screen. For an explanation of how the corpus can be used, see Antonette diPaolo Healey, "The *Dictionary of Old English Corpus* on the World-Wide Web," *Old English Newsletter* 33.1 (1999): 21–28 (reprinted from *Medieval English Studies Newsletter* 40 [1999]: 2–10). *Old English Corpus* is an incomparable resource for linguistic studies, thematic investigations, and stylistic analyses. It effectively supersedes the following:

> Venezky, Richard L., and Antonette diPaolo Healey, comps. *A Microfiche Concordance to Old English.* Newark: U of Delaware, 1980. Microfiche.
> Venezky, Richard L., and Sharon Butler, comps. *A Microfiche Concordance to Old English: The High-Frequency Words.* 1983. Microfiche.

> > An unlemmatized concordance based on an earlier version of *Old English Corpus*. Users should note that homographs are not differentiated. Editorial policies are explained and sources listed in the accompanying guides: Healey and Venezky, comps., *A Microfiche Concordance to Old English: The List of Texts and Index of Editions*, rpt. with revisions, Publications of the Dictionary of Old English 1 (Toronto: Pontifical Inst. of Mediaeval Studies for Dictionary of Old English Project, 1985, 202 pp.), and Venezky and Butler, comps., *A Microfiche Concordance to Old English: The High-Frequency Words*, Publications of the Dictionary of Old English 2 (1985, 20 pp.).

> Bessinger, J. B., Jr., ed. *A Concordance to* The Anglo-Saxon Poetic Records. Programmed by Philip H. Smith, Jr. Cornell Concordances. Ithaca: Cornell UP, 1978. 1,510 pp.

> > A concordance based on George Philip Krapp and Elliott Van Kirk Dobbie, eds., *The Anglo-Saxon Poetic Records: A Collective Edition*, 6 vols. (New York: Columbia UP, 1931–53), plus one other poem, "Instructions for Christians." Madeleine M. Bergman, "Supplement to *A Concordance to* The Anglo-Saxon Poetic Records," *Mediaevalia* 8 (for 1982): 9–52, adds 113 lines of verse and runic inscriptions. Review: Thomas Elwood Hart, *Computers and the Humanities* 13 (1979): 229–35 (an important discussion of limitations and uses).

> Cameron, Angus. "A List of Old English Texts." *A Plan for the Dictionary of Old English.* Ed. Roberta Frank and Angus Cameron. Toronto: U of Toronto P in association with Centre for Medieval Studies, U of Toronto, 1973. 25–306.

Prepared as a list of manuscripts and editions on which the *Dictionary of Old English* is based, this was the most complete record of extant Old English works. Each entry identifies the known manuscripts (or object, for inscriptions), facsimiles, and the most important editions. Except for the variant manuscripts Cameron records, the bibliographical records in the *Corpus* provides the most current information on editions.

THESAURUSES

M1707   Edmonds, Flora, Christian Kay, Jane Roberts, and Irené Wotherspoon. *Thesaurus of Old English*. University of Glasgow Online. 4 Dec. 2005 <http://libra.englang.arts.gla.ac.uk/oethesaurus>.
An online expanded version of Jane Roberts and Christian Kay, *A Thesaurus of Old English*, new impression, 2 vols., Costerus ns 131–32 (Amsterdam: Rodopi, 2000), that allows users to search the database by Old English word or phrase, modern English word, or tags (indicating that a word appears infrequently or only in poetry or in glosses or glossaries). Users can also browse a list of category headings. For suggestions about revising the *Thesaurus*, see Hideki Watanabe, "*A Thesaurus of Old English* Revisited," *Symposium on Lexicography X*, ed. Henrik Gottlieb, Jens Erik Mogensen, and Arne Zettersten, Lexicographica Ser. Maior 109 (Tübingen: Niemeyer, 2002) 313–24.
   Thesaurus of Old English is part of the *Historical Thesaurus of English* (M1420) project, which, when complete, will be a valuable resource for studying the evolution of meaning of words as well as for explicating literary works.

STUDIES OF LANGUAGE

M1710   Mitchell, Bruce. *Old English Syntax*. 2 vols. Oxford: Clarendon–Oxford UP, 1985.   PE213.M5   429'.5.
A detailed study of the principles of Old English syntax using "the formal descriptive approach and traditional Latin-based grammar." Vol. 1 examines concord, parts of speech, and sentence parts; vol. 2, subordinate clauses, other sentence elements and their order, and problems specifically related to poetry. An afterword (pp. 1000–05) prints additions to vol. 2. Throughout, Mitchell examines problems of interpretation in literary texts, emphasizes areas needing further study, and rigorously evaluates existing scholarship (which is more fully surveyed in his *Critical Bibliography of Old English Syntax* [below]). Includes a selective bibliography, a general index to each volume, and two cumulative indexes (words and phrases, passages discussed; authors are indexed in *Critical Bibliography* [below]). A seminal work, *Old English Syntax* admirably fulfills the author's intent to provide a basis for definitive studies of individual topics and eventually "an authoritative *Old English Syntax*." For Mitchell's response to reviews and a list of additions and corrections, see "*Old English Syntax*: A Review of the Reviews," *Neuphilologische Mitteilungen* 91 (1990): 273–93; lists of reviews and additions and corrections are also printed in *Critical Bibliography* 239–47 (below). Reviews: R. D. Fulk, *Philological Quarterly* 66 (1987): 279–83; Stanley B. Greenfield, *JEGP: Journal of En-*

glish and Germanic Philology 86 (1987): 392–99; Willem Koopman, *Neophilologus* 71 (1987): 460–66; T. A. Shippey, *TLS: Times Literary Supplement* 28 June 1985: 716.

   Old English Syntax must be used with Mitchell, *A Critical Bibliography of Old English Syntax to the End of 1984 Including Addenda and Corrigenda to* Old English Syntax (Oxford: Blackwell, 1990, 269 pp.), and Mitchell and Susan Irvine, "A Critical Bibliography of Old English Syntax: Supplement 1985–[96]," *Neuphilologische Mitteilungen* 93 (1992): 1–56; 97 (1996): 1–28, 121–61, 255–78; 103 (2002): 3–32, 179–204, 275–304 with entries organized chronologically within classified divisions that usually match the organization of *Old English Syntax*. As in *Old English Syntax*, Mitchell is forthright and blunt (or rancorous, in at least one reviewer's opinion) in his evaluations. Works that "can be safely disregarded by the general reader" are marked by a dagger and generally receive no further comment; a symbol resembling crossed swords identifies studies that are "written from a 'modern linguistic' viewpoint and often call for no further comment" (for Mitchell's prejudice against such studies see the introduction to *Old English Syntax* and "*Old English Syntax*: A Review of the Reviews" [above]); a double dagger indicates works evaluated in *Old English Syntax*. Entries not preceded by one of the symbols are usually accompanied by full (usually evaluative) annotations; some, though, are for studies that, despite their titles, have little relevance to Old English. Reviews are cited as part of entries for books. The main volume concludes with three appendixes: a list of reviews of *Old English Syntax*; additions and corrections to *Old English Syntax*; and comments by reviewers that Mitchell did not accept. Two indexes in both the main volume and the supplement: subjects; authors and reviewers (including citations in *Old English Syntax*; to obtain a revised index of authors and reviewers, see p. 56 of the supplement). Admirably thorough in coverage, *Critical Bibliography of Old English Syntax* certainly fulfills the promise of the "critical" in its title and, if used with due regard to the clearly articulated prejudices of the foremost scholar of the subject, is an invaluable guide to scholarship on Old English syntax.

M1715   Campbell, A. *Old English Grammar.* Oxford: Clarendon–Oxford UP,
         1959. 423 pp.   PE131.C3   429.5.
   A detailed historical grammar of Old English, covering phonology, morphology, and almost all other aspects and features of the language except syntax (for which, see Mitchell, *Old English Syntax* [M1710]). Concludes with a selective bibliography and an index of words discussed. *Old English Grammar* is the authoritative work on the subject. Reviews: C. E. Bazell, *Medium Ævum* 29 (1960): 27–30; Norman E. Eliason, *Speculum* 35 (1960): 435–38.
   More suitable for beginners is Bruce Mitchell and Fred C. Robinson, *A Guide to Old English*, 7th ed. (Oxford: Blackwell, 2007, 432 pp.).

Genres

POETRY

Histories and Surveys

M1735   Pearsall, Derek. *Old English and Middle English Poetry.* Vol. 1 of *The
         Routledge History of English Poetry.* Gen ed. R. A. Foakes. London:
         Routledge, 1977. 352 pp.   PR502.R58   821'.009.

Emphasizes poetry as a social, rather than artistic, phenomenon in a critical history of poetry to c. 1500. Ranging broadly through the poetic corpus, Pearsall offers chapters on "*Beowulf* and the Anglo-Saxon Poetic Tradition," "Anglo-Saxon Religious Poems," "Late Old English Poetry and the Transition," "Poetry in the Early Middle English Period," "Some Fourteenth-Century Books and Writers," "Alliterative Poetry," "Court Poetry," and "The Close of the Middle Ages." Concludes with an appendix listing technical terms (mostly describing metrics) and a chronology (with sections for historical events, poems by composition date, and the most important poetry manuscripts). Indexed by persons, anonymous works, and a few subjects. Although reviewers have pointed out errors in translations, objected to a number of interpretations, and faulted the density of many passages, they generally commend the breadth and learning of the work. Reviews: Daniel G. Calder, *Anglo-Saxon England* 10 (1982): 243–44; Margaret E. Goldsmith, *English* 27 (Spring 1978): 33–37; Stanley B. Greenfield, *Modern Philology* 77 (1979): 188–91; Fred C. Robinson, *Modern Language Review* 76 (1981): 651–54.

Guides to Scholarship and Criticism

See

Martinez, *Guide to British Poetry Explication*, vol. 1 (L1255a).

Middle English Literature

Many works listed in section M: English Literature/General are important to research in Middle English literature.

Research Methods

GENERAL GUIDES

M1755   Powell, James M., ed. *Medieval Studies: An Introduction.* 2nd ed. Syracuse: Syracuse UP, 1992. 438 pp.   D116.M4   940.1′072.

A collection of introductions to research in Latin paleography, diplomatics, numismatics, archaeology, prosopography, computer-assisted analysis of statistical documents, chronology, English literature (with some inaccuracies and errors of judgment in the discussions of reference works), Latin philosophy, law, science and natural philosophy, art, and music. Each essay outlines the historical development of its field, identifies major reference tools and important studies, explains research methods, and ends with a selective bibliography. Indexed by authors and anonymous works. Although addressed to "the beginner in medieval studies," the volume offers expert orientations to research in unfamiliar fields. Review: Charles T. Wood, *Speculum* 68 (1993): 554–55.

MANUSCRIPTS

M1760   *A Guide to Editing Middle English.* Ed. Vincent P. McCarren and Douglas
    Moffat. Ann Arbor: U of Michigan P, 1998. 338 pp.   PR275.T45 G85
    820.9'001.

A collection of essays that treat practical aspects of editing Middle English manuscripts. Although addressed to the neophyte, few experienced editors will fail to benefit
from the discussions of such topics as editing methods, parallel texts, using sources,
annotating a text, preparing a glossary, electronic editions, and editing kinds of literary
and nonliterary manuscripts. Of particular importance for both students and aspiring
editors is an admirably straightforward "Practical Guide to Working with Middle English Manuscripts." Indexed by subjects. Written by many of the top Middle English
scholars, *Guide to Editing Middle English* stands as a model for the kind of guide needed
for other periods and will—if thoroughly studied by aspiring editors—accomplish its
goal of "rais[ing] the standard of scholarly editing for Middle English texts." Review:
Eric Eliason, *Text: An Interdisciplinary Annual of Textual Studies* 13 (2000): 277–83.

This work supersedes Charles Moorman, *Editing the Middle English Manuscript*
(Jackson: UP of Mississippi, 1975, 107 pp.).

For a convenient (and effectively illustrated) guide to terminology, see Michelle
P. Brown, *Understanding Illuminated Manuscripts: A Guide to Technical Terms* (Malibu:
Getty Museum in association with the British Lib., 1994, 127 pp.).

Paleography

M1765   Johnson, Charles, and Hilary Jenkinson. *English Court Hand, A. D. 1066 to
    1500, Illustrated Chiefly from the Public Records.* 2 vols. Oxford: Clarendon–
    Oxford UP, 1915.   Z115.E5 J6   421'.7.

A manual for those learning to read English court hand. Vol. 1 traces the evolution
of the hand, outlines methods of abbreviations (with a helpful list of common ones),
offers practical hints on transcription, provides a selected bibliography, traces the development of individual forms (with valuable dated illustrations of letters, runes, abbreviations, signs, numerals, and other marks), and concludes with extensively annotated
transcriptions of the plates in vol. 2. The detailed illustrations of various forms make
this the best introduction to court hand and an essential companion for those who
work with medieval English documents.

Hands from the fifteenth through seventeenth centuries are described and illustrated in Jenkinson, *Later Court Hands in England* (entry M1965).

M1770   Parkes, M. B. *English Cursive Book Hands, 1250–1500.* Corrected rpt.
    Oxford Palaeographical Handbooks. Berkeley: U of California P, 1980.
    26 pp.   Z115.E5 P37   745.6'1.

    Wright, C. E. *English Vernacular Hands from the Twelfth to the Fifteenth
    Centuries.* Oxford Palaeographical Handbooks. Oxford: Clarendon–Oxford
    UP, 1960. 24 pp.   Z115.E5 W7   421.7.

Each work prints a series of plates with accompanying transcriptions and notes
that illustrate the different types of hands used in England for writing books. The plates
are arranged chronologically to show the development of each hand. Although lacking
a discussion of abbreviations used by scribes, Parkes and Wright are convenient sources
for identifying and learning to read the hands used for writing the majority of Middle

English literary manuscripts. Reviews: (Parkes) Ruth J. Dean, *Speculum* 46 (1971): 177–80; (Wright) A. I. Doyle, *Medium Ævum* 30 (1961): 117–20.

See also

Jenkinson, *Later Court Hands in England* (M1965).

Guides to Scholarship

M1775   Braswell, Laurel Nichols. *Western Manuscripts from Classical Antiquity to the Renaissance: A Handbook.* Garland Reference Library of the Humanities 139. New York: Garland, 1981. 382 pp.   Z105.B73   091.

A selective annotated bibliography of reference works and scholarship (published through the late 1970s) on the identification, study, and editing of early manuscripts from the ninth through the mid-fifteenth centuries, principally in Romance and Germanic languages, with particular attention to medieval English literary and scientific manuscripts. The 2,074 entries are listed alphabetically in 15 classified sections: bibliographies, libraries, microforms, incipits, subjects, paleography, diplomatics and archives, fragments and booklets, decoration and illumination, music, codicology, reference works, contexts of manuscripts, journals, and textual criticism. Although importance is the main criterion determining selection, a number of works of dubious value are admitted, and there are some notable omissions. The descriptive annotations are neither as precise nor as accurate as they might be, but there are some judicious brief evaluations. Indexed by persons and anonymous titles. Despite the errors and some lack of balance among sections, Braswell is a serviceable basic guide to scholarship on early manuscripts. Reviews: Revilo P. Oliver, *Classical Journal* 78 (1983): 367–69; Germaine Warkentin, *University of Toronto Quarterly* 52 (1983): 403–04.

Histories and Surveys

The best guides to earlier literary histories and surveys are Robert W. Ackerman, "Middle English Literature to 1400" (pp. 73–123), in Fisher, *Medieval Literature of Western Europe* (entry M1830), and John H. Fisher, "English Literature" (pp. 1–54), in Cooke, *The Present State of Scholarship in Fourteenth-Century Literature* (M1830a).

For an account of the emergence of Middle English studies as a scholarly discipline, see David Matthews, *The Making of Middle English, 1765–1910,* Medieval Cultures 18 (Minneapolis: U of Minnesota P, 1999, 231 pp.).

M1777   *The Cambridge History of Medieval English Literature.* Ed. David Wallace. New Cambridge History of English Literature. Cambridge: Cambridge UP, 1999. 1,043 pp.   PR255.C35   820.9′001.

A collaborative history of "literature composed or transmitted in the British Isles between 1066 and 1547." Although separately authored, the 31 chapters are designed to offer a continuous narrative (but not a grand récit) and attend to the conditions of the production and reception of a wide range of works. Unlike so many recent multiauthored literary histories, this one has a chronology and bibliography; unfortunately, the layout of the former makes it difficult to compare literary and historical events, and the lack of any topical organization in the bibliography of secondary works leaves a reader with 73 pages to skim. Two indexes: manuscripts; persons, subjects, and titles of anonymous works. Including contributions by many of the leading medieval scholars, *Cambridge History of Medieval English Literature* has exerted substantial influence on the study of medieval British literature. Review: Tom Shippey, *TLS: Times Literary Supplement* 14 May 1999: 18–19.

M1778   Simpson, James. *1350–1547: Reform and Cultural Revolution.* Vol. 2 of
    The Oxford English Literary History (M1310a). Gen. ed. Jonathan Bate.
    Oxford: Oxford UP, 2002. 661 pp.   PR85.O96   820.9.
    In a literary history of the progression from medieval to early modern, this work emphasizes the centralization of language and literature in chapters on genres and social, political, and religious contexts. Concludes with a series of author bibliographies and a selected bibliography; both omit many important works. Indexed by persons, subjects, and anonymous works. Because of the short shrift accorded several important authors and works (e.g., Thomas More and John Skelton), Simpson does not supplant the other literary histories in this section or Lewis, *English Literature in the Sixteenth Century Excluding Drama* (M1975).

M1780   Bennett, H. S. *Chaucer and the Fifteenth Century.* Corrected rpt. Vol. 2,
    pt. 1 of *The Oxford History of English Literature* (M1310). Gen. eds. John
    Buxton and Norman Davis. Oxford: Clarendon–Oxford UP, 1979. 348
    pp. (Reprinted in 1990 as vol. 2, with the title *Chaucer and Fifteenth-
    Century Verse and Prose.*)   PR255.B43   821.17.
    A critical history with chapters on fourteenth-century London, Chaucer, religion, the intellectual background, author-audience relationships, verse, and prose, as well as a chronology and selective bibliography (now outdated). Indexed by authors, anonymous works, and subjects. (The corrected reprint makes only minor corrections to the text of the 1947 edition but provides a much better index and updates the bibliography to c. 1970.) Bennett is an important history, although reviewers have argued with some interpretations and justifiably faulted the division of coverage between this volume and Chambers, *English Literature at the Close of the Middle Ages* (M1790) — a division that, for example, isolates Chaucer from his contemporaries. Reviews: *Times Literary Supplement* 17 Apr. 1948: 221; Francis Lee Utley, *Speculum* 26 (1951): 370–75.

M1785   Bennett, J. A. W. *Middle English Literature.* Ed. and completed by Douglas
    Gray. Vol. 1., pt. 2 of *The Oxford History of English Literature* (M1310).
    Gen. eds. John Buxton and Norman Davis. Oxford: Clarendon–Oxford
    UP, 1986. 496 pp. (Reprinted in 1990 as vol. 1, with the title *Middle
    English Literature, 1100–1400.*)   PR255.B45   820'.9'001.
    A critical history organized in chapters devoted to genres and major authors: pastoral and comedy, didactic and homiletic verse, Layamon, romances, poems of the Gawain manuscript, prose, lyrics, Gower, and Langland. Concludes with a chronology and selected bibliography through 1984 (but the latter excludes some important works). Indexed by persons and works. Although the volume lacks any synthesis and gives little attention to historical and intellectual contexts, most chapters offer substantial — and, depending on one's perspective, occasionally brilliant or opinionated — discussions of major authors and works. *Middle English Literature* is one of the standard works on the period. Reviews: Charles Blyth, *Essays in Criticism* 37 (1987): 321–29; A. J. Minnis, *TLS: Times Literary Supplement* 6 Feb. 1987: 140; A. C. Spearing, *Yearbook of Langland Studies* 2 (1988): 155–59.

M1790   Chambers, E. K. *English Literature at the Close of the Middle Ages.* 2nd
        impression with corrections. Vol. 2, pt. 2 of *The Oxford History of English
        Literature* (M1310). Gen. eds. F. P. Wilson and Bonamy Dobrée. Oxford:
        Clarendon–Oxford UP, 1947. 247 pp. (Reprinted in 1990 as vol. 3, with
        the title *Malory and Fifteenth-Century Drama, Lyrics, and Ballads.*)
        PR291.C5   820.902.

   Unlike other volumes of the *Oxford History of English Literature* (M1310), Chambers comprises four independent essays on the drama (an updated distillation of his
Mediaeval Stage [M1905]), the carol and fifteenth-century lyric, popular narrative poetry
and the ballad, and Malory. Concludes with a selective bibliography (now outdated).
Indexed by authors, anonymous works, and subjects. Although composed of erudite,
balanced discussions, the volume does not offer a literary history of the period. This
and Bennett, *Chaucer and the Fifteenth Century* (M1780), have been justifiably faulted
for the division of coverage. Reviews: A. C. Baugh, *JEGP: Journal of English and Germanic Philology* 46 (1947): 304–07; Beatrice White, *Modern Language Review* 41
(1946): 426–28.

See also

   Sec. M: English Literature/General/Histories and Surveys.

Literary Handbooks, Dictionaries, and Encyclopedias

M1795   *Dictionary of the Middle Ages.* Ed. Joseph R. Strayer. 13 vols. New York:
        Scribner's, 1982–89. *Supplement 1.* Ed. William Chester Jordan. New
        York: Scribner's–Gale, 2004. 722 pp.   D114.D5   909.07.

   Covers the intellectual, ecclesiastical, political, and literary history, material culture,
and geography of "the Latin West, the Slavic World, Asia Minor, the lands of the
caliphate in the East, and the Muslim-Christian areas of North Africa" from the period
500 to 1500. The approximately 5,000 entries, ranging from brief identifications and
definitions to major articles by established scholars, treat places, persons, art works,
events, literary forms and genres, national literatures, and a variety of miscellaneous
topics. Brief bibliographies, largely confined to English-language scholarship, conclude
most entries. Errata to all volumes are printed in vol. 13, pp. 607–13. The best approach to persons and subjects is through the detailed index (vol. 13). There is an
occasional imbalance in the treatment of similar topics, but readable discussions and
solid scholarship make this a useful source of quick information and basic surveys. The
Supplement emphasizes topics that have emerged since the 1970s, new evidence about
old topics, and areas outside northwestern Europe; its selective bibliographies include
more works in languages other than English. Complemented by *Lexikon des Mittelalters*
(M1800), which is more scholarly but less broad in coverage. Reviews: Charles T.
Wood, *Speculum* 60 (1985): 967–71; 66 (1991): 147–49.

M1800   *Lexikon des Mittelalters Online* (*LexMA*). Brepols. Online. 5 Feb. 2006
        <http://www.brepolis.net>.
        International Encyclopedia for the Middle Ages: A Supplement to LexMa
        Online (*IEMA*). Brepols. Online. 5 Feb. 2006 <http://www.brepolis.net>.
        Lexikon des Mittelalters. 10 vols. München: Lexma, 1977–99.
        D101.5.L49   940.1′05.

A dictionary of the history and culture of the Middle Ages in Europe and parts of North Africa and the Middle East from c. 300 to c. 1500. *Lexikon des Mittelalters Online* reproduces the entries in the original *Lexikon des Mittelalters*, adds a searchable and browsable list of English-language headwords, adds links to *BREPOLiS Medieval Bibliographies* (M1835), provides a translation tool (which accepts only one word at a time and does not work with a word including a diacritic mark), allows for keyword searches of the entire text (except the bibliographies appended to entries), and lets users download or print articles. Entries, ranging from brief definitions or identifications to lengthy articles by an international group of scholars, treat individuals, works, forms and genres, material culture, places, and events. Each concludes with a brief bibliography. (In the online version, users must click the *LexMA* link next to Bibliography to view the citations.) The extensive use of symbols and abbreviations makes for slow reading, and there is some imbalance in the treatment of similar topics. Three indexes: subjects (subdivided; see, e.g., Englische Sprache und Literatur subdivision); cross-references; contributors.

The online version supersedes the CD-ROM (ed. Charlotte Bretscher-Gisiger and Thomas Meier [Lachen: Coron, 2000]). *Lexikon des Mittelalters* is being supplemented in English by *International Encyclopedia for the Middle Ages*, which covers the same geographic area from 500 to 1500. *IEMA* and *LexMA* can be searched separately or simultaneously.

Authoritative and scholarly, *Lexikon des Mittelalters*, *International Encyclopedia for the Middle Ages*, and *Dictionary of the Middle Ages* (M1795) provide medievalists with essential information on a wide range of topics. Review: (vol. 1.1–5) Joseph R. Strayer, *Speculum* 55 (1980): 627–28.

Bibliographies of Bibliographies

M1805   Rouse, Richard H. *Serial Bibliographies for Medieval Studies.* Publications of
the Center for Medieval and Renaissance Studies 3. Berkeley: U of
California P, 1969. 150 pp.   Z6203.R66   016.016914'03'1.

A classified, descriptive guide to 294 current and defunct serial bibliographies covering medieval studies from the advent of Christianity to c. 1500. Rouse omits standard general indexes and national bibliographies but includes bibliographic essays, lists of contents of recent periodicals, accessions lists of special libraries, and reports of work in progress. Entries are classified in 11 divisions: general bibliographies; national and regional bibliographies; Byzantine, Islamic, and Judaic studies; archival and auxiliary studies; art and archaeology; ecclesiastical history; economic, social, and institutional history; intellectual history; literature and linguistics; music; science, technology, and medicine. Since the description of each bibliography is based primarily on a single volume published between 1964 and 1967, variations in scope, editorial policy, and organization are not always noted. An asterisk denotes an important work. Two indexes: title; editor. Although dated, Rouse remains useful for identifying essential serial bibliographies outside the field of literature (for which Wortman, *Guide to Serial Bibliographies* [G325], generally provides more-thorough coverage).

See also

Sec. D: Bibliographies of Bibliographies.

Guides to Primary Works

MANUSCRIPTS

M1810 Ker, N. R., and A. J. Piper. *Medieval Manuscripts in British Libraries.* 5 vols.
Oxford: Clarendon–Oxford UP, 1969–2002.   Z6620.G7 K4   011.

A catalog of manuscripts written before c. 1500 in Latin or Western European
languages and held in public collections that have not been previously or adequately
cataloged. Thus Ker does not include private collections or major libraries (such as the
British Library or the Bodleian), although researchers are directed to the standard catalogs of institutional collections. Vol. 1 covers London; vols. 2–4 list collections alphabetically by city; vol. 5 (ed. I. C. Cunningham and A. G. Watson) includes addenda
and 11 indexes (authors, subjects, and titles; other names; Bibles; liturgies; iconography;
languages other than Latin; origins and dates of manuscripts; secundo folios; incipits;
repertories cited; manuscripts cited [some of the preceding are subdivided]). The detailed descriptions of uncataloged items—informed by Ker's incomparable knowledge
of medieval manuscripts—include short title; date; contents; bibliographical, paleographical, and codicological information; and provenance. (Manuscripts adequately described elsewhere receive summary treatment and references to published catalogs.)
Besides making known for the first time a number of manuscripts, *Medieval Manuscripts*
is an invaluable source for finding iconographic and paleographical information, identifying texts and provenance, and locating manuscripts. One of the truly great catalogs.
Reviews: (vol. 2) Christopher de Hamel, *Medium Ævum* 50 (1981): 101–04; Jean F.
Preston, *Review* 1 (1979): 223–31; (vols. 3–4) *Book Collector* 41 (1992): 161–79.

M1815 Ricci, Seymour de. *Census of Medieval and Renaissance Manuscripts in the
United States and Canada.* 3 vols. New York: Wilson, 1935–40. C. U. Faye
and W. H. Bond. *Supplement.* New York: Bibliog. Soc. of Amer., 1962.
626 pp.   Z6620.U5 R5.

Essentially a finding list of Western manuscripts before 1600 owned by institutions
and private collectors. Except for Greek and Latin papyri, the work includes all written
documents, but because of their number, letters, charters, and deeds are usually not
described separately. Entries are organized alphabetically by state, then by city, then by
institution or collector; Canadian listings appear in vol. 2, pp. 2201–38, and are followed by a lengthy list of errata and corrections (vol. 2, pp. 2239–343). Since Ricci is
not intended to be a definitive catalog and since many descriptions are supplied by
owners, an entry provides only basic information: author, title or incipit, brief physical
description, place of composition, provenance, and references to scholarship. Vol. 3 is
made up of six indexes (general index of names, titles, and headings; scribes, illumi-
nators, and cartographers; incipits; Gregory numbers for Greek New Testament manuscripts; present owners; previous owners) but does not include the planned lists of
unlocated manuscripts or those held by dealers. The *Supplement* (compiled almost exclusively from questionnaires) adds new manuscripts, records changes in ownership, and
prints corrections. The most current information on manuscripts listed in *Census* and
Supplement can be found at the Uncatalogued Manuscript Control Center Web site
(http://members.aol.com/dericci/umcc/umcc.html). Although not comprehensive and
now dated, the work remains an important starting point for locating manuscripts in
collections that have not been fully cataloged and for tracing provenance.

A major desideratum is a descriptive catalog (such as Ker, *Medieval Manuscripts in British Libraries* [M1810]) for medieval manuscripts in North American collections — a need that might be met if the Uncatalogued Manuscript Control Center project is a success (see the URL above) or if institutions adopt the Electronic Access to Medieval Manuscripts (EAMMS) guidelines for cataloging manuscripts and contribute the records to *WorldCat* and RLG Union Catalog. For a discussion of the latter and an assessment of the *Census* and *Supplement,* see Gregory A. Pass, "Electrifying Research in Medieval and Renaissance Manuscripts," *Papers of the Bibliographical Society of America* 94 (2000): 507 – 30.

PRINTED WORKS

M1820   *Gesamtkatalog der Wiegendrucke* (*GKW*). Vols. 1 – 7. 2nd ed. 1968. Vol. 8 – .
Stuttgart: Hiersemann, 1972 – . (The second edition reprints, with additions and corrections, the volumes published 1925 – 38.)   Z240.G39.
Online. 1 Nov. 2005 <http://www.gesamtkatalogderwiegendrucke.de/NFuseEN.htm>.

An analytical bibliography that attempts to describe every extant edition printed in fifteenth-century Europe. Listed alphabetically by author or title of anonymous work, the detailed entries include author, short title, editor, translator, corrector, commentator, place of printing, printer, publisher, date, format, collation, notes on typography, transcription of title and colophon, contents, references to standard bibliographies, and locations of copies. (See vol. 8 for a description in English [pp. *101 – 08], German, French, Russian, and Italian of the parts of an entry; an updated version appears on the Help page of the *GKW* Web site.) Vols. 1 – 7 locate no more than 10 copies, but the later ones attempt a complete census. Since the editors must frequently work from photographic copies, format and collation are not always accurately described, and there are errors in the identification of printers. For the history of *GKW* and discussions of editorial procedure, see the essays in *Zur Arbeit mit dem* Gesamtkatalog der Wiegendrucke, Beiträge aus der Deutschen Staatsbibliothek 9 (Berlin: Deutsche Staatsbibliothek, 1989, 155 pp.). Although the prewar volumes now need revision, *GKW* is an essential source for identifying editions (and their contents and sometimes complex textual relationships), authors, and printers; for localizing and dating books; and for locating copies. Reviews: John L. Flood, *Library* 5th ser. 30 (1975): 339 – 44; Lotte Hellinga, *Library* 6th ser. 13 (1991): 268 – 71; Paul Needham, *TLS: Times Literary Supplement* 15 Aug. 1980: 922.

The online *GKW* is very much a work-in-progress. Currently the database is divided into two parts: A – H, which is an updated version of the print edition, and I – Z, which represents the working-copy for the bibliography (for the status of the database consult the Current Processing Status page). Because the search engine allows only literal searches (i.e., it is case sensitive and requires diacritics), users must consult the Help file before attempting a search. The database currently has four search interfaces: advanced (which allows keyword searches of the full text and the record fields, e.g., author, format, printer, collation, date, locations); printer, place, and date (with pull-down lists of the first two); bibliography; second quires. In addition, users can search indexes of authors, *GKW* numbers, personal names, printers (by city), titles, short titles, incipits, second quires, locations (by city), holdings (by city, then institution), and bibliography (by siglum). Users who take the time to master the search interfaces will be able to manipulate in sophisticated ways the massive amount of data in *GKW*.

Even when *GKW* is complete, existing general bibliographies of incunabula will remain valuable complements, especially for their fuller information on individual copies. Among the most important of these bibliographies are the following:

Bayerische Staatsbibliothek Inkunabelkatalog (*BSB-Ink*). Wiesbaden: Reichert, 1988–2005. Review: (vol. 1) John Goldfinch, *Library* 6th ser. 13 (1991): 275–78.

Catalogue des incunables. 2 vols. Paris: Bibliothèque Nationale, 1981– .

Catalogue of Books Printed in the XVth Century Now in the British Museum. Gay-Houten: HES and DeGraff, 1908– . Review: David McKitterick, *TLS: Times Literary Supplement* 30 Mar. 2007: 7–8.

Goff, Frederick R., comp. and ed. *Incunabula in American Libraries: A Third Census of Fifteenth-Century Books Recorded in North American Collections.* New York: Bibliog. Soc. of Amer., 1964. 798 pp. *Supplement.* 1972. 104 pp. A photographic reprint of Goff's annotated copy was published by Kraus in 1973. Although the annotated copy served as the working copy for the *Supplement,* the latter does not include Goff's notes on dealers' and auction prices. The entries, along with substantial additions and corrections, are incorporated into the *ISTC* database (see below).

Hain, Ludwig. *Repertorium Bibliographicum, in Quo Libri Omnes ab Arte Typographica Inventa usque ad Annum MD. Typis Expressi Ordine Alphabetico vel Simpliciter Enumerantur vel Adcuratius Recensentur.* 2 vols. in 4 pts. Stuttgart: Cotta; Paris: Lutetiae, 1826–38. The work is indexed by K. Burger, *Ludwig Hain's* Repertorium Bibliographicum*: Register,* Zentralblatt für Bibliothekswesen 8 (Leipzig: Harrassowitz, 1891, 427 pp.). Copinger, W. A. *Supplement to Hain's* Repertorium Bibliographicum. 2 pts. Berlin: Altmann, 1926 (with Index by Konrad Burger).

Incunabula Short-Title Catalogue (*ISTC*). British Library. Online. 1 Nov. 2005 <http://www.bl.uk/catalogues/istc/index.html>. An online catalog that intends to record every copy of every extant edition. Although the database is currently the single most comprehensive list of incunabula, entries are based largely on printed catalogs and do not provide the detail of *GKW.* The Simple Search screen allows for searching by keyword, author, title, place of publication, printer, bibliographical reference, *ISTC* number, format, locations of copies, date, language, and British Library shelf mark; the preceding fields can also be browsed. Advanced Search allows users to combine the preceding fields and to limit searches to country of publication. In addition, all fields can be browsed. Many titles in the database are being reproduced in microfiche in *Incunabula: The Printing Revolution in Europe, 1455–1500* (Woodbridge: Primary Source Microfilm, 1992–).

Proctor, Robert. *An Index to the Early Printed Books in the British Museum: From the Invention of Printing to the Year 1500. With Notes of Those in the Bodleian Library.* London: Holland, 1960. 908 pp. A convenient reprint of the original two volumes and four supplements, 1898–1906.

Reichling, Dietrich. *Appendices ad Hainii-Copingeri* Repertorium Bibliographicum: *Additiones et Emendationes.* 6 fascicles and index. München: Rosenthal, 1905–11. *Supplement.* Monasterii Guestphalorum, 1914. 109 pp.

See also

English Short Title Catalogue (M1377).
Pollard, *Short-Title Catalogue* (M1990).
Severs, *Manual of the Writings in Middle English* (M1825).

Guides to Scholarship and Criticism

SURVEYS OF RESEARCH

M1825   Severs, J. Burke, Albert E. Hartung, and Peter G. Beidler, gen. eds. *A Manual of the Writings in Middle English, 1050–1500.* 12 vols. New Haven: Connecticut Acad. of Arts and Sciences, 1967– .   PR255.M3 016.820'9'001.

Chapters are published as they are completed in consecutively paginated volumes:

Vol. 1: Romances. 1967. (Supplemented by Joanne A. Rice, *Middle English Romance: An Annotated Bibliography, 1955–1985,* Garland Reference Library of the Humanities 545 [New York: Garland, 1987, 626 pp.], although there are numerous omissions of studies published outside the United States.)

Vol. 2: *Pearl* Poet; Wyclyf and His Followers; Translations and Paraphrases of the Bible, and Commentaries; Saints' Legends; Instructions for Religious. 1970.

Vol. 3: Dialogues, Debates, and Catechisms; Thomas Hoccleve; Malory and Caxton. 1972.

Vol. 4: Middle Scots Writers; Chaucerian Apocrypha. 1973.

Vol. 5: Dramatic Pieces [miracle, mystery, morality, and folk plays]; Poems Dealing with Contemporary Conditions. 1975.

Vol. 6: Carols; Ballads; John Lydgate. 1980. (See A. S. G. Edwards, "Additions and Corrections to the Bibliography of John Lydgate," *Notes and Queries* ns 32 [1985]: 450–52.)

Vol. 7: John Gower; *Piers Plowman;* Travel and Geographical Writings; Works of Religious and Philosophical Instruction. 1986.

Vol. 8: Chronicles and Other Historical Writings. 1989.

Vol. 9: Proverbs, Precepts, and Monitory Pieces; English Mystical Writings; Tales. 1993.

Vol. 10: Works of Science and Information. 1998.

Vol. 11: Sermons and Homilies; Lyrics of MS Harley 2253. 2005.

Chapters are planned for letters, legal writings, lyrics, and miscellaneous prose.

The work is a survey of scholarship and bibliography that revises and expands John Edwin Wells, *A Manual of the Writings in Middle English, 1050–1400* (New Haven: Connecticut Acad. of Arts and Sciences, 1916, 941 pp.), and its nine supplements (1919–51). Each chapter (and sometimes sections thereof) has two parts: (1) the commentary, which for each work discusses content, manuscripts, date, dialect, source, and form and summarizes scholarship and critical trends; (2) a classified bibliography (with sections for manuscripts, editions, textual matters, language, versification, date, authorship, sources, literary criticism, and bibliography). Many entries are briefly annotated. Coverage is less thorough in vols. 1–3 ("all serious studies down through 1955 . . . and all important studies from 1955 to" one or two years before publication); the later volumes strive to include "all serious studies" up to one or two years before publication. (See the preface to each volume—especially vol. 5—for specific terminal dates.) Reviewers have, however, noted a number of omissions in some chapters; and following Wells's organization while expanding his scope has led to some inconsistent groupings in chapters. Indexed by authors, titles, early printers, and subjects; a master index is planned upon completion. Although the early chapters are now dated and some works and authors are now more exhaustively treated in separate bibliographies, Severs and Hartung remains an indispensable starting point for most research in medieval literature. Reviews: (vol. 1) Norman Davis, *Review of English Studies* ns 21 (1970): 72–74; (vol. 2) Anne Hudson, *Medium Ævum* 43 (1974): 199–201; (vol. 3) Davis, *Review of English Studies* ns 25 (1974): 67–69; (vol. 4) Davis, *Review of English Studies* ns 26 (1975): 325–27; (vol. 5) Hudson, *Yearbook of English Studies* 9 (1979): 361–62.

M1830   Fisher, John H., ed. *The Medieval Literature of Western Europe: A Review of Research, Mainly 1930–1960.* Revolving Fund Series 22. New York: New York UP for MLA; London: U of London P, 1966. 432 pp.   PN671.F5 809.02.

Surveys of research from c. 1930 to c. 1964 on medieval Latin, Old English, Middle English (to 1400), French, German, Old Norse, Italian, Spanish, Catalan, Portuguese, and Celtic literatures. Addressed to advanced graduate students and scholars not specializing in the literatures, chapters typically examine bibliographical and reference works; background, language, and general studies; literary histories; and research on major forms, works, and authors. (The essay "Middle English Literature to 1400" [pp. 73–123], by Robert W. Ackerman, has sections for bibliographies, general and background studies, works of religious instruction, mysticism, translations and didactic works, poetry, romance, drama, *Piers Plowman*, Chaucer, and Gower.) Indexed by scholars and authors. Although now badly dated, *Medieval Literature of Western Europe* is still useful for its sensible evaluations of important studies published during the period. Review: A. A. Heathcote, Johanna H. Torringa, and R. M. Wilson, *Modern Language Review* 63 (1968): 141–42.

Essential supplements are *Year's Work in English Studies* (G330), *Year's Work in Modern Language Studies* (S4855), and especially the surveys and bibliographies of English, French, German, Italian, Latin, and Spanish literature in Thomas D. Cooke, ed., *The Present State of Scholarship in Fourteenth-Century Literature* (Columbia: U of Missouri P, 1982, 319 pp.). The essay by John H. Fisher on English literature (pp. 1–54) surveys bibliographies and research tools, anthologies and translations, facsimiles, thematic studies, language, major authors, works, and genres and concludes with a selective classified bibliography of 386 books published since the early 1960s.

See also

YWES (G330): Chapters for Middle English Literature; Chaucer.

SERIAL BIBLIOGRAPHIES

M1835   *BREPOLiS Medieval Bibliographies: International Medieval Bibliography Online.* Brepols. Online. 3 Feb. 2006 <http://www.brepolis.net>. Updated regularly.

International Medieval Bibliography [1967–   ]: Multidisciplinary Bibliography of the Middle Ages/Bibliographie multidisciplinaire du Moyen Age/ Multidisziplinäre Bibliographie des Mittelalters/Bibliografia multidisciplinaria del Medioevo/Bibliografía multidisciplinaria la Edad Media/ Mul'tidistsdplinarnaya Bibliografiya Srednevekov'ya (300–1500) (IMB).

Turnhout: Brepols, 1968– . 2/yr. Subtitle varies.   Z6203.I63
016.914'03'1. CD-ROM.

An international bibliography of articles and notes in journals, Festschriften, and collections of essays that, through the bibliography for 1998, treated Europe and the Byzantine Empire from 450 to 1500; with the 1999 bibliography, coverage expanded to include the Middle East and North Africa and was extended back to 400 (and then to 300 with the 2003 bibliography). Single-author monographs, reviews, and (as of 1983) collections of previously published articles are excluded.

The *IMB Online* can be searched by keyword(s), author, article title, publication title (e.g., of a collection of essays), year, ISBN or ISSN, language (users should consult the information screen for languages listed as *unclassified*), index terms, subjects, places, persons, repositories of manuscripts, and century. There are separate expandable lists of subjects, places, and dates under an Index tab; clicking on one of the terms inserts it into the appropriate search box; the Wordlist tabs next to several boxes on the search screen do not work. Records, which are organized by date of publication (descending), can be marked for downloading or e-mailing.

In the print version, entries are classified by country or area under several divisions, which currently include ones for language; literature (with sections for general studies, drama, prose, and verse); manuscripts and paleography; folk studies; printing; historiography; and women's studies. Since these divisions have changed markedly over the years, users must consult the contents list in respective volumes. Many entries are now briefly annotated. Two indexes: scholars; subjects (selective). The CD-ROM, while cumulating the print version and offering basic search options, is hampered by a primitive search engine and less than user-friendly interface. Although the work is not comprehensive, its breadth makes it an important complement to the standard serial bibliographies and indexes in section G. Review: B. D. H. Miller, *Review of English Studies* ns 29 (1978): 78–79.

(A companion database—*Bibliographie de civilisation médiévale* (http://www.brepolis.net)—indexes single-author books, but its coverage of Medieval English literature is negligible.)

IMB is complemented by *Iter: Gateway to the Middle Ages and Renaissance* (*Iter*, online, 10 Nov. 2005 <http://www.itergateway.org>, updated daily), which covers studies of the period 400–1700. As of 10 November 2005, the database included more that 720,000 records for books, articles, book chapters, and reviews. The Basic Search screen allows for a keyword search of an entire record or of individual record fields (author, title, subject, publication title [i.e., title and series title], series title [i.e., journal title], or Dewey Decimal Classification). Advanced Search allows users to combine the preceding fields; to limit searches by language, date, and type of publication; and to sort records in a variety of ways. There is considerable disparity in the level of indexing of individual records, only a few records include summaries, and coverage of journals runs two to three years behind publication date; nevertheless *Iter* is a welcome resource, especially for its coverage of post-1500 topics. For a history of *Iter*, see William R. Bowen, "*Iter*: Where Does the Path Lead?" *Early Modern Literary Studies* 5.3 (2000): 26 pars. 5 March 2001 <http://purl.oclc.org/emls/05-3/bowiter.html>.

The following defunct serial bibliographies are still useful:

"Bibliography of American Periodical Literature." *Speculum* 9–47 (1934–72).

International Guide to Medieval Studies: A Continuous Index to Periodical Literature. 12 vols. Darien: Amer. Bibliog. Service, 1963–78. International coverage of articles from 1961 to 1973, with scholar and subject indexes.

> *Progress of Medieval and Renaissance Studies in the United States and Canada.*
> 25 nos. Boulder: U of Colorado, 1921–60. Lists publications, disserta-
> tions, and works in progress, 1922–59.

For other serial bibliographies, see Rouse, *Serial Bibliographies for Medieval Studies*
(M1805).

See also

> Sec. G: Serial Bibliographies, Indexes, and Abstracts.
> *ABELL* (G340): English Literature/Middle English through the volume for 1972;
> English Literature/Old and Middle English: Subsidiary through the volume
> for 1933; English Literature/Fifteenth Century in the volumes for 1927–72;
> and English Literature/Middle English and Fifteenth Century in later volumes.
> *MLAIB* (G335): English Language and Literature division in the volumes for
> 1921–25; English VI in the volumes for 1926–56; English V in the volumes
> for 1957–80; and English Literature/1100–1499: Middle English Period sec-
> tion (as well as any larger chronological sections encompassing the period) in
> the later volumes. Some studies treating Middle English literature appear in
> General/Medieval in the volume for 1928; General II: Medieval Literature in
> the volumes for 1929–32; General/Medieval Literature in the volumes for
> 1933–52; General VII: Literature, General and Comparative/Medieval Lit-
> erature in the volumes for 1953–55; General II: Literature, General and Com-
> parative/Medieval Literature in the volume for 1956; and General III: Litera-
> ture, General and Comparative/Medieval Literature in the volumes for 1957–
> 80. Researchers must also check the headings beginning "English Literature,"
> "Medieval," and "Middle Ages" in the subject index to post-1980 volumes and
> in the online thesaurus.

OTHER BIBLIOGRAPHIES

M1840   *The New Cambridge Bibliography of English Literature* (*NCBEL*). Vol. 1:
         600–1660. Ed. George Watson. Cambridge: Cambridge UP, 1974.
         2,476 cols.   Z2011.N45 [PR83]   016.82.
         (For a full discussion of *NCBEL*, see entry M1385.) The part devoted to the
Middle English period (1100–1500) has six major divisions, each subdivided and classified as its subject requires: introduction, Middle English literature to 1400 (with
sections for romances, literature, Chaucer, education), the fifteenth century (English
Chaucerians, Middle Scots poets, English prose, miscellaneous verse and prose), songs
and ballads, medieval drama, and writings in Latin. The general introduction for the
volume as a whole lists bibliographies, histories, anthologies, and works about prosody,
prose rhythm, and language important to the study of the Middle English period. Users
must familiarize themselves with the organization, remember that there is considerable
unevenness of coverage among subdivisions, and consult the index volume (vol. 5)
rather than the provisional index in vol. 1. Review: Fred C. Robinson, *Anglia* 97 (1979):
511–17.
         Vol. 1 of the *Cambridge Bibliography of English Literature* (M1385a) is still occa-
sionally useful for its coverage of the social and political background (which *NCBEL*
drops).

See also

> *Annotated Bibliographies of Old and Middle English Literature* (M1670a).
> Kallendorf, Latin *Influences on English Literature from the Middle Ages to the Eighteenth Century* (S4895).

RELATED TOPICS

M1845   Graves, Edgar B., ed. *A Bibliography of English History to 1485*. Oxford:
           Clarendon–Oxford UP, 1975. 1,103 pp.   Z2017.B5 [DA130]   016.942.
      An extensive, albeit selective, bibliography of primary works and scholarship on English (not British) history from prehistoric times to 1485 that revises Charles Gross, *The Sources and Literature of English History from the Earliest Times to about 1485*, 2nd ed. (London: Longmans, 1915, 820 pp.). Graves covers publications through December 1969 on the pre-Norman era and through December 1970 (along with some later works) on the period 1066–1485. Entries are organized in five classified divisions: general (with sections for bibliographies, journals, and ancillary areas such as philology, archaeology, and art); archives, source collections, and modern narratives (including a section on local history); prehistory to Anglo-Saxon conquest; Anglo-Saxon period; the period 1066–1485 (with sections on a variety of topics such as chronicles, public records, military and naval history, urban society, the church, and intellectual interests). Many annotations are evaluative or refer to related works; unfortunately, several entries are not annotated or inadequately so. Indexed by persons and subjects. The authoritative guide to historical scholarship on the period, Graves is especially useful for cross-disciplinary research.
      For broader geographical coverage, see Paetow, *Guide to the Study of Medieval History* (M1855), and Crosby, *Medieval Studies* (M1850). Convenient highly selective bibliographies are Bertie Wilkinson, *The High Middle Ages in England, 1154–1377*, Conference on British Studies Bibliographical Handbooks (Cambridge: Cambridge UP for the Conf. on British Studies, 1978, 130 pp.), and Delloyd J. Guth, *Late-Medieval England, 1377–1485*, Conf. on British Studies Bibliographical Handbooks (Cambridge: Cambridge UP for the Conf. on British Studies, 1976, 143 pp.). Guth is continued (but less selectively) by Joel T. Rosenthal, *Late Medieval England (1377–1485): A Bibliography of Historical Scholarship, 1975–1989* (Kalamazoo: Medieval Inst., Western Michigan U, 1994, 371 pp.) and *Late Medieval England (1377–1485): A Bibliography of Historical Scholarship, 1990–1999* (2003, 285 pp.).

M1850   Crosby, Everett U., C. Julian Bishko, and Robert L. Kellogg. *Medieval*
           Studies: A Bibliographical Guide. Garland Reference Library of the
           Humanities 427. New York: Garland, 1983. 1,131 pp.   Z5579.5.C76
           [CB351]   016.9401.
      A classified, annotated, selective bibliography of books and serials on all aspects of medieval studies from the period 200 to 1500. The approximately 9,000 entries are organized in 138 divisions covering reference works, the arts, sciences, social sciences, religion, laws, languages, literatures, numismatics, and heraldry. The broader topics have sections devoted to geographical areas, and each is subdivided as its subject requires. The brief annotations—many of them evaluative—are generally accurate and helpful. Two indexes: authors and editors; topics. Given the breadth of coverage, the organi-

zation of the work is clear and the selection judicious, but access is inhibited by the lack of a subject index. Still, *Medieval Studies* is useful for identifying important reference works and studies and for interdisciplinary research.

M1855   Paetow, Louis John. *A Guide to the Study of Medieval History.* Rev. and
          corrected ed. with errata by Gray C. Boyce and an addendum by Lynn
          Thorndike. Millwood: Kraus, 1980. 643 pp. Gray Cowan Boyce, comp.
          and ed. *Literature of Medieval History, 1930–1975: A Supplement to Louis
          John Paetow's* A Guide to the Study of Medieval History. 5 vols. Millwood:
          Kraus, 1981.   Z6203.P25 [D117]   016.9401.

A selective bibliography emphasizing studies in English, French, and German (with some in Spanish and Italian) published through 1975 on Western Europe. Entries are organized in three divisions, each elaborately classified: general works (with chapters for bibliographies, reference works, subjects related to the study of medieval history, general modern historical works, and collections of original sources), general history of the Middle Ages, and medieval culture (to 1300 in Paetow, 1500 in Boyce). In Paetow, most sections begin with an outline, followed by a list of the most important works and then a general bibliography. (See pp. xxi-li for errata and pp. liii-cxii for the addendum.) Indexed by scholars, collection titles, and subjects. Boyce generally follows Paetow's organization (omitting the introductory outlines and providing a straightforward author list of studies) but offers more-thorough coverage of scholarship and expands the section on medieval culture to 1500. Indexed by persons. Although poorly organized, both works are valuable guides to scholarship on literature-related subjects. Review (Boyce): C. Warren Hollister, *American Historical Review* 87 (1982): 1064–66.

See also

  Royal Historical Society Bibliography (M1400).

Language

GUIDES TO SCHOLARSHIP

See

  ABELL (G340): Middle English headings in the subdivisions of the English Language section in the volumes for 1934–84; in earlier and later volumes, studies treating Middle English appear throughout the English Language division.
  MLAIB (G335): English Language and Literature division in the volumes for 1922–25; Middle English headings in English I/Linguistics section of the volumes for 1926–66; Indo-European C/Germanic Linguistics IV/English/ Middle English section in the 1967–80 volumes; and the Indo-European Languages/Germanic Languages/West Germanic Languages/English Language/ English Language (Middle) section in pt. 3 of the later volumes. Researchers should also check the "English Language (Middle)" heading in the subject index to post-1980 volumes and in the online thesaurus.
  Tajima, *Old and Middle English Language Studies* (M1687).

DICTIONARIES

M1860   *Middle English Dictionary (MED)*. Ed. Hans Kurath et al. 13 vols. Ann
Arbor: U of Michigan P, 1952–2001.   PE679.M54   427.02. Online
through *Middle English Compendium*. 27 Sept. 2005. <http://
quod.lib.umich.edu/m/mec>.

A dictionary of Middle English from c. 1100 to 1475. Entries, based on the
Southeast Midland dialect, cite variant and grammatical forms, part of speech, etymology, meanings (grouped by semantic relationship), and illustrative quotations. The electronic version can be searched by headword (and its forms), by elements of an entry,
and by quotation and provides links to the HyperBibliography (which includes all of
the Middle English materials cited in the *Dictionary* and supersedes the printed bibliographies [see below]) and to texts in the *Corpus of Middle English Prose and Verse*; it
offers far more versatile access than the print volumes. The electronic version corrects
some obvious errors in the print version, revises numerous bibliographic citations, and
supplies definitions for a few entries lacking them; the editor plans to supply entries for
words originally intended for a supplement and for newly discovered words and meanings.

For a detailed description of editorial procedures and a bibliography of the manuscripts and printed editions from which passages are drawn, see *Plan and Bibliography*
(1954, 105 pp.) and *Plan and Bibliography: Supplement I* (1984, 36 pp.), which updates
the bibliography in the original *Plan*; for an overview of modifications of the *Plan*, see
Robert E. Lewis, "*The Middle English Dictionary* at 71," *Dictionaries* 23 (2002): 76–
94; for an account of compilation methods and procedures, see Sherman M. Kuhn,
"On the Making of the *Middle English Dictionary*," *Dictionaries* 4 (1982): 14–41; on
the history of the work, see N. F. Blake, "The Early History of, and Its Impact upon,
the *Middle English Dictionary*," *Dictionaries* 23 (2002): 48–75. Largely superseding the
Middle English entries in *Oxford English Dictionary* (M1410) and justly praised for
accuracy and reliability, *MED* is the indispensable source for the study of Middle English
and for explication of the literature of the period.

Representative of the numerous reviews that suggest additions and corrections are
those appearing in *Medium Ævum*: B. D. H. Miller, 37 (1968): 332–36; 42 (1973):
73–81; 44 (1975): 181–90; 46 (1977): 343–48; 47 (1978): 351–56; R. L. Thompson, 34 (1965): 269–74; Martyn Wakelin, 54 (1985): 292–95. *English Studies* and
Review of English Studies also regularly reviewed volumes. In addition, there are a number
of corrections and additions: F. Th. Visser, "Three Suggested Emendations of the *Mid-
dle English Dictionary*," *English Studies* 36 (1955): 23–24, and "*The Middle English
Dictionary* (Parts A, B1-4, E, and F)," *English Studies* 40 (1959): 18–27; Hans Kurath,
"Some Comments on Professor Visser's Notes on the *Middle English Dictionary*," *English
Studies* 41 (1960): 253–54 (with a response by Visser, 254–55); Hans Käsmann,
"Anmerkungen zum *Middle English Dictionary*," *Anglia* 77 (1959): 65–74; Autumn
Simmons, "*A Contribution to the Middle English Dictionary*: Citations from the English
Poems of Charles, Duc d'Orléans," *Journal of English Linguistics* 2 (1968): 43–56; Lilo
Moessner, "Some Remarks on the *MED*," *Neuphilologische Mitteilungen* 83 (1982):
150–51.

An important complement for the localization of English from c. 1350 to c. 1450
is Angus McIntosh, M. L. Samuels, and Michael Benskin, *A Linguistic Atlas of Late
Mediaeval English*, 4 vols. (Aberdeen: Aberdeen UP, 1986). Although full of information, it is a difficult work to use even with the accompanying *Guide* (1987, 23 pp.).
For examples of how the work can be used, see *Regionalism in Late Medieval Manuscripts*

and Texts: Essays Celebrating the Publication of A Linguistic Atlas of Late Mediaeval English, ed. Felicity Riddy, York Manuscripts Conferences: Proceedings Series 2 (Cambridge: Brewer, 1991, 214 pp.). Review: M. C. Seymour, *English Studies* 72 (1991): 73–80.

See also

> *Dictionary of Medieval Latin from British Sources* (M1700).

STUDIES OF LANGUAGE

M1865   Brunner, Karl. *An Outline of Middle English Grammar.* Trans. Grahame
         Johnston. Cambridge: Harvard UP, 1963. 111 pp.   PE531.B713   427.02.
   A basic overview of the phonology and inflections of Middle English from c. 1100 to c. 1500. Indexed by lexical items. Terse but clear, Brunner is a basic introductory outline of the language.
   Fernand Mossé, *A Handbook of Middle English*, trans. James A. Walker (Baltimore: Johns Hopkins P, 1952, 495 pp.), is a good complement because of its somewhat fuller explanations and generous selection of annotated illustrative texts. A more compact introduction for those new to the language is J. A. Burrow and Thorlac Turville-Petre, *A Book of Middle English*, 3rd ed. (Oxford: Blackwell, 2005, 419 pp.), with succinct discussions of pronunciation, vocabulary, inflections, syntax, and meter preceding selections from major texts.

Genres

DRAMA AND THEATER

Histories and Surveys

M1905   Chambers, E. K. *The Mediaeval Stage.* 2 vols. Oxford: Oxford UP, 1903.
         PN2152.C4   792.094.
   A history of the development of the stage to 1558, in four parts: minstrelsy, folk drama, religious drama, and interludes. A variety of appendixes print documents or extracts from dramatic works, amplify points in the text, or provide bibliographies. The pioneering, seminal work on the topic, Chambers has never been completely superseded but must be supplemented by later histories and specialized studies such as the following:

> Hardison, O. B., Jr. *Christian Rite and Christian Drama in the Middle Ages: Essays in the Origin and Early History of Modern Drama.* Baltimore: Johns Hopkins P, 1965. 328 pp.
> *Revels History of Drama*, vols. 1–2 (M1530) and a number of the works cited in the bibliographies (vol. 1, pp. 303–36; vol. 2, pp. 259–82).
> Wickham, *Early English Stages* (M1915).
> Young, Karl. *The Drama of the Medieval Church.* 2 vols. Oxford: Clarendon – Oxford UP, 1933. On the importance of Young's study, see C. Clifford Flanigan, "Karl Young and the Drama of the Medieval Church: An

Anniversary Appraisal," *Research Opportunities in Renaissance Drama* 27 (1984): 157–66.

For an updated distillation, see the essay on drama in Chambers, *English Literature at the Close of the Middle Ages* (M1790); continued by his *Elizabethan Stage* (M2115).

M1915   Wickham, Glynne. *Early English Stages, 1300 to 1660.* 4 vols. London: Routledge; New York: Columbia UP, 1963–2002.   PN2587.W53 792'.0941.

> Vol. 1: *1300 to 1576.* 2nd ed. 1980. 428 pp. (Originally published, 1959.)
> Vol. 2: *1576–1660.* 2 pts. 1963–72.
> Vol. 3: *Plays and Their Makers to 1576.* 1981. 357 pp.
> Vol. 4: *Requiem and an Epilogue.* 2002. 239 pp.

Traces the evolution of the drama, emphasizing visual elements in organizing the survey on the theory that festival is the basis for drama. Vol. 1 examines open-air and indoor entertainments and dramatic theory and practice; vol. 2, regulation of the theater, the emblematic tradition, playhouses and theaters, and stages and stage directions; vol. 3, the occasions of drama, emblems, and comedy and tragedy; vol. 4, the development of drama from 975 to 1580. A variety of appendixes print documents and texts. Indexed by persons, subjects, works, and places (in a single index in vols. 1, 2, and 4, but separately in 3). Reviewers note many factual errors but generally agree that Wickham is an important, provocative work. Reviews: (vol. 1) Hardin Craig, *Speculum* 34 (1959): 702–05; (vol. 2, pt. 1) *Times Literary Supplement* 15 Mar. 1963: 180; (vol. 3) Clifford Davidson, *Comparative Drama* 16 (1982): 86–88; Gordon Kipling, *Renaissance Quarterly* 36 (1983): 654–59.

Important complementary works are Chambers, *Mediaeval Stage* (M1905) and *Elizabethan Stage* (M2115); *Revels History of Drama,* vols. 1–4 (M1530); and Bentley, *Jacobean and Caroline Stage* (M2110).

Annals

See

> Harbage, *Annals of English Drama* (M1535).

Guides to Primary Works

M1920   *Records of Early English Drama* (*REED*). Exec. ed. Sally-Beth MacLean; dir. Alexandra F. Johnston. Toronto: U of Toronto P; London: British Lib., 1979– .   <http://www.reed.utoronto.ca/index.html>.

> *York.* Ed. Alexandra F. Johnston and Margaret Rogerson. 2 vols. 1979. (Covers 1370–1642.)   PN2596.Y6 Y6   790.2'09428'43.
> *Chester.* Ed. Lawrence M. Clopper. 1979. 591 pp. (Covers 1268–1642.) PN2596.C48 C4   790.2'09427'14.
> *Coventry.* Ed. R. W. Ingram. 1981. 712 pp. (Covers 1392–1642.) PN2596.C68 C6   790.2'09424'98.
> *Newcastle upon Tyne.* Ed. J. J. Anderson. 1982. 216 pp. (Covers 1427– 1641.)   PN2596.N4 N48   790.2'09428'76.

Norwich, 1540–1642. Ed. David Galloway. 1984. 501 pp.   PN2596.N6 N67
    790.2'09426'15.
Cumberland, Westmorland, Gloucestershire. Ed. Audrey Douglas and Peter
    Greenfield. 1986. 547 pp. (Covers 1345–1643, 1537–1642, 1283–
    1643, respectively.)   PN2589.C86   790.2'09427'8.
Devon. Ed. John M. Wasson. 1986. 623 pp. (Covers 1444–1637.)
    PN2596.D48 D48   790.2'09423'5.
Cambridge. Ed. Alan H. Nelson. 2 vols. 1989. (Covers 1342–1642.)
    PN2596.C3 C36   790.2'09426'59.
Herefordshire/Worcestershire. Ed. David N. Klausner. 1990. 734 pp. (Covers
    c. 1265–1643 and 1186–1643, respectively.)   PN2595.5.H47 R4
    792.094244.
Lancashire. Ed. David George. 1991. 471 pp. (Covers 1352–1668.)
    PN2595.5.L35 L35.
Shropshire. Ed. J. A. B. Somerset. 2 vols. 1994. (Covers 1269–1642.)
    PN2596.S67 S57   791'.09424'5.
Somerset and Bath. Ed. James Stokes and Robert J. Alexander. 2 vols. 1996.
    (Covers 1258–1642.)   PN2592.S65   790.2'09423'8.
Bristol. Ed. Mark C. Pilkington. 1997. 382 pp. (Covers 1255–1643.)
    PN2596.B75 R435   790.2'0942'2393.
Dorset/Cornwall. Ed. Rosalind Conklin Hays and C. E. McGee, and Sally L.
    Joyce and Evelyn S. Newlyn, respectively. 1999. 719 pp. (Covers
    1311–1642 and 1287–1642, respectively.)   PN2595.5.D67 R43
    791'.09423'3.
Sussex. Ed. Cameron Louis. 2000. 403 pp. (Covers 1245–1643.)
    PN2595.5.S87 R43   790.2'09422'5.
Kent: Diocese of Canterbury. Ed. James M. Gibson. 3 vols. 2002. (Covers
    1272–1641.)   PN2595.5.K46 R43   792'.09422'3.
Oxford. Ed. John R. Elliott, Jr., Nelson, Johnston, and Diana Wyatt. 2 vols.
    2004. (Covers 1284–1643.)   PN2596.O94 R43   791'.0942574.
Wales. Ed. Klausner. 2005. 528 pp. (Covers c. 540–1654.)
    PN2607.R43   790.2'09429'0902.
Bedfordshire. Ed. Greenfield. In progress.
Berkshire. Ed. Johnston. In progress.
Beverley. Ed. Wyatt. In progress.
Buckinghamshire. Ed. Johnston. In progress.
Clifford Family. Ed. Wasson. In progress.
Cambridgeshire. Ed. Anne Brannen. In progress.
Cheshire. Ed. Elizabeth Baldwin or David Mills. In progress.
Derbyshire. Ed. Wasson. In progress.
Dudley Family. Ed. Sally-Beth MacLean.
Durham. Ed. John McKinnell. In progress.
Essex. Ed. Nelson. In progress.
Hampshire. Ed. Jane Cowling or Greenfield. In progress.
Hertfordshire. Ed. Greenfield. In progress.
Huntingdonshire and the Soke of Peterborough. Ed. Brannen. In progress.
Ireland. Ed. Alan Fletcher. In progress.
Leicestershire. Ed. Alice Hamilton. In progress.
Lincolnshire. Ed. Stokes. In progress.
London: Corporation and Guilds. Ed. Anne Lancashire. In progress.
London: Inns of Court. Ed. Nelson. In progress.

London: Parishes and Middlesex. Ed. Mary Erler. In progress.
Norwich (to 1540). Ed. JoAnna Dutka. In progress.
Nottinghamshire. Ed. John Coldewey. In progress.
Oxfordshire. Ed. Johnston. In progress.
Percy Family. Ed. Alexander. In progress.
Rutland. Ed. Stokes. In progress.
Salisbury. Ed. Douglas. In progress.
Scotland. Ed. John McGavin or Eila Williamson. In progress.
Staffordshire. Ed. Somerset. In progress.
Suffolk. Ed. MacLean. In progress.
Surrey. Ed. MacLean. In progress.
Warwickshire. Ed. Somerset. In progress.
Westminster. Ed. Sheila Lindenbaum. In progress.
Wiltshire. Ed. Hays. In progress.
Yorkshire (West Riding). Ed. Barbara Palmer. In progress.

Almost all of the published volumes can be downloaded from the *Internet Archive* (http://www.archive.org); however, formatting has not been preserved in some instances and, as of mid-November 2005, the files have not been proofread for scanning errors. Corrected, supplemented data from published volumes are being added to a database (http://link.library.utoronto.ca/reed) that can be searched by patron, event, venue, and troupe (as well as by keyword).

Transcribes—but does not interpret—civic, guild, and ecclesiastical records, wills, and antiquarians' compilations that relate to dramatic, ceremonial, or minstrel activity before 1642. Each volume includes a general introduction to the urban center or county (with the latter following pre-1642 boundaries), its dramatic activities, and the nature of the records; transcriptions of the pertinent documents (arranged chronologically in the city volumes, by place in the county ones); various appendixes (including one with English translations of Latin-language documents); a glossary; and an index of persons, places, subjects, and titles.

These volumes are incomparable sources of raw material for theatrical, dramatic, and musical history, but they must be consulted with due regard for the sociohistorical context of the records transcribed. For a critique of the assumptions about historical scholarship that inform that project's editorial policies, see Theresa Coletti, "Reading *REED*: History and the Records of Early English Drama," *Literary Practice and Social Change in Britain, 1380–1530*, ed. Lee Patterson, New Historicism: Studies in Cultural Poetics 8 (Berkeley: U of California P, 1990) 248–84. For histories of *REED* and examples of uses of the data gathered by the project, see Douglas and MacLean, eds., REED *in Review: Essays in Celebration of the First Twenty-Five Years*, Studies in Early English Drama 8 (Toronto: U of Toronto P, 2006, 271 pp.). Reviews: (*York*) Barrie Dobson, *Renaissance and Reformation* ns 6 (1982): 47–55; Sheila Lindenbaum, *Modern Philology* 80 (1982): 80–83; (*Chester*) Peter Clark, *Renaissance and Reformation* ns 5 (1981): 237–39; Alan H. Nelson, *Modern Language Review* 78 (1983): 131–33; (*Newcastle*) Richard C. Kohler, *Shakespeare Studies* 18 (1986): 279–84; (*Cambridge*) Peter Happé, *Comparative Drama* 24 (1990): 78–82 (with an assessment of the entire project); Hilton Kelliher, *Library* 6th ser. 13 (1991): 360–63; (*Lancashire*) Richard Rastall, *Music and Letters* 74 (1993): 417–21, and *Comparative Drama* 27 (1993): 256–63.

The *Records of Early English Drama Newsletter* (*REEDN*) (1976–97) printed news of the project, additions and corrections to published volumes, transcriptions of records, and occasional updates of Lancashire, *Dramatic Texts and Records of Britain* (M1925).

M1925   Lancashire, Ian. *Dramatic Texts and Records of Britain: A Chronological Topography to 1558.* Studies in Early English Drama 1. Toronto: U of Toronto P, 1984. 633 pp.   PN2587.L36   792'.0941.

A calendar and finding list of references to "a text . . . or the record of a dramatic representation or show, a playing place, a playwright, visits of acting troupes, an official act of control over playing, or other evidence relating to plays and their production" from Roman times to 1558. Entries are organized chronologically under specific sites in separate sections for England, Wales, Scotland, and Ireland. An entry includes a brief summary of a record along with references to the most reliable printed editions or manuscript sources. The chronological list of published and unpublished dramatic works refers to editions and important scholarship. The mass of information is best approached through the several indexes: playing companies (two indexes: place; patron or player); playwrights; playing places and buildings (chronological); salient dates and entry numbers; general index of places, persons, and subjects. (Unfortunately, users must contend with five different number systems.) The emphasis is on collecting rather than interpreting evidence, but the introduction provides a brief history of dramatic activity and suggestions for further research. (Confusing, though, is the use of italic numbers to refer to the list of bibliographical abbreviations, since numbers in the list are hidden at the end of citations.) *Dramatic Texts and Records* is a valuable systematic guide to widely scattered primary evidence and scholarship that serves as an important complement to *Records of Early English Drama* (M1920).

Incorporates and is continued by the biennial "Annotated Bibliography of Printed Records of Early British Drama and Minstrelsy [for 1976–83]," *Records of Early English Drama Newsletter* (entry M1920a) 1978.1–9.2 (1978–84), and by Mary Blackstone, "A Survey and Annotated Bibliography of Records Research and Performance History Relating to Early British Drama and Minstrelsy for 1984–8," 15.1 (1990): 1–104, cont. in 15.2 (1990): 1–104.

M1927   Grantley, Darryll. *English Dramatic Interludes 1300–1580: A Reference Guide.* Cambridge: Cambridge UP, 2004. 427 pp.   Z2014.D7 G73 [PR643.I57]   016.822'041.

A bibliography of extant noncycle drama in English from 1300 to 1580; coverage extends to "saint plays, farces, early history plays and neoclassical drama" but excludes liturgical and closet drama and stray single plays that probably belonged to a larger cycle. The plays are listed alphabetically by title, with each entry including sections for date, authorship, and auspices; texts (including manuscripts) and editions (with modern editions keyed to the first part of the bibliography at the back of the book); sources; characters; plot summary; length; commentary; significant topics or narrative patterns; dramaturgical and rhetorical features (including verbal features, costume, stage directions and significant actions, songs and music, set and staging, and stage properties); place names and allusions; modern productions and recordings; and a list of critical studies (with some citations keyed to the second part of the bibliography at the back of the book). Concludes with indexes of characters and songs; biographical notes on authors; a list of closet plays and noncycle plays in languages other than English; a bibliography that confusingly separates lists of modern editions and critical studies cited by short form in the play entries; and recommendations for further reading. *English Dramatic Interludes* includes a wealth of information, but much of it is rendered frustratingly inaccessible by the inexcusable failure to index topics, narrative patterns, rhetorical features, costumes, stage directions, settings, stage properties, place names, and allusions.

Guides to Scholarship and Criticism

Surveys of Research

For a convenient overview of criticism and selective bibliography, see Peter Happé, "A Guide to Criticism of Medieval English Theatre" and Richard Beadle and Happé, "Select Bibliography," *The Cambridge Companion to Medieval English Theatre*, ed. Beadle (Cambridge: Cambridge UP, 1994) 312–67.

Other Bibliographies

M1930   Stratman, Carl J., C. S. V. *Bibliography of Medieval Drama.* 2nd ed. rev. and enl. 2 vols. New York: Ungar, 1972.   Z5782.A2 S8   016.80882'02.

A bibliography of manuscripts and editions and studies of liturgical, mystery, morality, and miracle plays, interludes, and folk drama written before c. 1600, principally in England; there is very selective coverage of Continental and Byzantine works. Entries are organized in 10 variously classified divisions: general studies; Festschriften; liturgical Latin; and English, Byzantine, French, German, Italian, Low Countries, and Spanish drama. The English division has sections for bibliographies, collections of plays, general studies, mystery and miracle plays, moralities and interludes, and folk drama. Plays are organized alphabetically by title, with listings for manuscripts, editions, and studies (with the last arranged chronologically and including theses and dissertations). Entries are not annotated, but important studies are marked by an asterisk, and library locations are provided for manuscripts and books. Indexed by scholars, dramatists, titles, and subjects. The lack of clear organization within some divisions is compounded by poor layout and typography. Although untrustworthy because of the numerous errors and omissions, the *Bibliography of Medieval Drama* is useful as a preliminary list of works published before 1970. Reviews: Lorrayne Y. Baird, *Speculum* 50 (1975): 155–58; J. W. Robinson, *Theatre Research International* 1 (1975): 47–48.

Stratman's coverage of English drama is continued to about 1986 by Sidney E. Berger, *Medieval English Drama: An Annotated Bibliography of Recent Criticism*, Garland Reference Library of the Humanities 956: Garland Medieval Bibliographies 2 (New York: Garland, 1990, 500 pp.). Coverage is reasonably thorough (except of dissertations not abstracted in *ProQuest Dissertations and Theses* [H465]), and most of the 1,744 entries are accompanied by adequate descriptive annotations; however, the rudimentary division into editions and criticism, coupled with insufficient, unrefined subject indexing, render *Medieval English Drama* much less accessible than it should be. Review: John C. Coldewey, *Speculum* 67 (1992): 377–78.

Stratman and Berger are supplemented by Jim Villani, Lorrayne Y. Baird, Alice Crosetto, and Mary Sandra Moller, "Musical Texts, Recordings, Films, and Filmstrips for Medi[e]val Drama," *Studies in Medieval and Renaissance Teaching* 10.1 (1983): 3–8. For a more complete and trustworthy guide to English drama c. 1495–1580, see White, *Early English Drama* (M2165).

Continued by Maria Spaeth Murphy and James Hoy, eds., "Bibliography of Medieval Drama, 1969–1972," *Emporia State Research Studies* 34.4 (1986): 44 pp.; Murphy, Carole Ferguson, and Hoy, "Bibliography of Medieval Drama, 1973–1976," 35.1 (1986): 41 pp.; and Ferguson and Hoy, "Bibliography of Medieval Drama, 1977–1980," 37.2 (1988): 53 pp. Entries are organized chronologically (with separate lists of books, articles, and dissertations under each year); most are accompanied by a descriptive annotation.

See also

> Lancashire, Dramatic *Texts and Records* (M1925).
> John Leyerle, "Medieval Drama," pp. 19–28, in Wells, *English Drama* (M1555).

POETRY

Histories and Surveys

See

> Pearsall, *Old and Middle English Poetry* (M1735).

Guides to Primary Works

M1940   Boffey, Julia, and A. S. G. Edwards. *A New Index of Middle English Verse.*
London: British Lib., 2005. 344 pp.   Z2014.P7   016.8211.

A first-line index to poems, for the most part in manuscripts and written before c. 1500 (but including copies after 1500 of poems written before that date). In revising, expanding, and correcting Carleton Brown and Rossell Hope Robbins, *The Index of Middle English Verse* (New York: Columbia UP for the Index Soc., 1943, 785 pp.) and its *Supplement* by Robbins and John L. Cutler (Lexington: U of Kentucky P, 1965, 551 pp.), Boffey and Edwards retain the Brown-Robinson-Cutler numbers (which are standard for referring to Middle English verse) but delete post-1500 entries, erroneous ones, those for extracts, and ones that are not verse; attempt to record significant variants; and insert some 1,500 new entries into the sequence. A typical entry includes first line, author, title, genre, length, verse form, a list of manuscripts including the verse, and early printed editions. Two indexes: manuscripts (with a list of entries included in each); authors, titles, and subjects (which the authors admit is not as comprehensive as that in the parent volumes). Based on firsthand examination of many of the entries and conflating, correcting, and expanding the original *Index* and its *Supplement, New Index of Middle English Verse* is the essential resource for investigating verse of the period.

For discussion of the questions and challenges the editors faced, see Edwards, "Towards a New Index of Middle English Verse," *Studies in Medieval English Language and Literature* 15 (2000): 51–75.

Complemented and continued by Ringler, *Bibliography and Index of English Verse Printed 1476–1558* (M2190) and *Bibliography and Index of English Verse in Manuscript 1501–1558* (M2190).

PROSE

Guides to Primary Works

M1945   *The Index of Middle English Prose.* Gen. ed. A. S. G. Edwards. In progress
since 1977.

An attempt to locate and identify all Middle English printed and manuscript prose texts (except letters and legal documents) composed between c. 1200 and c. 1500 (as well as later transcripts). The project and editorial procedures are outlined in A. S. G. Edwards, "Towards an *Index of Middle English Prose*," and Robert E. Lewis, "Editorial Technique in the *Index of Middle English Prose*," *Middle English Prose: Essays on Bibliographical Problems*, ed. A. S. G. Edwards and Derek Pearsall (New York: Garland, 1981) 23–41, 43–64. Preparation of the comprehensive index is proceeding in a number of stages:

> Lewis, R. E., N. F. Blake, and A. S. G. Edwards. *Index of Printed Middle English Prose*. Garland Reference Library of the Humanities 537. New York: Garland, 1985. 362 pp. An index of literary prose written from c. 1150 to c. 1500; entries include first line, title, and lists of printed editions and manuscripts.

A series of bibliographical catalogs of genres and authors.

Handlists to major collections, of which the following have appeared under the main title *The Index of Middle English Prose*:

> *Handlist I: A Handlist of Manuscripts Containing Middle English Prose in the Henry E. Huntingdon* [sic] *Library*. By Ralph Hanna III. Cambridge: Brewer, 1984. 81 pp.
>
> *Handlist II: A Handlist of Manuscripts Containing Middle English Prose in the John Rylands University Library of Manchester and Chetham's Library, Manchester*. By G. A. Lester. 1985. 112 pp.
>
> *Handlist III: A Handlist of Manuscripts Containing Middle English Prose in the Digby Collection, Bodleian Library, Oxford*. By Patrick J. Horner. 1986. 86 pp.
>
> *Handlist IV: A Handlist of Douce Manuscripts Containing Middle English Prose in the Bodleian Library, Oxford*. By Laurel Braswell. 1987. 110 pp. Reviewers have noted numerous errors in this volume.
>
> *Handlist V: A Handlist of Manuscripts Containing Middle English Prose in the Additional Collection (10001–[14000]), British Library, London*. By Peter Brown and Elton D. Higgs. 1988. 68 pp.
>
> *Handlist VI: A Handlist of Manuscripts Containing Middle English Prose in Yorkshire Libraries and Archives*. By O. S. Pickering and Susan Powell. 1989. 81 pp. Pickering. "A London Chronicle in Yorkshire: An Addendum to Handlist VI of the *Index of Middle English Prose*." *Notes and Queries* ns 40 (1993): 305–07.
>
> *Handlist VII: A Handlist of Manuscripts Containing Middle English Prose in Parisian Libraries*. By James Simpson. 1989. 38 pp.
>
> *Handlist VIII: A Handlist of Manuscripts Containing Middle English Prose in Oxford College Libraries*. By S. J. Ogilvie-Thomson. 1991. 198 pp.
>
> *Handlist IX: A Handlist of Manuscripts Containing Middle English Prose in the Ashmole Collection, Bodleian Library, Oxford*. By L. M. Eldredge. 1992. 164 pp.
>
> *Handlist X: Manuscripts in Scandinavian Collections*. By Irma Taavitsainen. 1994. 46 pp.
>
> *Handlist XI: Manuscripts in the Library of Trinity College, Cambridge*. By Lynne R. Mooney. 1995. 251 pp.
>
> *Handlist XII: Smaller Bodleian Collections: English Miscellaneous, English Poetry, English Theology, Finch, Latin Theology, Lyell, Radcliffe Trust*. By Hanna. 1997. 45 pp.

> *Handlist XIII: Manuscripts in Lambeth Palace Library, Including Those*
> *Formerly in Sion College Library.* By Pickering and V. M. O'Mara.
> 1999. 133 pp.
> *Handlist XIV: Manuscripts in the National Library of Wales (Llyfrgell*
> *Genedlaethol Cymru), Aberystwyth.* By William Marx. 1999. 100 pp.
> *Handlist XV: Manuscripts in Midland Libraries.* By Valerie Edden. 2000.
> 110 pp.
> *Handlist XVI: Manuscripts in the Laudian Collection, Bodleian Library,*
> *Oxford.* By Ogilvie-Thomson. 2000. 140 pp.
> *Handlist XVII: Manuscripts in the Library of Gonville and Caius College,*
> *Cambridge.* By Kari Anne Rand Schmidt. 2001. 168 pp.
> *Handlist XVIII: Manuscripts in the Library of Pembroke College,*
> *Cambridge, and the Fitzwilliam Museum.* By Kari Anne Rand. 2006.
> 129 pp.

Entries, organized by the library's shelf mark, include incipit and explicit (for each item in a collection), physical description, and references to other manuscripts, reference works, and scholarship. Users must watch for the peculiar alphabetization practices in the indexes (e.g., variant spellings are not regularized). For suggestions on the recording of recipes, see Rand Schmidt, *"The Index of Middle English Prose* and Late Medieval English Recipes," *English Studies* 75 (1994): 423–29. Reviews: (*Handlist III*) H. L. Spencer, *Studies in the Age of Chaucer* 11 (1989): 238–41 (noting several errors); (*Handlist IV*) Jeremy Griffiths, *Studies in the Age of Chaucer* 11 (1989): 191–94; Patricia Deery Kurtz, *Speculum* 65 (1990): 426–29 (both noting numerous inaccuracies); (*Handlist V*) Juris G. Lidaka, *Analytical and Enumerative Bibliography* ns 3 (1989): 171–74; (*Handlist IX*) Spencer, *Review of English Studies* 47 (1996): 73–75 (with several corrections); (*Handlist XI*) John B. Friedman, *JEGP: Journal of English and Germanic Philology* 98 (1999): 252–54.

If editorial problems involving dates of coverage and handling of items such as recipes and macaronic texts can be solved, the *Index* could exert an influence on the study of prose similar to that of Boffey and Edwards, *New Index of Middle English Verse* (entry M1940) on poetry.

Guides to Scholarship and Criticism

M1950   Edwards, A. S. G., ed. *Middle English Prose: A Critical Guide to Major*
         Authors and Genres. New Brunswick: Rutgers UP, 1984. 452 pp.
         PR255.M52   828'.108'09.
         Surveys of scholarship and editions, with essays on *Ancrene Wisse*, the Katherine Group, and the *Wohunge* Group; Richard Rolle and related works; *The Cloud of Unknowing* and Walter Hilton's *Scale of Perfection*; Nicholas Love; Julian of Norwich; Margery Kempe; John Mandeville; John Trevisa; minor devotional writings; sermon literature; historical prose; Wycliffite prose; romances; Chaucer; medical prose; utilitarian and scientific prose; Caxton; and works of religious instruction. (Malory is omitted because of the existence of recent author bibliographies such as Page West Life, *Sir Thomas Malory and the* Morte Darthur*: A Survey of Scholarship and Annotated Bibliography* [Charlottesville: UP of Virginia for Bibliog. Soc. of U of Virginia, 1980, 297 pp.].) Each essay concludes with a selective bibliography of manuscripts, editions, and studies. Indexed by authors, scholars, and anonymous works. Although the essays are uneven in covering dissertations and editions, their perceptive evaluations of scholarship and suggestions for further study make *Middle English Prose* an essential starting point

for research on prose works. Reviews: A. J. Colaianne, *Studies in the Age of Chaucer* 7 (1985): 188–91; Siegfried Wenzel, *Anglia* 104 (1986): 478–81.

Although *A Companion to Middle English Prose*, ed. Edwards (Cambridge: Brewer–Boydell and Brewer, 2004, 334 pp.), covers most of the same topics, few contributors survey editions or scholarship.

Renaissance Literature (1500–1660)

Many works listed in section M: English Literature/General are useful for research in Renaissance literature.

Research Methods

M1965 Jenkinson, Hilary. *The Later Court Hands in England from the Fifteenth to the Seventeenth Century: Illustrated from the Common Paper of the Scriveners' Company of London, the English Writing Masters, and the Public Records.* 2 vols. Cambridge: Cambridge UP, 1927.   Z115.E5 J57   745.6'1.

A manual for reading the hands used in documents from c. 1400 to c. 1700. Vol. 1 consists of succinct discussions of the development of the hands; forms of documents; languages used in English archives; the teaching and practice of handwriting in England; letter forms current in the fifteenth century; runes; abbreviations, ligatures, conjoined letters, and elisions; the letter forms of each of the hands; dating court hands; personal marks, paraphs, and signatures; symbols and ciphers; numerals; punctuation, accents, and the apostrophe; paragraph marks and other conventional divisions; alterations and corrections; decoration; and hints on reading, interpreting, transcribing, and describing hands. Concludes with a selective bibliography and annotated transcriptions of the plates in vol. 2. Among the plates are alphabets for each of the hands. Indexed in vol. 1 by persons and subjects. Although more detailed in its treatment of the fifteenth and sixteenth centuries, it remains the best introduction to the reading of the hands commonly used between 1400 and 1700. Also useful are Giles E. Dawson and Laetitia Kennedy-Skipton, *Elizabethan Handwriting, 1500–1650: A Manual* (New York: Norton, 1966, 130 pp.), and Jean F. Preston and Laetitia Yeandle, *English Handwriting, 1400–1650: An Introductory Manual* (Binghamton: Medieval and Renaissance Texts and Studies, 1992, 103 pp.); the illustrations of variant letter forms in the latter are especially useful. The National Archives offers an online tutorial for reading hands from 1500 to 1800 (http://www.nationalarchives.gov.uk/palaeography/default.htm). For earlier hands, see Johnson, *English Court Hand* (M1765).

Anthony G. Petti, *English Literary Hands from Chaucer to Dryden* (Cambridge: Harvard UP, 1977, 133 pp.), which emphasizes manuscripts after 1500, must be consulted with care because of its oversimplifications and errors (see the review by M. C. Seymour, followed by Petti's response, *Library* 5th ser. 33 [1978]: 343–49).

Useful for tracing the later development of English handwriting is P. J. Croft, comp. and ed., *Autograph Poetry in the English Language: Facsimiles of Original Manuscripts from the Fourteenth to the Twentieth Century,* 2 vols. (London: Cassell, 1973), which reproduces and transcribes examples from holograph manuscripts by 146 poets.

Histories and Surveys

M1970   Bush, Douglas. *English Literature in the Earlier Seventeenth Century, 1600–1660.* 2nd ed. rev. Vol. 5 of *The Oxford History of English Literature* (M1310). Gen. eds. Bonamy Dobrée, Norman Davis, and F. P. Wilson. Oxford: Clarendon–Oxford UP, 1962. 680 pp. (Reprinted in 1990 as vol. 7, with the title *The Early Seventeenth Century, 1600–1660: Jonson, Donne, and Milton.*)   PR431.B8   820.903.

A literary history of the period organized by "types of writing and modes of thought," with chapters on the background of the age; popular literature and translations; successors of Spenser, songbooks, and miscellanies; Jonson, Donne, and their successors; travel literature; essays and characters; history and biography; political thought; science; religion; heroic verse; and Milton. Concludes with a chronology and a now outdated selective bibliography (both omitted in the 1973 paperback edition). Indexed by authors and subjects. A magisterial work that fully merits its reputation as the best volume of the *Oxford History* and a model of traditional literary history. Review: Arthur E. Barker, *JEGP: Journal of English and Germanic Philology* 62 (1963): 617–28 (a detailed examination of revisions).

M1975   Lewis, C. S. *English Literature in the Sixteenth Century Excluding Drama.* Vol. 3 of *The Oxford History of English Literature* (M1310). Gen. eds. F. P. Wilson and Bonamy Dobrée. Oxford: Clarendon–Oxford UP, 1954. 696 pp. (Reprinted in 1990 as vol. 4, with the title *Poetry and Prose in the Sixteenth Century.*)   PR411.L4   820.903.

A literary history covering the latter part of the fifteenth century to 1600. After an initial chapter outlining the background of the age, divides the literature into three periods: late medieval, "drab," and "golden"—a division that has not gained wide acceptance. Includes a chronology and a now outdated selective bibliography (both omitted in the 1973 paperback edition). Indexed by authors, subjects, and anonymous works. A provocative, opinionated, sometimes brilliant work that has occasioned widespread controversy. Reviews: Donald Davie, *Essays in Criticism* 5 (1955): 159–64; Charles T. Harrison, *Sewanee Review* 63 (1955): 153–61; Yvor Winters, *Hudson Review* 8 (1955): 281–87.

M1977   *The Cambridge History of Early Modern English Literature.* Ed. David Loewenstein and Janel Mueller. New Cambridge History of English Literature. Cambridge: Cambridge UP, 2002. 1,038 pp.   PR421.C26   820.9'003.

A collaborative history of "English literature written in Britain between the Reformation and the Restoration." Although separately authored, the 26 chapters are designed to attend to "the aesthetic and generic features of early modern texts" as well as the conditions (especially political and religious) of their production and reception. Unlike many recent multiauthored literary histories, this one has a chronology and bibliography; unfortunately, the layout of the former makes it useless for comparisons of literary and historical events, and the lack of any topical organization will deter most readers from skimming the 40-page selective bibliography of secondary works (a curious mishmash that omits too much essential to the study of the period). Indexed by persons, subjects, and anonymous works. Including contributions by many of the leading early modern scholars, *Cambridge History of Early Modern English Literature* will likely exert substantial influence on the study of the period.

See also

    Sec. M: English Literature/General/Histories and Surveys.

Literary Handbooks, Dictionaries, and Encyclopedias

M1980   Ruoff, James E. *Crowell's Handbook of Elizabethan and Stuart Literature.*
    New York: Crowell, 1975. 468 pp. British ed.: *Macmillan's Handbook of
    Elizabethan and Stuart Literature.* London: Macmillan, 1975.   PR19.R8
    820'.9'003.

    A handbook to the period 1558–1660, with entries for authors, works, genres,
movements, and literary terms. Author entries include biographical information, a brief
career survey, and a summary critical evaluation. Entries for works note details of composition, date, and source and offer a brief synopsis and critical evaluation. Those for
genres survey major developments and works. Most entries conclude with a very brief
list of standard editions, reference works, and major critical studies. Indexed in *Biography
and Genealogy Master Index* (J565). Although a useful compendium, whose commentary
is frequently more illuminating than one expects in a handbook, the work must be used
with care, since there are inexplicable omissions, questionable evaluations, untrustworthy or outdated bibliographies, and numerous factual errors. Reviews: J. Max Patrick,
Seventeenth-Century News 35 (1977): 26–27; Warren W. Wooden, *Literary Research
Newsletter* 3 (1978): 135–37.

    Historical topics and persons are more fully covered in John A. Wagner, *Historical
Dictionary of the Elizabethan World: Britain, Ireland, Europe, and America* (Phoenix:
Oryx, 1999, 392 pp.).

Bibliographies of Bibliographies

For a survey and selected list of bibliographies published before 1700, see Archer Taylor,
Renaissance Guides to Books: An Inventory and Some Conclusions (Berkeley: U of California P, 1945, 130 pp.).

See also

    Secs. D: Bibliographies of Bibliographies and M: English Literature/General/
    Bibliographies of Bibliographies.

Guides to Primary Works

MANUSCRIPTS

For an overview of studies relating to codicology, paleography, attribution, and other
aspects of manuscripts, see Noel J. Kinnamon, "Recent Studies in Renaissance English
Manuscripts," *English Literary Renaissance* 27 (1997): 281–326.

M1985   *Index of English Literary Manuscripts* (M1365). Ed. P. J. Croft, Theodore
Hofmann, and John Horden. Vol. 1: *1450–1625.* 2 pts. Comp. Peter Beal.
Vol. 2: *1625–1700.* 2 pts. Comp. Beal. London: Mansell; New York:
Bowker, 1980–93. (In progress is *Catalogue of English Literary Manuscripts
1450-1700* [*CELM*], comp. Beal [http://ies.sas.ac.uk/cmps/Projects/
CELM].)   Z6611.L7 I5 [PR83]   016.82'08.

A descriptive catalog of extant literary manuscripts. Vol. 1 covers 72 British and
Irish authors who flourished between 1450 and 1625, with the bulk dating from the
latter years of the period; vol. 2 covers 52 authors from the years 1625–1700. The authors
are essentially those listed in *Concise Cambridge Bibliography of English Literature, 600–
1950* (M1365a). The emphasis is (rather loosely at times) on literary manuscripts, including scribal copies. Letters are excluded, although the introductions to individual authors list either individual ones or collections. Moreover, the introductions alert researchers to special problems and relevant scholarship, point out additional manuscripts, discuss
canon, and conclude with an outline of the arrangement of entries. A typical entry provides a physical description, identifies the hand(s), dates composition of the manuscript,
includes any necessary commentary (as well as references to editions or scholarship), and
identifies location (with shelf mark). Since some entries are based on inquiries to libraries
and collectors, bibliographies and other reference works, booksellers' and auction catalogs,
rather than personal examination by the compiler, descriptions vary in fullness and accuracy. Also, terminology and format vary somewhat from part to part.

Addenda to the list of Donne manuscripts can be found in Peter Beal, "More
Donne Manuscripts," *John Donne Journal* 6 (1987): 213–18; Ernest W. Sullivan II,
"Updating the John Donne Listings in Peter Beal's *Index of English Literary Manuscripts*," *John Donne Journal* 6 (1987): 219–34, and "Updating the John Donne Listings
in Peter Beal's *Index of English Literary Manuscripts* II," *John Donne Journal* 9 (1990):
141–48.

Although there are errors and omissions, and the scope is unduly restricted by
reliance on the *Concise Cambridge Bibliography*, these volumes have brought to light a
number of significant unrecorded manuscripts and are an essential, if limited, source
for the identification and location of manuscripts. They must, however, be supplemented by the works listed in section F: Guides to Manuscripts and Archives. Reviews:
(vol. 1) Hilton Kelliher, *Library* 6th ser. 4 (1982): 435–40; Anthony G. Petti, *Analytical
and Enumerative Bibliography* 5 (1981): 153–56.

Catalogue of English Literary Manuscripts 1450–1700, which will initially record
the surviving manuscripts of more than 200 authors, will eventually supersede Beal's
Index. The database will be searchable by "authors, patrons, scholars, compilers, composers, etc. (with the ability to distinguish by gender), titles of works, first lines of
poems and songs, and up-to-date locations."

See also

Sec. F: Guides to Manuscripts and Archives.
Ricci, *Census of Medieval and Renaissance Manuscripts* (M1815).

PRINTED WORKS

Bibliographies and Indexes

M1990   Pollard, A. W., and G. R. Redgrave, comps. *A Short-Title Catalogue of Books
Printed in England, Scotland, and Ireland, and of English Books Printed*

Abroad, 1475–1640 (*RSTC, NSTC*). Rev. Katharine F. Pantzer, W. A. Jackson, and F. S. Ferguson. 2nd ed., rev. and enl. 3 vols. London: Bibliog. Soc., 1976–91.   Z2002.P77   015'.42.

A bibliography of extant editions, impressions, issues, and occasionally states and variants of books and other printed matter published or printed in the British Isles and of books in English, Irish, or Welsh printed abroad from c. 1473 through 1640. Although it lists a few unique items seen by the compilers but now destroyed or untraceable, *RSTC* is not a bibliography of all works actually printed during the period. The work revises—more precisely, transforms—the venerable *Short-Title Catalogue* (*STC*), comp. Pollard and Redgrave (London: Bibliog. Soc., 1926, 609 pp.), by adding some 10,000 entries, including fuller transcriptions of titles, and providing considerably expanded bibliographical detail and helpful cross-references. (For a full account of the revision and the history of *STC* and *RSTC*, see the preface to vol. 1 and "*STC*: The Scholar's Vademecum," *Book Collector* 33 [1984]: 273–304.) As far as possible, *RSTC* retains the *STC* numbers, which have become the standard of reference for printed works of the period.

Entries, based largely on personal examination of copies or extensive correspondence with librarians and scholars, are arranged by author; corporate heading (with extensive sections such as "England" or "Liturgies" clearly subdivided); or, for anonymous works, by author's initials, proper noun or adjective, or first noun. (See vol. 1, pp. xxx–xxxi for a fuller explanation of the handling of anonymous works. A useful aid to locating entries for attributed works in English is Halkett, *Dictionary of Anonymous and Pseudonymous Publications* [U5110], which includes *RSTC* references as well as a concordance of *RSTC* numbers.) A typical entry includes author, title, format, imprint, Stationers' Register entry, locations, references to standard bibliographies, and editorial information (which offers sometimes extensive bibliographical detail and references to scholarship). Each volume concludes with a list of additions and corrections, which are cumulated, revised, and supplemented in vol. 3. Other addenda are printed in Stephen Tabor, "Additions to *STC*," *Library* 6th ser. 16 (1994): 190–207. Although the *ESTC* (M1377) once assumed responsibility for augmenting and amending *RSTC* records, the agreement with the Bibliographical Society has lapsed. (On the difficulties of identifying in *ESTC* works, editions, and issues not in *RSTC*, see David McKitterick, " 'Not in STC': Opportunities and Challenges in the ESTC," *Library* 7th ser. 6 [2005]: 178–94.) Users should study the admirably clear explanation of parts of an entry and procedures in the introduction to vol. 1.

Each entry lists up to five locations in Europe (principally in the British Isles) and five in North America (primarily), Australia, or New Zealand. A plus sign signifies that additional copies are known. Most locations are institutions or libraries, although a few private collections are listed. For the location "Private Owner," a query addressed to the secretary of the (London) Bibliographical Society will be forwarded to the owner where possible. (For the secretary's address, see the current issue of *Library* or the society's Web site [http://www.bibsoc.org.uk].) Additional locations for entries in the *STC* may be found in William Warner Bishop, comp., *A Checklist of American Copies of* Short-Title Catalogue *Books*, 2nd ed. (Ann Arbor: U of Michigan P, 1950, 201 pp.), and David Ramage, comp., *A Finding-List of English Books to 1640 in Libraries in the British Isles (Excluding the National Libraries and the Libraries of Oxford and Cambridge)* (Durham, Eng.: Council of the Durham Colls., 1958, 101 pp.). Researchers should also note that most *STC* works are available on microfilm through *Early English Books, 1475–1640* (Ann Arbor: UMI) and *Early English Books Online* (M2009). Reels are indexed by *STC* numbers, some of which are changed in *RSTC*, and there are instances where the filmed image does not match the *STC* record (see McKitterick, above).

Vol. 3 offers several invaluable indexes—printers and publishers; places of publication (other than London); London imprints; dates of publication (by Philip R. Rider)—that will make practicable numerous studies of publishing, printing, and intellectual history. As Pantzer cautions, users of vol. 3 must "remember to read the headnotes" to the indexes and their appendixes. Some title access is offered by A. F. Allison and V. F. Goldsmith, *Titles of English Books (and of Foreign Books Printed in England): An Alphabetical Finding-List by Title of Books Published under the Author's Name, Pseudonym, or Initials*, vol. 1: *1475–1640* (Hamden: Archon–Shoe String, 1976, 176 pp.). This source must be used with care, however, since it omits anonymous works and is based on unauthorized use of an unrevised draft of vol. 1 and proof of vol. 2 of *RSTC*. (For details, see the review by Peter Davison, *Library* 5th ser. 31 [1976]: 273.) Writers of prefatory matter and dedicatees are indexed in Franklin B. Williams, Jr., *Index of Dedications and Commendatory Verses in English Books before 1641* (London: Bibliog. Soc., 1962, 256 pp.), and "Dedications and Verses through 1640: Addenda," a 19-page supplement printed at the end of *Library* 5th ser. 30.1 (1975). Works of American interest are identified in Jackson Campbell Boswell, *A Check List of Americana in* A Short-Title Catalogue of Books Printed in England, Scotland, and Ireland and of English Books Printed Abroad, 1475–1640, Supplement to *Early American Literature* 9.2 (1974), 124 pp. Several of the preceding works are being superseded by *ESTC* (M1377). Provisional statistical analysis of the data in *RSTC* is offered by Maureen Bell and John Barnard, "Provisional Count of *STC* Titles 1475–1640," *Publishing History* 31 (1992): 48–64.

RSTC is the indispensable source for identifying and locating extant works (and various editions, issues, variants, and impressions). Exemplary thoroughness in searching out material and precision in its analysis make the *RSTC* one of the truly monumental reference works. Like its predecessor, *RSTC* is the essential basis for scholarship of the period; however, it is gradually being supplanted but not superseded by *ESTC*, which incorporates augmented, corrected, and new records and offers all the advantages of computer searching. Continued by Wing, *Short-Title Catalogue, 1641–1700* (M1995). Reviews: (vol. 1) *Book Collector* 35 (1986): 417–30; Arthur Freeman, *TLS: Times Literary Supplement* 13 Feb. 1987: 170; Freeman, *Library* 6th ser. 9 (1987): 289–92; (vol. 2): R. C. Alston, *Papers of the Bibliographical Society of America* 71 (1977): 391–95; James L. Harner, *Seventeenth-Century News* 36 (1978): 24–25; David Rogers, *TLS: Times Literary Supplement* 27 Aug. 1976: 1061; William P. Williams, *Review* 1 (1979): 249–54; (vol. 3): T. A. Birrell, *TLS: Times Literary Supplement* 13 Dec. 1991: 25; (vols. 1–3): Peter W. M. Blayney, *Papers of the Bibliographical Society of America* 88 (1994): 353–407.

A useful complement is M. A. Shaaber, *Check-list of Works by British Authors Printed Abroad, in Languages Other Than English, to 1641* (New York: Bibliog. Soc. of America, 1975, 168 pp.).

M1995 Wing, Donald, comp. *Short-Title Catalogue of Books Printed in England, Scotland, Ireland, Wales, and British America and of English Books Printed in Other Countries, 1641–1700* (Wing). 2nd ed., rev. and enl. 4 vols. New York: MLA, 1982–98.   Z2002.W52   015.42. CD-ROM: Alexandria: Chadwyck-Healey, 1996.

> Vol. 1: *A1–E2926L*. Rev. and ed. John J. Morrison and Carolyn W. Nelson. 1994. 954 pp.
> Vol. 2: *E2927–O1000*. Ed. Timothy J. Crist. 1982. 690 pp.
> Vol. 3: *P1–Z28*. Ed. Morrison. 1988. 766 pp.
> Vol. 4: *Indexes*. Comp. Nelson and Matthew Seccombe. 1998. 1,078 pp.

Continues the *Short-Title Catalogue* (M1990), employing the same basic organization but providing less comprehensive coverage and much less bibliographical detail. Like *RSTC*, Wing is an enumerative bibliography of extant works printed in the British Isles and North America, and in English elsewhere in the world. Vols. 2 and 3 do include a few unique items destroyed during World War II; other than annuals, periodicals, which are listed in Nelson, *British Newspapers and Periodicals* (M2060), are excluded.

Works are entered by author, corporate author, or title of anonymous work. A typical entry provides author, short title (several titles are truncated too much to indicate contents or subject), imprint, format, references to standard bibliographies, and locations. Researchers should note that "anr. ed." (another edition) refers indiscriminately to edition, issue, or state, and "var." merely indicates that undifferentiated variants exist. The revised vol. 3 provides somewhat fuller descriptions and is more precise in identifying editions and variants. There are occasional duplicate entries.

Up to 10 copies are located in libraries and a few private collections: five in the British Isles, and five in North America (primarily), New Zealand, Australia, or the Continent. (Several entries actually provide more than 10 locations.) Additions and corrections are printed in *Studies in Bibliography* 29 (1976): 386–87; 30 (1977): 276–80; 31 (1978): 266–71; and in works listed in vol. 1, p. ix. Like *RSTC*, Wing is not a census of copies; however, information on additional locations—as well as some details of bibliographical references, provenance, and auction records—can be obtained from the editor (Wing *STC* Revision Project, Yale U Lib., 130 Wall St., Box 208240, New Haven, CT 06520-8240).

The *Indexes* volume, which covers additions and corrections made to the CD-ROM version, provides an index of printers, publishers, and booksellers and a chronological list of non-London publications. The CD-ROM or *ESTC* (M1377) offers the best way to locate anonymous works, those listed by corporate author, and those for which a researcher knows only the titles.

Researchers must be certain to use only the 1994 revised edition of vol. 1, not the original revision (1972), because of serious flaws arising from the reassignment of 7–8% of the original numbers that serve as standard references in bibliographies, catalogs, studies, and editions and are essential to locating microfilmed works in University Microfilms International's *Early English Books, 1641–1700* collection. Several entries were canceled without notice or moved without cross-reference, and typographical errors abound. These problems are not fully redressed by the list of changes in vol. 2, pp. 669–90. Vol. 2 seldom reassigns numbers and the 1994 revision of vol. 1 and vol. 3 never does; all three scrupulously note canceled or moved entries.

The Wing *STC* has spawned a number of useful supplementary works:

> *Early English Books, 1641–1700: A Cumulative Index to Units 1–60 of the Microfilm Collection.* 8 vols. Ann Arbor: UMI, 1990. Author, title, subject, and reel-position-Wing-number indexes to the first 42,500 titles in the microfilm collection. The title index expands the short titles in Wing and is sometimes useful in locating anonymous works in the catalog; the subject index, based on Library of Congress headings, is not adequate for most narrow subject searches. The indexes must be used with the original edition of vol. 1. The handlists to the later microfilm units are not indexed. Works filmed are searchable through *WorldCat* (E225) and *Early English Books Online* (M2009).

> Allison, A. F., and V. F. Goldsmith. *Titles of English Books (and of Foreign Books Printed in England): An Alphabetical Finding-List by Title of Books*

> *Published under the Author's Name, Pseudonym, or Initials.* Vol. 2: *1641–1700*. Hamden: Archon–Shoe String, 1977. 318 pp. Only marginally useful because of the exclusion of anonymous works and the failure to include many entries in the revised vol. 1. Better title access to many entries is offered by the CD-ROM, title index to *Early English Books, 1641–1700*, and *ESTC.*

> Smith, *Women and the Literature of the Seventeenth Century: An Annotated Bibliography Based on Wing's* Short-Title Catalogue (M2007).

> Wing, Donald. *A Gallery of Ghosts: Books Published between 1641–1700 Not Found in the* Short-Title Catalogue. New York: Index Committee of the MLA, 1967. 225 pp. A catalog of works and editions listed in bibliographies and dealers' or auction catalogs but not identified or located. Those found are incorporated in the revised edition.

Despite its faults, Wing is an essential guide to the identification and location of works published during the period. The CD-ROM resolves many of the difficulties of searching Wing; much fuller records (with additional access points) are being added to the *ESTC,* which will eventually supplant but not completely supersede Wing.

For an account of the compilation of the first edition, see Donald G. Wing, "The Making of the *Short-Title Catalogue, 1641–1700,*" *Papers of the Bibliographical Society of America* 45 (1951): 59–69; for the revision, see Timothy Christ [i.e., Crist], "The Wing *STC* Revision Project: A Progress Report," *Literary Research Newsletter* 4 (1979): 67–72. Provisional statistical analysis of the data in Wing is offered by Maureen Bell and John Barnard, "Provisional Count of *Wing* Titles 1641–1700," *Publishing History* 44 (1998): 89–97.

Reviews: (vol. 1) *TLS: Times Literary Supplement* 26 Jan. 1973: 100 (and the subsequent correspondence by James M. Osborn and the reviewer, 23 Mar. 1973: 325; and Peter Grant, 6 Apr. 1973: 395); B. J. McMullin, *Papers of the Bibliographical Society of America* 72 (1978): 435–54 (with a reply by Timothy Crist, 73 [1979]: 273–75); (vol. 2) D. F. McKenzie, *TLS: Times Literary Supplement* 17 Dec. 1982: 1403; Alexandra Mason, *Papers of the Bibliographical Society of America* 80 (1986): 255–62; (vol. 3) Theodore Hofmann, *Library* 6th ser. 11 (1989): 383–88; David McKitterick, *Book Collector* 37 (1988): 461–78.

M2000   *A Transcript of the Registers of the Company of Stationers of London, 1554–1640 A. D.* Ed. Edward Arber. 5 vols. London and Birmingham: Privately printed, 1875–94.   Z2002.S69   655.442. Online. 24 June 2006 <http://www.archive.org/details/stationersregist01arberuoft>.

An edited transcript of part of the surviving records relating to the ownership of written works or to members of the company, as well as a number of miscellaneous documents. (See entry M1380 for a discussion of the records of the company.) Of principal interest to literary scholars are the registers of copies entered and records of fines for unlawful printing. In the registers, entries are listed chronologically according to the Old Style calendar and include the member entering the work (or being fined), a descriptive "title" (sometimes accompanied by the author's name), and registration fee. (For the typographical distinctions of parts of an entry, see vol. 1, pp. 27–30.) Users must remember that (1) the registers are records of ownership claims by members of the company; (2) they were never intended as a record of authorized publication; (3) an entry does not automatically mean the work actually existed at that date; (4) many works entered were never published (or intended to be, as in the case of "blocking entries" used to prevent unauthorized printing of plays) or are no longer extant; (5) many works were printed with a different title; (6) sometimes a year or more elapsed between entry and publication; (7) later editions, unless a transfer of ownership occurred, were typically not entered; (8) a considerable number of works actually printed were never entered; (9) Register B and Arber's transcript of it include entries forged by John Payne Collier (see Franklin Dickey, "The Old Man at Work: Forgeries in the Stationers' Registers," *Shakespeare Quarterly* 11 [1960]: 39–47).

The online version consists of DjVu or PDF files of OCR scans, some of which are difficult to read.

Because the *Transcript* is incomplete, confusingly organized, and inadequately indexed, it must be supplemented by the following:

> *Short-Title Catalogue* (M1990), which includes references to entries in the register and thus serves as a handy index to extant publications that were entered.
>
> Greg, *Bibliography of the English Printed Drama* (M2135), which prints a superior transcription of all entries relating to the drama.
>
> Greg, W. W., ed. *A Companion to Arber: Being a Calendar of Documents in Edward Arber's* Transcript . . . . Oxford: Clarendon–Oxford UP, 1967. 451 pp. A calendar and index to the illustrative documents scattered haphazardly through the *Transcript,* as well as documents from other sources.
>
> Greg, W. W., and E. Boswell, eds. *Records of the Court of the Stationers' Company, 1576 to 1602, from Register B.* London: Bibliog. Soc., 1930. 144 pp.
>
> Jackson, William A., ed. *Records of the Court of the Stationers' Company, 1602 to 1640.* London: Bibliog. Soc., 1957. 555 pp. This and the preceding work transcribe documents Arber was not allowed to publish.
>
> Rollins, Hyder E., comp. *An Analytical Index to the Ballad-Entries (1557–1709) in the Registers of the Company of Stationers of London.* 1924. Rpt., with some corrections in a foreword by Leslie Shepard. Hatboro: Tradition, 1976. 324 pp.

Of major value would be a published index to the early records. (Although one can search the DjVu or PDF files, the old-spelling transcription and abbreviations require considerable ingenuity to identify all possible spellings of a word, and there are errors in the OCR transcriptions, e.g. "Jonsox" for "Jonson".)

Despite its faults, the *Transcript* offers the most convenient access to records essential for identifying lost works, researching publishing history, and dating composition (but the evidence must be carefully evaluated, since entry in the register establishes only a possible terminus ad quem for composition and only a possible terminus a quo for publication). Some research will require the use of the original records at Stationers' Hall or the microfilm (M1380a). For a description of the records and a useful annotated list of published and unpublished catalogs, indexes, and transcripts, see Myers, *Stationers' Company Archive* (M1380a).

M2005   *A Transcript of the Registers of the Worshipful Company of Stationers from 1640–1708 A. D.* [Ed. George Edward Briscoe Eyre, Charles Robert Rivington, and Henry Robert Plomer.] 3 vols. London: Privately printed, 1913–14.   PR1105.R7.

A transcript that continues the 1554–1640 *Transcript* (M2000) to March 1709 and employs the same typographic conventions to print entries. See entry M2000 for a discussion of the organization and use of the registers and entry M1380 for the records of the Stationers' Company. Fortunately for scholars, the *Transcript* has been indexed by printers, publishers, authors, editors, translators, compilers, and titles in William P.

Williams, ed., *Index to the Stationers' Register, 1640–1708: Being an Index to* A Transcript of the Registers of the Worshipful Company of Stationers from 1640–1708 A. D., *Edited by Eyre, Rivington, and Plomer (1913–1914)* (La Jolla: McGilvery, 1980, 67 pp. and 2 microfiche). Ballad entries are indexed in Rollins, *Analytical Index to the Ballad-Entries* (M2000a).

M2007   Smith, Hilda L., and Susan Cardinale, comps. *Women and the Literature of the Seventeenth Century: An Annotated Bibliography Based on Wing's* Short-Title Catalogue. Bibliographies and Indexes in Women's Studies 10. New York: Greenwood, 1990. 332 pp.   Z2013.5.W6.S6 [PR113] 016.8208'09287.

An annotated bibliography of works, published between 1641 and 1700, by and about women. Although based on the revised edition of Wing, *Short-Title Catalogue* (M1995), Smith includes some works not in Wing, buried in collections unanalyzed in Wing or published after but written before 1700. The approximately 1,800 entries are listed alphabetically by author in three divisions: works by women (including some of indeterminate authorship and a few published after 1700 but written before that year); works about specific living or dead females (but excluding fictional characters); works discovered too late to be annotated and incorporated into the preceding divisions. A typical entry records author, title, publication information, number of pages, Wing number of the edition consulted, and reel and position location for the *Early English Books* (M1995a) or Thomason Tracts microfilm collections. The accompanying annotations—obviously based on a careful perusal of each work—offer a succinct, informative account of contents. The concluding list of women printers, publishers, and booksellers is rendered useless since it cites no page or entry numbers. Because the chronological and subject indexes cite page numbers, users must be certain to scan all entries on a given page.

Given the shortened titles in Wing, merely to have identified therein works by and about women would have rendered an important service to researchers; by offering informative annotations for all but 183 of the works, *Women and Literature* makes feasible a variety of studies of themes, subjects, social attitudes, groups of writers, and types of works that would otherwise daunt all but the hardiest scholar. Unfortunately, users must examine every entry because of utterly inadequate indexing: works in the third division are unindexed; the subject indexing of the other divisions is incomplete and inconsistent. Review: Mary Ann O'Donnell, *Analytical and Enumerative Bibliography* ns 4 (1990): 212–16.

Researchers can also use *EEBO* (M2009) to identify works about women, both real and fictional.

Text Archives

M2009   *Early English Books Online* (*EEBO*). Chadwyck-Healey. Online. 24 Mar. 2005 <http://eebo.chadwyck.com>. Updated regularly.

Digitized copies of approximately 106,000 of the 125,000 titles included in the two *Short-Title Catalogues* (M1990 and M1995), in the Thomason Collection (tracts, periodicals, broadsides, and other publications from 1640 through 1660), and (eventually) a group of tract volumes (bound collections of broadside ballads, proclamations, almanacs, some manuscripts, and ephemera). Although the images are captured from the microfilms that make up *Early English Books, 1475–1640* and *Early English Books, 1641–1700* (1990a and 1995a) and thus are not searchable, an increasing number of titles (approximately 8,000 of a planned 25,000) can be searched by keyword in a rekeyed full text. For the current status of the archive, click the About *EEBO* button on the *EEBO* homepage and follow the Status—What's Online Now? and Status of the Microfilm Project links; for information about the Text Creation Partnership that is producing the keyed full-text documents, see http://www.lib.umich.edu/tcp/eebo.

Users must understand that the microfilms that are the source of most of the images preserve some incomplete copies, include copies whose missing leaves were photographed from other copies, reproduce nineteenth-century type facsimiles of some copies, do not necessarily reproduce the most authoritative edition(s) of a work, and do not include multiple copies of an edition that exists in variant states. Although the *EEBO* record for a document records the owner of the copy filmed, it does not identify the specific copy among multiple copies in an institutional collection. Thus, like the majority of text archives, *EEBO* is a resource for text-based studies but cannot be relied upon for bibliographical analyses. (For particulars, see B. J. McMullin, "Getting Acquainted with *EEBO*," *Bibliographical Society of Australia and New Zealand Bulletin* 26.3–4 [2002]: 220–30.)

Users can browse or search the contents. The browse window allows users to browse by author (with the option of restricting the list to those with at least one work available in full text), to scan the Thomason Collection volume by volume (an important feature since the volumes are organized chronologically), and to peruse the periodicals by date. The Basic Search window allows users to search by full-text keyword, author, title keyword, subject (Library of Congress subject headings assigned to the MARC record for each title), and bibliographic record number (e.g., *RSTC* and Wing numbers); by default fields are combined with the Boolean "and". Searches can be limited by date and restricted to items with images or with keyed full text. Records can be sorted alphabetically, by author or title, or chronologically (with either the earliest or most recent first). The Advanced Search window offers additional options: users can search by record keyword, imprint, reel position in the *Early English Books* microfilm collections, and type of illustration; they can limit full-text keyword searches to genres or parts of texts (e.g., colophons, dedications, prefaces); and they can select additional limiters: UMI collections, libraries (i.e., owners—some of which are not libraries—of the digitized copies at the time they were microfilmed), language, and country of origin. Because the full-text transcriptions follow the spelling of the underlying original copies, searchers must be certain to use truncation or combine all variants with the Boolean "or" when performing a full-text keyword search (e.g., "book" or "boke" or "booke"). Periodicals, which have their own search screen, can be searched by keyword, date, author or editor, title, bibliographic record number, reel position, and type of illustration; records can be sorted by date, title, or chronologically by separate issue. Users can combine searches by clicking on Search History.

Images can be viewed on-screen (and resized or adjusted), printed, or downloaded as PDF files (users must save a title to the marked list before exporting it); full-text files are linked to each screen image of the transcribed text.

Although the digitized images vary in quality because of the condition of the copies originally microfilmed and although there are quirks in the search engine (e.g., locating a record by *RSTC* number requires the insertion of the Boolean "and" between "STC" and the number, but no "and" is required between "Wing" and the number; the addition of Library of Congress subject headings to records sometimes results in false hits, especially in author searches), the ability to search the database in such a variety of ways and the increasing number of keyed full-text documents make *EEBO* an incomparable resource, and studies—linguistic and topical—that would otherwise take a lifetime of searching and reading are now feasible. Review: John Jowett and Gabriel Egan, *Inter-*

active Early Modern Literary Studies (Jan. 2001) 1-13: http://purl.oclc.org/emls/iemls/reviews/jowetteebo.htm.

See also

> *New Cambridge Bibliography of English Literature*, vol. 1: *600–1660* (M2035).

Guides to Scholarship and Criticism

SURVEYS OF RESEARCH

M2010   "Recent Studies in the English Renaissance." *English Literary Renaissance* 1
(1971)– .   PR1.E43   920.9'002.
Most issues of *English Literary Renaissance* conclude with a survey of recent research on an author, topic, or group of related works from 1485 to 1665. Modeled on those in Logan and Smith (M2145) and based on *MLAIB* (G335), *ABELL* (G340), and *Year's Work in English Studies* (G330), the surveys typically examine biographical and general works, editions, studies of special topics and individual works, canon and text, and the current state of scholarship. Each survey concludes with a bibliography of works not discussed in the text. Coverage and evaluation vary with the individual contributor, but the general quality is high and the series treats a number of authors who are not the subject of a more comprehensive author bibliography. The individual surveys are conveniently indexed in *MLAIB* (G335) and *ABELL* (G340).

M2015   "Recent Studies in the English Renaissance." *Studies in English Literature,
1500–1900* 1 (1961)– . Annually in the Winter issue.   PR1.S82
820'.9.
A commissioned survey by an established scholar of studies on nondramatic literature, with recent ones emphasizing full-length critical and historical works and typically offering only cursory attention to editions or reference works. (The drama is covered in the Spring issue [M2150].) The essays vary considerably in soundness and rigor of assessment. Although it is the most current annual survey, the work is generally limited to books submitted for review and must be supplemented by the chapters in *Year's Work in English Studies* (G330) on the nondramatic literature of the period.
Some volumes of *Manuscripta* (7–28 [1963–84]) include "A Review of English Renaissance Textual Studies," a survey of editions and textual and bibliographical scholarship.
Broader authoritative surveys include the following:

> Hamilton, A. C. "The Modern Study of Renaissance English Literature: A
> Critical Survey." *Modern Language Quarterly* 26 (1965): 150–83.
> Schoeck, Richard J. "English Literature." *The Present State of Scholarship in
> Sixteenth-Century Literature.* Ed. William M. Jones. Columbia: U of Missouri P, 1978. 111–68.
> Summers, Joseph H. "Notes on Recent Studies in English Literature of the
> Earlier Seventeenth Century." *Modern Language Quarterly* 26 (1965):
> 135–49.
> Tuve, Rosemond. "Critical Survey of Scholarship in the Field of English
> Literature of the Renaissance." *Studies in Philology* 40 (1943): 204–55.

See also

> *YWES* (G330): Chapters for Sixteenth Century: Excluding Drama after 1550; Shakespeare; Renaissance Drama: Excluding Shakespeare; Earlier Seventeenth Century: Excluding Drama; Milton.

SERIAL BIBLIOGRAPHIES

M2020 *World Shakespeare Bibliography Online* [1962–] (*WSB Online*). Ed. James L. Harner. Johns Hopkins UP for the Folger Shakespeare Library. 2000– . Online. 10 Apr. 2006 <http://www.worldshakesbib.org>. Updated quarterly. An expanded cumulation and continuation of "World Shakespeare Bibliography [1949–2003]." *Shakespeare Quarterly* 1–55 (1950–2004). Annual. Title varies.   PR2885.S63   822.3'3. <http://www-english.tamu.edu/index.php?id=896>.

An annotated bibliography of Shakespearean scholarship and productions that lists a significant number of works important to Renaissance literature generally. The international coverage (118 languages) encompasses books, articles, dissertations, productions, films, computer software, and reviews of the foregoing—in short, anything that is related to the study of Shakespeare. Basic Search allows users to search by keyword; Advanced Search allows searches by keyword, title, author, persons other than authors, publisher or journal, date, type of document, language, and year. The Browse feature allows users to access records according to the taxonomy employed in the annual print version (e.g., users can skim all textual studies of *Hamlet*, translations of *Coriolanus*, or discussions of the sources of *As You Like It*). In all three search modes, records can be sorted in ascending or descending order by date, author, or title. Records can be marked for printing, exporting, or e-mailing. Coverage will eventually extend back to 1900. The extensive coverage, clear organization, numerous hyperlinks, and thorough indexing make this work the indispensable bibliography of Shakespeare studies and an important guide to scholarship on Renaissance literature generally.

Earlier Shakespeare scholarship can be located in:

> Ebisch, Walther, and Levin L. Schücking. *A Shakespeare Bibliography*. Oxford: Clarendon–Oxford UP, 1931. 294 pp.
>
> ———. *Supplement for the Years 1930–1935 to* A Shakespeare Bibliography. Oxford: Clarendon–Oxford UP, 1937. 104 pp.
>
> Sajdak, Bruce T., ed. *Shakespeare Index: An Annotated Bibliography of Critical Articles on the Plays, 1959–1983.* 2 vols. Millwood: Kraus, 1992. An admirably thorough guide to English-language articles that is noteworthy for its incisive annotations and its character, scene, and subject indexes.
>
> "Shakespeare." *Year's Work in English Studies* (G330).
>
> Smith, Gordon Ross. *A Classified Shakespeare Bibliography, 1936–1958.* University Park: Pennsylvania State UP, 1963. 784 pp.
>
> "The Year's Contributions to Shakespeare Studies." *Shakespeare Survey* 1 (1948–).

The best selective bibliographies of Shakespeare scholarship are David M. Bergeron and Geraldo U. de Sousa, *Shakespeare: A Study and Research Guide*, rev. 3rd. ed. (Lawrence: UP of Kansas, 1995, 235 pp.), and Larry S. Champion, *The Essential Shakespeare: An Annotated Bibliography of Major Modern Studies*, 2nd ed., Reference Publication in Literature (New York: Hall-Macmillan; Toronto: Maxwell, 1993, 568 pp.).

M2025   *Bibliographie Internationale de l'Humanisme et de la Renaissance (BIHR).*
Genève: Droz, 1966–. Annual.   Z6207.R4 B5   016.9402'1. Online.
12 Oct. 2006 <http://bihr.droz.org>. CD-ROM.

An international, interdisciplinary bibliography of scholarship on all aspects of humanism and the Renaissance that continues and expands "Bibliographie des articles relatifs à l'histoire de l'Humanisme et de la Renaissance [1956–64]," *Bibliothèque d'Humanisme et Renaissance* 20–27 (1958–65). Coverage in *BIHR* begins with 1963. Since vol. 34 (for 1998), entries are organized in a single alphabetized list followed by four indexes: subjects; geographical areas; persons and anonymous works; and document authors (largely superfluous given the alphabetized list of entries). Earlier volumes consisted of seven divisions: studies of individuals and anonymous works; general studies; history (including geography and political, social, and economic history); religion, philosophy, politics, and law; general literary studies, linguistics, and bibliography; the arts (including music and dance); science and technology. Except in the first division, which is organized alphabetically by writer, historical personage, or anonymous work, studies are grouped by country or geographical area, then listed alphabetically by author. Two indexes: scholars; writers and other individuals not separately classified in the first division. Researchers would benefit from a more refined classification system and greater currency (the lag is currently five years).

The online version can be searched by document author, title keyword, date, subject, geographical area, and persons; for the last three, records appearing in vols. 1–33 must be searched separately from those in later volumes. Except for title keyword and date searches, users must work through a cumbersome process that involves opening a separate window (click List), typing the search term, clicking OK, clicking the + button to move each term to a List of Selected Items, clicking Submit to add the term(s) to the main search box, and then clicking Submit and Search to bring records to the screen. Results can be sorted by author (ascending), date (descending), or theme (apparently, subject headings). Records can be printed or copied to a file but not e-mailed. Although the subject and geographical area searches are limited by the taxonomy of vols. 1–33 and by the indexes since vol. 34, although records for essays from edited collections lack a full citation and are (inexcusably) not linked to main-entry records, and although the search interface is cumbersome, the online version keeps searchers from having to slog through stacks of printed volumes.

The coverage of British literature is much less thorough than in *MLAIB* (G335) or *ABELL* (G340), but the interdisciplinary scope and more extensive survey of European publications make *BIHR* an essential complement to these standard serial bibliographies.

For a discussion of the editorial difficulties that have beset *BIHR* and the unsuccessful attempt to establish an *Annual Bibliography of Early Modern Europe*, see John B. Dillon, "Renaissance Bibliography in the Electronic Age: Recent Work on a Computer-Produced Annual Bibliography of Studies on Early Modern Europe," *Collection Development* 6.1–2 (1984): 217–26. Coverage must be complemented by *Iter: Gateway to the Middle Ages and Renaissance* (M1835a)

M2030   "Literature of the Renaissance in [1917–68]: A Bibliography." *Studies in Philology* 14–66 (1917–69).   P25.S8   405.

An annual bibliography originally limited to English literature but expanded in vol. 36 (1939) to encompass French, Germanic, Italian, Spanish, and Portuguese literature. At its demise, coverage was international and included dissertations and some reviews as well as books and articles. Entries in the English division are listed by author in nine sections: general; history, manners, and customs; drama and stage; Shakespeare;

nondramatic literature; More; Spenser; Donne; Milton. Indexed by persons. Although never comprehensive, it includes many works omitted from the other standard bibliographies such as *MLAIB* (G335) and *ABELL* (G340).

See also

> Secs. G: Serial Bibliographies, Indexes, and Abstracts and H: Guides to Dissertations and Theses.
> *ABELL* (G340): English Literature/Sixteenth Century and Seventeenth Century sections.
> *MLAIB* (G335): English Language and Literature division in the volumes for 1921–25; English VII and VIII in the volumes for 1926–56; English VI and VII in the volumes for 1957–80; and English Literature/1500–1599 and 1600–1699 sections (as well as any other larger chronological section encompassing either century) in the later volumes. Researchers must also check the headings beginning "Elizabethan," "Jacobean," and "Renaissance" in the subject index to post-1980 volumes and in the online thesaurus.
> *Progress of Medieval and Renaissance Studies* (M1835a).

OTHER BIBLIOGRAPHIES

M2035   *The New Cambridge Bibliography of English Literature* (*NCBEL*). Vol. 1:
        600–1660. Ed. George Watson. Cambridge: Cambridge UP, 1974.
        2,476 cols.   Z2011.N45 [PR83]   016.82.

(For a full discussion of *NCBEL*, see entry M1385.) The part devoted to Renaissance literature (1500–1660) has seven divisions, each subdivided and classified as its subject requires: introduction (general works, literary relations with the Continent, book production and distribution); poetry (general works, Tudor poetry, Elizabethan sonnet, minor Tudor poetry, Jacobean and Caroline poetry, Milton, minor Jacobean and Caroline poetry, emblem books, epigrams and formal satire, songbooks); drama (general works, theaters and actors, Puritan attack on the stage, moralities, early comedies, early tragedies, later Elizabethan drama, minor Elizabethan drama, Shakespeare, Jacobean and Caroline drama, minor Jacobean and Caroline drama, university plays); religion (humanists and reformers, English Bible, Prayer Book, versions of the Psalms, sermons and devotional writings, Richard Hooker, Marprelate controversy, Caroline divines); popular and miscellaneous prose (pamphleteers and miscellaneous writers, minor popular literature, character books and essays, prose fiction, news sheets and newsbooks, travel, translations into English); history, philosophy, science and other forms of learning (historians, biographers, and antiquaries; letters, diaries, autobiographies, and biographies; economics and politics; law; scholarship; literary criticism; philosophy; science; education); and Scottish literature (general works, poetry and drama, prose). The general introduction for the volume as a whole lists bibliographies, histories, anthologies, and works about prosody, prose rhythm, and language important to the study of the Renaissance period. Vol. 1 of the *Cambridge Bibliography of English Literature* (M1385a) is still occasionally useful for its coverage of the social and political background (which *NCBEL* drops).

Users must familiarize themselves with the organization, remember that there is considerable unevenness of coverage among subdivisions, and consult the index volume (vol. 5) rather than the provisional index in vol. 1. Despite its shortcomings (see entry

M1385), *NCBEL* offers the best general coverage of both primary and secondary works for the study of Renaissance literature, but it must be supplemented by the other works in this section and by *MLAIB* (G335), *ABELL* (G340), and *Year's Work in English Studies* (G330). Review: Fred C. Robinson, *Anglia* 97 (1979): 511–17.

M2040 Tannenbaum, Samuel A., and Dorothy R. Tannenbaum. *Elizabethan Bibliographies.* 10 vols. Port Washington: Kennikat, 1967. Z2012.T3 016.8208′003.

A convenient reprint of the 41 volumes and seven supplements privately printed in limited numbers between 1937 and 1950. The individual volumes—devoted to a variety of Renaissance writers, some of Shakespeare's works, and Mary Stuart—vary in organization but typically include sections for editions, selections, biography and commentary, and bibliography. Indexed by person and subject. The highly abbreviated entries rarely transcribe a title exactly, include a number of inessential passing notices, and are replete with errors.

The Tannenbaums also compiled the annual "Shakespeare and His Contemporaries (A Classified Bibliography for [1925–48])," *Shakespeare Association Bulletin* 1–24 (1924–45), which supplements their Elizabethan Bibliographies series. Many of the volumes are updated and new authors added in *Elizabethan Bibliographies Supplements,* gen. ed. Charles A. Pennel, 17 vols. (London: Nether, 1967–71). Entries are listed chronologically and indexed by scholar and title.

The Tannenbaum and Pennel volumes are convenient starting points for research on a writer who has not been the subject of a recent author bibliography. Neither series, however, offers comprehensive coverage.

See also

Kallendorf, *Latin Influences on English Literature from the Middle Ages to the Eighteenth Century* (S4895).

RELATED TOPICS

M2045 Davies, Godfrey, ed. *Bibliography of British History: Stuart Period, 1603–1714.* 2nd ed. Ed. Mary Frear Keeler. Oxford: Clarendon–Oxford UP, 1970. 734 pp. Z2018.D25 016.9142.

An extensive, albeit selective, bibliography of primary and secondary materials published for the most part before 1963. Entries are organized in 15 classified divisions: general reference works, politics, constitutional history, law, ecclesiastical history, military history, naval history, economics, social history, cultural history (e.g., fine arts, music, science, and education), local history, colonization, Wales, Scotland, and Ireland. Annotations are largely descriptive, with frequent references to related studies, but many entries lack annotation. Indexed by persons and subjects. The authoritative guide to historical studies on the period and a valuable resource for cross-disciplinary research. Review: J. P. Cooper, *English Historical Review* 89 (1974): 118–22.

A useful supplement because of its pointed evaluations and inclusion of works published to mid-1979 is J. S. Morrill, *Seventeenth-Century Britain, 1603–1714,* Critical Bibliographies in Modern History (Folkestone: Dawson; Hamden: Archon–Shoe String, 1980, 189 pp.). Coverage is highly selective and for articles does not extend before 1957.

M2050   Read, Conyers, ed. *Bibliography of British History: Tudor Period, 1485–
         1603*. 2nd ed. Oxford: Clarendon–Oxford UP, 1959. 624 pp.
         Z2018.R28   016.94205.

An extensive, albeit rigorously selective, bibliography of primary and secondary materials published largely before 1 January 1957. Entries are organized in 14 classified divisions: general studies (including reference works); political history; constitutional history; political theory; law; ecclesiastical history; economics; discovery, exploration, and colonization; military and naval history; cultural and social history (e.g., education, music, science, and fine arts); local history; Scotland; Ireland; and Wales. Several annotations are helpfully evaluative or refer to related studies; unfortunately, many entries are inadequately annotated or not at all. Indexed by persons and subjects (with several errors in the indexing). The authoritative guide to historical studies on the period and a valuable resource for cross-disciplinary research.

A very selective but useful supplement with coverage through 1 September 1966 is Mortimer Levine, *Tudor England, 1485–1603*, Conference on British Studies Bibliographical Handbooks (Cambridge: Cambridge UP, 1968, 115 pp.), with frequent brief but pointed annotations.

See also

  Royal Historical Society Bibliography (M1400).

Language

DICTIONARIES

See

  Bailey, *Early Modern English* (M1410a).
  ———. *Michigan Early Modern English Materials* (M1410a).
  Dictionary of Medieval Latin from British Sources (M1700). ·

Biographical Dictionaries

The *Oxford Dictionary of National Biography* (M1425) remains the standard general source of biographical information for the period. Additional details, especially about less prominent individuals, may be found in Mark Eccles, *Brief Lives: Tudor and Stuart Authors*, Texts and Studies, 1982, *Studies in Philology* 79.4 (1982): 135 pp.; and J. W. Saunders, *A Biographical Dictionary of Renaissance Poets and Dramatists, 1520–1650* (Brighton: Harvester; Totowa: Barnes, 1983, 216 pp.). The latter suffers from a lack of balance and numerous errors. Neither fulfills the need for a reliable and thorough biographical dictionary of Renaissance authors.

See also

  Bell, *Biographical Dictionary of English Women Writers, 1580–1720* (M1433a).
  Dictionary of Literary Biography (J600).
  Ruoff, *Crowell's Handbook of Elizabethan and Stuart Literature* (M1980).

Periodicals

GUIDES TO PRIMARY WORKS

M2060   Nelson, Carolyn, and Matthew Seccombe, comps. *British Newspapers and Periodicals, 1641–1700: A Short-Title Catalogue of Serials Printed in England, Scotland, Ireland, and British America.* Index Society Fund Publications. New York: MLA, 1987. 724 pp.   Z6956.G6 N44 [PN5115] 015.41034.

An enumerative bibliography and finding list of extant issues of serials printed between 1641 and 1700, with a supplementary checklist extending coverage through March 1702. The approximately 700 titles encompass newspapers, newsbooks, miscellanies, official journals, trade bulletins, and other publications with numbered or dated issues bearing uniform titles and formats and published at intervals of less than a year. (Annuals are included in Wing, *Short-Title Catalogue* [M1995].) The serials are organized alphabetically by title of the first number, followed by issues in chronological order, with separate entries for different editions or versions; variant, general, and later titles are thoroughly cross-referenced to main entries. Preceding the list of issues is a headnote that includes, when known, variant titles, inclusive dates, format, average length of issue, frequency, price, author or editor, notes on variants, and references to standard bibliographies. The entry for an issue cites, when appropriate, title, volume number, issue number, date (in New Style), imprint, variants, standard bibliographies, and up to 20 locations (with those in the British Isles to the left of the semicolon, and those elsewhere in the world to the right). An extensive appendix on variants identifies different typesettings of selected serials after June 1642; variants in earlier publications are described in the main list. Descriptions are based on personal examination of at least one copy of nearly every issue. Six indexes: chronological by month; publishers and printers; editors and authors; subjects; places of publication other than London; foreign languages. Users must be certain to study the full explanation of organization and editorial policies and remember that, like Wing, this work is not a census of copies and that the identification of authors and editors is based on *New Cambridge Bibliography of English Literature* (M2035 and M2255), which is not trustworthy in many of its ascriptions. The first reliable guide to the identification and location of issues, *British Newspapers and Periodicals* provides the necessary groundwork for further bibliographical investigations and studies of authorship, editorship, and content. For addenda and corrigenda, see Joad Raymond, "Some Corrections and Additions to *British Newspapers and Periodicals 1641–1700: A Short-Title Catalogue,*" *Notes and Queries* ns 42 (1995): 451–53. Review: Michael Harris, *Library* 6th ser. 11 (1989): 378–83.

For a preliminary analysis of publishing practices, along with suggestions for further research on serial publications, see Nelson and Seccombe, *Periodical Publications, 1641–1700: A Survey with Illustrations,* Occasional Papers of the Bibliographical Society 2 (London: Bibliog. Soc., 1986, 109 pp.).

GUIDES TO SCHOLARSHIP AND CRITICISM

See

Linton, *Newspaper Press in Britain* (M1455).
Weed, *Studies of British Newspapers and Periodicals* (M2285).

Genres

FICTION

Histories and Surveys

M2090   Salzman, Paul. *English Prose Fiction, 1558–1700: A Critical History.*
        Oxford: Clarendon–Oxford UP, 1985. 391 pp.   PR836.S24   823′.3′09.
    A critical history of the development of prose fiction, organized by genre or type
and including an extended critical analysis of at least one example of each. Concludes
with a two-part bibliography of extant works: pt. 1 is an author list of Elizabethan
fiction; pt. 2 classifies seventeenth-century fiction in 25 types. Although the bibliography is not comprehensive, it does complement Mish, *English Prose Fiction* (M2095),
and O'Dell, *Chronological List of Prose Fiction* (M2100). Indexed by persons, genres,
and titles (but with some inconsistencies in the last). Salzman is by far the best survey,
with especially perceptive treatment of seventeenth-century fiction. Reviews: Jerry C.
Beasley, *Studies in the Novel* 17 (1985): 303–10; John J. O'Connor, *Renaissance Quarterly* 39 (1986): 130–32.
    For fiction before 1558, Margaret Schlauch, *Antecedents of the English Novel,
1400–1600 (from Chaucer to Deloney)* (Warszawa: PWN; London: Oxford UP, 1963,
264 pp.), remains useful although colored by an anachronistic search for realism.

See also

    Baker, *History of the English Novel,* vols. 1–2 (M1505).

Guides to Primary Works

Bibliographies and Indexes

M2095   Mish, Charles C., comp. *English Prose Fiction, 1600–1700: A Chronological
        Checklist.* Charlottesville: Bibliog. Soc. of the U of Virginia, 1967. 110 pp.
        Z2014.F4 M5.
    A chronological short-title list of editions of original fictional works and transla-
tions that depends heavily on the *Short-Title Catalogues* (M1990 and M1995) and
Arundell Esdaile, *A List of English Tales and Prose Romances Printed before 1700* (London: Blades for the Bibliog. Soc., 1912, 329 pp.). Editions are listed alphabetically by
author or title of anonymous work under the year of publication (although the dating
of many editions is conjectural). Indexed by authors and titles. Although Mish is more
conservative than O'Dell (M2100) in defining fiction and generally superior to O'Dell
for editions after 1599, both works are bedeviled by the difficulty in determining what
constitutes prose fiction before the eighteenth century. Mish supersedes Esdaile but
must be supplemented by the bibliography in Salzman, *English Prose Fiction* (M2090).

M2100   O'Dell, Sterg. *A Chronological List of Prose Fiction in English Printed in
        England and Other Countries, 1475–1640.* Cambridge: Technology P of
        MIT, 1954. 147 pp.   Z2014.F5 O33   016.823.
    A chronological list of editions of original works and translations that is based
largely on *Short-Title Catalogue* (M1990), *Transcript of the Registers of the Company of*

Stationers (M2000), and Esdaile, *List of English Tales and Prose Romances* (M2095a). Editions are listed alphabetically by author or title of anonymous work under the year of publication (or entry in the Stationers' Register for nonextant editions). Entries include *Short-Title Catalogue* or Stationers' Register references, locations of copies (superseded by the revised *Short-Title Catalogue*), and occasional citations to modern editions (superseded by Harner, *English Renaissance Prose Fiction* [M2105]). Indexed by authors and anonymous works. Although it is the fullest bibliography of early fiction, O'Dell is swollen by the inclusion of many works that cannot qualify as fiction and several bibliographical ghosts. O'Dell supersedes Esdaile, but Mish, *English Prose Fiction* (M2095), is generally preferable as a guide to editions printed after 1599; see also the bibliography in Salzman, *English Prose Fiction* (M2090).

Text Archives

M2103   *Early English Prose Fiction.* ProQuest. Online. 14 June 2006 <http:// collections.chadwyck.com>.

An archive of rekeyed texts of about 211 works of English-language fiction printed between 1500 and 1700. Editions were selected by an editorial board to offer "a balanced and representative survey of fictional prose in English from the period 1500– 1700"; no other selection criteria are stipulated.

Simple keyword, first line or title, and author searches can be limited by date of publication, date during an author's lifetime, gender, nationality, and part of a work (e.g., front matter, epigraphs). Searchers must be certain to checkmark the Include Typographical Variants box but must be aware that this feature works on simple variants (e.g. "glove/gloue") but not more complicated ones ("dogs/dogges/doges"). Searchers can also browse an author list of the contents of the database. Results appear in ascending alphabetical order and cannot be re-sorted. Citations (but not the full text) can be marked for e-mailing, downloading, or printing; each citation includes a durable URL to the full text.

Some works are rekeyed from textually unsound editions; however, the bibliographic record for each work identifies the source of the text and any omissions (e.g., preliminary matter). Besides being a useful source for identifying an elusive quotation, *Early English Prose Fiction*'s text archive makes feasible a variety of kinds of studies (stylistic, thematic, imagistic, and topical).

The contents of *Early English Prose Fiction* can also be searched through *LiOn* (I527), which offers a less versatile search interface.

Guides to Scholarship and Criticism

M2105   Harner, James L. *English Renaissance Prose Fiction, 1500–1660: An Annotated Bibliography of Criticism.* A Reference Publication in Literature. Boston: Hall, 1978. 556 pp. *English Renaissance Prose Fiction, 1500–1660: An Annotated Bibliography of Criticism (1976–1983).* A Reference Publication in Literature. 1985. 228 pp. *1984–1990.* 1992. 185 pp. Z2014.F4 H37 [PR833]   016.823'009.

An annotated bibliography of studies and editions since 1800 of English-language fiction (including translations) written or printed in England from 1500 to 1660. The descriptively annotated entries are arranged in four divisions: bibliographies; anthologies; general studies; and authors, translators, and titles. The last is organized alphabetically, with anonymous works entered (sometimes awkwardly) by title of the earliest extant edition. Each author, translator, or title includes sections for bibliographies, editions, and studies. Indexed by persons, anonymous works, and subjects (with the supplements more fully indexed). Although conservative in defining prose fiction and overlooking some studies, *English Renaissance Prose Fiction* offers the most thorough coverage of international scholarship on the topic. Reviews: Jane Belfield, *Library* 6th ser. 3 (1981): 73–74; Charles C. Mish, *Seventeenth-Century News* 38 (1980): 10; Robert Yeager, *Studies in the Novel* 13 (1981): 340–41.

Selected recent studies (as late as 1994) are surveyed in Reid Barbour, "Recent Studies in Elizabethan Prose Fiction," *English Literary Renaissance* 25 (1995): 248–76.

DRAMA AND THEATER

Several works in sections L: Genres/Drama and Theater and M: English Literature/ General/Genres/Drama and Theater are useful for research in Renaissance literature.

Histories and Surveys

M2110   Bentley, Gerald Eades. *The Jacobean and Caroline Stage.* 7 vols. Oxford:
Clarendon–Oxford UP, 1941–68.   PN2592.B4   792.0942.

> Vols. 1–2: *Dramatic Companies and Players.* 1941.
> Vols. 3–5: *Plays and Playwrights.* 1956.
> Vol. 6: *Theatres.* 1968. 309 pp.
> Vol. 7: *Appendixes to Volume VI; General Index.* 1968. 390 pp.

A massive cumulation of factual information on all aspects of the stage from 1616 to 1642, designed to continue Chambers, *Elizabethan Stage* (M2115). Vols. 1–2 trace the history of each of the London dramatic companies (with lists of actors and repertory) and the career of each known actor (quoting in chronological order "every scrap of biographical evidence"); appendixes transcribe various documents. Vols. 3–5 collect biographical details on dramatists and bibliographical information on plays. A typical entry for a play lists editions, scholarship, and seventeenth-century records and evaluates what is known of its date, authorship, source(s), allusions, and performance. Vol. 6 examines the private and public London theaters. Vol. 7 prints appendixes to vol. 6 (among which is a chronology of theatrical affairs) and a detailed analytical index of plays, authors, scholars, actors, places, and subjects. The careful evaluation of primary evidence and scholarship makes Bentley the essential source for facts about acting companies, players, playwrights, plays, and theaters. Reviews: (vols. 1–2) K. M. Lea, *Review of English Studies* 18 (1942): 491–96; (vols. 3–5) Harold Jenkins, *Review of English Studies* ns 9 (1958): 196–202; (vols. 6–7) Jenkins, *Review of English Studies* ns 20 (1969): 222–24.

M2115   Chambers, E. K. *The Elizabethan Stage.* 4 vols. Rpt. with corrections.
Oxford: Clarendon–Oxford UP, 1951.   PN2589.C4   792.0942.

Continues his *Mediaeval Stage* (M1905) in a history of the development of the Elizabethan stage that emphasizes the social and economic conditions affecting the drama from 1558 to 1616. Detailed examinations of court entertainments, the control of the stage, acting companies, playhouses, and plays and playwrights are supplemented by extensive appendixes (a calendar of court entertainments, extracts from records and texts, and bibliographies of academic, printed, lost, and manuscript plays). For additions, see his "Elizabethan Stage Gleanings," *Review of English Studies* 1 (1925): 75–

78, 182–86. Four indexes: plays; persons; places; subjects; more fully indexed by Be-atrice White, comp., *An Index to* The Elizabethan Stage *and* William Shakespeare *by Sir Edmund Chambers* (Oxford: Clarendon–Oxford UP, 1934, 161 pp.). An indis-pensable source, *Elizabethan Stage* has never been superseded but must be supplemented with other histories (such as *Revels History of Drama* [M1530]) and specialized studies such as those listed in the bibliographies of the *Revels History*, vol. 2, pp. 259–82; vol. 3, pp. 475–508. Continued by Bentley, *Jacobean and Caroline Stage* (M2110).

M2117   Hunter, G. K. *English Drama, 1586–1642: The Age of Shakespeare.* Vol. 6
        [originally vol. 4, pt. 2] of *The Oxford History of English Literature*
        (M1310). Oxford: Clarendon–Oxford UP, 1997. 623 pp.   PR421.H86
        822′.309.
   A history of English drama from 1586 to 1642 that emphasizes the contradictory pressures—from audiences, censorship, profit-driven theatrical managers, and authors hoping for social or literary esteem—on the composition and production of plays. Following an introductory chapter on the "preconditions of Elizabethan drama," or-ganizes chapters around genres, and Shakespeare is central in the discussions. Concludes with brief biographies, a chronology, and a selective bibliography. Two indexes: play-wrights and plays; persons and subjects. Written by one of the foremost scholars of Renaissance drama, *English Drama, 1586–1642* seems destined to become one of the classic volumes in the *Oxford History*. Review(s): Paul Dean, *English Studies* 79 (1998): 441–46; Marion Trousdale, *Huntington Library Quarterly* 64 (2001): 237–44.

M2125   Wilson, F. P. *The English Drama, 1485–1585.* Ed. G. K. Hunter. Vol. 4,
        pt. 1 of *The Oxford History of English Literature* (M1310). Gen. eds.
        Bonamy Dobrée and Norman Davis. Oxford: Clarendon–Oxford UP,
        1969. 244 pp. (Reprinted in 1990 as vol. 5 of *OHEL.*)   PR641.W58
        822′.2′09.
   A critical history of the morality, interlude, masque, pageant, entertainment, sacred drama, comedy, and tragedy, with a chapter on the major dramatic companies. Includes a chronology and a now dated selective bibliography. Indexed by authors, titles, and subjects. A judicious, authoritative account that remains one of the better introductions to the drama of the period. Reviews: Norman Sanders, *Shakespeare Studies* 6 (1970): 389–91; S. Schoenbaum, *Yearbook of English Studies* 1 (1971): 226–27.

See also

   Chambers, *Mediaeval Stage* (M1905).
   Revels History of Drama in English (M1530)
   Wickham, *Early English Stages, 1300 to 1660* (M1915).

Annals

M2130   Kawachi, Yoshiko. *Calendar of English Renaissance Drama, 1558–1642.*
        Garland Reference Library of the Humanities 661. New York: Garland,
        1986. 351 pp.   PN2589.K36   792′.0941.
   A daily calendar of performances of plays, masks, entertainments, and other the-atrical presentations and of tours of acting companies in England. Modeled on Harbage, *Annals of English Drama* (M1535), and borrowing many of its conventions and symbols (along with a good bit of information), the *Calendar* presents details in tabular format,

with columns for date of production (according to the New Style calendar), information (such as licensing or entry in Stationers' Register [M1380 and M2000]) that qualifies the preceding date, acting company, location of performance or tour (including patrons or other important persons in the audience), title, type of play, author(s), date of manuscript or earliest printed text, and sources of information. Deciphering an entry requires constant reference to the explanations of abbreviations and symbols (pp. x–xvi). Three indexes: titles of plays; playwrights; dramatic companies (classified by types of companies). Although the lack of running heads makes the year difficult to ascertain and articles used as sources are not identified (e.g., the code "K" stands for 23 different journals), Kawachi is valuable for its compilation and organization of widely scattered scholarship. While the daily record of performances allows for more precise studies of dramatic trends, stage history, and repertory than does its complement, Harbage, *Annals of English Drama* (M1535), Kawachi must be used with due regard to the impreciseness and incompleteness of the records as well as the provisional dating of many plays and performances. Review: Carol Chillington Rutter, *Theatre Notebook* 42 (1988): 83–86.

See also

Harbage, *Annals of English Drama, 975–1700* (M1535).

Guides to Primary Works

M2135   Greg, W. W. *A Bibliography of the English Printed Drama to the Restoration.*
4 vols. Illustrated Monographs 24: 1–4. London: Bibliog. Soc., 1939–59.
Z2014.D7 G78   016.822.

A descriptive bibliography of all editions, issues, and variants to 1700 of dramatic works (including many translations) "written before the *end* of 1642 . . . and printed before the *end* of 1700 . . . together with those written after 1642 but printed before the *beginning* of 1660." After an initial section that transcribes extracts relating to drama from the records of the Stationers' Company (M1380), plays are described in four divisions: individual plays, Latin plays, lost plays, and collected editions. Individual and Latin plays are listed chronologically by publication date of the earliest extant edition (with issues, variants, and later editions following in order of printing); lost plays, by date of presumed publication; and collected editions, by author. Additions and corrections appear in vol. 4, pp. 1643–711.

An entry for a printed play includes the Greg number (now the standard reference number); a full analytical description for each edition, issue, and variant, with notes on bibliographical and textual matters; references to advertisements and bibliographies; and locations in a limited number of British and American libraries (see the revised *Short-Title Catalogue* [M1990], Wing, *Short-Title Catalogue* [M1995], and *English Short Title Catalogue* [M1377] for current and additional locations). Users must consult the lengthy introduction (vol. 4, pp. i–clxxiv) for a detailed explanation of scope, content, and procedures.

Vol. 3 prints several useful appendixes—advertisements in newspapers, prefatory matter and actor lists from editions, contemporary lists of plays—as well as 18 indexes (e.g., prologues and epilogues; acting companies; court performances; printers, publishers, and booksellers; and general indexes of persons and titles and of subjects mentioned in descriptions and commentary). Vol. 4 provides a title index to the entire work.

A cornucopia of historical, bibliographical, and textual detail derived from meticulous examination of copies, Greg is the authoritative source for information on the publication and identification of early texts and the foundation for much of the important research on Renaissance drama. Reviews: (vols. 3–4) *Times Literary Supplement* 15 Jan. 1960: 40; Harold Jenkins, *Review of English Studies* ns 12 (1961): 201–04.

M2140   Berger, Thomas L., William C. Bradford, and Sidney L. Sondergard. *An Index of Characters in Early Modern English Drama Printed Plays, 1500– 1660.* Rev. ed. Cambridge: Cambridge UP, 1998. 170 pp.   PR1265.3.B4 016.822009.

An index to characters (including animals and inanimate objects represented by actors, such as Wall in *Midsummer Night's Dream*) who appear in printed English and Latin plays listed in Greg, *Bibliography of the English Printed Drama* (M2135). Characters are indexed by surname, given name, alias, nationality, occupation, religion, psychological state (e.g., melancholic), and type (e.g., poisoner, tyrant, magician). Plays are identified by Greg number (a finding list is appended). Effective use requires close familiarity with the description of scope and procedures in the introduction. Although the indexing by psychological state and type is sometimes inexact, surname and given name are not indexed together, and variants of the same name are entered separately, the work is a valuable resource for character studies of the drama. Reviews: (first edition) G. K. Hunter, *Yearbook of English Studies* 9 (1979): 297–99; J. L. Simmons, *Research Opportunities in Renaissance Drama* 18 (1975): 25–28.

See also

Lancashire, *Dramatic Texts and Records* (M1925).
Records of *Early English Drama* (M1920).

Guides to Scholarship and Criticism

Surveys of Research

M2145   Logan, Terence P., and Denzell S. Smith, eds. *The Predecessors of Shakespeare.* Lincoln: U of Nebraska P, 1973. 348 pp.   Z2014.D7 L83 [PR646]   016.822′3′09.

———. *The Popular School.* 1975. 299 pp.   Z2014.D7 L82 [PR651] 016.822′3′09.

———. *The New Intellectuals.* 1977. 370 pp.   Z2014.D7 N29 [PR671] 016.822′3.

———. *The Later Jacobean and Caroline Dramatists.* 1978. 279 pp. Z2014.D7 L816 [PR671]   016.822′3′09.

(Each volume bears the subtitle *A Survey and Bibliography of Recent Studies in English Renaissance Drama.*)

Selective surveys of research and bibliographies for dramatists (excluding Shakespeare) and plays from 1580 to 1642. Coverage extends from 1923 to 1968–76, supplemented by some important earlier and later publications (see the preface to each volume for details of coverage). Each volume consists of chapters on individual major writers, anonymous works, and minor dramatists. Those on individual authors are in three parts: (1) a survey of biographical and general studies of the plays as well as nondramatic works; (2) a survey of criticism of individual plays (with plays awkwardly arranged in order of critical importance) and a summary of the state of scholarship; (3) a survey of scholarship on canon, dating, and textual studies, and a critique of editions. A selective bibliography of studies not discussed concludes each chapter. Anonymous plays are grouped by date of performance in a single chapter with sections, when necessary, on editions, authorship, date, source, genre, and general studies. The chapter on minor dramatists consists of an annotated bibliography of studies and editions. Two indexes: persons; plays. Although the extent and quality of evaluation vary from contributor to contributor and although many playwrights are now the subjects of more-thorough author bibliographies, these volumes remain important for their evaluative surveys of scholarship. Reviews: (*Popular School*) Michael Shapiro, *Literary Research Newsletter* 3 (1978): 79–83; (*New Intellectuals*) David M. Bergeron, *Shakespeare Quarterly* 31 (1980): 443–44; Philip R. Rider, *Analytical and Enumerative Bibliography* 2 (1978): 63–71; (*Later Jacobean*) Rider, *Analytical and Enumerative Bibliography* 4 (1980): 49–54.

Coverage should be supplemented with *Year's Work in English Studies* (G330), Wells, *English Drama* (M1555), "Recent Studies in Tudor and Stuart Drama" (M2150), *World Shakespeare Bibliography Online* (M2020), installments devoted to dramatists in the "Recent Studies in the English Renaissance" survey in *English Literary Renaissance* (M2010), and the following:

> Fordyce, Rachel. *Caroline Drama: A Bibliographic History of Criticism.* 2nd ed. A Reference Publication in Literature. New York: Hall; Toronto: Maxwell, 1992. 332 pp. Although occasionally useful for its inclusion of early scholarship, the work is badly marred by poor organization, superfluous entries in the divisions for reference works and textual studies, and numerous errors.
>
> Lidman, Mark J. *Studies in Jacobean Drama, 1973–1984: An Annotated Bibliography.* Garland Reference Library of the Humanities 597. New York: Garland, 1986. 278 pp. Updates Logan and Smith's coverage of English-language scholarship on Chapman, Dekker, Heywood, Tourneur, Marston, Middleton, Webster, Massinger, Ford, Brome, and Shirley.

The best (albeit dated) selective bibliography of studies of non-Shakespearean drama 1580–1642 is Brownell Salomon, *Critical Analyses in English Renaissance Drama: A Bibliographic Guide*, rev. 3rd ed., Garland Reference Library of the Humanities 1370 (New York: Garland, 1991, 262 pp.). The 936 informatively annotated entries are accompanied by an admirably thorough subject index of themes, images, topics, character types, forms, rhetorical figures, topoi, titles, critical approaches, dramatic and theatrical conventions, and individuals.

M2150   "Recent Studies in Tudor and Stuart Drama." *Studies in English Literature, 1500–1900* 1 (1961)– . Annually in the Spring issue.   PR1.S82. 820'.9.

A commissioned survey by an established scholar, with recent ones emphasizing full-length critical and historical studies and typically offering only cursory attention to editions and reference works. (Nondramatic literature is covered in the Winter issue [M2015].) The essays vary considerably in soundness and rigor of assessment. Although the most current annual survey, the work is generally limited to books received for review and must be supplemented by the chapters in *Year's Work in English Studies*

(G330) on Renaissance drama and Shakespeare. The broader surveys listed in entry M2015 also treat drama.

See also

> *YWES* (G330): Chapters for Shakespeare; Renaissance Drama: Excluding Shakespeare.

Other Bibliographies

M2155 Bergeron, David M. *Twentieth-Century Criticism of English Masques, Pageants, and Entertainments, 1558–1642.* With a supplement on the folk play and related forms by Harry B. Caldwell. Checklists in the Humanities and Education. San Antonio: Trinity UP, 1972. 67 pp.   Z2014.D7 B44 016.822′3.

A selective bibliography of English-language studies published through 1971. Entries are arranged alphabetically in five divisions: general studies, Ben Jonson (including works on Inigo Jones), Milton's *Comus*, other writers, and folk plays, with additions to the first four parts on pp. 39–40. Two indexes: authors; subjects. Although in need of updating, sometimes superseded by author bibliographies (especially the sections on Jonson and *Comus*), and limited by the exclusion of foreign-language criticism, Bergeron remains useful as a starting point for research on the masque and related dramatic forms.

Recent studies are selectively surveyed in Suzanne Gossett, "Recent Studies in the English Masque," *English Literary Renaissance* 26 (1996): 586–627.

M2160 Stevens, David. *English Renaissance Theatre History: A Reference Guide.* A Reference Guide to Literature. Boston: Hall, 1982. 342 pp. Z2014.D7 S78 [PN2589]   016.792′0942.

An annotated bibliography of scholarship published between 1664 and 1979 on theater history from 1558 through 1642. The descriptively annotated entries, arranged chronologically, include (for example) studies of acting, playhouses, the stage, audience, actors and other theater personnel, finance, government regulation, and music. Indexed by playwrights, scholars, and subjects. There are errors and omissions, and reviewers have criticized the inadequate coverage of music and repertory, but Stevens offers the best starting point for research on many aspects of theater history of the period. Reviews: David M. Bergeron, *Shakespeare Quarterly* 35 (1984): 253–54; Reavley Gair, *Analytical and Enumerative Bibliography* 7 (1983): 239–42.

M2165 White, D. Jerry. *Early English Drama, Everyman to 1580: A Reference Guide.* A Reference Guide to Literature. Boston: Hall, 1986. 289 pp. Z2014.D7 W48 [PR641]   016.822′2′09.

An extensive, although not comprehensive, bibliography of studies and scholarly editions (published from 1691 to 1982, with a few later items) on plays from c. 1495 to 1580 by British playwrights. Biographical material not related to plays is excluded, as are studies of folk drama, pageants, entertainments, masques, and John Skelton, since they are the subjects of other bibliographies (see Stevens, *English Renaissance Theatre History* [M2160], Bergeron, *Twentieth-Century Criticism of English Masques* [M2155], and Robert S. Kinsman, *John Skelton, Early Tudor Laureate: An Annotated Bibliography, c. 1488–1977,* A Reference Publication in Literature [Boston: Hall, 1979, 179 pp.]).

The succinctly annotated entries are listed chronologically in divisions for bibliographies, collections, general studies, and authors, translators, or anonymous works; the last has sections for bibliographies and editions and studies. Since there are few multiple listings, users must consult the index to locate all studies on an author or work. Indexed by authors, scholars, anonymous works, and subjects. Breadth, accuracy, and clear annotations make this an essential starting point for research on the early drama.

See also

> Berger, *Medieval English Drama* (M1930a).
> Kallendorf, *Latin Influences on English Literature from the Middle Ages to the Eighteenth Century* (S4895).
> Lancashire, *Dramatic Texts and Records* (M1925).
> Stratman, *Bibliography of Medieval Drama* (M1930).

POETRY

Many works in sections L: Genres/Poetry and M: English Literature/General/Genres/Poetry are important to research in Renaissance poetry.

Histories and Surveys

Lewis, *English Literature in the Sixteenth Century* (M1975), and Bush, *English Literature in the Earlier Seventeenth Century* (M1970), remain the best general histories of Renaissance poetry.

Guides to Primary Works

M2180   Case, Arthur E. *A Bibliography of English Poetical Miscellanies, 1521–1750.* London: Oxford UP for the Bibliog. Soc., 1935. 386 pp.   Z2014.P7 C3 016.8210822.

An analytical bibliography of 481 collections of miscellaneous verse (including translations) by British writers in any language and printed in any country. Case excludes song and hymn books but otherwise lists any volume with "a fairly considerable section devoted to miscellaneous verse." Collections are listed chronologically by date of earliest known edition, followed by later editions to 1750 (with additions on p. 344). An entry includes title, collation, brief indication of content (but not a list of individual poems), bibliographical notes, and a few locations (superseded by the *Short-Title Catalogues* [M1377, M1990, and M1995]); for additional locations of eighteenth-century editions, see Richard C. Boys, "A Finding-List of English Poetical Miscellanies, 1700–48, in Selected American Libraries," *ELH: A Journal of English Literary History* 7 (1940): 144–62. Five indexes: titles; chronological index of editions other than the earliest known ones; places of publication (other than London); persons; printers and publishers. The descriptions are accurate, but researchers would benefit from a published list of first lines (a first-line index compiled by Boys and Arthur Mizener is held by the Dept. of Special Collections, Kenneth Spencer Research Lib., U of Kansas, Lawrence 66045). Review: *Times Literary Supplement* 10 Oct. 1935: 626.

For 54 collections published before 1640, a first-line index to English-language poems is available in Frederic William Baue, *A Bibliographical Catalogue and First-Line*

Index of Printed Anthologies of English Poetry to 1640 (Lanham: Scarecrow, 2002, 282 pp.). Although Baue includes some miscellanies not in Case, his descriptions must be used with caution since the majority of his title-page transcriptions and collations are based on examination of a single microfilm copy. The disorganization of data and ineffective indexing means that most users will be reduced to scanning all entries. Review: T. H. Howard-Hill, *Papers of the Bibliographical Society of America* 97 (2003): 621–22.

Miscellanies published between 1640 and 1682 are more fully described and more easily searched in Adam Smyth, *Index of Poetry in Printed Miscellanies, 1640–1682* (online; 8 Apr. 2006 <http://www.adamsmyth.clara.net>). The 4,639 poems in 41 collections are arranged in fully searchable tables that include first- and last-line, title of miscellany, date, page number and title of poem, number of lines, and author. Developed as part of the research underlying Smyth's doctoral dissertation, *Index of Poetry in Printed Miscellanies, 1640–1682* serves as a fine example of how scholars can use the World Wide Web to share valuable data.

M2185   Frank, Joseph. *Hobbled Pegasus: A Descriptive Bibliography of Minor English Poetry, 1641–1660.* Albuquerque: U of New Mexico P, 1968. 482 pp. Z2014.P7 F7   016.821′4′08.

A bibliography of English-language poetry written and printed in the British Isles from March 1641 to 29 May 1660 (with a few additional works to June 1661). Frank excludes plays and any work of which more than half is in prose. The approximately 800 entries, listed chronologically by date of first publication, give Wing, *Short-Title Catalogue* (M1995), and Case, *Bibliography of English Poetical Miscellanies* (M2180), numbers; short title; author; length (see p. 29 for an explanation of the abbreviations); publication details; subsequent editions to 1700; political or religious classification, "literary category," and subject (see pp. 5–12 for an explanation); meter or stanza form; illustrative extract; content; an incomplete list of reprints; and references to related poems, scholarship, and bibliographies. Additions appear on p. 462. Two indexes: authors; titles. There are numerous inconsistencies and inaccuracies in transcribing details; the lack of a first-line index seriously inhibits use; and most editions are listed in Wing, *Short-Title Catalogue.* Even so, *Hobbled Pegasus* is a time-saving compilation for researchers interested in this body of mostly second-rate poetry. Review: Charles Clay Doyle, *Eighteenth-Century Studies* 2 (1969): 490–93.

M2190   Ringler, William A., Jr. *Bibliography and Index of English Verse Printed 1476–1558.* London: Mansell, 1988. 440 pp.   Z2014.P7 R56 [PR531] 016.811′208.

————. *Bibliography and Index of English Verse in Manuscript 1501–1558.* Prepared and completed by Michael Rudick and Susan J. Ringler. London: Mansell, 1992. 315 pp.   Z2014.P7 R55 [PR521]   016.821′208.

May, Steven W., and Ringler. *Elizabethan Poetry: A Bibliography and First-Line Index of English Verse 1559–1603.* 3 vols. London: Thoemmes Continuum, 2004.   Z2014.P7 M348 [PR531]   016.821′308.

Bibliography and Index of English Verse Printed 1476–1558 indexes more than 2,900 English-language poems or parts thereof. Books containing poems are organized by revised *Short-Title Catalogue* (M1990) number in separate lists for 1476–1500 and 1501–58. Each entry provides revised *STC* number; author; title; notes on authorship; publication information; copy consulted; reel number for editions available in University Microfilms International's *Early English Books, 1475–1640* (M1990a) series;

earliest, best, and most recent reprints and facsimiles; number of poems in the volume; and Brown-Robbins-Cutler (M1940a) or first-line index number of each poem. Each chronological list is followed by a first-line index, whose entries cite, when appropriate, Brown-Robbins-Cutler number, first line, author, title of poem, date of composition if different from publication date, total number of lines and verse form (as well as number of stresses or syllables per line, burdens, and refrains), revised *STC* number of the edition(s) printing the poem and its location in the first edition of each book, and genre and subject classifications. Two indexes (1475–1500, 1501–58); both have headings for refrains, verse forms, poets, authors translated, literary kinds and subjects, and titles; that for 1501–58 adds headings for burdens, rhyme schemes, historical persons and events, religious topics, and translations and adaptations (by language). Unfortunately, the volume is marred by numerous typographical errors and inconsistencies and is incompletely indexed. Review: Thomas Moser, *Papers of the Bibliographical Society of America* 84 (1990): 305–08.

Bibliography and Index of English Verse in Manuscript, 1501–1558 records 2,045 poems from nearly 400 documents, including manuscripts, printed books, and funeral monuments. Entries are grouped by libraries and other depositories. A typical entry cites shelf mark, describes the contents, lists printed versions, records the total number of poems and lines transcribed, and concludes with a sequential list (keyed to the first-line index) of poems transcribed. Entries in the first-line index cite collection and shelf mark, date of transcription, location of the poem within the manuscript or printed book, title or other identification of the poem (including author when known), number of lines in the copy, verse form, stanza form, rhyme scheme, verse measure, burden or refrain, other manuscript copies, references to standard bibliographies (including Brown-Robbins-Cutler number), and subject and genre categories under which the poem is indexed. Concludes with separate indexes for burdens, refrains, verse forms and rhyme schemes, poets, composers, historical persons and events, genres and kinds, subjects (including titles and fictional characters), and translations. An appendix offers a concordance of transcribed poems with Brown-Robbins-Cutler and *Bibliography and Index of English Verse Printed 1476–1558.*

Elizabethan Poetry covers verse printed or transcribed (including drama—with prologues, epilogues, and songs entered separately— as well as "a sampling of epitaphs from contemporary funeral monuments, poems from Elizabethan paintings, and one couplet from a wall painting") between 1559 and 1603 (though several works were composed well before 1559 and many poems written during the period were not published until after 1603). Coverage of printed verse is, understandably, much more complete than that in manuscript. Books containing verse are listed by *Short-Title Catalogue* (M1990) number, with each entry supplying the revised *STC* number; author; short title; date of publication; copy examined; details of facsimile reprints or modern editions (though this information is not intended to be exhaustive); reel number for editions available in University Microfilms International's *Early English Books, 1475-1640* series; number of poems in the volume; and the first-line index number for each poem in the volume. Manuscripts are listed alphabetically by sigla (largely those used in the *STC*), with an entry typically including shelf mark; number of folios or pages; date of transcription of the Elizabethan verse; contents; modern editions or facsimiles; references to scholarship on the manuscript; number of poems; and the first-line index number of each poem in the document. In the first-line index entries for poems in printed works typically consist of entry number, first line (in modern English to facilitate searching), *STC* number, date of publication, signature(s) on which the poem is printed, author, context in which the poem appears, title of book, number of lines, number of stanzas and lines per stanza, rhyme scheme and meter (and the number of lines, rhyme scheme, and meter of any burden, along with its first line), refrain, and subject matter and genre. The entry for a poem from a manuscript includes entry number, first line, symbol for the location of the manuscript, shelf mark, date of transcription, folios on which the poem is written, author, title, number of lines, rhyme scheme and meter, and subject matter and genre. Eleven indexes (some of which are subdivided): English poets; fictional names and topics; historical persons and events; literary kinds (genres and forms); poems set to music; rhyme schemes and verse forms; scribes and owners; subjects; subscriptions (i.e., a name, phrase, or pseudonym affixed to a poem); titles; and translations. Reviews: Brian Vickers, *TLS: Times Literary Supplement* 10 Feb. 2006: 7–8; Paul J. Voss, *Ben Jonson Journal* 12 (2005): 259–66.

    Bibliography and Index of English Verse in Manuscript, 1501–1558, Bibliography and Index of English Verse Printed 1476–1558, and—especially—*Elizabethan Poetry* are invaluable compilations. They complement and continue Brown, *Index of Middle English Verse* (M1940a), offer a nearly exhaustive finding list of English verse for the period (including a substantial amount hidden in unlikely volumes), and—by indexing of subjects, genres, rhyme schemes, and verse forms—make feasible a number of approaches to the study of early Tudor poetry (for valuable examples, see May, "Interdisciplinary Research with the Indexes of Tudor Verse," *Ben Jonson Journal* 11 [2004]: 89–101; for the value of the works to editors, see May, "Queen Elizabeth's 'Future Foes': Editing Manuscripts with the First-Line Index of Elizabethan Verse (a Future Friend)," *New Ways of Looking at Old Texts, III: Papers of the Renaissance English Text Society, 1997–2001,* ed. W. Speed Hill, Medieval and Renaissance Texts and Studies 270 [Tempe: Arizona Center for Medieval and Renaissance Studies in conjunction with Renaissance English Text Soc., 2004: 1–12]).

See also

    Crum, *First-Line Index of English Poetry, 1500–1800* (M1590).

Guides to Scholarship and Criticism

There is no adequate general bibliography of scholarship on Renaissance poetry; however, most poets, major and minor, are the subjects of author bibliographies, and studies of poetry are well covered in the guides to scholarship and criticism listed at the beginning of the Renaissance literature section.

See

    Brogan, *English Versification, 1570–1980* (M1600).
    Donow, *Sonnet in England and America* (L1250).
    Kuntz, *Poetry Explication* (L1255).
    Martinez, *Guide to British Poetry Explication,* vol. 2 (L1255a).

Restoration and Eighteenth-Century Literature

Many works listed in section M: English Literature/General are useful for research in Restoration and eighteenth-century literature.

Histories and Surveys

M2205   Butt, John. *The Mid-Eighteenth Century.* Ed. and completed by Geoffrey
Carnall. Vol. 8 of *The Oxford History of English Literature* (M1310). Gen.
eds. John Buxton and Norman Davis. Oxford: Clarendon–Oxford UP,
1979. 671 pp. (Reprinted in 1990 as vol. 10, with the title *The Age of
Johnson, 1740–1789.*)   PR441.B83   820'.9'006.

A literary history of the period 1740–89, with chapters on Johnson; poetry (1740–
60 and 1760–89); Scottish poetry; drama; history; travel literature, memoirs, and biography; essays, letters, dialogues, and speeches; major novelists (Richardson, Fielding,
Smollett, Sterne); and other prose fiction. Concludes with a chronology and a selective
bibliography. Indexed by authors, artists, and some subjects. *Mid-Eighteenth Century*
received a mixed reception, with its "traditional" approach to literary history eliciting
much of the negative criticism. Reviews: P. N. Furbank, *Listener* 12 July 1979: 61–
62; Donald Greene, *English Language Notes* 18 (1980): 139–46; Ronald Paulson, *Modern Language Review* 76 (1981): 674–75; Pat Rogers, *Review of English Studies* ns 32
(1981): 83–86; G. S. Rousseau, *Eighteenth-Century Studies* 14 (1980–81): 181–93.

M2207   *The Cambridge History of English Literature, 1660–1780.* Ed. John Richetti.
New Cambridge History of English Literature. Cambridge: Cambridge UP,
2005. 945 pp.   PR442.C26   820.9005.

A collection of 30 essays that address the "literary and cultural production" of the
long eighteenth century and that both exemplify and evaluate new approaches to the
literature of the period. The essays—written by a veritable who's who of Restoration
and eighteenth-century scholars—treat literary production and dissemination, genres,
literature and intellectual life, literature and social and institutional change, and new
forms of literary expression. Concludes with a chronology and a series of "bibliographies" (more properly, a list of works cited) for each essay. Indexed by authors, titles,
and subjects. As in other volumes in the New Cambridge History, there is frequently
little sense of relation among the essays, but the roster of contributors will likely make
this one of the more influential volumes in the series.

M2210   Dobrée, Bonamy. *English Literature in the Early Eighteenth Century, 1700–
1740.* Corrected rpt. Vol. 7 of *The Oxford History of English Literature*
(M1310). Gen. eds. Bonamy Dobrée and F. P. Wilson. Oxford:
Clarendon–Oxford UP, 1964. 701 pp. (Reprinted in 1990 as vol. 9, with
the title *The Early Eighteenth Century, 1700–1740: Swift, Defoe, and Pope.*)
PR445.D6   820.903.

Emphasizes Defoe, Swift, and Pope but does not scant minor figures, in a three-
part literary history of the period. Pt. 1 covers the period 1700–20 in chapters on the
background of the age, Defoe to 1710, Swift to 1709, essayists and controversialists,
poetry, and Pope to 1725; pt. 2 treats the period 1700–40 in chapters on drama (a
weak discussion), philosophers, critics and aestheticians, and miscellaneous prose; pt. 3
covers the period 1720–40 in chapters on Defoe (1715–31), Swift (1715–45), poetry,
and Pope (1725–44). Concludes with a chronology and an inadequate (and now outdated) selective bibliography. Indexed by authors and a few subjects. This work received
a mixed reception, with some reviewers praising its thoroughness and critical sympathy
and others censuring it as prejudiced and unreliable. Some of the numerous factual
errors are corrected in the 1964 printing. Reviews: Donald F. Bond, *Modern Philology*
60 (1962): 138–41; Kathleen Williams, *Modern Language Notes* 76 (1961): 356–59.

M2215   Sutherland, James. *English Literature of the Late Seventeenth Century.* Vol. 6
        of *The Oxford History of English Literature* (M1310). Gen. eds. Bonamy
        Dobrée and Norman Davis. Oxford: Clarendon–Oxford UP, 1969.
        589 pp. (Reprinted in 1990 as vol. 8, with the title *Restoration Literature,
        1660–1700: Dryden, Bunyan, and Pepys.*)   PR437.S9   820.9'004.
   A critical history of the period 1660–1700, with chapters on the background of
the age; drama; poetry; fiction; essays, letters, and journals; biography, history, and
travel writings; religious literature; philosophy, politics, and economics; science; and
criticism. Includes a chronology and a selective bibliography (with numerous errors and
now outdated). Indexed by author, anonymous work, and subject. A good, sensible
history but sometimes dated in its critical discussions. Review: *TLS: Times Literary
Supplement* 5 June 1969: 611–12.

See also

   Sec. M: English Literature/General/Histories and Surveys.

Literary Handbooks, Dictionaries, and Encyclopedias

M2218   *The Blackwell Companion to the Enlightenment.* Ed. John W. Yolton et al.
        Oxford: Blackwell, 1991. 581 pp.   CB411.B57   940.2'53'03.
   A dictionary of concepts, groups, movements, persons, places, events, professions,
activities, and other topics associated with the period 1720–80 in Europe and North
America. Many of the entries are signed and conclude with a brief bibliography. Indexed
by persons and subjects; entrants are also indexed in *Biography and Genealogy Master
Index* (J565). Although prefaced by an utterly inadequate discussion of editorial procedures, the uniformly high level of expertise of the contributors makes the *Companion*
an informative and authoritative resource.

Bibliographies of Bibliographies

M2220   Lund, Roger D. *Restoration and Early Eighteenth-Century English Literature,
        1660–1740: A Selected Bibliography of Resource Materials.* Selected
        Bibliographies in Language and Literature 1. New York: MLA, 1980.
        42 pp.   Z2012.L88 [PR43]   016.82.
   A highly selective list of important bibliographies, concordances, and current journals published through 1978. Entries are listed alphabetically by author, editor, or title
in divisions for current journals; annual bibliographies; general bibliographies; poetry;
drama; fiction; literary criticism and language study; translation; publishing and bookselling; newspapers and periodicals; art and music; history, biography, and autobiography; religious literature; miscellaneous bibliographies; and individual authors. A brief
descriptive annotation accompanies many works. Indexed by persons. A convenient,
judicious (but now dated) guide to essential reference sources. Review: J. M. Armistead,
Literary Research Newsletter 5 (1980): 189–91.

See also

   Secs. D: Bibliographies of Bibliographies and M: English Literature/General/
   Bibliographies of Bibliographies.

Guides to Primary Works

MANUSCRIPTS

M2225   *Index of English Literary Manuscripts* (M1365). Ed. P. J. Croft, Theodore
   Hofmann, and John Horden. Vol. 3: *1700–1800.* 4 pts. Comp. Margaret
   M. Smith and Alexander Lindsay. London: Mansell, 1986–97.
   Z6611.L7 I5 [PR83]   016.82'08.

A descriptive catalog of extant literary manuscripts by 57 major English, Scottish, and Irish authors. The emphasis is on literary manuscripts, including diaries, notebooks, marginalia, and some scribal copies. Letters are excluded, but the introductions to individual authors identify collections of them. In addition, the introductions alert researchers to special problems and relevant scholarship, point out additional manuscripts and transcripts, discuss canon, note the disposition of any personal library, and conclude with an outline of the arrangement of entries. A typical entry provides a physical description, dates composition of the manuscript, includes any necessary commentary (as well as references to sale catalogs, editions, or scholarship), and identifies location (with shelf mark). Pt. 4 prints a first-line index to verse in pts. 1–4. Additions and corrections will be printed in vol. 5. Since some entries are based on inquiries to libraries and collectors, bibliographies, other reference works, and booksellers' and auction catalogs rather than personal examination by the compiler, descriptions vary in fullness and accuracy.

Although there are errors and omissions, and the scope is unduly restricted by reliance on the *Concise Cambridge Bibliography* (M1365a), the *Index* is an essential, if limited, source for the identification and location of manuscripts. It must, however, be supplemented by the works listed in sections F: Guides to Manuscripts and Archives and M: English Literature/General/Guides to Primary Works/Manuscripts. Review: J. D. Fleeman, *Notes and Queries* ns 38 (1991): 390–92.

M2227   *Location Register of English Literary Manuscripts and Letters: Eighteenth and
   Nineteenth Centuries.* Ed. David C. Sutton. 2 vols. London: British Lib.,
   1995.   Z6611.L7 L629 [PR471]   016.82'08'0091.

A union catalog of manuscripts and letters by British literary figures (including immigrants and refugees) who wrote during the eighteenth and nineteenth centuries (the chronological limits are not clear: presumably, these volumes include persons who lived beyond 1699 and died before 1900; writers alive beyond 1900 are included in *Location Register of Twentieth-Century English Literary Manuscripts* [M2765]). Only items (including photocopies and microforms) available to the public (as of June 1994) in the British Isles are listed. Under each author, manuscripts are listed alphabetically by title, followed by editorial correspondence files, and then letters in chronological order (collections of letters are listed by date of the earliest one). A typical entry consists of title or description, date, physical description, location, shelf mark, and a note on access. Important recipients of letters are interfiled in the author list. When appropriate, an author section begins with a headnote on major collections (especially outside Great Britain), an author's policy on the disposition of his or her papers, or the destruction of manuscripts. Because of the descriptive titles given several items, researchers must read the entire section for an author. Although the descriptions vary in detail (and are frequently based on finding aids supplied by repositories rather than personal examination) and although letters in large collections are frequently undifferentiated, the

Location Register is an important resource and the most convenient tool for locating many eighteenth- and nineteenth-century literary manuscripts. All records are now part of RLG Union Catalog (E230); to identify *Location Register* records, users must first perform a search, then click on Limit (bottom left of the Eureka screen), select Location Code, and enter UKRV in the box.

Although the database from which the *Location Register* was printed is being augmented, there is unfortunately no plan for systematic updating.

PRINTED WORKS

Bibliographies and Indexes

M2235   Arber, Edward, ed. *The Term Catalogues, 1668–1709 A. D.; with a Number for Easter Term, 1711 A. D.* 3 vols. London: Privately printed, 1903–06.
Z2002.A31   015.42.

An edition of the quarterly lists of books printed in London, Oxford, and Cambridge for London booksellers. Since the catalogs are advertising lists, not all books published during the period are included. Works are classified under various headings, such as divinity, physic, histories (including novels), humanity, poetry and plays, Latin books, music, miscellanies, law, and reprints. Entries record title (frequently descriptive rather than exact), author (but only occasionally), size, price, and the bookseller(s) for whom the work was printed. Two indexes in each volume: titles (accompanied by author); names, places, and subjects. An important source for identifying works and editions no longer extant, researching publishing history, establishing approximate publication dates, and studying the environment of a work.

The catalog of Michaelmas Term 1695 is reproduced as *The "Missing" Term Catalogue: A Facsimile of the Term Catalogue for Michaelmas Term 1695 with a List of Identified Books*, Occasional Publication 20 (Oxford: Oxford Bibliog. Soc., 1987, n. pag.).

See also

English Short Title Catalogue (M1377).
New Cambridge Bibliography of English Literature, vol. 2: 1660–1800 (M2255).
Transcript of the Registers of the Worshipful Company of Stationers from 1640–1708 A. D. (M2005).
Wing, Short-Title Catalogue (M1995).

Text Archives

M2238   *Eighteenth Century Collections Online (ECCO)*. Thomson Gale. Online. 10 May 2005 <http://gale.cenage.com/EighteenthCentury>. Updated regularly.

A digital archive that will eventually include more than 150,000 works printed in Great Britain, North America, and elsewhere during the eighteenth century. Basic Search allows users to limit keyword searches of full text, authors, or titles by publication date and subject area; Advanced Search allows users to limit combined searches of authors, titles, full text, front matter, main text, indexes, publishers, and places of publication by date, subject areas, language, and kinds of illustrations. Advanced Search also allows for fuzzy searches—an especially valuable feature for searching documents in an era before spelling became normalized. Images (which vary in quality and legibility, as expected in archives produced from microfilm, and thus affect the accuracy of the search engine) can be saved to a disk, printed, or e-mailed. The breadth of coverage and the powerful search engine make possible numerous studies that heretofore would have consumed years of research or would have been simply untenable.

The ECCO Text Creation Partnership (http://www.lib.umich.edu/tcp/ecco) is producing SGML/XML fully searchable texts of 10,000 editions included in *ECCO.*

Guides to Scholarship and Criticism

SURVEYS OF RESEARCH

M2240   "Recent Studies in the Restoration and Eighteenth Century." *Studies in English Literature, 1500–1900.* 1 (1961)– . Annually in the Summer issue. PR1.S82   820'.9.

A commissioned survey by established scholars, with recent surveys emphasizing full-length critical and historical studies and typically offering only cursory attention to editions and reference works. The essays vary considerably in soundness and rigor of assessment. Although highly selective and now generally limited to books received for review, the work is the most current annual survey, but it must be supplemented by the chapters in *Year's Work in English Studies* (G330) on the period.

See also

YWES (G330): Later Seventeenth Century and Eighteenth Century chapters.

SERIAL BIBLIOGRAPHIES

M2245   *ECCB: The Eighteenth Century Current Bibliography for [1925–] (ECCB).* NS 1– . New York: AMS, 1978– . Annual. Former title: *The Eighteenth Century: A Current Bibliography for [1975–2000].* Z5579.6.E36 [CB411] 016.909. http://www.eccb.net.

1925–74: *Philological Quarterly* 5–54 (1926–75). (Title varies: [1925–26] "English Literature of the Restoration and Eighteenth Century: A Current Bibliography"; [1927–69] "English Literature, 1660–1800: A Current Bibliography"; [1970–74] "The Eighteenth Century: A Current Bibliography.")

(The bibliographies for 1925–70 are reprinted, with a few corrections and cumulative indexes in every second volume, as *English Literature, 1660–1800: A Bibliography of Modern Studies,* 6 vols. [Princeton: Princeton UP, 1950–72].)

A selective international bibliography of books, articles, and reviews that now offers interdisciplinary coverage of the period in Europe and the New World. Until the bibliography for 1970, *ECCB* emphasized English literature but always included numerous studies in other disciplines and national literatures. Both scope and criteria governing selection have varied over the years and within individual disciplines (see, e.g., the prefatory statements in the bibliographies for 1970 [50 (1971): 321–23]; for 1975 [ns 1: n. pag.]; for 1982 [ns 8: i–iv]; and for 2000 [ns 26: ix–xiii]) but have generally included important studies in English, French, German, Italian, and Spanish (with other languages covered less systematically).

Currently, entries are listed alphabetically by scholar in seven divisions: printing and bibliographical studies; historical, social, and economic studies; philosophy, science, and religion; fine arts; foreign literatures and languages; British literatures; and New World literatures and languages. Some articles are descriptively annotated (and frequently evaluated); significant books are stringently reviewed by specialists (although the quality and authoritativeness of the reviewing are uneven in the volumes for the 1980s). Indexed since 1970 by persons (since indexing is by page number, users sometimes have to scan several entries).

For a history of the bibliography, see Donald Greene, " 'More Than a Necessary Chore': *The Eighteenth-Century Current Bibliography* in Retrospect and Prospect," *Eighteenth-Century Studies* 10 (1976): 94–110; and O M Brack, "Curt Zimansky: A Reminiscence," *ECCB* ns 7 (for 1981): ix–xvii.

Although users would benefit from subject indexing and classified sections in the divisions (a shortcoming remedied beginning in ns 27 [for 2001]), *ECCB* is an indispensable resource. Unfortunately, while it long enjoyed a reputation as the best period serial bibliography, its importance and usefulness are compromised by delays in publication (the volume for 2001 was published in 2005); however, the editors are working to increase currency and the number of reviews. Review: (ns 3–4) Paula R. Backscheider, *Modern Language Review* 80 (1985): 681–84.

Since coverage is selective and omits dissertations, researchers must also consult the other bibliographies in this section as well as in sections G: Serial Bibliographies, Indexes, and Abstracts and H: Guides to Dissertations and Theses. Waldo Sumner Glock, *Eighteenth-Century English Literary Studies: A Bibliography* (Metuchen: Scarecrow, 1984, 847 pp.), a selective annotated list of studies from 1925 to 1980 on 25 authors, is an occasionally serviceable compilation of listings from *ECCB*, *MLAIB* (G335), *ABELL* (G340), and *Year's Work in English Studies* (G330). Earlier scholarship is selectively covered in James E. Tobin, *Eighteenth Century English Literature and Its Cultural Background: A Bibliography* (New York: Fordham UP, 1939, 190 pp.), with additions in a review by Donald F. Bond, *Library Quarterly* 10 (1940): 446–50.

The two general selective bibliographies compiled by Donald F. Bond for the Goldentree Bibliographies in Language and Literature series— *The Age of Dryden* (New York: Appleton, 1970, 103 pp.) and *The Eighteenth Century* (Northbrook: AHM, 1975, 180 pp.)—are too dated to be of much use. More current is Margaret M. Duggan, *English Literature and Backgrounds, 1660–1700: A Selective Critical Guide*, 2 vols., Garland Reference Library of the Humanities 711 (New York: Garland, 1990). Although coverage extends to a variety of general topics, genres, themes, related disciplines, and individual authors, the essay format—with commentary that is rarely "critical" and generally inadequate to describe content—results in a needlessly swollen compilation that cannot be efficiently consulted. In addition, *English Literature and Backgrounds* is plagued by errors and fails to indicate what criteria govern the inclusion of studies.

M2250 "Some Current Publications." *Restoration: Studies in English Literary Culture, 1660–1700.* 1 (1977–) 2/yr.   PR437.R47   820'.9'004.

A selective bibliography by a different compiler in each issue. The descriptively annotated entries are classified under sections for individual authors; bibliography; drama; nondramatic literature; economics, history, philosophy, politics, religion, and science; colonies; and sister arts. The criteria governing selection are unclear and the quality of annotations and coverage varies radically with the contributor (especially in recent installments), but the work is sometimes a useful source for identifying current scholarship.

Some additional studies can be found in the highly selective "Abstracts of Recent Articles," *Seventeenth-Century News* 6.3–51.1–2 (1948–93).

See also

> Secs. G: Serial Bibliographies, Indexes, and Abstracts and H: Guides to Dissertations and Theses.
> *ABELL* (G340): English Literature/Seventeenth Century and Eighteenth Century sections.
> *MLAIB* (G335): English Language and Literature division in the volumes for 1921–25; English VIII and IX in the volumes for 1926–56; English VII and VIII in the volumes for 1957–80; and English Literature/1600–1699 and 1700–1799 sections (as well as any larger chronological section encompassing either century) in the later volumes. Researchers must also check the headings beginning "Eighteenth-Century," "Enlightenment," and "Restoration" in the subject index to post-1980 volumes and in the online thesaurus.

OTHER BIBLIOGRAPHIES

M2255   *The New Cambridge Bibliography of English Literature* (*NCBEL*). Vol. 2: *1660–1800.* Ed. George Watson. Cambridge: Cambridge UP, 1971. 2,082 cols.   Z2011.N45 [PR83]   016.82.

(For a full discussion of *NCBEL*, see entry M1385.) Primary works and scholarship are organized in six major divisions (each subdivided and classified as its subject requires): introduction (general works, literary theory, literary relations with the Continent, medieval influences, book production and distribution), poetry (histories, collections, 1660–1700, 1700–50, 1750–1800), drama (theaters and actors, 1660–1700, 1700–50, 1750–1800, adaptations and translations), novel (principal novelists, minor fiction, children's books), prose (essayists and pamphleteers; periodicals; travel; English-language translations; sport; letters, diaries, autobiographies, and memoirs; religion; history; literary studies; classical and oriental studies; philosophy; science; law; education), and Scottish literature. Vol. 2 of the *Cambridge Bibliography of English Literature* (M1385a) is still occasionally useful for its coverage of the social and political background (most of which *NCBEL* drops).

Users must familiarize themselves with the organization, remember that there is considerable unevenness of coverage among sections, and consult the index volume (vol. 5) rather than the provisional index in vol. 2. Reviews: *TLS: Times Literary Supplement* 15 Oct. 1971: 1296; Eric Rothstein, *Modern Philology* 71 (1973): 176–86.

See also

> Kallendorf, *Latin Influences on English Literature from the Middle Ages to the Eighteenth Century* (S4895).

RELATED TOPICS

M2260   Pargellis, Stanley, and D. J. Medley, eds. *Bibliography of British History: The Eighteenth Century, 1714–1789.* Oxford: Clarendon–Oxford UP, 1951. 642 pp.   Z2018.P37 [DA498]   016.94207.

A selective bibliography, with significantly fuller coverage of primary than secondary materials, of publications before 1941 than after, and of books than articles. The 4,558 entries are variously organized under 17 extensively classified divisions: general reference works; political, constitutional, legal, ecclesiastical, economic, military, naval, social, cultural, and local history; Scotland; Ireland; Wales; American Colonies; India; and Historical Manuscripts Commission reports. Annotations are generally descriptive and cite numerous related studies, but many entries lack annotation. Indexed by persons and some subjects. Although now badly dated and marred by an inadequate explanation of selection criteria, the *Bibliography* is still useful as a starting point for cross-disciplinary research. Reviews: E. R. Adair, *Canadian Historical Review* 32 (1951): 384–86; D. B. Horn, *English Historical Review* 66 (1951): 594–97.

Convenient selective bibliographies are Robert A. Smith, *Late Georgian and Regency England, 1760–1837,* Conference on British Studies Bibliographical Handbooks (Cambridge: Cambridge UP for the Conf. on British Studies, 1984, 114 pp.), with coverage through 1980, and William L. Sachse, *Restoration England, 1660–1689,* Conference on British Studies Bibliographical Handbooks (Cambridge: Cambridge UP for the Conf. on British Studies, 1971, 115 pp.), with coverage through 1968.

M2263   Spector, Robert D., comp. *Backgrounds to Restoration and Eighteenth-Century English Literature: An Annotated Bibliographical Guide to Modern Scholarship.* Bibliographies and Indexes in World Literature 17. New York: Greenwood, 1989. 553 pp.   Z2012.S65 [PR441]   016.82'09.

An annotated guide to English-language books and articles published as late as 1987 that are important to the interdisciplinary study of English literature from 1660 to 1800. The entries are listed alphabetically by author in 12 divisions: bibliographies; publishing, printing, and journalism; history and politics; religion; philosophy; science, medicine, and technology; economics; crime and law; society, manners, customs, and attitudes (with sections on the family, on women, on sex, and on race, nationalities, and religion); education and scholarship; language and rhetoric; and literature and the arts (with sections on literary history; satire; music; painting, engraving, and sculpture; architecture, gardening, and decorative arts; and the sister arts). The brief but adequate descriptive annotations frequently incorporate an evaluative comment. Indexed by scholars. Several important works are omitted (while a number of superseded ones are included), the discussion of criteria governing selection and the explanation of scope are completely inadequate, several evaluations are inaccurate, and there are numerous typos; nevertheless, Spector is a starting place for identifying English-language works important to interdisciplinary research.

See also

Brown, *Bibliography of British History, 1789–1851* (M2515).
Davies, *Bibliography of British History: Stuart Period, 1603–1714* (M2045).
Royal Historical Society Bibliography (M1400).

Biographical Dictionaries

Although the *Oxford Dictionary of National Biography* (M1425) remains the standard general source of biographical information for the period, Highfill, *Biographical Dictionary* (M2400), generally offers superior treatment of Restoration and eighteenth-century theatrical personnel (including dramatists who were also actors or managers), and Todd, *Dictionary of British and American Women Writers* (M2265), provides fuller coverage of female authors.

M2265   Todd, Janet, ed. *A Dictionary of British and American Women Writers,*
       1660–1800. Totowa: Rowman, 1985. 344 pp.   PR113.D5   820′.9′9287.
    A biographical dictionary of women who wrote published or unpublished literary or nonliterary works between 1660 and 1800. A writer is entered under her most commonly used name or title, with index entries for a married or family name used in her writing. Entries provide biographical details, a list (usually complete) of known works, and a brief assessment that sometimes includes contemporary critical comments. Unfortunately, unpublished works are not located. Indexed by names, periodicals, and a few subjects; entrants are also indexed in *Biography and Genealogy Master Index* (J565). Fuller subject indexing—especially of genres—would improve the utility of the work. Although it is selective—especially for authors in prolific nonbelletristic genres—the *Dictionary* is an indispensable guide to Restoration and eighteenth-century women writers, few of whom are accorded entries in the standard biographical dictionaries such as *Oxford Dictionary of National Biography* (M1425) and *Dictionary of American Biography* (Q3380). Of special importance are the numerous discussions of unpublished writers.
    Important complements to Todd are Bell, *Biographical Dictionary of English Women Writers, 1580–1720* (M1433a), Todd, *British Women Writers* (M1433a), Blain, *Feminist Companion to Literature in English* (J593), and Schlueter, *Encyclopedia of British Women Writers* (M1433).

See also

    Valentine, *British Establishment, 1760–1784* (M1425a).

Periodicals

GUIDES TO PRIMARY WORKS

Bibliographies

M2270   Crane, R. S., and F. B. Kaye. *A Census of British Newspapers and Periodicals,*
       1620–1800. Chapel Hill: U of North Carolina P, 1927. 205 pp. (A reprint
       of *Studies in Philology* 24 [1927]: 1–205.)   Z6956.E5 C8.
    A preliminary checklist in two parts: a finding list based on the holdings of 37 United States libraries; a list, compiled largely from other works, of periodicals and newspapers not found in the United States. Organized alphabetically (with cross-references for variant titles), entries supply title, variants, place of publication, beginning and ending dates, editor(s), publisher(s), printer(s), frequency, and (in the first part) locations (occasionally specifying the length of runs). Two indexes: chronological; geo-

graphical (excluding London). Compiled largely from institutional reports and published bibliographies, the *Census* is not comprehensive and many entries are inaccurate
or incomplete. As the fullest single list of newspapers and periodicals of the period, it
remains a useful preliminary guide, but it has been superseded by the union lists in
section K: Periodicals for locations and by the following for various periods:

> Nelson, *British Newspapers and Periodicals, 1641–1700* (M2060).
>
> Ward, *Index and Finding List of Serials Published in the British Isles, 1789–
> 1832* (M2535).

A second edition was planned but never published, but several additions and
corrections by J. G. Muddiman et al. appear as "The History and Bibliography of
English Newspapers," *Notes and Queries* 160 (1931): 3–6, 21–24, 40–43, 57–59,
174–75, 207–09, 227–30, 264, 298–300, 336–38, 375–76, 391, 442–43; 161
(1931): 337. Several periodicals are reproduced in two microfilm series published by
University Microfilms International: *Early British Periodicals, 1681–1921* and *English
Literary Periodicals, 1681–1914.* Review: Walter Graham, *JEGP: Journal of English and
Germanic Philology* 28 (1929): 303–07.

See also

> Sec. K: Periodicals/Union Lists.
> *Bibliography of British Newspapers* (M1440).
> Sullivan, *British Literary Magazines*, vols. 1–2 (M1445).

Indexes

James E. Tierney is compiling *British Periodicals 1660–1800: An Electronic Index*, which
will be published by the Center for Electronic Texts in the Humanities at Rutgers
University (http://www.ceth.rutgers.edu). The *Index* will allow searches of the contents
of 136 periodicals by authors, editors, publishers, printers, booksellers, genre, price, and
frequency of publication.

M2275   Forster, Antonia. *Index to Book Reviews in England, 1749–1774.*
        Carbondale: Southern Illinois UP, 1990. 307 pp. *Index to Book Reviews in
        England, 1775–1800.* London: British Lib., 1997. 490 pp.
        Z1035.A1 F67   028.1'0942.
        An index to reviews of poetry, fiction, and drama that appear in 16 English pe-
riodicals between 1749 and 1774 and 27 between 1775 and 1800. Excludes newspapers
and reviews of dramatic productions. The 8,007 entries are listed alphabetically by
author, translator, adapter, or anonymous title of the work reviewed, with cross-references for original authors of translated works or adaptations; a female is entered under
her most generally used surname. A typical entry cites title, place and date of publication,
format, price, bookseller, location of copy examined, and reviews. For most works, the
title, place of publication, and date are based on personal examination of a copy; format,
price, and bookseller are taken from the reviews. The introductions examine the theory
and practice of reviewing during the respective periods. Although restricted to reviews
of literary works in 43 periodicals, the *Index* is an invaluable source for locating reviews
and studying the critical reception of belles lettres during the latter half of the eighteenth
century. Review: (*1749–1774*) James G. Basker, *Analytical and Enumerative Bibliography* ns 4 (1990): 148–50.

M2280   Ward, William S., comp. *Literary Reviews in British Periodicals, 1789–1797: A Bibliography: With a Supplementary List of General (Non-review) Articles on Literary Subjects.* Garland Reference Library of the Humanities 172. New York: Garland, 1979. 342 pp.   Z2013.W36 [PR442] 016.820'9'006.

A bibliography of reviews of books published between 1789 and 1797 by British and American literary authors. Works reviewed are organized alphabetically by author, then chronologically by date of publication, followed by reviews listed alphabetically by periodical title. Nonreview articles are divided among five appendixes: (A) general articles on contemporary authors and works; (B, which consists of five separate lists) volumes of general and genre criticism reviewed, general criticism, and articles on poetry, fiction, and drama and theater; (C) reviews of studies of contemporary authors and their works; (D) reviews of books and articles dealing with selected authors before 1789 (with separate sections for Shakespeare, Milton, Pope, and Johnson); (E) reviews of operas and musical dramas. The preface offers some general suggestions for further research. An essential source for investigating the contemporary critical reception of an author or work and for locating early criticism. Continued by Ward, *Literary Reviews in British Periodicals, 1798–1820* and *1821–1826* (M2550).

GUIDES TO SCHOLARSHIP AND CRITICISM

See James E. Tierney, "The Study of the Eighteenth-Century British Periodical," *Papers of the Bibliographical Society of America* 69 (1975): 165–86, for an assessment of the state of scholarship that surveys reference works, editions, and critical and historical studies; comments on difficulties researchers face; and offers detailed suggestions for topics needing investigation.

M2285   Weed, Katherine Kirtley, and Richmond Pugh Bond. *Studies of British Newspapers and Periodicals from Their Beginning to 1800: A Bibliography.* *Studies in Philology* extra ser. 2. Chapel Hill: U of North Carolina P, 1946. 233 pp.   P25.S82 no.2.

A bibliography of studies (essentially through 1940, but with some as late as 1945) of serials published through 1800 in Great Britain and a few other countries. The approximately 2,100 entries are organized alphabetically in seven divisions: bibliographies and bibliographical studies; corantos, newsbooks, and newsletters; general studies; works on individual newspapers and periodicals, editors, authors, publishers, towns, and counties (classified by newspaper, editor, etc.); subjects; newspapers and periodicals in Europe (classified by country); newspapers and periodicals in North America (classified by country, then province or state). The last three divisions are highly selective. Several entries are accompanied by brief descriptive annotations, which include citations to selected reviews. Indexed by authors (excluding those who appear as a heading in the fourth division). Although the work is badly dated, its coverage of pre-1941 scholarship on serials published before 1789 remains unsuperseded. For studies of periodicals published after 1789, see Ward, *British Periodicals and Newspapers, 1789–1832* (M2565). *New Cambridge Bibliography of English Literature* (M2255) and Linton, *Newspaper Press in Britain* (M1455), offer the best coverage of post-1940 scholarship. Review: Donald F. Bond, *Modern Philology* 45 (1947): 65–66.

See also

> White, *English Literary Journal to 1900* (M1460).

Genres

Several works in sections L: Genres and M: English Literature/General/Genres are useful for research in Restoration and eighteenth-century English literature.

FICTION

Some works in sections L: Genres/Fiction and M: English Literature/General/Genres/Fiction are useful for research in Restoration and eighteenth-century fiction.

Histories and Surveys

See

> Baker, *History of the English Novel,* vols. 3–5 (M1505).
> Salzman, *English Prose Fiction, 1558–1700* (M2090).

Literary Handbooks, Dictionaries, and Encyclopedias

See

> *Dictionary of British Literary Characters: 18th- and 19th-Century Novels* (M1507).

Guides to Primary Works

Bibliographies and Indexes

M2320 Beasley, Jerry C., comp. *A Check List of Prose Fiction Published in England, 1740–1749.* Charlottesville: UP of Virginia for the Bibliog. Soc. of the U of Virginia, 1972. 213 pp.   Z2014.F4 B37   016.823′5′08.
    An enumerative bibliography of original works, reprints, and English translations that continues McBurney, *Check List of English Prose Fiction, 1700–1739* (M2325). Although admitting histories, lives, voyages, or collections of letters with a narrative line, Beasley excludes chapbooks, jestbooks, and magazine fiction (for the last, see Mayo, "Catalogue of Magazine Novels" [M2330]). Works are organized by year of initial publication; under each year are separate alphabetical lists of anonymous publications, works of known authorship, and translations. A typical entry includes author, short title, imprint, pagination or number of volumes, format, price, location of at least one copy, a descriptive annotation that identifies subject matter and type of work, and a list of subsequent editions through 1749. Appendixes list unverified editions of authentic

works and unauthenticated titles. Indexed by titles, authors, and members of the book trade. Although limited to a decade, *Check List of Prose Fiction* is an accurate source for identifying works by subject or type, locating copies, and studying the environment of some of the major novels of the century. Several works are available on microfilm in *Early British Fiction: Pre-1750* (Woodbridge: Research, 1980). Beasley's checklist is complemented by his analysis of narrative forms in *Novels of the 1740s* (Athens: U of Georgia P, 1982, 238 pp.).

M2325   McBurney, William Harlin, comp. *A Check List of English Prose Fiction, 1700–1739.* Cambridge: Harvard UP, 1960. 154 pp.   Z2014.F4 M3 016.8235.

A bibliography of fictional prose narratives, by English writers or translators, first published in England between 1700 and 1739. McBurney omits reprints of earlier fiction, chapbooks, jestbooks, pamphlets, and periodical fiction. Works are listed chronologically by year of first publication; under each year are sections for original works and translations, each organized alphabetically by author or title of anonymous work. A typical entry includes author, complete title, imprint, pagination, format, price, location of at least one copy, translator and original title (for translations), miscellaneous notes, and a chronological list of subsequent editions through 1739. Dubious or unauthenticated titles occupy a separate section at the back. Indexed by authors, titles, translators, printers, publishers, and booksellers. The selection policy could be clearer and transcriptions more accurate, but McBurney is the standard bibliography for identifying and locating works, establishing the fictional environment of a novel, and charting trends in fiction (although the last two tasks are made difficult because subsequent editions are not cross-referenced to years of publication and because periodical fiction and reprints of pre-1700 works are excluded). Reviews: Donald F. Bond, *Modern Philology* 59 (1962): 231–34; C. J. Rawson, *Notes and Queries* ns 9 (1962): 468–71; Andrew Wright, *Library* 5th ser. 17 (1962): 273.

Several titles are available on microfilm in *Early British Fiction: Pre-1750* (Woodbridge: Research, 1980). Continued by Beasley, *Check List of Prose Fiction Published in England, 1740–1749* (M2320).

M2330   Mayo, Robert D. "A Catalogue of Magazine Novels and Novelettes, 1740–1815." *The English Novel in the Magazines, 1740–1815: With a Catalogue of 1,375 Novels and Novelettes.* Evanston: Northwestern UP; London: Oxford UP, 1962. 431–677.   PR851.M37   823.09.

A bibliography of narrative prose works of more than 5,000 words printed in serial publications (except newspapers). Includes translations, abridgments of and self-contained excerpts from novels, as well as travels, voyages, biographies, and histories that are predominantly fictional. Works are listed alphabetically by title (with identical texts listed under the title of the first magazine appearance); additions appear on p. 647. Entries identify the periodical, number of parts (and approximate number of words), and, when possible, author or translator, reprints, source, alternate titles, and related works. Users should note that the bibliography is indexed separately in three parts: authors, editors, translators, titles, alternative titles, and series titles; publication date; periodicals. Although not exhaustive, Mayo is the indispensable pioneering guide to fiction previously ignored in histories and bibliographies. Numerous additions and corrections are printed in Edward W. R. Pitcher, *Discoveries in Periodicals, 1720–1820: Facts and Fictions,* Studies in British and American Magazines 7 (Lewiston: Mellen, 2000) 357–421 (a cumulation and expansion of a series of articles and notes published 1976–97). Reviews: Richard D. Altick, *Library Quarterly* 34 (1964): 131–32; J. M. S. Tompkins, *Review of English Studies* ns 15 (1964): 208–10.

M2335   Raven, James. *British Fiction, 1750–1770: A Chronological Check-list of Prose Fiction Printed in Britain and Ireland.* Newark: U of Delaware P; London: Assoc. UP, 1987. 349 pp.   Z2014.F4 R34 [PR851] 016.823′6′08.

A checklist of editions of prose fiction—original works, reprints, and translations extant as well as lost—printed in the British Isles and Ireland between 1750 and 1770. Although emphasizing the novel, *British Fiction* includes representative examples of imaginary voyages, fictional biographies, and miscellanies; it excludes jestbooks, children's books, chapbooks, reports of crimes, and serial and magazine fiction. The 1,363 entries are organized by year of actual publication (which sometimes differs from imprint date); under each year, anonymous works are listed alphabetically by title, followed by works of known or attributed authorship (alphabetically by author, with translations listed by original author), and then a selection of miscellanies, imaginary voyages, and fictional biographies. A typical entry includes author, title, imprint, number of pages or volumes, format, price, references to reviews and standard bibliographies, notes on authorship, other editions, cross-references, and locations in selected British and American libraries. Two indexes: authors and translators; titles. Raven is an indispensable source for locating copies and charting trends in prose fiction during the two decades. It must, however, be supplemented with *ESTC* (M1377).

M2336   *The English Novel, 1770–1829: A Bibliographical Survey of Prose Fiction Published in the British Isles.* Ed. Peter Garside, James Raven, and Rainer Schöwerling. 2 vols. Oxford: Oxford UP, 2000.   Z2014.F4 E52 [PR851] 016.823′508.

> Vol. 1: *1770–1799.* Ed. Raven and Antonia Forster. 864 pp.
> Vol. 2: *1800–1829.* Ed. Garside and Schöwerling. 753 pp.

A bibliography of first editions of separately published works of English-language fiction printed in Britain and Ireland between 1770 and 1829 (with information on subsequent editions to 1850). Excludes chapbooks, religious tracts, short tales, and works written for young readers. Entries (which are organized chronologically by date in imprint, then alphabetically by title of anonymous work and then author) record full title and imprint, details of authorship attribution, format, price, references to contemporary reviews, locations of copies, call number of copy consulted, and notes (including details of subscription lists, dedications, advertisements, excerpts from reviews, and bibliographical matters; the notes are far more extensive in vol. 1 than in vol. 2, and in both volumes the extensive use of abbreviations inhibits readability). When no copy of the first edition exists, title and publication details are reconstructed from publishing records or later editions. Four indexes: authors and translators; titles; publishers and booksellers; notes (vol. 2 omits this). Based on the actual examination of at least one copy of extant works and boasting an admirably full account of scope and organization, *English Novel, 1770–1829* is an invaluable and trustworthy guide to six decades of English fiction.

An important complement to and extension of the *1800–1829* volume is Peter Garside et al., *British Fiction, 1800–1829: A Database of Production, Circulation, and Reception* (online; 24 June 2006 <http://www.british-fiction.cf.ac.uk/index.html>), which allows users to browse the records by author, title, or publisher; and to search by keyword, author and translator, title, gender, place of publication, publisher, publication date, and notes (with the option of restricting a search to titles with advertisements, reviews, contemporary library information, anecdotal information, publishing history, or subscription lists).

English Novel, 1770–1829 supersedes the two existing, but absolutely inadequate, bibliographies covering late-eighteenth-century fiction. Leonard Orr, *A Catalogue Checklist of English Prose Fiction, 1750–1800* (Troy: Whitston, 1979, 204 pp.), compiled almost exclusively from other sources, is riddled with errors and omissions. (See the reviews by Edward W. Pitcher, *Analytical and Enumerative Bibliography* 5 [1981]: 56–60; and Jerry C. Beasley, *Literary Research Newsletter* 5 [1980]: 140–47.) Andrew Block, *The English Novel, 1740–1850: A Catalogue Including Prose Romances, Short Stories, and Translations of Foreign Fiction*, rev. ed. (London: Dawsons, 1961, 349 pp.), is, as Richard Altick points out, "one of the worst such compilations published in modern times—inaccurate, incomplete, wholly dependent on secondary sources and not even using them in any systematic way" (*Librarianship and the Pursuit of Truth* [New Brunswick: Rutgers U, Graduate School of Lib. Science, 1974] 11). For particulars, see the following reviews: *Times Literary Supplement* 25 Mar. 1939: 180; Robert A. Colby, *Nineteenth-Century Fiction* 16 (1962): 354–59.

Text Archives

M2339   *Eighteenth-Century Fiction.* ProQuest. Online. 17 June 2006 <http://collections.chadwyck.com>.

An archive of rekeyed texts of 96 English-language works of fiction published in the British Isles between 1700 and 1780. First editions were selected for inclusion, but some extensively revised works are present in two versions. Selection was done by an editorial board. Simple keyword, title, and author searches can be limited by publication date, genre, date during an author's lifetime, gender, nationality, ethnicity, and to parts (e.g., front matter, epigraphs). Searchers can also browse an author list of the contents of the database. Results appear in ascending alphabetical order and cannot be re-sorted. Citations (but not the full text) can be marked for e-mailing, downloading, or printing; each citation includes a durable URL to the full text. Some works are rekeyed from textually unsound editions; however, the bibliographic record for each work identifies the source of the text and any omissions (e.g., preliminary matter). Besides being a useful source for identifying an elusive quotation or allusion, *Eighteenth-Century Fiction*'s text archive makes feasible a variety of kinds of studies (stylistic, thematic, imagistic, and topical).

The contents of *Eighteenth-Century Fiction* can also be searched through *LiOn* (I527), which offers a less versatile search interface.

Continued by *Nineteenth-Century Fiction* (M2663).

See also

Mish, *English Prose Fiction, 1600–1700* (M2095).

Guides to Scholarship and Criticism

M2340   Letellier, Robert Ignatius. *The English Novel, 1660–1700: An Annotated Bibliography.* Bibliographies and Indexes in World Literature 53. Westport: Greenwood, 1997. 448 pp.   Z2014.F4 L46 [PN3491]   016.823'408.

————. *The English Novel, 1700–1740: An Annotated Bibliography.*
Bibliographies and Indexes in World Literature 56. Westport: Greenwood,
2002. 625 pp.   Z2014.F4 L47 [PR851]   016.823′508.

Annotated bibliographies of editions and studies of prose fiction in English (including translations) published between 1660 and 1740. The 3,138 entries (through 1995 in *1660–1700*, through 1997 or 1999—depending on the section—in *1700–1740*) are organized in sections for bibliographies (including far too many works only tangentially related to the subject), anthologies, general studies, and individual authors. Entries for authors include sections for primary works, editions, bibliographies, and criticism (for many authors in *1700–1740* this section includes numerous studies that have no bearing on prose fiction); coverage for some writers (such as Behn, Bunyan, and Defoe) supplements existing bibliographies, and coverage for foreign writers is appropriately limited to discussions of English translations. Each volume concludes with a chronological list of fiction and two indexes: scholars; subjects. With full and informative annotations (though some are commentary and others, summary) and only a few studies listed as unseen, *English Novel, 1660–1700* and *1700-1740* offer the most current, thorough guide to scholarship on fiction of the period.

For 1660–1740, Letellier's two volumes supersede Jerry C. Beasley, *English Fiction, 1660–1800: A Guide to Information Sources,* American Literature, English Literature, and World Literatures in English: An Information Guide Series 14 (Detroit: Gale, 1978, 313 pp.), a highly selective annotated bibliography restricted largely to English-language scholarship published through the mid-1970s, and H. George Hahn and Carl Behm III, *The Eighteenth-Century British Novel and Its Background: An Annotated Bibliography and Guide to Topics* (Metuchen: Scarecrow, 1985, 392 pp.), which combines inadequate annotations with an unsuccessful attempt to index scholarship through 1984 by topic.

M2345   Spector, Robert Donald. *The English Gothic: A Bibliographic Guide to Writers from Horace Walpole to Mary Shelley.* Westport: Greenwood, 1984. 269 pp.   Z2014.H67 S66 [PR830.T3]   016.823′0872′09.

An evaluative survey of the most important English-language publications on the genre and major authors. After a lengthy introduction that treats the definition and development of the genre, an initial chapter examines bibliographies; genre, influence, and critical reception studies; and scholarship on several minor writers. The remaining four chapters range beyond Gothic fiction in evaluating biographies, editions, and scholarship on pairs of related authors: Walpole and Reeve, Charlotte Smith and Radcliffe, Lewis and Beckford, Maturin and Mary Shelley. The index of subjects and authors is seriously marred by inconsistencies and numerous omissions. Although highly selective and inadequately indexed, *English Gothic* is valuable for its extensive evaluations of studies and surveys of critical trends.

Less selective but provisionally complete through only 1971 is Dan J. McNutt, *The Eighteenth-Century Gothic Novel: An Annotated Bibliography of Criticism and Selected Texts* (New York: Garland, 1975, 330 pp.). There are numerous omissions in the background sections; foreign-language studies are relegated (unannotated) to an appendix; and the indexing is inadequate. Nevertheless, the clearly annotated entries include studies omitted by Spector.

See also

Frank, *Guide to the Gothic* (L875).

DRAMA AND THEATER

Many works in sections L: Genres/Drama and Theater and M: English Literature/
General/Genres/Drama and Theater are useful to research in Restoration and eighteenth-century drama and theater.

Histories and Surveys

M2355   Hume, Robert D. *The Development of English Drama in the Late Seventeenth
          Century.* Oxford: Clarendon–Oxford UP, 1976. 525 pp.   PR691.H8
          822'.4'09.
    A study of the development of the drama from 1660 to 1710 in two parts: an
examination of the dramatic types in theory and practice; and a decade-by-decade analysis of theatrical fashions, particularly as they are influenced by political and social
change. Two indexes: names and subjects; plays. A provocative, scholarly work on a
neglected period of the drama, but Hume's categorization of types of plays and individual readings have elicited some controversy. Reviews: Anne Barton, *TLS: Times
Literary Supplement* 10 Sept. 1976: 1110–11; Maximillian E. Novak, *Eighteenth-
Century Studies* 10 (1977): 512–16; Eric Rothstein, *Modern Language Quarterly* 38
(1977): 191–94.

M2360   Nicoll, Allardyce. *Restoration Drama, 1660–1700.* 4th ed. *Early Eighteenth
          Century Drama.* 3rd ed. *Late Eighteenth Century Drama, 1750–1800.* 2nd
          ed. Vols. 1–3 of *A History of English Drama, 1660–1900* (M1525).
          Cambridge: Cambridge UP, 1952.   PR625.N52   822.09.
    Emphasizing the history of the stage and dramatic forms, each volume includes
chapters on the theater, tragedy, comedy, and (except vol. 1) miscellaneous dramatic
forms. Appendixes treat playhouses and government documents related to the stage.
Each volume concludes with an author list of plays, operas, and other dramatic forms
written during the period, with information on performances, printed editions, and
manuscripts (although the last are sketchily treated). Revisions that could not be incorporated readily into the text are printed as supplementary sections. Indexed by persons and subjects; the lists of plays (excluding most Italian operas and "the repertoire
of the French and Italian comedians") are indexed and supplemented in vol. 6 (entry
M1545). (Further additions are printed in Raymond A. Biswanger, Jr., "Additions to
Allardyce Nicoll's 'Hand-List of Plays, 1700–1750,'" *Restoration and 18th Century
Theatre Research* 15.1 [1976]: 46–60; 15.2: 60.) Although in need of updating (most
notably by reference to *London Stage, 1660–1800* [M2370]), the volumes contain a
wealth of information not available elsewhere and the most complete bibliographies of
dramatic works for the period.

See also

      Revels History of Drama in English (M1530).

Annals

See

      Harbage, *Annals of English Drama, 975–1700* (M1535).

Guides to Primary Works

M2370   *The London Stage, 1660–1800: A Calendar of Plays, Entertainments, and
        Afterpieces Together with Casts, Box-Receipts, and Contemporary Comment:
        Compiled from the Playbills, Newspapers, and Theatrical Diaries of the Period.*
        5 pts. and index in 12 vols. Carbondale: Southern Illinois UP, 1960–79.
        PN1582.G72 L65   792'.09421.

> Part 1: *1660–1700.* Ed. William Van Lennep. 1965. 532 pp. (A revision
> by Judith Milhous and Robert D. Hume is in progress.)
> Part 2: *1700–1729.* 2 vols. Ed. Emmett L. Avery. 1960. (A revision by
> Judith Milhous and Robert D. Hume is in progress; a draft of the 1700–
> 11 calendar is available at http://www.personal.psu.edu/faculty/h/b/hb1/
> London%20Stage%202001.)
> Part 3: *1729–1747.* 2 vols. Ed. Arthur H. Scouten. 1961.
> Part 4: *1747–1776.* 3 vols. Ed. George Winchester Stone, Jr. 1962.
> Part 5: *1776–1800.* 3 vols. Ed. Charles Beecher Hogan. 1968.
> *Index to* The London Stage, 1660–1800. Comp. Ben Ross Schneider, Jr.
> 1979. 939 pp.

A calendar of spoken and in some instances sung dramatic entertainments, organized by theatrical season and then by date of performance. A typical entry identifies
date, theater, title, afterpiece, cast (a full list for the initial performance, with changes
noted for subsequent ones), prologues, epilogues, dancing, singing, music, or other
entertainment; a concluding section notes "benefits, requests for particular plays, box
office receipts, the presence of royalty and other persons named in the bills, and references to or quotations from contemporary documents which throw light upon the
evening's whole entertainment." Entries vary in fullness, depending on the available
information.

Each season is prefaced by a brief summary, and each part begins with an extensive
general introduction that typically examines the playhouses and their organization, fi-
nances, management, advertising, costumes, scenery, repertory, players, music, production details, audience, and contemporary criticism. (These important introductions have
been separately published as *The London Stage*, 5 vols. [Carbondale: Southern Illinois
UP; London: Feffer, 1968].)

Entries—but not the introductions—are indexed by titles, names, places, theaters,
and some subjects in Schneider's *Index*, which cumulates and expands the index in each
volume; however, the index volume must be used very cautiously, since there are in-
numerable errors and misidentifications. (For important strictures on the use of the
Index, see Langhans's review.)

Users must remember that (1) completeness and accuracy vary markedly from part
to part; (2) editorial policy changes somewhat from part to part; (3) performance records
are very incomplete in the early years; (4) before 1705, dates are frequently those of
publication rather than performance; (5) an advertised play or entertainment was not
necessarily performed or acted by the announced cast; (6) many additions and corrections have been made (see, for example, William J. Burling and Robert D. Hume,
"Theatrical Companies at the Little Haymarket, 1720–1737," *Essays in Theatre* 4
[1986]: 98–118; Burling, *Checklist of New Plays* [M2377]; Burling, "New London Cast
Listings, 1696–1737, with Other Additions and Corrections to *The London Stage*,"
Theatre Notebook 51 [1997]: 42–54; Rob Jordan, "An Addendum to *The London Stage,
1660–1700*," *Theatre Notebook* 47 [1993]: 62–75; and the following by Judith Milhous and Robert D. Hume in *Harvard Library Bulletin*: "Dating Play Premières from

Publication Data," 22 [1974]: 374–405; "Lost English Plays, 1660–1700," 25 [1977]: 5–33; and "Attribution Problems in English Drama, 1660–1700," 31 [1983]: 5–39). The revisions of pts. 1 and 2 will be based on a fresh examination of the primary sources, add several fringe performances, include texts or summaries of a substantial number of ancillary documents, distinguish among performers with the same name, and index fully all actors and actresses by role.

In spite of its flaws, *London Stage* is an indispensable source for research on theater and stage history, repertory, acting careers, theater personnel, trends in drama, reception history—in short, on nearly every aspect of the drama and stage of the period. Researchers must also consult Highfill, *Biographical Dictionary* (M2400), whose entries make numerous corrections and additions to *London Stage*. Until the revisions of pts. 1 and 2 are published, scholars should also see Milhous, *Register of English Theatrical Documents* (M2380). Reviews: (pt. 1) Arthur Sherbo, *JEGP: Journal of English and Germanic Philology* 65 (1966): 194–96; (pt. 2) Sherbo, 60 (1961): 299–305; (pt. 3) Sherbo, 61 (1962): 926–31; (pt. 4) Sherbo, 63 (1964): 365–69; (pt. 5) Robert D. Hume, *Philological Quarterly* 50 (1971): 389–90; (index) Edward A. Langhans, *Eighteenth-Century Studies* 14 (1980): 72–78 (including a list of entries in the *Biographical Dictionary* [M2400] corrected by the *Index*).

M2375   Bowers, Fredson. *A Bibliography of the English Printed Drama, 1660–1700.*
          Temporarily suspended.

A descriptive bibliography of all editions, impressions, issues, and states of plays published between 1660 and 1700 that are excluded from Greg, *Bibliography of the English Printed Drama* (M2135). Titles are arranged according to date of publication. Each entry provides a full bibliographical description based on personal examination of multiple copies, with extensive notes on printing, dating, advertisements, and identification of printers. Indexes include printers, publishers, dedicatees, writers of prologues and epilogues, first lines of epilogues and prologues, and first lines of songs. Since Bowers's death, David L. Vander Meulen (Dept. of English, U of Virginia, Charlottesville 22904–4121) has custody of the project until a suitable successor can be found.

M2377   Burling, William J. *A Checklist of New Plays and Entertainments on the
          London Stage, 1700–1737.* Rutherford: Fairleigh Dickinson UP; London:
          Assoc. UP, 1993. 235 pp.   PN2596.L6 B84   792'.09421'09033.

A chronological checklist—keyed to *London Stage* (M2370)—of plays, pantomimes, operas, ballad-operas, farces, afterpieces, and other entertainments first performed in London between 1700 and 1737. A typical entry includes "date of premiere, venue, title, author(s) or attribution, type of play (genre), printer or publisher, date of publication, and notes . . . on attribution, performance history, or secondary studies." The introduction offers a refreshingly clear explanation of scope and parts of an entry. Concludes with two appendixes: entertainments at minor London venues (such as taverns, fairs, and minor playhouses); plays not produced. Indexed by authors, titles, and subtitles. Combining a thorough synthesis of standard sources and recent scholarship with a fresh examination of primary sources—especially London newspapers—*Checklist of New Plays* complements (and frequently corrects) *London Stage* and offers an invaluable conspectus that makes feasible the systematic study of trends in and the milieu of London theatrical activity 1700–37.

M2380   Milhous, Judith, and Robert D. Hume, comps. and eds. *A Register of
          English Theatrical Documents, 1660–1737.* 2 vols. Carbondale: Southern
          Illinois UP, 1991.   Z6611.T28 M55 [PN2599]   016.792'0942'09032.

A chronological calendar of manuscript and printed documents related to the management and regulation of the theater, principally in London, from 1660 through 1737. Entries are organized by theatrical season, then by date (but users must study the introductory discussion of how certain kinds of documents, such as lawsuits, are dated). Each entry provides date, location, title (descriptive in the case of manuscripts), description of content (with a full transcription in many instances; some documents will be printed in full or excerpted in the revision of pts. 1 and 2 of *London Stage* [M2370]), and notes (amplifying location information, giving bibliographical details for printed works, and referring to other copies, published transcriptions, or scholarship). Four appendixes list undatable bills from Drury Lane (1714–16), documents spanning more than one season, documents misdated by earlier authorities, and Chancery suits by Public Record Office number. Indexed by persons, subjects, and play titles. An outgrowth of the editors' revision of *London Stage, 1660–1800*, pts. 1–2, the work is an invaluable compilation that carefully describes and locates a mass of widely scattered documents, corrects numerous published accounts, and adds much that is new. By ordering what is known, the *Register* should stimulate the identification and publication of additional material.

See also

Nicoll, *History of English Drama*, vols. 1–3 (M2360).

Guides to Scholarship and Criticism

Surveys of Research

M2385   Hume, Robert D. "English Drama and Theatre, 1660–1800: New Directions in Research." *Theatre Survey* 23.1 (1982): 71–100. PN2000.T716.
   A summary of the state of scholarship, with evaluations of reference works, bibliographies, critical studies, and histories; comments on research methodologies; and valuable suggestions for further research (many of which have not been taken up).

Serial Bibliographies

M2387   "Restoration and 18th Century Theatre Research Bibliography [1961–75]." *Restoration and 18th Century Theatre Research* 1–15 (1962–76). PN2592.R46 792.
   A descriptively annotated subject bibliography that resurfaced briefly as the unannotated "Selective Bibliography, [1986–90]" (2nd ser. 4.2–6.2 [1989–91]), but with no explanation of the criteria governing selection. The bibliographies for 1961–67 are incorporated into Stratman, *Restoration and Eighteenth Century Theatre Research* (M2395), and are cumulated in Carl J. Stratman, C. S. V., ed., and Edmund A. Napieralski and Jean E. Westbrook, comps., *Restoration and 18th Century Theatre Research Bibliography, 1961–1968* (Troy: Whitston, 1969, 241 pp.). Although subject headings are not as refined as they might be and coverage is not comprehensive, this work is a useful complement to *ECCB: The Eighteenth Century Current Bibliography* (M2245) and the serial bibliographies and indexes in section G.

Other Bibliographies

M2390   Link, Frederick M. *English Drama, 1660–1800: A Guide to Information
          Sources.* American Literature, English Literature, and World Literatures in
          English: An Information Guide Series 9. Detroit: Gale, 1976. 374 pp.
          Z2014.D7 L55 [PR701]   016.822.

A selective survey of "every substantial book and article" through 1973 (along with
a few from 1974). The emphasis is on English-language studies, and researchers must
read the prefatory list of topics excluded before consulting the guide. Unlike other
volumes in the series, this one consists of a series of surveys of research in two divisions.
The first examines general works in sections for reference works, collections, playhouses
and audience, biography, dramatic theory, history of drama, general criticism, and antecedents and influences. The second treats a variety of playwrights, major and minor.
The commentary tends toward brief description, with occasional incisive evaluations
and perceptive suggestions for research. The format—more effective for the treatment
of individual authors than for general topics—does not accommodate scanning. Two
indexes: persons; play titles. Accuracy, judicious selectivity and evaluation, clear organization, and broad coverage make *English Drama, 1660–1800* a useful starting point,
especially for minor writers, but it must be supplemented by Stratman, *Restoration and
Eighteenth Century Theatre Research* (M2395); *ECCB: The Eighteenth Century Current
Bibliography* (M2245); and *Year's Work in English Studies* (G330). Review: David Mann,
Analytical and Enumerative Bibliography 1 (1977): 246–50.

M2395   Stratman, Carl J., C. S. V., David G. Spencer, and Mary Elizabeth Devine,
          eds. *Restoration and Eighteenth Century Theatre Research: A Bibliographical
          Guide, 1900–1968.* Carbondale: Southern Illinois UP; London: Feffer,
          1971. 811 pp.   Z2014.D7 S854   016.822'5'09.

An annotated bibliography of editions and studies (including dissertations and
master's theses) through 1967 on all aspects of drama and theater in the British Isles.
The approximately 6,000 entries are listed chronologically under 780 alphabetically
arranged subject headings, with those for playwrights having separate lists of editions
and studies. By the editors' count, 81.6% of the entries are descriptively annotated. The
work is indexed by persons and subject headings, but because of the insufficiently refined
headings and lack of cross-references, it is difficult to locate studies of specific topics.
The numerous errors and omissions make this an untrustworthy source, yet it offers
the most extensive single list of scholarship on the topic. Reviews: Hilbert H. Campbell,
Papers of the Bibliographical Society of America 67 (1973): 200–03; D. F. McKenzie,
Notes and Queries ns 21 (1974): 237–39; Geoffrey Marshall, *Seventeenth-Century News*
31 (1973): 18–19.

This work incorporates the "Restoration and 18th Century Theatre Research Bibliography for [1961–67]" (M2387); for post-1967 publications, see "Restoration and
18th Century Theatre Research Bibliography" (M2387); "Some Current Publications,"
Restoration (M2250); *ECCB: The Eighteenth Century Current Bibliography* (M2245);
"Recent Studies in the Restoration and Eighteenth Century" (M2240); and the serial
bibliographies and indexes in section G. For a selective bibliography, see Link, *English
Drama, 1660–1800* (M2390).

See also

    "Restoration and 18th Century Theatre Research Bibliography" (M2387).

Biographical Dictionaries

M2400   Highfill, Philip H., Jr., Kalman A. Burnim, and Edward A. Langhans. *A Biographical Dictionary of Actors, Actresses, Musicians, Dancers, Managers, and Other Stage Personnel in London, 1660–1800.* 16 vols. Carbondale: Southern Illinois UP, 1973–93.   PN2597.H5   790.2'092'2.

A biographical dictionary of about 8,500 persons (and some animals) associated with professional dramatic entertainments. Entries include "actors and actresses, dancers, singers, instrumental musicians, scene painters, machinists, management officials, prompters, acrobats, contortionists, pyrotechnists, magicians, dwarfs, freaks, animal trainers, strong men, public orators, mimics, dressers, callers, concessionaires, and also members of certain trades operating on salary and within the physical confines of the theatres—such employees as tailors, carpenters, and barbers." Excludes dramatists except those who were also actors, managers, or otherwise connected with the theater. The informative, well-written entries, which vary from a single line to more than a hundred pages and include at least one portrait if any exists, are based on extensive research in primary sources. Although many biographies are the most authoritative available, entries lack full documentation—the only major flaw and one that will not be rectified by a bibliography volume. There are omissions and errors (but the majority of corrections and additions have come to light only because of the publication of the biographies); nevertheless, the *Biographical Dictionary* is undeniably a major achievement that, along with *London Stage* (M2370), has already stimulated much research. For an entertaining account of the research undergirding the *Biographical Dictionary*, see Highfill, "A Peep behind the Curtain: Mass Theatrical Biography," *In Search of Restoration and Eighteenth-Century Theatrical Biography*, by George Winchester Stone, Jr., and Highfill (Los Angeles: William Andrews Clark Memorial Lib., 1976) 33–66. Reviews: (vols. 1–2) Robert D. Hume, *Eighteenth-Century Studies* 8 (1975): 510–17; (vols. 3–4) Judith Milhous, *Eighteenth Century: A Current Bibliography* ns 2 (1976): 162–65.

POETRY

Some works in sections L: Genres/Poetry and M: English Literature/General/Genres/Poetry are useful for research in Restoration and eighteenth-century English poetry.

Histories and Surveys

M2410   Rothstein, Eric. *Restoration and Eighteenth-Century Poetry, 1660–1780.* Vol. 3 of *The Routledge History of English Poetry.* Gen. ed. R. A. Foakes. Boston: Routledge, 1981. 242 pp.   PR502.R58 [PR561]   821'.009.

A critical history that emphasizes the continuity of the period in chapters on poetry (1660–1720), style, uses of the past, and poetry (1720–80). A chronology features commentary on principal poems and collections by minor poets, and summaries of important historical events, especially political ones. Indexed by authors and anonymous works. Although sometimes lapsing into dense lists of authors and poems, the volume is overall an intelligent, well-organized, authoritative treatment of both major and minor writers. Reviews: John M. Aden, *Eighteenth Century: A Current Bibliography* ns 7 (for 1981): 371–72; James Engell, *Modern Philology* 79 (1982): 438–41.

Guides to Primary Works

M2415 Foxon, D. F. *English Verse, 1701–1750: A Catalogue of Separately Printed Poems with Notes on Contemporary Collected Editions.* 2 vols. Cambridge: Cambridge UP, 1975. Z2014.P7 F69 [PR551] 016.821.

A short-title catalog of separately published verse, translations, and collections by a single author, in any language, written and printed between 1701 and 1750 in the British Isles. Since Foxon is not a catalog of all poems written and printed during the period, it excludes miscellanies (see Case, *Bibliography of English Poetical Miscellanies* [M2180]), periodical verse, popular broadside ballads, slip songs, chapbooks, engraved sheets with music or cartoons, oratorios, and libretti (but see vol. 1, pp. xii–xiii, for some exceptions). Entries are listed alphabetically by author, translator, or title of anonymous work; under each author, collected editions are listed chronologically, with separately published poems following in alphabetical order. An entry for a single work includes short title, imprint, collation, bibliographical notes (which distinguish editions, issues, impressions, or states; describe watermark; and cite standard bibliographies), first line, notes on authorship and subject matter, and locations (up to five libraries in the British Isles and five in the United States). Collected editions receive abbreviated descriptions. Six indexes: first lines; first editions (listed chronologically); imprints; bibliographical notes; epithets describing authors of anonymous books; subjects (including forms and genres). Inevitably there are omissions, but the accuracy and detail of the descriptions (based almost exclusively on personal examination of multiple copies) make this an indispensable source for textual study, publishing history, and the identification and location of editions. Thorough coverage, detailed indexes (which open new approaches to the poetry), and numerous attributions render this a landmark catalog that lays the groundwork for definitive studies. For some additions and corrections, see Bryan Coleborne, "Some Notes on D. F. Foxon's *English Verse, 1701–1750*," *Bibliographical Society of Australia and New Zealand Bulletin* 7 (1983): 45–48, as well as the following reviews: L. J. Harris, *Library* 5th ser. 31 (1976): 158–64; James Woolley, *Modern Philology* 75 (1977): 59–73.

M2420 Jackson, J. R. de J. *Annals of English Verse, 1770–1835: A Preliminary Survey of the Volumes Published.* Garland Reference Library of the Humanities 535. New York: Garland, 1985. 709 pp. Z2039.P6 J32 [PR502] 016.821'6.

A chronological catalog of volumes of poems and verse drama published in the United Kingdom (along with a few volumes published elsewhere but intended for a British audience) in English and other languages except Gaelic and Welsh. Jackson excludes hymnbooks (except for some that print original hymns), books of songs not intended to be read, annuals, reprints of works originally published before 1770 (except for significant new editions), volumes of fewer than eight pages, "stage adaptations of plays, operas, textbooks, [and] foreign works in foreign languages." Entries, organized alphabetically by title under year of publication, record short title, editor or translator, publication information, edition if other than the first, format, number of volumes, pagination for single-volume works, price, author, and source(s) of the citation. Two indexes: authors; anonymous works.

Compiled from secondary sources (principally *Cambridge Bibliography of English Literature* [M1385a], *New Cambridge Bibliography of English Literature* [M1385], *British Museum General Catalogue of Printed Books* [E250a], and *National Union Catalog, Pre-56 Imprints* [E235]), *Annals of English Verse* is intended as a preliminary list. Although it repeats the errors of its sources, perpetuates ghosts, and omits works and editions, it is nonetheless a useful compilation for situating a play or volume of verse in its literary context and for preliminary identification of editions (especially of minor works). For the period 1770–1800, researchers should also consult *ESTC* (M1377). Review: Anne McWhir, *University of Toronto Quarterly* 56 (1986): 99–101.

Entries for women poets in *Annals of English Verse* is superseded by J. R. de J. Jackson, *Romantic Poetry by Women: A Bibliography, 1770–1835* (Oxford: Clarendon– Oxford UP, 1993, 484 pp.), a bibliography of separate volumes (of 8 pp. or more) of verse written or translated by women and published for the first time between 1770 and 1835. Works in languages other than English by authors whose first language is English are included; annuals and works intended for musical performance are excluded. Entries are organized alphabetically by author (under the surname most frequently used during the period), and works are listed chronologically by date of the first edition (subsequent editions follow thereunder). A typical entry consists of basic bibliographical information, page size, price, and copy examined or source of information. Concludes with appendixes on female pseudonyms used by men and on publication statistics. Four indexes: authors; titles; publishers; locations of publishers. Based on personal examination of copies and prefaced by an admirably detailed explanation of editorial procedures, *Romantic Poetry by Women* offers an invaluable guide to identifying poetry by women and to locating these frequently elusive volumes.

See also

Case, *Bibliography of English Poetical Miscellanies* (M2180).
Crum, *First-Line Index of English Poetry, 1500–1800* (M1590).

Guides to Scholarship and Criticism

M2425 Mell, Donald C., Jr. *English Poetry, 1660–1800: A Guide to Information Sources.* American Literature, English Literature, and World Literatures in English: An Information Guide Series 40. Detroit: Gale, 1982. 501 pp. Z2014.P7 M44 [PR551]   016.821.

A selective bibliography of English-language scholarship (primarily from the 1930s through 1979) organized in two divisions: general studies and individual authors. The first lists works in three classified sections: reference materials; background studies of English literature, 1660–1800; and general studies of poetry, 1660–1800 (with sub-sections for themes, genres, poetic forms and structures, and language and versification). The second is devoted to 31 poets, each with separate lists of major editions; correspondence; bibliographies, textual studies, and concordances; collections of studies; biographical works; and critical studies. Annotations to the 2,264 entries are occasionally evaluative (but not always reliably so). Indexed by persons and titles of works listed. The established canon is emphasized, and subject indexing is lacking; nonetheless, the judicious selection of studies and clear annotations make his work, as Mell says, "imperfect yet useful." Review: David L. Vander Meulen, *Literary Research Newsletter* 9 (1984): 29–31.

A useful complement, especially for its evaluations and coverage of studies through 1987, is David Nokes and Janet Barron, *An Annotated Critical Bibliography of Augustan Poetry,* Annotated Critical Bibliographies (Hemel Hempstead: Harvester; New York: St. Martin's, 1989, 158 pp.). Users should note that Nokes offers a highly selective guide to the most important or representative English-language scholarship; is marred by an organizational scheme that unnecessarily separates books, articles, and parts of books in the generally brief chronological lists under each author; omits Swift since he was to have been the subject of a separate volume in the series; and renders superfluous the needlessly complex entry number system by citing page numbers in the indexes of scholars and literary authors.

See also

> Donow, *Sonnet in England and America* (L1250).
> Kuntz, *Poetry Explication* (L1255).
> Martinez, *Guide to British Poetry Explication*, vol. 3 (L1255a).

PROSE

Some works in sections L: Genres/Prose and M: English Literature/General/Genres/ Prose are useful for research in Restoration and eighteenth-century prose.

Biography and Autobiography

Histories and Surveys

M2430   Stauffer, Donald A. *The Art of Biography in Eighteenth Century England.*
Princeton: Princeton UP; London: Oxford UP, 1941. 572 pp.
Bibliographical Supplement (entry M2435). 1941.   CT34.G7 S67   808.06.
    A critical history of eighteenth-century English biography that emphasizes its place in the literature of the period. Chapters are devoted to biography and the drama, biography and the novel, biography and the Romantic spirit, lives of eccentrics and antiquaries, inner life, major biographers, and trends of biography. Indexed by persons and a few titles. Although now dated, this work remains the fullest history of biography during the century. Reviews: James R. Sutherland, *Review of English Studies* 18 (1942): 350–54; René Wellek, *Modern Philology* 39 (1942): 432–36.
    Art of Biography continues Stauffer, *English Biography before 1700* (M1605). For the *Bibliographical Supplement*, see entry M2435.

Guides to Primary Works

M2435   Stauffer, Donald A. *The Art of Biography in Eighteenth Century England:*
Bibliographical Supplement. Princeton: Princeton UP; London: Oxford UP,
1941. 293 pp.   CT34.G7 S67   808.06.
    A bibliography of biographies written or translated in England from 1700 through 1800 and of important scholarship on the genre. The bulk of the work consists of an author list of biographies, with cross-references to subjects. Each entry cites editions through 1800, along with an occasional modern one. Works not discussed in the text of *Art of Biography in Eighteenth Century England* (M2430) are accompanied by a brief description of content or evaluative comment. The second part is a selective list of important studies. Concludes with a chronology of the most important biographies from 1700 through 1800. Although incomplete and including some works more prop-

erly classified as fiction, the *Supplement* remains the most complete list of biographies of the period.

Nineteenth-Century Literature

Many works listed in section M: English Literature/General are important for research in nineteenth-century literature. See also sections N: Irish Literature; O: Scottish Literature; P: Welsh Literature; and U: Literature-Related Topics and Sources/Children's Literature.

Research Methods

M2445   Keeran, Peggy, and Jennifer Bowers. *Literary Research and the British Romantic Era: Strategies and Sources.* Literary Research: Strategies and Resources 1. Lanham: Scarecrow, 2005. 255 pp. (Updates will appear at http://www.literaryresearchseries.org.)   PR457.K44   820.9′145′072.

A guide to research strategies and reference sources for the scholar working with British Romantic literature (here, 1775–1830). Following an admirably clear explanation of the basics of online searching are chapters on general literary reference sources (including some devoted to individual writers); library catalogs; print and electronic bibliographies, indexes, and annual reviews (again, with some devoted to individual writers); scholarly journals; contemporary reviews; contemporary journals and newspapers; microform and digital collections; manuscripts and archives; and Web resources. A final chapter demonstrates how to use many of the works and strategies previously discussed to develop a research plan. An appendix lists sources in related disciplines. Indexed by titles, authors, and subjects. Describing fully the uses of kinds of reference tools, providing illuminating examples in discussions of key individual resources, detailing techniques for finding kinds of information (including primary works), and illustrating research processes, *Literary Research and the British Romantic Era* admirably fulfills its intent: "to explain the best practices for conducting research in the British Romantic era and to address the challenges scholars working in this era face." It sets the benchmark for the volumes to follow in this important new series.

M2450   Storey, Richard, and Lionel Madden. *Primary Sources for Victorian Studies: A Guide to the Location and Use of Unpublished Materials.* London: Phillimore, 1977. 81 pp. Storey. *Primary Sources for Victorian Studies: An Updating.* Occasional Papers in Bibliography. Leicester: Victorian Studies Centre, U of Leicester, 1987. 38 pp.   Z2019.S86 [DA550]   016.941081.

A basic guide to the location and use of manuscripts and records. Except for a very brief discussion of guides to collections outside Britain, the work emphasizes British resources in chapters on the Royal Commission on Historical Manuscripts (F285a) and National Register of Archives (F285a), national repositories, local repositories, general published guides, and special topics (such as art, education, literature, and religious history), terminology, and practical hints to researchers. Indexed by subjects. A clear, practical introduction whose usefulness as a guide to locating and using unpublished materials extends well beyond the Victorian period.

Guides to Reference Works

M2453   Propas, Sharon W. *Victorian Studies: A Research Guide.* 2nd ed. High
        Wycombe: Rivendale, 2006. 267 pp.   Z2019.P76 [DA550]   016.941.

An annotated multidisciplinary guide to reference works published through 2004
that are important to research in the Victorian period (1832–1900) in Great Britain,
Ireland, and the British Empire. The 957 entries are organized by ascending date of
publication in seven classified divisions: guides and bibliographies; union lists, catalogs,
and guides to collections; manuscripts and archives; guides to museums and collections;
general reference works; multidisciplinary reference works; works devoted to a specific
discipline (including book arts, literature and language, and theater and drama). Indexed
by authors, titles, and subjects. Although commendably broad in its coverage, *Victorian
Studies* omits a number of revised editions or supplements published before its cutoff
date and is marred by numerous errors in citations and annotations (the latter typically
offer unsophisticated descriptions or evaluations).

Histories and Surveys

M2455   Jack, Ian. *English Literature, 1815–1832.* Vol. 10 of *The Oxford History of
        English Literature* (M1310). Gen. eds. Bonamy Dobrée, Norman Davis, and
        F. P. Wilson. Oxford: Clarendon–Oxford UP, 1963. 643 pp. (Reprinted in
        1990 as vol. 12, with the title *English Literature, 1815–1832: Scott, Byron,
        and Keats.*)   PR457.J24   820.903.

A history of the period, with chapters on the literary scene in 1815; Byron; Shelley;
Keats; Clare and minor poets; the Waverley romances; Peacock; Galt and minor prose
fiction; Hazlitt; Lamb; De Quincey; miscellaneous prose; history, biography, and autobiography; the interest in foreign and earlier English literature; and the literary scene
in 1832. Includes a chronology and an outdated selective bibliography. Indexed by
persons and a few titles. A solid but not critically adventuresome work, whose accuracy,
range, lucidity, and clarity of style cause reviewers to rate this work as one of the better
Oxford History volumes. Reviews: Geoffrey Carnall, *Essays in Criticism* 14 (1964): 310–
18; John Jones, *Review of English Studies* ns 16 (1965): 319–20.

The earlier Romantic writers are treated in a separate, unsatisfactory volume by
Renwick (M2460).

M2460   Renwick, W. L. *English Literature, 1789–1815.* Vol. 9 of *The Oxford
        History of English Literature* (M1310). Gen. eds. Bonamy Dobrée, Norman
        Davis, and F. P. Wilson. Oxford: Clarendon–Oxford UP, 1963. 293 pp.
        (Reprinted in 1990 as vol. 11, with the title *The Rise of the Romantics,
        1789–1815: Wordsworth, Coleridge, and Jane Austen.*)   PR447.R4
        820.903.

Covers the full careers of writers whose "most characteristic work was published
between 1789 and 1815" in eight chapters: background of the period; political works;
science and travel writing; novels; writers of the early 1790s; Wordsworth, Coleridge,
and Southey; Scottish literature; and drama and historical writing. Concludes with a
chronology and an outdated bibliography. Indexed (inadequately) by person. A frequently impenetrable style, imbalances in discussions of important figures, and a lack
of synthesis make this one of the least successful *Oxford History* volumes. Reviews: *Times*

Literary Supplement 1 Mar. 1963: 154; Robert Martin Adams, *Hudson Review* 16 (1963–64): 594–600; Anne Kostelanetz, *Minnesota Review* 4 (1964): 532–43.

The later Romantic writers are more adequately treated by Jack, *English Literature, 1815–1832* (M2455).

M2462 Davis, Philip. *1830–1880: The Victorians.* Vol. 8 of *The Oxford English Literary History* (M1310a). Gen. ed. Jonathan Bate. Oxford: Oxford UP, 2002. 631 pp.   PR85.O96   820.9.

A literary history devoted to the literature of the Victorian era, with chapters on the social and cultural background, nature, religion, the rise of psychology, literary production, the drama, the novel, biography, and poetry. Concludes with a selective bibliography that frequently offers evaluations of editions and studies. Indexed by persons and subjects.

This volume is meant to replace Turner, *English Literature, 1832–1890, Excluding the Novel* (M1310a), which favors critical evaluation at the expense of social-historical context, and Horsman, *The Victorian Novel* (M1310a), which remains useful for writers and works not discussed by Davis.

See also

Sec. M: English Literature/General/Histories and Surveys.

Literary Handbooks, Dictionaries, and Encyclopedias

M2463 Mitchell, Sally, ed. *Victorian Britain: An Encyclopedia.* Garland Reference Library of Social Science 438. New York: Garland, 1988. 986 pp. DA550.V53   941.081′03′21.

An encyclopedia covering individuals, events, groups, topics, places, and types of publications associated with the cultural, political, social, religious, literary, and intellectual milieu from 1837 to 1901. The signed entries range from about 100 to 3,600 words, include liberal cross-references, and end with a brief list of suggested readings. The volume begins with a chronology and concludes with an evaluative bibliography of important reference works. An especially useful feature is the index of persons, places, subjects, and anonymous works mentioned in entries; entrants are also indexed in *Biography and Genealogy Master Index* (J565). The entries vary in quality and the volume emphasizes lesser-known individuals and has more than its share of errors and inconsistencies, but *Victorian Britain* is a valuable encyclopedia of aspects of Victorian culture. Reviews: Bruce L. Kinzer, *Albion* 21 (1989): 650–52; William Thesing, *Victorian Studies* 33 (1990): 490–91.

The last decade of the nineteenth century is treated more extensively in *The 1890s: An Encyclopedia of British Literature, Art, and Culture,* ed. G. A. Cevasco, Garland Reference Library of the Humanities 1237 (New York: Garland, 1993, 714 pp.), whose approximately 800 signed entries cover topics of cultural interest (most entries are devoted to individuals).

The early part of the century is less satisfactorily treated in *Encyclopedia of Romanticism: Culture in Britain, 1780s–1830s,* ed. Laura Dabundo, Garland Reference Library of the Humanities 1299 (New York: Garland, 1992, 662 pp.). Few of the signed entries are written by top scholars in the field, there is no explanation of the selection criteria or editorial principles, and there are numerous errors.

Bibliographies of Bibliographies

See

> Secs. D: Bibliographies of Bibliographies and M: English Literature/General/
> Bibliographies of Bibliographies.

Guides to Primary Works

MANUSCRIPTS

M2465   *Index of English Literary Manuscripts* (M1365). Ed. P. J. Croft, Theodore
Hofmann, and John Horden. Vol. 4, *1800–1900.* Comp. Barbara
Rosenbaum and Pamela White. London: Mansell, 1982– .   Z6611.L7 I5
[PR83]   016.8208′008.

A descriptive catalog of extant literary manuscripts by a limited number of major
British and Irish authors drawn from among those in *Concise Cambridge Bibliography
of English Literature, 600–1950* (M1365a). The emphasis is on literary manuscripts,
including diaries, notebooks, and marginalia. Letters are excluded, although the
introductions to individual authors identify important collections. In addition, the
introductions alert researchers to special problems and relevant scholarship, point out
additional manuscripts, discuss canon, note the disposition of an author's library, and
conclude with an outline of the arrangement of entries. A typical entry provides a
physical description of the manuscript, dates its composition, includes any necessary
commentary (as well as references to editions, facsimiles, sale catalogs, or scholarship),
and identifies its location (with shelf mark). Additions and corrections appear in pt. 1,
pp. 825–31; others will be printed in vol. 5. Since some entries are based on inquiries
to libraries and collectors, bibliographies, other reference works, and booksellers' and
auction catalogs rather than personal examination by the compilers, the descriptions
vary in fullness and precision.

Although restricted in the number of authors covered, this volume is an essential
source for identifying and locating manuscripts. It must, however, be supplemented by
the works listed in sections F: Guides to Manuscripts and Archives and M: English
Literature/General/Guides to Primary Works/Manuscripts. Reviews: (pt. 1) T. A. J.
Burnett, *TLS: Times Literary Supplement* 4 Feb. 1983: 120; Philip Collins, *Library* 6th
ser. 5 (1983): 309–12; (pt. 2) Michael *Millgate*, Library 6th ser. 14 (1992): 66–68.

See also

> Secs. F: Guides to Manuscripts and Archives and M: English Literature/General/
> Guides to Primary Works/Manuscripts.
> *Location Register of English Literary Manuscripts and Letters: Eighteenth and Nine-
> teenth Centuries* (M2227).

PRINTED WORKS

M2466   *C19: The Nineteenth Century Index.* Chadwyck-Healey. Online. 31 July
2006 <http://c19index.chadwyck.com>. Updated regularly.

An electronic index that includes *Nineteenth Century Short Title Catalogue* (M2475), *Poole's Index to Periodical Literature* (Q4150), and *Wellesley Index to Victorian Periodicals, 1824–1900 on CD-ROM* (M2545); bibliographic records for Chadwyck-Healey's *The Nineteenth Century* microfiche collection; and selected records from *American Periodicals Series Online 1740–1900* (Q4050), *Periodicals Index Online* (G397), *Periodicals Archive Online* (G397), *ArchivesUSA* (F280), and *Palmer's Index to the* Times *Newspaper* (M1450a). Some records are linked to full text. The databases that make up *C19* can be searched together by keyword, title, author, and periodical title; searches can be limited by date and type of document and can be saved to a personal archive. Results can be sorted by author, title, or date (ascending and descending); records can be marked for printing, e-mailing, downloading, or saving to an archive. Each database can also be searched individually through its own search interface. In either case, users should check for spelling variants by using the pull-down lists associated with the search fields. *C19* is a valuable resource that allows the cross-searching of so many important resources for the study of nineteenth-century literature.

M2467   *The Cambridge Bibliography of English Literature (CBEL).* Vol. 4: *1800–1900.*
         3rd ed. Ed. Joanne Shattock. Cambridge: Cambridge UP, 1999. 2,995 cols.
         Z2001.N45 [PR83]   016.82.

(For a full discussion of *CBEL*—especially its limited coverage of secondary works—see entry M1376.) Primary and some secondary works are organized in 16 divisions: book production and distribution, literary relations with the Continent, poetry, novel (including children's literature), drama, prose, history, political economy, philosophy and science, religion, English studies, travel, household books, sport, education, and newspapers and magazines. Users must remember that there is considerable unevenness of coverage among authors and subjects and that, for secondary works, *CBEL* does not supersede vol. 3 of *NCBEL* (M2505). Review: Stefan Collini, *Notes and Queries* 48 (2001): 454–58.

For a discussion of the compilation of this volume, see Shattock, "Revising *The Cambridge Bibliography of English Literature*: Bibliographical Research in an Electronic Age," *European English Messenger* 10.2 (2001): 56–61.

M2470   *The English Catalogue of Books [1801–1968].* Irregular, with various
         cumulations and index volumes. London: Publishers Circular, 1858–1969.
         Z2001.E52   015.42.

An author, title, and subject list of books published in Great Britain, American books imported or issued in England, and English-language books published on the Continent. Since the lists are augmented compilations of various trade catalogs, there are several ghosts and coverage is not thorough, especially for provincial British, American, and Continental publications. Through 1905, series are listed in an appendix, as are publications of learned societies (through 1941). Subject indexing is largely confined to title keywords. Separate subject indexes were published through 1889; thereafter, subject heads appear in the main alphabetic sequence. Entries vary in details but usually cite publisher, edition, size, and price. Although superseded in many respects by the union and national library catalogs in section E, the *English Catalogue,* as the most complete record of books published in Great Britain during the nineteenth century, is occasionally useful as a limited subject guide and for identifying and dating editions. Beginning in 1874, *Reference Catalogue of Current Literature* (M2770) is an important supplement; after 1924, more thorough coverage of works published or issued in Great Britain is provided by *Whitaker's Cumulative Book List* (M2770a) and after 1950 by *British National Bibliography* (M2775).

M2475   *Nineteenth Century Short Title Catalogue* (*NSTC*). Online. 3 Oct. 2005
         <http://nstc.chadwyck.com>. *NSTC* can also be searched through *C19:*
         The Nineteenth Century Index (M2466). (Chadwyck-Healey plans to
         augment the database and add full text and digital images.)

    Series I, Phase I, 1801–1815. 6 vols. Newcastle-upon-Tyne: Avero, 1984–
    86. CD-ROM.
    Series II, Phase I, 1816–1870. 56 vols. 1986–95. CD-ROM.
    Series III, 1871–1919. 1996–2002. CD-ROM.

An attempt to record all books (and other unspecified letterpress material) printed between 1801 and 1919 in Great Britain, the colonies, and the United States; in English throughout the rest of the world; and in translation from English. *NSTC* plans a series of increasingly complete listings: the first phase is limited to a series of author catalogs based on the holdings of a few major libraries; phase two will draw upon the catalogs of specialist libraries.

Series I, Phase I, 1810–1815 is a union list derived from the published and in-house catalogs of the Bodleian; British Library; Library of Trinity College, Dublin; National Library of Scotland; and University Libraries of Cambridge and Newcastle. An entry cites *NSTC* number, author, short title, as many as three Dewey Decimal Classification numbers (the bases for the subject index), date and place of publication (but not printer or publisher), format, bibliographical notes, number of volumes, locations (with a complete list only in the main entry), and cross-references. Although cataloging generally follows the practices of the British Museum *General Catalogue of Printed Books* (see E250a), the entries are subject to the limitations, errors, and vagaries of the individual catalogs. Vols. 1–4 are author catalogs, each with imprint (i.e., place of publication only) and subject indexes (which are cumulated in vol. 5). Vol. 5 includes subject listings (essentially taken over from the British Museum *General Catalogue of Printed Books*) for England, Ireland, London, Scotland, directories, ephemerides, and periodical publications, with separate imprint and subject indexes for each; a title index to the subject listings; a supplement to vols. 1–4, listing British Library accessions from 1976 to 1984; imprint and subject indexes to the supplement; and cumulative imprint and subject indexes to the first four volumes. (London is omitted from all the imprint indexes.) Vol. 6 is a cumulative title index to vols. 1–4 and the supplement in vol. 5. Although five of the six libraries included are copyright deposit libraries, coverage of works published in Great Britain is not comprehensive (especially for provincial and ephemeral publications); that for the rest of the world is much less so. For United States imprints, bibliographies listed in section Q: American Literature/Nineteenth Century/ Guides to Primary Works offer superior coverage. Because of an inadequate explanation of scope, users cannot be certain what kinds of publications are excluded.

Series II, Phase I, 1816–1870 provides better coverage of American imprints by incorporating the catalogs of the Library of Congress and Harvard University Libraries and transcribes titles and imprints more fully, but otherwise retains the features of the first series. Subject and imprint (i.e., place of publication only) indexes appear in every fifth volume through vol. 35 and erratically thereafter; a cumulative title index for the regular entries occupies vols. 44–53.

Series III, which was published on CD-ROM only, offers fuller information (including printers and publishers and more numerous and precise subject headings). The main volumes are useful primarily as a union list (although it appears that locations are incomplete for many entries); the imprint indexes are important tools for identifying works printed in a locale other than London; and the title indexes are essential to locating entries for anonymous works; but the subject indexes, based on and organized by Dewey classifications, are too unrefined, especially for literary topics (e.g., the English Poetry entry in *1801–1815* consists of 10 densely packed columns of *NSTC* numbers).

If possible, researchers should ignore the print and CD-ROM versions in favor of the online one. (In the CD-ROMs the Boolean search process is hopelessly complicated and the help files are anything but helpful.) Users can search by keyword, author, dates during author's lifetime, title, publication date, place of publication, publisher, subject, language, source library, series, and *NSTC* number; most of the preceding have browsable lists. Results (which can be sorted by author, title, or ascending or descending date) can be marked for e-mailing, printing, downloading, or saving to a personal archive.

News of the project and progress reports were published in *Nineteenth Century Short Title Catalogue (NSTC) Newsletter* (1983–91, irregular). Chadwyck-Healey is publishing microform collections based on selected subject categories from the *NSTC*.

The larger scope, greater number of publications, and reliance on library catalog entries rather than examination of copies mean that *NSTC* will never attain the comprehensiveness, sophistication, and level of accuracy of the other *Short-Title Catalogues* (M1377, M1990, and M1995). Fortunately, with the move to electronic form the publishers have addressed some of the weaknesses of the *NSTC*, making it far more accessible. Reviews: (1801–15) Robin Alston, *TLS: Times Literary Supplement* 6 Apr. 1984: 381–82; Patricia Fleming, *Victorian Periodicals Review* 19 (1986): 68–69; Donald H. Reiman, *Studies in Romanticism* 28 (1989): 650–56; (1801–15 and 1816–70) David McKitterick, *TLS: Times Literary Supplement* 8 May 1987: 497; (CD-ROM) McKitterick, *TLS: Times Literary Supplement* 4 July 1997: 11; Joanne Shattock, *Historical Journal* 47 (2004): 511–13; (online) Angela Courtney, *Victorian Studies* 46 (2003–04): 682–84.

For a description of the use of *NSTC* in the quantitative study of publishing and book history, see Simon Eliot, "Patterns and Trends and the *NSTC*: Some Initial Observations," *Publishing History* 42 (1997): 79–105 and 43 (1998): 71–112.

See also

> Sec. E: Libraries and Library Catalogs.
> Halkett, *Dictionary of Anonymous and Pseudonymous English Literature* (U5110).
> *New Cambridge Bibliography of English Literature*, vol. 3 (M2505).
> Records of the Worshipful Company of Stationers (M1380).
> *Whitaker's Books in Print* (M2770).

Guides to Scholarship and Criticism

SURVEYS OF RESEARCH

M2477 O'Neill, Michael, ed. *Literature of the Romantic Period: A Bibliographical Guide.* Oxford: Clarendon–Oxford UP, 1998. 410 pp.   Z2013.L58 [PR457]   016.8209'007.

Separately authored surveys of research on major authors, groups, and genres associated with English Romanticism. Chapters typically treat editions, textual studies, bibliographies, biographies, and criticism and conclude with a list of works cited (that sometimes cites additional publications), but there is no consistency across chapters in the chronological span of studies included or in organization (some discussions are excessively subdivided). Although all the chapters are by established scholars, the depth of evaluation varies considerably: the better ones compare editions, place studies within the critical reception of (or controversies surrounding) the author, and isolate topics that need investigation; some chapters, though, are little more than lists; few subject reference works to more than a cursory comment. Indexed by names and a smattering of topics. Although needing a much firmer editorial hand and a clearer statement of the editorial policy that guided selection and organization, *Literature of the Romantic Period* offers generally authoritative guidance to the state of research on British Romantic writers.

M2480   "Recent Studies in the Nineteenth Century." *Studies in English Literature,*
        1500–1900. 1 (1961)– . Annually in the Autumn issue.   PR1.S82
        820'.9.

A commissioned survey by an established scholar, with recent issues emphasizing book-length critical and historical studies and typically offering only cursory attention to editions and reference works. The essays vary considerably in breadth as well as soundness and degree of assessment. Now generally limited to books received for review, this work must be supplemented by *Romantic Movement* (M2485) and the chapters in *Year's Work in English Studies* (G330) on the Romantic and Victorian periods.

See also

> *YWES* (G330): Chapters for Nineteenth Century: Romantic Period and Nineteenth Century: Victorian Period.

SERIAL BIBLIOGRAPHIES

M2485   *The Romantic Movement: A Selective and Critical Bibliography for [1936–*
        98]. West Cornwall: Locust Hill, 1980–99. Annual.   Z6514.R6 R63
        [PN603]   016.809'9145.

> 1964–78: Supplement to *English Language Notes* 3–17 (1965–79).
> 1949–63: *Philological Quarterly* 29–43 (1950–64).
> 1936–48: *ELH: A Journal of Literary History* 4–16 (1937–49).
> (The bibliographies for 1936–70 are reprinted, with cumulative indexes, as
>   A. C. Elkins and L. J. Forstner, eds., *The Romantic Movement Bibliography,*
>   *1936–1970: A Master Cumulation,* 7 vols. [Ann Arbor: Pierian in association with Bowker, 1973].)

A bibliography of significant books, articles, and reviews on the Romantic movement in Great Britain and Western Europe. Although this work includes minor items that fall outside the scope of *MLAIB* (G335) and studies of American Romanticism that relate to the European movement, it makes no attempt at comprehensiveness. The scope has altered over the years and within individual sections so that recent volumes are more critical and selective. (For an overview of changes, see David V. Erdman's foreword to the reprint of the 1936–70 bibliographies [vol. 1, pp. vii–xi].) Entries are organized in six major divisions: general, English, French, German, Italian, and Spanish (at various times there were divisions for other national literatures such as Portuguese, Russian, and Scandinavian); each national literature has sections for bibliographies, general studies, and individual authors (some have a section for the "environment"— art, philosophy, politics, religion, science, and society). The chronological scope varies from country to country and alters to reflect changes in critical perspectives (e.g., while the English section has remained fairly stable at 1789–1837, the German one has undergone some major shifts in chronological coverage). In the later volumes, most entries are annotated: many descriptively, several critically, with a number of books receiving full reviews. Recent volumes quote from other reviews. Since the 1961 bibliography, reviews of previously listed books, composite reviews, and review essays are grouped at the end of a section. Although the later annual volumes unfortunately provide only an index of critics, the reprint of the 1936–70 bibliographies offers three cumulative indexes: authors, main entries, reviewers; subjects: personal names; subjects: categories. Although the lack of a subject index is inexcusable and although coverage varies substantially among the national literatures (Italian and Spanish are so sketchily treated that their coverage should have been discontinued), timeliness and judicious evaluation made this before its unfortunate demise the best guide to significant scholarship on the Romantic movement. Since it made no attempt at comprehensiveness, scholars must also consult "Current Bibliography" in *Keats-Shelley Journal* (M2495) and the standard serial bibliographies in section G.

M2490   *Victorian Database Online [1945–].* Comp. and ed. Brahma Chaudhuri.
         LITIR Database. Online. 30 July 2005 <http://
         www.victoriandatabase.com>.
     This produces and subsumes a confusing array of print and CD-ROM products (with recent ones produced on demand):
     A Comprehensive Bibliography of Victorian Studies, 1970–1984. 3 vols. Edmonton: LITIR Database, 1984–85.
     Cumulative Bibliography of Victorian Studies, 1945–1969. Comp. and ed. Chaudhuri and Fred Radford. 2 vols. 2000. *1970–1984.* Comp. and ed. Chaudhuri. 2 vols. 1988. *1985–1989.* 1990. 1,037 pp. *1990–1994.* 1995. 880 pp. *1995–1999.* 1999. 825 pp. *1945–1969.* 2 vols. 2000. *1970–2000.* 3 vols. 2001. *2000–2004.* 2005. 726 pp.
     Annual Bibliography of Victorian Studies, [1976–]. Edmonton: LITIR Database, 1980– . Annual.   Z2019.A64 [DA533]   016.941.
     Victorian Database on CD-ROM: 1945–2004. 2005.
     Reviews, which are not included until 1995, can be located in Chaudhuri, *Cumulated Index to Reviews of Books on Victorian Studies, 1975–1989* (1990, 1,197 pp.).
     A database of books, articles, and dissertations, primarily in English, on Great Britain from c. 1830 to 1914. This work emphasizes studies of language and literature, with some attention to other subjects; for transitional authors, it includes only those studies treating the Victorian period. The online version can be searched only by author, title, and keyword (each limited by date; however, the date limitation sometimes malfunctions). Records (which are returned only in descending alphabetical order) can be marked for printing or downloading. In the print versions entries are listed alphabetically by scholar in seven classified divisions: general and reference works, fine arts, philosophy and religion, history, social sciences, science and technology, and language and literature. The last has sections for general works, reference works, drama and theater, poetry, prose, fiction, children's literature, and individual authors (with lists of general works, bibliographies, biography and correspondence, general criticism, and studies of individual works). A few entries are accompanied by brief descriptive annotations. Users searching the print versions for publications on a minor author must be sure to use the subject index, since writers who are the subject of fewer than three studies are lumped together under "Other Authors" in the classified listings. Four

indexes in each *Annual Bibliography* and the *Cumulated Index* (subjects; scholars; reviewers; titles of works); each volume of the *Comprehensive Bibliography* has three indexes (subjects; scholars; titles of works), and those in vol. 3 are cumulative; the *Cumulative Bibliography* offers the same three indexes. The subject indexing and keyword access in the online version, while useful, are limited to literary authors and title keywords (with some significant omissions); records do not consistently expand journal titles or other abbreviations (a list of journal abbreviations can be accessed through the Help screen). Much less accessible than it should be (especially the online version), reliant on secondary sources for citations to some books rather than firsthand examination, and far short of the comprehensiveness it claims, *Victorian Database Online* is nonetheless useful for its cumulation of studies. Researchers must also consult the other bibliographies listed in this section and in section G: Serial Bibliographies, Indexes, and Abstracts, as well as "RSVP Bibliography" (M2555) and "Guide to the Year's Work in Victorian Poetry" (M2720).

M2495   "Current Bibliography [1 July 1950–]." *Keats-Shelley Journal* 1 (1952)– .
    PR4836.A145   821.705.
    The work is cumulated as the following:

        Hartley, Robert A., ed. *Keats, Shelley, Byron, Hunt, and Their Circles: A Bibliography: July 1, 1962–December 31, 1974.* Lincoln: U of Nebraska P, 1978. 487 pp.
        Green, David Bonnell, and Edwin Graves Wilson, eds. *Keats, Shelley, Byron, Hunt, and Their Circles: A Bibliography: July 1, 1950–June 30, 1962.* Lincoln: U of Nebraska P, 1964. 323 pp.
        Current Bibliography: Keats-Shelley Journal [1994–99]. Online. 8 Jan. 2006 <http://www.rc.umd.edu/reference/ksjbib>. (The current bibliographer plans to make additional years available.)

    An annotated bibliography that attempts comprehensive coverage of Byron, Shelley, Keats, Hunt, and their circles. This excludes textbooks, but otherwise includes substantial references as well as reprints or translations of even a single poem and (between 1 July 1955 and 31 December 1972) phonograph recordings. The early numbers list publications from 1940 through 1950 that were omitted from other standard bibliographies. Entries in the print version are currently organized in five divisions: general works (with sections for bibliographies and general studies of English Romanticism), Byron, Hunt (Hunt and Hazlitt since the bibliography for 1984), Keats, and the Shelleys (until 41 [1992], only Percy Shelley); the online version separates Hunt and Hazlitt and Percy Bysshe and Mary Shelley. In the author sections, primary works appear first, followed by an alphabetical list of studies on the writer and his circle. In some years, entries are accompanied by brief descriptive annotations (with several works left unannotated in the early volumes; the annotations disappear altogether with the bibliography for 2000 in 50 [2001]) and review citations (in recent years, reviews are interspersed in the lists of studies). In the online version descriptions are longer (but journal acronyms are not expanded), some entries include links to a table of contents or other material, and reviews appear in a separate file. Indexed by names and works referred to in annotations or titles and by scholars. The two reprints cumulate the individual indexes. Because the makeup of the various circles is not consistent throughout the volumes, users should consult the index to locate studies of individuals other than the four principal authors. Searching the online version is limited to a Web browser's find function, and each year's bibliography must be searched separately. This offers fuller coverage of the six writers and their circles than *Romantic Movement* (M2485) or the serial bibliographies and indexes in section G.

M2500   *Victorian Studies Bibliography [1999–   ]*. Indiana UP, 2006–   . Online. 27 Jan. 2006 <http://www.letrs.indiana.edu/web/v/victbib/index.html>.
      "Victorian Bibliography for [1932–2001]." *Victorian Studies* 1–45 (1958–2003). (The bibliographies for 2000–01 are available only in electronic form through Project Muse [K705].)   PR1.V5   820'.9'008.
      1932–56: *Modern Philology* 30–54 (1933–57).
      Reprinted, with cumulative indexes, as follows:
         Tobias, Richard C., ed. *Bibliographies of Studies in Victorian Literature for the Ten Years 1975–1984*. New York: AMS, 1991. 1,130 pp.
         Freeman, Ronald E., ed. *Bibliographies of Studies in Victorian Literature for the Ten Years 1965–1974*. New York: AMS, 1981. 876 pp.
         Slack, Robert C., ed. *Bibliographies of Studies in Victorian Literature for the Ten Years 1955–1964*. Urbana: U of Illinois P, 1967. 461 pp.
         Wright, Austin, ed. *Bibliographies of Studies in Victorian Literature for the Ten Years 1945–1954*. Urbana: U of Illinois P, 1956. 310 pp.
         Templeman, William D., ed. *Bibliographies of Studies in Victorian Literature for the Thirteen Years 1932–1944*. Urbana: U of Illinois P, 1945. 450 pp.
      A selective international bibliography of "noteworthy" publications, including reviews, on Victorian England. Over the years, coverage has become more inclusive but with a corresponding decrease in annotations, so that recent bibliographies offer only an occasional brief explanation of an uninformative title. (Early volumes offer more substantial commentary, including some full reviews and quotations from others; however, evaluations during the first two decades are far less rigorous than they should be.) The bibliographies for 1932–74 list works alphabetically in four divisions: bibliographical materials; economic, political, religious, and social environment; movements of ideas, literary forms, and anthologies; individual authors. With the 1975 bibliography, entries appear in one of six divisions: bibliographical materials; history, historiography, and historical documents; economics, education, politics, religion, science, and social environment; architecture, fine arts, household arts, performing arts, and city planning; literary history, literary forms, literary ideas; individual authors. Since the bibliography for 1966, listings under transitional figures such as Conrad and Shaw are restricted to studies dealing with the Victorian period. Articles in author journals and newsletters are awkwardly grouped under a single entry for the periodical, in some volumes books are not listed unless they have been reviewed, and users would benefit from a more refined classification system and better cross-referencing. Until recently, the annual issues (and subsequent cumulations) are seriously marred by a multitude of typographical errors, inaccurate citations, and faulty cross-references. The five volumes of reprints provide useful—but incomplete—cumulative indexes: of Victorian authors in the 1932–44 volume; of scholars, Victorian figures, and some topics in those for 1945–74; and of scholars, authors (Victorian and otherwise), and subjects in that for 1975–84. The cumulation for 1965–74 corrects some errors (pp. 739–42) and provides an introductory statistical and narrative survey of trends in scholarship for the period. For the history of the print bibliography, see Edward H. Cohen, " 'Victorian Bibliography': Seventy Years after," *Victorian Studies* 44 (2001–2): 625–35.
      The online version can be searched by keyword, author (which also maps to reviewers), and title or browsed by the six divisions listed above. Because only the sub-

headings economics, education, politics, religion, science, and social environment are in separate lists, browsing bibliographical materials, individual authors, and literary history, literary forms, and literary ideas exceeds the search engine's sort limit. Records can be saved to a bookbag for downloading or e-mailing. Unfortunately, a substantial number of brief records are miscoded (e.g., a keyword search for *Shakespeare* returned 20 brief records, 8 of which omitted author and title; the full records are correctly coded); many journal acronyms are not expanded (and there is no key on the Web site); and related records are not linked.

Despite its faults (and the limited functionality of the online version), the work offers the fullest, most current list of scholarship on the period, but scholars must also consult *Victorian Database Online* (M2490), "RSVP Bibliography" (M2555), "Guide to the Year's Work in Victorian Poetry" (M2720), and the standard serial bibliographies and indexes in section G.

See also

> Sec. G: Serial Bibliographies, Indexes, and Abstracts.
> *ABELL* (G340): English Literature/Nineteenth Century section.
> *MLAIB* (G335): English Language and Literature division in the volumes for 1921–25; English X in the volumes for 1926–56; English IX in the volumes for 1957–80; and English Literature/1800–1899 (as well as any larger chronological sections encompassing the century) in later volumes. Researchers must also check the headings beginning "English Literature," "Romantic," and "Victorian" in the subject index to post-1980 volumes and in the online thesaurus.

OTHER BIBLIOGRAPHIES

M2505   *The New Cambridge Bibliography of English Literature* (*NCBEL*). Vol. 3:
          1800–1900. Ed. George Watson. Cambridge: Cambridge UP, 1969.
          1,948 cols.   Z2011.N45 [PR83]   016.82.

(For a full discussion of *NCBEL*, see entry M1385.) Primary works and scholarship are organized in six divisions (each subdivided and classified as its subject requires): introduction (general studies, book production and distribution, literary relations with the Continent), poetry (1800–35, 1835–70, 1870–1900), novel (1800–35, 1835–70, 1870–1900, children's books), drama (1800–35, 1835–70, 1870–1900), prose (1800–35, 1835–70, 1870–1900, history, philosophy, religion, English studies, travel, sport, education, periodicals), Anglo-Irish literature (through 1916). Vol. 3 of the *Cambridge Bibliography of English Literature* (M1385a) is still occasionally useful for its coverage of the intellectual, social, and political background; education; and Commonwealth literature (which *NCBEL* drops).

Users must familiarize themselves with the organization, remember that there is considerable unevenness of coverage among subdivisions, realize that the third edition of *CBEL* (M1376) does not supersede *NCBEL*'s coverage of secondary works, and consult the index volume (vol. 5) rather than the provisional index in vol. 3. Review: Richard D. Altick, *JEGP: Journal of English and Germanic Philology* 70 (1971): 139–45.

See also

> McKenna, *Irish Literature, 1800–1875* (N2985).

DISSERTATIONS AND THESES

M2510   Altick, Richard D., and William R. Matthews, comps. *Guide to Doctoral Dissertations in Victorian Literature, 1886–1958.* Urbana: U of Illinois P, 1960. 119 pp.   Z2013.A4   016.82'09'008.

A classified bibliography of 2,105 dissertations entirely or partly on British literature from c. 1837 to 1900. Coverage extends through 1957 for France, 1956 for the United Kingdom and Germany, and 1958 for Austria, Switzerland, and the United States. Dissertations are listed alphabetically by writer in nine sections: general topics, themes and intellectual influences, fiction, drama, poetry, literary criticism, periodicals, foreign relations, and individual authors. Indexed by dissertation writers. Although compiled largely from printed institutional and national lists (which are themselves not always accurate or complete), the *Guide* also includes several dissertations that have otherwise escaped notice. Thorough but not exhaustive, this work significantly reduces the time researchers would otherwise spend poring over the bibliographies in section H: Guides to Dissertations and Theses. A supplement would be welcomed by scholars.

See also

Sec. H: Guides to Dissertations and Theses.

RELATED TOPICS

M2515   Brown, Lucy M., and Ian R. Christie, eds. *Bibliography of British History, 1789–1851.* Oxford: Clarendon–Oxford UP, 1977. 759 pp.   Z2019.B76 [DA520]   016.94107'3.

An extensive, albeit rigorously selective, bibliography of primary and secondary materials published through the early 1970s. Because of the multitude of publications on the era, Brown emphasizes reference sources. The 4,782 entries are listed chronologically (for the most part) in 15 extensively classified divisions: general reference works; political, constitutional, legal, ecclesiastical, military, naval, economic, social, cultural, and local history; Wales; Scotland; Ireland; and British Empire. A majority of the entries are descriptively annotated and frequently cite several related studies. Indexed by persons and a few subjects. An essential guide for cross-disciplinary research. Review: John Saville, *Victorian Studies* 22 (1979): 203–04.

Continued by Hanham, *Bibliography of British History, 1851–1914* (M2520). A convenient, more selective bibliography is Smith, *Late Georgian and Regency England, 1760–1837* (M2260a).

M2520   Hanham, H. J., comp. and ed. *Bibliography of British History, 1851–1914.* Oxford: Clarendon–Oxford UP, 1976. 1,606 pp.   Z2019.H35 [DA530] 016.942.

A massive, yet selective, bibliography of primary and secondary works (through 1973) organized in 13 extensively classified divisions: general reference works and studies, political and constitutional history, colonies and foreign relations, armed forces, legal system, religion, economic history, social history, intellectual and cultural history, local history, Wales, Scotland, and Ireland. A majority of the entries are annotated, many with judicious evaluative comments and citations to related studies (which nearly double the 10,829 numbered entries). Indexed by persons and subjects. An indispensable guide to historical scholarship on the period (and one of the better volumes of this important series). The earlier half of the century is covered in Brown, *Bibliography of British History, 1789–1851* (M2515). Review: Josef L. Altholz, *Victorian Studies* 21 (1977): 108–09.

Convenient, more selective bibliographies are Josef L. Altholz, *Victorian England, 1837–1901*, Conference on British Studies Bibliographical Handbooks (Cambridge: Cambridge UP for the Conf. on British Studies, 1970, 100 pp.); and David Nicholls, *Nineteenth-Century Britain, 1815–1914*, Critical Bibliographies in Modern History (Folkestone: Dawson; Hamden: Archon, 1978, 170 pp.). Altholz is decidedly more thorough and authoritative, cites articles as well as books (through 1967), but offers only an occasional brief descriptive comment. Nicholls is current through 1977 and provides evaluative annotations, but it cites only books and is designed for the undergraduate.

See also

Royal Historical Society Bibliography (M1400).
Smith, *Late Georgian and Regency England, 1760–1837* (M2260a).

Biographical Dictionaries

The *Oxford Dictionary of National Biography* (M1425) remains the standard general source of biographical information for the nineteenth century; however, Boase, *Modern English Biography* (M1425a), is an important supplement.

See also

Sec. J: Biographical Sources.
Dictionary of Literary Biography (J600).

Periodicals

CONTEMPORARY PERIODICALS

Research Methods

M2525   Vann, J. Don, and Rosemary T. VanArsdel, eds. *Victorian Periodicals: A Guide to Research.* 2 vols. New York: MLA, 1978–89.   PN5124.P4 V5   052.

Vol. 1 is a guide to research methods and reference works (to 1977) essential to the study of periodicals (primarily elite British ones) from 1824 to 1900. Individual essays treat bibliographies and inventories, finding lists, biographical resources, general histories of the press, histories and studies of individual periodicals, identification of authors, and circulation and the Stamp Tax. Vol. 2 is both a companion and a supplement to the earlier one. Along with appendixes evaluating the *Wellesley Index* (M2545) and updating the essays on finding lists, biographical resources, general histories, and histories and studies of individual periodicals, it has chapters on Scottish, Welsh, feminist, religious, and children's periodicals; the radical and labor press; publishers' archives; periodicals of the 1890s; serialized novels; periodicals and art history; and desiderata to the twenty-first century. In both volumes, contributors typically outline their subject, describe (with occasional evaluative comments) essential reference sources (but without complete citations), discuss research strategies, and sometimes suggest topics for further work. Indexed by persons and titles. Individual essays vary in accuracy (in both citations and evaluations of reference works), but, overall, *Victorian Periodicals* is an essential guide for those working in this expanding field. Review: John Bush Jones, *Analytical and Enumerative Bibliography* 4 (1980): 107–23.

Some of the preceding essays are complemented by Vann and VanArsdel, eds., *Victorian Periodicals and Victorian Society* (Toronto: U of Toronto P, 1994, 370 pp.), a collection of 18 essays on law, medicine, architecture, the military, science, music, illustration, authorship and the book trade, theater, transport, the financial and trade press, advertising, agriculture, temperance, comic periodicals, sports, workers' journals, and student publications. Each contributor typically offers a general introduction to the subject, a discussion of available bibliographic tools (or the lack thereof), an annotated list of periodicals (with locations), and suggestions for further research. Indexed by persons and titles of periodicals.

For the state of research on nineteenth-century periodicals in Australia, Canada, India, New Zealand, southern Africa, and other former British colonies, see Vann and VanArsdel, eds., *Periodicals of Queen Victoria's Empire: An Exploration* (Toronto: U of Toronto P, 1996, 371 pp.).

See also

Latham, "The Rise of Periodical Studies" (A45).

Guides to Primary Works

For other guides, indexes, lists, and bibliographies, see Scott Bennett, "The Bibliographic Control of Victorian Periodicals" (vol. 1, pp. 35–51), in Vann, *Victorian Periodicals* (M2525). Many nineteenth-century periodicals have been reproduced in microfilm in two series by University Microfilms International: *Early British Periodicals, 1681–1921* and *English Literary Periodicals, 1681–1914*.

Union Lists

M2530   Fulton, Richard D., and C. M. Colee, gen. eds. *Union List of Victorian Serials: A Union List of Selected Nineteenth-Century British Serials Available in United States and Canadian Libraries.* Garland Reference Library of the Humanities 530. New York: Garland, 1985. 732 pp.   Z6956.G6 F85 [PN5124.P4]   011′.34.

A union list of periodicals published between 1824 and 1900 and listed in *New Cambridge Bibliography of English Literature* (M2505) (augmented by about 100 science and technology titles). Compiled from regional union lists, library lists, and reports by volunteers who examined actual holdings, the *Union List* records the holdings of 376 libraries (predominantly in the United States), especially major regional libraries and those with important Victorian serials collections. (There are some notable omissions, however.) A typical entry provides *Waterloo Directory of Victorian Periodicals* number (entry M2540a), *NCBEL* reference, bibliographical information, notes (which may include title, series, and volume changes; details of conflicting information in standard references; and numbering irregularities), and locations (with exact holdings—accurate and complete for 1824–1900 only for those periodicals published outside these dates—including microform copies or reprints and notes on special copies or cataloging problems). While many questions of dates and titles remain unsolved, entries alert researchers to conflicting information in standard reference sources. Although neither comprehensive nor definitive, this work is more thorough and reliable in its bibliographical descriptions and locations than *Union List of Serials* (K640a), *British Union-Catalogue of Periodicals* (K645a), or *New Cambridge Bibliography of English Literature*. See *WorldCat* (E225) and RLG Union Catalog (E230) for other locations; for serials after 1800 Fulton's descriptions are frequently superseded by *Waterloo Directory of English Newspaper and Periodicals* (M2540), *Waterloo Directory of Irish Newspapers and Periodicals* (N3000), and *Waterloo Directory of Scottish Newspapers and Periodicals* (O3103). Review: Kathryn Chittick, *Victorian Periodicals Review* 18 (1985): 149–51.

M2535   Ward, William S., comp. *Index and Finding List of Serials Published in the British Isles, 1789–1832*. Lexington: U of Kentucky P, 1953. 180 pp. Z6956.E5 W27   016.052.

———. "*Index and Finding List of Serials Published in the British Isles, 1789–1832*: A Supplementary List." *Bulletin of the New York Public Library* 77 (1974): 291–97.   Z881.N6B   027.47471.

A list of periodicals and newspapers held by some 475 libraries and newspaper offices in the United States and Great Britain. Serials are listed by title (or by institution or learned society for publications lacking a distinctive title) and accompanied by minimal bibliographical information. Ward is designed to be used with *Union List of Serials* (K640a); *Union Catalogue of the Periodical Publications in the University Libraries of the British Isles*, comp. Marion G. Roupell (London: Joint Standing Committee on Lib. Co-operation, Natl. Central Lib., 1937, 712 pp.); and *British Union-Catalogue of Periodicals* (K645a); therefore, only additional or corrected holdings are recorded (but imprecisely in many instances). Although it offers numerous additions to the standard union lists, Ward must be supplemented by *WorldCat* (E225), RLG Union Catalog (E230), and *Serials in the British Library* (K645). For serials after 1800, Ward is superseded by *Waterloo Directory of English Newspapers and Periodicals* (M2540), *Waterloo Directory of Irish Newspapers and Periodicals* (N3000), and *Waterloo Directory of Scottish Newspapers and Periodicals* (O3103). A new edition covering 1789–1800, with full bibliographical information and details of holdings, would be welcome.

See also

Sec. K: Periodicals/Union Lists.

Bibliographies

M2540   North, John S., ed. *The Waterloo Directory of English Newspapers and Periodicals, 1800–1900*. 5 sers. Waterloo: North Waterloo Academic P, 1994– .   Z6956.E5 W38 [PN5117]   015.42'035. Online. 29 June 2006 <http://www.victorianperiodicals.com/series2>. Updated daily.

A bibliography and finding list of approximately 125,000 serials (when complete) published in England during the nineteenth century. Publications are listed alphabetically by earliest title or issuing body for nonspecific titles (entries are repeated under absorbed or merged titles). Entries record, when possible, titles, alternative or later titles, subtitles, and title changes, along with reproductions of title pages for about 3,000 publications; series, volume, and issue numbering; publication dates; places of publication; editors; proprietors; publishers; printers; editorial or production staff; size; price; circulation; frequency of publication; illustrations; issuing bodies; indexing; departments; religious or political perspectives; miscellaneous notes; mergers; references to studies or bibliographies; and locations. Six indexes: titles; cities of publication; counties of publication; issuing bodies; persons; subjects. Much of the information is based on firsthand examination of representative issues. The online version and publication in a rolling series of printed sets (wherein each new set cumulates, integrates, expands, and corrects the preceding one) allows for continual revision and expansion as additional collections are visited.

The online version offers four search options: Basic Search (keyword searching of title, issuing body, persons, town, county or country, or subject); Advanced Search (combined keyword searching of title, issuing body, persons, subject, place of publication, date); Global Search (keyword searching of the entire text of all records); Browse (the six indexes included in the printed version [see above]). Results of a search can be printed or saved only through a Web browser.

Even though incomplete, *Waterloo Directory* already offers the most thorough and accessible accumulation of information on English serial publications. The flexibility of searching the online version provides ready access for the first time to essential sources for the study of nearly all facets of nineteenth-century English life. An indispensable work that—like its companions, *Waterloo Directory of Irish Newspapers and Periodicals* (N3000) and *Waterloo Directory of Scottish Newspapers and Periodical* (O3103)—stands as an example of the kind of guide needed for serials of other countries and periods. For a history of the *Waterloo Directory* project and explanation of its importance, see Rosemary T. Van Arsdel, "John North, the *Waterloo Directory*, and an RSVP History Lesson!" *Victorian Periodicals Review* 36 (2003): 100–108.

For a list of periodicals addressed to women and of articles about women in other serials, see E. M. Palmegiano, *Women and British Periodicals, 1832–1867: A Bibliography*, Garland Reference Library of the Humanities 55 (New York: Garland, 1976, 118 pp.)—also published as *Victorian Periodicals Newsletter* 9 (1976): 1–36—with additions in Anne Lohrli, "Women in British Periodicals," *Victorian Periodicals Newsletter* 9 (1976): 128–30.

See also

   Bibliography of British Newspapers (M1440).
   Sullivan, *British Literary Magazines* (M1445).

Indexes

M2545   Houghton, Walter E., Esther Rhoads Houghton, and Jean Harris
        Slingerland, eds. *Wellesley Index to Victorian Periodicals, 1824–1900 on
        CD-ROM*. Vers. 1.0. London: Routledge, 1999.

        ———. *Wellesley Index to Victorian Periodicals, 1824–1900*. 5 vols.
        Toronto: U of Toronto P; London: Routledge, 1966–89.   AI3.W45
        052'.016.

The print version is an index to the prose contents of 43 major periodicals. Poetry is excluded—unfortunately, but understandably so, because of the quantity and insurmountable problems in attributing authorship. Vols. 1 through 4 each consists of three parts. Organized by periodical, pt. A is an issue-by-issue list of contents that explains uninformative titles, identifies reprints, and attributes authorship (citing evidence) for individual articles and reviews. The list for each periodical is prefaced by a summary of publishing history and editorial policy, discussion of sources for attribution of authorship, and a bibliography. Pt. B is an author bibliography of works listed in pt. A. Pt. C indexes initials and pseudonyms. Unfortunately, authors and titles of books reviewed are not indexed, nor are subjects. Additions and corrections to vol. 1 appear in vol. 2, pp. 1181–221; to vols. 1 and 2, in vol. 3, pp. 977–1012; and to vols. 1–3, in vol. 4, pp. 765–826. Vol. 5 cumulates pts. B and C, prints additions and corrections to the preceding volumes, and identifies entries in pt. A that were subsequently altered in appendixes to vols. 1–4; users must be certain to check *Victorian Periodicals Review* beginning with 23.2 (1990) for important additions and corrections. In addition, Eileen M. Curran tracks addenda and corrigenda in *The Curran Index: Additions to and Corrections of* The Wellesley Index to Victorian Periodicals (http://victorianresearch.org/curranindex.html).

The CD-ROM adds coverage of two periodicals, incorporates some corrections and additions from the print volumes as well as *Victorian Periodicals Review* to the end of 1997, and provides hyperlinks among entries. The ability to search by periodical, contributor, pseudonym, and title keyword remedies some of the problems of access faced by users of the print volumes. The text of the CD-ROM is also searchable through *C19: The Nineteenth Century Index* (M2466), which offers a superior search interface that allows users to search by the preceding fields, to limit searches by date, and to sort results by author, periodical title, relevance, or date (ascending or descending). Records can be marked for e-mailing, printing, downloading, or saving to a personal archive. Because of spelling variants, users should check the pull-down lists associated with the search fields.

The high degree of accuracy and reliability makes the *Wellesley Index* an indispensable source for efficiently scanning the contents of journals (especially inaccessible ones), for gauging the spirit of the age as reflected in a range of leading periodicals, for comparing the contents of influential serials, for determining the authorship of a majority of the numerous unsigned or pseudonymous contributions (although attributions cannot be automatically accepted, since some are based on unauthenticated sources or internal evidence), and for identifying pseudonyms used in periodicals, which Halkett, *Dictionary of Anonymous and Pseudonymous English Literature* (U5110), does not cover. A monumental scholarly work that has revolutionized the study of Victorian periodicals. For a history of the work, see Rosemary T. VanArsdel, "The *Wellesley Index* Forty Years Later (1966–2006)," *Victorian Periodicals Review* 39 (2006): 257–65. Reviews: (vol. 1) Robert A. Colby, *Modern Philology* 65 (1968): 411–14; Ian Jack, *Review of English Studies* ns 19 (1968): 228–31; (vol. 2) Colby, *Modern Philology* 71 (1974): 455–59; Jack, *Review of English Studies* ns 25 (1974): 491–93; (vol. 3) William S. Ward, *JEGP: Journal of English and Germanic Philology* 79 (1980): 454–57; (vol. 4) Richard D. Altick, *Modern Philology* 87 (1989): 101–04; Barbara Quinn Schmidt, *Victorian Periodicals Review* 22 (1989): 71–74; P. L. Shillingsburg, *Analytical and Enumerative Bibliography* ns 2 (1988): 126–28.

The *Wellesley Index* archive, on deposit in the Wellesley College Archives, contains incomplete records of an additional 15 periodicals. For a brief description of the archive and evaluation of *Wellesley Index*, see VanArsdel, "The *Wellesley Index* to Victorian Periodicals, 1824–1900" (vol. 2, pp. 165–67), in Vann, *Victorian Periodicals* (M2525); further information and a guide are available from Wilma R. Slaight, Wellesley College Archives, Margaret Clapp Library, Wellesley, MA 02481 (wslaight@wellesley.edu).

M2550   Ward, William S., comp. *Literary Reviews in British Periodicals, 1798–*
        1820: A Bibliography: With a Supplementary List of General (Non-review)
        Articles on Literary Subjects. 2 vols. New York: Garland, 1972.
        ————. *Literary Reviews in British Periodicals, 1821–1826: A Bibliography:*
        With a Supplementary List of General (Non-Review) Articles on Literary
        Subjects. Garland Reference Library of the Humanities 60. New York:
        Garland, 1977. 301 pp.   Z2013.W36 [PR453]   016.809'034.

   A bibliography of reviews of belles lettres, criticism, and other writings by literary
authors published between 1798 and 1826. Books are organized alphabetically by author, then by publication date, with reviews following alphabetically by periodical title.
Nonreview articles are relegated to various appendixes. Appendix A includes general
articles about authors appearing in the reviews section. Appendix B is in five parts: (1)
volumes of general criticism reviewed, (2) general criticism articles, and articles on (3)
poetry, (4) fiction, and (5) drama and theater. Appendix C (in *1798–1820* only) lists
reviews of operas. The prefaces offer general suggestions for further research. These two
works are essential sources for investigating the contemporary critical reception of an
author or work and for locating early criticism. For earlier coverage, see Ward, *Literary
Reviews in British Periodicals, 1789–1797* (M2280).

   Most reviews published between 1793 and 1824 of books by Wordsworth, Coleridge, Byron, Shelley, and Keats (along with a few reviews of other writers) are conveniently reproduced in Donald H. Reiman, ed., *The Romantics Reviewed: Contemporary
Reviews of British Romantic Writers*, 9 vols. (New York: Garland, 1972).

See also

   Poole's Index to Periodical Literature (Q4150).
   Times Index (M1450).

Guides to Scholarship and Criticism

Serial Bibliographies

M2555   "RSVP Bibliography [1971–   ]." *Victorian Periodicals Review* 6 (1973)–   .
        Irregular. Title varies.   PN5124.P4 V52   052.

   An annotated author list of books, dissertations, articles, and reviews about periodicals published between 1800 and 1914 in the United Kingdom and its colonies
(with some coverage of English-language periodicals from the rest of the world). Unfortunately, annotations in recent installments rarely extend beyond a terse sentence.
Indexed by persons, subjects, and periodicals. Entries for 1972 through 1987 are cumulated and supplemented in Uffelman, *Nineteenth-Century Periodical Press in Britain*
(M2560). For earlier scholarship, see Madden, *Nineteenth-Century Periodical Press in
Britain* (M2560). Although this work is the standard serial bibliography, its coverage is
far from exhaustive.

Other Bibliographies

M2560   Madden, Lionel, and Diana Dixon, comps. *The Nineteenth-Century
        Periodical Press in Britain: A Bibliography of Modern Studies, 1901–1971.*

Supplement to *Victorian Periodicals Newsletter* 8.3 (M1975). Toronto: Victorian Periodicals Newsletter, 1975. 76 pp. Also published as Garland Reference Library of the Humanities 53. New York: Garland, 1976. 280 pp.   Z6956.G6 M3 [PN5117]   016.072.

Uffelman, Larry K., comp. *The Nineteenth-Century Periodical Press in Britain: A Bibliography of Modern Studies, 1972–1987.* Supplement to *Victorian Periodicals Review* 25 (1992): 124 pp.

An annotated bibliography of books, articles, dissertations, and theses devoted to the history, editing, and publication of general interest periodicals; Uffelman cumulates and expands "RSVP Bibliography" (M2555). Madden excludes examinations of a periodical's treatment of specific topics, literary history studies, and attributions of individual works (however, such exclusions are not rigorously observed); Uffelman is much less restrictive. The 4,717 entries are organized in four liberally cross-referenced divisions: reference works (listed chronologically), general histories of periodicals and newspapers (listed chronologically), studies of individual periodicals (listed alphabetically by the earliest nineteenth-century title, then chronologically), and studies and memoirs of proprietors, editors, journalists, and contributors (listed alphabetically by person, then chronologically). Indexed by names. Madden is carelessly compiled (there are numerous omissions, uneven annotations, inconsistencies in coverage, and far too many errors in the citations and index), Uffelman is more accurate but also offers uneven annotations (a substantial number of entries are unannotated) and overlooks numerous studies, and both are inefficiently organized and inadequately indexed; nevertheless, the two offer the most complete guide to scholarship on the topic. They must be supplemented, however, by the serial bibliographies and indexes in section G and by Ward, *British Periodicals and Newspapers, 1789–1832* (M2565). For studies published after 1987, see the annual "RSVP Bibliography" (M2555). Reviews: (Madden) Walter E. Houghton, *Library* 5th ser. 32 (1977): 386–87; John Bush Jones, *Analytical and Enumerative Bibliography* 4 (1980): 107–23 (with several additions and corrections).

M2565   Ward, William S. *British Periodicals and Newspapers, 1789–1832: A Bibliography of Secondary Sources.* Lexington: UP of Kentucky, [1972]. 386 pp.   Z6956.G6 W37   016.052.

A bibliography of books, articles, theses, and dissertations (through the late 1960s) about periodicals and newspapers listed in Ward, *Index and Finding List of Serials* (M2535). Entries are listed in six divisions: general bibliographies and bibliographical studies, general studies, periodicals, people, places, and special subjects. Brief descriptive annotations accompany some entries. Three indexes: scholars; subjects; library catalogs and union lists. Ward offers generally better coverage than Madden, *Nineteenth-Century Periodical Press* (M2560), of the early decades of the nineteenth century, especially for studies of topics and literary authors; however, the organization, paucity of cross-references, and utterly inadequate subject indexing make it a frustrating work to search. For recent scholarship, see "RSVP Bibliography" (M2555).

See also

Linton, *Newspaper Press in Britain* (M1455).
Vann, *Victorian Periodicals* (M2525).
White, *English Literary Journal to 1900* (M1460).

Genres

Many works in section L: Genres and most in section M: English Literature/General/ Genres are useful for research in nineteenth-century literature.

FICTION

Sections L: Genres/Fiction and M: English Literature/General/Genres/Fiction include several works useful for research in nineteenth-century fiction.

Literary Handbooks, Dictionaries, and Encyclopedias

M2633   Sutherland, John. *The Stanford Companion to Victorian Fiction.* Stanford: Stanford UP, 1989. 696 pp. British ed.: *The Longman Companion to Victorian Fiction.* Harlow: Longman, 1988. 696 pp.   PR871.S87 823'.809'03.

    An encyclopedia, whose 1,606 entries include novelists, publishers, illustrators, periodicals, genres, forms, schools, and more than 500 novels. Two appendixes: pseudonyms; maiden and married names of women. Indexed in *Biography and Genealogy Master Index* (J565). With its informative entries—leavened with wit, pithy judgments, and the significant detail or anecdote—Sutherland is an entertaining and generally trustworthy companion, especially to the lesser-known Victorian novelists and their works. Reviews: Miriam Allott, *Review of English Studies* ns 42 (1991): 130–32; Richard Jenkyns, *TLS: Times Literary Supplement* 28 July–3 Aug. 1989: 817.

See also

    Dictionary of British Literary Characters: 18th- and 19th-Century Novels (M1507).

Guides to Primary Works

Bibliographies and Indexes

Monica Correa Fryckstedt is compiling *A Guide to English Fiction of the 1860s*, a checklist, organized by title, of some 2,500 novels published in Great Britain during the 1860s, along with reviews of them in more than 50 periodicals. For a description of the project and sample entries, see Fryckstedt, "Compiling A Guide to English Fiction of the 1860s," *Publishing History* 39 (1996): 55–86.

M2635   Sadleir, Michael. *XIX Century Fiction: A Bibliographical Record Based on His Own Collection.* 2 vols. London: Constable; Berkeley: U of California P, 1951.   Z2014.F4 S16   016.8237.

    A descriptive catalog of Sadleir's collection—now at the University of California, Los Angeles—with some additions (identified by an asterisk) from other sources to complete the list of first editions for authors not previously subjects of bibliographies. Reflecting Sadleir's tastes and interests, the collection emphasizes rare and unusual editions of British authors between 1800 and 1899, especially "Silver Fork" novels and those published in two or three volumes; generally excludes major novelists and those who published fiction before 1800; and includes a few foreign writers notable for the rarity of their English editions and some British novels published after 1900. The novels are organized in three divisions: an author catalog of first editions as well as variant issues, later editions of textual significance, and multiple copies; the Yellow-Back collection (books issued in colored noncloth bindings); and principal series of fiction and novels. Only the author catalog fully describes editions by recording title, subtitle, number of volumes and pagination, imprint, binding, provenance, notes on bibliographical points, and references to other bibliographies. A headnote indicates the completeness of each author list. (Users should note that entry numbers skip from 2099 to 3000.) Indexed by titles in vol. 1, by titles and by authors in vol. 2. Although the catalog includes only a small fraction of the novels published during the century, the careful descriptions and numerous unique items make Sadleir a valuable source of bibliographical and textual information, a significant contribution to the much needed record of fiction published during the nineteenth century, and one of the monumental catalogs of a private collection. Supplemented by Wolff, *Nineteenth-Century Fiction* (M2660), which Sadleir's catalog inspired, and by *English Catalogue of Books* (M2470), which remains the most complete list of novels published during the century. The subject index described by Bradford A. Booth ("An Analytical Subject-Index to the Sadleir Collection," *Nineteenth-Century Fiction* 23 [1968]: 217–20) has apparently not survived. Reviews: Hugh G. Dick, *Nineteenth-Century Fiction* 6 (1951): 209–17; *Times Literary Supplement* 13 Apr. 1951: 234.

M2640   Grimes, Janet, and Diva Daims. *Novels in English by Women, 1891–1920:*
         A Preliminary Checklist. Garland Reference Library of the Humanities 202.
         New York: Garland, 1981. 805 pp.   Z2013.5.W6.G75 [PR1286]
         016.823'912.

An author list of 15,174 titles (including translations) by 5,267 authors, primarily published in England and the United States. Excludes most juvenile fiction and novels by joint authors when one is male. Entries are arranged by author in three divisions: verified entries, novels by anonymous or pseudonymous authors whose gender could not be determined, and unverified novels. Approximately 75% of the entries are annotated with what are aptly described as "working notes not originally intended for publication," which consist principally of quotations from or rough paraphrases of reviews. Indexed by titles. Although it is a reproduction of a printout of a minimally edited working copy based on secondary sources, *Novels in English by Women* does record the bulk of novels written by women during the period (as well as reviews of them in several major periodicals). Unfortunately, work on the checklist for 1781–1890 has been suspended.

The potential value of these working notes is illustrated by Daims and Grimes, *Toward a Feminist Tradition: An Annotated Bibliography of Novels in English by Women, 1891–1920*, Garland Reference Library of the Humanities 201 (New York: Garland, 1982, 885 pp.), which extracts entries for novels offering "unconventional treatment of women characters which focuses attention either on the efforts of women to control their lives or on social attitudes and conditions functioning as counterforces to that achievement." The annotations have been edited, but readers must consult *Novels in English* for sources of the reviews. Indexed by titles. Although neither comprehensive nor based on firsthand knowledge of the works, *Toward a Feminist Tradition* is nonetheless an important source for studying attitudes toward women, especially in British novels.

Intended as a companion to *Novels in English* and *Toward a Feminist Tradition,* Doris Robinson, *Women Novelists, 1891–1920: An Index to Biographical and Autobiographical Sources,* Garland Reference Library of the Humanities 491 (New York: Garland, 1984, 458 pp.), lists separately published autobiographies and biographies as well as entries in collective biographies for 1,565 of the women. Indexed in *Biography and Genealogy Master Index* (J565).

Additional works of fiction—along with poetry and drama—can be identified in R. C. Alston, *A Checklist of Women Writers, 1801–1900: Fiction, Verse, Drama* (Boston: Hall, 1990, 517 pp.); however, the title fails to make clear that coverage is limited to English-language works published in the British Isles or British territories and held in the British Library.

M2645 Harris, Wendell V. *British Short Fiction in the Nineteenth Century: A Literary and Bibliographic Guide.* Detroit: Wayne State UP, 1979. 209 pp. PR861.H35   823'.01.

The "Bibliographic Appendix" (pp. 164–203) is an author list of collections of short fiction made by the author, standard collections published after the author's death, and selected other collections. *British Short Fiction* lists contents of collections not analyzed in *New Cambridge Bibliography of English Literature* (M1385) or *Short Story Index* (L1085) and, for all authors, cites standard general and author bibliographies that list short fiction. Harris, *NCBEL,* and *Short Story Index* combined provide the best guide to the collected short fiction during the century. Review: Robert A. Colby, *Victorian Studies* 24 (1981): 254–55.

M2650 Snell, K. D. M. *The Bibliography of Regional Fiction in Britain and Ireland, 1800–2000.* Aldershot: Ashgate, 2002. 213 pp.   Z2014.F4 S64 [PR868.R45]   016.823'808032.

A bibliography of English-language fiction (loosely conceived) published between 1800 and 2000 that is set at least partly in a particular region of Great Britain or Ireland and that uses "recognizable and distinctive features of the life, customs, language, dialect or other aspects of that area's culture and people." Among the kinds of publications excluded are folktales, chapbooks, most temperance novels, and short fiction not collected in book form. Entries—which consist of author, title, and date of first publication—are generally listed under the county as it existed at the work's composition (though there are headings for some broader topographical regions [e.g., the Scottish Highlands and the Welsh borders], for cities that have inspired a large body of fiction, and for political categories [e.g., the northern Irish border]); there are separate lists for England, Ireland, Scotland, and Wales. Although a bare-bones listing that is difficult to consult because of the lack of author and title indexes, Snell offers the fullest and most current guide to the regional fiction of the United Kingdom and Republic of Ireland; it supersedes Lucien Leclaire, *A General Analytical Bibliography of the Regional Novelists of the British Isles, 1800–1950,* rev. ed., Collection d'histoire et de littérature étrangères (Paris: Belles Lettres, 1969, 399 pp.), and is an essential complement to Brown, *Ireland in Fiction* (N3025).

M2655 Vann, J. Don. *Victorian Novels in Serial.* Index Society Fund Publications. New York: MLA, 1985. 181 pp.   Z2014.F4 V36 [PR871]   016.823'8.

Identifies the date of publication and content of each installment of 192 serialized novels by Ainsworth, Collins, Dickens, Eliot, Gaskell, Hardy, Kingsley, Kipling, Bulwer-Lytton, Marryat, Meredith, Reade, Stevenson, Thackeray, Trollope, and Ward. Under each author, Vann lists novels by date of publication of the first part and for each installment cites date of publication and identifies, as precisely as possible, its content in relation to the separately published volume. The introduction discusses the history of serialization, its effect on authorship, the impact of the form on plot (especially the ending of an installment), and publishing practices. Concludes with a selected bibliography of scholarship on serial novels. Since the periodicals are frequently difficult to obtain and few modern editions identify installments, Vann offers essential information to those studying the initial reception and structure of the more important Victorian serial novels. Reviews: Michael Lund, *Studies in the Novel* 19 (1987): 503–05; Rosemary T. VanArsdel, *Victorian Periodicals Review* 19 (1986): 78–79.

M2660   Wolff, Robert Lee, comp. *Nineteenth-Century Fiction: A Bibliographical Catalogue Based on the Collection Formed by Robert Lee Wolff.* 5 vols. Garland Reference Library of the Humanities 261, 331–34. New York: Garland, 1981–86.   Z2014.F4 W64 [PR861]   016.823'8.

A descriptive author catalog of Wolff's extensive collection of novels published between 1837 and 1901 (as well as other works written by novelists during the period, novels before 1837 and after 1901 by novelists published between those years, and related manuscripts and letters). The collection—now owned by the Harry Ransom Humanities Research Center, University of Texas, Austin—complements Sadleir's, since Wolff sought the minor authors (especially women) not favored by collectors. Effective use of the catalog requires a copy of *XIX Century Fiction* (M2635) at hand, because Wolff assumes familiarity with Sadleir's procedures and records only significant variants and details of provenance for editions fully described by Sadleir. The 7,938 titles (plus numerous editions thereof and duplicates) are listed alphabetically by author, then title; there are separate alphabetic sequences for unattributed anonymous works, pseudonymous works, and multiple-author collections, annuals, and periodical fiction in vol. 5. Letters relating to novels are fully transcribed; manuscripts receive extensive descriptions. Entries vary in content but typically include title; imprint; description of binding; number of volumes and pagination; bibliographical notes, with information on condition, provenance, and references to standard bibliographies; and a variety of miscellaneous notes, including publishing history, content, and frequently eccentric critical observations. Indexed by title in vol. 5. Wolff corrected only the entries from A to mid-D before his death; hence, many errors and incomplete references remain, and most entries would benefit from considerable pruning. Although the work is not one of the monumental catalogs of a private collection, its emphasis on minor novels, the several corrections to standard author bibliographies, and descriptions of numerous unique items, variant editions, manuscripts, and association copies make Wolff an essential complement to Sadleir and an important contribution toward a much needed comprehensive list of Victorian novels. Review: (vol. 1) Walter E. Smith, *Papers of the Bibliographical Society of America* 76 (1982): 481–88.

See also

Bleiler, *Guide to Supernatural Fiction* (L860).
English Novels, 1770–1829: A Bibliographical Survey of Prose Fiction Published in the British Isles (M2336).
Hubin, *Crime Fiction, 1749–1980* (L915).
Mayo, *English Novel in the Magazines, 1740–1815* (M2330).
Sargent, *British and American Utopian Literature* (L1055).
Tymn, *Horror Literature* (L860a).

Wright, *[Author/Chronological/Title] Bibliography of English Language Fiction* (L1060).

Text Archives

M2663   *Nineteenth-Century Fiction.* ProQuest. Online. 18 June 2006 <http://collections.chadwyck.com>.

An archive of rekeyed texts of 250 English-language works of fiction published in the British Isles between 1782 and 1903. First editions were selected for inclusion, although some serialized versions and revised later editions are used. The About *Nineteenth-Century Fiction* page offers no explanation of the criteria used to select authors or works.

Simple keyword, title, and author searches can be limited by publication date, date during an author's lifetime, gender, nationality, ethnicity, and to parts (e.g., front matter, epigraphs). Searchers can also browse an author list of the contents of the database. Results appear in ascending alphabetical order and cannot be re-sorted. Citations (but not the full text) can be marked for e-mailing, downloading, or printing; each citation includes a durable URL to the full text.

Some works are rekeyed from textually unsound editions; however, the bibliographic record for each work identifies the source of the text and any omissions (e.g., preliminary matter). Besides being a useful source for identifying an elusive quotation or allusion, *Nineteenth-Century Fiction*'s text archive makes feasible a variety of kinds of studies (stylistic, thematic, imagistic, and topical).

The contents of *Nineteenth-Century Fiction* can also be searched through *LiOn* (I527), which offers a less versatile search interface.

Continues *Eighteenth-Century Fiction* (M2339).

Guides to Scholarship and Criticism

Surveys of Research

M2665   Ford, George H., ed. *Victorian Fiction: A Second Guide to Research.* New York: MLA, 1978. 401 pp.   PR871.V5   823'.8'09.

Stevenson, Lionel, ed. *Victorian Fiction: A Guide to Research.* Cambridge: Harvard UP, 1964. 440 pp.   PR873.S8   823.809.

Evaluative surveys of research on established novelists. The original volume covers scholarship from the 1930s through 1962 (with some important earlier and later studies) in chapters on general works, Disraeli and Bulwer-Lytton, Dickens, Thackeray, Trollope, the Brontës, Gaskell and Kingsley, Collins and Reade, Eliot, Meredith, Hardy, and Moore and Gissing. The *Second Guide* continues coverage through 1974 (along with some significant omissions from the earlier volume and a few 1975 publications) and adds chapters on Butler and Stevenson. The individual essays are variously subdivided but typically examine bibliographies, biographical studies, editions, collections of letters, and critical studies (with the sequel utilizing more subdivisions, giving more attention to manuscripts, and adding a discussion of film adaptations). Most include suggestions for further research (more consistently and fully in the 1978 volume). Indexed by persons. Marred only by incomplete citations, these volumes offer magisterial surveys that remain valuable guides to earlier scholarship. Reviews: (Stevenson) Geoffrey Tillotson and Kathleen Tillotson, *Nineteenth-Century Fiction* 19 (1965): 405–10;

(Ford) David J. DeLaura, *English Language Notes* 16 (1978): 178–91; Sylvère Monod, *Yearbook of English Studies* 11 (1981): 310–12.

See also

> Spector, *English Gothic* (M2345).

Other Bibliographies

There is no adequate bibliography of criticism of nineteenth-century British fiction. Although it does index parts of some monographs, Lynndianne Beene, *Guide to British Prose Fiction Explication: Nineteenth and Twentieth Centuries*, Reference Publication in Literature (New York: Hall-Simon; London: Prentice, 1997, 697 pp.), is plagued by too many serious deficiencies: an inadequate set of principles governing selection ("Pragmaticism, the availability of resources, and the author's sense of identification shaped the decisions to include or exclude a writer"); the inclusion of authors (such as Atwood, Mansfield, and Durrell) who hardly qualify as British; the citation of numerous reviews that cannot remotely be labeled "explication"; and the lack of an index.

See

> Albert, *Detective and Mystery Fiction* (L920).
> Frank, *Guide to the Gothic* (L875).
> Kirby, *America's Hive of Honey* (Q4190).
> *Twentieth-Century Short Story Explication* (L1090).

DRAMA AND THEATER

Sections L: Genres/Drama and Theater and M: English Literature/General/Genres/Drama and Theater include many works useful for research in nineteenth-century drama and theater.

Histories and Surveys

M2670   Nicoll, Allardyce. *Early Nineteenth Century Drama, 1800–1850.* 2nd ed.
       Late Nineteenth Century Drama, 1850–1900. 2nd ed. Vols. 4–5 of *A History of English Drama, 1660–1900* (M1525). Cambridge: Cambridge UP, 1955–59.   PR625.N52   822.09.
       Emphasizing the history of the stage and dramatic forms, vol. 4 includes chapters on the theater, dramatic conditions, the illegitimate drama (e.g., melodrama, farce, burlesque), the legitimate drama, and the poetic drama not intended for production; vol. 5 has chapters on the theater, dramatic conditions, and each decade of the last half of the century. Both volumes provide an appendix listing playhouses and an author list of plays and other dramatic forms written and produced during the respective period (with details of first performance, printed editions, and manuscripts, although the last are sketchily treated). Readers should note the supplementary sections that print revisions that could not be incorporated readily into the text. Although the history of the stage requires supplementing, the volumes assemble a wealth of information, and the lists of plays produced (although not exhaustive) are the most complete available. Indexed by persons and subjects in each volume; the lists of plays are indexed, with

additions and corrections, in vol. 6 (entry M1545). For further additions and corrections, see:

> Hauger, George. "English Musical Theatre 1830–1900." *Theatre Notebook* 36 (1982): 55–64, 122–25.
> Stratman, Carl J., C. S. V. "Additions to Allardyce Nicoll's Hand-List of Plays: 1800–1818." *Notes and Queries* 206 (1961): 214–17.
> ———. "English Tragedy: 1819–1823." *Philological Quarterly* 41 (1962): 465–74.

See also

> *Revels History of Drama in English* (M1530).

Guides to Primary Works

M2685   Gänzl, Kurt. *The British Musical Theatre.* 2 vols. New York: Oxford UP, 1986.   ML1731.8.L7.G36   782.81′0941.

> Vol. 1: *1865–1914.* 1,196 pp.
> Vol. 2: *1915–1984.* 1,258 pp.

A year-by-year account of original light musical theater produced in London's West End. Gänzl excludes operas, ballad operas, and burlesques, but otherwise encompasses a wide range of musical entertainments. Each year consists of two parts: (1) an extensive overview that combines plot summary with evaluation and comments on critical reception; (2) a list of productions, recording for each the author, librettist, producer, director, composer, theater, opening and closing dates, number of performances, original cast (along with understudies and replacements), revivals, adaptations in a different medium, some productions outside London (with cast lists for revivals and foreign productions), and touring dates. Each volume concludes with two appendixes: list of printed music; discography. Indexed separately in each volume by persons and titles of musicals. The massive and generally trustworthy accumulation of factual information makes Gänzl an indispensable source for the theater historian and should encourage a general critical history of the London musical theater as well as a host of specialized studies.

See also

> *Dramatic Compositions Copyrighted in the United States, 1870 to 1916* (Q4195).
> *Wearing, London Stage, 1890–1899* (M2865).

Guides to Scholarship and Criticism

M2690   Conolly, L. W., and J. P. Wearing. *English Drama and Theatre, 1800–1900: A Guide to Information Sources.* American Literature, English Literature, and World Literatures in English: An Information Guide Series 12. Detroit: Gale, 1978. 508 pp.   Z2014.D7 C72 [PR721] 016.822′7′08.

A selective bibliography of English-language scholarship (including dissertations) and editions through 1973. The 3,324 entries are arranged chronologically in 10 classified divisions: contemporary history and criticism; modern history and criticism; individual authors; reference works; anthologies; theaters; acting and management; critics; stage design, scenic art, and costume; and periodicals. The 110 authors have sections, when required, for collected works, major acted plays, unacted plays, bibliographies, biographies, critical studies, and author journals and newsletters. Annotations generally consist of brief descriptive comments. Since there are few cross-references, users must be certain to check the person, anonymous title, and selected subject index. Although lacking a clear statement of criteria governing selection, *English Drama and Theatre* is a convenient starting place, but coverage must be supplemented by Arnott, *English Theatrical Literature* (M1560), general bibliographies on the period (entries M2480– 510), "Nineteenth-Century Theatre Research: A Bibliography for [1972–81]" (in *Nineteenth Century Theatre* 1–10 [1973–83]), and the serial bibliographies and indexes in section G. Reviews: James Ellis, *Victorian Periodicals Review* 12 (1979): 146–49; Jan McDonald, *Theatre Notebook* 34 (1980): 42–44.

See also

  International Bibliography of Theatre (L1160).

POETRY

Many works in sections L: Genres/Poetry and M: English Literature/General/Genres/ Poetry are important to research in nineteenth-century poetry.

Histories and Surveys

For evaluative surveys of histories and general studies, see Frank Jordan, "The Romantic Movement in England" (pp. 1–112), in Jordan, *English Romantic Poets* (M2710), and Jerome H. Buckley, "General Materials" (pp. 1–31), in Faverty, *Victorian Poets* (M2715).

Guides to Primary Works

M2707   Reilly, Catherine W. *Late Victorian Poetry, 1880–1899: An Annotated Biobibliography.* London: Mansell, 1994. 577 pp.   Z2014.P7 R453 [PR581]   016.821'808.
     A bibliography of separately published volumes of poetry in English by 2,964 authors who lived in the United Kingdom between 1880 and 1899. Excluded are literal translations, verse drama, dialect poetry, songs, verse for children, books of fewer than eight leaves, publications that include the work of more than two poets, and volumes by poets dead before 1880. Entries, listed alphabetically by authors, begin with a biographical note, followed by a list of works that supplies standard bibliographical information and identifies the libraries holding the copies examined. (The few entries for works that the author could not examine are clearly identified.) The subtitle is misleading since very few entries are annotated and even there, the commentary is typically restricted to details of printing or publication. Indexed by titles. Although inevitably incomplete (only one library outside the United Kingdom was searched), *Late Victorian Poetry* brings under bibliographic control a substantial body of minor verse.

See also

Jackson, *Annals of English Verse, 1770–1835* (M2420).

Guides to Scholarship and Criticism

Surveys of Research

M2710   Jordan, Frank, ed. *The English Romantic Poets: A Review of Research and
Criticism.* 4th ed. New York: MLA, 1985. 765 pp.   PR590.E5
016.821′7′09.

An evaluative guide to important scholarship and criticism through the early
1980s, with chapters by major scholars on the Romantic movement in England, Blake,
Wordsworth, Coleridge, Byron, Shelley, and Keats. The organization of each chapter
varies, but all chapters except the first include sections for reference works, editions,
biographical studies, general criticism, and studies of individual works; all examine
trends and prospects in criticism as well as identify topics needing attention. As in other
MLA reviews of research, the failure to cite full publication information makes tracking
down articles (and some books) needlessly time-consuming. Indexed by persons (with
titles of works listed under the six poets). Clear organization, judicious selection and
evaluation, and authoritative commentary make this the indispensable guide to important earlier studies of English Romanticism and the six poets.

Although largely superseded, the third edition, ed. Frank Jordan (1972, 468 pp.),
is still occasionally useful for its evaluation of outdated works. A complementary volume
that has not been superseded but is now badly dated is Carolyn Washburn Houtchens
and Lawrence Huston Houtchens, eds., *The English Romantic Poets and Essayists: A
Review of Research and Criticism,* rev. ed., Revolving Fund Series 21 (New York: New
York UP for MLA; London: U of London P, 1966, 395 pp.). Essays survey bibliographies, editions, biographical studies, and criticism on Blake, Lamb, Hazlitt, Scott,
Southey, Campbell, Moore, Landor, Hunt, De Quincey, and Carlyle.

M2715   Faverty, Frederic E., ed. *The Victorian Poets: A Guide to Research.* 2nd ed.
Cambridge: Harvard UP, 1968. 433 pp.   PR593.F3   821′.8′09.

An evaluative guide to scholarship through 1966, with chapters on general works,
Tennyson, R. Browning, E. B. Browning, FitzGerald, Clough, Arnold, Swinburne, Pre-
Raphaelites (D. G. Rossetti, C. Rossetti, Morris, and minor poets), Hopkins, and later
Victorian poets (Patmore, Meredith, Thomson, Hardy, Bridges, Henley, Stevenson,
Wilde, Davidson, Thompson, Housman, Kipling, Johnson, and Dowson). The chapters
vary in organization but typically include sections for bibliographies, editions, biographies, and general criticism. Unfortunately, citations do not record full publication
information, and there are more than a few errors. The directness of evaluation varies
with the contributor, but all suggest topics for further research. Indexed by persons. A
trustworthy guide to significant research through 1966, but a new edition is needed.
Review: Kenneth Allott, *Victorian Poetry* 8 (1970): 82–91.

Supplemented by "Guide to the Year's Work in Victorian Poetry" (M2720).

Serial Bibliographies

M2720   "Guide to the Year's Work in Victorian Poetry: [1962–   ]." *Victorian Poetry*
1 (1963)–   .   PR500.V5   811.

An evaluative survey of important scholarship on poetry (with some attention to nonfiction prose). The surveys for 1962–71 are by R. C. Tobias; those since 1972 consist of brief essays on general studies, groups, and major authors by a variety of scholars. The surveys for 1972 through 1974 are titled "Guide to the Year's Work in Victorian Poetry and Prose" and intended to supplement DeLaura, *Victorian Prose* (M2740), but those since 1975 give less attention to nonfiction prose. (The guide for 1972, which was published as a supplement to vol. 10 [1974], covers studies published between 1966 and 1972.) The most authoritative annual survey and a valuable supplement to Faverty, *Victorian Poets* (M2715). Less satisfying surveys appear in *Studies in English Literature, 1500–1900* (M2480) and *Year's Work in English Studies* (G330).

Other Bibliographies

M2725   Reiman, Donald H. *English Romantic Poetry, 1800–1835: A Guide to Information Sources.* American Literature, English Literature, and World Literatures in English: An Information Guide Series 27. Detroit: Gale, 1979. 294 pp.   Z2014.P7 R46 [PR590]   016.821'7'09.
　　　A selective annotated bibliography, principally of English-language scholarship through the mid-1970s. Entries are organized in eight classified divisions: general and background studies, the Romantic movement, Wordsworth, Coleridge, Byron, Shelley, Keats, and secondary poets (Beddoes, Campbell, Clare, Hogg, Hood, Hunt, Landor, Moore, Peacock, Rogers, Scott, and Southey). The author divisions have sections for reference works, editions, biographical studies, and criticism. Most of the brief annotations offer pointed evaluations, and various symbols (see p. xiii) identify levels of use and audience. Three indexes: authors; titles; subjects. Judicious selection, evaluation, and subject indexing make Reiman a trustworthy starting point for research on the minor writers and one of the better volumes in this highly uneven series. Jordan, *English Romantic Poets* (M2710), is a more authoritative guide to scholarship on the major writers. Reviews: James H. Averill, *Analytical and Enumerative Bibliography* 5 (1981): 180–83; E. D. Mackerness, *Notes and Queries* ns 28 (1981): 438–40.

See also

　　　Brogan, *English Versification, 1570–1980* (M1600).
　　　Donow, *Sonnet in England and America* (L1250).
　　　Kuntz, *Poetry Explication* (L1255).
　　　Martinez, *Guide to British Poetry Explication* (L1255a).

PROSE

Some works in sections L: Genres/Prose and M: English Literature/General/Genres/ Prose are useful for research in nineteenth-century prose.

Guides to Scholarship and Criticism

M2740   DeLaura, David J., ed. *Victorian Prose: A Guide to Research.* New York: MLA, 1973. 560 pp.   PR785.D4   820'.9.'008.
　　　An evaluative survey of research through 1971 (with some publications from 1972) that includes chapters on general works, Macaulay, Thomas and Jane Carlyle, Newman,

Mill, Ruskin, Arnold, Pater, the Oxford Movement, the Victorian churches, critics (Lewes, Bagehot, Hutton, Dallas, Lee, Swinburne, Symonds, Moore, Saintsbury, Gosse, Wilde, and Symons), and the unbelievers (Harrison, T. Huxley, Morley, and Stephen). Individual chapters are variously subdivided (with headings listed in the table of contents), but typically cover bibliographies, editions, manuscripts, biographies, and general studies. Unfortunately, full publication details are not cited. Evaluations are fair-minded (sometimes trenchant), and all contributors point out topics needing further research. Indexed by persons. A trustworthy, essential guide to scholarship through 1971, but a new edition is needed. Supplemented in part by "Guide to the Year's Work in Victorian Poetry" (M2720). Reviews: Miriam Allott, *Victorian Studies* 19 (1975): 107–11; Alan Shelston, *Critical Quarterly* 16 (1974): 91–94; Vincent L. Tollers, *Papers of the Bibliographical Society of America* 69 (1975): 284–85.

This collection and its supplement are preferable to Harris W. Wilson and Diane Long Hoeveler, *English Prose and Criticism in the Nineteenth Century: A Guide to Information Sources*, American Literature, English Literature, and World Literatures in English: An Information Guide Series 18 (Detroit: Gale, 1979, 437 pp.), which is inadequately annotated and plagued by errors, omissions, and inconsistencies (for details, see the review by David J. DeLaura, *Analytical and Enumerative Bibliography* 5 [1981]: 61–63).

Twentieth-Century Literature

Many reference works devoted to twentieth-century literature are international in scope. Multinational works that emphasize British literature and those that treat British and American literature more or less equally appear in this part. Other works important to research in twentieth-century English literature are listed in sections G: Serial Bibliographies, Indexes, and Abstracts; M: English Literature/General; and Q: American Literature/General and American Literature/Twentieth-Century Literature.

Histories and Surveys

M2750   *The Cambridge History of Twentieth-Century English Literature.* Ed. Laura Marcus and Peter Nicholls. New Cambridge History of English Literature. Cambridge: Cambridge UP, 2004. 886 pp.   PR471.C36   820.9′0091.

A collection of 44 separately authored essays that address the development of English-language literature in the United Kingdom from late-nineteenth-century decadence through the avant-garde, modernism, and post–World War II culture to the millennium. The essays focus variously on movements, groups, sociocultural influences, genres, forms, and the interaction of media and literature. Unlike earlier volumes in this series, this one lacks a chronology but does include a 36-page selective bibliography organized unhelpfully by the five major divisions of the volume. The index of persons, subjects, and titles is, as John Sutherland points out, a "disaster"; although Cambridge University Press planned to make a revised index available at its Web site, the version there on 3 Sept. 2006 was uncorrected (http://www.cambridge.org/us/catalogue/catalogue.asp?isbn=0521820774&ss=ind). The volume is more valuable for its individual contributions than for any sense of narrative history. Review: John Sutherland,

TLS: Times Literary Supplement 4 Mar. 2005 (http://tls.timesonline.co.uk/article/0,,25370-1888565_1,00.html).

M2752   Baldick, Chris. *1910–1940: The Modern Movement.* Vol. 10 of *The Oxford English Literary History* (M1310a). Gen. ed. Jonathan Bate. Oxford: Oxford UP, 2004. 477 pp.   PR85.O96   820.9.

A literary history of the modernist phase of English literature, with sections devoted to its infrastructure (the literary marketplace, notions of authorship, and English language usage), its genres and forms, and topics that significantly engaged authors (Englishness, World War I, childhood and youth, and sexuality). Concludes with a series of author bibliographies that note standard editions and important critical studies and a selective survey of scholarship and reference works that is more evaluative than is typical in other volumes of *Oxford English Literary History.* Indexed by persons and subjects. *1910–1940: The Modern Movement* is a welcome replacement for Stewart, *Eight Modern Writers* (M1310a).

M2753   Stevenson, Randall. *1960–2000: The Last of England?* Vol. 12 of *The Oxford English Literary History* (M1310a). Gen. ed. Jonathan Bate. Oxford: Oxford UP, 2004. 624 pp.   PR85.O96   820.9.

A literary history of the latter part of the twentieth century, with sections devoted to forces that shaped literature of the era (including social pressures, the media, theory, and the book trade), poetry, drama, and narrative (with the latter three including chapters on movements and forms). Concludes with a series of descriptive author bibliographies, and a list of general studies. Indexed by persons and subjects. Fully aware of the inevitable ensuing shifts in perspectives on and judgments about English literature in the latter half of the twentieth century, Stevenson wisely offers "an account only of what seemed significant during the period itself."

Complemented by Bruce King, *1948–2000: The Internationalization of English Literature*, vol. 13 of *The Oxford English Literary History*, gen. ed. Jonathan Bate (Oxford: Oxford UP, 2004, 386 pp.), which examines how immigrants and their children changed the literary landscape in the United Kingdom during the second half of the twentieth century. Concludes with a series of descriptive author bibliographies and a selective survey of scholarship. Indexed by persons and subjects.

See also

Sec. M: English Literature/General/Histories and Surveys.

Literary Handbooks, Dictionaries, and Encyclopedias

M2755   *Encyclopedia of World Literature in the 20th Century.* Ed. Steven R. Serafin. 3rd ed. 4 vols. Farmington Hills: St. James, 2000.   PN771.E5   803.

Offers truly international coverage of significant twentieth-century literary activity in signed entries by established scholars on literary movements, ideas, the arts, national literatures, and authors who produced important work after 1900. Each entry concludes with a brief bibliography. The author entries—which constitute the bulk of the work—give basic biographical information, offer a general critical assessment of major works, list other publications, and provide a very selective bibliography of scholarship. Two indexes: writers by nationality; authors and subjects.

The overall reliability of the entries, breadth, critical commentary superior to what usually appears in encyclopedic compilations, balance, and currency make this source the best of the numerous encyclopedias of twentieth-century literature.

A useful complement is *The Oxford Companion to Twentieth-Century Literature in English*, ed. Jenny Stringer (Oxford: Oxford UP, 1996, 751 pp.), which contains entries on groups, movements, individual works, concepts, genres, and (predominantly) writers.

Entrants in both works are indexed in *Biography and Genealogy Master Index* (J565).

Bibliographies of Bibliographies

M2760 Mellown, Elgin W. *A Descriptive Catalogue of the Bibliographies of Twentieth Century British Poets, Novelists, and Dramatists.* 2nd ed., rev. and enl. Troy: Whitston, 1978. 414 pp.   Z2011.A1 M43 [PR471] 016.01682'08'00912.

An annotated bibliography of bibliographies (including articles and parts of books) published through 1977 of works by and about (1) British authors who were born after 1840 and published the majority of their work after 1890; (2) Scottish, Welsh, and Irish authors who were born before 1920, wrote in English, and are closely associated with English literature; and (3) a few Commonwealth writers. Under each author, entries appear in one of three sections: bibliographies of primary works, bibliographies of secondary works, and bibliographies in selected general reference sources (listed on pp. ix–xiv). Most annotations offer a detailed, but telegraphic, description of scope and content, as well as an incisive evaluation. Indexed by persons. Although the national scope is fuzzy, reasonably thorough coverage and helpful annotations make Mellown the principal bibliography of bibliographies for the period, but it must be supplemented with Howard-Hill, *Index to British Literary Bibliography* (M1355), and *Bibliographic Index* (D145). The first edition (*A Descriptive Catalogue of the Bibliographies of 20th Century British Writers* [1972, 446 pp.]) remains useful for its inclusion of nonliterary writers omitted from the second edition. Review: Peter Davison, *Analytical and Enumerative Bibliography* 3 (1979): 135–38.

Guides to Primary Works

MANUSCRIPTS

M2765 *Location Register of 20th-Century English Literary Manuscripts and Letters.* University of Reading Lib. Online. 12 Jan. 2005 <http:// www.reading.ac.uk/library/about-us/projects/lib-location-register.asp>. Updates will depend on the availability of funding.

A union catalog of manuscripts (including proofs, tape recordings, e-mail print-outs, and computer disks) and letters by British literary figures (including immigrants and refugees) who are currently alive or who died after 31 December 1899. Only items (including photocopies and microform copies) available for public consultation in the British Isles as of the end of 2002 are listed among the approximately 53,000-entries.

The database can be searched by author, title, and keyword or browsed by author or title. Author searches done through the browse screen will bring up cross-references (which are inexplicably absent from search results for a keyword author search); unfortunately, many of the cross-references are blind ones. Entries, which are unhelpfully listed by descending date of acquisition, typically consist of title or description, date, physical description, location, shelf mark, and a note on access. Because of the descriptive titles given several items, researchers must read the entire section for an author. Entries can be marked and downloaded by e-mail.

Because of the utterly inadequate description of the scope, content, and editorial policies offered at the Web site and because the help screen is for the library's OPAC, users need to consult the printed version: *Location Register of Twentieth-Century English Literary Manuscripts and Letters: A Union List of Papers of Modern English, Irish, Scottish, and Welsh Authors in the British Isles*, 2 vols. (London: British Lib., 1988). The print version is also useful since the database excludes the headnotes to author listings that describe major collections (especially outside Great Britain), an author's policy on the disposition of his or her papers, or the destruction of manuscripts. Otherwise, the 1988 version is superseded by the database.

Although the database offers only rudimentary access and lacks a remotely adequate description of contents and although descriptions vary in detail and letters are frequently undifferentiated in large collections, the *Register* is an important resource that presents the most convenient means of locating many twentieth-century British literary manuscripts.

Records in the printed *Location Register* are part of RLG Union Catalog (E230), which, however, does not include the additional or updated material added to the *Register*'s database.

PRINTED WORKS

M2770   *Whitaker's Books in Print: The Reference Catalogue of Current Literature.*
         Farnham: Nielsen BookData, 1874–2003. Annual. (Former titles: *British Books in Print*, 1962–87; *The Reference Catalogue of Current Literature*, 1874–1961.)   Z2001.R33   015.42. Online; CD-ROM; microfiche.

An author, title, and subject list of books in print and on sale in the United Kingdom, which cumulated and updated the weekly list in *Bookseller* (1858–). An entry cites author, title, size, number of pages, edition, series, price, publisher, date of publication, and ISBN. A directory of publishers concludes each annual compilation. Since *Whitaker's* was compiled from information supplied by publishers, it is neither comprehensive nor always accurate, but was the essential source for identifying books available for purchase in the United Kingdom. Earlier volumes, which until 1932 included publishers' catalogs, remain an important source of bibliographical information and book trade history.

For books currently in print or forthcoming in the British Isles, search *GlobalBooksinPrint.com* (Q4225) or the printed clone, *Bowker's British Books in Print* (Q4225a).

M2775   *British National Bibliography* (*BNB*). Boston Spa: British Lib., 1950– .
         Weekly with four-month, annual, and larger cumulations, including ones
         for 1950–84 and 1981–85; records since 1950 are cumulated monthly on
         CD-ROM.   Z2001.B75   015.42. CD-ROM.

A subject list (arranged by Dewey Decimal Classification) of books, electronic resources (since 2003), and new periodicals published in the British Isles. (For a current list of materials excluded, see the preface to the most recent four-month or annual cumulation or http://www.bl.uk/services/bibliographic/exclude.html.) Entries reproduce full cataloging information, but because they are prepared from books as well as Cataloguing-in-Publication (CIP) information received by the Legal Deposit Office of the British Library, there is sometimes a lag of a year or more between publication and listing, and ghosts occur when books for which CIP entries were prepared are never published. (The quarterly and annual cumulations do not include a CIP entry unless the book has actually appeared.) The subject and author-title indexes cite classification rather than page. For British books published simultaneously in the United States, *American Book Publishing Record* (Q4110) is usually a more timely source of information. For the genesis and early evolution of the *BNB*, see Andy Stephens, *The History of the* British National Bibliography, *1950–1973* (London: British Lib., 1994, 159 pp.).

See also

>   *Nineteenth Century Short Title Catalogue* (M2475).
>   Vrana, *Interviews and Conversations with 20th-Century Authors Writing in English* (Q4235).

Guides to Scholarship and Criticism

SURVEYS OF RESEARCH

See

>   *YWES* (G330): Twentieth Century chapter.

SERIAL BIBLIOGRAPHIES

M2780 "Annual Review [1970–2000]." *Journal of Modern Literature* 1-24 (1970–2001). PN2.J6 809'.04.

An annotated bibliography of English-language studies and other materials on the modernist period and those writers who achieved recognition after 1880 and before c. 1950. Entries are organized by form (books, "secondary books" [e.g., critical editions, study guides, and surveys], dissertations, articles, special issues of journals, and miscellaneous materials—an organizational scheme last explained in 18 [1993]: facing 165) in two divisions: general studies (with sections for reference works and bibliographies; literary history; themes and movements; regional, national, and ethnic literatures; comparative studies of two or more authors; general studies of modern literature; fiction; poetry; drama; and film and/as literature) and individual authors who were the subject of at least one book or several articles and dissertations. The first two bibliographies (and recent ones) include full-length reviews of some books; in other years, books frequently receive generous annotations (most of which are admirable for their precise descriptions and evaluative comments). The replacement of the name index beginning in the bibliography for 1991–92 with useless indexes of authors of books reviewed and of reviewers inexcusably hampers access to the contents. The cessation of the "Annual Review" deprived scholars of an important resource for research in the modernist period.

See also

> *ABELL* (G340): English Literature/Twentieth Century and Twenty-First Century sections.
> "Current Bibliography," *Twentieth Century Literature* (M2790a).
> *MLAIB* (G335): English Language and Literature division in the volumes for 1921–25; English XI in the volumes for 1926–56; English X in the volumes for 1957–80; and English Literature/1900–1999 and 2000–2099 sections (as well as any larger chronological sections encompassing the century) in later volumes. Researchers must also check the headings beginning "English" in the subject index to post-1980 volumes and in the online thesaurus.
> *Victorian Database Online* (M2490).

OTHER BIBLIOGRAPHIES

M2785   *The New Cambridge Bibliography of English Literature* (*NCBEL*). Vol. 4: *1900–1950.* Ed. I. R. Willison. Cambridge: Cambridge UP, 1972. 1,408 cols.   Z2011.N45 [PR83]   016.82.

(For a full discussion of *NCBEL*, see entry M1385.) Primary and secondary works are organized in six divisions (each subdivided and classified as its subject requires): introduction (with sections for general, book production and distribution), poetry (general, individual poets), novel (general, individual novelists, children's books), drama (general, individual dramatists), prose (critics and scholars; historians, political scientists; philosophers, theologians, scientists; travel and sport), and periodicals. Users must familiarize themselves with the organization, remember that there is considerable unevenness of coverage among subdivisions, and consult the index volume (vol. 5) rather than the provisional index in vol. 4. Despite its errors and omissions, the work offers the fullest general coverage of the period. Reviews: *TLS: Times Literary Supplement* 29 Dec. 1972: 1582; T. A. Birrell, *Neophilologus* 59 (1975): 306–15.

M2790   Pownall, David E. *Articles on Twentieth Century Literature: An Annotated Bibliography, 1954 to 1970: An Expanded Cumulation of "Current Bibliography" in the Journal* Twentieth Century Literature, *Volume One to Volume Sixteen, 1955 to 1970.* 7 vols. New York: KTO, 1973–80. Z6519.P66 [PN771]   016.809'04.

A descriptively annotated bibliography of some 40,000 journal articles (excluding review essays, popular journalism, and pedagogical discussions) printed between 1954 and 1970 on authors (regardless of nationality) who lived and published in the twentieth century. Pownall cumulates, verifies, and expands the quarterly "Current Bibliography," *Twentieth Century Literature* 1–16 (1955–70). Entries are organized alphabetically by literary authors; under each author, articles are listed alphabetically by scholar within sections for general studies and individual works. Although the volumes on comparative, national, and regional literature and general topics were never published, the work is an important compilation because it offers more extensive coverage of articles than the serial bibliographies and indexes in section G. For studies after 1970, see "Current Bibliography," *Twentieth Century Literature* 17–27.2 (1971–81), a descriptively annotated bibliography of journal articles on twentieth-century literature worldwide, and the serial bibliographies and indexes in section G.

M2795   Davies, Alistair. *An Annotated Critical Bibliography of Modernism.* Harvester
        Annotated Critical Bibliographies. Brighton: Harvester; Totowa: Barnes,
        1982. 261 pp.   Z2014.M6 D38 [PR478.M6]   016.82'09'0091.

A selective, classified guide to "major books and articles" on literary modernism (principally in England), with the bulk of the volume consisting of separate bibliographies of Yeats, Lewis, Lawrence, and Eliot. The general division on modernism includes sections for the theory, literary context, critique, and critical reception of the movement; fiction; poetry; drama; anthologies; general studies; and literary modernism and the arts. Entries (arranged chronologically within each section or division) are accompanied by evaluative annotations that clearly delineate content. Each division has two indexes: subjects; critics. There are numerous important omissions (especially of works published in the 1970s), the indexing system is poorly conceived, the chronological organization compromised by a failure to list numerous reprinted essays by their respective years of initial publication, and scholarship on the four principal authors is more adequately covered in separate author bibliographies. Still, Davies is useful as a starting point because of its evaluations and (in the general section) compilation of studies not readily identifiable in standard bibliographies such as *MLAIB* (G335) and *ABELL* (G340). Review: Edward Mendelson, *TLS: Times Literary Supplement* 26 Aug. 1983: 901.

M2800   Somer, John, and Barbara Eck Cooper. *American and British Literature,*
        1945–1975: An Annotated Bibliography of Contemporary Scholarship.
        Lawrence: Regents P of Kansas, 1980. 326 pp.   Z1227.S65 [PS221]
        016.820'9'00914.

An annotated bibliography of 1,060 English-language books published before 1975 on critical theory, trends, patterns, topics, and backgrounds of modern literature, with accompanying unannotated lists of 162 books published after 1975 and 456 bibliographies and reference works. Somer excludes books devoted to a single author. The annotated entries are divided among sections for general studies, genres, and critical theory. The list of bibliographies and reference works (which, like that of studies published after 1975, includes a number of volumes not examined by the authors) is classified by topic (e.g., minority literature, science fiction) or type (e.g., biographical guides, handbooks). The descriptive annotations are sometimes vague and depend too much on introductory matter or tables of contents, but they do cite authors or topics that receive substantial discussion. Indexed by authors and subjects (with specific headings that offer efficient access to the annotations). Although *American and British Literature* is a valuable source for locating discussions of authors and topics buried in books, users would benefit from a more refined classification of entries. Review: Martin Tucker, *Analytical and Enumerative Bibliography* 5 (1981): 127–29.

RELATED TOPICS

M2805   Robbins, Keith, comp. and ed. *A Bibliography of British History, 1914–*
        1989. Oxford: Clarendon–Oxford UP, 1996. 918 pp.   Z2020.R63
        [DA566]   016.941.

A massive, albeit selective bibliography of primary and secondary works (through 1989 and overwhelmingly in English) in 12 extensively classified divisions: general reference works and studies; constitutional and political history; economy and industry; British society; religion; external relations; armed forces and war; transport; urban and rural life and the environment; medicine and health; education; and culture, recreation, leisure, and sport. Each division begins with a discussion of scope, limitations, and organization. Entries are not annotated, unlike those in earlier volumes in the series (e.g., Hanham, *Bibliography of British History, 1851–1914* [M2520]). Indexed by authors (including titles). Although the bibliography is marred by an inadequate explanation of the selection criteria and by the lack of annotations, the breadth of coverage makes it a valuable resource for interdisciplinary research.

Although more selective, Peter Catterall, *British History, 1945–1987: An Annotated Bibliography* (Oxford: Blackwell for Inst. of Contemporary British History, 1990, 843 pp.), evaluates or annotates its 8,644 entries. Coverage extends through 1989, but the criteria governing selection of books and articles are unclear, and the intellectual and cultural history division omits numerous essential reference works.

See also

Hanham, *Bibliography of British History, 1851–1914* (M2520).
Royal Historical Society Bibliography (M1400).

Language

STUDIES OF LANGUAGE

M2810   Quirk, Randolph, et al. *A Comprehensive Grammar of the English Language.*
London: Longman, 1985. 1,779 pp. (The ninth impression [1991] was
ostensibly revised, but with no explanation of the nature of the revisions.)
PE1106.C65   428.2.

A detailed description of the constituents and categories of grammar in Modern British and American English. After a general discussion of the English language and outline of its grammar (which serves as a guide to the remainder of the work), successive chapters examine in extenso verbs and auxiliaries; the semantics of the verb phrase; nouns and determiners; pronouns and numerals; adjectives and adverbs; the semantics and grammar of adverbials; prepositions and prepositional phrases; the simple sentence; sentence types and discourse functions; pro-forms and ellipsis; coordination; complex sentences; the syntactic and semantic functions of subordinate clauses; complementation of verbs and adjectives; noun phrases; theme, focus, and information processing; and sentence and text. Each chapter begins with a detailed table of contents, offers a multitude of examples, and concludes with suggestions for further reading. Three appendixes: word formation; stress, rhythm, and intonation; punctuation. Indexed by lexical items, abbreviations for grammatical categories, and general concepts. A clear, thorough, nearly exhaustive description, *Comprehensive Grammar* is the essential resource for understanding the grammar of Modern English. It supersedes Quirk et al., *A Grammar of Contemporary English* (New York: Seminar-Harcourt, 1972, 1,120 pp.). Reviews: F. G. A. M. Aarts, *English Studies* 69 (1988): 163–73; Rodney Huddleston, *Language* 64 (1988): 345–54; John M. Sinclair, *TLS: Times Literary Supplement* 28 June 1985: 715–16.

A similar exhaustiveness marks Rodney Huddleston and Geoffrey K. Pullum, *Cambridge Grammar of the English Language* (Cambridge: Cambridge UP, 2002, 1,842 pp), "a synchronic, descriptive grammar of general-purpose, present-day [i.e, post World War II], international Standard English." Considering both the written and spoken language, chapters treat syntax, the verb, complementary clauses, nouns, adjectives and adverbs, prepositions, adjunct clauses, negation, clause type and illocutionary force, content clauses and reported speech, relative constructions and unbounded dependencies, comparative constructions, nonfinite and verbless clauses, coordination and supplementation, information packaging, deixis and anaphora, inflectional morphology, lexis, and punctuation. Errata and corrigenda are posted at http://people.ucsc.edu/~pullum/errata.html. Two indexes: lexical index; conceptual index. Although failing to distinguish between written and spoken English, this is the most exhaustive treatment of the grammar of contemporary English. Review: Peter W. Cullicover, *Language* 80 (2004): 127–41.

Biographical Dictionaries

See

> *Contemporary Authors* (J595).
> *Dictionary of Literary Biography* (J600).

Periodicals

GUIDES TO PRIMARY WORKS

See

> Sec. K: Periodicals/Little Magazines.
> *Bibliography of British Newspapers* (M1440).
> Sullivan, *British Literary Magazines* (M1445).

GUIDES TO SCHOLARSHIP AND CRITICISM

See

> Linton, *Twentieth-Century Newspaper Press in Britain* (M1455a).
> "RSVP Bibliography" (M2555).

Genres

Most works in sections L: Genres and M: English Literature/General/Genres are useful for research in twentieth-century English literature.

FICTION

Most works in sections L: Genres/Fiction and M: English Literature/General/Genres/ Fiction are useful for research in twentieth-century English fiction.

Histories and Surveys

M2830   Allen, Walter. *Tradition and Dream: The English and American Novel from the Twenties to Our Time.* With a new afterword. London: Hogarth, 1986. 358 pp.   PR881.A42   823.912′09.

A critical survey of the British and American novel from c. 1920 to 1960. Limited to works in English and excluding first novels published after 1955 as well as most historical fiction and short stories, *Tradition and Dream* emphasizes established authors. After an introduction outlining the relationship between the American and British novel, chapters are organized chronologically, then by country. Indexed by persons, titles, and a few subjects. A sequel to Allen, *English Novel* (M1505a), this work offers a basic overview of important modern British and American novels. In the afterword to the 1986 reprint, Allen reflects on changes in his perception of the novel, discusses how he might now alter the work, and comments on major novels from 1955 to the 1980s. Reviews: *Times Literary Supplement* 13 Feb. 1964: 126; Irving Malin, *American Literature* 36 (1964): 390–91; Harvey Curtis Webster, *Kenyon Review* 26 (1964): 571–76.

Literary Handbooks, Dictionaries, and Encyclopedias

See

> *Dictionary of British Literary Characters: 20th-Century Novels* (M1507).

Guides to Primary Works

See

> Grimes, *Novels in English by Women, 1891–1920* (M2640).
> Snell, *The Bibliography of Regional Fiction in Britain and Ireland, 1800–2000* (M2650).

Guides to Scholarship and Criticism

Although studies of modern fiction (to c. 1950) are covered in the following works, there is no satisfactory current bibliography of scholarship and criticism on fiction after 1950. Both Alfred F. Rosa and Paul A. Eschholz, *Contemporary Fiction in America and England, 1950–1970: A Guide to Information Sources,* American Literature, English Literature, and World Literatures in English: An Information Guide Series 10 (Detroit: Gale, 1976, 454 pp.), and Irving Adelman and Rita Dworkin, *The Contemporary Novel: A Checklist of Critical Literature on the British and American Novel,* 2nd ed. (Lanham: Scarecrow, 1997, 666 pp.), are too dated and narrow in scope to offer more than minimal guidance (*Contemporary Novel,* despite a 1997 publication date, inexcusably covers no studies after 1982). Horst W. Drescher and Bernd Kahrmann, *The Contemporary English Novel: An Annotated Bibliography of Secondary Sources* (Frankfurt: Athenäum, 1973, 204 pp.), is also outdated but still occasionally useful for its coverage of European (especially German) criticism. Until an adequate bibliography is published, those researching contemporary fiction will need to consult the following: *MLAIB* (G335), *ABELL* (G340), *Year's Work in English Studies* (G330), Pownall, *Articles on Twentieth Century Literature* (M2790), "Current Bibliography" in *Twentieth Century Literature* (M2790a), "Annual Review" in *Journal of Modern Literature* (M2780), Somer, *American and British Literature, 1945–1975* (M2800), serial bibliographies and indexes in section G, and the numerous author bibliographies.

M2835   Cassis, A. F. *The Twentieth-Century English Novel: An Annotated*
        Bibliography of General Criticism. Garland Reference Library of the
        Humanities 56. New York: Garland, 1977. 413 pp.   Z2014.F5 C35
        [PR881]   016.823'9'109.
   A bibliography of studies from 1900 to 1972 of more than one novelist, the theory or technique of the novel, or the genre. The 2,832 entries are listed alphabetically by author in three divisions: bibliographies, criticism (subdivided into books and articles), and dissertations and theses. The descriptive annotations give particular attention to novelists discussed (dissertations and theses are not annotated). Two indexes: novelists; selected topics and themes. Clear annotations and the full (but not comprehensive) international scope make Cassis the best available guide to discussions of novelists in general studies, but poor organization and inadequate subject indexing render the work much less accessible than it should be. Reviews: Melvin J. Friedman, *Literary Research Newsletter* 4 (1979): 95–98; J. K. Johnstone, *English Studies in Canada* 6 (1980): 257–60.

M2840   Rice, Thomas Jackson. *English Fiction, 1900–1950: A Guide to Information*
        Sources. 2 vols. American Literature, English Literature, and World
        Literatures in English: An Information Guide Series 20–21. Detroit: Gale,
        1979–83.   Z2014.F4 R5 [PR881]   016.823'9.
   A selective annotated bibliography of works by and about British novelists (including major writers, those who "made a significant contribution to modern fiction," and minor novelists who have been the subjects of a "significant amount" of scholarship, but omitting many who are listed in other guides in this series). Vol. 1 covers English-language studies published through 1976, vol. 2, through 1980; both exclude unpublished dissertations, but otherwise the criteria determining selection are unstated. Entries are organized in two divisions: general (with sections for bibliographies; literary histories; critical studies of modern English fiction; theory of fiction; short story; studies of major types; histories and memoirs; and art, film, and music) and individual authors. Under each author, primary works appear first (with a full list of fictional works and a selection of others); secondary works are divided among bibliographies, biographical studies, book-length critical works, general articles and chapters of books, and studies of individual works. Although an asterisk marks important works, the brief annotations rarely explain the significance of a study or offer an adequate description of content. Three indexes (scholars; titles; subjects) in vol. 1, but only an index of scholars in vol. 2. Insufficient explanation of the criteria determining selection of authors and scholarship, inadequate annotations, and the lack of a subject index in vol. 2 detract significantly from the work, which is primarily useful as a starting point for research. Review: Bruce E. Teets, *Conradiana* 14 (1982): 77–80.

Complementary, but less current, bibliographies include the following:

> Stanton, Robert J. *A Bibliography of Modern British Novelists.* 2 vols. Troy: Whitston, 1978. Although plagued by innumerable errors and omissions and restricted to only seventeen novelists, *Bibliography of Modern British Novelists* offers much fuller coverage of studies—especially popular journalism and reviews—and primary works (through c. 1976). Although unreliable, it is useful for its inclusion of material outside the scope of the standard serial bibliographies.
>
> Wiley, Paul L., comp. *The British Novel: Conrad to the Present.* Goldentree Bibliographies in Language and Literature. Northbrook: AHM, 1973. 137 pp. Although it is judicious in its selection, the work is current only through c. 1971.

See also

> Sec. M: English Literature/General/Genres/Fiction/Guides to Scholarship and Criticism.

Biographical Dictionaries

M2845   *Contemporary Novelists.* 7th ed. Ed. Neil Schlager and Josh Lauer. Contemporary Writers Series. Detroit: St. James–Gale, 2001. 1,166 pp. Online through *Biography Resource Center* (J572) and *Gale Virtual Reference Library* (I535).   PR883.C64   823′.91409.

A dictionary of 787 living English-language fiction writers, the majority of whom are established British, American, Australian, and Canadian authors. Each signed entry provides basic biographical details (including addresses), a list of books and uncollected short stories, and a brief critical essay; some entries include one or more of the following: critical studies and reviews recommended by the entrant, a personal comment by the writer, and a note on manuscript collections. Indexed by nationality and titles of novels and collections of short stories; entrants are also indexed in *Biography and Genealogy Master Index* (J565). Like other volumes in this series, *Contemporary Novelists* has improved markedly since its first edition and now deserves its reputation as a standard source for basic information. For lesser known writers, see *Contemporary Authors* (J595).

DRAMA AND THEATER

Many works in sections L: Genres/Drama and Theater and M: English Literature/General/Genres/Drama and Theater are useful for research in twentieth-century English drama and theater.

Histories and Surveys

M2855   Nicoll, Allardyce. *English Drama, 1900–1930: The Beginnings of the Modern Period.* Cambridge: Cambridge UP, 1973. 1,083 pp.   PR721.N45   016.822′9′1209.

Like *History of English Drama, 1660–1900* (M1525), which this work effectively continues, *English Drama, 1900–1930* focuses on the history of the stage and dramatic forms of legitimate and popular theater in chapters on the theatrical world; influences, patterns, and forms; popular entertainment (musicals, revues, and melodramas); minority drama (e.g., regional and social drama); and "general" drama (essentially that by major playwrights). Nicoll excludes operas, pantomimes, plays of unestablished authorship, and most revues and music hall sketches. The concluding author list of plays (based on extensive research in the lord chamberlain's records) provides details of performances and printed editions but must be supplemented by J. P. Wearing, "Additions and Corrections to Allardyce Nicoll's 'Hand-List of Plays 1900–1930,'" *Nineteenth Century Theatre Research* 14 (1986): 51–96. Indexed by persons and subjects. An essential source for the history of dramatic works of the period.

See also

Revels History of Drama in English (M1530).

Guides to Primary Works

Manuscripts

M2860   Innes, Christopher. *Twentieth-Century British and American Theatre: A Critical Guide to Archives.* Aldershot: Ashgate, 1999. 316 pp.   Z5782.I55 [PN2266]   792'.0973'0904.

Offers a guide to manuscripts and ephemera related to twentieth-century British and American theater held in 99 archives in Europe and North America. Organized by individuals (including performers, agents, designers, dramaturgs, directors, playwrights, and, occasionally, collectives), an entry begins with an overview of the surviving papers and their potential uses and then describes, by institution, significant holdings (with many descriptions including a critical assessment of the significance of the materials and suggestions for their use by theater historians). Indexed by play titles. Although necessarily selective in institutions covered, sometimes telegraphic in its descriptions (with no list of abbreviations), and inexplicably omitting persons and theaters from the index, the incisive assessments of material and suggestions for research make this essential reading for historians of twentieth-century British and American theater. It should indeed, as the author hopes, "generate research projects by other scholars and encourage graduate theses."

Calendars

M2865   Wearing, J. P. *The London Stage, 1890–1899: A Calendar of Plays and Players.* 2 vols. Metuchen: Scarecrow, 1976. *The London Stage, 1900–1909: A Calendar of Plays and Players.* 2 vols. 1981. *The London Stage, 1910–1919: A Calendar of Plays and Players.* 2 vols. 1982. *The London Stage, 1920–1929: A Calendar of Plays and Players.* 3 vols. 1984. *The London Stage, 1930–1939: A Calendar of Plays and Players.* 3 vols. 1990. *The London Stage, 1940–1949: A Calendar of Plays and Players.* 2 vols. 1991. *The London Stage, 1950–1959: A Calendar of Plays and Players.* 2 vols. 1993.   PN2596.L6 W37   792'.09421'2.

A calendar of first-night, professional, full-length productions in selected legitimate theaters (ranging in number from about 30 during 1890–99 to 56 during 1950–59). Available information varies, of course, with a full entry giving the following information for a first-night performance: title; genre and number of acts or scenes; author, translator, or adapter; theater; date, length of run, and number of performances; male and female casts (with changes in subsequent performances listed); production staff; selected list of first-night reviews; miscellaneous notes relating to the production or discrepancies in sources. Indexed by persons, titles, and theaters (a single index for 1890–99; a separate index of titles for the later decades). Because of the nature of the sources, some information is inaccurate, since advertisements include errors, performances were cancelled, productions were withdrawn, and substitutions were made in casts. Although not exhaustive, these works are valuable compilations for the study of trends in the legitimate theater; the popularity of genres, specific plays, and playwrights; and careers of theater personnel and players. Reviews: (1890–99) Trevor R. Griffiths, *Theatre Notebook* 31.3 (1977): 43–44; (1900–09) Griffiths, *Theatre Notebook* 37.3 (1983): 141–43; (1920–29) Margaret Watson, *Notes and Queries* ns 33 (1986): 564–65.

Guides to Scholarship and Criticism

Serial Bibliographies

M2870   "Modern Drama Studies: An Annual Bibliography." *Modern Drama* 17–42
        (1974–99).   PN1861.M55   809.2'005.

The expanded successor to "Modern Drama: A Selective Bibliography of Works Published in English in [1959–67]," 3–11 (1960–68), this covers studies published since 1972 on dramatic works by authors (with the exception of Büchner—through 35 [1992]—and Becque) who lived past 1899; emphasizes dramatic literature rather than theatrical history; and excludes reviews, unpublished dissertations, "graduate-student periodicals," and (in most years) works printed in non-Latin alphabets. Entries are organized in divisions for general studies and national literatures (or geographical areas); within the latter are sections for general studies and individual authors. Although the work is not comprehensive, the compiler claims that 35–40% of the entries in early volumes are not listed in *MLAIB* (G335); however, beginning in 37 (1994) coverage was drastically scaled back, and many books listed were not seen by the compilers. The bibliographies for 1966–90 are incorporated in Carpenter, *Modern Drama Scholarship and Criticism, 1966–1980* and *1981–1990* (M2875), which the annual bibliographies after 1980 correct and update.

Other Bibliographies

M2875   Carpenter, Charles A. *Modern Drama Scholarship and Criticism, 1966–*
        1980: An International Bibliography. Toronto: U of Toronto P, 1986. 587
        pp. *1981–1990.* 1997. 632 pp.   Z5781.C37 [PN1851]   016.8092'04.

A classified bibliography of studies of the drama worldwide since Ibsen. Excludes publications in non-Latin alphabets, discussions of theater not related to a dramatic text, unpublished dissertations, most reviews of productions, and most popular journalism; the degree of selectivity in the author lists varies with an individual's commitment to the drama. The approximately 50,000 entries are classified in divisions for general studies and national literatures or language groups (with the latter including sections for individual playwrights). Each division is prefaced by an outline of its organization. Under each dramatist are separate lists of primary works (including only critical editions of plays, essays, collections of letters, and interviews), reference works, collections of essays, and critical studies (including parts of books). A few entries are accompanied by very brief descriptive annotations. Indexed by persons. Although covering only 25 years and omitting dissertations, *Modern Drama Scholarship* is clearly a major contribution to the study of modern drama. Even with the exclusions, the scope is admirably full (Carpenter claims to double the *MLAIB* [G335] coverage before 1970 and add half again as many entries for 1970–80; however, his introductory comments in *1981–1990* suggest that the claim is based on a misunderstanding of the scope of *MLAIB*). The work must, however, be supplemented by section H: Guides to Dissertations and Theses; *MLAIB* (G335) and *ABELL* (G340) for scholarship in non-Latin alphabets; and "Modern Drama Studies: An Annual Bibliography" (M2870), which updates and corrects Carpenter.

Although the following pale in comparison, they are still useful—in varying degrees—for pre-1966 publications:

> Adelman, Irving, and Rita Dworkin. *Modern Drama: A Checklist of Critical Literature on 20th Century Plays.* Metuchen: Scarecrow, 1967. 370 pp. Occasionally useful for its indexing of parts of books, but for its deficiencies, see Carpenter's review, *Modern Drama* 12 (1969): 49–56.
>
> Breed, Paul F., and Florence M. Sniderman, comps. and eds. *Dramatic Criticism Index: A Bibliography of Commentaries on Playwrights from Ibsen to the Avant-Garde.* Detroit: Gale, 1972. 1,022 pp. Principally useful for its indexing of parts of books.
>
> Carpenter, Charles A., comp. *Modern British Drama.* Goldentree Bibliographies in Language and Literature. Arlington Heights: AHM, 1979. 120 pp. Although dated, this work remains the best overall of the selective bibliographies of modern British drama from c. 1860 to the 1970s, and is completely superior to the two padded, repetitive, poorly organized, and inadequately annotated bibliographies by E. H. Mikhail: *English Drama, 1900–1950: A Guide to Information Sources,* American Literature, English Literature, and World Literatures in English: An Information Guide Series 11 (Detroit: Gale, 1977, 328 pp.)—which actually covers British drama, but lists only bibliographies for authors—and *Contemporary British Drama, 1950–1976: An Annotated Critical Bibliography* (Totowa: Rowman, 1976, 147 pp.), which includes no listings for individual authors, no introduction, no index, almost nothing that is not in the preceding work, and which in no way merits "annotated critical" in the title.
>
> Coleman, Arthur, and Gary R. Tyler. *Drama Criticism.* Vol. 1: *A Checklist of Interpretation since 1940 of English and American Plays.* Vol. 2: *A Checklist of Interpretation since 1940 of Classical and Continental Plays.* Chicago: Swallow, 1966–71.
>
> Harris, *Modern Drama in America and England, 1950–1970* (Q4290).
>
> King, Kimball. *Twenty Modern British Playwrights: A Bibliography, 1956–1976.* Garland Reference Library of the Humanities 98. New York: Garland, 1977. 289 pp.
>
> Palmer, *European Drama Criticism* (L1170).

See also

Wildbihler, *The Musical: An International Annotated Bibliography* (Q4295).

Biographical Dictionaries

M2880   *Contemporary Dramatists.* 6th ed. Ed. Thomas Riggs. Contemporary Writers
Series. Detroit: St. James–Gale, 1999. 891 pp. Online through *Biography
Resource Center* (J572).   PR737.C57   822'.914'09.

A dictionary of 433 living English-language dramatists, the majority of whom are
established British, American, Australian, and Canadian writers. Each signed entry provides basic biographical details (including addresses), lists of primary works and theatrical activities, and a brief critical essay; some include one or more of the following: a
list of critical studies (recommended by the entrant), a personal comment by the dramatist, and a note on manuscript collections. Two indexes: nationality; titles of plays.
Entrants are also indexed in *Biography and Genealogy Master Index* (J565). Like other
volumes in this series, a standard source for basic information. For lesser known dramatists, see *Contemporary Authors* (J595).

See also

   Contemporary Theatre, Film, and Television (Q4305).

POETRY

Most works in sections L: Genres/Poetry and M: English Literature/General/Genres/
Poetry are useful for research in twentieth-century English poetry.

Histories and Surveys

M2890   Perkins, David. *A History of Modern Poetry.* 2 vols. Cambridge: Belknap–
Harvard UP, 1976–87.   PR610.P4   821'.009.
   Vol. 1: *From the 1890s to the High Modernist Mode.* 1976. 623 pp.
   Vol. 2: *Modernism and After.* 1987. 694 pp.

   A history of twentieth-century English and American poetry. Although emphasizing poets and their careers, chapters also consider "opposed and evolving assumptions
about poetry[,] . . . the effects on poetry of its changing audiences, . . . premises
and procedures in literary criticism, . . . publishing outlets, . . . and the interrelations of poetry with developments in the other arts—the novel, painting, film, music—
as well as in social, political, and intellectual life." Among contemporary poets, only
those whose reputations were of significance by the 1970s are examined in detail. Indexed in each volume by persons, titles, and a few subjects. These volumes, praised as
well as damned for their breadth and impartiality, remain the only reasonably full survey
of twentieth-century poetry. Review: (vol. 1) James E. Breslin, *Georgia Review* 31
(1977): 978–84.

Literary Handbooks, Dictionaries, and Encyclopedias

M2893   *The Oxford Companion to Twentieth-Century Poetry in English.* Ed. Ian
Hamilton. Oxford: Oxford UP, 1994. 602 pp.   PR601.O9
821'.9109'03. Online through *Oxford Reference Online* (I530).

A guide to individuals, magazines, movements, genres, and subjects involving poetry in English from 1900 to the 1990s. The bulk of the signed entries are for poets (about 1,500, most from Great Britain and the United States) who were born before 1964 and lived anytime during the twentieth century. A typical entry includes critical commentary and a brief overview of the poet's life, career, and publications. Entrants are indexed in *Biography and Genealogy Master Index* (J565). Although readers will inevitably find omissions, this *Oxford Companion* is a useful basic desktop reference on twentieth-century English-language poetry.

Guides to Primary Works

M2894   *Twentieth-Century English Poetry*. ProQuest. Online. 17 June 2006 <http://
        collections.chadwyck.com>.

An archive of rekeyed texts of more than 280 twentieth-century poets born or based in the British Isles. Editions were selected according to the following criteria: a collected edition; other editions for poets without a collected one. Selection seems to be based on the ability to secure rights for electronic publication.

Simple keyword, first line or title, and author searches can be limited by publication date, publisher, gender, date during a poet's lifetime, nationality, and to notes. Searchers can also browse an author list of the contents of the database. Results appear in ascending alphabetical order and cannot be re-sorted. Citations (but not the full text of poems) can be marked for e-mailing, downloading, or printing; each citation includes a durable URL to the full text.

Some works are rekeyed from textually unsound editions; however, the bibliographic record for each work identifies the source of the text and any omissions (e.g., preliminary matter). Besides being a useful source for identifying an elusive quotation or half-remembered line, the scope of *Twentieth-Century English Poetry*'s text archive makes feasible a variety of kinds of studies (stylistic, thematic, imagistic, and topical).

The contents of *Twentieth-Century English Poetry* can also be searched through *LiOn* (I527), which offers a less versatile search interface.

Continues *English Poetry* (M1593).

Guides to Scholarship and Criticism

The *New Cambridge Bibliography of English Literature* (M2785) offers the single best list of studies on modern poetry (to c. 1950), but its coverage must be supplemented by the works listed below under *See also*. Of the other available bibliographies, Charles F. Altieri, comp., *Modern Poetry*, Goldentree Bibliographies in Language and Literature (Arlington Heights: AHM, 1979, 129 pp.), emphasizes established poets who are more adequately covered in author bibliographies and is too selective and dated to be of much use. Because of its omissions, incomplete indexing, inadequate annotations, and numerous errors, Emily Ann Anderson, *English Poetry, 1900–1950: A Guide to Information Sources*, American Literature, English Literature, and World Literatures in English: An Information Guide Series 33 (Detroit: Gale, 1982, 315 pp.), cannot be recommended even for preliminary work. Those interested in contemporary poetry will have to turn to the serial bibliographies and indexes in section G, as well as the works listed below. An adequate bibliography of scholarship and criticism on twentieth-century English poetry is a major desideratum.

See also

> Gingerich, *Contemporary Poetry in America and England, 1950–1975* (Q4335).
> Kuntz, *Poetry Explication* (L1255).
> Martinez, *Guide to British Poetry Explication*, vol. 4 (L1255a).

Biographical Dictionaries

M2895   *Contemporary Poets.* 7th ed. Ed. Thomas Riggs. Contemporary Writers
Series. Detroit: St. James–Gale, 2001. 1,443 pp. Online through *Biography
Resource Center* (J572) and *Gale Virtual Reference Library* (I535).
PR603.C6   821'.91'09.

A dictionary of 787 living English-language poets, the majority of whom are established British, Indian, American, Australian, or Canadian writers. The signed entries provide basic biographical information (including address), a list of published books, and a basic critical evaluation; some include one or more of the following: a selective list of critical studies, a note on manuscript locations, and comments by the poet. Two indexes: nationality; titles of books of poetry listed in the publications section of each entry. Entrants are also indexed in *Biography and Genealogy Master Index* (J565). Like other volumes in this series, it is a standard source for basic information.

For lesser known poets, see *Contemporary Authors* (J595).

PROSE

Some works in sections L: Genres/Prose and M: English Literature/General/Genres/ Prose are useful for research in twentieth-century English prose.

Guides to Scholarship and Criticism

M2900   Brown, Christopher C., and William B. Thesing. *English Prose and
Criticism, 1900–1950: A Guide to Information Sources.* American Literature,
English Literature, and World Literatures in English: An Information Guide
Series 42. Detroit: Gale, 1983. 553 pp.   Z2014.P795 B76 [PR801]
016.828'91208'09.

A highly selective annotated bibliography of editions and studies (published in English before June 1982) of nonfictional prose by 37 authors (selected for the quality of their work or representativeness). Entries are organized in two divisions: general and period studies; and individual authors. The first division (which omits some important works) includes brief sections for bibliographies, literary histories, biography and autobiography, the essay and prose style, literary criticism, and travel writing. Under individual authors are separate lists of primary works (limited to books), editions, bibliographies, biographies, and critical studies. The brief annotations — essentially descriptive, with evaluative adjectives — are barely adequate to convey a sense of content. Two indexes: persons; titles. Although it is highly selective and partly superseded by author bibliographies, *English Prose and Criticism* does serve as a starting point for the study of nonfiction prose. Because of the increasing interest in the topic, a more thorough bibliography would be welcomed by scholars.

N

Irish Literature

This section is limited to works devoted exclusively to Irish literature (primarily in English). Because Irish writers are frequently included in works on English or British literature, researchers must also consult section M: English Literature. In addition, many works listed in sections G: Serial Bibliographies, Indexes, and Abstracts and H: Guides to Dissertations and Theses are useful for research in Irish literature.

Histories and Surveys

N2915   *The Cambridge History of Irish Literature.* Ed. Margaret Kelleher and Philip
         O'Leary. 2 vols. Cambridge: Cambridge UP, 2006.   PB1306.C36
         820.9′9417.

A history of Irish literature, principally in English and Irish, from the sixth century to 2000. The essays, which define *Irish* and *literature* expansively, consider cultural, social, and historical contexts and give particular attention to the role of literature in shaping Irish identity. Each chapter concludes with a select bibliography. Indexed in each volume by authors, titles, and subjects. Attending to canonical and marginalized writers, *Cambridge History of Irish Literature* is the fullest single account of the entire Irish literary tradition. Review Lucy McDiarmid, *TLS: Times Literary Supplement* 6 Oct. 2006: 3–4.

Literary Handbooks, Dictionaries, and Encyclopedias

N2925   *Dictionary of Irish Literature.* Rev. and expanded ed. Ed. Robert Hogan.
         2 vols. Westport: Greenwood, 1996.   PR8706.D5   820′.99415. Available
         on CD-ROM and online as part of *Studies in Irish Literature* <http://
         www.gem.greenwood.com/products/prod_irishlit.asp>.

A literary dictionary consisting primarily of entries (ranging from fewer than 25 to nearly 10,000 words) on some 500 English-language writers (including historians, editors, political writers, journalists, and the like) along with a few discussions of literature-related topics and two lengthy essays on Irish-language authors. Criteria governing the selection of authors or topics are decidedly vague. The author entries emphasize critical commentary but also provide basic biographical information and lists of book-length primary works and criticism. Concludes with a basic chronology of literary and historical events and a selected general bibliography. Indexed by titles, persons, and some subjects. Although something of a hodgepodge of entries of variable quality, the *Dictionary* does provide the fullest discussions of the handbooks devoted to Irish literature. Review: Patrick Crotty, *TLS: Times Literary Supplement* 30 May 1997: 15.

An essential complement is *The Oxford Companion to Irish Literature*, ed. Robert Welch (Oxford: Clarendon–Oxford UP, 1996, 614 pp.), which covers more movements, genres, institutions, historical events and figures, folklore, and groups than *Dictionary of Irish Literature* does. Unfortunately, it contains more factual and typographical errors than one expects in an *Oxford Companion.*

Entrants in both works are indexed in *Biography and Genealogy Master Index* (J565).

Bibliographies of Bibliographies

N2930   Eager, Alan R. *A Guide to Irish Bibliographical Material: A Bibliography of Irish Bibliographies and Sources of Information.* 2nd ed., rev. and enl. Westport: Greenwood, 1980. 502 pp.   Z2031.E16 [DA906] 016.0169415.

A bibliography of bibliographies, including books, articles, parts of books and articles, catalogs, unpublished materials, and works in progress through 1978. Although the majority of the 9,517 entries are for bibliographies wholly or substantially devoted to Irish topics, the *Guide* includes several that are printed in but not about the country, as well as many nonbibliographical works, for the sake of "balance." Entries are organized by Dewey Decimal Classification; a few are accompanied by a brief descriptive annotation. Supplementary entries are printed on pp. 379–81. Two indexes: scholars; subjects (including literary authors). Because of the organization, users should approach the work through the subject index (especially when searching for bibliographies about a person). Although it is not comprehensive, contains numerous errors, is marred by an inadequate description of limitations and organization, and includes several works outside its focus, the work is an essential source for identifying bibliographies on all Irish topics. For recent bibliographies, consult *Bibliographic Index* (D145).

Guides to Primary Works

There is no adequate bibliography of Irish literature. *The Cambridge Bibliography of English Literature* (M1376) and *New Cambridge Bibliography of English Literature* (N2965) list primary works by some writers, as does Frank L. Kersnowski, C. W. Spinks, and Laird Loomis, *A Bibliography of Modern Irish and Anglo-Irish Literature*, Checklists in the Humanities and Education: A Series (San Antonio: Trinity UP, 1976, 157 pp.). Although the latter cites bibliographies of primary and secondary works, its lists of books by 61 writers are highly selective and plagued by numerous errors.

Guides to Collections

N2935   Lester, DeeGee, comp. *Irish Research: A Guide to Collections in North America, Ireland, and Great Britain.* Bibliographies and Indexes in World History 9. New York: Greenwood, 1987. 348 pp.   Z2031.L47 [DA906] 016.9415′0025.

A guide to collections for the study of Irish culture and civilization, including biography, film, folklore, literature, and theater. Although the bulk of the entries are for libraries and museums, Lester also lists organizations and periodicals. Entries are grouped by country; then alphabetically by state, province, or county; then city; and then repository or organization. A typical entry consists of address, a brief description of the repository or organization, a note on general collections of Irish materials, a description of special collections, a list of finding aids, notes on access or restrictions, and tips for researchers. Since information is taken from questionnaires or published descriptions, the entries vary in accuracy and fullness of detail. Two appendixes: dealers specializing in Irish books; Irish local newspapers. Indexed by persons, subjects, and titles. Despite the omission of several important collections, the inclusion of many libraries that "may have" Irish material or whose holdings are essentially general, and insufficient detail of many descriptions, *Irish Research* can be a useful source for identifying collections of Irish literature and related works.

The standard guide to archives in Ireland is *Directory of Irish Archives*, 4th ed., ed. Seamus Helferty and Raymond Refaussé (Dublin: Four Courts, 2003, 217 pp.); however, it describes little of literary interest. Consequently, researchers must also consult the guides in sections E: Libraries and Library Catalogs/Research Libraries/Guides to Collections and F: Guides to Manuscripts and Archives/Guides to Repositories and Archives.

Manuscripts

N2940   Hayes, Richard J., ed. *Manuscript Sources for the History of Irish Civilisation.*
        11 vols. Boston: Hall, 1965. *First Supplement, 1965–1975.* 3 vols. 1979.
        Z2041.D85   016.9415.

An index to manuscripts relating to Ireland held in about 678 libraries and more than 600 private collections in 30 countries. Entries are organized in four sequences: persons and institutions (vols. 1–4), subjects (5–6), places in Ireland (7–8), and dates (9–10). An entry typically provides a brief description of a manuscript, location, and (usually) shelf number or citation to printed calendar or catalog. Vol. 11 consists of lists of manuscript catalogs of manuscripts, private collections, libraries, and various lists of Gaelic manuscripts. The supplement records newly acquired manuscripts. Although many entries are taken from other catalogs or sources and some private collections have been dispersed, Hayes is a valuable, time-saving compilation that includes numerous literary manuscripts.

See also

> Sec. F: Guides to Manuscripts and Archives.
> *Index of English Literary Manuscripts* (M1365).

Printed Works

N2945   *Irish Publishing Record [1967–94].* Dublin: Natl. Lib. of Ireland, 1967–
        [1995?]. Annual.   Z2034.I87   015'.415.

A national bibliography that records books, pamphlets, new periodicals, yearbooks, musical scores, and selected government publications published in Northern Ireland and the Republic of Ireland. Entries, which provide basic card catalog information, are organized by Dewey Decimal Classification. Two indexes: authors; titles. Since information is compiled from a variety of sources, details are not always accurate, but the work does offer the most thorough record of books published in the island from 1967 to 1994.

In January 2005, the National Library of Ireland began compiling a monthly list of new books and periodicals published in the Republic of Ireland (http://www.nli.ie/en/irish-publishing-record.aspx).

Guides to Scholarship and Criticism

Surveys of Research

N2950   Finneran, Richard J., ed. *Anglo-Irish Literature: A Review of Research.* New York: MLA, 1976. 596 pp.   PR8712.A5   820′.9′9415. *Recent Research on Anglo-Irish Writers: A Supplement to* Anglo-Irish Literature: A Review of Research. Modern Language Association of America Reviews of Research. 1983. 361 pp.   PR8712.R4   820′.9′9415.

Evaluative surveys of research on genres and dead authors of Anglo-Irish background who have been the subject of a substantial amount of scholarship. Coverage extends through 1974 in the first volume, through 1980 in the supplement, with the degree of selectivity varying with the contributor. The original volume has chapters on general works; nineteenth-century writers; Wilde; Moore; Shaw; Yeats; Synge; Joyce; four Revival figures: Lady Gregory, A. E., Gogarty, Stephens; O'Casey; and modern drama. The supplement adds modern fiction and poetry. The chapters are extensively classified, with most including sections on reference works, manuscripts, editions, biography, letters, general studies, and individual works. Each survey combines, in varying degrees, description and evaluation, with suggestions for further research. Indexed by persons. Like similar MLA surveys of research, this is marred by incomplete citations, and some reviewers have objected to a definition of Anglo-Irish background that admits Shaw and Wilde but excludes other similar writers. Still, Finneran is the indispensable, authoritative guide to earlier scholarship. Review: Ellsworth Mason, *James Joyce Quarterly* 15 (1978): 138–46.

Although the revised edition planned for 1990 publication was abandoned because some contributors were unable to complete their surveys, a few of the chapters fortunately have been published elsewhere:

> Kopper, Edward A., Jr. *Lady Gregory: A Review of the Criticism.* Modern Irish Literature Monograph Series 2. Butler: Kopper, 1991. 39 pp.
> ———. *Synge: A Review of the Criticism.* Modern Irish Literature Monograph Series 1. Lyndora: Kopper, 1990. 65 pp.
> Murphy, P. J., et al. *Critique of Beckett Criticism: A Guide to Research in English, French, and German.* Literary Criticism in Perspective. Columbia: Camden, 1994. 173 pp.

See also

> *YWES* (G330): Anglo-Irish writers are covered in several chapters.

Serial Bibliographies

N2955   "IASIL Bibliography Bulletin for [1970–]." *Irish University Review* 2 (1972)– . Former title: "IASAIL Bibliographic Bulletin for [1970–94]." PR8700.I73   820′.8′09415.

An international bibliography of studies of Anglo-Irish literature (along with some original poetry and short fiction). Since the bibliography for 1974 (6 [1976]), entries are organized in two sections: general studies and individual authors. In the earlier ones, studies are listed by country of origin. Although not comprehensive, the bibliography is useful because of its international coverage.

A useful complement is "Irish Literature in English: The Year's Work," *Études irlandaises* 1–17.2 (1972–92), with better coverage of Continental scholarship.

See also

> Secs. G: Serial Bibliographies, Indexes, and Abstracts and H: Guides to Dissertations and Theses.
>
> *ABELL* (G340): Entries on Anglo-Irish writers and literature are dispersed throughout.
>
> *Bibliotheca Celtica* (P3155).
>
> *MLAIB* (G335): Until the volume for 1981, Anglo-Irish literature was included in the English Literature division. Literature in Irish Gaelic was covered in the Celtic Languages and Literatures heading under the General division in the volumes for 1928–52; in General IV (later V or VI): Celtic Languages and Literatures in the volumes for 1953–66; and in Celtic VI: Irish Gaelic in the volumes for 1967–80. Since the volume for 1981, the Irish Literature section encompasses Irish literature in any language. Researchers must also check the headings beginning with "Irish" in the subject index to post-1980 volumes and in the online thesaurus.
>
> *Royal Historical Society Bibliography* (M1400).

Other Bibliographies

N2965   *New Cambridge Bibliography of English Literature* (*NCBEL*). Ed. George
        Watson and I. R. Willison. 5 vols. Cambridge: Cambridge UP, 1969–77.
        Z2011.N45 [PR83]   016.82.
(For a full discussion of *NCBEL*, see entry M1385.) Sections on Anglo-Irish literature are scattered throughout the four volumes:

> Vol. 1: *600–1660* has sections on Irish literature in Latin (cols. 341–44, 351–56) and Irish printing and bookselling (cols. 669–70), with Irish writers listed in various sections.
>
> Vol. 2: *1660–1800* has sections on Irish printing and bookselling (cols. 273–74) and periodicals (cols. 1377–90), with Irish writers listed in various sections.
>
> Vol. 3: *1800–1900* has a division for Anglo-Irish literature through 1916 (cols. 1885–948), with classified sections for Gaelic sources, general studies, poets, Yeats and Synge, and dramatists. Coverage of primary (but not secondary) works in vol. 3 is superseded by vol. 4 of the third edition of *CBEL* (M2467).
>
> Vol. 4: *1900–1950* has Anglo-Irish topics and writers listed throughout the various sections.

In each volume, many of the general sections list works important to the study of Anglo-Irish literature. Coverage extends through 1962–69, depending on the volume.

Users must familiarize themselves with the organization, remember that there is considerable unevenness of coverage among subdivisions, and consult the index volume (vol. 5) rather than the provisional indexes in vols. 1–4. Despite its shortcomings (see entry M1385), *NCBEL* offers the fullest single bibliography of primary works and scholarship for the study of Anglo-Irish literature.

N2970   Guilarte, Alexandre, comp. *Bibliography of Irish Linguistics and Literature 1972–*. School of Celtic Studies, Dublin Inst. for Advanced Studies. Online. 25 Sept. 2005 <http://bill.celt.dias.ie>.

Baumgarten, Rolf. *Electronic Bibliography of Irish Linguistics and Literature 1942-71*. Ed. Roibeard Ó Maolalaigh. School of Celtic Studies, Dublin Inst. for Advanced Studies, 2004. Online. 25 Sept. 2005 <http:// bill.celt.dias.ie/vol3/index1.html>; CD-ROM. An electronic, corrected version of *Bibliography of Irish Linguistics and Literature, 1942–71*. Dublin: Dublin Inst. for Advanced Studies, 1986. 776 pp.

Best, R. I. *Bibliography of Irish Philology and of Printed Irish Literature*. Dublin: HMSO, 1913. 307 pp. *Bibliography of Irish Philology and Manuscript Literature: Publications, 1913–1941*. Dublin: Dublin Inst. for Advanced Studies, 1942. 253 pp.   Z2037.D81   016.8916.

A bibliography of scholarship on Irish language and literature through the latter part of the nineteenth century but excluding the Irish Revival. *Bibliography of Irish Linguistics and Literature* is a draft version that includes only a limited number of articles and books and is cumbersome to search since the database is designed to produce future printed volumes. Users can search a series of static (but interlinked) indexes: authors (i.e., scholars); periodicals; book series; books; classifications (bibliography, manuscripts, linguistics, lexicography, grammar, literature and learning, mythology, verse, law and institutions, church history, history, prehistory and cultural history, and reviews; except for the last, each is extensively subdivided); authors and textual sources (i.e., literary authors and anonymous works); first lines of verse; manuscripts; and words and proper nouns. To view a full entry (which provides a citation, a brief annotation in most, and indexing and classification tags) users must click on the Details link at the bottom of a record. Entries are variously hyperlinked (though inconsistently and sometimes needlessly). Unfortunately, users can download only one record at a time as a LaTeX or PDF file. Still very much a work-in-progress and lacking a sufficient statement of scope and taxonomy, *Bibliography of Irish Linguistics and Literature* is at least a place to begin research.

In the volumes by Best, entries are variously organized in two divisions: philology and literature. The first has classified sections for general works, dictionaries and lexicography, etymology (combined with lexicography in the 1913–41 volume), phonology (combined with grammar in 1913–41), grammar, metrics, inscriptions, manuscripts, and Old Irish glosses; the second has sections for general studies, tales and sagas, poetry (only through the seventeenth century in the 1913–41 volume), religious works, history, legal works, and miscellaneous works. The original volume prints additions on pp. 273–74; in the volume for 1913–41 additions appear on pp. 193–94 and corrections to the earlier volume on pp. 253–54. Baumgarten organizes entries by publication date in extensively classified sections for general works, sources, linguistics, lexicology and onomastics, grammar, literature and learning, narrative literature, verse, society (a grab-bag section), Christianity, history and genealogy, and prehistory and cultural history. A few entries are accompanied by a brief descriptive annotation or list of reviews. In the online version, users must navigate through indexes that replicate the classification and indexes of the print edition. Entries can be saved to a list for down-loading or printing. The original volume is indexed by persons (with numerous omissions); the one for 1913–41 has indexes for words (with separate sections for personal names, place names, and other words, as well as an index to the earlier volume), first lines of poems, and persons and subjects; the most recent one has four indexes: words and proper names; first lines of verse; sources; authors of works cited (the electronic version adds an author and short-title index). Although confusingly organized, not comprehensive, and lacking any statement of scope and editorial policy in the 1942–71 volume, these volumes offer the fullest general coverage of scholarship on Irish language and literature through 1971.

N2975   Harmon, Maurice. *Select Bibliography for the Study of Anglo-Irish Literature and Its Backgrounds: An Irish Studies Handbook.* Port Credit: Meany, 1977. 187 pp.   Z2037.H32 [PR8711]   016.82.

A highly selective annotated guide, principally to reference works and important background studies published through the mid-1970s. Entries are organized in three divisions: general reference works, background materials, and literature. The background division has sections for reference works, history, biography, topography, folk culture and anthropology, theater, Anglo-Irish language, Irish language, Gaelic literature, and newspapers and periodicals. The literature division lists entries in sections for general studies, poetry, fiction, drama, bibliographies of individual authors, and literary periodicals. The brief descriptive annotations (sometimes including evaluative comments) too infrequently offer an adequate indication of contents or accurate evaluation. The chronology for 1765–1976 has numerous gaps. The lack of an index and numerous omissions make Harmon useful only insofar as it complements or updates the much fuller coverage in *New Cambridge Bibliography of English Literature* (N2965). Review: William T. O'Malley, *American Notes and Queries* 17 (1978): 66.

N2980   Hayes, Richard J., ed. *Sources for the History of Irish Civilisation: Articles in Irish Periodicals.* 9 vols. Boston: Hall, 1970.   Z2034.H35   016.91415′03.

A bibliography of articles, original literary works, and reviews in 152 periodicals, published in Ireland from c. 1800 through 1969, that print material useful for research in Irish intellectual and cultural life. Hayes excludes popular, trade, and current news periodicals as well as those in the Irish language. Entries (which record author, title, and publication information) are organized in four divisions: persons (vols. 1–5; library catalog main entries as well as persons as subjects and authors of books reviewed); subjects (vols. 6–8); places in Ireland (vol. 9); dates (vol. 9; works dealing with a specific date or period are organized in chronological order). Although the majority of the entries relate to Ireland, a significant number of articles and reviews on other topics, especially British literature, are also indexed. An essential source for locating works by and about Irish writers, and an important complement to the serial bibliographies and indexes in section G.

N2985   McKenna, Brian. *Irish Literature, 1800–1875: A Guide to Information Sources.* American Literature, English Literature, and World Literatures in English: An Information Guide Series 13. Detroit: Gale, 1978. 388 pp. Z2037.M235 [PR8750]   016.82.

A highly selective bibliography of works by and about Anglo-Irish authors. Coverage extends through 1974 and includes a few foreign-language studies. Entries are arranged chronologically in classified divisions for anthologies, periodicals, general studies, background studies, and individual authors (each with separate lists of bibliographies, biographies, criticism, and primary works). The brief annotations rarely offer an adequate indication of content or substantiate an evaluative comment. Three indexes: authors; titles; subjects. The lack of cross-references—especially to general studies—is not fully remedied by the subject index. Because of its selectivity (which results in some significant omissions) and the fuller treatment of major figures in author bibliographies, McKenna is principally useful as a starting point for work on minor writers. Review: James Kilroy, *Analytical and Enumerative Bibliography* 3 (1979): 62–67.

McKenna's volume for 1876–1950, although announced, was never published.

See also

Schwartz, *Articles on Women Writers* (U6605).

Dissertations and Theses

N2988   O'Malley, William T., comp. *Anglo-Irish Literature: A Bibliography of Dissertations, 1873–1989.* Bibliographies and Indexes in World Literature 26. New York: Greenwood, 1990. 299 pp.   Z2037.A54 [PR8711] 016.8209'9415.

An international bibliography of 4,359 dissertations on literature in English by 193 Irish writers (those born in Ireland or usually considered Irish, including a few critics, scholars, actors, and others) as well as "rhetorical, oratorical, and linguistic" studies of some nonliterary figures. Coverage extends through 1989 for United States and Canadian dissertations but ends considerably earlier or is not consecutive for most other countries. Entries—which consist of author, title, institution, and date—are organized in two divisions: individual authors; general and topical studies. Since each dissertation is listed only once, users must be certain to check the "See also" listings after each author section and the subject index for multiple-author studies. Two indexes: dissertation authors; subjects. Although incomplete, based largely on other bibliographies and lists of dissertations, and providing minimal information, O'Malley offers a useful preliminary compilation of dissertations on Anglo-Irish literature.

Language

Guides to Scholarship

See

ABELL (G340): See especially the Dialects section in the volumes for 1920–26; the English Dialects section in the volumes for 1927–72; and the Dialects/ British Isles section in the volumes since 1973.

Best, *Bibliography of Irish Philology* (N2970).

Bibliotheca Celtica (P3155).

Harmon, *Select Bibliography for the Study of Anglo-Irish Literature* (N2975).

MLAIB (G335): See especially the Dialectology section of the English Language division. (For an outline of this division, see p. 179.) Researchers must also check the heading "Irish English Dialect" in the subject index to post-1980 volumes and in the online thesaurus.

Biographical Dictionaries

Although there is no adequate, authoritative biographical dictionary for Ireland, the Royal Irish Academy is sponsoring the seven-volume *Dictionary of Irish Biography*, ed. Aidan Clarke et al., which will include about 9,000 noteworthy individuals (from the fifth century to the beginning of the twentieth century) who were natives or residents of Ireland or were thought of as Irish. Publication in print and online is scheduled for c. 2007 by Cambridge UP. Aidan Duggan, "A Dictionary of Irish Biography," *Scholarly Publishing* 20 (1988): 39–42, provides details of the project. For an overview of general and specialized biographical dictionaries through 1979, see C. J. Woods, "A Guide to Irish Biographical Dictionaries," *Maynooth Review* 6 (1980): 16–34.

N2990   Boylan, Henry. *A Dictionary of Irish Biography*. 3rd ed. Niwot: Rinehart,
         1998. 462 pp.   CT862.B69   920'.0415.
     A biographical dictionary of deceased individuals, principally of Irish birth (but also including some who were of Irish descent, "made a considerable contribution to Irish affairs," or had some lasting impact on Ireland). Each brief entry provides a basic chronological account of the entrant's life. Both earlier editions (New York: Barnes, 1978, 385 pp.; New York: St. Martin's, 1988, 420 pp.) and the new one are indexed in *Biography and Genealogy Master Index* (J565). Based heavily on *Dictionary of National Biography* (M1425a) and other sources, the *Dictionary* offers reasonably broad coverage. Brady, *Biographical Dictionary of Irish Writers* (N2995), includes a greater number of writers.

N2995   Brady, Anne M., and Brian Cleeve. *A Biographical Dictionary of Irish
         Writers*. New York: St. Martin's, 1985. 387 pp.   PR8727.B5
         820'.9'9415.
     A biographical dictionary of Irish writers, from St. Patrick to the present, that corrects many of the errors and omissions in Cleeve, *Dictionary of Irish Writers*, 3 vols. (Cork: Mercier, 1967–71). Brady and Cleeve includes numerous contemporary authors as well as scholars whose reputation extends beyond academe, but offers no statement of the criteria used to determine who qualifies as "Irish." The very brief entries—which provide basic biographical information, a list of major publications, and summary critical comments on major writers—are organized in two divisions: writers in English and writers in Irish and Latin. Additions appear on p. 254. Both editions are indexed in *Biography and Genealogy Master Index* (J565). This work offers the widest coverage (especially of contemporary authors) but the least information of the biographical dictionaries of Irish writers.

See also

   Dictionary of Irish Literature (N2925).
   Dictionary of Literary Biography (J600).
   Oxford Dictionary of National Biography (M1425).

Periodicals

Guides to Primary Works

N3000   North, John S. *The Waterloo Directory of Irish Newspapers and Periodicals,*
        1800–1900, Phase II. Phase 2, vol. 1 of Waterloo Directory Series of
        Newspapers and Periodicals: England, Ireland, Scotland, and Wales, 1800–
        1900. Waterloo: North Waterloo Academic, 1986. 838 pp.   Z6956.I7 N67
        011'.35'09415.

A bibliography and finding list of 3,932 serials published in Ireland during the nineteenth century. Publications are listed alphabetically by earliest title or issuing body for nonspecific titles; cross-references cite alternate titles, issuing bodies, and many subtitles. Main entries record, when possible, title; subtitles; title changes; series, volume, and issue numbering; publication dates; places of publication; editors; proprietors; publishers; printers; size; price; circulation; frequency of publication; illustrations; issuing bodies; indexing; subject matter; departments; religious or political stance; mergers; miscellaneous notes; references to studies or histories; and locations (in selected British and Irish collections). Three indexes: subjects; persons (including companies and issuing bodies); places of publication. The *Waterloo Directory,* a majority of whose entries are based on the actual examination of runs, offers the most accurate, complete accumulation of information on Irish serial publications. The extensive indexing makes essential sources for the study of nearly all facets of nineteenth-century Irish life and culture readily accessible for the first time. An indispensable work that supersedes all earlier bibliographies listing nineteenth-century Irish periodicals and newspapers and stands as an example of the kind of guide needed for serials of other countries and periods. Review: Rosemary T. VanArsdel, *Newsletter of the Victorian Studies Association of Western Canada* 13.1 (1987): 63–68.

Since locations are restricted to 50 British and Irish libraries, consult the following for additional holdings: Fulton, *Union List of Victorian Serials* (M2530); Ward, *Index and Finding List* (M2535); *Union List of Serials* (K640a); *British Union-Catalogue of Periodicals* (K645a); *WorldCat* (E225); and RLG Union Catalog (E230).

N3003   Clyde, Tom. *Irish Literary Magazines: An Outline History and Descriptive*
        Bibliography. Dublin: Irish Academic, 2003. 318 pp.   PR8711.C58
        820.9'9417.

An annotated bibliography of approximately 225 Irish literary magazines in English whose first issue was published in Ireland between 1710 and 1985 (with the early terminal date apparently determined by the scope of the doctoral dissertation on which this work is based). Entries, which proceed chronologically, include title, editorial address and printer, editor(s), inclusive dates of publication, total number of issues, frequency, average number of pages per issue, locations of copies (with details of microfilms and reprints), an evaluative (sometimes acerbic) description (hence the *Descriptive* of the subtitle), and citations to scholarship. Indexed by title. Based on firsthand examination of copies, the entries offer a wealth of detail. Unfortunately, the usefulness of *Irish Literary Magazines* is severely hindered by the absence of indexes of names and subjects, a flaw thrown into sharp relief by the suggestions for projects that conclude the preliminary outline history. Anyone taking on the recommended studies of publishers, editors, authors, censorship, or small presses will be relegated to reading large blocks of text.

Genres

Some works in section L: Genres are useful for research in Anglo-Irish literature.

Fiction

Some works in section L: Genres/Fiction are useful to research in Anglo-Irish fiction.

HISTORIES AND SURVEYS

N3023   Cahalan, James M. *The Irish Novel: A Critical History.* Twayne's Critical
        History of the Novel. Boston: Twayne, 1988. 365 pp.   PR8797.C34
        823′.009′89162.

   A history of Irish novels, written in Irish or English and set in Ireland, from the
eighteenth century to the late 1980s. The chapters, organized chronologically, examine
a variety of representative novelists and stress matters of language, genre, and history.
Indexed by persons and some subjects. The first single-volume history of the Irish novel,
Cahalan is especially valuable for its suggestions for further research (which are designed
to redress the neglect of Irish novelists other than Joyce). Review: Marilyn Thorne,
Studies in the Novel 21 (1989): 446–48.

GUIDES TO PRIMARY WORKS

N3025   Brown, Stephen J., S. J. *Ireland in Fiction: A Guide to Irish Novels, Tales,
        Romances, and Folklore.* New ed. Dublin: Maunsel, 1919. 362 pp. Brown
        and Desmond Clarke. Vol. 2. Cork: Royal Carberry, 1985. 290 pp.
        Z2039.F4 B8   016.823.

   An annotated author list of approximately 3,400 separately published fictional
works, through 1960, that treat Ireland or the Irish. Brown includes works by Anglo-
Irish as well as foreign writers, but excludes fiction written in Irish. Entries provide title,
pagination, publication information (usually for the most recent edition), and a synopsis
(including occasional comments on historical accuracy or representation of dialects and
quotations from reviews). Most Irish authors receive a brief biographical headnote.
Three appendixes in vol. 1 are worthy of note: appendix B is a list of series; appendix
C classifies works by type or subject matter (historical fiction by date of event depicted,
Gaelic epic and romantic literature, legends and folktales, fairy tales for children, Catholic clerical life, and humorous books); appendix D lists Irish periodicals publishing
fiction. Additions are printed in 1: 314–16. Indexed by titles and subjects in vol. 1,
by titles in vol. 2. Although the synopses are not always objective (especially for anti-
Irish, anti-Catholic, or "prurient" works) and coverage is incomplete, Brown provides
access to a wealth of examples of the treatment of Ireland and the Irish in fiction.
Unfortunately, vol. 2 is not widely held. Snell, *The Bibliography of Regional Fiction in
Britain and Ireland, 1800–2000* (M2650), is an essential supplement.

GUIDES TO SCHOLARSHIP AND CRITICISM

Diane Tolomeo, "Modern Fiction" (pp. 268–98), in Finneran, *Recent Research on Anglo-Irish Writers* (N2950), surveys scholarship and criticism.

Drama and Theater

Some works in section L: Genres/Drama and Theater are useful to research in Anglo-Irish drama and theater.

HISTORIES AND SURVEYS

N3030   Hogan, Robert, et al. *The Modern Irish Drama: A Documentary History.* 6 vols. Irish Theatre Series 6–8, 10, 12. Dublin: Dolmen; Atlantic Highlands: Humanities, 1975–84.   PR8789.H62 [PN2602.D82] 792'.09415.

> Vol. 1: *The Irish Literary Theatre, 1899–1901.* By Robert Hogan and James Kilroy. 1975. 164 pp.
> Vol. 2: *Laying the Foundations, 1902–1904.* By Hogan and Kilroy. 1976. 164 pp.
> Vol. 3: *The Abbey Theatre: The Years of Synge, 1905–1909.* By Hogan and Kilroy. 1978. 385 pp.
> Vol. 4: *The Rise of the Realists, 1910–1915.* By Hogan, Richard Burnham, and Daniel P. Poteet. 1979. 532 pp.
> Vol. 5: *The Art of the Amateur, 1916–1920.* By Hogan and Burnham. 1984. 368 pp.
> Vol. 6: *The Years of O'Casey, 1921–1926: A Documentary History.* By Hogan and Burnham. Newark: U of Delaware P; Gerrards Cross: Smythe, 1992. 437 pp. PR8789.H66 792'.0415'09042.

A year-by-year account of the drama and theater, with each volume attempting "to recreate the flavour of the period" through extensive quotations from contemporary documents, accounts or reviews of performances, letters, memoirs, and the like. Vols. 4–6, however, do offer considerable critical commentary. Each volume includes a chronological list of significant Anglo-Irish plays and the most important Irish-language ones. Organized by year of first production (or date of publication for unperformed plays), each entry records the first edition, original cast, and date and theater of the first production. Each volume is indexed by persons, titles, and a few subjects. A well-integrated re-creation of the modern Irish theatrical and dramatic milieu.

N3035   Maxwell, D. E. S. *A Critical History of Modern Irish Drama, 1891–1980.* Cambridge: Cambridge UP, 1984. 250 pp.   PR8789.M39 822'.91'099415.

A critical history of Anglo-Irish drama since the beginning of the Irish Literary Theatre. Organized chronologically, the 10 chapters chronicle periods and major dramatists. Concludes with a brief chronology and selected bibliography. Indexed by persons and subjects. The fullest critical history of the Irish drama, Maxwell supersedes earlier histories. Review: Ronald Ayling, *Essays in Theatre* 5 (1987): 139–44.

GUIDES TO PRIMARY WORKS

N3037   Greene, John C., and Gladys L. H. Clark. *The Dublin Stage, 1720–1745: A Calendar of Plays, Entertainments, and Afterpieces.* Bethlehem: Lehigh UP; London: Assoc. UP, 1993. 473 pp.   PN2602.D8 G7 792'.09418'3509033.

A calendar of theatrical performances in Dublin. Modeled on *London Stage, 1660–1800* (M2370), entries provide, where available, venue, date of performance, cast, production personnel, afterpiece(s) and other entertainment, details of benefit or command performances, and notes on box-office receipts and other details. Prefaced by an overview of such theatrical topics as the playhouses, the season, costume, music, and the repertory. Four indexes: stage personnel; playwrights and titles; main- and afterpieces; topics and persons not included in the preceding indexes. An essential guide to the history of the early Irish theater.

GUIDES TO SCHOLARSHIP AND CRITICISM

Despite the interest in Irish drama, there is no reasonably thorough bibliography of scholarship and criticism. The following do little more than provide a starting point for research.

Surveys of Research

Finneran, *Anglo-Irish Literature* and *Recent Research on Anglo-Irish Writers* (N2950) have chapters on the modern drama by Robert Hogan, Bonnie K. Scott, and Gordon Henderson (pp. 518–61) and Hogan (pp. 255–67), respectively.

Other Bibliographies

N3040   King, Kimball. *Ten Modern Irish Playwrights: A Comprehensive Annotated Bibliography.* Garland Reference Library of the Humanities 153. New York: Garland, 1979. 111 pp.   Z2039.D7 K56 [PR8789]   016.822'9'1408.

A partially annotated bibliography of primary and secondary works through 1977 for Behan, Boyd, Douglas, Friel, Keane, Kilroy, Leonard, McKenna, Murphy, and O'Brien. The list of primary works for each author includes all genres (as well as interviews); secondary works appear under one of three headings: criticism, dissertations (unannotated), and reviews (spottily annotated). Some of the descriptive annotations are misleading, and there are numerous other errors. Indexed by scholars. The exclusion of most reviews and several articles from Irish periodicals and newspapers along with other significant omissions render this work much less than the comprehensive bibliography claimed by the subtitle. As reviewers point out, a careful revision is needed if *Ten Modern Irish Playwrights* is to offer more than minimal guidance for research on the 10 playwrights. Reviews: Charles A. Carpenter, *Modern Drama* 24 (1981): 116–

19; Richard J. Finneran, *Analytical and Enumerative Bibliography* 3 (1979): 305–19 (with a lengthy list of additions and corrections).

N3045   Mikhail, E. H. *An Annotated Bibliography of Modern Anglo–Irish Drama.*
          Troy: Whitston, 1981. 300 pp.   Z2039.D7 M528 [PR8789]
          016.822′91′099415.
   A bibliography limited to general studies (from 1899 through 1977), organized in five divisions: bibliographies (a hodgepodge including several works of minimal importance to the subject), reference works, books, periodical articles, and dissertations. Concludes with an incomplete list of library collections. Few of the annotations are adequately descriptive. Two indexes: persons (including authors as subjects); subjects. Plagued by inadequate indexing and annotations, numerous errors and significant omissions, the inclusion of much that is trivial, and poor organization, *Bibliography of Modern Anglo-Irish Drama* is only marginally useful for identifying discussions of playwrights and a few subjects buried in general studies. This work supersedes Mikhail, *A Bibliography of Modern Irish Drama, 1899–1970* (Seattle: U of Washington P, 1972, 51 pp.) and *Dissertations on Anglo-Irish Drama: A Bibliography of Studies, 1870–1970* (Totowa: Rowman, 1973, 73 pp.).
   Complemented—somewhat—by Mikhail, *A Research Guide to Modern Irish Dramatists* (Troy: Whitston, 1979, 104 pp.), a bibliography of bibliographies of primary and secondary works. The annotations describe nothing more than the kind of bibliography, and nearly 70% of the entries refer to seven general selective bibliographies (e.g., *New Cambridge Bibliography of English Literature* [M1385]; Samples, *Drama Scholars' Index* [L1150a]; and Coleman, *Drama Criticism* [M2875a]).

Poetry

Some works in section L: Genres/Poetry are useful to research in Anglo-Irish poetry.

GUIDES TO SCHOLARSHIP AND CRITICISM

Mary M. FitzGerald, "Modern Poetry," pp. 299–334, in Finneran, *Recent Research on Anglo-Irish Writers* (N2950), surveys scholarship and criticism.

O

Scottish Literature

This section is limited to works devoted exclusively to Scottish literature (primarily in English). Because Scottish writers are frequently included in reference works on English or British literature, researchers must also consult section M: English Literature. Many works listed in sections G: Serial Bibliographies, Indexes, and Abstracts and H: Guides to Dissertations and Theses are useful for research in Scottish literature.

Histories and Surveys

O3060   *The History of Scottish Literature.* Gen. ed. Cairns Craig. 4 vols. Aberdeen: Aberdeen UP, 1987–88.   PR8511.H57   820′.9′89163.

Vol. 1: *Origins to 1660 (Mediaeval and Renaissance)*. Ed. R. D. S. Jack. 1988.
310 pp.
Vol. 2: *1660–1800*. Ed. Andrew Hook. 1987. 337 pp.
Vol. 3: *Nineteenth Century*. Ed. Douglas Gifford. 1988. 471 pp.
Vol. 4: *Twentieth Century*. Ed. Cairns Craig. 1987. 399 pp.

A collaborative history of Scottish literature in English, Scottish, and Gaelic that emphasizes its cultural, intellectual, and linguistic contexts. Each volume consists of essays by established scholars on cultural, social, and intellectual backgrounds, genres, and major writers. Most volumes conclude with a brief list of recommended readings. Indexed in each volume by persons and subjects. Although lacking the coherence and balance possible in a connected narrative, these volumes offer the most current and thorough history of Scottish literature. Reviews: (vols. 1, 2, and 4) Alastair Fowler, *TLS: Times Literary Supplement* 28 Oct.–3 Nov. 1988: 1198–99; (vol. 1) Elizabeth Archibald, *Scottish Literary Journal* supp. 31 (1989): 1–3; Roger A. Mason, *Scottish Historical Review* 69 (1990): 101–02; (vol. 3) Murray G. H. Pittock, *Scottish Literary Journal* supp. 31 (1989): 13–17; (vol. 4) Thomas Crawford, *Scottish Literary Journal* supp. 29 (1988): 19–23.

Still needed, however, is a history that will offer a thorough, coherent treatment of Scottish literature and supersede J. H. Millar, *A Literary History of Scotland*, Library of Literary History (London: Unwin, 1903, 703 pp.), whose chapters on periods, genres, and major authors exclude writers (such as Boswell and Carlyle) who belong more properly to English literature.

Literary Handbooks, Dictionaries, and Encyclopedias

O3065   Royle, Trevor. *Mainstream Companion to Scottish Literature*. Edinburgh: Mainstream, 1993. 335 pp. (Revision of *Companion to Scottish Literature* [Detroit: Gale, 1983, 322 pp.].)   PR8506.R692   820.9'9411'03.

A handbook with entries on authors writing in English, Scots, or Gaelic; movements; historical events and persons; publishing; manuscripts; places; and other topics of literary interest. The majority of the entries are for writers (including historians, philosophers, divines, and scholars) and provide basic biographical information, brief critical comments, and a list of major books (including standard editions) and citations to important scholarship. Entrants in the 1983 edition are indexed in *Biography and Genealogy Master Index* (J565). Despite occasional errors, this is a valuable, lucidly written source for quick reference.

O3067   Bold, Alan. *Scotland: A Literary Guide*. London: Routledge, 1989. 327 pp.
PR8531.B65   820.9'9411.

A guide to important locations with literary associations. Places are listed alphabetically; organized chronologically under each location are sections on authors, medieval to contemporary and foreigners as well as Scots, that describe the nature of the association, note specific buildings or monuments (without precise locations in too many instances), and usually offer an illustrative quotation. With more attention to local color than is usual in such works, *Scotland: A Literary Guide* is an entertaining resource for the literary tourist.

Guides to Scholarship and Criticism

Surveys of Research

O3070   *Scottish Literary Journal: The Year's Work in Scottish Literary and Linguistic Studies [1984–96].* 1987–2001. Annual.   PR8514.S3.

> 1973–83: "The Year's Work in Scottish Literary and Linguistic Studies [1973–83]." *Scottish Literary Journal: Supplement* 1–23 (1975–85). Annual.

Selective, essay reviews of scholarship based on *Annual Bibliography of Scottish Literature* (O3075). The separately authored essays on language, folk literature, the medieval period to 1650, 1650 to 1800, 1800 to 1900, and 1900 to the present are typically judicious in selecting and evaluating the most important scholarship. More thorough in its coverage of Scottish literature than *Year's Work in English Studies* (G330), this work was the best annual survey of scholarship on the field.

See also

> *YWES* (G330): Scottish writers are covered in several chapters.

Serial Bibliographies

O3075   *Annual Bibliography of Scottish Literature [1969–82].* Supplement to *Bibliotheck.* 1970–84.   Z2057.A65   011.

A bibliography of books, articles, and reviews organized in four classified divisions: general bibliographical and reference works; general literary criticism, anthologies, and collections; individual authors (subdivided by period); and ballads and folk literature. In each division or section, entries are listed alphabetically by author in three parts: books, reviews of previously listed books, and articles. Two indexes: literary authors; scholars. The *Annual Bibliography of Scottish Literature* was an important supplement to the serial bibliographies and indexes in section G.

O3080   *Bibliography of Scotland [1988–   ] (BOS).* Edinburgh: Natl. Lib. of Scotland, 1988–   . Online. 24 Sept. 2005 <http://www.nls.uk> path: Search other catalogues/Bibliography of Scotland (BOS): Go to search page/ Quick limits: BOS.

> *Bibliography of Scotland [1976–87].* 1978–90. Annual.   Z2069.B52 015.411.

A database of books (including chapters of books not primarily about Scotland), serials, and articles about Scotland published after 1987 (along with publications from 1976–87 cataloged after 1988). The entries from the print volumes will eventually be incorporated into the database. Coverage is based largely on acquisitions by the National Library and thus is full but not comprehensive. To limit a search to the *BOS* database, users must click on Quick Limits on the Simple Search screen or Limits on the Advanced Search screen. Simple Search allows for keyword searches of the entire record, author, title, journal title, shelf mark, subject, ISBN, ISSN, or a combination of author and title. Advanced Search allows combinations of keyword searches of the same fields (except journal title and shelf mark) along with date, series title, publisher, or personal name. Records can be sorted by author, title, or date, and marked for printing, saving, or e-mailing. Although the coverage of literary studies is not particularly thorough, *Bibliography of Scotland* is sometimes a useful complement to *Annual Bibliography of Scottish Literature* (O3075) and the serial bibliographies and indexes in section G.

For earlier books about Scotland, see the following:

> Hancock, P. D., comp. *A Bibliography of Works Relating to Scotland, 1916– 1950.* 2 vols. Edinburgh: Edinburgh UP, 1959–60. Of interest to literary scholars are the classified divisions for biography, folklore, books and printing, language, and literature. Coverage of literary studies is far from complete, however.
>
> Mitchell, Arthur, and C. G. Cash. *A Contribution to the Bibliography of Scottish Topography.* 2 vols. Publications of the Scottish History Society 2nd ser. 14–15. Edinburgh: Edinburgh UP for Scottish History Soc., 1917. Of interest to literary scholars are the divisions for bibliography, biography, folklore, place-names, and theater.

See also

> Secs. G: Serial Bibliographies, Indexes, and Abstracts and H: Guides to Dissertations and Theses.
>
> *ABELL* (G340): Entries on Scottish writers and literature are dispersed throughout.
>
> *Bibliotheca Celtica* (P3155).
>
> *MLAIB* (G335): Until the volume for 1981, Scottish literature in English was included in the English Literature division. Literature in Scottish Gaelic was covered in a Celtic Languages and Literatures heading under the General division in the volumes for 1928–52; in General IV (later V or VI): Celtic Languages and Literatures in the volumes for 1953–66; and in Celtic VIII: Scottish Gaelic in the volumes for 1967–80. Since the 1981 volume, the Scottish Literature section encompasses literature in whatever language. Researchers must also check the headings beginning "Scottish" in the subject index to post-1980 volumes and in the online thesaurus.
>
> *Royal Historical Society Bibliography* (M1400).

Other Bibliographies

O3085   *The New Cambridge Bibliography of English Literature* (*NCBEL*). Ed. George Watson and I. R. Willison. 5 vols. Cambridge: Cambridge UP, 1969–77. Z2011.N45 [PR83]   016.82.

(For a full discussion of *NCBEL*, see entry M1385.) Scottish literature is covered throughout the volumes:

> Vol. 1: *600–1660* has a section on Middle Scots poets (cols. 651–64) in the Middle English division and, in the Renaissance division, a section on Scottish printing and bookselling (cols. 967–70) and a subdivision on Scottish literature (cols. 2419–76), with classified listings for general studies, poetry and drama, and prose. Scottish writers also appear in other sections.

> Vol. 2: *1660–1800* has sections on Scottish printing and bookselling (cols. 271–72) and periodicals (cols. 1369–78), and a separate division for Scottish literature (cols. 1955–2082) with sections for general studies, poetry and drama, and prose.
>
> Vols. 3: *1800–1900* and 4: *1900–1950* treat Scottish literature and writers throughout their various divisions. Coverage of primary (but not secondary) works in vol. 3 is superseded by vol. 4 of the third edition of *CBEL* (M2467).

In addition, many of the general sections list works important to the study of Scottish literature. Coverage extends through 1962–69, depending on the volume.

Users must familiarize themselves with the organization, remember that there is considerable unevenness of coverage among sections, and consult the index volume (vol. 5) rather than the provisional indexes in vols. 1–4.

Despite its shortcomings (see entry M1385), *NCBEL* offers the fullest overall bibliography of primary works and scholarship on Scottish literature in English.

For authors omitted from *NCBEL* or scholarship published after the cutoff dates of volumes, W. R. Aitken, *Scottish Literature in English and Scots: A Guide to Information Sources*, American Literature, English Literature, and World Literatures in English: An Information Guide Series 37 (Detroit: Gale, 1982, 421 pp.)—a highly selective and only partially annotated bibliography—is sometimes useful as a supplement.

Language

Guides to Scholarship

See

> *ABELL* (G340): See especially the Dialects section in the volumes for 1920–26; the English Dialects section in the volumes for 1927–72; and the Dialects/British Isles section in later volumes.
>
> *MLAIB* (G335): See especially the Dialectology section of the English Language division. (For an outline of the division, see p. 179.) Researchers must also check the heading "Scots English Dialect" in the subject index to post-1980 volumes and in the online thesaurus.
>
> "Year's Work in Scottish Literary and Linguistic Studies" (O3070).

Dictionaries

O3090   *Dictionary of the Scots Language* (*DSL*). Online. 4 Sept. 2006 <http://www.dsl.ac.uk/dsl/index.html>. An electronic version of:

> *A Dictionary of the Older Scottish Tongue from the Twelfth Century to the End of the Seventeenth* (*DOST*). Ed. William A. Craigie et al. 12 vols. Oxford: Oxford UP, 1931–2002.   PE2116.C7   427′.9411. <http://www.arts.ed.ac.uk/dost>.
>
> *The Scottish National Dictionary: Designed Partly on Regional Lines and Partly on Historical Principles, and Containing All the Scottish Words Known to Be in Use or to Have Been in Use since c. 1700* (*SND*). Ed. William Grant

and David D. Murison. 10 vols. Edinburgh: Scottish Natl. Dictionary Assn., 1931–76. Reduced print ed.: *The Compact Scottish National Dictionary: Containing All the Scottish Words Known to Be in Use or to Have Been in Use since c. 1700, Arranged Partly on Regional Lines and Partly on Historical Principles.* 2 vols. Aberdeen: Aberdeen UP, 1986. PE2106.S4   427.9.

Dictionary of the Scottish Language consists of five data files: *DOST* main file, *DOST Additions* (the data published at the end of vol. 10), *SND* main file, *SND Supplement* (data from the supplements in the firsts three volumes, but with the completely new entries integrated into the *SND* main file), and *SND New Supplement.* Users can search text or browse headwords in a single file, in both *DOST* or the three *SND* files, or in all five files simultaneously (the default). Users can perform keyword or phrase searches in the full entry for a word (the default) or limit searches to headwords, geographic label abbreviations, citations, illustrative quotations, works cited, authors cited, etymologies, senses, or dates. Users must be certain to read the Search the *DSL* page for information about the search engine's handling of Boolean operators, right truncation, diacritics, special characters, and punctuation. Since abbreviations have not been expanded, users will need frequent recourse to the lists of abbreviations (hidden away in *DOST* Prelims and *SND Introduction* [scroll to the bottom of the Go To pull-down menu]). Effective use of the *DSL* requires an understanding of the scope and editorial practices of the two dictionaries it digitizes.

DOST is a historical dictionary of the Scottish language based on literary works, documents, records, and other manuscript materials. Because of the nature of the sources and changes in the language, the fullest coverage is for 1375–1600 (with words after 1600 confined to those no longer current or not coinciding with English usage), and because of changes in editorial policies and procedures, entries after vol. 2 are much more thorough. Typical entries record parts of speech, selected variant spellings (with a full index of these variants in each volume), etymologies, definitions, and illustrative quotations. Users should note that additions and corrections are collected at the end of each volume. Accuracy and thoroughness make this the essential source for the historical study of the language and interpretation of Scottish literature to 1700 and a necessary complement to the *Oxford English Dictionary* (M1410). For a discussion of the excerpting procedures, editing, and editorial problems, see A. J. Aitken, "*DOST*: How We Make It and What's in It," *Dictionaries* 4 (1982): 42–64; for an overview of changes in editorial practices, see Margaret G. Dareau, "*DOST*: Its History and Completion," *Dictionaries* 23 (2002): 208–31. Reviews: (pt. 1) Percy W. Long, *JEGP: Journal of English and Germanic Philology* 32 (1933): 235–38; (pts. 1–2) Bruch Dickins, *Modern Language Review* 28 (1933): 243–44; (pt. 17) Hans Heinrich Meier, *English Studies* 43 (1962): 444–48; (pts. 19–21) A. Fenton, *Scottish Studies* 10 (1966): 198–205.

SND is a historical and dialectal dictionary of the Scottish language from c. 1700 to the mid-twentieth century that includes the following:

(1) Scottish words that do not occur in St[andard] Eng[lish] except as acknowledged loan words; (2) Scottish words the cognates of which occur in St[andard] Eng[lish]; (3) words which have the same form in Sc[ottish] and St[andard] Eng[lish] but have a different meaning in Sc[ottish] . . . ; (4) legal, theological or ecclesiastical terms which . . . have been current in Scottish speech . . . ; (5) words borrowed since c. 1700 (from other dialects or languages) which have become current in Gen[eral] Sc[ottish], or in any of its dialects . . . .

A typical entry records variant spelling, part(s) of speech, status (e.g., obsolete, archaic, dialectal), meaning(s), pronunciation, inflections, etymology, and illustrative quotations (for the order of these, see vol. 1, pp. xlvi–xlvii; pp. 35–36 in the *SND* Introduction at the *DSL* site). Vol. 10 includes various appendixes (Scottish forms of personal names, place names, fairs and markets, and a table of Scottish weights and measures, pp. 299–317); a list of abbreviations used in entries (pp. 318–23); additions and corrections (pp. 325–536); a list of works quoted (pp. 537–74; click on the Search Bibliographies link at the *DSL* site); and scientific terms with Scottish connections (pp. 575–91). For the history and significance of *SND*, see A. J. Aitken, R. W. Burchfield, and Hugh MacDiarmid, "*The Scottish National Dictionary*: Three Comments on the Occasion of Its Completion," *Scottish Review* 1 (1975): 17–25. Like *Dictionary of the Older Scottish Tongue*, which it continues, *SND* is an essential source for the historical study of the language and interpretation of Scottish literature, and an important complement to the *Oxford English Dictionary* (M1410). Review: W. F. H. Nicolaisen, *Archiv* 214 (1977): 403–05.

The preceding are complemented by J. Y. Mather and H. H. Speitel, eds., *The Linguistic Atlas of Scotland: Scots Section* (London: Croom Helm, 1975–). The best concise dictionary is Mairi Robinson, ed., *The Concise Scots Dictionary* (Aberdeen: Aberdeen UP, 1985, 819 pp.). For its potential uses, see Mairi Robinson, "*The Concise Scots Dictionary* as a Tool for Linguistic Research," *The Nuttis Schell: Essays on the Scots Language Presented to A. J. Aitken*, ed. Caroline Macafee and Iseabail Macleod (Aberdeen: Aberdeen UP, 1987) 59–72.

Biographical Dictionaries

John Horden's plan for a Dictionary of Scottish Biography was never realized.

See

> Sec. J: Biographical Sources.
> *Oxford Dictionary of National Biography* (M1425).
> Royle, *Companion to Scottish Literature* (O3065).

Periodicals

Guides to Primary Works

O3103   North, John S. *The Waterloo Directory of Scottish Newspapers and Periodicals, 1800–1900*. Phase II of the Waterloo Directory Series of Newspapers and Periodicals, England, Ireland, Scotland, and Wales, 1800–1900. 2 vols. Waterloo: North Waterloo Academic, 1989.   Z6956.S3 W38 011'.34'09411.

A bibliography and finding list of several thousand serials published in Scotland during the nineteenth century. Publications are listed alphabetically by earliest title or issuing body for nonspecific titles; liberal cross-references cite alternate titles, issuing bodies, wrapper titles, nicknames, and many subtitles. Main entries record, when possible, titles; subtitles and title changes; series, volume, and issue numbering; publication dates; places of publication; editors; proprietors; publishers; printers; size; price; circulation; frequency of publication; illustrations; issuing bodies; indexing; departments; religious or political perspectives; miscellaneous notes; mergers; references to studies or histories; subject matter; and locations in about 111 collections in England and Scotland. Many entries are accompanied by a facsimile of a title page. Three indexes: subjects; persons (including corporate names); places of publication. The *Waterloo Directory*, about 85% of whose entries are based on the actual examination of runs, offers the most accurate and complete accumulation of information on Scottish serial publications. The extensive indexing makes essential sources for the study of nearly all facets of nineteenth-century Scottish life and culture readily accessible for the first time. An indispensable work that supersedes all earlier bibliographies listing nineteenth-century Scottish periodicals and newspapers, and that—like its companion, *Waterloo Directory of Irish Newspapers and Periodicals* (N3000)—stands as an example of the kind of guide needed for serials of other countries and periods.

Since locations are restricted to selected English and Scottish collections, consult the following for additional holdings: Fulton, *Union List of Victorian Serials* (M2530); Ward, *Index and Finding List* (M2535); *Union List of Serials* (K640a); *British Union-Catalogue of Periodicals* (K645a); *WorldCat* (E225); and RLG Union Catalog (E230).

Genres

Many works in sections L: Genres and M: English Literature/General/Genres are useful for research in Scottish literature.

Fiction

Some works in sections L: Genres/Fiction and M: English Literature/General/Genres/ Fiction are useful for research in Scottish fiction.

HISTORIES AND SURVEYS

O3120   Hart, Francis Russell. *The Scottish Novel from Smollett to Spark*. Cambridge: Harvard UP, 1978. 442 pp. British ed.: *The Scottish Novel: A Critical Survey*. London: Murray, 1978.   PR8597.H37   823'.03.

A critical history of the development of the novel in Scotland from c. 1760 to the 1970s. In discussing approximately 200 works by some 50 novelists, Hart offers generally full descriptions of content and emphasizes distinctively Scottish motifs and methods but gives only limited attention to social context and style. Chapters are organized more or less chronologically, with a separate section on the novel of the Highlands and a concluding chapter on the theory of Scottish fiction. Indexed by persons and a few subjects. Praised for its scope and command of the topic, this work is the standard history of the Scottish novel. Reviews: John Clubbe, *JEGP: Journal of English and Germanic Philology* 78 (1979): 439–42; Cairns Craig, *Studies in Scottish Literature* 15 (1980): 302–10; David Daiches, *Nineteenth-Century Fiction* 34 (1979): 75–78.

Poetry

GUIDES TO PRIMARY WORKS

Priscilla Bawcutt has ceased working on the first-line index described in "A First-Line Index of Early Scottish Verse," *Studies in Scottish Literature* 26 (1991): 254–69.

GUIDES TO SCHOLARSHIP AND CRITICISM

O3130   Glen, Duncan. *The Poetry of the Scots: An Introduction and Bibliographical Guide to Poetry in Gaelic, Scots, Latin, and English.* Edinburgh: Edinburgh UP, 1991. 149 pp.   PR8561.G58   016.8091.

A highly selective bibliography of works, through 1990, by and about Scottish poets. Entries are organized in eight divisions: background studies (including sections for dictionaries, bibliographies, general and social histories of Scotland, general background studies, histories of Scottish literature, studies of languages, general studies of Scottish poetry, general critical studies of Scottish literature); anthologies and magazines; early Scots poetry (to the mid-sixteenth century); Renaissance poets; ballads; eighteenth-century poets; nineteenth-century poets; and twentieth-century poets. The sections on individual poets (which are variously organized within the period divisions) typically cite the best and other important editions, recordings, and a very few studies; some entries are accompanied by brief evaluative comments, with the best edition or recording usually followed by a lengthy assessment of the poet's canon. Two indexes: poets; persons, anonymous works, subjects. Although highly selective and idiosyncratically organized, Duncan offers a starting point for those unfamiliar with Scottish poetry (especially of the twentieth century).

P

Welsh Literature

This section is limited to works devoted exclusively to Welsh literature (primarily in English). Because Welsh writers are frequently included in reference sources on English or British literature, researchers must consult section M: English Literature. Many works listed in sections G: Serial Bibliographies, Indexes, and Abstracts and H: Guides to Dissertations and Theses are useful for research in Welsh literature.

Histories and Surveys

P3135   *A Guide to Welsh Literature.* 7 vols. Cardiff: U of Wales P, 1976–2003.
      PB2206.G8   891'.6'6'09.

     Vol. 1. Rev. ed. Ed. A. O. H. Jarman and Gwilym Rees Hughes. 1992.
       295 pp. (Sixth century to c. 1300.)
     Vol. 2. Ed. Jarman and Hughes. 1979. 400 pp. (c. 1300 to 1527.)
     Vol. 3. Ed. R. Geraint Gruffydd. 1997. 293 pp. (c. 1530 to 1700.)
     Vol. 4. Ed. Branwen Jarvis. 2000. 342 pp. (c. 1700 to 1800.)
     Vol. 5. Ed. Hywel Teifi Edwards. 2000. 247 pp. (c. 1800 to 1900.)
     Vol. 6. Ed. Dafydd Johnston. 1998. 308 pp. (c. 1900 to 1996.)
     Vol. 7. Ed. M. Wynn Thomas. 2003. 348 pp. (Welsh Writing in English.)

A descriptive, interpretative history of Welsh literature from the sixth century to 1996. Each volume is made up of essays by major scholars on important works or writers, forms, genres, and historical background; each essay concludes with a highly selective bibliography of editions and studies. Indexed by persons, titles, and subjects in each volume. The failure to identify sources of passages and references to scholarship renders the *Guide* less useful than it might be. Although frequently offering more detailed analyses than Parry but lacking his continuity and breadth, *Guide to Welsh Literature* complements rather than supersedes his *History of Welsh Literature* (P3140). Reviews: (vol. 1) Patrick K. Ford, *Speculum* 54 (1979): 812–17; Margaret Charlotte Ward, *Medium Ævum* 47 (1978): 333–37.

P3140   Parry, Thomas. *A History of Welsh Literature*. Trans. H. Idris Bell. Corrected rpt. Oxford: Clarendon–Oxford UP, 1962. 534 pp. (Trans. of *Hanes llenyddiaeth Gymraeg hyd 1900*. Cardiff: U of Wales P, 1944. 323 pp.)   PB2206.P33   820.9.
   A history of Welsh literature from the sixth century to 1900, with an appendix by the translator carrying the record forward to c. 1950. Organized chronologically, chapters treat genres, forms, major works or authors; beginning with the nineteenth century, chapters include a section on literary, linguistic, and historical scholarship. Concludes with a highly selective bibliography of English-language scholarship. Two indexes: Welsh authors; subjects (including scholars cited). Although the translation incorporates Parry's modified views on some topics, the Welsh edition is still useful for its fuller bibliography. Authoritative but not definitive, this is the standard history of Welsh literature; it is complemented, but not superseded, by *Guide to Welsh Literature* (P3135). Review: *Times Literary Supplement* 23 Dec. 1955: 778.

Literary Handbooks,
Dictionaries, and Encyclopedias

P3145   *The New Companion to the Literature of Wales*. Comp. and ed. Meic Stephens. Cardiff: U of Wales P, 1998. 841 pp. Welsh ed.: *Cydymaith i lenyddiaeth Cymru*. Cardiff: Gwasg Prifysgol Cymru, 1997. 831 pp. PB2202.N49.
   Covers Welsh literary culture from the sixth century through the late 1990s in some 3,300 entries on authors (including hymn writers, historians, antiquaries, critics, scholars, translators, journalists, and the like, but excluding anyone born after 1950); prosody (less fully than in the Welsh edition); genres; motifs; manuscripts; periodicals; literary works; folk songs; hymns; mythical, historical, and literary figures as well as a host of other individuals (even rugby players); folklore and legend; historical events; societies; movements; English authors important to Welsh culture; music—in short, just about anything of significance to Welsh literature. Entries emphasize factual information rather than interpretation, and many cite standard scholarly works; author entries focus on biographical details and major works but do offer occasional evaluative comments. Concludes with a chronology of Welsh history. Although some entries have no discernible connection with Welsh literature, the *New Companion* is an essential work for quick reference. A revision of *The Oxford Companion to the Literature of Wales*, ed. Stephens (Oxford: Oxford UP, 1986, 682 pp.); Welsh edition: *Cydymaith i lenyddiaeth Cymru* (1986, 662 pp.).

Guides to Primary Works

For an overview of bibliographies covering works printed in Wales and Welsh manuscripts, see Eiluned Rees, "From Autograph to Automation: Welsh Bibliography," *The Book Encompassed: Studies in Twentieth-Century Bibliography*, ed. Peter Davison (Cambridge: Cambridge UP, 1992) 193–99.

P3150   Jones, Brynmor. *A Bibliography of Anglo-Welsh Literature, 1900–1965.*
         Swansea: Wales and Monmouthshire Branch of the Lib. Assn., 1970.
         139 pp.   Z2013.3.J64   016.8209′0091.

A selective bibliography of poetry, drama, and fiction in English by Welsh writers, of some works set in Wales by foreign authors, and of studies of Anglo-Welsh literature. Since only works utilizing a Welsh locale, characters, or idiom are included, many important plays and fictional works by Welsh writers are omitted. (The requirement for Welsh content is less strictly applied to poetry.) Entries are organized in three parts. The list of primary works includes sections for anthologies and individual authors. In the latter, works are grouped by genre, with entries citing editions, translations, and excerpts, and identifying locale in fiction and plays. The highly selective list of secondary works has sections for bibliographies and indexes, general criticism, and individual authors; some entries are briefly annotated. A concluding list of children's stories is unannotated. Two indexes: settings; persons (excluding authors of studies of individual writers). Although its value as a record of twentieth-century Anglo-Welsh literature is seriously marred by the ill-considered editorial policy that excludes works lacking a Welsh background, this work remains a useful pioneering effort. It must be supplemented, however, by other sources such as *Cambridge Bibliography of English Literature* (M1376), *New Cambridge Bibliography of English Literature* (M1385), *British Library Integrated Catalogue* (E250), *WorldCat* (E225), and RLG Union Catalog (E230). Review: *TLS: Times Literary Supplement* 4 Dec. 1970: 1428.

Guides to Scholarship and Criticism

Serial Bibliographies

P3155   *Llyfryddiaeth Cymru/A Bibliography of Wales.* National Library of Wales.
         Online. 22 Sept. 2005 <http://cat.llgc.org.uk>. Updated regularly.

         Llyfryddiaeth Cymru/A Bibliography of Wales [1985–94]. Aberystwyth: Natl.
         Lib. of Wales, 1992–99. Biennial.   Z2071.L57 [DA708]   016.9429.

         *Bibliotheca Celtica: A Register of Publications Relating to Wales and the Celtic
         Peoples and Languages [1909–84].* Aberystwyth: Natl. Lib. of Wales, 1910–
         90.   Z2071.B56   016.9429.

         Welsh Publications 1801–1919. National Library of Wales. Online. 22 Sept.
         2005 <http://cat.llgc.org.uk>.

Bibliography of Wales is a bibliographic database of publications in Welsh, published in Wales, or relating to Wales. In Simple search, users can search title, series title, author, subject, keyword (i.e., the four preceding fields), place of publication, publisher, notes, ISSN, or ISBN fields; Advanced search allows uses to combine two of the preceding fields and to sort results by author, title, or date. Both Simple and Advanced search allow users to limit searches by date, language, and type of material. Users can also Browse several record fields. Records—which supply basic bibliographical information—can be marked for e-mailing, printing, or saving.

The printed *Bibliography of Wales* combines and continues *Bibliotheca Celtica* and *Subject Index to Welsh Periodicals* [1931–84] (Aberystwyth: Natl. Lib. of Wales, 1934–89). Entries (which provide full bibliographic information and cite reviews of books) are listed in two parts: subjects and authors.

Bibliotheca Celtica is a classified bibliography of books, dissertations, theses, and articles of Welsh interest and acquired by the National Library. Since the volume covering 1929–33 (1939), entries are organized by Library of Congress classification system. The language and literature division includes sections for biography, Celtic languages, Celtic literature, Welsh language, Welsh literature, Anglo-Welsh literature, and Arthurian literature (for many years this last section appeared at the end of the classified list). (Until the volume for 1973–76 [1981], *Bibliotheca Celtica* also includes Irish and Scottish Gaelic language and literature.) Indexed by names.

Welsh Publications 1801–1919 is an ongoing union catalogue of materials printed in Wales between 1801 and 1919 designed to fill a major gap in the national bibliographies of the country and to redress the underrepresentation of Welsh publications in the *Nineteenth Century Short Title Catalogue* (M2475).

While *Bibliography of Wales* and *Bibliotheca Celtica* offer the fullest general coverage of scholarship on Welsh literature, they must be supplemented by *ABELL* (G340), *MLAIB* (G335), and the other serial bibliographies and indexes in section G.

P3156   "Welsh Writing in English: A Bibliography of Criticism [1993–]." *Welsh Writing in English* 1– (1995–).   PR8950.W35.

An unannotated list of publications and some dissertations and theses on Welsh writers writing in English, along with some English-language studies of Welsh-language authors and some Welsh-language works on English-language authors. Entries are divided between two divisions, general criticism and individual authors (organized by literary author). Users must skim all entries since essays on individual authors included in collective entries for yearbooks and collections of essays in the general criticism division usually are not listed in the second division and since essays on two or more authors frequently appear under only one author heading.

See also

>   Secs. G: Serial Bibliographies, Indexes, and Abstracts and H: Guides to Dissertations and Theses.
>   *ABELL* (G340): Entries on Anglo-Welsh writers and literature are dispersed throughout.
>   *MLAIB* (G335): Until the volume for 1981, Welsh literature in English was included in the English Literature division. Welsh-language literature was covered in the Celtic Languages and Literatures heading under the General division in the volumes for 1928–52; in General IV (later V or VI): Celtic Languages and Literatures in the volumes for 1953–66; and in Celtic IX: Welsh in the volumes for 1967–80. Since the 1981 volume, the Welsh Literature section encompasses Welsh literature in whatever language. Researchers must also check the headings beginning with "Welsh" in the subject index to post-1980 volumes and in the online thesaurus.
>   *Royal Historical Society Bibliography* (M1400).
>   *YWES* (G330).

Other Bibliographies

P3157   Harris, John. *A Bibliographical Guide to Twenty-Four Modern Anglo-Welsh Writers.* Cardiff: U of Wales P, 1994. 387 pp.   Z2077.H37 [PR8951] 016.8209'9429.

A bibliography of works by and about 24 modern Anglo-Welsh writers. Coverage extends through 1991 (along with a few later publications). Following sections for anthologies and general criticism (with subdivisions for bibliographies and reference works, general studies, poetry, prose, regional guides, and pedagogy), the writers appear alphabetically; under each are chronological lists of primary works and alphabetical lists of studies of the writer (with contributions to books and periodicals covered selectively and a headnote outlining the organization of primary and secondary works). Several entries are taken unverified from other sources. Where a reliable bibliography exists, coverage in *Bibliographical Guide* is meant to supplement it. Some entries are accompanied by an explanatory phrase. Although inexcusably lacking an index, *Bibliographical Guide* offers the most thorough list of works about the selected authors (and, for some, the most complete list of primary works). For post-1991 studies, see *MLAIB* (G335) and *ABELL* (G340)—though neither is very thorough in covering Anglo-Welsh literature.

Biographical Dictionaries

P3160   *Y Bywgraffiadur Arlein (YBA)/Welsh Biography Online (WBO).* National Library of Wales. Online. 19 Apr. 2005 <http://yba.llgc.org.uk>. A digitized, XML-encoded version of:

Y Bywgraffiadur Cymreig hyd 1940. Ed. John Edward Lloyd and R. T. Jenkins. London: n.p., 1953. 1,110 pp.   DA710.A1 B9.

The Dictionary of Welsh Biography down to 1940. [Ed. Lloyd and Jenkins.] London: Honourable Soc. of Cymmrodorion, 1959. 1,157 pp. DA710.A1 B9.

Bywgraffiadur Cymreig hyd 1941-1950: Gydag Atodiad i'r Bywgraffiadur Cymreig Hyd 1940. [Ed. Lloyd, Jenkins, and W. Llewelyn Davies.] London: Anrhydeddus Gyndeithas y Cymmrodorion, 1970. 179 pp. DA710.A1 B9.

Y Bywgraffiadur Cymreig, 1951-1970: Gydag atodiad i'r Bywgraffiadur Cymreig hyd 1940 *a'r* Bywgraffiadur Cymreig 1941–1950. Ed. Jones and Brynley F. Roberts. London: Anrhydeddus Gymdeithas y Cymmrodorion, 1997. 304 pp.   DA710.A1 B9.

The Dictionary of Welsh Biography, 1941–1970: Together with a Supplement to The Dictionary of Welsh Biography down to 1940. Ed. Jenkins, Jones, and Roberts. London: Honourable Soc. of Cymmrodorion, 2001. 449 pp. DA710.A1 B9.

A biographical dictionary of deceased persons of Welsh birth or parentage and of foreigners important to the country's history. The signed entries—several of which are devoted to families—offer factual accounts of notorious and eminent persons from all walks of life (including a considerable number of writers). Although less discursive than in *Oxford Dictionary of National Biography* (M1425), the articles incorporate much important recent research and conclude with a list of sources. The digitized version allows users to browse page by page or to search by entries (a process that requires clicking through four screens) or full text (a particularly welcome feature since the lack of indexes in the print volumes made it virtually impossible to identify individuals associated with professions, places, organizations, educational institutions, and the like). Users should note that the additions and corrections in the print volumes have not been incorporated into main entries; an icon at the head of an entry links to corrections or supplemental information. The National Library of Wales plans to update the data and to "add portraits, other images, multimedia audio, video, etc. and Internet links." Scholarly and authoritative, this work is the standard biographical dictionary of Wales—one that in its electronic form can be more widely disseminated and far more easily mined for its wealth of data. Review: Penry Williams, *English Historical Review* 75 (1960): 706–08.

See also

    Sec. J: Biographical Sources.
    New Companion to the Literature of Wales (P3145).
    Oxford Dictionary of National Biography (M1425).

Periodicals

Guides to Primary Works

P3165   Walters, Huw. *Llyfryddiaeth Cylchgronau Cymreig 1735–1850/ A Bibliography of Welsh Periodicals, 1735–1850*. Aberystwyth: Natl. Lib. of Wales, 1993. 109 pp.   Z6956.W25 W35 [PN5157.P4]   015.429.

        —————. *Llyfryddiaeth Cylchgronau Cymreig 1851–1900/A Bibliography of Welsh Periodicals, 1851–1900*. Aberystwyth: Natl. Lib. of Wales, 2003. 501 pp.   PN5157.P4 W35.   015.429.

    A bibliography of periodicals (excluding newspapers and almanacs) published in Wales or associated with the country but published elsewhere. Entries—listed alphabetically (according to the Welsh alphabet) by title—include alternative titles and subtitles, date of first and last issue, editors, printers, publishers, frequency of publication, list of appendixes, illustrations, price, size, indexes, notes, and indication of the source of the description; English-language periodicals are described in English, Welsh-language periodicals in Welsh. Five indexes: editors and authors; publishers; printers; places of publication; places of printing. *1851–1900* includes a chronological list of periodicals by date of founding as well as a 2-page addenda to *1735–1850*. Although *Llyfryddiaeth Cylchgronau Cymreig* cites only a limited number of locations of runs and bases some descriptions on sources other than firsthand examination, it offers the fullest record of Welsh periodicals established before 1900.

Q

American Literature

This division includes works devoted primarily to the literatures—in whatever language—of the United States.

General

Researchers should also consult sections Q: American Literature/Regional Literatures and American Literature/Ethnic and Minority Literatures for other general reference works.

Guides to Reference Works

LITERATURE

Q3175   Brogan, Martha L. *A Kaleidoscope of Digital American Literature.*
            Washington: Council on Lib. and Information Sources, Digital Lib.
            Federation, 2005. 176 pp.   PS51.B76   025.06′81. Online. 23 Mar. 2007
            <http://www.diglib.org/pubs/dlf104>.
    An evaluative survey of electronic resources—databases, digital archives, gateways, Web sites, and pedagogical tools—for the study of American literature. Using extensive interviews with experts in the field, Brogan illustrates the potential, pitfalls, and lacunae in digital resources. The wealth of information and astute observations have led those working with other literatures to wish for a similar guide.

Q3180   Gohdes, Clarence, and Sanford E. Marovitz. *Bibliographical Guide to the Study of the Literature of the U. S. A.* 5th ed., rev. and enl. Durham: Duke UP, 1984. 256 pp.   Z1225.G6 [PS88]   016.81.
    A selective, interdisciplinary guide to reference works, histories, critical studies, and discussions of research methods (published through early 1983) important to the study of American literature and its historical background. Entries are organized in 35 divisions: general reference works, philosophy and methodology of literary and historical study, technical procedures in literary and historical research, definitions of literary and related terms, preparation of manuscripts for publication, national bibliographies, periodical indexes, American studies or civilization (including popular culture), general works on American history, specialized studies of American history, biography, peri-

odicals, newspapers, book trade and publishing, history of ideas, psychology, philosophy (including transcendentalism), religion, women's studies, general bibliographies of American literature, histories of American literature, poetry, drama (including theater and film), fiction, criticism, humor and other special genres (including children's literature), seventeenth- and eighteenth-century literature, twentieth-century literature, themes and topics, regionalism, minorities, relations with other countries, American language, folklore, and comparative and general literature. The generally brief descriptive annotations frequently cite related works. An appendix lists the principal biographies of 135 authors. Two indexes: subjects; names. Many divisions would benefit from more refined classification or organization; some annotations have not been revised to reflect changes in scope or organization of serial publications or revised editions; and a few outdated works or superseded editions should be excised. Especially valuable for its interdisciplinary scope, this onetime standard guide to reference works and scholarship essential to research in American literature is now in need of wholesale revision and updating. Review: David Van Leer, *Resources for American Literary Study* 16 (1986–89): 49–52.

Less useful guides are the following:

> Fenster, Valmai Kirkham. *Guide to American Literature.* Littleton: Libraries Unlimited, 1983. 243 pp. Designed for undergraduates, but untrustworthy because of numerous inaccuracies and omissions.
>
> Kolb, Harold H., Jr. *A Field Guide to the Study of American Literature.* Charlottesville: UP of Virginia, 1976. 136 pp. A poorly organized compilation, whose annotations consist largely of quotations from prefatory matter.
>
> Leary, Lewis. *American Literature: A Study and Research Guide.* New York: St. Martin's, 1976. 185 pp. Designed for undergraduates and plagued by numerous errors, but more evaluative than Gohdes or Kolb.

See also

> *American Literary Scholarship* (Q3265): In addition to the chapter on general reference sources, most of the other chapters evaluate reference works.
>
> Bateson, *Guide to English and American Literature* (B85).
>
> *Literary History of the United States: Bibliography* (Q3300).
>
> Marcuse, *Reference Guide for English Studies* (B90).

RELATED TOPICS

Q3185   Perrault, Anna H., and Ron Blazek. *United States History: A Multicultural, Interdisciplinary Guide to Information Sources.* 2nd ed. Westport: Libraries Unlimited, 2003. 661 pp.   Z1236.P45 [E178]   016.973.

A guide to reference sources (through 2002) on American history and culture to c. 2002. The 1,250 entries are listed alphabetically by title in six classified divisions: general works; politics and government; economic history; diplomatic history and foreign affairs; military history; and social, cultural, and intellectual history (with sections for genealogy, ethnic and gender issues, education, theater, and popular culture). Indexed by authors and titles. The evaluative annotations are quite full and frequently cite related works.

Because the second edition of *United States History* emphasizes social history, a useful complement is Francis Paul Prucha, *Handbook for Research in American History: A Guide to Bibliographies and Other Reference Works*, 2nd ed. (Lincoln: U of Nebraska

P, 1994, 214 pp.), which is organized by kind of reference work (with coverage extending through c. 1993). Works are described in chapters on electronic resources; library catalogs and guides; general bibliographies of American history; catalogs of books; book review indexes; guides to periodical literature; guides to manuscripts; guides to newspapers; dissertations and theses; biographical sources; oral history materials; printed documents of the federal government; the National Archives; state and local materials; legal sources; atlases, maps, and geographical guides; encyclopedias, handbooks, and dictionaries; statistics; and picture sources. Unfortunately, the second edition drops the coverage of specific topics such as political history, social history, ethnic groups, women, blacks, American Indians, religion, regional material, and travel accounts. Works are described—but too rarely evaluated—in narrative fashion, a practice that makes scanning difficult; coverage of electronic resources is inadequate; and there are more errors and lapses in judgment than one would like in an introductory guide. Indexed by persons, titles, and subjects. The original edition of the *Handbook* was once the best guide to reference works on American history and included much of importance to literary scholarship; unfortunately, the same cannot be said of the new edition.

Q3190   Sears, Jean L., and Marilyn K. Moody. *Using Government Information Sources, Electronic and Print.* 3rd ed. Phoenix: Oryx, 2001. 536 pp. Z1223.Z7 S4 [J83]   015.73′053.
    A guide to searching United States government publications. Along with describing how to use the basic indexes, databases, and numerous Web sites, Sears and Moody explain the Superintendent of Documents Classification system and outline research strategies. Of particular interest to literary researchers are the sections on copyright, genealogy, and the National Archives. Indexed by subjects and titles. This work is the best introduction for those needing to search government publications. Prucha, *Handbook for Research in American History* (Q3185a), also has a useful chapter on locating printed documents of the federal government.
    For a representative list of GPO publications on the humanities, see Donna L. Burton, "Government Document Resources for the Humanities: A Representative Bibliography," *Bulletin of Bibliography* 49 (1992): 93–100.

Histories and Surveys

Useful lists of histories and surveys appear in Gohdes, *Bibliographical Guide to the Study of the Literature of the U. S. A.*, pp. 95–101 (entry Q3180); Kolb, *Field Guide to the Study of American Literature*, pp. 25–87 (Q3180a); and Leary, *American Literature: A Study and Research Guide*, pp. 11–27 (Q3180a). For a detailed account and assessment of major histories from 1829 through 1948, see Vanderbilt, *American Literature and the Academy* (Q3209); for a comparison of *Columbia Literary History of the United States* (Q3195), *Literary History of the United States* (Q3200), and *Cambridge History of American Literature* (Q3205a), see Hans-Joachim Lang, "From the Old *Cambridge History of American Literature* to the New *Columbia Literary History of the United States*," *Reconstructing American Literary and Historical Studies*, ed. Günter H. Lenz, Hartmut Keil, and Sabine Bröck-Sallah (Frankfurt: Campus; New York: St. Martin's, 1990) 110–27.
    The announcements of *Columbia Literary History of the United States* (Q3195) and *Cambridge History of American Literature* (Q3205) elicited considerable discussion of canon and approach. See, for example, the following articles in *American Literature*: Annette Kolodny, "The Integrity of Memory: Creating a New Literary History of the

United States," 57 (1985): 291–307; William C. Spengemann, "American Things/
Literary Things: The Problem of American Literary History," 57 (1985): 456–81;
Emory Elliott, "New Literary History: Past and Present," 57 (1985): 611–21; Sacvan
Bercovitch, "America as Canon and Context: Literary History in a Time of Dissensus,"
58 (1986): 99–107.

Q3195   *Columbia Literary History of the United States* (*CLHUS*). Gen. ed. Emory
         Elliott. New York: Columbia UP, 1988. 1,263 pp.   PS92.C64   810'.9.
   A collaborative history of literature in English and other languages from twelfth-
century painted cave narratives to the 1980s. Organized by traditional periods (the
beginnings to 1810, 1810 to 1885, 1885 to 1910, 1910 to 1945, 1945 to the present),
each section begins with a discussion of cultural and intellectual contexts and includes
essays on genres, movements, major writers, regions, groups, or historical developments.
Rather than attempt a consensus or an integrated narrative, the chapters (each by a
distinguished scholar) employ a variety of critical approaches and reflect the diversity
of the country's literary heritage by treating ethnic, minority, regional, and Native
American literatures and works by women as well as established writers, and popular as
well as elite literature. Since many writers are discussed in several chapters, users must
be certain to consult the index of subjects, persons, and titles. Admirably fulfilling the
editor's criteria for a good literary history ("that it have a good index, readable type,
sensible chapter divisions, and interesting and informative essays, and that it be inexpensive, durable, and not too heavy"), this is a worthy, much-needed successor to
Literary History of the United States (Q3200). Unfortunately, it includes no bibliography
volume, and the essays lack documentation or a list of suggested readings. For an outline
of the project, see Emory Elliott, "New Literary History: Past and Present," *American
Literature* 57 (1985): 611–21.
   While the *Columbia Literary History*'s critical reception has been deservedly favor-
able, it has been criticized for its handling of regional, especially western, literature by
James H. Maguire, "The Canon and the 'Diminished Thing,'" *American Literature* 60
(1988): 643–52. Review: Larzer Ziff, *American Quarterly* 42 (1990): 102–07.

Q3200   *Literary History of the United States: History* (*LHUS*). Ed. Robert E. Spiller
         et al. 4th ed. New York: Macmillan; London: Collier, 1974. 1,556 pp.
         PS88.L522   810'.9.
   A collaborative history by leading scholars and critics of the literature of the United
States through the early 1970s (but emphasizing the nineteenth and early part of the
twentieth centuries) and accompanied by a separate *Bibliography* volume (Q3300). Organized more or less chronologically, the 11 sections include chapters on cultural and
historical background, genres, major authors, regions, and movements. Except for new
chapters on Emily Dickinson and literature since World War II, the fourth edition
essentially preserves the text of the first (1948). The *History* and *Bibliography* are complementary volumes and must be used together (the highly selective bibliography at the
end of the *History* is meant for the "general" reader). Indexed by persons and some
subjects.
   Criticized for its unevenness in scale and quality, the formulaic nature of many
chapters, and emphasis on history at the expense of criticism, but recognized for many
years as the indispensable literary history of the United States, *LHUS* exerted a major
influence on scholarship for many years after its publication and served as a godsend
for two generations of doctoral candidates studying for preliminary examinations. Although superseded by *Columbia Literary History of the United States* (Q3195), it remains
a major document in the historiography of American literary history. For the inception,

organization, composition, and editing of *LHUS*, see Robert E. Spiller, "History of a History: A Study in Cooperative Scholarship," *PMLA* 89 (1974): 602–16; and especially Vanderbilt, *American Literature and the Academy* (Q3209), which also examines the academic politics behind the work, traces its critical reception, and offers a detailed assessment (pp. 413–60, 499–531, passim). Reviews: (1st ed.) Daniel Aaron, Leslie A. Fiedler, and R. A. Miller, *American Quarterly* 1 (1949): 169–83; Ralph L. Rusk, *American Literature* 21 (1950): 489–92; René Wellek, *Kenyon Review* 11 (1949): 500–06; (4th ed.) Larzer Ziff, *Review of English Studies* ns 27 (1976): 363–66.

Q3205   *The Cambridge History of American Literature.* Gen. ed. Sacvan Bercovitch. 8 vols. Cambridge: Cambridge UP, 1994–2005.   PS92.C34   810.9.

> Vol. 1: *1590–1820.* 1994. 829 pp.
> Vol. 2: *Prose Writing, 1820–1865.* 1995. 887 pp.
> Vol. 3: *Prose Writing, 1860–1920.* 2005. 813 pp.
> Vol. 4: *Nineteenth-Century Poetry, 1800–1910.* 2004. 562 pp.
> Vol. 5: *Poetry and Criticism, 1910–1950.* 2003. 624 pp.
> Vol. 6: *Prose Writing, 1910–1950.* 2002. 620 pp.
> Vol. 7: *Prose Writing, 1940–1990.* 1999. 795 pp.
> Vol. 8: *Poetry and Criticism, 1940–1995.* 1996. 545 pp.

A collaborative history of American literature from the colonial period to the 1990s. The overall organization is chronological, the approach historical and contextual rather than biographical and canonical or "totalizing or encyclopedic" with lengthy sections by major scholars (e.g., Emory Elliott on Puritan literature, Wendy Steiner on postmodern fiction, Frank Lentricchia on modern poetry, and Gerald Graff on modern criticism) who incorporate minority, popular, Native American, and ethnic literature in treating genres, themes, representative authors, and the literary marketplace. For a discussion of the broad principles underlying the *History,* see Sacvan Bercovitch, "America as Canon and Context: Literary History in a Time of Dissensus," *American Literature* 58 (1986): 99–107, and "The Problem of Ideology in American Literary History," *Critical Inquiry* 12 (1986): 631–53 (subsequently revised in *The Rites of Assent: Transformations in the Symbolic Construction of America* [New York: Routledge, 1993] 353–76).

Each volume concludes with a chronology and a virtually useless list of "especially influential" books; unfortunately, the essays lack notes and there is no bibliography volume planned. Indexed by persons, subjects, and titles of anonymous works. Like so many recent literary histories, the *Cambridge History of American Literature* eschews continuity in favor of polyphony, pluralism, and—inevitably—imbalance. Yet the quality of the contributors ensures that it will assume an influential—perhaps canonical—place among histories of American literatures. Reviews: (vol. 1) Mitchell Breitweiser, *Modern Language Quarterly* 56 (1995): 197–206; Philip F. Gura, *New England Quarterly* 68 (1995): 118–38; William S. Spengemann, *Early American Literature* 29 (1993): 276–94; Leonard Tennenhouse, *Modern Language Quarterly* 56 (1995): 207–20; Larzer Ziff, *Modern Language Quarterly* 56 (1995): 189–96; (vol. 2) Freddie Baveystock, *English* 45 (1996): 157–63.

The *New Cambridge History* replaces the outdated *Cambridge History of American Literature* (*CHAL*), ed. William Peterfield Trent et al., 4 vols. (New York: Putnam's; Cambridge: Cambridge UP, 1917–21; online as *The Cambridge History of English and American Literature* <http://www.bartleby.com/cambridge>). For a detailed account of the genesis, editing, publication, and reception—as well as an assessment—of *CHAL*, see Vanderbilt, *American Literature and the Academy* (Q3209), pp. 3–28, 153–83, 221–36, passim.

Q3209   Vanderbilt, Kermit. *American Literature and the Academy: The Roots,*
         Growth, and Maturity of a Profession. Philadelphia: U of Pennsylvania P,
         1986. 609 pp.   PS62.V28   8109.791273.

A history of the origins and development of the study of American literature in
the United States from 1829 through 1948. Organized in three periods (1829–1921,
1921–39, 1939–48), chapters examine in detail the professional lives, publications,
and other contributions of major scholars; the genesis, production, critical reception,
and importance of major literary histories (especially *Cambridge History of American
Literature* [Q3205a] and *Literary History of the United States* [Q3200]), scholarly works,
and journals (particularly *American Literature* and *PMLA*); the introduction of American literature into secondary and higher education; the development of professional
organizations (especially the American Literature Group of the MLA); and the academic
politics that shaped the profession. An appendix lists the leaders of the American Literature Group from 1921 through 1948. Drawing extensively on unpublished materials,
Vanderbilt offers a fascinating, critical (but not always impartial) account of the evolution of the academic study of American literature in the United States. Organizers of
a major cooperative scholarly venture will find the accounts of *CHAL* and *LHUS* both
instructive and sobering. Readers who are English literature specialists will wish for a
similar history of their profession.

See also

> *History of Southern Literature* (Q3615).
> *Literary History of the American West* (Q3660).
> Ruoff, *Redefining American Literary History* (Q3695).

Literary Handbooks, Dictionaries, and Encyclopedias

Q3210   Hart, James D. *The Oxford Companion to American Literature.* 6th ed. with
         revisions and additions by Phillip W. Leininger. New York: Oxford UP,
         1995. 779 pp.   PS21.H3   810.9′003. Online through *Oxford Reference
         Online* (I530).

A wide-ranging encyclopedia, with more than 5,000 entries on authors and other
persons, works, literary terms, characters, movements and groups, awards, organizations,
periodicals, historical and cultural events, foreign writers, and a host of other topics
related to American literature. The bulk of the entries are for authors (recording basic
career information) and plot summaries of elite as well as popular works. Concludes
with a chronology of literary and social history, 1578–1994. Entries for individuals in
the fourth through sixth editions are indexed in *Biography and Genealogy Master Index*
(J565). Breadth, accuracy, judicious selection, and wealth of detail have made the
Oxford Companion the essential source of quick reference for beginning student through
accomplished scholar.

A good supplement because of its inclusion of numerous minor writers is W. J.
Burke and Will D. Howe, *American Authors and Books: 1640 to the Present Day,* 3rd
rev. ed., rev. Irving Weiss and Anne Weiss (New York: Crown, 1972, 719 pp.). Besides
writers of all kinds, it has entries for works, literary characters, periodicals, newspapers,
publishers, literary terms, associations, book collectors, libraries, places, and literature-
related subjects. (Entrants are indexed in *Biography and Genealogy Master Index* [J565].)
The first edition—*American Authors and Books, 1640–1940* (New York: Gramercy,
1943, 858 pp.)—remains useful for the numerous entries omitted in later editions.

HarperCollins Reader's Encyclopedia of American Literature, 2nd ed., ed. George Perkins, Barbara Perkins, and Phillip Leininger (New York: Harper, 2002, 1,126 pp.) and *The Continuum Encyclopedia of American Literature,* ed. Steven R. Serafin (New York: Continuum, 1999, 1,305 pp.) offer somewhat more lengthy entries on writers, works, genres, groups, movements, and other topics than is typical in literary encyclopedias. The latter, with some 1,300 entries, is neither "a comprehensive survey" nor "the most extensive single-volume treatment of its subject available" as its editor claims. *The Oxford Encyclopedia of American Literature,* ed. Jay Parini, 4 vols. (New York: Oxford UP, 2004; online, 17 Aug. 2006 <http://www.oxford-americanliterature .com>) offers even lengthier entries, but its more than 350 authors, works, movements, institutions, ethnic literatures, and literary forms are obviously chosen and written about with the targeted student or general reader in mind. The electronic version (available as part of *The Oxford Digital Reference Shelf* [http://www.oxford-digitalreference.com]) can be searched by keyword or browsed by entry; entries can be e-mailed.

Q3211   *Encyclopedia of American Studies.* Ed. Miles Orvell. Johns Hopkins UP.
        Online. 17 Feb. 2006 <http://eas-ref.press.jhu.edu>. Updated quarterly.

        Encyclopedia of American Studies. Ed. George T. Kurian, Miles Orvell,
        Johnnella E. Butler, and Jay Mechling. 5 vols. New York: Grolier, 2001.
        E169.1.E625   973'.03.

An encyclopedia for the student of the cultures of the United States. Ranging across folk, vernacular, elite, regional, sectarian, and mass cultures, the approximately 660 entries (which range from 500 to 5,000 words and which are, for the most part, written by established scholars) use an interdisciplinary approach to a topic and its relation to American culture in encompassing such areas as communication, economics, ethnicity, the arts, gender, national identity, the environment, religion, and technology—in short, virtually any area of interest to the discipline of American studies. The online version, which expands and updates the print version but does not reproduce its illustrations, can be browsed by individual entries or by broad subject areas and their subheadings. Keyword searches can be limited to title, contributors, or bibliographies within articles only or biographies only. Entries can be formatted for printing, or citations to entries can be saved (in MLA or Chicago style) for e-mailing. Although the database will be updated quarterly, there is currently no provision for identifying new or updated entries.

Because of the broad scope of the majority of entries, readers of the print version should begin with the subject index in vol. 4 (e.g., while Amish, Civilian Conservation Corps, and Works Progress Administration lack individual entries, they are discussed under broader ones). Sporting readable discussions and aptly chosen illustrations in the print version, *Encyclopedia of American Studies* is a browser's delight and a source of authoritative overviews of aspects of American culture.

Q3213   *The Oxford Companion to Women's Writing in the United States.* Ed. Cathy
        N. Davidson and Linda Wagner-Martin. New York: Oxford UP, 1995.
        1,021 pp.   PS147.094   810.9'9287'03. Online through *Oxford Reference
        Online* (I530).

A dictionary of United States women writers, literary forms (including fiction, poetry, and drama as well as such forms as travel writing, recipe books, and spiritual narratives), literary periods, regions, themes, ethnic literatures, concepts and issues associated with feminism and women writers, cultural and historical issues, and publishing. The 771 signed entries (by an impressive array of contributors) range from brief pieces to extensive essays; they usually conclude with a selective bibliography (though these are not always as current as one should expect) and, frequently, with a note on the location of the subject's papers. A chronology of social history, everyday life, and women's writing and a selective bibliography end the volume. Indexed by persons and subjects; entrants are also indexed in *Biography and Genealogy Master Index* (J565). The judicious selectivity, extensive coverage and quality of entries, and efficient cross-refer-encing and indexing give *Oxford Companion to Women's Writing* pride of place among the dictionaries of women writers in the United States.

Q3215   Ehrlich, Eugene, and Gorton Carruth. *The Oxford Illustrated Literary Guide to the United States.* New York: Oxford UP, 1982. 464 pp.   PS141.E74 917.3'04.

An illustrated dictionary and gazetteer to 1,586 cities, towns, and villages associated with more than 1,500 writers from colonial times to the present. The towns are orga-nized alphabetically within region, then state; the entry for each locality describes its associations with writers or its use as setting and locates buildings, graves, and other sites of literary interest. Indexed by states and towns at the front, by authors at the back. Although the descriptions are not always based on firsthand investigation, some im-portant sites are omitted, and the volume is too unwieldy to carry on a literary tour, this book is the most current and comprehensive guide to places in the United States that are associated with an author or literary work. Review: John Russell, *TLS: Times Literary Supplement* 10 June 1983: 608.

See also

Sec. C: Literary Handbooks, Dictionaries, and Encyclopedias.
Franklin, *Dictionary of American Literary Characters* (Q3472).

Annals

Q3220   Ludwig, Richard M., and Clifford A. Nault, Jr., eds. *Annals of American Literature, 1602–1983.* New York: Oxford UP, 1986. 342 pp.   PS94.L83 810.2'02.

A chronology of important and representative literary works. The main column cites author, date of birth, title, and genre for each work. The secondary column lists historical and cultural events, the founding of serial publications, births and deaths of authors, and major foreign publications. (Beginning in 1783, this column is in two parts: American and foreign.) Although the arts are slighted in the secondary column, breadth and judicious selection make *Annals of American Literature* the best source for placing a work in its literary and historical context. It supersedes the treatment of American literature in *Annals of English Literature* (M1345).

The *Chronology of American Literature: America's Literary Achievements from the Colonial Era to Modern Times*, ed. Daniel S. Burt (Boston: Houghton, 2004, 805 pp.) is more current (with coverage extending through 1999) and offers 3–4-sentence sum-maries of or commentaries on the importance of works, but the two-column layout (with works grouped by genre, type, or subject—e.g., drama and theater, poetry, non-fiction, literary criticism and scholarship, essays and philosophy, sermons and religious writing, and publications and events—and lists of births and deaths, popular books or bestsellers, and awards and prizes [including the "Noble Prize"] scattered at intervals throughout the text) and the lack of information on historical and social events make it impossible to contextualize a work (the principal purpose for which one consults a work such as this). Dates of birth and death appear only the first time an author is listed. The indexes of authors and titles exclude entries in the lists noted above unless a work also appears in the chronology proper.

Women writers and their social and historical contexts are more fully documented in Cynthia J. Davis and Kathryn West, *Women Writers in the United States: A Timeline of Literary, Cultural, and Social History* (New York: Oxford UP, 1996, 488 pp.).

Bibliographies of Bibliographies

Although purporting to be an evaluative history of the bibliographical control of American belles lettres, Vito Joseph Brenni, *The Bibliographic Control of American Literature, 1920–1975* (Metuchen: Scarecrow, 1979, 210 pp.), is too incomplete, poorly organized, inaccurately descriptive, uncritically evaluative, badly written, and inadequately indexed to be of much use.

Q3225   Nilon, Charles H. *Bibliography of Bibliographies in American Literature.* New
           York: Bowker, 1970. 483 pp.   Z1225.A1 N5   016.01681.
    A bibliography of books, parts of books, and articles (published before 1970) that list works by and about authors, about genres, and about subjects related to literature. Entries are classified in four divisions: bibliography, authors (organized by century, then alphabetically), genres (including literary history and criticism), and ancillary subjects (including various forms, types, and topics such as children's literature, dissertations, humor, regionalism, and travels). Occasional brief annotations comment on scope or publishing information. Indexed by titles and persons. Poor design makes scanning entries difficult. Nilon must be used with caution, since there are numerous omissions and inconsistencies in organization and since many works were not examined by the compiler. A major desideratum is an up-to-date, thorough bibliography of bibliographies of American literature. Review: *TLS: Times Literary Supplement* 2 July 1971: 788.
    A few additional bibliographies published in periodicals are listed in Patricia Pate Havlice, *Index to American Author Bibliographies* (Metuchen: Scarecrow, 1971, 204 pp.).

See also

    Sec. D: Bibliographies of Bibliographies.
    Tanselle, *Guide to the Study of United States Imprints* (U5290).

Guides to Primary Works

MANUSCRIPTS

Q3230   *American Literary Manuscripts: A Checklist of Holdings in Academic,
           Historical, and Public Libraries, Museums, and Authors' Homes in the United
           States* (*ALM*). 2nd ed. Comp. and ed. J. Albert Robbins et al. Athens: U of
           Georgia P, 1977. 387 pp.   Z6620.U5 M6 [PS88]   016.81.

A finding list of manuscripts—including journals, diaries, correspondence, galley and page proofs, documents, audio and video recordings, books with marginalia, and memorabilia—held in about 600 institutions in the United States. Among the approximately 2,800 Americans are all the major authors, selected minor ones, and several quasi-literary writers such as editors, publishers, theatrical performers and producers, literary critics and scholars, and a few public figures also known (sometimes remotely) as writers. Following each author, holdings are listed alphabetically by institutional symbol, with manuscripts identified only by type and item count. (Symbols for libraries and types of manuscripts are identified on pp. xxvii–liii.) A few institutional holdings are keyed to a list (on pp. 367–77) of calendars, inventories, checklists, and other finding aids. Concludes with two appendixes (pseudonyms and alternative names, and authors for whom no holdings were reported; both should have been integrated into the main list of authors) and a bibliography of catalogs and guides, including ones listing American manuscripts held abroad. The introduction is refreshingly frank about the limitations of the checklist, with the Notes on Coverage (pp. xxii–xxvi) listing institutions whose holdings are not covered or are incompletely reported. Although the dense pages of symbols and numbers are initially forbidding, researchers soon appreciate how much drudgery this checklist can save them. Even so, much work is left for users: they must write or visit institutions that have no published or online finding aids to determine their exact holdings, and they must consult the works listed in section F: Guides to Manuscripts and Archives to locate additional American manuscripts. Review: John C. Broderick, *Review* 1 (1979): 295–300.

Q3235   Cripe, Helen, and Diane Campbell, comps. and eds. *American Manuscripts,*
        1763–1815: An Index to Documents Described in Auction Records and
        Dealers' Catalogues. Wilmington: Scholarly Resources, 1977. 704 pp.
        Z1237.C89 [E195]   016.973.
An index to manuscript material written between 1763 and 1815 and described in catalogs of booksellers, autograph dealers, and auction houses in the United States. *American Manuscripts* covers selected dealers' catalogs through 1970 but auction catalogs only before 1895, when publication of *American Book Prices Current* (U5415) began. Organized by date of manuscript, entries identify the catalog and note what kind of description it supplies (e.g., a summary, transcription, or reproduction). Dealers' catalogs are keyed to a list in the back; auction catalogs are cited by the number used in McKay, *American Book Auction Catalogues* (U5400). Indexed by names. Although the bulk of the manuscripts are historical, Cripe and Campbell does index a considerable number of items of literary interest. Coverage of dealers' catalogs is not comprehensive and the decision to omit auction catalogs after 1895 is unfortunate, since *American Book Prices Current* is far from thorough; nevertheless, *American Manuscripts* is an important work that will save researchers a few of the hours that must be spent in tracking down and poring through these scarce catalogs. Scholars need many more such indexes to manuscripts listed in catalogs.

Q3240   Raimo, John W., ed. *A Guide to Manuscripts Relating to America in Great*
        Britain and Ireland. [Rev. ed.] Westport: Meckler for British Assn. for
        Amer. Studies, 1979. 467 pp.   Z1236.C74 [E178]   016.973.
A guide to manuscripts and some rare printed works relating to the American colonies and the United States and held by libraries, county and local record offices, organizations, and some private collectors in Great Britain. Raimo excludes the Public Record Office, British Library, Oxford and Cambridge libraries, and London Archives, since all have separate guides (identified in the introduction). Organized alphabetically

by country, then county, city, and owner, the descriptions of collections identify groups
of papers or individual manuscripts and cite transcriptions, catalogs, and other finding
aids. The descriptions vary in detail, but most are helpfully precise. Locations are not
cited for collections identified through the National Register of Archives (F285a) to
encourage scholars to consult the finding aids held there. Indexed by subjects, persons,
and places. Users must remember that this work is not comprehensive and that inclusion
of a collection does not mean it is accessible to researchers. Although the bulk of the
papers are historical or political, Raimo locates a significant number of literary manuscripts and thus is an important preliminary source for tracking down items in British
collections.

Q3245   *Women's History Sources: A Guide to Archives and Manuscript Collections in
the United States.* Ed. Andrea Hinding and Ames Sheldon Bower. 2 vols.
New York: Bowker, 1979.   Z7964.U49 W64 [HQ1410]
016.30141′2′0973.

A guide to 18,026 collections in 1,586 repositories holding manuscripts by or
related to women in the United States since colonial times. Organized alphabetically
by state, city, repository, and then collection title, entries record types of documents,
inclusive dates, size, information on access, repository, existence of finding aids, contents, and published guides. Based on printed descriptions, responses to questionnaires,
or on-site inspections, the descriptions vary considerably in sophistication, specificity,
and accuracy. Indexed in vol. 2 by persons (including all forms of a woman's name),
subjects, occupations, and places. Although many libraries were unable to provide a
thorough description of their holdings, *Women's History Sources* is the essential guide
to a wealth of little-known material, a decent portion of which is of literary interest. A
revised edition—or supplement—is needed. Review: Gerda Lerner, *Library Quarterly*
51 (1981): 102–04.

See also

Sec. F: Guides to Manuscripts and Archives.
American Book Prices Current (U5415).
Book Auction Records (U5420).

PRINTED WORKS

For a survey deploring the state of the bibliography of American imprints, recom-
mending standards and procedures, and suggesting needed research, see G. Thomas
Tanselle, "The Bibliography and Textual Study of American Books," *Proceedings of the
American Antiquarian Society* 95 (1985): 113–51, with a commentary (pp. 152–60)
by Norman Fiering.

Tanselle, *Guide to the Study of United States Imprints* (U5290) is the best source
for locating works that identify or locate a particular book printed or published in the
United States.

Q3250   Blanck, Jacob, comp. *Bibliography of American Literature* (*BAL*). Completed
by Michael Winship and Virginia L. Smyers. 9 vols. New Haven: Yale UP,
1955–91.   Z1225.B55 [PS88]   016.81. Online. 14 Mar. 2006 <http://
collections.chadwyck.com/bal>. CD-ROM.

Bibliography of American Literature: *A Selective Index*. Comp. Winship.
  Golden: North American–Fulcrum, 1995. 325 pp.   Z1255.B55   016.81.
Epitome of Bibliography of American Literature. Comp. Winship. Golden:
  North American–Fulcrum, 1995. 325 pp.   Z1255.B55   016.81.

A bibliography of works by 281 authors (from the Federal period to those who
died before 1931) "who, in their own time at least, were known and read" and who
primarily published belles lettres. Limited to separate publications (including books,
broadsides, anthologies, and ephemera) and emphasizing initial appearances, *BAL* excludes altogether "periodical and newspaper publications, . . . unrevised reprints . . . , translations into other languages, [and] volumes containing isolated correspondence." First American editions (along with variant issues and states) and
English-language foreign editions preceding the first American one receive a full description; briefer descriptions are accorded volumes containing the first printing of a
prose work (excluding letters) or poem, textually significant reprints or revised editions,
nonbelletristic works, and edited texts. Authors are listed alphabetically, with works
normally organized by date of publication in three parts: first or revised editions of
books wholly or substantially by an author and books by others containing the first
book publication of a work; reprints of an author's own books; and books by others
containing material by an author reprinted from earlier books, followed by a selection
of bibliographies, biographies, and -ana. Some authors, because of the variety or com-
plexity of their output, require a different organization (outlined in a headnote). A full
entry includes title page, imprint, pagination, type of paper, size of leaf, collation,
description of binding (including variants and notes on inserted ads, endpapers, binder's
and fly leaves), publication notes (citing copyright deposit date when possible and early
advertisements), locations of copies examined, and miscellaneous notes, especially dealing with publishing history. These parts are repeated as necessary within an entry for
each state or issue. The entry numbers have become the standard references for identifying an edition, state, or issue. Indexed by initials, pseudonyms, and anonyms in each
volume. The *Selective Index* covers separately published works in three indexes: titles
(with separate list of main titles and series titles); dates; publishers (organized by city).
Entrants in vols. 1–8 are indexed in *Biography and Genealogy Master Index* (J565).

Users must study carefully the prefatory explanation of scope, limitations, organization, terminology, and parts of an entry (especially descriptive conventions); consult
the headnote to an author for information on special limitations or organization; and
remember that *BAL* does not list everything written by an author and is not a census
of copies.

The online version allows users to browse the contents or search by a combination
of keyword, title, imprint, author, location of copy (although this does not function
properly), date of publication, and *BAL* number. Searches can be restricted to principal
works, reprints and contributions, or references and -ana. Unfortunately, the only way
to print or save records is by screen capture. The CD-ROM version is becoming obsolete
since the search interface must be installed from 3.5-inch disks.

Additions and corrections once regularly appeared in the notes section of *Papers
of the Bibliographical Society of America*; published additions and corrections through
1969 are listed in vol. 1, pp. 163–64, in Tanselle, *Guide to the Study of United States
Imprints* (U5290). On the form for reporting additions and corrections, see G. Thomas
Tanselle, "A Proposal for Recording Additions to Bibliographies," *Papers of the Bibliographical Society of America* 62 (1968): 227–36; "Additions to Bibliographies: With
Notes on Procedure for *BAL*," 73 (1979): 123–25. The *BAL* working papers and files,
which contain much fuller descriptions and notes, additions, and corrections, can be

consulted in the Manuscript Department, Houghton Library. Separately published main works are listed in the *Epitome*, but it does not incorporate additions or corrections to the original nine volumes.

Although not comprehensive (especially in listing reprints), inconsistent in treating some kinds of works (such as foreign editions and reprints), and emphasizing nineteenth-century authors, *BAL* remains — for writers not the subject of a more recent, separately published descriptive bibliography — an indispensable source for identifying and locating first editions and appearances as well as important revised editions, for obtaining details of publishing and textual history, and for dating publication. For a history of the work, see W. H. Bond, "Jacob Blanck and *BAL*," *Papers of the Bibliographical Society of America* 86 (1992): 129–45. For the uses of *BAL* by those who are not primarily bibliographers, see Joseph R. McElrath, Jr., "From the *Bibliography of American Literature* to 'The Pittsburgh Series in Bibliography': Our Progressive Tradition," *Literary Research* 14 (1989): 5–12; and Lawrence Buell, "The Bibliographical Conscience," *Papers of the Bibliographical Society of America* 86 (1992): 191–98. For the importance of *BAL* to British and American book-trade history, book collecting, and critical editing, see *Papers of the Bibliographical Society of America* 86.2 (1992), a special issue that prints papers from a 1992 conference on *BAL*.

The meticulous examination of copies in public as well as private collections, extensive research in copyright records and publishers' archives, and a remarkable degree of accuracy make *BAL* one of the monumental bibliographies of the twentieth century. Reviews: (vol. 1) John D. Gordan, *Papers of the Bibliographical Society of America* 50 (1956): 201–04; James D. Hart, *American Literature* 28 (1956): 378–81; (vol. 7) Joel Myerson, *Papers of the Bibliographical Society of America* 78 (1984): 45–56 (an important evaluation of the general strengths and shortcomings of *BAL*); (vols. 8–9) Richard Layman, *Papers of the Bibliographical Society of America* 87 (1993): 259–63.

Much less satisfactory is Matthew J. Bruccoli et al., eds., *First Printings of American Authors: Contributions toward Descriptive Checklists*, 5 vols. (Detroit: Gale, 1977–87), an ambitious but flawed, inadequately descriptive record of the first American and English printings of separate publications by some 336 collectible authors from the seventeenth century through the 1970s. Given the paucity of information and inconsistencies in its presentation, *First Printings* is only occasionally useful for those few authors not in *BAL* or the subject of an author bibliography. For a detailed critique of the work, see William Matheson, "American Literary Bibliography—*FPAA* Style," *Review* 1 (1979): 173–81.

Q3255   *Literary Writings in America: A Bibliography.* 8 vols. Millwood: KTO, 1977.
      Z1225.L8 [PS88]   016.81.
A reproduction of the card file prepared as a Works Progress Administration project whose goal was to compile a list of creative works and reviews published by Americans between 1850 and 1940. No record exists, however, of what or how many sources were actually examined. The approximately 250,000 cards are organized by author, then alphabetically by title within sections for bibliographies, collected works, separately published works, periodical publications, biographical sources, and critical studies (including reviews) about the author. Reviews are listed under both the reviewer and the author of the book reviewed. Each card usually records author, title, publication information (omitting publishers of books), and genre or type of work. Far from complete, haphazard in its coverage (especially of books), inconsistent in format, including numerous errors, and largely unedited, *Literary Writings* is only occasionally useful for identifying periodical contributions (especially of minor authors) that are not indexed

elsewhere. Review: George Monteiro, *Papers of the Bibliographical Society of America* 73 (1979): 498–502.

Q3260   Tanselle, G. Thomas. "Copyright Records and the Bibliographer." *Studies in Bibliography* 22 (1969): 77–124.   Z1008.V55.

A discussion of the value of copyright records in literary and bibliographical research. The focus is the United States, with a summary of major provisions of copyright law and description of surviving records, published and unpublished, from 1793 through the 1960s. Concludes with a brief commentary on English copyright law. A clear introduction to these underutilized records that are valuable for establishing publication dates, authorship of anonymous and pseudonymous publications, and details of nonextant works.

See also

> Sec. U: Literature-Related Topics and Sources/Anonymous and Pseudonymous Works/Dictionaries.

Guides to Scholarship and Criticism

SURVEYS OF RESEARCH

Q3265   *American Literary Scholarship: An Annual [1963–   ]* (*ALS, AmLS*).
        Durham: Duke UP, 1965– . Annual. Online. 4 Sept. 2006 <http://als.dukejournals.org>.   PS3.A47   810.

A selective, evaluative survey of important studies, editions, biographies, and reference works. Currently, the volumes are divided into 22 chapters, each by an established scholar: Emerson, Thoreau, Fuller, and transcendentalism (Fuller was added in 1994); Hawthorne; Melville; Whitman and Dickinson (the latter was added in 1967); Mark Twain; James; Wharton and Cather (since 1997); Pound and Eliot (since 1974); Faulkner; Fitzgerald and Hemingway; literature to 1800; early-nineteenth-century literature; late-nineteenth-century literature (before 1994 a single chapter covered 1800–1899); fiction, 1900 to 1930s; fiction, 1930s to 1960s; fiction, 1960s to the present; poetry, 1900 to 1940s; poetry, 1940s to the present; drama; themes, topics, and criticism; foreign scholarship (since 1973, with separate essays on various countries); and general reference works (since 1977). Some earlier volumes include chapters on folklore (1965–74), Poe (1973–96), and black literature (1977–88). The scope of some chapters has changed over the years, and the organization varies with the subject. Two indexes: scholars; subjects.

Judicious selectivity, currency, and frank, authoritative evaluations (usually much fuller and more critical than in typical surveys of research) make *ALS* an indispensable guide to the year's important scholarship and an essential source for keeping abreast of the increasing number of publications, especially in areas outside one's immediate fields of interest. Together, the volumes offer an incomparable source for studying trends in American literary scholarship and an important complement to *MLAIB* (G335) and *ABELL* (G340), especially for the superior coverage of books.

Since vol. 35 (for 1954), *Year's Work in English Studies* (G330) includes American literature; however, *ALS* offers much fuller, more authoritative coverage.

Q3275   Duke, Maurice, Jackson R. Bryer, and M. Thomas Inge, eds. *American
Women Writers: Bibliographical Essays.* Westport: Greenwood, 1983. 434 pp.
Z1229.W8 A44 [PS147]   016.81'09'9287.
Evaluative surveys of scholarship published through c. 1981 on 24 writers: Brad-
street, Rowlandson, Knight, Jewett, Freeman, Murfree, Chopin, Wharton, Stein,
Barnes, Nin, Glasgow, Porter, Welty, O'Connor, McCullers, Hurston, Rourke, Buck,
Rawlings, Mitchell, Moore, Sexton, and Plath. Each of the 14 chapters, which treat
individuals or groups of authors, devotes sections to bibliographies, editions, manuscripts and letters (noting locations as well as scholarship), biographies, and criticism
(with the last variously subdivided). Indexed by persons. The individual essays vary in
selectivity and suggest topics for further research. The volume as a whole, however,
would benefit from a statement of scope and policies governing the selection of scholarship and writers.

Q3280   Harbert, Earl N., and Robert A. Rees, eds. *Fifteen American Authors before
1900: Bibliographical Essays on Research and Criticism.* Rev. ed. Madison: U
of Wisconsin P, 1984. 531 pp.   PS55.F53   016.81'09.
Evaluative surveys of research by established scholars on H. Adams, Bryant,
Cooper, Crane, Dickinson, Edwards, Franklin, Holmes, Howells, Irving, Longfellow,
Lowell, Norris, Taylor, and Whittier. The original edition (1971, 442 pp.) included
two additional essays, on southern literature. The surveys vary in selectivity, coverage
of foreign scholarship and dissertations, currency (generally citing publications through
1980, with some as late as 1983), and organization. All have sections for bibliography,
editions, manuscripts and letters, biographical studies, and criticism and offer suggestions for further research. The Dickinson essay treats recent studies separately; others
incorporate new scholarship in the commentary. Unfortunately, citations do not provide
full bibliographical information. Indexed by persons. An authoritative guide to winnowing the important studies from the mass published on the 15 authors. Review:
David Timms, *Notes and Oueries* ns 33 (1986): 276–77.
For evaluative surveys of recent scholarship on these authors, see *American Literary
Scholarship* (Q3265).

Q3283   Kopley, Richard, ed. *Prospects for the Study of American Literature: A Guide
for Scholars and Students.* New York: New York UP, 1997. 347 pp.
PS25.P76   810.9.
Surveys of research that assess the current state of scholarship but emphasize studies—biographical, bibliographical, critical, historical, and archival—needed on Emerson, Thoreau, Poe, Melville, Douglass, Stowe, Whitman, Twain, James, Wharton,
Cather, T. S. Eliot, Hemingway, Hurston, Faulkner, and Wright. Additional surveys
(thus far on Howells, Malamud, Fuller, Dickinson, London, Dreiser, Louisa May Al-
cott, and Fitzgerald) appear in the ongoing *Resources for American Literary Study* "Prospects" essays (some of which are reprinted in this current volume). Two indexes: persons; subjects. Written for the most part by seasoned scholars, these essays offer
invaluable guides for graduate students searching for dissertation topics and for junior
faculty members ready to move beyond a dissertation; as a whole *Prospects for the Study
of American Literature* serves as an admirable model for more such collections on American and British writers.

See also

Dorson, *Handbook of American Folklore* (U5860).
Greenblatt, *Redrawing the Boundaries* (M1383).

Greenwood Guide to American Popular Culture (U6295).

Horner, *Present State of Scholarship in Historical and Contemporary Rhetoric* (U5565).

SERIAL BIBLIOGRAPHIES

Q3285 "Publications in American Studies from German-Speaking Countries [1945–]." *Amerikastudien/American Studies* 1 (1956)– . Title varies. E169.1 973.92′05.

An irregularly published list of German, Swiss, and Austrian scholarship on American culture. Entries are currently organized alphabetically in 10 divisions: general works and bibliographies; linguistics; literature and culture; history; politics, economics, and society; education; the arts and the media; philosophy, psychology, and religion; culture; and geography. Indexed by scholars. A useful complement to *American Literary Scholarship* (Q3265) and the standard serial bibliographies and indexes in section G, which typically overlook much scholarship published in Germany, Switzerland, and Austria.

Among the defunct serial bibliographies of American literature are:

> "Articles in American Studies [1954–72]." *American Quarterly* 7–25 (1955–73). A selective annotated interdisciplinary list, which was succeeded in vols. 26–38 (1974–86) by a yearly bibliography issue composed of surveys of research and discussions of methodology on a theme or topic. The annual bibliographies for 1954–68 are reprinted with cumulative scholar and personal name indexes as Hennig Cohen, ed., *Articles in American Studies, 1954–1968: A Cumulation of the Annual Bibliographies from American Quarterly*, 2 vols., Cumulated Bibliography Series 2 (Ann Arbor: Pierian, 1972).

> "A Selected, Annotated List of Current Articles on American Literature." *American Literature* 54–62 (1982–90). A timely and rigorously selective guide to the most important recent scholarship. Its predecessor, "Articles on American Literature Appearing in Current Periodicals" (vols. 1–53 [1929–82]), offered a much fuller classified list whose entries through 1975 are incorporated in Leary, *Articles on American Literature* (Q3295).

See also

> Sec. G: Serial Bibliographies, Indexes, and Abstracts.
> *ABELL* (G340): Entries on American writers and literature are dispersed throughout.
> *MLAIB* (G335): American Literature division in the volumes for 1922 to the present. Researchers must also check the headings beginning "American" in the subject index to post-1980 volumes and in the online thesaurus.

OTHER BIBLIOGRAPHIES

Q3290 Jones, Steven Swann. *Folklore and Literature in the United States: An Annotated Bibliography of Studies of Folklore in American Literature*. Garland Reference Library of the Humanities 392: Garland Folklore Bibliographies 5.

New York: Garland, 1984. 262 pp.   Z1225.J66 [PS169.F64]
016.81'09'3.

A bibliography of books, articles, master's theses, and doctoral dissertations through 1980 that explicitly examine the influence of folklore on American literature and demonstrate "clear folkloristic competence." Jones includes a few works whose titles erroneously suggest that they treat folklore but excludes discussions of organized religions and general works on literary humor. Listed alphabetically by scholar, entries are accompanied by full descriptive annotations, a few of which point out shortcomings in folklore methodology. (Most theses are not annotated.) Six indexes: literary authors; folklore genres; general theoretical studies (a single list with no headings); regional and ethnic studies (with headings only for Afro-American and general regional and ethnic studies); humor (a single list with no headings); dialect, themes, and characters (again, with no headings). Although selective, *Folklore and Literature* gathers and clearly annotates studies that are not readily identifiable in the standard serial bibliographies and indexes in section G and that are frequently omitted from folklore bibliographies. Unfortunately, the utterly inadequate subject indexing means that users in search of studies of other than specific literary authors must skim all entries.

Q3295   Leary, Lewis. *Articles on American Literature, 1900–1950.* Durham: Duke
            UP, 1954. 437 pp. Leary, with Carolyn Bartholet and Catherine Roth,
            comps. *1950–1967.* 1970. 751 pp. Leary and John Auchard, comps.
            1968–1975. 1979. 745 pp.   Z1225.L49   016.81.

A bibliography of periodical articles, significant reviews, and review articles compiled from "Articles on American Literature Appearing in Current Periodicals" (Q3285a), *MLAIB* (G335), other bibliographies, and some journals not covered by the preceding. The 1900–50 compilation is limited primarily to English-language studies; the later volumes admit more foreign-language articles but are also more selective. Entries are listed alphabetically in divisions for individual authors; almanacs, annuals, and gift books (1900–50 only); American literature, aims and methods; serial bibliographies; other bibliographies; biography (in the 1968–75 edition, the four preceding divisions became subdivisions—along with ethnic groups—under American literature); fiction; foreign influences and estimates; frontier; humor; Indian literature (in 1968–75, a classified section under American literature); language and style (added in 1950–67); libraries and reading; criticism; literary history; literary trends and attitudes (added in 1950–67); Negro literature (in 1968–75, a classified section under American literature); newspapers and periodicals; philosophy and philosophical trends; poetry; printing, publishing, and bookselling; prose (1900–50 only); regionalism; religion; science; social and political topics; societies; theater; and women (added in 1968–75). Since each volume includes additions and corrections to the preceding one(s), all three must be used together. There are numerous errors and inconsistencies (especially in recording dates and essential issue numbers), and articles treating more than one author or topic do not always receive multiple entries. (Thaddeo K. Babiiha discusses these problems in "The Faulkner Section in Leary's *Articles on American Literature, 1968–1975*," *Papers of the Bibliographical Society of America* 75 [1981]: 93–98, but his generalizations are not completely accurate.) Although access would be enhanced by a more refined and detailed classification system, the volumes are a time-saving compilation. Because of their limitations, however, they must be supplemented by *American Literary Scholarship* (Q3265) and the serial bibliographies and indexes in section G. Review: (1950–67) J. Albert Robbins, *Papers of the Bibliographical Society of America* 65 (1971): 417–19.

Q3300   *Literary History of the United States: Bibliography (LHUS).* Ed. Thomas H.
        Johnson and Richard M. Ludwig. 4th ed. New York: Macmillan; London:
        Collier, 1974. 1,466 pp. (The fourth edition consists of corrected reprints
        of the 1948 bibliography and the supplements of 1959 and 1972, with a
        cumulative index.)   PS88.L522   810′.9.

A series of selective, usually evaluative bibliographical essays organized in four
extensively classified divisions: general resources and reference works, general literature
(with subdivisions for periods, background studies, American language, folk literature,
Indian lore and antiquities, and popular literature), movements and influences, and 239
individual authors (covering primary works, editions, biographies, criticism, bibliographies, and public collections of manuscripts). Throughout, the emphasis is on guiding
readers to the best editions and studies; in addition, many essays point out topics
needing study. The supplements are keyed to the original volume, and the *Bibliography*
must be used in conjunction with the *History* (Q3200), even though the organization
frequently differs. Indexed by authors, titles, and some subjects. Confusingly organized,
with numerous errors, badly dated, and largely superseded by author, subject, and period
bibliographies, *LHUS* is now principally useful as a guide to older scholarship. Review:
R. A. Miller, *American Quarterly* 1 (1949): 180–83.

See also

   Sec. U: Literature-Related Topics and Sources/Folklore and Literature/Guides to
       Scholarship and Criticism.
   Bailey, *English Stylistics* (U6080).
   Flanagan, *American Folklore: A Bibliography, 1950–1974* (U5870).
   Gohdes, *Literature and Theater of the States and Regions of the U. S. A.* (Q3570).
   Haywood, *Bibliography of North American Folklore and Folksong* (U5875).
   Horner, *Historical Rhetoric* (U5600).
   Huddleston, *Relationship of Painting and Literature* (U5160).
   Literary Writings in America (Q3255).
   Ross, *Film as Literature, Literature as Film* (U5800).
   Schwartz, *Articles on Women Writers* (U6605).
   Tanselle, *Guide to the Study of United States Imprints* (U5290).

ABSTRACTS

Q3310   *America: History and Life.* Santa Barbara: ABC-Clio, 1964– . 5/yr.,
        including a cumulative index.   Z1236.A48   016.917. Online. 19 Apr.
        2006 <http://serials.abc-clio.com>. Updated monthly.

Abstracts of articles and citations to book reviews and dissertations in *ProQuest
Dissertations and Theses* (H465) on the history and culture of the United States and
Canada, including some studies of American, Native American, and Canadian literature
and language. A retrospective volume (designated vol. 0) covers 1954–63 (1972), and
a *Supplement* (2 vols., 1980) adds entries to vols. 1–10. Because of changes in organization over the years (especially beginning with vol. 26 [1989]), the online version
offers the best approach to listings. Users can search by keyword, subject, author or
editor, title, language, journal, date, time period, and entry number; most of the preceding fields are linked to browsable lists. Searches can be limited to kinds of documents;

results can be sorted by author, date, journal, language, or type of document (however, the sort options were not functioning on 19 April 2006). Records can be tagged for printing, e-mailing, or exporting into bibliographic software programs. An important source for identifying literary and language scholarship in historical journals, few of which are covered by the standard serial bibliographies and indexes in section G.

DISSERTATIONS AND THESES

Q3315   Howard, Patsy C., comp. *Theses in American Literature, 1896–1971.* Ann
         Arbor: Pierian, 1973. 307 pp.   Z1225.H67   016.8109.
    A list of baccalaureate and master's theses accepted by American and some foreign institutions. Howard covers a limited number of institutions (whether completely is unclear) and apparently only theses devoted to an identifiable author. Entries are organized alphabetically under literary authors, with cross-references for studies of multiple authors. Two indexes: subjects (inadequate); thesis authors. Although marred by a completely inadequate explanation of scope and coverage, *Theses in American Literature* will save some hunting through elusive institutional lists. Theses on southern writers are more fully covered in Emerson, *Southern Literary Culture* (Q3630). A companion volume is devoted to *Theses in English Literature* (M1395).

Q3320   Woodress, James. *Dissertations in American Literature, 1891–1966.* Rev.
         and enl. Durham: Duke UP, 1968. 185 pp.   Z1225.W8   016.8109.
    A bibliography of American, British, French, New Zealand, Indian, German, Austrian, and Canadian dissertations, completed or once in progress. The approximately 4,700 entries, most of which are taken from standard national dissertation bibliographies or other published lists, are organized alphabetically by author in 34 divisions: individual authors; almanacs, gift books, and annuals; American Revolution; Civil War; criticism; drama; economic studies; education and scholarship; fiction; fine arts; folklore; foreign relationships; humor and satire; Indians; language; libraries and reading; literary history; literary nationalism; lyceum; Negro literature; nonfictional prose; periodicals and journalism; philosophy and intellectual history; poetry; politics and government; printing, publishing, and censorship; psychology and literature; Puritanism; regionalism; religion; science and technology; transcendentalism; travel; and writers and writing. Those for genres, foreign relationships, language, literary history, periodicals and journalism, and regionalism are further classified. Each division or section concludes with cross-references to related dissertations. An entry cites author, title, institution, department (if other than English), and year and indicates when a dissertation has been published. Indexed by dissertation writers. Although not comprehensive and citing dissertations never completed, this is a time-saving compilation from standard bibliographies (especially because of the inclusion of studies accepted by departments other than English). It must be supplemented, however, by works listed in section H: Guides to Dissertations and Theses.

See also

    Sec. H: Guides to Dissertations and Theses.

RELATED TOPICS

For other bibliographies of American history, see the chapter on general bibliographies in Prucha, *Handbook for Research in American History* (Q3185a).

Q3325   Basler, Roy P., Donald H. Mugridge, and Blanche P. McCrum. *A Guide to the Study of the United States of America: Representative Books Reflecting the Development of American Life and Thought.* Washington: Lib. of Congress, 1960. 1,193 pp. Basler and Oliver H. Orr, Jr. *Supplement, 1956–1965.* 1976. 526 pp.   Z1215.U53   016.9173.

A selective, albeit extensive, annotated bibliography of books published through 1965 that are important to the understanding of the United States. The approximately 9,400 entries — most accompanied by extensive descriptive annotations that typically cite related works — are classified in 32 chapters covering all aspects of history; culture; the humanities; the arts; and social, natural, and physical sciences. The best approach to the contents is through the extensive index of persons, titles, and subjects. Although dated, this study remains the fullest general guide to works essential for investigating life and thought before 1965 in the United States. Review: *Times Literary Supplement* 8 Sept. 1961: 594.

Q3330   *Harvard Guide to American History.* 2 vols. Rev. ed. Ed. Frank Freidel. Cambridge: Belknap–Harvard UP, 1974.   Z1236.F77   016.9173′03.

A guide to important primary and secondary works published to 30 June 1970 on the political, social, constitutional, economic, cultural, and diplomatic history of the United States. The books and articles, selected on the basis of "potential usefulness," are variously organized in divisions for research methods and materials (with sections on reference works, printed public documents, and unpublished primary sources), biographies and personal records (with sections on travels and descriptions, and biographies), comprehensive and area histories (with a section on regional, state, and local histories), and numerous subjects. The first division consists of a narrative interspersed with lists of works; the other divisions are made up of classified lists. Two indexes: authors (with titles following each author); subjects. Once a standard resource, *Harvard Guide to American History* is now useful primarily as a guide to studies published before mid-1970. Review: Justus D. Doenecke, *History Teacher* 8 (1975): 317–21.

Q3335   Salzman, Jack, ed. *American Studies: An Annotated Bibliography.* 3 vols. Cambridge: Cambridge UP, 1986. *1984–1988.* 1990. 1,085 pp. Z1361.C6 A436 [E169.1]   016.973.

An annotated bibliography of English-language books and collections of essays through 1988 on the culture of the United States. Salzman excludes journal articles, theoretical and methodological studies, and reference works, as well as most studies of single authors and, in *1984–1988*, books published outside the United States. In the three-volume compilation, the 7,634 entries are listed alphabetically by author in 11 variously classified divisions: anthropology and folklore (including sections on minorities, ethnic groups, and linguistics); art and architecture; history (with sections on women, ethnicity, black history, and Native Americans); literature (with sections on general surveys, historical periods, and themes); music; political science; popular culture (with sections on general studies, literature, various genres and types of popular fiction, comics, entertainment, film, media, and material culture); psychology; religion; science, technology, and medicine; and sociology. Introducing each division are a brief overview of important reference works (including some published as late as 1986) and, in too few instances, a discussion of criteria determining scope and selection. All but a few annotations are full and accurate descriptions of content. Three indexes in vol. 3: authors; titles; subjects.

The supplement for 1984–88 separates anthropology and folklore, adds a division for autobiographies and memoirs, omits science, lacks the introductory overviews of reference sources, offers a brief statement of general editorial policy but an inadequate explanation of the scope of individual divisions, and inexplicably omits several entries that appeared in the continuation of the original bibliography in *Prospects: An Annual of American Cultural Studies* 10–11 (1987). Two indexes: scholars; titles (with numbers referring to pages rather than entries). The lack of a subject index is inexcusable, especially since so many of the books (each of which is listed in only one section) cover several topics. The volumes for journal articles and books published outside the United States never appeared. Although divisions vary considerably in quality and authoritativeness (with many lacking a clear focus and effective organization), the work offers the most extensive general guide to books through 1988 on several aspects of American culture. Review: (1986 ed.) Lawrence H. Fuchs, *American Quarterly* 39 (1987): 292–95.

Salzman's compilation does not completely supersede its parent, Murray G. Murphey, gen. ed., *American Studies: An Annotated Bibliography of Works on the Civilization of the United States*, 4 vols. (Washington: US Information Agency, 1982), which lists articles in several divisions but which is not widely available in the United States. Basler, *Guide to the Study of the United States of America* (Q3325), remains useful for its breadth and inclusion of many earlier books. The same cannot be said for David W. Marcell, *American Studies: A Guide to Information Sources*, American Studies Information Guide Series 10 (Detroit: Gale, 1982, 207 pp.), which is incomplete, poorly organized, and uninformatively annotated.

Q3340   *Writings on American History [1973–90]: A Subject Bibliography of Articles.*
          Washington: Amer. Historical Assn.; Millwood: Kraus, 1974–91. Annual.
          Z1236.L331   016.97.

          Writings on American History, 1962–73: A Subject Bibliography of Articles.
          4 vols. Washington: Amer. Historical Assn.; Millwood: KTO, 1976.
          Z1236.W773 [E178]   016.973.

          Writings on American History, 1962–73: A Subject Bibliography of Books and Monographs. 10 vols. Washington: Amer. Historical Assn.; White Plains:
          Kraus, 1985.   Z1236.W773 [E178]   016.973.

          Writings on American History [1902–61]. Millwood: KTO, 1904–78.

A bibliography of scholarship on all aspects of American history. Until the volumes for 1962–73, the work annotated books, articles, and dissertations, but subsequent volumes are unannotated and limited to journal articles and dissertations (with the majority of the former taken from *Recently Published Articles* [Washington: Amer. Historical Assn., 1976–90], which originally appeared in various forms in each issue of *American Historical Review* 1–80.3 [1895–1975]). The volumes for 1904–05 and 1941–47 were never published. In the volumes for 1962–1985/86, entries are listed by scholar in three classified divisions: periods (including a section for bibliographies), regions, and subjects (including sections for literature, theater, and popular culture). Later volumes have an additional division for general works (with the bibliography section relocated to here) and a section for language in the subjects division. Several works receive multiple listings. Indexed by authors. Earlier volumes are variously organized, with the later ones having a tripartite division: the historical professions; national history (with literature, theater, and folklore sections in the cultural history sub-division); and regional, state, and local history. Indexed by names, places, and subjects (although not all volumes have subject indexing); cumulative index, 1902–40: *Index to the* Writings on American History, *1902–1940* (Washington: Amer. Historical Assn., 1956, 1,115 pp.). Although the post-1961 volumes would benefit from a more refined classification system in the first two divisions as well as subject indexing, this work includes literary studies from periodicals not covered by the standard bibliographies and indexes in section G. For historical studies, it must be supplemented by the other bibliographies and abstracts in section U: Literature-Related Topics and Sources/Social Sciences and Literature/History and Literature/Guides to Scholarship.

Language

GUIDES TO SCHOLARSHIP

Surveys of Research

Q3345   *Needed Research in American English (1983). Publication of the American Dialect Society* 71 (1984): 76 pp.   PE2841.A75   427.

Needed Research in American Dialects. Ed. Dennis R. Preston. *Publication of the American Dialect Society* 88 (2003): 261 pp.   PE2841.N44   427'.973.

Collections of reports on the state of research and projects needed in linguistic geography, regional speech, usage, new words, proverbs, non-English American languages, the history of American English, discourse studies, social variation, slang, folk speech, and language change. Particularly valuable are Raven I. McDavid, Jr., "Linguistic Geography" (pp. 4–31 in *American English*) and William A. Kretzschmar, Jr., "Linguistic Atlases of the United States and Canada" (pp. 25–48 in *American Dialects*), which offer overviews of publications, work in progress, location of archives, and status for each of the regional linguistic atlases.

Serial Bibliographies

See

> *ABELL* (G340): See the Dialect section of the English Language division in the volumes for 1920–26, the American English section in the volumes for 1927–33, the English Dialects section in the volume for 1934, the American English section in the volumes for 1935–72, and the Dialects/Dialects of [North] America section in later volumes.
>
> *MLAIB* (G335): English Language and Literature division in the volumes for 1922–25; American Literature I: Linguistics in the volumes for 1926–40; English Language and Literature I: Linguistics in the volumes for 1941–55; English Language and Literature I: Linguistics/American English in the volumes for 1956–66; Indo-European C: Germanic Linguistics IV: English/Modern English/Dialectology in the volumes for 1967–80; and Indo-European Languages/Germanic Languages/West Germanic Languages/English Language (Modern)/Dialectology in later volumes. Researchers must also check the headings beginning "American English" in the subject index to volumes since 1981 and in the online thesaurus.

Other Bibliographies

See

Leary, *Articles on American Literature* (Q3295).
Literary History of the United States: Bibliography (Q3300).
McMillan, *Annotated Bibliography of Southern American English* (Q3635).
Salzman, *American Studies: An Annotated Bibliography* (Q3335).

DICTIONARIES

Q3350   *Dictionary of American Regional English* (*DARE*). Ed. Frederic G. Cassidy
and Joan Houston Hall. 6 vols. Cambridge: Belknap–Harvard UP,
1985– .   PE2843.D52   427'.973. <http://polyglot.lss.wisc.edu/dare/
dare.html>.
A dictionary of words and phrases of folk usage or whose form or meaning is
confined to a region or regions of the United States or to a social group. Includes Black
English, Gullah, Hawai'ian pidgin, and the language of children's games, but excludes
artificial forms, criminal argot, trade jargon, and restricted occupational vocabularies.
Information is drawn from 1,002 lengthy *DARE* questionnaires, other oral sources, and
written works, with the heaviest reliance on the last. A typical entry consists of headword, part of speech, pronunciation, variant spellings, etymology for words not treated
in standard dictionaries, geographical distribution, usage labels (including frequency,
currency, type of user, and manner of use), cross-references, definition, and illustrative
quotations from printed and oral sources. Some entries are accompanied by maps that
illustrate regional distribution. The admirably clear introduction in vol. 1 outlines the
history of the dictionary; explains the editorial policy, maps, and regional labels; discusses language changes especially common in American folk speech; provides a guide
to pronunciation; and prints the questionnaire and data about the informants. Vol. 6
will include a bibliography, series of maps illustrating social distribution, and a summary
of data from the questionnaires. For explanations of the regional and social labels, see
Luanne von Schneidemesser, "Regional Labels in *DARE*," *Dictionaries* 18 (1997): 166–
77, and George H. Goebel, "Social Labels in *DARE*," *Dictionaries* 18 (1997): 178–89.
Invaluable access to *DARE* entries is offered by *An Index by Region, Usage, and Etymology
to the* Dictionary of American Regional English, *Volumes I and II*, Publication of the
American Dialect Society 77 (Tuscaloosa: U of Alabama P for Amer. Dialect Soc.,
1993, 178 pp.) and Luanne von Schneidemesser, *An Index by Region, Usage, and Etymology to the* Dictionary of American Regional English, *Volume III*, Publication of the
American Dialect Society 82 (Durham: Duke UP for Amer. Dialect Soc., 1999, 82
pp.); further installments are planned. Copies of DARE *Newsletter* are available at the
DARE Web site. Justifiably praised by reviewers for its substantial scholarship, *DARE*
is a major contribution to dialect studies, sociolinguistics, and areal linguistics in the
United States; an essential source for the explication of regional and folk terms in
American literature; and a delight to browse in. Reviews: (vol. 1) Hugh Kenner, *TLS:
Times Literary Supplement* 9 May 1986: 490–91; Walt Wolfram, *American Speech* 61
(1986): 345–52; (vol. 2) Thomas L. Clark, *American Speech* 69 (1994): 306–11; (vol.
3) Natalie Schilling-Estes, *Dictionaries* 21 (2000): 125–35.
For a survey of the status (as of 1983) of the regional linguistic atlas projects in
the United States, see Raven I. McDavid, Jr., "Linguistic Geography," *Needed Research*

in American English (Q3345) and William A. Kretzschmar, Jr., "Linguistic Atlases of the United States and Canada," in *Needed Research in American Dialects* (Q3345).

Q3355   *A Dictionary of American English on Historical Principles* (*DAE*). Ed.
         William A. Craigie and James R. Hulbert. 4 vols. Chicago: U of Chicago P,
         1938–44.   PE2835.C72   427.9.

A dictionary of words originating in the United States, having greater currency in that nation than elsewhere, or "denoting something which has a real connection with the development of the country and the history of its people." Slang and dialect terms are limited to early or prominent examples. Although the cutoff date for new words is the end of the nineteenth century, illustrative quotations extend to c. 1925. A typical entry consists of headword, definitions arranged by part of speech, illustrative dated quotations from printed sources for each meaning, combined forms, and, occasionally, pronunciation and etymology. Vol. 4 concludes with a bibliography of sources. Although far from complete, this pioneering work remains an essential source for the history of American English and the explication of American literary works. It must be complemented by *Dictionary of Americanisms* (Q3360), which is more current and accurate, and *Dictionary of American Regional English* (Q3350). Supplemented by Joseph A. Weingarten, *Supplementary Notes to the* Dictionary of American English (New York: n.p., 1948, 95 pp.); additions, corrections, and antedatings are also indexed in Wall, *Words and Phrases Index* (U6025).

For an account of the genesis, compilation, and editing of *DAE*, see Craigie, "Sidelights on the *Dictionary of American English*," *Essays and Studies* 30 (1944): 100–13. For a different perspective, however, see M. M. Mathews, "George Watson and the *Dictionary of American English*," *Dictionaries* 7 (1985): 214–24, with a response by Allen Walker Read, "Craigie, Mathews, and Watson: New Light on the *Dictionary of American English*," 8 (1986): 160–63.

Q3360   *A Dictionary of Americanisms on Historical Principles* (*DA*). Ed. Mitford M.
         Mathews. 2 vols. Chicago: U of Chicago P, 1951.   PE2835.D5   427.9.

A dictionary of words originating in the United States, other words with a particular American meaning, and foreign terms adopted in American English through c. 1950. A typical entry consists of headword, pronunciation and etymology for words originating in the United States and foreign terms, definitions organized by part of speech, dated illustrative quotations from printed sources for each meaning, combined forms, and occasionally a line drawing. Vol. 2 concludes with a bibliography of sources. Some additions, corrections, and antedatings are indexed in Wall, *Words and Phrases Index* (U6025). More restrictive than other dictionaries in defining "Americanism" (and unfortunately vague in delineating criteria governing inclusion of certain kinds of words), this work corrects several attributions of Americanisms in *Dictionary of American English* (Q3355), *Oxford English Dictionary* (M1410), and *English Dialect Dictionary* (M1415). Although *DA* is generally more accurate in recording Americanisms than the preceding, these dictionaries are complementary and, along with *Dictionary of American Regional English* (Q3350) and updates in *The Barnhart Dictionary Companion* (Q3365a), essential sources for the historical study of American English and explication of American literary works. Much remains to be done, however, before we have an adequate record of Americanisms. Reviews: Norman E. Eliason, *Modern Language Review* 48 (1952): 565–67; Archibald A. Hill, *Virginia Quarterly Review* 28 (1952): 131–35.

The abridgment as Mathews, *Americanisms: A Dictionary of Selected Americanisms on Historical Principles* (Chicago: U of Chicago P, 1966, 304 pp.), is of little value for scholarly research.

Q3365   *Webster's Third New International Dictionary of the English Language Unabridged* (*Webster's Third*). Ed. Philip Babcock Gove. Springfield: Merriam, 1961. 2,662 pp.   PE1625.W36   423. Online through *Literature Online* (I527); CD-ROM.

A dictionary "of the current vocabulary of standard written and spoken English," especially in the United States. The approximately 450,000 words blend entries from the second edition with new words and meanings, but unlike its predecessor the third edition omits proper names that are not generic, terms obsolete before 1775, and "comparatively useless or obscure words." A typical main entry includes selected variant spellings; pronunciation, with variants used by educated speakers; part of speech; inflectional forms; a note on capitalization practices; etymology; status label; subject label; definitions, in historical order; illustrative quotations largely from twentieth-century sources; usage notes; cross-references; synonyms; and combined forms. Those consulting the third edition for more than a quick definition must study the detailed prefatory explanation of parts of a main entry. The preliminary matter also includes a section on forms of address.

Some later printings list additions before the main alphabet. These words are incorporated into occasional supplements, the most recent of which is *12,000 Words: A Supplement to* Webster's Third New International Dictionary (Springfield: Merriam, 1986, 212 pp.). Other sources for new words and meanings include the following:

> Ayto, John. *The Longman Register of New Words.* 2 vols. Harlow: Longman, 1989–90. Covers new words and phrases, 1986–90, primarily in American and British English.
>
> *The Barnhart Dictionary of New English since 1963.* Ed. Clarence L. Barnhart, Sol Steinmetz, and Robert K. Barnhart. Bronxville: Barnhart, 1973. 512 pp. Continued by: *The Second Barnhart Dictionary of New English* (1980, 520 pp.); *Third Barnhart Dictionary of New English* (Bronx: Wilson, 1990, 565 pp.).
>
> *The Barnhart Dictionary Companion: A Quarterly of New Words.* Springfield: Merriam, 1982–2001. Quarterly. Updates a variety of standard dictionaries, including, at various times, the preceding, *Dictionary of Americanisms* (Q3360), *Dictionary of American English* (Q3355), *Dictionary of American Regional English* (Q3350), *New Dictionary of American Slang* (see below), *Oxford English Dictionary* (M1410), *Oxford Dictionary of New Words* (see below), *Random House Dictionary of the English Language* (see below), *Merriam-Webster's Collegiate Dictionary* (see below), and *12,000 Words* (see above). Index: vols. 1–4, David K. Barnhart, The Barnhart Dictionary Companion *Index (1982–1985)* (1987, 102 pp.).
>
> *The Oxford Dictionary of New Words.* Ed. Elizabeth Knowles. [New ed.] Oxford: Oxford UP, 1997. 357 pp.

Webster's Third has received a decidedly mixed reception, with the popular press generally condemning the work but linguists and lexicographers considerably more positive toward many of its innovations (especially definition style) and departures from the venerable second edition. Features that have drawn the most criticism include the typographical design; the lowercasing of all proper names (except one sense of God) used as headwords, with some confusing notes on capitalization practices; unnecessary citations; deletion of obsolete words; flaws in etymologies; omission of usage labels (the major criticism of those who mistakenly think that a dictionary should arbitrate usage); a confusing system for recording pronunciation; and definitions that are frequently too abridged.

However one judges its lexicographical practices, *Webster's Third* is an essential, if flawed, source for the study of the vocabulary of its time (especially in the United States). For the explication of American literary works, it must be used with the unsuperseded second edition, *Webster's New International Dictionary of the English Language* (*Webster's Second*), 2nd ed., unabridged, ed. William Allan Neilson (Springfield: Merriam, 1934, 3,210 pp.). Reviews: R. W. Burchfield, *Review of English Studies* ns 14 (1963): 319–23; Robert L. Chapman, *American Speech* 42 (1967): 202–10; Albert H. Marckwardt, "The New Webster Dictionary: A Critical Appraisal," *Readings in Applied English Linguistics*, ed. Harold B. Allen, 2nd ed. (New York: Appleton, 1964) 476–85; James Sledd, *College English* 23 (1962): 682–87. Several reviews in the popular press are reprinted in James Sledd and Wilma R. Ebbitt [eds.], *Dictionaries and THAT Dictionary: A Casebook on the Aims of Lexicographers and the Targets of Reviewers* (Chicago: Scott, 1962, 274 pp.). Reviews and responses to *Webster's Third* are listed in Ted Haebler, "The Reception of the *Third New International Dictionary*," *Dictionaries* 11 (1989): 165–218. For an overview of the controversy, of its place within the history of lexicography, and of the editorial decisions underlying the edition, see Herbert C. Morton, *The Story of* Webster's Third: *Philip Gove's Controversial Dictionary and Its Critics* (Cambridge: Cambridge UP, 1994, 332 pp.).

As an authority for spelling, most American publishers and style manuals (including Chicago [U6395] and MLA [U6400]) recommend the latest edition of *Merriam-Webster's Collegiate Dictionary* (currently the 11th ed. [Springfield: Merriam-Webster, 2003, 1,623 pp.; also published on CD-ROM and searchable online at http://www .m-w.com/home.htm]).

Important complementary dictionaries and other works include the following:

> *Random House Webster's Unabridged Dictionary.* 2nd ed. New York: Random, 1998. 2,230 pp. (A revised, updated edition of *The Random House Dictionary of the English Language*, 2nd ed., unabridged, ed. Stuart Berg Flexner [New York: Random, 1987, 2,478 pp.; CD-ROM].) This has much fuller notes on usage; however, the standard general guide to usage in American English is Wilson Follett, *Modern American Usage: A Guide*, rev. Erik Wensberg (New York: Hill-Farrar, 1998, 362 pp.).
>
> *New Dictionary of American Slang.* 3rd ed. Ed. Robert L. Chapman. New York: Harper, 1995. 617 pp.
>
> *New Oxford American Dictionary.* 2nd ed. Ed. Erin McKean. New York: Oxford UP, 2005. 2,051 pp. Emphasizes the modern American lexicon, including numerous quotations illustrating terms in actual use.

See also

> *English Dialect Dictionary* (M1415).
> *Oxford English Dictionary* (M1410).

STUDIES OF LANGUAGE

Q3370   Mencken, H. L. *The American Language: An Inquiry into the Development of English in the United States.* 4th ed., corrected, enl., and rewritten. New York: Knopf, 1936. 769 pp. *Supplement I.* 1945. 739 pp. *Supplement II.* 1948. 890 pp. The fourth edition and its supplements are abridged and

updated by Raven I. McDavid, Jr. (New York: Knopf, 1963, 777 pp.).
PE2808.M4   427.9.

A detailed account of the development of American English and its divergence from British English. The multitude of examples are loosely organized in chapters on historical developments, influences on American English, its relationship with British English, pronunciation, spelling, the common speech, proper names, slang, and the future of American English. *Supplement I* updates chapters through the relationship with British English; *Supplement II*, from pronunciation through slang. Non-English dialects are briefly discussed in an appendix to the fourth edition. Two indexes in each volume: words and phrases; persons, subjects, and titles. Stylistically entertaining but hardly impartial, full of errors, weak in organization, and emphasizing description and accumulation of examples rather than analysis, *American Language* has had a mixed reception. (For the origins, evolution, and reception of the work, see Raymond Nelson, "Babylonian Frolics: H. L. Mencken and *The American Language*," *American Literary History* 11 [1999]: 668–98.) It remains the fullest account of American English, even if one disagrees with Mencken's argument for its status as a language. Reviews: (supplements) Raven I. McDavid, Jr., *Language* 23 (1947): 68–73; 25 (1949): 69–77.

Biographical Dictionaries

Q3378   *American National Biography Online* (*ANB*). American Council of Learned Societies and Oxford UP. Online. 14 Mar. 2006 <http://www.anb.org>. Updated quarterly. CD-ROM.

American National Biography (*ANB*). Ed. John A. Garraty and Mark C. Carnes. 24 vols. New York: Oxford UP, 1999. *Supplement 1*. Ed. Paul Betz and Carnes. 2002. 926 pp. *Supplement 2*. Ed. Carnes. 2005. 835 pp. CT213.A68   920.073.

A biographical dictionary of more than 17,400 individuals who died before 1996 and whose achievement, fame, or notoriety occurred while living in what is now the United States or who "directly influenced the course of American history." Entries, which range from 750 to 7,500 words, chronicle the subject's life and career; most conclude with a note on the location of the individual's papers and a selected bibliography. Four indexes: biographees; contributors (with a list of contributions); state or country of birth; occupation or realm of renown. *Supplement 2* ends with a cumulative, updated index of occupations or realms of renown classified under 17 topical areas. Biographees are also indexed in *Biography and Genealogy Master Index* (J565). The supplements include individuals who died after 1996 (admitting "a few people of admittedly ephemeral significance") as well as notable persons overlooked in the main volumes.

The online version is updated quarterly with new biographies, illustrations, internal and external hyperlinks, and revisions to existing entries and bibliographies; unfortunately, the Web site does not identify revised articles. (A 6 July 2006 e-mail communication from M. Carnes suggests that revisions will be limited to factual matters.) Users can search by a combination of full-text keyword, name, realm of renown, occupation, birth date, death date, United States state of birth, country of birth outside the United States, and contributor; searches can be restricted to the text of an article or to a bibliography, to articles with illustrations or online resources, and by gender and update. Articles can be printed or e-mailed. An impressive editorial achievement that numbers a legion of major scholars among the contributors, *American National Biography* is a fully worthy successor to *Dictionary of American Biography* (Q3380) and will remain the country's standard national biography for the foreseeable future. Review: Edmund S. Morgan and Marie Morgan, *New York Review of Books* 9 Mar. 2000: 38–43.

Q3380 *Dictionary of American Biography (DAB).* Ed. Allen Johnson and Dumas
       Malone. Corrected rpt. 11 vols. New York: Scribner's, 1964. (A corrected
       reprint of the original 20 volumes and the first 2 supplements, 1928–58.)
       E176.D563   920′.073.

> *Supplement One: To December 31, 1935.* Ed. Harris E. Starr. 1944. 718 pp.
> *Supplement Two: To December 31, 1940.* Ed. Robert Livingston Schuyler
>   and Edward T. James. 1958. 745 pp.
> *Supplement Three: 1941–1945.* Ed. James et al. 1973. 879 pp.
> *Supplement Four: 1946–1950.* Ed. John A. Garraty and James. 1974.
>   951 pp.
> *Supplement Five: 1951–1955.* Ed. Garraty. 1977. 799 pp.
> *Supplement Six: 1956–1960.* Ed. Garraty. 1980. 769 pp.
> *Supplement Seven: 1961–1965.* Ed. Garraty. 1981. 854 pp.
> *Supplement Eight: 1966–1970.* Ed. Garraty and Mark C. Carnes. 1988.
>   759 pp.
> *Supplement Nine: 1971–1975.* Ed. Kenneth T. Jackson. 1994. 952 pp.
> *Supplement Ten: 1976–1980.* Ed. Jackson. 1995. 928 pp.
> *Comprehensive Index.* 1996. 1,091 pp.
> The preceding are online through *Biography Resource Center* (J572).

A biographical dictionary of dead individuals who have resided in what is now the United States and "have made some significant contributions to American life." British officers serving in the colonies after the Declaration of Independence are excluded. The 19,173 entries encompass the eminent and the notorious, although the scope is less catholic than that of its model, the *Dictionary of National Biography* (M1425a). Written by established authorities, the sketches range from 500 to 16,500 words in the original dictionary, but are limited to 5,000 words after the fourth supplement; combine factual information and interpretation based on extensive original research; and conclude with a short list of sources, which frequently locates unpublished materials. With *Supplement Five,* much of the extensive family and other personal data are recorded only on forms stored in the *DAB* archives in the Library of Congress. Errata to the original 20 volumes are printed in vol. 1, pp. xxii–xxxvi, of the 1964 reprint, which also makes some corrections within entries. The *Comprehensive Index* indexes the corrected reprint and the supplements by biographees, contributors, birthplaces, schools and colleges, occupations, and topics. The history of the work is outlined in vol. 1, pp. vii–xvi, of the 1964 reprint. Although there are errors and notable omissions (especially of women, who account for only 625 of the 13,633 entries in the original 20 volumes) and although the *American National Biography Online* (Q3378) supersedes many entries, the *DAB* remains useful for its historical perspective and for the biographies of individuals not included in the *ANB*. Reviews: Arthur M. Schlesinger, *American Historical Review* 35 (1929–30): 119–26, 624–25; 36 (1931): 402–05; 37 (1932): 353–56; 38 (1933): 336–38; 39 (1934): 337–38; 40 (1935): 343–47; 41 (1936): 344–46, 761–63; 42 (1937): 769–73.

The following are important, if much less trustworthy, sources for information on persons excluded from *DAB* or *ANB*:

Appleton's Cyclopædia of American Biography. Ed. James Grant Wilson and John Fiske. 6 vols. and supplement. New York: Appleton, 1887–1900. *The Cyclopedia of American Biography: Supplementary Edition.* Vols. 7–10. Ed. James E. Homans, L. E. Dearborn, and Herbert M. Linen. New York: Press Assn., 1918–26. Because of numerous fictitious biographies and fabricated publications, the original six volumes must be used with caution; see Margaret Castle Schindler, "Fictitious Biography," *American Historical Review* 42 (1937): 680–90, and John Blythe Dobson, "The Spurious Articles in *Appleton's Cyclopædia of American Biography*—Some New Discoveries and Considerations," *Biography* 16 (1993): 388–408, for accounts of these deliberate falsifications.

The National Cyclopedia of American Biography. 76 vols. Clifton: White, 1898–1984. Includes a considerable number of persons not in the *DAB*. Because of the nonalphabetic organization, the cumulative *Index* (1984, 576 pp.) is essential for locating entries.

The *DAB*, its supplements, *Appleton's Cyclopædia*, and *National Cyclopedia* are indexed in *Biography and Genealogy Master Index* (J565).

Q3385   *Notable American Women, 1607–1950: A Biographical Dictionary.* Ed. Edward T. James. 3 vols. Cambridge: Belknap–Harvard UP, 1971.

Notable American Women: The Modern Period: A Biographical Dictionary. Ed. Barbara Sicherman and Carol Hurd Green. Cambridge: Belknap–Harvard UP, 1980. 773 pp.

Notable American Women: A Biographical Dictionary Completing the Twentieth Century. Ed. Susan Ware. Cambridge: Belknap–Harvard UP, 2004. 729 pp.   CT3260.N57   920.72'0973.

A biographical dictionary of American and foreign-born residents who died before 31 December 1999 and who achieved more than local eminence or notoriety. Wives of presidents are the only women included on the basis of a husband's credentials (and only in *1607–1950*). The 2,262 entries, ranging from 400 to 7,000 words, are based on extensive research and combine factual information with interpretation. Each entry concludes with a list of sources that typically locates manuscript and archival material. A classified list of occupations, avocations, groups, and interests concludes each *Dictionary*. Entrants are indexed in *Biography and Genealogy Master Index* (J565). Although there are some notable omissions, *Notable American Women* is the most authoritative biographical dictionary of American women (many of whom receive their first and only scholarly discussion here) and a valuable source for literary scholars because of its inclusion of so many authors. Reviews: Ray Ginger and Victoria Ginger, *Canadian Historical Review* 55 (1974): 106–09; Helen Vendler, *New York Times Book Review* 17 Sept. 1972: 11; Barbara Welter, *William and Mary Quarterly* 3rd ser. 30 (1973): 518–22.

For basic biographical data (including addresses) for living women, see *Marquis Who's Who on the Web* (Q3395).

Q3390   *American Women Writers: A Critical Reference Guide from Colonial Times to the Present.* Ed. Taryn Benbow-Pfalzgraf. 2nd ed. 4 vols. Detroit: St. James–Gale, 2000. Online through *Gale Virtual Reference Library* (I535).   PS147.A4   810'.9'9287'03.

A dictionary of about 1,300 women writers of belles lettres as well as popular forms, diaries, letters, autobiographies, and children's books. Listed under the name used by the Library of Congress, the signed entries, which range from one to five pages,

provide biographical information, an overview of major works, a general critical estimate, a "complete" bibliography of primary works, and a selected list of studies. (Neither
bibliography cites full publication information, however.) Indexed in vol. 4 by persons
and subjects (including vocations and ethnic groups). Entrants in the second edition—
as well as those in the first edition and its *Supplement* (see below)—are also indexed in
Biography and Genealogy Master Index (J565). The second edition updates some entries
and adds a few new ones but for the most part merely reprints entries from the first
edition (ed. Lina Mainiero and Langdon Lynne Faust, 4 vols. [New York: Ungar, 1979–
82] and the *Supplement* (ed. Carol Hurd Green and Mary Grimly Mason, 2 vols. [New
York: Continuum-Ungar, 1994]), in many instances not even revising the bibliographies. The second edition in no way bears out the claim that "the explosion of feminist
scholarship has enriched each subsequent edition of *American Women Writers*"; indeed,
the entries for Nella Larsen and Frances Watkins Harper—two writers singled out as
examples of how much new information has been discovered about women writers—
are unchanged from the first edition (but for updated bibliographies). The essays vary
considerably in quality (with many full of errors and hardly penetrating in analysis).
Once the most inclusive single guide to female writers in the United States, it is now
useful only for those few writers not profiled in other biographical dictionaries.

Q3395   *Marquis Who's Who on the Web*. New Providence: Marquis. Online. 12
        Sept. 2005 <http://search.marquiswhoswho.com>. Updated daily. (Also
        online through *Biography Resource Center* [J572] and SilverPlatter [I523].)
        Who's Who in America [1899–]. New Providence: Marquis, [1899–].
        E176.W642   920.073. CD-ROM.

A biographical database of citizens of the United States, Canada, and Mexico (and
some other countries) who are (or were) nationally prominent for their positions or
achievements and who were listed since 1985 in *Who's Who in America [1899–]* or
one or more of the complementary regional or topical *Who's Who*. In addition, the
database includes entries from *Who Was Who in America: With World Notables [1897–]*
(1943–) and *Who Was Who in America: Historical Volume, 1607–1896*, rev. ed. (1967),
689 pp.

The compact entries—largely compiled from information supplied by entrants—
supply basic biographical, family, and career data; a list of significant publications and
awards; and home or office address.

Users can limit name searches by the city of mailing address, state or province of
mailing address, zip or postal code, country (outside the United States), occupation,
gender, college or university, degrees, year of graduation, hobbies and special interests,
political party, religion, or keyword; all of the preceding fields can also be searched
separately. In addition, users can search only the current or the historical bibliographies.

Although the entries offer minimal information and are not always accurate or
complete, *Marquis Who's Who on the Web* is among the best sources for current information and addresses of prominent Americans. For many entrants, however, *American
National Biography Online* (Q3378) offers fuller, more accurate information.

See also

    Sec. J: Biographical Sources.
    Allibone, *Critical Dictionary of English Literature* (M1430).
    Dictionary of Literary Biography (J600).
    Hart, *Oxford Companion to American Literature* (Q3210).

Periodicals

HISTORIES AND SURVEYS

Q3400   Mott, Frank Luther. *A History of American Magazines, [1741–1930]*.
5 vols. Cambridge: Harvard UP, 1930–68.   PN4877.M63   051'.09.

>   Vol. 1: *1741–1850*. New York: Appleton, 1930. 848 pp.
>   Vol. 2: *1850–1865*. Cambridge: Harvard UP, 1938. 608 pp.
>   Vol. 3: *1865–1885*. 1938. 649 pp.
>   Vol. 4: *1885–1905*. 1957. 858 pp.
>   Vol. 5: *Sketches of 21 Magazines: 1905–1930*. Cambridge: Belknap–
>   Harvard UP, 1968. 595 pp.

A history of the development of English-language periodicals in the United States to c. 1905, with individual studies of important magazines through 1930. Excludes newspapers and annuals but otherwise surveys a representative sample of magazines. Vols. 1 through 3 include a chronological list of periodicals mentioned in the text. Indexed in each volume by persons, titles, and subjects; however, the cumulative index in vol. 5 is more thorough. For a history of the project, see "Unfinished Story; or, The Man in the Carrel" (vol. 5, pp. 341–50). Justly praised for its erudition and style, Mott is the monumental history of periodicals in the country. Vols. 2 and 3 were awarded the Pulitzer Prize in History (1939). Some literary magazines are more fully described in Chielens, *American Literary Magazines* (Q3410).

For a more succinct and current history, especially of mass market publications, see John Tebbel and Mary Ellen Zuckerman, *The Magazine in America, 1741–1990* (New York: Oxford UP, 1991, 433 pp.), which emphasizes social and cultural history in chapters on such topics as magazines for women, African American periodicals, male audiences, and pulps and science fiction magazines.

GUIDES TO PRIMARY WORKS

Union Lists

Q3405   *United States Newspaper Program National Union List*. 5th ed. Dublin,
Ohio: OCLC Online Computer Lib. Center, 1999. Microfiche.

A bibliography and union list of newspapers derived from the database being compiled by participants in the United States Newspaper Program, which is attempting to catalog and eventually microfilm the more than 300,000 newspapers published in the United States and its territories. (For a description of the program and its status, see http://www.neh.gov/projects/usnp.html.) Listed alphabetically by title, entries include publication information and exact holdings. Four indexes: date; subjects; geographic area; place of publication or printing. Entries can also be searched by title through *WorldCat* (E225), whose records are more current than the published version. The *National Union List* is especially useful for locating runs and identifying newspapers by locale.

This work largely supersedes Winifred Gregory, ed., *American Newspapers, 1821– 1936: A Union List of Files Available in the United States and Canada* (New York:

Wilson, 1937, 791 pp.); for newspapers before 1820, Brigham, *History and Bibliography of American Newspapers* (Q4035), frequently supplies fuller information and locations.

See also

Sec. K: Periodicals/Union Lists.

Bibliographies

Q3410 Chielens, Edward E., ed. *American Literary Magazines: The Eighteenth and Nineteenth Centuries.* Historical Guides to the World's Periodicals and Newspapers. New York: Greenwood, 1986. 503 pp.   Z1231.P45 A43 [PS201]   810′.9′003.

————. *American Literary Magazines: The Twentieth Century.* Historical Guides to the World's Periodicals and Newspapers. Westport: Greenwood, 1992. 474 pp.   Z1231.P45 A44 [PS221]   016.8108′005.

A collection of separately authored profiles of 168 of the most important American magazines that print a significant amount of literature (including criticism) or are otherwise important in literary history. The essays, organized by periodical title, typically discuss publishing history, audience, and significant literary content, and conclude with a list of studies, indexes, reprints, and a few locations, as well as details of publishing history (including title changes, numbering and dating of volumes and issues, frequency, publishers, and editors). Each volume concludes with an annotated list of minor literary magazines (and in the earlier volume nonliterary ones that have literary content) and with a chronology of American literary magazines and literary and social events; the later volume also prints a valuable overview, by Willard Fox, of little-magazine collections in the United States and Canada. Indexed by persons, magazine titles, and subjects. Although the essays vary in quality, *American Literary Magazines* is a useful compendium of information on the publishing history and contents of a small group of significant literary magazines.

See also

Kelly, *Children's Periodicals of the United States* (U5510).

Indexes

Although many clipping files and unpublished indexes exist for local and regional newspapers, there is no trustworthy guide to these important sources. Because Anita Cheek Milner, *Newspaper Indexes: A Location and Subject Guide for Researchers,* 3 vols. (Metuchen: Scarecrow, 1977–82), is incomplete, poorly organized, inadequately indexed, and full of errors, researchers attempting to locate a clipping file or an unpublished index cannot depend on the work as a guide. Instead, they will usually have to contact the newspaper office and area libraries and historical societies. For other indexes, bibliographies, and union lists of newspapers, see the chapter on guides to newspapers in Prucha, *Handbook for Research in American History* (Q3185a). For a convenient guide to online indexes, archives, and morgues see *U.S. News Archives on the Web* (http://www.ibiblio.org/slanews/internet/archives.html).

Q3415   *The* New York Times *Index.* Current Series. Ann Arbor: ProQuest,
         1913– . 3/mo., with quarterly and annual cumulations. Prior Series
         [covering Sept. 1851–1912]. 15 vols. 1967–74.   AI21.N45   071′.47′1.

A subject index with abstracts of articles and features in the late city edition and regional Sunday supplements. Abstracts are listed chronologically under a heading; reviews appear under "Books and Literature" ("Book Reviews," in earlier volumes), "Theater," and "Motion Pictures," with cross-references to authors and directors. Besides providing excellent access to the contents of the country's leading newspaper, the *Index* can be used to determine the approximate date of stories in newspapers not indexed. The *Index* is hardly complicated enough to require anyone to endure the wretched prose and belabored explanation of Grant W. Morse, *Guide to the Incomparable New York Times* Index (New York: Fleet, 1980, 72 pp.). Issues since 1851 can be searched at http://www.nytimes.com; other online providers—including *ProQuest* (I519) and *19th Century Masterfile* (Q4147)—offer full-text access to the *Times.*

Four specialized indexes also provide access to the *Times:*

> Falk, Byron A., Jr., and Valerie R. Falk. *Personal Name Index to* The *New York Times* Index, *1851–1974.* 22 vols. Verdi: Roxbury Data Interface, 1976–83. *1975–2001 Supplement.* 9 vols. Sparks: Roxbury Data Interface, 2004–05. The supplement includes names overlooked in the index to *1851–1974.*
>
> New York Times Book Review *Index, 1896–1970.* 5 vols. New York: Arno, 1973.
>
> *The* New York Times *Obituaries Index, 1858–1968.* New York: New York Times, 1970. 1,136 pp. *The* New York Times *Obituaries Index, II: 1969–1978.* 1980. 131 pp.
>
> *The* New York Times *Obituary Index [1988].* Westport: Meckler, 1990. (The index was to be annual, but it apparently lasted only one year.)

See also

> *Literary Writings in America* (Q3255).

Genres

Most works in section L: Genres are useful for research in American literature.

FICTION

Most works in section L: Genres/Fiction are important to research in American fiction.

Histories and Surveys

Q3470   *The Columbia History of the American Novel.* Gen. ed. Emory Elliott. New
         York: Columbia UP, 1991. 905 pp.   PS371.C7   813.009.

A collection of separately authored essays on the development of the novel in the United States, Canada, the Caribbean, and Latin America. Organized within four chronological divisions (the beginnings to the mid-nineteenth century, the late nineteenth century, the early twentieth century, the late twentieth century), the chapters emphasize a thematic rather than biographical approach, treating such topics as autobiography and the early novel, the book marketplace, romance, race and ethnicity, realism, gender, popular forms, regions, and movements. Varied in their approaches, the essays—all by established scholars—range from broad surveys to extended examinations of representative works, and they encompass the well-known as well as the newly discovered novelists. Concludes with brief biographies of about 200 novelists and a selected bibliography of criticism (more useful, however, would be a selected bibliography accompanying each chapter). Indexed by persons and subjects. Although generally authoritative and provocative, the *Columbia History* does not fulfill the pressing need for a unified history of fiction in the United States. Reviews: Paul Bauer, Russell J. Reising, and Ellen Weinauer, *Dictionary of Literary Biography Yearbook: 1992* (1993): 178–86; Marc Dolan, *Modern Fiction Studies* 38 (1993): 459–61.

Although now dated, the following general histories remain useful:

> Chase, Richard. *The American Novel and Its Tradition.* Garden City: Doubleday, 1957. 266 pp. A critical survey from Brown to Faulkner that emphasizes major writers in exploring the relationship of the romance to the development of the American novel.
>
> Cowie, Alexander. *The Rise of the American Novel.* American Literature Series. New York: American Book, 1948. 877 pp. A critical history of the evolution of the American novel during the eighteenth and nineteenth centuries, with a concluding chapter on the first four decades of the present century. Organized chronologically, chapters on groups and major authors also treat representative minor writers. Indexed by titles and authors. Although now dated, this is among the fuller surveys and remains useful for its detailed consideration of several minor novelists.
>
> Quinn, Arthur Hobson. *American Fiction: An Historical and Critical Survey.* New York: Appleton, 1936. 805 pp. A critical history of American fiction from the eighteenth century to the 1930s, excluding juvenile, dime, and detective fiction as well as works by authors who were first published after 1920. Although it is dated, offers some questionable evaluations, and is superseded in many parts by specialized surveys, Quinn remains one of the few works covering both novels and short fiction. Review: Fred Lewis Pattee, *American Literature* 8 (1937): 468–70.
>
> Wagenknecht, Edward. *Cavalcade of the American Novel from the Birth of the Nation to the Middle of the Twentieth Century.* New York: Holt, 1952. 575 pp. A critical history through the 1940s.

A major desideratum remains an adequate history of fiction in the United States.

Literary Handbooks, Dictionaries, and Encyclopedias

Q3472   Franklin, Benjamin, V, ed. *Dictionary of American Literary Characters.* 2nd ed. Rev. American BookWorks Corp. 2 vols. New York: Facts on File, 2002.   PS374.C43 D5   813.009′27′03.

A dictionary of "major characters" from "significant American novels," "some uncelebrated ones," and a "sampling of best-sellers" published between 1789 and 2000; the second edition adds more "literary, popular, and genre fiction." Ranging from 10 to approximately 100 words (those added in the second edition lack the terseness of the original edition), entries identify a character and the novel in which he, she, or it appears. Two indexes in each volume: titles; authors (for users who cannot recall a character's name, the author index lists novels and then characters included under each author). Although misleadingly titled, lacking any explanation of the criteria employed to define "major" characters or select the "uncelebrated" novels and best sellers through 1979 (the cut-off date of the first edition; the revised edition relies on best seller and award lists and "several literature professors" for additions and deletions), and including few major scholars in the list of contributors, the *Dictionary* is a convenient source of factual details about several thousand fictional characters.

Guides to Primary Works

Q3473   Davis, Gwenn, and Beverly A. Joyce, comps. *Short Fiction by Women to 1900: A Bibliography of American and British Writers.* Bibliographies of Writings by American and British Women to 1900 4. London: Mansell, 1999. 413 pp.   Z1229.W8 D4 [PS374.W6]   016.813'01089287.

A bibliography of short fiction—including novellas, short stories, prose characters, "narrative tracts and brief stories intended to teach religious lessons," sketches, "moral tales, collections of legends and folklore, prose allegories, and proverb stories" of less than 150 pages and directed to an adult audience—published separately, for the most part, before 1900 by American and British women writers. The 6,185 entries (listed alphabetically by author) typically provide alternate forms of an author's name, nationality, birth and death dates, title, publication information for the first edition, source(s) for the entry, and a brief annotation (that sometimes notes forms, genres, subject matter, and revised editions). Authors are sorted into chronological groups in an appendix; however, beginning with 1850, the groupings are too broad to be of much value. Indexed by subjects. As in the other volumes in this series—*Drama by Women to 1900* (Q3513), *Poetry by Women to 1900* (Q3534), and *Personal Writings by Women to 1900* (Q3545a)—the indexing is too unrefined to allow adequate access to the entries. Although based primarily on other sources—notably *National Union Catalog, Pre-1956 Imprints* (E235), the British Museum *General Catalogue of Printed Books* (see E250), and *WorldCat* (E225)—rather than firsthand examination of copies, *Short Fiction by Women to 1900* at least offers a starting place for identifying fiction written by women writers before 1900.

Guides to Scholarship and Criticism

Q3474   *Facts on File Bibliography of American Fiction through 1865.* Ed. Kent P. Ljungquist. New York: Facts on File, 1994. 326 pp.   Z1231.F4 F33 016.813.

Facts on File Bibliography of American Fiction, 1866–1918. Ed. James Nagel and Gwen L. Nagel. New York: Facts on File, 1993. 412 pp. Z1231.F4 B46 [PS377]   016.813'4.

Facts on File Bibliography of American Fiction, 1919–1988. Ed. Matthew J. Bruccoli and Judith S. Baughman. 2 vols. New York: Facts on File: 1991. Z1231.F4 B47 [PS379]   016.813'508.

Separately authored bibliographies of important works by and about established and popular United States writers born before 1 January 1941. Coverage of primary and secondary works extends through 1988, but later publications are included in each volume's prefatory lists of reference works essential to the study of United States literature and of general studies, reference works, and journals important to the authors in the volume. Assignment to a period is determined by the date of the author's first major work. Writers are listed alphabetically; following a headnote describing the author's reputation or influence are sections for bibliographies, first and revised second editions of separately published works (except for pamphlets and ephemera) written in or translated into English, standard editions, major repositories of manuscripts, concordances, biographies, interviews, and the most important studies (subdivided into books, collections of essays, special issues of journals, and essays). Each volume ends with a chronology, list of journal acronyms, and index of scholars. There are numerous inconsistencies in citation form and some disconcerting editorial practices, such as the omission of periods after initials and abbreviations and the reduction of the subject author's name to initials in book and article titles. Both the trustworthiness and degree of the selection vary widely from bibliography to bibliography: some are written by "scholar-specialists" (as the series introduction claims); many, though, are signed by persons whose names do not appear in the list of studies on the author, some are contributed by graduate students, and at least one is by the subject author. Despite these shortcomings, *Facts on File Bibliography of American Fiction* offers a convenient starting place for research on American fiction writers; indeed, many minor writers find their most complete bibliographies in these volumes.

Some bibliographies from *Facts on File Bibliography of American Fiction* have been adapted and updated for the series Essential Bibliography of American Fiction, ed. Matthew J. Bruccoli and Judith S. Baughman:

> *Modern African American Writers.* 1994. 92 pp.
> *Modern Classic Writers.* 1994. 99 pp.
> *Modern Women Writers.* 1994. 100 pp.

The volumes of *Facts on File Bibliography of American Fiction* were the only ones published of the Facts on File Bibliography Series, a project designed to fulfill the long-standing need for a general bibliography — comparable to *New Cambridge Bibliography of English Literature* (M1385) — for the literature of the United States.

Q3475   Gerstenberger, Donna, and George Hendrick. *The American Novel, 1789–1959: A Checklist of Twentieth-Century Criticism.* 2nd ed. Swallow Checklists of Criticism and Explication. Denver: Swallow, 1961. 333 pp.

——. *The American Novel: A Checklist of Twentieth Century Criticism on Novels Written since 1789.* Vol. 2: *Criticism Written 1960–1968.* Chicago: Swallow, 1970. 459 pp.   Z1231.F4 G4   016.813'03.

Glitsch, Catherine, comp. *American Novel Explication, 1991–1995.* North Haven: Archon–Shoe String, 1998. 319 pp. *1969–1980.* 2000. 575 pp. Z1231.F4 G58 [PS371]   016.813009.

A selective checklist of articles, parts of books, and bibliographies published between 1900 and 1980 and between 1991 and 1995. Gerstenberger and Hendrick favor standard works and periodicals but exclude general literary histories and almost all reviews. Entries are organized in two divisions: authors and general studies. Under each author are sections for individual novels, general studies (of two or more works but with no cross-references under specific titles), and bibliographies. The second part has sections for general studies and centuries. Entries for parts of books and essays from collections are keyed to a list at the back. The two *Checklists* are time-consuming, frustrating works to use because of the lack of cross-references and indexing and a layout that prevents easy identification of sections. Highly selective in coverage and now dated, *The American Novel* is principally useful for the indexing of parts of books published before 1969. Superior coverage of articles is offered by Leary, *Articles on American Literature* (Q3295).

American Novel Explication indexes books and articles, primarily in English, that explicate (i.e., interpret "the significance and meaning" of) novels by United States and English- and French-Canadian writers. Entries are organized alphabetically by novelist and then by novel; entries for parts of books are keyed to a list at the back. Indexed by novelists and titles of novel. Although lacking a sufficient explanation of the criteria governing selection, *American Novel Explication* is useful for its indexing of single-author monographs.

Q3480   Weixlmann, Joe. *American Short-Fiction Criticism and Scholarship, 1959–*
         1977: A Checklist. Chicago: Swallow–Ohio UP, 1982. 625 pp.
         Z1231.F4 W43 [PS374.S5]   016.813′01′09.

A classified list of English-language articles, interviews, and bibliographies from some 325 journals and of sections in about 5,000 books on the short fiction of more than 500 authors from the eighteenth through the twentieth century. Weixlmann makes an effort to include minority writers. Entries are organized in divisions for general studies and individual authors; under the latter are sections for individual works, general studies, interviews, and bibliographies. The omission of page references in entries for parts of books and the lack of an index mar this otherwise useful compilation.

Weixlmann continues the coverage of American writers in Jarvis Thurston, O. B. Emerson, Carl Hartman, and Elizabeth B. Wright, *Short Fiction Criticism: A Checklist of Interpretation since 1925 of Stories and Novelettes (American, British, Continental), 1800–1958,* Swallow Checklists of Criticism and Explication (Denver: Swallow, 1960, 265 pp.), which is only marginally useful because of its exclusion of studies "dealing with the 'environmental' circumstances of literature (biography, genesis, source, etc.)."

See also

Leary, *Articles on American Literature* (Q3295).

DRAMA AND THEATER

Most works in section L: Genres/Drama and Theater are important to research in American drama and theater.

Histories and Surveys

Q3490   Meserve, Walter J. *An Emerging Entertainment: The Drama of the American*
         People to 1828. Bloomington: Indiana UP, 1977. 342 pp.   PS332.M39
         812′.009.

         ———. *Heralds of Promise: The Drama of the American People during the*
         Age of Jackson, 1829–1849. Contributions in American Studies 86. New
         York: Greenwood, 1986. 269 pp.   PS343.M47   812′.3′09.

The only volumes published of a projected six-volume critical history of plays written and published in America from its colonization to the present. After a discussion of what constitutes American drama, chapters survey the plays of a period, emphasizing their "relationship . . . to the cultural and historical progress of the country," offering a brief synopsis of each work and biographical information on important authors, and tracing "the development of American drama as a literary genre and its contribution to

American theatre." Each volume concludes with a selective bibliography that (depending on the volume) lists studies of the cultural and historical background, theater histories, general bibliographies and studies, works on individual dramatists, periodicals and newspapers, manuscript and theater collections, and dissertations. The second volume lists playwrights and plays of the period in appendixes. Indexed by names and plays (separately in the first volume). Although plagued by numerous factual errors, the thoroughness of coverage and attention to the social and political conditions affecting drama make Meserve's work the best general history of American drama through 1849. Reviews: (*Emerging Entertainment*) Thomas F. Marshall, *American Literature* 50 (1978): 519–21; Kenneth Silverman, *Early American Literature* 14 (1979): 125–26.

Because it treats popular and "paratheatrical forms," *The Cambridge History of American Theatre*, ed. Don B. Wilmeth and Christopher Bigsby, 3 vols. (Cambridge: Cambridge UP, 1998–2000) is an important complement to Meserve. Chapters are devoted to such topics as management, plays and playwrights, actors, directors, theatrical groups, musical theater, stagecraft, and popular entertainment; many contributors are among the leading scholars in the field. Unlike so many recent multiauthored literary histories, *Cambridge History of American Theatre* provides a bibliographical survey at the end of each chapter (although full citations can be found only in the bibliography that concludes each volume). In addition, a useful chronology is hidden away after the front matter to each volume. Indexed in each volume by persons, subjects, and titles.

Because of their emphasis on theater, the preceding works do not completely supersede Arthur Hobson Quinn, *A History of the American Drama from the Beginning to the Civil War*, 2nd ed. (New York: Crofts, 1943, 530 pp.), and *A History of the American Drama from the Civil War to the Present Day*, rev. ed., 2 vols. in 1 (1936, 296 and 432 pp.).

See also

Revels History of Drama in English (M1530).

Literary Handbooks, Dictionaries, and Encyclopedias

Q3499   *Cambridge Guide to American Theatre.* Ed. Don B. Wilmeth and Tice L. Miller. Updated paperback ed. Cambridge: Cambridge UP, 1996. 463 pp. PN2220.C35   792'.0973.

Emphasizes American theater "in the broadest possible terms" from its beginnings through early 1992 (with updated, corrected, and approximately 50 new entries in the paperback edition; further updates appear in Wilmeth, comp., "Updates to the *Cambridge Guide to American Theatre*," *Theatre History Studies* 22 [2002]: 79–81). Like Bordman, *Oxford Companion to American Theatre* (Q3500), the *Cambridge Guide* includes entries on performers, theatrical personnel, theaters, organizations, and individual works (many taken from *Cambridge Guide to Theatre* [L1125]). Although fewer in number and generally more concise than entries in the *Oxford Companion*, entries in the *Cambridge Guide* are signed, and many conclude with suggestions for further reading. Indexed by persons who do not have separate entries. In general, the *Cambridge Guide* offers broader, more balanced, and more accurate coverage of American theater than does the *Oxford Companion*, but ultimately the two must be used together.

Q3500   Bordman, Gerald, and Thomas S. Hischak. *The Oxford Companion to American Theatre.* 3rd ed. New York: Oxford UP, 2004. 681 pp.

PN2220.B6   792'.0973'03. Online through *Oxford Reference Online* (I530) and *North American Theatre Online* (Q3512).

Although still emphasizing popular Broadway theater (through early 2003) in entries on plays, musicals, actors, actresses, producers, directors, designers, other notable theatrical people, theaters, organizations, and periodicals, the 3rd edition extends its reach outside New York City to include regional theatrical companies and historic theater buildings, admits more off-Broadway and regional works, adds people from the earlier days of American theater, but shortens many entries from the 2nd edition (1999, 735 pp.) to make room for the new ones. In less depth, Bordman covers other entertainment, such as minstrelsy, vaudeville, circus, and Wild West and tent shows. The bulk of the entries are for plays (with length of New York run the main criterion governing selection), recording place and date of original production, length of run, and cast, and providing a brief synopsis and critical commentary. Entries for people give an overview of career. Entrants in the original edition (1984, 734 pp.) are indexed in *Biography and Genealogy Master Index* (J565). The first two editions are plagued by numerous inaccuracies, and the emphasis on popular Broadway entertainment distorts the picture of the American theatrical scene; nevertheless, the *Oxford Companion* is the single fullest handbook designed for quick reference. It does not offer the balance one expects in an *Oxford Companion*, however, and it must be used in conjunction with *Cambridge Guide to American Theatre* (Q3499). Reviews: (1st ed.) John Simon, *TLS: Times Literary Supplement* 26 Apr. 1985: 477 (an important discussion of weaknesses); Don B. Wilmeth, *Theatre History Studies* 5 (1985): 116–19.

A useful supplement for plays is Edwin Bronner, *The Encyclopedia of the American Theatre, 1900–1975* (San Diego: Barnes, 1980, 659 pp.), which covers plays written or adapted by Anglo-American authors and produced on and off Broadway. Entries cite date and place of original production, length of run, cast, producer, director, and screen adaptations and include a brief synopsis.

Q3505   Durham, Weldon B., ed. *American Theatre Companies, 1749–1887.* New York: Greenwood, 1986. 598 pp. *1888–1930.* 1987. 541 pp. *1931–1986.* 1989. 596 pp.   PN2266.A54   792'.0973. All are online through *North American Theatre Online* (Q3512).

A collection of separately authored discussions of theatrical companies that produced more than one nonmusical play while in residence in one place for a minimum of 20 consecutive weeks. Organized alphabetically by company (with cross-references for alternative names), entries consist of two parts: a discussion of the history, commercial and artistic significance, and repertory of the company; lists of personnel (including managers, designers, technicians, and performers), works produced (selective if a full list has been published), and selected scholarship and manuscript or archival material. Each volume concludes with two appendixes: a chronology of theater companies; a list by state. Indexed in each volume by persons and play titles. Although the essays vary in quality and some companies are more extensively treated in separate studies, *American Theatre Companies* is the fullest single compendium of information on American theater companies. Review: (*1749–1887* and *1888–1930*) Walter J. Meserve, *Theatre Survey* 28 (1987): 108–10.

Annals

Q3510   Odell, George C. D. *Annals of the New York Stage.* 15 vols. New York: Columbia UP, 1927–49.   PN2277.N5 O4   792'.097471. Online through *North American Theatre Online* (Q3512).

A narrative calendar of theatrical entertainment (including opera, ballet, vaudeville, minstrelsy, circus, and concert) in New York City from 1699 through 1894. Organized by season, then by theater or troupe, the commentary draws on newspapers, unpublished manuscripts and archival materials, autobiographies, playbills, and other documents to record performances (along with cast lists) as well as discuss critical reception, performers, and theater architecture. Indexed in each volume by persons, titles, subjects, and theaters; the numerous illustrations are indexed in *Index to the Portraits in Odell's Annals of the New York Stage* (N.p.: Amer. Soc. for Theatre Research, 1963, 179 pp.). Odell offers a full, if at times discursive, record of activity in the country's major theatrical center. Reviews: Arthur Hobson Quinn, *American Literature* 1 (1929): 89–92; 3 (1931): 335–39; 8 (1937): 472–74; 9 (1937): 382–84; 10 (1938): 362–64; 12 (1940): 123–24; 13 (1941): 177–78; 14 (1943): 453–55; 22 (1950): 88–89; *Modern Language Notes* 61 (1946): 138–39.

Complemented by Gerald Bordman, *American Theatre: A Chronicle of Comedy and Drama, 1869–1914* (New York: Oxford UP, 1994, 793 pp.), Bordman, *1914–1930* (1995, 446 pp.), Bordman, *1930–1969* (1996, 472 pp.), and Thomas S. Hischak, *1969–2000* (2001, 504 pp.), a narrative of nonmusical plays produced in New York City. Like Odell, *American Theatre* draws on a range of documents to discuss cast and reception. Two indexes: plays (with a subsection for sources of plays); persons. Unfortunately, theaters are not indexed. All four volumes are searchable in *North American Theatre Online* (Q3512).

Q3511   Norton, Richard C. *A Chronology of American Musical Theater.* 3 vols. New York: Oxford UP, 2002.   ML1711.8.N3.N67   782.1'4'097471.

A chronicle of the "popular American Musical Theatre as presented on first-class stages in New York City [i.e., Manhattan]" with selective coverage from 1750 to 1850 and full coverage from 1850 through 2001. Musical theater is broadly defined to include such forms as operetta, dance drama, and rock opera and is not limited to English-language works. Productions are listed chronologically by season; when possible, each entry includes title, opening and closing dates, venue changes, number of performances and details of revivals, author (and relationship to literary works), production credits, full cast list (with only notable changes recorded), descriptions of acts and scenes, and a list of songs or other musical sketches. Three indexes: titles; names (limited to principal performers); titles of songs (those within double quotation marks in the entries). Based on an encyclopedic knowledge of the subject and extensive examination of opening night programs, advertisements, sheet music, and reviews, *Chronology of American Musical Theater* offers a seemingly inexhaustible wealth of detail; unfortunately, the restrictions on indexing will leave users hopelessly frustrated by being unable to extract efficiently information about production personnel, venues, genres or forms, authors, composers, and adaptations of literary works. This is an impressive resource that stands ready to encourage important research on Broadway musical theater, but to do so the data herein must be available in an electronic format.

Guides to Primary Works

Bibliographies and Indexes

Q3512   *North American Theatre Online* (*NATO*). Alexander Street P. Online. 14 Feb. 2006 <http://www.alexanderstreet6.com/atho/index.shtml>. Updated quarterly.

A database of reference works that treat North American theater, texts of plays (along with bibliographic records for those the publisher cannot license), a bibliography of published and unpublished plays, image files, biographical data on theater personnel, details of major North American productions, and information on theaters and acting companies. As of early 2006, the database included data on more than 30,000 plays. Coverage of the United States is far more extensive than that for Canada and the rest of North America. Users can browse indexes of people, theaters, acting companies, "resources" (i.e., images), plays, productions, dates, reference works (an uncritical listing of separate chapters or entries from reference works, with hundreds of lines beginning "Chapter" or "Entry"), and subjects; several of the preceding include subindexes and sort options, but the only way to search is through a Web browser's search function. Users can also search (via Quick Search or Search [i.e., Advanced Search]) subsets of data: people, scenes, theaters, production companies, plays, characters, productions, and resources and reference works. Each subset allows searchers to combine a variety of fields and limit searches; for example, the Advanced Search screen for searching plays has fields for full text keyword, title, availability of full text, unpublished plays, date of composition, playwright, gender, nationality, race, translator, lyricist, composer, librettist, author of book for a musical, conceiver, all contributors, publication date, year of first production, medium, genre, original language, setting, performers, character names, theater, production company, subject, and record code; that for characters has fields for full-text keyword, character name, gender, occupation, nationality, race, sexual orientation, marital status, person on whom a character is based, type, author, play title, genre, year of composition, performer, record code. Most of the preceding have lists associated with them, but some lists are alphabetized by first name or initial or with an initial definite article not inverted.

Although the source of the full text of a play can be identified only in the bibliographical record (search or browse Plays) and although some indexes are created by an uncritical sorting of record fields, the indexing of the data herein allows for some very precise and sophisticated searches. And, unlike most databases, the publisher provides a way for users to report errors or omissions.

Q3513   Davis, Gwenn, and Beverly A. Joyce, comps. *Drama by Women to 1900: A Bibliography of American and British Writers.* Bibliographies of Writings by American and British Women to 1900 3. Toronto: U of Toronto P, 1992. 189 pp.   Z1231.D7 D38   016.812.

A bibliography of published (both separately and in collections), unpublished, and nonextant English-language dramatic works (including dramatic poems and poems intended for recitation) written by British or American women before 1900. The 2,828 entries (listed alphabetically by author) typically provide alternative forms of an author's name, nationality, birth and death dates, title, publication information for the first edition, source(s) for the entry, and a brief annotation (that sometimes notes forms, genres, subject matter, and revised editions). Playwrights are sorted into chronological groups in an appendix; however, beginning with 1850, the groupings are too broad to be of much value. Three indexes: actresses; subjects (including genres, forms, and a few historical persons); translations and adaptations. As in the other volumes in this series— *Short Fiction by Women to 1900* (Q3473), *Poetry by Women to 1900* (Q3534), and *Personal Writings by Women to 1900* (Q3545a)—the indexing is too unrefined to allow adequate access to the entries. Although based primarily on other sources—notably *National Union Catalog, Pre-1956 Imprints* (E235), the British Museum *General Catalogue of Printed Books* (see E250), and *WorldCat* (E225)—rather than firsthand examination of copies, *Drama by Women to 1900* at least offers a starting place for identifying dramatic works written by women writers before 1900.

Coverage is continued—at least cursorily—by Frances Diodato Bzowski, comp., *American Women Playwrights, 1900–1930: A Checklist*, Bibliographies and Indexes in Women's Studies 15 (Westport: Greenwood, 1992, 420 pp.), which lists published and some unpublished plays alphabetically by author, with entries including date of production or publication, type of play, number of acts, and locations in anthologies, periodicals, or libraries. Indexed in *Biography and Genealogy Master Index* (J565). The lack of full bibliographical information and of title and subject indexes—coupled with the secondhand nature of much of the information—makes this little more than a place to begin identifying plays by American women of the period.

Text Archives

Q3514   *American Drama 1714–1915*. ProQuest. Online. 17 June 2006 <http://collections.chadwyck.com>.

An archive of rekeyed texts of more than 1,500 English-language dramatic works by American playwrights (including African Americans). The About *American Drama 1714–1915* is uncharacteristically silent about the criteria used to select editions for rekeying. Simple keyword, first line or title, and author searches can be limited by speaker, place of first performance, date of first performance, publication date, publisher, genre, gender, nationality, ethnicity, to verse or prose drama, to notes, and to parts (e.g., epilogues, stage directions). Searchers can also browse an author list of the contents of the database. Results appear in ascending alphabetical order and cannot be re-sorted. Citations (but not the full text) can be marked for e-mailing, downloading, or printing; each citation includes a durable URL to the full text.

Some works are rekeyed from textually unsound editions; however, the bibliographic record for each work identifies the source of the text and any omissions (e.g., preliminary matter). Besides being a useful source for identifying an elusive quotation or half-remembered line, the scope of *American Drama*'s text archive makes feasible a variety of kinds of studies (stylistic, thematic, imagistic, generic, and topical).

The contents of *American Drama 1714–1915* can also be searched through *LiOn* (I527), which offers a less versatile search interface.

Guides to Scholarship and Criticism

Surveys of Research

For an evaluative survey of histories and general studies (mostly after 1950), see Charles A. Carpenter, "American Drama: A Bibliographical Essay," *American Studies International* 21.5 (1983): 3–52.

See also

   American Literary Scholarship (Q3265): Chapter on drama.

Other Bibliographies

Q3515   Archer, Stephen M. *American Actors and Actresses: A Guide to Information Sources.* Performing Arts Information Guide Series 8. Detroit: Gale, 1983. 710 pp.   Z5784.M9 A7 [PN1998.A2]   016.79143'028'0922.

A bibliography of English-language scholarship on actors and actresses who were associated with the legitimate stage, had substantial careers, and have been the subject of scholarly study. Some foreigners important to the American theatrical tradition or who had substantial careers in the country before 1900 are included; most living persons are omitted. Archer excludes dissertations, theses, newspapers, fan magazines, and reviews of specific performances. The 3,263 entries are organized alphabetically in seven divisions: general reference works; bibliographies and indexes; general histories, surveys, and regional studies; books that discuss several performers; articles that treat several performers; biographies and autobiographies of performers not among those in the next division; 226 individual performers. The lists for individual performers conclude with cross-references to the general divisions. The brief (but adequate) descriptive annotations sometimes offer evaluative comments. Three indexes: persons; titles; subjects (including performers). Although selective, *American Actors and Actresses* offers the fullest single compilation of scholarship on significant American actors and actresses.

Q3517   Silvester, Robert. *United States Theatre: A Bibliography from the Beginning to 1990.* Motley Bibliographies 2. New York: Hall; Romsey: Motley, 1993. 400 pp.   Z5781.S55 [PN2221]   016.792'0973.

A bibliography of separately published works (through 1990) on English-language and Native American drama and theater in the United States and on the musical in other countries. Includes theses and dissertations; periodicals not in Stratman, *American Theatrical Periodicals* (Q3530), or C. Edwards, *World Guide to Performing Arts Periodicals* (London: Intl. Theatre Inst., 1982, 66 pp.); and texts of plays with substantial historical or biographical material. Entries, which cite the best or most recently revised edition, are organized chronologically by date of edition cited in three classified divisions: theater; drama; music. The first has variously classified sections for general reference works; federal and state intervention; religion; theater arts; theater history; regional studies; theater companies, clubs, and societies; biography; criticism; revue, vaudeville, and showboats; community and university theater; and pedagogy. The second has sections for general studies, history, foreign influences, and biography and criticism. The third is devoted to the musical. Users should study the admirably clear explanation (pp. 6–8) of the scope and coverage of individual sections. Some entries are accompanied by brief annotations that provide bibliographical information, list contents, or elucidate an obscure title; for all but the most obscure works, locating the copy described at one of 16 institutions is superfluous. Two indexes: subjects; authors. Although it excludes periodical articles, includes little beyond proper nouns in the subject index, and omits numerous non-English-language titles, *United States Theatre* is especially valuable for its coverage of publications of limited distribution, is attractively printed, and offers the best general list of separately published works on all aspects of United States theater. Review: Don B. Wilmeth, *Theatre Survey* 35 (1994): 143–46.

Q3520   Eddleman, Floyd Eugene, comp. *American Drama Criticism: Interpretations, 1890–1977.* 2nd ed. Hamden: Shoe String, 1979. 488 pp. *Supplement I.* 1984. 255 pp. *Supplement II.* 1989. 269 pp. *Supplement III.* 1992. 436 pp. *Supplement IV.* Comp. LaNelle Daniel. 1996. 239 pp.   Z1231.D7 P3 [PS332]   016.812'009.

A selective bibliography of studies published between 1890 and 1993 on plays by Americans (along with a few works by Canadian and Caribbean writers whose plays were performed in the United States). Eddleman initially excludes interviews, biographical studies, and author bibliographies; however, *Supplement IV* admits nearly anything (even master's theses), including much that hardly merits being called criticism. Under each playwright, plays are organized alphabetically by title, with each play followed by a list of studies and then reviews (*Supplement IV* mixes studies and reviews indiscriminately). The supplements add a section of general studies for each author. Entries for parts of books are keyed to a list at the back. Four indexes: scholars; adapted works and their authors; titles of plays; playwrights. Excluding most author bibliographies until *Supplement IV* (which would lead users to fuller lists of scholarship), plagued by numerous errors, and consisting largely of unverified entries copied from other sources, *American Drama Criticism* is primarily useful for its identification of parts of books that discuss a play and as an incomplete (and in *Supplement IV* erratic) compilation of entries from several of the standard bibliographies and indexes in section G.

Even more unsatisfactory is Rosalie Otero, *Guide to American Drama Explication*, Reference Publication in Literature (New York: Hall-Simon, 1995, 431 pp.), a guide to explications—including some reviews, interviews, and dissertations published in or translated into English between 1942 and 1994—of "American" (i.e., United States) drama. Entries are organized alphabetically by playwright, then by play, and then by critic; entries for books including five or more explications are keyed to a list of sources consulted at the end of the book. The criteria governing selection of dramatists and studies are inexcusably vague ("those that most effectively use explication as a critical tool, those that seem to us most essential to scholars as well as students in the field, and those that might be difficult to find in existing bibliographies"), and most of the entries have been gleaned from readily available sources (although the *Annual Bibliography of English Language and Literature* [G340] is conspicuously absent from the list of indexes consulted). But the guide—like others of its ilk—is useful for identifying discussions of plays buried in single-author monographs.

Fuller, more accurate coverage of scholarship published between 1966 and 1980 on twentieth-century American drama is offered by Carpenter, *Modern Drama Scholarship* (M2875); of post-1980 scholarship, by "Modern Drama Studies" (M2870); and of scholarship before c. 1977 on plays before 1900, by Meserve, *American Drama to 1900* (Q4200).

An adequate annotated bibliography of studies of twentieth-century American drama is a major desideratum.

Q3525   Wilmeth, Don B. *The American Stage to World War I: A Guide to Information Sources.* Performing Arts Information Guide Series 4. Detroit: Gale, 1978. 269 pp.   Z1231.D7 W55 [PN2221]   016.792'0973.

A highly selective annotated guide to English-language scholarship (through c. 1974) on the legitimate professional stage to c. 1915. Wilmeth excludes newspaper articles, popular magazines, works exclusively on playwrights or plays, dissertations, theses, and general histories of the theater. The 1,480 entries are listed alphabetically by author in 13 divisions: general reference works; bibliographies; indexes; general histories, surveys, and regional studies; state and local histories (listed by state); general sources on actors and acting on the American stage; individuals in American theater (listed by person); scenery, architecture, and lighting; foreign-language theater in America; paratheatrical forms; guides to theater collections; suspended periodicals and serials; current periodicals and serials. The brief descriptive annotations are frequently accompanied by evaluative comments, but many annotations inadequately describe content or establish the significance of a work. Three indexes: authors; titles; subjects. Wilmeth is occasionally useful only as a preliminary guide, since most topics are more fully covered in other sources, including Stratman, *American Theatrical Periodicals* (Q3530); Gohdes, *Literature and Theater of the States and Regions of the U. S. A.* (Q3570); Larson, *American Regional Theatre History* (Q3575); Meserve, *American Drama to 1900* (Q4200); and Archer, *American Actors and Actresses* (Q3515).

For a highly selective guide to reference works and scholarship (through April 1978) on popular theater and other live entertainments established before motion pictures, see Don B. Wilmeth, *American and English Popular Entertainment: A Guide to Information Sources*, Performing Arts Information Guide Series 7 (Detroit: Gale, 1980, 465 pp.); continued by Wilmeth, "Stage Entertainment," vol. 3, pp. 1297–328, in Inge, *Handbook of American Popular Culture* (U6295a). It emphasizes American forms in covering circus and Wild West exhibitions, outdoor amusements, variety forms, optical and mechanical entertainments, musical theater and review, pantomime, music hall, and popular theater. There are, however, numerous inaccuracies and omissions.

See also

> Gohdes, *Literature and Theater of the States and Regions of the U. S. A.* (Q3570).
> Larson, *American Regional Theatre History to 1900* (Q3575).
> Leary, *Articles on American Literature* (Q3295).
> Stratman, *Bibliography of the American Theatre Excluding New York City* (Q3580).

Biographical Dictionaries

See

> Wearing, *American and British Theatrical Biography* (L1175).

Periodicals

Guides to Primary Works

Q3530   Stratman, Carl J., C. S. V. *American Theatrical Periodicals, 1798–1967: A Bibliographical Guide.* Durham: Duke UP, 1970. 133 pp.   Z6935.S75 016.7902.

A preliminary bibliography of some 685 periodicals and newspapers published in the United States and devoted to the theater (defined broadly to encompass most stage entertainment, including folk performance, magic, opera, puppetry, and vaudeville but excluding television, cinema, and radio). Although the focus is American theater, Stratman includes periodicals that cover other countries as well. Organized chronologically by year of first publication, entries provide (when available) original title; editor(s); publication information; number of volumes or issues; date of first and last issues; title changes; frequency; miscellaneous notes on content, bibliographical matters, or source of information for works not examined; and locations, with exact holdings of incomplete runs. Additions are printed on pp. 86–87. A tabular overview of publication spans in the appendix offers a convenient means of identifying periodicals published during a period. Indexed by titles, subtitles, cities of publication, and sponsoring organizations. Although not comprehensive, it is the fullest single list of theatrical periodicals published in the United States.

POETRY

Most works in section L: Genres/Poetry are useful for research in American poetry.

Histories and Surveys

Q3533   *The Columbia History of American Poetry.* Ed. Jay Parini. New York:
         Columbia UP, 1993. 894 pp.   PS303.C64   811.009.

A collection of thirty separately authored essays on groups, forms, and individual
poets that consider poetry in the United States from Anne Bradstreet to Charles Wright.
Employing a variety of critical approaches, the contributors examine neglected and well-
known poets; each essay concludes with suggestions for further reading. Indexed by
authors, subjects, and titles. Sporting a distinguished roster of contributors, the *Columbia History* demands the attention of those interested in the relation of poetry to American culture. But it is poorly proofread and marred by some rather surprising omissions;
it also concentrates on the twentieth century and, like other recent literary histories,
subordinates history to other concerns. Reviews: Ed Folsom, *American Literature* 66
(1994): 832–33; Mark Jarman, *Hudson Review* 47 (1995): 641–47; John Piller, *Virginia
Quarterly Review* 71 (1995): 362–66; Jed Rasula, *Resources for American Literary Study*
23 (1997): 263–67; Willard Spiegelman, *Kenyon Review* 17.3–4 (1995): 219–24.

The following, while dated, are important complements to the *Columbia History*:

> Pearce, Roy Harvey. *The Continuity of American Poetry.* 3rd printing, with
> corrections and revisions. Princeton: Princeton UP, 1965. 442 pp. A crit-
> ical survey, from the seventeenth century through Wallace Stevens, that
> emphasizes cultural history in chapters on periods, forms, and major writers.
> Waggoner, Hyatt H. *American Poets from the Puritans to the Present.* Rev.
> ed. Baton Rouge: Louisiana State UP, 1984. 735 pp. A critical survey of
> representative writers, from the Puritans through the 1970s, that argues
> for the centrality of Emerson to the development of American poetry.

Guides to Primary Works

Bibliographies and Indexes

Q3534   Davis, Gwenn, and Beverly A. Joyce, comps. *Poetry by Women to 1900: A
         Bibliography of American and British Writers.* Bibliographies of Writings by
         American and British Women to 1900 2. Toronto: U of Toronto P, 1991.
         340 pp.   Z2013.5.W6.D38 [PR508.W6]   016.821008'09287.

A bibliography of separately published first and extensively revised editions of
English-language poems or poetry collections published between 1573 and 1900 by
American and British women writers. The 6,017 entries, listed alphabetically by author,
typically provide alternate forms of an author's name, nationality, birth and death dates,
title, publication information, source(s) for the entry, and an annotation (that sometimes notes subject matter or revised editions). Authors are sorted into chronological
groups in an appendix; however, beginning with 1750, the groupings are too broad to
be of much value. Indexed by a few general subjects and poetic forms. Although based
primarily on other sources—notably *National Union Catalog, Pre-1956 Imprints*
(E235), the *British Museum General Catalogue of Printed Books* (see E250), and *WorldCat*
(E225)—rather than firsthand examination of copies, *Poetry by Women to 1900* at least
offers a starting place for identifying separately published books of poetry by women
writers before 1900. What is needed, however, are works such as Smith, *Women and
the Literature of the Seventeenth Century* (M2007), for other periods of British and
American literature.

Text Archives

Q3536   *American Poetry.* ProQuest. Online. 14 June 2006 <http://collections
       .chadwyck.com>.
       A text archive of rekeyed texts of about 40,000 English-language poems by Amer-
ican poets from the colonial era to the early twentieth century. Editions were selected
according to the following criteria: editions "contemporary with their authors were
preferred, and, when available, collected editions"; "reliable later editions" in the case
of "poets whose established canon could not be covered by contemporary printings."
Poets were chosen on the basis of their inclusion in Blanck, *Bibliography of American
Literature* (Q3250), or the recommendation of the editorial board.
       Simple keyword, first line or title, and author searches can be limited by date
during an author's lifetime, gender, ethnicity, literary period, rhymed or unrhymed
poems, and parts of a poem (e.g., epigraphs, notes). Searchers can also browse an author
list of the contents of the database. Results appear in ascending alphabetical order
and cannot be re-sorted. Citations (but not the full text of poems) can be marked for
e-mailing, downloading, or printing; each citation includes a durable URL to the
full text.
       Some works are rekeyed from textually unsound editions; however, the biblio-
graphic record for each work identifies the source of the text and any omissions (e.g.,
preliminary matter), and the site is refreshingly forthcoming in its explanations of editorial procedures and revision history. Besides being a useful source for identifying an
elusive quotation or half-remembered line, the scope of *American Poetry*'s text archive
makes feasible a variety of kinds of studies (stylistic, thematic, imagistic, and topical).
       The contents of *American Poetry Database* can also be searched through *LiOn*
(I527), which offers a less versatile search interface.
       Continued by *Twentieth-Century American Poetry* (Q4333).

Guides to Scholarship and Criticism

See

       Brogan, *English Versification, 1570–1980* (M1600).

PROSE

Most works in section L: Genres/Prose are useful for research in American prose.

Biography and Autobiography

Histories and Surveys

Q3538   Kagle, Steven E. *American Diary Literature, 1620–1799.* Twayne's United
       States Authors Series 342. Boston: Twayne, 1979. 203 pp.   PS409.K3
       818'.103.

       ———. *Early Nineteenth-Century American Diary Literature.* Twayne's
       United States Authors Series 495. 1986. 166 pp.   PS409.K33   818'.203.

————. *Late Nineteenth-Century American Diary Literature.* Twayne's
United States Authors Series 524. 1988. 177 pp.   PS409.K33
818'.403'09.

A study of the diary tradition in America that attempts to establish a canon of
works of literary merit and a methodology for their study. The volumes are organized
by type of diary (e.g., spiritual journals, travel diaries, diaries of romance and courtship,
war diaries, life diaries, transcendentalist journals), with each chapter offering an extended analysis of selective examples. Each volume concludes with a selected annotated
list of diaries and scholarship. Indexed by persons and a few subjects. Although it is
highly selective in coverage, Kagle's work is valuable for its methodology of the literary
study of diaries. Review: (1620–1799) Richard C. Davis, *Canadian Review of American
Studies* 12 (1981): 301–11.

Guides to Primary Works

Q3540   Arksey, Laura, Nancy Pries, and Marcia Reed. *American Diaries: An
         Annotated Bibliography of Published American Diaries and Journals.* 2 vols.
         Detroit: Gale, 1983–87.   Z5305.U5 A74 [CT214]   016.92'0073.
         Vol. 1: *Diaries Written from 1492 to 1844.* 1983. 311 pp.
         Vol. 2: *Diaries Written from 1845 to 1980.* 1987. 501 pp.

A bibliography of approximately 6,000 English-language diaries or journals (including translations) written between 1492 and 1980 (and published as late as 1986)
by American citizens anywhere in the world and by foreigners while resident in what
is now the United States or treating events regarded as American. Along with traditional
diaries and journals, *American Diaries* includes some expedition narratives and ships'
logs that record more than weather or position. Except for some Canadian diaries, this
work incorporates everything in William Matthews, *American Diaries: An Annotated
Bibliography of American Diaries Written Prior to the Year 1861* (Berkeley: U of California P, 1945, 383 pp.). Organized by year of initial entry, then alphabetically by
author, entries provide title, publication information, and annotation, which typically
notes dates of coverage, place of birth or residence, major emphases, categories of persons
discussed, occupations, historic events, modes of travel, religious affiliation, people,
places, ships, customs, social milieu, and type of diary or journal. Annotations taken
from Matthews frequently add comments on language and the quality of the work.
Three indexes in each volume: names of writers and persons mentioned in annotations;
subjects; places. The thorough annotations and detailed subject indexing make *American
Diaries* an invaluable source for locating diaries on a topic or associated with a specific
place, event, or group. It offers the fullest coverage of published American diaries, many
of which appeared in limited editions or obscure periodicals. Many of the entries in
Arksey and Matthews are repeated or revised in Handley, *An Annotated Bibliography of
Diaries Printed in English* (M1615a). Review: (vol. 1) Steven E. Kagle, *Early American
Literature* 20 (1985): 174–77.

A few additional published diaries are listed in Patricia Pate Havlice, *And So to
Bed: A Bibliography of Diaries Published in English* (Metuchen: Scarecrow, 1987, 698
pp.); however, the best feature of this work is its combined index of diarists in Matthews,
American Diaries (see above), *British Diaries* (M1615), and *Canadian Diaries* (R4765).

For a list of about 5,000 unpublished diaries and journals held in libraries and
other institutions, see William Matthews, *American Diaries in Manuscript, 1580–1954:
A Descriptive Bibliography* (Athens: U of Georgia P, 1974, 176 pp.). The entries are
organized chronologically by initial date of entry (with a separate alphabetical list of

undated works) and note location along with a brief description of content; unfortunately, works are indexed only by author. Many manuscript diaries are listed in *National Union Catalog of Manuscript Collections* (F295) and in other works in sections F: Guides to Manuscripts and Archives and Q: American Literature/General/Guides to Primary Works/Manuscripts.

A rekeyed full text of some of the diaries, print and manuscript, listed in the preceding works can be searched in *North American Women's Letters and Diaries: Colonial to 1950* (Alexander Street P, online, 15 Feb. 2006 <http://www.alexanderstreet2.com/ NWLDLive>). In the current version, c. 605 documents can be browsed by author, source, date of composition, geographical location in North America, historical event, and personal event; unfortunately, the source and historical event lists are organized in no apparent order. Sources, authors, letters, and diaries can also be searched separately through fielded search screens. The Advanced Search screen allows users to combine a number of fields—full-text keyword, author, age when writing, marital status, maternal status, age at marriage, number of marriages, age at first childbirth, number of children, nationality, race, religion, occupation, year of composition, month of composition, document type, where written (setting, geographical region), historical events, personal events, and subjects—in order to construct very sophisticated searches. (Unfortunately, the list of authors associated with the author field is alphabetized by first name or initial.) Search results can be printed or saved only through a Web browser's print or save functions. Although the selection criteria and plans for expanding the content could be more precisely explained, this archive—if it continues to grow—will provide unprecedented access to the documents herein.

Q3545   Kaplan, Louis, comp. *A Bibliography of American Autobiographies*. Madison: U of Wisconsin P, 1961. 372 pp.   Z1224.K3   016.920073.

Briscoe, Mary Louise, ed. *American Autobiography, 1945–1980: A Bibliography*. Madison: U of Wisconsin P, 1982. 365 pp.   Z5305.U5 A47 [CT220]   016.92'0073.

Together, these two volumes provide a bibliography of more than 11,000 separately published autobiographies (through 1980) of American citizens and foreigners resident for an appreciable time in the United States. Kaplan excludes Indian captivity, travel, and slave narratives; journals; diaries; collections of letters; manuscripts; genealogical works; fiction; and general reminiscences. Briscoe, however, broadens the scope to admit published memoirs, journals, diaries, and nonfiction works that include substantial autobiographical material. Briscoe also includes reprints of autobiographies published before 1945 as well as some works omitted in Kaplan. Kaplan cites the most convenient edition; Briscoe typically refers to the first edition. Entries, organized alphabetically by author, include birth date (and death date in Briscoe), title, publication information, pagination, location of one copy (only in Kaplan), and annotation. Kaplan's annotations rarely extend beyond occupation and principal areas of residence, but Briscoe's are much fuller, typically offering an evaluative comment and citing occupation, main focus, precise geographical locations, and important persons and events. In Briscoe, an asterisk denotes a female author. Both offer valuable subject indexes that cite occupations, places, historical events, names, and ethnic and religious groups; however, Briscoe's index is more precise, detailed, and effectively organized. Together, Kaplan and Briscoe list the majority of the separately published autobiographies of American citizens and long-time foreign residents.

Additional separately published autobiographical works (in print by 1900) are listed in Gwenn Davis and Beverly A. Joyce, comps., *Personal Writings by Women to 1900: A Bibliography of American and British Writers* (Norman: U of Oklahoma P,

1989, 294 pp.), with most entries drawn from *WorldCat* (E225), *National Union Catalog, Pre-1956 Imprints* (E235), and the British Museum *General Catalogue of Printed Books* (see E250). Concludes with an appendix listing writers by chronological period and an index of places, occupations, types of works, and a few miscellaneous topics. For details of the unsatisfactory coverage of pre-1800 works, see the review by Alexandra Barratt, *Library* 6th ser. 12 (1990): 360–62.

Guides to Scholarship and Criticism

See

> Leary, *Articles on American Literature* (Q3295).

Regional Literature

This section includes works limited to or emphasizing a region of the United States.

Most states and some cities have bibliographies of works by native or resident authors. For such bibliographies published through 1970, see vol. 1, pp. 164–68, in Tanselle, *Guide to the Study of United States Imprints* (U5290); for later ones, see *Bibliographic Index* (D145).

General

GUIDES TO SCHOLARSHIP AND CRITICISM

Q3570 Gohdes, Clarence. *Literature and Theater of the States and Regions of the U. S. A.: An Historical Bibliography.* Durham: Duke UP, 1967. 276 pp.
Z1225.G63   016.8109.

A checklist of studies through 1964 on regional belles lettres and theater in the United States and its possessions. Gohdes excludes theses and dissertations as well as most newspaper articles, foreign scholarship, and studies of individual writers or theater personnel. Within divisions for states, possessions, and geographic regions, entries are listed alphabetically in sections for literature and theater. Two appendixes: western literature (for studies dealing with this area, as distinct from the Midwest or West); general studies of regionalism. Because there are no indexes or cross-references and few duplicate entries, users must be certain to search the regional as well as state divisions for studies of a locale. Although superseded by Larson, *American Regional Theatre History* (Q3575), for studies of theater before 1900, and offering less extensive coverage than Stratman, *Bibliography of the American Theatre* (Q3580), Gohdes remains an indispensable compilation of general studies of regional literature. It must be supplemented by works in sections G: Serial Bibliographies, Indexes, and Abstracts and H: Guides to Dissertations and Theses.

See also

> "Annual Review," *Journal of Modern Literature* (M2780).
> Leary, *Articles on American Literature* (Q3295).
> Woodress, *Dissertations in American Literature, 1891–1966* (Q3320).

PERIODICALS

Guides to Scholarship and Criticism

See

> Chielens, *Literary Journal in America to 1900* (Q4145).

GENRES

Drama

Guides to Scholarship and Criticism

Q3575   Larson, Carl F. W., comp. *American Regional Theatre History to 1900: A Bibliography.* Metuchen: Scarecrow, 1979. 187 pp.   Z5781.L34 [PN2221] 016.792'0973.

A bibliography of books, articles, dissertations, theses, newspaper articles, and some manuscripts (through 1976) on regional theater outside New York City. Larson emphasizes English-language theater and studies of a specific geographical area; it excludes publications before 1900 unless their focus is historical and studies of actors, actresses, and theatrical personnel unless they emphasize a specific region. The 1,481 entries are organized chronologically by date of coverage in four divisions: states (with sections for cities and general studies), regions, miscellaneous works, and bibliographies. The chronology of numerous entries is imprecise because the compiler did not examine many items or relied on secondhand information. Three indexes: foreign-language theater; subjects (limited to persons); authors. Although no locations are provided for manuscripts, subject indexing is inadequate, the chronological placement is not reliable, and scope is insufficiently defined (especially what "theatre history" encompasses), Larson does offer the best general coverage of regional theater for the period. It corrects several errors in Stratman, *Bibliography of the American Theatre* (Q3580), and Gohdes, *Literature and Theater of the States and Regions* (Q3570), but does not completely supersede either. Review: Don B. Wilmeth, *Nineteenth Century Theatre Research* 8 (1980): 109–10.

Q3580   Stratman, Carl J., C. S. V. *Bibliography of the American Theatre Excluding New York City.* Chicago: Loyola UP, 1965. 397 pp.   Z1231.D7 S8 016.7920973.

A bibliography of studies through c. 1964 on the stage and theater, encompassing a wide range of theatrical activity and types of entertainment such as ballet, minstrel shows, opera, and puppetry and extending to high school and university theater. Stratman excludes general theater and stage histories, newspaper articles, manuscripts, local or state histories, and critical studies of plays. The 3,856 entries are organized by state or region, then by city, then by publication date. Each state section concludes with a list of general works. Except for theses and dissertations, each work is located in at least one library (an especially helpful feature in the case of ephemeral publications); only periodical articles are accompanied by brief descriptive annotations. Indexed by persons and subjects. Although now dated and superseded in part by Larson, *American Regional*

Theatre History (Q3575), Stratman remains a valuable guide to studies of the theatrical activity of a city or region and offers fuller coverage than Gohdes, *Literature and Theater of the States and Regions* (Q3570).

Eastern Literature

Most works in section Q: American Literature/Early American Literature (to 1800), and many in American Literature/Nineteenth-Century Literature emphasize eastern writers.

HISTORIES AND SURVEYS

Q3583   Westbrook, Perry D. *A Literary History of New England.* Bethlehem: Lehigh
         UP; London: Assoc. UP, 1988. 362 pp.   PS243.W42   810′.9′974.
    A literary history devoted to belles lettres and other writings by natives or residents and treating "some subject, place, or persons — imaginary or not — connected with New England and its culture." The chapters on major authors, groups, movements, and genres cover 1620 to 1950, with some recent writers mentioned in an epilogue. Concludes with a highly selective bibliography. Indexed by persons and subjects. *Literary History of New England* offers a balanced overview of literature associated with the region.

Midwestern Literature

LITERARY HANDBOOKS, DICTIONARIES, AND ENCYCLOPEDIAS

Q3592   *Dictionary of Midwestern Literature.* Ed. Philip A. Greasley. 3 vols.
         Bloomington: Indiana UP, 2001 – .   PS273.D53   810.9′977′03.
            Vol. 1: *The Authors.* 2001. 666 pp.
    A dictionary and history of the literature of the Midwest (Michigan, Ohio, Indiana, Illinois, Wisconsin, Minnesota, Iowa, Missouri, Kansas, Nebraska, and North and South Dakota). Vol. 1 covers the lives and writings of more than 400 established and "emerging" poets, fiction writers, dramatists, journalists, and critics with an "extended connection" with the Midwest who have published English-language works that depict the region. The signed entries typically provide basic biographical information, a critical assessment, a list of major works, and suggestions for further reading. Indexed by persons and titles; entrants are also indexed in *Biography and Genealogy Master Index* (J595). Although readers will wish for regional headings in the index and although the connection to the literature of the Midwest is tenuous for some writers (e.g., T. S. Eliot and Donald Hall), *Dictionary of Midwestern Literature* offers the best guide to midwestern writers.
    Vol. 2 will cover places, movements, themes, genres, and other topics; vol. 3 will be a literary history of the Midwest.

GUIDES TO PRIMARY WORKS

There is no adequate guide to the literature of the Midwest. For example, Donald W. Maxwell, *Literature of the Great Lakes Region: An Annotated Bibliography*, Garland Reference Library of the Humanities 1252 (New York: Garland, 1991, 485 pp.), offers 1,707 entries on novels, plays, short stories, and poems about locales in Ohio, Indiana, Illinois, Michigan, Wisconsin, and Minnesota; however, few of the brief annotations are based on the author's direct knowledge of the books (as he confesses, "I haven't read many of these works"), and the inexcusable lack of a subject index means that users must scan every entry when searching for works about a place or an event.

GUIDES TO SCHOLARSHIP AND CRITICISM

Bibliographies on a variety of midwestern writers and subjects appear in issues of *Great Lakes Review* 1–10 (1974–84); with the title change to *Michigan Historical Review* (12 [1986]), the journal narrowed its focus to that state.

Serial Bibliographies

Q3595   "Annual Bibliography of Midwestern Literature [1973–]." *Midamerica* 2
      (1975)– .   PS273.M53.
      A list of primary and secondary publications relating to authors born or resident in the Midwest as well as of fiction with a midwestern setting. Currently, entries are organized in three divisions: primary sources (an alphabetic list — by writer — of literary works and the names of authors of secondary works, with a cross-reference to the secondary sources division); secondary sources (with subdivisions for general studies and literary authors); and new periodicals. Early installments of the bibliography are unnecessarily difficult to read because they are reproduced from a much-reduced uppercase printout, and the cross-referencing system in the primary works division is cumbersome. Although not comprehensive (especially for major authors), the "Annual Bibliography" does assimilate a considerable amount of the year's work on midwestern literature and serves as a useful complement to the standard bibliographies and indexes in section G. Unfortunately, coverage is far in arrears (the installment for 2002 appeared in 2006, although the volume bears 2004 as the date of publication).

See also

> *MLAIB* (G335): See the headings beginning "Midwestern" in the subject index
> to post-1980 volumes and in the online thesaurus.

Other Bibliographies

Q3600   Nemanic, Gerald, gen. ed. *A Bibliographical Guide to Midwestern Literature.*
      Iowa City: U of Iowa P, 1981. 380 pp.   Z1251.W5 B52 [PS273]
      016.81′08′0977.

A selective bibliography of studies of the literature and culture of the midwestern states (Illinois, Indiana, Iowa, Michigan, Minnesota, Missouri, Ohio, Wisconsin, and the eastern part of Kansas, Nebraska, and the Dakotas) and of about 150 authors whose works reflect the cultural life of the region. Entries are organized in two divisions: subjects and individual authors. The first grouping consists of extensively classified subdivisions listing primarily books on literature and language, history and society, folklore, personal narratives, architecture and graphics, Chicago, black literature, Indians, and literary periodicals. Each subdivision is preceded by a helpful evaluative overview of scholarship; most entries are succinctly and clearly annotated. Each author bibliography consists of a headnote that briefly comments on the writer's stature, notes important studies, suggests topics for research, and identifies major manuscript collections; a chronological list of major primary works; and a selective, unannotated list of scholarship. Two appendixes: brief biographical notes on an additional 101 writers; a list of 101 fictional narratives on the Midwest by writers not associated with the region. Individual bibliographies are uneven in quality; the lack of cross-references in the first part and the failure to provide a subject index substantially reduce usability; articles are generally excluded from the subject lists; and major writers are more adequately treated in separate author bibliographies; even so, the usually judicious selection and evaluative comments in the headnotes make Nemanic the first source to consult in the study of midwestern literature generally and minor writers associated with the region. Reviews: Craig S. Abbott, *Analytical and Enumerative Bibliography* 6 (1982): 135–37; Michael J. Bresnahan, *Resources for American Literary Study* 12 (1982): 111–16.

Southern Literature

HISTORIES AND SURVEYS

Q3615   *The History of Southern Literature.* Gen. ed. Louis D. Rubin, Jr. Baton
          Rouge: Louisiana State UP, 1985. 626 pp.   PS261.H53   810'.9'975.
A collection of essays, on authors, movements, genres, and topics, that makes a concerted effort to include African American literature and emphasizes twentieth-century writers. Unfortunately the essays exclude references to scholarship, a deficiency not compensated for by M. Thomas Inge's brief appendix surveying anthologies, reference sources, surveys, bibliographies, literary histories, and general critical studies (pp. 589–99). The quality of the essays and breadth of coverage make this work the standard literary history for the region, although Jay B. Hubbell's monumental *The South in American Literature, 1607–1900* (Durham: Duke UP, 1954, 987 pp.) remains valuable for its encyclopedic treatment of the literature before 1865. Reviews: Melvin J. Friedman, *American Literature* 58 (1986): 427–30; Jan Nordby Gretlund, *Resources for American Literary Study* 16 (1986–89): 52–57; Michael Kreyling, *American Literature* 60 (1988): 83–95; Ellen M. Weinauer, *Nineteenth-Century Contexts* 16 (1992): 91–96.
Women writers are more fully treated in *The History of Southern Women's Literature*, ed. Carolyn Perry and Mary Louise Weaks (Baton Rouge: Louisiana State UP, 2002, 689 pp.); however, most of the essays read like extended entries in a literary encyclopedia.

LITERARY HANDBOOKS, DICTIONARIES, AND ENCYCLOPEDIAS

Q3617   *Companion to Southern Literature: Themes, Genres, Places, People, Movements, and Motifs.* Ed. Joseph M. Flora and Lucinda H. Mackethan. Southern Literary Studies. Baton Rouge: Louisiana State UP, 2002. 1,054 pp. PS261.C55   810.9'975.

A dictionary of authors, institutions, places, customs, historical events and persons, genres, movements, periodicals, scholars, themes, and stereotypes associated with Southern literature (here "broadly defined as constituting a cultural territory that has been imaginatively created by all kinds of 'makers'"). Focusing on approaches that are not author-centered, the work includes only those few writers who are pioneers or seminal influences and works that are essential for defining the southern mind. The approximately 500 signed entries—many by established scholars or creative writers—provide full, readable, informative treatments of their respective topics and their manifestations in or importance to the literature of the South (see, for example, "bourbon," "hog," "K Mart fiction," "mammy," and "whoopin'"); most conclude with a selective bibliography. Broad but representative in its coverage and guided by attentive editorial judgment (except for the lapse that allowed the starkly insubstantial "Sears catalog" entry), *Companion to Southern Literature*—an essential desktop companion for specialists in the literature of the South—is a resource that will captivate readers into turning leaves long after perusing the entry that brought them to this work.

GUIDES TO SCHOLARSHIP AND CRITICISM

Surveys of Research

See

Harbert, *Fifteen American Authors before 1900*, 1971 edition (Q3280a).

Serial Bibliographies

Q3620   *SSSL Bibliography: A Checklist of Scholarship on Southern Literature [1968–].* Online. 4 Sept. 2005 <http://www.missq.msstate.edu/sssl>.
"A Checklist of Scholarship on Southern Literature for [1968–96]." Supplement to *Mississippi Quarterly* 22–50 (1969–1996-1997). AS30.M58 A2   051.

An annotated bibliographic database of books and articles published since 1968 about southern writers. This cumulates, expands, and continues the annual "A Checklist of Scholarship on Southern Literature for [1968–96]." Users can search entries by keyword or browse lists of writers (either by surname or by period: colonial [1607–1800], antebellum [1800–65], postbellum [1865–1920], modern [1920–50], contemporary [1950 to the present], and unassigned [which includes both writers as well as lists of general and miscellaneous studies, though the distinction between the two is not clear]), scholars, and journals. Results of keyword searches, which are ranked by relevance, provide author, title, and brief descriptive annotation; results of browse searches, which are listed in ascending chronological order, then alphabetically by title within a year, provide title, author, and year as well as links to related Web sites. In both kinds of searches, users must click on a result to view the full citation; since journal acronyms are not expanded, users must click on the acronym to identify the journal.

Although it is not comprehensive and although the search interface is unsophisticated, *SSSL Bibliography* is an essential continuation of Rubin, *Bibliographical Guide to the Study of Southern Literature* (Q3625), and supplement to the standard serial bibliographies and indexes in section G.

The first eight "Checklists" are cumulated and supplemented in Jerry T. Williams, ed., *Southern Literature, 1968–1975: A Checklist of Scholarship*, Reference Publication in Literature (Boston: Hall, 1978, 271 pp.).

See also

> *MLAIB* (G335): See the headings beginning "Southern American(s)" in the subject index to post-1980 volumes and in the online thesaurus.

Other Bibliographies

Q3625   Rubin, Louis D., Jr., ed. *A Bibliographical Guide to the Study of Southern Literature*. Southern Literary Studies. Baton Rouge: Louisiana State UP, 1969. 351 pp.   Z1225.R8   016.81.

A collection of selective bibliographies compiled by specialists on southern literature and confined largely to English-language scholarship published through the late 1960s. The bibliographies are organized in two divisions: 23 topics (including general works, periods, themes, local color, periodicals, southern speech, drama, folklore, manuscript collections, and bibliographies) and 135 individual authors. An appendix covers 68 writers of the colonial South. Each bibliography is in two parts: an evaluative summary of scholarship (ranging from a few lines to several pages and sometimes commenting on the stature of the writer) and a selective list of studies (variously classified in the topics division). The appendix has no summaries. An asterisk denotes works including a useful bibliography. The lack of an index significantly reduces usability, there is considerable overlapping among the bibliographies, and the coverage (originally too selective for major writers) is now dated, but this remains a useful guide to the best scholarship before c. 1968 on southern literature generally and on minor writers. Review: Hensley C. Woodbridge, *Papers of the Bibliographical Society of America* 63 (1969): 332–36.

Coverage must be supplemented with *SSSL Bibliography* (Q3620), *American Literary Scholarship* (Q3265), and Jack D. Wages, *Seventy-Four Writers of the Colonial South*, Reference Publication in Literature (Boston: Hall, 1979, 252 pp.). The last work, however, is marred by omissions, frequently uninformative annotations, and cryptic abbreviations of authors' names in the index.

Dissertations and Theses

Q3630   Emerson, O. B., and Marion C. Michael, comps. and eds. *Southern Literary Culture: A Bibliography of Masters' and Doctors' Theses*. Rev. and enl. ed. University: U of Alabama P, 1979. 400 pp.   Z1251.S7 C3 [PS261] 016.810'9'975.

Wages, Jack D., and William L. Andrews, comps. "Southern Literary Culture: 1969–1975." *Mississippi Quarterly* 32 (1978–79): 13–214. AS30.M58 A2   051.

The revised edition lists about 8,000 American and foreign theses and dissertations, accepted through winter 1969, on southern literature and writers (i.e., those who "flourished" in the South). Entries are listed alphabetically by thesis or dissertation author in three classified divisions: individual writers; cultural, historical, and social background (with sections for general studies, folklore, education, theater, libraries and lyceums, onomastics, language, and southern culture through others' eyes); and general literary studies (with sections for studies that include the South, studies restricted to southern literature, bibliographies and checklists, comparative studies, newspapers and periodicals, and original works written at southern universities). Each entry provides author, title, institution, year, degree, and department; occasionally a note identifies authors or works discussed. Since a thesis or dissertation is listed only once, the lack of cross-references and an index seriously mars the usability of the work. Although not comprehensive—especially in its coverage of foreign theses and dissertations on Twain—*Southern Literary Culture* is valuable for its extensive coverage, especially of studies written in a variety of departments other than English.

The supplement is more closely restricted to literary studies and omits foreign theses and dissertations. Its approximately 3,000 entries are listed alphabetically by author in 13 divisions: individual authors, multiple author studies, general culture, education, folklore, history, journalism, libraries, linguistics, music, politics, religion, and speech and theater. Only the first division is classified and includes cross-references for multiple-author studies. Except for the omission of department, entries include the same information as in the revised edition. Indexed by dissertation or thesis writers. Although lacking the breadth of coverage of its predecessor, Wages and Andrews's work remains a useful compilation but must be supplemented by section H: Guides to Dissertations and Theses.

LANGUAGE

Guides to Scholarship

Q3635   McMillan, James B., and Michael B. Montgomery. *Annotated Bibliography of Southern American English.* [2nd ed.] Tuscaloosa: U of Alabama P, 1989. 444 pp.   Z1251.S7 M37 [PE2922]   016.427'975.

A bibliography of studies (some as late as 1989 and all but a few in English) of English used in the District of Columbia and the "states south and west of the Mason-Dixon Line from the Delaware Bay to [and including] Texas." McMillan includes theses, dissertations, research reports, ERIC documents, and scholarly reviews of books, but excludes popular journalism, general works on American English, and studies of folklore, foreign languages, language of children under nine, language contact, and literature unless of interest to students of dialect. The approximately 3,800 entries are listed alphabetically by author in 12 divisions: general studies; historical and creole studies; lexical studies; phonology and phonetics; morphology and syntax; place names; personal and miscellaneous names; figurative language, exaggerations, and wordplay; literary dialect; language attitudes and speech perception; speech acts and style; and bibliographies. Unlike in the first edition (Coral Gables: U of Miami P, 1971, 173 pp.), a majority of the approximately 3,800 entries are adequately annotated; entries for books cite reviews. Indexed by scholars. Although there are cross-references, the lack of a subject index seriously impedes access to what is otherwise a valuable compilation, especially for those interested in scholarship on the use of southern dialects in literary works. Review: Edgar W. Schneider, *English World-wide* 10 (1989): 345–48.

Recent studies can be identified by searching "Southern American English dialect" in the subject index to post-1981 volumes of *MLAIB* (G335) and in the online thesaurus.

See also

> Emerson, *Southern Literary Culture* (Q3630).
> Rubin, *Bibliographical Guide to the Study of Southern Literature* (Q3625).

BIOGRAPHICAL DICTIONARIES

Q3640   *Southern Writers: A New Biographical Dictionary.* Ed. Joseph M. Flora and
        Amber Vogel. Baton Rouge: Louisiana State UP, 2006. 468 pp.
        PS261.S595   810.9′975′03.

A biographical dictionary of more than 600 writers associated (sometimes loosely) with the southern United States (not herein geographically defined). The signed entries (which range from 300 to c. 1,000 words depending on the eminence of the subject) offer a basic overview of a subject's life and career, and conclude with a chronological list of books. Informative and sometimes witty, *Southern Writers* will likely assume pride of place among biographical dictionaries of the region.

Western Literature

HISTORIES AND SURVEYS

Q3660   *A Literary History of the American West.* Ed. in chief J. Golden Taylor. Fort
        Worth: Texas Christian UP, 1987. 1,353 pp.   PS271.L58   810′.99978.
        Online. 23 Mar. 2007 <http://www.prs.tcu.edu/lit_west_full.pdf>.

A collaborative critical history whose 75 chapters employ a variety of approaches to encompass major writers; regions; historical periods; genres; types of characters; ethnic and non-English literatures; folklore; nature writing; and movies, television, and radio. Most chapters conclude with a selective bibliography (several of which are evaluatively annotated). The volume also includes chronologies of historical (1507–1980) and literary (1510–1984) events; an appendix that surveys the development of criticism of western literature; and an incomplete and sometimes inaccurate list of major reference sources. Indexed by persons and subjects. Although uneven in execution, the impressive scope and quality of the contributors make this collection the essential starting point for research on western literature.

Updating the Literary West, ed. in chief Thomas J. Lyon (1997, 1,031 pp.), updates (through 1996) and expands *Literary History of the American West* in 106 essays that survey developments in criticism; canonicity; and the study of genres, regions, groups, and individual authors. As in the earlier volume, there is a chronology (of events and texts, 1980–96), the authors employ a variety of approaches, and essays conclude with a selective bibliography (with only a few bearing annotations). Indexed by persons, titles, and subjects. Although *Updating the Literary West* stretches West to include Hawaiʻi and the Midwest and although the essays are uneven, it—like *Literary History of the American West*—is an essential starting point for research on western literature.

GUIDES TO SCHOLARSHIP AND CRITICISM

Serial Bibliographies

Q3665   *Bibliography of Studies in Western American Literature [1998–2000].*
          Western Lit. Assn. Online. 10 Jan. 2006 <http://www.usu.edu/westlit/
          research.htm>.
          "Annual Bibliography of Studies in Western American Literature [1965–
          97]." *Western American Literature* 1–32.4 (1966–98).   PS271.W46
          810.9'978.

An unannotated list of books and articles on western literature. Entries are divided among two divisions: literary authors; subjects (though many studies appear in both). A substantial number of entries are taken from other sources (see Angela Ashurst-McGee, "From the Bibliographic Editor," *Western American Literature* 33 [1999]: 342–44). Although it offers better subject access than its print predecessor, the electronic version is a static list that is searchable only through a Web browser's find function. Even so, the *Bibliography* was a helpful compilation of the year's work on western writers, a continuation of Etulain, *Bibliographical Guide* (Q3670), and an essential complement to the bibliographies and indexes in section G. Its unfortunate demise deprived scholars of an essential resource for the study of western literature.

Dissertations and theses are listed in the annual *Research in Western American Literature* (online, 10 Jan. 2006 <http://www.usu.edu/westlit/research.htm>), which formerly included work in progress and which appeared in *Western American Literature* until the list for 1996–97 in 32.4 (1998); thereafter, only the overview of trends appears in the journal. "Western American Literary Scholarship [2001]: The Year in Review"—a review essay—lasted one year (37.1 [2002]).

See also

> *MLAIB* (G335): See the headings beginning "Western American" in the subject index to post-1980 volumes and in the online thesaurus.

Other Bibliographies

Q3670   Etulain, Richard W., and N. Jill Howard, eds. *A Bibliographical Guide to
          the Study of Western American Literature.* 2nd ed. Albuquerque: U of New
          Mexico P, 1996. 471 pp.   Z1251.W5 E8 [PS271]   016.8109'978.

A selective bibliography of studies on trans-Mississippi western literature and authors (including a few major nonfiction writers), as well as outsiders who have written on the area or influenced its literature. It is limited to important scholarship (largely in English through 1994) and emphasizes recent studies; the second edition omits master's theses and several briefer or outdated items included in the original edition (by Etulain

[Lincoln: U of Nebraska P, 1982, 317 pp.]). Coverage is especially selective for major authors such as Cooper, Cather, Clemens, and Steinbeck. The 6,494 entries are listed alphabetically in five divisions: bibliographies and reference works, anthologies, general works (unhelpfully divided into books and dissertations, and articles—special issues of journals unaccountably appear in both sections), special topics (local color and regionalism, dime novels and the western, film, Indian literature and Indians in western literature, Mexican American literature and Chicanos in western literature, the environment and western literature, women and families in western literature, the Beats, and Canadian western literature), and individual authors. A very few entries are briefly annotated. Indexed by scholars. The lack of cross-references and subject indexing means that researchers looking for studies on a writer must skim the general works and special topics divisions. Although several authors are more fully covered in separate author bibliographies, *Bibliographical Guide to the Study of Western American Literature* is the essential starting point for research on the region.

Because coverage is selective (indeed, there are some inexplicable omissions), the guide must be supplemented with "Annual Bibliography of Studies in Western American Literature" (Q3665), *Bibliography of Studies in Western American Literature* (Q3665), and the serial bibliographies and indexes in section G.

As a guide to studies of twentieth-century western literature, Richard W. Etulain, ed., *The American West in the Twentieth Century: A Bibliography* (Norman: U of Oklahoma P, 1994, 456 pp.) is virtually useless: the criteria governing selection are impossibly vague ("earlier major studies as well as . . . recent burgeoning scholarship"); there are significant omissions in the section on bibliographies and reference works; the division on literature and theater is utterly inadequate, and coverage of individual authors is erratic and incomplete (e.g., the 366 entries include 6 on Willa Cather); and there is no subject indexing. If the divisions on reference works and literature are representative, *American West in the Twentieth Century* can hardly claim to be "the most comprehensive bibliography now available on the history and culture of the twentieth-century West."

Ethnic and Minority Literatures

Many works in sections G: Serial Bibliographies, Indexes, and Abstracts; H: Guides to Dissertations and Theses; L: Genres; and, especially, Q: American Literature/General are important for research in minority and ethnic literatures of the United States.

General

HISTORIES AND SURVEYS

Q3690   Di Pietro, Robert J., and Edward Ifkovic, eds. *Ethnic Perspectives in American Literature: Selected Essays on the European Contribution.* New York: MLA, 1983. 333 pp.   PN843.E8   810'.9.
        Surveys of Franco-American New England writers and the literatures of Americans of German, Greek, Hungarian, Italian, Jewish, Polish, Portuguese, Romanian, Russian, Scandinavian, and South Slavic ancestry. Organized chronologically, thematically, or

by genre, the essays typically offer a basic historical overview of the development of a literature and of its major authors; some essays briefly comment on important scholarship and suggest topics for research. Indexed by persons and titles. Although the surveys vary in breadth and quality, the collection overall serves as a handy (but dated) introduction to some ethnic literatures of the United States.

Q3695   Ruoff, A. LaVonne Brown, and Jerry W. Ward, Jr., eds. *Redefining American Literary History.* New York: MLA, 1990. 406 pp.
PS153.M56 R4   810.9'920693.

A collection of essays that seeks to redefine American literary history by "expanding the canon, forging new critical perspectives, and scrutinizing underlying cultural and ideological assumptions" through a focus on African American, American Indian, Asian American, Chicano, and Puerto Rican literature. The essays are organized in three divisions: discussions of "various ways of redefining the American literary canon and its relation to the literatures of minorities and white women"; the oral dimensions of American literature; critical and historical perspectives. Following the essays are selected, annotated bibliographies through 1989—with sections for bibliographies, anthologies, primary works, general criticism, and major authors—of multiethnic, African American, American Indian (superseded by Ruoff, *American Indian Literatures* [Q3880]), Asian American, Chicano, and Puerto Rican literatures. Concluding the work is a list of selected presses and journals. The lack of an index hampers access, and some of the essays originally prepared for a 1981 convention do not reflect the debate over and changes in the canon during the past decade; however, *Redefining American Literary History* is an important contribution to the continuing evaluation of the canon of the literature of the United States.

See also

Cambridge History of American Literature (Q3205).
Columbia Literary History of the United States (Q3195).
Literary History of the American West (Q3660).

GUIDES TO SCHOLARSHIP AND CRITICISM

Q3700   Miller, Wayne Charles. *A Comprehensive Bibliography for the Study of American Minorities.* 2 vols. New York: New York UP, 1976.
Z1361.E4 M529 [E184.A1]   016.973'04.

Minorities in America: The Annual Bibliography [1976–78]. 3 vols. University Park: Pennsylvania State UP, 1985–86. Annual.
Z1361.E4 M57 [E184.A1]   016.973'04.

A bibliography of English-language materials on minority groups in America. The *Comprehensive Bibliography* covers studies through c. 1973; the *Annual Bibliography* covers 1976 through 1978. Entries are organized by area of origin (Africa and Middle East, Europe, Eastern Europe and Balkans, Asia, Puerto Rico and Cuba, and America [including Indians and Mexican Americans]), then by minority group, and then by subject. Most groups include sections for language, general literary criticism, fiction, poetry, drama, folklore, and some individual writers. Entries in the annual bibliographies are accompanied by descriptive annotations; although only a few are annotated in the *Comprehensive Bibliography*, each minority group is preceded by an introduction that identifies important studies and reference works. Two indexes: authors; titles. Although the *Comprehensive Bibliography* is hardly comprehensive, it—along with the *Annual Bibliography*—offers the fullest single record of scholarship before 1978 on minority groups in the United States.

See also

"Annual Review," *Journal of Modern Literature* (M2780).
Greenwood Guide to American Popular Culture (U6295).
Lcary, *Articles on American Literature* (Q3295).
Ruoff, *Redefining American Literary History* (Q3695).
Salzman, *American Studies: An Annotated Bibliography* (Q3335).

GENRES

Prose

Q3705   Stuhr-Rommereim, Rebecca. *Autobiographies by Americans of Color, 1980–1994: An Annotated Bibliography.* Troy: Whitston, 1997. 262 pp.
Z5305.U5 S78 [CT220]   016.92.

Iwabuchi, Deborah Stuhr, and Rebecca Stuhr. *Autobiographies by Americans of Color, 1995–2000: An Annotated Bibliography.* Albany: Whitston, 2003. 565 pp.   Z5305.U5 [CT220]   973.049016.

An annotated bibliography of more than 1,100 separately published autobiographies by Americans of color that were printed, reprinted, or digitized between 1980 and 2000. Defining *autobiography* loosely (to include oral narratives, family histories, and "as told to" accounts), both volumes exclude interviews, dissertations, and journal articles. More than half of the works are by African Americans. Entries, which are organized alphabetically by author (and preceded in *1995–2000* by entries for 21 anthologies), include a bibliographical citation (with references to editions preceding 1980 and later reprints) and a lengthy annotation. Indexed by subject (including ethnic group); the subject indexing is much fuller in *1995–2000*. The admirably full annotations (clearly based on an actual reading of the works) and coverage of a number of elusive publications not easily identified in standard catalogs make *Autobiographies by Americans of Color* the standard resource for identifying recently published autobiographies by ethnic Americans. For earlier works, see Brignano, *Black Americans in Autobiography* (Q3850) and Brumble, *An Annotated Bibliography of American Indian and Eskimo Autobiographies* and its supplements (Q3925).

African American Literature

Many works in the other sections on American literature are important to research in African American literature.

Because the Library of Congress subject headings—used in many library catalogs, databases, and printed bibliographies—were until recently inadequate for analyzing African American resources, scholars doing extensive subject searching will find Doris H. Clack, *Black Literature Resources: Analysis and Organization*, Books in Library and

Information Science 16 (New York: Dekker, 1975, 207 pp.) and Lorene Byron Brown, *Subject Headings for African American Materials* (Englewood: Libraries Unlimited, 1995, 118 pp.) valuable guides to Library of Congress subject headings and classification numbers in this field.

GUIDES TO REFERENCE WORKS

Q3710   *The Harvard Guide to African-American History.* Ed. Evelyn Brooks
         Higginbotham. Cambridge: Harvard UP, 2001. 923 pp. CD-ROM.
         E185.H326   973'.0496073.

A guide to reference works on and studies about African American history and culture, with coverage extending through 1999 in some sections. The first part consists of a series of essays on reference works; of most interest to users of this *Guide* are the ones on general bibliographies, general reference resources, manuscript collections, and film and television. The essays tend to be descriptive rather than evaluative, and some are not as current as users might expect. The second part is a series of classified lists of publications: following a section on general works are ones for ten chronological periods (with that for 1831–65 giving separate treatment to the North and South) and for subjects (women, geographical areas, and autobiography and biography). In each section language, literature, and related topics appear under the Thought and Expression heading. Indexed by authors. The CD-ROM (which is not mentioned in the front matter) provides PDF files of the lists and some of the front matter, as well as a contents file (whose links to other files were nonfunctioning in the two copies I consulted). The first part of *Harvard Guide* offers the best overview of reference sources for the study of African American culture.

Some additional resources are covered in Nathaniel Davis, comp. and ed., *Afro-American Reference: An Annotated Bibliography of Selected Sources*, Bibliographies and Indexes in Afro-American and African Studies 9 (Westport: Greenwood, 1985, 288 pp.), an annotated guide to 642 reference sources (some published as recently as 1985) that are important to research in all aspects of African American life. Entries are listed alphabetically in 17 classified divisions: general reference works; journal abstracts, bibliographies, and guides; newspaper indexes, bibliographies, and guides; genealogy; history; slavery (with a section on slave narratives); social sciences (including linguistics); humanities; literature; mass media; education and multimedia; family and related studies; psychology; medicine; sports; armed forces; and Latin America and the Caribbean. An appendix incongruously lists works on African Americans in Los Angeles and the rest of California. The descriptive annotations typically describe scope, content, and organization. Because of some significant omissions, inclusion of several superseded works, and errors of fact and judgment in annotations, this work cannot always be trusted.

For an exacting (but now dated) survey of reference sources devoted to African American literature and the inadequate treatment of African American writers in some standard reference works in American literature, see Richard C. Tobias, "A Matter of Difference: An Interim Guide to the Study of Black American Writing," *Literary Research Newsletter* 1 (1976): 129–46. Still valuable because of its broad topical coverage of scholarship through 1970 on African American culture and history is James M. McPherson et al., *Blacks in America: Bibliographical Essays* (Garden City: Doubleday, 1971, 430 pp.).

See also

>   Perrault, *United States History: A Multicultural, Interdisciplinary Guide to Information Sources* (Q3185).

HISTORIES AND SURVEYS

For an evaluative survey of literary histories and general critical studies through 1987, see the "Bibliographical Essay" (pp. 401–50) in Jackson, *History of Afro-American Literature: The Long Beginning* (Q3713).

Q3713   *A History of Afro-American Literature.* 4 vols. Baton Rouge: Louisiana State
>   UP, 1989– .   PS153.N5 J33   810'.9'896073.
>   Vol. 1: Jackson, Blyden. *The Long Beginning, 1746–1895.* 1989. 461 pp.
>   Vol. 2: *The Transition Years, 1895–1930.*
>   Vol. 3: *The Golden Age, 1930–1965.*
>   Vol. 4: *The Present and the Future, 1965– .*

A history of African American literature from 1746 to the present. Vol. 1 treats poetry and novels as well as slave narratives, historical works, sermons, folk literature, spirituals, journalism, and pamphlets. Although the discussions of both major and lesser-known writers favor the biographical and historical, few works escape stringent evaluation. Vol. 1 concludes with a valuable bibliographical essay that evaluates general historical studies, literary histories, critical books, and anthologies. Indexed by persons, literary forms, and titles of anonymous works. A balanced, thorough account of the development of African American literature that stresses racial protest as its common factor, vol. 1 sets a high standard for a work that will fill a major void in the history of literatures of the United States and promises to become the standard work in its field. Despite the death of Blyden Jackson, the press intends to go forward with the project. Reviews: John Lowe, *Southern Literary Journal* 22.2 (1990): 134–39; Edward Margolies, *Mississippi Quarterly* 45 (1991–92): 105–10.

See also

>   *History of Southern Literature* (Q3615).

LITERARY HANDBOOKS, DICTIONARIES, AND ENCYCLOPEDIAS

Q3714   *Encyclopedia of African-American Culture and History.* Ed. Colin A. Palmer.
>   2nd ed. 6 vols. Black Experience in the Americas. Detroit: Gale, 2006.
>   Online through *Gale Virtual Reference Library* (I535).   E185.E54
>   973'.0496073'003.

An encyclopedia of a few individuals, events, movements, sports, places, professions, legal cases, and other topics important to the African diaspora in the United States, Canada, Latin America, and the Caribbean. Besides extending the scope beyond the United States, the second edition omits most of the biographies that dominated the first edition (ed. Jack Salzman, David Lionel Smith, and Cornel West, 5 vols. [New York: Macmillan Lib. Reference; London: Simon, 1996]), reprints a third of the original entries with no changes or minor ones, revises another third of the original entries, and claims that the remaining third of the entries are new. Concludes with statistical information and an index of names and subjects. This is the most wide-ranging of encyclopedias devoted to blacks in North America and the Caribbean.

More compact but equally impressive is *The Oxford Companion to African American Literature*, ed. William L. Andrews, Frances Smith Foster, and Trudier Harris (New York: Oxford UP, 1997, 866 pp.), which contains entries on writers and other persons, genres, literary and other works, characters and character types, customs, concepts, groups, periodicals and newspapers, and other topics of importance to African American literature. Most entries conclude with suggestions for further reading. Indexed by persons, titles, and subjects; entrants are also indexed in *Biography and Genealogy Master Index* (J565).

Hazel Arnett Ervin, *The Handbook of African American Literature* (Gainesville: UP of Florida, 2004, 236 pp.), is an important complement to the preceding works because it explains literary terminology particularly associated with African American literature (e.g., def-jam poetry and ring shout) as well as defines common terms (such as euphony and free verse) as they are used by African American writers. Some entries include suggestions for further reading. In addition to the alphabetic list of terms, there is a section of longer essays on terms of particular importance: ambiguity, influence, literary history, memory, repetition, representation, signifying and signification, and collective unconsciousness. One appendix provides a chronology of African American, African, and anglophone Caribbean literary history from 1657 to 2002. The index of terms (which unnecessarily replicates the alphabetic list) does not include the longer essays.

BIBLIOGRAPHIES OF BIBLIOGRAPHIES

Q3715   Newman, Richard, comp. *Black Access: A Bibliography of Afro-American Bibliographies*. Westport: Greenwood, 1984. 249 pp.   Z1361.N39 N578 [E185]   016.016973′0496073.

A bibliography of bibliographies through c. 1982 on all aspects of African American history, culture, and life in the United States and Canada. The approximately 3,000 works include books, pamphlets, articles, chapters in books, exhibition catalogs, calendars and guides to manuscripts, works on library collections and book collecting, and discographies; they exclude book dealers' catalogs, bibliographies appended to monographs, and works on the Civil War, the Caribbean, Latin America, and Africa. Organized in a single alphabetical list by author or title of anonymous work, entries generally provide basic publication information but no annotations. Several citations seem to be taken unverified from other sources. In the introduction, Dorothy Parker reflects on her development of the Afro-American collection at Howard University. Two indexes: chronological (by date of coverage); subjects. Although users would be better served by a classified organization—a deficiency not remedied by the subject index, which is insufficiently thorough and precise—the international scope and inclusion of numerous little-known works make *Black Access* the best source for identifying bibliographies on all African American topics. For recent bibliographies, see *Bibliographic Index* (D145).

GUIDES TO PRIMARY WORKS

Q3720   *Dictionary Catalog of the Schomburg Collection of Negro Literature and*
        History. 9 vols. Boston: Hall, 1962. *First Supplement.* 2 vols. 1967. *Second*
        Supplement. 4 vols. 1972. *Supplement 1974.* 1976. 580 pp. Continued by
        G. K. Hall Interdisciplinary Bibliographic Guide to Black Studies [1975–].
        Detroit: Gale, 1976– . Annual. (Title varies.)   Z881.N592 S35.
        CD-ROM.

A reproduction of the card catalog of the most important and extensive collection
of material by and about people of African descent. Along with printed material, the
collection includes art objects, recordings, sheet music, photographs, and manuscripts.
Manuscripts are listed only in the supplements; photographs and vertical file materials
are excluded in all volumes. Since the supplements and *G. K. Hall Interdisciplinary
Bibliographic Guide to Black Studies* record material newly acquired—not just recently
published—users must search the supplements and the *G. K. Hall Interdisciplinary
Bibliographic Guide* as well as the original *Catalog.* An indispensable, but frequently
overlooked, source for identifying authors and titles, the *Dictionary Catalog* is especially
valuable for the detailed subject access it offers to works relating to all aspects of African
American culture. The CD-ROM (*Black Studies on Disc,* 1995–) includes the *Dictionary Catalog,* supplements, and *Index to Black Periodicals* (Q3740); however the data
is difficult to extract because the primitive search interface offers limited search and
export options.

Other published catalogs of important collections include the following:

> *Afro-Americana, 1553–1906: Author Catalog of the Library Company of Phil-
> adelphia and the Historical Society of Pennsylvania.* Boston: Hall, 1973.
> 714 pp.
> *Dictionary Catalog of the Arthur B. Spingarn Collection of Negro Authors,
> Howard University Library, Washington, D.C.* 2 vols. Boston: Hall, 1970.
> *Dictionary Catalog of the George Foster Peabody Collection of Negro Literature
> and History, Collis P. Huntington Memorial Library, Hampton Institute,
> Hampton, Virginia.* 2 vols. Westport: Greenwood, 1972.
> *Dictionary Catalog of the Jesse E. Moorland Collection of Negro Life and History,
> Howard University Library, Washington, D.C.* 9 vols. Boston: Hall, 1970.
> *First Supplement.* 3 vols. 1976.
> *Dictionary Catalog of the Negro Collection of the Fisk University Library, Nash-
> ville, Tennessee.* 6 vols. Boston: Hall, 1974.
> *Dictionary Catalog of the Vivian G. Harsh Collection of Afro-American History
> and Literature, the Chicago Public Library.* 4 vols. Boston: Hall, 1978.

Many of these collections—at least a portion of them—can be searched through their
respective library's OPAC.

The holdings of 65 southern libraries are the basis for Geraldine O. Matthews,
comp., *Black American Writers, 1773–1949: A Bibliography and Union List* (Boston:
Hall, 1975, 221 pp.). Although entries are frequently incomplete and only about 60%
cite locations, Matthews is occasionally useful for tracking down an elusive work.

To identify other catalogs and collections, see section E: Libraries and Library
Catalogs/Library Catalogs.

Q3723   Jordan, Casper LeRoy, comp. *A Bibliographical Guide to African-American
        Women Writers.* Bibliographies and Indexes in Afro-American and African

Studies 31. Westport: Greenwood, 1993. 387 pp.   Z1229.N39 J67
[PS153.N5]   016.8108'09287'08996.

A bibliography of works in English by and about black American women writers.
Coverage extends to "poetry, memoirs, biographies, criticisms, autobiographies, essays,
short fiction, novels, diaries and journals" written between 1746 and 1991. Entries are
organized in three divisions: individual authors; anthologies; general works. In the first,
authors are listed alphabetically; under each are sections for primary works and for
studies (the former listed alphabetically by title and the latter by author), and some
sections are followed by a "1988–1991 Supplement," the inconsistent placement of
which is decidedly confusing (e.g., the additional list of works by an author sometimes
follows the primary works section and sometimes follows the secondary works section).
In addition, a separate "Supplement: Additional Writers and Sources, 1988–1991"
follows the general-works division. Coverage of primary works seems much fuller than
that of studies, especially for post-1987 publications (e.g., the "1988–1991 Supplement" under Toni Morrison lists only 20 works about her). The inexcusably haphazard
organization, failure to include names in running heads, and poorly designed index
make this book needlessly difficult to use. And the numerous omissions—especially in
the coverage of critical studies—unfortunately render it untrustworthy.

Q3725   Kallenbach, Jessamine S., comp. *Index to Black American Literary
Anthologies.* Boston: Hall, 1979. 219 pp.   Z1229.N39 K34 [PS153.N5]
016.8108'0896.

An author list of African American poetry, fiction, essays, and plays in some 140
literary anthologies designed for adults, primarily by African American authors, and
published through c. 1975. Under each author, works are organized by genre, then
alphabetically by title. Indexed by titles. The *Index* is frequently useful for locating texts,
although it is limited in scope.

Chapman, *Index to Poetry by Black American Women* (Q3840a) and *Index to Black
Poetry* (Q3840a) index, by subject, poems in collections.

Q3730   Schatz, Walter, ed. *Directory of Afro-American Resources.* New York: Bowker,
1970. 485 pp.   Z1361.N39 R3   917.3'06'96073.

A guide to about 5,365 collections of books, manuscripts, documents, and other
materials held by 2,108 organizations, libraries, institutions, and private and government agencies. Entries are organized alphabetically by state, then city, then institution.
Entries typically include organization or institution, address and telephone, name of
contact person (now outdated), services provided for researchers, purpose of organization, publications (especially guides and indexes to collections), description of individual
collections (identifying subject, size, inclusive dates, scope, and content), and restrictions
on use. Since entries are based on responses to questionnaires and on printed sources,
they vary in accuracy and sophistication; the most complete are taken from *National
Union Catalog of Manuscript Collections* (F295) through 1968 or submitted by libraries,
and the skimpiest are from local organizations and agencies. Two indexes: persons,
subjects, institutions, and places; supervisors and administrators of organizations and
collections. Although the *Directory* is now dated and omits several important institutions
and organizations, its focus and extensive coverage make it still useful for identifying
subject collections and locating manuscripts. The work must, however, be supplemented
by *ArchivesUSA* (F280), *National Union Catalog of Manuscript Collections*, and works
in section E: Libraries and Library Catalogs/Library Catalogs.

GUIDES TO SCHOLARSHIP AND CRITICISM

Surveys of Research

Q3735   Inge, M. Thomas, Maurice Duke, and Jackson R. Bryer, eds. *Black
American Writers: Bibliographical Essays.* 2 vols. New York: St. Martin's,
1978.   PS153.N5 B55   016.810'9'896073.

Selective surveys of research through mid-1970, with chapters devoted to major
eighteenth-century writers, slave narratives, nineteenth-century polemicists, early modern authors, the Harlem Renaissance, Hughes, Wright, Ellison, Baldwin, and Baraka.
The chapters are variously organized, but each has sections for bibliographies, editions,
manuscripts and letters, biographical studies, and criticism; a few offer suggestions for
further research. Indexed by persons in each volume; also indexed in *Biography and
Genealogy Master Index* (J565). Although the essays vary in selectiveness and rigor of
evaluation, most provide authoritative assessments of scholarship before mid-1970.
What is needed is a revised edition that would evaluate recent scholarship and devote
chapters to general reference works and studies. Review: R. Baxter Miller, *Black American Literature Forum* 13 (1979): 119–20.

For an evaluative survey of general histories, studies of slavery, and critical volumes
through 1987, see the "Bibliographical Essay" (pp. 401–50) in Jackson, *History of Afro-
American Literature: The Long Beginning* (Q3713).

See also

> *American Literary Scholarship* (Q3265): Chapter on black literature in the vols.
> for 1977–88.

Serial Bibliographies

Q3740   *G. K. Hall Index to Black Periodicals: [1950–].* Detroit: Gale, 1950– .
Annual, with cumulations for 1950–59 and 1960–70; the volumes since
1989 are included in *Black Studies on Disc* (CD-ROM, 1995– , annual).
Former titles: *Index to Black Periodicals* (1988–99); *Index to Periodical
Articles by and about Blacks* (1973–86); *Index to Periodical Articles by and
about Negroes* (1966–72); *Index to Selected Periodicals* (1954–65); *Index to
Selected Negro Periodicals* (1950–54).   AI3.O4   974.

An author and subject index to the contents of general and scholarly periodicals
(currently 38) devoted to African American topics. Literary works are listed by title
under genre headings; reviews are indexed by author, reviewer, and title (the last only
under headings such as "Book Reviews" and "Drama Reviews"). Because of its highly
selective coverage, the work is primarily useful for its indexing of a few periodicals
excluded from the serial bibliographies and indexes in section G.

The data from *G. K. Hall Index* in *Black Studies on Disc* is difficult to extract
because of the primitive search interface that offers limited search and export options.

Some additional studies are included in "Studies in African-American Literature:
An Annual Annotated Bibliography [1983–89]," *Callaloo* 7–13 (1984–90) and in
"An Annual Bibliography of Afro-American Literature, [1975–76], with Selected Bibliographies of African and Caribbean Literature," *CLA Journal* 20–21 (1976–77). For
earlier publications, some coverage is offered by *A Guide to Negro Periodical Literature*,
4 vols. (Winston-Salem: n.p., 1941–46).

Some additional periodicals and newspapers are indexed by subject—though idiosyncratically and incompletely—in *The Kaiser Index to Black Resources, 1948–1986: From the Schomburg Center for Research in Black Culture of the New York Public Library*, 5 vols. (Brooklyn: Carlson, 1992), an edited version of a card index at the Schomburg Center.

International Index to Black Periodicals Full Text (http://iibp.chadwyck.com) provides the full text of 37 periodicals since the mid-1990s and indexes several others. The major gaps in coverage of many journals and the limitation of subject searches to documents dated 1988 or later mean that anyone extracting information from this database must also search all the preceding works in this entry.

See also

> Secs. G: Serial Bibliographies, Indexes, and Abstracts and H: Guides to Dissertations and Theses.
>
> *MLAIB* (G335): American Literature division through the volume for 1969; Afro-American heading in American Literature sections in the volumes for 1970–80; in later volumes, researchers must consult the headings beginning "African American" or "Afro-American" in the subject index and "African American" in the online thesaurus.

Other Bibliographies

Q3750   Perry, Margaret. *The Harlem Renaissance: An Annotated Bibliography and Commentary*. Garland Reference Library of the Humanities 278: Critical Studies on Black Life and Culture 2. New York: Garland, 1982. 272 pp. Z5956.A47 P47 [NX511.N4]   016.81'09'97471.

A bibliography of works (published through 1980) by and about writers associated with the Harlem Renaissance. Perry includes authors who identified themselves with the movement as well as those who lived during the 1920s through early 1930s, and covers published works as well as dissertations, theses, manuscripts, and films in English or French. The 913 entries are organized alphabetically by author in eight divisions: bibliographies and reference works (including author bibliographies), histories of African American literature that include significant discussion of the Harlem Renaissance, general studies (with sections for works on the period, and for reviews of books and plays), 19 major authors (with selected primary works listed by genre, followed by criticism), miscellaneous materials (a hodgepodge), anthologies, library and special collections (organized by institution, with descriptions of individual collections), and an unannotated list of theses and dissertations. The reasonably full annotations are largely descriptive, although some include evaluative comments. Two indexes: persons (regrettably not indexing references to writers in divisions other than that for individual authors); titles of works cited. Poor and inconsistent organization, incomplete cross-references, and inadequate indexing mean that users searching for single-author studies must skim all entries. These shortcomings, together with the lack of clarity about criteria governing the selection of both primary and secondary works and the exclusion of most foreign scholarship, render *Harlem Renaissance* much less useful and accessible than it should be. Review: Hensley C. Woodbridge, *American Notes and Queries* 20 (1982): 159–60.

Q3755   Turner, Darwin T., comp. *Afro-American Writers*. Goldentree Bibliographies in Language and Literature. New York: Appleton, 1970. 117 pp.   Z1361.N39 T78   016.8108'091'7496.

A selective bibliography of primary and secondary works (chiefly in English and published through 1969) that are important to the study of African American literature. Theses, dissertations, book reviews, and general literary histories are excluded. Entries are organized in four classified divisions: aids to research (with sections for bibliographies, guides to library collections, other reference works, and periodicals); background studies (with highly selective lists of autobiographies and collections of essays; slave narratives; studies of historical, social, and intellectual backgrounds; and works on art, journalism, music, and theater); literary history and criticism (with sections for anthologies, general studies, drama, fiction, poetry, and folklore); and individual writers who have been the subject of critical or popular attention, or are otherwise important (with lists of primary works, bibliographies, and biographical studies and criticism for most authors). Additional entries appear in a supplement on pp. 105–17. Studies of African Americans as characters appear in an appendix. Important works are marked with an asterisk. Indexed by persons. Although now dated, *Afro-American Writers* remains the best selective guide to scholarship before 1970.

Theressa Gunnels Rush, Carol Fairbanks Myers, and Esther Spring Arata, *Black American Writers Past and Present: A Biographical and Bibliographical Dictionary*, 2 vols. (Metuchen: Scarecrow, 1975), offers a fuller—but much less accurate—list of works by and about some 2,000 writers. Although it is incomplete, lacks any indexes (however, writers are indexed in *Biography and Genealogy Master Index* [J565]), and frequently is based on other sources, the work is useful for its inclusion of parts of books and a host of minor authors.

Modern African American culture through c. 1974 is the subject of Charles D. Peavy, *Afro-American Literature and Culture since World War II: A Guide to Information Sources*, American Studies Information Guide Series 6 (Detroit: Gale, 1979, 302 pp.), but the poor organization, inadequate definitions of scope and criteria determining selection, frequent errors, and omission of numerous significant works make it virtually useless as a selective guide. (For the numerous inadequacies, see the review by Jill Warren, *Analytical and Enumerative Bibliography* 4 [1980]: 78–85.)

A major desideratum is an authoritative and current selective bibliography of scholarship on African American literature.

See also

>   *Harvard Guide to African-American History* (Q3710).
>   Leary, *Articles on American Literature* (Q3295).
>   Nemanic, *Bibliographical Guide to Midwestern Literature* (Q3600).
>   Ruoff, *Redefining American Literary History* (Q3695).
>   Szwed, *Afro-American Folk Culture* (U5880).
>   Woodress, *Dissertations in American Literature, 1891–1966* (Q3320).

LANGUAGE

Guides to Scholarship

Q3760   Brasch, Ila Wales, and Walter Milton Brasch. *A Comprehensive Annotated Bibliography of American Black English.* Baton Rouge: Louisiana State UP, 1974. 289 pp.   Z1234.D5 B7   016.427'973.

An author list of publications, dissertations, theses, and unpublished papers (through c. 1973 and primarily in English) on Black English, as well as a few literary and folklore works that use black speech. About 80% of the approximately 2,300 entries are accompanied by brief descriptive annotations. The work is marred by an inadequate explanation of scope (especially regarding the selection of works illustrating Black English), lacks an index and cross-references (thus one must skim all entries to locate studies of a particular topic), and falls far short of the comprehensiveness claimed in the title; nevertheless, Brasch offers the fullest single list of scholarship through c. 1973. It must be supplemented—even for studies before 1973—by *MLAIB* (G335), *ABELL* (G340), *Bibliographie linguistique* (U6010), *LLBA: Linguistics and Language Behavior Abstracts* (U6015), and most works in sections G: Serial Bibliographies, Indexes, and Abstracts and H: Guides to Dissertations and Theses. A major desideratum is a current, thorough, adequately indexed bibliography of scholarship on Black English. Review: J[ohn] A[lgeo], *American Speech* 49 (1974): 142–46.

See also

> *ABELL* (G340): Dialect section of the English Language division in the volumes for 1920–26; the American English section in the volumes for 1927–33; the English Dialects section in the volume for 1934; the American English section in the volumes for 1935–72; and the Dialects/Dialects of [North] America section in later volumes.
>
> *MLAIB* (G335): English Language and Literature division in the volumes for 1922–25; American Literature I: Linguistics in the volumes for 1926–40; English Language and Literature I: Linguistics in the volumes for 1941–55; English Language and Literature I: Linguistics/American English in the volumes for 1956–66; Indo-European C: Germanic Linguistics IV: English/ Modern English/Dialectology in the volumes for 1967–80; and Indo-European Languages/Germanic Languages/West Germanic Languages/English Language (Modern)/Dialectology in the volumes since 1981. Researchers must also check the heading "Black English Dialect" in the subject index to post-1980 volumes and in the online thesaurus.

BIOGRAPHICAL DICTIONARIES

Indexes

Q3765   *AABD: African American Biographical Database.* Chadwyck-Healey. Online. 24 June 2005 <http://aabd.chadwyck.com>. Updated bimonthly.

A database of biographical information that incorporates Randall K. Burkett, Nancy Hall Burkett, and Henry Louis Gates, Jr., eds., *Black Biography, 1790–1950: A Cumulative Index,* 3 vols. (Alexandria: Chadwyck-Healey, 1991) and the microform collection *Black Biographical Dictionaries, 1790–1950* (Alexandria: Chadwyck-Healey, 1987) as well as other resources (almost all of which are out-of-copyright texts or Web sites). The title of the database is misleading since it includes numerous entries for Africans who have no connection with North America (e.g., Amenotep III and Haile Selassie I). Entries can be searched by any combination of name, state or country, city or county, occupation, religion, date of birth, date of death, and gender; in addition, full-text documents can be searched by keyword. A typical entry (which can be downloaded by e-mail) includes date of birth and of death, birthplace, occupation, religion, and a hyperlinked list of dictionaries in which a biographical sketch or illustration appears. Although supposedly updated bimonthly, there is no record of updates on the site. The lack of coverage of printed sources published after the late 1940s and the reliance on Web sites for living individuals means that *AABD* must be complemented by *Biography and Genealogy Master Index* (J565) and Dorothy W. Campbell, *Index to Black American Writers in Collective Biographies* (Littleton: Libraries Unlimited, 1983, 162 pp.), a name index to biographical sketches of about 1,900 black writers in 267 collective biographies that focus on African Americans and were published between 1837 and 1982. *AABD, Black Biography,* and *Index to Black American Writers* are essential starting points for locating biographical information on African Americans; the three resources index a number of works not covered by *Biography and Genealogy Master Index* (J565), which should also be checked, since it offers broader, more current coverage.

See also

    Sec. J: Biographical Sources/Biographical Dictionaries/Indexes.

Dictionaries

Q3770   *African American National Biography (AANB).* Ed. Henry Louis Gates, Jr., and Evelyn Brooks Higginbotham. New York: Oxford UP, in progress. <http://www.fas.harvard.edu/~aanb>.

    A biographical dictionary that will include more than 10,000 African Americans "in all fields, from all periods of North American history, and from all stations of life"; a searchable list of entrants is available at the *AANB* Web site (as are sample entries). The signed entries (typically ranging from 750 to 1,500 words) will conclude with a selective bibliography. This will undoubtedly become the most authoritative biographical dictionary of African Americans. A preliminary collection appears as *African American Lives,* ed. Gates and Higginbotham (New York: Oxford UP, 2004, 1,025 pp.). Modeled on *American National Biography* (Q3378), from which *AANB* reprints 257 entries, the 611 biographees (living and dead) represent the broad range of the African American experience. Appendices include lists of entrants by category or area of renown, of prize winners, of medalists, of members of Congress, and of judges. Indexed by persons, titles, and subjects.

    Although now dated, Rayford W. Logan and Michael R. Winston, eds., *Dictionary of American Negro Biography* (New York: Norton, 1982, 680 pp.), treats 636 African Americans who died before 1970. Entrants, chosen on the basis of historical significance, represent a variety of walks of life. The separately authored entries provide essential details of an entrant's life and career, a brief estimate of the person's significance, and references to biographical sources and collections of papers. Entrants are indexed in *Biography and Genealogy Master Index* (J565). Review: Henry Louis Gates, Jr., *New York Times Book Review* 1 May 1983: 13, 29.

    For basic biographical information about living African Americans, see the most recent edition of *Who's Who among African Americans* (Detroit: Gale, 1975– ; online through *Biography Resource Center* [J572] and *Gale Virtual Reference Library* [I535]), which is indexed in *Biography and Genealogy Master Index* (J565). The fullest biographical coverage of writers is offered by *Dictionary of Literary Biography* (J600).

See also

> *Contemporary Authors* (J595).
> Rush, *Black American Writers Past and Present* (Q3755a).

PERIODICALS

Guides to Primary Works

Q3775   Danky, James P., and Maureen E. Hady, eds. *African-American Newspapers and Periodicals: A National Bibliography.* Harvard University Press Reference Library. Cambridge: Harvard UP, 1998. 740 pp.   Z6944.N39 A37 [PN4882.5]   015.73′035′08996073.

A census of more than 6,500 newspapers and periodicals published, for the most part, in the United States and edited by or published by or for blacks between 1827 and 1997. Organized alphabetically by title, entries (which are based on personal examination by the editors, their research assistants, librarians, and archivists) typically cite current title; beginning and cessation dates; frequency; current editor and address; subscription rate; publisher(s); number of pages in final issue or the last one examined; content (line drawings, photographs, commercial advertising); size; previous editor(s); variations in title, place of publication, or frequency; bibliographies that index the work; availability in microform; ISSN, *WorldCat*, and LC catalog numbers; subject focus and special features; and libraries that hold the title (with volumes or issues held and location within the library). Four indexes: subjects and features; editors; publishers; places of publication. Although lacking an adequate discussion of scope and editorial procedure and failing to index or cross-reference variant titles, *African-American Newspapers and Periodicals* is an important resource that provides the basis for the recovery and assessment of the rich tradition of African American periodical fiction and poetry. The editors hope to update the bibliography and make it available electronically.

A rekeyed text of seven newspapers can be searched through *African-American Newspapers: The 19th Century*, which is part of *Accessible Archives* (online, 18 May 2006 <http://www.accessible.com>). Only basic keyword searches can be performed, and records are sorted by newspaper, then in descending chronological order.

GENRES

Some works in sections L: Genres and Q: American Literature/General/Genres are useful for research in African American literature.

Fiction

Some works in sections L: Genres/Fiction and Q: American Literature/General/Genres/ Fiction are useful for research in African American fiction.

Histories and Surveys

Q3805   Bell, Bernard W. *The Afro-American Novel and Its Tradition.* Amherst: U of
         Massachusetts P, 1987. 421 pp.   PS153.N5 B43   813'.009'896.
     A "sociopsychological, sociocultural" history of extended prose narratives from
1853 through 1983. Organized chronologically, chapters emphasize the place of about
150 works in their respective historical, cultural, and literary contexts, with particular
attention given to the relationship to oral and literary, European and African traditions.
Indexed by persons, titles, and subjects. The most thorough, balanced, and sympathetic
history of the African American novel, Bell supersedes earlier histories (especially Robert
Bone, *The Negro Novel in America*, rev. ed. [New Haven: Yale UP, 1965], 289 pp.).
     Short fiction awaits comparable treatment. Robert Bone, *Down Home: Origins of
the Afro-American Short Story*, rpt. with a new pref. (New York: Columbia UP, 1988,
328 pp.)—a critical survey of African American short fiction (primarily the short story)
from 1885 to 1935 that emphasizes its debts to oral tradition as well as to mainstream
Western literary forms, the Protestant tradition, the rural South, the anxiety about the
role of the African American writer in American society, and (in the preface to the
reprint) the blues tradition—is too restrictive in coverage and controversial in its underlying critical assumptions to serve as an adequate history of African American short
fiction. For an important disagreement with these assumptions, see the review by Darwin T. Turner, *American Literature* 48 (1976): 416–18.

Guides to Primary Works

Q3815   Margolies, Edward, and David Bakish. *Afro-American Fiction, 1853–1976:
         A Guide to Information Sources.* American Literature, English Literature, and
         World Literatures in English: An Information Guide Series 25. Detroit:
         Gale, 1979. 161 pp.   Z1229.N39 M37 [PS374.N4]   016.813'008'0352.
     A highly selective list of novels, short story collections, and scholarship through c.
1976. Entries are organized in four divisions: novels for adults (listed alphabetically by
author, then chronologically by publication date), short story collections (with separate
lists of single-author collections and anthologies), 15 major novelists chosen for their
historical or literary importance (authors are listed chronologically by publication date
of their first novels, with separate lists of bibliographies and critical studies), and bibliographies and general studies. Only entries in the third and fourth divisions are annotated, with many works inadequately described. The appendix lists fictional works
by publication date. Three indexes: authors; titles; and subjects. Because it is highly
selective in all but the first division, inefficiently organized, and marred by an inadequate
explanation of scope and criteria governing selection, *Afro-American Fiction* is primarily
useful for its list of novels. Review: Jill Warren, *Analytical and Enumerative Bibliography*
4 (1980): 78–85.
     Somewhat better—although also selective—coverage of novels published between
1965 and 1975 is offered by Helen Ruth Houston, *The Afro-American Novel, 1965–
1975: A Descriptive Bibliography of Primary and Secondary Materials* (Troy: Whitston,
1977, 214 pp.), which is an annotated list—not a "descriptive" bibliography—of
novels, studies, and reviews.
     More than 850 short stories published between 1950 and 1982 in collections,
anthologies, and periodicals are indexed by author, title, collection, and year of publication in Preston M. Yancy, comp., *The Afro-American Short Story: A Comprehensive,
Annotated Index with Selected Commentaries*, Bibliographies and Indexes in Afro-American

and African Studies 10 (Westport: Greenwood, 1986, 171 pp.). Coverage is far short of "comprehensive," and the work is confusingly organized and repetitive.

See also

>   Fairbanks, *Black American Fiction: A Bibliography* (Q3820).

Guides to Scholarship and Criticism

Q3820   Fairbanks, Carol, and Eugene A. Engeldinger. *Black American Fiction: A Bibliography.* Metuchen: Scarecrow, 1978. 351 pp.   Z1229.N39 F34 [PS153.N5]   016.813.

A selective list of novels, short fiction, and English-language studies (including dissertations) through c. 1976. Under each fiction writer are sections, when appropriate, listing novels, short fiction, collections, biographical studies and criticism, and reviews (by work reviewed). General studies of African American fiction appear in a concluding list. There is no explanation of criteria governing selection and no index; many entries are copied from unidentified sources; significant omissions and incomplete citations occur; and relevant pages of parts of books are not cited. In spite of these serious deficiencies, *Black American Fiction* provides the single fullest list of works by and about African American fiction writers. The work must, though, be supplemented by Margolies, *Afro-American Fiction* (Q3815), as well as the serial bibliographies and indexes in section G.

See also

>   Margolies, *Afro-American Fiction, 1853–1976* (Q3815).
>   Weixlmann, *American Short-Fiction Criticism and Scholarship, 1959–1977* (Q3480).

Drama and Theater

Some works in sections L: Genres/Drama and Theater and Q: American Literature/ General/Genres/Drama and Theater are useful for research in African American drama.

Histories and Surveys

Q3823   Hill, Errol G., and James V. Hatch. *A History of African American Theatre.* Cambridge: Cambridge UP, 2003. 608 pp.   PN2270.A35 H55 792'.089'96073.

A history of African American theater from 1821 to 2000 that includes the legitimate stage as well as minstrelsy, spectacles, musicals, operas, and educational theater. With the issue of racism at their center, chapters proceed more or less chronologically to examine the principal works, performers, theater personnel, playwrights, and acting companies. An appendix surveys broadly the scholarship on African American theater. Indexed by persons, titles, and subjects. Written by the preeminent scholars in the field, *History of African American Theatre* offers a masterful survey of African American theater and provides the basis for the "thoroughly integrated American theatre history" that remains to be written. Review: Harry Elam, *Theatre Survey* 46 (2005): 127–29.

Guides to Primary Works

Q3825   Hatch, James V., and OMANii Abdullah, comps. and eds. *Black Playwrights, 1823–1977: An Annotated Bibliography*. New York: Bowker, 1977. 319 pp.   Z1231.D7 H37 [PS338.N4]   016.812′009′352.

An author bibliography of about 2,700 plays by approximately 900 African Americans, along with some foreigners whose plays have been produced in the United States. Although a majority of the works are published and unpublished stage plays, some film, television, and radio dramas are also included. Each entry provides (when available) title, date of composition and copyright, genre, a brief summary (sometimes based on reviews or written by the playwright or an agent), cast (by race and sex), location of at least one copy, and permission information. Concludes with selected bibliographies of books, anthologies, and dissertations and theses and three appendixes: a list of taped interviews on the African American theater and held in Hatch-Billops archives; awards; addresses of playwrights, agents, and agencies (although more-current addresses are usually available in *Contemporary Authors* [J595]). Indexed by titles. Superior in coverage to the drama part of French, *Afro-American Poetry and Drama* (Q3845), *Black Playwrights* is the fullest record of plays by African Americans and an invaluable source for locating copies of obscure works.

It must, however, be supplemented by Bernard L. Peterson, Jr., *Contemporary Black American Playwrights: A Biographical Directory and Dramatic Index* (New York: Greenwood, 1988, 625 pp.) and *Early Black American Playwrights and Dramatic Writers: A Biographical Directory and Catalog of Plays, Films, and Broadcasting Scripts* (New York: Greenwood, 1990, 298 pp.), with entries on about 900 "black American and U. S. resident dramatists, screenwriters, radio and television scriptwriters, musical theatre collaborators, and other originators of theatrical and dramatic works, written, produced, and published" through 1985. Each entry provides biographical information, address, and a list of dramatic works (noting genre, production or publication information, and source; providing a brief synopsis and production history; and locating scripts or recordings). Indexed in *Biography and Genealogy Master Index* (J565). Although not the "comprehensive" work claimed in the preface and necessarily incomplete in many entries, Peterson is an invaluable source for identifying and locating frequently unpublished dramatic works by African American writers. The preceding are complemented by Peterson, *The African American Theatre Directory, 1816–1960: A Comprehensive Guide to Early Black Theatre Organizations, Companies, Theatres, and Performing Groups* (1997, 301 pp.).

For additional theatrical works (by blacks and whites) with black characters, see James V. Hatch, *Black Image on the American Stage: A Bibliography of Plays and Musicals, 1770–1970* (New York: DBS, 1970, 162 pp.), with additions by Joseph N. Weixlmann, "Black Portraiture on the Eighteenth-Century American Stage: Addenda," *Analytical and Enumerative Bibliography* 1 (1977): 203–06.

Guides to Scholarship and Criticism

There is no adequate bibliography devoted to studies of African American drama. Esther Spring Arata and Nicholas John Rotoli, *Black American Playwrights, 1800 to the Present: A Bibliography* (Metuchen: Scarecrow, 1976, 295 pp.), and Arata, *More Black American Playwrights: A Bibliography* (1978, 321 pp.), are too error-ridden, poorly organized, incomplete, and inconsistent to recommend to researchers. French, *Afro-American Poetry and Drama* (Q3845), is so selective that it is barely a place to begin research. And Dana A. Williams, *Contemporary African American Female Playwrights: An Annotated*

Bibliography, Bibliographies and Indexes in Afro-American and African Studies 37 (Westport: Greenwood, 1998, 124 pp.), is ineffectively organized, incompletely indexed (e.g., authors of critical studies of individual playwrights are excluded from the name index), and—despite its subtitle—offers annotations for fewer than one-third of its entries (the annotations that do exist are hardly informative).

Poetry

Some works in section L: Genres/Poetry are useful for research in African American poetry.

Histories and Surveys

Q3830   Sherman, Joan R. *Invisible Poets: Afro-Americans of the Nineteenth Century.* 2nd ed. Urbana: U of Illinois P, 1989. 288 pp.   PS153.N5 S48 811′.009′896073.

A series of essays on 26 poets born between 1796 and 1883 and representative of nineteenth-century African American poets, who are virtually ignored in literary histories and anthologies. The individual essays, organized by birthdate of authors, consist of a biography, critical appraisal, and selective list of sources (including manuscripts). The essays are complemented by a series of bibliographies and appendixes: a bibliography of primary works that includes manuscripts and locations of printed copies; a bibliographical essay that evaluates the bibliographies, periodical guides and indexes, biographical and critical works, anthologies, and manuscript collections important to research in nineteenth-century African American literature; a list of 35 writers who published a significant amount of poetry and who need further research; a list of other, less prolific poets who need further research; anonymous and pseudonymous poets; turn-of-the-century writers who did not publish before 1900; poets erroneously identified as African American; Creole poets of *Les Cenelles*; and selected bibliographies of Wheatley and Harmon. The bibliographical essay and selective bibliographies appended to discussions of individual poets are updated through c. 1987 in the second edition (pp. 237–53), which is otherwise a reprint of the first edition (1974). Indexed by persons, subjects, and anonymous titles; unfortunately, the index in the second edition is not revised to reflect the repagination of the latter part of the work. Besides providing the fullest history of nineteenth-century African American poets, *Invisible Poets* is an essential guide to research on the topic and a valuable source for identifying writers who need further attention. Review: Duncan MacLeod, *TLS: Times Literary Supplement* 13 June 1975: 675.

Q3835   Wagner, Jean. *Black Poets of the United States: From Paul Laurence Dunbar to Langston Hughes.* Trans. Kenneth Douglas. Urbana: U of Illinois P, 1973. 561 pp. (Originally published as *Les poètes nègres des Etats-Unis: Le sentiment racial et religieux dans la poésie de P. L. Dunbar à L. Hughes [1890–1940].* Paris: Istra, 1963. 637 pp.)   PS153.N5 W313   811′.009.

A detailed critical history of African American poetry that emphasizes "the interdependence of racial and religious feeling" in the works of major poets from 1890 to 1940. The chapters on early nineteenth-century African American poets, Dunbar, his contemporaries, the African American renaissance, McKay, Toomer, Cullen, Johnson, Hughes, and Brown consider biography, cultural and social contexts, and themes. The selective bibliography, extended to c. 1972 by Keneth Kinnamon, is now outdated. Indexed by persons, subjects, and titles. An encyclopedic work noteworthy for its scrupulous scholarship, it remains the standard history. Review: Robert Penn Warren, *Études anglaises* 28 (1975): 241–42.

Guides to Primary Works

Bibliographies and Indexes

Q3840   *Columbia Granger's Index to African-American Poetry.* Ed. Nicholas Frankovich and David Larzelere. New York: Columbia UP, 1999. 302 pp. Z1229.N39 C65 [PS153.N5]   016.811008'0896073.

A title, first-line, last-line, author, and subject index to 7,983 poems by 659 poets that appear in 55 anthologies or collected works ("the poetry books most likely to be found on library shelves"). As in its model, *Columbia Granger's Index to Poetry* (L1235), the indexes are cumbersome to use because the author and subject listings are keyed to the title, first-line, and last-line entries, which are in turn keyed to the list of anthologies and collections at the front of the volume; however, the subject indexing in this work goes beyond title keywords, forms, and genres. (The most efficient way to search this resource is through *Columbia Granger's World of Poetry* database [L1235].) Although the most current source for identifying poems by African American writers on a topic or in anthologies, *Columbia Granger's Index to African-American Poetry* must be supplemented by Dorothy Hilton Chapman, comp., *Index to Poetry by Black American Women*, Bibliographies and Indexes in Afro-American and African Studies 15 (New York: Greenwood, 1986, 424 pp.), a title, first-line, and subject index to about 4,000 poems in 120 single-author collections and 83 anthologies (through c. 1984) by more than 400 African American women. Also included are about 185 anonymous poems, several of which may be by males. The title and first-line index is keyed to a list of collections. The subject index extends beyond title keywords. Although lacking an adequate explanation of the criteria governing the choice of collections and omitting some significant anthologies, the *Index* is a useful source for locating texts and identifying poems on topics. Since her projected volume on African American male poets was never published, Chapman's *Index to Black Poetry* (Boston: Hall, 1974, 541 pp.) remains useful. Additional anthologies are indexed by title and author in Kallenbach, *Index to Black American Literary Anthologies* (Q3725). Some poems by African Americans are indexed in *Columbia Granger's Index to Poetry* (L1235), *Poetry Index Annual* (L1235a), and *Index of American Periodical Verse* (Q4325).

Q3845   French, William P., et al. *Afro-American Poetry and Drama, 1760–1975: A Guide to Information Sources.* American Literature, English Literature, and World Literatures in English: An Information Guide Series 17. Detroit: Gale, 1979. 493 pp.   Z1229.N39 A37 [PS153.N5]   016.810'9'896073.

A bibliography of primary works and selected studies in two parts: poetry from 1760 through 1975, compiled by French, Michael J. Fabre, and Amritjit Singh; drama from 1850 through 1975, by Geneviève E. Fabre.

Poetry. This part attempts comprehensive coverage of separately published volumes of more than four pages by African Americans born in the United States as well as a few foreign-born residents. Although emphasizing written works, the part includes some folk and oral poetry. Coverage of scholarship is highly selective, especially for major writers. Entries are organized in two divisions: general studies (with sections for bibliographies and reference works, general studies, and anthologies) and individual authors (organized in three periods—1760–1900, 1901–45, 1946–75—with separate lists of primary works, bibliographies, and biographical studies and criticism for each poet). Few entries are annotated. Although coverage of scholarship is highly selective, *Afro-American Poetry and Drama* offers the fullest list of separately published volumes of poetry by African Americans and is especially valuable for its identification of numerous privately printed and ephemeral publications.

Drama. This part attempts comprehensive coverage of published plays by African Americans born or resident in the United States, includes some unpublished works, and lists selected scholarship. Entries are organized in two divisions: general studies (with sections for library collections, periodicals, bibliographies, collections of plays, and criticism) and individual authors (organized in three periods—1850–1900, 1901–50, 1951–75—with separate lists of published plays, unpublished ones, collections, and biographical studies and criticism for each playwright). Published plays are accompanied by summaries and details of first production; otherwise, few entries are annotated. Because Hatch, *Black Playwrights* (Q3825), offers more extensive and informative coverage of published and unpublished plays, this section is only marginally useful as a preliminary guide to scholarship. A single index of persons, titles, and subjects encompasses both parts. Left unexplained are the justification for publishing the two parts as a single volume and the criteria governing the selection of studies. Review: Joe Weixlmann, *Black American Literature Forum* 14 (1980): 44–46.

Text Archives

Q3848   *African American Poetry.* ProQuest. Online. 14 June 2006 <http://
         collections.chadwyck.com>.

A text archive of rekeyed texts of about 3,000 English-language poems by eighteenth- and nineteenth-century African American poets. Editions were selected according to the following criteria: first editions or more-inclusive later editions; poems originally appearing in periodicals are also included. Apparently only poets listed in French, *Afro-American Poetry and Drama, 1760–1975* (Q3845), merited inclusion.

Simple keyword, first line or title, and author searches can be limited by date during a poet's lifetime, gender, nationality, literary period, rhymed or unrhymed poems, and parts. Searchers can also browse an author list of the contents of the database. Results appear in ascending alphabetical order and cannot be re-sorted. Citations (but not the full text of poems) can be marked for e-mailing, downloading, or printing; each citation includes a durable URL to the full text.

Some works are rekeyed from textually unsound editions; however, the bibliographic record for each work identifies the source of the text and any omissions (e.g., preliminary matter). Besides being a useful source for identifying an elusive quotation or half-remembered line, the scope of *African American Poetry*'s text archive makes feasible a variety of kinds of studies (stylistic, thematic, imagistic, and topical).

Coverage is continued by *Twentieth-Century African American Poetry* (ProQuest; online; 17 June 2006 <http://collections.chadwyck.com>), which includes more than 9,000 poems by 70 poets. Editions were selected according to the following criteria: a collected edition; other editions for poets without a collected one. Selection seems to be based on the ability to secure rights for electronic publication.

Twentieth-Century African American Poetry uses the same search interface as *African American Poetry* but with some differences in ways of limiting a search. The contents of both archives can also be searched through *LiOn* (I527), which offers a less versatile search interface.

Prose

Some works in sections L: Genres/Prose and Q: American Literature/General/Genres/ Prose are useful for research in African American prose.

Guides to Primary Works

Q3850 Brignano, Russell C. *Black Americans in Autobiography: An Annotated Bibliography of Autobiographies and Autobiographical Books Written since the Civil War.* Rev. and expanded ed. Durham: Duke UP, 1984. 193 pp. Z1361.N39 B67 [E185.96] 016.973′0496073022.

An annotated bibliography of book-length autobiographical works by African Americans through 1982. The 710 entries are listed in four divisions: autobiographies (i.e., "volumes describing appreciable spans of the authors' lives"); autobiographical books that address a phase of the author's life; works that the compiler could not locate or read; autobiographical works published before 1865 and reprinted since 1945. Entries provide publication information, details of reprints, locations in up to 10 libraries, and, in the first two parts, a descriptive annotation. Five indexes: activities, experiences, occupations, and professions; organizations; geographical locations and educational institutions; chronological listing of works by date of first publication; titles. Except for the rare volumes that have not been reprinted, citing library locations is unnecessary (especially since there is no logic to the choice of locations for commonly available books). Although the value of including post-1945 reprints of pre-1865 publications and the reasons for separating post-1865 works into three lists are unclear, Brignano offers valuable subject access to an important body of African American writing.

For earlier works, see "Annotated Bibliography of Afro-American Autobiography, 1760–1865" in William L. Andrews, *To Tell a Free Story: The First Century of Afro-American Autobiography, 1760–1865* (Urbana: U of Illinois P, 1986), 333–42, a selective list of separately published autobiographies; the annotations, however, consist of pagination and publication details for a few translations or later editions. In the same volume is "Annotated Bibliography of Afro-American Biography, 1760–1865" (343–47), which is drawn from Andrews, "Annotated Bibliography of Afro-American Biography, Beginnings to 1930," *Resources for American Literary Study* 12 (1982): 119–33; the annotations are minimal in both lists.

For autobiographies published or reprinted between 1980 and 2000, see Stuhr-Rommereim, *Autobiographies by Americans of Color, 1980–1994*, and Iwabuchi, *Autobiographies by Americans of Color, 1995–2000* (Q3705).

American Indian Literatures

Some works in section Q: American Literature/General are useful for research in American Indian literatures.

GUIDES TO REFERENCE WORKS

Q3860 Hirschfelder, Arlene B., Mary Gloyne Byler, and Michael A. Dorris. *Guide to Research on North American Indians.* Chicago: Amer. Lib. Assn., 1983. 330 pp. Z1209.2.N67.H57 [E77] 016.970004′97.

A highly selective annotated bibliography of important reference works and studies of Indians of the United States and Alaska, along with a few major works on the rest of the Americas. The approximately 1,100 entries encompass English-language books, articles, and government documents published through 1979 (with a few as late as 1982) but exclude ethnographies. Entries are organized in four divisions: general works (with sections for general bibliographies and general studies); history (including sections for descriptive narratives and autobiographies and biographies); economic and social topics (including a section for language); and religion, arts, and literature (with sections for religion and philosophy, music and dance, education, the arts, science, law, and literature). Each section begins with an essay overview of sources, followed by a list of general studies, then works devoted to a specific region, and then bibliographies. The full annotations offer detailed descriptions of contents. Two indexes: authors and titles; subjects. Superficial and inconsistent in its coverage of specialized studies (especially in the literature and literature-related sections) and now dated, it is primarily useful as a guide to important reference works before 1980.

It is far superior, however, to Marilyn L. Haas, *Indians of North America: Methods and Sources for Library Research* (Hamden: Lib. Professional–Shoe String, 1983, 163 pp.), an elementary guide that is frequently inaccurate and misleading. Review (Hirschfelder and Haas): G. Edward Evans, *American Indian Culture and Research Journal* 8.4 (1984): 66–70.

HISTORIES AND SURVEYS

Q3865   Wiget, Andrew. *Native American Literature.* Twayne's United States
         Authors Series 467. Boston: Twayne, 1985. 147 pp.   PM155.W54
         810'.9'897.
    A critical history of the oral and narrative literatures of Native Americans of North America and Mesoamerica. The six chapters—organized variously by genre, group, or author—offer basic surveys of oral narrative (especially creation myths); oratory and oral poetry; the beginnings of a written literature; modern fiction; contemporary poetry; and recent nonfiction, autobiography, and drama. Concludes with a selected bibliography of primary and secondary works (the latter are accompanied by terse evaluative comments). Indexed by persons, works, and subjects. Although it is an introductory survey that emphasizes representative works and major authors, Wiget is currently the fullest history of Native American literatures. Given the level of interest, the time is ripe for a more comprehensive history.

See also

   Cambridge History of American Literature (Q3205).
   Columbia Literary History of the United States (Q3195).

LITERARY HANDBOOKS, DICTIONARIES, AND ENCYCLOPEDIAS

Q3867   *Dictionary of Native American Literature.* Ed. Andrew Wiget. Garland
         Reference Library of the Humanities 1815. New York: Garland, 1994.
         598 pp. (Reprinted as *Handbook of Native American Literature* [1996].)
         PM155.D53   897.

A collection of 73 essays by various authors on oral and written Native American literature, organized into three sections: oral literatures (with essays on geographical areas, genres, and topics [e.g., the trickster figure, myth and religion]); the historical emergence of Native American writing (with a historical overview, discussions of genres, and essays on individual writers); Native American renaissance (with a historical overview, discussions of critical approaches, European responses, pedagogy, genres, Native Americans in Anglo-American literature, and essays on individual authors). Written mostly by established authorities, the essays offer essential biographical and bibliographical information and critical estimates; all but a few conclude with a selective bibliography. Indexed by persons, titles, and subjects; entrants are also indexed in *Biography and Genealogy Master Index* (J565). *Dictionary of Native American Literature* is the best single compendium of biographical and bibliographical information on Native American literature.

Q3868   *Handbook of North American Indians.* Gen. ed. William C. Sturtevant. 20 vols. Washington: Smithsonian Inst., 1978– .   E77.H25   970′.004′97.

  Vol. 1: *Introduction.*
  Vol. 2: *Indians in Contemporary Society.*
  Vol. 3: *Environment, Origins, and Population.*
  Vol. 4: *History of Indian-White Relations.* Ed. Wilcomb E. Washburn. 1988. 838 pp.
  Vol. 5: *Arctic.* Ed. David Damas. 1984. 829 pp.
  Vol. 6: *Subarctic.* Ed. June Helm. 1981. 837 pp.
  Vol. 7: *Northwest Coast.* Ed. Wayne Suttles. 1990. 777 pp.
  Vol. 8: *California.* Ed. Robert F. Heizer. 1978. 800 pp.
  Vol. 9: *Southwest.* Ed. Alfonso Ortiz. 1979. 701 pp.
  Vol. 10: *Southwest.* Ed. Ortiz. 1983. 868 pp.
  Vol. 11: *Great Basin.* Ed. Warren L. d'Azevedo. 1986. 852 pp.
  Vol. 12: *Plateau.* Ed. Deward E. Walker, Jr. 1998. 791 pp.
  Vol. 13: *Plains.* Ed. Raymond J. DeMallie. 2001. 2 pts.
  Vol. 14: *Southeast.* Ed. Raymond D. Fogelson. 2004. 1,042 pp.
  Vol. 15: *Northeast.* Ed. Bruce G. Trigger. 1978. 924 pp.
  Vol. 16: *Technology and Visual Arts.*
  Vol. 17: *Languages.* Ed. Ives Goddard. 1996. 957 pp. (A rev. ed. of the map in the back pocket was published in 1999.)
  Vols. 18–19: *Biographical Dictionary.*
  Vol. 20: *Index.*

An encyclopedic treatment of the history and culture of North American Indians. The volumes devoted to geographical areas typically include essays by established scholars on ethnography, languages, archaeology, tribal groups, art, and—occasionally—literature, religion, and mythology. The extensive list of works cited in each volume constitutes a valuable bibliography of major studies. Indexed in each volume by names and subjects. Although the essays are uneven in quality and some ignore controversies about their subject matter, the *Handbook* will eventually be the most authoritative general source of information on American Indian history, ethnography, and culture. Reviews: (vol. 4) J. R. Miller, *Canadian Historical Review* 72 (1991): 241–44; (vol. 5) Steve Talbot, *American Indian Culture and Research Journal* 11.1 (1987): 123–27; (vol. 7) Michael Harkin, *Ethnohistory* 39 (1992): 172–78; (vol. 9) Bernard L. Fontana, *Arizona Quarterly* 38 (1982): 81–85.

BIBLIOGRAPHIES OF BIBLIOGRAPHIES

Q3869   White, Phillip M., comp. *Bibliography of Native American Bibliographies.*
Bibliographies and Indexes in Ethnic Studies 11. Westport: Praeger, 2004.
241 pp.   Z1209.2.N67.W55 [E77]   016.970004'97.

A selective bibliography of bibliographies (including books, articles, and Web sites published by 2003) about Native Americans of the United States and Canada. The 843 entries—which exclude outdated material, textbooks, and most dissertations—are organized under a variety of subject headings, of which the following will be of most interest to users of this *Guide*: archives, authors, biographies and autobiographies, children's literature, languages and linguistics, libraries, literature, performing arts, periodicals, and stage (the theater). Literature researchers must check both the author and literature sections since there are a number of publications on individual authors in the literature section and vice versa. Entries are accompanied by brief, descriptive, woodenly written annotations. Excluding coverage of annotations in the index of persons, tribes, and subjects seriously hampers access to the work. Despite these shortcomings, White is a serviceable guide to bibliographies of Native American topics.

GUIDES TO PRIMARY WORKS

Q3870   Littlefield, Daniel F., Jr., and James W. Parins. *A Biobibliography of Native American Writers, 1772–1924.* Native American Bibliography Series 2.
Metuchen: Scarecrow, 1981. 343 pp. *Supplement.* Native American Bibliography Series 5. 1985. 339 pp.   Z1209.2.U5.L57 [E77]   016.973'0497.

An author list of works published between 1772 and 1924 and written in English by Native Americans of the United States (including Alaska). Except for writers known only by pseudonyms, coverage is limited to individuals definitely identified as Native Americans and to writings composed by the authors themselves. Each volume is made up of three parts: writers of established identity, writers known only by pseudonyms, and biographical notices. Under an author, entries are listed by publication date (a practice that needlessly separates later editions, reprints, and revisions from an original edition or version). A code system identifies the genre of each work, and in the *Supplement* brief descriptive annotations explain unclear titles. The biographical notices offer basic factual details; only in the *Supplement* do these cite sources. Two indexes in each volume: writers by tribal affiliation; subjects. In addition, the biographical notices are indexed in *Biography and Genealogy Master Index* (J565). Although not comprehensive, Littlefield is an indispensable guide to these early writings, the majority of which are indexed nowhere else. Review: A. LaVonne Brown Ruoff, *Arizona Quarterly* 38 (1982): 272–74.

GUIDES TO SCHOLARSHIP AND CRITICISM

Other Bibliographies

Q3875   Marken, Jack W., comp. *The American Indian: Language and Literature.*
Goldentree Bibliographies in Language and Literature. Arlington Heights:
AHM, 1978. 205 pp.   Z7118.M27 [PM181]   016.497.

A selective bibliography of scholarship and some primary works (through c. 1976) for the study of the languages and literatures of Indians (other than the Eskimo) in the United States and Canada. The 3,695 entries are organized alphabetically by author in 16 divisions. The first four are devoted to general topics: bibliography, autobiography (both primary and secondary works), general literature (with sections for collections and anthologies, general studies of Indian authors, types of Indian literature, and general studies of Indian literature), and language (with sections for general studies; lexicography, grammar, and morphology; language classification; glottochronology and lexicostatistics; language and culture; linguists, collecting, recording, and transcribing; interrelationships of Indian languages and their relationships to other languages; sign language). The remaining divisions are devoted to regions, each with sections for literature, language, and tribal groups; under the last heading are separate alphabetical lists for literature and language. An asterisk denotes an important work. Because of the overlapping of regions and tribal groups, users should check the index to locate studies of a particular tribe. Indexed by authors, tribal groups, and subjects, but because of the organization, the subject indexing does not provide adequate access to the entries. Although selective, dated, and emphasizing written literature, this work remains the best general guide to research before 1977 on Indian languages and literatures. Review: Dennis R. Hoilman, *Old Northwest* 4 (1978): 180–82.

Q3880   Ruoff, A. LaVonne Brown. *American Indian Literatures: An Introduction,*
         Bibliographic Review, and Selected Bibliography. New York: MLA, 1990.
            200 pp.   PM155.R86   897.
    A three-part introduction to American Indian literatures. The first is an introduction to the kinds of oral forms and a history of written literatures. The second is an essay review of reference works, anthologies and collections, general studies, scholarship on selected writers, and materials for teaching. The third is a selected bibliography, whose organization copies that of the essay review. Although the essay review and bibliography supersede Ruoff's selective bibliography in *Redefining American Literary History* (Q3695), the latter has the advantage of being annotated (and actually includes most entries in the newer version). The index of subjects and authors unfortunately excludes the selected bibliography. Although selective, this is the most current guide to scholarship on American Indian literatures.

See also

> Etulain, *Bibliographical Guide to the Study of Western American Literature* (Q3670).
> Leary, *Articles on American Literature* (Q3295).
> *Literary History of the United States: Bibliography* (Q3300).
> *MLAIB* (G335): American Literature division through the volume for 1973; American Indian heading in American Literature sections in the volumes for 1974–80; in later volumes, researchers must consult the headings beginning "Native American(s)" and related terms in the subject index and in the online thesaurus.
> Woodress, *Dissertations in American Literature* (Q3320).

Related Topics

Q3885   Clements, William M., and Frances M. Malpezzi, comps. *Native American*
         Folklore, 1879–1979: An Annotated Bibliography. Athens: Swallow, 1984.
            247 pp.   Z1209.C57 [E98.F6]   016.398'08997073.

An annotated bibliography of about 5,500 English-language books and articles (mostly published between 1879 and 1979) on the "oral narratives, songs, chants, prayers, formulas, orations, proverbs, riddles, word play, music, dances, games, and ceremonials" of Native Americans living north of Mexico. Clements and Malpezzi exclude newspaper articles, works for children, and reviews. Entries are listed alphabetically in 12 classified divisions. The first covers general studies in sections for bibliographies and reference works, collections of essays, collections of primary works in various genres, and general studies of genres. Each of the remaining divisions is devoted to a cultural area, with sections for general studies and individual tribal groups. The descriptive annotations (sometimes accompanied by evaluative comments) are succinct yet admirably clear. Two indexes: subjects; scholars. The indispensable guide to scholarship on the folklore of the Native Americans of North America. For recent studies, see section U: Literature-Related Topics and Sources/Folklore and Literature/Guides to Scholarship and Criticism.

See also

America: History and Life (Q3310).
Haywood, *Bibliography of North American Folklore and Folksong* (U5875).
Historical Abstracts (U6500).
Miller, *Folk Music in America* (U5910).
Ruoff, *Redefining American Literary History* (Q3695).
Salzman, *American Studies: An Annotated Bibliography* (Q3335).

PERIODICALS

Guides to Primary Works

Q3895   Littlefield, Daniel F., Jr., and James W. Parins, eds. *American Indian and Alaska Native Newspapers and Periodicals, [1826–1985]*. 3 vols. Historical Guides to the World's Periodicals and Newspapers. Westport: Greenwood, 1984–86.   PN4883.L57   051.

Vol. 1: *1826–1924*. 1984. 482 pp.
Vol. 2: *1925–1970*. 1986. 553 pp.
Vol. 3: *1971–1985*. 1986. 609 pp.

A collection of profiles of "newspapers and periodicals edited or published by American Indians or Alaska Natives and those whose primary purpose was to publish information about contemporary Indians or Alaska Natives." Excludes ethnological, archaeological, historical, Mexican, and Canadian publications. Organized alphabetically by most recent title (or title used when under the control of Indians or Alaska Natives), entries provide a publishing history and overview of content, and cite scholarship, indexing sources, location sources (noting a few actual locations and availability in microform collections), publication information, and editors. Alternate and earlier titles are cross-referenced to main entries. Three appendixes list titles by date of original publication, place of publication, and tribal affiliation. Indexed by persons and subjects.

Complemented by James P. Danky, ed., and Maureen E. Hady, comp., *Native American Periodicals and Newspapers, 1828–1982: Bibliography, Publishing Record, and Holdings* (Westport: Greenwood, 1984, 532 pp.), which is more exhaustive in its coverage and precise in recording holdings but lacks the useful overviews of publishing history and is less thorough and precise in its subject indexing.

Together, these works on Native American periodicals are the essential guides to extensive but underutilized sources, many of which are omitted from standard union lists.

See also

> Sec. K: Periodicals/Directories, and Periodicals/Union Lists.
> *United States Newspaper Program National Union List* (Q3405).

GENRES

Fiction

Some works in sections L: Genres/Fiction and Q: American Literature/General/Genres/Fiction are useful for research on fiction by American Indians.

Guides to Scholarship and Criticism

Q3920   Colonnese, Tom, and Louis Owens. *American Indian Novelists: An Annotated Critical Bibliography.* Garland Reference Library of the Humanities 384. New York: Garland, 1985. 161 pp.   Z1229.I52 C65 [PS153.I52]   016.813′009′897.

A selective annotated bibliography of works (published through c. 1983) by and about 21 novelists. Under each novelist are sections for book-length primary works (with separate chronological lists of novels and other books), selected shorter works (organized by genre, then alphabetically by title), and selected studies (with separate lists of criticism — organized by primary work and including reviews — and biographical sources). Novels are accompanied by plot summaries, and studies of novels are accompanied by descriptive annotations; both are wordy and wooden. Indexed by novelists and titles. Highly selective and marred by an inadequate discussion of criteria governing selection of both novelists and studies, *American Indian Novelists* does little more than offer a place to begin research. Review: Jerome Klinkowitz, *American Indian Culture and Research Journal* 8.2 (1984): 58–60.

Prose

Guides to Primary Works

Q3925   Brumble, H. David, III. *An Annotated Bibliography of American Indian and Eskimo Autobiographies.* Lincoln: U of Nebraska P, 1981. 177 pp. Z1209.B78 [E89]   016.970004′97.

———. "A Supplement to *An Annotated Bibliography of American Indian and Eskimo Autobiographies*." *Western American Literature* 17 (1982): 243–60.

———. *American Indian Autobiography.* Berkeley: U of California P, 1988. 211–58.   E89.5.B78   970.004′97.

A bibliography of some 600 first-person narratives written by North American Indians and Eskimos or transcribed and edited by other persons. Although largely confined to published autobiographies (through c. 1987), the work includes a few in manuscript or on tape. Organized alphabetically by the commonly used name of the auto-biographer, entries provide collaborator, editor, or amanuensis; gender, if not apparent from the name; title; publication information or location of tape or manuscript; birth-date; date of composition; tribal affiliation; an account of how the narrative was com-posed; and a detailed description of content. Three indexes: editors, anthropologists, ghostwriters, and amanuenses; tribes; subjects. Although it is imprecise and insufficiently detailed in subject indexing and incomplete in cross-referencing Indian and Anglo names, Brumble's compilation offers the fullest record of these autobiographical nar-ratives, many of which are hidden in anthropological or historical studies. Review: Ralph Maud, *Canadian Review of American Studies* 14 (1983): 71–77.

For autobiographies published or reprinted between 1980 and 2000, see Stuhr-Rommereim, *Autobiographies by Americans of Color, 1980–1994*, and Iwabuchi, *Auto-biographies by Americans of Color, 1995–2000* (Q3705).

Asian American Literature

GUIDES TO SCHOLARSHIP AND CRITICISM

Q3940   Cheung, King-Kok, and Stan Yogi. *Asian American Literature: An Annotated Bibliography.* New York: MLA, 1988. 276 pp.   Z1229.A75 C47 [PS153.A84]   016.81′08′089507.

A bibliography of works (through July 1987) by and about writers of Asian descent resident in the United States and Canada as well as those living elsewhere who have written about the experiences of Asians in North America. Includes autobiographies, essays, and popular fiction but excludes publications by native Pacific Islanders, works in Asian languages not translated into English, individual poems in anthologies or periodicals, manuscripts, and works in student publications. The approximately 3,400 entries are organized in seven divisions: bibliographies and reference works, anthologies, periodicals, primary works (with sections for national groups and children's literature; each national group has separate lists of prose, poetry, and drama), scholarship and criticism (with the sections for general studies and national groups divided into three parts: books, theses, and dissertations; articles; and interviews, profiles, and commen-tary), fiction about Asians or Asian Americans by non-Asians, and background studies. Some works have descriptive annotations that sometimes cite reviews; unfortunately, most of the annotations are too brief to convey an adequate sense of content. Four indexes: writers; scholars; reviewers; editors, translators, and illustrators. Although it is frustratingly brief in its annotations and less accessible than it should be because of the lack of a subject index, *Asian American Literature* fills a major gap in reference sources for the literatures of the United States and Canada.

Recent work by and studies of Asian American writers can be found in *An Inter-ethnic Companion to Asian American Literature*, ed. Cheung (Cambridge: Cambridge UP, 1997, 414 pp.). The surveys, covering literature by Americans of Chinese, Filipino, Japanese, Korean, South Asian, and Vietnamese descent, are complemented by a selec-tive bibliography.

See also

> *MLAIB* (G335): See the headings beginning "Asian American(s)" in the subject index to post-1980 volumes and in the online thesaurus.
> Ruoff, *Redefining American Literary History* (Q3695).

Hispanic American Literature

Some works in section Q: American Literature/General are useful to research in Hispanic American literatures.

GUIDES TO REFERENCE WORKS

Q3970 Robinson, Barbara J., and J. Cordell Robinson, *The Mexican American: A Critical Guide to Research Aids.* Foundations in Library and Information Science 1. Greenwich: JAI, 1980. 287 pp. Z1361.M4 R63 [E184.M5] 016.973'046872.

A selective, annotated guide to reference works (in English and Spanish, and published between 1857 and 1978) on the cultural, historical, social, political, artistic, or economic milieu of Mexican Americans. The authors cover both published and unpublished works (including dissertations, theses, and mimeographed material) and emphasize the nineteenth and twentieth centuries. The 668 entries are listed alphabetically by author in two classified divisions: general works and subject bibliographies. The first has sections for general bibliographies, library guides, biographical sources, genealogical sources, statistical sources, directories, dictionaries, newspaper and periodical guides, and audiovisual sources; the second for education, folklore, history, labor, linguistics, literature, social and behavioral sciences, and women. Each section is preceded by an evaluative overview of the reference sources. The full annotations are largely descriptive and focus on scope, content, and organization. Three indexes: authors; titles; subjects. Although it is now dated, includes several ephemeral and superseded works, and lacks an adequate explanation of criteria governing selection, this work remains a useful guide to important reference sources for the study of Mexican Americans.

Julio A. Martínez and Ada Burns, *Mexican Americans: An Annotated Bibliography of Bibliographies* (Saratoga: R and E, 1984, 132 pp.), is an important complement because of its full evaluative annotations and coverage of works through 1983.

Less thorough than *Mexican Americans* but including Cuban American and continental Puerto Rican literature as well as sociolinguistics is David William Foster, ed., *Sourcebook of Hispanic Culture in the United States* (Chicago: Amer. Lib. Assn., 1982, 352 pp.). Coverage is very selective and rarely extends beyond 1975.

GUIDES TO SCHOLARSHIP AND CRITICISM

Serial Bibliographies

Q3973 *HAPI Online.* UCLA Latin American Center. Online. 9 Jan. 2006 <http://hapi.gseis.ucla.edu>. Updated monthly.

> *HAPI: Hispanic American Periodicals Index [1970–].* Los Angeles: U of California, Los Angeles, Latin Amer. Center 1977– . Annual. Z1605.H16 [F1408] 016.98'0005. CD-ROM.
>
> *HAPI: Hispanic American Periodicals Index: Articles in English, 1976–1980.* Ed. Barbara G. Valk. Los Angeles: U of California, Los Angeles, Latin Amer. Center; Westwood: Faxon, 1984. 403 pp. Z1605.H6 [F1408] 016.98'0005.

A database that indexes the content of about 500 periodicals on Latin Americans and Hispanics in the United States, with coverage extending to all areas except the hard sciences and technology. Records can be searched by keyword, document author, title, subject (based on a thesaurus), and journal; searches can be limited by date and language and to articles with full-text links or about United States Hispanics only. Records can be exported by e-mail or downloaded into bibliographic software programs. In the print version, entries are currently organized in two parts: subjects; authors of articles and literary works (coverage of book reviews was discontinued after the volume for 2001). The substantial coverage of literary periodicals makes *HAPI* the best source for identifying current studies of Hispanic American literature.

Chicano Database (U of California, Berkeley, Chicano Studies Collection, Ethnic Studies Lib., [online through RLG Union Catalog (E230)]; updated quarterly), includes records (a few with abstracts) for books, dissertations, and articles since the 1960s on Hispanic American literature, language, and folklore. Its coverage is much less current than that by *HAPI*.

Other Bibliographies

Q3975   Eger, Ernestina N. *A Bibliography of Criticism of Contemporary Chicano Literature.* Berkeley: Chicano Lib., U of California, 1982. 295 pp.
Z1229.M48 E36 [PS153.M4]   016.81'08'086872073.

A bibliography of books, articles, theses, dissertations, commercial audio- and videotapes, reviews, newspaper articles, unpublished convention papers, and some works in progress from 1960 to mid-1979 on Chicano and Mexican American literature of the same period. The 2,181 entries are organized alphabetically in 12 divisions: collections of critical essays; bibliographies; general studies; the Chicana as writer, critic, or literary character; general criticism; linguistic studies; poetry; fiction; theater (with sections for general studies, Teatro Campesino and Luis Valdez, other *teatros*, and theater festivals); literary festivals; individual authors; and anthologies. Studies of literature before 1960 are listed in a brief appendix; another appendix serves as a directory of Chicano literary periodicals. Two indexes: scholars; titles. Although there are several omissions as well as duplicate entries for subsequently published convention papers, Eger is the fullest list of scholarship through mid-1979. Review: Hensley C. Woodbridge, *Bilingual Review/Revista bilingüe* 10 (1983): 69–72.

Some recent general studies—but not those of individual authors—are listed in Roberto G. Trujillo and Andres Rodriguez, comps., *Literatura Chicana: Creative and Critical Writings through 1984* (Oakland: Floricanto, 1985, 95 pp.); however, numerous omissions, poor organization, and a confusing description of scope make this source an unsatisfactory guide to critical works. More useful as a supplement to Eger is Julio A. Martínez and Francisco A. Lomelí, eds., *Chicano Literature: A Reference Guide* (Westport: Greenwood, 1985, 492 pp.), a collection of essays with selective bibliographies on established authors and some literary periods, genres, and topics, along with a chronology of Chicano literature from 1539 to 1982 and a glossary of Chicano literary terms. Entrants are indexed in *Biography and Genealogy Master Index* (J565). Unfortunately, principles governing selection are not clearly stated, and many entries are poorly written.

See also

Secs. G: Serial Bibliographies, Indexes, and Abstracts and H: Guides to Dissertations and Theses.
Etulain, *Bibliographical Guide to the Study of Western American Literature* (Q3670).

> *MLAIB* (G335): Until the volume for 1972, see the American Literature division; in the volumes for 1972–80, see the Mexican American heading in American Literature sections; in later volumes, see the headings beginning "Hispanic American(s)" and "Mexican American(s)" (and related headings) in the subject index and in the online thesaurus.
>
> Ruoff, *Redefining American Literary History* (Q3695).

LANGUAGE

Guides to Scholarship

Q3980   Teschner, Richard V., gen. ed. *Spanish and English of United States Hispanos: A Critical, Annotated, Linguistic Bibliography.* Arlington: Center for Applied Linguistics, 1975. 352 pp.   Z2695.D5 T47 [PC4826] 016.467'9'73.

> Bills, Garland D., Jerry R. Craddock, and Richard V. Teschner. "Current Research on the Language(s) of U. S. Hispanos." *Hispania* 60 (1977): 347–58. PC4001.H7   460'.5.

A bibliography of publications, dissertations, theses, and some unpublished papers and reports (through January 1977 in the supplement) on the Spanish and English used by Hispanic citizens or residents of the mainland United States. Excludes most discussions of language teaching. In the 1975 volume, entries are organized alphabetically in divisions for general studies, Mexican Americans (subdivided by region), Puerto Ricans, Cubans, Louisiana Canary Islanders, Spaniards, and Sephardic Jews. Each division has sections, when appropriate, for bibliographies, general studies, sociolinguistics, textbooks, Spanish phonology, Spanish grammar, Spanish lexicon, onomastics, English influence on Spanish, Spanish influence on English, English as used by the group, and code-switching. Each section begins with lists of the most important works and cross-references. Annotations typically combine detailed description with trenchant evaluation, and the introduction surveys trends in research. The author index utilizes a confusing system of sigla. (The supplement is merely an unannotated author list.) The extensive evaluative annotations in the 1975 volume make it a valuable guide to scholarship on Spanish and English as used by Hispanics in the United States. For recent studies, see *MLAIB* (G335), *Bibliographie linguistique* (U6010), and *LLBA: Linguistics and Language Behavior Abstracts* (U6015). Review: Hensley C. Woodbridge, *Modern Language Journal* 60 (1976): 316.

See also

> Eger, *Bibliography of Criticism of Contemporary Chicano Literature* (Q3975).

GENRES

Fiction

Guides to Primary Works

Q3985   Leonard, Kathy S. *Bibliographic Guide to Chicana and Latina Narrative.* Bibliographies and Indexes in Women's Studies 31. Westport: Praeger, 2003. 273 pp.   Z1229.M48 L46 [PS153.M4]   016.8109'9287'08968.

An index to short fiction in anthologies or collections, novels, and biographies or autobiographies written by Latina or Chicana authors for an adolescent or older audience and published in English or Spanish between the early 1940s and 2002. The approximately 2,745 works by nearly 600 authors are organized alphabetically in five indexes: authors and titles; titles and authors; anthologies; novels; autobiographies and biographies. The lists of titles and authors (alphabetized according to English-language conventions) are keyed to the other three indexes; novels and autobiographies and biographies include a one- or two-sentence description of content. The list of novels inconsistently cites translations and editions (e.g., the two entries for Sandra Cisneros's *The House on Mango Street* are for the 1999 Knopf edition and a 1994 Spanish translation; the German, Italian, and Chinese translations and earlier English-language editions are not included); the practice of listing translations separately with virtually the same annotation wastes space. The autobiographies and biographies list is something of a hodgepodge that includes interviews and biographical dictionaries with entries on — not by — Chicana and Latina authors. Although marred by inconsistencies and omissions and a lack of explanation of what denominates Chicana and Latina, in need of a good copyediting, and stronger in its coverage of works published in the United States, *Bibliographic Guide to Chicana and Latina Narrative* offers a serviceable guide to the subject.

Jewish American Literature

GUIDES TO SCHOLARSHIP AND CRITICISM

Q3990   Nadel, Ira Bruce. *Jewish Writers of North America: A Guide to Information Sources.* American Studies Information Guide Series 8. Detroit: Gale, 1981. 493 pp.   Z1229.J4 N32 [PS153.J4]   016.810'8'08924.

A selective bibliography of works by and about American and Canadian Jewish writers chosen for their "literary excellence, cultural significance, and historical importance." Coverage extends through the late 1970s. The 3,291 entries are organized in four divisions: general works (with sections for bibliographies, biographical sources, indexes, library and manuscript collections, literary history, general criticism, and anthologies), poets, fiction writers, and dramatists (with sections for reference works and criticism and theater history). Each division or section has separate lists for American and Canadian literature and writers. Under each author are lists of bibliographies, primary works (chronologically by genre), and criticism. Appendix A is devoted to Yiddish literature in English translation, appendix B to a list of other Jewish writers. The descriptive annotations are brief but generally adequate; however, many entries are not annotated. Three indexes: authors; titles; subjects. Users should note that some writers appear under more than one genre. Although marred by an inadequate explanation of scope and the failure to index authors and topics mentioned in annotations to the first division, this work offers the fullest single guide to North American Jewish writers. Many studies of American and Canadian Jewish literature can be identified through the headings beginning with "Jewish" in the subject index to post-1980 volumes of *MLAIB* (G335) or in the online thesaurus.

Additional English-language studies of and works by (published through 1988) 62 Jewish American fiction writers of the nineteenth and twentieth centuries can be found in Gloria L. Cronin, Blaine H. Hall, and Connie Lamb, *Jewish American Fiction*

Writers: An Annotated Bibliography, Garland Reference Library of the Humanities 972 (New York: Garland, 1991, 1,233 pp.). A majority of the entries have been culled from standard databases and indexes, and the excessive number of pages needlessly consumed by annotations of book reviews (while dissertations and general studies are listed without comment) should instead be devoted to an index.

Early American Literature (to 1800)

Many works in section Q: American Literature/General are important to research in early American literature.

Guides to Reference Works

For a selective overview of World Wide Web resources for the study and teaching of early American literature and culture, see Joanna Brooks, "New Media's Prospect: A Review of Web Resources in Early American Studies," *Early American Literature* 39 (2004): 577–90.

Literary Handbooks, Dictionaries, and Encyclopedias

See

> *Blackwell Companion to the Enlightenment* (M2218).

Guides to Primary Works

Q4000 Alden, John, and Dennis Channing Landis, eds. *European Americana: A Chronological Guide to Works Printed in Europe Relating to the Americas, 1493–1776 [i.e., 1750].* 6 vols. New Canaan: Readex, 1980–97. Z1203.E87 [E18.82]   016.97.

> Vol. 1: *1493–1600.* 1980. 467 pp.
> Vol. 2: *1601–1650.* 1982. 954 pp.
> Vol. 3: *1651–1675.* 1996. 682 pp.
> Vol. 4: *1676–1700.* 1997. 711 pp.
> Vol. 5: *1701–1725.* 1987. 597 pp.
> Vol. 6: *1726–1750.* 1988. 852 pp.

A chronological guide to separately published works and editions thereof printed in Europe and related to the Americas (here defined as North and South America, Greenland, and the Caribbean islands). Based on the holdings of important North American and European collections and listings in several bibliographies, *European Americana* includes in vol. 1 many literary and other works with only incidental references to the area; in later volumes, the scope narrows to exclude most works that have only a passing mention of the New World. Users must consult the Guide to Use in vol. 4 to find the fullest discussion of scope and editorial principles. Organized alphabetically within each year by author, corporate author, or title of anonymous work, entries provide title, imprint, final page number, format, a note on American content if not clear from the title, references to standard bibliographies, and locations. Users must remember that much information is taken unverified from other sources and that titles and imprints are frequently edited rather than exact transcriptions. Additions are printed in vol. 1, pp. 261–66, and vol. 2, pp. 526–27. Each volume has three indexes: geographical index of printers and booksellers; alphabetical index of printers and booksellers; authors, titles, and subjects. The Alden-Landis *European Americana* supersedes Henry Harrisse, *Bibliotheca Americana Vetustissima: A Description of Works Relating to America Published between the Years 1492 and 1551* (New York: Philes, 1866, 519 pp.), and *Additions* (Paris: Tross, 1872, 199 pp.), and, for the volumes published, represents a major improvement in coverage, organization, and accuracy over Sabin, *Bibliotheca Americana* (Q4015); for example, supposedly fewer than one-quarter of the entries in volumes 3–4 also appear in Sabin. Although such a work cannot be comprehensive and inevitably perpetuates many of the errors of its sources, its coverage, organization, and indexing make *European Americana* the indispensable source for studying the impact of the Americas on Europe. Reviews: (vol. 1) David B. Quinn, *Renaissance Quarterly* 34 (1981): 570–72; (vols. 1–2) J. A. Leo Lemay, *Resources for American Literary Study* 13 (1983): 26–32; Edwin Wolf 2nd, *Papers of the Bibliographical Society of America* 78 (1984): 91–95.

Q4005   *Early American Imprints, Series I: Evans, 1639–1800.* Readex. Online. 26 Jan. 2005 <http://infoweb.newsbank.com>.

Evans, Charles. *American Bibliography: A Chronological Dictionary of All Books, Pamphlets, and Periodical Publications Printed in the United States of America from the Genesis of Printing in 1639 down to and Including the Year 1820 [i.e., 1800]* (Evans). 14 vols. (vols. 1–12) Chicago: Privately printed, 1903–34; (vols. 13–14) Worcester: Amer. Antiquarian Soc., 1955–59. (Vol. 13 is by Clifford Shipton; vol. 14, by Roger Pattrell Bristol.) Z1215.E92   015.73.

A bibliographical database and digital archive based on Evans, *American Bibliography*, and Bristol's *Supplement* (see below), that reproduces the c. 36,000 works in the original microprint and microform version of *Early American Imprints* along with about 1,200 additional titles. Users can view digitized facsimiles of pages as well as search ASCII text generated by Optical Character Recognition scanning. In the basic search mode, documents can be searched by citation, full text, title, subject (i.e., Library of Congress subject headings), genre, author, place of publication, publisher, document number (i.e., Evans number), and date of publication; the advanced search mode allows users to combine up to two fields with full text and date. Given the treatment of attributions of authorship, users should search for an author in both the Author and Citation Text fields. Because of the spelling practices in the period covered and because of scanning errors in the ASCII text underlying the digital images, users must read the discussion of Irregular Spelling under Search Hints before attempting a full-text search. Users can also browse by author, place of publication, history of printing (with separate lists of publishers, printers, and booksellers), language, and selected genres and subjects.

A search returns records in Evans number order (i.e., chronologically—but see the discussion below of problems with the chronological sequence in Evans); an individual record reformats the enhanced cataloging copy created for the microform version of *Early American Imprints* (which cites Evans number along with other standard bibliographies, albeit in abbreviated forms that will mystify the majority of users). The original Evans entry (along with identification of the copy reproduced) is hidden under a Document Source link at the end of the Table of Contents.

Copies can be downloaded as PDF files (file transfer can be slow, and a maximum of 25 pages can be downloaded at a time), printed, or saved to a personal collection for later access.

Inevitably, many of the images are only partly legible because of flaws in the underlying copy or problems with the original filming, and thus keyword searches of the full text frequently return false hits (e.g., in a search for *Macbeth*, three of the first ten records show false hits on *teacheth* or *toucheth*), but this resource brings to the computer screen the text of thousands of rare volumes and, because of the search capabilities, makes possible studies that would otherwise be unfeasible because of the time it would take to identify and acquire the necessary books. Review: Norman Desmarais, *Charleston Advisor* 6.2 (2004): 15–17, 27 Jan. 2005 <http://www.charlestonco.com>.

While *Early American Imprints* vastly improves access to information hidden away in Evans (especially anonymous works), it replicates silently many of the limitations and quirks of its progenitor. Thus a thorough familiarity with *American Bibliography* is a prerequisite for informed use of the digital archive. And the user of any digital archive must be aware that a copy reproduced may have leaves supplied from another copy, be of an edition that is extant in more than one issue or state, or be incomplete.

American Bibliography is a preliminary retrospective national bibliography of printed works (excluding tickets, invitations, circulars, and forms designed to be completed in manuscript). Organized by year of publication, then alphabetically by author, corporate author, or title of anonymous work, the 39,162 entries typically cite title, imprint, pagination, size or format, locations, and contemporary auction values. A few are accompanied by bibliographical, biographical, or historical notes.

Each volume has two indexes (authors and anonymous titles; subjects). However, the author and title indexes are superseded by the *Index* (vol. 14), which lists pseudonyms, corporate authors, and authors; includes titles (as well as running titles and half titles recorded by Evans); and adds names of people, ships, and Indian tribes mentioned in titles. Because of inconsistencies in the treatment of main headings for some kinds of works, erroneous dating, and incorrect attributions of authorship, the *Index* frequently offers the only convenient way to locate unsigned publications. The History of Printing tab in *Early American Imprints* offers far better access to individuals in the book trade than do the lists of printers and publishers in vols. 1–12 or in Bristol, *Index of Printers, Publishers, and Booksellers Indicated by Charles Evans in His* American Bibliography (Charlottesville: Bibliog. Soc. of the U of Virginia, 1961, 172 pp.). Items in Evans and *Early American Imprints* containing printed musical notation are indexed in Donald L. Hixon, *Music in Early America: A Bibliography of Music in Evans* (Metuchen: Scarecrow, 1970, 607 pp.).

To make effective use of Evans, researchers must be aware of its major deficiencies:

1. Because of numerous typographical errors and because much information is copied without verification from secondary sources — including other bibliographies, advertisements, and booksellers', auction, and library catalogs — as many as 30% of the entries are inaccurate, especially in recording titles, publication information, and date. Particularly vexing is Evans's practice of supplying descriptive titles based on advertisements. Although Evans does not identify secondhand entries, Shipton encloses within brackets titles not seen

or "described by a careful bibliographer" and derives entries from booksellers'
or auction catalogs only when a title page is reproduced.

2. Anonymous works are difficult to locate because Evans frequently misattri-
butes authorship, place, publisher, or date, or lists such works under inconsistent or peculiar corporate author headings without supplying title cross-
references. Only vol. 13 identifies attributions (within brackets) and
cross-references titles of anonymous works. By utilizing more accurate, consistent corporate headings and listing short titles, the *Index* (vol. 14) allows
for the location of many anonymous publications.

3. Regardless of the number of copies extant, Evans typically locates only one or
two and sometimes omits locations to save an additional line of type. (Vol.
13 provides more locations.) To decipher Evans's location symbols, see John
C. Munger, "Evans's *American Bibliography:* Tentative Check List of the Library Location Symbols," *Bulletin of the New York Public Library* 40 (1936):
665–68. (In *Early American Imprints*, this information is hidden away at
Help/How to Search/Advanced Search Tips/Owning Sources.)

4. Several works are listed out of chronological sequence because they were discovered after publication of the appropriate volume. And many undatable
publications are grouped under "1800."

Not surprisingly, there are numerous ghosts and duplicate entries. Also, many works
or editions identified in studies and catalogs as "not in Evans" are actually there but
difficult to locate.

The following works supplement Evans:

"American Bibliographical Notes." *Proceedings of the American Antiquarian
Society* 82 (1972): 45–64; 83 (1973): 261–73; 87 (1977): 409–15; 88
(1978): 90–119, 327–28; 89 (1979): 155–57; 93 (1983): 197–221. A
series of variously authored notes and lists that provide numerous additions
and corrections to Evans.

Bristol, Roger P. *Supplement to Charles Evans' American Bibliography.* Charlottesville: UP of Virginia for Bibliog. Soc. of Amer. and Bibliog. Soc. of
U of Virginia, 1970. 636 pp. Collects from a variety of sources some
11,200 additions, with locations and entry numbers for those reproduced
in the Readex microfilm series. Addenda appear on pp. 631–34. Separately indexed as *Index to* Supplement to Charles Evans' *American Bibliography* (Charlottesville: UP of Virginia for Bibliog. Soc. of U of Virginia,
1971, 191 pp.). Review: J. A. Leo Lemay, *Early American Literature* 8
(1973): 66–77.

Federal Copyright Records, 1790–1800. Ed. James Gilreath. Comp. Elizabeth
Carter Wills. Washington: Lib. of Congress, 1987. 166 pp. A transcript
of surviving records for the period.

Shipton, Clifford K., and James E. Mooney. *National Index of American
Imprints through 1800: The Short-Title Evans.* 2 vols. Worcester: Amer.
Antiquarian Soc. and Barre, 1969. An index to the microform version of
Early American Imprints that makes numerous corrections to Evans and
in some instances cites the sources of his errors. It is particularly useful
for identifying duplicate entries. Review: J. A. Leo Lemay, *Early American
Literature* 8 (1973): 66–77.

American imprints are also included in the *Short-Title Catalogues* (M1377, M1990,
and M1995), which are typically more thorough and accurate than Evans. Book catalogs

are more thoroughly covered in Winans, *Descriptive Checklist of Book Catalogues* (U5410).

Despite its manifold deficiencies and incompleteness, Evans, and its supplements currently offer the fullest record of early American imprints; provide an invaluable resource for investigating the intellectual milieu of works, surveying publishing trends, identifying works and editions by standard reference number, and locating copies; and form the basis for a fuller, more sophisticated and accurate retrospective bibliography. Only because of this preliminary bibliography has it been possible to make readily available in digital form a majority of works printed before 1801 in the United States. Scholars should also search the North American Imprints Program database (Q4010), which will eventually supersede Evans and its supplements.

The chronological record is continued by Shaw, *American Bibliography* (Q4125), and Shoemaker, *Checklist of American Imprints* (Q4130).

Bibliography of American Imprints to 1901, 92 vols. (New York: Saur, 1993), conflates entries from the American Antiquarian Society catalog and RLG Union Catalog (E230) into a title list with separate author, subject, place, and date indexes; it is notable only for the amount of shelf space it wastes.

Q4010   North American Imprints Program (NAIP). Amer. Antiquarian Soc.
　　　　<http://www.americanantiquarian.org/naip.htm>.

A machine-readable union catalog whose goal is to record all extant books, pamphlets, and broadsides (but not periodicals, newspapers, and engraved materials) printed through 1876 in what is now the United States and Canada. Entries for works examined by NAIP staff contain a full transcription of title page and imprint, detailed statement of pagination, collation, notes, and references to published bibliographies. Descriptions based on reports by cooperating libraries, *Early American Imprints* (Q4005), or published bibliographies are less detailed. Records are being incorporated into the *ESTC* (M1377) database and can be searched through the American Antiquarian Society's OPAC (http://catalog.mwa.org), which supports special indexes that allow searching by genre, series, illustrator, printer, publisher, bookseller, place, and date.. Eventually the database will supersede Tremaine, *Bibliography of Canadian Imprints* (R4615), and Evans, *American Bibliography* and its various supplements (Q4005) and continuations.

Q4015   Sabin, Joseph, Wilberforce Eames, and R. W. G. Vail, eds. *Bibliotheca*
　　　　Americana: A Dictionary of Books Relating to America, from Its Discovery to
　　　　the Present Time (Sabin). 29 vols. New York: Sabin, 1868–1936.
　　　　(Originally issued in parts.) Z1201.S2 015.73.

A bibliography of publications related to the political, governmental, economic, social, intellectual, and religious history of the Western Hemisphere since 1492. Until vol. 21 (1929–31), Sabin includes potentially anything even remotely touching on the Americas published up to the date of publication of a part (except that post-1800 newspapers and broadsides are generally excluded); in succeeding volumes, both scope and coverage are substantially reduced. With vol. 21, the cutoff date becomes 1876; with pt. 130 (in vol. 22 [1931–32]), the cutoff date is 1860 (earlier for certain kinds of publications—e.g., 1800 for most literary works, but 1830 for those "of historical importance"); with pt. 141 (in vol. 24 [1933–34]), virtually nothing published after 1840 is included. Researchers must be certain to read the explanation in vol. 29, pp. x–xi, of the successive narrowing in scope and coverage.

Entries are listed alphabetically by author or, for anonymous works, by title, locale, or subject. An entry includes title; publication information; size or format; pagination; occasional notes on content, editions, related titles, scholarship, reviews, other works by the author, or references to booksellers' or auction catalogs; and locations (more consistently and fully in the later volumes; location symbols are listed in vol. 29, pp. 299–305). References in the notes more than double the 106,413 numbered entries.

Users must be aware of the deficiencies of Sabin: there are numerous omissions; the volumes through 13 (1881) admit many works that can hardly be classified as Americana, but with Eames's editorship (beginning in pt. 83 [1884]), standards defining coverage are tighter; many errors exist because of Sabin's reliance on unsound secondary sources and frequent use of wrappers as sources for titles (accuracy improves under Eames's editorship); entries are not standardized and there are several duplicate entries.

John Edgar Molnar, comp., *Author-Title Index to Joseph Sabin's* Dictionary of Books Relating to America, 3 vols. (Metuchen: Scarecrow, 1974), remedies many of the difficulties in locating works in Sabin by indexing authors, editors, compilers, illustrators, corporate authors, main titles, series titles, and selected subtitles and alternative titles, as well as by identifying several anonymous and pseudonymous authors.

Despite its incompleteness and manifold deficiencies, Sabin remains the single most extensive bibliography of early works related to the Western Hemisphere.

Many works in Sabin are included in the digital archive *American History and Culture Online: Sabin Americana 1500–1926* (Thomson Gale; online; 26 Feb. 2006 <http://infotrac.galegroup.com/galenet>). Basic Search allows users to limit keyword searches of full text, authors, or titles by publication date; Advanced Search allows users to search by document number (MARC, Sabin, or Thomson Gale number) or to limit combined searches of authors, titles, full text, front matter, main text, indexes, subjects, persons as subjects, geographic subjects, publishers, and places of publication by date, language, serial title, and kinds of illustrations. Advanced Search also allows for fuzzy searches—an especially valuable feature for searching documents published before spelling became normalized. Users can also browse lists of authors and titles. Images (which vary in quality and legibility as expected in archives produced from microfiche) can be saved as PDF files or printed. The breadth of coverage and the powerful search engine make possible numerous studies that heretofore would have consumed years of research or would have been simply untenable.

For more thorough coverage of European imprints through 1750, see Alden, *European Americana* (Q4000); some areas are more fully treated in bibliographies devoted to a region or country (consult Besterman, *World Bibliography of Bibliographies* [D155], and *Bibliographic Index* [D145]).

Lawrence S. Thompson, *The New Sabin: Books Described by Joseph Sabin and His Successors, Now Described Again on the Basis of Examination of Originals, and Fully Indexed by Title, Subject, Joint Authors, and Institutions and Agencies*, 10 vols. and cumulative index (Troy: Whitston, 1974–86), is misleadingly titled. Rather than a revision of Sabin, the work is merely a set of separate lists of and indexes to large-scale microform collections (including Wright, *American Fiction* [Q4180]). The entries consist of information taken from catalog cards prepared for the collections (and not from the compiler's personal examination of original copies). Cumulatively indexed by subjects, titles, joint authors, and corporate bodies. Although restricted to publications available in microform collections, awkwardly organized, and lacking cross-references to Sabin, *New Sabin* adds as well as corrects numerous entries and offers useful, but limited, subject access to works about the Americas.

See also

Boswell, *Check List of Americana in* A Short-Title Catalogue (M1990a).
English Short Title Catalogue (M1377).

Pollard, *Short-Title Catalogue, 1475–1640* (M1990).
Wing, *Short-Title Catalogue, 1641–1700* (M1995).

Guides to Scholarship and Criticism

SURVEYS OF RESEARCH

See

> *American Literary Scholarship* (Q3265): chapter on literature to 1800.
> Harbert, *Fifteen American Authors before 1900* (Q3280).

SERIAL BIBLIOGRAPHIES

See

> *ABELL* (G340): English Literature/Seventeenth Century and Eighteenth Century
> sections.
> *ECCB: The Eighteenth Century Current Bibliography* (M2245).
> *MLAIB* (G335): American Literature division in the volumes for 1922–25;
> American III: Seventeenth and Eighteenth Centuries (1607–1815) in the vol-
> umes for 1926–28; American III: Seventeenth and Eighteenth Centuries in
> the volumes for 1929–40; American II: Seventeenth and Eighteenth Centuries
> in the volumes for 1941–80; and American Literature/1600–1699 and 1700–
> 1799 (or any larger chronological section that encompasses either century) in
> volumes after 1980. Researchers must also check the headings beginning
> "American" and "Colonial" in the subject index to post-1980 volumes and in
> the online thesaurus.
> "Some Current Publications," *Restoration* (M2250).

OTHER BIBLIOGRAPHIES

See

> Rubin, *Bibliographical Guide to the Study of Southern Literature* (Q3625).
> Wages, *Seventy-Four Writers of the Colonial South* (Q3625a).

THESES AND DISSERTATIONS

Q4020   Montgomery, Michael S., comp. *American Puritan Studies: An Annotated
        Bibliography of Dissertations, 1882–1981.* Bibliographies and Indexes in
        American History 1. Westport: Greenwood, 1984. 419 pp.
        Z1251.E1 A54 [F7]   016.974′02.
     An annotated bibliography of 940 dissertations accepted through 1981 by Amer-
ican, Canadian, British, and German universities on American Puritanism from c. 1620 to
c. 1730. Besides literature and language, this work encompasses philosophy, psychology,

politics, history, geography, religion, recreation, economics, sociology, law, education, music, art, science, medicine, and military affairs. Arranged chronologically by date of degree, entries record author, title, degree, institution, and pagination. The typically full annotations cite *ProQuest Dissertations and Theses* (H465); identify full, partial, or revised publication as a monograph (but not article); and note when a dissertation is not extant. Descriptions, which consist largely of quotations from introductions or abstracts and/or a list of contents, are derived (in order of preference) from published versions, printed abstracts, or the dissertations themselves, and frequently note parts not appearing in a published version. Four indexes: authors; short titles; institutions; subjects. *American Puritan Studies* is valuable for its compilation and indexing of entries in the standard national lists of dissertations, annotation of numerous works not abstracted elsewhere, and identification of published versions. For dissertations after 1981, see section H: Guides to Dissertations and Theses.

RELATED TOPICS

Q4025   Gephart, Ronald M., comp. *Revolutionary America, 1763–1789: A Bibliography.* 2 vols. Washington: Lib. of Congress, 1984.   Z1238.G43 [E208]   016.9733.

A selective, yet extensive, bibliography of primary and secondary works (through December 1972) related to the Revolutionary period. Although journal articles, theses, and dissertations are included, selection is limited to holdings of the Library of Congress. The 14,810 entries are organized alphabetically by author or title of anonymous work in most of the 12 extensively classified divisions: bibliographies and reference works (with sections for subject bibliographies, catalogs of eighteenth-century imprints, and guides to manuscript collections); general studies; the British Empire and the American Revolution; the colonies on the eve of independence; the West; the war, 1775–83; loyalists; diplomacy and other international aspects of the Revolution; confederation and consolidation of the Revolution; the Constitution, 1787–89; economic, social, and intellectual life (with sections on printers, newspapers, books, and libraries; literature; and fine arts); and biographical sources. Fewer than 40% of the entries are accompanied by descriptive annotations that frequently cite related works. The work is indexed by names and some subjects, but users must study the explanation of indexing procedures on p. 1,469 before searching the index. Restricting coverage to Library of Congress holdings and works published before 1973 results in the omission of some important studies, especially in the sections related to literature, and the inclusion of several works of dubious value; even so, Gephart provides an important guide to scholarship and primary materials that range well on either side of the period 1763–89.

See also

Pargellis, *Bibliography of British History: The Eighteenth Century* (M2260).

Biographical Dictionaries

Q4030   Levernier, James A., and Douglas R. Wilmes, eds. *American Writers before 1800: A Biographical and Critical Dictionary.* 3 vols. Westport: Greenwood, 1983.   PS185.A4   810'.9'001.

A collection of biographical-bibliographical-critical essays on 786 representative writers. Each essay consists of four parts: a list of major works, biography, critical estimate, and list of selected studies (to c. 1982). Concluding the work are a chronology (1492–1800) and three appendixes (lists of writers by year of birth, place of birth, and principal residence). Indexed by persons and subjects; entrants are also indexed in *Biography and Genealogy Master Index* (J565). Although the essays are uneven in quality, several incorporate recent discoveries. Overall this is a generally trustworthy compilation of information, especially for minor writers; for authors in common, the *Dictionary of Literary Biography* (J600) volumes on the period are generally superior. Reviews: Norman S. Grabo, *Eighteenth-Century Studies* 19 (1985): 130–35; J. A. Leo Lemay, *Early American Literature* 19 (1984): 215–17.

See also

> Dictionary of Literary Biography (J600).
> Todd, *Dictionary of British and American Women Writers* (M2265).

Periodicals

GUIDES TO PRIMARY WORKS

Bibliographies

Q4035   Brigham, Clarence S. *History and Bibliography of American Newspapers, 1690–1820.* 2 vols. Worcester: Amer. Antiquarian Soc., 1947. Z6951.B86   016.071.

————. "Additions and Corrections to *History and Bibliography of American Newspapers, 1690–1820.*" *Proceedings of the American Antiquarian Society* 71 (1961): 15–62.   E172.A35   973'.0519.

Lathem, Edward Connery, comp. *Chronological Tables of American Newspapers, 1690–1820: Being a Tabular Guide to Holdings of Newspapers Published in America through the Year 1820.* Barre: Amer. Antiquarian Soc., 1972. 131 pp.   Z6951.L3   016.071'3.

A bibliography of 2,120 newspapers published through 1820 in what is now the United States. Organized alphabetically by state, then by original title (with cross-references for later ones), entries include notes on the date of establishment and cessation, frequency, title changes, printer(s), and publisher(s), followed by a list of holdings; both the notes and locations are generally fuller than those in *United States Newspaper Program National Union List* (Q3405). Concludes with lists of libraries and private owners. Two indexes in vol. 2: titles; printers, publishers, and editors. The *Chronological Tables*, which includes Brigham's additions, is organized by state, then city, then newspaper. A monumental work, Brigham is still the best general source for information about and locations of early American newspapers, which remain understudied by literary scholars. For other holdings, see *WorldCat* (E225) and RLG Union Catalog (E230).

Q4040   Kribbs, Jayne K., comp. and ed. *An Annotated Bibliography of American Literary Periodicals, 1741–1850.* Reference Publication in Literature. Boston: Hall, 1977. 285 pp.   Z1219.K75 [PS1]   016.81'05.

A bibliography of 940 periodicals of "distinctly literary interest," excluding dailies, almanacs, and gift books. Entries are organized alphabetically by original title, with cross-references for subtitles and later titles. The amount of detail varies depending on available information, but a full entry cites title, date of first and last issue, frequency, editor(s), publisher(s), and up to two locations. (For a more complete list of locations, see section K: Periodicals/Union Lists; *WorldCat* [E225]; and RLG Union Catalog [E230].) Most entries conclude with a summary of literary content organized by genre and noting representative poets, types of prose works, subjects of biographies, titles of fiction and plays, and miscellaneous topics. Five indexes: chronological index of periodicals; geographical list of periodicals; editors and publishers; literary authors; titles of fiction and plays. Some information is taken from *Union List of Serials* (K640a) and other standard sources rather than personal examination of runs. Although Kribbs's work is not comprehensive, cites publication information incompletely, and is highly selective in recording contents, it is nevertheless an important pioneering effort that is especially valuable for the access its indexes offer. Review: Benjamin Franklin Fisher IV, *Literary Research Newsletter* 5 (1980): 149–52.

Indexes

Q4045   *Index to Early American Periodicals to 1850.* Ed. Nelson F. Adkins. New
York: Readex, 1964. Micropaque.

A reproduction of a card index to some 340 American magazines published between 1730 and 1850. The cards are divided into six parts:

1. General prose, with separate alphabetical sequences for authors and titles of anonymous works;
2. Fiction, also with sequences for authors and anonymous works;
3. Poetry, with alphabetical lists of authors, titles, and first lines;
4. Book reviews, with sequences for authors of books reviewed and titles of anonymous books;
5. Songs, with lists for authors, composers, titles of anonymous works, and first lines;
6. Subject index to pt. 1.

A card typically records author, title, periodical, publication information, and an occasional note on content. The illegibility of many of the handwritten cards and poor quality of the reproduction, incomplete coverage of many periodicals, numerous inconsistencies in recording information, a multitude of inaccuracies, and uneven, idiosyncratic indexing render the volume an exasperating work to consult. Yet as the only index to many of the periodicals, it remains a useful source of American literary and cultural history. A major desideratum is an index similar to the *Wellesley Index* (M2545).

Text Archives

Q4050   *American Periodicals Series Online 1740–1900.* ProQuest. Online. 18 May
2006 <http://proquest.umi.com>.

A digitized collection of more than 1,100 periodicals that were microfilmed for the *American Periodicals* microform collection. For an evaluation of the ProQuest search interface used by the archive, see entry I519. Users must remember to search for variant spellings. Unfortunately, there is no way to limit searches to illustrations. As is true of any text archive, the digital images vary widely in legibility, but the ability to search by keyword such a large amount of text will save searchers years of reading through bound printed volumes.

Selected records can be searched through *C19: The Nineteenth Century Index* (M2466).

GUIDES TO SCHOLARSHIP AND CRITICISM

See

Chielens, *Literary Journal in America to 1900* (Q4145).

Genres

Most works in section Q: American Literature/General/Genres and some in L: Genres are important to research in early American literature.

FICTION

Most works in section Q: American Literature/General/Genres/Fiction and some in L: Genres/Fiction are useful for research in early American fiction.

Histories and Surveys

Q4055   Petter, Henri. *The Early American Novel.* Columbus: Ohio State UP, 1971. 500 pp.   PS375.P4   813'.03.

A descriptive, critical survey of American fiction (excluding that published in magazines) from the 1780s to 1820. Organized by subject matter (didactic, satiric, or polemical fiction; love stories; novels of adventure), the discussions of individual works typically incorporate lengthy synopses. Additional summaries are printed in an appendix. Concludes with a bibliography of primary and secondary works (although the latter is superseded by Parker, *Early American Fiction* [Q4065]). Indexed by persons and titles. The standard survey of early American fiction, Petter is more valuable for its description of works than for critical commentary. Reviews: Alexander Cowie, *American Literature* 43 (1971): 485–86; John Duffy, *New England Quarterly* 45 (1972): 133–34.

Guides to Primary Works

Q4060   Pitcher, Edward W. R., comp. *Fiction in American Magazines before 1800: An Annotated Catalogue.* [Rev. ed.] 3 vols. Studies in British and American Magazines 17-18. Lewiston: Mellen, 2002.   Z1231.F4 P58 [PS375] 016.813'108005.

A catalog of fiction (broadly conceived) of more than 500 words in 77 American magazines before 1800. Organized alphabetically by story title, entries cite publication information and typically include notes on authorship, source, reprints, related works, content, and scholarship. (Users must be certain to check the supplementary notes (book

1, pt. 2: 727–45.) Concludes with an index of authors, pseudonyms, and a few subjects; a register of fiction by magazine; and chronological lists of fiction by American authors and of translations. Based on extensive research on sources and authorship, *Fiction in American Magazines before 1800* is an indispensable catalog that will make feasible and encourage studies of a neglected area of early American fiction.

See also

Wright, *American Fiction, 1774–1850* (Q4180).

Guides to Scholarship and Criticism

Q4065   Parker, Patricia L. *Early American Fiction: A Reference Guide. Reference Guide to Literature.* Boston: Hall, 1984. 197 pp.   Z1231.F4 P25 [PS375] 016.813′2.

A descriptively annotated bibliography of studies (through 1980, with a few as late as 1982) on American fiction before 1800. Entries are listed by year of publication within divisions for general and thematic studies, anonymous works, and 28 individual authors (excluding Brown, who is the subject of her *Charles Brockden Brown: A Reference Guide*, Reference Publication in Literature [Boston: Hall, 1980, 132 pp.]). Reprints are needlessly given separate entries; dissertations actually read by the compiler appear under date of acceptance but others, incongruously, under the year an abstract was published in *ProQuest Dissertations and Theses* (H465). Although several works receive multiple listings, users should check the name index to locate all studies treating an author. Annotations are adequately descriptive. Two indexes: names; titles and subjects. The fullest guide to scholarship on early American fiction.

See also

Holman, *American Novel through Henry James* (Q4185).
Kirby, *America's Hive of Honey* (Q4190).

DRAMA AND THEATER

Most works in section Q: American Literature/General/Genres/Drama and Theater and some in L: Genres/Drama and Theater are important to research in early American drama and theater.

Guides to Primary Works

Q4070   Hill, Frank Pierce, comp. *American Plays Printed, 1714–1830: A Bibliographical Record.* Stanford: Stanford UP; London: Oxford UP, 1934. 152 pp.   Z1231.D7 H6   061.812.

A bibliography of original plays and translations written and published between 1714 and 1830 by American authors, either resident in the country or abroad, and foreigners living in America. Although admitting a broad range of works, Hill excludes dialogues with fewer than three characters and grand opera libretti. Entries, listed by author or title of anonymous work, include title, publication information, pagination, size, locations (restricted to the holdings of 10 United States libraries), and occasional notes (on, for example, productions, sources, authorship, and dedicatee). Works not located are listed separately on pp. 117–20. Two indexes: titles; dates of publication. Although it includes several inaccurate descriptions, much unverified information, and many works that can hardly be considered plays or are not by Americans or foreign residents, Hill remains the standard guide. It must be used with the extensive corrections and additions recorded in four articles by Roger E. Stoddard: "Some Corrigenda and Addenda to Hill's *American Plays Printed 1714–1830*," *Papers of the Bibliographical Society of America* 65 (1971): 278–95; "Further Corrigenda and Addenda to Hill's *American Plays Printed 1714–1830*," 77 (1983): 335–37; "Third Addenda to Hill's *American Plays Printed 1714–1830*," 93 (1999): 519–20; "United States Dramatic Copyrights, 1790–1830: A Provisional Catalogue," *Essays in Honor of James Edward Walsh on His Sixty-Fifth Birthday*, [ed. Hugh Amory and Rodney G. Dennis] (Cambridge: Goethe Inst. and Houghton Lib., 1983) 231–54.

Although superseded in its listing of published plays, Oscar Wegelin, *Early American Plays, 1714–1830: Being a Compilation of the Titles of Plays by American Authors Published and Performed in America Previous to 1830*, ed. John Malone (New York: Dunlap Soc., 1900, 113 pp.), remains useful for its attempt to cover all plays, published or not.

Q4073   Johnson, Odai, and William J. Burling. *The Colonial American Stage,*
         1665–1774: A Documentary Calendar. Madison: Fairleigh Dickinson UP;
         London: Assoc. UP, 2001. 519 pp.   PN2237.J64.   792'.0973'09032.

A calendar of performances by professional or amateur theatrical companies and solo performers in the British American Colonies and British West Indies between 1665 and 1774. Depending on the available information, a typical entry for a performance includes date; venue; title of play(s), afterpiece(s), or entertainment(s) performed (in bold print for the first known performance); author(s); cast; theatrical company; benefits; details from advertisements or reviews; source of information; ticket prices; and related financial or legal information. Other entries provide details of building contracts and financial records, moral opposition to the theater, laws governing theatrical activity, and the formation and movement of acting companies. Three indexes: persons; subjects and places; titles and authors of theatrical works (the lack of running heads makes it difficult to identify an index).

In consolidating, correcting, and adding substantial new data from an impressive array of published and primary resources, *Colonial American Stage* is an indispensable source for research on stage and theater history, acting careers, repertory, theater personnel, reception history, and trends in theatrical taste—in short, on every aspect of the theatrical life of colonial America.

Guides to Scholarship and Criticism

For a survey of scholarship (through the mid-1980s) and suggestions for future research, see Carla Mulford, "Re-Presenting Early American Drama and Theatre," *Resources for American Literary Study* 17 (1990): 1–24.

See

Meserve, *American Drama to 1900* (Q4200).
Wilmeth, *American Stage to World War I* (Q3525).

POETRY

Some works in section L: Genres/Poetry are useful for research in early American poetry.

Guides to Primary Works

Q4075   Jantz, Harold S. "The First Century of New England Verse." *Proceedings of the American Antiquarian Society* 53 (1944): 219–508. Also separately published: Worcester: Amer. Antiquarian Soc., 1944. 292 pp.   PS312.J3 811.109.

A historical survey, anthology, and bibliography of early New England verse, including fragments and epitaphs from gravestones. The bibliography lists all known verse, printed and manuscript, by New England writers born up to the 1670s, by immigrants before their arrival in the colonies, and written in or about New England by transients. Under each author, individual poems or collections are listed by composition or publication date; a chronological list of anonymous verse through 1700 follows the author section. An entry typically provides title, first line, or descriptive heading, number of lines, publication information, location of manuscript or a particularly rare printed work, reprints, and occasional notes on textual or bibliographical matters. Although in need of revision and updating, Jantz remains an essential guide to identifying and locating early American verse.

Q4080   Lemay, J. A. Leo. *A Calendar of American Poetry in the Colonial Newspapers and Magazines and in the Major English Magazines through 1765.* Worcester: Amer. Antiquarian Soc., 1972. 353 pp.   Z1231.P7 L44   016.811′1′08.

A chronological list of American poetry (that is, English-language poems of five or more lines by American residents as well as poems about the country by foreigners) published in 52 periodicals between 1705 and 1765. Because of difficulties in establishing authorship, as many as 20% of the 2,091 entries may represent poems by foreign writers. A typical entry provides date and publication information, first line, title, number of lines, author or pseudonym, and notes (including a list of reprints, biographical information, or commentary on subject matter). Four indexes: first lines; names, pseudonyms, and titles; subjects and genres; periodicals. Because of its numerous attributions of authorship and the access to subject and genre it provides, the *Calendar* is the indispensable guide to the previously uncharted body of early American poetry.

Separately published verse is recorded in Wegelin, *Early American Poetry* (Q4085).

Q4085   Wegelin, Oscar. *Early American Poetry: A Compilation of the Titles of Volumes of Verse and Broadsides by Writers Born or Residing in North America North of the Mexican Border [1650–1820].* 2nd ed., rev. and enl. 2 vols. New York: Smith, 1930.   Z1231.P7 W4   016.81.

A bibliography of separately published British and American editions of verse by residents of what is now the United States. Wegelin includes broadsides, pamphlets, and verse dialogues but excludes plays. Vol. 1 covers 1650 to 1799, vol. 2, 1800 to 1820; each volume consists of separate alphabetical lists of works of known or ascribed authorship and of anonymous publications. Under each author, works are organized chronologically by date of earliest known edition. For the earliest known edition, a description includes title, format, pagination, a limited number of locations, and occasional notes on content, other editions, and bibliographical matters; for subsequent editions, only publication information is usually given. Indexed by titles in vol. 2.

Roger E. Stoddard is preparing *A Bibliographical Description of Books and Pamphlets of American Verse Printed from 1610 through 1820*, which will exclude music books, drama, and works for children. Entries, organized by year of publication then alphabetically by author, record author, title, imprint, collation, number of pages, height of leaf, location of up to five copies, description of publisher's binding, bibliographical references, and notes. Nineteenth-century reprints will have briefer descriptions. Until the revision appears, scholars must consult the following by Stoddard:

> *A Catalogue of Books and Pamphlets Unrecorded in Oscar Wegelin's Early American Poetry, 1650–1820.* Providence: Friends of the Lib. of Brown U, 1969. 84 pp. (Reprinted from *Books at Brown* 23 [1969]: 1–84.) Review: J. A. Leo Lemay, *Early American Literature* 8 (1973): 66–77.
>
> "Further Addenda to Wegelin's *Early American Poetry.*" *Papers of the Bibliographical Society of America* 65 (1971): 169–72.
>
> "More Addenda to Wegelin's *Early American Poetry.*" *Proceedings of the American Antiquarian Society* 88 (1978): 83–90.
>
> "Fourth Addenda to Wegelin's *Early American Poetry.*" *Proceedings of the American Antiquarian Society* 90 (1981): 387–90.
>
> "A Provisional List of U. S. Poetry Copyrights, 1786–1820, and a Plea for the Recovery of Unlocated Copyright Registers." *Papers of the Bibliographical Society of America* 75 (1981): 450–83.
>
> "Lost Books: American Poetry before 1821." *Papers of the Bibliographical Society of America* 76 (1982): 11–41.
>
> "Poet and Printer in Colonial and Federal America: Some Bibliographical Perspectives." *Proceedings of the American Antiquarian Society* 92 (1983): 265–361.
>
> "Fifth Addenda to Wegelin's *Early American Poetry.*" *Proceedings of the American Antiquarian Society* 100 (1990): 251–53.
>
> "Sixth Addenda to Wegelin's *Early American Poetry.*" *Proceedings of the American Antiquarian Society* 107 (1997): 389–93.

Together, these works provide the fullest guide to separately published early American verse. For poetry in periodicals, see Lemay, *Calendar of American Poetry* (Q4080).

Guides to Scholarship and Criticism

Q4090   Scheick, William J., and JoElla Doggett. *Seventeenth-Century American Poetry: A Reference Guide.* Reference Guides in Literature 14. Boston: Hall, 1977. 188 pp.   Z1227.S3 [PS312]   016.811'1.

Rainwater, Catherine, and William J. Scheick. "*Seventeenth-Century American Poetry: A Reference Guide* Updated." *Resources for American Literary Study* 10 (1980): 121–45.   Z1225.R46   016.81.

An annotated bibliography of scholarship through 1979 on poetry by American immigrants or transients born before 1680. Excludes bibliographies and general literary histories. Following a division for general and thematic studies, literary influences, and aesthetics are sections for individual authors and almanacs; broadsides, ballads, and anonymous verse; and elegies. Within each division, works are listed by publication date under separate headings for books, shorter writings (including parts of books), and dissertations. (As in other early Hall Reference Guides, these headings are repeated even when no book, shorter writing, or dissertation appears in a year.) Entries are accompanied by full descriptive annotations. Although many works are given multiple entries, users should consult the index to locate all studies of a writer or type of verse. An asterisk marks the few works not seen. The index of persons and selected topics is difficult to use because of the abbreviations identifying the section in which an entry appears. Despite the omission of bibliographies and general literary histories, *Seventeenth-Century American Poetry* is an essential compilation for identifying scholarship on early American verse.

See also

> Donow, *Sonnet in England and America* (L1250).
> Kuntz, *Poetry Explication* (L1255).
> Ruppert, *Guide to American Poetry Explication*, vol. 1 (L1255a).

PROSE

Most works in section Q: American Literature/General/Genres/Prose and some in L: Genres/Prose are important to research in early American prose.

Guides to Scholarship and Criticism

Q4095   Yannella, Donald, and John H. Roch. *American Prose to 1820: A Guide to Information Sources.* American Literature, English Literature, and World Literatures in English: An Information Guide Series 26. Detroit: Gale, 1979. 653 pp.   Z1231.P8 Y36 [PS367]   016.818'08.

A selective bibliography of studies and editions through 1975 (but with some works as late as 1978) of nonfiction prose. Yannella and Roch emphasizes twentieth-century scholarship but excludes most dissertations and foreign-language studies. Entries are organized alphabetically by author in five divisions: general studies and reference works (with sections for printing and publishing, anthologies and collections, bibliographies and checklists, genres and rhetoric, studies in period criticism, studies of periodicals and newspapers, African American slave narratives, and Indian captivity narratives), colonial period, Revolutionary and early national period (both with sections for literary and cultural studies, anthologies and collections, and bibliographies and checklists), principal authors (with separate lists of editions, bibliographies, and biographical and critical studies under each), and other authors. Indexed by persons, titles, and selected subjects. The guide is a useful starting place for research on early prose, even though it is selective, lacks a clear explanation of criteria governing selection, and is awkwardly organized (with many sections unnecessarily split into books and articles).

Nineteenth-Century Literature

Most works in section Q: American Literature/General are important to research in nineteenth-century American literature.

Literary Handbooks, Dictionaries, and Encyclopedias

Q4105   *Encyclopedia of Transcendentalism.* Ed. Wesley T. Mott. Westport:
         Greenwood, 1996. 280 pp.   PS217.T7 E53   810.9'384.
   An encyclopedia of the "major philosophical concepts, antecedents, genres, institutions, organizations, movements, periodicals, events, and places associated with transcendentalism in the United States." The 145 signed entries employ a history-of-ideas approach and focus on New England; each concludes with a list of suggested readings. *Encyclopedia of Transcendentalism* has somewhat fuller discussions than is typical for such a compendium and offers a convenient guide to the aesthetic, intellectual, and social background of the movement.

Guides to Primary Works

Q4110   *American Book Publishing Record (ABPR).* New Providence: Bowker,
         1960– . Monthly, with annual, quinquennial, and retrospective
         cumulations for 1876–1949, 1950–77, and 1876–1981 (microfiche).
         Z1219.A515   015.
   Originally an augmented, corrected cumulation of the alphabetical lists in *Weekly Record* (in *Publishers Weekly* from 1876 through 26 August 1974; after that, published separately by Bowker through 23 December 1991), *ABPR* is now a classified list of books published or distributed in the United States that have been cataloged by the Library of Congress. Excluded are "federal and other governmental publications, subscription books, dissertations, new printings as distinct from reprints, reissue[s] and other periodicals, pamphlets under 49 pages, specialized publications of a transitory nature or intended as advertising and most elementary and high school textbooks." Books are organized by Dewey Decimal Classification (with separate alphabetical lists of adult and juvenile fiction). In addition to basic library catalog information, entries usually list price and the address of an obscure publisher or distributor. Corrected entries are substituted in the various cumulations, and the ones for 1950–77 and 1876–1981 add thousands of records taken from the *NUC* (E235 and E240). Each issue and cumulation has author, title, and Library of Congress subject-tracing indexes; in addition, there are cumulative indexes covering 1876–1981 (1982, microfiche). Unfortunately the indexes cite Dewey Decimal Classification rather than page number; thus, in the cumulations users must frequently scan several columns to locate an entry. The title index offers quicker access than the author index to books by someone with a common name such as "Susan Jones" or "John Smith." Although not comprehensive and including several ghosts and errors, *ABPR* is the most convenient source for keeping abreast of new works, editions, or reprints published or distributed in the United States; and, within the limitations of the Dewey Decimal Classification, the cumulations provide a subject guide to a majority of the books published since 1876 in the country. Review: (1950–77 cumulation) Ruth P. Burnett, *College and Research Libraries* 40 (1979): 358–62.
   Works for children that are listed in *ABPR* also appear in *Fiction, Folklore, Fantasy, and Poetry for Children, 1876–1985* (U5475). The 1876–1950 cumulation supersedes E. Leypoldt and R. R. Bowker, eds., *American Catalogue: Author and Title Entries of Books in Print and for Sale (Including Reprints and Importations), July 1, 1876–December 31, 1910*, 8 vols. in 13 pts. (New York: Publishers Weekly, 1880–1911).

Q4115   *Bibliotheca Americana: Catalogue of American Publications, Including Reprints and Original Works, from 1820 to 1852, Inclusive.* Comp. O. A. Roorbach. New York: Roorbach, 1852. 652 pp. Supplements: *October, 1852, to May, 1855.* 1855. 220 pp. *May, 1855, to March, 1858.* New York: Wiley; London: Trubner, 1858. 256 pp. *March, 1858, to January, 1861.* New York: Roorbach; London: Trubner, 1861. 162 pp.   Z1215.A3   015.73.

An author and title list of books published in the United States. Biographies are entered under subject rather than author; legal publications and periodicals occupy separate lists in the 1820–52 collection. An entry records author, title, number of volumes, size, binding, price, and publisher. The original compilation gives publication dates for only historical and travel literature; the first and second supplements, for most works; the last supplement, for none. Although incomplete, frequently inaccurate, and inconsistent in providing both author and title entries, *Bibliotheca Americana* remains the most comprehensive general list of works published in the country during the period. It is partly superseded, however, by Shoemaker, *Checklist of American Imprints* (Q4130).

Q4120   Kelly, James, comp. *The American Catalogue of Books (Original and Reprints) Published in the United States from Jan., 1861, to Jan., [1871], with Date of Publication, Size, Price, and Publisher's Name.* 2 vols. New York: Wiley, 1866–71.   Z1215.A5   015.73.

An author and title list that continues *Bibliotheca Americana* (Q4115) and includes some pre-1861 works omitted from it. Most author and title entries cite editor, illustrator, translator, edition, size, binding, price, publication information, and date. Three appendixes: (vol. 1) pamphlets, sermons, and addresses on the Civil War; other sermons and addresses (giving topic but neither title nor publication information); (both vols.) publications of learned societies. The *American Catalogue* is incomplete (especially for works published in the South during the Civil War), frequently inaccurate, and inconsistent in supplying title entries. Nevertheless, it provides the fullest general list of works published in the country during the 10 years. Continued by *American Book Publishing Record* (Q4110).

Q4125   *Early American Imprints, Series II: Shaw-Shoemaker, 1801–1819.* Readex. Online. 30 Aug. 2005 <http://infoweb.newsbank.com>. Updated monthly.

Shaw, Ralph R., and Richard H. Shoemaker, comps. *American Bibliography: A Preliminary Checklist for [1801–19]* (Shaw-Shoemaker). 22 vols. New York: Scarecrow, 1958–66.   Z1215.S48   015.73.

A bibliographical database and digital archive based on Shaw, *American Bibliography,* that will eventually reproduce the c. 36,000 works in the original microprint and microform version of *Early American Imprints, Series II: Shaw-Shoemaker* (New Canaan: Readex) along with about 3,600 additional titles (however, the microprint and microform collection omits serial publications listed in Shaw-Shoemaker). Users can view digitized facsimiles of pages as well as search ASCII text generated by Optical Character Recognition scanning. In the basic search mode, documents can be searched by citation, full text, title, subject (i.e., Library of Congress subject headings), genre, author, place of publication, publisher, document number (i.e., Shaw-Shoemaker number), and date of publication; the advanced search mode allows users to combine up to two fields with full text and date. Given the treatment of attributions of authorship, users should search for an author in both the Author and Citation Text fields. Because of the spelling practices in the period covered and because of scanning errors in the ASCII text underlying the digital images, users must read the discussion of Irregular Spelling under Search Hints before attempting a full text search. Users can also browse by author, place of publication, history of printing (with separate lists of publishers, printers, and booksellers), language, and selected genres and subjects.

A search returns records in ascending chronological order; an individual record reformats the enhanced cataloging copy created for the microform version of *Early American Imprints, Series II* (which cites Shaw-Shoemaker number along with other standard bibliographies, albeit in abbreviated forms that will mystify the majority of users). The original Shaw-Shoemaker entry (along with identification of the copy reproduced) is hidden under a Document Source link at the end of the Table of Contents.

Copies can be downloaded as PDF files (file transfer can be slow, and a maximum of 25 pages can be downloaded at a time), printed, or saved to a personal collection for later access. Inevitably, many of the images of pages are only partly legible because of flaws in the underlying copy or problems with the original filming (and thus keyword searches of the full text generally return some false hits), but this resource brings to the computer screen the text of thousands of rare volumes and, because of the search capabilities, makes possible studies that would otherwise be unfeasible because of the time it would take to identify and acquire the necessary books. Review: Norman Desmarais, *Charleston Advisor* 6.2 (2004): 15–17, 27 Jan. 2005 <http://www.charlestonco.com>.

While *Early American Imprints, Series II* vastly improves access to information hidden away in Shaw-Shoemaker (especially anonymous works), it replicates silently many of the limitations and quirks of its progenitor. Thus a thorough familiarity with *American Bibliography* is a prerequisite for informed use of the digital archive. And the user of any digital archive must be aware that a copy reproduced may have leaves supplied from another copy, be of an edition that is extant in more than one issue or state, or be incomplete.

Shaw-Shoemaker continues Evans, *American Bibliography* (Q4005), with each volume devoted to a single year. The 51,960 entries—listed alphabetically by author, corporate author, or title of anonymous work—record title, imprint, pagination, and locations. Corrections appear in vol. 22 and in the list of omitted entries in Frances P. Newton, comp., *Printers, Publishers, and Booksellers Index; Geographical Index* (Metuchen: Scarecrow, 1983, 443 pp.). Indexed by titles in vol. 21, by authors in vol. 22. *Early American Imprints, Series II: Shaw-Shoemaker* (New Canaan: Readex) reproduces in microform a majority of the nonserial publications.

A preliminary bibliography based entirely on secondary sources (with discrepancies resolved by reliance on what the compilers determined was the "best" source), Shaw-Shoemaker is subject to many of the same deficiencies and limitations as Evans, including misattributions of authorship, publication information, or date; inaccurate titles; and duplicate entries. Like its predecessor, however, Shaw-Shoemaker offers the fullest record of printing during the period; is a useful resource for investigating the intellectual milieu of works, surveying publishing trends, identifying works or editions by standard reference number, and locating copies; and forms part of the basis for a fuller, more sophisticated and accurate retrospective bibliography. Some additions appear in "American Bibliographical Notes," *Proceedings of the American Antiquarian Society* 82 (1972): 53–64; 83 (1973): 273–76; 84 (1974): 399–402, 404–06.

The chronological record is continued by Shoemaker, *Checklist of American Imprints* (Q4130).

Q4130   Shoemaker, Richard H., Gayle Cooper, Scott Bruntjen, and Carol Rinderknecht [Bruntjen], comps. *A Checklist of American Imprints for*

[1820–46] (Shoemaker). Metuchen: Scarecrow, 1964–97. (Publication has been suspended.)   Z1215.S5   015.73.

A continuation of Shaw, *American Bibliography* (Q4125). Like its predecessor, Shoemaker devotes a volume to each year; lists entries alphabetically by author, corporate author, or title of anonymous work; and records title, imprint, pagination, and locations of copies. Unlike Evans, *American Bibliography* (Q4005), and Shaw-Shoemaker, it excludes serial publications. Indexed by decade:

> Cooper, M. Frances, comp. *A Checklist of American Imprints, 1820–1829: Author Index, Corrections, and Sources.* Metuchen: Scarecrow, 1973. 172 pp.
>
> ———. *A Checklist of American Imprints, 1820–1829: Title Index.* Metuchen: Scarecrow, 1972. 556 pp.
>
> Newton, Frances P., comp. *A Checklist of American Imprints, 1820–1829: Printers, Publishers, and Booksellers Index; Geographical Index.* Lanham: Scarecrow, 2000. 391 pp.
>
> Rinderknecht, Carol, comp. *A Checklist of American Imprints, 1830–1839: Author Index.* Metuchen: Scarecrow, 1989. 173 pp.
>
> ———. *A Checklist of American Imprints, 1830–1839: Title Index.* 2 vols. Metuchen: Scarecrow, 1989.

Although some entries are based on examination of copies, the majority are derived from secondary sources; thus Shoemaker is subject to many of the same limitations and deficiencies as Evans and Shaw-Shoemaker, including misattributions of authorship, publication information, or date; inaccurate titles; and duplicate entries. (Corrections are printed in Cooper, *Author Index* [see above].) Like its predecessors, however, Shoemaker offers the most thorough record of printing during the period; is a useful resource for investigating the intellectual milieu of works, surveying publishing trends, identifying works or editions by standard reference number, and locating copies; forms part of the basis for a fuller, more sophisticated and accurate retrospective bibliography; and supersedes, for the volumes published, *Bibliotheca Americana* (Q4115) and *American Imprints Inventory*, 52 nos. (Washington: Historical Records Survey, 1937–42).

Complementing Shoemaker is *American Broadsides and Ephemera* (Readex; online; 17 Feb. 2006 <http://infoweb.newsbank.com>), a digital archive of c. 30,000 documents from the collections of the American Antiquarian Society. Part of Readex's *Archive of Americana*, *American Broadsides and Ephemera* uses the same search interface as *Early American Imprints, Series I* (Q4005) and *II* (Q4125).

See also

> *Literary Writings in America* (Q3255).
> *Nineteenth Century Short Title Catalogue* (M2475).

Guides to Scholarship and Criticism

SURVEYS OF RESEARCH

Q4135   Myerson, Joel, ed. *The Transcendentalists: A Review of Research and Criticism.* Modern Language Association of America Reviews of Research. New York: MLA, 1984. 534 pp.   Z7128.T7 T7 [B905] 016.141'3'0973.

A collection of evaluative surveys of research (from the nineteenth century through 1981), with individual essays on general topics (the transcendentalist movement, its historical background, relation to Unitarianism, communities, and periodicals), 28 transcendentalists, and the contemporary reaction of 11 authors. The essays on transcendentalist writers (varying from 2 to 28 pages) include sections on bibliographies, manuscripts, editions, biographical studies, and criticism (with the last variously subdivided); the essays on major authors such as Emerson and Thoreau focus on the transcendentalist period of their careers. The other essays are variously organized, with those on contemporary writers limited to their relation to the movement. Most essays offer suggestions for further research. Unlike other MLA surveys of research, this work records full publication information in a list of works cited. Indexed by persons, anonymous titles, and some subjects. Judicious evaluation, accuracy, and thoroughness make *The Transcendentalists* the indispensable guide to the movement. Review: Kenneth Walter Cameron, *Analytical and Enumerative Bibliography* ns 1 (1987): 92–97.

For evaluations of recent scholarship, see the chapters "Emerson, Thoreau, and Transcendentalism" and "19th-Century Literature" in *American Literary Scholarship* (Q3265).

Q4140   Woodress, James, ed. *Eight American Authors: A Review of Research and Criticism.* Rev. ed. New York: Norton, 1972. 392 pp.   PS201.E4 810'.9'003.

Evaluative surveys of research on Poe, Emerson, Hawthorne, Thoreau, Melville, Whitman, Twain, and James, in a collection that revises the work by Floyd Stovall, ed. (New York: MLA, 1956, 418 pp.; rpt., with a bibliographic supplement by J. Chesley Mathews, New York: Norton, 1963, 466 pp.). Coverage extends through 1969, is selective (especially for articles), and excludes dissertations and foreign scholarship in some chapters. The essays — by established scholars but not necessarily specialists in the respective authors — are variously organized within a general framework that encompasses bibliographies, editions, biographical studies, and criticism. The failure to provide complete bibliographical information sometimes results in delays in tracking down an article. Indexed by persons. While *Eight American Authors* is now badly dated, its thoughtful and exacting evaluations make it an indispensable guide to studies published before 1970. For evaluative surveys of later scholarship, see *American Literary Scholarship* (Q3265), which has chapters on each author.

See also

>   *American Literary Scholarship* (Q3265): Chapters on Emerson, Thoreau, and transcendentalism; Hawthorne; Poe; Melville; Whitman and Dickinson; Mark Twain; James; and the nineteenth century.
>   *Romantic Movement: A Selective and Critical Bibliography* (M2485).

SERIAL BIBLIOGRAPHIES

See

>   *ABELL* (G340): English Literature/Nineteenth Century section.
>   *MLAIB* (G335): American Literature division in the volumes for 1922–25; American IV: Romantic Period (1815–1890) and V: 1890 to the Present in the volume for 1926; American III: Seventeenth and Eighteenth Centuries

(1607–1815) in the volumes for 1926–28; American IV: Nineteenth Century in the volumes for 1929–34; American IV: Nineteenth Century, 1800–1870 and V: Nineteenth Century, 1870–1900 in the volumes for 1935–40; American III: Nineteenth Century, 1800–1870 and IV: Nineteenth Century, 1870–1900 in the volumes for 1941–80; and American Literature/1800–1899 (as well as any larger chronological section encompassing the century) in volumes after 1980. Researchers must also check the heading beginning with "American" in the subject index to post-1980 volumes and in the online thesaurus.

Biographical Dictionaries

See

Dictionary of Literary Biography (J600).

Periodicals

GUIDES TO PRIMARY WORKS

See

Brigham, *History and Bibliography of American Newspapers, 1690–1820* (Q4035).
Index to Early American Periodicals to 1850 (Q4045).
Kribbs, *Annotated Bibliography of American Literary Periodicals, 1741–1850* (Q4040).

GUIDES TO SCHOLARSHIP AND CRITICISM

Q4145   Chielens, Edward E. *The Literary Journal in America to 1900: A Guide to Information Sources.* American Literature, English Literature, and World Literatures in English: An Information Guide Series 3. Detroit: Gale, 1975. 197 pp.   Z6951.C57 [PN4877]   016.81'05.

A selective annotated bibliography of English-language studies (through the early 1970s) of literary periodicals as well as other periodicals that were influential in the development of American literature. Chielens excludes dailies and annuals as well as any work that has not been the subject of at least one dissertation, book, chapter, or article. Entries are listed alphabetically by author in seven divisions (some of which have sections for general studies and individual periodicals): general studies, New England, Middle Atlantic states, the South, the West, bibliographies and checklists (including sections for some of the preceding divisions), and background studies. Studies of literary materials in nonliterary periodicals and of Poe and American literary periodicals are relegated to appendixes. The work is flawed by a narrow focus, inadequate explanation of scope, and inefficient organization, but it is a serviceable compilation of studies that are sometimes difficult to locate in the standard serial bibliographies and indexes in section G. Continued by Chielens, *Literary Journal in America, 1900–1950* (Q4250).

INDEXES

Q4147   *19th Century Masterfile.* Paratext. Online. 23 Aug. 2005 <http://
poolesplus.odyssi.com>. (Former title: *Poole's Plus.*)

An electronic index to printed author, subject, and title indexes of nineteenth-century periodicals, newspapers, and patents, including *Poole's Index to Periodical Literature* (Q4150); *"A.L.A." Index* (G380a); New York Times *Index* (1863–1905; entry Q3415); *Palmer's Index to the* Times *Newspaper* (1880–1890; entry M1450a); and individual indexes to such periodicals as *North American Review, Putnam's Monthly,* and *Atlantic Monthly.* The overwhelming majority of the publications indexed were printed in the United States. Users can search by keyword(s) in all fields, document authors, article titles, or index terms (though several searches of the last yielded no results). Searchers must try variant forms of names in keyword searches (e.g., a search for "Shakespeare" yielded only two hits in *Poole's,* while a search for "William Shakespeare" returned 45 hits). Some records can be browsed by title or author. Search results are broken down by printed source, then by relevancy rank within each source; results can be sorted by date, author, title, language, or classification (though it is unclear what the last entails). Although the content of a record is determined by its printed source (and thus frequently lacks full bibliographical details), some records have been enhanced. Records marked for downloading must first be saved to a list. Although subject to most of the limitations of the sources it reproduces, *19th Century Masterfile* does allow users to extract information expeditiously from a wide range of printed indexes.

Q4150   *Poole's Index to Periodical Literature.* By William Frederick Poole et al.
6 vols. Boston: Houghton, 1888–1908.   AI3.P7   016.05.

1802–81. 2 pts. Rev. ed. By William Frederick Poole and William I. Fletcher. 1891.

First Supplement: 1882–87. By William Frederick Poole and Fletcher. 1888. 483 pp.

Second Supplement: 1887–92. By Fletcher. 1895. 476 pp.

Third Supplement: 1892–96. By Fletcher and Franklin O. Poole. 1897. 637 pp.

Fourth Supplement: 1897–1902. By Fletcher and Mary Poole. 1903. 646 pp.

Fifth Supplement: 1902–07. By Fletcher and Mary Poole. 1908. 714 pp.

A subject index to 479 British and (predominantly) American periodicals published between 1802 and 1 January 1907. The supplements provide current as well as retrospective coverage for periodicals newly added. Although entries cite an abbreviated title, author (with many unauthenticated attributions), periodical title, volume, and initial page number, researchers accustomed to modern subject indexes will find Poole's a frustrating work to consult because (1) subject headings, derived largely from title words, are capricious and inconsistent and offer few cross-references to related headings; (2) the imposition of uniform periodical titles and volume numbers that ignore title changes and a publisher's numbering system means that Dearing (see below) must be consulted to locate many articles; (3) literary contributions are listed by title; (4) reviews of literary works appear under the author of the work reviewed, but reviews of nonfiction books appear under the subject of the work; (5) the numerous attributions of unsigned articles must be authenticated in more reliable sources. Some of these defects are remedied in the following:

Dearing, Vinton A. *Transfer Vectors for* Poole's Index to Periodical Literature: *Number One: Titles, Volumes, and Dates.* Los Angeles: Pison, 1967. 95 pp. (The projected key to subject headings was never published.) Because it expands title abbreviations, lists title changes, provides volume-year correspondences, and converts assigned volume numbers to those used in periodicals, this work is essential for ascertaining the actual publication details for citations. Dearing is easier to use than Marion V. Bell and Jean C. Bacon, Poole's Index *Date and Volume Key,* ACRL Monographs 19 (Chicago: Assn. of College and Reference Libraries, 1957, 61 pp.).

Wall, C. Edward, comp. and ed. *Cumulative Author Index for* Poole's Index to Periodical Literature, *1802–1906.* Ann Arbor: Pierian, 1971. 488 pp. Provides access to authors listed in *Poole's,* but users must search all possible variants because Wall does not regularize names.

Additions and corrections appear in Thorvald Solberg, "Authors of Anonymous Articles Indexed in *Poole,*" *Bulletin of Bibliography* 1 (1898): 91–93, 105–07, and in a series of variously authored "Errata in *Poole's Index* and Supplements," 2 (1900): 24–25, 40–41, 56–58, 75–76; (1901): 107–08, 133–34; 3 (1902): 25–26; 4 (1904): 11–12, 72.

Despite its manifold deficiencies, *Poole's* offers the only available indexing of numerous periodicals and—if approached with patience, an awareness of its limitations, and inventiveness—can yield valuable access to more than 590,000 articles. For an instructive discussion of search strategies, see vol. 1, pp. 37–40 in Vann, *Victorian Periodicals* (M2525).

Some of the frustrations of searching *Poole's* are alleviated by the electronic versions included in *19th Century Masterfile* (Q4147) and *C19: The Nineteenth Century Index* (M2466); however, researchers should first consult Robert Balay's evaluation of the *19th Century Masterfile* version (pp. 25–28) in *Early Periodical Indexes* (G327).

More accurate indexing of a limited number of periodicals can be found in *Nineteenth Century Readers' Guide* (G400a) and *Wellesley Index* (M2545); however, neither approaches the breadth of *Poole's.* Reviews published between 1880 and 1900 in 13 popular American periodicals not in *Poole's* are indexed in Patricia Marks, *American Literary and Drama Reviews: An Index to Late Nineteenth Century Periodicals,* Reference Publication in Literature (Boston: Hall, 1983, 313 pp.).

Q4155   Wells, Daniel A., and Jonathan Daniel Wells. *The Literary and Historical Index to American Magazines, 1800–1850.* Bibliographies and Indexes in American Literature 32. Westport: Praeger, 2004. 506 pp.   Z1225.W37 [PS214]   016.8108′004.

Wells, Daniel A. *The Literary Index to American Magazines, 1850–1900.* Bibliographies and Indexes in American Literature 22. Westport: Greenwood, 1996. 441 pp.   Z1225.W38 [PS214]   016.8108′004.

An author and rudimentary subject indexes to articles, excerpts, reviews, and regular columns of literary, cultural, or historical (the last only in *1800–1850*) interest in c. 90 important or representative literary magazines between 1800 and 1900. Entries for authors consist of three parts: general references to the life or career; references to books and pamphlets by the author; works by the author. Anonymous contributors are identified only for *Dial.* Although coverage is limited and the subject indexing is minimal, the *Literary Index* is a useful preliminary source for locating works by several minor authors and for studying the American reception of writers, native and some foreign, of the period.

See also

> *Literary Writings in America* (Q3255).

Genres

Most works in sections L: Genres and Q: American Literature/General/Genres are useful for research in nineteenth-century American literature.

FICTION

Most works in sections L: Genres/Fiction and Q: American Literature/General/Genres/ Fiction are useful for research in nineteenth-century American fiction.

Histories and Surveys

See

> Petter, *Early American Novel* (Q4055).

Guides to Primary Works

Bibliographies and Indexes

Q4180   Wright, Lyle H. *American Fiction, 1774–1850: A Contribution toward a Bibliography.* 2nd rev. ed. San Marino: Huntington Lib., 1969. 411 pp. Z1231.F4 W9   016.812′3.
——. *American Fiction, 1851–1875: A Contribution toward a Bibliography.* Rpt., with additions and corrections. 1965. 438 pp. Z1231.F4 W92   016.8133.
——. *American Fiction, 1876–1900: A Contribution toward a Bibliography.* 1966. 683 pp.   Z1231.F4 W93   016.8134.

A bibliography of American editions of separately published American fiction, including novels, romances, tall tales, allegories, and fictitious biographies and travels but excluding juvenile fiction, jestbooks, Indian captivity narratives, periodicals, annuals, gift books, folklore, tracts published by religious societies, dime novels, and subscription series. The 1774–1850 volume attempts to include all editions; the later volumes are limited to first or earliest located editions. Organized alphabetically by author, unidentified pseudonym, or title of anonymous work, entries provide title, publication information, pagination, format, list of contents for collections of stories, copyright deposit information, occasional notes on subject matter, and locations in selected major libraries and private collections. Stories in collections are cross-referenced to the collection. Indexed by titles in all volumes and by dates in the 1774–1850 volume. Although not comprehensive, Wright offers an incomparable record of American fiction through 1900. A number of corrections appear in Edward W. Pitcher,

"Some Emendations for Lyle B. [sic] Wright's *American Fiction, 1774–1850*," *Papers of the Bibliographical Society of America* 74 (1980): 143–45. Reviews: (1774–1850) John S. Van E. Kohn, *Papers of the Bibliographical Society of America* 42 (1948): 324–30; (1876–1900) Roger E. Stoddard, *New England Quarterly* 41 (1968): 600–04.

All but a few of the works in Wright have been microfilmed in *American Fiction, 1774–1910* (Woodbridge: Research, 1967–84). Post-1900 editions were compiled from the Library of Congress shelflist of American adult fiction. *American Fiction, 1774–1900: Cumulative Author Index to the Microfilm Collection* (New Haven: Research, 1974, 416 pp.) and *American Fiction, 1901–1910: Cumulative Author Index to the Microfilm Collection* (Woodbridge: Research, 1984, 217 pp.) are essential for locating individual titles on the microfilm reels. *Wright American Fiction, 1851–1875* (Committee on Institutional Cooperation; online; 26 Apr. 2006 <http://www.letrs.indiana.edu/web/w/wright2>) allows keyword searches of digitized copies of 2,887 volumes from the microfilm; as of 26 April 2006, 1,124 of these texts had been fully encoded and edited. Keyword, Boolean, or proximity searches can be limited to titles, authors, place of publication, publisher, date, bibliographical citation, or idno (which is not explained at the site). In addition, users can browse a word index. Like other archives of encoded digitized texts, *Wright American Fiction, 1851–1875* makes feasible studies of style, imagery, subjects, and intellectual history that would otherwise require years of reading texts cover to cover.

Coverage is continued by American Fiction Database (Q4267).

See also

> *Early American Fiction, 1789–1875* (Q4183).
> Grimes, *Novels in English by Women, 1891–1920* (M2640).

Text Archives

Q4183   *Early American Fiction, 1789–1875.* ProQuest. Online. 18 June 2006
          <http://collections.chadwyck.com>.

An archive of rekeyed texts and digital images of more than 730 first editions of novels and collections of short stories published by American writers between 1789 and 1875. To be included a first edition must be owned by the University of Virginia Library and be listed in Wright, *American Fiction, 1774–1850* (Q4180) or its author included in *BAL* (Q3250). Each book is photographed from front cover to back cover (along with the spine and top, front, and bottom edges).

Simple keyword, title, and author searches can be limited by publication date, place of publication, publisher, date during an author's lifetime, gender, and to parts (e.g., front matter, epigraphs). Searchers can also browse an author list of the contents of the database. Results appear in ascending alphabetical order and cannot be re-sorted. Citations (but not the full text) can be marked for e-mailing, downloading, or printing; each citation includes a durable URL to the full text.

Besides being a useful source for identifying an elusive quotation or allusion, *Early American Fiction*'s text archive makes feasible a variety of kinds of studies (stylistic, thematic, imagistic, and topical). This archive incorporates all of the content of *Early American Fiction, 1789–1850* (http://collections.chadwyck.com).

The contents of *Early American Fiction* can also be searched through *LiOn* (I527), which offers a less versatile search interface.

See also

   Wright American Fiction, 1851–1875 (Q4180a).

Guides to Scholarship and Criticism

Q4185   Holman, C. Hugh, comp. *The American Novel through Henry James.* 2nd
        ed. Goldentree Bibliographies in Language and Literature. Arlington
        Heights: AHM, 1979. 177 pp.   Z1231.F4 H64 [PS371]   016.813.
   A highly selective bibliography of English-language scholarship through 1976 that
emphasizes nineteenth-century novelists. Holman excludes most studies before 1900
and most general literary histories as well as dissertations and bibliographies of bibliographies. Entries are organized in divisions for the novel as form, histories of the
American novel, special studies (with sections for periods, genres, and themes or subjects), major novelists (with sections for editions, bibliographies, biographical and critical books, and essays), and lesser novelists. The supplement (pp. 141–57) is similarly
organized. A few entries are accompanied by brief descriptive annotations. Indexed by
scholars.
   A similar work is David K. Kirby, *American Fiction to 1900: A Guide to Information
Sources,* American Literature, English Literature, and World Literatures in English: An
Information Guide Series 4 (Detroit: Gale, 1975, 296 pp.), with highly selective cov-
erage through c. 1975 and an inadequate explanation of scope and criteria governing
both the selection of authors and scholarship.
   Highly selective and dated, *The American Novel* and *American Fiction* together
offer only a preliminary guide to scholarship.
   For reviews of late nineteenth-century fiction, see Clayton L. Eichelberger, comp.,
A Guide to Critical Reviews of United States Fiction, 1870–1910, 2 vols. (Metuchen:
Scarecrow, 1971–74). Unfortunately, because of its numerous errors and inconsistencies, omission of significant periodicals, inclusion of many nonfictional works, and
inadequate editing, Eichelberger's *Guide* cannot be trusted. (For the deficiencies of this
work, see the review by Blake Nevius, *Nineteenth-Century Fiction* 27 [1972]: 245–47.)

Q4190   Kirby, David. *America's Hive of Honey; or, Foreign Influences on American
        Fiction through Henry James: Essays and Bibliographies.* Metuchen: Scarecrow,
        1980. 214 pp.   Z1231.F4 K573 [PS374.F64]   813'.009'3.
   A selective annotated bibliography of studies of 16 major influences on the fiction
of Brown, Irving, Cooper, Poe, Hawthorne, Melville, Twain, James, Howells, Norris,
and Crane. The work is limited to studies (through 1976 and primarily in English) that
identify specific sources. Within divisions for Oriental sources, classical literature, the
Bible, Dante and the Middle Ages, Spenser, Cervantes, Shakespeare and the Renaissance, Milton and his age, the eighteenth century, Austen, Gothic novelists, the Romantics, Scott, the Victorians, realists, and scientific thinkers and naturalists, entries are
listed alphabetically by author in sections for general studies and individual American
writers. Each division begins with a headnote assessing generally the influence of the
author, period, group, movement, or work. Two brief appendixes list general studies
of the influence of foreign cultures on American fiction and of the reading habits of
individual authors. Indexed by persons and titles of primary works. The detailed annotations make *America's Hive of Honey* a useful guide to source studies, few of which
are readily identifiable in standard bibliographies and indexes.

DRAMA AND THEATER

Most works in sections L: Genres/Drama and Theater and Q: American Literature/General/Genres/Drama and Theater are useful for research in nineteenth-century American drama and theater.

Guides to Primary Works

Q4195   *Dramatic Compositions Copyrighted in the United States, 1870 to 1916.*
        2 vols. Washington: GPO, 1918.   Z5781.U55 [PN1851]   016.812.
    A list of the approximately 60,000 plays registered for copyright between 1870 and 1916. Works are listed alphabetically by title, with cross-references for alternate titles or subtitles. Because of changes in copyright law, entries vary in content but typically record (when appropriate) title; author; translator; copyright claimant; and date of registration, publication, and deposit of copy. (Users should study the explanation of the sample entries on pp. iii–iv.) Plays registered during part of 1915 and all of 1916, along with additions and corrections, appear in a supplementary list (pp. 2,659–833). Indexed by persons (with titles following each name). Copies of about 20,000 works registered before 1 July 1909 were never deposited; however, *Dramatic Compositions* is an underutilized but indispensable record of plays that were copyrighted in the United States. Since some deposit copies—many of which are unpublished manuscripts or printed acting copies—are held by the Library of Congress, the work also serves as a valuable source for locating otherwise unobtainable materials. Researchers should note that printed copies selected for the Library of Congress collection are included in the library's online catalog; other printed copies and manuscripts must be located by consulting the card file in the Copyright Office Public Record Reading Room. After obtaining the copyright registration number for an unpublished manuscript or typescript, researchers may consult microfilm copies of many of the deposits for this period in the Manuscript Reading Room. Some notes about prefilming transfers of certain twentieth-century scripts may be found in the Manuscript Division's evolving, internal finding aid for selected plays from the Copyright Deposit Drama Collection. For other copyright records, see Tanselle, "Copyright Records and the Bibliographer" (Q3260).

See also

    Hill, *American Plays Printed, 1714–1830* (Q4070).

Guides to Scholarship and Criticism

Q4200   Meserve, Walter J. *American Drama to 1900: A Guide to Information*
        Sources. American Literature, English Literature, and World Literatures in
        English: An Information Guide Series 28. Detroit: Gale, 1980. 254 pp.
        Z1231.D7 M45 [PS345]   016.812.
    A bibliography of English-language scholarship and selected editions through c. 1977. Meserve excludes studies of theater because of the presence of Wilmeth, *American Stage to World War I* (Q3525), in a related Gale series. Entries are listed alphabetically by author in two divisions: general studies and major authors. The first has sections for bibliographies, indexes, library and microform collections, anthologies and

collections, general histories, and history and criticism (with the last organized by period and including studies of minor authors and anonymous plays). Each of the 34 important playwrights (most of whom date from the nineteenth century) has separate lists of editions, nondramatic works, bibliographies, biographical studies, and criticism. Generous cross-references guide users to related studies. The generally brief descriptive annotations are uneven, with many failing to convey a sense of content. Three indexes: persons; titles; subjects. Although selective and lacking an adequate explanation of scope and criteria governing selection, Meserve offers the best preliminary guide to studies of American drama before 1900 and is far superior to Eddleman, *American Drama Criticism* (Q3520). It must be supplemented by the serial bibliographies and indexes in section G and in section Q: American Literature/General/Guides to Scholarship and Criticism.

For an overview of recent scholarship and suggestions for future research, see Brenda Murphy, "Breaking the Constraints of History: Recent Scholarly Treatment of Nineteenth-Century American Drama," *Resources for American Literary Study* 17 (1990): 25–34.

See also

Wilmeth, *American Stage to World War I* (Q3525).

POETRY

Some works in section L: Genres/Poetry are useful for research in nineteenth-century American poetry.

PROSE

Many works in sections L: Genres/Prose and Q: American Literature/General/Genres/ Prose are useful for research in nineteenth-century American prose.

Guides to Scholarship and Criticism

Q4205   Partridge, Elinore Hughes. *American Prose and Criticism, 1820–1900: A Guide to Information Sources.* American Literature, English Literature, and World Literatures in English: An Information Guide Series 39. Detroit: Gale, 1983. 575 pp.   Z1231.P8 P37 [PS368]   016.818'08.
          A highly selective list of editions and studies through c. 1981 of nonfiction prose. Entries are organized in three divisions: general studies (with sections for bibliographies and reference works; periodicals and annual bibliographies; cultural, historical, and literary studies; and anthologies), prose (with sections for literary theory and criticism; autobiographies, memoirs, and diaries; essays and sketches; works of travel and description; educational, religious, philosophical, and scientific writings; and history and politics—each with lists of primary works and studies), and 45 individual authors (with lists of principal works; letters and journals; editions, selections, and reprints; bibliographies; biographical studies and criticism; and related general studies). The descriptive annotations sometimes include brief evaluative comments. Indexed by persons and

titles. Because of the inadequate explanation of scope and criteria governing selection, poor organization of the first division, exclusion of most articles in the lists of studies, and numerous inconsistencies, Partridge offers little more than a place to begin research on prose of the period.

See also

Yannella, *American Prose to 1820* (Q4095).

Twentieth-Century Literature

Most works in section Q: American Literature/General and some in section M: English Literature/Twentieth-Century Literature are important to research in twentieth-century American literature.

Histories and Surveys

Q4220   Hoffman, Daniel, ed. *Harvard Guide to Contemporary American Writing.* Cambridge: Belknap–Harvard UP, 1979. 618 pp.   PS221.H357 810'.9'0054.
    A critical history of trends and movements in American literature from 1945 to c. 1978 that emphasizes established writers and literature as an exposition of culture. Separate essays consider intellectual backgrounds; literary criticism; realists, naturalists, and novelists of manners; southern fiction; Jewish writers; experimental fiction; African American literature; women's literature; drama; and poetry. Although not a connected history and not always balanced in its treatment, the *Harvard Guide* offers the fullest overview of the period. Reviews: Nina Baym, *JEGP: Journal of English and Germanic Philology* 79 (1980): 271–75; Jerome Klinkowitz, *College English* 42 (1980): 382–89.

Literary Handbooks, Dictionaries, and Encyclopedias

See

    Encyclopedia of World Literature in the 20th Century (M2755).

Guides to Primary Works

Q4225   *GlobalBooksinPrint.com.* Bowker. Online. 20 Aug. 2005 <http://www.globalbooksinprint.com>. Updated weekly. CD-ROM. Updated monthly. (A variety of specialist databases and CD-ROMs are cloned from the *GlobalBooksinPrint.com* database, including *BooksinPrint.com Professional, ChildrensBooksinPrint.com* [U5470], *Books in Print on Disc,* and *Global Books in Print on Disc.* For a full list of electronic permutations, click on the Products & Services tab at http://www.bowker.com.)

A database of English- and Spanish-language books, e-books, audio books, and videos published or distributed in the United States, United Kingdom, Canada, Australia, South Africa, and New Zealand and available for general purchase. *Global BooksinPrint.com* excludes music and a host of ephemeral publications (though the Web site does not specify kinds of publications that are not covered). In the Quick Search screen, keyword, author, title, or ISBN/ISSN searches can be limited by format, status (in print, out of print, forthcoming), and market; in addition, users can browse a list of subjects or a variety of indexes (e.g., author, title, and publisher). Advanced Search allows users to combine keyword searches of a variety of record fields and to limit searches by format, status, market, date, country of publication, language, audience level, and date. Advanced Search also allows users to sort results in a variety of ways (including author, date, or Library of Congress classification). Records can be marked for downloading, printing, or e-mailing. Users can also set up alerts. Each entry records author, title, publication information, market, LC and ISBN numbers, binding, status, price, subject descriptors, Library of Congress and Dewey classification, distributor, and price; many records also include a synopsis or review(s). Because names are not standardized, users must check all forms of an author's name. Compiled from information supplied by publishers, *GlobalBooksinPrint.com* is neither comprehensive nor always accurate, but it is the most convenient source for determining what books are currently available for sale from publishers and distributors in the major English-speaking countries.

The following are useful related Bowker publications:

> *Books in Print* (*BIP*). New Providence: Bowker, 1948– . Annual, with supplement between editions. Online. 22 Aug. 2005 <http://www .booksinprint.com>. CD-ROM. Currently published in four parts— authors, titles, subjects, and publishers— *BIP* lists books printed or published in the United States.
>
> *Bowker's British Books in Print.* 2005– . Annual.
>
> *Children's Books in Print* (U5470).
>
> *Forthcoming Books.* 1966– . 3/yr. Compiled from information supplied by publishers, these volumes are far from complete and inevitably list books that will be delayed or will never appear.
>
> *Publishers' Trade List Annual* (*PTLA*). 1873–2001. Annual. A compilation of publishers' catalogs (of four or more pages) along with a yellow-page section comprising smaller lists. Although far from comprehensive, *PTLA* was once a useful supplement to *BIP*, especially for a description of a book or list of titles within a series. Since few libraries have extensive holdings of publishers' catalogs, *PTLA* is a valuable resource for studying publishing history and reconstructing a firm's list.

For author, title, publisher, and subject lists of books published by small and private presses, see the current edition of *Small Press Record of Books in Print*, CD-ROM (Paradise: Dustbooks, 1969– , irregular). Coverage is international but emphasizes English-language works printed in the United States.

Reprints are conveniently listed in *Guide to Reprints* (Munich: Saur, 1967– , annual; subtitle varies).

Q4230 Lepper, Gary M. *A Bibliographical Introduction to Seventy-Five Modern American Authors.* Berkeley: Serendipity, 1976. 428 pp. Z1227.L46 [PS221] 016.81.

Checklists of first printings of separately published works through 1975 by 75 authors who achieved prominence after 1945. Lepper includes signed and revised editions, ephemera (such as broadsides and mimeographed or photocopied material), and some bound proofs and advance review copies; he excludes sheet music, recordings, and edited books. Authors are listed alphabetically; works, chronologically. Entries include title, publication information, type of binding or method of reproduction, format, notes on priority of issues, identifying marks of first printings, illustrator, and series. The descriptions are not bibliographically sophisticated; criteria governing selection of authors are unstated; there are some notable omissions; and coverage is sometimes inconsistent. Nonetheless, the *Bibliographical Introduction* offers a useful and reasonably accurate preliminary guide to first printings of works by writers who are not the subject of separate author bibliographies. Some other contemporary authors are treated in Bruccoli, *First Printings of American Authors* (Q3250a). Review: Patricia McLaren-Turner, *Book Collector* 28 (1979): 449–50, 453.

Q4235   Vrana, Stan A. *Interviews and Conversations with 20th-Century Authors Writing in English: An Index.* Metuchen: Scarecrow, 1982. 239 pp. *Series II.* 1986. 288 pp. *Series III.* 1990. 435 pp.   Z2013.V73 [PR471] 016.82′09′0091.

A selective author index to interviews and similar works from 1900 through 1985 in periodicals, newspapers, and books (the majority of which are published in the United States and involve American authors). Entries are listed chronologically under an author and include citations to reprints. Authors in *Series II* are indexed in *Biography and Genealogy Master Index* (J565); *Series III* includes addenda for 1900–80. Although not at all comprehensive—since it omits recordings and numerous serials—*Interviews and Conversations* is a useful starting point for locating interviews; however, the inadequate explanation of scope and failure to record the years or volumes actually searched for periodicals and newspapers in the list of sources consulted mean that a user will frequently end up having to duplicate much of Vrana's research.

Reviews in selected little magazines are listed in "Little Magazine Interview Index," *Serials Review* 11.2 (1985–). A card file covering 1976–83 is available in the Department of Rare Books and Special Collections, University of Wisconsin, Madison.

Researchers with access to the *MLAIB* (G335) database can identify additional interviews.

See also

> *American Book Publishing Record* (Q4110).
> *Literary Writings in America* (Q3255).
> *Nineteenth Century Short Title Catalogue* (M2475).

Guides to Scholarship and Criticism

SURVEYS OF RESEARCH

Q4240   Bryer, Jackson R., ed. *Sixteen Modern American Authors: A Survey of Research and Criticism.* New York: Norton, 1973. 673 pp.   PS221.F45 810′.9′0052.

———. *Sixteen Modern American Authors: A Survey of Research and Criticism since 1972.* Durham: Duke UP, 1989. 810 pp.   PS221.S625 810.9′0052.

Evaluative surveys of research and criticism on Anderson, Cather, Crane, Dreiser, Eliot, Faulkner, Fitzgerald, Frost, Hemingway, O'Neill, Pound, Robinson, Steinbeck, Stevens, William Carlos Williams, and Wolfe. The first volume revises *Fifteen Modern American Authors* (Durham: Duke UP, 1969, 493 pp.), correcting errors, extending coverage through 1971–72, and adding the essay on Williams. The second volume continues coverage through 1985, with most essays having an addendum that superficially treats publications from late 1985 through mid-1988. Although each chapter consists of five parts—bibliographies, editions, manuscripts and letters, biographical studies, and criticism, with a supplementary section for each—there is considerable variation in the extent of coverage, especially of dissertations and foreign-language scholarship (with very little attention to either in the second volume). A majority of the contributors are frank in their evaluations but seldom offer suggestions for further research and do not provide full publication information for articles. These authoritative surveys remain indispensable for their winnowing of pre-1986 scholarship. For evaluative surveys of recent scholarship, see *American Literary Scholarship* (Q3265). Review: (1st ed.) Willard Thorp, *American Literature* 42 (1970): 122–24.

See also

> *American Literary Scholarship* (Q3265): Chapters on Pound and Eliot; Faulkner; Fitzgerald and Hemingway; fiction: 1900–1930s; fiction: 1930s–1960s; fiction: 1960s–present; poetry: 1900–1940s; and poetry: 1940s–present.
> *Contemporary Authors: Bibliographical Series* (J595a).

SERIAL BIBLIOGRAPHIES

See

> *ABELL* (G340): English Literature/Twentieth Century and Twenty-First Century sections.
> "Annual Review," *Journal of Modern Literature* (M2780).
> "Current Bibliography," *Twentieth Century Literature* (M2790a).
> *MLAIB* (G335): American Literature division in the volumes for 1922–25; American V: 1890 to the Present in the volumes for 1926–28; American V: Contemporary Literature (occasionally called Twentieth Century) in the volumes for 1929–34; American VI: Contemporary in the volumes for 1935–40; American V: Twentieth Century (also called Contemporary in 1941–56) in the volumes for 1941–80; and American Literature/1900–1999 and 2000–2099 (as well as any larger chronological section encompassing either century) in later volumes. Researchers must also check the headings beginning with "American" in the subject index to post-1980 volumes and in the online thesaurus.

OTHER BIBLIOGRAPHIES

See

> *Contemporary Authors: Bibliographical Series* (J595a).
> Pownall, *Articles on Twentieth Century Literature* (M2790).
> Somer, *American and British Literature, 1945–1975* (M2800).

Language

See

> Quirk, *Comprehensive Grammar of the English Language* (M2810).

Biographical Dictionaries

See

> *Contemporary Authors* (J595).
> *Dictionary of Literary Biography* (J600).

Periodicals

GUIDES TO PRIMARY WORKS

See

> Sec. K: Periodicals/Little Magazines.
> Chielens, *American Literary Magazines: The Twentieth Century* (Q3410).

GUIDES TO SCHOLARSHIP AND CRITICISM

Q4250   Chielens, Edward E. *The Literary Journal in America, 1900–1950: A Guide to Information Sources.* American Literature, English Literature, and World Literatures in English: An Information Guide Series 16. Detroit: Gale, 1977. 186 pp.   Z6951.C572 [PN4877]   016.051.

An annotated, selective bibliography of English-language studies (through the early 1970s) of periodicals devoted to creative works or criticism. Chielens excludes weeklies and annuals, and includes only those publications that have been the subject of at least one dissertation, book, chapter, or article. Entries are listed alphabetically by author in eight divisions (most of which have sections for general studies and individual titles): general works, general mass circulation periodicals, little magazines, regional publications, politically radical literary periodicals, academic quarterlies of scholarship and criticism, bibliographies and checklists (including sections for some of the preceding divisions), and background studies. Scholarship on literary material in nonliterary periodicals is listed in an appendix. Most annotations are helpfully descriptive. Indexed by persons and titles. While *Literary Journal in America* is not comprehensive, is inefficiently organized, and lacks an adequate explanation of scope, it is a useful compilation of studies that are sometimes difficult to locate in standard serial bibliographies and indexes. This work continues Chielens, *Literary Journal in America to 1900* (Q4145).

INDEXES

See

> *Literary Writings in America* (Q3255).

Genres

Most works in sections L: Genres and Q: American Literature/General/Genres are important to research in twentieth-century American literature.

FICTION

Most works in sections L: Genres/Fiction and Q: American Literature/General/Genres/ Fiction are useful to research in twentieth-century American literature.

Histories and Surveys

Q4260   Karl, Frederick R. *American Fictions, 1940–1980: A Comprehensive History and Critical Evaluation.* New York: Harper, 1983. 637 pp.   PS379.K24 813'.54'09.

────. *American Fictions: 1980–2000: Whose America Is It Anyway?* N.p.: Xlibris, 2001. 535 pp.   PS379.K244.

A critical history of American fiction that emphasizes its relationship to modernism and favors experimental works (in *1940–1980*) and its reflection of "a cultural mosaic of so many conflicting ideas and efforts" that precludes any sense of direction or judgment of achievement (in *1980–2000*). Indexed by persons, titles, and subjects in the first installment; by persons only in the second. An encyclopedic and polemical work, it is especially valuable for placing fiction in cultural contexts. Review: Sanford Pinsker, *Georgia Review* 38 (1984): 891–93.

See also

Allen, *Tradition and Dream: The English and American Novel from the Twenties to Our Time* (M2830).

Bibliographies of Bibliographies

Q4265   McPheron, William, and Jocelyn Sheppard. *The Bibliography of Contemporary American Fiction, 1945–1988: An Annotated Checklist.* Westport: Meckler, 1989. 190 pp.   Z1231.F4 M36 [PS379] 016.813'54'09.

An annotated bibliography of bibliographies of works by or about writers of adult fiction (including science fiction, fantasy, crime, historical, regional, ethnic, and small-press authors) who have achieved prominence since 1945 (along with a few whose reputations were established earlier and who continued to publish into the late 1970s). Coverage extends to books, articles, dissertations, and parts of books published through 1986 (but with some as late as 1988). The 613 entries are organized in two divisions: multiauthor bibliographies (listed alphabetically by editor, author, or title of anonymous work, and excluding serial bibliographies, highly selective checklists, and outdated works); single-author bibliographies (listed by publication date, then alphabetically by compiler, under each fiction writer [except, unaccountably, Baldwin]). Many of the informative annotations are evaluative (but not always rigorously so, especially in the first division) and point out the importance of a work. Two indexes: fiction writers; authors of bibliographies. An essential guide because so many bibliographies of contemporary fiction writers appear in obscure journals or parts of books or are published by little-known presses—and thus not indexed in the standard serial bibliographies and indexes in section G.

Guides to Primary Works

Q4267   American Fiction Database. Rare Books Room, Ohio State University
         Libraries.
    A database of American fiction based on—but not limited to—the William Charvat Collection of American Fiction at Ohio State University. The focus is 1901–50 (but includes works before and after); selection generally follows Lyle H. Wright's criteria for *American Fiction, 1774–[1900]* (Q4180). Records for 1901–25—for which coverage is virtually complete—are published as Geoffrey D. Smith, *American Fiction, 1901–1925: A Bibliography* (Cambridge: Cambridge UP, 1997, 1,038 pp.); work on 1926–50 is ongoing. Although the database, which is housed in the Rare Books Room, is not publicly accessible, individual volumes can be identified through the Rare/Charvat Catalog (http://library.ohio-state.edu/search~S6), which can be searched by author, title, subject (including genre), keyword, call number, *WorldCat* number, and other standard numbers (such as ISBN). Cataloging records for books that are in the database can be identified by searching for "Bibliography of American Fiction" as a keyword and restricting the location to Charvat Collection. Because of the depth of coverage and multiple points of access, the database is a key resource for the study of twentieth-century American fiction—one that makes possible a multitude of subject and genre studies. For a description of the project, see Smith, "Literary Databases: Some Thoughts on Standards," *Literary Research* 13 (1988): 5–12.

See also

> Facts on File Bibliography of American Fiction, 1919–1988 (Q3474).
> Grimes, *Novels in English by Women, 1891–1920* (M2640).

Guides to Scholarship and Criticism

Q4270   Woodress, James. *American Fiction, 1900–1950: A Guide to Information
         Sources.* American Literature, English Literature and World Literatures in
         English: An Information Guide Series 1. Detroit: Gale, 1974. 260 pp.
         Z1231.F4 W64   016.813'03.
    A selective guide to scholarship (mostly in English and published before c. 1972) on 44 authors who have received substantial critical attention. Entries are organized in two divisions: general works and individuals authors. The first division consists of inadequately annotated lists of references works (including general historical and critical studies), general works on the novel (with sections for history and criticism, types, themes, and regionalism), studies of the short story, and collections of interviews. Individual authors are treated in essays, with sections for bibliographies and manuscripts, primary works, editions and reprints, biographical studies, and criticism. The commentary here is much fuller and judiciously evaluative, with important works marked by an

asterisk; however, the essay form prevents skimming. Indexed by persons. Although now dated, *American Fiction* is superior to Blake Nevius, comp., *The American Novel: Sinclair Lewis to the Present,* Goldentree Bibliographies in Language and Literature (New York: Meredith-Appleton, 1970, 126 pp.), and remains useful for its guidance to important scholarship before c. 1972 on authors not included in Bryer, *Sixteen Modern American Authors* (Q4240). For evaluative surveys of recent scholarship, see *American Literary Scholarship* (Q3265).

See also

> *American Literary Scholarship* (Q3265): Chapters on fiction: 1900–1930s; fiction: 1930s–1960s; and fiction: 1960s–present.
> Martine, *American Novelists* (J595a).

Biographical Dictionaries

See

> *Contemporary Novelists* (M2845).

DRAMA AND THEATER

Most works in sections L: Genres/Drama and Theater and Q: American Literature/General/Genres/Drama and Theater are useful for research in twentieth-century American drama and theater.

Guides to Reference Works

Although there is no general guide to reference tools for the study of twentieth-century American theater, the musical theater of this century is more than adequately treated in Paul Metzger, "American Musical Theater: A Guide to Information Sources," *Bulletin of Bibliography* 49 (1992): 251–61 and "American Musical Theater: Supplement 1992–1996," *Bulletin of Bibliography* 54 (1997): 181–86. The annotations are very brief, but several are helpfully evaluative.

Histories and Surveys

Histories and general studies are surveyed in Jackson R. Bryer and Ruth M. Alvarez, "American Drama, 1918–1940: A Survey of Research and Criticism," *American Quarterly* 30 (1978): 298–330, and C. W. E. Bigsby, "Drama as Cultural Sign: American Dramatic Criticism," 331–57; these are updated by Mark W. Estrin, "The American Drama 1900–1940: Areas of Recent Scholarly Achievement and Critical Neglect," *Resources for American Literary Study* 17 (1990): 35–49, and Thomas P. Adler, "American Dramatic Scholarship, 1940–Present: The Contours and Some Items for an Agenda," 51–61 (both with useful suggestions for future research).

Q4275   Bigsby, C. W. E. *A Critical Introduction to Twentieth-Century American Drama.* 3 vols. Cambridge: Cambridge UP, 1982–85.   PS351.B483 812'.52'09.

A critical rather than historical survey of major playwrights, theater groups, and — in vol. 3 — types of drama that emphasizes alienation as the central theme of modern American drama. Vol. 1 has several appendixes listing productions by important theater groups; in vol. 3, an appendix traces the growth of not-for-profit professional theater. Indexed in each volume by persons, titles, and theater groups. Densely written and omitting some important writers, Bigsby nonetheless is the best survey of the topic. Reviews: Peter L. Hays, *Theatre Research International* 8 (1983): 265–67; Myron Matlaw, *Essays in Theatre* 5 (1986): 77–81.

Literary Handbooks, Dictionaries, and Encyclopedias

Q4280   *Notable Names in the American Theatre.* Rev. ed. [Ed. Raymond D. McGill.] Clifton: White, 1976. 1,250 pp.   PN2285.N6   790.2'0973.

An accumulation of biographical and other information on the American stage through c. 1974 that revises Walter Rigdon, ed., *The Biographical Encyclopaedia and Who's Who of the American Theatre* (New York: Heinemann, 1966, 1,101 pp.). *Notable Names* is organized in nine divisions:

> A title list of New York productions since 1900, with entries providing theater, opening date, and number of performances;
>
> A title list of premieres in America since 1968, with entries citing author, date of first performance, producing group, and theater and with an author index following;
>
> A chronological list of premieres of American plays abroad from 9 December 1948 through 8 April 1974, with entries noting date, title, author, director, producer, theater, and location;
>
> An alphabetical list of active and defunct American theater groups, with entries giving address, major personnel, and a brief history;
>
> An alphabetical list of active and defunct American theaters, with entries citing address and opening date;
>
> An alphabetical list of theater awards, with a chronological list of recipients of each;
>
> A subject bibliography of biographies and autobiographies of American and foreign theater persons;
>
> An alphabetical necrology of American and foreign theater persons, with entries providing birth and death dates;
>
> A biographical dictionary of notable persons in the American theater, with stylistically wooden entries providing basic biographical information, address, and lists of credits, publications, and awards.

While the work lacks an adequate statement of scope for most of the lists, fails to provide a general index, and is sometimes inaccurate, it does bring together a significant amount of useful detail about the American stage. (Biographies in *Notable Names* and *Biographical Encyclopedia* are indexed in *Biography and Genealogy Master Index* [J565].)

Guides to Primary Works

Q4285   Leiter, Samuel L., ed. *The Encyclopedia of the New York Stage, 1920–1930.* 2 vols. Westport: Greenwood, 1985. *1930–1940.* 1989. 1,299 pp. *1940–*

1950. 1992. 946 pp.   PN2277.N5 L36   792.9'5'097471. All are online through *North American Theatre Online* (Q3512).

A description of Broadway and off-Broadway plays (as well as foreign-language and ethnic theater productions reviewed in the English-language press) staged from mid-June 1920 through the end of May 1950. Productions are organized alphabetically by title. For each production, a typical entry includes (where appropriate) genre, subject categories, language if other than English, author, translator or adapter, reviser, librettist, music composer, lyricist, source, director, choreographer, set and costume designers, producer, theater, opening date, length of run, plot synopsis, and notes on critical reception. Concludes with a selected bibliography and 10 appendixes: chronological calendar of productions, with length of run; classified lists by genre, subject, and language (but confusingly organized by subcategories); awards; sources of plays; institutional theaters, with a list of plays produced; foreign companies and stars; longest running shows; critics cited; seasonal statistics; theaters. Two indexes: proper names; titles. The inclusion of cast lists and the provision of clearer subject access would increase the *Encyclopedia*'s utility; it is still, however, a valuable compendium of information on the New York theater.

See also

    Bzowski, *American Women Playwrights, 1900–1930* (Q3512a).
    Dramatic Compositions Copyrighted in the United States, 1870 to 1916 (Q4195).
    Harris, *Modern Drama in America and England, 1950–1970* (Q4290).

Guides to Scholarship and Criticism

Surveys of Research

Q4287   Kolin, Philip C., ed. *American Playwrights since 1945: A Guide to Scholarship, Criticism, and Performance.* New York: Greenwood, 1989. 595 pp.   Z1231.D7 A53 [PS350]   016.812'54'09. Online through *North American Theatre Online* (Q3512).

A collection of separately authored bibliographic essays on 40 playwrights who have written for the American stage since 1945. Each essay consists of six parts: a brief overview of the playwright's critical reputation, achievements, and important contributions to American theater; a classified list of published and unpublished primary works (including interviews); a history of productions and their critical reception; an evaluative survey of scholarship and criticism (with separate sections for bibliographies, biographies, source studies, general studies, and analyses of individual plays); suggestions for further research; and a checklist of all sources cited in the essay. Two indexes: persons; titles of plays and screenplays. Coverage is selective—too much so for major playwrights—and limited to English-language publications, and some contributors are cryptic or insufficiently rigorous in assessing secondary works; yet, *American Playwrights* offers a convenient introduction to the reputation of and scholarship on several contemporary dramatists and is especially valuable for its numerous suggestions for further research. Still needed, however, is a full bibliography of studies of contemporary American drama and theater.

Other Bibliographies

Q4289   Gavin, Christy. *American Women Playwrights 1964–1989: A Research Guide and Annotated Bibliography.* Garland Reference Library of the Humanities 879. New York: Garland, 1993. 493 pp.   Z1231.D7 G38 [PS338.W6] 016.812′54099287.

A selective bibliography of plays by and publications about American women playwrights "who have demonstrated a sustained record of achievement and who have produced at least one play on Broadway, Off Broadway, or Off-Off Broadway from the early 1960s through 1989." Following a prefatory survey of feminist scholarship (which concludes with suggestions for future research), the 4,214 entries are organized in two divisions: general studies of contemporary women dramatists and feminist theater; playwrights (with sections for selected plays, profiles and interviews, and reviews and studies of individual plays). Entries for profiles, interviews, and studies (as well as a few reviews) are accompanied by annotations that are often evaluative (and usually wordy). Indexed by authors of annotated entries only. An utterly inadequate (and incomplete as well as frequently erroneous) index, lack of an explanation of the criteria governing selection of works by and about the playwrights, omission of *International Bibliography of Theatre* (L1160) and *ABELL* (G340) from the serial bibliographies searched for entries, and poor design (e.g., the failure to include names of dramatists in running heads makes locating sections on individuals needlessly difficult) make *American Women Playwrights* frustrating to consult; that is unfortunate since the volume offers the best available guide to the widely scattered literature about contemporary American women playwrights.

Q4290   Harris, Richard H. *Modern Drama in America and England, 1950–1970: A Guide to Information Sources.* American Literature, English Literature, and World Literatures in English: An Information Guide Series 34. Detroit: Gale, 1982. 606 pp.   Z1231.D7 H36 [PS351]   016.822′914.

A selective bibliography of editions of British and American plays published for the first time between 1950 and 1975, and of English-language scholarship through 1975 on plays published between 1950 and 1970. Excludes plays produced during the period but published after 1975, musicals, and works by African American playwrights (presumably because such works are included in French, *Afro-American Poetry and Drama* [Q3845], in the same Gale series). Entries are organized in three divisions: bibliographies; general criticism; and 255 authors, each with sections for editions of plays, collaborative works, bibliographies, selected nondramatic works, and criticism. Annotations typically combine description with evaluative comment, but several are inaccurate or inadequately descriptive. Three indexes: persons; titles; subjects (including playwrights). There are significant omissions and the description of scope is confusing and incomplete; thus Harris is useful only for preliminary work. Review: Albert Wertheim, *Literary Research Newsletter* 8 (1983): 38–41. Carpenter, *Modern Drama Scholarship and Criticism, 1966–1980* (M2875), offers more thorough coverage of studies after 1965.

Superior coverage of works (through c. 1981) by and about Albee, Baraka, Bullins, Gelber, Kopit, Mamet, Rabe, Shepard, Simon, and Lanford Wilson can be found in Kimball King, *Ten Modern American Playwrights: An Annotated Bibliography,* Garland Reference Library of the Humanities 234 (New York: Garland, 1982, 251 pp.), which is particularly valuable for its full annotations, coverage of foreign scholarship, lists of reviews, and inclusion of translations of primary works.

Q4295   Wildbihler, Hubert, and Sonja Völklein. *The Musical: An International
        Annotated Bibliography/Eine internationale annotierte Bibliographie.*
        München: Saur, 1986. 320 pp.   ML128.M78 W56   016.78281'09.

A bibliography of studies through 1985 on the musical (including stage and film
productions, extravaganzas, vaudeville and variety shows, and operettas), primarily in
North America but also in Great Britain, the Federal Republic of Germany, and a few
other countries. Most reviews of individual productions are excluded. The approximately 3,600 entries are organized by publication date in five classified divisions: general
reference works (with sections for encyclopedias and guides, review and song indexes,
bibliographies, yearbooks, and discographies); stage musical in North America (predecessors, history and development, elements of the musical [such as music and dance],
production, and public reception); stage musical in other countries (Great Britain, Federal Republic of Germany and Austria, socialist countries, and other countries); film
musical (general studies, essays and short criticism, special effects, adaptations of stage
musicals, and dance); and people (general biographical works; composers, lyricists, and
librettists; directors, choreographers, and producers; performers). The subtitle is misleading, since only about one-fourth of the entries are accompanied by descriptive
annotations, a few of which incorporate an evaluative comment; none of the entries in
the people divisions is annotated. Two indexes: scholars; subjects and titles of musicals.
Despite the incomplete annotation, this work provides the fullest list of scholarship on
the musical and is especially valuable for its international coverage of scholarship.

See also

> Carpenter, *Modern Drama Scholarship and Criticism, 1966–1980* (M2875).
> "Modern Drama Studies: An Annual Bibliography," *Modern Drama* (M2870).
> Roudané, *American Dramatists* (J595a).
> Wilmeth, *American Stage to World War I* (Q3525).

Review Indexes

Q4300   Salem, James M. *A Guide to Critical Reviews.* 4 pts. Metuchen: Scarecrow,
        1971–91.   Z5781.S16 [PN2266]   016.8092.
> Pt. 1: *American Drama, 1909–1982.* 3rd ed. 1984. 657 pp.
> Pt. 2: *The Musical, 1909–1989.* 3rd ed. 1991. 820 pp.
> Pt. 3: *Foreign Drama, 1909–1977.* 2nd ed. 1979. 420 pp.
> Pt. 4: *The Screenplay from* The Jazz Singer *to* Dr. Strangelove. 2 vols. 1971.
>   *Supplement One: 1963–1980.* 1982. 698 pp.

A selective checklist of reviews in general-circulation American and Canadian periodicals and the *New York Times* of productions on the New York stage and of movie
and television screenplays. Salem excludes productions of plays written before the late
nineteenth century (but the precise cutoff date is unclear). Plays are listed alphabetically
by author; screenplays and musicals, by title. Under each work, reviews are organized
alphabetically by periodical title. Each part includes a list of major awards; lists of
popular or long-running plays appear in pts. 1–3. Indexes: pt. 1 (names; titles); pt. 2
(authors, composers, lyricists; directors, designers, choreographers; original works and
authors); pt. 3 (authors, adapters, translators; titles). Limited in scope, the series is
principally useful as a compilation of reviews indexed in the standard general indexes
in section G.

Biographical Dictionaries

Q4305   *Contemporary Theatre, Film, and Television: A Biographical Guide Featuring Performers, Directors, Writers, Producers, Designers, Managers, Choreographers, Technicians, Composers, Executives, Dancers, and Critics in the United States, Canada, Great Britain, and the World.* Detroit: Gale, 1984– . Annual. (Subtitle varies.)   PN2285.C58   791'.092'2. Online through *Biography Resource Center* (J572).

The expanded continuation of *Who's Who in the Theatre* (Detroit: Gale, 1912–81) that emphasizes established, active individuals but also includes some major figures who are inactive or who died after 1960. Entries, which are modeled after *Contemporary Authors* (J595), provide biographical information; career data; publications; screen credits; recordings; memberships; awards; miscellaneous details; and home, office, or agent address. All but a few entries are based on information supplied or checked by the entrant or an agent. Succeeding volumes print updated or revised entries. Cumulative index in each volume; beginning with vol. 2, the cumulative index also covers all 17 editions of *Who's Who in the Theatre* and *Who Was Who in the Theatre: A Biographical Dictionary of Actors, Actresses, Directors, Playwrights, and Producers of English-Speaking Theatre*, 4 vols., Gale Composite Biographical Dictionary Series 3 (Detroit: Gale, 1978). All these volumes are also indexed in *Biography and Genealogy Master Index* (J565). Although the guide is not comprehensive and although the information supplied by entrants or agents is not always accurate or complete, *Contemporary Theatre* is a useful source of biographical and career information (as well as addresses) of important persons connected with American or British theater, film, or television.

See also

> *Contemporary Dramatists* (M2880).
> *Notable Names in the American Theatre* (Q4280).

POETRY

Most works in section L: Genres/Poetry are important to research in twentieth-century American poetry.

Histories and Surveys

See

> Perkins, *History of Modern Poetry* (M2890).

Bibliographies of Bibliographies

Q4315   McPheron, William. *The Bibliography of Contemporary American Poetry, 1945–1985: An Annotated Checklist.* Westport: Meckler, 1986. 72 pp. Z1231.P7 M37 [PS323.5]   016.811'54.

A bibliography of bibliographies of works by or about American poets whose reputations were established since 1945. Coverage includes separately published bibliographies, articles, dissertations, theses, and parts of books through 1984. The 267 entries are listed in two divisions: multiple-author bibliographies (organized alphabetically by compiler or editor and including bibliographies of private presses) and single-author bibliographies (listed by publication date under each author). The annotations offer a clear description of scope and (usually) a succinct evaluation of a work's utility or quality. The introduction provides an overview of the bibliography of contemporary poetry. Although the first division includes some works that hardly qualify as bibliographies and although access is hampered by the lack of a subject index or cross-references to multiple-author bibliographies, McPheron includes a number of works not indexed in the standard serial bibliographies and indexes in section G and is the essential guide to bibliographies of contemporary poets.

Guides to Primary Works

Bibliographies and Indexes

Q4320   Davis, Lloyd, and Robert Irwin. *Contemporary American Poetry: A Checklist.* Metuchen: Scarecrow, 1975. 179 pp. Davis. *Second Series, 1973–1983.* 1985. 297 pp.   Z1231.P7 D38 [PS323.5]   016.811'5'4.
An author list of books of poetry by Americans born after 1900 and still publishing after 1950. The original volume covers 1950 through 1972 (as well as some earlier publications by established poets); the latter, 1973 through 1983. Both exclude vanity press books, collaborations, translations, children's books, broadsides, reprints, and most publications of fewer than 10 pages, although exceptions are made for established writers. Books are listed by publication date under each poet. Indexed by titles. Because the works are far from complete, include many errors, list several non-American writers, and take many entries unverified from unidentified sources, they are useful only as a preliminary guide to volumes of poetry published after 1950 by writers who are not the subject of an author bibliography. For most others, *WorldCat* (E225) and RLG Union Catalog (E230) will provide a more accurate, thorough list of separate publications.
Kirby Congdon, *Contemporary Poets in American Anthologies, 1960–1977* (Metuchen: Scarecrow, 1978, 228 pp.), is virtually useless since it indexes poets but not poems.

Q4325   *Index of American Periodical Verse: [1971–   ].* Lanham: Scarecrow, 1973–   . Annual.   Z1231.P7 I47   016.811'5'4.
An author list of poems appearing in selected periodicals, primarily English-language little magazines, university reviews, and scholarly journals published in North America (although a few Spanish-language publications have been indexed since the volume for 1981). Coverage currently encompasses about 300 periodicals and includes poets from all periods and countries, although the majority are contemporary American writers. Entries are listed alphabetically by author; cross-references cite variant forms of names. Indexed by titles. Compilations since 1982 are also available as digital files from the editors. Although the criteria governing selection of periodicals are vague ("a broad cross section" and "recommendations of poets, librarians, literary scholars, and publishers") and although coverage is far from comprehensive, this work is a useful source for locating poems by contemporary poets in periodicals indexed nowhere else.
Some additional periodicals—along with a variety of single-author collections—are indexed by author, title, and first line in *Roth's American Poetry Annual [1988–90]:*

A Reference and Guide to Poetry Published in the United States during [1987–89] (Great Neck: Roth, 1989–91, annual), which continues *Annual Index to Poetry in Periodicals [1984–86]* (Great Neck: Poetry Index, 1985–88) and *American Poetry Index: An Author, Title, and Subject Index to Poetry by Americans in Single-Author Collections [1981–86]* (Great Neck: Granger, 1983–88). None of the preceding explains the criteria governing the selection of periodicals or collections.

For earlier publications, see the following:

> Caskey, Jefferson D., comp. *Index to Poetry in Popular Periodicals, 1955–1959.* Westport: Greenwood, 1984. 269 pp. *1960–1964.* 1988. 232 pp. Author, title, first-line, and subject indexes to poems in periodicals covered by *Readers' Guide* (G400), which does not index poems after 1957.
>
> *Index to Poetry in Periodicals, 1925–1929: An Index of Poets and Poems Published in American Magazines and Newspapers.* Great Neck: Granger, 1984. 265 pp. Covers about 450 periodicals and newspapers.
>
> *Index to Poetry in Periodicals, 1920–1924: An Index of Poets and Poems Published in American Magazines and Newspapers.* Great Neck: Granger, 1983. 178 pp. Covers 302 periodicals and newspapers.
>
> *Index to Poetry in Periodicals: American Poetic Renaissance, 1915–1919: An Index of Poets and Poems Published in American Magazines and Newspapers.* Great Neck: Granger, 1981. 221 pp. An author index to 122 American magazines and newspapers.

Q4330   Reardon, Joan, and Kristine A. Thorsen. *Poetry by American Women, 1900–1975: A Bibliography.* Metuchen: Scarecrow, 1979. 674 pp. Reardon. *Poetry by American Women, 1975–1989: A Bibliography.* 1990. 232 pp.
Z1229.W8 R4 [PS151]   016.811'008.

An author bibliography of about 12,380 separately published volumes of poetry by some 7,065 female United States citizens who published significant works between 1900 and 1989. Both compilations exclude mixed-genre works, foreign-language editions, and most broadsides; reprints and collaborative works are excluded in the 1900–75 volume but not in the supplement. Entries—listed by publication date under an author—cite title, publication information, and pagination. Indexed by titles. Although the authors base most entries on standard bibliographical resources rather than the examination of copies and are inconsistent in citing later editions and providing cross-references for pseudonyms and variant forms of names, *Poetry by American Women* is a serviceable compilation.

See also

> Baughman, *American Poets* (J595a).
> *Poetry Index Annual* (L1235a).

Text Archives

Q4333   *Twentieth-Century American Poetry.* ProQuest. Online. 17 June 2006
<http://collections.chadwyck.com>.

An archive of rekeyed texts of more than 50,000 English-language poems by twentieth-century American poets. Editions were selected according to the following criteria: a collected edition; other editions for poets without a collected one. Selection is based on an attempt to present "a broad representative collection that reflects the diversity of

modern American literary traditions, including . . . major figures alongside histori-
cally important writers and younger emergent poets" and on the ability to secure rights
for electronic publication.

Simple keyword, first line or title, and author searches can be limited by publication date, publisher, gender, date during a poet's lifetime, ethnicity, literary movement, to rhymed or unrhymed poems, and to notes. Searchers can also browse an author
list of the contents of the database. Results appear in ascending alphabetical order and
cannot be re-sorted. Citations (but not the full text of poems) can be marked for
e-mailing, downloading, or printing; each citation includes a durable URL to the full
text.

Some works are rekeyed from textually unsound editions; however, the bibliographic record for each work identifies the source of the text and any omissions (e.g.,
preliminary matter). Besides being a useful source for identifying an elusive quotation
or half-remembered line, the scope of *Twentieth-Century American Poetry*'s text archive
makes feasible a variety of kinds of studies (stylistic, thematic, imagistic, and topical).

The contents of *Twentieth-Century American Poetry* can also be searched through
LiOn (I527), which offers a less versatile search interface.

Continues *American Poetry* (Q3536).

Guides to Scholarship and Criticism

Q4335   Gingerich, Martin E. *Contemporary Poetry in America and England, 1950–*
         1975. American Literature, English Literature, and World Literatures in
         English: An Information Guide Series 41. Detroit: Gale, 1983. 453 pp.
         Z1231.P7 G56 [PS303]   016.811'5.

An annotated selective bibliography of English-language studies (published
through 1978, but with some additions through 1981) on contemporary British and
American poetry. The approximately 100 poets (two-thirds of them American) are
selected on the basis of having been the subject of a reasonable amount of criticism,
although writers who appear in other volumes in the series are excluded. The studies
included seem to represent what the compiler found in standard bibliographies and
indexes. The descriptively annotated entries are organized alphabetically in eight divisions: bibliographies and reference works, contemporary culture and sociology, general
aesthetics and poetic theory, general studies of poetry and poets, general studies of
American poets and literature, general studies of British poets and literature, studies of
two or more poets, and individual authors (each with sections, when needed, for books
of poetry, bibliographies, biographies, books about, and articles about). Users must
consult existing author bibliographies, since Gingerich supplements but does not duplicate listings in them, and use the name index to locate general studies that discuss
an author, since there are no cross-references. Two indexes: names; titles of works cited.
The considerable gaps in coverage and lack of a subject index leave this work far short
of the sorely needed bibliography of scholarship and criticism on contemporary poetry.
It is, however, far superior to Phillis Gershator, *A Bibliographic Guide to the Literature
of Contemporary American Poetry, 1970–1975* (Metuchen: Scarecrow, 1976, 124 pp.),
which relies extensively on other sources, is far from complete, is inadequately indexed,
and includes only books published between 1970 and 1975.

See also

     Sec. M: English Literature/Twentieth Century Literature/Genres/Poetry/Guides
     to Scholarship and Criticism.

American Literary Scholarship (Q3265): Chapters on poetry: 1900–1940s and poetry: 1940s–present.
Baughman, *American Poets* (J595a).
Kuntz, *Poetry Explication* (L1255).
Leo, *Guide to American Poetry Explication*, vol. 2 (L1255a).

Biographical Dictionaries

See

   Contemporary Poets (M2895).

PROSE

Some works in sections L: Genres/Prose and Q: American Literature/General/Genres/Prose are useful for research in twentieth-century American prose.

Guides to Scholarship and Criticism

Q4345   Brier, Peter A., and Anthony Arthur. *American Prose and Criticism, 1900–1950: A Guide to Information Sources.* American Literature, English Literature, and World Literatures in English: An Information Guide Series 35. Detroit: Gale, 1981. 242 pp.   Z1231.P8 B74 [PS362] 016.81′08′0052.

A bibliography of works (through the mid-1970s) by and about prose writers "who transcend the idiom and intention of purely journalistic or academic writing." The entries are organized in two separate parts: prose and criticism. The first is composed of two divisions: general works (with sections for handbooks, bibliographies and checklists, intellectual background, rhetorical studies, anthologies, and studies of periodicals) and individual authors, who are categorized as entertainers, teachers, or reporters, and then ranked in three groups: A, who receive an annotated list of primary and secondary works; B, for whom selected primary works and studies are summarized in a few paragraphs; and C, who are given a couple sentences each. The criticism part is composed of three divisions: general works (with sections for bibliographies, general histories of criticism, studies of schools and movements, and literary histories important to the history of criticism), collections of critical essays, and major critics (with separate lists of bibliographies and critical works, an essay discussion of representative studies, and a list of other sources). In both parts, annotations or discussions are largely descriptive. Three indexes: scholars; titles; subjects. Because of the incomplete coverage and lack of criteria governing the selection of both writers and studies, *American Prose and Criticism* is only marginally useful as a starting point for research and must be supplemented by the serial bibliographies and indexes in section G.

R

Other Literatures in English

This section includes works devoted exclusively to literatures in English outside of England, Scotland, Wales, Ireland, and the United States. Because writers in some of these literatures are included in reference works on English or British literature, researchers must consult section M: English Literature. Many works listed in sections G: Serial Bibliographies, Indexes, and Abstracts and H: Guides to Dissertations and Theses cover these literatures.

General

Literary Handbooks, Dictionaries, and Encyclopedias

R4355   *Encyclopedia of Post-colonial Literatures in English.* Ed. Eugene Benson and
L. W. Conolly. 2nd ed. 2 vols. London: Routledge–Taylor and Francis,
2005.   PR9080.A52 E53   820.9′917124′09045.

An encyclopedia of genres, subjects, national literatures, and writers associated with
the English-language literatures of Australia, Bangladesh, Canada, the Caribbean, East
Africa, Gibraltar, Hong Kong, India, Malaysia, Malta, New Zealand, Pakistan, the
Philippines, Saint Helena, Singapore, South Africa, South Central Africa, the South
Pacific, Sri Lanka, and West Africa. The more than 1,800 signed entries (with coverage
to 2002–03) combine factual information with critical commentary and frequently end
with suggestions for further reading (many entries on genres run to several thousand
words). Concludes with an admirably detailed index of titles, subjects, and persons.
Encyclopedia of Post-colonial Literatures in English is easily the most extensive general
encyclopedia of the newer literatures in English.

See also

Cambridge Guide to Literature in English (C125).

Guides to Primary Works

See

GlobalBooksinPrint.com (Q4225).

Guides to Scholarship and Criticism

SERIAL BIBLIOGRAPHIES

R4375   "Annual Bibliography of Commonwealth Literature [1964–]." *Journal of
Commonwealth Literature* 1 (1965)– .   PR1.J67   820.05.

A classified bibliography of primary and secondary works with divisions for general
studies, East and Central Africa, Western Africa, Southern Africa, Australia (with Papua
New Guinea), Canada, India, Malaysia and Singapore, New Zealand (including the
South Pacific islands), Sri Lanka, West Indies, Pakistan, and South Africa; some divisions—notably those for East and Central Africa, Western Africa, Southern Africa, and
the West Indies—appear irregularly, and the first three disappear after 26 (1991). Each
division is prefaced by an overview of the year's publications and has sections for bibliographies, research aids, primary works (by genre), criticism (classified by general works
and individual authors), nonfiction, and new periodicals. Even though "Annual Bibliography of Commonwealth Literature" is not comprehensive, it offers the best coverage
of current studies of English-language literature in several of the countries or areas.

Some additional publications are listed in "Bibliography of Books and Articles Published in English on Colonialism and Imperialism in [1999–]," *Journal of Colonialism and Social History* 1 (2000–), which currently organizes journal articles, books, and essays from collections or chapters from books in separate alphabetized, unannotated lists. See New, *Critical Writings on Commonwealth Literatures* (R4380), for scholarship before 1964.

See also

> Secs. G: Serial Bibliographies, Indexes, and Abstracts and H: Guides to Dissertations and Theses.
> *ABELL* (G340): Entries on English-language writers and literatures are dispersed throughout.
> *MLAIB* (G335): English Literature division (especially English III: General) through the volume for 1956; English XI: Australia, Canada, Etc. section in the volumes for 1957–66; English II: Australia, Canada, Etc. section in the volumes for 1967–80; and the [British] Commonwealth Literature/Canadian Literature section in later volumes. Researchers must also check the headings beginning with "Commonwealth" in the subject index to post-1980 volumes and in the online thesaurus.
> *YWES* (G330): African, Caribbean, and Canadian Literatures in English chapter since vol. 63 (for 1982); expanded to include Australian, New Zealand, and Indian literatures in vol. 64 (for 1983).

OTHER BIBLIOGRAPHIES

R4380   New, William H. *Critical Writings on Commonwealth Literatures: A Selective Bibliography to 1970, with a List of Theses and Dissertations.* University Park: Pennsylvania State UP, 1975. 333 pp.   Z2000.9.N48 [PR9080] 016.82'09.

A selective bibliography of scholarship on Commonwealth literatures in English. The 6,576 entries are organized in two parts: published works; theses and dissertations. In each part, entries are listed alphabetically by author in classified divisions for general works and countries or areas (East and West Africa, Australia, Canada, New Zealand, South Africa and Rhodesia, South Asia [India, Pakistan, and Ceylon], Southeast Asia [Malaysia, Singapore, and Philippines], and West Indies). Where appropriate, each division has sections for reference works, general studies, and individual authors. Indexed by scholars. Unfortunately, *Critical Writings on Commonwealth Literatures* separates published works from theses and dissertations—an unnecessary distinction; moreover, it is superseded in parts by recent bibliographies of a national literature or area. Still, the work remains an indispensable source that includes a significant number of studies overlooked by the standard bibliographies and indexes in section G. For scholarship since 1964, see "Annual Bibliography of Commonwealth Literature" (R4375).

Portions of New are continued in a regrettably short-lived series edited by Alan Lawson: *Post-colonial Literatures in English*, Reference Publication in Literature (New York: Hall-Simon 1996–97):

> Lawson, Alan, Leigh Dale, Helen Tiffin, and Shane Rowlands. *Post-colonial Literatures in English: General, Theoretical, and Comparative, 1970–1993.* 1997. 374 pp.

Lever, Richard, James Wieland, and Scott Findlay. *Post-colonial Literatures in English: Australia, 1970–1992.* 1996. 361 pp.

Williams, Mark. *Post-colonial Literatures in English: Southeast Asia, New Zealand, and the Pacific, 1970–1992.* 1996. 370 pp.

Each volume offers a selective annotated guide to scholarship. Although organization varies from title to title, all but *General, Theoretical, and Comparative* have a section for reference works, general studies, and publications about individual authors. Two indexes: persons; subjects (the latter needs considerable improvement, e.g., that in *Southeast Asia, New Zealand, and the Pacific* consists primarily of names and cannot be trusted to index those; that in *Australia* is inconsistent in its coverage). Despite the inadequate subject indexing (except in *General, Theoretical, and Comparative*), these volumes, with their typically full annotations and judicious selectivity, offer some of the best guidance to recent studies of newer literatures in English.

Periodicals

GUIDES TO PRIMARY WORKS

R4385   Warwick, Ronald, comp. and ed. *Commonwealth Literature Periodicals: A Bibliography, Including Periodicals of Former Commonwealth Countries, with Locations in the United Kingdom.* London: Mansell, 1979. 146 pp. Z2000.9.W37 [PR9080]   016.805.

A bibliography and finding list of English-language scholarly and literary journals published through mid-1977 in or about current and former Commonwealth countries (excluding the United Kingdom). Journals are placed according to focus rather than country of publication, in divisions for general works, Africa, Australia, Canada, Caribbean, Hong Kong, Malaysia and Singapore, Mediterranean, New Zealand, Pacific Islands, South Asia, and former Commonwealth nations. Many are subdivided by region or genre. A typical entry cites title, frequency of publication, date of first and last issue, place of publication, publisher, editor, variant titles, and holdings in United Kingdom libraries. (North American scholars will want to consult *WorldCat* [E225], RLG Union Catalog [E230], *Union List of Serials* [K640a], and *New Serial Titles* [K640] for locations.) Although the inevitable omissions and errors appear in this first attempt at a comprehensive list of Commonwealth literary journals, it is an essential source for identifying and locating frequently elusive publications.

An essential complement for nineteenth-century periodicals is Vann, *Periodicals of Queen Victoria's Empire: An Exploration* (M2525a).

INDEXES

See

Index to Commonwealth Little Magazines (K795).

African Literatures in English

Works in section R: Other Literatures in English/General are important to research in African literatures in English.

Guides to Primary Works

R4420   Jahn, Janheinz, and Claus Peter Dressler. *Bibliography of Creative African Writing*. Nendeln: KTO, 1971. 446 pp.   Z3508.L5 J28   016.8088.

A bibliography of works by and about African authors writing in English and in a variety of other European and African languages. Jahn and Dressler include all books published before 1900 but only creative works from 1910 to c. 1970 (along with some manuscripts ready for publication); except for plays, they exclude separate works in periodicals and anthologies. Coverage of scholarship (including reviews) is selective but international in scope. Entries are organized alphabetically by author within five classified divisions: general (with sections for bibliographies, journals, general studies, negritude, and general anthologies), Western Africa, Central Africa, Eastern Africa, and Austral Africa. Within each region are sections for general studies, anthologies, and individual works; general studies of an author precede the list of his or her primary works, and studies of a specific work are listed after the work. Additions appear on pp. 376–77. Forgeries are listed in an appendix. Four indexes: books by African language (classified according to the four regions); translations, organized by language of the translation; books, by country; persons. Users should study the introductory discussion of limitations and editorial practices. Impressive in its accuracy and breadth, *Bibliography of Creative African Writing* remains the best single list of creative works published before 1970. Parts have now been superseded by more recent author and regional bibliographies, however.

See also

"Annual Bibliography of Commonwealth Literature" (R4375).

Guides to Scholarship and Criticism

SERIAL BIBLIOGRAPHIES

R4423   *South African Studies*. Baltimore: Natl. Information Services Corp. (NISC). Quarterly. Online. 6 Dec. 2006 <http://biblioline.nisc.com>; CD-ROM. (Also available as part of *Africa-Wide: NiPAD* <http://biblioline.nisc .com>.)

A group of databases that provide access to documents about South Africa or produced in the country. Of most interest to literary researchers are the *Index to South African Periodicals* (1987–), the *South African National Bibliography* (1988–), and— especially—the National English Literary Museum (NELM) databases (with coverage extending back to the nineteenth century, though that for 1990–present is more thorough): *Select Index to South African Literature in English, Critical Writings* (which currently includes more than 27,800 books, articles, dissertations, and reviews), *Select Index to South African Literature in English, Creative Writings* (with more than 141,600 records), the NELM catalog (more than 18,500 records), the NELM manuscripts catalog (more than 34,800 records), and *A Bibliography of Anglophone Literature and Literary Criticism by Black South Africans* (which covers first printings of creative and critical writing by South Africans of color between 1800 and 1990). Many records include abstracts. Currency, depth of coverage, and well-designed search menus at all levels make *South African Studies* an essential resource for research in South African literature.

For those unable to access *South African Studies,* the NELM will do searches of its databases for a small fee (http://www.ru.ac.za/affiliates/nelm/nelmhome.html).

OTHER BIBLIOGRAPHIES

R4425   Lindfors, Bernth. *Black African Literature in English: A Guide to Information Sources.* American Literature, English Literature, and World Literatures in English: An Information Guide Series 23. Detroit: Gale, 1979. 482 pp. *Black African Literature in English, 1977–1981: Supplement.* New York: Africana, 1986. 382 pp. *Black African Literature in English, 1982–1986.* London: Zell, 1989. 444 pp. *Black African Literature in English, 1987– 1991.* Bibliographical Research in African Literatures 3. London: Zell, 1995. 682 pp. *Black African Literature in English, 1992–1996.* Oxford: Zell-Currey, 2000. 654 pp. *Black African Literature in English, 1997–1999.* Oxford: Zell-Currey, 2003. 457 pp.   Z3508.L5 L56 [PR9340]   016.82.

A bibliography of important scholarship and critical editions from 1936 through 1999. Lindfors excludes reviews, political biographies, and newspaper articles on nonliterary activity by authors. Entries are organized in two divisions: genres, topics, and reference sources; individual authors. The first division has sections for bibliographies, biographical sources, interviews with critics and multiple authors, general studies, fiction, drama, media (in 1992–99), poetry, criticism, autobiography, children's literature, popular literature, language and style, literature and commitment, role of the writer, folklore and literature, image of the African, audience, craft of writing, periodicals, publishing, censorship, research (dissertation guides, surveys of research, and discussions of reference works), teaching, organizations and associations, conferences, and festivals; most of these sections have separate lists of bibliographies and studies. Bibliographies, biographical works, interviews, and criticism are listed separately under each author. Most sections conclude with a lengthy list of cross-references. Only a few entries are briefly annotated, principally with a list of authors discussed but sometimes with a note on content or evaluative comment. Four indexes: persons; titles of works cited; subjects; regions. Authoritative in its selection of the most important scholarship and including numerous works omitted from the standard bibliographies and indexes in section G, Lindfors is the indispensable guide to the topic; however, users will wish for more extensive annotations by one of the foremost scholars of black African literature in English.

For a statistical analysis of the studies listed in the first four volumes, see Lindfors, "Counting Caliban's Curses: A Statistical Inventory," *Language, Literature, and Society: A Conference in Honour of Bessie Head,* spec. issue of *Marang* (1999): 57–63.

See also

> Lindfors, "Researching African Literatures" (S4865).
> *MLAIB* (G335): See the English Literature division, especially English III: General, in volumes through 1956; English XI: Australia, Canada, Etc./Africa section in the volumes for 1957–66; English II: Australia, Canada, Etc./Africa section in the volumes for 1967–80; and the African Literature division in later volumes. For African literatures in other languages, see General VII: Oriental and African section in the volumes for 1965–66; Oriental and African Literatures III: Africa in the volume for 1967; and the African Literature division in later volumes. Researchers must also check the headings beginning with "African(s)" in the subject index to post-1980 volumes and in the online thesaurus.
> New, *Critical Writings on Commonwealth Literatures* (R4380).
> Schwartz, *Articles on Women Writers* (U6605).
> *YWES* (G330): African literature has been covered in the African, Caribbean, Canadian, Australian, New Zealand, and Indian Literatures in English chapter since vol. 63 (for 1982).

Australian Literature

Works in section R: Other Literatures in English/General are important to research in Australian literature.

Guides to Reference Works

R4440   Lock, Fred, and Alan Lawson. *Australian Literature: A Reference Guide.*
2nd ed. Australian Bibliographies. Melbourne: Oxford UP, 1980. 120 pp.
Z4011.L6 [PR9604.3]   016.82.

A selective guide to reference sources important to research in Australian literature. The 417 entries—which comprise general works as well as those specific to Australia— are variously organized in seven classified divisions: bibliographies; other reference works (including encyclopedias, language dictionaries, guides to quotations and proverbs, biographical dictionaries, literary handbooks, and literary and cultural histories); individual authors (limited to bibliographies, textual studies, and biographies); periodicals; library resources (with informative descriptions of important collections of Australian literature in the country's libraries); general guides to literary, bibliographical, and biographical research; and professional associations. Many sections are preceded by headnotes that compare works and offer helpful tips on research procedures. The full annotations clearly describe and frequently evaluate works. Judiciously selective and informative but now dated, this is the essential guide to research in Australian literature. A new edition is a major desideratum. Review: Laurie Hergenhan, *Australian Literary Studies* 9 (1980): 542–47.

Horst Priessnitz and Marion Spies, *Neuere Informationsmittel zur Literatur Australiens: Ein bibliographischer Essay,* Anglophone Literaturen: Hamburger Beiträge zur Erforschung neuer englischsprachiger Literaturen/Anglophone Literatures: Hamburg

Studies in the New Literatures in English 3 (Hamburg: Lit, 1996, 67 pp.)—with coverage through 1995 and including some works in progress—is an essential complement to *Australian Literature*. Each section begins with a list of reference sources, the majority of which are described in an accompanying essay (with numerous additional works cited in footnotes). Unfortunately, the lack of an index and the essay format make *Neuere Informationsmittel zur Literatur Australiens* less accessible than it should be.

The best general guide to reference works (through 1974) on Australia is D. H. Borchardt, *Australian Bibliography: A Guide to Printed Sources of Information* [3rd ed.] (Rushcutters Bay: Pergamon, 1976, 270 pp.). The descriptive surveys, keyed to a list of works cited and accompanied by an inadequate subject index, are difficult to scan, however.

Histories and Surveys

R4445   Green, H. M. *A History of Australian Literature Pure and Applied: A Critical Review of All Forms of Literature Produced in Australia from the First Books Published after the Arrival of the First Fleet until 1950.* Rev. by Dorothy Green. 2 vols. Sydney: Angus, 1984–85.   PR9604.3.G74   820'.9'994.

A critical history of belletristic, philosophical, biographical, theological, historical, and scholarly writing by Australian residents or those influenced by their stay in the country. The history is organized in four periods (1789–1850, 1850–90, 1890–1923, and 1923–50), each divided in two parts—belles lettres and applied literature—with chapters on genres or types of works. Vol. 3, which was to cover 1950–80, was never published. Indexed in vol. 2 by persons, titles, and some subjects. Although in need of updating and superseded in parts by more specialized studies, Green remains the seminal history of Australian literature. Review: (vols. 1–2) Bruce Bennett, *Australian Literary Studies* 12 (1986): 542–46 (includes a comparison with Goodwin, *History of Australian Literature* [below]).

The best short histories are Ken Goodwin, *A History of Australian Literature* (New York: St. Martin's, 1986, 322 pp.), which extends to 1984; Laurie Hergenhan, gen. ed., *The Penguin New Literary History of Australia* (Victoria: Penguin, 1988, 620 pp.; also published as *Australian Literary Studies* 13.4 [1988]), with chapters on periods, genres, groups, culture, and literary production; and Bruce Bennett and Jennifer Strauss, eds., *The Oxford Literary History of Australia* (Melbourne: Oxford UP, 1998, 488pp.), which replaces (but for Joy Hooton's bibliographical survey, pp. 427–90) the less satisfactory *The Oxford History of Australian Literature*, ed. Leonie Kramer (Melbourne: Oxford UP, 1981, 509 pp.).

Literary Handbooks, Dictionaries, and Encyclopedias

R4450   Wilde, William H., Joy Hooton, and Barry Andrews. *The Oxford Companion to Australian Literature.* 2nd ed. Melbourne: Oxford UP, 1994. 833 pp.   PR9600.2.W55   820'.9'944. Online through *Oxford Reference Online* (I530).

Covers all aspects of Australian literary culture in about 3,000 entries on authors (including historians, critics, and journalists, but with very selective coverage of con-

temporary writers), major works, literary and scholarly journals, awards, societies, movements, publishers, literary characters and types, cultural and scholarly organizations,
Australian life and history, places, other literature-related topics, and foreign writers
who visited the continent or had an impact on its literature. Author entries (which
predominate in the listings) include basic biographical information, a brief overview of
important works, appreciative commentary in some instances, and (for major writers)
a selective list of criticism. Entrants are indexed in *Biography and Genealogy Master Index*
(J565). Although the *Oxford Companion* is a useful source for quick reference, several
reviewers have noted significant omissions, numerous contradictions in editorial guidelines, and several errors and have questioned the overall balance of the work. Reviews:
Overland 102 (1986): 6–15; Miriam J. Shillingsburg, *Review* 9 (1987): 231–39; (2nd
ed.) Brian Kiernan, *Antipodes* 9 (1995): 168–70; Marion Spiess, *Australian Literary
Studies* 17 (1996): 310–17 (with numerous additions for nineteenth-century literature).

R4455   *The Dictionary of Australian Quotations.* Ed. Stephen Murray-Smith. 2nd
         ed. Port Melbourne: Mandarin, 1992. 493 pp.   PN6081.D496   828'.02.
    A dictionary of quotations ranging from aboriginal times to the late 1980s and
encompassing "anything worth retrieving and repeating that has been said by outsiders
about Australia, and anything worth collecting that Australians have said about anything." Quotations are organized alphabetically by author. Two indexes: keywords;
subjects. The corrected reprint of the original edition (Richmond: Heinemann, 1987,
464 pp.) remains useful for quotations deleted in the second edition. The *Dictionary* is
the best source for locating quotations from Australian authors or about the country.
    Additional quotations can be found in *The Macquarie Dictionary of Australian
Quotations,* ed. Stephen Torre ([Sydney]: Macquarie Lib., 1990, 431 pp.).

Annals

R4460   Hooton, Joy, and Harry Heseltine. *Annals of Australian Literature.* 2nd ed.
         Melbourne: Oxford UP, 1992. 367 pp.   Z4021.H66 [PR9604.3]
         016.8208'0994.
    A chronology from 1784 through 1988 of Australian literary works (interpreted
broadly to include historical, biographical, political, anthropological, popular, critical,
and philological works). Under each year the main column lists author, year of birth,
literary work (primarily books), and genre; the secondary column notes births and
deaths of writers, the founding of newspapers and periodicals, and publication of nonliterary books by Australians and of significant foreign works referring to Australia.
Indexed by authors. Interpreting entries requires continual reference to the key to abbreviations and symbols (p. viii). The introductory discussion of editorial principles is
utterly inadequate: for a full understanding of the inclusion and presentation of material
readers are expected to consult the original edition (Grahame Johnston, *Annals of Australian Literature* [Melbourne: Oxford UP, 1970, 147 pp.]). Hooton and Heseltine
merely note that their selection of entries is "based on an even broader idea of literature"
than Johnston's and inexcusably provide only "an abbreviated version" of his "principles
of presentation." The exclusion of political, cultural, and historical events, and limitation to books make *Annals of Australian Literature* less useful than it could be for placing
a work or author in an intellectual context. Reviews: *Australian Literary Studies* 4 (1970):
421–24; S. J. Routh, *Meanjin Quarterly* 29 (1970): 555–59.

The chronology in Goodwin, *History of Australian Literature* (R4445a), is a useful supplement.

Guides to Primary Works

Lock, *Australian Literature* (R4440), has a valuable discussion of how to identify and locate Australian books (pp. 15–17) and descriptions of Australian library collections (pp. 90–97).

MANUSCRIPTS

R4462   *Register of Australian Archives and Manuscripts* (*RAAM*). National Library of Australia. Online. 10 Sept. 2005 <http://www.nla.gov.au/raam>. Updated regularly.

A union register of manuscript collections and individual manuscripts held by Australian libraries and archives. The register covers collections (including those not directly related to Australia), individual manuscripts of primary material, photocopies or microfilms of documents related to the continent, and personal papers in government archives; it excludes unpublished copies of secondary material (e.g., conference papers or theses), media, microfilms or photocopies of non-Australian material, and government records. Since data is taken from a variety of printed and other sources as well as from information submitted by repositories, individual records vary in amount of information and extent of description. A full record includes *RAAM* number, name of the creator of the collection (e.g., an author or the individual or organization responsible for forming the collection), title of collection, date(s) covered by the collection, physical format, size, occupation, keyword subject descriptors, summary (i.e., a description of the content of the collection), biographical note (on the creator), names of individuals represented in the collection, access information, finding aids, finding aid URL, location (with the URL of the collection's home page), call number, immutable and source numbers (tags that allow updating from the source of the record), date created, and date of last update.

In the basic search screen, users can search by creator, creator and names, occupation, or keyword (among all indexed words); in advanced search, users can combine the preceding fields, along with National Union Catalog symbol and location, and limit a search by date created or last updated. Users can also search by *RAAM* number, or browse lists of repositories, creators, names, and occupations. Searching returns records in alphabetic order (by creator); browsing, in *RAAM* number order.

Register of Australian Archives and Manuscripts is the place to begin when searching for Australian manuscript materials. Researchers looking for literary manuscripts should also search *Guide to Australian Literary Manuscripts* (U of Western Australia; online; 10 Sept. 2005 <http://findaid.library.uwa.edu.au>), a database of detailed guides to 80 collections. Although some of the guides are not cited in *RAAM*, *Guide to Australian Literary Manuscripts* does not appear to have been updated since its creation c. 2000.

PRINTED WORKS

R4463   *AustLit: The Resource for Australian Literature.* Online. 8 Sept. 2005 <http://
       www.austlit.edu.au>. Updated daily.

A database of print and electronic creative and critical writing and literary nonfiction published since c. 1780 by Australians (including expatriates and visitors with
"significant . . . involvement in Australian literary activity") and about Australian literature. General discussions of Australian studies, language, or culture are excluded; self-
published works are given minimal treatment.

The database includes three kinds of records: biographical (names[s], birth and
death dates, ethnicity, summary of life and literary career, links to archival resources,
and links to kinds of works by and about the author); organizational (name[s], dates
and places of activity, place in and contribution to Australian literature, and selected
references); bibliographical (title, publication information, list of editions, content
notes, subject headings, translations, and tables of contents for anthologies and collected
works). Many bibliographical records include a Library Holdings link. Since *AustLit*
employs the Functional Requirements for Bibliographic Records (FRBR) model, records are contextualized, e.g., a record for a work will include versions of it as well as
individual editions or printings. For a discussion of the importance of such contextualized records, see Carol Hetherington, "Setting the Record Straight: Bibliography
and Australian Literature," *Australian Literary Studies* 21 (2003): 198–208.

In Basic Search users can search by name (i.e., creator of a work), title, subject
(i.e., terms included in the *AustLit* thesaurus), date, type of work (e.g., anthology, Web
site), form (e.g., autobiography, interview), and genre (e.g., fantasy, thriller—the Form
pull-down menu includes several genres [e.g., drama, novel]); searches can be limited
to full text records or separately published works (i.e., books); results can be ordered
by date, title, book, or electronic resource (i.e., books or electronic resources will appear
at the head of the list, followed by other records in descending chronological order).
The Advanced Search screen allow users to construct a custom search form by selecting
attributes in the author, work, and subject fields (e.g., the work field allows users to
select such subfields as title; publication details, type, form, or genre; awards; source;
first line of poem, notes, or role; all but the title field have subfields).

Users can restrict searches to several Specialist Research Subsets (some of which
are independently produced databases):

> *Aboriginal and Torres Strait Islander Writers.*
> *Australian Children's Literature and the Lu Rees Archives.*
> *Australian Drama.*
> *Australian Literary Responses to 'Asia.'* An expansion of Lyn Jacobs and Rick
>   Hosking, *A Bibliography of Australian Literary Responses to 'Asia,'* Flinders
>   Library Publication Series 2 (Adelaide: Lib., Flinders U of South Australia,
>   1995, 160 pp.).
> *Australian Magazines* (see the description of the database for instructions on
>   searching—path: Home/AustLit Subsets/Australian Magazines).
> *Australian Multicultural Writers.* An updated version of Gunew Sneja, Loló
>   Houbein, Alexandra Karakostas-Seda, and Jan Mahyuddin, comps., *A Bib-
>   liography of Australian Multicultural Writers* (Geelong: Centre for Studies
>   in Literary Educ., Humanities, Deakin U, 1992, 291 pp.).
> *South Australian Women Writers.*
> *Western Australian Literature.*
> *Writers of Tropical Queensland.*

Because the names of search fields are not always clear, users should read the *AustLit* Fields page before searching. Records can be marked for e-mailing or screen display (and thence downloaded or printed).

Neither the Basic nor the Advanced Search interface is intuitive, but both allow for sophisticated searches of the database. Its currency (records for many works appear within days of their publications), contextualization of a work, and breadth of coverage make *AustLit* the essential resource for identifying Australian literary works and writings about them. *AustLit* supersedes *Austlit: The Australian Literary Database* (Canberra: U Coll. Lib., Australian Defence Force Acad.).

Bibliography of Australian Literature, ed. John Arnold and John Hay (Saint Lucia: U of Queensland P, 2001–)—which is intended to supersede Miller, *Australian Literature from Its Beginnings to 1935* (R4475) and Macartney's *Australian Literature* (R4475a)—is now being compiled within *AustLit*. Coverage is limited to separately published books of creative writing (including poetry, fiction, drama, and collections of short stories) by Australian authors addressed to readers of all ages and published through 2000 (an appendix will eventually extend coverage in vol. 1 through 2000). Books for an adult audience must be by a single author; those for children may contain the work of no more than four writers. Included are authors who were born in Australia and resident there for a substantial part of their lives or during their formative years as well as writers born overseas but now considered Australian or who resided in the country "and produced a work of creative literature reflecting their experiences." Entries provide a full description of the first edition and location of copy examined and brief citations to selected later editions. The compilers attempt to see a copy of all titles except romance and pulp fiction.

R4465   *Australian National Bibliography* (*ANB*). Canberra: Natl. Lib. of Australia, 1961–96. Monthly, with four-month, eight-month, and annual cumulations. Available since 1980 on microfiche.   Z4015.A96   015.94.

A national bibliography of Australian publications deposited for copyright in the National Library, as well as of some foreign works by Australian authors or about the country. At its demise *ANB* was published in four parts: a subject list organized by Dewey Decimal Classification (with full cataloging information for each entry); author, title, and series index; subject index; and list of periodicals. Both indexes cite classification rather than page. Once the fullest record of current Australian publications, *ANB* was absorbed by *Libraries Australia* (Natl. Lib. of Australia; online; 28 Feb. 2006 <http://librariesaustralia.nla.gov.au/apps/kss> [formerly *Kinetica*]).

ANB continues the *Annual Catalogue of Australian Publications [1936–60]*, 25 vols. (Canberra: Natl. Lib. of Australia, 1937–61), a combined main entry and subject list of books deposited for copyright and foreign publications about Australia. Retrospective coverage is offered by *Australian National Bibliography, 1901–1950*, 4 vols. (Canberra: Natl. Lib. of Australia, 1988), which includes Australian imprints, as well as foreign publications by Australians or about the country.

Since works by ethnic writers were frequently not submitted for copyright, researchers must also consult:

> *Bibliography of Australian Multicultural Writers* (R4463a).
> *Ethnic Writings in English from Australia: A Bibliography*. 3rd ed. Adelaide A. L. S. Working Papers. Adelaide: Australian Literary Studies, 1984. 124 pp.
> Lumb, Peter, and Anne Hazell, eds. *Diversity and Diversion: An Annotated Bibliography of Australian Ethnic Minority Literature*. Richmond, Victoria: Hodja, 1983. 123 pp.

R4470   Ferguson, John Alexander. *Bibliography of Australia.* Facsimile ed. 7 vols.
        Canberra: Natl. Lib. of Australia, 1975–77. *Addenda, 1784–1850*
        (Volumes I to IV). 1986. 706 pp.   Z4011.F47 [DU96]   016.994.

A retrospective national bibliography covering 1784 to 1900 that attempts to
record for the period 1784–1850 all Australian imprints as well as foreign publications
"relating in any way" to the country; for the years 1851–1900, excludes belles lettres,
periodicals, and governmental papers, as well as legal, scientific, technical, and certain
ephemeral publications. Works by Australians published elsewhere and lacking a reference to the country are sometimes mentioned in notes. In vols. 1–4 (1784–1850),
entries are organized by year of publication, then alphabetically by author, corporate
author, or title of anonymous work; vols. 5–7 (1851–1900) consist of a single alphabetical list. Entries provide a transcription of title page; size; pagination; list of contents
or description of content relating to Australia; publication information (if not on the
title page); occasionally extensive notes on content, reprints and other editions, related
scholarship, and bibliographical matters; and locations of copies (with a list of supplementary locations inserted in vols. 1–2 of the facsimile edition). Vol. 2 prints additions
to 1; vol. 4, additions and corrections to 1–3. The *Addenda* incorporates these additions
and corrections, adds new entries, revises some existing ones, and lists additional locations; the National Library no longer plans to publish addenda to vols. 5–7 and a
cumulative index. Indexed by titles, authors, and corporate authors in each of the first
four volumes. Book trade personnel are indexed in Ian Morrison, *The Publishing Industry in Colonial Australia: A Name Index to John Alexander Ferguson's* Bibliography of
Australia 1784–1900, BSANZ Occasional Publication 6 (Melbourne: Bibliog. Soc. of
Australia and New Zealand, 1996, 162 pp.).

While the numerous omissions, errors, and inconsistencies make Ferguson untrustworthy as a descriptive bibliography, it remains the most complete guide to Australian literature through 1850; the record is continued, although less satisfactorily, to
1950 by Macartney, *Australian Literature* (R4475a). Review: Brian McMullen, *Australian Library Journal* 25 (1976): 39–40.

Books by female Australian writers are more thoroughly covered in Debra Ade-
laide, *Bibliography of Australian Women's Literature: A Listing of Fiction, Poetry, Drama,
and Non-fiction Published in Monograph Form Arranged Alphabetically by Author* (Port
Melbourne: Thorpe in association with Natl. Centre for Australian Studies, 1991, 270
pp.), an author list of about 11,500 titles culled, for the most part, from other sources
rather than personal examination.

R4475   Miller, E. Morris. *Australian Literature from Its Beginnings to 1935: A
        Descriptive and Bibliographical Survey of Books by Australian Authors in
        Poetry, Drama, Fiction, Criticism, and Anthology with Subsidiary Entries to
        1938.* Facsimile rpt., with corrections and additions. 2 vols. Sydney: Sydney
        UP, 1975.   Z4021.M5   016.82'08.

A bibliography of separately published works by Australian natives or residents
who wrote or commenced at least one book in the country. Although the focus is belles
lettres, the notes cite a substantial number of other books by philosophers, artists,
historians, and scientists who published at least one literary work. Entries are organized
by genre: poetry, drama, fiction, and criticism (with sections for essays and reviews;
English, Australian, classical, and modern literature; anthologies and miscellanies).
Within each section, authors are listed chronologically by date of first publication in
the genre. A typical author entry consists of a list of separately published literary works
(and some editions thereof) accompanied by bibliographical notes and, for fiction, a

one- or two-sentence summary; references to scholarship, bibliographies, and manuscripts; reprints and excerpts in anthologies and some periodical contributions; and
major nonliterary works. (The amount and organization of information vary from author to author, however.) Each genre division is prefaced by a lengthy historical introduction composed largely of biographical and critical discussions of authors. In the
facsimile reprint, the separately issued additions and corrections appear on pp. 1075–
78. An appendix lists novels associated with Australia by foreign authors. Three indexes:
subjects of fiction; subjects of Australian literature and persons not in the general index
of Australian authors; Australian authors.

Australian Literature: A Bibliography to 1938, extended to 1950 and ed. Frederick
T. Macartney (Sydney: Angus, 1956, 503 pp.), extends coverage to 1950, incorporates
Miller's corrections and rearranges entries into a straightforward author list, but deletes
nonbelletristic works, children's books, translations, critical and scholarly works except
those about Australian literature, anthologized reprints, contributions to periodicals,
references to scholarship and bibliographies, introductions, and indexes. A few corrections and additions to the enlarged edition are listed in Clive Hamer, " 'Not in Miller,'"
Meanjin 15 (1956): 419, which is followed by Miller's brief description of his compilation of the original bibliography (pp. 420–21). Macartney's defense of his reworking
of Miller and rejoinder to several negative reviews (such as Russel Ward, Meanjin 15
[1956]: 212–14) make up An Odious Comparison: Considered in Its Relation to Australian Literature (Black Rock: Bulldozer Booklets, 1956, 15 pp.).

Although Macartney's revision is more current and consolidates an author's separately published literary works, the original edition includes much more complete
information and provides some subject access. Together, the two offer the single fullest
record of separately published Australian literary works from 1850 to 1950. Before
1850, more thorough and accurate coverage is offered by Ferguson, Bibliography of
Australia (R4470), and the Bibliography of Australian Literature database (R4463a) is
designed to supersede Miller and Macartney.

See also

Andrews, Australian Literature to 1900 (R4485).
"Annual Bibliography of Commonwealth Literature" (R4375).
"Annual Bibliography of Studies in Australian Literature" (R4480).

Guides to Scholarship and Criticism

SERIAL BIBLIOGRAPHIES

R4480   "Annual Bibliography of Studies in Australian Literature [1963–]."
        Australian Literary Studies 1 (1964)– .   PR9400.A86   820'.9'994.
   A selective list of studies of Australian literature, language, and area studies, along
with "new books (with reviews of them) by contemporary writers whose work has
attracted substantial discussion." Electronic journals are not covered. In the bibliographies for 1989–92 (14–16 [1990–93]) coverage of most North American publications
was unwisely ceded to Antipodes (see below), which—even after the bibliography for
1992—offers fuller coverage of North American publications. Entries—drawn partly
from other bibliographies—are listed in two divisions: general studies and individual authors; some entries are accompanied by a brief annotation. Entries from the

individual-authors division in the bibliographies for 1963–95 are cumulated and augmented in *The* ALS *Guide to Australian Writers: A Bibliography, 1963–1995*, 2nd ed., ed. Martin Duwell, Marianne Ehrhardt, and Carol Hetherington (Saint Lucia: Queensland UP, 1997, 489 pp.).

An essential complement is "Bibliography of Australian Literature and Criticism Published in North America [1985–]," *Antipodes* 3– (1989–), whose unannotated entries are organized in two divisions: works by and about individual authors; general studies. Many of the entries are taken from other serial bibliographies, and there are gaps in coverage of years.

Although not comprehensive, the "Annual Bibliography" and "Bibliography of Australian Literature" provide more current coverage of scholarship than the Australia division of "Annual Bibliography of Commonwealth Literature" (R4375)—which offers fuller coverage of primary works, especially by new writers—and the standard serial bibliographies and indexes in section G.

See also

> Secs. G: Serial Bibliographies, Indexes, and Abstracts and H: Guides to Dissertations and Theses.
>
> *ABELL* (G340): Entries on Australian writers and literature are dispersed throughout.
>
> *MLAIB* (G335): English Literature division (especially English III: General) through the volume for 1956; English XI: Australia, Canada, Etc./Australia section in the volumes for 1957–66; English II: Australia, Canada, Etc./Australia section in the volumes for 1967–80; and the [British] Commonwealth Literature/Australian Literature section in later volumes. Researchers must also check the headings beginning with "Australian(s)" in the subject index to post-1980 volumes or in the online thesaurus.
>
> *YWES* (G330): Australian literature has been covered in the chapter for African, Caribbean, Canadian, Australian, New Zealand, and Indian Literatures in English since vol. 64 (for 1983).

OTHER BIBLIOGRAPHIES

R4485   Andrews, Barry G., and William H. Wilde. *Australian Literature to 1900: A Guide to Information Sources*. American Literature, English Literature, and World Literatures in English: An Information Guide Series 22. Detroit: Gale, 1980. 472 pp.   Z4021.A54 [PR9604.3]   016.82.

A selective, annotated bibliography of primary and secondary works (published through 1976) on Australian literature from 1788 to 1900. Andrews and Wilde include 72 authors who had significant work published before 1900 or who clearly belong to the 1890s but generally exclude their publications not related to the country. The 1,576 entries—augmented by numerous others cited in annotations or headnotes—are organized in three divisions: general works (including sections for bibliographies, reference works, literary history and criticism, Australian English, nineteenth-century periodicals, and anthologies), individual authors (including a biographical headnote and sections for bibliographies, primary works—by genre, with a note on manuscript collections—and studies), and selected nonfiction (with sections for exploration, transportation, travel, history and biography, and literary and theatrical autobiographies). Although a work is entered only once, cross-references are provided in headnotes to sections. The typically full annotations are generally informative and frequently evaluative. Two indexes: persons; titles. Judicious selection, accuracy, and helpful annotations make this a valuable guide to the study of Australian literature before 1900. Reviews: L. T. Hergenhan, *Australian Literary Studies* 10 (1981): 137–39; Alan Lawson, *Modern Language Review* 78 (1983): 692–94.

R4488   Ross, Robert L. *Australian Literary Criticism, 1945–1988: An Annotated Bibliography.* Garland Reference Library of the Humanities 1075. New York: Garland, 1989. 375 pp.   Z4024.C8 R67 [PR9604.3]   016.82'09.

A selective annotated bibliography of English-language studies and anthologies (the majority published between 1945 and June 1988), dissertations abstracted in *ProQuest Dissertations and Theses* (H465), and—incongruously—novels about the convict period. The 1,397 entries are organized by publication date in most of the seven classified divisions: general works, international views (including comparative studies), special topics (such as aborigines, fiction about the convict period, film, language, and women's studies), fiction, poetry, drama, and 42 major writers (with sections for published books, special issues of journals, interviews, critical studies, and bibliographies). Although brief, the annotations generally offer an adequate description of content. Two indexes: scholars; literary authors and subjects; also indexed in *Biography and Genealogy Master Index* (J565). The subject indexing is inadequate and the criteria governing selection are too vague; however, Ross offers a useful preliminary guide to criticism from 1945 through mid-1988 of Australian literature. Researchers must supplement coverage with other works in this Guides to Scholarship and Criticism section. Review: Ken Goodwin, *World Literature Written in English* 29 (1989): 85–87.

See also

    AustLit (R4463).
    Boos, *Bibliography of Women and Literature* (U6600).
    Lever, *Post-colonial Literatures in English: Australia, 1970–1992* (R4380a).
    New, *Critical Writings on Commonwealth Literatures* (R4380).
    Oxford History of Australian Literature (R4445a).
    Schwartz, *Articles on Women Writers* (U6605).

Language

GUIDES TO SCHOLARSHIP

See

    ABELL (G340): Dialects section of the English Language division in the volumes for 1920–26; the English Dialects section in the volumes for 1927–72; the Dialects/Australia and New Zealand section in the volumes for 1973–84; the Dialects/Australasia section in the volumes for 1985–86; and the Dialects/Dialects of the Rest of the World section in later volumes.
    Andrews, *Australian Literature to 1900* (R4485).
    "Annual Bibliography of Studies in Australian Literature" (R4480).
    Day, *Modern Australian Prose, 1901–1975* (R4530).

MLAIB (G335): See the English I: Linguistics section through the volume for 1966; the Indo-European C: Germanic Linguistics IV: English/Modern English/Dialectology section in the volumes for 1967–80; and the Indo-European Languages/Germanic Languages/West Germanic Languages/English Language (Modern)/Dialectology section in later volumes. Researchers must also check the "Australian English Dialect" heading in the subject index to post-1980 volumes and in the online thesaurus.

DICTIONARIES

R4490   *The Australian National Dictionary: A Dictionary of Australianisms on Historical Principles* (*AND*). Ed. W. S. Ramson. Melbourne: Oxford UP, 1988. 814 pp. (A revised edition is tentatively scheduled for 2008.) PE3601.Z5 A865.

A historical dictionary of terms distinctly or prominently Australian. The approximately 6,000 main entries provide pronunciation; part(s) of speech; variant spellings; a note on history and derivation, with a cross-reference, where appropriate, to the *Oxford English Dictionary* (M1410); definition(s) organized by part of speech; and illustrative quotations, arranged chronologically, for each definition. *AND* is an essential complement to the *Oxford English Dictionary* and the indispensable source for the historical study of Australian English and explication of literary works by Australian writers. For the history of the *AND*, see Ramson, *Lexical Images: The Story of the* Australian National Dictionary (Victoria: Oxford UP, 2002, 255 pp.). Review: David Bradley, *Australian Journal of Linguistics* 9 (1989): 191–95.

The best treatment of colloquial language is G. A. Wilkes, *A Dictionary of Australian Colloquialisms*, 4th ed. (Melbourne: Oxford UP, 1996, 426 pp.), with dated quotations accompanying definitions. Also useful is *The Macquarie Dictionary*, ed. C. Yallop et al., [rev. ed.] (Sydney: Macquarie Lib., 2005, 1,676 pp.).

Biographical Dictionaries

R4495   *Australian Dictionary of Biography Online* (*ADB Online*). Australian National University. Online. 11 Sept. 2006 <http://www.adb.online.anu.edu.au/adbonline.htm>. Updated regularly.

Australian Dictionary of Biography (*ADB*). Gen. eds. Douglas Pike, Bede Nairn, Geoffrey Serle, and John Ritchie. Carlton: Melbourne UP, 1966– . CT2802.A95   920.094. CD-ROM (vols. 1–12). <http://adb.anu.edu.au>.

   Vols. 1–2: *1788–1850.*
   Vols. 3–6: *1851–90.*
   Vols. 7–12: *1891–1939.*
   Index: Volumes 1 to 12, 1788–1939. Ed. Hilary Kent. 1991. 326 pp.
   Vols. 13–16: *1940–1980.*
   Vols. 17–18: *1918–1990.* In progress.

A biographical dictionary that includes entries on important and representative Australians. (Other than vetting by various committees, selection criteria are undefined.)

Placement in vols. 1–12 is determined by the period of the individual's most important work; placement in later volumes is by date of death. A typical entry summarizes basic biographical and career information and concludes with a brief list of important scholarship and unpublished papers. Separate lists of corrections are tipped in all volumes; those for vols. 1–12 are consolidated in the *Index*, which includes separate indexes for persons, places of birth, and occupations (superseded by *ADB Online*). H. J. Gibbney and Ann G. Smith, comps. and eds., *A Biographical Register, 1788–1939: Notes from the Name Index of the* Australian Dictionary of Biography, 2 vols. (Canberra: Australian Dictionary of Biography, 1987), is a more rudimentary index to individuals and their occupations (but provides basic biographical and bibliographical information on numerous individuals not in *ADB*). *ADB Online* renders superfluous Julie G. Marshall and Richard C. S. Trahair, *Occupational Index to the* Australian Dictionary of Biography *(1788–1890), Volumes I–VI*, La Trobe Working Papers in Sociology 43 (Bundoora: Dept. of Sociology, La Trobe U, 1979, 139 pp.), and *Occupational Index to the* Australian Dictionary of Biography *(1891–1939), Volumes VII–IX, A-Las*, La Trobe Working Papers in Sociology 71 (1985, 100 pp.). The *ADB* headquarters at the Australian National University (Research School of Social Sciences, Canberra ACT 0200; fax: [02] 6125 3644; adb@coombs.anu.edu.au) maintains a research file on each entrant and a biographical register with information on more than 300,000 persons not in the *Dictionary*.

As volumes are published, entries are incorporated into *Australian Dictionary of Biography Online*, which is adding portraits to entries, expanding the bibliographies, and providing hyperlinks. In Advanced Search, users can search by biographee, keyword in full text, date during lifetime, date of birth, date of death, birthplace, place of death, cultural heritage, religious affiliation, occupation (users much work from nested lists and remember to click Add Term), date during career, place of occupation, and printed volume number. Users can also browse lists of people, occupations, and contributors. Results—which can be sorted (in ascending or descending order) by surname, date of birth, or date of death—can be printed or downloaded only through a Web browser's print or save commands. *ADB Online* allows for sophisticated retrieval of information in the standard general source for biographical information on Australians.

For persons not in *ADB*, consult Percival Serle, *Dictionary of Australian Biography*, 2 vols. (Sydney: Angus, 1949), and the current edition of *Who's Who in Australia* (North Melbourne: Crown Content, 1922– , annual).

Periodicals

GUIDES TO PRIMARY WORKS

R4500   Stuart, Lurline. *Australian Periodicals with Literary Contents, 1821–1926: An Annotated Bibliography*. Melbourne: Australian Scholarly, 2003. 178 pp. Z6962.A8 S78   [PN5517.P4].

A bibliography of periodicals (excluding newspapers) of some literary interest published in Australia through 1925. The 576 entries, arranged alphabetically by original title, include (when possible) title, subtitle, motto or epigraph, printer, publisher, editor(s), frequency, dates of publication and title changes, size, average number of pages, price, presence of illustrations, locations in Australian collections, description of content, and important writers and articles published. Concludes with a chronological list of periodicals. Indexed by persons, publishers, and printers. Although a subject index would greatly increase its usefulness, Stuart is the essential guide to identifying and locating these frequently scarce and ephemeral periodicals.

See also

Vann, *Periodicals of Queen Victoria's Empire: An Exploration* (M2525a).

Genres

Some works in section L: Genres are useful for research in Australian literature.

FICTION

Some works in section L: Genres/Fiction are useful for research in Australian fiction.

Guides to Primary Works

R4525   Torre, Stephen. *The Australian Short Story, 1940–1980: A Bibliography.*
Sydney: Hale, 1984. 367 pp.   Z4024.S5 T67 [PR9612.5]
016.823'01'08994.
An index to English-language short fiction (along with selected criticism) by writers born, resident in, or otherwise associated with Australia and first published between 1940 and 1980 in anthologies, single-author collections, or 12 major Australian periodicals. Torre excludes fiction for children and transcriptions of oral narratives, but otherwise defines "short story" broadly. The entries are organized in five divisions: an author bibliography of short stories and criticism (with sections for single-author collections, including the contents of each; individual short stories, with the publishing history of each in the periodicals, collections, and anthologies selected for indexing; anthologies and miscellanies edited by the author; other publications by the author that are of some importance to his or her short fiction; and critical studies, including reviews); a list of periodicals that publish short fiction by Australian authors, including the 12 selected for full indexing; a title list of anthologies and miscellanies indexed; a superfluous list of single-author collections indexed; and general studies of short stories and reference works, the bulk of which are on Australian short fiction. An appendix provides a chronological list of the journals that hosted *Tabloid Story.* Although the work is not comprehensive, especially for periodical fiction, and although much information is taken secondhand, Torre is the single best source for identifying Australian short stories and critical studies of them.

Guides to Scholarship and Criticism

R4530   Day, A. Grove. *Modern Australian Prose, 1901–1975: A Guide to Information Sources.* American Literature, English Literature, and World Literatures in English: An Information Guide Series 29. Detroit: Gale, 1980. 462 pp.   Z4011.D38 [PR9604.3]   016.82.

A highly selective, annotated bibliography of primary and secondary works that also includes a brief section on drama. Limited to works (generally published between 1901 and 1975) about Australia by citizens and others resident in the country, *Modern Australian Prose* excludes some important publications by Australian authors. The general cutoff for studies is 1976 (although a few later publications are admitted). Entries are organized in four classified divisions: general works (with sections for bibliographies, reference works, literary history and criticism, Australian English, periodicals, and anthologies), fiction (organized by author, with sections under each for bibliographies, primary works, and criticism), nonfiction (a highly selective list organized by genre or topic and including a section on aborigines), and drama (with sections for bibliographies, studies, and primary works). Most of the annotations are adequately descriptive. Three indexes: scholars; book titles; subjects (including authors). Because of the degree of selectivity (recent authors are slighted) and numerous errors, Day is useful primarily as a starting point for research on prose. (The drama section, seemingly an afterthought, is completely inadequate.) Reviews: Laurie Hergenhan, *Australian Literary Studies* 10 (1982): 407–08; Alan Lawson, *Modern Language Review* 78 (1983): 692–94.

For fiction before 1901, see Andrews, *Australian Literature to 1900* (R4485). Supplement coverage with Rose Marie Beston and John B. Beston, "Critical Writings on Modern New Zealand and Australian Fiction: A Selected Checklist," *Modern Fiction Studies* 27 (1981): 189–204; New, *Critical Writings on Commonwealth Literatures* (R4380); and "Annual Bibliography of Commonwealth Literature" (R4375).

DRAMA AND THEATER

Some works in section L: Genres/Drama and Theater are useful for research in Australian drama and theater.

Histories and Surveys

R4535   Love, Harold, ed. *The Australian Stage: A Documentary History.* Kensington: New South Wales UP with Australian Theatre Studies Centre School of Drama, U of New South Wales, 1984. 383 pp.   PN3011.A97 792'.0994.

A collection of extracts from documents (including reviews, articles, autobiographies, manuscripts, illustrations, and photographs) that depict the history of the Australian stage to 1980. The emphasis is on Australian drama professionally produced in Sydney and Melbourne, with less attention to foreign-language, amateur, and educational theater, and excluding opera, film, and television. The heart of the work is the extensive extracts, which describe productions of both Australian and foreign plays. The extracts are organized chronologically in four periods (1788–1853, 1854–1900, 1901–50, and 1950–80), followed by a section reproducing pictorial documents depicting productions, theaters, sets, and performers. Each period begins with a summary of theatrical activity and includes one or two essays on aspects of the theater of the time (e.g., theater of the convict era, dramatic criticism from 1850 to 1890, Australian plays on Australian topics, vaudeville, state theater companies, and alternative theater). Most essays conclude with an evaluative guide to further reading, and the last section of the book is an extensive bibliography of studies of Australian theater. Indexed by persons, titles, and subjects. Valuable for its extensive documentation, this is the most trustworthy source of information on the Australian stage. More extensive but less factually reliable coverage of Australian drama is offered by Rees, *History of Australian Drama* (R4540). Review: Veronica Kelly, *Australian Literary Studies* 12 (1986): 546–50.

R4540   Rees, Leslie. *A History of Australian Drama.* Rev. and enl. ed. 2 vols.
         Sydney: Angus, 1978–87.   PR9611.2.R43   822'.009.

> Vol. 1: *The Making of Australian Drama from the 1830s to the Late 1960s.*
> Rev. ed. 1978. 435 pp. (Rpt. of *The Making of Australian Drama: A
> Historical and Critical Survey from the 1830s to the 1970s.* 1973. 510 pp.)
> Vol. 2: *Australian Drama, 1970–1985.* 1987. 400 pp. (Rev. of *Australian
> Drama in the 1970s.* 1978. 270 pp.)

A critical history of the development of Australian drama from the colonial period through 1985. Encompasses stage as well as radio and television plays by Australians, resident or not, and—in early chapters—about the country by foreign authors. The overall organization is chronological, with chapters devoted to types of plays, major authors, periods, movements, and topics. Among the various appendixes are, in vol. 1, a history of the Playwrights Advisory Board; in vol. 2, a chronology of selected plays published since 1936; chronological lists (by decade) of radio (since 1935) and television plays (since 1955) produced by the Australian Broadcasting Commission; and a discussion of Australian noncommercial theaters. Vol. 2 concludes with a selective bibliography. Each volume is indexed by persons, titles, and topics. Although frequently unreliable in factual matters and impressionistic in judgment, Rees's work represents the fullest history of the country's drama.

More accurate but less thorough in covering Australian drama is Love, *Australian Stage* (R4535).

Guides to Primary Works

See

> *From Page to Stage: An Annotated Bibliography of Australian Drama* (R4463a).

Guides to Scholarship and Criticism

See

> Day, *Modern Australian Prose, 1901–1975* (R4530).

POETRY

Guides to Primary Works

R4545   Webby, Elizabeth. *Early Australian Poetry: An Annotated Bibliography of
         Original Poems Published in Australian Newspapers, Magazines, and
         Almanacks before 1850.* Sydney: Hale, 1982. 332 pp.   Z4008.P63 W42
         [PR9610.4]   016.821.

A bibliography of original periodical verse. Entries are organized by Australian state, medium of publication, city, periodical, and then date of publication. A typical entry consists of title, author (if known) or pseudonym, date of publication, page, and a brief note on content. Indexed by poets and titles of newspapers, magazines, and almanacs. Webby is the essential source for identifying Australian periodical verse before 1850.

Guides to Scholarship and Criticism

There is no adequate guide to studies of Australian poetry. Herbert C. Jaffa, *Modern Australian Poetry, 1920–1970: A Guide to Information Sources*, American Literature, English Literature, and World Literatures in English: An Information Guide Series 24 (Detroit: Gale, 1979, 241 pp.) — which is not actually a guide to information sources — has too many omissions to serve even as a starting point. (For the multiple deficiencies of this work, see the review by Alan Lawson, *Analytical and Enumerative Bibliography* 5 [1981]: 130–34.)

PROSE

Guides to Primary Works

R4550   Walsh, Kay, and Joy Hooton. *Australian Autobiographical Narratives: An Annotated Bibliography.* 2 vols. Canberra: Australia Scholarly Editions Centre, Australian Defence Force Acad., and Natl. Lib. of Australia, 1993–98. Z5303.A8 W35 [CT2802]   016.920094.

An annotated bibliography of published autobiographies that treat life in Australia to 1900 (vol. 1 covers the beginnings to 1850; vol. 2, 1850–1900). Listed alphabetically by author, entries cite publication information (variously the first edition or the most accessible one), include a summary of the Australian content, and conclude with the date span and, if possible, a citation to the *Australian Dictionary of Biography* (R4495). Three indexes: names; places; subjects. The generous summaries make *Australian Autobiographical Narratives* an important resource for studies of Australian culture and for autobiography as a genre.

Canadian Literature

This section includes works devoted exclusively to Canadian literature (in whatever language). Many works in sections Q: American Literature and R: Other Literatures in English/General are also important to research in Canadian literature.

Guides to Reference Works

GENERAL GUIDES

R4555   *Canadian Reference Sources: An Annotated Bibliography: General Reference Works, History, Humanities/Ouvrages de référence canadiens: Une bibliographie annotée: Ouvrages de référence généraux, histoire, sciences humaines.* Ed. and comp. Mary E. Bond; comp. Martine M. Caron. Vancouver: UBC P, 1996. 1,076 pp.   Z1365.B57 [F1008]   016.971.

A selective, annotated guide to reference sources available through January 1995 for Canadian topics. Entries are organized alphabetically by author, editor, or title of anonymous work in three extensively classified divisions: general reference works, history and related subjects, and humanities. The literature subdivision includes sections for general works, children's literature, diaries and autobiographies, drama, fiction, film, poetry, and quotations (theater is included under performing arts). The linguistics subdivision includes sections for general works, Canadian English, and French and native languages. The annotations, in English and French, are descriptive. Four indexes: names; titles; subjects (English); subjects (French). Although researchers would benefit from more evaluative annotations and some refinements in organization (e.g., the literary history and criticism section mixes bibliographies and literary histories, and the alphabetic lists frequently separate related works), *Canadian Reference Sources* is the essential general guide to reference sources on Canadian topics.

Guide to Reference Books (B60) and *Walford's Guide to Reference Material* (B65) list numerous Canadian reference sources.

LITERATURE GUIDES

R4557   Jones, Joseph. *Reference Sources for Canadian Literary Studies.* Toronto: U of Toronto P, 2005. 464 pp.   Z1375.J66   016.8109.

A guide to reference works (published through early 2003) that treat Canadian literature in English (with selective coverage of resources for other languages); "reference work," "Canadian," and "literature" are interpreted broadly. Entries are divided among classified sections for reference guides (i.e., general guides to reference works, guides to reference works on Canadian literature, and some general bibliographies of Canadian literature); dictionaries, encyclopedias, and handbooks; serial bibliographies; closed bibliographies of Canadian literature; closed bibliographies of general Canadian topics; catalogs; special collections and archives; periodical indexes; periodicals; dissertations and theses; anthologies; literary histories and surveys; biography; directories; children's literature; translation; language; miscellaneous topics; and other sources.

Sections—which typically have subdivisions for works covering Canadian literature generally, for genres, for works devoted to specific topics, and for works devoted to Canada generally—begin with a discussion of the type(s) of work(s) included, a comparative overview of the listings, and a comment on related sources. Individual entries include brief annotations (with those for electronic resources rarely extending beyond two sentences) that are primarily descriptive, but several refer to complementary or related works; a handful cite reviews. Four indexes: names; titles; subjects (with titles listed in reverse chronological order under 14 main headings, some of which are subdivided); chronology (but without distinctions between dates of publications and of coverage). Although *Reference Sources for Canadian Literary Studies* offers the fullest guide to reference tools for Canadian literature, its multitude of serious deficiencies— many descriptions are too brief to offer any sense of a work's importance to research in Canadian literature (e.g., the description of *ABELL*), many superseded or elementary works are given space (e.g., entries D-004 and D-005), rigid adherence to a reverse chronological order within most subdivisions separates supplements from their parent works, cross-reference numbers are omitted, entries are organized by type of reference work, and an utterly inadequate subject index will leave many users unable to locate resources—will quickly frustrate most researchers.

See also

Beugnot, *Manuel bibliographique des études littéraires* (S4905).

Histories and Surveys

For a history of Canadian literary histories through the mid-1990s and analysis of their political, national, ideological, and theoretical underpinnings, see E. D. Blodgett, *Five-Part Invention: A History of Literary History in Canada* (Toronto: U of Toronto P, 2003, 371 pp.).

R4560   Grandpré, Pierre de, ed. *Histoire de la littérature française du Québec.*
         Corrected rpt. 4 vols. Montréal: Beauchemin, 1971–73.   PQ3917.G7   840.
    A collaborative history of French-language literature from 1534 to the 1960s, with three of the volumes devoted to the twentieth century. Organized chronologically, with chapters on intellectual and social life, genres, history, journalism, the essay, and literary criticism, the volumes emphasize historical and intellectual contexts. Two indexes in each volume: persons; titles. Vol. 4 concludes with a selective bibliography of studies on French Canadian literature. Despite poor organization and inconsistency in the quality of chapters, Grandpré offers the fullest history of French Canadian literature. Reviews: (vol. 1) David M. Hayne, *Canadian Historical Review* 49 (1968): 415–16; (vols. 2–4) Hayne, *Canadian Historical Review* 51 (1970): 459–61.

R4565   *Literary History of Canada: Canadian Literature in English.* Corrected rpt. of
         2nd ed. Gen. eds. Carl F. Klinck and W. H. New. 4 vols. Toronto: U of
         Toronto P, 1976–90.   PR9184.3.K5   810′.9′005.
    A critical history, from the seventeenth century to 1984, of English Canadian literature. Chapters, usually by major scholars, treat philosophy, history, the social and natural sciences, religion, literary criticism and scholarship, travel writing, translation, publishing and the book trade, and children's literature, as well as fiction, poetry, and drama. Some include a highly selective bibliography. Vols. 1–3 conclude with a very brief general bibliography; each volume has an index of names, anonymous works, and subjects (vol. 4 cites all titles). The volumes comprise the most comprehensive history of English Canadian literature, although belles lettres are frequently overshadowed by the extensive treatment accorded nonliterary topics (especially in vol. 3). Reviews: John Ferns, *Modern Language Review* 74 (1979): 186–88; W. J. Keith, *University of Toronto Quarterly* 46 (1977): 461–66.
    Good complements are W. J. Keith, *Canadian Literature in English*, Longman Literature in English Series (London: Longman, 1985, 287 pp.), which emphasizes major writers and concludes with a useful chronology and selective bibliography; and W. H. New, *A History of Canadian Literature*, 2nd ed. (Montreal: McGill–Queen's UP, 2003, 464 pp.), which also concludes with a chronology and selective bibliography.

See also

Wiget, *Native American Literature* (Q3865).

Literary Handbooks, Dictionaries, and Encyclopedias

R4567   *Encyclopedia of Literature in Canada.* Ed. William H. New. Toronto: U of
          Toronto P, 2002. 1,347 pp.   PR9180.2.E64   810.9'971'03.
    An encyclopedia of literatures, written and oral, in Canada, with entries on writers,
awards and prizes, motifs, genres, events, places, regions, groups, periodicals, organizations, institutions, allusions, and a very select few individual works. While the bulk
of the entries (which inconsistently conclude with suggestions for further reading) are
for individuals, topics not usually encountered in literary encyclopedias are also given
their due, such as archives, book history, editors and editing, libraries, and publishing
industry. Concludes with a chronology and three indexes: contributors; authors; persons
and subjects not accorded separate entries. Although many entries for common literary
terms (e.g., allusion, burlesque, lyric, prosody) should be jettisoned, others (e.g.,
Bloomsbury Group, muscular Christianity, renga) strain to make a Canadian connection, and there are a substantial number of misprints and errors in dates, the breadth
and depth of coverage make *Encyclopedia of Literature in Canada* an important desktop
companion to the literary culture of the country. Reviews: Stephen Henighan, *TLS:
Times Literary Supplement* 19 Sept. 2003: 26; John J. O'Connor, *University of Toronto
Quarterly* 73 (2003–4): 161–62.
    The Oxford Companion to Canadian Literature, gen. eds. Eugene Benson and Wil-
liam Toye, 2nd ed. (Toronto: Oxford UP, 1997, 1,199 pp.; online through *Oxford
Reference Online* [I530]), remains a useful complement. The approximately 1,100 signed
entries primarily treat authors and genres, emphasize modern literature (mostly French
and English), and are more extensive, evaluative, and exclusively literary than in the
typical *Oxford Companion.* As in *Encyclopedia of Literature in Canada,* author entries
combine biographical and bibliographical information with critical commentary. Review: Colin Hill, *Essays on Canadian Writing* 65 (1998): 76–81.

R4570   *Dictionnaire des œuvres littéraires du Québec.* Ed. Maurice Lemire et al.
          7 vols. Saint Laurent: Fides, 1980–2003.   PQ3901.D5   840'.9.

    Vol. 1: *Des origines à 1900.* 2nd ed., rev. and corrected. 1980. 927 pp.
    Vol. 2: *1900–1939.* 1980. 1,363 pp.
    Vol. 3: *1940–1959.* 1982. 1,252 pp.
    Vol. 4: *1960–1969.* 1984. 1,123 pp.
    Vol. 5: *1970–1975.* 1987. 1,133 pp.
    Vol. 6: *1976–1980.* 1994. 1,087 pp.
    Vol. 7: *1981–1985.* 2003. 1,229 pp.

    A dictionary of literary works by Québec authors or related to the province. Or-
ganized by title, the signed entries, which range from 250 to 3,000 words, typically
provide a summary, discussion of the work's place in its author's canon, critical commentary, and (sometimes lengthy) lists of editions and studies. A brief biographical
notice precedes the entry for an author's first work. Each volume includes a chronology;
selective bibliographies of literary works, reference works, and critical studies; and an
index of persons. The entries vary in quality, of course, but the *Dictionnaire* offers
impressively thorough coverage of the bulk of French Canadian literature through 1985.
Reviews: (vol. 4) B.-Z. Shek, *University of Toronto Quarterly* 54 (1985): 471–74; (vol.
5) Shek, *University of Toronto Quarterly* 5 (1989): 172–75; (vol. 7) Marcel Olscamp,
University of Toronto Quarterly 76 (2007): 61–64.

R4575   Hamilton, Robert M., and Dorothy Shields. *The Dictionary of Canadian Quotations and Phrases.* Rev. and enl. ed. Toronto: McClelland, 1979. 1,063 pp.   PN6081.H24   818'.02.

A dictionary of about 10,300 quotations and phrases from Canadian sources (and some British, French, and American ones) on distinctly Canadian topics, as well as by Canadians about other subjects. Organized by subject, then chronologically under a heading, an entry consists of quotation and citation to a printed source. Indexed by authors. To locate cross-references, users must consult the prefatory list of subject headings. This is the best source for locating and identifying Canadian quotations.

An essential complement is John Robert Colombo, *The Dictionary of Canadian Quotations* (Toronto: Stoddart, 1991, 671 pp.), the majority of whose 6,000 quotations date from 1970 and reportedly are not in any other dictionary. The quotations are organized by topic; notes on sources neglect to cite page number, however. Indexed by author or speaker.

Bibliographies of Bibliographies

R4585   Ingles, Ernie, ed. and comp. *Bibliography of Canadian Bibliographies/ Bibliographie des bibliographies canadiennes.* 3rd ed., updated, rev., and enl. Toronto: U of Toronto P, 1994, 1,178 pp.   Z1365.A1 I54   016.016971.

A bibliography of bibliographies — including periodical articles and theses — from 1789 to mid-1993 that have "substantial Canadian content or interest." The 7,375 entries are listed chronologically by date of publication (then alphabetically) in seven divisions: general bibliographies, geographical areas, arts and humanities (including sections for performing arts, literature, children's literature, and linguistics and translation), social sciences (including sections for women's, native, and ethnic studies), sciences, types of bibliographies (which includes a fair number of works that should be included in the preceding subject divisions), and catalogs (though other catalogs appear in the preceding subject divisions). A typical entry provides a bibliographical citation, notes (on content, scope, number of entries, and previous editions), and location of at least one copy. Three indexes: authors; titles; subjects (with separate ones for English and French headings). Concludes with a "short entry listing" — a list, by author or title of anonymous work, of all 7,375 entries — that merely wastes a substantial amount of paper and contributes to the unwieldy size of the volume. Although access is marred by the use of both subject and type-of-document organization, *Bibliography of Canadian Bibliographies* is a substantial improvement over the second edition (Douglas Lochhead, comp., *Bibliography of Canadian Bibliographies/Bibliographie des bibliographies canadiennes* [Toronto: U of Toronto P, 1972, 312 pp.]), which absurdly admitted a number of works that had nothing to do with Canada simply because they were by Canadians or published in the country. Impressively broad and comprehensive, *Bibliography of Canadian Bibliographies* is an essential starting point for research on Canadian topics. Review: Linda M. Jones, *Papers of the Bibliographical Society of Canada* 33.1 (1995): 189–92.

For more recent bibliographies, see *Bibliographic Index* (D145).

See also

Sec. D: Bibliographies of Bibliographies.
Kempton, *French Literature: An Annotated Guide to Selected Bibliographies* (S4905a).
Newman, *Black Access: A Bibliography of Afro-American Bibliographies* (Q3715).

Guides to Primary Works

MANUSCRIPTS

R4590   *Archives Canada: Canadian Archival Information Network/Réseau canadien
         d'information archivistique.* Canadian Council of Archives/Conseil canadien
         des archives. Online. 14 Aug. 2005 <http://www.archivescanada.ca/
         index2.html>. Updated regularly.
   A database of archival collections housed in Canadian institutions. The Basic
Search mode allows users to search by keyword anywhere or in the provenance or
collection title fields; users can also browse the provenance and title indexes. In Advanced Search, users can combine keyword searches of several additional fields (e.g.,
scope and content note, repository name). Search results are returned in unsorted order
but can be re-sorted by collection title; records can be saved to a list for e-mailing. A
typical record includes record number, collection title, physical description of the collection, dates of holdings, administrative history (for organizations) or biographical
sketch (for individuals), notes on scope and content, repository (with a link to the
repository's Web site), restrictions on access, terms governing use and reproduction,
finding aids (with a link to online ones), history of the collection, indication whether
additions may be made, miscellaneous notes, provenance (i.e., name of the creator of
the records), and subjects. Users must remember that this is a database of collections
(not individual manuscripts), that the sophistication and accuracy of descriptions vary
depending on the reporting institution, and that in large collections individual writers,
especially of letters, go unmentioned in the description.
   Essential complements to *Archives Canada* are:

> *ArchiviaNet.* Library and Archives Canada/Bibliothèque et archives Canada.
> Online. 15 Aug. 2005 <http://www.collectionscanada.gc.ca/archivianet>.
> This offers access to some individual manuscripts; unfortunately, the
> search interface (which is being upgraded) is not very sophisticated and
> searches tend to return several records minimally related to a search term.
> *Union List of Manuscripts in Canadian Repositories/Catalogue collectif des man-
> uscrits des archives canadiennes.* Ed. E. Grace Maurice. Rev. ed. 2 vols.
> Ottawa: Public Archives, 1975. Supplements (with French title as *Cata-
> logue collectif des manuscrits conservés dans les dépôts d'archives canadiennes*):
> *1976.* 1976. 322 pp. *1977–1978.* 1979. 236 pp. *1979–1980.* Ed. Grace
> Maurice Hyam. 1982. 243 pp. *1981–1982.* Ed. Peter Yurkiw. 1985. 616
> pp. A union list of significant collections of manuscripts and records held
> by Canadian institutions. Entries are listed alphabetically by the author or
> corporate body who created or accumulated the collection. A typical entry
> includes location, a brief description of content, size, dates covered, and,
> when necessary, restrictions on use and finding lists or other aids. Two
> indexes: repositories; names, corporate bodies, places, and selected subjects
> mentioned in annotations. As is usual in other national union lists of
> manuscripts, the sophistication and accuracy of descriptions vary depend-
> ing on the reporting institution, and in large collections individual writers,
> especially of letters, go unmentioned in the annotations (and thus in the
> index). Since this work is a list of collections (with only a few entries for
> individual manuscripts), users searching for writings by an author should

begin with the name, place, and subject index. This remains useful since *Archives Canada* and *ArchiviaNet* apparently do not index everything in the *Union List.*

See also

Sec. F: Guides to Manuscripts and Archives.

PRINTED WORKS

R4595   *Canadiana: The National Bibliography/La bibliographie nationale.* Library and Archives Canada/Bibliothèque et archives Canada. Online. 14 July 2005 <http://www.collectionscanada.gc.ca/amicus/index-e.html>. CD-ROM. <http://www.collectionscanada.gc.ca/canadiana/index-e.html>.

A database of Canadian imprints and foreign publications (printed and electronic, published and forthcoming) that were written by Canadian citizens and residents or that are of Canadian interest. Coverage depends heavily on copyright deposits and acquisitions by the National Library: films and some ephemeral material are excluded. Since this incorporates the print version of *Canadiana: Canada's National Bibliography/ La bibliographie nationale du Canada* (Ottawa: Natl. Lib. of Canada, 1951–2000) and *Canadiana Pre–1901: Monographs/Canadiana d'avant 1901: Monographies* (Ottawa: Natl. Lib. of Canada, 1980–94; title varies) as well as records from *Early Canadiana* (Ottawa: Canadian Inst. for Historical Microreproductions, 1980– ; http:// www.canadiana.org/eco/index.html), coverage for 1920–49 is not very thorough. (For a discussion of changes in scope in the early print volumes, see Dorothy E. Ryder, *Canadian Reference Sources: A Selective Guide,* 2nd ed. [Ottawa: Canadian Lib. Assn., 1981] 235–39.) Although not exhaustive (especially for foreign imprints relating to the country), *Canadiana* offers the fullest coverage of recent Canadian imprints and is a useful source of books about Canadian topics.

Less thorough and accurate is *Canadian Books in Print* (Toronto: U of Toronto P, 1967– ; the *Author and Title Index* appears quarterly in microfiche, with an annual hardcover cumulation; the *Subject Index* is published annually in hardcover), which excludes most French-language titles. Earlier coverage is offered by Dorothea D. Tod and Audrey Cordingley, comps., *A Check List of Canadian Imprints/Catalogue d'ouvrages imprimés au Canada, 1900–1925: Preliminary Checking Edition/Liste à vérifier* (Ottawa: Canadian Bibliog. Centre and Public Archives of Canada, 1950, 370 pp.), and by *The Canadian Catalogue of Books Published in Canada, about Canada, as Well as Those Written by Canadians [1921–49],* 28 nos. (Toronto: Toronto Public Lib., 1923–50). A cumulation of listings for English-language titles in the latter was published as *The Canadian Catalogue of Books Published in Canada, about Canada, as Well as Those Written by Canadians, with Imprint 1921–1949,* 2 vols. (Toronto: Toronto Public Lib., 1959). For additional retrospective bibliographies, see *Canadian Reference Sources* (R4555), pp. 28–47.

R4605   Lecker, Robert, and Jack David, eds. *The Annotated Bibliography of Canada's Major Authors (ABCMA).* 8 vols. Toronto: ECW, 1979–94.   Z1375.A56 [PR9184.3]   016.81.

A collection of author bibliographies of works by and about important English Canadian and French Canadian writers, with half of the volumes devoted to poets and half to prose writers. Each volume attempts comprehensive coverage (up to one to three years before publication) of primary works (all editions, reprints, translations, excerpts, audiovisual materials, manuscripts, but only selected contributions to anthologies) and secondary materials. The overall organization is chronological. Under primary works, separate publications—classified by genre, form, or medium—appear first (with later editions and translations listed under the first edition), followed by manuscripts (by collection, with a description of contents), then other publications (by type or form). Secondary works—accompanied by descriptive annotations—are classified by form: books, articles and parts of books, theses and dissertations, interviews, awards and honors, and selected reviews. Through vol. 3 an introduction to each author offers a cursory survey of criticism and a necessary discussion of limitations in coverage. Each author section is separately indexed by persons. Numerous reviewers have objected to the choice of major authors and to the poetry and prose division. The individual bibliographies vary widely in accuracy, and many are far short of the comprehensive coverage (especially for secondary works) the editors claim for the work; moreover, there is rarely any logic to groupings in volumes, and inconsistencies abound. However, *ABCMA* is an important contribution to Canadian literary scholarship and an essential starting point for research on many of the authors. Several bibliographies have been reprinted as volumes in the Canadian Author Bibliographies series. Reviews: (vol. 1) David Jackel, *Canadian Literature* 88 (1981): 147–50; Donald Stephens, *English Studies in Canada* 8 (1982): 96–100; (vol. 2) R. G. Moyles, *Analytical and Enumerative Bibliography* 6 (1982): 49–51; (vols. 1–2) D. G. Lochhead, *Canadian Poetry* 9 (1981): 100–03, with a reply by Lecker and David, 10 (1982): 132–36, and a response by Lochhead, pp. 136–37; (vol. 3) Terry Goldie, *Canadian Literature* 96 (1983): 153–55; (vols. 5–6) David Staines, *Literary Research* 11 (1986): 188–91.

R4610   "Letters in Canada/Lettres canadiennes [1935–]." *University of Toronto*
         Quarterly 5 (1936)– .   AP5.U55   378.1.
     An annual selective review of English Canadian and French Canadian literary, critical, and scholarly works. Beginning with vol. 56 (1986–87), one issue is devoted entirely to the survey. Separate signed essays examine fiction, poetry, drama, and translations; the humanities section now consists of individual signed reviews of critical and scholarly books by Canadian authors on a wide range of topics and national literatures. The early surveys include selective checklists of titles. Indexed by books reviewed. For the history of "Letters in Canada," see W. J. Keith and B.-Z. Shek, "A Half-Century of *UTQ*," *University of Toronto Quarterly* 50 (1980): 146–54. Although selective in coverage, "Letters in Canada" is the best annual evaluative survey of books by Canadians.

R4613   Miska, John. *Ethnic and Native Canadian Literature: A Bibliography.*
         Toronto: U of Toronto P, 1990. 445 pp.   Z1376.E87 M57
         016.8088'9971.
     A partly annotated bibliography of literary works by and studies about the literature of native peoples and Canadian immigrants (excluding those from the United States, France, Great Britain, Australia, and New Zealand), as well as some Canadian-born authors writing in languages other than English or French. Coverage of literary works is limited to separately published books of fiction, poetry, or drama written as late as 1989 while the author resided in Canada. The 5,497 entries are organized in three divisions: reference works (with sections for bibliographies, general book-length studies, general articles and review essays, and anthologies; within each, the briefly annotated entries are listed alphabetically by author); 65 national or language groups (listed alphabetically, each group begins, where appropriate, with lists of reference works, general

studies, and anthologies; sections on individual authors follow, with each typically including a biographical note and separate lists of books by and writings about the author); minorities in Canadian literature (with sections for immigrants and native peoples, each with separate annotated lists of secondary and primary works). Indexed by authors and subjects. Although lacking any statement about the terminal date of coverage, inconsistent in defining "ethnic" and "native," limited to separately published literary works, and overlooking some studies, Miska is the essential starting place for research on the ethnic and native literatures of Canada. Scholars must, however, consult both *MLAIB* (G335) and *ABELL* (G340) to identify additional studies. Review: Joanne Henning, *Papers of the Bibliographical Society of Canada* 30 (1992): 61–62.

R4615   Tremaine, Marie. *A Bibliography of Canadian Imprints, 1751–1800.*
Toronto: U of Toronto P, 1952. 705 pp.   Z1365.T7   015.71.

Fleming, Patricia Lockhart, and Sandra Alston. *Early Canadian Printing: A Supplement to Marie Tremaine's* A Bibliography of Canadian Imprints, 1751–1800. Toronto: U of Toronto P, 1999. 629 pp.   Z1365.T7 015.71.

A retrospective national bibliography of Canadian imprints (including newspapers and magazines) from 1751 through 1800. The 1,240 entries of the 1952 volume are divided in two parts. The first is devoted to books, pamphlets, broadsides, handbills, and other separately printed matter. Organized by year of printing, then alphabetically by author, corporate author, or title of anonymous work, the detailed entries consist of a quasi-facsimile transcription of the title page; collation; list of contents; extensive notes on the printer, author, subject matter, advertisements, printing or publishing records, related scholarship, and post-1800 editions; and locations in public and private collections. The second part lists newspapers by province and then magazines. Each entry provides thorough notes on printing and publishing history and a list of locations with exact holdings. Concludes with descriptions of Canadian printing offices. Thoroughly indexed by authors, titles, subjects, and types of printed matter.

The *Supplement* extends the scope to "all the products of the press" in updating Tremaine's entries, verifying locations, describing publications unknown to her (altering some of Tremaine's practices to accord with the current conventions of analytical bibliography), and transcribing records of the Brown-Neilson printing shop and printers' vouchers in the Audited Public Accounts. The five indexes (names; titles; genres, languages, and subjects; printers; copies located) cover both the *Supplement* and the original volume (except for the chapters on newspapers and magazines and on printing offices and biographical notes on printers).

The detailed, careful descriptions of both volumes and the expanded scope of the *Supplement* make *Bibliography of Canadian Imprints* and *Early Canadian Printing* the essential record of Canadian imprints and publishing history for the latter half of the eighteenth century.

Coverage is both supplemented and continued by Fleming, *Upper Canadian Imprints, 1801–1841: A Bibliography* (Toronto: U of Toronto P, with the Natl. Lib. of Canada and the Canadian Government Publishing Centre, 1988, 555 pp.), and *Atlantic Canadian Imprints, 1801–1820: A Bibliography* (Toronto: U of Toronto P, 1991, 189 pp.), whose admirably detailed entries include a quasi-facsimile transcription of the title page; collation; list of contents and illustrations; details of paper, typography, and binding; notes on authorship or publishing history; copies examined; and references to standard bibliographies. Newspapers, journals, and unlocated publications are listed in appendixes in *Upper Canadian Imprints*; *Atlantic Canadian Imprints* includes a single appendix for unlocated imprints. Six indexes: names; titles; genres and subjects; trades; places of publication; languages. Thoroughness and attention to detail make these admirable bibliographies important contributions to the retrospective national bibliography of Canadian imprints.

R4620   Watters, Reginald Eyre. *A Checklist of Canadian Literature and Background Materials, 1628–1960.* 2nd ed., rev. and enl. Toronto: U of Toronto P, 1972. 1,085 pp.   Z1375.W3   013′.971.

A bibliography of separately published English Canadian literary and related works by some 7,000 Canadian authors (with "Canadian" broadly inclusive). The approximately 16,000 titles are organized alphabetically by author in two parts. Pt. 1 is meant to be a comprehensive list of literary works, with entries divided among sections for poetry, poetry and prose mixed, fiction, and drama. Pt. 2 is a selective list of books important as backgrounds to Canadian literature, with entries grouped by topics: biography, essays and speeches, local history and description, religion and morality, social history, scholarship and criticism on literature and the humanities, and travel and description. In both parts, works published before 1951 are located in up to five libraries (primarily in Canada). Two indexes: titles of anonymous works; authors, initials, and pseudonyms. Users must remember that (1) this is a list of works, not an exhaustive bibliography of editions; (2) there are numerous errors and inconsistencies, since the majority of entries were compiled from library catalogs and other sources rather than personal examination of copies; (3) pt. 2 includes several works only marginally related to Canadian literature; (4) the reliance on library call numbers to identify genre or subject matter means there will be classification errors. Although unsophisticated as a bibliography, Watters offers the fullest record of English Canadian literature. Reviews: (1st ed.) H. P. Gundy, *Queen's Quarterly* 66 (1959): 326–28; (2nd ed.) Robert L. McDougall, *Queen's Quarterly* 81 (1974): 120–22; Peter C. Noel-Bentley, *Humanities Association Review* 24 (1973): 340–41.

For literary works, Watters supersedes Vernon Blair Rhodenizer, *Canadian Literature in English* (Montreal: Privately printed, 1965, 1,055 pp.), a poorly organized compilation of miscellaneous information on books by Canadian citizens and residents that must be used with Lois Mary Thierman, comp., *Index to Vernon Blair Rhodenizer's Canadian Literature in English* (Edmonton: La Survivance, [1968], 469 pp.). For post-1960 works, see *Canadiana* (R4595). Wagner, *Brock Bibliography of Published Canadian Plays* (R4725), provides fuller coverage of drama but does not list locations.

See also

"Annual Bibliography of Commonwealth Literature" (R4375).
Canadian Literary Periodicals Index (R4630).
Canadian Literature Index (R4630a).
Canadian Periodical Index (R4635).
Cheung, *Asian American Literature* (Q3940).
English Short Title Catalogue (M1377).
Lecker, *Canadian Writers and Their Works* (R4645).
Moyles, *English-Canadian Literature to 1900* (R4650).
Nineteenth Century Short Title Catalogue (M2475).
North American Imprints Program (Q4010).
Sabin, *Bibliotheca Americana* (Q4015).

Guides to Scholarship and Criticism

SERIAL BIBLIOGRAPHIES

R4630   *Canadian Literary Periodicals Index: Cumulative Index to [1992, 1997]
         Publications.* Teeswater: Reference, 1997–98. Annual.   Z1375.C36
         016.81′05. (The online version is no longer available.)

An author, subject, and title index to literary materials published in Canadian
literary periodicals (96 in number at its demise, with the majority in English). Book
reviews are indexed by reviewer, author, and title of book reviewed and listed by title
under headings for kinds of books reviewed (e.g., "Anthologies—Reviews"); poems,
plays, and short stories are indexed by author and listed by title under headings for each
of the genres; subject headings are all in English. Modeled after the short-lived *Canadian
Literature Index*, *Canadian Literary Periodicals Index* scraps the former's two-part structure, improves its subject indexing, and intends to be more current, but like its predecessor it is vague about what constitutes "Canadian" and is limited in coverage. Nonetheless, it fills an important gap in the indexing of Canadian literature.

Three important serial bibliographies for earlier scholarship are:

> *Canadian Literature Index: A Guide to Periodicals and Newspapers [1985–
> 88].* Canadian Index Series. Toronto: ECW, 1987–92. Quarterly, with
> annual cumulation. An index of creative works by Canadian authors, stud-
> ies of Canadian literary works, and reviews of books by Canadians and
> about the country's literature—all published in some 100 periodicals and
> newspapers, the majority of which originate in Canada. The entries are
> organized in two parts: an author list of publications indexed and a subject
> list, with headings for writers, literary works, and some topics (with subject
> heads in English only). Vague titles are usually accompanied by a phrase
> indicating content. Despite *Canadian Literature Index*'s drawbacks—it
> lacks an explanation of the criteria used to determine "Canadian," need-
> lessly separates literary works from their authors in the subject division (a
> practice that occasions unnecessary duplicate entries), employs subject
> headings that are usually too broad, is limited in coverage and appeared
> about four years after the date of coverage—it was a welcome addition to
> Canadian reference sources.
>
> "Canadian Literature/Littérature canadienne [1959–74]: An Annotated Bib-
> liography/Une bibliographie avec commentaire," [for 1959–70] *Cana-
> dian Literature/Littérature canadienne* 3–48 (1960–71); [for 1971] *Essays
> on Canadian Writing* 9 (1977–78): 190–326; [for 1972–74] *Journal of
> Canadian Fiction* 2–23 (1973–79). A bibliography of primary and sec-
> ondary works (including dissertations, theses, and reviews) related to En-
> glish Canadian and French Canadian literature. The bibliographies for
> 1959–63 are cumulated and slightly expanded in Inglis F. Bell and Susan
> W. Port, eds., *Canadian Literature, 1959–1963: A Checklist of Creative
> and Critical Writings/Littérature canadienne, 1959–1963: Bibliographie de
> la critique et des œuvres d'imagination* (Vancouver: U of British Columbia,
> 1966, 140 pp.).
>
> *Bibliography of Comparative Studies in Canadian, Québec, and Foreign Litera-
> tures/Bibliography d'études comparées des littératures canadiennes, québécoise et
> étrangères.* Département des lettres et communications, Université de

Sherbrooke. Online. 13 Mar. 2005 <http://compcanlit.usherbrooke.ca/ index.html>. Updated regularly. A database of publications (since c. 1930) that "contain a significant comparison or discussion of Canadian and/or Québécois literatures, including their production, reception, study, histories, effects and influences, in relation to each other, or each or both in relation to other literatures of the world." Although the Web site offers no explanation of the scope, editorial principles underlying the selection of documents, frequency of updating, or record structure, much of the data is drawn from Antoine Sirois et al., *Bibliography of Comparative Studies in Canadian, Québec, and Foreign Literatures/Bibliographie d'études comparées des littératures canadienne, québécoise et étrangères 1930–1995* (Sherbrooke: U de Sherbrook and Editions G.G.C., 2001)—which expands and updates A. Sirois, Jean Vigneault, Maria van Sundert, and David M. Hayne, *Bibliography of Studies in Comparative Canadian Literature, 1930–1987/Bibliographie d'études de littérature canadienne comparée, 1930–1987*, Cahiers de littérature canadienne comparée 1 (Sherbrooke: Département des Lettres et Communications, U de Sherbrooke, 1989, 130 pp.), itself a cumulation and expansion of "Preliminary Bibliography of Comparative Canadian Literature (English-Canadian and French-Canadian)," *Canadian Review of Comparative Literature/Revue canadienne de littérature comparée* 3–13 (1976–86), but which omits the divisions for translation and language and style included in the annual bibliography through vol. 14 (1987)—Sirois and Sundert, "Supplementary Bibliography of Comparative Canadian Literature (English-Canadian and French-Canadian): First Supplement 1988–1989," *Canadian Review of Comparative Literature* 16 (1989): 170–76; and Sirois et al., "Supplementary Bibliography of Comparative Canadian Literature (English-Canadian and French-Canadian): 2nd Supplement 1990–95/Bibliographie de la littérature canadienne comparée (Littératures canadienne-anglaise et canadienne-française): 2e supplément 1990–95," 23 (1996): 126–38. The 2,460 records (as of 13 Mar. 2005)—which include fields for author; title; publication information; index terms; and authors, translators, and geographical areas discussed—can be searched in Advanced Search by titles, authors, keywords, or geographical areas discussed. Before performing Boolean searches, users should read the instructions in the Advanced Search screen. Records are sorted in descending chronological order and can be marked for printing or e-mailing. For studies of translations, see Kathy Mezei, *Bibliography of Criticism on English and French Literary Translations in Canada, 1950–1986: Annotated/Bibliographie de la critique des traductions littéraires anglaises et françaises au Canada de 1950 à 1986: Avec commentaires*, Cahiers de traductologie 7 (Ottawa: U of Ottawa P and Canadian Federation for the Humanities, 1988, 177 pp.); however, the volume is awkwardly organized by type of publication (e.g., books, interviews, review essays, reviews, theses).

R4635   *CPI.Q.* Thomson Gale. Online. 27 July 2005
<http://web6.infotrac.galegroup.com>.

Canadian Periodical Index: An Author and Subject Index/Index de périodiques canadiens: Un index auteurs/sujets (*CPI*). Detroit: Gale, 1928–32, 1938– 2003. Monthly, with annual and larger cumulations. Former titles: *Canadian Periodical Index* (1928–47); *Canadian Index to Periodicals and*

Documentary Films: An Author and Subject Index/Index de périodiques et de films documentaires canadiens: Auteurs et sujets (1948–63).   AI3.C242 051.

An index to reviews, original literary works, and articles with significant Canadian content in some 415 (as of July 2005) scholarly and popular periodicals and newspapers published in Canada (along with a few United States publications that treat North American or international topics). Selection is largely determined by subscribers. Entries since 1988 (along with content from other Gale databases) can be searched through *CPI.Q*; full-text coverage begins in 1995. The database can be searched in four modes:

> Subject Search, which maps to subject terms (that are, however, masked in the record display).
> Relevance Search, which selects records based on the frequency and density of the appearance of a search term within a record. Searchers must use this search form with care, especially when searching for a term (e.g., Shakespeare) that generates several hundred hits: the algorithm frequently places records without full text at the top, and the limit of records returned is 200.
> Keyword Search.
> Advanced Search, which allows users to restrict searches to specific record fields.

Searches of each of these can be limited to full-text articles, refereed publications, date(s), journal(s), and additional terms. Except for a Relevance Search, records are returned in descending chronological order and cannot be sorted otherwise. A maximum of 50 records can be marked for printing or e-mailing; some full-text records can be downloaded as PDF files.

The print version is an author and subject index. Subject headings are in English (with French-language cross-references; all headings and cross-references are listed in the current edition of *Canadian Thesaurus/Thésaurus canadien*). Articles are usually indexed under only one subject heading; book reviews are grouped under "Book Reviews"; poems appear under "Poems"; short stories, under "Short Stories"; and art works, under the name of the artist. Like *Readers' Guide* (G400), which it resembles, this series is useful for its coverage of periodicals not indexed in the bibliographies and indexes in this section and in section G.

See also

> Sec. G: Serial Bibliographies, Indexes, Abstracts.
> *ABELL* (G340): Entries on Canadian writers and literature are dispersed throughout.
> "Annual Bibliography of Commonwealth Literature" (R4375).
> "Letters in Canada" (R4610).
> *MLAIB* (G335): For English Canadian literature see the English Literature division, especially English III: General, in volumes through 1956; English XI: Australia, Canada, Etc./Canada section in the volumes for 1957–66; English II: Australia, Canada, Etc./Canada section in the volumes for 1967–80; and the [British] Commonwealth Literature/Canadian Literature section in later volumes. For French Canadian literature, see the French division (especially French II) in the pre-1981 volumes and the French Literature/French Canadian section in the later ones. Researchers must also check the headings beginning with "Canadian(s)" and "French Canadian(s)" in the subject index to post-1980 volumes and in the online thesaurus.

YWES (G330): Canadian literature has been covered in the African, Caribbean, Canadian, Australian, New Zealand, and Indian Literature in English chapter since vol. 63 (for 1982).

OTHER BIBLIOGRAPHIES

R4643   Dionne, René, and Pierre Cantin. *Bibliographie de la critique de la littérature québécoise et canadienne-française dans les revues canadiennes [1760–1899, 1974–1978, 1979–1982, 1983–1984].* 4 vols. Histoire littéraire du Québec et du Canada français. Ottawa: P de l'U d'Ottawa, 1988–94. Z1377.F8 D56   016.8409′971.

Cantin, Pierre, Normand Harrington, and Jean-Paul Hudon. *Bibliographie de la critique de la littérature québécoise dans les revues des XIXe and XXe siècles.* 5 vols. Documents de travail du Centre de recherche en civilisation canadienne-française 12–16. Ottawa: Centre de Recherche en Civilisation Canadienne-Française, U d'Ottawa, 1979.   Z1377.F8 C36 [PQ3901] 016.84′09.

Bibliographies of articles on French Canadian literature published in Canadian periodicals. The unannotated entries are listed alphabetically within year of publication in three classified divisions: general studies; genres; individual authors. Three indexes: scholars; journals covered; chronology (a useless agglomeration rendered superfluous by the chronological organization). The bibliographies covering 1974–83 cumulate and expand the articles (but not books) included in "Bibliographie de la critique [1974–83]," *Revue d'histoire littéraire du Québec et du Canada français* 1–10 (1979–85). Unfortunately, the authors had to suspend their work before completing the volumes for 1900–73 and 1984–90. Although the bibliographies are admirably extensive in their coverage, the insufficiently refined taxonomy, chronological organization, and lack of cross-references or subject indexes render them far less accessible than they should be.

Some additional studies—almost all of which are published by Canadian publishers or in Canadian serials—are listed in Réjean Beaudoin, Annette Hayward, and André Lamontagne, *Bibliographie de la critique de la littérature québécoise au Canada anglais (1939–1989),* Convergences 31 (Québec: Nota Bene, 2004, 253 pp.). The 2,696 entries are needlessly swollen by separate listings for entries in literary dictionaries (such as *Oxford Companion to Canadian Theatre* [R4717]). Unfortunately, the organization by decade then by type of publication and a single index of Québec authors render this resource maddeningly inaccessible.

Because the foregoing are restricted to Canadian publications, researchers must also consult the serial bibliographies and indexes in section G.

R4645   Lecker, Robert, Jack David, and Ellen Quigley, eds. *Canadian Writers and Their Works (CWTW).* [22 vols.] Toronto: ECW, 1983–93. PR9192.2.C38   810′.9′971.

A collection of chapters on major writers of the last 200 years, with 10 volumes devoted to fiction and 10 to poetry (and a cumulative index to each). Each volume treats four or five authors or related groups in essays that include a biography, discussion of milieu, survey of major studies, critical commentary on important works, and selected bibliographies of primary works and scholarship. Indexed by persons and titles of primary works in each volume and in separate cumulative indexes for the fiction and poetry volumes. Although there is considerable unevenness in the quality of individual essays, *CWTW* is a useful introduction to the work of and scholarship on major Canadian writers. Each essay is also published separately in the series ECW Canadian Author Studies.

R4650   Moyles, R. G. *English-Canadian Literature to 1900: A Guide to Information Sources.* American Literature, English Literature, and World Literatures in English: An Information Guide Series 6. Detroit: Gale, 1976. 346 pp. Z1375.M68 [PR9184.3]   016.81'08.

A selective bibliography of primary and secondary works (published through the early 1970s) important to the study of nineteenth-century English Canadian literature. Entries are listed in seven divisions: reference works (including sections for bibliographies; biographical sources; indexes to serials, theses, and microforms; and library catalogs), general literary history and criticism, anthologies, 12 major authors, 36 minor authors, travel writing, and nineteenth-century literary periodicals. Under each author are sections for bibliographies and manuscripts, collected works, biographical materials, primary works (by genre), and criticism. Less than half of the entries are descriptively annotated. Two indexes: persons; titles (incomplete). Although marred by an inadequate explanation of scope and criteria governing selection, Moyles is an essential supplement to Watters, *On Canadian Literature* (R4655), and Watters, *Checklist of Canadian Literature* (R4620); as a selective bibliography, it is superior to Michael Gnarowski, *A Concise Bibliography of English-Canadian Literature*, rev. ed. (Toronto: McClelland, 1978, 145 pp.), which is restricted to major authors and too dated to be of much use.

R4655   Watters, Reginald Eyre, and Inglis Freeman Bell, comps. *On Canadian Literature, 1806–1960: A Check List of Articles, Books, and Theses on English-Canadian Literature, Its Authors, and Language.* Rpt., with corrections and additions. Toronto: U of Toronto P, 1973. 165 pp. Z1375.W33   016.8109.

A classified list of biographical, critical, and scholarly studies, published between 1806 and 1960, on English Canadian literature and language. Entries are organized alphabetically in two divisions: general and topical studies; individual authors. The first has sections for general bibliographies; Canadian culture and background; language and linguistics; general studies on Canadian literature; drama and theater; fiction; poetry; general criticism; literary history; regionalism; songs, folksongs, and folklore; journalism, publishing, and periodicals; libraries and reading; and censorship and copyright. The work's flaws—it lacks an index, is not comprehensive, includes several unverified entries taken from other sources, and is superseded in parts—do not outweigh its usefulness as a starting point for identifying studies published before 1961. Review: Gordon Roper, *University of Toronto Quarterly* 36 (1967): 411–13.

For scholarship on theater, see Ball, *Bibliography of Canadian Theatre History* (R4735).

See also

Boos, *Bibliography of Women and Literature* (U6600).
Cheung, *Asian American Literature* (Q3940).
Etulain, *Bibliographical Guide to the Study of Western American Literature* (Q3670).
Lecker, *Annotated Bibliography of Canada's Major Authors* (R4605).
Marken, *American Indian: Language and Literature* (Q3875).

Miska, *Ethnic and Native Canadian Literature* (R4613).
Nadel, *Jewish Writers of North America* (Q3990).
New, *Critical Writings on Commonwealth Literatures* (R4380).
Pownall, *Articles on Twentieth Century Literature* (M2790).
Schwartz, *Articles on Women Writers* (U6605).
Watters, *Checklist of Canadian Literature and Background Materials, 1628–1960*
    (R4620).

DISSERTATIONS AND THESES

R4660   Gabel, Gernot U. *Canadian Literature: An Index to Theses Accepted by*
         Canadian Universities, 1925–1980. Köln: Gemini, 1984. 157 pp.
         Z1375.G32 [PR9184.3]   016.81'09'005.
    A classified bibliography of baccalaureate, master's, and doctoral theses accepted
by Canadian institutions and treating English or French Canadian literature. The 1,531
entries are organized by degree candidate in two divisions: general literary history (with
sections for general studies, poetry, fiction, drama and theater, and periodicals), and
individual literary authors. An entry cites title, degree, university, and date. Two indexes:
authors of theses; subjects.
    An essential complement for English Canadian literature is Apollonia Steele,
comp., *Theses on English-Canadian Literature: A Bibliography of Research Produced in*
Canada and Elsewhere from 1903 Forward (Calgary: U of Calgary P, 1988, 505 pp.),
an author and subject list of baccalaureate, master's, and doctoral theses accepted by
and in progress (as of early 1988) at Canadian, British, Italian, United States, and a
few other European and Indian institutions. Coverage excludes pedagogy, folklore, and
Canadian theater (as distinct from drama). Besides providing author, title, institution,
source of the citation, and, frequently, location of a copy, entries helpfully identify
theses that were listed as in progress in other sources but that were never completed or
that underwent a change of title. The subject indexing is quite full for Canadian authors
and topics, but there are no headings for foreign writers, literatures, or movements.
Three indexes: universities; types of degree; dates.
    Together, Gabel and Steele supersede Michael Gnarowski, *Theses and Dissertations*
in Canadian Literature (English): A Preliminary Check List (Ottawa: Golden Dog, 1975,
41 pp.), and save users from having to search Namaan, *Répertoire des thèses littéraires*
canadiennes (H470a), *Canadian Graduate Theses* (H470a), and *Canadian Theses* (H470).
For post-1986 theses accepted by Canadian universities, see *Canadian Theses* and
ProQuest Dissertations and Theses (H465); for dissertations on Canadian literature from
non-Canadian institutions, see section H: Guides to Dissertations and Theses.

RELATED TOPICS

R4665   Fowke, Edith, and Carole Henderson Carpenter, comps. *A Bibliography of*
         Canadian Folklore in English. Toronto: U of Toronto P, 1981. 272 pp.
         Z5984.C33 F68 [GR113]   016.39'000971.
    A selective bibliography of English-language studies (along with a very few in
French) published through 1979. The 3,877 entries are listed by author in variously
classified divisions for reference works, periodicals, general studies, genres (folktale,

music and dance, folk speech and names, minor genres, superstition and popular belief, folk life and customs, and art and material culture), biographies and appreciations of folklorists, records, films, and theses and dissertations. The genre divisions include sections for general studies and ethnic groups. An elaborate, rather confusing code (see p. xx) identifies audience, quality, content, or type of work in most entries. Users must study the discussion of classification and limitations in the introduction, which also surveys broadly the scholarship and identifies topics needing attention. Indexed by scholars. It is selective (with several unverified entries from other sources) and lacks a subject index; nevertheless, the *Bibliography of Canadian Folklore* is the most complete list of English-language studies of Canadian folklore. Review: Gerald Thomas, *Canadian Literature* 95 (1982): 161–65.

See also

>   Sec. U: Literature-Related Topics and Sources/Folklore and Literature.
>   *America: History and Life* (Q3310).
>   Clements, *Native American Folklore, 1879–1979* (Q3885).

Language

GUIDES TO SCHOLARSHIP

R4670   Avis, Walter S., and A. M. Kinloch. *Writings on Canadian English, 1792–1975: An Annotated Bibliography.* Toronto: Fitzhenry, [1978]. 153 pp. Z1379.A88 [PE3208]   016.427'9'71.

>   Lougheed, W. C. *Writings on Canadian English, 1976–1987: A Selective, Annotated Bibliography.* Strathy Language Unit Occasional Papers 2. Kingston: Strathy Language Unit, Queen's U, 1988. 66 pp.   Z1379.L68 [PE3208]   016.42'0971.

Bibliographies of popular and scholarly studies (including dissertations, theses, and reviews) published through 1987. The two volumes exclude works concerned solely with onomastics, the influence of Canadian English on other languages, or pedagogy. In both works, entries are organized in a single alphabetical sequence; in *1792–1975*, this material is followed by a section listing additions, including selected publications through 1977. The annotations clearly describe the scope and contents of works. Indexed in *1792–1975* by coauthors and coeditors, and in *1976–1987* by persons and subjects. The lack of a classified organization, cross-references, or subject index in the original volume means that users interested in a specific topic must skim all entries; however, *Writings on Canadian English* represents the most complete single list of studies through 1987. For later scholarship, see *MLAIB* (G335) and *ABELL* (G340).

See also

>   *ABELL* (G340): Dialect section of the English Language division in the volumes for 1920–26; the American English section in the volumes for 1927–33; the English Dialects section in the volume for 1934; the American English section in the volumes for 1935–72; and the Dialects/Dialects of [North] America section in later volumes.

MLAIB (G335): English Language and Literature division in the volumes for 1922–25; English Language and Literature I: Linguistics section in the volumes for 1926–66; the Indo-European C: Germanic Linguistics IV: English/ Modern English/Dialectology section in the volumes for 1967–80; and the Indo-European Languages/Germanic Languages/West Germanic Languages/ English Language (Modern)/Dialectology section in the later volumes. Researchers must also check the headings "Canada" and "Canadian English Dialect" in the subject index to post-1980 volumes and in the online thesaurus. Watters, *On Canadian Literature, 1806–1960* (R4655).

DICTIONARIES

R4675   *A Dictionary of Canadianisms on Historical Principles.* Ed. Walter S. Avis et al. Toronto: Gage, 1967. 927 pp.   PE3243.D5   427′.9′71.

A dictionary of words, expressions, and meanings "native to Canada or . . . distinctively characteristic of Canadian usage." A typical entry includes headword, pronunciation, part of speech, etymology, usage labels (for vocation, locale, or currency), definition, dated illustrative quotations from printed works, and, occasionally, a line drawing. Concludes with a bibliography of sources. The essential dictionary for the historical study of Canadian English and for the explication of Canadianisms in literary works. Canadian English is also included in *Dictionary of American English* (Q3355), *Dictionary of Americanisms* (Q3360), and *Oxford English Dictionary* (M1410). For contemporary Canadian English, see *The Canadian Oxford Dictionary*, ed. Katherine Barber, reissue with supp. (Toronto: Oxford UP, 2001, 1,710 pp.); however, it includes a number of personal names and geographic terms that have no discernible relation to Canada.

Biographical Dictionaries

R4680   *Dictionary of Canadian Biography (DCB).* Gen. eds. Ramsay Cook, George W. Brown, David M. Hayne, and Francess G. Halpenny. Toronto: U of Toronto P, 1966– . French ed.: *Dictionnaire biographique du Canada (DBC).* Gen. eds. Marcel Trudel, André Vachon, and Jean Hamelin. Québec: P de l'U Laval, 1966– .   F1005.D49 [FC25]   920′.071.

Vol. 1: *1000 to 1700.* 1966. 755 pp.
Vol. 2: *1701 to 1740.* 1969. 759 pp.
Vol. 3: *1741 to 1770.* 1974. 782 pp.
Vol. 4: *1771 to 1800.* 1979. 913 pp.
Index: *Volumes I to IV, 1000 to 1800.* 1981. 254 pp.
Vol. 5: *1801 to 1820.* 1983. 1,044 pp.
Vol. 6: *1821 to 1835.* 1987. 960 pp.
Vol. 7: *1836 to 1850.* 1988. 1,088 pp.
Vol. 8: *1851 to 1860.* 1985. 1,129 pp.
Vol. 9: *1861 to 1870.* 1976. 967 pp.

Vol. 10: *1871 to 1880.* 1972. 823 pp.
Vol. 11: *1881 to 1890.* 1982. 1,092 pp.
Vol. 12: *1891 to 1900.* 1990. 1,305 pp.
Index: *Volumes I to XII, 1000–1900.* 1991. 557 pp.
Vol. 13: *1901 to 1910.* 1994. 1,295 pp.
Vol. 14: *1911 to 1920.* 1998. 1,247 pp.
Vol. 15: *1921 to 1930.* 2005. 1,266 pp.

Dictionary of Canadian Biography Online/Dictionnaire biographique du Canada en ligne. Library and Archives Canada/Bibliothèque et archives Canada. Online. 11 Sept. 2006 <http://www.biographi.ca/EN/index.html>. Updated regularly. CD-ROM.

A biographical dictionary encompassing a broad range of Canadians and others who at least set foot in the country. Entries are listed alphabetically, with placement in a volume determined by the date of an entrant's death. The biographies, ranging from 200 to 10,000 words, combine facts with interpretation and conclude with a bibliography of works by and about the individual (frequently citing unpublished material). Each volume includes a general bibliography and index of names; volumes published or reprinted since 1979 include occupation or vocation and geographical indexes. The cumulative index to vols. 1–4 has four indexes (subjects of biographies; occupations or vocations; geographical area; names); that for vols. 1–12 has only two (biographees and names). In addition, entrants are indexed in *Biography and Genealogy Master Index* (J565).

Dictionary of Canadian Biography Online includes all entrants in the published volumes as well as selected biographies from the forthcoming one. The Quick Biography Search screen allows keyword searching and browsing by surname; the Advanced Search screen allows searches to be restricted by gender or date range of death and—for some biographees—by geographical area, profession, or race (consult the respective help screens for details). The results of a search can be organized in ascending or descending order by date range of death or alphabetically by surname. The editors plan to make all entrants searchable by geography and profession or race, to add portraits to selected entries, and to provide links to sections of *Library and Archives Canada* (http://www.collectionscanada.ca/). Although searchers would benefit from being able to combine fields in Advanced Search, *Dictionary of Canadian Biography Online* offers free access to a major resource.

DCB is a well-edited, authoritative, scholarly source that fully deserves the praise accorded it by reviewers and its rank among the great biographical dictionaries such as *Oxford Dictionary of National Biography* (M1425) and *American National Biography* (Q3378); it is especially useful to the literary researcher for its biographies of Canadian writers and historical figures depicted in Canadian literature as well as for the numerous citations to unpublished materials. Reviews: (vol. 1) H. P. Gundy, *Dalhousie Review* 46 (1966): 405–11; (vol. 4) Carl F. Klinck, *English Studies in Canada* 7 (1981): 496–500; (vol. 9) Clara Thomas, *English Studies in Canada* 5 (1979): 227–31; (vol. 11) Shirley Neuman, *Canadian Literature* 101 (1984): 82–83.

A useful basic biographical dictionary is W. Stewart Wallace, ed., *The Macmillan Dictionary of Canadian Biography,* rev. W. A. McKay, 4th ed. (Toronto: Macmillan, 1978, 914 pp.). For living persons, see the current edition of *Canadian Who's Who* (Toronto: U of Toronto P, 1910– ; online and CD-ROM). Entrants in both works are indexed in *Biography and Genealogy Master Index* (J565). *Marquis Who's Who on the Web* (Q3395) also includes Canadians.

See also

> Sec. J: Biographical Sources.
> *Dictionary of Literary Biography* (J600).

Periodicals

GUIDES TO PRIMARY WORKS

See

> Sec. K: Periodicals/Directories and Periodicals/Union Lists.
> Warwick, *Commonwealth Literature Periodicals* (R4385).

INDEXES

See

> Goode, *Index to Commonwealth Little Magazines* (K795).

Genres

Some works in section L: Genres are useful for research in Canadian literature.

FICTION

Some works in section L: Genres/Fiction are useful for research in Canadian fiction.

Guides to Primary Works

There is no adequate bibliography devoted solely to English Canadian fiction. Margery Fee and Ruth Cawker, *Canadian Fiction: An Annotated Bibliography* (Toronto: Martin, 1976, 170 pp.), a selection aid for teachers, is too incomplete to be of much use. Until an adequate bibliography appears, researchers will have to make do with Watters, *Checklist of Canadian Literature* (R4620).

R4703   Weiss, Allan, comp. *A Comprehensive Bibliography of English-Canadian Short Stories, 1950–1983.* Toronto: ECW, 1988. 973 pp.   Z1375.W46 [PR9192.52]   016.813'01.

An author list of 14,314 short stories written in English for adults and published 1950–83 in nearly 1,700 periodicals, anthologies, and author collections or broadcast on radio programs. Although foreign-language translations are cited, English-language translations of stories originally written in other languages are excluded. The 4,966 authors include Canadian citizens living in the country and abroad, landed immigrants, and permanent residents as of 1983. Under each author, collections appear first, followed by an alphabetical title list of short stories; along with publication information, entries sometimes cite the source for unverified details, note an alternative title, or indicate that the work might be something other than a short story. Indexed by titles. Although many entries are derived from other indexes or author questionnaires and although it is hardly "a comprehensive bibliography"—it omits most regional and student publications outside Ontario and is weak in the coverage of crime and science fiction—*English-Canadian Short Stories* does identify scores of works in frequently elusive publications and offers the best guide to English Canadian short stories (and their publishing history) during the period. Review: Helen Hoy, *Papers of the Bibliographical Society of Canada* 28 (1991): 100–02.

R4705   Hayne, David M., and Marcel Tirol. *Bibliographie critique du roman canadien-français, 1837–1900*. Toronto: U of Toronto P, 1968. 144 pp. Z1377.F8 H3   016.843.

A bibliography of French-language novels published separately before 1901 by Canadian citizens or permanent residents, and of selected scholarship and criticism through 1966. Entries are organized in three divisions: bibliographies, general biographical and critical works, and individual novelists. Under each author, novels are listed alphabetically, with editions, translations, and extracts in periodicals following in chronological order (with locations in Canadian libraries and the Library of Congress). Concluding each author section is a selective list of studies. Although its record of secondary works is far from complete, this remains an essential source for the study of the early French Canadian novel. Unfortunately, there is no comparable bibliography of twentieth-century French Canadian novels.

See also

> Wright, *[Author/Chronological/Title] Bibliography of English Language Fiction* (L1060).

Guides to Scholarship and Criticism

R4710   Hoy, Helen. *Modern English-Canadian Prose: A Guide to Information Sources*. American Literature, English Literature, and World Literatures in English: An Information Guide Series 38. Detroit: Gale, 1983. 605 pp. Z1377.F4 H69 [PR9192.5]   016.818'508.

A selective bibliography of primary and secondary works through 1980 that emphasizes fiction writers but also includes essayists, nature writers, critics, and biographers. Of the 78 authors, 10 are nonfiction writers and all were born before 1942; those in Moyles, *English-Canadian Literature to 1900* (R4650), are excluded. The approximately 5,250 entries are organized in three divisions: reference works (with sections for bibliographies and general reference works, biographical dictionaries, periodical and dissertation indexes, and guides to manuscripts and special collections), general studies (divided into books and articles), and individual authors (with separate sections for fiction and nonfiction). Under each author, primary works are divided into books and shorter pieces (each classified by genre) and include a list of manuscript collections; secondary works are listed in three sections: bibliographies, criticism, and book reviews (from major periodicals). Only reference works and a few general studies are annotated (the majority inadequately so). Three indexes: persons; book titles; subjects. Although the criteria governing inclusion of authors are vague, the bases for selection of secondary works are unstated, and many entries appear to be copied without verification from other sources, Hoy is at least a starting point for research on established fiction writers. Review: W. J. Keith, *Essays on Canadian Writing* 30 (1984–85): 136–39.

Biographical Dictionaries

See

    Contemporary Novelists (M2845).

DRAMA AND THEATER

Some works in section L: Genres/Drama and Theater are useful for research in Canadian drama and theater.

Literary Handbooks, Dictionaries, and Encyclopedias

R4717   *The Oxford Companion to Canadian Theatre.* Ed. Eugene Benson and L. W. Conolly. Toronto: Oxford UP, 1989. 662 pp.   PN2300.O94   792′.0971.
    An encyclopedia of Canadian theatrical activity from its first appearance in native cultures through 1988. The 703 signed entries — most of which are far lengthier than one expects in an *Oxford Companion* and which usually combine factual information and interpretation or evaluation — encompass individuals, 50 major plays, genres and forms, theaters, theatrical companies, and festivals; many conclude with suggestions for further reading. Indexed by persons, titles, and subjects; entrants are also indexed in *Biography and Genealogy Master Index* (J565). The full, authoritative entries and thorough indexing rank *Canadian Theatre* among the best of the *Oxford Companions.* For suggestions for a revision of *Canadian Theatre,* see the omnibus review by Bruce Barton, Catherine Graham, Jennifer Harvie, Shawn Huffman, Shemina Keshvani, and Marlene Moser, *Theatre Research in Canada* 18 (1997): 208–19.

See also

    Sec. L: Genres/Drama and Theater/Literary Handbooks, Dictionaries, and Encyclopedias.

Guides to Primary Works

R4720   Rinfret, Edouard G. *Le Théâtre canadien d'expression française: Répertoire analytique des origines à nos jours.* 4 vols. Collection Documents. Ottawa: Leméac, 1975–78.   PQ3911.R5   792′.09714.
    An annotated author bibliography of published and unpublished French Canadian plays (including radio and television drama) written through the early 1970s. A typical entry gives title, type of play, number of acts or scenes or playing time, cast, setting,

synopsis (usually lengthy), first production, and (for published works) publication information and locations of copies in Canadian libraries. Television dramas are listed separately in vol. 4. Indexed by titles in vol. 4. A valuable compendium of information on French Canadian drama, much of which is unpublished.

R4722   McCallum, Heather, and Ruth Pincoe, comps. *Directory of Canadian*
         Theatre Archives. Occasional Papers Ser. 53. Halifax: School of Lib. and
         Information Studies, Dalhousie U, 1992. 217 pp.   Z5785.M29
         [PN2308.5]   792'.02571.
    A guide to collections of Canadian theater materials (including "playbills, programs, posters, scrapbooks, stage designs, playscripts, prompt and stage managers' scripts, audio and video recordings," and manuscripts) held by Canadian institutions, libraries, theater companies, museums, and collectors. Entries, based on responses to a questionnaire, are organized by province, then by city, then by institution or theater (with named collections then listed in no apparent order). Indexed by persons, titles, and subjects. Although admittedly incomplete, McCallum offers the fullest guide to Canadian theatrical archives.
    Additional materials can be found through *ArchiviaNet* (http://www.collectionscanada .gc.ca/archivianet [which is being phased out]) and, especially, *Archives Canada: Canadian Archival Information Network/Réseau canadien d'information archivistique* (http://www.archivescanada.ca/index2.html).

R4725   Wagner, Anton, ed. *The Brock Bibliography of Published Canadian Plays in*
         English, 1766–1978. Toronto: Playwrights, 1980. 375 pp.
         Z1377.D7 B75 [PR9191.2]   016.812.
    A bibliography of plays (including some radio and television dramas) written by Canadians — native, naturalized, or landed immigrants — primarily while resident in the country. Wagner includes only extant dramatic works published separately or in periodicals or newspapers. Entries are organized by century of composition, then alphabetically by author, and then by title. Each entry provides publication information (but not a list of all editions), number of acts, number of male and female characters, genre, plot summary, and date and place of first production. Indexed by short titles. The organization by century (which is too gross to indicate trends) results in the placement of several authors in two places, and the lack of author, subject, and genre indexes make the bibliography much less accessible than it should be. There are several omissions and errors (especially in bibliographical details), but the *Brock Bibliography* is the fullest single source of information on published English Canadian plays. Review: Ron Davies, *Canadian Theatre Review* 31 (1981): 144–45.
    An essential complement because of its broader definition of what constitutes Canadian drama and its inclusion of unpublished works is Patrick B. O'Neill, "A Checklist of Canadian Dramatic Materials to 1967," *Canadian Drama* 8 (1982): 173–303; 9 (1983): 369–506. Although offering a less complete list of dramatic works, Watters, *Checklist of Canadian Literature* (R4620), is still useful, since it provides locations of copies. For plays published after 1978, see *Canadiana* (R4595); for recent televised plays, see Richard Bruce Kirkley, "A Catalogue of Canadian Stage Plays on English Canadian Television, 1952 to 1987," *Theatre Research in Canada* 15 (1994): 96–108. Recent English-language Canadian plays can be searched through the Playwrights Guild of Canada catalog (http://www.playwrightsguild.com/pgc/main.asp), which attempts to include every published or professionally produced Canadian play (many of which are unpublished).

Guides to Scholarship and Criticism

Surveys of Research

R4730   Wagner, Anton. "From Art to Theory: Canada's Critical Tools." *Canadian Theatre Review* 34 (1982): 59–83.   PN2009.C35   792'.05.
     A survey of the state of research that evaluates bibliographies and reference works, discusses problems facing researchers in Canadian drama, identifies needed reference works, and concludes with a selective list of bibliographies and guides.

Other Bibliographies

R4735   Ball, John, and Richard Plant, eds. *Bibliography of Theatre History in Canada: The Beginnings through 1984/Bibliographie d'histoire du théâtre au Canada: Des débuts–fin 1984.* Toronto: ECW, 1993. 445 pp. PN2301.B28   016.792'0971. Online. 29 Apr. 2006 <http:// www.lib.unb.ca/Texts/Theatre/Bib> (the URL is case sensitive).
     A bibliography of studies through 1984 on Canadian theater history, both English and francophone, with selective coverage of radio and television and the theatrical activities of native peoples. Excludes almost all newspaper articles as well as discussions of ballet, opera, and music. Entries are organized alphabetically (in two sequences: titles of anonymous works; authors) in the following classified divisions—general surveys; theater history to 1900; twentieth-century theater; little theater; festivals; radio and television drama; architecture and facilities; stage design and lighting; stagecraft; biographies and criticism of actors, actresses, and playwrights; theater education; theater for young people; puppetry; periodicals; and theses and dissertations. A few entries are accompanied by one-sentence annotations. Indexed by persons, theaters, subjects, and associations, but regrettably not by titles. There are unaccountable omissions (the editors did not search a source as basic as the *MLAIB* [G335]), but *Bibliography of Theatre History in Canada*—which represents a major improvement over its predecessor, *A Bibliography of Canadian Theatre History, 1583–1975* (Toronto: Playwrights Co-op, 1976, 160 pp.), and the *Supplement, 1975–76* (1979, 75 pp.)—is nonetheless the essential starting place for research on Canadian theater. Coverage is updated in "Bibliography Up-Date/Mise à jour de la bibliographie" in *Association for Canadian Theatre Research/Association de la recherché théâtrale au Canada: Newsletter/Bulletin de liaison,* which is incorporated into the bibliography's Web site. Unfortunately, as of 15 July 2005 the site offers a primitive search interface that allows only single-keyword searches, includes numerous records with citations so incomplete that users will be unable to locate publications, and provides no key to periodical title abbreviations or acronyms. In short, this is one of the most ineptly designed and poorly edited databases listed in this *Guide. A Preliminary Bibliography and Database of Canadian Theatre Reviews 1900– 1992* (which is housed at the same site) offers a similar lack of sophistication in its design.

See also

     Carpenter, *Modern Drama Scholarship and Criticism, 1966–1980* (M2875).
     Eddleman, *American Drama Criticism* (Q3520).
     International Bibliography of Theatre (L1160).
     "Modern Drama Studies" (M2870).
     Wildbihler, *Musical: An International Annotated Bibliography* (Q4295).

Biographical Dictionaries

See

Contemporary Dramatists (M2880).

POETRY

Some works in section L: Genres/Poetry are useful for research in Canadian poetry.

Guides to Primary Works

Bibliographies and Indexes

R4750   McQuarrie, Jane, Anne Mercer, and Gordon Ripley, comps. and eds. *Index
to Canadian Poetry in English*. Toronto: Reference, 1984. 367 pp.
Z1377.P7 M35 [PR9190.2]   016.811′008′0971.
Title and first-line, author, and subject indexes to about 7,000 poems (including
some translations of French Canadian works) from 51 collections. The title and first-
line index is keyed to a list of anthologies; the author and subject indexes are keyed to
the title and first-line index. Although highly selective, this is a convenient source for
locating the text of a poem or for identifying works about a topic or theme. *Columbia
Granger's Index to Poetry* (L1235), *Index of American Periodical Verse* (Q4325), and
Poetry Index Annual (L1235a) also index some English Canadian poems.
Some additional poems are included in the 44 anthologies indexed by author, title,
first line, and translator in *Canadian Poetry in Selected English-Language Anthologies: An
Index and Guide*, ed. Margery Fee, Dalhousie University Libraries and Dalhousie School
of Library Service Occasional Papers Series 36 (Halifax: Dalhousie U, School of Lib.
Service, 1985, 257 pp.).

Text Archives

R4753   *Canadian Poetry*. ProQuest. Online. 17 June 2006 <http://collections
.chadwyck.com>.
An archive of rekeyed texts of more than 19,000 English-language poems by Canadian writers from the seventeenth to the early twentieth century. Poems published
in book form, as broadsheets, or in periodicals have been included up to 1850; post-
1850 broadsheets and periodical publications have been included if recommended by
the editorial board (a practice at odds with the site's claim to include the complete
canon up to 1900). Editions were selected according to the following criteria: "Reliable
modern critical editions have been used as copy text where these are available. Where
no suitable modern edition exists, the policy has been to use reliable collected works
editions or editions published during the author's lifetime reflecting his or her final
intentions."
Simple keyword, first line or title, and author searches can be limited by date
during an author's lifetime, gender, literary period, and to parts (e.g., dedications, epigraphs). Searchers can also browse an author list of the contents of the database. Results
appear in ascending alphabetical order and cannot be re-sorted. Citations (but not the

full text of poems) can be marked for e-mailing, downloading, or printing; each citation includes a durable URL to the full text.

Some works are rekeyed from textually unsound editions; however, the bibliographic record for each work identifies the source of the text and any omissions (e.g., preliminary matter). Besides being a useful source for identifying an elusive quotation or half-remembered line, the scope of *Canadian Poetry*'s text archive makes feasible a variety of kinds of studies (stylistic, thematic, imagistic, and topical).

The contents of *Canadian Poetry* can also be searched through *LiOn* (I527), which offers a less versatile search interface.

Guides to Scholarship and Criticism

R4755   Stevens, Peter. Modern *English-Canadian Poetry: A Guide to Information Sources*. American Literature, English Literature, and World Literatures in English: An Information Guide Series 15. Detroit: Gale, 1978. 216 pp. Z1377.P7 S79 [PR9184.3]   016.811'5.

A highly selective bibliography of primary and secondary works (published almost exclusively in English through the early 1970s) for the study of English Canadian poetry. Entries are organized in classified divisions for reference sources (with sections for bibliographies; biographical sources; indexes to serials, theses, and microforms; and manuscript and special collections), literary histories and general studies, anthologies, periodicals, and 60 poets. The poets are grouped by period (1900–40, 1940–60, and 1960–70s), and each has separate lists of primary works and criticism. Several annotations are inadequately or imprecisely descriptive; few entries in the author division are annotated. Three indexes: persons; book titles; subjects. Because of its inadequate explanation of scope and criteria governing selection of both poets and secondary works, significant omissions, and numerous unverified entries, Stevens is only marginally useful as a guide to modern English Canadian poetry. Review: R. G. Moyles, *Essays on Canadian Writing* 16 (1979–80): 229–33.

Some additional studies can be identified through "The Year's Work in Canadian Poetry Studies [1976–86]," *Canadian Poetry* 2–20 (1978–87; 29 Apr. 2006 <http://www.uwo.ca/english/canadianpoetry/journpage.htm>), a selective, partly annotated bibliography of studies on English Canadian poetry.

Biographical Dictionaries

See

     Contemporary Poets (M2895).

PROSE

Some works in section L: Genres/Prose are useful for research in Canadian prose.

Guides to Primary Works

R4765   Matthews, William, comp. *Canadian Diaries and Autobiographies*. Berkeley: U of California P, 1950. 130 pp.   Z5305.C3 M3   016.920071.

An author list of 1,276 published and manuscript diaries, journals, travel accounts, reminiscences, autobiographies, and the like by Canadians or relating to Canada. Users should note the list in the preface of kinds of material excluded (e.g., French works before the French and Indian Wars, journals by world explorers, and writings by American travelers—for the last, see Arksey, *American Diaries* [Q3540]). A typical entry includes birth and death dates, occupation, title of published work and publication information or type of manuscript, and time span; a brief description of content; and location and number of pages for a manuscript. Additions appear on pp. 129–30. Indexed by subjects (but inadequately so, since only major or broad topics are included). While far from comprehensive, emphasizing the better known published works and manuscripts in major libraries, and including several errors, Matthews is still a useful place to begin a search for autobiographical material of Canadian interest. It must be supplemented, however, by *Union List of Manuscripts in Canadian Repositories* (R4590) and the works in section F: Guides to Manuscripts and Archives. Review: Marie Tremaine, *Canadian Historical Review* 33 (1952): 78–79.

Many of the entries in *Canadian Diaries* are repeated or revised in Handley, *An Annotated Bibliography of Diaries Printed in English* (M1615a). Some additional published Canadian diaries are listed in Patricia Pate Havlice, *And So to Bed: A Bibliography of Diaries Published in English* (Metuchen: Scarecrow, 1987, 698 pp.); however, its chief feature is a combined index of diarists in Matthews, *Canadian Diaries*; *British Diaries* (M1615); and *American Diaries* (Q3540a).

Unpublished English-language diaries written by women are more fully covered in Kathryn Carter, *Diaries in English by Women in Canada, 1753–1995: An Annotated Bibliography*, F. V. 4 (Ottawa: Canadian Research Inst. for the Advancement of Women/Institut Canadien de Recherches sur les Femmes, 1997, 106 pp.). Annotations identify the location of the manuscript, describe in a sentence or two the subject matter, and cite published versions and studies of the diary. The lack of a subject index hampers access to the more than 500 entries.

See also

> Brumble, *Annotated Bibliography of American Indian and Eskimo Autobiographies* (Q3925).
> Hoy, *Modern English-Canadian Prose* (R4710).

Guides to Scholarship and Criticism

See

> Hoy, *Modern English-Canadian Prose* (R4710).

Caribbean-Area Literatures in English

Works in section R: Other Literatures in English/General are important to research in Caribbean-area literatures.

Guides to Reference Works

R4775   Hallewell, L. "English-Speaking Caribbean Literature." *Latin America and the Caribbean: A Critical Guide to Research Sources.* Ed. Paula H. Covington. Bibliographies and Indexes in Latin American and Caribbean Studies 2. New York: Greenwood, 1992. 495–501.   Z1601.L3225 [F1408] 016.98.

An annotated guide to bibliographies, biographical resources, and other reference works for the study of English-language Caribbean literature. Hallewell's clear annotations frequently point up strengths and weaknesses of a resource; the list offers the best guide to reference sources for this literature.

Literary Handbooks, Dictionaries, and Encyclopedias

R4780   Herdeck, Donald E., ed. *Caribbean Writers: A Bio-Bibliographical-Critical Encyclopedia.* Washington: Three Continents, 1979. 943 pp.   PN849.C3 C3   809'.89729.

A biographical and bibliographical guide to Caribbean literature in four parts: anglophone literature, francophone literature, Netherlands Antilles and Suriname, and Spanish-language literature. Each part begins with an overview of the social, linguistic, and literary history of the area and a list of writers by country or region; each concludes with various bibliographies of primary works and studies. The bulk of the work consists of author entries that provide basic biographical and career information, occasional critical comments, and an incomplete list of primary works and a highly selective list of studies. Because of the organization and incomplete cross-referencing of pseudonyms and variant forms of names, an author index would make entries much easier to locate. The work is inconsistent in places and stylistically wooden but is packed with information; it offers the fullest general guide to Caribbean writers and their work. Review: Marian Goslinga, *Revista interamericana de bibliografía* 30 (1980): 183–84.

More current information on the writers included can be found in Daryl Cumber Dance, ed., *Fifty Caribbean Writers: A Bio-Bibliographical Critical Sourcebook* (New York: Greenwood, 1986, 530 pp.). Each essay provides a biography, discussion of major works, survey of important scholarship, and selected bibliography of primary and secondary sources. Indexed in *Biography and Genealogy Master Index* (J565).

Neither of the preceding is superseded by *Encyclopedia of Caribbean Literature*, ed. D. H. Figueredo, 2 vols. (Westport: Greenwood, 2006), which—as Michael Dash point out—omits important writers and topics, ignores important scholarship, and is sometimes superficial or incorrect. Review: Michael Dash, *TLS: Times Literary Supplement* 23 June 2006: 28.

Bibliographies of Bibliographies

R4785   Jordan, Alma, and Barbara Comissiong. *The English-Speaking Caribbean: A Bibliography of Bibliographies.* Reference Publication in Latin American Studies. Boston: Hall, 1984. 411 pp.   Z1595.J67 [F2161]   016.0169729.

A bibliography of published and unpublished national, regional, and topical bibliographies available through April 1981 on British Caribbean territories. Works are listed alphabetically by author, editor, or sponsoring organization under variously classified divisions, with the following of most interest to language and literature researchers: library catalogs; regional, national, and general bibliographies; biography (including several literary authors); folklore; history; language and linguistics; and literature. The literature division includes sections for general works, criticism, drama, fiction, indexes, periodicals, poetry, and countries or areas. Entries are accompanied by full descriptions of content and locations of copies (principally in Caribbean libraries). Two indexes: names; subjects. Although some classifications could be more refined and the coverage of parts of books is weak, *English-Speaking Caribbean* is an essential source for the identification and location of bibliographies treating the Caribbean (many of which are mimeographed works of severely limited distribution). A quick perusal will reveal how much basic bibliographical work remains to be done on Caribbean literatures.

Guides to Scholarship and Criticism

SERIAL BIBLIOGRAPHIES

R4787   "Select Bibliography of the Literature of the English-Speaking West Indies [1986–]." *Journal of West Indian Literature* 3.1 (1989)– . Irregular. PR9214.5.J6   820.6.
A selective, unannotated bibliography of primary and secondary works relating to the literatures of the English-speaking Caribbean. Entries are listed alphabetically in divisions for anthologies, drama, fiction, essays and nonfiction, poetry, bibliography, interviews, reviews, and criticism (with sections for general studies and individual authors). Although selective, this is the best current guide to English-language literature in the West Indies.
Some additional studies are included in "Studies in Caribbean and South American Literature: An Annual Annotated Bibliography [1985–92]," *Callaloo* 9–16 (1986–93), and in "An Annual Bibliography of Afro-American Literature, [1975–76], with Selected Bibliographies of African and Caribbean Literature," *CLA Journal* 20–21 (1976–77).

See also

> Secs. G: Serial Bibliographies, Indexes, and Abstracts and H: Guides to Dissertations and Theses.
> *ABELL* (G340): Entries on Caribbean writers and literature are dispersed throughout.
> "Annual Bibliography of Commonwealth Literature" (R4375).
> *MLAIB* (G335): English Literature division (especially English III: General) through the volume for 1956; English XI: Australia, Canada, Etc. section in the volumes for 1957–66; English II: Australia, Canada, Etc. section in the volumes for 1967–80; and the English Caribbean Literature division in later volumes. Researchers must also check the headings beginning "Caribbean" and "English Caribbean" in the subject index to post-1980 volumes and in the online thesaurus.

YWES (G330): Caribbean-area literatures have been covered in the chapter "African, Caribbean, Canadian, Australian, New Zealand, and Indian Literature in English" since vol. 63 (for 1982).

OTHER BIBLIOGRAPHIES

R4790   Allis, Jeannette B. *West Indian Literature: An Index to Criticism, 1930–1975.* Reference Publication in Latin American Studies. Boston: Hall, 1981. 353 pp.   Z1502.B5 A38 [PR9210]   016.820′9′9729.
    A highly selective bibliography of English-language books, a very few collections of essays, and articles from 77 journals and newspapers (with some coverage extending beyond 1975). Entries are organized in three divisions: the first includes studies of specific writers (with sections for general criticism and individual works); the last lists general studies by date of publication. The middle division repeats the entries in the other two as a scholar/critic list; a simple name index would accomplish the same in one-tenth of the 120 pages. General books on West Indian literature are relegated to an appendix. Only the entries in the third division are descriptively annotated, but the lack of an index means one must search through the entire list to find works that treat a particular writer or topic. The high degree of selectivity, lack of an adequate statement of criteria governing selection, poor organization, and lack of indexing make *West Indian Literature* useful only as an occasional supplement to New, *Critical Writings on Commonwealth Literatures* (R4380), and "Annual Bibliography of Commonwealth Literature" (R4375). Some additional studies can be found in Lambros Comitas, *The Complete Caribbeana, 1800–1975: A Bibliographic Guide to the Scholarly Literature,* 4 vols. (Millwood: KTO, 1977). In particular, see the following chapters in vol. 2: 22, "Creative Arts and Recreation" (including literature); 24, "Folklore"; and 25, "Language and Linguistics." Theses and dissertations are listed in Samuel B. Bandara, "A Checklist of Theses and Dissertations in English on Caribbean Literature," *World Literature Written in English* 20 (1981): 319–34.

See also

    New, *Critical Writings on Commonwealth Literatures* (R4380).
    Szwed, *Afro-American Folk Culture* (U5880).

Genres

POETRY

Guides to Scholarship and Criticism

R4797   Williams, Emily Allen. *Anglophone Caribbean Poetry, 1970–2001: An Annotated Bibliography.* Bibliographies and Indexes in World Literature 57. Westport: Greenwood, 2002. 191 pp.   Z1524.P6 W45 [PR9205.2] 016.821′54099729.

An annotated bibliography of English-language primary and secondary resources for the study of English-language poetry by authors resident in or originating from the former British Caribbean territories and the Virgin Islands of the United States. Entries are organized in seven sections: anthologies, reference works, conference proceedings, collected works by individual poets, criticism, interviews, and audio and audiovisual recordings. The brief descriptive annotations generally offer a minimal sense of a work's content or thesis. Three indexes: authors (of both documents and as subjects); titles; subjects. The subject indexing—both in the authors and subjects indexes—is completely inadequate; users will simply have to skim all entries. Even skimming all the entries will give users only a limited sense of the published studies on a topic and affirm the author's assertion that the primary criterion governing selection was "the accessibility of the material": the reference works section omits such basic tools as "Select Bibliography of the Literature of the English Speaking West Indies" (R4787) and Allis, *West Indian Literature* (R4790); the conference proceedings section does not cite titles of essays (only a few of which are included in the criticism section); a five-minute search of the *MLAIB* (G335) identified numerous studies omitted from the criticism section. In short, *Anglophone Caribbean Poetry, 1970–2001* offers only the most basic starting point for research in the field.

Indian Literature in English

Most works in section R: Other Literatures in English/General are important to research in Indian literature in English.

Guides to Primary Works

R4800   Singh, Amritjit, Rajiva Verma, and Irene M. Joshi. *Indian Literature in English, 1827–1979: A Guide to Information Sources.* American Literature, English Literature, and World Literatures in English: An Information Guide Series 36. Detroit: Gale, 1981. 631 pp.   Z3208.L5 S56 [PR9484.3] 016.82.

A bibliography of English-language creative works and translations by Indian writers and of selected studies of these works. Except for some plays, coverage of primary works is limited to separate publications (attempting but not achieving comprehensiveness). Entries are organized in two divisions: general studies (with sections for philosophy, religion, and the arts; history, society, and politics; reference works; criticism and literary history; and anthologies) and individual writers (organized by genre, then by author, with primary works followed by studies). Selected lists of Indian periodicals and publishers appear as appendixes. Many entries are copied from other sources; a very few works are annotated (inadequately) in the first division. Three indexes: literary authors listed in the second division (with a separate alphabet for each genre); other persons; titles. The work is hard to use because of the poor organization of the individual-writers part and its corresponding index (which requires checking four alphabets for some writers) and because of a design and typography that make sections difficult to distinguish. Still, it is the fullest bibliography of primary and secondary works representing Indian writing in English, and is especially valuable for its coverage of ephemeral and limited-circulation publications. Review: Prabhu S. Guptara, *Yearbook of English Studies* 16 (1986): 311–13.

Guides to Scholarship and Criticism

See

> Secs. G: Serial Bibliographies, Indexes, and Abstracts and H: Guides to Dissertations and Theses.
> *ABELL* (G340): Entries on English-language Indian writers and literature are dispersed throughout.
> "Annual Bibliography of Commonwealth Literature" (R4375).
> *MLAIB* (G335): English Literature division (especially English III: General) through the volume for 1956; English XI: Australia, Canada, Etc./Indian section in the volumes for 1957–66; English II: Australia, Canada, Etc./Indian section in the volumes for 1967–80; and the Asian Literature/South Asian Literature/Indian Literature section in later volumes. Researchers must also check the headings beginning "Indian" in the subject index to post-1980 volumes and in the online thesaurus.
> New, *Critical Writings on Commonwealth Literatures* (R4380).
> *YWES* (G330): Indian literature has been covered in the chapter African, Caribbean, Canadian, Australian, New Zealand, and Indian Literature in English since vol. 64 (for 1983).

New Zealand Literature in English

Works in section R: Other Literatures in English/General are important to research in New Zealand literature.

Guides to Reference Works

For an evaluative survey of some basic general reference sources, see J. E. Traue, *New Zealand Studies: A Guide to Bibliographic Resources* (Wellington: Victoria UP for Stout Research Centre for the Study of New Zealand Society, History, and Culture, 1985, 27 pp.). Literary reference works are more fully treated by John Thomson, "Bibliography," pp. 737–865, in Sturm, ed., *The Oxford History of New Zealand Literature in English* (R4805).

Histories and Surveys

R4805   Sturm, Terry, ed. *The Oxford History of New Zealand Literature in English.* 2nd ed. Auckland: Oxford UP, 1998. 890 pp.   PR9624.3.O94 820.9'993.

A collection of separately authored essays—devoted to genres as well as nonfiction, children's literature, popular fiction, publishing and literary magazines, Maori literature, literary criticism and theory, and reference works—on the history of New Zealand literature, primarily in English, through c. 1996. The chapters on literature proceed chronologically, with due attention to social, political, and cultural contexts. Some chapters offer the first detailed consideration of their respective subject; the evaluative bibliographical survey is the best guide now available to reference works and general studies (published and unpublished) important to research in English-language New Zealand literature. Indexed by persons, subjects, and titles of anonymous works. The breadth, depth, and balance of coverage make Sturm the most comprehensive and authoritative history of New Zealand literature in English. Review: Alex Calder, *Landfall* 46.1 (1992): 98–109.

Literary Handbooks, Dictionaries, and Encyclopedias

R4807   *The Oxford Companion to New Zealand Literature.* Ed. Roger Robinson and
         Nelson Wattie. Melbourne: Oxford UP, 1998. 608 pp.   PR9620.2.O94
         820.9′993′03. Online through *Oxford Reference Online* (I530).
    A dictionary of New Zealand literature in English, Maori, and other languages. The majority of the signed entries, which range from fewer than 100 to more than 2,000 words, are for individuals, but works, publishers, collectors, children's literature, periodicals, libraries, films, relations with other national literatures, and topics of significance to New Zealand literature are included. Readable, informative, and reliable, *Oxford Companion to New Zealand Literature* goes well beyond the typical *Oxford Companion* to treat many topics and writers for the first time and thus offers researchers a plethora of subjects worthy of fuller discussion. Review: Iain Sharp, *Landfall* ns 7 (1999): 117–20.

Guides to Primary Works

MANUSCRIPTS

R4808   *National Register of Archives and Manuscripts/Te Rārangi Pūranga, Tuhinga
         Ake o te Motu* (*NRAM*). Archives New Zealand. Online. 20 July 2005
         <http://www.nram.org.nz>. Updated regularly.
    A database register of manuscript collections held by repositories in New Zealand that includes most entries in *National Register of Archives and Manuscripts in New Zealand* (Wellington: Alexander Turnbull Lib., 1979–93) as well as descriptions contributed after cessation of the print volumes; collections in the Alexander Turnbull Library are excluded from the database but can be searched through *TAPUHI* (http://tapuhi.natlib.govt.nz). Entries, based on information contributed by archives and libraries, can be searched by keyword; in addition, searchers can browse four lists: collection titles; *NRAM* accession number; repositories and owners; subjects. A typical entry includes title of collection; author of the documents; holder of the collection (with shelf list and contact information); type of materials; dates covered; description; quantity; information on access; finding aids; places, persons, and institutions figuring prom-

inently in the collection; and date of last update. The descriptions vary considerably in their informativeness, like those in any register based on institutional contributions, but *National Register of Archives and Manuscripts* offers the best guide to locating manuscript collections in New Zealand.

PRINTED WORKS

R4810   Bagnall, A. G., ed. and comp. *New Zealand National Bibliography to the Year 1960.* 5 vols. Wellington: Govt. Printer, 1969–85.   Z4101.B28 015.931.

A retrospective national bibliography of books and pamphlets published in New Zealand or containing "significant references" to the country. (For a full discussion of kinds of publications excluded, see vol. 1, pt. 1, p. vii, and vol. 2, pp. viii–ix.) Vol. 1 covers 1663–1889; vols. 2–4, 1890–1960. Listed alphabetically by author, corporate author, or title of anonymous work, entries supply title, imprint, pagination, size, and an occasional note on content. A double asterisk denotes a work not seen by the compiler; a title set in italic identifies a work that is outside the bibliography's scope but that researchers might expect to find listed. Vol. 1, pt. 2 prints additions (pp. 1159–70) and two indexes: chronological; subjects, titles, joint authors. Vol. 5 includes additions and corrections to vol. 1 (pp. 619–37) and vols. 2–4 (pp. 1–279), as well as a subject, title, and joint author index to entries for 1890–1960. Bagnall offers the fullest guide to works published in and about the country.

Although largely superseded by Bagnall, T. M. Hocken, *A Bibliography of the Literature Relating to New Zealand* (Wellington: Mackay, 1909, 619 pp.), is still useful because of its inclusion of articles and newspapers, classified organization (with sections for language and literature), and extensive notes. See also A. H. Johnstone, comp., *Supplement to Hocken's Bibliography of New Zealand Literature* (Auckland: Whitcombe, 1927, 73 pp.), and L. J. B. Chapple, *A Bibliographical Brochure Containing Addenda and Corrigenda to Extant Bibliographies of N. Z. Literature* (Dunedin: Reed, 1938, 47 pp.).

R4815   *New Zealand National Bibliography [1966–]* (*NZNB*). Wellington: Natl. Lib. of New Zealand, 1968– . Monthly, with some annual cumulations and one for 1983–93. Microfiche only, 1983–99; *Microsoft Word* or PDF files since 2000 (http://www.natlib.govt.nz/catalogues/national-bibliography).

A national bibliography of publications and electronic materials published in New Zealand, by New Zealanders, or having significant New Zealand content that were deposited since 1966 under the country's copyright act or acquired by the National Library of New Zealand. After the bibliography for 1985, nonbook print publications are omitted. The printed volumes were single author, title, and subject lists. The microfiche edition was published in four parts: register (with entries listed by National Library card number), subject list, author and title list, and publishers' addresses; only the first provides full cataloging information. Currently, catalog records are listed alphabetically by title under the main Dewey Decimal Classification schedules (with separated sections for New Zealand literature and publications without Dewey Decimal classifications). Each issue concludes with an author index. Records since 1983 can be searched by subscribers through *Te Puna* (<http://tepuna.natlib.govt.nz>). *New Zealand National Bibliography* offers the most complete record of current New Zealand publications. Works published before 1966 are listed in *Index to New Zealand Periodicals and Current National Bibliography of New Zealand Books and Pamphlets Published in*

[1950–65] (Wellington: Natl. Lib. of New Zealand, 1951–66) and before 1960 in Bagnall, *New Zealand National Bibliography* (R4810).

See also

"Annual Bibliography of Commonwealth Literature" (R4375).

Guides to Scholarship and Criticism

R4820   Thomson, John. *New Zealand Literature to 1977: A Guide to Information Sources.* American Literature, English Literature, and World Literatures in English: An Information Guide Series 30. Detroit: Gale, 1980. 272 pp. Z4111.T45 [PR9624.3]   016.82.

A bibliography of primary and secondary works (including theses, dissertations, popular journalism, and numerous unpublished checklists and ephemeral items) covering literature in English and Maori. Entries are organized in seven classified divisions: bibliographies and reference works (with sections for general works, biographical dictionaries, indexes to serial publications, guides to special collections, and New Zealand English), literary history and criticism, anthologies, individual authors (with sections for bibliographies, collected works, biographical materials, primary works, and criticism), other writers (listing works by minor or unestablished authors), periodicals, and nonfiction prose (by New Zealanders as well as foreigners) about the country. A headnote outlines the scope and organization of each division. Most annotations are full, with many offering evaluative comments; however, several entries are left unannotated. Two indexes: persons; titles. Although the coverage of nineteenth-century literature is weak, Thomson is the most complete single guide to scholarship on New Zealand literature. Review: Shaun F. D. Hughes, *Modern Fiction Studies* 27 (1981): 173–88. Some additional studies of prose fiction are recorded in Rose Marie Beston and John B. Beston, "Critical Writings on Modern New Zealand and Australian Fiction: A Selected Checklist," *Modern Fiction Studies* 27 (1981): 189–204.

See also

> Secs. G: Serial Bibliographies, Indexes, and Abstracts and H: Guides to Dissertations and Theses.
> *ABELL* (G340): Entries on English-language New Zealand writers and literature are dispersed throughout.
> "Annual Bibliography of Commonwealth Literature" (R4375).
> Boos, *Bibliography of Women and Literature* (U6600).
> *MLAIB* (G335): English Literature division (especially English III: General) through the volume for 1956; English XI: Australia, Canada, Etc./New Zealand section in the volumes for 1957–66; English II: Australia, Canada, Etc./New Zealand section in the volumes for 1967–80; and the [British] Commonwealth Literature/New Zealand Literature section in later volumes. Researchers must also check the headings beginning "New Zealand" in the subject index to post-1980 volumes and in the online thesaurus.
> New, *Critical Writings on Commonwealth Literatures* (R4380).
> Schwartz, *Articles on Women Writers* (U6605).

Thompson, John, "Bibliography," pp. 737–865, in Sturm, ed., *The Oxford History of New Zealand Literature in English* (R4805).

Williams, Mark, "Literary Scholarship, Criticism, and Theory," pp. 695–736, in Sturm, ed., *The Oxford History of New Zealand Literature in English* (R4805).

————, *Post-colonial Literatures in English: Southeast Asia, New Zealand, and the Pacific, 1970–1992* (R4380a).

YWES (G330): New Zealand literature has been covered in the chapter African, Caribbean, Canadian, Australian, New Zealand, and Indian Literature in English since vol. 64 (for 1983).

Language

GUIDES TO SCHOLARSHIP

See

ABELL (G340): Dialects section of the English Language division in the volumes for 1920–26; the English Dialects section in the volumes for 1927–72; the Dialects/Australia and New Zealand section in the volumes for 1973–84; the Dialects/Australasia section in the volumes for 1985–86; and the Dialects/Dialects of the Rest of the World section in later volumes.

MLAIB (G335): See the English I: Linguistics section through the volume for 1966; the Indo-European C: Germanic Linguistics IV: English/Modern English/Dialectology section in the volumes for 1967–80; and the Indo-European Languages/Germanic Languages/West Germanic Languages/English Language (Modern)/Dialectology section in later volumes. Researchers must also check the heading "New Zealand English Dialect" in the subject index to post-1980 volumes and in the online thesaurus.

Thomson, *New Zealand Literature to 1977* (R4820).

DICTIONARIES

R4823   *Dictionary of New Zealand English: A Dictionary of New Zealandisms on Historical Principles* (*DNZE*). Ed. H. W. Orsman. Auckland: Oxford UP, 1997. 965 pp.   PE3602.Z5 D53   442′.0993.

A historical dictionary of terms originating in New Zealand, "words used elsewhere but having in New Zealand a significantly different meaning, words of special significance to the history of the country, and terms shared with Australia." Entries consist of headword, pronunciation, part of speech, descriptive label (e.g., "obsolete"), variant spellings, etymology, definitions, cross-references, and illustrative quotations. Like other historical dictionaries, *DNZE* is an essential tool for explicating New Zealand literary works.

Biographical Dictionaries

R4825   *The Dictionary of New Zealand Biography/Nga Tangata Taumata Rau* (*DNZB*). Auckland: Auckland UP with Bridget Williams Books and Dept.

of Internal Affairs, 1990– .   CT2882.D53   920.093. New Zealand
Historical Association. Online. 19 July 2005 <http://www.dnzb.govt.nz/
dnzb>.

> Vol. 1: *1769–1869.* 1990. 674 pp.
> Vol. 2: *1870–1900.* 1993. 664 pp.
> Vol. 3: *1901–1920.* 1996. 649 pp.
> Vol. 4: *1921–1940.* 1998. 650 pp.
> Vol. 5: *1941–1960.* 2000. 679 pp.
> Vol. 6: *1961–1980.*
> Future volumes are planned.

A biographical dictionary, in English and Maori, of persons who "flourished" in
New Zealand. Entrants are chosen for their eminence or representativeness (with due
attention given to ethnic group, gender, region, and activity), or for balance within a
volume (e.g., in vol. 1, 30% of the biographees are Maori and 20% are women). The
signed entries provide a basic biography and conclude with a selected bibliography of
published and unpublished sources. Three indexes in vol. 1: occupations, activities,
vocations, tribal leaders; tribes and hapu; persons (vol. 2 adds a regional index).

The online version includes all the biographies in the printed volumes—some of
which have been corrected and some of which include additional images or sound
files—as well as ones for people who died after 1960 (the cutoff date of the last printed
volume). The basic search mode allows users to search by keyword or browse lists of
biographees or entry authors; the advanced search screen allows searches by occupation,
region, gender, Maori or non-Maori, decade of activity, decade of death, decade of
birth, tribal affiliation, and country of birth. Unfortunately, the text of an entry is
displayed in a very small window that cannot be resized.

Admirably broad in coverage, the *DNZB* is the standard biographical dictionary
for New Zealanders. On the background of the project, see W. H. Oliver, "The *Dictionary of New Zealand Biography* and the State of New Zealand Historical Studies,"
Australian and New Zealand Studies, ed. Patricia McLaren-Turner, British Library Occasional Papers 4 (London: British Lib., 1985) 30–40; for current information about
the project, consult the *Dictionary*'s Web site.

Genres

FICTION

Guides to Primary Works

R4835   Burns, James. *New Zealand Novels and Novelists, 1861–1979: An Annotated
Bibliography.* Auckland: Heinemann, 1981. 71 pp.   Z4114.F4 B83
[PR9632.2]   016.823′008′09931.
    A chronological list of novels by New Zealanders, including those resident abroad,
and some by foreigners that are set in New Zealand; Burns excludes works for children.
Listed by date of first publication, the approximately 1,000 entries cite author, title,
publication information, number of pages or volumes, translations, and appearances in
periodicals. The very brief (and frequently inadequate) annotations describe content.
Two indexes: titles; authors. *New Zealand Novels and Novelists* offers the fullest list of
New Zealand novels, but a subject index would enhance its usefulness.

S

Foreign-Language Literatures

This section is limited to guides to reference works that will direct researchers to essential sources, along with a very few important bibliographies of bibliographies or major serial bibliographies. For a basic list of specialized bibliographies, literary dictionaries and encyclopedias, and other reference works on a particular literature, consult Thompson, *Key Sources in Comparative and World Literature* (S4850), *Guide to Reference Books* (B60), or *Walford's Guide to Reference Material* (B65).

   Users should also remember that studies of all literatures (except classical Greek and Latin) are covered by *MLAIB* (G335).

General

Guides to Reference Works

S4850   Thompson, George A., Jr. *Key Sources in Comparative and World Literature.*
New York: Ungar, 1982. 383 pp.   Z6511.T47 [PN523]   016.809.

A highly selective, annotated guide to reference works on a variety of literatures, but emphasizing those in English and Western European languages. Entries are organized in 11 extensively classified divisions: comparative, general, and international literatures; classical; Romance; French; Italian; Hispanic; German; literatures in English; other European literatures; Oriental literatures; and related fields. Many sections list bibliographies and concordances for major authors. The annotations are typically descriptive, noting scope, organization, related works, and (sometimes) reviews. While some are full, many of the annotations inadequately detail the content or significance of a work. Poor layout makes skimming difficult. Three indexes: names; selected titles and institutions; subjects. Although it does not really emphasize comparative literature, omits several essential works, and is frequently uncritical in selection or annotation, Thompson is the best general guide to essential bibliographies, handbooks, histories, and other reference works for foreign literatures.

Guides to Scholarship and Criticism

S4855   *Year's Work in Modern Language Studies* (*YWMLS*). Leeds: Maney for Mod.
Humanities Research Assn., 1931– . Annual.   PB1.Y45   405.8. <http://
www.mhra.org.uk/Publications/Journals/ywmls.html>.

A selective, evaluative review of research on Romance, Celtic, Germanic, and Slavonic languages and literatures. Currently organized by language or geographic area within five divisions (Latin, Romance, Celtic, Germanic, and Slavonic languages), with essays on language and literary periods as required by the extent of the scholarship. For example, in vol. 65 (for 2003) French Studies takes 13 essays whereas Swedish Studies needs only two.

The necessarily selective coverage depends on availability of material, individual contributors, the extent of coverage in other bibliographies, and—since vol. 45 (for 1983)—the number of pages allocated by the editors to a chapter. As in *Year's Work in English Studies* (G330), the quality and objectivity of individual essays vary depending on the contributor(s), but most (until the mid-1990s) attempt judicious evaluations of the significant scholarship. Recent volumes have been published within a year or two following that of the scholarship covered. Indexed by persons (including authors discussed); a cumulative author index beginning with 61 (for 1999) can be downloaded from the *YWMLS* Web site. The inexcusable elimination of the subject index beginning in 58 (1996) leaves *YWMLS* less accessible than it should be.

Although some topics are covered more exhaustively in other sources, *YWMLS* was for many years the single most comprehensive evaluative survey of scholarship on European and Latin American languages and literatures. Since the mid-1990s, however, the majority of the essays are little more than lists of citations accompanied by one-sentence descriptions of content; many essays in recent volumes are listed as "Postponed." Taken together, the annual volumes offer an incomparable record of scholarly and critical trends as well as of the fluctuations of academic reputations of literary works and authors.

African Literatures

S4865   Lindfors, Bernth. "Researching African Literatures." *Literary Research Newsletter* 4 (1979): 171–80.   PN73.L57   809.19.

An evaluative overview of bibliographies, biographical sources, and other reference works (through early 1979) important for the study of African literatures. Although now dated, it remains a useful guide, since many of the works have not been superseded. Additional bibliographies are listed in Yvette Scheven, ed., *Bibliographies for African Studies, 1970–1986* (London: Zell, 1988, 615 pp.), *Bibliographies for African Studies, 1987–1993* (1994, 176 pp.), and Alfred Kagan, *Reference Guide to Africa: A Bibliography of Sources*, 2nd ed. (Lanham: Scarecrow, 2005, 222 pp.).

A useful introduction to important scholarship on selected literatures is B. W. Andrzejewski, S. Piłaszewicz, and W. Tyloch, eds., *Literatures in African Languages: Theoretical Issues and Sample Surveys* (Cambridge: Cambridge UP; Warszawa: Wiedza Powszechna, 1985, 672 pp.).

See also

Sec. R: Other Literatures in English/African Literatures in English.

Asian Literatures

S4875   Anderson, G. L. *Asian Literature in English: A Guide to Information Sources.* American Literature, English Literature, and World Literatures in English: An Information Guide Series 31. Detroit: Gale, 1981. 336 pp.
Z3001.A655 [PR9410]   016.895.

A bibliography of English-language translations and important studies (published through c. 1978) of East Asian literature. Indian literature, which is the subject of Singh, *Indian Literature in English* (R4800), is excluded. The 2,224 entries are organized in 16 divisions: Far East, China, Japan, Korea, Southeast Asia, Burma, Cambodia, Indonesia, Laos, Malaya and Singapore, Thailand, Vietnam, Mongolia, Tibet, Turkic and other literatures, and periodicals about Central Asian literature. The divisions are variously classified, but most have sections for bibliographies, reference works, anthologies, general literary history and criticism, periodicals, genres, earlier literature, and modern literature, as well as individual authors and anonymous works. About half of the very brief annotations are descriptive, with the remainder offering an evaluative comment; however, few adequately describe the content or significance of a work. Indexed by persons and English-language titles of literary works. Users should be sure to note the explanation on p. xiv of conventions governing names (however, the use of brackets around variant pen names and parentheses around real names is not consistently followed). Although marred by an insufficient explanation of scope and criteria governing selection, omitting several important studies, and inadequately annotated, Anderson is useful as a preliminary compilation of English-language translations and studies of East Asian literature.

Some additional studies on Burma, Thailand, Cambodia, Laos, Vietnam, Malaysia, Indonesia, the Philippines, and China are listed in Patricia Herbert and Anthony Milner, eds., *South-east Asia Languages and Literatures: A Select Guide* (Honolulu: U of Hawai'i P, 1989, 182 pp.).

Classical Literatures

Guides to Reference Works

S4885   Jenkins, Fred W. *Classical Studies: A Guide to the Reference Literature*. 2nd ed. Reference Sources in the Humanities Series. Westport: Libraries Unlimited, 2006. 401 pp.   Z7016.J4 [PA91]   016.48.

A guide to book-length and electronic reference sources, available through 2004, for the study of classical Greece and Rome (from the Bronze Age through AD 599). Entries are organized by type of resource or topic, with chapters on general bibliographies, abstracts and indexes, review journals, periodicals, general dictionaries and encyclopedias, general Internet resources, biographical works, history, primary sources in translation, geography, art and archaeology, language, general works on literature, genres, Greek authors, Latin authors, philosophy, religion and mythology, related disciplines, scholarly societies, research centers, and directories. The annotations offer full descriptions, reliably alert users to revisions or related works in progress, and usually offer some kind of evaluative comment (less so in the case of electronic resources). Two indexes: authors and titles; subjects. More effectively organized than the first edition (1996), Jenkins is a solid guide to basic reference sources for classical studies.

It must, however, be supplemented by Thomas P. Halton, *Classical Scholarship: An Annotated Bibliography* (White Plains: Kraus, 1986, 396 pp.), a guide to important reference works and scholarship (through c. 1980) for the study of classical Greek and Roman civilization. Entries are organized alphabetically by author in 15 classified divisions: bibliographies and reference works; literary history and criticism; history and influence of the classical tradition; transmission of the classics (including sections on books and libraries, paleography, and textual criticism); language and style; metrics, song, and music; epigraphy; political and cultural history; numismatics; art and archaeology; religion, mythology, and magic; philosophy; science and technology; teaching aids; and collections. Most entries include a list of reviews and an annotation that describes scope and contents, identifies the work's importance to classical scholarship, and evaluates its quality. Two indexes: subjects; scholars. *Classical Scholarship* is marred by an inadequate explanation of scope and criteria governing selection and by several annotations that are less precisely descriptive and evaluative than one expects in a critical bibliography.

Guides to Scholarship and Criticism

S4890   *APh: L'année philologique*. Société Internationale de Bibliographie Classique. Online. 10 May 2005 <http://www.annee-philologique.com/aph>. CD-ROM.

L'année philologique: Bibliographie critique et analytique de l'antiquité gréco-latine [1924–]. Collection de bibliographie classique. Paris: Belles Lettres, 1928– . Annual.   Z7016.M35A.

An international bibliography of scholarship on all aspects of the Greco-Latin world to c. AD 800. Entries are organized in two parts: authors and anonymous works; subjects. Under each author or anonymous work are separate lists of bibliographies, collections of essays, editions, and studies. The second part consists of 10 variously classified divisions: literary history (with sections for genres; folklore and mythology; and Judeo-Christian, Byzantine, and medieval literature); linguistics and philology (with sections for grammar; onomastics; metrics, rhythm, and prosody; and chants, music, and choreography); history of texts (including paleography, papyrology, and textual criticism); antiquities; history; law; philosophy and history of ideas; science, technology, and work; the study of the classics; and collections of essays. Entries are accompanied by descriptive annotations (predominantly in French but also in English, Italian, and German) and citations to reviews. The type and number of indexes vary, with recent volumes providing four: subject headings; names from antiquity; names of authors and others since the Middle Ages; scholars. The international scope and impressive degree of coverage make this the indispensable guide to scholarship on Greek and Latin language and literature to c. AD 800. Despite its poorly designed search interface, *APh* offers the best access to records since vol. 20 (1949). Users can search by Modern Author (i.e., document author), full text, Ancient Authors, subjects (i.e., the taxonomy of the print volumes), date, and Other Criteria (title, publisher, edited collection details, language, accession number, and reviews [by periodical or by reviewer]); searches can be combined or limited only through the Search History window. Records, which are organized by accession number and cannot be otherwise sorted, aggregate book reviews spread over multiple print volumes but inexplicably do not expand abbreviations; hence, users downloading search results must remember to expand by hand unfamiliar abbreviations or acronyms for journal titles. Exporting search results by e-mail or direct download requires clicking through three screens. Fortunately, *APh* supersedes *DCB: Database of Classical Bibliography* (CD-ROM), a user-unfriendly electronic resource plagued by virtually incomprehensible or woefully inadequate help screens. Complemented by *MLAIB* (G335) for studies of Greek and Latin language of all ages and for studies of literature after c. 800.

Scholarship before 1924 is covered in the following:

> Engelmann, Wilhelm, ed. *Bibliotheca Scriptorum Classicorum.* Rev. E. Preuss. 8th ed. 2 vols. Leipzig: Engelmann, 1880–82. (Covers 1700–1878.)
>
> Klussman, Rudolf, ed. *Bibliotheca Scriptorum Classicorum et Graecorum et Latinorum.* 4 pts. in 2 vols. Leipzig: Reisland, 1909–13. (Covers 1878–96.)
>
> Lambrino, Scarlat. *Bibliographie de l'antiquité classique, 1896–1914.* Collection de bibliographie classique. Paris: Belles Lettres, 1951. 761 pp. (The second volume, which was to cover subjects, will not be published.)
>
> Marouzeau, J. *Dix années de bibliographie classique: Bibliographie critique et analytique de l'antiquité gréco-latine pour la période 1914–1924.* 2 vols. Paris: Belles Lettres, 1927–28.

Researchers will find a useful key to acronyms and abbreviations of book, series, and journal titles in Jean Susorney Wellington, *Dictionary of Bibliographic Abbreviations Found in the Scholarship of Classical Studies and Related Disciplines,* rev. and expanded ed. (Westport: Praeger, 2003, 684 pp.)

S4893   Carlsen, Hanne. *A Bibliography to the Classical Tradition in English
         Literature.* Anglica et Americana 21. Copenhagen: [Dept. of English, U of
         Copenhagen], 1985. 164 pp.   Z2014.C55 C37 [PR127]   016.82′09′3.

A classified bibliography of scholarship, published between 1900 and 1983, on
the relationship of English literature to the Greek and Latin classical tradition. The
1,692 entries include studies published in English (for the most part), French, German,
Italian, and the Scandinavian languages but exclude dissertations. Entries are listed
alphabetically by author in 16 sections: general studies, Middle Ages, Chaucer, sixteenth
century excluding Shakespeare, Shakespeare, seventeenth century excluding Milton,
eighteenth century, nineteenth century, twentieth century, Greek authors, Latin authors, myths and themes, literary genres, translation, philology, and art. The lack of
cross-references means that users must consult the index to locate all listed works on a
literary author or anonymous work. A few entries are annotated with a phrase that is
seldom adequate to describe the content of a study. Indexed by literary authors, anonymous titles, and some subjects. Although broader in scope than Kallendorf, *Latin
Influences on English Literature* (S4895), and claiming to include all entries therein,
Carlsen is less helpfully annotated and less thoroughly indexed, and it overlooks a
considerable number of studies. It is, though, a time-saving compilation that, for post-
1900 scholarship, supersedes Huntington Brown, "The Classical Tradition in English
Literature: A Bibliography," *Harvard Studies and Notes in Philology and Literature* 18
(1935): 7–46; and the brief bibliography and notes (pp. 550–705) in Gilbert Highet,
The Classical Tradition: Greek and Roman Influences on Western Literature (New York:
Oxford UP, 1949, 763 pp.).

Some additional studies can be found in "Bibliography of the Classical Tradition
for [1980–89]," *Classical and Modern Literature* 5–12 (1985–91), an annotated bibliography of books, articles, and dissertations on the relation of classical and postclassical
literature, art, life, and thought. Entries are cross-indexed in two subject lists: classical
topics (including persons, genres, and subjects); postclassical references (including subjects, a few major authors, and national literatures [subdivided by period]). Most entries
in the first division are accompanied by a very brief descriptive annotation. Two indexes:
mythological figures (since the bibliography for 1984); scholars. Although the layout
prevents effective skimming and subject headings in the second part tend to be too
general, this bibliography is useful for its international coverage.

S4895   Kallendorf, Craig. *Latin Influences on English Literature from the Middle Ages
         to the Eighteenth Century: An Annotated Bibliography of Scholarship, 1945–
         1979.* Garland Reference Library of the Humanities 345. New York:
         Garland, 1982. 141 pp.   Z2012.K34 [PR127]   016.82′09.

A selective bibliography of books and articles (in English, French, German, Italian,
and Dutch) that clearly focus on the influence of classical Latin authors on English
literature. Thus, discussions of medieval and Neo-Latin authors, technical studies of
translation, and purely linguistic scholarship are excluded. Entries are organized in seven
variously classified divisions: basic works on the classical tradition; rhetoric and English
prose style; medieval literature; Renaissance literature; English Literature, 1600–60;
Elizabethan, Jacobean, and Caroline drama; and Restoration and eighteenth-century
literature. The descriptive annotations are sometimes too brief to convey an adequate
sense of content, but they are more informative than those in Carlsen, *Bibliography to
the Classical Tradition in English Literature* (S4893). Indexed by authors and subjects.
Although there are notable omissions, Kallendorf is a time-saving compilation that
brings together widely scattered studies. Review: Fram Dinshaw, *Notes and Queries* ns
31 (1984): 265–66.

French-Language Literatures

S4905   Beugnot, B., and J.-M. Moureaux. *Manuel bibliographique des études*
         littéraires: Les bases de l'histoire littéraire, les voies nouvelles de l'analyse
         critique. Nathan-Université. Paris: Nathan, 1982. 478 pp.   Z6511.B48
         [PN544]   016.809.

A guide to reference works (through c. 1980) important to the study of French-
language literature. The approximately 3,400 entries are listed by publication date
within extensively classified divisions: general reference works (with sections for general
works, bibliographies, periodicals, surveys of research, and textual criticism and major
editions), literary history and criticism (history of criticism, literary history, literature
and other arts, ideas and themes, genres, poetic theory, imagery and myth, literature
and psychoanalysis, and literature and sociology), and new areas of study (French-
language literature outside France and children's and popular literature). Few entries
are annotated, but each division, section, and subsection is preceded by a brief overview
of reference works. Two indexes: scholars (at the end of the book); subjects (at the
beginning). This is the fullest guide to reference works on French literature, but users
would benefit from more annotations.

Although more selective, Fernande Bassan, Donald C. Spinelli, and Howard A.
Sullivan, *French Language and Literature: An Annotated Bibliography*, Garland Reference
Library of the Humanities 954 (New York: Garland, 1989, 365 pp.), is an important
complement since it covers publications through early 1988 and offers brief—but
generally adequate and accurate—descriptive annotations for more than 1,250 reference works and critical studies. Even more selective—but also more current—is Michel
Brix, *Guide bibliographique des études d'histoire de la littérature française*, 3rd ed. rev.
and aug., Bibliothèque Universitaire Moretus Plantin 2 (Namur: Bibliothèque Universitaire Moretus Plantin, 1992, 138 pp.).

A judiciously selective, evaluative guide to bibliographies is Richard Kempton,
French Literature: An Annotated Guide to Selected Bibliographies, Selected Bibliographies
in Language and Literature 2 (New York: MLA, 1981, 42 pp.), which includes brief
sections on French Canadian and other French-language literatures.

German Literature

S4915   Hansel, Johannes, and Lydia Kaiser. *Literaturrecherche für Germanisten:*
         Studienausgabe. 10th ed. Berlin: Schmidt, 2003. 280 pp. (Former title:
         Bücherkunde für Germanisten: Studienausgabe.)   Z2235.A2 H3 [PT84]
         016.43.

An annotated guide to reference works (primarily in German) important to the
study of German language and literature. The approximately 1,528 entries are organized
in two classified divisions: Internet sites; print and electronic resources. The latter has
subdivisions for general reference works on linguistics and literary history and scholarship (with sections for general literary and linguistic studies, German language and
literature, and general reference works), closed bibliographies (general bibliographies of
scholarship on language and literature, German language and literature, general topics),
serial bibliographies of scholarship (general bibliographies of scholarship on language
and literature, German language and literature, bibliographies of bibliographies), other

serial bibliographies (national bibliographies, dissertation bibliographies, bibliographies of periodical articles), periodicals, and professional topics. Each subdivision is preceded by a comparative overview of works, but the annotations tend to be very brief descriptions of scope and content. Two indexes: persons and titles; subjects.

Italian Literature

S4925   Baroni, Giorgio, and Mario Puppo. *Manuale critico-bibliografico per lo studio della letteratura italiana*. 5th ed. Torino: Internazionale, 2002. 673 pp. Z2354.C3 P87   [PQ4037].

A guide to reference works (through c. 2000) that are important to the study of Italian language and literature. The first division lists general guides to Italian literature, bibliographies, journals, collections and anthologies, encyclopedias and dictionaries, and literary histories. The remaining divisions consist of essay overviews accompanied by selective bibliographies on literary criticism and philology (with discussions of textual criticism, criticism, literary history, and metrics); linguistics and stylistics (language, grammar, and vocabulary; the Italian language; and the history of language in Italy); literary periods or movements; and 30 major authors. Indexed by persons. Although more descriptive than evaluative, with access hampered by the lack of subject indexing, Baroni and Puppo is the standard guide to Italian literary scholarship.

Latin-Language Literatures (Medieval and Neo-Latin)

S4935   IJsewijn, Jozef, and Dirk Sacré. *Companion to Neo-Latin Studies*. 2nd ed. 2 vols. Humanistica Lovaniensia Supplementa 5, 14. Leuven: Leuven UP, 1990–98.   PA8020.I37   870'.9'003.

A survey and bibliography of Latin-language works written between 1300 and 1990. Vol. 1 offers a country-by-country history of Neo-Latin literature; each chapter concludes with a selective list of bibliographies, general works, cultural and literary histories, studies of genres, anthologies, and journals. Vol. 2 provides selective bibliographies of genres, language and style, prosody and metrics, texts and editions, and the development of Neo-Latin studies. Five indexes in each volume: persons; places; literary subjects; other subjects; manuscripts. Written for the most part by one of the foremost Neo-Latinists, the *Companion* is the essential guide to the subject, important for its historical surveys as well as its compilation of widely dispersed scholarship and editions.

S4940   Strecker, Karl. *Introduction to Medieval Latin*. Trans. and rev. Robert B. Palmer. 4th ed. Dublin: Weidmann, 1967. 174 pp.   PA2816.S87.

A survey of reference sources, editions, and scholarship (principally through 1955, with some additions through 1961) that describes and occasionally evaluates general reference works, dictionaries, literary histories, periodicals, libraries, paleographical guides, and studies of language, poetry, and prose. Additions and corrections appear on pp. 161–74. Two indexes: subjects; scholars. Although poorly organized in places and now dated, the *Introduction* remains a standard guide. Supplement coverage with

IJsewijn, *Companion to Neo-Latin Studies* (S4935); Albert C. Friend, "Medieval Latin Literature," pp. 1–33, in Fisher, *Medieval Literature of Western Europe* (M1830); and *Medieval Latin: An Introduction and Bibliographical Guide*, ed. F. A. C. Mantello and A. G. Rigg (Washington: Catholic U of America P, 1996, 774 pp.). The first part of the last work lists reference works; however, the descriptions and evaluations are sometimes inaccurate (e.g., *Bibliographie internationale de l'Humanisme et de la Renaissance* (M2025) is deemed "comprehensive"), and the lack of a subject index makes the work much less accessible than it should be.

Portuguese-Language Literatures

S4950   Chamberlain, Bobby J. *Portuguese Language and Luso-Brazilian Literature: An Annotated Guide to Selected Reference Works*. Selected Bibliographies in Language and Literature 6. New York: MLA, 1989. 95 pp. Z2725.A2 C45 [PC5041]   016.869.

A selective guide to reference works, for the most part published since 1945, for the study of the Portuguese language and Luso-Brazilian literature. The approximately 538 entries (including numbered cross-references) are organized in extensively classified divisions for Portuguese language, Portuguese literature, Brazilian literature, and Luso-African and other lusophone literatures. The annotations are largely descriptive, although some offer evaluations. Indexed by authors. Given the relatively small number of separate works cited, *Portuguese Language and Luso-Brazilian Literature* includes a disconcerting number of errors and amount of outdated information.

Russian Literature

S4960   Zalewski, Wojciech. *Fundamentals of Russian Reference Work in the Humanities and Social Sciences*. Russica Bibliography Series 5. New York: Russica, 1985. 170 pp.   Z2491.A1 Z3   016.016947.

———. *Russian Reference Works*. SULAIR (Stanford University Libraries and Academic Information Resources). Online. 17 July 2005 <http://www-sul .stanford.edu/depts/hasrg/slavic/3refint.html>.

A guide to important reference works for the study of the humanities and social sciences in Russia. The essay overviews (interspersed with lists of works) are organized in two divisions: general works (with sections for publishing; theory and history of bibliography; libraries, archives, and museums; general bibliographies; other reference sources) and subject bibliographies (with sections for bibliographic institutions, history, literature, linguistics and languages, social sciences, law, and the humanities). Particularly helpful are the evaluations and comparisons of works, descriptions of Russian bibliographical networks, and suggestions for search strategies. Concludes with a list of numbered monographic series published in the West. Indexed by persons.

Russian Reference Works, which emphasizes post-1970 publications, updates the coverage of *Fundamentals of Russian Reference Works* but offers few evaluations or comparisons. Entries are organized in three sections: general bibliographies, nonbibliographic reference sources, and subject bibliographies (humanities and social sciences); the humanities subdivision includes sections for book history, history, language, literature, philosophy, religion, and the arts. Because each subdivision is a static Web page with hyperlinks to subheads, users cannot search the entire file. Although hampered by its lack of navigability, *Russian Reference Works* and *Fundamentals* are indispensable guides to the identification and effective use of reference sources for research in the humanities and social sciences in Russia.

Spanish-Language Literatures

S4970   Woodbridge, Hensley C. *Guide to Reference Works for the Study of the Spanish Language and Literature and Spanish American Literature.* 2nd ed. New York: MLA, 1997. 236 pp.   Z2695.A2 W66 [PC4071]   016.46.

A selective, annotated bibliography of reference works essential in the study of Spanish language and literature in Europe and the Western Hemisphere. Woodbridge emphasizes works published between 1950 and c. 1996, gives preference to annotated bibliographies, and includes works devoted to a single author. The 1,230 entries are organized in five extensively classified (and variously organized) divisions: general bibliographies, Spanish of Spain, American Spanish, Spanish literature of Europe, and Spanish literature of the Western Hemisphere. The brief annotations are largely descriptive, although some offer evaluative comments. Three indexes: authors, editors, compilers, and translators; literary authors; titles. Judicious selection and clear annotations make Woodbridge a valuable guide to the major print reference works in its field; the second edition unaccountably ignores electronic resources.

Woodbridge's coverage of resources for the study of the Spanish language and Spanish-language literature in Latin America and the Caribbean is frequently superior in his "Bibliography," *Latin America and the Caribbean: A Critical Guide to Research Sources,* ed. Paula H. Covington. Bibliographies and Indexes in Latin American and Caribbean Studies 2 (New York: Greenwood, 1992) 457–93. Here, annotations are more evaluative than in his *Guide.*

Broader in scope, but less trustworthy in its selection and accuracy, is Donald W. Bleznick, *A Sourcebook for Hispanic Literature and Language: A Selected, Annotated Guide to Spanish, Spanish-American, and United States Hispanic Bibliography, Literature, Linguistics, Journals, and Other Source Material,* 3rd ed. (Lanham: Scarecrow, 1995, 310 pp.).

T

Comparative Literature

General Introductions 4990
Guides to Scholarship and Criticism 5000–05
  Serial Bibliographies
  Other Bibliographies 5000–05

This section is highly selective and emphasizes those works likely to be of most value to researchers whose primary interest is literatures in English. For additional reference works in comparative literature, consult Thompson, *Key Sources in Comparative and World Literature* (S4850).

General Introductions

For an evaluative survey of introductions to comparative literature, see Ulrich Weisstein, "Assessing the Assessors: An Anatomy of Comparative Literature Handbooks," *Sensus Communis: Contemporary Trends in Comparative Literature/Panorama de la situation actuelle en littérature comparée*, ed. János Riesz, Peter Boerner, and Bernhardt Scholz (Tübingen: Narr, 1986) 97–113.

T4990   Weisstein, Ulrich. *Comparative Literature and Literary Theory*. Trans.
         William Riggan. Bloomington: Indiana UP, 1973. 339 pp. (Translation and
         partial revision of *Einführung in die Vergleichende Literaturwissenschaft*
         [Stuttgart: Kohlhammer, 1968], 256 pp.)   PN874.W4   809.
         ———. *Vergleichende Literaturwissenschaft: Erster Bericht, 1968–1977*.
         Jahrbuch für Internationale Germanistik, Reihe C: Forschungsberichte 2.
         Bern: Lang, 1981. 218 pp.   PN874.W4   430.5.
         An introduction to the history and theory of comparative literature, with chapters
on the definition of the discipline and its study of influence and imitation; reception
and survival; epoch, period, generation, and movement; genre; thematology; and relations of literature to the other arts. Concluding the study are two appendixes (a history

of comparative literature and an evaluation of the major bibliographies) and a selected bibliography (through June 1973). Indexed by persons and anonymous works. The supplement updates the chapters and selective bibliography and adds discussions of publications and projects of the Association Internationale de Littérature Comparée, new periodicals and Festschriften, and national images. The volumes remain a useful general introduction to the theory and methodology of comparative literature. Review: (German ed.) Richard Bjornson, *Monatshefte* 62 (1970): 186–88.

Covering much the same ground—but less authoritatively—are S. S. Prawer, *Comparative Literary Studies: An Introduction* (London: Duckworth, 1973, 180 pp.), and Susan Bassnett, *Comparative Literature: A Critical Introduction* (Oxford: Blackwell, 1993, 183 pp.).

See also

   Barricelli, *Interrelations of Literature* (U5955).

Guides to Scholarship and Criticism

Serial Bibliographies

Unfortunately there is no remotely adequate serial bibliography of comparative literature. Some studies by British and Irish scholars and foreigners at British universities are listed in "Bibliography of Comparative Literature in Britain and Ireland," *Comparative Criticism: An Annual Journal* 1–20 (1979–98), a very selective list that never seems to have migrated to the Web as planned; and for a time the "Revue des revues" section of *Canadian Review of Comparative Literature/Revue canadienne de littérature comparée* (1–15 [1974–88]) printed abstracts of selected general comparative studies. The best current coverage—by no means adequate—is offered by *ABELL* (G340) and *MLAIB* (G335).

For an overview of the development of comparative literature and assessment of the current state of the discipline, see J. Michael Holquist, "Comparative Literature" (pp. 194–208), in Nicholls, *Introduction to Scholarship in Modern Languages and Literatures* (A25).

See also

   ABELL (G340): Comparative Literature division in the volumes for 1923–60.
   "Bibliography on the Relations of Literature and the Other Arts" (U5965).
   MLAIB (G335): General VII: Literature, General and Comparative/Other General and Comparative section in the volumes for 1953–55; General II: Literature, General and Comparative/Other General and Comparative section in the volume for 1956; General III: Literature, General and Comparative/Comparative Literature section in the volumes for 1957–80; Professional Topics/Comparative Literature section in the volumes for 1981–99; and Comparative Literature division in later volumes. Researchers must also check the "Comparative Literature" heading in the subject index to post-1980 volumes and in the online thesaurus.

Other Bibliographies

T5000   Baldensperger, Fernand, and Werner P. Friederich. *Bibliography of
        Comparative Literature.* New York: Russell, 1960. 705 pp. (A reprint of the
        1950 edition with a revision of the Scandinavian section by P. M.
        Mitchell.)   Z6514.C7 B3   016.809.

A selective bibliography of publications and "significant" American dissertations
through 1949 on comparative and world literature (principally of the Western Hemisphere). Although international in scope, *Bibliography of Comparative Literature* emphasizes scholarship from Western Europe and North America. The approximately
33,000 entries are organized in four extensively classified divisions:

> general topics (with sections for comparative, world, and European literatures;
> literature and politics; literature and arts and sciences; intermediaries; compar-
> isons, sources, and imitations; themes; collective motifs; and genres and forms);
> Orient, classical antiquity, Judaism, early Christianity, and Mohammedanism
> (with sections for the Orient, classical antiquity, Greek literature, Latin liter-
> ature, and Hebraism and Christianity);
> aspects of Western culture (with sections for modern Christianity, various literary
> movements, and international literary relations);
> the modern world (with sections for Celtic and Arthurian, Provençal, Italian,
> Spanish, Portuguese, Dutch and Belgian, French, English, Swiss, German,
> North and South American, Scandinavian, and East European literatures).

Most sections are extensively subdivided. Entries for books usually omit subtitles;
those for articles, page numbers. Users must remember that (1) coverage varies considerably from section to section (e.g., the treatment of genres, literary theory, and Oriental
and East European literatures is especially weak; in many sections, selection seems ar-
bitrary); (2) because the classification is heavily dependent on titles, works are frequently
inappropriately classified; (3) influence studies are listed under the influencer; (4) effective use requires close familiarity with the classification system outlined on pp. v–x.
The lack of any index or sufficient cross-references, the classification practices, and
inconsistencies mean that users must exercise considerable ingenuity to track down
studies (and will usually end up searching entry by entry through several sections).
Although it lacks an adequate explanation of scope, limitations, and principles of organization and selection, omits many important works, and is frustrating to use because
of its classification practices and lack of indexing, the work remains the most complete
bibliography of comparative scholarship before 1950. (Scholars would thank the selfless
person who compiles a subject index to this bibliography.) Reviews: B. Munteano, *Revue
de littérature comparée* 26 (1952): 273–83; Sigmund Skard, *JEGP: Journal of English
and Germanic Philology* 52 (1953): 229–42.

Although the supplement planned for 1955 was never published, the "Annual
Bibliography [1949–69]," *YCGL: Yearbook of Comparative and General Literature*
1–19 (1952–70), continued coverage through 1969. Until the bibliography for 1960
(10 [1961]), the organization followed Baldensperger. Then, until the bibliography's
unfortunate demise, entries were organized in eight classified divisions: comparative,
world, and general literature; translations, translators, correspondents, travelers, and
other intermediaries; themes, motifs, and topoi; genres, types, forms, and techniques;
epochs, currents, periods, and movements; Bible and classical antiquity and larger geographic and linguistic groups; individual countries; individual authors.

Some additional coverage is offered by *Bibliographie générale de littérature comparée* [1949–58] (Paris: Didier, 1950–59), with sections for bibliographies, theory, stylistics, genres, themes and types, general studies, intermediaries, movements and periods, and individual countries. (This work is essentially a cumulation of the bibliographies for 1949 through 1958 in *Revue de littérature comparée*.)

T5005   Dyserinck, Hugo, and Manfred S. Fischer, eds. *Internationale Bibliographie zu Geschichte und Theorie der Komparatistik.* Hiersemanns Bibliographische Handbücher 5. Stuttgart: Hiersemann, 1985. 314 pp.   Z6514.C7 I6 [PN870.5.].

A bibliography of studies (from 1800 through autumn 1982) on the history, theory, and teaching of comparative literature. The entries are placed by publication date in one of two divisions: 1800–99 and 1900–82. In the first division, entries are organized alphabetically by author in three sections: general works on the theory of comparative literature; bibliographies and studies of special topics, terminology, and the relationship to other disciplines; and works on the history of comparative literature. The 1900–82 division is organized chronologically, with each year divided into the same three sections as in the 1800–99 division. Two indexes: proper names and subjects (with headings in German); scholars. The *Bibliographie* is confusing and inconsistent in organization and omits some important works but is still the most complete guide to scholarship on the history and theory of comparative literature. Reviews: Adrian Marino, *Archiv für das Studium der neueren Sprachen und Literaturen* 224 (1987): 124–28; Ulrich Weisstein, *YCGL: Yearbook of Comparative and General Literature* 34 (1985): 161–63.

U

Literature-Related Topics and Sources

Acronyms

U5045   *Acronyms, Initialisms, and Abbreviations Dictionary: A Guide to Acronyms,
         Abbreviations, Contractions, Alphabetic Symbols, and Similar Condensed
         Appellations.* Detroit: Gale, 1960– . Biennial. (Title varies.) Online
         through *Gale Virtual Reference Library* (I535).   P365.A28   423'.1.

   The work is currently published in three volumes:

   Vol. 1: *Acronyms, Initialisms, and Abbreviations Dictionary.* 4 pts.
   Vol. 2: *New Acronyms, Initialisms, and Abbreviations.* 2 pts. (An interedition
      supplement.)
   Vol. 3: *Reverse Acronyms, Initialisms, and Abbreviations Dictionary.* 4 pts.

   A guide to acronyms and the like—derived from English-language terms and
foreign ones in international use—from a variety of fields, including academic degrees,
associations, books of the Bible, brand names, American and British government and
military terms, colleges and universities, Library of Congress library symbols, *WorldCat*
(E225) symbols, personal names, religious orders, titles and forms of address, television
and radio call letters, and online databases. Vol. 1 is an acronym list; vol. 3, a list by
source or phrase; vol. 2 includes both. Although not comprehensive, the work is the
fullest guide to these frequently indecipherable coinages.

   For foreign acronyms not in common international use, see *International Acronyms,
Initialisms, and Abbreviations Dictionary: A Guide to Over [number] International Acronyms, Initialisms, Abbreviations, Alphabetic Symbols, Contractions, and Similar Condensed Appellations in All Fields*, 2 vols. (Detroit: Gale, 1985– , irregular).

Addresses

Individuals

U5060   Directory. *PMLA: Publications of the Modern Language Association of
         America* (*PMLA*). 1886– . Published annually as the Sept. issue.
         PB6.M6   809.2.

   An annual directory of names and addresses of members of the Modern Language
Association (MLA members can now search this data, which is updated daily, through
the MLA Web site [http://www.mla.org]); administrators (by institution) in literature
and language departments of four-year colleges and universities and of junior and community colleges, ethnic studies programs, language and area studies programs, women's
studies programs, and comparative literature programs; organizations of independent

scholars; humanities research centers; and selected publishers and learned and professional societies. In addition, it identifies members of the MLA staff, Delegate Assembly, and committees and commissions, as well as executive committees of divisions and discussion groups; includes a concise guide to association activities and services; describes selected fellowships and grants available to language and literature scholars; and outlines the procedure for organizing meetings at the MLA Annual Convention. Although the Directory is a useful general source of information and addresses, the following are more comprehensive: *National Faculty Directory* (U5070) for addresses of faculty members; *Grants Register* (U5940) for grants; and *Publishers' International Directory* (U5090) for addresses of publishers.

U5065   *A Directory of American Poets and Fiction Writers: Names and Addresses of*
         Over [number] Contemporary Poets, Fiction Writers, and Performance Writers.
         New York: Poets and Writers, 1980– . Biennial. (Title varies.)
         PS129.D55   810'.25'73. Online. 30 Apr. 2006 <http://www.pw.org/
         directory>.

A directory of published fiction writers and poets who are citizens or permanent residents of the United States. The *Directory* also includes a few writers who perform their works rather than rely on print but excludes children's authors, playwrights, and nonfiction writers. Entries are organized by state or foreign country of residence (with countries grouped after the state lists), then alphabetically by name. An entry can include address, URL, and e-mail; phone number; identification as a poet, fiction writer, or performer; and a few recent publications. The online version includes only those writers requesting inclusion. Six indexes: writers; performance poets; language fluency; race, gender, group identity; audience preference; literary agents. Through the 2001–02 edition, entrants are also indexed in *Biography and Genealogy Master Index* (J565). This is the most current source for addresses of American writers published by legitimate (rather than vanity) presses.

U5070   *National Faculty Directory: An Alphabetical List, with Addresses, of More*
         Than [number] Members of Teaching Faculties at Junior Colleges, Colleges, and
         Universities in the United States and at Selected Canadian Institutions.
         Detroit: Gale, 1970– . Annual. (Title varies.)   L901.N34
         378.1'2'02573.

A list of teaching faculty members at United States and Canadian institutions "that use instructional materials primarily in English." Based on institutional catalogs and course lists and compiled from a database designed to generate mailing lists for textbook and academic publishers, the *Directory* excludes faculty members who do not have teaching responsibilities or who cannot be identified with a specific subject area. Entries provide name, department, institutional address, and telephone number. Although incomplete, this work is the most comprehensive source for addresses of faculty members at United States and several Canadian institutions.

Another source of addresses is *Directory of American Scholars*, 10th ed., ed. Caryn E. Klebba, 6 vols. (Detroit: Gale, 2002; online through *Biography Resource Center* [J572]). Although less current and comprehensive, it does offer compact biographical entries that allow for the differentiation between persons of the same name. Since the sixth edition, entrants are indexed in *Biography and Genealogy Master Index* (J565).

For addresses of faculty members at institutions outside the United States and Canada, consult *Commonwealth Universities Yearbook: A Directory to the Universities of the Commonwealth and the Handbook of Their Association* (London: Assn. of Commonwealth Universities, 1941– ; annual). The increased use of first names rather than initials makes differentiating common last names less maddening.

Faculty and staff directories are also available at many university Web sites.

See also

Sec. U: Literature-Related Topics and Sources/Book Collecting/Directories of
   Book Dealers.
Arts and Humanities Citation Index (G365).
Contemporary Authors (J595).
Contemporary Dramatists (M2880).
Contemporary Novelists (M2845).
Contemporary Poets (M2895).
Contemporary Theatre, Film, and Television (Q4305).
Current Biography (J585).
International Authors and Writers Who's Who (J595a).
International Who's Who (J590).
Marquis Who's Who on the Web (Q3395).
Twentieth-Century Children's Writers (U5505).
Who's Who (M1435).

Institutions

U5080   *World of Learning.* London: Taylor and Francis, 1947–. Annual.   AS2.W6
    060.25.
    World of Learning: The International Guide to the Academic World.
    Routledge–Taylor and Francis. Online. 7 Aug. 2005 <http://
    www.worldoflearning.com>. Updated regularly.

A guide to learned organizations and institutions throughout the world. Following a list of international organizations, entries are organized by country, then classified as learned societies (by subject), research institutes (by subject), libraries and archives (including government, public, and university ones, organized by location), museums and art galleries (by location), or universities and colleges (by type, then alphabetically). An entry typically includes a brief description of the organization or institution, address (along with e-mail and Web site), officers, and list of serial publications; entries for universities and colleges usually list major administrators and sometimes faculty members. Indexed by organizations and institutions. At the basic level the online version can be searched by keyword or browsed by country, institution, or subject; advanced search allows users to limit a full-text search by institution, person, or location or to search by institutions, people, or publication title. Although the online version is ostensibly updated throughout the year, the site offers no indication of when or how. The lists are selective and entries vary considerably in detail (with no explanation of the criteria governing selection or reasons for variation) and currency of data (e.g., the Texas A&M University entry is four years out-of-date); however, *World of Learning* is a handy source of addresses of and basic information about a variety of learned organizations and institutions throughout the world.

See also

Sec. E: Libraries and Library Catalogs/Research Libraries/Guides to Libraries and
   Libraries and Library Catalogs/Research Libraries/Guides to Collections.

ArchivesUSA (F280).
Foster, *British Archives* (F283).

Organizations

U5085   *Associations Unlimited.* Thomson Gale. Online. 24 June 2005 <http://
infotrac.galegroup.com/galenet>. Updated quarterly. CD-ROM.
A database of not-for-profit associations that incorporates:

> *Encyclopedia of Associations: A Guide to More than [number] National and
> International Organizations, Including: Trade, Business, and Commercial;
> Environmental and Agricultural; Legal, Governmental, Public Administra-
> tion, and Military; Engineering, Technological, and Natural and Social Sci-
> ences; Educational; Cultural; Social Welfare; Health and Medical; Public
> Affairs; Fraternal, Nationality, and Ethnic; Religious; Veterans', Hereditary,
> and Patriotic; Hobby and Avocational; Athletic and Sports; Labor Unions,
> Associations, and Federations; Chambers of Commerce and Trade and Tour-
> ism; Greek Letter and Related Organizations; and Fan Clubs.* Detroit: Gale,
> 1956– . Annual. (Title varies.) CD-ROM.

The work is currently published in three volumes:

> Vol. 1: *National Organizations of the U. S.* 3 pts.
> Vol. 2: *Geographic and Executive Indexes.*
> Vol. 3: *Supplement.* (Interedition supplement to vol. 1.)

A directory primarily of not-for-profit organizations of more than regional or local
interest. Entries are compiled from questionnaires as well as from other sources for
organizations that could not be contacted directly.

Vol. 1, pts. 1–2 consist of descriptions of United States associations organized
alphabetically by title within subdivisions of the subject areas listed in the subtitle.
Entries provide organization name, acronym, address of permanent national headquarters or chief official, telephone and fax numbers, e-mail, Web site, chief official and
title, founding date, number of members, annual budget, a brief description of purpose
and activities, computerized and telecommunications services, official publications, af-
filiated organizations, name changes, and details of upcoming conventions and meetings. Entries from these two parts—along with organizations that are inactive or defunct
and additional groups that might qualify as not-for-profit and are listed in other standard
directories—are indexed by name and keyword in vol. 1, pt. 3.

Vol. 2 indexes entries in vol. 1 by geographic area and by chief executive.

Vol. 3 lists new organizations (accompanied by a keyword and title index) and
updates some information in vol. 1.

The best way to locate entries is through the keyword and title indexes because of
the organization by keywords (many of which are added to accord with Gale's system
of classification) and because of the inclusion in this index of entries for organizations
that are defunct, inactive, or described in other standard directories but not accorded
entries in vols. 1 or 3. See also *Encyclopedia of Associations: Regional, State, and Local
Organizations*, 5 vols. (1987– , biennial), and *Encyclopedia of Associations: International
Organizations*, 3 pts. (1983– , Annual).

The database (which also includes IRS data on not-for-profit organizations) can
be searched by association name, address, subject category, keyword, and a variety of
other fields. Updated quarterly (annually, for the IRS data), *Associations Unlimited* offers
the most comprehensive source of information on not-for-profit organizations.

For associations in the British Isles, see the current edition of *Directory of British Associations and Associations in Ireland* (Beckenham: CBD, 1965– , irregular; CD-ROM). Organized alphabetically by title, entries provide address and other basic information. Indexed by abbreviations and subjects.

Publishers

U5090 *Publishers' International ISBN Directory.* Handbook of International Documentation and Information 7. München: Saur; Berlin: Internat. ISBN Agency; New Providence: Bowker, 1964– . Biennial. Z282.P8 070.5′025. CD-ROM.

A directory of periodical and book publishers, including small presses, alternative presses, institutions, organizations, and even some individuals; the CD-ROM includes defunct publishers, authors who are publishers, and United States publishers without ISBNs. Publishers are organized by country, then alphabetically by official name. An entry includes address, telephone, fax, e-mail, Web site, and ISBN. Indexed by ISBN prefixes (a useful feature when one knows a publisher's ISBN but not official name). As the most comprehensive source for addresses of publishers (especially outside the United States), the *Directory* is an essential resource for the addresses of publishers without Web sites.

The following works are less thorough but offer fuller information about United States and Canadian publishers:

> *Canadian Books in Print* (R4595a).
>
> *GlobalBooksinPrint.com* (Q4225).
>
> *Literary Market Place: The Directory of the American Book Publishing Industry with Industry Yellow Pages* (*LMP*). Medford: Information Today, 1940– . Annual. Title varies. Online. 16 Aug. 2005 <http://www .literarymarketplace.com>. Although it is a trade publication, some parts are of interest to literary researchers: a highly selective alphabetical list of United States and Canadian publishers (recording address, telephone and fax numbers, e-mail, Web site, major editorial personnel, and subject interests), with the United States section indexed by states, kinds of publishers or types of books, and subjects; literary agents (with submission instructions); literary awards, contests, and grants; and book review and index journals. Criteria determining inclusion are unstated (except for the exclusion of vanity presses), and all lists are seriously incomplete. The online version (updated "continuously") includes *International Literary Market Place* (Medford: Information Today, 1972– ; annual).
>
> *Publishers Directory: A Guide to New and Established, Commercial and Nonprofit, Private and Alternative, Corporate and Association, Government and Institution Publishing Programs and Their Distributors.* Detroit: Gale, 1977– . Annual. Organized alphabetically by official name, entries list address, telephone and fax numbers, e-mail, Web site, number of new titles and total titles in print, major editorial personnel, and subject interests of United States and Canadian publishers. Three indexes: publishers, imprints, and distributors; broad subjects; geographical location (by state or province, then city). The subject index can sometimes be helpful in identifying places to submit a manuscript.

Many publishers also maintain Web sites.

See also

> Association of American University Presses Directory (U6383).
> MLA Directory of Periodicals (K615).

Anonymous and Pseudonymous Works

General Introductions

U5105   Taylor, Archer, and Fredric J. Mosher. *The Bibliographical History of*
        Anonyma and Pseudonyma. Chicago: U of Chicago P for Newberry Lib.,
        1951. 289 pp.   Z1041.T3.
        A history of the study from the early Christian era to the mid-twentieth century
of anonymous and pseudonymous writings. Especially valuable is the selective, annotated bibliography of dictionaries and lists of anonyma and pseudonyma. The list concludes with a guide classified by language or geographical area and subject. The text,
but not the bibliography, is indexed by persons and anonymous works. *Bibliographical
History* is now dated, but it remains a valuable guide to extensive early scholarship,
much of which has not been superseded.

Dictionaries

U5110   Halkett, Samuel, and John Laing. *A Dictionary of Anonymous and*
        Pseudonymous Publications in the English Language (Halkett and Laing). Vol. 1:
        1475–1640. 3rd rev. and enl. ed. Ed. John Horden. London: Longman,
        1980. 271 pp. (Work on the 3rd edition has apparently been suspended.)
        Z1065.H18   014′.2.

        ———. *Dictionary of Anonymous and Pseudonymous English Literature*
        (Halkett and Laing). New and enl. ed. Ed. James Kennedy et al. 9 vols.
        Edinburgh: Oliver, 1926–62.   Z1065.H17   014′.2.

   Vols. 1–6: A–Z and Supplement. Ed. James Kennedy, W. A. Smith, and
      A. F. Johnson. 1926–32.
   Vol. 7: *Index and Second Supplement.* Ed. Kennedy, Smith, and Johnson.
      1934. 588 pp.
   Vol. 8: *1900–1950.* Ed. Dennis E. Rhodes and Anna E. C. Simoni. 1956.
      397 pp.
   Vol. 9: *Addenda to Volumes I–VIII.* Ed. Rhodes and Simoni. 1962. 477 pp.
        A title list of English-language works (including translations and bilingual or multi-
lingual publications with a significant portion in English) that were published anonymously or pseudonymously and whose authorship has been ascribed.
        Second edition (1926–62). The second edition lists about 75,000 titles from 1475
through 1949 and includes some works of unattributed authorship. Entries, listed alphabetically by title, cite attributed author, format, pagination, source of the entry, and
place and date of publication. Two indexes in vols. 7–9: authors; initials and pseudonyms. Since the indexes cite volume and page, locating an entry is usually time-consuming, since researchers must hunt through a title entry to find a name or initials.

Users should keep several points in mind: (1) because many entries are taken from other sources—especially the British Museum *General Catalogue of Printed Books* (see E250) and *Dictionary of National Biography* (M1425a), both notoriously inaccurate in attributing authorship—there are numerous errors in transcription of titles (thus making impossible the location of some works), identification of authorship, and inclusion of works not truly anonymous; (2) although the source of an entry is usually recorded, evidence for attribution is not; thus, there is no immediate way of assessing the accuracy of an ascription; (3) because of the organization, books published between 1475 and 1900 are included in vols. 1–6 as well as the supplements in vols. 6, 7, and 9, and books published between 1900 and 1949 are in vols. 8 and 9. Although incomplete, inaccurate, and time-consuming to use, Halkett and Laing remains an essential, if untrustworthy, source for identifying the author of an anonymous or pseudonymous publication. It is partly superseded by the much improved third edition. For a history of the first and second editions, see the preface to vol. 1 of the third edition.

Third edition. The third edition—which was to have become *Dictionary of Concealed Authorship: Publications in English, 1475–1700*—is limited to separately published English-language works (including translations and bilingual or multilingual publications with a substantial portion in English) that appeared anonymously or pseudonymously between 1475 and 1700 and for which authorship has been established or ascribed. It excludes works falsely attributed or unattributed, although exceptions are made for any works listed in the second edition.

The new edition is a major improvement over its predecessor: along with defining scope more precisely, adding numerous works, correcting many errors, and basing descriptions on the actual examination of copies, the third edition records the evidence and its source for attributions, along with title, place and date of publication, and references to standard bibliographies. Editorial practices are clearly and fully explained in the introduction (pp. xxii–xliv) to vol. 1. Additions and corrections to vol. 1 appear on p. 221. Indexed by writers' names, with a list of pseudonyms keyed to the index; in addition, vol. 1 prints useful concordances for entry numbers in Greg, *Bibliography of the English Printed Drama to the Restoration* (M2135); *Short-Title Catalogue* (M1990; although references are not based on the final version of the second edition of vol. 1); and A. F. Allison and D. M. Rogers, *A Catalogue of Catholic Books in English Printed Abroad or Secretly in England, 1558–1640*, 2 pts., Bibliographical Studies 3.3–4 (Bognor Regis: Arundel, 1956).

The careful assimilation and evaluation of widely scattered evidence for attributions and many new ascriptions make this new edition of Halkett and Laing the indispensable starting point for identifying the authors of anonymously and pseudonymously published works (before 1700), and the worthy successor to a venerable but flawed reference work.

The *National Union Catalogs* (E235, E240, and E245) and *British National Bibliography* (M2775) are also useful sources for identifying the author of an anonymous or pseudonymous work.

U5115   *Pseudonyms and Nicknames Dictionary: A Guide to 80,000 Aliases, Appellations, Assumed Names, Code Names, Cognomens, Cover Names, Epithets, Initialisms, Nicknames, Noms de Guerre, Noms de Plume, Pen Names, Pseudonyms, Sobriquets, and Stage Names of 55,000 Contemporary and Historical Persons, Including the Subjects' Real Names, Basic Biographical Information, and Citations for the Sources from Which the Entries Were Compiled.* Ed. Jennifer Mossman. 3rd ed. 2 vols. Detroit: Gale, 1987.

New Pseudonyms and Nicknames. 1988. 306 pp. (Gale has no plans to publish further supplements or editions.)   CT120.P8   920'.02.

A dictionary of pseudonyms and the like of prominent individuals from all ages and walks of life, with the bulk of the entries for authors, entertainers, and athletes. Names are listed in a single alphabetical sequence, with the main entry (giving birth and death dates, sources for further information, nationality, occupation, and assumed names) under the real name and cross-references for other names. Although this is the fullest single international source for identifying assumed names, the following works include additional literary ones:

> Atkinson, Frank. *Dictionary of Literary Pseudonyms: A Selection of Popular Modern Writers in English.* 4th ed. London: Lib. Assn.; Chicago: Amer. Lib. Assn., 1987. 299 pp. Indexed in *Biography and Genealogy Master Index* (J565).
>
> Carty, T. J. *A Dictionary of Literary Pseudonyms in the English Language.* 2nd ed. London: Mansell; Chicago: Fitzroy, 2000. 844 pp.
>
> Marshall, Alice Kahler. *Pen Names of Women Writers from 1600 to the Present: A Compendium of the Literary Identities of 2,650 Women Novelists, Playwrights, Poets, Diarists, Journalists, and Miscellaneous Writers.* Camp Hill: Alice Marshall Collection, 1985. 181 pp. Indexed in *Biography and Genealogy Master Index* (J565).
>
> Sharp, Harold S., comp. *Handbook of Pseudonyms and Personal Nicknames.* 2 vols. Metuchen: Scarecrow, 1972. *First Supplement.* 2 vols. 1975. *Second Supplement.* 1982. 289 pp.

Art and Literature

For an introduction to the interdisciplinary study of literature and art, see Ulrich Weisstein, "Literature and the Visual Arts" (pp. 251–77), in Barricelli, *Interrelations of Literature* (U5955). Several works in section U: Literature-Related Topics and Sources/ Interdisciplinary and Multidisciplinary Studies treat the relationship of art and literature.

Guides to Reference Works

U5130   Arntzen, Etta, and Robert Rainwater. *Guide to the Literature of Art History.* Chicago: Amer. Lib. Assn.; London: Art Book, 1980. 616 pp.   Z5931.A67 [N380]   016.709.

Marmor, Max, and Alex Ross. *Guide to the Literature of Art History 2.* Chicago: Amer. Lib. Assn., 2005. 899 pp.   Z5931.M37   016.7'09.

A guide to reference works, general studies, and exhibition catalogs (through 1977 in the original edition and 1998 in the supplement) important in the study of art history, especially architecture, sculpture, drawing, painting, prints, photography, and decorative and applied arts. Although international in coverage, *Guide to the Literature of Art History* emphasizes works in Western languages and excludes studies of individual artists. Entries are organized alphabetically by author in four divisions: general reference sources (including sections for bibliographies, visual resources, dictionaries and encyclopedias, and iconography); general primary and secondary sources (with a section on histories and handbooks); the individual arts; and serials. Most sections are extensively classified, generally by period and country. The annotations fully describe content (sometimes listing the table of contents of a work), and most include helpful evaluative comments. Two indexes in the first edition: authors and titles; subjects (however, the subject indexing is incomplete and frequently vague); the supplement has only an index of authors and titles. Arntzen and Marmor are the best general guides to reference works and important studies, but the absence of a subject index renders the supplement less accessible than it should be. Reviews: Margaret Girvan, *Art Libraries Journal* 6.3 (1981): 73–79; Alex Ross, *Art Bulletin* 65 (1983): 169–72.

Handbooks, Dictionaries, and Encyclopedias

U5135   *Grove Art Online.* Oxford UP. Online. 24 June 2005 <http://
  groveart.com>. Updated four times per year.
  A database that continually expands and revises *The Dictionary of Art*, ed. Jane Turner, 34 vols. (New York: Grove, 1996) and includes *The Oxford Companion to Western Art*, ed. Hugh Brigstocke (Oxford: Oxford UP, 2001, 820 pp.). Extensively illustrated and encompassing the visual arts (except for film) of all eras and countries, the more than 45,000 entries from *Dictionary of Art* and several hundred new ones — all by internationally recognized scholars, and many extending to several hundred pages — cover cultures, nations, schools, periods, artists, theories, methodologies, materials, places, theoretical issues, techniques, artistic genres, and related topics. Many of the lengthy entries consist of separately authored parts; all entries (and some parts) conclude with a bibliography. Entries can be searched by full text (and limited to biographies, bibliographies, or contributors) or browsed by title or contributor; images can be searched by artist, title, date, and location. Although many images in *Dictionary of Art* are not available digitally or are more clearly reproduced therein than in *Grove Art Online*, the latter allows users to download, print, or e-mail images. A masterly achievement, *Grove Art Online/Dictionary of Art* is the most authoritative and comprehensive of the numerous general encyclopedias of art.
  The most comprehensive dictionary of artists is *Allgemeines Künstlerlexikon: Die bildenden Künstler aller Zeiten und Völker*, ed. Günter Meissner (München: Saur, 1992–); however, as of mid-2005 coverage had progressed only to vol. 43: *Fosnes– Francone*. For parts of the alphabet not yet covered, see Ulrich Thieme and Felix Becker, eds., *Allgemeines Lexikon der bildenden Künstler von der Antike bis zur Gegenwart* (Thieme-Becker), 37 vols. (Leipzig: Seeman, 1907–50), and Hans Vollmer, ed., *Allgemeines Lexikon der bildenden Künstler der XX. Jahrhunderts*, 6 vols. (Leipzig: Seeman, 1953–62).

Guides to Scholarship and Criticism

SERIAL BIBLIOGRAPHIES

U5138   *BHA: Bibliography of the History of Art/Bibliographie d'histoire de l'art.*
  Vandœuvre: Centre National de la Recherche Scientifique, Institut de

l'Information Scientifique et Technique; Los Angeles: Getty Research Inst., 1991– .   Z5937.B53 [N7510]   016.7. Online; CD-ROM.

A bibliographic database of studies of European art from the fourth century AD to the present, American art from c. 1492 to the present, and non-Western art insofar as it influences European or American art; contemporary art, however, is selectively covered throughout the world. The result of a merger of *Répertoire d'art et d'archéologie* (U5150) and *RILA* (U5155), *BHA* both continues and expands the coverage of its predecessors. Entries are accompanied by abstracts in English or French. The CD-ROM includes records since the inception of the print version of *BHA* (9 vols., 1991–2000); the online version (available through RLG Union Catalog [E230], CSA [I510], Ovid [I515], and SilverPlatter [I523]) includes records for 1973–89 from *Répertoire d'art et d'archéologie* (U5150) and for 1975–89 from *RILA* (U5155). *BHA* now offers the fullest, most accessible—but not the most current—coverage of the major art bibliographies.

U5140   *ARTbibliographies Modern* [1969–]. Oxford: CSA, 1969– . 2/yr. Former
         title: *LOMA (Literature on Modern Art: An Annual Bibliography)* (1969–
         71).   Z5935.L64   016.709′04. Online. 28 June 2005 <http://
         ca1.csa.com>. CD-ROM.

A bibliography of dissertations, exhibition catalogs, and other scholarship on art and related topics since 1900. (Vols. 4–18 [1973–87] cover 1800 to the present.) Since vol. 4 (1973), entries—accompanied by brief nonevaluative abstracts—are organized in a single subject list, which incorporates generous cross-references. (The earlier volumes are organized by artist, have little other subject access, and are limited to twentieth-century art.) Two indexes in each issue: authors; museums and galleries. Cumulative indexes (with expanded coverage of artists): vols. 1–5 (1984); vols. 6–10 (1982, 264 pp.); vols. 11–15 (1987, 336 pp.); vols. 16–18 (1989, 232 pp.). Although *ARTbibliographies* offers the best coverage of modern and contemporary art, the lack of thorough subject indexing—especially of the abstracts—means that researchers looking for studies involving literary works or authors should search one of the electronic versions, both of which include entries since vol. 5 (1974). (For an evaluation of the CSA interface, see entry I510.) Review: Patricia E. Johner, *Charleston Advisor* 2.1 (2001). 19 Feb. 2003 <http://www.charlestonco.com>.

U5145   *Art Full Text.* Wilson. Online. 28 June 2005 <http://
         vnweb.hwwilsonweb.com/hww>. Updated daily. CD-ROM. Updated
         monthly.
         Art Index [1929–]. New York: Wilson, 1930– . Quarterly, with annual
         and larger cumulations.   Z5937.A78   016.7. Online; CD-ROM.

An author and subject index to articles in about 276 art periodicals, yearbooks, and museum bulletins (as of late June 2005), with coverage extending to archaeology, architecture, art history, crafts, films, graphic arts, industrial design, interior design, landscape architecture, museology, photography, and related fields. The serials indexed are determined by subscriber vote, but coverage is reasonably international. Articles are indexed by author and subject; exhibitions and reproductions by artist. Since vol. 22 (1973–74), book reviews are listed separately at the end. Entries since September 1984 can be searched most effectively in the electronic version and in two related Wilson databases (online; CD-ROM): *Art Abstracts* (with abstracts beginning in spring 1994) and *Art Full Text* (which offers full text of some articles beginning in 1997); entries from 1929–84 can be searched in *Art Index Retrospective: 1929–1984* (online; CD-

ROM). See entry I525 for an evaluation of the WilsonWeb search interface, which all of the *Art Index* databases use. Although the work is the most selective in coverage and limited to articles, it is also the broadest, most current, and easiest to use of the art indexes and is particularly useful for locating a reproduction of an art work.

U5150   *Répertoire d'art et d'archéologie (de l'époque paléochrétienne à 1939)* (*RAA*). 93 vols. Paris: Centre National de la Recherche Scientifique, 1910–89. Z5937.R4   016.7. Online; CD-ROM.
A bibliography of books, articles, and exhibition and auction catalogs on the history of art from the early Christian era through 1939. The scope and organization have altered considerably since 1910. Books are excluded until vol. 24 (1920); coverage of primitive and popular art is discontinued with the combined vols. 49–51 (1945–47), and Oriental, Islamic, and classical art since ns 1 (1965). *RAA* was originally composed of a list of contents of journals organized by country of publication; since ns 9 (1973), entries are organized in five extensively classified divisions: general works (including sections for reference works, theory of art, and iconography); general art history; Middle Ages; Renaissance and seventeenth and eighteenth centuries; and nineteenth and twentieth centuries. The period divisions have sections for general studies, architecture, sculpture, painting and graphic arts, and decorative arts, with each subdivided by country. Three indexes in each issue since ns 9 (1973): artists; subjects; authors (each cumulated annually); earlier volumes are variously indexed by authors, artists, and places. Many entries in recent volumes are accompanied by brief descriptive annotations in French. Entries since 1973 can be searched through the online *BHA* (U5138) or on CD-ROM. Of the major art bibliographies, *RAA* offered the fullest coverage before its merger with *RILA* (U5155) to form *BHA*.

U5155   *RILA: International Repertory of the Literature of Art/Répertoire international de la littérature de l'art* (*RILA*). 15 vols. Williamstown: Getty Art History Information Program, 1975–89.   Z5937.R16 [N7510]   016.7. Online; CD-ROM.
An abstracting service for publications (including dissertations and reviews of books and exhibitions from 1974 through 1988) on the history of Western art from the fourth century to the present. Entries are organized in seven classified divisions: reference works; general studies; medieval; Renaissance, baroque, and rococo; neoclassicism and modern (to 1945); modern (1945 to the present); collections and exhibitions. Where appropriate, each division has sections for general studies; architecture; sculpture; pictorial arts; decorative arts; and artists, architects, and photographers. The abstracts are descriptive, with several by document authors. Two indexes in each issue: authors; subjects; cumulative indexes: *1975–1979* (1982, 837 pp.); *1980–1984* (1987, 1,318 pp.); *1985–1989* (2 vols., 1990). Entries can be searched through the online *BHA* (U5138) and on CD-ROM. Until its merger with *RAA* (U5150) to form *BHA*, *RILA* offered the most thorough subject indexing of the major art bibliographies.

See also

Humm, *Annotated Critical Bibliography of Feminist Criticism* (U6170).

OTHER BIBLIOGRAPHIES

U5160   Huddleston, Eugene L., and Douglas A. Noverr. *The Relationship of Painting and Literature: A Guide to Information Sources.* American Studies

Information Guide Series 4. Detroit: Gale, 1978. 184 pp.   Z5069.H84
[N66]   016.75913.

A checklist of paintings and analogous works of American literature and of English-language studies, through c. 1976, of the relationship between the two. Entries are organized in six divisions: analogous American paintings and American poems (organized by artist in six chronological periods, with a numbering system defining the closeness of the analogy); American poems on paintings (organized by poet); American poems on painters; American poems on unspecified paintings, painters, and related subjects; studies of the relationship between poetry and painting; studies of the relationship between fiction and painting. Additions to the last two divisions appear on pp. 147–49. A very few entries are annotated, and those are done inadequately. Three indexes: authors; painters; paintings, books, and poems. Highly selective and misleadingly titled, *Relationship of Painting and Literature* is only marginally useful as a starting point for research.

U5165   Lambrechts, Eric, and Luc Salu. *Photography and Literature: An
           International Bibliography of Monographs.* 2 vols. London: Continuum,
           1992–2000.   Z1023.L33   016.096′1.

A bibliography of approximately 5,966 books, dissertations, photonovels, catalogs, and special issues of magazines published between 1839 and 1999 that treat the relation between photography and literature, contain portraits of writers or places with literary associations, or print a literary text accompanied by photographs. Entries, listed alphabetically by photographer or author (with generous cross-references, including ones for editors and writers of prefatory matter in vol. 1), provide basic bibliographical information, an occasional note identifying type of work, number of photographs, and language. Two indexes: names; broad subject categories (users must be certain to consult the subheadings under Geographical Studies and Topical Studies). Although including only separately published works, *Photography and Literature* is the essential starting point for locating studies of the subject as well as identifying editions of literary works illustrated with photographs.

See also

"Bibliography on the Relations of Literature and the Other Arts" (U5965).
MLAIB (G335): See the headings beginning "Art," "Painting," and "Sculpture"
     in the subject index to post-1980 volumes and in the online thesaurus.
Rice, *English Fiction, 1900–1950* (M2840).

Author Bibliographies

All major and numerous minor authors are the subject of at least one author bibliography. Because of their number, wide variation in quality, and ease of identification (in library catalogs, bibliographies of bibliographies, and serial bibliographies and indexes), individual author bibliographies are not listed in this *Guide.* (For a convenient list of separately published author bibliographies, consult Bracken, *Reference Works in British and American Literature* [M1357].)

Although it is generally the best place to begin extensive research on an author or specific work, an author bibliography, like any other reference work, must be used with due regard for its scope, limitations, and accuracy. As I point out in *On Compiling an Annotated Bibliography* (A30):

> Several of these bibliographies are models of their kind: intelligent, accurate, thorough, efficiently organized works that foster scholarship by guiding readers through accumulated studies as well as implicitly or explicitly isolating dominant scholarly concerns, identifying topics that have been overworked, and suggesting needed research. Unfortunately, many are flawed in either conception or execution, and some are downright shoddy. (1)

Before searching out entries, users must study the prefatory explanation of scope and organization, become familiar with the index(es), and assess the accuracy of the work. A good bibliography will begin with a precise statement of what it includes and excludes, its chronological span, organization and content of entries, and relationship to other bibliographies. (Because many bibliographies are inexcusably vague about some or all of these matters, researchers will have no immediate way of determining how complete a work is.) An efficient, effective search of an author bibliography requires an understanding of the organization of entries and the nature of the index(es). For example, when searching for scholarship on a specific work in an author bibliography with sections for individual literary works, it is essential to know whether general studies are cross-referenced, accorded multiple listings, or accessible only through an index. Because judging accuracy is best accomplished through repeated use, researchers consulting a bibliography for the first time should search out reviews; unfortunately, too few author bibliographies are subjected to rigorous reviewing.

Because no bibliography is comprehensive and every one is outdated even before the last keystroke of the final draft is saved, researchers will also have to consult appropriate serial bibliographies and indexes listed throughout this *Guide.*

Bibliography and Textual Criticism

This section is devoted to analytical bibliography and the Anglo-American tradition of textual criticism. Several closely allied works appear in the immediately following section, Book Collecting.

Handbooks, Dictionaries, and Encyclopedias

U5190 Glaister, Geoffrey Ashall. *Encyclopedia of the Book.* 2nd ed. with new introd. New Castle: Oak Knoll; London: British Lib., 1996. 551 pp. Z118.G55 686.2'03.

A dictionary of technical terms, presses, binderies, organizations, awards, periodicals, printers, publishers, binders, calligraphers, booksellers, and other persons associated with the book, paper, printing, and publishing trades. The 3,932 entries, which range from a few lines to several pages, offer clear definitions or biographies, cite important scholarship, and provide extensive cross-references to related entries. Several are accompanied by illustrations; unfortunately, many of the black-and-white ones are unclear. Four appendixes: selected type specimens; Latin place names in imprints of early books; British proof correction symbols; a selected bibliography. Generally authoritative and accurate, Glaister is the essential glossary of terminology related to the history and production of books and manuscripts. The 1996 edition reprints the second edition (*Glaister's Glossary of the Book: Terms Used in Papermaking, Printing, Bookbinding, and Publishing, with Notes on Illuminated Manuscripts and Private Presses*, 2nd ed. [London: Allen, 1979, 551 pp.]) with an introduction by Donald Farren on the genesis and evolution of the encyclopedia; the first edition — *An Encyclopedia of the Book* (Cleveland: World, 1960, 484 pp.); *Glossary of the Book* (London: Allen, 1960, 484 pp.) — remains useful for entries and illustrations subsequently dropped. Reviews: (1st ed.) *Times Literary Supplement* 3 Feb. 1961: 78; (2nd ed.) Paul S. Koda, *Papers of the Bibliographical Society of America* 75 (1981): 219–21; G. Thomas Tanselle, *Printing History* 4 (1982): 78–79.

Occasionally useful complements are the following:

> Feather, John. *A Dictionary of Book History.* New York: Oxford UP, 1986. 278 pp. Entries cover the book trade, printers, publishers, booksellers, bibliographers, presses, libraries, collectors, printing, paper, binding, periodicals, reference books, organizations, and bibliographical terminology. The selection is miscellaneous and the explanations less thorough and far less reliable than in Glaister, but the entries typically cite related sources or studies.

> Peters, Jean. *The Bookman's Glossary.* 6th ed., rev. and enl. New York: Bowker, 1983. 223 pp. The entries for terms used in publishing, book manufacturing, bookselling, and the antiquarian trade are much briefer than those in Glaister or Feather.

U5193   *Lexikon des gesamten Buchwesens* (*LGB2*). 2nd ed. Ed. Severin Corsten et al. Stuttgart: Hiersemann, 1985– . (Published in fascicles.)   Z1006.L464 020′.331.

An encyclopedia of all aspects of the history of the book, including its production, distribution, reception, and related topics. The approximately 16,000 signed entries cover illustration and illustrators, publishers, printers, bibliographers, libraries, associations and societies, periodicals, booksellers, terminology, technical processes, book collectors, and binding. Most entries conclude with a brief list of additional sources. Although the most extensive and thorough of the encyclopedias of the book, *Lexikon des gesamten Buchwesens* (which reached *Schuhe bauen-Sicherheitsverfilmung* in mid-2005) will not be complete for several more years.

See also

> Carter, *ABC for Book Collectors* (U5340).

General Introductions

U5194   Greetham, D. C. *Textual Scholarship: An Introduction.* Corr. rpt. Garland Reference Library of the Humanities 1417. New York: Garland, 1994. 561 pp. (A second edition was announced for 2005 but has not appeared as of March 2007.)   Z1001.G7   010′.44.

A historical and methodological introduction to textual scholarship. Following an introductory discussion of terminology, successive chapters focus on the process of textual scholarship: finding the text (enumerative and systematic bibliography); making manuscript and printed books (analytical bibliography); describing the text (descriptive bibliography); reading the text (paleography and typography); evaluating the text (textual bibliography, i.e., ways in which the process of making a manuscript or printed book can affect content of the text); criticizing the text (textual criticism); editing the text. Concludes with an appendix illustrating types of scholarly editions and an extensive selected bibliography (updated and substantially enlarged in the corrected reprint). Indexed by persons, titles, and subjects. Firmly grounded in the history, theory, and practice of each area it treats and replete with examples and illustrations, *Textual Scholarship* offers the best introduction to the field. Reviews: T. H. Howard-Hill, *Papers of the Bibliographical Society of America* 86 (1992): 477–79; B. J. McMullin, *Bibliographical Society of Australia and New Zealand Bulletin* 19.1 (1995): 52–60, with a reply by Greetham, 167–93.

U5195   Gaskell, Philip. *A New Introduction to Bibliography.* Rpt. with corrections. Oxford: Clarendon–Oxford UP, 1985. 438 pp. (Readers should avoid the uncorrected second printing of the American edition [New York: Oxford UP, 1975], since it omits several passages and duplicates others. The corrected second printing begins with "were" rather than "for" on p. 11.) Z116.A2 G27   686.2'09.

An introduction to the technical processes of book production from 1500 to 1950 in Great Britain and America. The bulk of the work consists of a history of book production organized in two extensively illustrated divisions: the handpress period (1500–1800) and the machine press period (1800–1950). The first discusses the technical details of printing type, composition, paper, imposition, presswork, the warehouse, binding, decoration and illustration, patterns of production, and the English book trade; the second, plates, type from 1800 to 1875, paper, edition binding, printing machines, processes of reproduction, mechanical composition and type from 1875 to 1950, printing practices, and the book trade in Britain and America. Following the history is a too-brief section on bibliographical applications: the identification of edition, impression, issue, and state; bibliographical description (with sample descriptions printed as an appendix); and textual bibliography (with two analyses of transmission of texts in an appendix). Another appendix reprints McKerrow's discussion of Elizabethan handwriting (see below). Concludes with a useful, but now dated, selected bibliography that evaluates important scholarship through the early 1970s. Thoroughly indexed by persons and subjects. Although it is better in its treatment of the machine press era and the eighteenth century than the earlier period, inadequate in its attention to analytical bibliography and demonstration of the applications of physical bibliography to the transmission of texts, and densely written in many places, this work provides the best basic introduction to the technical aspects of book production and a necessary prelude to Bowers, *Principles of Bibliographical Description* (U5205), and Gaskell, *From Writer to Reader* (U5220). For the inception and evolution of the *Introduction,* see David McKitterick's introduction to the 1994 reprint (Winchester: St. Paul's Bibliographies; New Castle: Oak Knoll, 1994). Reviews: Fredson Bowers, *Papers of the Bibliographical Society of America* 67 (1973): 104–24; Albert H. Smith, *Library* 5th ser. 28 (1973): 341–44; G. Thomas Tanselle, *Costerus* ns 1 (1974): 129–50.

(Researchers who must use the uncorrected second printing should obtain *Corrections to the 1975 "Second Printing" American Edition of Gaskell's* New Introduction to Bibliography, Occasional Publication 4 [New York: Book Arts, School of Lib. Science, Columbia U, 1975, 3 pp.].)

Although now dated in some respects, Ronald B. McKerrow, *An Introduction to Bibliography for Literary Students,* 2nd impression with corrections (Oxford: Clarendon–

Oxford UP, 1928, 359 pp.), has not been superseded in its integration of the history of book production, bibliographical theory, and application to textual matters in hand-press books of the period 1560–1660. McKerrow and Gaskell must be read together.

U5200   Williams, William Proctor, and Craig S. Abbott. *An Introduction to Bibliographical and Textual Studies.* 3rd ed. New York: MLA, 1999. 179 pp. Z1001.W58   010′.42.

An introduction to the methods and applications of twentieth-century Anglo-American textual and bibliographical scholarship. Chapters discuss analytical bibliography, descriptive bibliography, transmission of texts, and textual criticism; a selective bibliography concludes the work. Particularly informative are the description of the process of preparing a critical edition and the appendix on textual notation, a convenient guide for readers puzzled by the symbols and lists in the editorial apparatus of a critical edition. Although not a substitute for Gaskell, *New Introduction to Bibliography* (U5195), and McKerrow, *Introduction to Bibliography* (U5195a), this is a serviceable introduction for the reader who needs a basic understanding of bibliography and textual criticism. Reviews: Hugh Amory, *Papers of the Bibliographical Society of America* 80 (1986): 243–53; John Feather, *Library* 6th ser. 9 (1987): 196–97.

See also

Tanselle, "Copyright Records and the Bibliographer" (Q3260).

Descriptive Bibliography

U5205   Bowers, Fredson. *Principles of Bibliographical Description.* 1949. Winchester: St. Paul's Bibliographies; New Castle: Oak Knoll, 1994. 505 pp. Z1001.B78   010.1.

A detailed guide to the principles and methods of descriptive bibliography that consolidates scattered scholarship, offers a rationale for the field, and establishes norms for bibliographical description. The 12 chapters provide exacting, detailed treatment of the nature of descriptive bibliography; edition, issue, and state and ideal copy in the handpress period; the bibliographical description of books of the sixteenth through eighteenth centuries; the transcription of title pages and other features; format and collation formula; reference notation; statement of signing, pagination and foliation, and other elements of a description; special considerations for the description of eighteenth-century books; incunabula; the bibliography of nineteenth- and twentieth-century books; the determination of publication, edition, impression, issue, and state in the machine press period; and the description of nineteenth- and twentieth-century books. Three important appendixes conclude the work: a digest of the collation and pagination or foliation formulas; sample descriptions of books of different periods; collation formulas for incunabula. Indexed by persons, subjects, and titles. *Principles of Bibliographical Description* is more thorough in its treatment of books published before 1700 and has been modified and extended in some areas by recent scholarship; nevertheless, it remains the indispensable guide to the theory and practice of descriptive bibliography. The 1994 reprint includes an introduction by G. Thomas Tanselle, who traces the inception, reception, and reputation of the book and notes important recent studies.

Essential complements are Tanselle, "A Sample Bibliographical Description, with Commentary," *Studies in Bibliography* 40 (1987): 1–23, which consolidates and illustrates modifications made to Bowers's principles; David L. Vander Meulen, "The History and Future of Bowers's *Principles*," *Papers of the Bibliographical Society of America* 79 (1985): 197–219, which surveys modifications and extensions, as well as summarizes the reception and impact of this magisterial work; B. J. McMullin, "Bowers's *Principles of Bibliographical Description*," *Bibliographical Society of Australia and New Zealand Bulletin* 15.2 (1991): 53–59, which identifies portions needing revision and which is supplemented by Tanselle, "Bowers's *Principles:* Supplementary Notes on Issue, Format, and Insertions," *Bibliographical Society of Australia and New Zealand Bulletin* 23 (1999): 107–09; and by Vander Meulen, "Revision in Bibliographical Classics: 'McKerrow' and 'Bowers,'" *Studies in Bibliography* 52 (1999): 215–45, an examination of the changes, usually unidentified, that occurred in reprintings of *Principles* and McKerrow's *Introduction to Bibliography* (U5195a).

Because *Principles of Bibliographical Description* requires a sound knowledge of printing practices and bibliographical techniques, readers should first master Gaskell, *New Introduction to Bibliography* (U5195), and McKerrow, *Introduction to Bibliography*. Those daunted by Bowers's detailed instructions for transcribing title pages and other parts of a book, determining format, and recording collation and pagination will find M. J. Pearce, *A Workbook of Analytical and Descriptive Bibliography* (London: Bingley, 1970, 110 pp.), a helpful beginning guide. (Gaskell's section on bibliographical description is also helpful, but it adopts several modifications to Bowers that have not gained wide acceptance.)

Textual Criticism

Leah S. Marcus, "Textual Scholarship" (pp. 143–59), in Nicholls, *Introduction to Scholarship in Modern Languages and Literatures* (A25), offers a succinct, balanced overview of textual criticism and associated activities.

U5210   Greg, W. W. "The Rationale of Copy-Text." *Studies in Bibliography* 3
         (1950–51): 19–36. Reprinted with minor changes in Greg, *Collected
         Papers*, ed. J. C. Maxwell (Oxford: Clarendon–Oxford UP, 1966) 374–91.
         The classic formulation of the theory of copy-text (a text chosen as an expedient guide in formal matters for a critical edition) and the distinction between substantive readings (those "that affect the author's meaning or the essence of his expression") and accidental readings (those that affect mainly the formal presentation of the text). Although sometimes misunderstood and misapplied, Greg's theory, its subsequent modifications, and the debates engendered by the theory are central to modern Anglo-American textual editing. For a history and critique of the responses and modifications to Greg's theory and evaluation of writings on textual theory, see G. Thomas Tanselle, "Greg's Theory of Copy-Text and the Editing of American Literature," *Studies in Bibliography* 28 (1975): 167–229; "Recent Editorial Discussion and the Central Questions of Editing," *Studies in Bibliography* 34 (1981): 23–65; "Historicism and Critical Editing," *Studies in Bibliography* 39 (1986): 1–46; "Textual Criticism and Literary Sociology," *Studies in Bibliography* 44 (1991): 83–143; "Textual Instability and Editorial Idealism," *Studies in Bibliography* 49 (1996): 1–60; and "Textual Criticism at the Millennium: 1995–2000," *Studies in Bibliography* 54 (2001): 1–80. (The preceding are

conveniently reprinted in *Textual Criticism since Greg: A Chronicle, 1950–2000* [Charlottesville: Bibliog. Soc. of the U of Virginia, 2005, 373 pp.].)

U5215   Committee on Scholarly Editions (CSE). MLA, 26 Broadway, 3rd Floor,
             New York, NY 10004-1789. <http://www.mla.org>.

The Committee on Scholarly Editions, the successor to the Center for Editions of American Authors (CEAA; see below), was established in 1976 to encourage the highest standards in scholarly editing of all kinds of works or documents by distributing information about scholarly editing and editorial projects (a list of CSE- or CEAA-approved volumes is available at the MLA Web site [path: Professional Resources/Surveys, Reports, and Other Documents/CSE Approved Editions]); advising and consulting with editors on request; awarding emblems to qualified volumes submitted for review; and promoting dissemination of reliable texts for classroom use and among general readers.

The standards and procedures for obtaining the CSE emblem are described in "Guidelines for Editors of Scholarly Editions" (path: Professional Resources/Surveys, Reports, and Other Documents/Guidelines for Editors of Scholarly Editions; also printed in *Electronic Textual Editing* [U5217] on pp. 23–49), which includes a list of the guiding questions for vetters of editions. Although the committee does not prescribe an editorial methodology or procedure, it does insist that an editor "establish and follow a proofreading plan that serves to ensure the accuracy of the materials presented," strongly recommend that an edition include a textual essay and apparatus, and require that the edition undergo formal inspection by a CSE representative.

The CEAA was established to oversee the preparation of critical editions of American literature (primarily of the nineteenth century). Standards and procedures that governed CEAA-approved editions are explained in *Statement of Editorial Principles and Procedures: A Working Manual for Editing Nineteenth-Century American Texts*, rev. ed. (New York: MLA, 1972, 25 pp.). Although it is addressed to those editing nineteenth-century American literary works and although the principles underlying CEAA editions engendered considerable debate, the manual remains a valuable source of practical advice for those editing literary texts.

U5217   *Electronic Textual Editing.* Ed. Lou Burnard, Katherine O'Brien O'Keeffe,
             and John Unsworth. New York: MLA, 2006. 419 pp. and CD-ROM.
             PN162.E55   808'.027.

A collection of essays addressing the applications, principles, and procedures of electronic textual editing, especially in projects that adhere to the Text Encoding Initiative (TEI) guidelines (provided on the accompanying CD-ROM). Along with case studies are discussions of methods of inputting text; using levels of transcription; maintaining textual reliability; managing documents and files; representing special characters; documenting markup choices; storing, retrieving, and rendering text; knowing when not to use TEI; transforming a printed editorial project into an electronic one; dealing with rights and permissions; and preserving an electronic edition. Full of sound practical advice from many of the leading practitioners in the field, *Electronic Textual Editing* is required reading for those contemplating an electronic edition or evaluating one.

U5220   Gaskell, Philip. *From Writer to Reader: Studies in Editorial Method.* Oxford:
             Clarendon–Oxford UP, 1978. 268 pp.   PN162.G3   808'.02.

A collection of case studies that demonstrate how textual evidence can be used to produce editions for various kinds of audiences. The 12 examples—which range from 1591 to 1974 and encompass poetry, drama, nonfiction prose, and fiction—are effectively chosen to illustrate the kinds of problems that confront an editor and to show that each textual situation is unique. For each example, Gaskell characterizes the surviving forms and their relationship, discusses the choice of copy-text, proposes emendations, and suggests an appropriate kind of edition or examines an existing one. The introduction briefly discusses authorial intention, copy-text, techniques of presentation and annotation, regularization, and works not intended for publication as a printed book. Indexed by persons and subjects. Designed to complement *New Introduction to Bibliography* (U5195), *From Writer to Reader* presumes a knowledge of the history of printing and the basic concepts and theories underlying textual criticism. Although reviewers have raised serious objections to several of Gaskell's assertions, this work is a valuable illustration of the range of problems facing editors. Reviews: Vinton A. Dearing, *Analytical and Enumerative Bibliography* 3 (1979): 105–16; D. F. Foxon, *Review of English Studies* ns 30 (1979): 237–39; Daniel Karlin, *Essays in Criticism* 30 (1980): 71–78; G. Thomas Tanselle, *Library* 6th ser. 2 (1980): 337–50 (essential reading for its exposure of numerous weaknesses in the work).

U5225   Kline, Mary-Jo. *A Guide to Documentary Editing.* 2nd ed. Baltimore: Johns
        Hopkins UP, 1998. 300 pp.   Z113.3.K55   808'.027.

A guide to the principles and practices of editing documents, especially unpublished materials such as letters, journals, diaries, speeches, and ledgers. Following an overview of American documentary and critical editing, chapters proceed more or less in order of the tasks facing an editor: organizing a project, locating, collecting, and organizing materials, and maintaining records; determining the scope and organization of an edition; evaluating and transcribing the source text; deciding on the presentation of the text, with discussions of type facsimiles, diplomatic transcriptions, electronic publication, and inclusive, expanded, and clear texts; using editorial symbols (for interlineations, deletions, and the like, with a helpful list on pp. 148–52 of symbols that have been employed) and writing textual notes; understanding general rules and their exceptions, emending the text, and handling variant forms of a document; dealing with the mechanics of establishing a text; preparing an edition for the printer (including writing annotations, indexing, and drafting a statement of editorial method); and handling relations with the publisher (with attention to electronic publication). Each chapter concludes with a helpful list of suggested readings. An appendix prints sample inquiries addressed to librarians, booksellers, and auction houses. Based on a solid command of editorial theory and extensive familiarity with related scholarship and published editions, this work combines theory and practical advice to produce the best overall guide to documentary editing. The discussion of transcription must be supplemented by David L. Vander Meulen and G. Thomas Tanselle, "A System of Manuscript Transcription," *Studies in Bibliography* 52 (1999): 201–12. Kline is addressed primarily to those working with historical documents, but editors of all kinds will benefit from the sound advice about all aspects of the organization, preparation, and production of an edition. Review: Esther Katz and Ann D. Gordon, *Documentary Editing* 21 (1999): 29–32.

For examples of how editors have handled transcription, presentation, annotation, and indexing, see Michael E. Stevens and Steven B. Burg, *Editing Historical Documents: A Handbook of Practice*, American Association for State and Local History Book Series (Walnut Creek: Alta Mira–Sage, 1997, 264 pp.). While the photographic reproduction of examples of solutions to transcription and presentation problems is quite effective, the agglomeration of fonts and point sizes in the discussion of other topics is disconcerting and constitutes a serious flaw in the design of the book.

Robert Halsband, "Editing the Letters of Letter-Writers," *Studies in Bibliography* 11 (1958): 25–37, remains the best general introduction to the editing of correspondence.

U5230   Shillingsburg, Peter L. *Scholarly Editing in the Computer Age: Theory and Practice.* 3rd ed. Editorial Theory and Literary Criticism. Ann Arbor: U of Michigan P, 1996. 187 pp.   PN162.S45   808'.027.

An introduction to the use of computers in the preparation of scholarly editions. The first part surveys the principles underlying textual criticism in chapters on the concept of textual authority, the forms (or details of presentation) of a text, authorial intention, the "ontological status of literary works," authorial expectations (in relation to editing by a publisher), artistic closure, and the concept of ideal text. The second part discusses the selection of copy-text, emendation, and types and arrangement of apparatus. Using the CASE programs developed for the Thackeray edition as an example, the last part addresses the practical applications of computers to collation, manuscript preparation, typesetting, and electronic editions. Indexed by persons and subjects. *Scholarly Editing* is not a manual, but it does offer substantial practical advice on using a computer to prepare a critical edition. Review: T. H. Howard-Hill, *Analytical and Enumerative Bibliography* ns 2 (1988): 73–77.

U5240   Thorpe, James, *Principles of Textual Criticism.* San Marino: Huntington Lib., 1972. 209 pp.   PR65.T5   801'.959.

A discussion of the importance and imperfection of textual criticism that stresses the need for aesthetic judgment by an editor. Successive chapters draw on a wide range of examples from British and American literature to examine basic principles of textual criticism: the aesthetics of textual criticism (favoring the argument that textual criticism is a system of perfectible details rather than a science); the ideal of textual criticism ("to present the text which the author intended"); the province of textual criticism (especially its relations to bibliography); the basic principles of textual analysis; the treatment of accidentals; and the establishment of the text. Indexed by persons and subjects. Although some of Thorpe's assertions have occasioned disagreement among textual critics, this work is essential reading for those who would edit or use critical editions.

Other important discussions are in the following:

> Bowers, Fredson. *Bibliography and Textual Criticism.* The Lyell Lectures, Oxford, Trinity Term, 1959. Oxford: Clarendon–Oxford UP, 1964. 207 pp. In his argument for the importance of analytical bibliography in textual analysis, Bowers emphasizes the assessment of textual evidence.
>
> Dearing, Vinton A. *Principles and Practice of Textual Analysis.* Berkeley: U of California P, 1974. 243 pp. A highly technical discussion of mathematical methods for determining relations among forms of a text.
>
> McGann, Jerome J. *A Critique of Modern Textual Criticism.* Chicago: U of Chicago P, 1983. 146 pp. McGann argues that many principles of modern textual criticism—especially the emphasis on an author's final intentions—ignore the complex social nature of literary production. An important critique of McGann is David J. Nordloh, "Socialization, Authority, and Evidence: Reflections on McGann's *A Critique of Modern Textual Criticism,*" *Analytical and Enumerative Bibliography* ns 1 (1987): 3–12, with a response by Craig S. Abbott (13–16).
>
> Tanselle, G. Thomas. *A Rationale of Textual Criticism.* Philadelphia: U of Pennsylvania P, 1989. 104 pp. Explores the nature of texts and the distinctions between texts of documents and of works.

See also

> *Guide to Editing Middle English* (M1760).

Book Trade, History of the Book, and Publishing History

Suggestions for research are offered in "Research Opportunities in the Early English Book Trade," *Analytical and Enumerative Bibliography* 3 (1979): 165–200, a special section consisting of three articles on the sixteenth through eighteenth centuries, and in David D. Hall and John B. Hench, eds., *Needs and Opportunities in the History of the Book: America, 1639–1876* (Worcester: Amer. Antiquarian Soc., 1987, 280 pp.), which reprints surveys of research on printing, publishing, distribution, books and popular culture, and bibliography and textual study from *Proceedings of the American Antiquarian Society* 94.2–96.1 (1984–86).

Wallace Kirsop, "Booksellers and Their Customers: Some Reflections on Recent Research," *Book History* 1 (1998): 283–303, surveys the state of research on bookselling (primarily in France and English-speaking countries) and offers suggestions for future work. Mirjam J. Foot does the same for bookbinding in "Bookbinding Research: Pitfalls, Possibilities, and Needs," *Eloquent Witnesses: Bookbindings and Their History*, ed. Foot (London: Bibliog. Soc.; London: British Lib.; New Castle: Oak Knoll, 2004): 13–29.

RESEARCH METHODS

U5241   Finkelstein, David, and Alistair McCleery. *An Introduction to Book History.* New York: Routledge–Taylor and Francis, 2005. 160 pp.   Z4.F49 002'.09.

An introduction to the developing field of book history, with chapters on major theories and debates, the history of writing, continuities between manuscript and print culture, changes in concepts of authorship, cultural agents that affect book production, the reader and reading, and the future of the book. Includes a selective bibliography. Indexed by names, titles, and subjects. Each chapter formulaically states its thesis, maps the evolution of its topic while introducing major or representative scholarship, and summarizes conclusions. Addressed to readers new to the field (many of whom would benefit from more attention to methodology), the work fulfills the promise of its title.

The same cannot be said of Ronald J. Zboray and Mary Saracino Zboray, *A Handbook for the Study of Book History in the United States* (Washington: Center for the Book, Lib. of Congress, 2000, 155 pp.), which offers little in the way of actual guidance on how to go about research in the field. In addition, glaring errors (e.g., the "685 volumes" of the "*National Union Catalog* [i.e., *NUC, Pre-56* (E235)] . . . represent the book, pamphlet, map, atlas, and music holdings in the Library of Congress") and omissions (e.g., *WorldCat* [E225] and RLG Union Catalog [E230]) hardly inspire confidence. Review: Daniel Traister, *Papers of the Bibliographical Society of America* 96 (2002): 310–15.

ARCHIVES

U5242   Albinski, Nan Bowman. "Guide to the Archives of Publishers, Journals, and
        Literary Agents in North American Libraries." *Dictionary of Literary
        Biography Yearbook: 1993* (1994): 202–25.   PS221.D5.

Locates the archives of publishers, journals, and literary agents—primarily from
the United States and Great Britain—held in North American libraries. The list is
updated—albeit telegraphically and without any indication of when the file was last
revised—on the Web site of the Society for the History of Authorship, Reading, and
Publishing (SHARP; http://www.sharpweb.org).

Much of Albinski's information on twentieth-century United States publishers is
subsumed in Martha Brodersen, Beth Luey, Audrey Brichetto Morris, and Rosanne
Trujillo, *A Guide to Book Publishers' Archives* (New York: Book Industry Study Group,
1996, 140 pp.; the updated electronic copy formerly at http://www.bookwire.com/bisg/
archives is no longer available, though a copy may eventually be posted on http://
www.sharpweb.org.). In covering company archives as well as papers of editors, foun-
ders, and others closely associated with the publisher, the authors interpret "book,"
"publisher," "archive," and "United States" inclusively. The approximately 600 publishers are listed alphabetically (with cross-references for alternative names, imprints,
and corporations). A full description includes details about size, years covered, contents,
finding aids, restrictions on use, and location, but since descriptions are based on a
variety of sources, the amount of information varies (with unverified details noted).
Indexed by persons and imprints, but the indexing is not thorough. Review: Barbara
A. Brannon, *Papers of the Bibliographical Society of America* 91 (1997): 249–54.

Archives of many English-language Canadian publishers can be found in the *Canadian Publishers' Records* database (accessible through the list of databases at http://
www.lib.sfu.ca). The search engine is primitive, but this database offers the fullest guide
to archives of Canadian publishers, editors, and organizations.

U5243   Weedon, Alexis, and Michael Bott. *British Book Trade Archives, 1830–
        1939: A Location Register.* History of the Book: On Demand Series 5.
        Bristol: Eliot, 1996. 75 pp. (A revision is in progress for publication on
        http://www.sharpweb.org.)   Z325.W444   381.450020941.

A location register of book trade archives in Britain and Dublin (and a few in the
United States). Entries are organized alphabetically in six sections: publishers and printers, stationers and booksellers, literary agents, professional associations, bookbinders,
and Dublin book trade archives. A typical entry includes the location of the archive,
dates of coverage, references to microforms or catalog entries, cross-references to other
entries, source for the entry, and locations of related material. Indexed by names. Admittedly a preliminary survey, *British Book Trade Archives* nevertheless offers the fullest
guide to the location of archives essential to the history of publishing in Britain.

INDEXES

U5245   *British Book Trade Index* (*BBTI*). U of Birmingham. Online. 3 Feb. 2005
        <http://www.bbti.bham.ac.uk>. Updated regularly.

A database of individuals active by 1851 in the book trade in England and Wales.
Records can be searched through two search screens: the Normal Search Page (any

combination of personal name, date, county, town, trade, or trade descriptor); the Advanced Search Page (the preceding combination of options plus non-book trade descriptors and keywords in the notes to records). Users should read the Important Search Information page (click the Search BBTI button). A typical record includes name, address(es), biographical and trading dates, trade (both book trade and non-book trade occupations), notes, and the source(s) of information. The database is still very much a work in progress (users are invited to contribute or amend data). This work will eventually incorporate (and render more accessible) most of the standard published indexes as well as information from archival materials and private files; however, since external funding ended in March 2005, additions to the database will slow. *Quadrat: A Periodical Bulletin of Research in Progress on the History of the British Book Trade* (1995– ; title varies) provides updates on the project.

The *Scottish Book Trade Index* (which can be downloaded as a series of PDF files from http://www.nls.uk/catalogues/resources/sbti) covers the Scottish book trade to c. 1850. Still very much a work in progress, the index draws from the National Library of Scotland collection as well as city directories and bibliographies of Scottish books.

SURVEYS OF RESEARCH

U5255   Tanselle, G. Thomas. "The Historiography of American Literary
         Publishing." *Studies in Bibliography* 18 (1965): 3–39.   Z1008.V55.
An evaluative survey of scholarship about and sources for the history of literary publishing in the United States. In emphasizing how to reconstruct a list of works by a publisher, Tanselle treats national, regional, and other bibliographies; unpublished papers; reminiscences of publishers; and histories of firms. Authoritative evaluations, practical advice, and numerous suggestions for research make "The Historiography of American Literary Publishing" an essential introduction to a neglected area of scholarship.

HISTORIES

U5258   Feather, John. *A History of British Publishing.* London: Croom Helm, 1988.
         292 pp.   Z325.F414   070.5′0941.
A history from 1476 to the 1980s of the development of publishing in Great Britain that stresses the organizational role of the publisher, the importance of copyright laws, the marketing of books, and censorship. Indexed by subjects. Rather cursory in its treatment of several aspects of publishing, Feather is principally useful as an overview.

A much fuller history will be available in *The Cambridge History of the Book in Britain,* ed. Don McKenzie, David McKitterick, and Ian Willison (Cambridge: Cambridge UP, 1999–):

> Vol. 1: *The Early Middle Ages.* Ed. Michael Lapidge.
> Vol. 2: *The Later Middle Ages.* Ed. Nigel Morgan.
> Vol. 3: *1400–1557.* Ed. Lotte Hellinga and J. B. Trapp. 1999. 743 pp.
> Vol. 4: *1557–1695.* Ed. John Barnard and D. F. M. Mackenzie. 2002. 891
>   pp.
> Vol. 5: *The Eighteenth Century.*

Vol. 6: *The Nineteenth Century.* Ed. Simon Eliot and David McKitterick.
Vol. 7: *The Twentieth Century.* Ed. Ian Willison.

Offers essays by major scholars on all aspects of the book trade, collecting and ownership, audiences, book production, and the use of books. Each volume concludes with
a bibliography; some include statistical appendixes. Variously indexed. Review: (vol. 3)
Alexandra Gillespie, *Notes and Queries* 48 (2001): 11–14.

U5260   Tebbel, John. *A History of Book Publishing in the United States.* 4 vols. New
York: Bowker, 1972–81.   Z473.T42   070.5'0973.

Vol. 1: *The Creation of an Industry, 1630–1865.* 1972. 646 pp.
Vol. 2: *The Expansion of an Industry, 1865–1919.* 1975. 813 pp.
Vol. 3: *The Golden Age between Two Wars, 1920–1940.* 1978. 774 pp.
Vol. 4: *The Great Change, 1940–1980.* 1981. 830 pp.

An extensive history of book publishing from 1630 to 1980, with discussions of
printing, bookselling, economics of the trade, publishers, copyright, bestsellers, illustration, production, censorship, and specialized types of publishing (especially religious,
children's, music, private press, book club, and university press). In some volumes, these
topics are broken down by geographical area. Five appendixes: (in vol. 2) a year-by-year
breakdown by category of American publishing from 1880–1918, tables depicting book
publication, and directory of publishers for 1888, 1900, and 1919; (in vol. 3) an economic overview and a list of bestsellers. Indexed in each volume by persons, places,
titles, subjects, and publishers. More valuable for its accumulation of information than
its interpretation, the *History* presents the fullest account of book publishing in the
United States. It must be used cautiously, however, because of uncritical reliance on
sources and numerous errors. Reviews: (vol. 3) Gordon B. Neavill, *Publishing History*
6 (1979): 107–11; Susan O. Thompson, *Papers of the Bibliographical Society of America*
75 (1981): 230–33.

A less extensive but more scholarly history is Hellmut Lehmann-Haupt, *The Book
in America: A History of the Making and Selling of Books in the United States,* 2nd ed.
(New York: Bowker, 1951, 493 pp.). The first edition— *The Book in America: A History
of the Making, the Selling, and the Collecting of Books in the United States* (1939, 453
pp.)—remains useful for its additional material, especially a history of book collecting
and libraries, by Ruth Shepard Granniss.

Tebbel will eventually be superseded by *A History of the Book in America* (Worcester: Amer. Antiquarian Soc.; Cambridge: Cambridge UP, 2000–):

Vol. 1: *The Colonial Book in the Atlantic World.* Ed. Hugh Amory and David
D. Hall. 2000. 638 pp.
Vol. 2: *An Extensive Republic: Print, Culture, and Society in the New Nation.*
Ed. Robert A. Gross and Mary Kelley.
Vol. 3: *The Industrial Book, 1840–1880.* Ed. Stephen W. Nissenbaum and
Michael Winship.
Vol. 4: *Print in Motion: Books and Reading in the United States, 1880–1945.*
Ed. Carl F. Kaestle and Janice Radway.
Vol. 5: *The Enduring Book, 1945–1995.* Ed. David Paul Nord, Joan Shelley
Rubin, and Michael Schudson.

Each volume is made up of individually authored essays on printing, publishing, bookselling, reading, and literary culture organized chronologically (and, in some cases, re-
gionally); each concludes with a selective bibliography and statistical appendixes.

Guides to Scholarship

SURVEYS OF RESEARCH

U5273   Greetham, D. C., ed. *Scholarly Editing: A Guide to Research.* New York:
         MLA, 1995. 740 pp.   PN162.S24   808'.027.
    A collection of surveys of the state of textual criticism in several literatures, classical
to modern. Following an initial chapter on the varieties of scholarly editing, individual
treatment is accorded the Hebrew Bible, the Greek New Testament, Greek literature
(classical to the Renaissance), classical Latin literature, Old English literature, Middle
English literature, Renaissance nondramatic literature, non-Shakespearean Renaissance
drama, Shakespeare, eighteenth-century British literature, nineteenth-century British
poetry and prose, nineteenth-century British fiction, colonial and nineteenth-century
American literature, twentieth-century British and American literature, Old French literature, early modern French literature, Italian literature, Medieval Spanish literature,
German literature, Russian literature, Arabic literature, Sanskrit literature, and folk
literature. The chapters—by major scholars in the fields—typically survey the editorial
tradition, consider theoretical and practical problems peculiar to the literature or period,
comment on major editions, and conclude with a bibliography. Two indexes: subjects;
names and titles. *Scholarly Editing* admirably fulfills its intent of providing the neophyte
with an authoritative introduction to the state of scholarly editing within a national
literature or period.

SERIAL BIBLIOGRAPHIES

G. Thomas Tanselle, "The Periodical Literature of English and American Bibliography,"
Studies in Bibliography 26 (1973): 167–91, identifies where English-language bibliographical journals are indexed. Tanselle's survey is complemented by B. J. McMullin,
"Indexing the Periodical Literature of Anglo-American Bibliography," *Studies in Bibliography* 33 (1980): 1–17, an evaluation of the indexing of bibliographical scholarship
in the 1974 volumes of *ABHB: Annual Bibliography of the History of the Printed Book*
(U5275), *Bibliographic Index* (D145), *British Humanities Index* (G370), *Essay and General Literature Index* (G380), *Humanities Index* (G385), *Internationale Bibliographie der
geistes- und sozialwissenschaftlichen Zeitschriftenliteratur* (G390), *Library Literature*,
ABELL (G340), and *MLAIB* (G335). McMullin's conclusion that *ABELL* is "the most
satisfactory index to Anglo-American bibliography" must be modified because of the
introduction of subject indexing with the *MLAIB* for 1981. However, there is still no
serial bibliography that thoroughly covers bibliographical scholarship.
    For an evaluation of the indexing of studies in the history of the book, see John
Van Hook, "The Indexes to Current Work on the History of the Book: A Review
Article," *Analytical and Enumerative Bibliography* ns 6 (1992): 10–19.

U5275   *ABHB: Annual Bibliography of the History of the Printed Book and Libraries:
         [1970–] (ABHB).* Dordrecht: Kluwer, 1973– . Annual.   Z117.A55
         016.00155'2.

Book History Online. Koninklijke Bibliotheek. Online. 18 June 2005 <http://www.kb.nl/bho/index.html>. Updated regularly.

A bibliography of scholarship (including dissertations and reviews) on the history of the printed book since the fifteenth century and the arts, crafts, and techniques involved in its production, distribution, and description throughout the world. *ABHB* excludes discussions of manuscripts before the invention of printing and modern technical processes, as well as most textual studies. Entries are organized in 12 divisions: general; paper, inks, printing materials; calligraphy, type design, type founding; layout, composition, printing, presses; illustration; binding; book trade and publishing; book collecting; libraries and librarianship; legal, economic, and social aspects of book history; newspapers, periodicals, and journalism; other subjects. Except for the last—which is organized by Dewey Decimal Classification—each division has sections for general studies and countries, with the latter subdivided by century and then persons, places, or subjects, depending on the topic of the division. Two indexes: scholars and anonymous titles; geographical and personal names discussed. Cumulative index: vols. 1–17, *Cumulated Subject Index,* ed. Hendrik D. L. Vervliet, vol. 17a (1989): 209 pp. Records since 1989 (including those from volumes of *ABHB* in preparation) can be searched by author, title, keyword, country, and date through *Book History Online.* Since the site does not provide a way to mark records for export, users must rely on their Web browser to print or save screens one at a time. *ABHB* is sometimes far behind in coverage (with volumes typically including several retrospective entries), inconsistent in indexing journals ostensibly scanned on a regular basis, and frequently inaccurate in transcription and classification (though its accuracy in both areas has improved in recent volumes). With the demise of *Bibliographie der Buch- und Bibliotheksgeschichte* (U5280), *ABHB* is the only reasonably complete and current bibliography of international scholarship on the history of the printed book; unfortunately, it does not adequately fill the need for a thorough, trustworthy bibliography of the topic. For a detailed evaluation of *ABHB,* see B. J. McMullin, "Indexing the Periodical Literature of Anglo-American Bibliography," *Studies in Bibliography* 33 (1980): 1–17.

Selected studies before 1970 are listed in these works:

> Myers, Robin. *The British Book Trade from Caxton to the Present Day: A Bibliographical Guide Based on the Libraries of the National Book League and St. Bride Institute.* London: Deutsch, 1973. 405 pp. Although this work is a highly selective and sometimes idiosyncratic list of English-language books, it is far superior to Paul A. Winckler, *History of Books and Printing: A Guide to Information Sources,* Books, Publishing, and Libraries Information Guide Series 2 (Detroit: Gale, 1979, 209 pp.), which omits too many significant works and is replete with errors.
>
> "A Selective Check List of Bibliographical Scholarship for [1949–72]." *Studies in Bibliography* 3–27 (1950–74). A list of works on printing and publishing history, bibliography, and textual criticism, with an emphasis on Western literature, especially English and American. Although selective, it is the best general bibliography of pre-1970 scholarship. The bibliographies for 1949 through 1955 are reprinted with corrections and a cumulative index as vol. 10 (1957); those for 1956 through 1962 are reprinted with a cumulative index as *Selective Check Lists of Bibliographical Scholarship, Series B, 1956–1962,* ed. Howell J. Heaney and Rudolf Hirsch (Charlottesville: UP of Virginia for Bibliog. Soc. of the U of Virginia, 1966, 247 pp.).

Additional reviews are listed in *Index to Reviews of Bibliographical Publications: An International Annual [1976–85]* (Troy: Whitston, 1977–91; vol. 1 was also published as *Analytical and Enumerative Bibliography* 1.4 [1977]), an index of reviews (published in 300 to 400 journals) of general bibliographical books and articles; studies of the book trade and printing history and of bibliographies, editions, concordances; and manuscript studies of English and American literature.

U5280   *Bibliographie der Buch- und Bibliotheksgeschichte [1980–2003]* (*BBB*). Bad Iburg: Meyer, 1982–2004. Annual.   Z4.B54   016.002.

A bibliography of books, articles, and reviews on bibliography and the history of the book and libraries. Although originally limited to scholarship on German-speaking countries, coverage was international at its demise. Entries are organized in eight variously classified divisions: general studies (including sections for bibliographies of bibliographies, national bibliographies, and analytical and descriptive bibliography); individual authors; book production (including sections for handwriting and typography, composition, printing, paper, illustration, and binding); types of printed works (including children's books, periodicals, newspapers, and ephemera); bookselling, publishing, book collecting, libraries, and bookplates; readers and reading; curiosa; and reviews. Five indexes: scholars; reviewers; persons as subjects; places; subjects. Although it overlaps considerably with *ABHB: Annual Bibliography of the History of the Printed Book* (U5275), *BBB* was somewhat more current and accurate (however, like *ABHB*, it contains numerous errors, misclassifications, and omissions). The two should be used together. Reviews: B. J. McMullin, *Papers of the Bibliographical Society of America* 79 (1985): 260–62; 80 (1986): 263–65; 81 (1987): 81–82.

See also

Secs. G: Serial Bibliographies, Indexes, and Abstracts and H: Guides to Dissertations and Theses.

ABELL (G340): Bibliography division.

MLAIB (G335): See the Bibliographical heading in the General division in volumes for 1935–52; General III: Bibliographical in the volumes for 1953–55; General IX: Bibliographical in the volumes for 1956–66; General VI: Bibliographical in the volumes for 1967–69; General V: Bibliographical in the volumes for 1970–80; and the Bibliographical division in pt. 4 of the later volumes. Researchers must also consult the headings beginning "Analytical Bibliography," "Bibliographical," "Bibliography" "Textual," "Print," "Printed," "Printer's," "Printing," and "Publishing" in the subject index to post-1980 volumes or in the online thesaurus.

YWES (G330): Chapter on Reference, Literary History, and Bibliography since vol. 66 (for 1985).

OTHER BIBLIOGRAPHIES

U5283   Baker, William, and Kenneth Womack, comps. *Twentieth-Century Bibliography and Textual Criticism: An Annotated Bibliography.* Bibliographies and Indexes in Library and Information Science 13. Westport: Greenwood, 2000. 262 pp.   Z1002.B28   016.011.

A selective, annotated bibliography of twentieth-century English-language studies (published through 1998) relating to Anglo-American bibliography and textual studies. The 769 entries are organized alphabetically by author under six divisions: general bibliographical or textual studies; analytical bibliography; descriptive bibliography; textual criticism; historical bibliography; and enumerative bibliography. The annotations are descriptive, though the ones for collections of essays simply list authors and titles; most users would benefit from more attention to how a particular work fits into developments in editorial theory, bibliographical concepts (such as copy-text), and textual issues (e.g., authorial intention). Selection is generally judicious, except in the enumerative bibliography division, which includes an unsystematic sprinkling of enumerative bibliographies among works about the subject. Three indexes: authors; titles; subjects (which offers the best access to works about a topic). Although the lack of a list of journal acronyms will prevent some users from locating articles, *Twentieth-Century Bibliography and Textual Criticism* provides a much-needed guide to the theory and method of bibliography and textual criticism.

The fullest lists of publications on bibliography and textual criticism are G. Thomas Tanselle, *Introduction to Scholarly Editing: Seminar Syllabus*, 18th rev. (Charlottesville: Book Arts, 2002, 257 pp.) and *Introduction to Bibliography: Seminar Syllabus*, 19th rev. (2002, 370 pp.). Neither is widely held, however.

U5285   *Index to Selected Bibliographical Journals, 1933–1970.* London: Bibliog.
      Soc., 1982. 316 pp.   Z1002.I573   016.002.

      Barr, Bernard. "The Bibliographical Society: *Index to Selected Bibliographical Journals* (Addenda)." *Library* 6th ser. 9 (1987): 44–52.

      Feather, John. *An Index to Selected Bibliographical Journals, 1971–1985.* Occasional Publication 23. Oxford: Oxford Bibliog. Soc., 1991. 134 pp. Z1002.I5732   016.002.

An author and subject index to signed articles, notes, and some letters—but not reviews—published for the most part from 1933 through 1969 in 11 major bibliographical journals, with coverage for 6 continued for 1971–85 in Feather's supplement. Under each author or subject, *1933–1970* lists entries alphabetically by journal, then chronologically by publication date; Feather lists entries alphabetically by title under author heads, by author under subject heads. Because *1933–1970* is derived from a Bodleian Library card index that was compiled over several years by various persons, there are numerous errors in transcriptions, oversights (e.g., an entire volume of *Library* was omitted, although it is indexed in Barr's addenda), and inconsistencies in subject headings. Subject indexing is frequently superficial or inaccurate because of the reliance on title keywords. Feather offers superior subject indexing but unaccountably fails to continue coverage of *Studies in Bibliography* and *Papers of the Bibliographical Society of America*—two of the most important bibliographical journals—or to replace journals no longer published with *AEB: Analytical and Enumerative Bibliography* or *TEXT: An Interdisciplinary Annual of Textual Studies*. The general untrustworthiness of *1933–1970*, the failure to index volumes published in 1970, and the unacceptable reduction in coverage offered by *1971–1985* underscore Feather's prefatory remark that "bibliography has not been well served by indexers." Indeed, it is unfortunate to have to say that *1933–1970*, Barr's addenda, and Feather constitute the single best index to this body of publications. They must, however, be supplemented by the serial bibliographies in section U: Literature-Related Topics and Sources/Bibliography and Textual Criticism/ Guides to Scholarship/Serial Bibliographies. Review: (*1933–1970*) B. J. McMullin,

Papers of the Bibliographical Society of America 78 (1984): 57–67. A major desideratum remains a full and accurate index to bibliographical publications.

U5288   Luey, Beth. *Editing Documents and Texts: An Annotated Bibliography.*
         Madison: Madison House, 1990. 289 pp.   Z5165.L83 [PN162]
         016.808′027.
    A highly selective bibliography of English-language publications (through 1988) on the editing of postclassical historical documents and literary texts. Although prefatory matter to editions is excluded, some reviews of editions are listed. The approximately 900 entries are organized in a single alphabetical author list. Each entry consists of the citation, a list of keywords that serve as headings in the subject index, and a brief descriptive annotation. There is a list of mystery novels in which documents, manuscripts, or editors figure prominently. Indexed by subject. Several entries are for inconsequential or outdated discussions, there are some significant omissions, most annotations are too brief or general to convey an adequate sense of a work's content or place in the controversy over a topic or the development of scholarly editing, readers would benefit from more cross-references, and through-numbering would allow for easier location of entries; yet Luey serves as a convenient preliminary guide to the basic works on the theory and practice of textual editing. The prefatory "Suggestions for Teaching" offers useful advice for those preparing a course in editing. Review: Mary Ann O'Donnell, *Analytical and Enumerative Bibliography* ns 4 (1990): 134–37.

U5290   Tanselle, G. Thomas. *Guide to the Study of United States Imprints.* 2 vols.
         Cambridge: Belknap–Harvard UP, 1971.   Z1215.A2 T35   016.015′73.
    A bibliography of published research through 1969 on printing and publishing in the United States. Entries are organized geographically and then chronologically by date of coverage or publication in most of the nine divisions: regional lists; genre lists (by type, form, or subject); author lists (limited essentially to descriptive bibliographies or lists of editions); published copyright records; important or representative auction, booksellers', exhibition, and library catalogs; retrospective book trade directories; studies of individual printers and publishers; general studies; checklists of secondary material. Some entries cite selected reviews. An appendix lists 250 essential works on printing and publishing in the United States. Indexed by persons, publishers, and subjects. Users must be certain to read the introduction, which clearly outlines the scope and organization of each division, cites additional sources, and offers valuable advice on the uses of each type of work listed and on research procedures. Tanselle, while not comprehensive, nonetheless offers the fullest list of published research through 1969 on printing and publishing in the country and is an important source for locating reference works that will identify a particular printed book. For studies published after 1969, consult *ABHB: Annual Bibliography of the History of the Printed Book* (U5275). Review: Hensley C. Woodbridge, *Papers of the Bibliographical Society of America* 67 (1973): 351–56.

See also

   Howard-Hill, *Index to British Literary Bibliography* (M1355).
   Leary, *Articles on American Literature* (Q3295).
   New Cambridge Bibliography of English Literature (M1385).
   Woodress, *Dissertations in American Literature, 1891–1966* (Q3320).

Book Collecting

The preceding section, Bibliography and Textual Criticism, includes many works closely allied to book collecting.

Scholars needing to consult materials in private collections will benefit from the advice in Gordon N. Ray, "The Private Collector and the Literary Scholar," *The Private Collector and the Support of Scholarship: Papers Read at a Clark Library Seminar, April 5, 1969*, by Louis B. Wright and Ray (Los Angeles: William Andrews Clark Memorial Lib., 1969) 25–84, and conveniently reprinted in Ray, *Books as a Way of Life*, ed. G. Thomas Tanselle (New York: Grolier Club and Pierpont Morgan Lib., 1988) 233–77.

Research Methods

U5330   Pearson, David. *Provenance Research in Book History.* Rpt. with new introd. British Library Studies in the History of the Book. London: British Lib.; New Castle: Oak Knoll, 1998. 326 pp.   Z994.G7 P43   002.0941.

A guide to identifying ownership marks—including signatures, mottoes, bookplates, armorial binding stamps, and other marks in books—and to tracing the location, at some point in time, of a book owned by an individual or institution. Although the focus is on books from the fifteenth through the nineteenth century in British collections, works related to foreign provenance are also recorded. Following an overview of problems involved in establishing provenance, devotes chapters to identifying inscriptions, mottoes, and other manuscript marks (including booksellers' codes); bookplates, labels, and bookstamps; armorial and other bindings; auction catalogs; booksellers' catalogs; private library catalogs; provenance indexes (published and unpublished); and works on heraldry, paleography, biography, book collecting, and library history useful in provenance research. Most chapters include helpful illustrations and annotated bibliographies (the introduction to the 1998 reprint cites additional sources). A wonderfully practical handbook, *Provenance Research* is the essential starting point for anyone interested in identifying ownership marks in a book or a volume from the library of an individual or institution in Britain. A similar guide is needed for North America. Review: Nigel Ramsay, *Library* 6th ser. 19 (1997): 73–75.

Handbooks, Dictionaries, and Encyclopedias

U5340   Carter, John, and Nicolas Barker. *ABC for Book Collectors.* 8th ed. New Castle: Oak Knoll; London: British Lib., 2004. 232 pp.   Z1006.C37 002'.075.

A dictionary of terms used by book collectors and the antiquarian book trade in Great Britain and the United States. Carter excludes foreign-language terms except for those in common use or without an English equivalent. The sometimes detailed entries, based on Carter's years of experience as collector and member of the trade and on Barker's experience as editor of *Book Collector*, offer clear definitions (frequently leavened with wit) and make effective use of the book itself for illustrating some terms.

Instructive and entertaining, *ABC for Book Collectors* is the essential companion for collectors or occasional readers of auction and booksellers' catalogs.

For foreign-language terms, see Menno Hertzberger, ed., *Dictionnaire à l'usage de la librairie ancienne pour les langues française, anglaise, allemande, suédoise, danoise, italienne, espagnole, hollandaise, japonaise/Dictionary for the Antiquarian Booktrade in French, English, German, Swedish, Danish, Italian, Spanish, Dutch, and Japanese* ([Paris?]: Int. League of Antiquarian Booksellers, 1978, 202 pp.).

U5345   Zempel, Edward N., and Linda A. Verkler, eds. *First Editions: A Guide to Identification: Statements of Selected North American, British Commonwealth, and Irish Publishers on Their Methods of Designating First Editions.* 4th ed. Peoria: Spoon River, 2001. 669 pp.   Z1033.F53 F57   016.094'4.

A guide to the phrases, devices, symbols, and other marks used by about 4,200 American, British, and Irish publishers to designate a first printing or impression. Organized alphabetically by firm, entries consist of publishers' statements outlining practices through 2000 or 2001. A section on book club editions concludes the work. Although incomplete and not always accurate, Zempel is the best guide to identifying a first printing or impression.

Henry S. Boutell, *First Editions of Today and How to Tell Them: American, British, and Irish*, 4th ed., rev. and enl. by Wanda Underhill (Berkeley: Peacock, 1965, 227 pp.), remains an important complement for practices between 1947 and 1964. Statements from earlier editions no longer protected by copyright are reprinted in Zempel.

See also

Sec. U: Literature-Related Topics and Sources/Bibliography and Textual Criticism/Handbooks, Dictionaries, and Encyclopedias.

General Introductions

U5350   Carter, John. *Taste and Technique in Book Collecting.* Rpt. with additions. London: Private Libraries Assn., 1970. 242 pp.   Z987.C35   020'.75'08.

A study of the relationship between taste and technique in book collecting. Following a prefatory definition of *book collector*, chapters (replete with examples) are divided between two parts: the evolution of book collecting from 1812 to the early 1900s in Great Britain and the United States; a discussion of method, including the education of a collector, tools and terminology, bookstores and auction rooms, the concept of rarity, and the importance of condition. The 1970 reprint has corrections and notes on pp. 203–05, and an epilogue covering 1928–69 (pp. 209–42). Because *Taste and Technique* presumes a familiarity with the terminology of bibliography and book collecting, the beginning collector should have a copy of Carter, *ABC for Book Collectors* (U5340), in hand. Although not a manual, *Taste and Technique* remains the classic introduction to book collecting.

Among the numerous manuals, the best complements to Carter are the following:

Peters, Jean, ed. *Book Collecting: A Modern Guide.* New York: Bowker, 1977. 288 pp. A collection of essays on buying from dealers and auctions; the antiquarian book market; manuscript collecting; descriptive bibliography; fakes, forgeries, and facsimiles; the physical care of books and manuscripts;

organizing a collection; appraisal; the book collector and the world of scholarship; and the literature of book collecting (for the last, see entry U5355).

———, ed. *Collectible Books: Some New Paths.* New York: Bowker, 1979. 294 pp. A series of essays that describe unexplored and nontraditional areas for collecting.

Rees-Mogg, William. *How to Buy Rare Books: A Practical Guide to the Antiquarian Book Market.* Christie's Collectors Guides. Oxford: Phaidon, 1985. 159 pp. A practical guide for the beginning collector; topics include catalogs, relations with dealers, tastes and trends in collecting (with emphasis on the traditional subjects and expensive books), the physical makeup of a book, and care and conservation.

Winterich, John T., and David A. Randall. *A Primer of Book Collecting.* 3rd rev. ed. New York: Crown, 1966. 228 pp. Emphasizes the fundamentals of collecting, with discussions of kinds of collectible books, rarity, condition, the mechanics of collecting, bibliographical points, and reference works.

Beginning collectors should be especially wary of the numerous publications that stress book collecting as an investment. None of these works is adequate as a guide to either collecting or investing.

The best introduction to the related field of manuscript collecting remains Charles Hamilton, *Collecting Autographs and Manuscripts* (Santa Monica: Modoc, 1993, 425 pp.). Among the extensively illustrated chapters are discussions of building a collection, making finds, detecting forgeries, and collecting various kinds of materials, including literary manuscripts. Although it is addressed to the beginning collector and emphasizes American manuscripts, Hamilton is an entertaining and instructive introduction by one of the foremost dealers. Also useful is Mary A. Benjamin, *Autographs: A Key to Collecting*, corrected and rev. ed. (New York: Benjamin, 1963, 313 pp.).

Guides to Scholarship

U5355   Tanselle, G. Thomas. "The Literature of Book Collecting." *Book Collecting: A Modern Guide* (entry U5350a). Ed. Jean Peters. New York: Bowker, 1977. 209–71.   Z987.B68   020'.75.

An evaluative survey of general introductions and manuals; glossaries; histories of printing and allied trades; histories of collecting and bookselling; guides to and studies of collectors; periodicals; bibliographies; auction, booksellers', exhibition, and library catalogs; guides to prices; directories of dealers and collectors; works on conservation, bookplates, and manuscripts; and guides to further reading. Unfortunately, many of the authors and works cited are excluded from the index to the volume. Judicious selection and authoritative evaluation make Tanselle's survey the best guide to works about or essential in book collecting. An important complement is Tanselle's essay review of six book-collecting manuals in *Papers of the Bibliographical Society of America* 72 (1978): 265–81.

See also

ABELL (G340): Bibliography division in volumes for 1920–33; Bibliography/ Book Production, Selling, Collecting, Librarianship, the Newspaper (with var-

iations in the title) in the volumes for 1934–72; Bibliography/Booksellers',
Exhibition, and Sale Catalogues in the volumes for 1973–84; and Bibliogra-
phy/Collecting and the Library in the volumes for 1973–present.

ABHB: Annual Bibliography of the History of the Printed Book (U5275).

Bibliographie der Buch- und Bibliotheksgeschichte (U5280).

MLAIB (G335): In volumes before 1981, studies of collecting and collectors are
sometimes listed with bibliographical scholarship (see p. 627 for an outline of
that section). In volumes after 1980, researchers must consult the "Book Collecting," "Book Collection," "Book Collectors," and "Collection Study" headings in the subject index and in the online thesaurus.

Directories of Book Dealers

Individuals searching for a specific book should log on to http://used.addall.com or
http://www.bookfinder.com, which search the major Internet bookseller sites, or to
http://www.ilab-lila.com, which searches the inventory of members of the International
League of Antiquarian Booksellers.

For early dealers in the United States, see Madeleine B. Stern, *Antiquarian Bookselling in the United States: A History from the Origins to the 1940s* (Westport: Greenwood, 1985, 246 pp.), which concludes with a brief survey of primary sources and
scholarship.

U5360   *American Book Trade Directory.* Medford: Information Today, 1915– .
         Biennial.   Z475.A5   655.473.

A directory of the retail and wholesale book trade in the United States and its
territories and in Canada. Of most interest to literary scholars is the division listing
retail and antiquarian booksellers. Organized alphabetically by state (with United States
territories and Canadian provinces following the list of states), city, then store or bookseller, entries note kind of store, address, telephone and fax numbers, e-mail address,
Web site, name of owner, number of volumes in stock, subject specializations, and
services (such as searching for specific titles). Other divisions list auctioneers, appraisers,
and dealers in foreign-language books. Two indexes: types of stores; dealers. Although
American Book Trade Directory offers the fullest list of United States and Canadian
antiquarian booksellers, inadequate indexing makes it nearly impossible to identify
stores specializing in an author, period, or subject.

Members of the International League of Antiquarian Booksellers can be identified
by specialization at the league's Web site (http://www.ilab-lila.com).

U5365   *Sheppard's Book Dealers in the British Isles: A Directory of Antiquarian and
         Secondhand Book Dealers in the United Kingdom, the Channel Islands, the Isle
         of Man, and the Republic of Ireland.* Torrington: Joseph, 1952– . Irregular.
         Z327.D57   070.5'025'41.

         *Sheppard's Book Dealers in North America: A Directory of Antiquarian and
         Secondhand Book Dealers in the U.S.A. and Canada.* Farnham: Joseph,
         1954– . Irregular.   Z475.B63.

         Sheppard's Book Dealers in Europe. Farnham: Joseph, 1967– . Irregular.
         (Title varies.)   Z291.5.E96.

Sheppard's Book Dealers in Australia and New Zealand: A Directory of Antiquarian and Secondhand Book Dealers in Australia, New Zealand, and Parts of the Pacific. Farnham: Joseph, 1991– . Irregular.   Z533.4.S48 381'.45002'02594.

Geographical directories of bookstores and private dealers. A typical entry includes name of business, address, proprietor, Web site, e-mail address, telephone and fax numbers, hours, a very general indication of size and nature of stock, specializations, and number of catalogs issued each year. Among the indexes are ones for business names, proprietors, and subject specializations. Although the subject specialization headings are too broad, these are important guides to book dealers, especially the smaller shops and private dealers.

Biographical Dictionaries of Collectors

U5370   Dickinson, Donald C. *Dictionary of American Book Collectors.* New York: Greenwood, 1986. 383 pp.   Z989.A1 D53   002'.075'0922.

A biographical dictionary of 359 American book collectors who died before 31 December 1984 and whose collections were "distinguished by the quality, unity, . . . superior physical condition," and intrinsic importance of the books. An entry notes the disposition of the collection by auction or by sale or gift to an institution; provides basic biographical information; comments on the collector's major interests, the development and influence of the collection, and noteworthy items; and concludes with a selective bibliography of catalogs and studies of the collection as well as works by or about the collector. Two appendixes: a list of collectors by areas of specialization; a chronological list of important American book auctions from 1860 through 1984. Indexed by persons, titles, and subjects; entrants are also indexed in *Biography and Genealogy Master Index* (J565). As the most complete biographical dictionary of important American collectors, Dickinson is a valuable source for tracing the disposition of a collection and thus locating individual copies. Review: Madeleine B. Stern, *American Book Collector* ns 7.9 (1986): 39–41.

Carl L. Cannon, *American Book Collectors and Collecting from Colonial Times to the Present* (New York: Wilson, 1941, 391 pp.), treats additional collectors, but the topical organization and essay format make it difficult to locate information on minor collectors. Some collectors are profiled in two collections edited by Joseph Rosenblum: *American Book-Collectors and Bibliographers: First Series,* Dictionary of Literary Biography 140 (Detroit: Gale, 1994, 408 pp.) and *American Book Collectors and Bibliographers: Second Series,* Dictionary of Literary Biography 187 (Detroit: Gale, 1997, 431 pp.).

U5375   Quaritch, Bernard, ed. *Contributions towards a Dictionary of English Book-Collectors: As Also of Some Foreign Collectors Whose Libraries Were Incorporated in English Collections or Whose Books Are Chiefly Met with in England.* 14 pts. London: Quaritch, 1892–1921.   Z989.Q1   020'.75.

A collection of separately authored profiles of 78 collectors from the thirteenth through nineteenth centuries. The individual entries, which appear in no particular order, typically consist of two parts: (1) a biography of the collector and discussion of the nature, highlights, and dispersal of the collection; (2) a list of important manuscripts and printed works, a few of which record current owners. Many of the entries, which vary considerably in informativeness and length, were written by dealers involved in the formation of the collection or individuals acquainted with the collector. Part 12 is a preliminary list of several hundred collectors from 1316 to 1898. Quaritch remains the most comprehensive guide to English book collectors and is still valuable for tracing the provenance of important items. Additional collectors are treated in Seymour de Ricci, *English Collectors of Books and Manuscripts (1530–1930) and Their Marks of Ownership* (New York: Macmillan; Cambridge: Cambridge UP, 1930, 203 pp.) and in three collections edited by William Baker and Kenneth Womack: *Nineteenth-Century British Book Collectors and Bibliographers*, Dictionary of Literary Biography 184 (Detroit: Gale, 1997, 531 pp.), *Pre-Nineteenth-Century British Book Collectors and Bibliographers*, Dictionary of Literary Biography 213 (1999, 487 pp.), and *Twentieth-Century British Book Collectors and Bibliographers*, Dictionary of Literary Biography 201 (1999, 393 pp.). The time is ripe, however, for a dictionary of British book collectors similar to Dickinson, *Dictionary of American Book Collectors* (U5370).

See also

> Lehmann-Haupt, *Book in America* (U5260a).
> Tanselle, "The Literature of Book Collecting" (U5355), lists additional directories (pp. 266–67).

Booksellers' and Auction Catalogs

Booksellers' and auction catalogs are among the most underutilized scholarly resources. Although they are frequently difficult to locate (even in libraries that hold major collections) and (in the case of booksellers' catalogs) are rarely indexed, these catalogs are valuable for identifying hitherto unrecorded printed works, editions, or manuscripts; finding descriptions (and sometimes reproductions or transcriptions) of unique items no longer locatable; tracing the provenance of a copy (and thus possibly locating it); and reconstructing an individual's library.

For a discussion of the importance of auction catalogs and the pitfalls involved in using them, see Michael Hunter, "Auction Catalogues and Eminent Libraries," *Book Collector* 21 (1972): 471–88. On the use of catalogs and other resources for tracing provenance, see Robert Nikirk, "Looking into Provenance," *A Miscellany for Bibliophiles*, ed. H. George Fletcher (New York: Grastorf, 1979) 15–45; and Pearson, *Provenance Research* (U5330), with advice on identifying and locating auction and booksellers' catalogs. Of major value would be a series of indexes to manuscript material and association copies in catalogs issued by at least the major booksellers.

HISTORIES AND SURVEYS

U5395   Taylor, Archer. *Book Catalogues: Their Varieties and Uses.* 2nd ed. Rev. by
        Wm. P. Barlow, Jr. New York: Beil, 1987. 284 pp.   Z1001.T34   011'.3.
        An examination of the types, history, and uses of catalogs of booksellers, auction houses, private collections, institutions, and publishers. Taylor emphasizes catalogs published before 1900 of printed books, and for the most part excludes unpublished catalogs and those of manuscripts. The revised edition reprints the first edition (Chicago: Newberry Lib., 1957, 284 pp.), with a prefatory list of corrections and additions that

unfortunately does not incorporate scholarship since the mid-1950s. The first chapter describes the kinds of catalogs—especially their varieties and historical development—and surveys bibliographies based on them; the second details the uses of catalogs in scholarly research; the third surveys bibliographies of catalogs, emphasizing their uses and historical development; the last chapter prints an annotated list of important private library catalogs published before 1824. Four indexes: dealers, institutions, owners, and publishers; kinds of books and subjects listed in catalogs; subjects treated in catalogs and compilations based on them; compilers, editors, collectors, and bibliographers of catalogs. Although now dated, Taylor remains important as a general history of early catalogs, an account of individual ones, and a guide to their uses in research.

GUIDES TO PRIMARY WORKS

Bibliographies

U5400   McKay, George L., comp. *American Book Auction Catalogues, 1713–1934: A Union List.* Rpt. with supplements. Detroit: Gale, 1967. 560 pp. Z999.M15   018.3.

A chronological list of about 10,000 book auction catalogs (including some miscellaneous catalogs having more than five pages of books) issued in the United States from 1713 through 1934. Organized chronologically by opening date of sale, entries cite (when known) date, owner(s), auction firm, number of pages and lots, and locations of copies (noting priced or marked ones) or source of information for those unlocated. Many entries for eighteenth-century catalogs are based on newspaper advertisements or other sources, and a sizable number probably are for manuscript inventories. A separate grouping of auctions listed in newspaper advertisements that do not specify issuance of a catalog appears on pp. 461–91; additions and corrections to the main list are printed on pp. 493–95; the two supplements from *Bulletin of the New York Public Library* (50 [1946]: 177–84; 52 [1948]: 401–12) are reprinted after the index. An introduction, by Clarence S. Bingham, is entitled "History of Book Auctions in America" (pp. 1–37). Indexed by owners. Despite flaws—the work is incomplete, records a limited number of locations, and offers no indication of contents—it does provide the fullest list of United States auction catalogs from 1801 through 1934. Earlier catalogs are more thoroughly and accurately described by Winans, *Descriptive Checklist of Book Catalogues Separately Printed in America* (U5410).

U5405   Munby, A. N. L., and Lenore Coral, comps. and eds. *British Book Sale Catalogues, 1676–1800: A Union List.* London: Mansell, 1977. 146 pp. (*1801–1900* is in progress.)   Z999.5.M86   011.

A union list of extant auction catalogs and some retail lists with prices fixed by a dealer. Munby excludes catalogs of sales open to only members of the book trade. Catalogs are listed chronologically by date of commencement of the sale; those not datable by at least the month are grouped alphabetically by consignor or title at the end of a year. A typical entry provides consignor, short title, details of the conduct of the sale if not an auction, auctioneer or bookseller, location of the sale, locations of copies (including some shelf numbers) in about ninety public and private collections in the United States and Great Britain, references to other bibliographies, and information about reprints. Two indexes: consignors; auctioneers and booksellers. On the history and progress of the work see Coral, "Towards the Bibliography of British Book Auction Catalogues, 1801–1900," *Papers of the Bibliographical Society of America* 89 (1995): 419–25. The most thorough list of extant auction catalogs of the period, Munby is invaluable for identifying a catalog of the library of an individual and for locating copies (which are not only scarce but also difficult to identify in most library catalogs). Review: R. J. Roberts, *Library* 5th ser. 33 (1978): 336–38 (with additions and corrections).

Until the volume for 1801–1900 of *British Book Sale Catalogues* appears, *List of Catalogues of English Book Sales, 1676–1900, Now in the British Museum* (London: British Museum, 1915, 523 pp.) offers the most complete list of nineteenth-century auction catalogs. (According to Pearson, *Provenance Research* [U5330], Munby's marked copy of the British Museum list is in Cambridge University Library, with photocopies held by the British Library and the Bodleian Library [p. 140].) Although these publications are easier to identify in the online *British Library Integrated Catalogue* (E250) than in the British Library *General Catalogue of Printed Books* (see E250), *List of Catalogues* remains an important source of shelf numbers for the extensive collection, which includes several auctioneers' priced sets.

U5410   Winans, Robert B. *A Descriptive Checklist of Book Catalogues Separately Printed in America, 1693–1800.* Worcester: Amer. Antiquarian Soc., 1981. 207 pp.   Z1029.W56   018.

A chronological list of 689 separately published booksellers', publishers', and auction catalogs and circulating, private, social, and college library catalogs. The catalogs are listed by year of publication, then alphabetically by author, auctioneer, bookseller, or title of anonymous work. The 278 located catalogs have full entries that include author; title; publication information; collation; pagination; list of contents; notes on the type of catalog, number and kind of entries, organization, and other matters, including the presence of prices and the basis for dating undated publications; references to other bibliographies and scholarship; reprints; and locations of copies (primarily in East Coast libraries). Entries for unlocated items are, of course, much briefer, and cite references in other sources; entries for what are probably manuscript inventories listed in McKay, *American Book Auction Catalogues* (U5400), merely cite McKay. Thoroughly indexed by authors, owners, printers, cities, and subjects. Complemented by Winans, "The Beginnings of Systematic Bibliography in America up to 1800: Further Explorations," *Papers of the Bibliographical Society of America* 72 (1978): 15–35. Admirably thorough and accurate in its bibliographical descriptions but insufficiently informative in notes on contents, Winans supersedes McKay, *American Book Auction Catalogues*, for auction catalogs before 1801 and is an invaluable source for identifying and locating catalogs essential in bibliographical research, book trade history, and cultural studies. Review: Stephen Botein, *Papers of the Bibliographical Society of America* 76 (1982): 223–26.

See also

SCIPIO: Art and Rare Book Sales Catalogs (E230a).
Taylor, *Book Catalogues* (U5395).

Indexes

U5415   *ABPC on CD-ROM.* CD-ROM. Washington, CT: Bancroft-Parkman. Annual.

American Book Prices Current [1894–2004] (*ABPC*). Washington, CT: Bancroft-Parkman, 1895–2005. Annual.   Z1000.A51   018′.3. <http://www.bookpricescurrent.com>.

A list of books and manuscripts sold in the principal European and North American auction houses. Until vol. 64 (1958), *ABPC* covers only auctions in the United States; after vol. 73 (1967), it gradually becomes more international but is still selective in reporting sales outside North America and the United Kingdom. Recent volumes exclude items that bring less than $50 or the equivalent in another currency (those from vols. 76–85 [1970–79], less than $20; and earlier volumes, less than $10), most works in non-Western languages that sell for less than $100, books in lots, and incomplete sets and runs of periodicals. Entries are organized in two parts: autographs and manuscripts (including original illustrations for books, documents, letters, corrected proofs, and signed photographs) and books (including single sheets, broadsides, and uncorrected proofs). Works are listed alphabetically by author; title of anonymous work; or (when it is the main interest) private press, publisher, or printer. Entries record title, place and date of publication, edition, size, binding, condition, important features (such as provenance, bibliographical points, inscriptions, or marginalia), auction house, date of sale and lot number, price, and (since vol. 66 [1960]) purchaser (when reported on a price list). The publisher claims that entries for books have been independently verified, but the nature of this verification is not made clear. The fastest access to entries is through the CD-ROM (for volumes since September 1975) or the cumulative indexes: 1916–22, comp. Philip Sanford Goulding and Helen Plummer Goulding (1925, 1,397 pp.); 1923–32, comp. Eugenia Wallace and Lucie E. Wallace (1936, 1,007 pp.); 1933–40, comp. and ed. Edward Lazare (1941, 765 pp.); 1941–45, comp. and ed. Colton Storm (1946, 1,126 pp.); 1945–50, comp. and ed. Lazare (1951, 1,404 pp.); 1950–55, ed. Lazare (1956, 1,709 pp.); 1955–60, ed. Lazare (1961, 1,533 pp.); 1960–65, ed. Lazare (1968, 2,085 pp.); 1965–70, ed. William James Smith, 2 pts. (1974, 2,545 pp.); 1970–75, ed. Katharine Kyes Leab and Daniel J. Leab, 2 pts. (1976, 2,061 pp.); 1975–79, ed. Leab and Leab, 2 pts. (1980, 2,325 pp.); 1979–83, ed. Leab and Leab, 2 pts. (1984, 2,246 pp.); 1983–87, ed. Leab and Leab, 2 pts. (1988, 2,286 pp.); 1987–91, ed. Leab and Leab, 2 pts. (1992, 2,320 pp); 1991–95, ed. Leab and Leab, 2 pts. (1996, 2,335 pp.).

ABPC on CD-ROM includes records since 1975 divided among two files: books and other print material; autographs, manuscripts, documents, and other handwritten material. To navigate the poorly designed search interface, users will need to read the Help screen. Users can either search (by keyword, year of sale, date of publication, title, or author) or browse indexes of the preceding (except keyword) and editor or illustrator. Records can be sorted by year of sale, publication date, author, or title.

Although *ABPC* is more scholarly, current, comprehensive, and trustworthy than *Book Auction Records* (U5420), the two are ultimately complementary works and invaluable as indexes to auction catalogs and as aids for identifying and tracing unique items (especially manuscripts and association copies). Those using *ABPC* or *Book Auction Records* to evaluate books must remember that prices now do not reflect buyers' premiums or taxes (denominated for each auction house in the explanatory notes to individual volumes of *ABPC*) and depend on condition and other factors.

Some additional British and American sales (with coverage of the latter beginning in vol. 30 [1916]) are indexed in *Book-Prices Current: A Record of the Prices at Which Books Have Been Sold at Auction, from [December, 1886 to August, 1956]*, 64 vols. (London: Witherby, 1888–1957, with cumulative indexes for vols. 1–10, 11–20, and 21–30). Beginning in vol. 35 (1921), *Book-Prices Current* includes some manuscripts.

The early volumes are organized by auction house, then sale, with entries providing minimal information. Later volumes consist of a single alphabetical list, with entries citing author, title, publisher, condition, important features, auction house, date of sale, lot number, price, and sometimes buyer. If more than one copy was sold during the season, those copies with noteworthy features have full entries; for others, only auction house, date, and price are recorded. Because so many copies receive truncated entries, *American Book Prices Current* and *Book Auction Records* are superior indexes to sales covered in common.

Those searching for manuscripts should also consult the annual "Manuscripts at Auction: [January 1986–]" (*English Manuscript Studies, 1100–1700*, 1 [1989–]), a selective list of manuscripts sold at the principal London and New York auction houses or (beginning with vol. 2 [1990]) listed in major booksellers' catalogs.

U5420   *Book Auction Records: A Priced and Annotated Annual Record of International
        Book Auctions [1902–97]* (*BAR*). Folkestone: Dawson, 1903–99. Annual.
        Z1000.B65   017.3.

An index to books, other printed materials, and some manuscripts sold at auction, originally in London, then in Great Britain, the United States (vols. 12–18 [1915–21], 37–95 [1940–97]), and, since vol. 64 (1968), other countries. Only items selling for more than £95, $200, or the equivalent of £150 in foreign currencies are included in the later volumes. Entries are listed alphabetically by author, title of anonymous work, press, or subject heading. Vols. 77–94 (1981–96) divide entries between two parts: printed books and atlases; printed maps, charts, and plans. Early volumes are organized by sale; those from vol. 43 (1945–46) through vol. 50 (1952–53) place important manuscripts in a separate section. A typical entry records author, title, date of publication, press, important features such as provenance or binding, auction house, date of sale, lot number, price, and (sometimes) buyer. Early volumes provide significantly less information. The most convenient access is through the cumulative indexes: vols. 1–9, William Jaggard (1924, 1,142 pp.); vols. 10–20, ed. Kathleen L. Stevens (1928, 1,467 pp.); vols. 21–30, ed. Stevens (1935, 1,314 pp.); vols. 31–40, ed. Henry Stevens and Henry R. Peter Stevens (1948, 1,022 pp.); vols. 41–45, ed. Patricia B. Sargent (1951, 955 pp.); vols. 46–55, ed. Henry Stevens and J. G. Garratt (1962, 1,536 pp.); vols. 56–60, ed. Virginia Clarke and Garratt (1966, 1,146 pp.); vols. 61–65 (1971, 1,739 pp.); vols. 66–69, ed. D. Batho (1977, 1,129 pp.); vols. 77–81, ed. Dorothy C. Batho (1985, 1,008 pp.); no index is planned for vols. 70–76.

Although *BAR* is less accurate than *American Book Prices Current* (U5415), the two must be used together, since *Book Auction Records* covered more European and provincial English sales.

U5425   *Bookman's Price Index: A Guide to the Values of Rare and Other Out of Print
        Books* (*BPI*). Detroit: Gale, 1964– . 2–4/yr., with cumulative indexes for
        vols. 1–6, 7–12, 13–19, 20–26, 27–36, 37–46, 47–54, 55–61, 62–67,
        68–73, and 74–79.   Z1000.B74   018'.4.

A list of selected rare and antiquarian books offered for sale in recent catalogs of a small group of established dealers, in Great Britain and North America. Each volume selectively indexes the catalogs of 40 to 180 dealers, which change over the course of the volumes. Books are listed alphabetically by author or title of anonymous work, then alphabetically by title, with editions following in chronological order. Each entry provides author, title, place and date of publication, a brief description of the copy offered (noting, for example, provenance, binding, condition, and important bibliographical points), dealer's name, catalog and item number, and selling price. Since vol. 32 (1986), there are separate lists of association copies, bindings, and fore-edge paintings. A directory of dealers prefaces each volume. *BPI* covers only a small number of the thousands of dealers (and omits many of the more important ones), lacks any statement of principles governing the selection of dealers or books listed, and is full of misprints; still, it is the only index of frequently valuable but ephemeral sources of information and is an essential source for tracking down inscribed or annotated copies, books owned by authors or important collectors, and other unique items. Researchers using *BPI* as a source for evaluating the worth of a book must remember that the retail prices quoted vary widely among dealers and are based on a variety of factors such as condition, provenance, and edition. Reviews: (vol. 1) Walter Goldwater, *Papers of the Bibliographical Society of America* 60 (1966): 110–14; (vols. 1–12) Paul S. Koda, *Analytical and Enumerative Bibliography* 2 (1978): 76–80.

   Bookman's Price Index: Subject Series lasted for only one volume: *Modern First Editions* (1987), a cumulation of entries from the 1984–86 volumes of *BPI*.

See also

> Cripe, *American Manuscripts, 1763–1815: An Index to Documents Described in Auction Records and Dealers' Catalogues* (Q3235).
> Tanselle, "The Literature of Book Collecting" (U5355), lists additional indexes and price guides (pp. 259–64).

Children's Literature

Guides to Reference Works

U5440   Haviland, Virginia. *Children's Literature: A Guide to Reference Sources.*
         Washington: Lib. of Congress, 1966. 341 pp. Haviland and Margaret N.
         Coughlan. *First Supplement.* 1972. 316 pp. *Second Supplement.* 1977. 413
         pp. (Although some reference guides cite a *Third Supplement* [1982], no
         such supplement was ever published.)   Z1037.A1 H35   016.8098′928′2.
   A guide to reference works and general studies (including dissertations) through 1974 that are important to the study of children's literature. Although the work is international in scope, Haviland emphasizes British and North American literature. Entries are listed alphabetically by author, editor, or title in eight classified divisions: history and criticism, authorship (including sections on writing for children, individual authors, and biographical dictionaries), illustration (including studies of illustrators), bibliographies, books and children (including storytelling, folklore, nursery rhymes, poetry, and magazines; a section on pedagogy was added in the first supplement), libraries and children's books, international studies, and national studies (with sections on Western Europe, Eastern Europe, Latin America, South Africa, and Asia; ones for the Near East and Africa were added in the first supplement, and for French Canada in the second supplement). Concludes with a directory of associations and agencies. The full annotations are largely descriptive, although some offer evaluative comments. Indexed by persons and some titles. Haviland is now dated but remains the best guide to reference works and international scholarship through 1974.
   For recent publications, see Rahn, *Children's Literature* (U5485); *Hendrickson, Children's Literature* (U5480); Margaret W. Denman-West, *Children's Literature: A*

Guide to Information Sources, Reference Sources in the Humanities (Englewood: Libraries Unlimited, 1998, 187 pp.), which focuses on works published 1985–97 but which must be consulted with an awareness that the evaluative comments—which typically read like blurbs—are usually too generous and frequently erroneous; John T. Gillespie, *The Children's and Young Adult Literature Handbook: A Research and Reference Guide,* Children's and Young Adult Literature Reference Series (Westport: Libraries Unlimited–Greenwood, 2005, 393 pp.), which omits many essential reference works, is poorly organized, and lacks rigor in its evaluations; and the serial bibliographies and indexes in section G. A major desideratum remains a current, trustworthy guide to reference sources for the study of children's literature.

See also

>   Beugnot, *Manuel bibliographique des études littéraires* (S4905).
>   Gohdes, *Bibliographical Guide to the Study of the Literature of the U. S. A.* (Q3180).

Histories and Surveys

U5445   Darton, F. J. Harvey. *Children's Books in England: Five Centuries of Social Life.* 3rd ed. rpt. with corrections. Rev. Brian Alderson. London: British Lib.; New Castle: Oak Knoll, 1999. 398 pp.   PR990.D3   011'.62.

A social history of literature written to entertain children. Ranging from the Middle Ages to c. 1901, the chapters on periods, major types of children's literature, topics, publishers, and authors emphasize social, historical, literary, and commercial contexts. Each chapter concludes with an annotated list for further reading. While retaining Darton's text as much as possible, the third edition makes numerous factual corrections and provides fuller documentation, additional illustrations, and supplementary appendixes, including one devoted to late nineteenth-century works. Concludes with a selected, annotated bibliography (which is updated in the 1999 reprint). Fully indexed by persons, subjects, and titles. The classic history of children's literature in England before 1900, this is especially strong in its treatment of the eighteenth century. Reviews: Julia Briggs, *TLS: Times Literary Supplement* 26 Mar. 1982: 341–42; Andrea Immel, *Library* 7th ser. 1 (2000): 446–48.

See also

>   *Literary History of Canada* (R4565).
>   Tebbel, *History of Book Publishing in the United States* (U5260).

Literary Handbooks, Dictionaries, and Encyclopedias

U5450   Watson, Victor, ed. *The Cambridge Guide to Children's Books in English.* Cambridge: Cambridge UP, 2001. 814 pp. Online through *Gale Virtual Reference Library* (I535).   PR990.C36   820.9'9282'03.

An encyclopedia of authors, illustrators, and works published in English since pre-Norman times that have had significant influence, anywhere in the world, on young readers or that have "in some way influenced the production of children's books." Ranging well beyond what is thought of as "children's literature" and the *Books* in the title, the signed entries include critics, technical terms, topics (e.g., movable books, child authors, and superheroes), drama, television series, comics, media texts, illustration techniques, awards, genres, organizations, folktales, fairy tales, periodicals, and genres. An appendix lists winners of selected literary prizes. Although ostensibly limited to works in English, there are entries for several Anglo-Saxon authors of Latin works (e.g. Ælfric and Aldhelm), whereas *Beowulf* only appears as a cross-reference. Impressive in its breadth of coverage and attention to the political, social, and commercial forces affecting what young persons read and view, *Cambridge Guide to Children's Books in English* is now the standard desktop companion in its field.

It readily supplants Humphrey Carpenter and Mari Prichard, *The Oxford Companion to Children's Literature* (Oxford: Oxford UP, 1984, 587 pp.), a dictionary of British and North American children's literature, as well as foreign works important to the English-language tradition, through May 1983 (although coverage is less thorough for post-1945 publications and persons). The approximately 2,000 entries encompass works, authors, genres, critics, scholars, publishers, illustrators, organizations, characters, magazines, awards, fairy tales, folklore, and children's literature in various foreign languages and countries. Entrants are indexed in *Biography and Genealogy Master Index* (J565). Entries are sometimes uneven, inaccurate, or conservative in their criticism, and there are notable omissions (especially for North American writers and works). Reviews: Brian Alderson, *Library* 6th ser. 8 (1986): 187–89; Hugh Brogan, *TLS: Times Literary Supplement* 4 May 1984: 505–06; Irving P. Cummings, *Children's Literature* 14 (1986): 187–93.

U5453   *International Companion Encyclopedia of Children's Literature.* Ed. Peter
         Hunt. 2nd ed. 2 vols. London: Routledge–Taylor and Francis, 2004.
         PN1008.5.I57   809'.89282'03.

A compendium of 112 separately authored essays on children's literature worldwide. Organized in five parts—theoretical and critical approaches, forms and genres, contexts (a hodgepodge treating publishing, scholarly journals, censorship, television, film, research collections, and statements about the field by authors), applications (e.g., teaching, selecting books, and librarianship), and national surveys—variously address the history or development of a topic, explain methodologies, survey the state of research, or illustrate applications; most conclude with a list of suggested readings. Although the essays inevitably vary in quality and accuracy (e.g., in "Bibliography," Matthew Grenby erroneously asserts that there are "only two full-scale print-format bibliographies of children's literature studies") and, for historical reasons, many are anglocentric, *International Companion Encyclopedia* offers an important overview of the current state of the field of children's literature.

A valuable complementary work is *The Oxford Encyclopedia of Children's Literature*, ed. Jack Zipes, 4 vols. (New York: Oxford UP, 2006; online, 17 Aug. 2006 <http://www.oxford-childrensliterature.com>). International in scope (but emphasizing the Anglo-American tradition from the Middle Ages to the present), its more than 3,200 signed entries cover forms, genres, regions, groups, terms, characters, periodicals, illustrators, and—predominantly—authors; many conclude with a selective bibliography. Indexed by persons, titles, and subjects. The electronic version (available as part of *The Oxford Digital Reference Shelf* [http://www.oxford-digitalreference.com]) can be searched by keyword or browsed by cntry; entries can be e-mailed.

Annals

U5455 Bingham, Jane, and Grayce Scholt. *Fifteen Centuries of Children's Literature: An Annotated Chronology of British and American Works in Historical Context.* Westport: Greenwood, 1980. 540 pp. Z1037.A1 B582 [PN1009.A1] 028.52.

An annotated chronology of important or representative books written for or appropriated by children in Great Britain and the United States from 523 to 1945. The entries are organized in six periods, each of which is prefaced by a superficial and frequently inaccurate discussion of historical background, the development of books, and attitudes toward and treatment of children. English-language books are listed by date of publication; a foreign work is listed by the year it was introduced into Great Britain or the United States; works by a prolific or popular author are grouped under the year of his or her first important or popular publication (a practice that results in some lengthy, incomplete, and generally useless lists). A typical entry includes author, illustrator, translator, or editor; title; publisher or printer; annotation (with a brief description of content and list of other books by the person); and locations of copies in a limited number of collections. Three appendixes: a chronological list of American periodicals for children, 1789–1941; a chronological list of British periodicals for children, 1757–1941; an incomplete list of facsimiles and reprints of works cited in the chronology (which should have been incorporated into the individual entries). A selective bibliography of scholarship concludes the work. Two indexes: persons; titles. Marred by the uncritical inclusion of numerous works that hardly qualify as children's literature, uneven annotations, incomplete publication information for several works, numerous factual errors, and the unfortunate practice of grouping works by an author under one year, *Fifteen Centuries of Children's Literature* is useful for isolating only very broad trends (especially after 1800). Scholars still need an adequate chronology of children's literature. Reviews: Brian Alderson, *Phaedrus* 8 (1981): 87–88; Irving P. Cummings, *Children's Literature* 14 (1986): 187–93.

Bibliographies of Bibliographies

See

Ingles, *Bibliography of Canadian Bibliographies* (R4585).
Nilon, *Bibliography of Bibliographies in American Literature* (Q3225).

Guides to Primary Works

GUIDES TO COLLECTIONS

U5460 *Special Collections in Children's Literature.* Ed. Dolores Blythe Jones. 3rd ed. Chicago: Amer. Lib. Assn., 1995. 235 pp. Z688.C47 S63 026.8088'99282.

A subject guide to collections of children's literature in various media held by 419 public institutions in the United States, Canada, and forty other countries. Entries are divided into two parts: United States collections; international collections. Entries (organized alphabetically by state or country, then city, then name of institution) typically provide address information, contact person, details of cataloging or finding aids, and a description of holdings (usually fuller for United States collections). Since entries are based on responses to questionnaires, descriptions vary in accuracy and depth. Only the first part is indexed by subjects and persons (but the absurd decision to use *National Union Catalog* abbreviations for libraries makes locating entries unnecessarily time-consuming since one must either know a symbol or find it in a prefatory list); the concluding index of collections is more sensibly indexed by page number. Although the descriptions tend to be brief and the subject indexing is utterly inadequate, Jones offers the fullest guide to specialized collections of children's literature. Coverage is supplemented by Karen Nelson Hoyle, "Libraries, Research Collections, and Museums," pp. 722–30 in *International Companion Encyclopedia of Children's Literature* (U5453). To identify other collections, see section E: Libraries and Library Catalogs/Research Libraries/Guides to Collections.

MANUSCRIPTS

U5465   Fraser, James H., comp. *Children's Authors and Illustrators: A Guide to Manuscript Collections in United States Research Libraries.* Phaedrus Bibliographic Series 1. New York: Saur, 1980. 119 pp.   Z6611.L76 F73 [PN1009.A1]   028.52.

A guide to collections of manuscripts and original illustrations held in United States libraries and other institutions. Organized alphabetically by author or artist, the descriptions typically indicate the general kind and amount of manuscript material and describe the content of a collection. (Additions appear on p. 83.) There is a separate list of authors represented in the Kerlan Collection, University of Minnesota. Since they are based on reports from institutions, published descriptions, or entries in *National Union Catalog of Manuscript Collections* (F295), the entries vary considerably in detail and sophistication. (To understand the descriptions, users must become familiar with the explanation of terminology on p. x.) Concludes with a directory of institutions. Indexed by titles. Although Fraser is incomplete, cites collections of adult material for some writers, is based almost solely on reports or secondary sources, and emphasizes American writers, it at least offers an initial guide to the location of manuscripts and illustrations by children's authors. It must be supplemented with *National Union Catalog of Manuscript Collections* and other works listed under the heading "Manuscripts" in the various sections of this *Guide.*

For the Kerlan Collection, see Karen Nelson Hoyle, comp., *The Kerlan Collection: Manuscripts and Illustrations for Children's Books: A Checklist* (Minneapolis: Kerlan Collection, U of Minnesota Libraries, 1985, 432 pp.) and vol. 2: *1986–2001* (2002; http://special.lib.umn.edu/clrc/vol2/volume2.php); inventories of some papers can be searched through the collection's Web site (http://special.lib.umn.edu/clrc/kerlan/index.php).

See also

Sec. F: Guides to Manuscripts and Archives.

PRINTED WORKS

For an overview of bibliographies of primary works, see Matthew Grenby, "Bibliography," pp. 202–21 in *International Companion Encyclopedia of Children's Literature* (U5453).

U5470   *Children's Books in Print.* New Providence: Bowker, 1969– . Annual.
        Z1037.A1 C482   028.52. Online. 11 Aug. 2005 <http://
        www.childrensbooksinprint.com>; <http://www.globalbooksinprint.com>.
        Updated daily.
    Author, title, illustrator, and subject indexes to currently available children's books published or distributed in the United States. Produced from *BooksinPrint.com, Children's Books in Print* excludes textbooks, toybooks, and workbooks but otherwise leaves the definition of "children's book" to the publishers who supply information; the online database includes DVDs, e-books, videotapes, and audio books and offers access to reviews in selected library journals. In the search mode, users can search by keyword, title, author, publisher, subject, and source of reviews; searches can be limited by format, status (in print, out of print, forthcoming), date, price, audience age, lexile range, market (i.e., countries), award winners, award nominees, and type (fiction or nonfiction). (In *GlobalBooksinPrint.com* click on Children's Room; since the Advanced Search screen searches the entire database, uses must check Children under the Audience header.) Both search modes allow several options for sorting results. Entries typically cite author, editor, illustrator, translator, title, number of volumes, pagination, language (when other than English), LC control number, grade range, year of publication, price, ISBN, and publisher or distributor; in the print version, a few entries include, as a paid advertisement, a boldface description of contents. Since entries are based on information supplied by publishers, some are incomplete or inaccurate, and names and titles are not standardized. Identifying books about a topic is much easier and faster in the online versions than in *Subject Guide to Children's Books in Print*, which utilizes some broad or inexact headings. The print version also includes a directory of publishers. Although not exhaustive and lacking any explanation of the kinds of materials included or excluded, this work is the standard guide to children's books currently for sale in the United States. Most entries for imaginative works through 1985 are incorporated into *Fiction, Folklore, Fantasy, and Poetry for Children* (U5475).

U5473   *Children's Literature Comprehensive Database* (*CLCD*). Online. 13 Feb.
        2005 <http://clcd.odyssi.com>. Updated regularly.
    A database that currently includes MARC records for about 1,200,000 "children's books, video and audio recordings, film strips, and other children-focused media" and c. 200,000 reviews. The search screen allows users to limit keyword full-text searches by category (i.e., fiction or nonfiction), genre, record field, audience age, grade level, illustrator, language, publisher, and date (and combinations of the preceding). The browse screen allows keyword searches to be limited to author, reviewer, subject, Library of Congress classification, Dewey classification, or full text. The source of the MARC records is not specified (probably the Library of Congress); the database includes a substantial number of records for works that can hardly be classified as books for children (e.g., search *Shakespeare* and sort the results by ascending date); many of the older records offer minimal details; there is no explanation of editorial principles and practices; there is no indication of the date when coverage of publications or reviews begins (c. 1900 and c. 1989, respectively, it seems). In short, *Children's Literature Comprehensive*

Database is an unsophisticated resource that relies on automatic reproduction of cataloging records to populate its database and map searches; its chief value for literature researchers lies in its reproduction of reviews and ability to isolate works for children by subject, genre, illustrator, or prizes. Children's literature scholars deserve a far more sophisticated resource.

U5475   *Fiction, Folklore, Fantasy, and Poetry for Children, 1876–1985.* 2 vols. New
         York: Bowker, 1986.   Z1037.A2 F53 [PN1009.A1]   016.80806'8.

Author, title, and illustrator lists of editions and reprints of imaginative books for children published or distributed in the United States between 1876 and 1985. Incorporates records in the *American Book Publishing Record* (Q4110) and *Children's Books in Print* (U5470) databases—as well as from other sources—with selection largely determined by Library of Congress classifications and subject tracings. The author and title indexes provide full entries that, when the information is available, cite author, editor, illustrator, title, series, pagination, size, publication date, grade level, edition, LC card number, ISBN, publisher, and selected list of awards. Details vary with changes in Library of Congress cataloging rules and are frequently incomplete for early works. Entries in the illustrator index cite title, author, publisher, date, and selected awards. A separate list of winners of 20 children's books awards is also included. Although incomplete in its coverage and sometimes inaccurate (and subject to many of the same shortcomings as the cumulative *American Book Publishing Record*), *Fiction, Folklore, Fantasy, and Poetry* is the fullest single list of imaginative works for children published in the United States between 1876 and 1985.

Although limited to the "best" books (as determined by panels of librarians), the following are useful for their descriptive annotations and subject indexing of books for children as well as about children's literature, all but a few of which are in print:

> *Children's Catalog.* Ed. Anne Price and Juliette Yaakov. 18th ed. Standard
> Catalog Series. New York: Wilson, 2001. 1,265 pp. (Annual supplements
> between editions.) Online. 29 June 2006 <http://vnweb.hwwilsonweb
> .com/hww>.
> *Middle and Junior High School Library Catalog.* Ed. Price and Yaakov. 8th
> ed. Standard Catalog Series. New York: Wilson, 2000. 1,021 pp. (Annual
> supplements between editions.) Online. 29 June 2006 <http://
> vnweb.hwwilsonweb.com/hww>.
> *Senior High School Library Catalog.* Ed. Yaakov. 16th ed. Standard Catalog
> Series. New York: Wilson, 2002. 1,243 pp. (Annual supplements between
> editions.) Online. 29 June 2006 <http://vnweb.hwwilsonweb.com/hww>.

Each work organizes nonfiction by Dewey Decimal Classification, followed by an author list of fiction, and then short story collections. An entry is accompanied by a description of contents or quotations from reviews. Indexed by authors, titles, and subjects. Earlier editions remain useful for their subject access to works subsequently dropped.

Each online version of the *Catalogs* consists of two files: the current *Catalog* and a *[Children's Catalog] Archive.* Each of the *Archives* includes noncurrent entries from preceding editions (although it is not clear from the Web site if data from all editions are included).

See also

> *Australian Children's Literature and the Lu Rees Archives* (R4463a).
> Cheung, *Asian American Literature* (Q3940).
> *New Cambridge Bibliography of English Literature,* vols. 2–4 (M1385).

Guides to Scholarship and Criticism

SURVEYS OF RESEARCH

U5477   *Children's Literature Research: International Resources and Exchange.*
        München: Saur, 1991. 247 pp.   PN1008.3.C45   809'.89282.
        A series of reports, prepared for the first International Youth Library conference
in 1988, that assess the state of research in more than 25 countries or geographic areas.
The individual reports vary considerably in content, but many survey available reference
tools, historical or critical studies, and current periodicals; describe current projects and
research needs; note research centers; and conclude with a selective bibliography. Although the surveys are far from systematic and highly variable in the adequacy of their
coverage, the collection is valuable for its international perspective.

SERIAL BIBLIOGRAPHIES

Unfortunately, work on the CLIP (Children's Literature in Periodicals) database sponsored by the Swedish Institute for Children's Books has been suspended. For a description of the project, see Lena Törnqvist and Anne de Vries, "The CLIP Project; or,
Coming of Age as a Discipline," *Bookbird* 31.4 (1993): 20–23. Some journal articles
and essays in edited collections published after 1998 can be identified through *ELSA*,
the institute's online catalog (http://www.sbi.kb.se/index.html).

U5478   "Bibliography [1982, 1987–97]." *Children's Literature Association Quarterly*
        8 (1983), 14–24 (1989–99). Title varies.   PN1008.2.C48   809'.89282.
        An annotated bibliography of studies of children's and young adult literature that
is primarily derived from *Children's Literature Abstracts* (U5490). The entries are listed
in 18 divisions (only a few of which are subdivided): authors and illustrators, awards,
prizes, and organizations; bibliographies, reading lists, and reference works; canon, censorship, and stereotypes; collections, exhibitions, and libraries; critics and critical approaches; curriculum, instruction, and bibliotherapy; fantasy and science fiction; folklore, fable, fairy tale, myth, and storytelling; historical and sociological studies;
illustration, design, comics, and picture books; media and theater; mimetic fiction and
series; national and minority literatures and multiculturalism; nonfiction; periodicals;
poetry; publishing and bookselling; and young adult. Indexed by critics. Although several entries are taken from other bibliographies, the majority are accompanied by descriptive annotations; unfortunately, however, the lack of a subject index—coupled
with minimal cross-referencing and subclassification—renders the bibliography much
less accessible than it should be. Once the most important serial bibliography in children's literature, its coverage and annotations were scaled down so drastically with the
bibliography for 1990 (17 [1992]) that researchers were far better served by *Children's
Literature Abstracts.*

See also

        Secs. G: Serial Bibliographies, Indexes, and Abstracts and H: Guides to Disser-
        tations and Theses.

ABELL (G340): English Literature/General/Literature for Children in volumes since that for 1975, and the Literature for Children section in period divisions since the volume for 1985.

Bibliographie der Buch- und Bibliotheksgeschichte (U5280).

MLAIB (G335): General IV/Children's Literature in the volumes for 1976–80. In later volumes, researchers must consult the "Children—as Audience" or "Children's Literature" headings in the subject index and "Children's Literature" in the online thesaurus.

Victorian Database Online (M2490).

OTHER BIBLIOGRAPHIES

U5480   Hendrickson, Linnea. *Children's Literature: A Guide to the Criticism.* Reference Publication in Literature. Boston: Hall, 1987. 664 pp. Z2014.5.H46 [PR990]   011'.62. Online. 3 May 2006 <http://www.unm.edu/~lhendr>.

An annotated bibliography of significant English-language books, articles, and dissertations (through the mid-1980s) on imaginative works written for or read by children. (The online version includes "a few corrections.") Although the work is international in scope and covers some classics published before 1900, Hendrickson emphasizes twentieth-century works in English. The entries are organized alphabetically in two divisions: individual authors (with highly selective lists for those who are not principally children's authors); subjects, themes, genres, and national literatures (along with a substantial section on critical theory). The brief descriptive annotations frequently do not offer clear outlines of content. Two indexes: critics; authors, subjects, and titles of children's books. Hendrickson is wider in scope, fuller in coverage (especially of twentieth-century literature), and more current than Rahn, *Children's Literature* (U5485). However, the principles governing the selection of both primary authors and scholarship are unclear; subject headings and the classification of entries are frequently imprecise; and there are numerous significant omissions. Hendrickson and Rahn should be used together (especially because of the latter's superior annotations and coverage of older scholarship).

Although dated, Anne Pellowski, *The World of Children's Literature* (New York: Bowker, 1968, 538 pp.), remains a useful complement to Hendrickson and Rahn, *Children's Literature*, because of its annotations of foreign scholarship.

U5485   Rahn, Suzanne. *Children's Literature: An Annotated Bibliography of the History and Criticism.* Garland Reference Library of the Humanities 263. New York: Garland, 1981. 451 pp.   Z1037.R15 [PR990]   011'.62.

A selective bibliography of important English-language scholarship published through c. 1979 on imaginative works written expressly for children. Rahn excludes dissertations and theses, as well as studies of educational works and adult literature appropriated by children. The 1,328 entries are organized alphabetically in four divisions: discussions of the definition and aims of children's literature, historical studies and annotated catalogs of collections (inadequately organized in sections for general histories and specialized ones), genres (extensively classified by type and including magazines), and important authors (with sections for individuals and for multiple-author studies and collections of essays). An appendix describes important scholarly journals. The full descriptive annotations usually include comments on the quality or importance of a work. Indexed by persons. The cross-references that conclude each section do not compensate for the lack of subject indexing and the imprecise classification system. Although selective and insufficiently precise and detailed in its classification of entries, Rahn is nevertheless valuable for its judicious annotations. It must be supplemented by Haviland, *Children's Literature* (U5440), Hendrickson, *Children's Literature* (U5480), and the serial bibliographies and indexes in section G. Review: Selma K. Richardson, *Children's Literature Association Quarterly* 9 (1984): 44–45.

See also

> Boos, *Bibliography of Women and Literature* (U6600).
> *Greenwood Guide to American Popular Culture* (U6295).
> Haviland, *Children's Literature* (U5440).
> Lindfors, *Black African Literature in English* (R4425).
> *New Cambridge Bibliography of English Literature*, vols. 2–4 (M1385).

ABSTRACTS

U5490   *Children's Literature Abstracts.* Austin: Intl. Federation of Lib. Assns., Children's Libraries Sect., 1973–2001. Quarterly, with cumulative index and two supplements.   Z1037.C5446 [PN1009.A1]   028.52.

An abstract service for scholarship on children's literature. The international coverage extends to a wide range of journals and a few newspapers; beginning in late 1984, books and pamphlets are abstracted in two supplements each year. Entries are organized in classified divisions for authors and illustrators; awards, prizes, and organizations; bibliographies, reading lists, and reference works; canon, censorship, and stereotyping; collections, exhibitions, and libraries; critics and analytical approaches; curriculum, instruction, and bibliotherapy; environment; fantasy and science fiction; folklore, fable, fairy tale, myth, and storytelling; historical and cultural studies; illustration, design, picture books, and comics; media and theater; mimetic fiction, school stories, and historical novels; national and minority literatures; nonfiction; poetry; publishing, bookselling, and periodicals; and young adult literature. The English-language abstracts, prepared by a team of international contributors, tend to be brief but adequately descriptive. On the history of *Children's Literature Abstracts*, see Gillian Adams, "Halfway to the Future: *Children's Literature Abstracts*," *Bookbird* 31.4 (1993): 15–19. Although it is not comprehensive—especially in its coverage of books—its international scope made *Children's Literature Abstracts* the most important source for identifying studies of children's literature. It should be used with the surveys in *Phaedrus: An International Annual of Children's Literature Research* (1973–88), which are sometimes more comprehensive for individual countries.

With the demise of *Children's Literature Abstracts* and of the *Children's Literature Association Quarterly* "Bibliography" (U5478), researchers face a field with no adequate bibliographical control of its scholarship.

REVIEW INDEXES

U5495   *Children's Book Review Index.* Detroit: Gale, 1975– . Annual, with cumulation for 1965–84.   Z1037.A1 C475   028.52. Online through *Book Review Index* (G415).

An author or editor list of reviews of children's books and "book-related electronic media" that is cloned from *Book Review Index* (G415), which offers more current information on recent titles. Although it is restricted in its coverage of periodicals and does not distinguish between substantive reviews and brief descriptive notices, *Children's Book Review Index* does index the important serials that regularly review books for children.

Biographical Dictionaries

INDEXES

U5500   *Children's Authors and Illustrators: An Index to Biographical Dictionaries.* Ed. Joyce Nakamura. 5th ed. Gale Biographical Index Series 2. New York: Gale, 1995. 811 pp.   Z1037.A1 N18   016.809.

An index to some 200,000 biographies of about 30,000 writers and illustrators of English-language children's books (including translations) in approximately 650 standard biographical dictionaries, including several not confined to children's literature. Each entrant is followed by a coded list of dictionaries that include entries about him or her. Cloned from *Biography and Genealogy Master Index* (J565) and suffering from many of the same editorial shortcomings, *Children's Authors and Illustrators* provides some additional entries and attempts to differentiate those of the same name and to cross-reference pseudonyms (but without eliminating duplicate entries). Although lacking an explanation of the criteria governing the selection of works indexed and not discriminating between substantial biographical discussions and brief entries, this work is a time-saving source for determining what dictionaries to consult for biographical information about children's authors and illustrators.

Complemented by *Writers for Young Adults: Biographies Master Index: An Index to Sources of Biographical Information about Novelists, Poets, Playwrights, Nonfiction Writers, Songwriters and Lyricists, Television and Screenwriters Who Are of Interest to High School Students and to Teachers, Librarians, and Researchers Interested in High School Reading Materials,* ed. Joyce Nakamura, 3rd ed., Gale Biographical Index Series 6 (Detroit: Gale, 1989, 183 pp.). It indexes some 16,000 entries from about 600 dictionaries but suffers from a lack of clear focus and criteria governing selection of entrants.

Entries in these two indexes that also appear in *Biography and Genealogy Master Index* can be searched more efficiently through the online version of *BGMI*.

See also

Sec. J: Biographical Sources/Biographical Dictionaries/Indexes.

BIOGRAPHICAL DICTIONARIES

U5505   *St. James Guide to Children's Writers.* 5th ed. Ed. Sara Pendergast and Tom Pendergast. St. James Guide to Writers Series. Detroit: St. James-Gale, 1999. 1,406 pp.   PN1009.A1 T9   820.9'9282.

A biographical, bibliographical, and critical dictionary of established twentieth-century writers and illustrators of English-language literature for children. A typical entry consists of three parts: biographical information, including address or agent; a list of separately published works (including those for adults); a signed critical essay. Some entries also note the location of manuscript collections, list selected criticism, and print a comment by the entrant. Important nineteenth-century writers are grouped in an appendix. Concludes with a very selective list of foreign authors whose works have been translated into English. Indexed by titles of books for children; entrants are indexed in *Biography and Genealogy Master Index* (J565). The brief critical commentaries vary considerably in quality, but *St. James Guide to Children's Writers* is a useful source of basic biographical and bibliographical information about established children's authors. The *Dictionary of Literary Biography* (J600) volumes on children's literature are superior sources of information for those writers and illustrators in common.

See also

> Sec. J: Biographical Sources/Biographical Dictionaries/General Biographical Dictionaries.
> *Dictionary of Literary Biography* (J600).

Periodicals

GUIDES TO PRIMARY WORKS

U5510   Kelly, R. Gordon, ed. *Children's Periodicals of the United States*. Historical Guides to the World's Periodicals and Newspapers. Westport: Greenwood, 1984. 591 pp.   PN4878.C48   051'.088054.

A collection of separately authored profiles of about 100 representative American children's periodicals from 1789 to 1980. Entries, listed alphabetically by title, typically provide an overview of contents and publishing history; a selected list of scholarship, indexing sources, and locations; and a record of title changes, frequency, publisher(s), place(s) of publication, and editor(s). The preface surveys the state of general scholarship on children's periodicals. Three appendixes: title, chronological, and geographic lists of 423 American children's periodicals. Indexed by persons, titles, and subjects. While the work is flawed—it lacks an adequate statement of criteria governing selection, is admittedly weak in coverage of religious publications, excludes foreign-language periodicals, and is uneven in the quality of individual essays—it still offers some of the fullest discussions of children's periodicals published in the United States.

Genres

POETRY

Guides to Primary Works

U5540   *Index to Children's Poetry: A Title, Subject, Author, and First Line Index to Poetry in Collections for Children and Youth*. Comp. John E. Brewton and Sara W. Brewton. New York: Wilson, 1942. 965 pp. *First Supplement.*

1957. 405 pp. *Second Supplement.* 1965. 451 pp. *Index to Poetry for Children and Young People, 1964–1969.* Comp. Brewton, Brewton, and G. Meredith Blackburn III. 1972. 574 pp. *1970–1975.* Comp. J. E. Brewton, G. M. Blackburn, and Lorraine A. Blackburn. 1978. 472 pp. *1976–1981.* 1984. 317 pp. *1982–1987.* Comp. G. M. Blackburn. 1989. 408 pp. *1988–1992.* Comp. G. M. Blackburn. 1994. 358 pp. *1993–1997.* Comp. G. M. Blackburn. 1999. 461 pp.   PN1023.B7   821.0016.

An author, title, subject, and first-line index to English-language poems and translations for readers through grade 12 and printed in single-author collections and anthologies published from the early twentieth century through 1997. Selection is by vote of a committee of consulting librarians and teachers. The title entries cite author or translator, variant titles, and first line when needed to differentiate poems with the same title; other entries are more abbreviated; all refer by code to a prefatory list of collections indexed. Although limited in scope, the *Index* is a convenient source for identifying children's poems on a subject and locating texts.

Subject access to some additional poems is offered by *Subject Index to Poetry for Children and Young People*, comp. Violet Sell et al. (Chicago: Amer. Lib. Assn., 1957, 582 pp.); supplement, *1957–1975*, comp. Dorothy B. Frizzell Smith and Eva L. Andrews (1977, 1,035 pp.).

Composition and Rhetoric

This section is limited to works that emphasize composition at the postsecondary level and to reference sources in historical rhetoric of value in composition research or literary criticism.

Research Methods

U5550   Kirsch, Gesa, and Patricia A. Sullivan, eds. *Methods and Methodology in Composition Research.* Carbondale: Southern Illinois UP, 1992. 354 pp. PE1404.M47   808'.042'072.

An introduction to the theory and techniques of research in composition, with individual chapters on historical, feminist, linguistic, socioethnographic, case study, ethnographic, cognitive, teacher-research, experimental, pluralistic, and collaborative approaches. Contributors generally address epistemological assumptions, practical matters, and ideological issues, illustrating their discussions with examples from their own research. Indexed by persons, titles, and subjects. Blending theory and practice, the collection offers researchers a solid introduction to both traditional and new approaches. Review: Mary Minock, *Rhetoric Society Quarterly* 22.3 (1992): 70–73.

More general overviews of research methods in composition can be found in Lillian Bridwell-Bowles, "Research in Composition: Issues and Methods," *An Introduction to Composition Studies*, ed. Erika Lindemann and Gary Tate (New York: Oxford UP, 1991), 94–117, and David Bartholomae, "Composition" (pp. 103–25), in Nicholls, *Introduction to Scholarship in Modern Languages and Literatures* (A25); both offer an overview of objects of inquiry, types of research, major methodological approaches, and issues that need to be addressed.

See also

    Olson, *Publishing in Rhetoric and Composition* (U6381).

Guides to Reference Works

U5555   Scott, Patrick, and Bruce Castner. "Reference Sources for Composition
        Research: A Practical Survey." *College English* 45 (1983): 756–68.
        PE1.C6   820′.7′1173.

        Scott. "Bibliographical Resources and Problems." *An Introduction to
        Composition Studies.* Ed. Erika Lindemann and Gary Tate. New York:
        Oxford UP, 1991. 72–93.   PE1404.I57   808′.042′07.

    Evaluative surveys of reference sources essential to research in historical rhetoric
and composition. In both, the detailed evaluations are accompanied by valuable advice
on research procedures and searching serial bibliographies. Until someone produces the
much-needed detailed guide to research methods and reference sources in composition,
"Reference Sources" and "Bibliographical Resources" offer the best introduction.

    In describing the obstacles hindering bibliographic control of composition research
and the need for systematic coverage, Scott, "Bibliographical Problems in Research on
Composition," *College Composition and Communication* 37 (1986): 167–77, provides
valuable, if implicit, guidance on techniques for identifying scholarship.

Handbooks, Dictionaries, and Encyclopedias

U5557   *Encyclopedia of Rhetoric and Composition: Communication from Ancient Times
        to the Information Age.* Ed. Theresa Enos. Garland Reference Library of the
        Humanities 1389. New York: Garland, 1996. 803 pp.   PN172.E53
        808′.003.

    An encyclopedia of persons, concepts, terms, methodologies, historical periods,
and applications associated, in American higher education, with the history and practice
of rhetoric and composition. Many of the 467 signed entries are written by established
scholars and most conclude with a selective bibliography. Although lacking any explanation of how topics were selected, *Encyclopedia of Rhetoric and Composition* offers the
best guide to rhetoric and composition as understood and practiced in the United States.
Review: Gerard A. Hauser, *Quarterly Journal of Speech* 83 (1997): 243–46.

U5560   *Historisches Wörterbuch der Rhetorik.* Ed. Gerd Ueding. 8 vols. Tübingen:
        Niemeyer, 1992– .   PF3410.H5   808.003.

    A dictionary of rhetorical terms and concepts from classical antiquity to the
present. The signed essays—many of them quite extensive—include an etymology and
equivalents in languages other than German, a definition, a historical overview (with
several entries subdivided by period), and, when appropriate, uses in specific disciplines
or geographic areas; most conclude with a bibliography and liberal cross-references. For
an outline of the work and its editorial principles, see Ueding, "Das Historische Wörterbuch der Rhetorik," *Archiv für Begriffsgeschichte* 37 (1994): 7–20. Impressive in its
breadth and the quality of its contributors, *Historisches Wörterbuch der Rhetorik* is the

best dictionary of rhetorical terminology. Review: (vol. 1) Brian Vickers, *Rhetorica* 13 (1995): 345–58.

Until the work is complete, *Encyclopedia of Rhetoric*, ed. Thomas O. Sloane (Oxford: Oxford UP, 2001, 837 pp.), offers the best general guide to elements of rhetoric, schema, related subjects, strategies and principles, and the history of the subject. The approximately 200 signed entries (ranging from about 100 to 16,000 words) emphasize depth over breadth, favor the traditional aspects of the discipline over the new and unconventional, and conclude with a selective bibliography (that frequently offers evaluative comments). Review: Glen McClish, *Rhetoric Society Quarterly* 32.4 (2002): 117–20.

Bernard Dupriez, *A Dictionary of Literary Devices: Gradus, A–Z*, trans. and adapt. Albert W. Halsall (Toronto: U of Toronto P, 1991, 545 pp.), offers a fuller guide to rhetorical terms, classical through contemporary, that draws from linguistics, prosody, rhetoric, and philology. A typical entry consists of a definition and citations to important studies, followed by one or more sections devoted to examples, definitions proposed by others, synonyms, antonyms, analogous terms, and remarks (e.g., on usage, characteristics, or explanations by others; many entries include several separate remarks, each accompanied by examples). Concludes with a bibliography. Indexed by terms and persons. The full (but occasionally idiosyncratic) discussions, extensive use and range of examples, and liberal cross-references make this one of the best guides to rhetorical devices.

Students needing less extensive discussions will find Richard A. Lanham, *A Handlist of Rhetorical Terms*, 2nd ed. (Berkeley: U of California P, 1991, 205 pp.; also available as *A Hypertext Handlist of Rhetorical Terms for Macintosh Computers*, 1997), a useful handlist of basic rhetorical terms, most of them classical but extending through the mid-seventeenth century. In the alphabetical list, a typical entry indicates pronunciation, offers a brief definition or cross-reference to a synonymous term, summarizes differing interpretations when necessary, and sometimes cites an example. Following the alphabetical list are sections that outline the divisions of rhetoric and classify the terms by type. Clear, brief explanations make Lanham a useful desktop companion for the interpretation of rhetorical terminology.

Guides to Scholarship

SURVEYS OF RESEARCH

U5565   Horner, Winifred Bryan, ed. *The Present State of Scholarship in Historical and Contemporary Rhetoric*. Rev. ed. Columbia: U of Missouri P, 1990. 260 pp.   PN183.P7   016.808.

Surveys of scholarship accompanied by selective bibliographies on rhetoric, classical to contemporary. Essays focus on periods—classical, Middle Ages, Renaissance, eighteenth century, nineteenth century, and twentieth century—with all but the first two emphasizing British and American traditions. Although varying in organization, essays typically survey primary works (noting editions and translations), bibliographies, and important scholarship; provide an overview of major concerns in the period; suggest areas for research; and conclude with a selective bibliography. Indexed by persons, anonymous works, and a few subjects. Addressed specifically to the literature scholar, Horner is a valuable introductory survey of the most important primary works and scholarship. It should, however, be supplemented with Horner, *Historical Rhetoric* (U5600). Reviews: (1st ed.) Donald F. Reid, *Rhetoric Society Quarterly* 14 (1984): 145–51; (rev. ed.) Arthur Walzer, *Rhetoric Society Quarterly* 21.2 (1991): 57–59, with a reply by Horner, 60–61.

U5570   *Research on Composition: Multiple Perspectives on Two Decades of Change.* Ed.
        Peter Smagorinsky. Language and Literacy Series. New York: Teachers Coll.
        P, 2006. 308 pp.   PE1404.S596   808'.042'071.

Surveys of scholarship from 1984 through 2003 designed to continue the coverage by Hillocks and Braddock (see below). Individual essays assess the state of scholarship on, theoretical bases of, and research methods for preschool through elementary writing, middle and high school composition, postsecondary level writing, teacher research in writing classrooms, second-language composition and teaching, rhetoric, family and community literacies, writing in the professions, and historical studies of composition. Each concludes with what is intended to be a complete bibliography of published research during the two decades. Boasting contributions by leading scholars of their respective topics, *Research on Composition* is an essential first source for anyone working in the field.

Earlier scholarship is surveyed in the following:

> Braddock, Richard, Richard Lloyd-Jones, and Lowell Schoer. *Research in Written Composition.* Champaign: NCTE, 1963. 142 pp. (Covers the early twentieth century through 1962.)
>
> Hillocks, George, Jr. *Research on Written Composition: New Directions for Teaching.* Urbana: Natl. Conf. on Research in English, 1986. 369 pp. (Surveys empirical studies from 1963 through c. 1982 and concludes with an extensive bibliography.)
>
> McClelland, Ben W., and Timothy R. Donovan, eds. *Perspectives on Research and Scholarship in Composition.* New York: MLA, 1985. 266 pp. (Coverage extends through c. 1984.)
>
> Moran, *Research in Composition and Rhetoric* (U5575).
>
> Tate, *Teaching Composition* (U5580).

U5575   Moran, Michael G., and Ronald F. Lunsford, eds. *Research in Composition
        and Rhetoric: A Bibliographic Sourcebook.* Westport: Greenwood, 1984.
        506 pp.   Z5818.E5 R47 [PE1404]   016.808'042'07.

Selective surveys of scholarship (through c. 1982) designed to complement the first edition of Tate, *Teaching Composition* (U5580). The 16 essays cover the writing process; psychology of composition; writing blocks, anxiety, and apprehension; philosophy and rhetoric; literature, literary theory, and the teaching of composition; reading and writing; research methods; grading and evaluation; preparing assignments; basic writing; the sentence; the role of spelling in composition for older students; vocabulary development; punctuation; usage; and the paragraph. The chapters vary in organization, depth, and rigor of evaluation; some suggest topics for further research. Appendixes evaluate textbooks and usage manuals. Two indexes: authors; subjects. Along with Tate (which is less thorough and accessible), this is an important overview of early research in rhetoric and composition. Reviews: Kenneth Dowst, *Rhetoric Review* 4 (1986): 239–43; Richard Fulkerson, *Teaching English in the Two-Year College* 13.1 (1986): 51–57; Nancy Shapiro, *Literary Research* 11 (1986): 71–73.

U5580   Tate, Gary, ed. *Teaching Composition: Twelve Bibliographical Essays.* Rev.
         and enl. ed. Fort Worth: Texas Christian UP, 1987. 434 pp.   PE1404.T39
         808'.042'07.
    A collection of selective surveys of scholarship (through c. 1985) on rhetoric and
composition that revises *Teaching Composition: Ten Bibliographical Essays* (1976, 304
pp.). Chapters by leading scholars examine rhetorical invention; structure and form in
nonnarrative prose; approaches to the study of style; aims, modes, and forms of discourse; tests of writing ability; basic writing; language varieties and composition; literacy,
linguistics, and rhetoric; literary theory and composition; the study of rhetoric and
literature; writing across the curriculum; and computers and composition. The essays
vary considerably in organization, rigor of assessment, and scope, with some authors
merely updating rather than revising their original contributions. Three indexes: persons; subjects; titles. Because of the difficulty in determining which essay treats a particular topic, users should generally approach the work through the subject index. As
Tate points out in his preface, both this work and Moran, *Research in Composition*
(U5575), "are unsystematic and incomplete," yet both are important overviews of early
research in rhetoric and composition. In general, Moran is more effectively organized
and thorough than Tate. Review: Chris Anderson, *Rhetoric Review* 6 (1988): 220–24.
    Although the essays in *A Guide to Composition Pedagogies,* ed. Tate, Amy Rupiper,
and Kurt Schick (New York: Oxford UP, 2001, 256 pp.), focus on pedagogy, each
concludes with a selective bibliography that supplements coverage of parts of Tate and
Moran.

See also

    Greenblatt, *Redrawing the Boundaries* (M1383).

SERIAL BIBLIOGRAPHIES

U5583   *ComPile: An Ongoing Inventory of Publications in Post-secondary Composition,*
         Rhetoric, ESL, and Technical Writing: 1939-1999. Comp. Rich Haswell.
         Online. 19 Sept. 2006 <http://comppile.tamucc.edu>. Updated regularly.
    A database of books, articles, and essays from collections, published in English
about composition and rhetoric and related fields between 1939 and 1999 (although a
few stray 2000–01 publications have crept in). The 82,992 records (as of Sept. 2006)
can be searched by keyword in boxes for Author, Title, Book (that is, publisher as well
as editor[s] and title of an edited collection of essays), Journal, Pages, and Keyword
(which maps to a record field of index terms; it does not search the preceding fields);
filling in more than one box automatically triggers the Boolean *and.* Because of the
search engine's processing of punctuation, use of special symbols, treatment of multiple
words within one search box, and automatic wildcarding of the beginning and end of
a keyword (e.g., searching *direct* in the Title box will return records with *directions, co-
directors, indirect,* etc., in the title field), users must be certain to read the Search Tips
page. Although still very much a work in progress and needing a less idiosyncratic search
interface, *ComPile* offers the best access to the scholarship on composition and rhetoric
before 2000, when *MLAIB* (G335) began coverage of the fields.
    Although less thorough in its coverage, *CCCC Bibliography of Composition and
Rhetoric 1984–1999,* ed. Todd Taylor (online, 9 Feb. 2005 <http://www.ibiblio.org/

ccc>), does index video and audio recordings and electronic resources, offers brief abstracts (though some information is supplied by publishers rather than contributors' personal examinations), and provides a more sophisticated search interface. The ability to search by keyword remedies the utterly inadequate subject indexing of the printed *CCCC Bibliography of Composition and Rhetoric [1984–95]* (Carbondale: Southern Illinois UP, 1987–99; former title: *Longman Bibliography of Composition and Rhetoric [1984–86]* [1987–88]).

Some additional publications are listed in the following:

> "Current Bibliography from *American Book Publishing Record*" (title varies) in most issues of *Rhetoric Society Quarterly* 3.3–24.1–2 (1973–94), a minimally classified list of books copied from *American Book Publishing Record* (Q4110).

> "Selected Bibliography of Scholarship on Composition and Rhetoric [1973–78, 1986–87]," *College Composition and Communication* 26–30, 38–39 (1975–79, 1987–88), a highly selective annotated bibliography on composition and rhetoric at the postsecondary level.

U5585   "Annotated Bibliography of Research in the Teaching of English [1966–]." *Research in the Teaching of English* 1 (1967)– .   PE1066.R47   420.07.

A highly selective bibliography of research on all aspects of the teaching of English; installments once appeared in the May and November issues, but beginning in vol. 38 (2004) only the November issue includes the bibliography. The taxonomy has changed considerably over the years (most notably with vol. 18 [1984], 26.2 [1992], 31.2 [1997], and 38.2 [2003]); entries are currently organized in divisions whose titles are prone to change without notice or explanation: recent ones include assessment, bilingual/foreign language/second language instruction, classroom discussion/interaction, curriculum, discourse analysis, exceptional learners, literacy, literary response, professional development, reading, research methodology, technology/media uses, and writing. Beginning with 38.2 (2003), the annotated entries in each division are followed by an unannotated list headed Other Related Research. Until vol. 26.2 (1992), many of the descriptive annotations are too brief to offer an adequate sense of content. Although coverage of books and articles is not especially thorough (in some issues most entries come from *ProQuest Dissertations and Theses* [H465], and there is no explanation of the criteria governing selection) and classification seems haphazard at times, this was, for many years, the only serial bibliography that systematically covered research in composition.

U5590   ERIC [Education Resources Information Center]. United States Department of Education, Institute of Education Sciences. Online. 6 June 2005 http://www.eric.ed.gov. Updated weekly.

An information network established in 1966 to index, abstract, and disseminate research in education, ERIC is now a digital library of journal articles and reviews, books, dissertations, and unpublished material such as conference papers, curriculum guides, and research reports. The citations and abstracts in the ERIC database are available in printed form as the following:

> *CIJE: Current Index to Journals in Education* (*CIJE*). Phoenix: Oryx, 1969–2001. Monthly, with semiannual cumulations; available on CD-ROM as *CIJE on Disk*. An index to education and related journals (currently about 980). Organized by subject area, then in order of processing, entries consist of ERIC document number, bibliographical citation, a list of descriptors

(based on the current edition of *Thesaurus of ERIC Descriptors*) and identifiers (terms not in the *Thesaurus*) used to create the subject index, and an abstract. Three indexes in each issue and cumulation (subjects; authors; journal contents); cumulative index: *CIJE: Current Index to Journals in Education: Cumulated Author Index, 1969–1984* (1985, 2,218 pp.).

Resources in Education (*RIE*). Washington: GPO, 1967–2002. Monthly, with annual cumulation. (Former title: *Office of Education Research Reports [1956–65]*, 1967.) An index to books, dissertations, theses, audiovisual materials, computer programs, and a variety of unpublished materials such as conference papers, research reports, and curriculum guides — in short, material on education not indexed in *CIJE*. Organized like *CIJE*, entries include ERIC document number, bibliographical information, type of document, subject descriptors and identifiers, and abstract. Four indexes: subject; author; institution; and document type. Because ERIC abstracts virtually all of the unpublished materials submitted, *RIE* includes far too many substandard papers, reports, guides, and the like. Many documents (but not journal articles) can be downloaded as PDF files from the ERIC database; in addition, several libraries maintain a collection of all ERIC documents reproduced in microfiche.

Because of their lack of organization, the print versions of *CIJE* and *RIE* — if one has to consult ERIC in this form — must be approached through their thorough subject indexes, which should be consulted with the current edition of *Thesaurus of ERIC Descriptors* in hand. Much more effective and efficient is an electronic search of the ERIC database: access is free through the ERIC Web site, and many libraries offer access through one or more of the major Internet providers. For a comparison of the interfaces offered by SilverPlatter (I523), FirstSearch (E225a), AskERIC (now defunct), and SearchERIC.org, see Janet Dagenais Brown, "The ERIC Database: A Comparison of Four Versions," *Reference Services Review* 31.2 (2003): 154–74; these four and the interfaces for EBSCO, Ovid, ProQuest, and CSA are compared in Christina Cicchetti, "A Comparative Review of the ERIC Database," *Charleston Advisor* 2.4 (2001): 5–8 and 3.2 (2002): 12–15.

The ERIC database is of interest to language and literature scholars for its indexing of works on composition and rhetoric — and occasionally on literature in journals not covered by the standard serial bibliographies and indexes in section G.

Although less extensive in coverage, *Education Index* (New York: Wilson, 1929– , 10/yr., with annual and larger cumulations; online, 22 Feb. 2006 <http://vnweb .hwwilsonweb.com/hww>, updated daily; CD-ROM, updated monthly) and *Education Index Retrospective: 1929–1983* (online, 22 Feb. 2006 <http:// vnweb.hwwilsonweb.com/hww>) offer author and subject indexing of publications before 1966 and are much more accessible than *CIJE* and *RIE* for post-1966 works. See entry I525 for an evaluation of the WilsonWeb search interface, which all the *Education Index* databases use.

See also

> *MLAIB* (G335): Literary Forms/Rhetoric section in the General part, Stylistics/ Rhetoric (as well as the Stylistics/Rhetoric section in individual language divisions) in the Linguistics part since 1981, and the Rhetoric and Composition division in pt. 4 since 2000. Researchers must also check the headings beginning "Composition," "Rhetoric," or "Rhetorical" in the subject index to post-1980 volumes and in the online thesaurus.

OTHER BIBLIOGRAPHIES

Although the Conference on College Composition and Communication planned a bibliography that would cover 1900 through 1973, the project has been abandoned. However, the result of the search of one decade is available as Nancy Jones, ed., *Bibliography of Composition, 1940–1949*, Rhetoric Society Quarterly Bibliographies in the Teaching of Composition 1, *Rhetoric Society Quarterly*, special issue 2 (1987), 75 pp., an author list and subject classification of 612 works in the theory, practice, and teaching of composition.

U5600   Horner, Winifred Bryan, ed. *Historical Rhetoric: An Annotated Bibliography of Selected Sources in English.* Reference Publication in Literature. Boston: Hall, 1980. 294 pp.   Z7004.R5 H57 [PN187]   016.808.
    A highly selective bibliography of primary works and scholarship (through c. 1978) important to the study of rhetoric through the nineteenth century. Although encompassing some classical and European writers, Horner emphasizes English-language works on English and American literature. The entries are listed in five separately compiled divisions (classical, Middle Ages, Renaissance, eighteenth century, and nineteenth century), each with separate lists of primary and secondary works preceded by an introductory overview and statement of scope and limitations. The divisions vary considerably in their coverage (especially of foreign-language scholarship) and in the quality of their descriptive annotations. Indexed by persons, primary works, and subjects (but there are omissions and inaccuracies). Addressed to the novice, *Historical Rhetoric* is a convenient source for identifying the major primary works and studies, but it must be supplemented with Horner, *Present State of Scholarship* (U5565). Review: Victor J. Vitanza, *Analytical and Enumerative Bibliography* 6 (1982): 25–28.

Periodicals

GUIDES TO PRIMARY WORKS

U5605   Anson, Chris M., and Bruce R. Maylath. "Searching for Journals: A Brief Guide and 100 Sample Species." *Teacher as Writer: Entering the Professional Conversation.* Ed. Karin L. Dahl. Urbana: NCTE, 1992. 150–87.
    PN147.T328   808'.02'024372.
    A title list of 100 journals devoted to the study and teaching of composition. A typical entry includes title, auspices or organization responsible for publication, frequency, audience and circulation, areas of emphasis, subscription price, address for submissions, subscription address, degree of interest in publishing articles on writing and literacy, ratio of articles on writing and literacy to total number of articles published during the past five years, and advice from the editor on submitting manuscripts. For information on editorial policies and submission requirements, researchers should check a recent issue. The inclusion of major as well as regional periodicals makes this useful to those wanting to identify journals specializing in a particular area or searching for an appropriate place to submit an article.
    For an evaluative survey of major periodicals, see Robert J. Connors, "Journals in Composition Studies," *College English* 46 (1986): 348–65.

Computers and the Humanities

Surveys

U5650   *A Companion to Digital Humanities.* Ed. Susan Schreibman, Ray Siemens,
        and John Unsworth. Blackwell Companions to Literature and Culture.
        Malden: Blackwell, 2004. 611 pp.   AZ105.C588   001.3′0285.

A multidisciplinary collection of essays intended to document the evolution of
humanities computing and its present state and to suggest future directions for research
and applications. Of most interest to users of this *Guide* will be the essays on literary
studies, performing arts, databases, marking up texts, text encoding, audiences for and
purposes of electronic texts, stylistic analysis and authorship studies, preparation and
analysis of linguistic corpora, electronic editing, textual analysis, thematic digital collections, print scholarship and digital resources, digital media and the analysis of film,
cognitive stylistics, designing sustainable projects and publications, converting primary
sources to digital form, tools for text analysis, and interfaces. Predictably, the essays vary
in quality: the best offer clear, practical introductions or overviews ("Text Tools"), but
some are too heavily theoretical at the expense of the historical ("Literary Studies"),
others are too technical ("Databases") or simplistic ("How the Computer Works"), and
some are ponderous ("History of Humanities Computing"); even so, *Companion to
Digital Humanities* offers the best general introduction to this amorphous field.

Despite its title, Willard McCarty, *Humanities Computing* (Basingstoke: Palgrave,
2005, 311 pp.), never moves much beyond an unsuccessful attempt to theorize the
field.

See also

> Sec. I: Internet Resources.
> *Electronic Textual Editing* (U5217).
> Howard-Hill, *Literary Concordances* (U5680).
> Shillingsburg, *Scholarly Editing in the Computer Age* (U5230).

Guides to Scholarship

U5657   *Humanities Computing Yearbook [1988–90]: A Comprehensive Guide to
        Software and Other Resources.* Oxford: Clarendon–Oxford UP, 1988–91.
        Annual.   Z699.5.H8.H85   016.0013′0285.

A survey of scholarship, software, and other resources for computing in the humanities. The first volume covers materials through 1987. Entries are divided among
29 divisions: archaeology; art history; biblical studies; computational linguistics; creative
writing; dance; drama; English-language instruction; folklore; historical studies; law;
lexicography; linguistics; musicology; natural languages and literatures (classified by
language, with English subdivided by historical period); philosophy; bibliographic
databases; editing and publishing; information management; programming languages;
second-language instruction; statistics; text analysis; text-processing techniques; bibliographies; electronic texts; general guides and history; optical character recognition;
people and places. Each division or section consists of three parts: an overview of the

topic; a selected, descriptively annotated bibliography of publications; and a list of software and databases. Several entries are annotated, some extensively; however, descriptions of software are usually based on information from vendors rather than independent evaluation. Many software entries helpfully cite reviews or related materials. Indexed by persons, product names, companies, and subjects. The volume for 1989–90 successfully addressed many of the problems that plagued the one for 1988: inadequate indexing, inconsistencies in classifying entries, use of several nonmutually exclusive sections, lack of cross-references, and generally shoddy editing. *Humanities Computing Yearbook* offered admirably broad coverage of software and publications (scholarly as well as technical and popular), with vol. 1 the best available guide to the important early work involving computers and the humanities. With the yearbook's unfortunate demise a serial bibliography of computing in the humanities became again a major desideratum. Review: (1988) Joseph Raben, *Computers and the Humanities* 24 (1990): 111–13 (however, many of the shortcomings identified by Raben were remedied).

See also

Sec. G: Serial Bibliographies, Indexes, and Abstracts.

ABELL (G340): Language, Literature, and the Computer division since the volume for 1971.

MLAIB (G335): General IV: Themes and Types/Computer-Assisted [Literary] Research in the volumes for 1966–80; Professional Topics/Computer-Assisted Research in pt. 4 of the volumes for 1981–99; and Research Tools/Computer-Assisted Research in the later volumes. Researchers must also check the headings beginning "Computation," "Computational," or "Computer" in the subject index to post-1980 volumes and in the online thesaurus.

Computer Programs

U5659   *TACT [Text-Analysis Computing Tools]*. Version 2.1. Online. 5 June 2005
         <http://www.chass.utoronto.ca/tact>.

A shareware text-analysis program that is useful for detecting patterns in a writer's use of words, phrases, or themes; for attributing authorship; for producing concordances (though *Oxford Concordance Program* [U5685] is better for preparing camera-ready copy for a printed concordance); and for comparing usage in two texts. Users must begin with Ian Lancashire, *Using* TACT *with Electronic Texts: A Guide to Text-Analysis Computing Tools Version 2.1 for MS-DOS and PC DOS* (New York: MLA, 1996, 361 pp.), which is accompanied by a CD-ROM with the most recent version and sample literary texts and which includes a chapter on how the program can be used in studying a text.

For a description of other text-analysis tools, see John Bradley, "Text Tools," pp. 505–22, in *A Companion to Digital Humanities* (U5650).

Concordances

Although it is an essential tool for analyzing imagery, themes, and style as well as for locating specific passages, a concordance must be used with due regard for its editor's choice and handling of the base text(s). Specifically, researchers must evaluate the following:

> which edition(s) are used as base text(s), since a corrupt base text will result in a worthless concordance;
> which words or forms, if any, have been excluded;
> how variant spellings are recorded;
> how variant readings and cancelled passages are handled;
> whether homographs are differentiated;
> what the bases for the frequency counts are (e.g., if homographs are undifferentiated, a frequency count is of no value).

Those using a concordance for extensive analysis of an author or work will do well to spend an hour with Howard-Hill, *Literary Concordances* (U5680).

Some concordances are listed in Brewer, *Dictionaries, Encyclopedias, and Other Word-Related Books* (U6020).

General Introductions

U5680   Howard-Hill, T. H. *Literary Concordances: A Guide to the Preparation of Manual and Computer Concordances.* Oxford: Pergamon, 1979. 97 pp. Z695.92.H68   802′.8′5.

An examination of the principles and practices of editing a concordance, with discussions of selection and preediting of a base text, arrangement of entries, organization of entries under headwords, selection of entries, statistical information, preliminary and subsidiary matter (such as statistical tables), and special forms of concordances. Concludes with an appendix by Robert L. Oakman on the now-outdated *COCOA* program, a selective bibliography, and a glossary. Indexed by persons and subjects. Although now dated in its treatment of computer hardware and software, Howard-Hill remains the best introduction to the principles and techniques of editing a concordance and is essential reading for both prospective editors and those evaluating published concordances. Reviews: Serge Lusignan, *Computers and the Humanities* 14 (1980): 129–30; Michael J. Preston, *English Language Notes* 18 (1981): 321–24.

See also

> Sec. U: Literature-Related Topics and Sources/Computers and the Humanities.

Computer Programs

U5685   Hockey, Susan, and Ian Marriot. *Oxford Concordance Program (OCP).* Version 2.0. Oxford: Oxford U Computing Service, 1987.

Hockey, Susan. *Micro-OCP (Oxford Concordance Program).* Oxford: Oxford UP, 1987. (The manual was reprinted with corrections in 1989.) QA76.9.T48   410.

A natural language program designed for the production of concordances, word lists, and frequency counts for use in analyzing style, vocabulary, grammatical forms, and rhyme schemes. The program has the advantages of being flexible, inexpensive, machine-independent, and accompanied by an intelligible user's manual (a rarity in this genre). Version 2.0 runs more quickly and economically than the original. Although *OCP* is superior to *COCOA* or *CLOC*, two other widely used concordance programs, some computer centers that had problems installing version 1.0 (1980) report that Oxford University Computing Service offered virtually no technical support. For a description of *OCP* 2.0, see S. Hockey and J. Martin, "The Oxford Concordance Program Version 2," *Literary and Linguistic Computing* 2 (1987): 125–31. Reviews: (version 1.0) Frank O'Brien, *Computers and the Humanities* 20 (1986): 138–41 (with comments and evaluations by a variety of users); (*Micro-OCP*) Randall L. Jones, *Computers and the Humanities* 23 (1989): 131–35.

Users should watch the journals *Computers and the Humanities* and *Literary and Linguistic Computing* for notices of new concordance programs.

Copyright

Whether writing for publication or hire, quoting from or editing published or manuscript works, engaging in desktop or Web publishing, or reproducing printed material for classroom use, scholars must be aware of the basic provisions (as well as subsequent administrative guidelines or regulations) in appropriate national copyright acts that govern literary property rights.

Researchers needing to identify the holder of a copyright should first check *WATCH: Writers, Artists, and Their Copyright Holders* (http://tyler.hrc.utexas.edu), an invaluable database "of copyright holders or contact persons for authors whose archives are housed, in whole or in part, in libraries and archives in North America and the United Kingdom." *WATCH* also provides valuable guides for identifying copyright holders in the United States and United Kingdom. Researchers will also find helpful basic advice in *How to Investigate the Copyright Status of a Work*, circular R-22 (http:// www.copyright.gov/circs/circ22.html or http://www.copyright.gov/circs/circ22.pdf).

General Introductions

U5700   Strong, William S. *The Copyright Book: A Practical Guide.* 5th ed.
            Cambridge: MIT P, 1999. 376 pp.   KF2994.S75   346.7304'82.
            An explanation of United States copyright law, with chapters devoted to the kind of material that can be copyrighted; ownership of copyright (with discussion of work for hire); transferring copyright; copyright notice; registration of copyright; rights conferred under copyright; compulsory licenses; infringement of copyright and fair use; copyright status of works created before 1978; tax treatment of copyright; and international copyright protection. The planned updates were never posted at the MIT Press Web site. The clear organization and explanations make this work essential reading for owners of copyrights and those producing copyrightable material. Review: Kenneth D. Crews, *Library Quarterly* 71 (2001): 405–08.

Sample permission agreements (and straightforward explanations of how to request permission) can be found in Richard Stim, *Getting Permission: How to License and Clear Copyrighted Materials Online and Off,* 2nd ed. (Berkeley: Nolo, 2004, n. pag.).

For recent developments in copyright law, see *Journal of the Copyright Society of the USA.* For a clear, concise explanation of provisions affecting literature scholars, see the discussion by Arthur F. Abelman in Gibaldi, *MLA Style Manual* (U6400), 33–48.

British copyright law is conveniently summarized in J. M. Cavendish and Kate Pool, *Handbook of Copyright in British Publishing Practice*, 3rd ed. (London: Cassell, 1993, 239 pp.).

Cultural Studies

Histories and Surveys

U5710   During, Simon. *Cultural Studies: A Critical Introduction.* London:
          Routledge–Taylor and Francis, 2005. 244 pp.   HM623.D87   306'.071.
    Defining cultural studies "as the engaged analysis of contemporary cultures," offers an introduction to the field's "core topics": the discipline itself; time (past, present, future); space (local to global); media (television, popular music, and the Internet and technoculture); identity (multiculturalism and race); sexuality and gender (including queer culture); and value (high and low culture). Combining historical overviews, summaries of representative scholarship, descriptions of methodologies, and considerations of how cultural studies is demarcated from such related disciplines as literary studies, art history, and sociology, During offers an accessible overview of the evolving discipline of cultural studies.

Environmental Studies

Guides to Scholarship and Criticism

U5737   *ASLE Online Bibliography [2000–].* Assn. for the Study of Literature and
          the Environment. Online. 2 June 2005 <http://www.biblioserver.com/
          asle/>. Updated regularly.
          *ISLE Working Bibliography of Recent Scholarship in Literature and
          Environment (1999–2001).* Online. 2 June 2005 <http://www.unr.edu/cla/
          engl/isle/Bib.htm>.
          ASLE Bibliography: Books for Which We Need Abstracts and Keywords.
          Online. 3 June 2005 <http://people.cohums.ohio-state.edu/ulman1/asle/
          Books_A2E.htm>. (Includes books in the 1998–2000 *ISLE Working
          Bibliography* that have not been added to the *ASLE Online Bibliography.*)
          ASLE Bibliography [1990–97]. Online. 19 Sept. 2006 <http://
          etext.lib.virginia.edu/osi/ASLE/asle.html>. Electronic version of *Association
          for the Study of Literature and the Environment: Bibliography [1990–97]*
          (Knoxville: U of Tennessee, Knoxville, Libraries, [1994–99]).
    An annotated bibliography of English-language studies (including dissertations, creative works, and film and other media) involving the relationship of literature and the environment and related topics. Entries in the *ASLE Online Bibliography* can be searched by author, index term, title, and periodical title from the simple search screen; the advanced search screen allows Boolean combinations of the preceding fields. Users who browse the entire set of records by title or author will be disconcerted by the numerous entries alphabetized by an author's forename rather than surname. The ma-

jority of records are accompanied by an uninformative, brief summary or are not annotated, and many of the existing annotations are merely tables of contents. Since the site depends on contributions by members of Association for the Study of Literature and the Environment and contributing editors, coverage is, inevitably, uneven and citation style inconsistent. The *ISLE Working Bibliography* and the *ASLE Bibliography* are alphabetical lists that can be searched by a Web browser's find function (*ISLE*) and by rudimentary search screens (*ASLE*); only the latter includes brief annotations, and the former lists books only. Books from the *ISLE Working Bibliography* are added to the *ASLE Online Bibliography* as annotations are submitted. The online *ASLE Bibliography* is a decided improvement over its print counterpart, whose taxonomy was cumbersome. Although coverage is not comprehensive (and several entries are taken from secondhand sources in the *ASLE Bibliography*), these online bibliographies currently offer the fullest guide to studies of nature writing and literature and the environment. Researchers must also search "ecocriticism," "ecofeminism" and "environment," and "environmental" (and related terms) in the subject index to post-1980 volumes of *MLAIB* (G335) and in the online thesaurus.

Film and Literature

This section is limited to reference works of particular value to the study of the relationship between English-language film and literature. Because of the nature of the film industry and its documentation, factual information about individual films and persons is sometimes contradictory or unavailable; thus researchers must exercise more than usual care when consulting film reference sources.

Many drama and theater reference works include film (e.g., see section L: Genres/ Drama and Theater) as do some in section U: Literature-Related Topics and Sources/ Interdisciplinary and Multidisciplinary Studies.

For an introduction to the interdisciplinary study of literature and film, see Gerald Mast, "Literature and Film" (pp. 278–306), in Barricelli, *Interrelations of Literature* (U5955).

Research Methods

U5741   Hill, John, and Pamela Church Gibson, eds. *The Oxford Guide to Film
         Studies.* Oxford: Oxford UP, 1998. 624 pp.   PN1995.O93   791.43′01′5.
   A guide to critical approaches to the study of cinema, with separately authored essays devoted to "the main disciplinary approaches and theoretical frameworks which have been employed in the study of film, the main concepts and methods involved in film analysis, and the main issues involved in the discussion of specific areas (such as national cinemas)." Each essay typically identifies key terms, issues, debates, and unresolved questions related to its topic and closes with a selective bibliography; interspersed throughout are illustrative case studies and readings. Of particular value is the section on critical approaches, with essays on such topics as film and psychoanalysis, feminism and film, queer theory, and cultural studies and film. Indexed selectively by persons and film titles. The overall clarity of the essays and their blend of theory and illustration make *Oxford Guide to Film Studies* an indispensable handbook for anyone writing or reading film criticism.

For practical advice on doing research in film archives, see Eric Schaefer and Dan Streible, "Archival News," *Cinema Journal* 40.1 (2000): 127–33; for candid advice on working with printed materials related to cinema in major United States, British, and French libraries, see Stephen Bottomore, "A Critical View of Some Major Libraries: The Perspective of an Early Cinema Historian," *Moving Image* 4.2 (2004): 86–110.

Guides to Reference Works

U5745   Fisher, Kim N. *On the Screen: A Film, Television, and Video Research Guide.* Reference Sources in the Humanities Series. Littleton: Libraries Unlimited, 1986. 209 pp.   Z5784.M9 F535 [PN1994]   016.7914.

A guide to English-language reference sources, for the most part published in the United States between 1960 and 1985. Entries are organized in 14 classified divisions, most of which have separate sections for film and television: bibliographical guides; dictionaries and encyclopedias; indexes, abstracts, and databases; biographical sources; credits; film reviews and television programming; catalogs; directories and yearbooks; filmographies and videographies; bibliographies; handbooks and miscellaneous sources; periodicals; research centers and archives; societies and associations. The full annotations are accompanied by generally rigorous evaluations. Two indexes: authors and titles; subjects. Although the classification system is not as refined as it could be, judicious selection and evaluation make *On the Screen* the best guide to reference sources for the study of film in the United States. What is still needed is a similar guide that is international in scope.

See also

Joseph Milicia and Michael Klossner, "Science Fiction in Film, Television, and Radio" (pp. 678–734), in Barron, *Anatomy of Wonder* (L1015).

Handbooks, Dictionaries, and Encyclopedias

There is no satisfactory general encyclopedia of film. Of those available, the least objectionable is Ephraim Katz, *The Film Encyclopedia*, 5th ed., rev. Fred Klein and Ronald Dean Nolen (New York: Harper, 2005, 1,542 pp.), but the bulk of its entries are biographies. For an evaluation of encyclopedias through the early 1980s, see Daniel A. Greenberg, "The Reference Shelf Shuffle," *Film Quarterly* 36.2 (1982–83): 5–16.

U5750   Beaver, Frank Eugene. *Dictionary of Film Terms: The Aesthetic Companion to Film Art.* New York: Lang, 2006. 289 pp.   PN1993.45.B33   791.43'03.

A dictionary of genres, styles, techniques, and concepts associated with film. The full definitions are accompanied by specific examples and sometimes by illustrations. Four indexes: terms; film and television titles; persons; and general topics (such as camera movement, criticism, editing). Clear and concise, Beaver is a useful reference for those writing as well as reading film studies and supersedes *Dictionary of Film Terms: The Aesthetic Companion to Film Analysis*, 2nd ed., Twayne's Filmmakers Series (New York: Twayne, 1994, 410 pp.).

See also

    Enciclopedia dello spettacolo (L1130).

Bibliographies of Bibliographies

U5755 Wulff, Hans Jürgen, comp. and ed. *Bibliography of Film Bibliographies/ Bibliographie der Filmbibliographien.* München: Saur, 1987. 326 pp. Z5784.M9 W84 [PN1994] 016'.01679143.

    A bibliography of bibliographies, including those appended to books and articles as well as booksellers' and library catalogs. The approximately 1,200 entries are in two parts (works in Germanic and Romance languages; those in Slavic languages, compiled by Andrzej Gwóźdź and Anna Wastkowska). Each part is organized in nine extensively classified divisions: formal bibliographies (including filmographies and discographies), general bibliographies of film literature, film theory and research, special topics, history of the cinema, genre studies, national cinemas, persons, and related fields (including communications research and television). Most entries are accompanied by brief descriptive annotations. Two indexes: authors and editors; subjects. Impressive in its international coverage, Wulff is the essential source for identifying film bibliographies.

Guides to Primary Works

FILMOGRAPHIES

U5760 *AFI Catalog.* Chadwyck-Healey. Online. 1 Aug. 2006 <http:// afi.chadwyck.com>. Updated regularly. (The American Film Institute maintains a separate site [http://www.afi.com] that includes the same data but has different search capabilities; the site is restricted to AFI members.)

    The American Film Institute Catalog of Motion Pictures Produced in the United States. Berkeley: U of California P, 1971– . PN1998.A57 016.79143'75'0973.

        Vol. A: *Film Beginnings, 1893–1910: A Work in Progress.* Comp. Elias Savada. 2 pts. Metuchen: Scarecrow, 1995.
        Vol. F1: *Feature Films, 1911–1920.* Ed. Patricia King Hanson. 2 pts. 1988.
        Vol. F2: *Feature Films, 1921–1930.* Ed. Kenneth W. Munden. 2 pts. New York: Bowker, 1971.
        Vol. F3: *Feature Films, 1931–1940.* Ed. Hanson. 3 pts. 1993.
        Vol. F4: *Feature Films, 1941–1950.* Ed. Hanson. 3 pts. 1999.
        Vol. F6: *Feature Films, 1961–1970.* Ed. Richard P. Krafsur. 2 pts. New York: Bowker, 1976.
        (Because of funding issues and the presence of *AFI Catalog,* it is unlikely that the other projected volumes will appear in printed form.)

    A catalog of films produced for public showing in the United States. Although the criteria governing inclusion vary from volume to volume, each utilizes a combination of length, audience, and country of origin. Assignment to a volume is based on release date (or, lacking that information, date of copyright, initial showing, or licensing by a state commission). Within a volume, films are listed alphabetically by original title (with cross-references to alternative and variant titles). A typical entry consists of four parts, with the components of each depending on the period and kind of film: identification and physical description (citing title, country of origin, producer or production company, original distributor, date of release, copyright date, audio information, color, gauge and length, and MPAA rating); production credits (including persons, groups, companies, and organizations); cast (both performers and their roles); and description of contents (including genre, source, lengthy synopsis, and subject indexing terms). Notes explain any conflicts in sources. Because many films are not extant or available for screening and sources vary considerably in completeness and accuracy, several entries are necessarily incomplete or inaccurate in some details (many of these unavailable films are described in the reviews and articles reprinted in *The New York Times Encyclopedia of Film [1896–1979]*, ed. Gene Brown, 13 vols. [New York: Times, 1984]). Volumes F2 and F6 have two indexes: credits (including all personal and corporate names, with a separate alphabetic list for literary source credits); subjects (including headings for genres, character types, themes, dates and seasons, historical events and persons, places, institutions, physical objects, cinematic devices, animals, and literary works enacted). Volumes A, F1, F3, and F4 have seven to eleven indexes: chronological list of titles, personal names, corporate names, subjects, genres, places, foreign countries, series, foreign languages, songwriters and composers, and literary and dramatic sources. Inevitably there are errors, but the thoroughness of coverage, assimilation of widely scattered factual information, detailed synopses, and excellent indexes make the published volumes indispensable sources that supersede other catalogs for the respective periods. Unfortunately, work on the remaining years proceeds slowly, with priority going to the cataloging of feature films. Review: (vol. F2) Herman G. Weinberg, *Film Quarterly* 25.2 (1971–72): 59–65.

AFI Catalog, which corrects and updates the printed catalogs, currently covers films from 1893–1958 and 1961–70. It can be searched by keyword (in simple search mode) or (in advanced search) by combinations of keyword, title, director, character name, cast, crew, source of screenplay, year of release, country of origin, subject, songs, genre, or miscellaneous information; each field in advanced search includes a browsable list of terms. The list of abbreviations used in records is hidden at the bottom of the *AFI Catalog* FAQ page. Records, which include the same kinds of information as in the printed volumes, can be sorted alphabetically or chronologically and can be exported only by e-mail. *AFI Catalog*—which not only supersedes its printed ancestors but also offers a more efficient, thorough way of searching and manipulating a massive amount of data on American films—is the most authoritative filmography in its field, but *IMDb* (U5767) offers far broader coverage.

AFI Catalog and *Film Index International* (U5767a) can be cross-searched through *Film Indexes Online* (Chadwyck-Healey; online; 1 Aug. 2006 <http://film.chadwyck .com>).

U5765   Gifford, Denis. *The British Film Catalogue*. 3rd ed. 2 vols. London: Fitzroy Dearborn, 2000.   PN1993.5.G7   016.791430941.

> Vol. 1: *Fiction Film, 1895–1994*. 1,097 pp.
> Vol. 2: *Non-fiction Film, 1888–1994*. 625 pp.

A catalog of films produced for public entertainment and made in the British Isles or by British subjects elsewhere in the world between 1888 and 1994. Gifford includes both feature length and short films but excludes amateur productions, films made for and shown exclusively on television, and animations. The 28,158 films are listed chronologically by month of initial exhibition. Depending on the information available, entries include original title (and title changes), length, censor's rating, sound, color system, screen ratio, production company, distributor, reissues (with date and any title changes), producer, director, author and source of story, author and source of screenplay, narrator, important members of the cast (with roles), type of film (see 1: xiii–xiv for an explanation of categories), a synopsis, and awards. Entries after 1970 identify additional technical and artistic personnel. Indexed by titles in each volume. According to Bottomore, "A Critical View of Some Major Libraries" (U5741a) the Cataloguing Department of the British Film Institute Library holds a card index to persons. Although not exhaustive (especially in the case of shorts, pre-1927 releases, and films covered in vol. 2), Gifford is a monumental accumulation of information, but one whose value is considerably diminished by the lack of subject and person indexes. Much fuller information on many films listed herein can be found in *IMDb* (U5767).

Researchers should avoid the second edition of Gifford— *The British Film Catalogue, 1895–1985: A Reference Guide* (New York: Facts on File, 1986, n. pag.)—which grafts entries covering 1971–85 to a corrected reprint of Gifford, *The British Film Catalogue, 1895–1970: A Reference Guide* (New York: McGraw, 1973, n. pag.), hides a second introduction (which identifies additional abbreviations and notes some important modifications of scope and parts of an entry) after the 1970 listings, and prints two title indexes (that for 1895–1970 has a separate alphabetic sequence at the end for additions).

U5767   *Internet Movie Database* (*IMDb*). Online. 2 June 2005 <http://
         www.imdb.com>. Updated daily.

A database of more than 448,752 titles (as of June 2005) from throughout the world dating from the beginnings of cinema to the newest releases. There are apparently no restrictions on what is included: silent films, classics, trash, x-rated, and made-for-television films are all here (as are television series and video games). The ten search screens give users sophisticated options for searching by title, person, character, keyword, and plot summary. Records vary in content, with full ones including complete production details, cast and crew, awards, reviews, plot summaries, technical specifications, merchandising details, and formats; much of the information is helpfully hyperlinked. Of particular importance to literature researchers is the ability to retrieve full details of films based on a literary work. Although much information is supplied by users, *IMDb* offers the fullest, most accessible guide to films worldwide. Sporting fully documented help screens, well-designed search pages (from simple to advanced), and easily navigable displays, *IMDb* fully deserves its many accolades and serves as an example of the kind of free database the Web too seldom delivers. (*IMDbpro*—the subscription version— offers additional data primarily of interest to entertainment industry professionals.)

IMDb is occasionally supplemented by the following databases:

> *Film Index International.* Chadwyck-Healey. Online. 1 Aug. 2006 <http://
> film.chadwyck.com>. Updated twice a year. Although it covers only
> about one-quarter of the number of films in *IMDb*, it cites some studies
> of individual films. It and *AFI Catalog* (U5760) can be cross-searched
> through *Film Indexes Online* (Chadwyck-Healey; online; 1 Aug. 2006
> <http://film.chadwyck.com>).

> *TVGuide.com.* Online. 3 June 2005 <http://www.TVguide.com>. Updated
> daily. The Movies database at *TVGuide.com* incorporates some data from
> (and continues) Jay Robert Nash and Stanley Ralph Ross, *The Motion
> Picture Guide*, 12 vols (Chicago: Cinebooks, 1985–87), and *The Motion*

Picture Guide Annual (New York: Cinebooks, 1987–99; CD-ROM [1995]). The primitive search interface allows searching only by person or title (not both).

GUIDES TO LITERARY SOURCES

U5775   Dimmitt, Richard Bertrand. *A Title Guide to the Talkies: A Comprehensive Listing of 16,000 Feature-Length Films from October, 1927, until December, 1963.* 2 vols. New York: Scarecrow, 1965. Andrew A. Aros. *A Title Guide to the Talkies, 1964 through 1974.* 1977. 336 pp. *1975 through 1984.* 1986. 347 pp.   PN1998.D55   791.438.

A guide to plays, short stories, novels, poems, screen stories, story ideas, and other sources of feature films since 1927. Although the original compilation is limited to American films, the continuations include foreign ones exhibited in the United States and extend coverage to novelizations. Organized by film title, each entry consists of a brief note on the source of the script, screenplay, or idea. Indexed by authors. Although many entries fail to record exact publication details or are frustratingly vague in identifying a source merely as "a story by" someone, no other work covers so many kinds of sources or as many movies.

While not as thorough in coverage, the following list additional films or sometimes identify sources more precisely:

> Daisne, Johan. *Dictionnaire filmographique de la littérature mondiale/Filmographic Dictionary of World Literature/Filmographisches Lexikon der Weltliteratur/Filmografisch Lexicon der Wereldliteratuur.* 2 vols. Gand: Story-Scientia, 1971–75. *Supplement.* 1978. 638 pp. The only guide offering decent coverage of sources of foreign films (through 1977).
>
> Emmens, Carol A. *Short Stories on Film and Video.* 2nd ed. Littleton: Libraries Unlimited, 1985. 337 pp. Unlike Dimmitt and Aros, Emmens cites titles of short stories.
>
> *Enser's Filmed Books and Plays: A List of Books and Plays from Which Films Have Been Made, 1928–2001.* Comp. Ellen Baskin. Aldershot: Ashgate, 2003. 1,203 pp. Includes made-for-television movies, series, and animated films. All but a few of the entries are for English-language films.
>
> Gifford, Denis. *Books and Plays in Films, 1896–1915: Literary, Theatrical, and Artistic Sources of the First Twenty Years of Motion Pictures.* London: Mansell; Jefferson: McFarland, 1991. 206 pp. International in coverage, with films organized under headings for authors and artists.
>
> Langman, Larry. *Writers on the American Screen: A Guide to Film Adaptations of American and Foreign Literary Works.* Garland Reference Library of the Humanities 658. New York: Garland, 1986. 329 pp. Limited to American film adaptations of printed works and marred by an inadequate explanation of scope; includes some films not in Enser (and vice versa).

See also

> *AFI Catalog* (U5760).
> Hubin, *Crime Fiction, 1981–1985* (L915).
> *Internet Movie Database* (U5767).

Guides to Scholarship and Criticism

SERIAL BIBLIOGRAPHIES

U5780   *Film Literature Index [1973–]: A Quarterly Author-Subject Index to the International Periodical Literature of Film and Television/Video.* Albany: Film and Television Documentation Center, SU of New York at Albany, 1973– . Quarterly, with annual cumulation. (Subtitle varies.) Z5784.M9 F45   791.43'01'6.

     Film and Television Literature Index. EBSCO. Online. 26 Aug. 2006 <http://web.ebscohost.com/ehost>. Updated regularly. (A full text version is in progress.)

     Film Literature Index Online. Version 1.1. Indiana University Digital Library Program. Online. 10 June 2006 <http://webapp1.dlib.indiana.edu/fli/index.jsp>.

An author and subject index to material on film, television, and video published in some 300 periodicals worldwide. Excludes fan magazines and technical journals. Expanded coverage of television begins in vol. 5 (1977), of video in vol. 14 (1986). Since vol. 14, entries are organized in two parts: film; television and video. Each part consists of a single author and subject index, with liberal cross-references and with subject headings including titles of films or television programs, persons, geographical areas, and corporate bodies. With its inclusion of television and broader coverage of periodicals that print only occasional material on film or television, this is an important complement to *International Index to Film Periodicals* (U5785). Since each work indexes journals omitted by the other, the two together offer the best coverage of periodicals since 1972 and are essential sources for identifying articles on film and television adaptations of literary works as well as reviews of films, programs, and related books.

Film and Television Literature Index, which incorporates data since 1987 from *Film Literature Index* with entries generated by EBSCO (presumably from its other databases), uses the standard EBSCO search interface (see entry I512 for an evaluation) with the following differences: Basic Search allows users to limit a search to a specific publication; Advanced Search does not allow searches of specific record fields but users can limit a search by type of publication and document. The earliest document is from 1926, but extensive coverage does not begin until the late 1980s. Unfortunately, the Web site lacks a sufficient explanation of scope and editorial practices.

Film Literature Index Online covers 1976–2001; there is currently no plan to add additional records. The Basic Search screen allows users to search by keyword, production title, or person. Advanced Search searches by keyword, production title, person, person as subject, title, journal, subject, and corporate name to be limited by date, format (film or TV), document type, document features (e.g., biography, filmography), language, and peer-reviewed journals. Users can also browse lists of subjects, persons, production titles, and corporate names. Results, which appear in descending chronological order, can be e-mailed, saved, or printed.

The indexing of periodicals before the advent of *Film Literature Index* and *International Index to Film Periodicals* is unsatisfactory. Although there is considerable overlap among the following, each must be checked either because of its scope or its organization:

Batty, Linda. *Retrospective Index to Film Periodicals, 1930–1971.* New York: Bowker, 1975. 425 pp. An index to articles and reviews in only 14 English-language film periodicals (each of which is indexed in both Gerlach and MacCann—see below) and the *Village Voice.* The dates in the title are misleading, since only two of the journals were being published before 1950. The best that can be said for this work is that it includes reviews and that its subject indexing is better than in MacCann.

Bowles, Stephen E., comp. and ed. *Index to Critical Film Reviews in British and American Periodicals, Together with Index to Critical Reviews of Books about Film.* 3 vols. in 2. New York: Franklin, 1974–75. A title index to reviews of films (vols. 1–2) and books (vol. 3) in 31 major British and American film periodicals through 1971. Entries indicate the approximate number of words. Unfortunately, not all issues of some journals are indexed and few of those covered were published before 1950. Since the other retrospective indexes seldom include reviews (especially of books), this is an essential, if limited, source.

The Film Index: A Bibliography. 3 vols. White Plains: Kraus, 1941–85. A subject guide to English-language materials published through 1935 (with occasional later entries). *Film Index* includes fan and trade magazines, reviews of films and books, but excludes newspaper articles. In vol. 1, *The Film as Art* (1941, 723 pp.), the approximately 8,600 entries are organized in two extensively classified divisions: history and technique; types of films (including a section on adaptations). Vols. 2 and 3 — *The Film as Industry* (1985, 587 pp.) and *The Film in Society* (1985, 507 pp.) — include, respectively, sections on the history of the industry and censorship. Vol. 1 is indexed by persons, titles, and a few subjects; vols. 2–3, by persons. The fullest guide to pre-1936 publications, *Film Index* is particularly useful for its descriptive annotations.

Gerlach, John C., and Lana Gerlach. *The Critical Index: A Bibliography of Articles on Film in English, 1946–1973, Arranged by Names and Topics.* New Humanistic Research Series. New York: Teachers College P, 1974. 726 pp. An annotated list of articles from 22 British, American, and Canadian film journals and about 60 general periodicals. The approximately 5,000 entries are organized in two parts: works about persons; subjects. Although overlapping considerably with MacCann and difficult to use, Gerlach does index some additional articles.

MacCann, Richard Dyer, and Edward S. Perry. *The New Film Index: A Bibliography of Magazine Articles in English, 1930–1970.* New York: Dutton, 1975. 522 pp. An annotated bibliography of articles from both film and general-interest periodicals. The approximately 12,000 entries are organized chronologically within classified subject divisions. Although the work is incomplete and less than accessible because of its poor subject organization, MacCann offers the broadest coverage of the retrospective indexes.

U5785   *FIAF International FilmArchive Database.* International Federation of Film Archives. Online. 29 June 2006 <http://web5s.silverplatter.com>. Updated regularly. CD-ROM.

FIAF International Index to Film Periodicals. Chadwyck-Healey. Online. 1 Aug. 2006 <http://fiaf.chadwyck.com>. Updated regularly.

International Index to Film Periodicals [1972–]: An Annotated Guide. Brussels: Intl. Federation of Film Archives, 1973– . Annual. Z5784.M9 I49   016.79143.

A subject index that currently covers about 79 periodicals published worldwide. Since the volume for 1983, entries are organized in three divisions: general subjects (with many headings subdivided by country; discussions of film versions of literary works are grouped under "adaptations" but are not indexed by literary author), individual films (organized alphabetically by original title), and biographical discussions (organized by biographee). Each entry is accompanied by a brief descriptive annotation. Two indexes: authors; directors. The best access is through the electronic versions, which are more current than the print volumes. *FIAF International FilmArchive Database* can be searched by subjects, titles of films, persons, directors, authors of articles, periodicals, and keywords; searches can be limited by country of publication, country in which the film originated, journal, language, date of publication, and date of film. Records (which are returned in no apparent order and cannot be sorted) can be marked for e-mailing, downloading, or printing. *FIAF International Index to Film Periodicals* can be searched by keyword, title of article, subject, film title, persons, journal title, author, ISSN, date of publication, country of publication, language, and type of publication. Results are returned in descending chronological order and can be sorted only by journal title. Records can be e-mailed, printed, downloaded, or saved to a personal archive. Both versions cover television (and incorporate *International Index to Television Periodicals [1979–90]* [London: Intl. Federation of Film Archives, 1983–93]). Although it covers fewer journals than *Film Literature Index* (U5780) and the print version is unacceptably far in arrears in indexing many of them, the *International Index* does annotate entries. Since each work indexes journals omitted by the other, the two together offer the best coverage of film periodicals since 1972 and are essential sources for identifying articles on film adaptations of literary works and reviews of films.

See also

Sec. G: Serial Bibliographies, Indexes, and Abstracts.
"Annual Review," *Journal of Modern Literature* (M2780).
Art Index (U5145).
"Bibliography on the Relations of Literature and the Other Arts" (U5965).
MLAIB (G335): General IV/Cinema in the volumes for 1975–80; General Literature/Film in pt. 4 of the volumes for 1981–91; and Dramatic Arts/Film in the later volumes. In the post-1980 volumes, several national literature divisions have a Film heading in the 1900–1999 section, and there are listings for individual directors. Researchers must also consult the headings beginning "Film" in the subject index to post-1980 volumes and in the online thesaurus.
RILM Abstracts (U6240).

OTHER BIBLIOGRAPHIES

U5790   Rehrauer, George. *The Macmillan Film Bibliography.* 2 vols. New York: Macmillan, 1982.   Z5784.M9 R423 [PN1993.5.A1]   016.79143'09.

An annotated selective bibliography of English-language books published through c. 1980 on all aspects of film. Rehrauer includes reference works, biographies, and published filmscripts, but excludes novelizations and fictional works about the film industry. Listed alphabetically by title, most of the 6,762 entries are accompanied by full descriptions of content and brief evaluative commentary. Because of the organization, users should generally approach the work through the subject, author, and filmscript indexes; however, they are sometimes inconsistent and lack sufficient cross-references. The criteria governing selection are insufficiently explained; the evaluations are frequently bland or too generous; and there are numerous typographical errors. Still, Rehrauer is the most complete bibliography of English-language books about the subject and an especially valuable resource for identifying discussions of a film, performer, or film-related subjects. Review: Raoul Kulberg, *Journal of Popular Film and Television* 10 (1983): 183–84.

This work supersedes Rehrauer, *Cinema Booklist* (Metuchen: Scarecrow, 1972, 473 pp.), *Supplement One* (1974, 405 pp.), and *Supplement Two* (1977, 470 pp.).

Although less complete than Rehrauer, the following works list a few additional books:

> Armour, Robert A. *Film: A Reference Guide.* American Popular Culture. Westport: Greenwood, 1980. 251 pp. A selective guide to some 1,500 English-language books published through c. 1979 and principally concerned with American film.
>
> Dyment, Alan R. *The Literature of the Film: A Bibliographical Guide to the Film as Art and Entertainment, 1936–1970.* London: White Lion, 1975. 398 pp. An annotated, highly selective subject list of English-language books.
>
> Ellis, Jack C., Charles Derry, and Sharon Kern. *The Film Book Bibliography, 1940–1975.* Metuchen: Scarecrow, 1979. 752 pp. An annotated list of English-language books and dissertations organized by subject.

U5793   Manchel, Frank. *Film Study: An Analytical Bibliography.* 4 vols. Rutherford: Fairleigh Dickinson UP; London: Assoc. UP, 1990.   Z5784.M9 M34 [PN1994]   016.79143.

A massive (albeit selective), extensively annotated guide to English-language works and films (through 1988) illustrating representative approaches to the study of film. The extended evaluations of some 500 books, annotated entries for about 2,000 additional books and several hundred films, and several thousand citations to other books and articles are organized in seven extensively subdivided chapters: film as film (with a section on film criticism and theory); genres; stereotyping in film (with sections on feminist approaches to film, psychoanalysis and film, and Jews and African Americans in American films); thematic approaches; comparative literature (with sections on Hollywood and literature, literature and film, novels and film, and film adaptations of stage plays); the period approach (with American film, 1913–19, as its focus); history of film (with sections on reference works, histories, and national traditions). Chapters and subdivisions are introduced by extensive commentary. Seven indexes: article titles; authors of articles; authors of books; book titles; film personalities; subjects; film titles. Because of the book's size and organization, users must study the list of contents in vol. 1 and make continual use of the indexes. Although omitting several important reference works, *Film Study* is valuable not only for the extent of its coverage but also for its uncompromising evaluation of so many studies.

DISSERTATIONS AND THESES

U5795 Fielding, Raymond, comp. *A Bibliography of Theses and Dissertations on the Subject of Film, 1916–1979.* University Film Association Monograph 3. Houston: Univ. Film Assn., 1979. 70 pp. Z5784.M9.

A list of theses and dissertations accepted by academic institutions in the United States between 1916 and 1979, although coverage after 1976 is incomplete. The 1,420 entries are listed alphabetically by author, with each entry recording title, degree, institution, and date of graduation. Indexed by subject at the beginning. Although the subject headings are usually too broad to be of much use, Fielding does bring together dissertations and theses accepted in a variety of departments. Researchers should also consult the works in section H: Guides to Dissertations and Theses.

LITERATURE AND FILM

U5800 Ross, Harris. *Film as Literature, Literature as Film: An Introduction to and Bibliography of Film's Relationship to Literature.* Bibliographies and Indexes in World Literature 10. New York: Greenwood, 1987. 346 pp. Z5784.M9 R66 [PN1995.3] 016.79143′01′5.

A bibliography of about 2,500 English-language books and articles published between 1908 and 1985. Most reviews and newspaper articles are excluded. Entries are organized alphabetically by author in divisions for general studies of literature and film, language and film (including linguistic approaches), prose fiction and film, drama and film, poetry and film, general studies of adaptation, writers and the film industry, American writers, writers of the United Kingdom, Shakespeare and film, classical writers, European writers, Latin American writers, published scripts by literary figures and scripts of adaptations, pedagogy, and bibliographies and filmographies. The divisions treating writers have sections for individual authors; that for Shakespeare has sections for individual plays. Entries are accompanied by a list of writers or films discussed only when a title needs clarification. Although the introductory survey of basic issues involving the relationship between literature and film comments on numerous works, it is no substitute for annotations. Two indexes: scholars; subjects. *Film as Literature* is marred by the failure to annotate all entries and is restricted to English-language works; nevertheless, it is the best guide to scholarship on literature and film.

Jeffrey Egan Welch, *Literature and Film: An Annotated Bibliography, 1909–1977,* Garland Reference Library of the Humanities 241 (New York: Garland, 1981, 315 pp.) and *1978–1988,* Garland Reference Library of the Humanities 1114 (1993, 341 pp.), is useful for its brief annotations of English-language scholarship on film adaptations of literary works, the relationship of film and literary genres, and the teaching of literature and film.

See also

Etulain, *Bibliographical Guide to the Study of Western American Literature* (Q3670).
Fishburn, *Women in Popular Culture* (U6590).
Frank, *Guide to the Gothic* (L875).
Gilbert, *Women's Studies: A Bibliography of Dissertations, 1870–1982* (U6615).

Humm, *Annotated Critical Bibliography of Feminist Criticism* (U6170).
Rice, *English Fiction, 1900–1950* (M2840).
Salem, *Guide to Critical Reviews* (Q4300).
Salzman, *American Studies: An Annotated Bibliography* (Q3335).
Wildbihler, *The Musical: An International Annotated Bibliography* (Q4295).

Biographical Dictionaries

See

Sec. J: Biographical Sources/Biographical Dictionaries.
Contemporary Theatre, Film, and Television (Q4305).

Periodicals

GUIDES TO PRIMARY WORKS

U5805   Slide, Anthony, ed. *International Film, Radio, and Television Journals.*
Historical Guides to the World's Periodicals and Newspapers. Westport:
Greenwood, 1985. 428 pp.   Z5784.M9 I485 [PN1993]   016.79143'05.
A collection of signed profiles of about 190 important or representative scholarly
and popular film periodicals from throughout the world, but emphasizing those published in the United States and Great Britain. Organized alphabetically by periodical
title, each profile consists of two parts: a discussion of the history, general contents, and
quality of the work; and a list of indexing sources, reprints, selected locations, title
changes, volume and issue data, publisher(s) and place(s) of publication, and editor(s).
Six appendixes: fan club journals; fan magazines (mostly American, since some British
ones are given regular profiles); in-house journals; national film journals; a list of journals
by country; a list by subject. Indexed by persons, journal titles, and some subjects.
Although the profiles vary in quality, Slide is a convenient source of descriptions and
evaluations of major film periodicals.

Folklore and Literature

This section is limited to reference works of particular importance to the investigation
of the relationship between literatures in English and folklore; consequently, special
attention is accorded works on narrative folklore genres in Great Britain and North
America. Works devoted to the relationship between folklore and a specific literature
are listed with the appropriate national literature.

For an introduction to the interdisciplinary study of literature and folklore, see
Bruce A. Rosenberg, "Literature and Folklore" (pp. 90–106), in Barricelli, *Interrelations
of Literature* (U5955).

Guides to Reference Works

U5825   Steinfirst, Susan. *Folklore and Folklife: A Guide to English-Language Reference Sources.* 2 vols. Garland Reference Library of the Humanities 1429: Garland Folklore Bibliographies 16. New York: Garland, 1992.   Z5981.S74 [GN66]   016.398.

An annotated guide to reference works for the study of folklore throughout the world, with most of the 2,577 entries for English-language books or serial bibliographies published before 1988 (although some works in other languages and published after 1987 are included). The descriptively annotated entries are organized in eight classified divisions: introduction to folklore and folklife (with sections for bibliographies, abstracts and indexes, catalogs, dictionaries and encyclopedias, and guides and handbooks), history and study of folklore, folk literature, ethnomusicology, folk belief systems, folk rituals and rites, material culture, and journals and societies; the organization of each division (except the first and last) generally follows that of the folklore volume of the *MLAIB* (G335). Many sections are prefaced by a headnote that identifies pertinent surveys, histories, and general studies. Annotations are generally descriptive, although several offer helpful comparative and evaluative comments or cite related works. Three indexes: authors; titles; subjects. Although it is not as current as it should be, although it includes several works that are not reference sources, and although it is mostly restricted to English-language publications, *Folklore and Folklife* is the best available guide to reference works for the study of folklore.

See also

Gohdes, *Bibliographical Guide to the Study of the Literature of the U. S. A.* (Q3180).

Webb, *Sources of Information in the Social Sciences* (U6460), whose section on anthropology (pp. 332–402) encompasses folklore.

Handbooks, Dictionaries, and Encyclopedias

U5830   *Enzyklopädie des Märchens: Handwörterbuch zur historischen und vergleichenden Erzählforschung.* Ed. Kurt Ranke et al. 14 vols. and supplements. Berlin: de Gruyter, 1977– .   GR72.E58.

A comparative, historical dictionary that ranges beyond folktales to include animal stories, jests, fairy tales, novelle, and legends. The signed articles by major scholars emphasize the religious, social, psychological, and historical backgrounds of European, Mediterranean, and Asian oral and written narratives, with those of the rest of the world treated in regional or national surveys. The approximately 3,600 planned entries include extensive articles on theories, methods, genres, major tale-types and motifs, figures, themes, scholars, nations, and regions. Each entry concludes with a selected bibliography. (Articles scheduled for future parts are listed in a periodic *Sprichwortliste.*) An extensive, authoritative compilation, *Enzyklopädie des Märchens* is especially valuable for its attention to literary works.

Hans-Jörg Uther, "The Encyclopedia of the Folktale," *Fairy Tales and Society: Illusion, Allusion, and Paradigm,* ed. Ruth B. Bottigheimer (Philadelphia: U of Pennsylvania P, 1986) 187–93, outlines the history and scope of the work.

U5835   *Funk and Wagnalls Standard Dictionary of Folklore, Mythology, and Legend.*
         Ed. Maria Leach. [Corrected rpt.] New York: Funk, 1972. 1,236 pp.
         GR35.F82   398′.042.

A dictionary of mythological and folk figures, dances, festivals, rituals, food, games, customs, riddles, rhymes, witchcraft, magic, folk beliefs, folktales, regions, scholars, motifs, material culture, and a host of other topics related to folklore, especially of the Americas. Entries range from a sentence to several pages; some are signed, and a few conclude with a selective bibliography. The brief index of countries, regions, cultures, tribes, and groups added in the 1972 reprint does not offer adequate access to topics and persons not accorded separate entries. (A full analytic index and bibliography was promised but never published.) Although the work is seriously flawed because of numerous errors, inadequate cross-referencing and indexing, many uneven and unrepresentative entries, and generally slipshod editing, it remains the fullest English-language general dictionary of folklore. Superior coverage of classical mythology is offered by *Oxford Classical Dictionary* (C115); for scholars and topics related to narrative folklore, *Enzyklopädie des Märchens* (U5830) is the essential source. Reviews: (original printing) Wayland D. Hand, *Midwest Folklore* 1 (1951): 267–72; Stanley Edgar Hyman, *Journal of American Folklore* 64 (1951): 325–28; Hyman, *Kenyon Review* 12 (1950): 721–30; Branford P. Millar, *Southern Folklore Quarterly* 14 (1950): 123–28, 15 (1951): 171–72.

Fuller, more authoritative entries on forms and methods of analysis associated with North American and European folklore are offered in Thomas A. Green, ed., *Folklore: An Encyclopedia of Beliefs, Customs, Tales, Music, and Art*, 2 vols. (Santa Barbara: ABC-CLIO, 1997).

U5837   *American Folklore: An Encyclopedia.* Ed. Jan Harold Brunvand. Garland
         Reference Library of the Humanities 1551. New York: Garland, 1996.
         794 pp.   GR101.A54   398.2′0973.

An encyclopedia of North American folklore (excluding that associated with Native Americans), with entries for genres, scholarly approaches, regions, occupations, groups, organizations, performers, and dead folklorists. The signed entries are generously full and typically conclude with a list of additional resources and cross-references. As with most encyclopedias of this type, entries are uneven in quality (e.g., "Bodylore" is nearly incomprehensible in its jargon and "Cow Tipping" fails in its attempted cuteness, but the majority—such as "Dozens" and "Paper Cutting"—are clear discussions replete with examples that place the topic within its historical and scholarly contexts). Indexed by persons and subjects. Although lacking an explanation of selection criteria and emphasizing the United States, *American Folklore* is the best encyclopedia of folklore and folklorists of the region.

U5838   Simpson, Jacqueline, and Steve Roud. *A Dictionary of English Folklore.*
         Oxford: Oxford UP, 2000. 411 pp.   GR141.S59   398.20942003. Online
         through *Oxford Reference Online* (I530).

A dictionary of "oral genres, performance genres, calendar customs, life-cycle customs, supernatural, . . . 'superstitious' beliefs," everyday lore (e.g., the Vanishing Hitchhiker), topics formerly regarded as unpleasant (e.g., sex and menstruation), groups, and deceased folklorists associated with the folklore of England. Excludes material culture, "traditional foods, sports, games, fairs, . . . most obsolete customs," and much children's lore. The approximately 1,250 entries are factual rather than interpretative; many conclude with a list of additional readings (several citations are keyed to the bibliography at the end of the book). Although excluding some topics treated by most folklore dictionaries, *Dictionary of English Folklore* offers a sure-handed, entertaining guide to the folklore of England.

Guides to Primary Works

TYPE- AND MOTIF-INDEXES

For a critique of tale-type– and motif-indexes, see the special issue of *Journal of Folklore Research* 34.3 (1997). Of particular importance is Alan Dundes, "The Motif-Index and the Tale Type Index: A Critique" (195–202). On standards for compiling these indexes, see Jason, *Motif, Type, and Genre: A Manual for Compilation of Indices and a Bibliography of Indices and Indexing* (U5840a).

Bibliographies

U5840   Azzolina, David S. *Tale Type- and Motif-Indexes: An Annotated Bibliography.*
        Garland Reference Library of the Humanities 565: Garland Folklore
        Bibliographies 12. New York: Garland, 1987. 105 pp.   Z5983.L5 A98
        [GR74.6]   016.3982.

   An annotated bibliography of type- and motif-indexes published worldwide through 1985. Azzolina cites dissertations and theses as well as books and articles but excludes indexes of proverbs and most ballad indexes. The 186 entries are listed alphabetically by author or editor. Each is accompanied by a descriptive annotation that frequently cites reviews or related scholarship as well. Three indexes: subjects; geographic areas; additional authors. Admirably broad in coverage, Azzolina is the essential guide to type- and motif-indexes. Review: Hans Jörg Uther, *Journal of American Folklore* 102 (1989): 479–84 (with several additions and corrections).

   For additional indexes, see Heda Jason, *Motif, Type, and Genre: A Manual for Compilation of Indices and a Bibliography of Indices and Indexing*, FF Communications 273 (Helsinki: Suomalainen Tiedeakatemia, 2000, 279 pp.), and the additions in Azzolina's review (*Journal of American Folklore* 116 [2003]: 236–37).

Indexes

U5845   Thompson, Stith. *Motif-Index of Folk-Literature: A Classification of Narrative*
        Elements in Folktales, Ballads, Myths, Fables, Mediaeval Romances, Exempla,
        Fabliaux, Jest-Books, and Local Legends. Rev. and enl. ed. 6 vols.
        Bloomington: Indiana UP, 1955–58.   GR67.T52   398.012. Online.
        24 Feb. 2005 <http://www.library.nlx.com>. CD-ROM (Charlottesville:
        Intelex).

   A systematic classification of motifs occurring in traditional oral and written narratives throughout the world. Thompson excludes "superstitions, customs, religious beliefs, riddles, or proverbs except as they happen to form an organic part of a narrative"; and it silently ignores nearly everything sexual or scatological. The motifs are organized in 23 broad subject divisions (e.g., animals, ogres, mythological motifs, captives and fugitives, the dead) that are extensively subdivided (with each division prefaced by a detailed outline). Where possible, individual motifs are accompanied by references to locations, collections, lists of variants, scholarship, related motifs, and Aarne-Thompson tale-types (U5850a). Thompson's citations are more fully and accurately identified in Polly Grimshaw, ed., Motif-Index of Folk-Literature: *Bibliography and Abbreviations* (N.p.: n.p., [1976?], 38 pp.). Indexed by subjects. To locate specific motifs, users should begin with the outline prefacing each division or the thorough analytical subject index. A monumental compilation that is underutilized by literature scholars, Thompson is the indispensable source for identifying, locating, cataloging, and referring (by Thompson numbers) to motifs in oral and written literatures worldwide. Review: Kurt Ranke, *Journal of American Folklore* 71 (1958): 81–83.

While the electronic versions correct several cross-references, provide some 150,000 hyperlinks between motifs, and offer keyword searching of a static text, the brief citations are not linked to the full entries in the bibliography, the help screens of the CD-ROM are decidedly unhelpful, and the explanation of how to search the online text is in sore need of editing for clarity and of basic proofreading. Users unfamiliar with the Folio search engine must begin with the manual.

An important complementary source for identifying motifs and tale-types in English-language literature in Great Britain and North America is Ernest W. Baughman, *Type and Motif-Index of the Folktales of England and North America*, Indiana U Folklore Series 20 (The Hague: Mouton, 1966, 606 pp.). The organization of the tale-type–index is modeled on Aarne-Thompson (U5850a) and the motif-index on Thompson, with entries similar to the latter's in content. Although Baughman lacks its own subject index, users can locate individual types and motifs by consulting the one in Thompson.

U5850   Uther, Hans-Jörg. *The Types of International Folktales: A Classification and Bibliography (ATU)*. 3 vols. FF Communications 284–86. Helsinki: Suomalainen Tiedeakatemia, 2004.   GR1.F55   398'.012.

A classification by tale-type of folktales from throughout the world but emphasizing Europe, Western Asia, and areas settled by peoples from these regions. *Types of International Folktales* revises Antti Aarne, *The Types of the Folktale: A Classification and Bibliography* (Aarne-Thompson), trans. and enl. Stith Thompson, 2nd revision, FF Communications 184 (Helsinki: Suomalainen Tiedeakatemia, 1961, 558 pp.), adding some 250 new types, sharpening the descriptions, and establishing numerous connections among tales but retaining as far as possible the Aarne-Thompson numbers. Unlike a motif-index, which focuses on elements within tales, *ATU* classifies entire works. Organized within divisions for animal tales, tales of magic, religious tales, realistic tales, tales of the stupid ogre, jokes and anecdotes, and formula tales, entries provide a brief summary; notes on literary sources, origin, and distinctive features; citations to scholarship; and evidence of the geographic spread of the tale. Because these tales lack formal titles and exist in numerous variants, the best approach to the contents is through the subject index. An index to motifs would improve access. A model for tale-type classifications of other regions, *Types of International Folktales* is the standard source for locating texts of traditional oral narratives (especially of Europe) and for identifying tale-types (Aarne-Thompson—now *ATU*—numbers are the standard for citing tale-types).

OTHER GUIDES

U5855   Briggs, Katharine M. *A Dictionary of British Folk-tales in the English Language: Incorporating the F. J. Norton Collection*. 4 vols. Bloomington: Indiana UP, 1970–71.   GR141.B69   398.2'0942.

Pt. A: *Folk Narratives.* 2 vols. 1970.
Pt. B: *Folk Legends.* 2 vols. 1971.

A dictionary of English-language folk narratives and legends of the British Isles. Pt. A has divisions for fables and exempla, fairy tales, jocular tales, novelle, and nursery tales; pt. B, for black dogs, bogies, devils, dragons, fairies, ghosts, and giants. In each division, tales are organized by title, with the full text or extensive summary followed by source(s); Aarne-Thompson (U5850a) tale-type number; Thompson (U5845), Baughman (U5845a), or other motif-index numbers; cross-references; and commentary. Each part is prefaced by two indexes: tale-types; titles. Although an index of motifs would be welcome, *Dictionary of British Folk-tales* is an important compilation that saves researchers from hunting out widely scattered texts.

Guides to Scholarship and Criticism

SURVEYS OF RESEARCH

U5860   Dorson, Richard M., ed. *Handbook of American Folklore.* Bloomington:
         Indiana UP, 1983. 584 pp.   GR105.H36   398'.0973.

A collection of essays that describe the state of research (as of c. 1978) in various areas of American folklore. Organized in divisions for topics of research (with sections on ethnic groups and movements, cultural myths, settings, entertainments, and forms and performers), interpretation of research, research methods (including an essay on folklore and American literature and an inadequate overview of bibliographies and indexes), and the presentation of research. The essays variously outline a topic, comment on important scholarship, discuss methodology, and suggest topics for further research. Indexed by persons, titles, and subjects. The brief essays vary considerably in quality, but together they offer a useful, if flawed, introduction to the study of American folklore. Review: Bruce Jackson, *New York Folklore* 10.1–2 (1984): 99–112.

For a history of folklore studies in the United States, see Simon J. Bronner, *American Folklore Studies: An Intellectual History* (Lawrence: UP of Kansas, 1986, 213 pp.); for European folkloristics, see Giuseppe Cocchiara, *The History of Folklore in Europe*, trans. John N. McDaniel, Translations in Folklore Studies (Philadelphia: Inst. for the Study of Human Issues, 1981, 703 pp.).

See also

"Year's Work in Scottish Literary and Linguistic Studies" (O3070).

SERIAL BIBLIOGRAPHIES

U5865   *Internationale volkskundliche Bibliographie/International Folklore Bibliography/*
         Bibliographie internationale d'ethnologie [1917–] (IVB). Bonn: Habelt,
         1919– . Annual. Title varies.   Z5982.I523   016.398.

A selective bibliography of important or representative scholarship on the folklore of Europe, North and South America, and South Africa. Although the scope has broadened over the years (with the early volumes emphasizing Europe), the organization has remained fairly consistent. Entries are now listed alphabetically by author in 24 extensively classified divisions: the study of folklore; regional studies; ethnicity, identity, and living styles; age, gender, and social groups; economy, work, and occupations; folk art; tokens, symbols, and gestures; dress; food; settlement and cultural landscape; architecture; objects (including furniture and implements); customs, festivals, games, and leisure activities; religion; popular beliefs; health, illness, and the body; law; folk literature; songs; music and dance; popular literature (including fairy tales, legends, fables, and oral genres); language; theater, circus, and spectacle; and media. (The division for names was dropped with the volume for 1975–76.) Three indexes: authors; subjects (in German, but with separate ones in English, in the volumes for 1979–80 through 1983–84, and in French in the volumes for 1981–82 and 1983–84); geographic places (added in the bibliography for 1999). For the history of the work, see Rolf Wilhelm Brednich, "*The International Folklore Bibliography*," *International Folklore Review* 1 (1981): 17–21.

Although *IVB* now offers the most extensive coverage of any serial bibliography of folklore scholarship on the four continents, publication is far in arrears (the volume for 1999 was published in 2004) and there is no sign of the long-promised electronic version. It must be supplemented by the Folklore division of *MLAIB* (G335), which is more timely and truly international but less thorough in covering some regions the works have in common. For a discussion of *MLAIB*'s coverage of folklore, see entry G335 and Michael Taft, "The Folklore Section of the *MLA International Bibliography*," *International Folklore Review* 2 (1982): 61–64.

For earlier scholarship, the following defunct serial bibliographies and abstracts remain important:

> *Abstracts of Folklore Studies.* 13 vols. Austin: U of Texas P for Amer. Folklore Soc., 1963–75. Coverage is selective—more precisely, inconsistent—with the descriptive abstracts varying considerably in detail and quality. Because entries are organized by journal, the annual index of authors, subjects, and titles is essential for locating specific articles.

> "Annual Bibliography of Folklore [c. 1948–62]." *Journal of American Folklore* 62–76 (1949–63). (The earlier bibliographies are called "Folklore in Periodical Literature" and are scattered throughout issues; the bibliographies in later years appear in a supplement to the journal.) Continued by: "Annual Bibliography [1963–64]." *Abstracts of Folklore Studies* 2–3 (1964–65). Coverage is selective, with works organized in divisions for general studies; material culture; customs, beliefs, and superstitions; linguistic folklore; prose narratives; folk song and folk poetry; music; dance; games; drama; folklore and literature; and peripheral materials.

> "Folklore Bibliography for [1937–72]." *Southern Folklore Quarterly* 2–37 (1938–73). Continued by: *Folklore Bibliography for [1973–76].* Comp. Merle E. Simmons. Indiana U Folklore Institute Monograph Series [28–29, 31, 33]. Philadelphia: Inst. for the Study of Human Issues, 1975–81. The scope has varied considerably over the years, but with the bibliography for 1967 (32 [1968]), it narrows to works about the Americas, Spain, Portugal, and other Spanish- or Portuguese-speaking areas, as well as studies by folklorists in those regions. The descriptively annotated entries are listed in 10 divisions: general folklore; prose narrative; song, game, and dance; drama; ritual and festival; belief and practice; material culture; speech; proverbs; and riddles. Indexed by authors.

See also

Sec. G: Serial Bibliographies, Indexes, and Abstracts.

ABELL (G340): Ancillary Studies/Mythology, Legend, and Folklore section in the volumes for 1934–72; Folklife division in the volume for 1973; Folklore and Folklife division in the volumes for 1974–84; and Traditional Culture, Folklore, and Folklife division in later volumes.

L'année philologique (S4890).

Annual Bibliography of Scottish Literature (O3075).

International Medieval Bibliography (M1835).

Minorities in America (Q3700).

MLAIB (G335): Through the volume for 1980, many national literature divisions have a Folklore heading or section. See also the Folklore heading in the General division in the volume for 1928; General VII [or V]: Folklore and Folklore Motifs in Literature section in the volumes for 1929–32; the Folklore heading in the General division in the volumes for 1933–54; General V [or VIII]: Folklore in the volumes for 1955–68; and the Folklore division in later volumes. Researchers must also check the headings beginning "Folk-" in the subject index to post-1980 volumes and in the online thesaurus.

"Publications in American Studies from German-Speaking Countries," *Amerikastudien* (Q3285).

OTHER BIBLIOGRAPHIES

U5870   Flanagan, Cathleen C., and John T. Flanagan. *American Folklore: A Bibliography, 1950–1974*. Metuchen: Scarecrow, 1977. 406 pp. Z5984.U6 F55 [GR105]   016.398'0973.

A bibliography of publications on the verbal folklore of the United States. Flanagan excludes notes, newspaper articles, and most reviews. The 3,639 or so entries are listed alphabetically by author in 15 divisions (only a few of which are minimally classified): collections of essays; reference works; study and teaching of folklore; general studies; ballads and songs; tales and narrative material; legends; myth; beliefs, customs, superstitions, and cures; folk heroes; folklore in literature; proverbs, riddles, Wellerisms, and limericks; speech, names, and cries; minor genres; and obituaries of folklorists. Many entries are accompanied by brief descriptive annotations, a few of which include evaluative comments. Indexed by authors. There are numerous errors in citations, inconsistencies in classification, and significant omissions, and the insufficiently classified divisions, lack of cross-references, and inexcusable failure to provide a subject index make *American Folklore* a time-consuming work to consult. Yet this and Haywood, *Bibliography of North American Folklore* (U5875), remain essential sources principally because they offer the most thorough coverage of scholarship before 1975 on most genres of American folklore; fortunately, parts are gradually being superseded by bibliographies of individual genres. Reviews: Jan Harold Brunvand, *Western Folklore* 38 (1979): 66–70; Robert W. Halli, Jr., *Tennessee Folklore Society Bulletin* 44 (1978): 45–47.

U5875   Haywood, Charles. *A Bibliography of North American Folklore and Folksong*. 2nd rev. ed. 2 vols. New York: Dover, 1961.   Z5984.U5 H32   016.398.

Vol. 1: *The American People North of Mexico, Including Canada*.
Vol. 2: *The American Indians North of Mexico, Including the Eskimos*.

A bibliography of primary and secondary works (including some fiction) through‑ mid-1948 related to the folklore of North America (along with a few works on the British Isles). The second edition is actually an uncorrected reprint of the original one (New York: Greenberg, 1951, 1,291 pp.) with a new index of composers, arrangers, and performers. The approximately 40,000 entries are organized in seven variously classified divisions: (vol. 1) general studies, regions, ethnic groups, occupations, and miscellaneous; (vol. 2) general studies and cultural areas. Each of the various subdivisions typically includes sections for folklore and folk song. A few entries are accompanied by brief descriptive or evaluative annotations. Two indexes: authors, subjects, and titles of folk works; composers, arrangers, and performers. A conglomeration of entries that is confusingly organized, admits much that is inconsequential or outside the realm of folklore, includes numerous errors, and has major gaps in coverage, Haywood is, how- ever, an essential source for identifying studies before mid-1948 on North American folklore. Fortunately, it is now being superseded in many areas by bibliographies on individual genres. Reviews: (1951 ed.) Richard M. Dorson, *Southern Folklore Quarterly* 15 (1951): 263–66; MacEdward Leach, *Journal of American Folklore* 65 (1952): 98– 101; (2nd ed.) Dorson, *Southern Folklore Quarterly* 27 (1963): 346.

U5880   Szwed, John F., and Roger D. Abrahams. *Afro-American Folk Culture: An Annotated Bibliography of Materials from North, Central, and South America, and the West Indies.* 2 vols. Publications of the American Folklore Society: Bibliographical and Special Series 31–32. Philadelphia: Inst. for the Study of Human Issues, 1978.   Z5984.A44 S95 [GR103]   016.909′04′96.

A bibliography of published scholarship, some literary works, and record notes (through 1973) on Afro-American folk culture. The entries are listed alphabetically in six divisions: bibliographies, general studies, North America, Caribbean, Central Amer- ica, and South America (with the last three subdivided by region or country). Many of the very brief annotations are inadequately descriptive, and several works are unanno- tated. Two cumulated indexes in each volume: subjects; places. Annotations are fre- quently uninformative; there are significant omissions; and studies about a particular topic are difficult to locate because of the unrefined organization and inadequate, in- complete subject indexing. Even so, *Afro-American Folk Culture* is useful because of its breadth of coverage.

See also

> Baer, *Folklore and Literature of the British Isles* (M1390).
> Clements, *Native American Folklore, 1879–1979* (Q3885).
> Comitas, *Complete Caribbeana, 1800–1975* (R4790a).
> Fowke, *Bibliography of Canadian Folklore in English* (R4665).
> Jones, *Folklore and Literature in the United States* (Q3290).
> Jordan, *English-Speaking Caribbean* (R4785).
> Kiell, *Psychoanalysis, Psychology, and Literature* (U6540).
> Lindfors, *Black African Literature in English* (R4425).
> *Literary History of the United States: Bibliography* (Q3300).
> Miller, *Comprehensive Bibliography for the Study of American Minorities* (Q3700).
> Nemanic, *Bibliographical Guide to Midwestern Literature* (Q3600).
> Rubin, *Bibliographical Guide to the Study of Southern Literature* (Q3625).
> Salzman, *American Studies: An Annotated Bibliography* (Q3335).
> Watters, *On Canadian Literature, 1806–1960* (R4655).

DISSERTATIONS AND THESES

U5885   Dundes, Alan, comp. *Folklore Theses and Dissertations in the United States.*
         Publications of the American Folklore Society: Bibliographical and Special
         Series 27. Austin: U of Texas P for Amer. Folklore Soc., 1976. 610 pp.
         Z5981.D85 [GR65]   016.398.
    A bibliography of master's theses and doctoral dissertations on folklore accepted
between 1860 and 1968 by institutions in the United States. Organized chronologically
by year of acceptance, then alphabetically by author, entries cite title, degree, department, institution, and number of pages. Three indexes: subjects; authors; institutions.
Because of the chronological organization, the best approach to contents is through the
detailed analytic subject index (which, however, is based on titles). The introduction
discusses the importance of folklore theses and dissertations. Coverage is less complete
after 1964, and the nature of the sources means that there are inevitably omissions,
errors, and incomplete entries; however, Dundes is a time-saving compilation of theses
and dissertations from a variety of sources.

See also

    Sec. H: Guides to Dissertations and Theses.
    Emerson, *Southern Literary Culture: A Bibliography of Masters' and Doctors' Theses*
       (Q3630).
    Woodress, *Dissertations in American Literature, 1891–1966* (Q3320).

Genres

Coverage here is limited to genres that have reference sources of interest to literary
researchers.

BALLAD

U5902   Richmond, W. Edson. *Ballad Scholarship: An Annotated Bibliography.*
         Garland Reference Library of the Humanities 499: Garland Folklore
         Bibliographies 4. New York: Garland, 1989. 356 pp.   Z7156.P7 R5
         [PN6110.B2]   016.80881'44.
    A selective bibliography of studies published from 1898 through 1986 on the folk
ballads of northern and western Europe, England, Scotland, and North America. The
approximately 1,656 entries are organized alphabetically in 13 unclassified divisions:
general introductions; collections of essays; journals devoted to folk music; reference
works and bibliographies; studies of ballads generally; ballads and literature; ballads and
history; language; prosody and metrics; studies of individual ballad types and cycles;
music; collectors, editors, and histories of ballad scholarship; major ballad collections.
The descriptive annotations offer generally brief but adequate descriptions of content;
however, poor layout makes scanning entries difficult. Two indexes: authors; subjects.
But for "elective and subjective" the criteria governing the selection of studies remain
unexplained; yet *Ballad Scholarship* usefully identifies major studies in a variety of
languages.

FABLE

U5905   Carnes, Pack. *Fable Scholarship: An Annotated Bibliography.* Garland
         Reference Library of the Humanities 367: Garland Folklore Bibliographies
         8. New York: Garland, 1985. 382 pp.   Z5896.C37 [PN980]   016.3982.
   An international bibliography of books, articles, and dissertations, for the most
part published between 1880 and 1981 (with some works from 1982). Listed alphabetically by scholar, the 1,457 entries are accompanied by full descriptive annotations
that frequently include evaluative comments and cite Aarne-Thompson (U5850a),
Thompson (U5845), and Perry numbers. Three indexes: names and subjects; fables (by
Perry number); tale-types (by Aarne-Thompson number). Although *Fable Scholarship*
is selective, the full annotations, international coverage, and thorough indexing make
it the essential starting point for research on the fable.

MUSIC

U5910   Miller, Terry E. *Folk Music in America: A Reference Guide.* Garland
         Reference Library of the Humanities 496. New York: Garland, 1986.
         424 pp.   ML128.F74 M5   016.781773.
   An annotated bibliography of books, articles, and dissertations through 1984 on
folk music in the United States. Miller emphasizes recent ethnomusicological
publications; it excludes articles in newspapers and popular magazines, record notes,
and reviews, as well as most master's theses, articles of fewer than nine pages, and works
published before 1900. The 1,927 entries are organized in nine variously classified
divisions: general works (including bibliographies, discographies, reference works, and
general studies), music of the American Indians and Eskimos, Anglo-American folk
songs and ballads, later developments in Anglo-American folk music (especially blue-
grass, country and western, folk song revival, and protest music), traditional instruments
and instrumental music, American psalmody and hymnody, singing school and shape-
note traditions, Afro-American music, and music of various ethnic traditions. Several
of the descriptive annotations, which sometimes include an evaluative comment, inadequately summarize contents. Two indexes: scholars; subjects. Confusing in its explanation of criteria governing inclusion and omitting numerous studies, *Folk Music in
America* is only a starting point for research on folk music in the United States.
   Some additional studies can be found in "Current Bibliography" in each issue of
Ethnomusicology: Journal of the Society for Ethnomusicology, 1–44 (1953–2000); installments since 37.1 (1993) to the present can be found at http://webdb.iu.edu/sem/scripts/
publications/ographies.cfm.

PROVERB

Dictionaries

U5915   *The Oxford Dictionary of English Proverbs.* Rev. F. P. Wilson. 3rd ed.
         Oxford: Clarendon–Oxford UP, 1970. 930 pp.   PN6421.O9
         398.9′2′03.

A dictionary of selected proverbs used in written works in England since the fourteenth century. Listed alphabetically by the first significant word, with cross-references for other words, each proverb is followed by a chronological list of dated examples and variants. For some additions and corrections, see Robert D. Dunn, "Corrections to *The Oxford Dictionary of English Proverbs*," *American Notes and Queries* 24 (1985): 52–54. Although this is the best overall dictionary for identifying proverbs in English, it must be supplemented by the following:

> Mieder, Wolfgang, Stewart A. Kingsbury, and Kelsie B. Harder, eds. *A Dictionary of American Proverbs*. New York: Oxford UP, 1992. 710 pp. Includes about 15,000 proverbs in actual use in the contiguous United States and Canada. Entries, based on field research by numerous contributors, record regional distribution as well as appearance in standard collections.
>
> Stevenson, Burton. *The Home Book of Proverbs, Maxims, and Familiar Phrases*. New York: Macmillan, 1948. 2,957 pp. (Reprinted as *The Macmillan Book of Proverbs, Maxims, and Famous Phrases*, 1965.)
>
> Taylor, Archer, and Bartlett Jere Whiting. *A Dictionary of American Proverbs and Proverbial Phrases, 1820–1880*. Cambridge: Belknap–Harvard UP, 1958. 418 pp.
>
> Tilley, Morris Palmer. *A Dictionary of the Proverbs in England in the Sixteenth and Seventeenth Centuries: A Collection of the Proverbs Found in English Literature and the Dictionaries of the Period*. Ann Arbor: U of Michigan P, 1950. 854 pp. Much of this material is incorporated in *Oxford Dictionary*.
>
> Whiting, Bartlett Jere. *Early American Proverbs and Proverbial Phrases*. Cambridge: Belknap–Harvard UP, 1977. 555 pp.
>
> ———. *Modern Proverbs and Proverbial Sayings*. Cambridge: Harvard UP, 1989. 709 pp. Coverage extends from c. 1930 to the early 1980s and emphasizes popular sources.
>
> Whiting, Bartlett Jere, and Helen Wescott Whiting. *Proverbs, Sentences, and Proverbial Phrases from English Writings Mainly before 1500*. Cambridge: Belknap–Harvard UP, 1968. 733 pp.

Guide to Reference Books (B60), *Walford's Guide to Reference Material* (B65), and "International Bibliography of New and Reprinted Proverb Collections [1975–]," *Proverbium: Yearbook of International Proverb Scholarship* 1– (1984–) list additional dictionaries.

See also

> Bartlett, *Bartlett's Familiar Quotations* (U6315).

Guides to Scholarship

U5920   Mieder, Wolfgang. *International Proverb Scholarship: An Annotated Bibliography*. Garland Reference Library of the Humanities 342: Garland Folklore Bibliographies 3. New York: Garland, 1982. 613 pp. *Supplement I (1800–1981)*. Garland Reference Library of the Humanities 1230: Garland Folklore Bibliographies 15. 1990. 436 pp. *Supplement II (1982–1991)*. Garland Reference Library of the Humanities 1655: Garland Folklore Bibliographies 20. 1993. 927 pp. *Supplement III (1990–2000)*. New York: Lang, 2001. 457 pp.   Z7191.M543 [PN6401]   016.398'9.

An international bibliography of books, articles, and dissertations from 1800 through 2000 on proverbs. Mieder excludes collections of proverbs, literary studies that are lists unaccompanied by critical analysis, and most brief notes. Listed alphabetically by scholar, the first 4,599 entries are accompanied by full descriptive (and sometimes evaluative) annotations; in *Supplement III*, the 2,769 entries include a list of keywords. Three indexes: names; subjects; specific proverbs. Thoroughly indexed, clearly annotated (through *Supplement II*), and admirably broad in coverage, *International Proverb Scholarship* is the essential guide to international paroemiological scholarship (including numerous studies of proverbs in literary works), but it must be supplemented by *MLAIB* (G335). Continued in "International Proverb Scholarship: An Updated Bibliography [1981–]" in *Proverbium: Yearbook of International Proverb Scholarship* 1– (1984–).

Studies of proverbs in literary works are listed in Mieder and George B. Bryan, *Proverbs in World Literature: A Bibliography* (New York: Lang, 1996, 305 pp.). The 2,654 unannotated entries are organized by literary author.

Gay, Lesbian, Bisexual, and Transgendered Studies

Handbooks, Dictionaries, and Encyclopedias

U5928   *Encyclopedia of Lesbian and Gay Histories and Cultures.* 2 vols. Garland Reference Library of the Social Sciences 1002, 1008. New York: Garland, 2000.   HQ75.13   306.766.

> Vol. 1: *Lesbian Histories and Cultures: An Encyclopedia.* Ed. Bonnie Zimmerman. 862 pp.   HQ75.5.L4395   306.76′63′03.
>
> Vol. 2: *Gay Histories and Cultures: An Encyclopedia.* Ed. George E. Haggerty. 986 pp.   HQ75.13.G37   306.76′6′03.

An encyclopedia of lesbian, gay, bisexual, transgendered, and queer culture, including entries on persons, organizations, cultural identities, places, terms, media, popular culture, literature, film, theater, theory, and sexual practices. Each entry concludes with a selected bibliography. The two volumes share a common introduction and treat some of the same topics but are separated to ensure "that both histories receive full and unbiased attention." *Lesbian Histories* includes a valuable entry on bibliographies and reference works; *Gay Histories*, unfortunately, does not. Indexed in each volume by persons, titles, and subjects. The impressive range of readable, informative entries makes this the standard encyclopedia of lesbian and gay culture.

Although somewhat more current, *LGBT: Encyclopedia of Lesbian, Gay, Bisexual, and Transgender History in America*, ed. Marc Stein, 4 vols. (New York: Scribner's-Gale, 2004; online through *Gale Virtual Reference Library* [I535]), restricts its coverage to the United States. Entrants are indexed in *Biography and Genealogy Master Index* (J565).

Guides to Primary Works

U5930   Grier, Barbara. *The Lesbian in Literature.* 3rd ed. rev. Tallahassee: Naiad, 1981. 168 pp.   Z5866.L4 D3 [PN56.L45]   016.8088′0353.

A list of approximately 7,000 English-language works (including translations) published through 1979 that deal with lesbians or lesbianism. The majority are novels, short stories, poems, plays, biographies, autobiographies, or anthologies, though some nonfiction (primarily after 1967) is included. Listed alphabetically by author, some entries are accompanied by brief annotations that identify the lesbian content; all are coded for the amount and quality of lesbian content (see pp. xix-xx for the coding system). The lack of any subject index substantially hampers accessibility, but this is the fullest list of English-language literary works about lesbians. A new edition or supplement would be welcomed by those working on lesbianism in literature.

Guides to Scholarship and Criticism

SURVEYS OF RESEARCH

U5932   *Reader's Guide to Lesbian and Gay Studies.* Ed. Timothy F. Murphy.
        Chicago: Fitzroy Dearborn, 2000. 720 pp.   HQ75.15.R43   305.90664.
   A selective, evaluative guide to scholarship, primarily in English, on gay or lesbian culture. The approximately 440 signed entries treat culture, health and medical issues, art and artists, ethnic groups, geographical areas, education, gender studies, history, legal matters, literature (including authors, genres, and national literatures), media, music and the performing arts, philosophy, politics, psychology, religion, social and cultural issues, and transgender studies. Each entry begins with a list of studies, provides a brief overview of the subject, and then summarizes each study (frequently evaluating and comparing approaches and conclusions). Two indexes: author index of books and articles discussed; subjects. Several entries are by graduate students, but the generally judicious selection of scholarship accompanied by evenhanded summaries and by evaluations makes *Reader's Guide* a valuable introduction to the state of scholarship on gay and lesbian topics.

OTHER BIBLIOGRAPHIES

U5933   Nordquist, Joan, comp. *Queer Theory: A Bibliography.* Social Theory: A
        Bibliographic Series 48. Santa Cruz: Reference and Research Services, 1997.
        64 pp.   Z7164.H74 N67 [HQ76.25]   016.30676'6.
   A bibliography of English-language writings (through mid-1997) about queer theory. Entries are unnecessarily separated into books and articles under divisions for theory (with subdivisions for general works, lesbian theory, bisexuality, transsexualism and transgenderism, and race), pedagogy, academic disciplines (with subdivisions for language and linguistics, literature, film, and drama and theater), politics, personal accounts, and bibliographies. Although restricted to English-language publications, taking several entries from other sources rather than a firsthand examination, and lacking an index, this bibliography does offer a place to begin when searching for discussions of queer theory. However, researchers must also consult the serial bibliographies in section G, especially *MLAIB* (G335), which the compiler claims to have searched but which includes a substantial number of works that were apparently overlooked.

ABSTRACTS

U5935   *Sexual Diversity Studies: Gay, Lesbian, Bisexual, and Transgender Abstracts.*
Baltimore: Natl. Information Services Corp. Former title: *Gay and Lesbian
Abstracts.* Online. 6 Aug. 2005 <http://biblioline.nisc.com>. CD-ROM.
   Abstracts of articles, reviews, books, dissertations, electronic resources, and media
that treat issues of interest to the gay, lesbian, bisexual, and transgendered community.
As of 6 August 2005, the database included more than 80,500 records, the majority in
English and published since 1997. Although claiming to cover more than 3,500 serials,
several of these journals yield only one or two records, with many taken from Medline
and ERIC (U5590). Users can restrict keyword searches by author, date, and journal
title or publisher. Records (many of which lack abstracts) can be sorted by author,
journal, date, or title and can be marked for e-mailing, exporting into bibliographic
software programs, saving, or printing. For literature researchers, the primary value of
this database lies in its coverage of periodicals addressed to gays, lesbians, transsexuals,
and transgendered individuals.

Grants

U5940   *The Grants Register.* Basingstoke: Palgrave, 1969– . Biennial.   LB2338.G7
378.34.
   A guide to grants, fellowships, exchange programs, awards, and honoraria sponsored by foundations, institutions, and government agencies worldwide. Listed alphabetically by sponsor, entries consist of name of the grant, purpose, subjects, number
offered, frequency, value, tenability, country of study, eligibility requirements, deadline,
notes on application procedure and selection process, and address for further information. Four indexes: subjects and eligibility (the subject arrangement is nearly impenetrable; most users of this *Guide* will want to turn immediately to the "arts and humanities" subhead); name of grant/award; discontinued grants; organizations. The
fullest international guide, *Grants Register* describes several grants of interest to literature
and language scholars but is marred by ineffective indexing and an utterly inadequate
explanation of scope and criteria governing inclusion.
   Other sources for locating grants of interest to literary scholars include these works:

> *Annual Register of Grant Support: A Directory of Funding Sources.* Medford:
> Information Today, 1969– . Annual. Restricted to sources that fund
> applicants from the United States or Canada or otherwise benefit either
> country. The literature division lists numerous prizes and awards that are
> not grants.
> *Directory of Grants in the Humanities.* Westport: Oryx-Greenwood, 1986–.
> Biennial. Online; CD-ROM. Covers grants available worldwide (with the
> majority from United States and Canadian organizations). Access is ham-
> pered by insufficient subject indexing.
> *The Foundation Directory.* New York: Foundation Center, 1960– . 2 pts.
> and interedition supplement. Annual. Online. <http://fconline.fdncenter
> .org>; CD-ROM. A directory of the 20,000 largest private or
> community foundations in the United States.
> *PMLA,* Directory issue (U5060).

Interdisciplinary and Multidisciplinary Studies

This section is limited to reference works that treat the relation of literature to several other arts, disciplines, or fields of knowledge. Works devoted to a single art, discipline, or field appear in one of the following divisions of section U: Art and Literature, Film and Literature, Medicine and Literature, Music and Literature, Philosophy and Literature, Religion and Literature, Science and Literature, and Social Sciences and Literature.

General Introductions

U5955   Barricelli, Jean-Pierre, and Joseph Gibaldi, eds. *Interrelations of Literature.*
New York: MLA, 1982. 329 pp.   PN45.8.I56   809.

A collection of introductions to the interdisciplinary study of literature and linguistics, philosophy, religion, myth, folklore, sociology, politics, law, science, psychology, music, visual arts, and film. Although the emphasis varies from essay to essay, each essay typically outlines the nature of the relation, provides a historical overview, comments on important studies, describes major theories and approaches, suggests areas for research, and concludes with a selective, briefly annotated bibliography. A glossary covers all essays. Indexed by persons and anonymous titles. Written by distinguished scholars, the essays provide the nonspecialist with informed introductions to the study of literature in relationship to other fields.

James Thorpe, ed., *Relations of Literary Study: Essays on Interdisciplinary Contributions* (New York: MLA, 1967, 151 pp.), with essays on history, myth, biography, psychology, sociology, religion, and music, remains useful for its historical perspective.

Handbooks, Dictionaries, and Encyclopedias

U5960   *New Dictionary of the History of Ideas.* Ed. Maryanne Cline Horowitz.
6 vols. Detroit: Scribner's-Gale, 2005. Online through *Gale Virtual Reference Library* (I535).   CB9.N49 903.

Interdisciplinary, cross-cultural, and transnational examinations of seminal concepts and topics in intellectual history. Written by major scholars, the more than 500 signed articles include several on literary forms, techniques, movements, themes, and aesthetics. Each article concludes with a selected bibliography and cross-references to related articles. Prefacing each volume is a Reader's Guide that outlines entries under four subjects: communication, geography, chronology, and liberal arts disciplines and professions (with a subsection on literature). Indexed by persons and subjects. A monumental work, *New Dictionary of the History of Ideas* is especially valuable to literary researchers for its interdisciplinary coverage.

Since *New Dictionary of the History of Ideas* is a completely new work, *Dictionary of the History of Ideas*, ed. Philip P. Weiner, 5 vols. (New York: Scribner's, 1973; http://etext.lib.virginia.edu/DicHist/dict.html), remains useful for its historical perspective.

Guides to Scholarship and Criticism

U5965   "Bibliography on the Relations of Literature and Other Arts [1952–97]."
YCGL: Yearbook of Comparative and General Literature 34–45/46 (1985–
1997/98).   PN851.Y4.

> 1959–84: *A Bibliography on the Relations of Literature and the Other Arts.*
> Hanover: Dept. of German, Dartmouth Coll., 1959–[85?]. Annual.
>
> 1973–75: "Bibliography on the Relations of Literature and the Other Arts."
> *Hartford Studies in Literature* 6–8 (1974–76).
>
> 1952–67: *A Bibliography on the Relations of Literature and the Other Arts,
> 1952–1967.* New York: AMS, 1968. (A reprint of the issues covering
> 1952–67.)
>
> 1952–58: Neumann, Alfred E., comp. *Literature and the Other Arts: A Select
> Bibliography, 1952–1958.* Ed. David V. Erdman. New York: New York
> Public Lib., 1959. 37 pp.

An annual bibliography of studies involving literature and music, the visual arts,
or dance; those for 1974 through 1984 include film and literature. Entries are organized
by author in four divisions: general and theoretical studies, music and literature, visual
arts and literature, and dance or performance art and literature. Except for the first,
each division has sections for general studies and historical periods appropriate to the
subject. A few entries are accompanied by brief descriptive annotations. Two indexes:
scholars; subjects (beginning in vol. 35 [1986]). The supplement to volume 38 was
never published; instead, coverage was gradually caught up in vols. 39 and 43–44.
Although not comprehensive, this work was the single best source for identifying those
interdisciplinary studies that are frequently impossible to locate in the standard serial
bibliographies and indexes in section G. Because few libraries hold complete runs of
the annual volumes through 1984, an augmented cumulation—or at least a collected
reprint—would be welcomed by researchers.

For a few years, coverage of literature and dance was more thorough in "Bibliography: Dance and Literature, [1989–95]," *Dance Research Journal* 26.2–28.1(1994–
96), an author list of articles, books, and dissertations, with some entries accompanied
by a brief annotation.

For studies on the philosophical, scientific, or theoretical study of the arts see
"Selective Current Bibliography for Aesthetics and Related Fields," *Journal of Aesthetics
and Art Criticism* 1–31 (1941–73).

See also

> Sec. G: Serial Bibliographies, Indexes, and Abstracts.
> Baldensperger, *Bibliography of Comparative Literature* (T5000).

Linguistics and Literature

This section is limited to reference works of use to researchers interested in linguistic
approaches to and aspects of literature. It also includes some essential reference works
on the English language. For an introduction to the interdisciplinary study of literature
and linguistics, see Jonathan Culler, "Literature and Linguistics" (pp. 1–24), in Barricelli, *Interrelations of Literature* (U5955). Paul J. Hopper provides a succinct overview

of the field in "Linguistics" (pp. 20–47) in Nicholls, *Introduction to Scholarship in Modern Languages and Literatures* (A25).

Guides to Reference Works

U5980   DeMiller, Anna L. *Linguistics: A Guide to the Reference Literature.* 2nd ed.
         Reference Sources in the Humanities Series. Englewood: Libraries
         Unlimited, 2000. 396 pp.   Z7001.D45 [P121]   016.41.

An annotated guide to reference sources, for the most part published or reprinted between 1957 and 1998. Entries are organized within three classified divisions: general linguistics (with sections for dictionaries, encyclopedias, and guides; biographical dictionaries of linguists; indexes, abstracts, serial bibliographies, and databases; Internet metasites; bibliographies of bibliographies; general bibliographies; bibliographies of specific topics; bibliographies of individual linguists; directories and lists; professional associations and societies; research centers; and important periodicals); allied areas (with sections for anthropological linguistics, applied linguistics, mathematical and computational linguistics, psycholinguistics, semiotics, and sociolinguistics); and languages (with classified sections for general works and language families). Three indexes: authors; titles; subjects. As in the first edition, the annotations are wordy and frequently unevaluative, but DeMiller is the best available guide to essential reference sources for the study of language and linguistics.

General Introductions

U5990   Fowler, Roger. *Linguistic Criticism.* 2nd ed. OPUS Book. New York:
         Oxford UP, 1996. 262 pp.   P302.5.F68   410.

An introduction to the study of literature as social discourse that "demonstrate[s] the value to criticism of an analytic method drawn from linguistics." The chapters on semantic processes, textual structure and construction, contexts of communication, dialogue, point of view, and ordering of experience employ a variety of examples from literary works. Indexed by subjects, persons, and literary works. The work, which presumes a basic knowledge of linguistics on the reader's part, is a handy introduction to the linguistic criticism of literature by one of its leading theorists.

For a more detailed introduction to stylistic criticism, see Anne Cluysenaar, *Aspects of Literary Stylistics: A Discussion of Dominant Structures in Verse and Prose* (New York: St. Martin's, 1975, 160 pp.).

U5995   Traugott, Elizabeth Closs, and Mary Louise Pratt. *Linguistics for Students of Literature.* New York: Harcourt, 1980. 444 pp.   P123.T67   410.

An introductory guide to the application of linguistics in literary study, with chapters on linguistics and literary analysis, phonetics and phonology, morphemes and words, syntax, semantics, speech acts and speech genres (actually a conglomeration of topics), discourse, varieties of English, and English in contact with other languages. Using a generative model, each chapter describes an aspect of language, demonstrates its applications in literary study, and concludes with a list of suggested readings. Three indexes: literary authors; authors of linguistic and critical works; subjects. Although Traugott emphasizes linguistics more than literature and is not always successful in demonstrating applications in literary study, the work is useful as an introductory overview. Reviews: Peter C. Collins, *General Linguistics* 22 (1982): 65–70; Herbert Penzl, *Language* 57 (1981): 782–83.

See also

> Sec. U: Literature-Related Topics and Sources/Computers and the Humanities.

Histories of the English Language

U6000   *The Cambridge History of the English Language.* Ed. Richard M. Hogg.
        6 vols. Cambridge: Cambridge UP, 1992–2001.   PE1072.C36   420.'9.
        Vol. 1: *The Beginnings to 1066.* Ed. Hogg. 1992. 609 pp.
        Vol. 2: *1066–1476.* Ed. Norman Blake. 1992. 703 pp.
        Vol. 3: *1476–1776.* Ed. Roger Lass. 1999. 771 pp.
        Vol. 4: *1776–1997.* Ed. Suzanne Romaine. 1998. 783 pp.
        Vol. 5: *English in Britain and Overseas: Origins and Development.* Ed. Robert
            Burchfield. 1994. 656 pp.
        Vol. 6: *English in North America.* Ed. John Algeo. 2001. 625 pp.

A history of the English language, throughout the world, from its beginnings to the present. The lengthy essays—most of which are by eminent scholars—typically combine diachronic and synchronic approaches and conclude with suggestions for further reading. The volumes devoted to chronological periods include essays on phonology and morphology, orthography and punctuation, dialectology, syntax, lexis and semantics, onomastics, and—of particular interest to literature scholars—the literary language. Each volume concludes with a glossary and bibliography. Indexed by persons and subjects. *Cambridge History of the English Language* offers the most authoritative introduction to English worldwide. Reviews: (vol. 1) E. G. Stanley, *Review of English Studies* 45 (1994): 526–35; (vols. 1–2) R. Hamer, *Medium Ævum* 63 (1994): 313–16.

For those needing a more succinct introduction, the best one-volume histories are N. F. Blake, *A History of the English Language* (New York: New York UP, 1996, 382 pp.), and Thomas Pyles and John Algeo, *The Origins and Development of the English Language*, 4th ed. (Fort Worth: Harcourt, 1992, 381 pp.).

Handbooks, Linguistic Dictionaries, and Encyclopedias

U6005   *Encyclopedia of Language and Linguistics.* Ed. Keith Brown. 2nd ed. 14 vols.
        Amsterdam: Elsevier, 2006.   P29.E48   403. Online. 23 Aug. 2006
        <http://www.sciencedirect.com>.
        An encyclopedia of languages, both human and animal, and linguistics that covers all aspects of the field, giving particular attention to interdisciplinary relations. The c. 3,000 entries—which cover individual languages, language families, concepts, theories, persons, and the language situation in specific geographical areas—are signed and

conclude with suggestions for further reading. Vol. 14 includes an extensive glossary, a list of languages, language maps, a classified list of entries (but with no section on literature and the arts), an index of names, and an extensive subject index.

In the online version, Basic Search allows users to perform keyword searches of a combination of fields (all fields, abstracts, authors, entry titles, subheadings, references, full text); Advanced Search merely allows searchers to join terms with Boolean operators. The content can also be browsed by classification, authors, entries, or subjects; the list of languages and the glossary can also be browsed, but there are no links to entries. There is, unfortunately, no easy way to identify what entries have supplementary audio, video, or text files, and the online version does not reproduce the language maps in the print edition. The publisher does plan to include updates.

There are, of course, inconsistencies, omissions, and variations in the quality of entries, as in any large-scale encyclopedia. Counting an impressive array of established scholars among its contributors, *Encyclopedia of Language and Linguistics* offers the broadest and most thorough and authoritative overview of current knowledge about linguistics.

Although they do not match the magisterial stature of *Encyclopedia of Language and Linguistics*, the following serve as sometimes useful complements:

> Crystal, David. *A Dictionary of Linguistics and Phonetics.* 5th ed. Language Library. Oxford: Blackwell, 2003. 508 pp. A dictionary of terminology used in twentieth-century linguistic and phonetic scholarship. The fifth edition is less strict than its predesessors in admitting terms from related areas such as applied linguistics, acoustics, comparative philology, and language study before 1900.

> Frawley, William J., ed. *International Encyclopedia of Linguistics.* 2nd ed. 4 vols. New York: Oxford UP, 2003. Online. 17 Aug. 2006 <http://www.oxford-linguistics.com>. An encyclopedia of languages and linguistics that covers the major branches of the field—descriptive, historical, comparative, typological, functional, and formalist—and devotes special attention to their interrelations as well as their relations with other disciplines (e.g., the Language and Literature entry includes subentries on stylistics, rhetoric and literature, pragmatics and literature, metaphor, semiotics and literature, the language of prose fiction, the language or poetry, the language of drama, and language and literary history). The approximately 957 signed entries (some as lengthy as 5,000 words) summarize the state of knowledge on a topic and conclude with a selective bibliography; those on a language family include a list of living and selected extinct languages in the family. Indexed by subjects and persons. The electronic version (available as part of *The Oxford Digital Reference Shelf* [http://www.oxford-digitalreference.com]) can be searched by keyword or browsed by entry; entries can be e-mailed. For discussion of the uses literary and cultural critics can make of the work, see the review by Laurence M. Porter, *SubStance* 34.3 (2005): 139–48.

> McArthur, Tom, ed. *The Oxford Companion to the English Language.* Oxford: Oxford UP, 1992. 1,184 pp. Treats themes, places, persons, institutions, concepts, works, events, and technology associated with literary, common, and colloquial English worldwide.

> Richards, Jack C., and Richard Schmidt. *Longman Dictionary of Language Teaching and Applied Linguistics.* 3rd ed. Harlow: Longman-Pearson, 2002. 595 pp.

General Linguistics

GUIDES TO SCHOLARSHIP

A major need is a judiciously selective, current bibliography of scholarship on linguistics and the English language. Among available ones, Harold B. Allen, comp., *Linguistics and English Linguistics*, 2nd ed., Goldentree Bibliographies in Language and Literature (Arlington Heights: AHM, 1977, 175 pp.), is outdated; and Minoru Yasui, comp., *Current Bibliography on Linguistics and English Linguistics, 1960–1978* (Tokyo: Kaitakusha, 1979, 269 pp.) and *1978–1982* (1983, 887 pp.) are based on no clear principles governing selection, omit numerous essential works, and are either imprecise (*1960–1978*) or uncontrolled (*1978–1982*) in subject organization.

Surveys of Research

See

> Sec. U: Literature-Related Topics and Sources/Composition and Rhetoric/Guides to Scholarship/Surveys of Research.
> *Year's Work in Modern Language Studies* (S4855): General Linguistics division.
> *YWES* (G330): Chapter on English language.

Serial Bibliographies

U6010   *BL Online: The Bibliographical Database of Linguistics.* Instituut voor Nederlandse Lexicologie. Online. 1 Jan. 2007 <http://www.blonline.nl>. Updated regularly.

> *Bibliographie linguistique de l'année [1939–] et complément des années précédentes/Linguistic Bibliography for the Year [1939–] and Supplement for Previous Years.* Dordrecht: Springer, 1949– . Annual.   Z7001.P4 [P121] 016.41.

An international bibliography of scholarship (including book reviews and dissertations) on linguistics and languages worldwide. Entries are organized alphabetically by author in classified divisions for general works (including bibliographies), general linguistics, and major language families or areas. The General Linguistics division and individual languages with sufficient scholarship now have sections for bibliographies and general studies, phonetics and phonology, grammar, lexis, semantics and pragmatics, stylistics, metrics and versification, translation, script and orthography, psycholinguistics and neurolinguistics, sociolinguistics and dialectology, historical and comparative linguistics, mathematical and computational linguistics, and onomastics. Under languages not needing subdivision, bibliographies appear first, followed by other studies in alphabetical order. Indexed by scholars (including reviewers since the volume for 1993). Cross-referencing has improved in recent volumes, but the lack of subject indexing hinders access to many works, especially those treating more than one concept, topic, or language.

BL Online (with coverage beginning with records from the *Bibliographie linguistique* volume for 1993) is far more current that its print counterpart (the volume covering 2000 was published in 2004), but it has not dramatically improved accessibility.

Effective searching requires familiarity with the taxonomy and terminology of the print version. The Search screen allows for searches by keyword, title, subject (i.e., the subject classification terms used in the print version; click on Lists), object language (i.e., the language studied; click on Lists), author, editor, reviewer, person as subject, name, document language, journal, or publisher; searches can be limited by document type and date. Advanced Search allows users to combine the preceding fields. Both search screens allow a user to work from pull-down lists after at least one character has been keyboarded in the search box. The 1,000-record limit on records returned means that users wanting to browse the large classifications (e.g., syntax, lexicography, stylistics) will have to conduct multiple searches limited by year ranges. Records, which are listed only in descending chronological order, cannot be marked for downloading or printing.

Although the number of entries in each volume is swollen by the inclusion of works listed earlier and subsequently reviewed, *Bibliographie linguistique* offers generally fuller coverage of linguistic scholarship — especially that published outside North America — than *MLAIB* (G335) and *LLBA* (U6015), both of which offer superior access because of their more extensive subject indexing and the flexibility they allow in managing searches.

Although not as accessible as they should be, *Bibliographie linguistique* and *BL Online* are essential sources for identifying current linguistic scholarship; for the literature researcher, they are valuable for their inclusion of numerous studies — especially of stylistics and metrics — that are omitted from the standard serial bibliographies and indexes in section G.

U6015   *Linguistics and Language Behavior Abstracts.* Online. 7 Mar. 2005 <http://www-mi10.csa.com>. Updated monthly.

LLBA: Linguistics and Language Behavior Abstracts (LLBA). Bethesda: Cambridge Scientific Abstracts, 1967– . 5/yr. Former title: *LLBA: Language and Language Behavior Abstracts* (1967–84).   Z7001.L15   016.

Nonevaluative abstracts of books, articles, and dissertations since 1966 (print) or 1973 (electronic) on language behavior, linguistics, and related topics; a separate list of book reviews was added in vol. 24 (1990). Except for dissertations, which are generally limited to those in *ProQuest Dissertations and Theses* (H465), after 1985 coverage is international and, especially for journals, encompasses several disciplines. The scope has expanded somewhat since the initial volume, and the organization has become more refined. Since vol. 11 (1977) entries are listed alphabetically by author in 28 classified divisions: psycholinguistics, applied linguistics, phonology, syntax, semantics, morphology, discourse analysis and text linguistics, theory of linguistics, history of linguistics, anthropological linguistics, descriptive linguistics, lexicography, orthography and writing systems, language classification, interpersonal behavior and communication, sociolinguistics, poetics and literary theory (with sections for poetics, literary criticism, literary theory, and historical text studies), nonverbal communication, semiotics, philosophy of language, phonetics, hearing and speech physiology, pathological and normal hearing, pathological and normal language, learning disabilities, mental retardation, linguistics and psychiatry, and special education. A typical entry in the print version consists of author(s), address of primary author, title and publication information, LC and ISBN numbers for books, and a detailed abstract; the online version adds fields for ISSN, CODEN, language, type of publication, country of publication, descriptors, classification fields, update code, and accession number. Three indexes in each issue: authors; journals and issues indexed; subjects. (The last is a detailed analytic index based on a controlled thesaurus, with each entry providing essentially an abstract of the abstract.) The indexes are cumulated annually; there is also a cumulative index for vols. 1–5 (2 pts., 1971). In addition to the thesaurus and author and journal indexes, the online version has indexes of languages and publication types. The online version is available through CSA; see entry I510 for an evaluation of the search interface. The multidisciplinary coverage and full subject indexing make *LLBA* (especially in its electronic form) a useful source for identifying studies of stylistics, literary theory, and literary criticism, especially in journals not covered (or accessibly indexed) in the standard serial bibliographies and indexes in section G.

Although limited to the theory and practice of general linguistics rather than to applied studies or articles on individual languages, *Linguistics Abstracts* (Oxford: Blackwell, 1985– , quarterly; online; 7 June 2006 <http://www.linguisticsabstracts.com>; updated regularly) does abstract some journals not covered by *LLBA*. The best access is offered by the online version, which allows three types of searches: Quick Search (keyword); Browse (titles); Abstract Search (full text, title, author, journal, date, volume and issue, and subdiscipline). Results can be sorted by relevance, title, journal, subdiscipline, author (ascending), or date (descending).

See also

> Sec. H: Guides to Dissertations and Theses.
> *ABELL* (G340): English Language division.
> *L'année philologique* (S4890).
> Bullock, *Guide to Marxist Literary Criticism* (U6175).
> *MLAIB* (G335): See the national literature divisions in the volumes for 1921–32; General/Linguistics and the linguistics section in national literature divisions in the volume for 1933; General/Linguistics, General/Experimental Phonetics, and linguistics sections in national literature divisions in the volumes for 1934–45; General/General Linguistics, General/Experimental Phonetics, and linguistics sections in national literature divisions in the volumes for 1946–50; General/ Linguistics, General/Semantics, and linguistics sections in national literature divisions in the volumes for 1951–52; General VI: Language and linguistics sections in national literature divisions in the volumes for 1953–55; General III: General Language and Linguistics and linguistics sections in national literature divisions in the volume for 1956; General I: General Language and Linguistics and linguistics sections in national literature divisions in the volumes for 1957– 66; and the Linguistics division in later volumes (especially General Linguistics IV: Stylistics/Linguistics and Literature in the volumes for 1968–80). Researchers must also check the headings beginning "English Language" and "Linguistic(s)" in the subject index to post-1980 volumes and in the online thesaurus.
> *Psychological Abstracts* (U6530).
> *RILM Abstracts* (U6240).

Special Topics

LEXICOGRAPHY

Research Methods

U6017   Landau, Sidney I. *Dictionaries: The Art and Craft of Lexicography.* 2nd ed. Cambridge: Cambridge UP, 2001. 477 pp.   P327.L3   413'.028.

A guide to the principles and practices of the construction of English-language dictionaries. Offering an extensive range of examples, chapters are devoted to the definition of *dictionary* and the kinds of special-purpose dictionaries, a brief history of English lexicography, parts of a dictionary and the entries therein, the practice of definition, usage information, the uses of corpora, the process of commercial dictionary making, and legal and ethical concerns in lexicography. The second edition replaces the evaluative selective bibliography of monolingual dictionaries with a list that refers readers to significant commentary or evaluation in the text. Indexed by persons, titles of anonymous works, and subjects; titles of dictionaries are indexed under editors. Emphasizing practice rather than theory and combining illustration with sometimes trenchant (but fair) evaluation, *Dictionaries* is an essential introduction for aspiring lexicographers as well as readers interested in learning how to judge the dictionaries they rely on. Review: Henri Béjoint, *International Journal of Lexicography* 15 (2002): 169-73.

Ladislav Zgusta, *Manual of Lexicography*, Janua Linguarum: Series Maior 39 (Prague: Academia; The Hague: Mouton, 1971, 360 pp.), is more advanced and inclusive in its coverage but is now badly dated.

Individual aspects of the theory and practice of lexicography are treated at length in Franz Josef Hausmann et al., eds., *Wörterbücher/Dictionaries/Dictionnaires: Ein internationales Handbuch zur Lexikographie/An International Encyclopedia of Lexicography/Encyclopédie internationale de lexicographie*, 3 vols., Handbücher zur Sprach- und Kommunikationswissenschaft/Handbooks of Linguistics and Communication Science/Manuels de linguistique et des sciences de communication 5 (Berlin: de Gruyter, 1989–91).

Bibliographies of Bibliographies

U6018   Cop, Margaret. *Babel Unravelled: An Annotated World Bibliography of Dictionary Bibliographies, 1658–1988.* Lexicographica: Series Maior 36. Tübingen: Niemeyer, 1990. 195 pp.   Z7004.D5 C63 [P327] 016.01603.

A bibliography of bibliographies—including separately published works, contributions to periodicals, parts of books, booksellers' catalogs, and catalogs of collections, as well as some manuscript lists and databases—of language and subject dictionaries, including wordbooks, word lists, lexicons, vocabularies, thesauruses, glossaries, concordances, and syllabaries. Although the majority of the 619 bibliographies date from 1658–1988, some works published as late as 1990 are included. The entries (organized alphabetically by author, editor, or title of anonymous work) consist of a citation and locations of copies—principally in German libraries—or source of information, followed, in most cases, by information on languages, kinds of annotations, organization, chronological span, indexes, and number of items in and types, content, and time periods of dictionaries covered. Several entries conclude with helpful evaluative or historical notes (that also cite reviews). Indexed, at the beginning, by languages, types of dictionaries, subjects, Universal Decimal Classification numbers, types of bibliographies, and persons. Nearly one-third of the entries were not seen by the author, several works included (e.g., general guides to reference books, journals that merely review dictionaries, and miscellaneous bibliographies that happen to list some dictionaries) hardly can be classified as bibliographies of dictionaries, and coverage is better for European publications than for North American ones; yet *Babel Unravelled* is the best starting place for identifying lists of dictionaries. Researchers must, however, search serial bibliographies such as *Bibliographie linguistique* (U6010), *ABELL* (G340), and *MLAIB* (G335) for additional bibliographies.

Guides to Primary Works

Bibliographies

U6020   Brewer, Annie M., ed. *Dictionaries, Encyclopedias, and Other Word-Related Books: A Classified Guide to Dictionaries, Encyclopedias, and Similar Works, Based on Library of Congress MARC Records, and Arranged According to the Library of Congress Classification System.* 4th ed. 2 vols. Detroit: Gale, 1988. Z5848.D52 [AE5]   016.03.

A subject list of dictionaries, encyclopedias, concordances, glossaries, lexicons, thesauruses, vocabularies, and similar works. Since the entries, organized by LC classification, are derived from Library of Congress cataloging records prepared between 1966 and the end of 1986, the two volumes potentially include any "word-related" book published or reprinted during that period as well as numerous pre-1966 publications for which LC cards or MARC and REMARC records were prepared. The uncritical reliance on Library of Congress cataloging records leads to considerable duplication of entries (especially of unrevised reprints), serious gaps in coverage (especially of books published before 1966), the inclusion of many works that are only remotely "word-related," and inconsistencies in the classification of works. The fourth edition improves upon its predecessors by printing a title and subject index, but users will find it less than helpful because of the citation of LC classifications rather than page numbers and the reproduction of frequently imprecise LC subject headings from MARC records. Although seriously flawed and incomplete, Brewer is the most extensive single list of "word-related books." What would be welcome is a thorough, carefully organized, effectively indexed annotated bibliography based on personal examination of these kinds of publications.

For an evaluative survey of important dictionaries through the late 1960s, see Robert L. Collison, *Dictionaries of English and Foreign Languages: A Bibliographical Guide to Both General and Technical Dictionaries with Historical and Explanatory Notes and References,* 2nd ed. (New York: Hafner, 1971, 303 pp.). Organized by language or geographical area, chapters typically comment on the history and use of general, etymological, slang, dialect, specialist, and bilingual dictionaries. Technical dictionaries are listed by field in an appendix. Collison remains useful for its evaluations of dictionaries published before 1970.

More current (but not rigorous in selection or evaluation) are the sections on dictionaries in *Walford's Guide to Reference Material* (B65), and *Guide to Reference Books* (B60).

Indexes

U6025   Wall, C. Edward, and Edward Przebienda, comps. *Words and Phrases Index: A Guide to Antedatings, New Words, New Compounds, New Meanings, and Other Published Scholarship Supplementing the* Oxford English Dictionary, Dictionary of Americanisms, Dictionary of American English, *and Other Major Dictionaries of the English Language.* 4 vols. Ann Arbor: Pierian, 1969–70.   PE1689.W3   016.423.

An index to additions, antedatings, and corrections published in *American Notes and Queries* 1–8 (1941–49) and 1–5 (1962–67); *American Speech* 1–41 (1925–66); *Britannica Book of the Year* (1945–67); *California Folklore Quarterly* 1–6 (1942–47); *College English* 1–29 (1939–68); *Dialect Notes* 1–6 (1890–1939); *Notes and Queries* 148–211 (1925–66); *Publication of the American Dialect Society* 1–47 (1944–67); and

Western Folklore 7–26 (1948–67). Vols. 1 and 3 are word indexes; vols. 2 and 4, keyword-out-of-context indexes to phrases. Wall is a useful source for identifying scholarship on individual words and phrases, since few of the standard serial bibliographies and indexes in section G provide this kind of information.

Guides to Scholarship

U6027   Zgusta, Ladislav. *Lexicography Today: An Annotated Bibliography of the Theory of Lexicography.* Lexicographica: Series Maior 18. Tübingen: Niemeyer, 1988. 349 pp.   Z7004.L48 Z47 [P327]   016.413'028.

An international bibliography of publications, from c. 1962 through early 1987, on the procedures, methods, and theory of lexicography. Works listed in Zgusta, *Manual of Lexicography* (U6017a), are excluded as are recent studies treating "the history of lexicography, . . . etymological, historical, and encyclopedic lexicography," individual dictionaries, computational linguistics, and artificial intelligence—unless directly related to the theory or methodology of lexicography. Organized alphabetically by author, entries are accompanied by succinct descriptive annotations. Four indexes: second and other authors and editors; persons appearing in titles and annotations; selected languages discussed; subjects. Although not exhaustive, Zgusta is impressive in its international coverage and offers the best record of scholarship on lexicographical theory before 1987.

METAPHOR

Guides to Scholarship

U6035   *Bibliography of Metaphor and Metonymy (MetBib).* Ed. by Sabine de Knop. Benjamins. Online. 18 Aug. 2006 <http://www.benjamins.com/online/met>. Updated annually.

Noppen, J. P. van, S. de Knop, and R. Jongen, comps. *Metaphor: A Bibliography of Post-1970 Publications.* Amsterdam Studies in the Theory and History of Linguistic Science, Series 5: Library and Information Sources in Linguistics 17. Amsterdam: Benjamins, 1985. 497 pp.

Noppen, Jean-Pierre van, and Edith Hols, comps. *Metaphor II: A Classified Bibliography of Publications, 1985 to 1900* [i.e., *1990*]. Amsterdam Studies in the Theory and History of Linguistic Science, Series 5: Library and Information Sources in Linguistics 20. Amsterdam: Benjamins, 1990. 350 pp.   Z7004.M4 N66 [P301.5.M48]   016.808.

Shibles, Warren A. *Metaphor: An Annotated Bibliography and History.* Whitewater: Language P, 1971. 414 pp.   Z7004.M4 S5   011.

International bibliographies of books, articles, dissertations, and theses on metaphor in a variety of disciplines and periods. *Bibliography of Metaphor and Metonymy,* which covers 1990–2004, includes some unpublished papers and frequently takes abstracts from other bibliographic resources or quotes a publisher's description. The database uses the same interface as *Bibliography of Pragmatics Online* (with the addition of a field for title as subject in Advanced Search); see entry U6050 for an evaluation of the interface. Although lacking any explanation of editorial procedures and depending too much on other sources rather than firsthand examination of documents, *MetBib* offers the most current guide to studies of metaphor. The print volumes are organized alphabetically by author (then by title in Shibles, by date in Noppen), with some entries accompanied by descriptive annotations: in Shibles, the annotations vary considerably in quality, and most foreign-language works are not annotated; Noppen offers few annotations, but they tend to be fuller. Both appear to take many entries unverified from other sources. Noppen, *Post-1970*, concludes with a list of recommended works for beginners. Shibles has three indexes: extensive works on metaphor; general subjects; aspects of metaphor. However, the indexing is uncontrolled, inconsistent, and imprecise. Noppen, *Post-1970*, also has three indexes: general subjects; uses and theory of metaphor; tenors, vehicles, and their semantic fields (which is useful for locating studies of types of imagery or specific images); Noppen, *Metaphor II*, replaces the general subject index with indexes of disciplines and persons. Although Noppen's indexing is superior, the combination of entry number and date in *Post-1970* is extremely confusing and the additions (pp. 486–97 in *Post-1970*, pp. 345–50 in *Metaphor II*) are excluded. Noppen, *Metaphor II*, is inconsistent in citing reviews: some appear only in a list following the book reviewed, some appear in a list of reviews and have separate entries as well, and some have separate entries but are not cross-referenced to the book reviewed. Both Shibles and Noppen, *Post-1970*, suffer from an inadequate statement of scope and coverage. Although they are plagued by errors, inconsistent in annotations, include much that seems only vaguely related to metaphor, omit significant works, and are inadequately indexed in the case of Shibles, the three volumes together encompass an impressive range of international scholarship. For additions to Shibles, see the anonymous, untitled contribution in *Newsletter: Rhetoric Society of America* 4.3 (1974): 5–13. Reviews: (Shibles) Rosemarie Gläser, *Zeitschrift für Anglistik und Amerikanistik* 23 (1975): 170–71; Winfried Schleiner, *Comparative Literature Studies* 10 (1973): 394–95.

ONOMASTICS

Guides to Scholarship

U6040   Rajec, Elizabeth M. *The Study of Names in Literature: A Bibliography.* New York: Saur, 1978. 261 pp. *Supplement.* 1981. 298 pp.   Z6514.N35 R34 [PN56.N16]   016.809′92.

An international bibliography of selected reference sources on onomastics in general and of studies (including dissertations and reviews through 1979) of the use of names in literature. The 3,023 entries are listed alphabetically by author, but their number is swollen by separate listings of book reviews. Few of the brief annotations adequately convey a sense of contents. Except for literary authors and titles of anonymous works, the headings in the subject index are generally too broad (especially in the 1978 volume). The inadequate explanation of criteria governing selection, uninformative annotations, numerous errors, omissions, and ineffective subject indexing in the original volume make Rajec little more than a place to begin research on literary onomastics.

Some additional studies can be identified in two serial bibliographies formerly published in *Names: A Journal of Onomastics*: "Bibliography of Personal Names, [1952–75]," 1–24 (1953–76), and "Place-Name Literature, [1946–79]," irregularly in 3–27 (1955–79).

PRAGMATICS

Guides to Scholarship

U6050 *Bibliography of Pragmatics Online.* Ed. Frank Brisard, Michael Meeuwis, and Jef Verschueren. Benjamins. Online. 18 Aug. 2006 <http://www.benjamins.com/online/bop>. Updated annually.

A bibliographic database of publications (including reviews) through 2003 on pragmatics, including "accommodation theory, analytical philosophy and anthropological linguistics, . . . cognitive linguistics, construction grammar, conversation analysis, discourse analysis, literary pragmatics, neurolinguistics, psycholinguistics, relevance theory, sociolinguistics, speech act theory, and universal and transcendental pragmatics." Coverage is most complete for works written in English, French, German, or Dutch and incorporates the entries from Jan Nuyts and J. Verschueren, comps., *A Comprehensive Bibliography of Pragmatics,* 4 vols. (Amsterdam: Benjamins, 1987).

Basic Search offers keyword searching of all record fields; Advanced Search allows users to combine searches of the following fields: keyword (thesaurus terms), author or editor, title, annotation, publisher, document language, language as subject, person as subject, series title, journal, and date. In addition, users can browse lists of authors, journals, keywords, languages, persons, and series. Those who want to search through the Thesaurus should first consult the Instructions file. Results are listed in descending chronological order and cannot be sorted otherwise; several records lack a date and thus sort out of order. The only options for downloading data are to e-mail the entire results list or to download full records one at a time (the only way to retrieve the informative descriptive annotations that most records include). Although not comprehensive, not as current as one would expect, and in need of an interface that offers more flexibility in downloading records, *Bibliography of Pragmatics Online* is the fullest guide to scholarship on the subject.

SEMANTICS

Guides to Scholarship

U6055 Gordon, W. Terrence. *Semantics: A Bibliography, 1965–1978.* Metuchen: Scarecrow, 1980. 307 pp. *1979–1985.* 1987. 292 pp. *1986–1991.* 1992. 280 pp. Z7004.S4 G67 [P325] 016.415.

A bibliography of scholarship (including dissertations) in English, French, German, Italian, Spanish, and Portuguese on semantics. Although Gordon's work encompasses studies from linguistics, philosophy, psychology, and anthropology, it excludes several topics of particular interest to literary researchers: general semantics, history of semantics, semiotics, meaning and style, discourse analysis, lexicology, and logical semantics. The approximately 7,400 entries are listed alphabetically by author in divisions for books; general surveys; definitions and models of meaning; reference and pragmatics; ambiguity, indeterminacy, and generic meaning; synonymy; antonymy; polysemy; homonymy; morphosemantics; associative senses in the lexicon; semantic fields and componential analysis; kinship terminology; color terms; semantics of parts of speech; syntax; negation; idioms; case grammar; child language; comparative semantics; and semantic universals. In *1965–1978* and *1979–1985* a very few entries are accompanied by brief descriptive (occasionally evaluative) annotations; in *1986–1991* most entries are annotated. Although each division concludes with cross-references, the unrefined classification system and lack of subject indexing make locating works difficult. Two indexes: lexical terms; authors. The exclusion of so many areas of study and numerous omissions of works falling within its scope make Gordon little more than a starting point for identifying studies of semantics.

SEMIOTICS

Handbooks, Dictionaries, and Encyclopedias

U6065   *Encyclopedic Dictionary of Semiotics.* Gen. ed. Thomas A. Sebeok. 2nd ed.
        rev. and updated. 3 vols. Approaches to Semiotics 73. Berlin: Mouton de
        Gruyter, 1994.   P99.E65   302.2.

An encyclopedia of terms (treating both historical background and current uses), dead semioticians and others important in the development of the field, and the relationship of semiotics to other areas (including a 15-page article titled "Literature"). The 426 signed entries, ranging from 1 to 32 pages, refer extensively to the combined bibliography in vol. 3. The new edition reprints the text of the first and relegates the spotty revisions — most of which are one- or two-item additions to the bibliographies — to separately paginated supplements at the end of each volume. Although purchasers of this expensive set should rightfully expect (and would be better served by) a more thorough and integrated revision, *Encyclopedic Dictionary* remains the essential work for clarifying — and codifying — the sometimes abstruse terminology used in semiotics.

An important complement is *Encyclopedia of Semiotics*, ed. Paul Bouissac (New York: Oxford UP, 1998, 702 pp.), which treats terminology, schools and movements, persons, major publications, and applications associated with semiotics and aspects of cultural theory. The signed entries conclude with a bibliography. Indexed by persons, subjects, and some titles. Although lacking a sufficient explanation of the principles governing the selection of topics (and consequently including some rather surprising ones, e.g., baseball, database, gossip, military, and postage stamp), *Encyclopedia of Semiotics* gives, as a good encyclopedia should, clear, authoritative guidance to the field.

Fuller treatment of the theory, history, scope, structure, and application of sign theory is offered by *Semiotik/Semiotics: Ein Handbuch zu den zeichentheoretischen Grundlagen von Natur und Kultur/A Handbook on the Sign-Theoretic Foundations of Nature and Culture*, ed. Roland Posner, Klaus Robering, and Thomas A. Sebeok, 4 vols., Handbücher zur Sprach- und Kommunikationswissenschaft/Handbooks of Linguistics and Communication Science/Manuels de linguistique et des sciences de communication 13: 1–4 (Berlin: de Gruyter, 1997–2004). Each of the 178 essays, written in German or English by leading scholars, concludes with an extensive bibliography. Two indexes: persons; subjects.

Guides to Scholarship

U6070   Eschbach, Achim, and Viktória Eschbach-Szabó, comps. *Bibliography of
        Semiotics, 1975–1985.* 2 vols. Amsterdam Studies in the Theory and
        History of Linguistic Science, Series 5: Library and Information Sources in

Linguistics 16. Amsterdam: Benjamins, 1986.   Z7004.S43 E76 [P99]
016.00151.

Eschbach, Achim, and Wendelin Rader. *Semiotik-Bibliographie I.* Frankfurt:
Syndikat, 1976. 221 pp.   Z7004.S43 E77   [P99].

Eschbach, Achim. *Zeichen-Text-Bedeutung: Bibliographie zu Theorie und
Praxis der Semiotik.* Kritische Information 32. München: Fink, 1974.
508 pp.   Z7004.S43 E78.

International bibliographies of publications with some connection to semiotics.
Bibliography of Semiotics includes book reviews but excludes works published in the
Soviet Union. The 10,839 entries are listed alphabetically by author. Two indexes: book
reviews; subjects. *Semiotik-Bibliographie* organizes about 4,000 works (published between 1965 and June 1976) in 12 unclassified divisions: architecture, film, semiotic
theory and terminology, history of semiotics, art, literature, music, nonverbal communication, pragmatics, semantics, sociosemantics, and miscellaneous works. Two indexes: scholars; subjects. *Zeichen-Text-Bedeutung* includes dissertations. Entries are listed
alphabetically by author in six classified divisions: general studies, systematic studies
(syntax, semantics, and pragmatics), communication theory and text analysis, background studies, interdisciplinary studies, and works by and about individual semioticians. Indexed by scholars. Although all include a considerable number of studies of
literary works, locating these studies is frequently impossible except in *Semiotik-Bibliographie: Zeichen-Text-Bedeutung* lacks a subject index, and the one in *Bibliography of
Semiotics* is nothing more than an uncritical alphabetic list of title keywords (with no
attempt to reconcile equivalent terms in various languages). In all three compilations,
the heavy reliance on other bibliographies leads to the inclusion of numerous works
only remotely related to semiotics. The lack of any stated criteria governing what constitutes semiotic scholarship results in a hodgepodge that would benefit from judicious
organization and indexing.

STYLISTICS

Guides to Scholarship

Surveys of Research

U6073   "The Year's Work in Stylistics [1998–]." *Language and Literature* 8–
(1998–). Irregular.   P301.L32.

A highly selective review essay, with evaluations that tend to be fuller than one
typically finds in surveys of research these days. The organization of each essay is determined by the topics of the studies reviewed.

Serial Bibliographies

U6075   "Stylistics Annotated Bibliography [1966–90]." *Style* 1–25 (1967–91).
PE1.S89   805.

A highly selective annotated bibliography of books, dissertations in *ProQuest
Dissertations and Theses* (H465), and articles. Since the bibliography for 1979 (vol. 15
[1981]), entries are listed alphabetically by author in six divisions: bibliographies; general
theory; culture, history, and style—period, nation, and genre; the author; the text; and

the reader. The last four have subdivisions for theoretical and applied studies, with the latter classified by elements of style. Three indexes: scholars (beginning with the bibliography for 1987–88, in vol. 23 [1989]); subject terms (since the bibliography for 1980, in vol. 16 [1982]); persons as subjects (since that for 1981, in vol. 17 [1983]). Although not comprehensive (especially since the bibliography for 1987–88 [vol. 23 (1989)], when coverage was drastically scaled back), the bibliography was once the best source for identifying stylistic scholarship published between 1967 and 1986. Beginning in 26 (1992) "Stylistics Annotated Bibliography" was replaced with a bibliography issue that prints checklists and annotated bibliographies of individuals and subjects; the last of these issues appeared in vol. 34 (2000).

Other Bibliographies

U6080   Bailey, Richard W., and Dolores M. Burton, S. N. D. *English Stylistics: A Bibliography.* Cambridge: MIT P, 1968. 198 pp.   Z2015.S7 B2   016.808.
       A bibliography of primary works and scholarship (including dissertations) through c. 1966 on the stylistic study of English and American literary texts since 1500. Bailey also includes highly selective coverage of classical and medieval literature. The approximately 2,000 entries are organized in three divisions: bibliographies, language and style before 1900 (with each period subdivision including sections for primary works and related scholarship and general studies), and the twentieth century (with sections on creativity and style, modes of stylistic investigation, statistical approaches, translation, prose stylistics, and poetry). A few entries are accompanied by brief descriptive annotations. Two indexes: literary authors as subjects; scholars. The rather confusing organization, the lack of cross-references, and the failure to provide a subject index seriously impede locating studies on topics, stylistic features, or methodologies. Despite these drawbacks and the incomplete coverage, Bailey is useful because it represents the fullest list of stylistic studies before 1966 of English and American literature. Review: Louis T. Milic, *Style* 2 (1968): 239–43.
       More comprehensive coverage of statistical studies is offered by Richard W. Bailey and Lubomír Doležel, comps. and eds., *An Annotated Bibliography of Statistical Stylistics* (Ann Arbor: Dept. of Slavic Languages and Literatures, U of Michigan, 1968, 97 pp.). For some additions, see the review by Robert S. Wachal, *Style* 6 (1972): 66–70.
       Louis T. Milic, *Style and Stylistics: An Analytical Bibliography* (New York: Free; London: Collier, 1967, 199 pp.), whose approximately 800 entries are mostly English-language studies of literatures in English, is much less thorough than Bailey but it does cite some works omitted in Bailey and is more accessible, thanks to a subject index. Review: Richard W. Bailey, *Style* 2 (1968): 233–38.
       Because stylistic studies are virtually impossible to locate readily in most of the standard serial bibliographies and indexes in section G, these three bibliographies and Bennett, *Bibliography of Stylistics* (U6085), are indispensable guides to scholarship.

U6085   Bennett, James R. *A Bibliography of Stylistics and Related Criticism, 1967–83.* New York: MLA, 1986. 405 pp.   Z6514.S8 B46 [PN203]   016.809.
       A selective bibliography of works on the stylistic criticism of literature. Bennett covers studies published between 1967 and 1983 (along with a few from 1984) but excludes dissertations, theoretical studies that do not involve literary application, most psychoanalytic works as well as those about film and literature, and all articles (except for bibliographies and a few in collections of essays). The approximately 1,500 entries are organized by publication date in six classified divisions: bibliographies and reference

works (with sections for annual bibliographies and journals, and other bibliographies and reference works); general studies and concepts of style; works on period, national, and genre style (with sections for theoretical studies; diction, imagery, and tropes; syntax and schemes; prosody and sound patterns in prose; and studies involving several linguistic levels); single-author studies (with the same sections as the preceding division); studies of individual texts (again, with the same sections as the preceding division); and the phenomenology of readers (with sections for theoretical and practical studies). A majority of the entries are descriptively annotated (although the annotations too often rely on quotations from the works) and accompanied by citations to reviews (with frequent quotations from reviews). Three appendixes: a chronology of important works and events in stylistics from 1878 to early 1985; a classification of critics by theoretical or methodological approach; a suggested reading list on aspects of stylistic criticism. Four indexes: terms; literary authors and anonymous works; critics and theorists; authors of works cited. Although Bennett is limited by its exclusion of articles and dissertations, unevenly and incompletely annotated (especially for foreign-language works), and incomplete in its coverage of studies of individual authors and works, its international coverage and clear indexing make the *Bibliography* an essential preliminary guide to book-length theoretical studies and practical applications of stylistic criticism and theory. Users will have to supplement coverage with "Stylistics Annotated Bibliography" (U6075), Bailey, *English Stylistics* (U6080), *MLAIB* (G335), *Arts and Humanities Citation Index* (G365), the bibliographies and indexes in section G, and works in section H: Guides to Dissertations and Theses.

SYNTAX

General Introductions

U6100   Visser, F. Th. *An Historical Syntax of the English Language.* 4 vols. Leiden:
         Brill, 1963–73. (Vol. 1 has been published in a corrected second
         impression, 1970.)   PE1361.V5.
         A diachronic study of the development, in written language, of syntactic constructions with a verb form as a nucleus. Organized according to the number of verbs in a phrase, then by syntactic unit, the detailed analysis and history of each structural pattern is accompanied by numerous illustrations from Old English to the present century. Indexed by word in vols. 1 and 2, with a cumulative index in 4. The organization is confusing at times, and there are numerous typographical errors. Although reviewers have disagreed with some interpretations, all admit that this is a monumental contribution to the study of English syntax. Literary researchers will find it particularly useful in interpreting syntactic structures in literary works. Reviews: Norman Davis, *Review of English Studies* ns 17 (1966): 73–75, 20 (1969): 196–200, 22 (1971): 64–66, 26 (1975): 454–58.

Guides to Scholarship

U6105   Scheurweghs, G., et al. *Analytical Bibliography of Writings on Modern English
         Morphology and Syntax,* 1877–1960. 5 vols. Louvain: Nauwelaerts, 1963–
         79.   Z2015.A1 S33.

Vol. 1: Scheurweghs. *Periodical Literature and Miscellanies of the United States of America and Western and Northern Europe.* 1963. 293 pp. (With an appendix by Hideo Yamaguchi on Japanese publications.)

Vol. 2: Scheurweghs. *Studies in Bookform, Including Dissertations and Programmabhandlungen, Published in the United States of America and Western and Northern Europe.* 1965. 232 pp. (With appendixes on Japanese and Czechoslovak publications by Yamaguchi and Ján Simko, respectively.)

Vol. 3: Scheurweghs. *Soviet Research on English Morphology and Syntax.* Ed. G. C. Pocheptsov. *English Studies in Bulgaria, Poland, Rumania, and Yugoslavia.* By M. Mincoff et al. Ed. Pocheptsov. 1968. 267 pp.

Vol. 4: Scheurweghs and E. Vorlat. *Addenda and General Indexes.* 1968. 123 pp.

Vol. 5: Vorlat, ed. *Articles in Periodicals, 1961–1970.* 1979. 416 pp.

Bibliographies of publications and dissertations from several countries on English morphology and syntax since c. 1500. Pedagogical studies and popular journalism are excluded. Vols. 1–4 are organized by country, then by type of publication (journal articles, books, dissertations), then alphabetically by author; vol. 5 is organized by periodical, with articles following in order of publication. The individual volumes vary considerably in the thoroughness of their coverage. Some entries in vols. 1–4 are accompanied by descriptive annotations; vol. 5 offers extensive descriptions of each article. Vol. 4 prints additions to vols. 1 and 2. Two indexes (scholars and subjects) in each volume; the appendixes and the five countries in vol. 3 are separately indexed, and vol. 5 has an additional index of literary authors and works referred to. Vols. 1–3 are cumulatively indexed in five indexes in vol. 4: scholars; authors discussed; dissertations (by country, then institution); subjects of articles and books; subjects of dissertations. Although the *Analytical Bibliography* is valuable for its extensive (but not complete) coverage of foreign-language scholarship and inclusion of several studies of literary works, the lack of effective organization and insufficiently thorough indexing make locating works sometimes difficult.

Literary Criticism and Theory

This section is limited to important reference works and histories.

Histories and Surveys

U6120   Wellek, René. *A History of Modern Criticism, 1750–1950.* 8 vols. New Haven: Yale UP, 1955–92.   PN86.W4   801.95′09.

Vol. 1: *The Later Eighteenth Century.* 1955. 358 pp.
Vol. 2: *The Romantic Age.* 1955. 459 pp.
Vol. 3: *The Age of Transition.* 1965. 389 pp.
Vol. 4: *The Later Nineteenth Century.* 1965. 671 pp.
Vol. 5: *English Criticism, 1900–1950.* 1986. 343 pp.
Vol. 6: *American Criticism, 1900–1950.* 1986. 345 pp.

Vol. 7: *German, Russian, and Eastern European Criticism, 1900–1950.* 1991. 458 pp.

Vol. 8: *French, Italian, and Spanish Criticism, 1900–1950.* 1992. 369 pp.

A history of Western literary theory and criticism, with excursions into aesthetics, literary history, and practical criticism. Initially restricted to England, Scotland, France, Germany, and Italy, coverage expands to the United States and Russia in vol. 3. Volumes are organized around chapters devoted to major critics, groups, movements, or countries, with each chapter providing summaries of works and theories along with considerations of their place in Western critical thought. Vols. 1–6 and 8 conclude with a chronology, by country, of critical works. Two indexes in vols. 1–6: persons; topics and terms; vol. 7 is indexed by persons. Although some reviewers have objected to Wellek's definition of criticism, most agree that this is a masterful, balanced, indispensable exposition of modern critical thought. Reviews: (vols. 1–2) Erich Auerbach, *Romanische Forschungen* 67 (1956): 387–97; George Watson, *Essays in Criticism* 7 (1957): 81–84; (vols. 3–4) Roger Sale, *Hudson Review* 19 (1966): 324–29; (vols. 5–6) Jonathan Culler, *Journal of the History of Ideas* 49 (1988): 347–51; (vol. 8) Victor Brombert, *TLS: Times Literary Supplement* 2 July 1993: 25.

U6123   *The Cambridge History of Literary Criticism.* Ed. Peter Brooks, H. B. Nisbet, and Claude Rawson. 9 vols. Cambridge: Cambridge UP, 1989– . PN86.C27   801′.95′09.

Vol. 1: *Classical Criticism.* Ed. George A. Kennedy. 1989. 378 pp.

Vol. 2: *The Middle Ages.* Ed. Alastair Minnis and Ian Johnson. 2005. 865 pp.

Vol. 3: *The Renaissance.* Ed. Glyn P. Norton. 1999. 758 pp.

Vol. 4: *The Eighteenth Century.* Ed. Nisbet and Rawson. 1997. 951 pp.

Vol. 5: *Romanticism.* Ed. Marshall Brown. 2000. 493 pp.

Vol. 6: *The Nineteenth Century.* Ed. M. A. R. Habib.

Vol. 7: *Modernism and the New Criticism.* Ed. A. Walton Litz, Louis Menand, and Lawrence Rainey. 2000. 565 pp.

Vol. 8: *From Formalism to Poststructuralism.* Ed. Raman Selden. 1995. 487 pp.

Vol. 9: *Twentieth-Century Historical, Philosophical, and Psychological Perspectives.* Ed. Christa Knellwolf and Christopher Norris. 2001. 482 pp.

A history of Western literary theory and criticism from classical antiquity to the present. Each volume typically consists of separately authored essays on major theorists, groups, movements or schools, periods, and genres and concludes with a bibliography of primary and secondary sources. Indexed by persons and subjects. *Cambridge History of Literary Criticism* offers an authoritative, balanced overview of its subject. Review: (vol. 1) Steven Shankman, *Modern Philology* 90 (1992): 80–83.

The best single-volume introduction to Western literary theory and criticism is M. A. R. Habib, *A History of Literary Criticism* (Malden: Blackwell, 2005, 838 pp.), with chapters devoted to theorists, periods, schools, and movements from Plato to the present. In each chapter, it explains the philosophical and historical context, offers a close reading of keys texts, and places them within the critical tradition. Indexed by persons and subjects. With its admirably clear explanation of concepts and terminology, *History of Literary Criticism* admirably fulfills the promise of its title.

Handbooks, Dictionaries, and Encyclopedias

U6130   *The Johns Hopkins Guide to Literary Theory and Criticism.* Ed. Michael
Groden, Martin Kreiswirth, and Imre Szeman. Baltimore: Johns Hopkins
UP, 2005. 985 pp.   PN81.J554   801'.95'0922. (An online version is in
progress.)

An encyclopedia of literary theory from Plato to the present (the twentieth century
is "deliberately foreshortened"). The 241 signed entries (most by major scholars) consider "critics and theorists, critical and theoretical schools and movements, and the
critical and theoretical innovations of specific countries and historical periods" from a
North American perspective. Entries tend to be rather fuller than one expects in an
encyclopedia and conclude with selective bibliographies (although some have not been
adequately updated, e.g., Arnold, Matthew; Bloom, Harold [the list of secondary stud-
ies], and Drama Theory [especially the list of secondary studies]). Two indexes: individuals discussed in entries; topics. Review: (first ed.) Leroy F. Searle, *Yearbook of
Comparative and General Literature* 41 (1993): 228–32; (second ed.) Christopher
Hitchens, *New York Times Book Review* 22 May 2005: 18–19. Although among the
best of the numerous encyclopedias and dictionaries of theory and criticism, *Johns
Hopkins Guide* is not for readers unconversant with recent debates in the field, and
it must be supplemented by some of the following for twentieth-century developments.

Another of the best of the recent guides, *Literary Theory and Criticism: An Oxford
Guide*, ed. Patricia Waugh (Oxford: Oxford UP, 2006), complements *Johns Hopkins
Guide* by emphasizing twentieth-century critical practices, schools and movements, and
emerging theories. Each of the 37 essays typically addresses the history of its topic,
explains key concepts or debates, introduces key figures, and concludes with a selected
bibliography. Indexed by persons and subjects.

Equally valuable is *The Continuum Encyclopedia of Modern Criticism and Theory*,
gen. ed. Julian Wolfreys (New York: Continuum, 2002, 882 pp.), which offers 107
lengthy, signed essays on philosophers, critics, schools, groups, and theories important
in the history and development of literary theory and cultural studies in Europe, Britain,
and North America. An essay typically addresses cultural, intellectual, theoretical, ideological, and historical contexts in assessing the importance of its subject to institutional
criticism; each essay concludes with a selective bibliography. Featuring an impressive
array of contributors, *Continuum Encyclopedia of Modern Criticism and Theory* offers
accessible introductions to the current preoccupations of literary and cultural theory.

Anglo-American and French feminist theory in literary studies, psychology, sociology, history, and the arts is more fully treated in Maggie Humm, *The Dictionary of
Feminist Theory*, 2nd ed. (Columbus: Ohio State UP, 1995, 354 pp.).

Offering the best interdisciplinary coverage of recent cultural theory is *A Dictionary
of Cultural and Critical Theory*, ed. Michael Payne (Oxford: Blackwell, 1996, 644 pp.).
The preponderance of the signed entries are devoted to individuals and isms.

Terms associated with contemporary theoretical schools are more thoroughly covered in Jeremy Hawthorn, *A Glossary of Contemporary Literary Theory*, 4th ed. (London:
Arnold; New York: Oxford UP, 2000, 400 pp.), which is notable for its succinct,
admirably clear (and occasionally witty) explanations and generous cross-references and
for its overview of other glossaries and dictionaries of criticism and theory (xiii–xvi).
Hawthorn is complemented by *The Columbia Dictionary of Modern Literary and Cul-*

tural Criticism, ed. Joseph Childers and Gary Hentzi (New York: Columbia UP, 1995, 362 pp.; online <http://lion.chadwyck.co.uk/marketing/index.jsp>), which also offers clear, succinct explanation of terms, groups, and schools of thought. The approximately 450 entries are not signed, but most of them helpfully cite related studies. More extensive discussion of 28 key terms can be found in Frank Lentricchia and Thomas McLaughlin, eds., *Critical Terms for Literary Study*, 2nd ed. (Chicago: U of Chicago P, 1995, 486 pp.); however, entries from the first edition are—inexcusably—not revised to reflect recent scholarship. The best international coverage is offered by Leonard Orr, *A Dictionary of Critical Theory* (New York: Greenwood, 1991, 464 pp.), which covers Chinese, French, German, Greek, Japanese, Latin, Russian, Sanskrit, and English terms important in critical theory, ancient to contemporary.

See also

Cuddon, *A Dictionary of Literary Terms and Literary Theory* (C107).

Guides to Scholarship and Criticism

SURVEYS OF RESEARCH

U6133   *Year's Work in Critical and Cultural Theory [1991–] (YWCCT)*. Oxford: Oxford Journals–Oxford UP for the English Assn., 1993– . Annual. PN80.Y43   801'.95'05. Online. 20 Sept. 2006 <http://ywcct.oxfordjournals.org>. Updated regularly.

A selective, evaluative survey of critical and cultural theory that emphasizes literature but also includes media and cultural studies. Chapter topics randomly appear and disappear without explanation. Those showing up with some consistency include psychoanalysis, feminism, colonial discourse and postcolonial theory, and Marxism and post-Marxism. Those that appear less consistently include semiotics, historicism, queer theories and culture, deconstruction, theories of reading and reception, discourse analysis, popular culture, popular music, virtual cultures, film theory, aboriginal identity, culture, art, narrative, testimony, religion, Irish studies, Continental philosophy, science, poststructuralism, immanence, anthropology, media studies, art histories, visual culture studies, cultural policy, multiculturalism, law and culture, technology (sometimes called technics), sexual difference, genetics, and—unaccountably—Australian popular culture and media studies and Australian Pacific cultural theory. Indexed (inadequately) by persons and subjects. In the chapters that appear randomly, there is little attempt to offer any continuity of coverage. The online version, with coverage beginning with the first volume, publishes chapters as they are copyedited and typeset. The surveys vary in quality and extent of coverage and a print volume appears 3–4 years after its date of coverage, but *Year's Work* offers the only regular, albeit inconsistent, guide to critical and cultural theory.

See also

Greenblatt, *Redrawing the Boundaries* (M1383).

SERIAL BIBLIOGRAPHIES

Given that the New Literary History *International Bibliography of Literary Theory and Criticism* [1984] (Baltimore: Johns Hopkins UP, 1988) lasted for only one volume, it is unlikely that one of the major lacunae in literary reference works—a serial bibliography devoted to literary theory and criticism—will ever be filled. The lack of remotely adequate bibliographic control of works on theory and criticism is, ironically, a direct consequence of the hegemonic privileging in academe of theory and the resultant marginalization of such scholarly pursuits as enumerative bibliography.

OTHER BIBLIOGRAPHIES

U6135   Marshall, Donald G. *Contemporary Critical Theory: A Selective Bibliography.*
          New York: MLA, 1993. 201 pp.   Z6514.C97 M37 [PN81]   016.801'95.
      A selective bibliography of English-language books (published through 1992) important to the understanding of critical theory and major theorists since c. 1965. Although emphasizing contemporary theory in the United States, Marshall also includes works by important foreign theorists and about earlier theory. Following a section on general studies (including reference works and journals), entries are organized by schools or approaches: Russian formalism and Prague structuralism; new criticism; structuralism and semiotics; poststructuralism and deconstruction; hermeneutics and phenomenology; reader-response theory; psychological and psychoanalytic critical theory; cultural criticism; Marxist critical theory; poststructuralist cultural criticism; literacy, orality, and printing; myth, anthropology, and critical theory; ethnic and postcolonial criticism; and feminist and gender criticism. Each division or subdivision has up to four parts: bibliographies; introductory works; general books and collections; works by and about major theorists of the field. A headnote briefly surveys the development and major figures of each school or movement, or—for theorists—summarizes his or her leading ideas and career. Some entries are briefly annotated with notes on content and an occasional evaluative comment; most, however, are too terse to offer an adequate sense of the substance or importance of a work. Indexed by persons. Although some works have not been examined by Marshall (and although series titles are omitted in citations), *Contemporary Critical Theory* will provide a convenient guide to those unfamiliar with the cross-currents of recent theory.
      Some additional coverage is offered by William Baker and Kenneth Womack, comps., *Recent Work in Critical Theory, 1989–1995: An Annotated Bibliography*, Bibliographies and Indexes in World Literature 51 (Westport: Greenwood, 1996, 585 pp.). The entries for 1,876 English-language books (including collections of essays) are organized by author or editor in seven divisions: general criticism; semiotics, narratology, rhetoric, and language systems; postmodernism and deconstruction; reader-response and phenomenological criticism; feminist criticism and gender studies; psychoanalytic criticism; and historical criticism. Two indexes: authors; subjects. Although *Recent Work in Critical Theory* covers a limited range of years, its succinct but pointed annotations helpfully identify not only works about theory but also those that apply particular theories or approaches.

U6137   Orr, Leonard, comp. *Research in Critical Theory since 1965: A Classified Bibliography.* Bibliographies and Indexes in World Literature 21. New York: Greenwood, 1989. 465 pp.   Z6514.C97 O77 [PN81]   016.801'95.

A bibliography of books, articles, and American dissertations about critical theory since the mid-1960s. Coverage spans works published in English, French, or German between 1965 and 1987, along with a few major studies through August 1988. The majority of these works are discussions of theory, although "representative" examples of applied studies are included. The approximately 5,500 unannotated entries are listed alphabetically by author in 12 divisions: structuralism; semiotics (excluding narrative semiotics); narratology, narrative text-grammar, and narrative semiotics; psychological criticism; sociological criticism, literature and society; Marxist criticism, literature and politics; feminist criticism and gender criticism; reader-response criticism; reception aesthetics; phenomenological criticism; hermeneutics; and deconstruction, poststructuralist criticism, and postdeconstructive criticism. Since there is no list of the noncurrent *MLAIB* journal acronyms and abbreviations used, users sometimes will have to search several back volumes of *MLAIB* (G335) or the online *MLA Directory of Periodicals* (K615). Three indexes: subjects and major theorists (with each division separately indexed); a general index to the 12 division indexes; authors. Although the volume claims "near comprehensive" coverage, there are many omissions (especially of works listed in *MLAIB* [G335] and *ABELL* [G340], both of which the compiler purportedly searched). In fact, the bulk of the entries seem to be copied out of a few major serial bibliographies—but uncritically and without full awareness of where to search in each. Inefficiently and incompletely indexed, inconsistent in citation form, poorly proofread, and seriously incomplete, *Research in Critical Theory* must be used cautiously, even in preliminary searches for works about modern critical theories.

See also

> Secs. G: Serial Bibliographies, Indexes, and Abstracts; H: Guides to Dissertations and Theses; and U: Literature-Related Topics and Sources/Composition and Rhetoric/Guides to Scholarship/Surveys of Research.
>
> *ABELL* (G340): Literature, General/Literary Criticism in the volumes for 1922–67; Literature, General/Literary Criticism/General in the volumes for 1968–72; Literary History and Criticism/General in the volume for 1973; English Literature/General/Literary History and Criticism in the volumes for 1974–84; and English Literature/General/Literary Theory in later volumes.
>
> Brier, *American Prose and Criticism, 1900–1950* (Q4345).
>
> Brown, *English Prose and Criticism, 1900–1950* (M2900).
>
> *LLBA: Linguistics and Language Behavior Abstracts* (U6015).
>
> *MLAIB* (G335): General/Aesthetics and Literary Criticism in the volumes for 1933–50; General/Aesthetics, and General/Literary Criticism in the volumes for 1951–53; General I: Aesthetics and Literary Criticism in the volumes for 1954–56; General II: Aesthetics, Literary Criticism, and Literary Theory [or Aesthetics and Literary Criticism] in the volumes for 1957–66; General I: Aesthetics, and General II: Literary Criticism and Theory in the volumes for 1967–80; Criticism and Literary Theory divisions in pt. 4 of the volumes for 1981–89; and the Literary Theory and Criticism division in pt. 4 of the later volumes. Researchers must also consult the "Criticism," "Literary Theory," and "Literary Theory and Criticism" headings (along with those beginning with "Critical") in the subject index to post-1980 volumes and in the online thesaurus.
>
> Partridge, *American Prose and Criticism, 1820–1900* (Q4205).
>
> Somer, *American and British Literature, 1945–1975* (M2800).
>
> *YWES* (G330): Chapters on literary history and criticism and (since vol. 62 [1981]) on literary theory.

Types, Schools, and Movements

FEMINIST CRITICISM

For a succinct overview of recent developments in feminist and gender criticism, see Anne Donadey and Françoise Lionnet, "Feminisms, Genders, Sexualities" (pp. 225–44), in Nicholls, *Introduction to Scholarship in Modern Languages and Literatures* (A25).

Guides to Reference Works

For an important discussion of the obstacles facing researchers in feminist criticism and women's studies, an evaluation of their treatment in standard bibliographies, and a list of bibliographic resources, see Marlene Manoff, "Tools for Feminist and Women's Studies Scholars in Literature: Issues and Problems," *Bibliography in Literature, Folklore, Language, and Linguistics: Essays on the Status of the Field*, ed. David William Foster and James R. Kelly (Jefferson: McFarland, 2003) 48–69.

Handbooks, Dictionaries, and Encyclopedias

U6167   *Encyclopedia of Feminist Literary Theory*. Ed. Elizabeth Kowaleski-Wallace. Garland Reference Library of the Humanities 1582. New York: Garland, 1997. 449 pp.   PN98.W64 E53   801′.95′082.

A dictionary of concepts, terms, and persons important to Anglo-American feminist literary theory, especially since 1970. The signed entries are generously full, and each concludes with a selective bibliography (unfortunately current only through 1994). Although a substantial number of contributions are by graduate students rather than established scholars, *Encyclopedia of Feminist Literary Theory* offers a solid overview of the field as of the mid-1990s.

Guides to Scholarship and Criticism

U6169   Nordquist, Joan, comp. *Feminist Literary Theory: A Bibliography*. Social Theory: A Bibliographic Series 52. Santa Cruz: Reference and Research Services, 1998. 64 pp.   Z6514.C97 N67 [HQ76.25]   016.30676′6.

A bibliography of English-language writings (through 1997) about feminist literary theory. Entries are unnecessarily separated into books and articles under divisions for general works, Latinas, African American women, Asian American women, Native American women, women of color, Third World women, other ethnic groups and countries, lesbian literary theory, and reference works. Although restricted to English-language publications, taking several entries from other sources rather than a firsthand examination, and lacking an index, this bibliography does offer a place to begin when searching for discussions of feminist theory. However, researchers must also search the serial bibliographies in section G, especially *MLAIB* (G335), which the compiler claims to have searched but which includes a substantial number of works that were apparently overlooked.

U6170   Humm, Maggie. *An Annotated Critical Bibliography of Feminist Criticism*. Harvester Annotated Critical Bibliographies. Boston: Hall, 1987. 240 pp. Z7963.F44 H85 [HQ1206]   016.3054′2.

A selective bibliography of books and articles, through 1985, representing feminist criticism in England and the United States. Although Humm includes numerous fugitive and limited circulation items, the criteria determining selection are unclear. Entries are organized by publication date in divisions for theory and sexual politics; literary criticism; sociology, politics, and economics; arts, film, theater, media, and music; psychology; history; anthropology and myth; and education and women's studies. Unfortunately, many of the descriptive annotations do not convey an adequate sense of content. Two indexes: subjects; scholars. Although the work is valuable for its breadth, the high degree of selectivity means that Humm is only a place to begin research.

Additional English-language articles utilizing a feminist approach are listed in Wendy Frost and Michele Valiquette, *Feminist Literary Criticism: A Bibliography of Journal Articles, 1975–1981*, Garland Reference Library of the Humanities 784 (New York: Garland, 1988, 867 pp.). The approximately 1,950 entries, culled from 450 scholarly and popular periodicals, are accompanied by lists of indexing terms that are the bases for the indexes of subjects, literary authors, and scholars. Although far from complete even within its seven-year period of coverage, with the choice of many journals depending more on availability than on other criteria, this work does isolate a considerable number of studies using a feminist approach.

See also

Gilbert, *Women's Studies: A Bibliography of Dissertations, 1870–1982* (U6615).

MARXIST CRITICISM

U6175   Bullock, Chris, and David Peck, comps. *Guide to Marxist Literary Criticism.*
          Bloomington: Indiana UP, 1980. 176 pp.   Z2014.C8 B84 [PR77]
          801'.95.
          An annotated bibliography of English-language studies (published through mid-1979) of English, English Canadian, and American literature and culture. Bullock also includes non-Marxist criticism (identified by the acronym NM) on Marxist works or writers as well as studies important in the development of Marxist criticism. The unevenly and inconsistently annotated entries are classified in sections for bibliographies; collections; journals; general Marxist criticism; national literatures (genre and period studies); individual authors; teaching English; language, linguistics, and literacy; literature and society (sociology and literature); and mass culture. Most unfortunate, however, is the failure to include studies already listed in published bibliographies of Marxist criticism on an author or critic. Users must study the introduction to understand the organization, the confusing numbering system, and the cross-listings practices. Not explained in the introduction is that journal acronyms are identified only in the section listing journals (pp. 6–7). The two indexes are inexplicably restricted to critics "who have at least three separate items in different sections" and to topics "that are treated in at least three items." Despite these shortcomings and several significant omissions, *Guide to Marxist Literary Criticism* is a useful compilation of studies not easily identified in standard bibliographies. Reviews: James Steele, *English Studies in Canada* 9 (1983): 527–32 (with numerous additions); Michael Wilding, *Modern Language Review* 73 (1983): 632–34.

POSTCOLONIAL CRITICISM

Handbooks, Dictionaries, and Encyclopedias

U6180   Thieme, John. *Post-colonial Studies: The Essential Glossary*. London: Arnold–
Hodder Headline, 2003. 303 pp.   JV22.T45   325.303.

An interdisciplinary guide to concepts, major figures, movements, historical events, cultural forms, journals, organizations, and terms associated with postcolonial studies. Entries (which tend to be longer than is usual in such handbooks) typically conclude with suggestions for further reading. *Post-colonial Studies* is a serviceable guide to the terminology of a still-emerging field.

Guides to Scholarship and Criticism

U6183   Nordquist, Joan, comp. *Postcolonial Theory: A Bibliography*. Social Theory:
A Bibliographic Series 50. Santa Cruz: Reference and Research Services,
1998. 60 pp.   Z7164.C7 N67   016.325'3.

————. *Postcolonial Theory (II): Literature and the Arts*. Social Theory: A
Bibliographic Series 55. Santa Cruz: Reference and Research Services, 1999.
63 pp.   Z7164.C7 N675.

A bibliography of English-language writings (through 1999) about postcolonial theory and by and about three prominent theorists and three critics of postcolonialism. Entries are unnecessarily separated into books and articles under divisions for general studies, postcolonial theory and women, Gayatri Spivak, Edward Said, Homi Bhabha, Aijaz Ahmad, Arif Dirlik, and Epifanio San Juan, Jr. (all in the 1998 volumes) and (in the 1999 volume) under divisions for general works, specific countries and nationalities (followed by an index), women's literature (followed by an index), drama, film, art and architecture, music, education, psychology and psychoanalysis, and bibliographies. Although restricted to English-language publications, taking many entries from other sources rather than a firsthand examination, and lacking an index to all the entries, Nordquist offers a place to begin when searching for discussions of postcolonial theory.

However, researchers must also consult the serial bibliographies in section G, especially *MLAIB* (G335), which the compiler claims to have searched but which includes a substantial number of works that were apparently overlooked.

Researchers interested in the development of postcolonial theory should consult *Postcolonial Theory: The Emergence of a Critical Discourse: A Selected and Annotated Bibliography*, ed. Dieter Riemenschneider, ZAA Studies: Language, Literature, Culture 17 (Tübingen: Stauffenburg, 2004, 211 pp.), which offers a chronological, annotated bibliography of studies through 1990 important to the development of postcolonial theory. Studies from 1991–99 are relegated to a bibliographical essay.

POSTMODERNIST CRITICISM

Handbooks, Dictionaries, and Encyclopedias

U6187   *Encyclopedia of Postmodernism*. Ed. Victor E. Taylor and Charles E.
Winquist. London: Routledge, 2001. 466 pp.   B831.2.E63   149'.97'03.

An encyclopedia of terms, disciplines, and individuals associated with postmodernist studies in the arts, social sciences, and humanities. The signed entries, which typically conclude with a selective bibliography, emphasize postmodernism as an ongoing process. Entries on concepts helpfully summarize the history and positions of key theorists, but some definitions suffer from a lack of clarity (e.g., "desire," "indeterminacy," and "margin") and most would benefit from more attention to how a concept is applied. Indexed by persons and subjects; entrants are also indexed in *Biography and Genealogy Master Index* (J565). Although lacking an adequate explanation of principles governing the selection of entries, *Encyclopedia of Postmodernism* offers readers an adequate introduction to the terminology and theorists central to postmodernist studies.

PSYCHOLOGICAL CRITICISM

See

     Kiell, *Psychoanalysis, Psychology, and Literature* (U6540).

Medicine and Literature

For an introduction to the interdisciplinary study of medicine and literature, see G. S. Rousseau, "Literature and Medicine: The State of the Field," *Isis* 72 (1981): 406–24.

Guides to Primary Works

U6190   *Literature, Arts, and Medicine Database.* Hippocrates Project, New York University School of Medicine. Online. 24 Apr. 2005 <http://litmed.med.nyu.edu>. Updated quarterly.

     A database of films and works of literature and art, classical to contemporary, that treat medical topics. The 3,131 entries (as of Apr. 2005) provide a summary or description of the work; cite and provide a hyperlink to an accessible text, reproduction, or video or audio version; and list searchable descriptors. Many records include a critical commentary that emphasizes medical themes. Records can be browsed by author or artist and title; all records can be searched by keyword. The literature entries can be searched through lists of descriptors, titles, genres, historical periods, and groups (Special Authors); to access these lists, searchers must first click on one of the links under Literature. Users performing more than basic keyword searches should consult the Help file for protocols peculiar to the search engine. Well-edited and constantly expanding, *Literature, Arts, and Medicine Database* is the best resource for identifying medical topics depicted in English-language literature published after 1800.

     Several additional works are included in Joanne Trautmann and Carol Pollard, *Literature and Medicine: An Annotated Bibliography*, rev. ed., Contemporary Community Health Series (Pittsburgh: U of Pittsburgh P, 1982, 228 pp.). As in *Literature, Arts, and Medicine Database*, coverage ranges from classical to contemporary and includes some works from Western Europe, but the majority are published after 1800 in Great Britain and the United States. Organized alphabetically by author within period divisions, the 1,396 entries include publication information for an accessible text, a list of medical topics treated, and a lengthy critical synopsis focusing on medical themes. Works added in the revised edition are grouped in an author list after the twentieth-century division. Indexed by 39 topics. *Literature and Medicine* must be used with care since it includes some works only remotely treating medical themes, omits some important titles, provides much dubious critical commentary, and is vague in some of the topics indexed.

See also

> *MLAIB* (G335): See the headings beginning "Medical" and "Medicine" in the subject index to post-1980 volumes and in the online thesaurus.
> *Relations of Science to Literature and the Arts* (U6440).
> Schatzberg, *Relations of Literature and Science* (U6445).

Microforms

Although despised by researchers who must hunch over a poorly designed, ill-lit reader, microforms are essential components of any research library. Once essentially a medium for reproducing a document, rare book, thesis, or dissertation needed by a distant scholar, microform now provides a means for preserving deteriorating materials, for making organized collections of research materials widely available at a fraction of the cost in hard copy, and for conserving space in overcrowded libraries; fortunately, many microform collections have been digitized. Scholars realize that any photographic copy must be used with due regard for the pitfalls surveyed by G. Thomas Tanselle, "Reproductions and Scholarship," *Studies in Bibliography* 42 (1989): 25–54.

U6210   *Guide to Microforms in Print: Incorporating International Microforms in Print.* München: Saur, 1978– . Annual.   Z1033.M5 G8   016.099.

Separate subject and title lists of books, serials, collections, and other materials (except theses and dissertations) available in microform from publishers worldwide. The title list includes cross-references for authors and editors. The subject index, organized by broad Dewey class, is too general to be of much use. A typical entry includes author, title, number of volumes, date, price, publisher, type of microform, and, for collections, a brief description. Because microform publications are rarely included in the national books in print volumes, the *Guide* is the essential source for locating works currently available. For fuller descriptions of collections, see *Microform Research Collections* (U6215).

U6215   *Microform Research Collections: A Guide.* Ed. Suzanne Cates Dodson. 2nd ed. Meckler Publishing Series in Library Micrographics Management 9. Westport: Meckler, 1984. 670 pp.   Z1033.M5 D64   011.36.

A selective guide to microform collections, not reproductions of individual works (for those, see *Guide to Microforms in Print* [U6210]). Organized alphabetically by collection title, descriptions typically include publisher, format, technical specifications, size, review citations, arrangement, finding aids, and a description of scope and content. Because many do not have official or fixed titles, the best way to locate collections is through the index of authors, editors, titles of finding aids, subjects, and collection titles and variants. Although based almost exclusively on publishers' descriptions (which are notoriously unreliable for microform collections), reviews, questionnaires, and printed guides, Dodson's compilation is currently the best general guide to collections.

For recently published collections, see *Guide to Microforms in Print* (U6210). For evaluations of collections, the best source is *Microform and Imaging Review* (1972– , quarterly).

Music and Literature

For an introduction to the interdisciplinary study of literature and music, see Steven Paul Scher, "Literature and Music" (pp. 225–50), in Barricelli, *Interrelations of Literature* (U5955). Researchers should note that many reference works on drama and theater cover musical theater and opera (see, e.g., section L: Genres/Drama and Theater) as do several in section U: Literature-Related Topics and Sources/Interdisciplinary and Multidisciplinary Studies.

Guides to Reference Works

U6230   Duckles, Vincent H., and Ida Reed. *Music Reference and Research Materials: An Annotated Bibliography.* 5th ed. rev. New York: Schirmer-Simon; London: Prentice, 1997. 812 pp.   ML113.D83   016.78.

A selective international guide to reference sources (through 1995) important in the study of music worldwide. The entries are organized alphabetically by author, editor, or title in variously classified divisions for dictionaries and encyclopedias, histories and chronologies, guides to systematic and historical musicology, bibliographies of music literature, bibliographies of music, reference works on individual composers, catalogs of music libraries and collections, catalogs of musical instrument collections, histories and bibliographies of music printing and publishing, discographies, yearbooks and directories, electronic resources and bibliography, the music business, and library science. Most entries are accompanied by succinct but informative annotations that cite important reviews and are frequently trenchant in evaluating works. Indexed by persons, titles, and subjects. Duckles is the indispensable guide to reference sources for the study of music. The fifth edition, although more selective than its predecessors and offering fewer cross-references, draws on the expertise of several contributors and is far more accurate and trustworthy than the ineptly revised fourth edition and its so-called revision. Review: John Wagstaff, *Notes: Quarterly Journal of the Music Library Association* 54 (1997–98): 911–13.

Handbooks, Dictionaries, and Encyclopedias

U6235   *Grove Music Online.* Oxford UP. Online. 22 Apr. 2005 <http://www.grovemusic.com>. Updated two or three times a year.
An updated electronic version of:
   The New Grove Dictionary of Music and Musicians (*New Grove II*). Ed. Stanley Sadie. 2nd ed. 29 vols. New York: Grove, 2001.

> *The New Grove Dictionary of Opera.* Ed. S. Sadie. 4 vols. London: Macmillan;
> New York: Grove's Dictionaries of Music, 1992.
> *The New Grove Dictionary of Jazz.* Ed. Barry Kernfeld. 2nd ed. 3 vols. New
> York: Grove, 2002.

An encyclopedia of music and musicians from all periods and countries. Although encompassing non-Western and folk music, *New Grove Dictionary of Music and Musicians* (which is the principal component of *Grove Music Online*) emphasizes the European art tradition in Western music, with more than half of the approximately 29,000 entries devoted to composers and the rest to performers of international achievement, writers about music, other persons of importance in musical history, terminology, genres and forms, instruments, places with a significant musical tradition, institutions and organizations, concepts, and countries. Written by major scholars, the articles range from a paragraph to more than 160 pages; most conclude with a selective bibliography. Some articles are taken unaltered from the 1980 edition; earlier editions remain valuable for the historical perspective they offer as well as for entries on individuals and topics dropped from subsequent editions. Those on major composers provide a complete list of compositions (including locations of manuscripts); those on lesser figures, a selected list. On the development of *New Grove*, see Sadie, "*The New Grove*, Second Edition," *Notes: Quarterly Journal of the Music Library Association* 57 (2000-2001): 11–20.

Grove Music Online not only allows for the continual updating of the *New Grove*s but also is beginning to exploit the potential for multimedia enhancements, most notably audio clips illustrating musical concepts or composers' styles and links to image files on other Web sites. While the search interface has improved since its initial release in 2001, it essentially allows users to do little more than perform keyword searches or browse indexes and offers no download options beyond a Web browser's print function (since the text associated with each head or subhead loads separately, printing lengthy articles is time-consuming; e.g., printing the Shakespeare entry from *New Grove Dictionary of Opera* requires one to load and print 46 separate screens). Although plagued by misprints and some uneven coverage (especially of pop music), *Grove Music Online* and *New Grove* are, overall, authoritative guides that are noteworthy for their scholarship, breadth, and general impartiality. Reviews: (print) Andrew Porter, *TLS: Times Literary Supplement* 23 Nov. 2001: 3–4; Charles Rosen, *New York Review of Books* 21 June 2001: 29–32; (electronic) Lenore Coral, *Notes: Quarterly Journal of the Music Library Association* 58 (2001–02): 406-08; C. Michael Phillips, *Charleston Advisor* 2.4 (2001) online; 23 Apr. 2005 <http://www.charlestonco.com>; (print and electronic) Peter Phillips, *Musical Times* 143 (Summer 2002): 74–77.

Several related Grove products offer fuller treatment of groups, topics, and kinds of music:

> *The Norton/Grove Dictionary of Women Composers.* Ed. Julie Ann Sadie and
> Rhian Samuel. New York: Norton, 1995. 548 pp. (Some entries have
> been incorporated into *Grove Music Online.*)
> *The New Grove Dictionary of American Music.* Ed. H. Wiley Hitchcock and
> Stanley Sadie. 4 vols. London: Macmillan, 1986. Review: Peter Dickinson,
> *Music and Letters* 70 (1989): 233–36.
> *The New Grove Dictionary of Musical Instruments.* Ed. S. Sadie. 3 vols. London: Macmillan, 1984.

New Grove Dictionary of American Music, New Grove Dictionary of Opera, and the first edition of *New Grove Dictionary of Music and Musicians* are indexed in *Biography and Genealogy Master Index* (J565).

The other major general dictionary of music and an essential complement to *New Grove* is *Die Musik in Geschichte und Gegenwart: Allgemeine Enzyklopädie der Musik*

(*MGG*), ed. Ludwig Finscher, 27 vols. (Kassel: Bärenreiter; Stuttgart: Metzler, 1994–); until publication is complete, the earlier edition—ed. Friedrich Blume, 17 vols. (Kassel: Bärenreiter, 1949–86)—remains useful.

Because of the length of many articles, *New Grove* is frequently unsuitable for quick reference. On those occasions, one of the following will offer better service:

> *Baker's Biographical Dictionary of Musicians.* Ed. Nicolas Slonimsky and Laura Kuhn. Centennial [i.e., 9th] ed. 6 vols. New York: Schirmer-Gale, 2001. Online through *Biography Resource Center* (J572). Entrants, from classical, rock, jazz, and other forms, include the famous and obscure among composers, performers, musicologists, critics, scholars, conductors, patrons—in short, nearly anyone (even bibliographers) connected with music. The typically succinct entries offer essential as well as merely interesting biographical details, a list of important works, and a selected bibliography of scholarship. Indexed by musical genre, nationality, and women composers and musicians. The sixth through ninth editions are indexed in *Biography and Genealogy Master Index* (J565). Although still accurate and reliable, the current edition edits out much of Slonimsky's irreverence, opinionated commentary, and wit that made *Baker's* one of the most entertaining biographical dictionaries of any field.
>
> *The Harvard Dictionary of Music.* Ed. Don Michael Randel. 4th ed. Cambridge: Belknap–Harvard UP, 2003. 978 pp. Although it includes both non-Western and popular music, *New Harvard Dictionary* emphasizes Western art music in entries on terms, concepts, instruments, genres, national and ethnic traditions, styles, major works, and movements. It excludes separate entries on composers and musicians. Many of the longer articles are signed and conclude with a selective bibliography.
>
> *The Oxford Companion to Music.* Ed. Alison Latham. Oxford: Oxford UP, 2002. 1,434 pp. Online (*Oxford Reference Online* [I530]). Emphasizing the Western tradition (and including non-Western and popular musics only as they influenced that tradition), the work treats a wide range of topics (with composers and compositions predominating). A few entries are signed and conclude with a brief list of selected readings. Indexed in *Biography and Genealogy Master Index* (J565). The broadest in coverage of the compact music dictionaries.

For a fuller list of music dictionaries and encyclopedias, see pp. 1–114 in Duckles, *Music Reference and Research Materials* (U6230).

See also

> Gänzl, *Encyclopedia of the Musical Theatre* (L1145a).
> Piper's *Enzyklopädie des Musiktheaters* (L1145).

Guides to Scholarship

U6240   *RILM Abstracts of Music Literature* [1967–]. New York: RILM, 1967– . Annual, with five-year cumulative indexes.   ML1.I83   780'.5. Online. 21 Apr. 2005 <http://www.rilm.org>. Updated monthly. CD-ROM. Updated quarterly.

Abstracts of significant books, articles, reviews, dissertations, and other materials produced since 1967. Entries are organized alphabetically by author within classified divisions; of most interest to literature researchers are those for reference materials, music and other arts (including sections for dramatic arts and poetry and other literature), and music and related disciplines (including linguistics and semiotics, printing and publishing). The descriptive abstracts tend to be brief but adequate. Indexed by authors and subjects in each volume. The subject indexes should be consulted with a copy of the most recent *RILM Thesaurus* in hand. The electronic versions (in which coverage begins with 1969) are far easier to search and more current than the print version (see the publisher's Web site for a list of vendors); however, some recently added records are placeholders awaiting an abstract or include an abstract marked "unedited." Its breadth of coverage and thorough subject indexing make *RILM* the best source for identifying music scholarship that treats literary works or authors. For a comparison of the interfaces of five vendors that offer the online version, see Donna Arnold et al., "RILM Online: A Comparison of Vendors," *Notes: Quarterly Journal of the Music Library Association* 61 (2004-5): 197–205.

Although *The Music Index: A Subject-Author Guide to Current Music Periodical Literature [1949–]* (Warren: Harmonie Park, 1949– , quarterly, with annual or biennial cumulations; online, 21 Apr. 2005 <http://www.hppmusicindex.com>, updated regularly) does not approach the breadth of *RILM*, it offers better coverage of popular music. The subject indexing has improved in recent cumulations, but it still remains less refined, thorough, and consistent than it should be. Since cross-references appear only in the cumulations (which are now two years in arrears), users must approach each quarterly issue with the annual *Subject Heading List* in hand. Coverage begins with 1978 in the online version (*Music Index Online*), which is hampered by an unsophisticated search interface that uses a Web browser's e-mail or print functions to download records.

Scholars doing extensive research in music and literature should consult the following comparisons of the coverage of *RILM, Music Index Online*, and *International Index to Music Periodicals* (ProQuest; online; 20 Sept. 2006 <http://music .chadwyck.com>): Leslie Troutman, "Comprehensiveness of Indexing in Three Music Periodical Index Databases," *Music Reference Services Quarterly* 8.1 (2001): 39–51, and Alan Green, "Keeping Up with the Times: Evaluating Currency of Indexing, Language Coverage, and Subject Area Coverage in the Three Music Periodical Index Databases," *Music Reference Services Quarterly* 8.1 (2001): 53–68.

For a fuller list of bibliographies, see pp. 163–233 in Duckles, *Music Reference and Research Materials* (U6230).

See also

"Bibliography on the Relations of Literature and the Other Arts" (U5965).
Brogan, *English Versification, 1570–1980* (M1600).
Haywood, *Bibliography of North American Folklore and Folksong* (U5875).
Humm, *Annotated Critical Bibliography of Feminist Criticism* (U6170).
Miller, *Folk Music in America* (U5910).
MLAIB (G335): See the headings beginning "Music" in the subject index to post-1980 volumes and in the online thesaurus.
Rice, *English Fiction, 1900–1950* (M2840).
Salzman, *American Studies: An Annotated Bibliography* (Q3335).
Wildbihler, *The Musical: An International Annotated Bibliography* (Q4295).

Philosophy and Literature

For an introduction to the interdisciplinary study of literature and philosophy, see Thomas McFarland, "Literature and Philosophy" (pp. 25–46), in Barricelli, *Interrelations of Literature* (U5955). Some works in section U: Literature-Related Topics and Sources/Interdisciplinary and Multidisciplinary Studies treat literature and philosophy.

Guides to Reference Works

U6260   Bynagle, Hans E. *Philosophy: A Guide to the Reference Literature.* 3rd ed. Reference Sources in the Humanities Series. Westport: Libraries Unlimited, 2006. 385 pp.   Z7125.B97 [B72]   016.1.

A selective, annotated guide to reference works, published through October 2005, on philosophy. The 866 entries are variously classified within 24 chapters covering general sources, the history of philosophy, the branches of philosophy, and miscellaneous topics. The annotations are admirably full and occasionally evaluative. Three indexes: authors; titles; subjects. Substantially expanded and more effectively organized than the second edition (1997), Bynagle offers the most current and evaluative guide to reference works on philosophy.

Handbooks, Dictionaries, and Encyclopedias

U6265   *Routledge Encyclopedia of Philosophy Online (REP Online).* Ver. 2.0. Routledge. Online. 14 Mar. 2006 <http://www.rep.routledge.com>. Updated quarterly.

Routledge Encyclopedia of Philosophy. Gen. ed. Edward Craig. 10 vols. London: Routledge, 1998.   B51.R68   100.21. CD-ROM.

A dictionary of philosophy, ancient through modern, Eastern and Western, with analytic and historical discussions of philosophers; branches of the discipline; and concepts, theories, schools, and movements. Written by major scholars and vetted by specialist editors, the 2,054 signed entries are of three kinds: "signpost" ones that offer an overview of a subdiscipline or region, thematic ones, and biographical ones. Each begins with a concise summary of the topic, followed by a table of contents for the entry (if more than 1,000 words), a full discussion with liberal cross-references, and an annotated bibliography. Since many persons, concepts, theories, and terms are treated within entries, the index of terms, concepts, and names in vol. 10 is frequently the best place to begin unless one has access to the online version, which is updated quarterly (click What's New for lists of new and revised articles). Users can browse articles, use the Subject Guides (which offer nested lists of articles), or search by keyword in full text, contributor, and subject fields (the pull-down menu includes language and philosophy and literature). The record display window provides a pane on the left that helpfully specifies how search results can be viewed by subject or article type. Unfortunately, printing or downloading is possible only through a Web browser's functions. Although there is some regional and theoretical imbalance, this authoritative, admirably edited compilation is the best encyclopedia of the subject. Reviews: (online version) Tom

Gilson, *Charleston Advisor* 2.4 (2001), online, 20 Apr. 2005 <http://www.charlestonco
.com>; (print version) George Steiner, *New York Times Book Review* 5 July 1998:
12–13.

Guides to Scholarship

U6275   *The Philosopher's Index: An International Index to Philosophical Periodicals
and Books.* Bowling Green: Philosopher's Information Center, 1969– .
Quarterly, with annual cumulation. Former title: *The Philosopher's Index: An
International Index to Periodicals* (1969–82).   Z7127.P47   016.105.
Online. 20 Apr. 2005 <http://www.philinfo.org>. Updated regularly.

  The Philosopher's Index: A Retrospective Index to U. S. Publications from 1940.
  3 vols. 1978.
  *The Philosopher's Index: A Retrospective Index to Non–U. S. English Language
  Publications from 1940.* 3 vols. 1980.

An index to major philosophical journals (currently about 550) in English, French,
German, Spanish, Italian, and selected other languages, some interdisciplinary journals,
English-language books (since the volume for 1980), and selected foreign-language ones
(beginning in the volume for 1984). Entries are now organized in three parts: (1) a
subject index, with headings for persons, historical periods, major fields of philosophy
and their branches, and topics; (2) an author index, with descriptive abstracts of several
works (beginning with the volume for 1969); (3) a book review index (since the volume
for 1970; coverage of book reviews in the database begins with vol. 28 [1994]). The
organization, subject indexing, and design have improved markedly over the years;
unfortunately, a substantial number of publications—especially in foreign languages—
in each annual volume are not abstracted, and some documents indexed have not been
seen by the editorial staff. *The Retrospective Index to Non-U. S. English Language
Publications* covers books published between 1940 and 1978 and articles between 1940
and 1966; *U. S. Publications* includes books from 1940 through 1976 and articles from
1940 through 1966. Both have separate subject and author indexes, but the majority
of the works in each lack abstracts. The records have (inexcusably) not been edited for
consistency in the database; thus, many entries before 1990 appear distractingly in
uppercase, recent abstracts adhere to no consistent style and mix summary and para-
phrase, and the subject-headings index needs to be transformed into something other
than a keyword list. For a list of vendors, see the publisher's Web site. Although not
comprehensive, *Philosopher's Index* series offers the most complete coverage of current
philosophical scholarship and cites numerous literary studies omitted from the standard
serial bibliographies and indexes in section G.

See also

  MLAIB (G335): See the headings beginning "Philosophical" or "Philosophy" in
  the subject index to post-1980 volumes and in the online thesaurus.

Popular Culture

Although "popular culture" embraces multifarious aspects of culture, this section is
limited to reference sources that focus on written works.

Guides to Primary Works

GUIDES TO COLLECTIONS

U6290   Geist, Christopher D., et al. *Directory of Popular Culture Collections.*
        Phoenix: Oryx, 1989. 234 pp.   E169.1.D54   973'.025.
    A guide to collections held by libraries, institutions, businesses, organizations, and some individuals in the United States and Canada. Organized by country, state or province, city, then owner, entries provide address, information on accessibility and special requirements for admission, and a description of holdings. Two indexes: subjects; institutions and collection titles. Based on questionnaires, the descriptions vary considerably in thoroughness and sophistication. Although far from complete, Geist offers the best guide to collections in the field and (because it ranges beyond libraries and museums) is an important complement to Ash, *Subject Collections* (E205).

Guides to Scholarship and Criticism

There is no satisfactory general guide to scholarship and criticism in popular culture, and, given the breadth and eclecticism of the field, there likely never will be. Researchers interested in a particular kind of popular literature will do better to consult reference works devoted to genres or periods.

U6295   *The Greenwood Guide to American Popular Culture.* Ed. M. Thomas Inge
        and Dennis Hall. 4 vols. Westport: Greenwood, 2002.   E169.1.H2643
        306.4'0973.
    A survey of research devoted to selected aspects of mass culture in the United States. Among the topics are a considerable number that are of literary interest: children's literature, film, Gothic novels, illustration, verse and popular poetry, pulps, science fiction, the western, best sellers, romantic fiction, popular literature, minorities in popular culture, and magazines. Each essay provides a historical outline of its subject; surveys important reference sources, research collections, and scholarship; and concludes with a selected bibliography (through c. 1999) and list of periodicals. Indexed by persons. Although the surveys vary considerably in completeness, rigor of evaluation, and overall quality, many offer the best introductions to research in their respective topics. Collectively, they form the most trustworthy and systematic guide to reference sources and studies in the major areas of popular culture. The two works that *Greenwood Guide* revises—Inge, ed., *Handbook of American Popular Culture*, 2nd ed., rev. and enl., 3 vols. (New York: Greenwood, 1989), and Inge, ed., *Handbook of American Popular Literature* (New York: Greenwood, 1988, 408 pp.)—remain useful for their coverage of detective and mystery novels, musical theater, stage entertainments, historical fiction, and women in popular culture. The following works are occasionally worth consulting:

        Landrum, Larry N. *American Popular Culture: A Guide to Information
            Sources.* American Studies Information Guide Series 12. Detroit: Gale,
            1982. 435 pp. The 2,173 descriptively annotated works—few of them
            published after 1979 and some inaccurately described—are organized in
            divisions for general bibliographies, indexes, and abstracts; general studies;

anthologies and collections; aspects of everyday life; ideology; heroes and celebrities; material culture; games; sports; music; dance; public art; advertising; theater; entertainments; literature (classified by types of popular literature); and media. The lack of clear principles of selection and organization turns *American Popular Culture* into a conglomeration that omits numerous important works and indiscriminately mixes reference works, histories, critical studies, anthologies, and miscellaneous publications in most divisions.

Wertheim, Arthur Frank, ed. *American Popular Culture: A Historical Bibliography.* Clio Bibliography Series 14. Santa Barbara: ABC-Clio, 1984. 246 pp. The 2,719 abstracts are listed alphabetically by author in seven divisions: popular culture in historical perspective; popular arts (including sections on literature and theater); mass media and communications; folk culture; customs, behavior, and attitudes; science and religion; and theory, research, and pedagogy. A miscellaneous, poorly organized hodgepodge that is completely dependent on the *America: History and Life* (Q3310) database for 1973–80, Wertheim is useless for any systematic guidance to popular culture scholarship and doesn't even come near to being the "comprehensive research tool" that the preface claims. Similarly miscellaneous is the short-lived *Abstracts of Popular Culture: A Biannual Publication of International Popular Phenomena,* 7 nos. (Bowling Green: Bowling Green U Popular P, 1976–82).

See also

Fishburn, *Women in Popular Culture* (U6590).
MLAIB (G335): See the "Popular Culture" heading in the subject index to post-1980 volumes and in the online thesaurus.
Salzman, *American Studies: An Annotated Bibliography* (Q3335).
Writings on American History (Q3340).

Quotations

Research Methods

U6310   Shipps, Anthony W. *The Quote Sleuth: A Manual for the Tracer of Lost Quotations.* Urbana: U of Illinois P, 1990. 194 pp.   PN6081.S44 080′.72.

A guide to tracing unidentified, misidentified, modified, or mistranscribed quotations. Advice on techniques alternates with evaluations of and hints on using standard resources in chapters treating general dictionaries of quotations; subject and special category quotation books; single-author quotation books; English-language dictionaries; concordances and word indexes to English and American literary works; indexes to first lines, last lines, opening words, and keywords; clues to authorship within quotations; and classical and foreign quotations. Concludes with axioms of a quote sleuth, a brief section on journals that print queries on untraced quotations, and an extensive, evaluatively annotated bibliography whose organization follows chapter divisions. Indexed by persons and subjects. Embodying the experience of the foremost practitioner of the craft, *Quote Sleuth* is the indispensable guide for anyone needing to identify or verify a quotation.

Dictionaries

U6315   Bartlett, John. *Bartlett's Familiar Quotations: A Collection of Passages, Phrases, and Proverbs Traced to Their Sources in Ancient and Modern Literature.* 17th ed. Ed. Justin Kaplan. Boston: Little, 2002. 1,431 pp. PN6081.B27   808.88′2.

Bartlett's Familiar Quotations: Expanded Multimedia Edition. Multimedia ed. Thomas Hine. Boston: Little, 1993. CD-ROM.

A collection of some 22,000 quotations chosen for their familiarity "as well as for their literary power, intellectual and historical significance, originality, and timeliness" from literary works, sacred writings, and other sources (written and recorded) throughout the world. The approximately 2,550 authors or sources are listed by date of birth, publication, or initial broadcast (ranging from c. 2650–2600 BC, for the author of "Song of the Harper," to 1969, for *Sesame Street*, although the most recent passage included is from George W. Bush's 20 Sept. 2001 address to a joint session of Congress); anonymous works follow the author list. Under each author, passages are organized by publication date; sources are identified by act, scene, line, stanza, or chapter whenever possible. Footnotes occasionally provide the original text for a translation, identify the translator, explain the context, or cite related quotations. Indexed by authors and titles of anonymous works at the front, by keywords (with context) at the back. The multimedia edition adds audio, video, and still-photo "quotations" (e.g., the smile face, the peace symbol, the *William Tell Overture*, and a video clip of Martin Luther King's "I Have a Dream" speech). Long a standard source, this is the fullest, most accurate, representative, and thoroughly indexed dictionary of quotations. The 16th edition (1992, 1,405 pp.) broadened the cultural base of the work, and was less hesitant than its predecessors to admit profanities and unpleasant topics. Because passages are dropped, earlier editions remain useful. For the genesis and publishing history (through the 16th ed.) of *Familiar Quotations* (along with a selective bibliography of studies and reviews), see Kerry L. Cochrane, "'The Most Famous Book of Its Kind': *Bartlett's Familiar Quotations*," *Distinguished Classics of Reference Publishing*, ed. James Rettig (Phoenix: Oryx, 1992) 9–17; on the various electronic versions, see Joseph Yue, "How Familiar Is It Any More? Bartlett's *Familiar Quotations* Goes Digital," *Reference and User Services Quarterly* 42 (2002–03): 26–29.

An essential complement to Bartlett, which retains an American emphasis, is *The Oxford Dictionary of Quotations*, 6th ed., ed. Elizabeth Knowles (Oxford: Oxford UP, 2004, 1,140 pp.; online through *Oxford Reference Online* [I530]; CD-ROM). *The Oxford Dictionary* is more current, more thorough in covering literary works and women writers, and cites some passages in their original languages (with English translations). Because each new edition is extensively revised, earlier editions (especially the second [1953, 1,003 pp.]) remain important sources; for an overview of the changes in each edition, see the introduction to the 6th edition. Review: (4th ed.) E. S. Turner, *TLS: Times Literary Supplement* 11 Dec. 1992: 7–8.

Most reference collections stock an array of other general and specialized dictionaries of quotations. For convenient lists, see *Guide to Reference Books* (B60); *Walford's*

Guide to Reference Material (B65); the bibliography (pp. 122–85) in Shipps, *Quote Sleuth* (U6310); and Patricia McColl Bee and Walter Schneider, *Quotation Location: A Quotation Seeker's Source Guide* (Ottawa: Canadian Lib. Assn., 1990, 73 pp.), with valuable evaluations and descriptions of differences between editions of the more popular dictionaries. If none of these yields the source, consult one or more of the following:

1. a concordance to the Bible (King James version) or Shakespeare, the two most frequently quoted sources;
2. historical dictionaries—such as *Oxford English Dictionary* (M1410), *Dictionary of American English* (Q3355), *Dictionary of Americanisms* (Q3360), or *Webster's Third* (Q3365)—that cite illustrative quotations;
3. first-line indexes to poems such as *Columbia Granger's Index to Poetry* (L1235);
4. dictionaries of proverbs (see section U: Literature-Related Topics and Sources/ Folklore and Literature/Genres/Proverb/Dictionaries);
5. Web search engine (use the advanced search screen and search for an exact phrase).
6. digital archives, such as *Eighteenth Century Collections Online* (M2238) and *Early American Imprints* (Q4005 and Q4125).

If these fail, send a query to the journal *Notes and Queries.*

See also

> *Dictionary of Australian Quotations* (R4455).
> Hamilton, *Dictionary of Canadian Quotations and Phrases* (R4575).

Religion and Literature

This section is limited to reference works of use to researchers seeking information on the relationships between religion (especially Christianity) and literature. Other reference works on religion are listed in Gorman, *Theological and Religious Reference Materials* (U6330), *Guide to Reference Books* (B60), and *Walford's Guide to Reference Material* (B65). Some works in section U: Literature-Related Topics and Sources/Interdisciplinary and Multidisciplinary Studies treat religion and literature.

For an introduction to the interdisciplinary study of literature and religion, see Giles Gunn, "Literature and Religion" (pp. 47–66), in Barricelli, *Interrelations of Literature* (U5955).

Guides to Reference Works

U6330   Gorman, G. E., Lyn Gorman, and S. Daniel Breslauer. *Theological and Religious Reference Materials.* 3 vols. Bibliographies and Indexes in Religious Studies 1–2, 7. Westport: Greenwood, 1984–86.   Z7770.G66 [BS511.2] 016.2.

> Vol. 1: *General Resources and Biblical Studies.* 1984. 526 pp.
> Vol. 2: *Systematic Theology and Church History.* 1985. 401 pp.
> Vol. 3: *Practical Theology.* 1986. 388 pp.

An international, interdenominational guide to reference works in Western languages for the study of theology and religion, but with a decided emphasis on English-language works treating Christianity (the projected volume on Judaism was canceled). The entries are listed alphabetically by author, editor, or title in divisions for general reference works, biblical studies, systematic theology and ethics, church history, missions and ecumenicism, religious orders, practical theology, liturgy and worship, homiletics, education, counseling, and sociology; each division is subdivided by type of reference works (usually bibliographies, dictionaries, and handbooks), a system that does not allow for a sufficiently refined organization of many sections. The annotations are uneven: at their best they provide hints on uses, pointed evaluations, and cross-references to related works; many, however, are too brief to offer either an adequate description of contents or guidance on use. The lack of judicious selectivity leads to extensive lists that indiscriminately mix the scholarly and the popular, the authoritative and the untrustworthy. Moreover, several superseded works and editions are cited. Three indexes in each volume: authors; titles; subjects. Vol. 1 prints an introduction on the study and use of theological literature. Despite its faults, however, Gorman is the best guide to the extensive body of reference material on theology and religion.

Complemented by William M. Johnston, *Recent Reference Books in Religion: A Guide for Students, Scholars, Researchers, Buyers, and Readers*, rev. ed. (Chicago: Fitzroy Dearborn, 1998, 329 pp.), which evaluates about 300 reference works published since 1970 and, for the most part, in English. Apportioned among five headings (world's religions, Christianity, other prophetic religions, Asian religions, and alternative approaches), works are listed under subheadings by date—beginning with the earliest but with later editions under the date of the first edition. Works published 1996–97 are relegated to an appendix. Each entry describes the scope, stringently assesses strengths and weaknesses, points out related works, and concludes with a summary comment. An appendix describes reference works that need to be written. Although virtually ignoring electronic resources and so poorly designed that skimming is impossible, *Recent Reference Books in Religion* is valuable for its trenchant evaluations and comparisons of works.

Handbooks, Dictionaries, and Encyclopedias

For a much fuller list of general dictionaries, see Gorman, *Theological and Religious Reference Materials* (U6330), vol. 1, pp. 123–53.

U6333   *A Dictionary of Biblical Tradition in English Literature.* David Lyle Jeffrey,
        gen. ed. Grand Rapids: Eerdmans, 1992. 960 pp.   PR149.B5 D53
        820.9′382′03.
        A dictionary of biblical names, common nouns, concepts, quotations, allusions, parables, and terms (in Hebrew, Greek, or Latin) that appear in literatures in English (primarily British and American). The approximately 900 entries by different authors describe how a term is used in the Bible and in exegetical tradition, trace chronologically its significant appearances in literature since the Middle Ages, and end with a selective bibliography. Concludes with three selective annotated bibliographies: biblical studies for the student of literature; the history of biblical interpretation; the biblical tradition in English literature (with sections for general studies and individual authors). Unfortunately, there is no index. Much information is taken uncritically from other reference works and, as David Jasper points out, the Dictionary represents an "unashamedly

Christian" conservative evangelical perspective and includes a "paucity of contemporary authors"; yet it is a valuable guide to the identification, interpretation, and history of biblical references in English-language literatures. Reviews: David Jasper, *Literature and Theology* 7 (1993): 306–07; Jay Macpherson, *University of Toronto Quarterly* 65 (1995-1996): 147–51.

U6335   **EJ: Encyclopaedia Judaica CD-ROM Edition.** Jerusalem: Judaica Multimedia, 1997. CD-ROM. An updated, integrated, multimedia version of: *Encyclopaedia Judaica.* 16 vols. Jerusalem: Encyclopaedia Judaica; New York: Macmillan, 1971–72. *Decennial Book, 1973–1982* (n.d.), *1983–1992* (1994); Yearbook, *1983/5[–90/91]* (1985–92).

An encyclopedia of persons, places, concepts, doctrines, sects, beliefs, practices, rituals, and terminology associated with Judaism. The approximately 25,000 signed entries range from a few sentences to nearly a volume, and most conclude with a selected bibliography. The CD-ROM integrates the yearbooks and decennial books with the main entries, updates (haphazardly) selected entries to 1996, adds hyperlinks and numerous multimedia enhancements, and allows searching by keyword or by subject category. The introduction to the electronic version offers an overview of encyclopedias of Judaism and describes the development of the print and CD-ROM versions of *Encyclopaedia Judaica.* Although it contains numerous biographies of decidedly minor individuals and abounds in typographical errors, this work is the standard English-language encyclopedia of Judaism. Review: *TLS: Times Literary Supplement* 23 Mar. 1973: 309–11.

U6340   **Encyclopedia of Religion.** Ed. Lindsay Jones. 2nd ed. 15 vols. Detroit: Macmillan-Gale, 2005. Online through *Gale Virtual Reference Library* (I535).   BL31.E46   200′.3.

An encyclopedia of the theoretical, practical, and sociological dimensions of popular, primitive, and traditional religions throughout the world from Paleolithic times to the present. The signed articles by major scholars emphasize the history of religion in covering beliefs, archaeological finds, myths, systems, practices, rituals, symbols, traditions, deities, cults, areas of the world, and relationships with other fields (including, e.g., an entry for "Literature"). Each article concludes with cross-references and a selected bibliography. Besides an analytic subject index, vol. 15 prints a synoptic outline of contents by religion and religious phenomena. Impressive in scope and scholarship, this is the best general guide to religion.

U6345   **New Catholic Encyclopedia.** Ed. Berard L. Marthaler. 2nd ed. 15 vols. Detroit: Gale in assn. with Catholic U of America, 2003. Online through *Gale Virtual Reference Library* (I535).   BX841.N44   282′.03.

An encyclopedia of the institutions, important dead individuals, history, places, terminology, religious orders, symbolism, canon law, theology, teachings, doctrines, and rituals associated with the Catholic church, as well as philosophies, religions, movements, and scientific and intellectual developments that have affected Catholicism. Although international in scope, *New Catholic Encyclopedia* emphasizes English-speaking countries, especially the United States. The signed articles are by major scholars, several of whom are not Catholic; most entries conclude with cross-references and a selected bibliography. Indexed by subject in vol. 15. The articles, while Catholic in perspective, are rarely partisan.

In many respects *New Catholic Encyclopedia* is an authoritative guide to Catholicism and related topics; unfortunately, though, most of the entries on writers and literary subjects have seen only minor revisions (consisting for the most part of inadequate updates of the selected bibliographies; see, e.g., the entries on Donne, Milton, and Shakespeare).

The most authoritative and balanced compact dictionary is *The Oxford Dictionary of the Christian Church*, ed. F. L. Cross, 3rd ed. rev., ed. E. A. Livingstone (Oxford: Oxford UP, 2005, 1,800 pp.), which emphasizes Christianity in Europe.

Guides to Scholarship

U6350 *ATLA Religion Database*. American Theological Library Association. Online. 16 Apr. 2005 <http://www.atla.com>. Updated four times a year. CD-ROM. Updated twice in a year.

Religion Index One: Periodicals (RIO). Chicago: Amer. Theological Lib. Assn., 1952– . 2/yr., including annual cumulation. (Vols. 1–4, rev. and expanded ed., 1985.) Former title: *Index to Religious Periodical Literature* (1952–77). Z7753.A5 [BL1]   016.2.

Religion Index Two: Multi-author Works (RIT). 1976–2001. Annual. Z7751.R35 [BL48]   016.2.

> *Religion Index Two: Festschriften, 1960–1969*. Ed. Betty A. O'Brien and Elmer J. O'Brien. 1980. 741 pp.
> *Religion Index Two: Multi-author Works, 1970–1975*. Ed. G. Fay Dickerson. 2 vols. 1982. *1976–1980*. Ed. Erica Treesh. 2 vols. 1989.

Index to Book Reviews in Religion (IBRR). Quarterly. 1986–2000. Z7753.I5 [BL1.A1]   016.2. Online.

> *Index to Book Reviews in Religion, 1949[–74]*. 3 vols. 1990–93. (A revised cumulation of book reviews in *Index to Religious Periodical Literature*.)

Subject indexes to articles in periodicals (currently about 650) and collections of essays on religion, especially in the West. Indexed by authors and editors (with the indexes in vols. 12–18 [for 1975–85] of *RIO* including abstracts) and by scripture passages. With vol. 18 (for 1986) of *RIO*, abstracts are discontinued and book reviews relegated to *Index to Book Reviews in Religion. Religion Index Two: Multi-author Works, 1976–1980* cumulates and augments the annual volumes for those years, adds some publications from 1970–75, and cites in its preliminary list of titles and series indexed books in *1970–1975*. A Retrospective Indexing Project is extending coverage back to the nineteenth century for selected periodicals. Although far from comprehensive, *Religion Index* is generally accounted the best serial bibliography devoted to articles on religion. The thorough subject indexing makes it an important source for identifying numerous literary studies in journals not covered by the standard serial bibliographies and indexes in section G. (See particularly the "Literature," "Language," and "Linguistic(s)" heads.) The best access to entries in *RIT, IBRR,* and *RIO* is through *ATLA Religion Database* on CD-ROM and online (for a discussion of vendors' search interfaces see CSA [I510], EBSCO [I512], Ovid [I515], FirstSearch [E225], and SilverPlatter [I523]; for a comparison of the database on EBSCO, SilverPlatter, and FirstSearch, see the review by Christina Cicchetti, *Charleston Advisor* 4.2 [2002]: 12–16, online; 23 Apr. 2006 <http://www.charlestonco.com>).

Researchers should also skim the "Bibliography [1957–c. 1988]" in each issue of *Christianity and Literature* 9.2–37.4 (1958–88). Books and articles – all but a few of which are in English and on American and British literature—are listed alphabetically by scholar in eight unclassified divisions: general studies, ancient and medieval biblical literature to 1500, ancient and medieval nonbiblical literature to 1500, and then by century. The accompanying descriptive annotations vary in fullness, and several are based on other abstracts rather than the works themselves. Highly incomplete and inconsistent, coverage seems dictated by what the compilers discover rather than by any clear principles of selection. Although the "Bibliography" is sometimes useful for isolating studies that treat aspects of Christianity in literature, the inconsistency in coverage and lack of indexing mean that users are in for an issue-by-issue search for discussions of authors or topics.

For other serial bibliographies, see Gorman, *Theological and Religious Reference Materials* (U6330), vol. 1, pp. 60–123.

See also

> *MLAIB* (G335): See the headings beginning "Religion" or "Religious" in the subject index to post-1980 volumes and in the online thesaurus.
> Woodress, *Dissertations in American Literature, 1891–1966* (Q3320).

Scholarly Writing and Publishing

This section is limited to works related to scholarly writing and publishing in literature and language. Persons preparing their first articles or books will benefit from the description of the process of scholarly publishing (and the suggestion for standards to govern it) in "Advice for Authors, Reviewers, Publishers, and Editors of Scholarly Books and Articles" (*ADE Bulletin* 132 [2002]: 107–11; PDF file: <http://www.mla.org/advice_for_authors>), prepared by the MLA Committee on Academic Freedom and Professional Rights and Responsibilities.

Anyone delivering a paper should heed Peter Barry's practical advice on preparing and reading the text ("The Editorial Commentary," *English* 53 [2004]: 151–56).

Guides to Scholarship

U6370   "A Bibliography of Books and Journal Articles on Scholarly Publishing
[2000–]." *Journal of Scholarly Publishing* 37– (2005–).   Z286.S37 S33
070.5'94.
A selective, unannotated bibliography of "significant" books, articles, and working papers on scholarly publishing (excluding those published in the host journal).

Handbooks and Guides to Publishing

U6375   McKerrow, R. B. "Form and Matter in the Publication of Research."
Review of English Studies 16 (1940): 116–21.   PR1.R4   820'.9.
A plea, largely unheeded, for "precision and intelligibility" in organizing and presenting research. Full of sensible advice (e.g., provide a title that describes what the

article or book is about; avoid ambiguity) and pithy asides ("'pedant' is merely the name which one gives to anyone whose standard of accuracy happens to be a little higher than one's own"), this should be read or reread before submitting the next article or book. Frequently reprinted (e.g., *PMLA* 65.3 [1950]: 3–8).

U6380   Germano, William. *Getting It Published: A Guide for Scholars and Anyone Else Serious about Serious Books.* Chicago Guides to Writing, Editing, and Publishing. Chicago: U of Chicago P, 2001. 197 pp.   PN161.G46 070.5'2.

A guide to the publishing practices of American university presses and trade publishers of scholarly books that explains how manuscripts are selected and published, how authors can increase their chance for acceptance of a manuscript, and "how the process from submission to publication can be made to work, and work well, for both publisher and author." Addressed primarily to the publish-or-perish American academic, chapters explain what publishers do, offer advice on writing (with a valuable excursus on bad titles), describe how to select a publisher (with a section on the pros and cons of publishing in a series) and contact an editor (the chapter on writing a letter of inquiry and description of a book offers the best available guide to submitting a proposal and is, alone, worth the price of this book), reveal what editors look for in a manuscript, advise how to survive the review process (with essential counsel on how to respond to a reader's report), anatomize contract provisions, enumerate problems associated with editing a collection of essays or an anthology (required reading for any potential editor), outline the permissions process and how to deliver a manuscript, detail the process of turning the accepted manuscript into a book, and delineate what makes a book a success. Indexed by topics. Written by an experienced and respected former humanities editor at Columbia University Press and Routledge who understands how books "count" in tenure and promotion reviews, *Getting It Published* is the essential advice manual for the academic looking to publish a first (or subsequent) book.

Beth Luey, *Handbook for Academic Authors*, 4th ed. (Cambridge: Cambridge UP, 2002, 320 pp.) is addressed to the same audience and covers, albeit with less wit and a more jaundiced attitude toward tenure and promotion review, the same topics (along with practical advice on publishing journal articles and revising a dissertation as articles or a book and fuller treatment of electronic publishing).

For a more succinct discussion of many of the same points, see Gibaldi, *MLA Style Manual* (U6400); R. C. Reynolds, "Luck and Pluck: A Practical Guide to Publishing in the Humanities," *Editors' Notes* 8.2 (1989): 13–23; and Richard G. Barlow, "Literary Research and the Preparation of Scholarly Manuscripts," *Literary Research* 15 (1990): 5–17 (the last two address how to publish articles—although few editors will approve of Reynolds's advice on multiple submission).

Anyone hoping to publish a dissertation should first consult Germano, *From Dissertation to Book*, Chicago Guides to Writing, Editing, and Publishing (Chicago: U of Chicago P, 2005, 141 pp.) for its straightforward explanation of how to turn an academic exercise into a readable book. Also valuable are parts of Beth Luey, ed., *Revising Your Dissertation: Advice from Leading Editors* (Berkeley: U of California P, 2004, 209 pp.) and Eleanor Harman et al., eds., *The Thesis and the Book: A Guide to First-Time Academic Authors*, 2nd ed. (Toronto: U of Toronto P, 2003, 104 pp.). Both Germano and Luey are especially cognizant of the pressure on untenured American faculty members to publish the first book.

Anyone contemplating the editing of a journal should consult Gillian Page, Robert Campbell, and Jack Meadows, *Journal Publishing* (Cambridge: Cambridge UP, 1997, 407 pp.). Although emphasizing science and technology and rather naive about the humanities (asserting, for example, that in this field "the pressure to publish is less acute" than in the sciences and medicine), the authors provide a practical—and sobering—overview of editing, producing, marketing, and managing a journal.

Along with discussions of marketing, technology, copyediting, and publishing, *Journal of Scholarly Publishing* includes several essays offering practical advice to the scholar:

> Schoeck, R. J. "The Publication of Group Scholarship." 2 (1971): 255–64.
> Halpenny, Francess G. "The Thesis and the Book." 3 (1972): 111–16.
> Holmes, Olive. "Thesis to Book: What to Get Rid Of." 5 (1974): 339–49; 6 (1974): 40–50.
> ———. "Thesis to Book: What to Do with What Is Left." 6 (1975): 165–76.
> Klemp, P. J. "Reviewing Academic Books: Some Ideas for Beginners." 12 (1981): 135–39.
> Wolper, Roy S. "On Academic Reviewing: Ten Common Errors." 16 (1985): 269–75.
> Meyers, Jeffrey. "On Editing Collections of Original Essays." 17 (1986): 99–108.
> Horowitz, Irving Louis. "The Place of the Festschrift." 21 (1990): 77–83.
> Henige, David. "Reviewing Reviewing." 33 (2001–02): 23–36.
> Pasco, Allan H. "Basic Advice for Novice Authors." 33 (2001–02): 75–89.

U6381   Olson, Gary A., and Todd W. Taylor, eds. *Publishing in Rhetoric and Composition.* Albany: State U of New York P, 1997. 247 pp.
PE1405.U6 P83   808'.042'07.

A collection of sixteen essays by prominent scholars (many of them editors of journals in the field) who address the "politics, conventions, and procedures" of publishing in rhetoric and composition. Replete with practical advice about how and why one goes about publishing, the essays treat such topics as breaking into print, integrating pedagogy and scholarship, transforming a dissertation into a monograph, editing a collection of essays, planning and producing a textbook, and negotiating electronic scholarship. Given that a newly minted PhD must have publications to make the shortlist for most tenure-track positions and that assistant professors must publish at ever-increasing levels (quantitatively and qualitatively) to secure tenure, this is a timely collection—one that will make scholars in other disciplines wish that they could consult a similar resource.

See also

> Sec. U: Literature-Related Topics and Sources/Copyright.
> Hartman, *Women in Print* (U6595).

Directories of Publishing Opportunities

U6383   *Association of American University Presses Directory.* New York: Assn. of Amer. UP, 1952– . Annual.   Z475.A88   070.5'94.

A directory of members of the American Association of University Presses (AAUP), which includes some learned societies and organizations not associated with a university and a few publishers located outside the United States. A typical entry provides address, phone and fax numbers, e-mail, URL, names and contact information for editorial personnel, number of titles published for the preceding two years, titles in print, series published, and a description of publishing interests. A grid at the front outlines publishing interests of members but does not compensate for the lack of a good subject index. With the discontinuation of *MLA Directory of Scholarly Presses in Language and Literature*, ed. James L. Harner (New York: MLA, 1991 and 1996), the AAUP directory is now the best resource for scholars to identify scholarly presses that might be interested in their manuscript or proposal. Before contacting an editor, scholars should visit the publisher's Web site to search for a fuller description of its publishing program and for special instructions on submitting a letter of inquiry or prospectus.

Along with journals, the publishing interests and submission requirements of some series are more fully described in *MLA Directory of Periodicals* (K615). *Publishers' ISBN Directory* (U5090), *Literary Market Place* (U5090a), and *Publishers Directory* (U5090a) also indicate publishing interests of some scholarly publishers (but none is adequately indexed).

Guides to Writing

U6385   Strunk, William, Jr. *The Elements of Style* (Strunk and White). With
            revisions and additions by E. B. White. 4th ed. Boston: Allyn, 2000.
            105 pp.   PE1408.S772   808'.042.
            A guide to the fundamentals of usage and basic principles of composition. The rules and guidelines are concisely presented in five sections: elementary rules of usage, elementary principles of composition, matters of form, words and expressions commonly misused, and matters of style. Each rule or entry on usage is clearly explained and accompanied by illustrative examples. A model of the clarity, accuracy, and brevity it expounds, Strunk and White is the classic guide to style and a work that repays frequent rereading. For a contrary view, see the review by Robert S. Wachal, *American Speech* 75 (2000): 199–207. On the evolution of the work (particularly the changes made in the fourth edition), see Richard H. Minear, "E. B. White Takes His Leave, or Does He? *The Elements of Style*, Six Editions (1918–2000)," *Massachusetts Review* 45 (2004): 51–71.

Style Manuals

The following are the major style manuals used by North American and British publishers of literary scholarship and criticism. For manuals in other fields, see John Bruce Howell, *Style Manuals of the English-Speaking World: A Guide* (Phoenix: Oryx, 1983, 138 pp.).

Researchers who prepare manuscripts by using bibliographic software (such as EndNote) programs, style manuals built into word processing programs, or styled files created by databases must still master the requirements of the style they use. This is especially true when preparing endnotes or a list of works cited: computer programs merely format data; the writer must know what information must be input or deleted.

GENERAL MANUALS

U6395   *The Chicago Manual of Style* (*Chicago*). 15th ed. Chicago: U of Chicago P,
2003. 956 pp.   Z253.U69   808'.027'0973.

> *The Chicago Manual of Style Online.* Online. 18 Oct. 2006 <http://www.chicagomanualofstyle.org>.

A manual for authors and editors that explains all aspects of manuscript preparation, editing, and publication. The 18 chapters and two appendixes are grouped around three topics:

> bookmaking, which covers the parts of a book and journal (print and electronic), manuscript preparation and copyediting (with a section on how a copyeditor marks a manuscript), proofs (with a table of proofreaders' marks), and rights and permissions (with an excellent sample letter for requesting permission to reprint copyrighted material in a scholarly book);
>
> style, with chapters on grammar and usage (new to this edition); punctuation; spelling and distinctive treatment of words (such as foreign words, slang, and letters used as words); names and terms; numbers; foreign languages (including capitalization, word division, and special characters); quotations; illustrations and captions; tables; mathematics in type; abbreviations; documentation (with illustrations of two styles); indexes (see entry U6415); and
>
> production and the publishing process, appendixes which are of interest primarily to editors.

Each chapter is preceded by a detailed outline of content and includes a wealth of examples and illustrations. Concludes with a selective bibliography. Thoroughly and admirably indexed by subjects.

In addition to a searchable text of the print version, *Chicago Manual of Style Online* includes Chicago-Style Citation Quick Guide, a Tools page (with sample correspondence and proofreaders' marks), and Chicago Style Q&A (with sometimes witty and irreverent responses to users' questions).

Thoroughness, clarity, and general good sense make this the long-time standard that both reflects and determines the practices of most American publishers. For those writing for publication, *Chicago* is an indispensable desktop companion. For a history of the work, see Catharine Seybold, "A Brief History of *The Chicago Manual of Style*," *Scholarly Publishing* 14 (1983): 163–77.

Kate L. Turabian, *A Manual for Writers of Term Paper, Theses, and Dissertations*, 6th ed., rev. John Grossman and Alice Bennett, Chicago Guides to Writing, Editing, and Publishing (Chicago: U of Chicago P, 1996, 308 pp.), is a commonly used distillation of *Chicago Manual of Style* and sometimes offers clearer explanations of basic points.

The British equivalents of *Chicago* are Judith Butcher, Caroline Drake, and Maureen Leach, *Butcher's Copy-editing: The Cambridge Handbook for Editors, Copyeditors, and Proofreaders*, 4th ed. (Cambridge: Cambridge UP, 2006, 543 pp.), which addresses copyediting in an electronic environment, and R. M. Ritter, *The Oxford Guide to Style* (Oxford: Oxford UP, 2002, 623 pp.).

One Book/Five Ways: The Publishing Practices of Five University Presses, 1994 ed. (Chicago: U of Chicago P, 1994, 330 pp.), offers an instructive comparison of how five North American university presses handled the same manuscript from submission through manufacture.

U6400   *MLA Style Manual and Guide to Scholarly Publishing.* 3rd ed. New York:
     MLA, 2008. 337 pp.   PN147.G444   808′.027.
     A guide to "the more formal modes of academic publishing in the field of language
and literature." Besides the expected sections treating the most recent version of the
MLA documentation system, abbreviations, proofreading symbols, and mechanics (such
as punctuation, personal names, capitalization, titles, quotations, and transliteration),
MLA Style Manual provides detailed advice on the preparation of a manuscript (including requirements for preparing a machine-readable one) along with a helpful overview of scholarly publishing (with advice on placing a journal article and book manuscript and a description of the production and publishing processes), legal issues
(including copyright and publishing contracts), and preparing a thesis or dissertation.
Indexed by subject. Complemented by Joseph Gibaldi, *MLA Handbook for Writers of
Research Papers,* 6th ed. (2003, 361 pp.; 7th ed. scheduled for 2008), which is addressed
to the undergraduate. Although *Chicago Manual of Style* (U6395) is more wide-ranging
and detailed in its treatment of matters of manuscript style, *MLA Style Manual* is
required reading for those who submit manuscripts for publication, since so many
literature journals and some academic presses (especially in the United States) follow it.
Updates to and FAQs about MLA style are posted on the MLA Web site (http://
www.mla.org).
     For scholars needing to cite unusual forms of electronic documents, the standard
guide is Janice R. Walker and Todd Taylor, *The Columbia Guide to Online Style,*
2nd ed. (New York: Columbia UP, 2006, 288 pp.), which also offers guidance on the
preparation of electronic manuscripts. Basic *CGOS* style is outlined at http://
www.columbia.edu/cu/cup/cgos2006/basic.html, which also will include updates.
     Many British journals follow *MHRA Style Guide: A Handbook for Authors, Editors,
and Writers of Theses* (London: Mod. Humanities Research Assn., 2002, 85 pp.; also
available as a free PDF file at http://www.mhra.org.uk/Publications/Books/StyleGuide/
index.html; EndNote style filters for MHRA style can be downloaded from this site),
with sections on preparing a manuscript for the press, styling a manuscript, footnotes
and endnotes, documentation form, indexing, and the preparation of theses and dissertations. Concludes with a table of proofreading symbols.

COPYEDITING GUIDES

U6405   Cook, Claire Kehrwald. *[The MLA's] Line by Line: How to Edit Your Own
     Writing.* Boston: Houghton, 1985. 219 pp.   PE1441.C66   808′.042.
     A handbook designed by the MLA's head copyeditor to "show writers how to edit
their own work." Chapters address major style problems (needless words, word order,
parallelism, agreement, and punctuation) with clear explanations illustrated by apt examples. Two appendixes: the parts of a sentence; a glossary of questionable usage.
Indexed by subjects. Replete with practical advice on detecting and correcting errors,
Line by Line should be a constant companion for anyone who writes.

ELECTRONIC MANUSCRIPTS

Submitting an electronic manuscript can save considerable time and money in the
publishing process, but authors must be aware of the potential for errors in the final

version. More than one printed text has been garbled by electronic interference, and at least one article has been deliberately altered by someone who came upon an untended screen while the author was entering copyediting changes on a disk (see *Early American Literature* 22 [1987]: 230).

U6410   *Chicago Guide to Preparing Electronic Manuscripts for Authors and Publishers.*
          Chicago Guides to Writing, Editing, and Publishing. Chicago: U of
          Chicago P, 1987. 143 pp.   Z286.E43 U54   070.5′028′5.

A general overview of the procedures and requirements for preparing and publishing a computer-readable manuscript. Of most interest to authors are the first two parts: (1) general instructions for authors, with discussions of hardware and software, typing (including important warnings about the disastrous effects of using "el" for the numeral 1 and instituting ill-considered global substitutions), preparing the text for a publisher, editing, proofing, and indexing; (2) generic coding (with a handy list of codes as one of the appendixes). Although most publishers have specific requirements for electronic manuscripts, the *Chicago Guide* remains a useful general introduction to the advantages and pitfalls of preparing, submitting, and publishing an electronic manuscript.

INDEXING GUIDES

U6415   "Indexes." Chapter 18 of *The Chicago Manual of Style* (entry U6395). 15th
          ed. Chicago: U of Chicago P, 2003. 755–801. (Also published separately as
          Indexes: A Chapter from The Chicago Manual of Style *15th Edition.*
          Chicago: U of Chicago P, 2003. 53 pp.)   Z253.U69   686.2′24.

A succinct, straightforward, practical guide to the mechanics and principles of preparing an index. Major sections explain indexing definitions, the step-by-step process of preparing an index, general principles (such as determining what to index, choosing terms for entries, and deciding between variants in names and titles), and alphabetization practices. Each point is illustrated with clear examples. Essential reading for an author required to index a book. Review: Bella Hass Weinberg, *Indexer* 19 (1994): 105–09.

Other authoritative guides are G. Norman Knight, *Indexing, the Art of: A Guide to the Indexing of Books and Periodicals* (London: Allen, 1979, 218 pp.), which includes chapters on indexing periodicals and preparing cumulative indexes (as well as a delightful survey of humor in indexes), and Nancy C. Mulvany, *Indexing Books*, 2nd ed., Chicago Guides to Writing, Editing, and Publishing (Chicago: U of Chicago P, 2005, 315 pp.), which provides a clear, thorough description of the process of indexing, extensively illustrated suggestions for resolving the myriad problems facing an indexer, an overview of computer-aided indexing, and a balanced examination of whether authors should index their own books.

Book Reviewing

U6420   Hoge, James O., ed. *Literary Reviewing.* Charlottesville: UP of Virginia,
          1987. 139 pp.   PN441.L487   808′.066028.

A collection of essays that address the need for greater rigor in the reviewing of literary scholarship. The bulk of the contributions are devoted to the theory and practice of evaluating kinds of books: works of literary theory; literary histories; literary biographies; editions of letters, journals, and diaries; enumerative bibliographies; and descriptive bibliographies. Other essays discuss factors that affect the quality of reviews. Dedicated to improving the quality and prestige of book reviewing, these essays are required reading for both the seasoned and the novice reviewer.

Klemp, "Reviewing Academic Books" (U6380a), and Wolper, "On Academic Reviewing: Ten Common Errors" (U6380a), are also full of sound practical advice. Much less useful is A. J. Walford, ed., *Reviews and Reviewing: A Guide* (Phoenix: Oryx, 1986, 248 pp.), which unsuccessfully attempts to provide guidelines for reviewing in a variety of disciplines.

Science and Literature

For an introduction to the interdisciplinary study of science and literature, see George Slusser and George Guffey, "Literature and Science" (pp. 176–204), in Barricelli, *Interrelations of Literature* (U5955).

Handbooks, Dictionaries, and Encyclopedias

U6435   *Encyclopedia of Literature and Science.* Ed. Pamela Gossin. Westport: Greenwood, 2002. 575 pp.   PN55.E53   809′.93356.

An encyclopedia of themes, writers, theories, concepts, organizations, objects, and scientific fields important to the interdisciplinary study of literature and science. The approximately 650 signed entries (ranging from 50 to about 3,500 words) emphasize the scientific aspects of literary topics and the literary aspects of scientific ones; most conclude with suggestions for further reading. The bulk of the entries are for individuals (including several literary authors with a tenuous connection to science [e.g., Aristophanes, Victor Hugo, and Philip Sidney]); several entries not on individuals are too brief to offer a clear explanation of their subject (e.g., anthroposophy and colonialism) and several on scientific topics establish no discernible relation to literature (e.g., biophilia, black box, chaos and chaotic systems, Schrödinger's cat, and scientific textbooks). Concludes with a selected bibliography. Indexed by persons, titles, and subjects (the fuller Web-based index will not be posted). Although needing a firmer editorial hand, the better entries are useful entry points into the study of science and literature and thus make *Encyclopedia of Literature and Science* a useful resource in this emerging field.

Guides to Scholarship

SERIAL BIBLIOGRAPHIES

U6440   *Relations of Science to Literature and the Arts [1950–].* Society for Literature, Science, and the Arts. Online. 14 Apr. 2005 <http://www.litsci.org>.

1989–99: *Configurations: A Journal of Literature, Science, and Technology* 1–9 (1993–2001).

1984–88: *PSLS: Publication of the Society for Literature and Science* 1–5 (1986–90).

1980–83: *Relations of Literature and Science: A Bibliography of Scholarship [1980–83]*. Ed. Walter Schatzberg. 4 vols. Worcester: Clark UP, 1982–84.

1972–79: *Clio: A Journal of Literature, History, and the Philosophy of History* 4–10 (1974–80).

1950–66: *Symposium: A Quarterly Journal in Modern Foreign Literatures* 5–21 (1951–67).

An international bibliography of scholarship (including dissertations) treating in some fashion the relation between science and literature, the visual arts, or music. Originally "Relations of Literature and Science," the title was changed in 1999 to reflect the actual scope. Entries (which provide merely basic bibliographical information) are now listed alphabetically by author in 15 divisions: collections of essays, biological sciences, computers and digital technology, environmental sciences, exploration/discovery/travel, medicine, occult sciences, physical and mathematical sciences, popular science, psychological and cognitive sciences, rhetoric of science, science and technology, social sciences, technology, and theory. Three indexes: scholars; subjects (i.e., persons); topics. The electronic version merely reproduces a static word-processing file: essays from a collection are not linked to the entry for the collection, users must search a separate file to expand abbreviations and acronyms, and searching can be done only through a Web browser's search feature. The subject indexing is primitive in both the print and electronic version; researchers with access to Project Muse (K705) can search the bibliographies for 1989–99 through their Web browser. There are omissions, coverage is in arrears (the bibliography for 2000 was still identified as under construction in Apr., 2005; all links in the 2001 bibliography were dead ends), and Schatzberg, *Relations of Literature and Science* (U6445), supersedes the bibliographies through 1980, but *Relations of Science to Literature and the Arts* is the best source for identifying scholarship on literature and science. Researchers should also check "Science" and related headings in the subject index of post-1980 volumes of and in the online thesaurus to *MLAIB* (G335).

OTHER BIBLIOGRAPHIES

U6445   Schatzberg, Walter, Ronald A. Waite, and Jonathan K. Johnson, eds. *The Relations of Literature and Science: An Annotated Bibliography of Scholarship, 1880–1980*. New York: MLA, 1987. 458 pp.   Z6511.R44 [PN55] 016.809'93356.

An annotated bibliography of scholarship (including dissertations) on the relation between science and Western literature (primarily English, American, French, and German). International in scope, the work covers studies that treat a specific aspect of the relation between the two areas, including the literary qualities of scientific works, scientific and literary discourse, and the representation of science or pseudoscience in literary works. Studies of medicine in literature are limited to those dealing with scientific aspects of the field, and studies of science fiction are restricted to those examining the treatment of science per se. Schatzberg excludes general works on cultural history and the history of science.

The approximately 2,500 entries are organized alphabetically by author in eight divisions: general works (with sections for the interactions of literature and science, and surveys), antiquity, Middle Ages, Renaissance, then by century. Each period division has sections for general studies and individual authors (but to locate all studies on an author, one must consult the subject index). Annotations clearly describe the focus and content of works and cite reviews of books. Two indexes: scholars; subjects. Thorough within its limits, clearly annotated, and effectively indexed, the *Annotated Bibliography* is the essential source for identifying studies of the treatment of individual scientists and scientific themes, theories, and disciplines in literature. Review: Eric S. Rabkin, *YCGL: Yearbook of Comparative and General Literature* 37 (1988): 215–17.

Schatzberg incorporates and expands the annual "Relations of Literature and Science" and Fred A. Dudley, ed., *The Relations of Literature and Science: A Selected Bibliography, 1930–1967* (Ann Arbor: UMI, 1968, 137 pp.). For studies after 1980, see *Relations of Science to Literature and the Arts* (U6440).

See also

Woodress, *Dissertations in American Literature, 1891–1966* (Q3320).

Social Sciences and Literature

For introductions to the interdisciplinary study of literature and the social sciences, see Priscilla B. P. Clark, "Literature and Sociology" (pp. 107–22), and Richard Weisberg and Jean-Pierre Barricelli, "Literature and Law" (pp. 150–75), in Barricelli, *Interrelations of Literature* (U5955). Several works in section U: Literature-Related Topics and Sources/Interdisciplinary and Multidisciplinary Studies treat literature and the social sciences.

General

GUIDES TO REFERENCE WORKS

U6460 *The Social Sciences: A Cross-Disciplinary Guide to Selected Sources.* Ed. Nancy L. Herron. 3rd ed. Library and Information Science Text Series. Greenwood Village: Libraries Unlimited–Greenwood, 2002. 494 pp. Z7161.S648 [H61] 016.3.

A guide to reference sources for the social sciences generally as well as political science, economics, business, history, law, anthropology, sociology, education, psychology, geography, and communication. Each subject division begins with a brief essay on the nature of the discipline (with some including a discussion of the "reference environment") and then proceeds to an annotated classified list of reference works variously organized as the subject requires. Although the annotations vary widely in fullness, quality, accuracy, currency, and rigor of assessment, Herron offers the most complete overall guide to reference sources in the social sciences.

HANDBOOKS, DICTIONARIES, AND ENCYCLOPEDIAS

U6465   *International Encyclopedia of the Social and Behavioral Sciences.* Ed. Neil J.
   Smelser and Paul B. Baltes. 26 vols. Amsterdam: Elsevir, 2001.   H41.I58
   300'.3 Online. 17 Aug. 2005 <http://www.sciencedirect.com>. Updated
   irregularly.

   An encyclopedia of concepts, processes, doctrines, persons, disciplines, forms, and
methodologies in anthropology, archaeology, demography, economics, education, geography, history, law, linguistics, philosophy, political science, psychiatry, psychology,
and sociology. The signed articles by major scholars conclude with selective bibliographies. Although there are liberal cross-references, the subject index offers the best access
to contents of the print version. The online version allows users to browse the subject
index as well as lists of classifications, authors, and titles of entries. The basic search
screen lets searchers limit keyword searches to specific fields; advanced search offers
command-line searching. Articles can be viewed as full text with links or as PDF files
and can be marked for e-mailing. Although the online version is being updated, the
site does not identify new entries. Besides the articles under the headings "Language"
and "Linguistics," the work is useful for background on the treatment of social science
concepts in literary works.

   The Encyclopaedia of the Social Sciences, ed. Edwin R. A. Seligman and Alvin Johnson, 15 vols. (New York: Macmillan, 1930–35), and *International Encyclopedia of the
Social Sciences*, ed. David L. Sills, 19 vols. (New York: Macmillan, 1968–91), remain
useful for their historical perspective.

GUIDES TO SCHOLARSHIP

Serial Bibliographies

U6470   *Social Sciences Full Text.* Wilson. Online. 10 Apr. 2005 <http://
   vnweb.hwwilsonweb.com/hww>. Updated daily.

   Social Sciences Abstracts. Online. <http://vnweb.hwwilsonweb.com/hww>.
   Updated daily. CD-ROM. Updated monthly.

   Social Sciences Index. New York: Wilson, 1974– . Quarterly, with annual
   cumulation. Preceded by *Social Sciences and Humanities Index* (entry G385).
   AI3.S62   016.3. Online. <http://vnweb.hwwilsonweb.com/hww>.
   Updated daily. CD-ROM. Updated monthly.

   Humanities and Social Sciences Index Retrospective. Online. <http://
   vnweb.hwwilsonweb.com/hww>. See entry G385.

   An author and subject index to about 521 (currently) English-language periodicals
in a variety of fields, including anthropology, economics, geography, political science,
psychology and psychiatry, sociology, women's studies, and minority studies; full-text
access is available for about 191 journals. Like other Wilson indexes, periodicals are
chosen by subscriber vote. *Social Sciences Full Text* also includes abstracts and index
entries from *Social Sciences Abstracts*, which in turn incorporates the index entries since
February 1983 in *Social Sciences Index.* See entry I525 for an evaluation of the
WilsonWeb search interface, which all of the *Social Sciences* databases use. Although
Social Sciences Index is limited in coverage, its subject indexing and extensive cross-

references make it a good source for locating articles on literary topics and authors in journals not covered by the standard bibliographies and indexes in section G.

See also

>Bullock, *Guide to Marxist Literary Criticism* (U6175).
>*MLAIB* (G335): See the headings "Social Sciences" and "Sociology" as well as those beginning "Sociological" and "Socio-" in the index to post-1980 volumes and in the online thesaurus.

History and Literature

The following is a highly selective listing of major general reference sources of particular use in literary research. Works limited to a country are listed in appropriate national literature divisions.

GUIDES TO REFERENCE WORKS

There is no adequate general guide to reference works in history. The most current guide is Ronald H. Fritze, Brian E. Coutts, and Louis A. Vyhnanek, *Reference Sources in History: An Introductory Guide*, 2nd ed. (Santa Barbara: ABC-Clio, 2004, 334 pp.), but coverage is inconsistent, evaluations are hardly rigorous, and there are numerous errors and significant omissions. Despite its promising title, R. C. Richardson, comp., *The Study of History: A Bibliographical Guide*, 2nd ed., History and Related Disciplines Select Bibliographies (Manchester: Manchester UP, 2000, 140 pp.), lists almost no bibliographies, historical encyclopedias, guides, databases, or other reference sources. Helen J. Poulton, *The Historian's Handbook: A Descriptive Guide to Reference Works* (Norman: U of Oklahoma P, 1972, 304 pp.) is outdated; and *American Historical Association's Guide to Historical Literature* (U6497) does not cover reference works thoroughly enough. Both *Guide to Reference Books* (B60) and *Walford's Guide to Reference Material* (B65) have extensive sections on history; however, neither is sufficiently rigorous in selection or evaluation of works. For American history, see Blazek, *United States History: A Selective Guide to Information Sources* (Q3185).

HANDBOOKS, DICTIONARIES, ENCYCLOPEDIAS, AND ATLASES

U6480   *An Encyclopedia of World History: Ancient, Medieval, and Modern*
            Chronologically Arranged. Ed. Peter N. Stearns. 6th ed. rev. and updated.
            Boston: Houghton, 2001. 1,243 pp. CD-ROM.   D21.E578   902'.02.
     An encyclopedia of world history through 2000. Organized by era, then by country or region, and then by periods, subjects, or peoples, the brief paragraphs on individuals, events, and groups appear in chronological sequence. While earlier editions emphasized political, military, and diplomatic matters in Western Europe and North America, the current one is much more global in its outlook, gives more attention to ordinary people,

and increases coverage of economic, cultural, and intellectual history. Throughout are numerous maps and genealogical charts of ruling dynasties. Indexed by places, persons, and subjects. The accompanying CD-ROM allows users to search by keyword or browse a detailed outline of contents. Not the typical encyclopedia, it is primarily useful for placing an individual or event in its chronological context.

U6485   *The Times Atlas of World History.* 4th ed. Ed. Geoffrey Barraclough and
         Geoffrey Parker. London: Times-Harper, 1993. 360 pp.   G1030.T54
         911.

A historical atlas with maps depicting political geography, social history, migrations, invasions, empires, towns, trade routes, battles, and the spread of civilizations and religions. The numerous plates and accompanying commentary are organized in seven chronological divisions that emphasize broad movements rather than specific events from prehistory to the early 1990s. Concludes with a glossary. Indexed by place names. This is now the most thorough and current historical atlas in English; however, William R. Shepherd, *Shepherd's Historical Atlas*, 9th ed., rev., updated, and rpt. with revisions (Totowa: Barnes, 1980, n. pag.), remains useful for its more precise maps of some topics. Review: J. H. Elliott, *New York Review of Books* 7 Dec. 1978: 14–15.

BIBLIOGRAPHIES OF BIBLIOGRAPHIES

U6490   Henige, David, comp. *Serial Bibliographies and Abstracts in History: An
         Annotated Guide.* Bibliographies and Indexes in World History 2. Westport:
         Greenwood, 1986. 220 pp.   Z6201.A1 H45 [D20]   016.9.

A guide to currently published serial bibliographies and abstracts, appearing separately or in periodicals, on historical topics. Encompassing "bibliographies which address in whole or part *any* aspect of the past," Henige covers several areas tangential to history. It excludes most bibliographies that list only books. The 874 entries are ostensibly organized by library catalog main entry but are actually entered inconsistently under title, journal, or organization. A typical entry includes title; journal; notes on scope, organization, size, and currency as of the early 1980s, along with occasional evaluative or comparative commentary; ISSN and *WorldCat* numbers; and cross-references to related works. Indexed by subjects. The inclusion of numerous works only loosely related to the study of history, failure to provide adequate publication information (especially the titles of bibliographies in periodicals) or to indicate when coverage began or important changes in scope or taxonomy, frequently inaccurate evaluations, poor organization, and barely adequate subject indexing mean that this work must be used with care to identify serial bibliographies in history.

GUIDES TO SCHOLARSHIP

Serial Bibliographies

See

> *MLAIB* (G335): See the headings beginning "Historical" or "History" in the
> subject index to post-1980 volumes and in the online thesaurus.

Other Bibliographies

U6497   *The American Historical Association's Guide to Historical Literature.* 3rd ed.
Gen. ed. Mary Beth Norton. 2 vols. New York: Oxford UP, 1995.
Z6201.A55 [D20]   016.9.

A bibliography "of the finest and most useful books and articles available in every field of historical scholarship." Designed to foster broad comparative perspectives rather than serve the needs of specialized inquiry, the *Guide*'s selection policy emphasizes "reliable syntheses and reference works that provide entry into a historical field," the essential studies that establish the standards of excellence in fields, and representatives of major alternative approaches to fields. The 26,926 entries—most for English-language books published between 1961 and 1992—are divided among 48 sections, most of which are prefaced by an overview of key historical issues and which begin with sections for reference works and general studies and then are organized in a way appropriate to each field. Entries—listed alphabetically within subsections—consist of a bibliographic citation and a brief annotation, most of which are helpfully evaluative. Two indexes: authors; subjects (unfortunately, titles of anonymous publications are not indexed, making it virtually impossible to locate a work such as *Historical Abstracts*). Although massive, the *Guide* is selective and thus will encourage sniping about inclusion and omissions (e.g., many of the subsections on reference works seemed rather thin or exclude essential works). Despite an organization that requires constant reference to the table of contents and to the outline (sans entry numbers, unfortunately) that prefaces each section, the *Guide*, with its thorough subject indexing and crisp, evaluative annotations, succeeds admirably in its purpose: to direct scholars to studies that will provide a reliable entrée into a subject and lead to more specialized publications. Because the sheer number of entries and the difficulties posed by the organization, users would be better served by an electronic version that offered keyword searching and hyperlinks between related entries.

Because of the emphasis on works published after 1961, users will still need to consult the first edition, ed. George Frederick Howe et al. (New York: Macmillan, 1961, 962 pp.).

Abstracts

U6500   *Historical Abstracts.* Santa Barbara: ABC-Clio, 1955– . Currently issued in
two parts. A: Modern History Abstracts, 1450–1914; B: Twentieth
Century Abstracts, 1914–[current year]. Quarterly, including cumulative
index.   D299.H5   909.8082. Online. 9 Apr. 2005 <http://serials
.abc-clio.com>. Updated regularly.

Nonevaluative abstracts of scholarship on history and related topics. Originally restricted to articles on the period 1775–1945, *Historical Abstracts* now covers books and dissertations, and has undergone several changes in scope: with vol. 16 (1970), coverage of the United States and Canada was transferred to *America: History and Life* (Q3310); in vol. 17 (1971), chronological coverage was extended from 1775 to the present; in vol. 19 (1973), chronological coverage was extended back to 1450. Quinquennial indexes cover 1955–89. The electronic version offers the most efficient access to literature- and language-related entries, many of which are from journals not covered in the serial bibliographies in section G.

Political Science and Literature

For an introduction to the interdisciplinary study of literature and political science, see Matei Calinescu, "Literature and Politics" (pp. 123–49), in Barricelli, *Interrelations of Literature* (U5955).

GUIDES TO REFERENCE WORKS

U6515   Green, Stephen W., and Douglas J. Ernest, eds. *Information Sources of Political Science.* 5th ed. Santa Barbara: ABC-Clio, 2005. 593 pp.
Z7161.I543 [JA71]   016.32.

A guide to English-language reference sources from the 1980s to early 2004 useful for the study of political topics. The 2,423 entries are organized by type of work within classified divisions for general reference sources; social sciences (with sections for anthropology, economics, education, geography, history, American history, world history, biography, psychology, and sociology); general political science; political theory; United States politics and government; international relations; comparative politics and government; public administration and policy studies; and biography. Many entries are accompanied by full annotations that provide helpful descriptive comments. Four indexes: authors; titles; subjects; Web sites. Although users would benefit from more incisive evaluative comments, the full descriptions and advice on research procedures make Green and Ernest the essential guide to reference sources for the study of political science.

The fourth edition by Frederick L. Holler (1986, 417 pp.) remains useful for its coverage of works published before the 1980s.

See also

Social Sciences: A Cross-Disciplinary Guide to Selected Sources (U6460).

GUIDES TO SCHOLARSHIP

U6520   *International Political Science Abstracts/Documentation politique internationale [1950–].* Paris: Intl. Political Science Assn., 1951– . 6/yr.   JA36.I5
320.82. Online. 16 May 2005 <http://www.ipsa.ca>. Updated regularly. CD-ROM.

Nonevaluative abstracts, in English or French, of articles in journals and yearbooks. Coverage is selective, emphasizing scholarly and "scientific" studies in major political science journals and omitting popular or "redundant" articles. Indexed by authors and subjects in each issue; cumulative author and subject indexes in each volume. The electronic versions (with coverage beginning in 1989) offer the best way to locate discussions of literary topics and authors. The database (in the WebSPIRS version) can be searched by keyword or by a combination of keyword, accession number, author, descriptors, ISSN, journal, or title. There is an inadequate explanation of the scope and editorial principles attached to the Web site. Although coverage is far from complete, the abstracts and subject indexing make *International Political Science Abstracts* the best source for identifying articles on literary topics published in political science journals and rarely included in the standard serial bibliographies and indexes in section G.

See also

Baldensperger, *Bibliography of Comparative Literature* (T5000).
MLAIB (G335): See the headings beginning "Political" or "Politics" in the subject index to post-1980 volumes and in the online thesaurus.

Psychology and Literature

For an introduction to the interdisciplinary study of literature and psychology, see Murray M. Schwartz and David Willbern, "Literature and Psychology" (pp. 205–24), in Barricelli, *Interrelations of Literature* (U5955).

GUIDES TO REFERENCE WORKS

See

Social Sciences: A Cross-Disciplinary Guide to Selected Sources (U6460).

HANDBOOKS, DICTIONARIES, AND ENCYCLOPEDIAS

U6525   *Encyclopedia of Psychology.* Ed. Alan E. Kazdin. 8 vols. Washington: Amer.
Psychological Assn.; Oxford: Oxford UP, 2000.   BF31.E52   150.3.
An encyclopedia of concepts, terms, theories, and other topics related to psychology. The c. 1,500 entries offer fuller treatment and selective bibliographies than the typical encyclopedia does (though the bibliography accompanying the literary and psychology entry is an outdated mishmash). Indexed by names and subjects.
An essential complement is *Corsini Encyclopedia of Psychology and Behavioral Science*, ed. W. Edward Craighead and Charles B. Nemeroff, 3rd ed., 4 vols. (New York: Wiley, 2001), which offers briefer entries and selective bibliographies but broader coverage of concepts, terms, theories, persons, and other topics. Two indexes: names of authors cited; subjects. Together, these encyclopedias will provide literature researchers some of the best introductions to psychological concepts and theories.

GUIDES TO SCHOLARSHIP

Abstracts

U6530   *PsycINFO.* American Psychological Association. Online. 8 Apr. 2005
<http://www.apa.org/psycinfo>. Updated weekly.

Psychological Abstracts: Nonevaluative Summaries of the Serial and Book Literature in Psychology and Related Disciplines (Psych Abstracts; PA). Washington: Amer. Psychological Assn., 1927– . Monthly, with annual, triennial, and larger expanded cumulated author and subject indexes. Title varies.   BF1.P65   150'.5.

A database of nonevaluative abstracts of research in psychology. In the print version coverage of books begins with vol. 79 (1992); in the online version coverage extends to 1887 (for a list of online providers, see the *PsycINFO* Web site; for an evaluation of searching the database on six platforms, see Michael Lackey, "*PsycINFO* on Ovid, SilverPlatter, OCLC New FirstSearch, and Cambridge Scientific Abstracts," *Charleston Advisor* 1.3 [2000], online, 10 Apr. 2005 <http://www.charlestonco.com> and "*PsycINFO* on InfoTrac and EBSCOHost," *Charleston Advisor* 2.1 [2000], online, 10 Apr. 2005 <http://www.charlestonco.com>). Coverage on the CD-ROM begins with 1974. Although recent issues have a Linguistics and Language and Speech section and a Literature and Fine Arts section, the best approach to contents is through the online version or the printed subject indexes. For the most efficient and precise subject searching, consult the current edition of *Thesaurus of Psychological Index Terms.* A valuable source for identifying studies of psychological topics in and approaches to literary works and language.

Literature and Psychology

U6540   Kiell, Norman, ed. *Psychoanalysis, Psychology, and Literature: A Bibliography.* 2nd ed. 2 vols. Metuchen: Scarecrow, 1982. *Supplement to the Second Edition.* 1990. 587 pp.   Z6514.P78 K53 [PN56.P93]   016.801'92.

An international bibliography of scholarship (including some dissertations) treating any aspect of psychology or psychoanalysis and literature. Although Kiell covers studies from 1790 through 1987, the bulk of the works date from the twentieth century. The approximately 27,400 entries are organized alphabetically by author in 14 unclassified divisions: autobiographies, biographies, diaries, and letters; literary, psychoanalytical, and psychological criticism; drama; fairy tales and fables; fiction; film; folklore and folktales; myths and legends; poetry; Scriptures; technical studies (dropped in the supplement); therapy; wit, humor, and jokes; ancillary topics. Three indexes in vol. 2: literary authors as subjects; titles of literary works; general subjects; the indexes of authors and titles are combined in the supplement. Because of the imprecise and unrefined classification system, the subject indexes offer the best access to contents. Although several entries appear to be taken without verification from other sources and the supplement is peppered with typographical and other errors, *Psychoanalysis, Psychology, and Literature* is the most thorough guide to studies of psychology and literature and is particularly valuable for its coverage of journals in psychology and psychoanalysis. It does, however, admit numerous studies only remotely connected with psychology.

Some more recent studies can be located in *IPSA Abstracts and Bibliography in Literature and Psychology,* 11 vols. (Gainesville: Inst. for Psychological Study of the Arts, 1986–96), with coverage from 1985 through March 1996; the bibliographies for 1993–96 are also available at http://www.clas.ufl.edu/ipsa/ipsabib.htm. The unfortunate discontinuation of this work left the field without a serial bibliography.

Some additional studies, especially in German, are included in Joachim Pfeiffer, ed., *Literaturpsychologie 1945–1987: Eine systematische und annotierte Bibliographie*

(Würzburg: Königshausen, 1989, 516 pp.), which is continued by "Literaturpsychologie 1987–1990: Eine systematische und annotierte Bibliographie: Erste Forsetzung und Nachträge," *Literatur und Sexualität*, ed. Johannes Cremerius et al., Freiberger literatur-psychologische Gespräche 10 (Würzburg: Königshausen, 1991) 221–309; "Literatur-psychologie 1990–1992: Eine systematische und annotierte Bibliographie: Zweite Forsetzung und Nachträge," *Trennung*, ed. Cremerius et al., Freiberger literatur-psychologische Gespräche 13 (Würzburg: Königshausen, 1994) 215–323; "Literatur-psychologie 1992–1996: Eine systematische und annotierte Bibliographie: Dritte Forsetzung und Nachträge," *Widersprüche Geschlechtlicher Identität*, ed. Cremerius et al., Freiberger literaturpsychologische Gespräche: Jahrbuch für Literatur und Psycho-analyse 17 (Würzburg: Königshausen, 1998) 227–355; and "Literaturpsychologie 1997–1999: Eine systematische und annotierte Bibliographie: Vierte Forsetzung und Nachträge," *Frank Wedekind*, ed. Ortrud Gutjahr, Freiberger literaturpsychologische Gespräche: Jahrbuch für Literatur und Psychoanalyse 20 (Würzburg: Königshausen, 2001) 301–56. The annotations, however, consist of indexing tags, and there are numerous omissions.

An essential complement for English-language Jungian criticism of English-language literary texts is Jos van Meurs and John Kidd, *Jungian Literary Criticism, 1920–1980: An Annotated, Critical Bibliography of Works in English (with a Selection of Titles after 1980)* (Metuchen: Scarecrow, 1988, 353 pp.). The 902 entries are accompanied by quite full annotations (including evaluations of "particularly perceptive or particu-larly inept" studies).

Joseph Natoli and Frederik L. Rusch, comps., *Psychocriticism: An Annotated Bib-liography*, Bibliographies and Indexes in World Literature 1 (Westport: Greenwood, 1984, 267 pp.), focuses more clearly on the relation between formal psychology and literature; covers a wide range of literatures, ancient to modern; offers annotated entries; and provides a good subject index. However, coverage is incomplete and limited to English-language books and articles published between 1969 and 1982.

See also

> *MLAIB* (G335): See the headings beginning "Psychoanalysis," "Psychoanalytic," "Psychological," and "Psychology" in the subject index to post-1980 volumes and in the online thesaurus.
>
> Woodress, *Dissertations in American Literature, 1891–1966* (Q3320).

Sociology and Literature

HANDBOOKS, DICTIONARIES, AND ENCYCLOPEDIAS

U6557   *Encyclopedia of Sociology.* Ed. Edgar F. Borgatta and Rhonda J. V.
         Montgomery. 2nd ed. 5 vols. New York: Macmillan Gale, 2000.
         HM425.E5   301'.03.

An encyclopedia of concepts, subfields, movements, research methods, theories, and other topics associated with sociology. Each of the 397 signed entries—including one on "Literature and Society"—concludes with a selective bibliography. The *Ency-clopedia of Sociology* offers literary scholars a solid introduction to the theories and practices of sociology.

GUIDES TO SCHOLARSHIP

U6560   *Sociological Abstracts.* Bethesda: CSA, 1953– . 6/yr., plus cumulative index
and supplement.   HM1.S67   301. Online. 9 May 2005 <http://
www.csa.com>. Updated monthly.

Nonevaluative abstracts of books, essays in edited collections, and articles from
selected sociological and related journals; beginning in vol. 36 (1988), dissertations
abstracted in *ProQuest Dissertations and Theses* (H465) are also cited; and, since vol. 37
(1989), a supplement prints abstracts of conference papers. Although recent issues include the classified section Sociology of Language and the Arts, the best approach to
contents is through the online version or the annual subject index. Records since 1963
can be searched online through CSA (J570), FirstSearch (E225a), and SilverPlatter
(I523); see the entries for discussion of the search interface for each. A useful source
for identifying studies on sociological topics in and approaches to literature.

Translations

Guides to Primary Works

U6565   *Index Translationum [1979–].* Paris: UNESCO, 1994– . Online. 24 Feb.
2005 <http://portal.unesco.org/culture/en/ev.php-URL_ID=7810&URL_
DO=DO_TOPIC&URL_SECTION=201.html>. Updated regularly.
CD-ROM.

*Index Translationum [1932–40, 1948–86]: Répertoire international des
traductions/International Bibliography of Translations/Repertorio internacional
de traducciones.* Paris: UNESCO, 1932–40, 1949–92. Annual.
Z6514.T7 I42   011'.7.

A bibliographic database of translated books published for the most part in
UNESCO member countries. As of 24 Feb. 2005 coverage extended to c. 1,500,000
volumes in more than 500 languages. Entries can be searched by author, title (original
or translated), target language, original language, translator, editor, country of publication, place of publication, publisher, year (specific year or range), and 9 predefined
subject areas (or by any combination of the preceding). Entries—which a search returns
in no apparent order—cite author, title of translation, editor, target language, edition,
translator, publication information, source language, and original title (both target and
source language are abbreviated, but the site provides no key to abbreviations).

Coverage varies in the print volumes, ranging from 6 to more than 70 countries.
Organized alphabetically by country of publication (using the French form of name),
then by Universal Decimal Classification main category, then alphabetically by author
or editor, entries cite title of translation, translator, publication information, and—if
known—language of the source and original title. (Organization by original author
would be more convenient for most literature researchers.) The print version is indexed
by original authors; some early volumes have indexes of translators and publishers (both
classified by country). Although it is compiled from a variety of sources that vary widely
in accuracy and is necessarily incomplete and cumbersome to use (especially in the
online version since the results of a search cannot be ordered, saved [except by cutting
and pasting 10 records at a time], or exported), *Index Translationum* does provide the

fullest list of translations published each year. Researchers should, however, also search *WorldCat* (E225) and RLG Union Catalog (E230).

U6570   *The Oxford Guide to Literature in English Translation.* Ed. Peter France.
        Oxford: Oxford UP, 2001. 656 pp.   PR131.O94   809.21.

An evaluative guide to English-language translations and related scholarship. The first part consists of essays on theoretical issues, historical development, and types of texts (poetry, theater and opera, sacred texts, children's literature, and oral literature); the second part, which surveys translations, is organized by individual languages, language families, or geographic area, with each subdivided by essays on a language, genre, or author. Each essay assesses both the accuracy and literary quality of translations and concludes with a bibliography of translations and criticism. Indexed by persons and titles of anonymous works. Impressive in scope and enlightening in its evaluations, *Oxford Guide to Literature in English Translation* is the essential resource for readers needing to understand the shortcomings of a translation or choose among competing ones.

A valuable complement is *Encyclopedia of Literary Translation into English*, ed. Olive Classe, 2 vols. (London: Fitzroy Dearborn, 2000), although it is less efficient to consult. Entries—which typically run to c. 1,000 words and cover topics associated with translation; the history, theory, and practice of translation; and authors or works translated—are organized alphabetically and end with a list of suggested readings. As in *Oxford Guide to Literature in English Translation*, assessments of individual translations can be trenchant. Three indexes: titles of source texts and target texts; translators; subjects.

Guides to Scholarship and Criticism

For an overview of recent developments in translation research, see Lawrence Venuti, "Translation Studies" (pp. 294–311), in Nicholls, *Introduction to Scholarship in Modern Languages and Literatures* (A25).

U6575   *Translation Studies Bibliography* (*TSB*). Ed. Yves Gambier and Luc van
        Doorslaer. Benjamins. Online. 26 Aug. 2006 <http://www.benjamins.com/
        online/tsb>. Updated annually.

An interdisciplinary database of documents (including unpublished material) treating translating or interpreting; coverage currently emphasizes 1993–2005. The c. 10,000 entries exclude translations and dictionaries unless they are germane to translation or interpretation research.

The database uses the same interface as *Bibliography of Pragmatics Online* but with different searchable fields in Advanced Search: author or editor, title, keyword (i.e., subject term), abstract, publisher, document language, source language, pivot language, target language, person and subject, title as subject, series, journal title, and date. It is subject to the same limitations in sorting and exporting results of a search. (See entry U6050 for an evaluation of the interface.) The current version does not include a thesaurus, but users can browse a list of subject keywords. International and interdisciplinary in scope but in need of an interface that offers more flexibility in downloading records, *Translation Studies Bibliography* is the fullest guide to scholarship on translation and interpretation studies.

Women and Literature

This section includes works encompassing women writers in several national literatures, as well as interdisciplinary women's studies sources that have a substantial literature component. Numerous works on women writers appear in appropriate national literature and other divisions.

Guides to Reference Works

For a survey of the pre-1980 bibliographical resources for the study of English and American women writers, see the appendix to Deborah S. Rosenfelt, "The Politics of Bibliography: Women's Studies and the Literary Canon" (vol. 1, pp. 11–35), in Hartman, *Women in Print* (U6595).

For an important discussion of the obstacles facing researchers in feminist criticism and women's studies, an evaluation of their treatment in standard bibliographies, and a list of bibliographic resources, see Marlene Manoff, "Tools for Feminist and Women's Studies Scholars in Literature: Issues and Problems," *Bibliography in Literature, Folklore, Language, and Linguistics: Essays on the Status of the Field*, ed. David William Foster and James R. Kelly (Jefferson: McFarland, 2003) 48–69.

U6580   Carter, Sarah, and Maureen Ritchie. *Women's Studies: A Guide to Information Sources.* Jefferson: McFarland; London: Mansell, 1990. 278 pp. Z7961.C37 [HQ1206]   016.3054.
A guide to reference sources, all but a few published between 1978 and 1988 and exclusively about women. (A few 1989 publications are included, with most described from publicity releases.) The annotated entries are organized in three divisions: general works (with sections for general reference works, biographical resources, and women's studies as a discipline); women in the world (with variously organized sections for broad geographical areas); and subjects (including extensively classified sections for arts and media, black women, and literature and language). A concluding page lists resources for men's studies. Indexed by persons, subjects, and titles; in addition, generous cross-references lead users to multidisciplinary resources. Although the succinct annotations too rarely alert researchers to weaknesses or major limitations of works, the international coverage makes Carter the best single guide to reference works through 1988 devoted solely to women.

An essential complement—because it covers general reference works not devoted solely to women but nonetheless essential to research in women's studies—is Susan E. Searing, *Introduction to Library Research in Women's Studies*, Westview Guides to Library Research (Boulder: Westview, 1985, 257 pp.), a highly selective guide addressed to the undergraduate. Of most value is the annotated guide to commonly available English-language sources. Although the annotations are sometimes helpfully evaluative and, for general works, focus on their value to women's studies, the numerous errors in citations and annotations render Searing untrustworthy.

See also

Gohdes, *Bibliographical Guide to the Study of the Literature of the U. S. A.* (Q3180).

Literary Handbooks, Dictionaries, and Encyclopedias

U6583   *The Bloomsbury Guide to Women's Literature.* Ed. Claire Buck. New York:
        Prentice Hall, 1992. 1,171 pp.   PN471.B57   809'.89287'03.
   A guide to women writers from the earliest times to the present. The coverage is
international and extends to popular forms, letters, and diaries as well as belles lettres.
Most of the more than 5,000 unsigned entries are for writers and individual works, but
cultural practices and beliefs, concepts, terms, periodicals, genres and forms, and other
topics are also included. Because of peculiar labels derived from the prefatory essays (see
below) and a lack of cross-references, some entries are simply not locatable (e.g., "Early
North American narratives of witchcraft cases," "Early North American Quaker
women's writings," and "Learned literature in Sweden"). Entries on forms and genres
include subdivisions for only a few of the national literatures covered. Entries for authors
include basic biographical and career information and a brief commentary on important
works; several conclude with a short list of studies. (Entrants are indexed in *Biography
and Genealogy Master Index* [J565].) Prefacing the work are 37 brief essays on national
literatures, geographical areas, and critical approaches designed to provide a context for
the entries. Impressive in its chronological and geographical breadth, and for the amount
of information packed into its readable entries, *Bloomsbury Guide* is clearly the best
single source for basic information about women writers and their works. A browser's
delight, it is especially valuable for the inclusion of many authors and titles virtually
unknown to North American scholars.

Bibliographies of Bibliographies

U6585   Ballou, Patricia K. *Women: A Bibliography of Bibliographies.* 2nd ed.
        Women's Studies Publications. Boston: Hall, 1986. 268 pp.   Z7961.B32
        [HQ1121]   016.0163054.
   A bibliography of bibliographies, surveys of research, library catalogs, and guides
to archives or manuscript repositories published as books, parts of books, articles, or
databases from 1970 through June 1985. Although international in scope, it emphasizes
works about the United States and Canada, and includes a very few publications not
in English. Basing selection on "scope, availability, organization, and commentary,"
Ballou excludes bibliographies of individuals and small groups, nonprint media, auction
and booksellers' catalogs, and most out-of-print publications. The 906 entries are organized in four divisions: general and interdisciplinary works, bibliographies devoted to
a type of publication or format (including library catalogs, biographical sources, and
guides to archives and manuscript collections), geographical areas, and subjects (including sections for history, literature, mass media and popular culture, performance art,
and anthropology, which encompasses folklore). The literature section includes subdivisions for general works; American, Canadian, English, French, Spanish and Latin
American, and other literatures; feminist criticism; and children's literature. Except for
studies involving the United States or Canada, a geographical focus takes precedence
over a topical one in organizing works; hence, users should generally begin with the
subject index. Entries are accompanied by full descriptive annotations, but only a few
offer an evaluative comment. Three indexes: persons; titles; subjects. Although the work
is limited in its coverage and now dated, it is the fullest bibliography of bibliographies
devoted to women's studies.

Jane Williamson, *New Feminist Scholarship: A Guide to Bibliographies* (Old Westbury: Feminist, 1979, 139 pp.), remains an important complement, since it cites works before 1970 and others omitted in Ballou.

See also

Ingles, *Bibliography of Canadian Bibliographies* (R4585).

Guides to Primary Works

See

Davis, *Drama by Women to 1900* (Q3512).
Davis, *Personal Writings by Women to 1900* (Q3545a).
Davis, *Poetry by Women to 1900* (Q3534).
Grimes, *Novels in English by Women, 1891–1920* (M2640).
Marshall, *Pen Names of Women Writers from 1660 to the Present* (U5115).
Reardon, *Poetry by American Women, 1900–1975* (Q4330).
Smith, *Women and the Literature of the Seventeenth Century* (M2007).
Women's History Sources (Q3245).

Guides to Scholarship and Criticism

For a valuable introduction to searching women's studies topics in the online versions of *Arts and Humanities Citation Index* (G365), *Humanities Index* (G385), *Essay and General Literature Index* (G380), *English Short Title Catalogue* (M1377), *America: History and Life* (Q3310), *Historical Abstracts* (U6500), *MLAIB* (G335), *Philosopher's Index* (U6275), *Religion Index* (U6350), *Art Index* (U5145), and *ARTbibliographies Modern* (U5140), see Joyce Duncan Falk, "Humanities," *Women Online: Research in Women's Studies Using Online Databases*, ed. Steven D. Atkinson and Judith Hudson, Haworth Series on Library and Information Science 3 (New York: Haworth, 1990) 7–72.

For an assessment of the indexing of women's studies journals by women's studies bibliographies and general serial bibliographies, see Kristin H. Gerhard, Trudi E. Jacobson, and Susan G. Williamson, "Indexing Adequacy and Interdisciplinary Journals: The Case of Women's Studies," *College and Research Libraries* 54 (1993): 125–35; and Deborah Mesplay and Loretta Kock, "An Evaluation of Indexing Services for Women's Studies Periodical Literature," *RQ* 32 (1993): 404–10.

SURVEYS OF RESEARCH

U6590   Fishburn, Katherine. *Women in Popular Culture*. American Popular Culture.
Westport: Greenwood, 1982. 267 pp.   HQ1426.F685   305.4'0973.
A survey of scholarship through c. 1980 on the role and image of women in popular culture. Although Fishburn does not provide any explanation of scope or criteria governing selection, she emphasizes recent studies in chapters on histories of women in popular culture; women in popular literature; women in magazines and magazine fic-

tion; women in film; women in television; women in advertising, fashion, sports, and comics; and theories of women in popular culture. The essays vary in organization and breadth, but most conclude with a brief commentary on important reference works and a selective bibliography. Five appendixes: selected periodicals; special issues of periodicals; selected reference works; a chronology; a list of research centers and institutions. Indexed by persons, subjects, and titles. Despite the lack of a statement of editorial policy, *Women in Popular Culture* is valuable for its detailed descriptions and sometimes trenchant evaluations of studies.

U6595   Hartman, Joan E., and Ellen Messer-Davidow, eds. *Women in Print: Opportunities for Women's Studies Research in Language and Literature.* New York: MLA, 1982. 198 pp.   PN481.W656   809'.89287.

A collection of surveys of areas needing research. The essays on bibliography, archival research, and language and on lesbian, black, working-class, and national literatures selectively survey scholarship as well as define topics for further research. Although now dated in their particulars, the essays remain full of solid practical suggestions for needed research.

See also

Duke, *American Women Writers: Bibliographical Essays* (Q3275).
Inge, *Handbook of American Popular Culture* (U6295a).

OTHER BIBLIOGRAPHIES

U6600   Boos, Florence, ed. *Bibliography of Women and Literature: Articles and Books [1974–81] by and about Women from 600 to 1975.* 2 vols. New York: Holmes, 1988.   Z2014.W65 B66 [PR111]   016.82'09'9287.

A bibliography of English-language books, articles, dissertations, and reviews on literature by and about women. Coverage supposedly extends from 1974 through 1981, but a few later studies are included. Vol. 1 (1974–78) is a revised, enlarged cumulation of the annual bibliographies published in 1976 through 1978 as supplements to *Women and Literature*; vol. 2 ostensibly extracts entries from *MLAIB* (G335) and *ABELL* (G340) "for 1979–81," but it actually cites only a very few works published after 1979. Although emphasizing British and American writers, Boos includes some of the other literatures in English (especially Canadian, Australian, and New Zealand). The approximately 10,000 entries are organized in divisions for general works, British literature (before 1660, 1660–1800, 1800–1900, and 1900–75), American literature (before 1800, 1800–1900, 1900–75), Canadian literature, other literatures in English, and (in vol. 1) foreign-language writers; each is subdivided by genre (including children's literature and one subdivision for the treatment of women by male writers), then by literary author. Some entries in vol. 1 are accompanied by brief descriptive annotations. Three indexes: scholars; literary authors; genres; unfortunately, the poorly conceived numbering system makes locating entries unduly difficult (and quite impossible unless one remembers that S identifies an entry to be found in vol. 2). Although error-ridden, covering a limited span of years and a restricted number of journals, and less accessible than it should be because of two sequences of entries, the separation of reviews from the work reviewed, and poorly conceived indexes, Boos at least serves as a preliminary guide to studies of women authors and women in literature, and demonstrates the need for both retrospective and current serial bibliographies of scholarship and criticism on women and literature. Review: Isobel Grundy, *Review of English Studies* ns 42 (1991): 235–36.

U6605   Schwartz, Narda Lacey. *Articles on Women Writers: A Bibliography [1960–84].* 2 vols. Santa Barbara: ABC-Clio, 1977–86.   Z2013.5.W6.S37 [PR111]   016.82'09'9287.

A checklist of English-language articles and dissertations listed in *ProQuest Dissertations and Theses* (H465) on women since the Middle Ages writing in English in the United States, Great Britain, Ireland, Australia, Canada, New Zealand, and Africa. Vol. 1 covers studies appearing between 1960 and 1975; vol. 2, between 1976 and mid-1984. Writers are listed alphabetically by the most commonly used name (but without cross-references for other forms); under each, studies are organized in up to three sections: bibliographies, general studies, and individual works. Indexed by scholars; writers in vol. 2 are indexed in *Biography and Genealogy Master Index* (J565). Limited in scope, omitting numerous studies, and taking most entries from other bibliographies rather than the journals themselves, *Articles on Women Writers* is principally useful as a starting place and must be supplemented by the serial bibliographies and indexes in section G.

Including works about women in literature as well as about female writers, two books by Carol Fairbanks (Myers)—*Women in Literature: Criticism of the Seventies* (Metuchen: Scarecrow, 1976, 256 pp.) and *More Women in Literature: Criticism of the Seventies* (1979, 457 pp.)—cover only 1970 through 1976, are riddled with errors, omit numerous studies, and are generally useless because of a lack of subject indexing. Some additional publications are listed in Linda K. Lewis, "Women in Literature: A Selected Bibliography," *Bulletin of Bibliography* 35 (1978): 116–22, 131.

See also

> Humm, *Annotated Critical Bibliography of Feminist Criticism* (U6170).
> *International Medieval Bibliography* (M1835).
> *MLAIB* (G335): See the headings beginning "Woman" or "Women" in the subject index to post-1980 volumes or in the online thesaurus.
> Salzman, *American Studies: An Annotated Bibliography* (Q3335).

ABSTRACTS

U6610   *Women Studies Abstracts.* New Brunswick: Transaction Periodicals Consortium for National Information Services Corp., 1972– . Quarterly, with annual cumulated index.   Z7962.W65   016.30141'2'05.

Nonevaluative abstracts and lists of studies on a wide range of topics relating to women. The organization varies widely over the years, with recent issues including unclassified divisions for literature, language, theater and films, biography and criticism, and book reviews. Although subject indexing is now very thorough, the early indexes are not reliable for locating literary authors or works mentioned in abstracts or titles. Many articles are listed without abstracts.

The best access to *Women Studies Abstracts* is through the *Gender Studies Database* or *Women's Studies International* database (online, 28 Mar. 2005 <http://biblioline.nisc

.com>; CD-ROM). The Quick Search screen allows users to limit keyword searches by author, date, journal, publisher, ISSN, and ISBN. The Advanced Search screen offers additional ways to limit searches: by title, author's institutional affiliation, type of publication, and reviewer. Expert Search Mode offers command-line searching. Results can be sorted by author, title, periodical, or date. The Biblioline interface is clumsy to navigate (e.g., viewing an index requires that the cursor be placed in the search field before clicking the Index button), explanations in many pop-up windows are not especially clear, and the Web site does not provide a remotely adequate explanation of the scope of, selection criteria for, or editorial principles governing the individual subfiles. Although inconsistent in coverage and annotations, *Women Studies Abstracts* is useful for its inclusion of numerous works overlooked by the standard bibliographies and indexes in section G.

In addition to *Women Studies Abstracts, Gender Studies Database* includes *Men's Studies Database* (which indexes print and electronic documents produced since 1990); *Women's Studies Database* (which indexes about 125 journals since 1972 devoted to women or feminism); *New Books on Women and Feminism* (which indexes books and essays in edited collections, beginning in 1987); and *Women, Race, and Ethnicity* (a selective bibliography of 2,458 publications dating from 1970–90).

G. K. Hall Women's Studies Index [1988–2002] (New Haven: Hall-Gale, 1991–2003, annual; title varies), includes more popular periodicals among the c. 80 titles indexed by author and subject in each volume. *Women's Studies on Disc*, the CD-ROM version, suffers from a rudimentary search engine and minimal help screens.

Studies on Women and Gender Abstracts (London: Routledge–Taylor and Francis, 1983– , 6/yr.; title varies; online, 7 June 2006 <http://informaworld.com/smpp/title~content=t714859056>) offers fuller abstracts of journal articles, essays in collections, and books but covers very few works on literature and suffers from rudimentary subject indexing.

For a comparative assessment of *Women Studies Abstracts, G. K. Hall Women's Studies Index*, and *Studies on Women and Gender Abstracts*, see Linda A. Krikos, "Women's Studies Periodical Indexes: An In-Depth Comparison," *Serials Review* 20.2 (1994): 651.

DISSERTATIONS AND THESES

U6615   Gilbert, V. F., and D. S. Tatla. *Women's Studies: A Bibliography of*
         Dissertations, 1870–1982. Oxford: Blackwell, 1985. 496 pp.   Z7961.G55
         [HQ1180]   016.3054.

A classified list of dissertations and some theses accepted through 1982 by British, Irish, Canadian, and United States institutions. Gilbert excludes North American master's theses as well as most studies of gender difference, marriage, and motherhood. The works are organized in 23 variously classified divisions, among which are ones for the arts (including film), language, and literature (with subdivisions for comparative and general studies, feminist criticism, and then national literatures, some of which are broken down by period and individual authors). An entry cites author, title, degree, institution, and date. Indexed by subjects. Because of a classification based on titles, a lack of cross-references, and an insufficiently thorough subject index (which has more than its share of errors), researchers are generally better served by *ProQuest Dissertations and Theses* (H465) for North American dissertations. Despite its faults, however, *Women's Studies* is a convenient compilation.

See also

> Sec. H: Guides to Dissertations and Theses.

Biographical Dictionaries

See

> *American Women Writers* (Q3390).
> Bell, *Biographical Dictionary of English Women Writers, 1580–1720* (M1433a).
> Blain, *Feminist Companion to Literature in English* (J593).
> *Notable American Women* (Q3385).
> Schlueter, *Encyclopedia of British Women Writers* (M1433a).
> Todd, *British Women Writers* (M1433a).
> Todd, *Dictionary of British and American Women Writers, 1660–1800* (M2265).

Index of Names

The index of names includes all authors, editors, compilers, translators, revisers, and other persons responsible for any of the works in citations or annotations. It excludes reviewers, compilers of indexes to scholarly journals, literary authors, and other names mentioned in passing in annotations. Entries are alphabetized letter by letter. Numbers generally refer to entry numbers; *a* following a number means that the name will be found in the annotation rather than the citation; *p.* or *pp.* preceding a number indicates a page reference.

Index of Titles

This index includes the current, former, and variant titles of all books, essays, and periodicals (cited as a separate work) in the citations and annotations. Titles used as cross-references, nondistinctive titles (such as "Bibliography" or "History and Criticism"), and indexes to journals are not indexed. To conserve space, shortened titles are listed when possible.

As in the other indexes, entries are alphabetized letter by letter; numbers are entry numbers (a number followed by the letter *a* means that the title will be found in the annotation; a number preceded by *p.* or *pp.* is a page number).

Subject Index

Along with subjects treated in a substantial way by the works cited, this index includes types of reference works. Numbers generally refer to entry numbers; page references are preceded by *p.* or *pp.* Users should also note that there are extensive cross-references in most sections.